RULERS AND GOVERNMENTS OF THE WORLD

Volume 1
Earliest Times to 1491

Compiled by
MARTHA ROSS

BOWKER
LONDON & NEW YORK

First published in Great Britain 1978 by Bowker Publishing Company Limited, Epping, Essex and published in the United States of America by R. R. Bowker Co., 1180 Avenue of the Americas, New York, NY 10036

British Library cataloguing in publication data

Rulers and governments of the world.
Vol. 1: Earliest times to 1491.
1. Kings and rulers 2. Cabinet system – History
I. Title II. Allen, Charles Geoffry III. Ross, Martha
909 D107

ISBN 0-85935-021-5
ISBN 0-85935-051-7 Set of 3 vols.

Library of Congress catalog card number 77-723-42

Printed in Great Britain by Thomson Litho Ltd, East Kilbride, Scotland

Contents

Preface

A generation of reference librarians has found in Bertold Spuler's *Regenten und Regierungen der Welt*, first published in 1953, a handy and comprehensive guide to those in power in the modern world. But Part 1 of the German original, designed to cover the ancient and medieval periods, has not yet appeared. While, therefore, Volumes 2 and 3 of this English version correspond substantially to Part 2 of the original, Volume 1 is an entirely new compilation.

Inevitably, in a volume covering eras which saw migrations and conquests, the dissolution of empires, the establishment of innumerable fiefs of varying size and degree of independence, and the gradual emergence of modern states, it is impossible to include every state or dynasty that has some claim to independent existence, nor can we hope that the work is free from error. The publishers will be grateful therefore for corrections and suggestions for improvement.

The compilers gratefully acknowledge the generous help of the libraries of the School of Slavonic and East European Studies, the School of Oriental and African Studies, the Institute of Historical Research and University College London, the British Library of Political and Economic Science, the British Library and the Department of Western Asian Antiquities at the British Museum. They also wish to place on record their appreciation of the invaluable help rendered throughout by the managing editor, Mr Derek French, and the copy editor, Mr Neil Saunders.

C. G. Allen

Introduction to Volume 1

The present volume contains for the most part lists of the more important rulers from the beginning of recorded history up to 1491 – emperors, kings and princes and their equivalents and a selection of lesser rulers. Among these last their degree of independence has been the principal criterion of inclusion, but in view of their numbers the historical importance of the territory in question has been taken into consideration. Inevitably, some dynasties will be missing which this or that reader would have preferred to find included, but it is hoped that in general the selection will be acceptable. Unlike Volumes 2 and 3, this one does not contain lists of 'governments' – a concept, for most of this period, of uncertain validity.

Most lists are entered under the English name of a territory, and in a few instances, e.g. China, Korea, Wales, dynasties which ruled over different parts of the territory have been grouped together and not scattered under Wei, Silla or Gwynedd, for example, as major headings. About a fifth of the entries, however, are under the names of dynasties, peoples or hordes, for the territories they ruled varied in extent from time to time and often had no single name, so that the notion of a state is inapplicable. This is particularly so in the case of Islamic rulers.

The territories, ecclesiastical sees, dynasties, peoples and hordes are arranged in one alphabetical sequence, irrespective of time and place.

All the pre-colonial African regimes are included in this volume, irrespective of date, and not in Volumes 2 and 3. Also a number of Islamic and other dynasties are continued in this volume beyond 1491: they had not been included in the German original, for from the point of view of the modern world they seemed no doubt of minor importance; but as their earlier rulers were included in this volume, it seemed reasonable to continue the lists to the end and not break off arbitrarily at 1491. Without unduly delaying the publication of Volume 2 it would have been impossible to include the appropriate portions in it, and in any case it was considered undesirable to make too many alterations in the content of what was basically a translation.

The entries are arranged as uniformly as possible, granted the very different conditions that obtained at different times and in different eras.

For each ruler, the date of accession, nomination, election or usurpation, if known, is given in the left-hand column, and unless otherwise stated, the period of office extends to the date next below. Where it can be done with reasonable consistency, the month and day are given, but for many states and periods we have had to be content with the year alone. (As indicated below, even this is not always possible.)

Uncertain dates are accompanied by a question mark, applicable to the whole date or to some part of it. Where a limited choice of dates exists, or there are alternative criteria for their establishment, two dates are given, and in some cases, as for instance when converting the years of other calendars, a pair of years. Periods of foreign domination, resulting in gaps in the sequence or the presence of rival claimants, are noted at the appropriate point, in the text or in a footnote.

Against the date stands the name of the ruler, with date of birth and nature of kinship with (unless otherwise stated) the preceding ruler, if known. If a reign is terminated by the death of the ruler, the date of death is not given separately but may be inferred from the closing date of the reign or the accession of the successor. If it is not so terminated, some such note as 'abdicated' or 'expelled' is given, and the date of death, if known, is recorded. In view of the complications of accession in many states we have preferred in these cases to give an exact closing date and a vague date of accession, rather than assume that the two always coincide. As medieval rulers were often mobile and pluralist, we have been more generous in giving the place of birth and death than in the later volumes.

A compilation of this sort must necessarily rely on existing sectional lists: lists of classes of rulers such as Zambaur's *Manuel de généalogie et de chronologie pour l'histoire de l'Islam*, lists accompanying major historical works, lists of rulers of single countries appearing in archival publications or numismatic catalogues. The more important of these sources are mentioned in the Bibliography. But in a good many cases such a list has been only the starting point, and the data have been checked by reference to reliable histories, major encyclopedias and specialized genealogical treatises. Biographical information has had to be sought elsewhere, usually in vain where dates of birth are in question.

Available lists vary in reliability: at one extreme there are those that are based on accurate and well-preserved records, at the other the almost legendary. At these extremes there is little scope for argument, and where the list is basically archival but there are gaps in the records, problems arise only at those points where the record is deficient. But some of the middle ground is occupied by lists which have had to be painfully reconstructed from conflicting native traditions, often stated in terms of variously interpreted chronological systems, from foreign testimony and from intermittent epigraphic or numismatic evidence. To make a credible list it may be necessary to postulate alternative names for rulers, overlapping of reigns, errors of transmission, or some combination of these. That these phenomena all occur there is no doubt: the argument is whether any of them should be postulated in this or that particular case. Furthermore, in default of synchronisms, such as the dating of the fall of Jerusalem to the 11th year of Zedekiah, King of Judah, and the 19th of Nebuchadnezzar, King of Babylon, individual bodies of chronological data may float, as it were, and even at the best there remains a good deal of play in the system. Thus there are 'high' and 'low' datings for events in the ancient Near East, and the highest dating for the end of the first Babylonian dynasty, for instance, is some 170 years earlier than the lowest one. (The date adopted here is middle to low.) Dates such as these should neither be naïvely accepted nor scouted as guesses. They rest on honest historical research and discussion and are generally accepted as the most probable. Where no sort of continuous chronological record is available, we have had to content ourselves with the insertion of occasional data, usually in the form of a '*floruit*'.

For medieval Europe the basic chronological framework is reliable enough, but individual data may be equivocal, depending as they sometimes do on the interpretation of the numbering of the year; or they may be deficient, so that an event can only be located within broader or narrow limits, or can be dated to the day and the month (because of some commemoration) but not to the exact year. The dates here given will be found to differ sometimes from those in other authorities, just as those authorities will at times be found to differ among themselves.

Additional evidence or more ingenious argument may one day eliminate some of these uncertainties, but some will undoubtedly remain.

The treatment of names has occasioned us a certain amount of perplexity. The old practice of using English forms, regardless of nationality, where equivalents exist, and contenting oneself with roughly phonetic adaptations of names in non-Latin alphabets has given way gradually and unevenly to the partial acceptance of vernacular forms. By now there is no universally accepted norm, and writers differ from each other in the extent of their anglicization, and within the compass of their own works will sometimes be found anglicizing one form while leaving another unaltered. We have not ventured to depart from the conventional forms of classical names, fearing, for instance, that if we entered Roman emperors under their official styles, they might not easily be identified. But we have added the official style in parentheses. We have also left in their conventional dress the names of Eastern rulers known to us through classical sources. In general, however, we have taken the vernacular forms, minimizing the occurrence of diacritical marks by accepting the type of transcription favoured by historians rather than those proper to linguistic study, and adding conventional forms in parentheses where it seemed desirable. It should be noted that a number of ancient Near Eastern names contain cuneiform ideograms which cannot at present be read, at any rate with certainty, in the language concerned. In such cases the standard Sumerian value is substituted, printed wholly in capitals, irrespective of language, e.g. DU-Teshub, King of Amurru.

In the Middle Ages the temptation to revert to English forms all round is peculiarly strong, for it is often difficult, if not impossible, in the case of men who ruled in more than one state, to fix on one vernacular form as the only correct one, to the exclusion of all others. Here we have accepted the fact that no one form can be found and have used in each case the one proper to the country or territory concerned, modernizing it in the normal way if it has become traditional, and adding the other forms in parentheses. Thus under Denmark we have: *Knud I*, the Great (known in England as *Cnut* or *Canute*). There is also a general conspectus of alternative forms on pages xli – lxiii.

A peculiar difficulty arises with Islamic names, which often contain a number of different elements, any one of which can become accepted as a man's principal name, the name under which he would be listed. Thus *Abu'l-Qasim Muhammad ibn Isma'il ibn Quraish ibn 'Abbad al-Qadi*, the first ʻAbbadid king at Seville, is best known as *Muhammad I ibn ʻAbbad*, but *Abu'l-ʻAbbas ʻAbdallah al-Saffah ibn Muhammad*, the first ʻAbbasid caliph, is known as *Abu'l-ʻAbbas al-Saffah*. We have indicated these differences by enclosing all elements neglected in the short form of the name in parentheses, so that the two names appear respectively as *(Abu'l-Qasim) Muhammad I (ibn Isma'il ibn Quraish) ibn ʻAbbad (al-Qadi)* and *Abu'l-ʻAbbas (ʻAbdallah) al-Saffah (ibn Muhammad)*. In this way it will be easier for the reader to find the names in other reference books, though as authorities differ, all uncertainty is not removed. The selection of the entry word rests wherever possible on the *Encyclopaedia of Islam* or the Turkish *İslâm ansiklopedisi*.

C. G. Allen

Acknowledgements

Grateful acknowledgement is made to the following for permission to use copyright material:

Athlone Press of the University of London: list of the kings of Kush from A. J. Arkell's *A history of the Sudan from the earliest times to 1821*;

Baker Book House: list of the kings of Nabathea from John Irving Lawlor's *The Nabataeans in historical perspective*;

B. T. Batsford Ltd: list of the high-kings of Ireland from Francis John Byrne's *Irish kings and high-kings*;

Cambridge University Press: lists concerning the ancient Near East from *The Cambridge ancient history* (1st and 3rd editions); lists concerning medieval Greek, Venetian and Armenian rulers from *The Cambridge medieval history*, vol. 4, part 1 (2nd edition), and for material concerning the Eldigüzids from *The Cambridge history of Iran*, vol. 5;

Edinburgh University Press: for the use of material from C. E. Bosworth's *The Islamic dynasties*;

Faber and Faber Ltd: lists of the rulers of Bornu, Sokoto and Oyo from Michael Crowder's *The story of Nigeria*; lists of the rulers of the Akan States from Eva L. R. Meyerowitz's *Akan traditions of origin* and *The Akan of Ghana*;

International African Institute: list of the rulers of Nupe from S. F. Nadel's *A black Byzantium*;

Longman Group Ltd: list of the rulers of Buganda from N. S. M. Semakula Kiwanuka's *A history of Buganda*; list of the rulers of Bulozi from Mutumba Maina's *Bulozi under the Luyana kings*; and list of the rulers of the Ashanti from W. E. Ward's *A short history of Ghana*;

Macmillan Ltd: lists of the rulers of Burma, Thailand and Viet Nam from D. G. E. Hall's *A history of south-east Asia*;

Marican and Sons: list of the sultans of Malacca from Richard O. Winstedt's *A history of Malaya*;

Oxford University Press: list of the Ottomans from A. D. Alderson's *The structure of the Ottoman dynasty*; list of the sultans of Kilwa from G. S. P. Freeman-Grenville's *The French at Kilwa Island*; lists of the rulers of the Hausa States from S. J. Hogben and A. H. M. Kirk-Greene's *The emirates of northern Nigeria*; list of the rulers of Judaea from W. O. E. Oesterley's *A history of Israel*, vol. 2; list of the rulers of Tibet from H. E. Richardson's *Tibet and its history*; materials from Vincent A. Smith's *Oxford history of India* (3rd edition; edited Percival Spear); and lists of the rulers of Mali and Songhay from J. Spencer Trimingham's *A history of Islam in west Africa*;

Routledge and Kegan Paul Ltd: lists of the rulers of Korea from *Hulbert's history of Korea*, vol. 2;

University of Wisconsin Press: lists of the rulers of the Luba/Lunda States from Jan Vansina's *Kingdoms of the savanna*;

Professor Jan Vansina: list of the rulers of Rwanda from *L'évolution du royaume rwanda*.

Bibliography

Academia Republicii Populare Romîne. *Documente privind istoria Romîniei: introducere*. vol. 1. Bucureşti: Editura Academiei RPR, 1956.

Acharyya, N. N. *The history of medieval Assam (from the thirteenth to the seventeenth century)*. Gauhati, Assam: Dutta Baruah and Co., 1966.

Alderson, A. D. *The structure of the Ottoman dynasty*. Oxford: Clarendon Press, 1956.

Alpers, Edward A. 'Dynasties of the Mutapa-Rowzi complex', *Journal of African History*, II (1970) 2.

Alpers, Edward A. 'A revised chronology of the sultans of Kilwa in the eighteenth and nineteenth centuries', *Azania: The Journal of the British Institute of History and Archaeology in East Africa*, II (1967).

Anderson, Marjorie Ogilvie. *Kings and kingship in early Scotland*. Edinburgh: Scottish Academic Press, 1973.

Annuario Pontificio per l'anno 1976. Vatican City: Tipografia Poliglotta Vaticana, 1976.

Arbusow, L. *Grundiss der Geschichte Liv-, Est- und Kurlands*. 3rd ed. Riga: Jonck und Poliewsky, 1908.

Arkell, A. J. *A history of the Sudan from the earliest times to 1821*. London: Athlone Press, 1955.

Barrow, Geoffrey Wallis Stewart. *Robert Bruce*. 2nd ed. Edinburgh: Edinburgh University Press, 1976.

Barthold, W. *Turkestan down to the Mongol invasion*. rev. 2nd ed. transl. H. A. R. Gibb. London: Luzac and Co., 1958.

Bartrum, P. C. (ed.) *Early Welsh genealogical tracts*. Cardiff: University of Wales Press, 1966.

Barua, Kanaka Lal. *Early history of Kamarupa*. 2nd ed. Gauhati: Lawyers' Book Stall, 1966.

Benninghoven, Friedrich. *Der Orden der Schwertbrüder*. Köln: Böhlau, 1965.

Bol'shaya sovetskaya éntsiklopediya. Moskva, 1970–. 26 vol. to 1977.

Bosworth, Clifford Edmund. *The Islamic dynasties: a chronological and genealogical handbook*. Edinburgh: Edinburgh University Press, 1967.

Bosworth, Clifford Edmund. 'The titulature of the early Ghaznavids', *Oriens*, XV (1962).

Boyle, J. A. (ed.) *The Cambridge history of Iran*. vol. 5. London: Cambridge University Press, 1968.

Bright, John. *A history of Israel*. 2nd ed. Philadelphia and London: Westminster Press and SCM Press, 1972.

Brockhaus Enzyklopädie. Wiesbaden: F. A. Brockhaus, 1966–76. 24 vol.

Brooke, Z. N. *A history of Europe from 911 to 1198*. rev. 3rd ed. London: Methuen and Co., 1956.

Brunschvig, Robert. *La Berberie orientale sous les hafsides, des origines à la fin du XV siècle*. vol. 2. Paris: Adrien-Maisonneuve, 1947.

Budge, Sir E. A. Wallis. *A history of Ethiopia, Nubia and Abyssinia (according to the hieroglyphic inscriptions of Egypt and Nubia, and the Ethiopian chronicles)*. vol. 1. London: Methuen and Co., 1928.

Bury, J. B. et al. *The Cambridge ancient history*. London: Cambridge University Press, 1923–39. 12 vol.

Buxton, David. *The Abyssinians*. London: Thames and Hudson, 1970.

Byrne, Francis John. *Irish kings and high-kings*. London: B. T. Batsford, 1973.

Chadwick, Hector Munro. *Early Scotland*. London: Cambridge University Press, 1949.

Charles-Picard, Gilbert *and* Collette. *The life and death of Carthage*. transl. Dominique Collon. London: Sidgwick and Jackson, 1968.

Colledge, Malcolm A. R. *The Parthians*. London: Thames and Hudson, 1967.

Crawford, O. G. S. *The Fung kingdom of Sennar*. Gloucester: John Bellows, 1951.

Crowder, Michael. *The story of Nigeria*. London: Faber and Faber, 1962.

Cuvelier, Mgr J., *and* Jadin, L. *L'ancien Congo d'après les archives romaines (1518–1640).* Bruxelles: Académie Royale des Sciences Coloniales, 1954.

Davis, Norman, *and* Kraay, Colin M. *The Hellenistic kingdoms: portrait coins and history.* London: Thames and Hudson, 1973.

Deanesly, Margaret. *A history of early medieval Europe from 476 to 911.* 2nd ed. London: Methuen and Co., 1974.

Dickinson, William Croft. *Scotland from the earliest times to 1603 (A new history of Scotland, vol. 1).* London and Edinburgh: Nelson, 1961.

Dicţionar enciclopedic român. Bucureşti: Editura Politică, 1962–6. 4 vol.

Doresse, Jean. *L'empire du Prêtre-Jean.* Paris: Librairie Plon, 1957. 2 vol.

Duda, Franciszek. *Rozwój terytoryalny Pomorza polskiego, wiek XI–XIII.* w Krakowie: Akademia Umiejętności, 1909.

Dworzaczek, Włodzimierz. *Genealogia: tablice.* Warszawa: Państwowe Wydawnictwo Naukowe, 1959.

Edwards, I. E. S., Gadd, C. J., *and* Hammond, N. G. L. (ed.) *The Cambridge ancient history.* 3rd ed. London: Cambridge University Press, 1970–. 2 vol. to 1973.

Enciclopedia italiana. Milano: Istituto Giovanni Treccani, 1929–37. 24 vol.

Enciklopedija Jugoslavije. Zagreb: Leksikografski Zavod, 1955–71. 8 vol.

Encyclopædia Britannica. 14th ed., 1970 printing. Chicago: Encyclopædia Britannica, Inc., 1970. 23 vol.

Encyclopædia Britannica. 15th ed. Chicago: Encyclopædia Britannica, Inc., 1974. 30 vol.

Encyclopaedia of Islām. London: Luzac and Co., 1913–38. 4 vol. and 1 suppl.

Encyclopaedia of Islam. 2nd ed. London: Luzac and Co., 1960–. 3 vol. to 1971.

Encyclopedia Lituanica. Boston: 1970–6. 5 vol.

Engel, Arthur, *and* Serrure, Raymond. *Traité de numismatique du moyen âge.* Paris: Ernest Leroux, 1891–1905. 3 vol.

Eubel, Conrad. *Hierarchia catholica medii aevi, sive summorum pontificum, S.R.E. cardinalium, ecclesiarum antistitum series, ab anno 1198 usque ad annum 1431 (ab anno 1431 usque ad annum 1503) perducta.* Editio altera. vol. 1 and 2. Monasterii, sumptibus . . .

Librariae Regensbergianae, 1913–14.

Evans, Stanley G. *A short history of Bulgaria*. London: Lawrence and Wishart, 1960.

Freeman-Grenville, G. S. P. *The French at Kilwa Island: an episode in eighteenth-century east African history*. Oxford: Clarendon Press, 1965.

Freeman-Grenville, G. S. P. *The medieval history of the coast of Tanganyika*. Berlin: Akademie-Verlag, 1962.

Furdoonjee, D. J. Paruck. *Sasanian coins*. Bombay: Times Press, 1924.

Gait, Sir Edward Albert. *A history of Assam*. Calcutta: Thacker, Spink, 1906.

Gajdukevič, V. F. *Das bosporanische Reich*. Berlin: Akademie-Verlag (in Arbeitsgemeinschaft mit Adolf M. Hakkert, Amsterdam), 1971.

Gardiner, Sir Alan H. *Egypt of the pharoahs: an introduction*. Oxford: Clarendon Press, 1961.

La Grande Encyclopédie. Paris: H. Lamirault et Cie, 1887–1902. 30 vol.

Grand Larousse encyclopédique. Paris: Librairie Larousse, 1960–4. 10 vol.

Haig, T. W. 'The chronology and genealogy of the Muhammedan kings of Kashmir', *Journal of the Royal Asiatic Society* (1918).

Hall, D. G. E. *A history of south-east Asia*. 3rd ed. London and Basingstoke: Macmillan and Co., 1968.

Hall, H. R. H. *The ancient history of the Near East, from the earliest times to the battle of Salamis*. 8th ed. ed. C. J. Gadd. London: Methuen and Co., 1932.

Hama, Boubou, *Histoire du Gobir et de Sokoto*. Paris: Présence Africaine, 1967.

Harvey, G. E. *History of Burma: from the earliest times to 10 March 1824, the beginning of the English conquest*. London: Longmans, Green and Co., 1925.

Hauck, Albert. *Kirchengeschichte Deutschlands*. Leipzig: Hinrich, 1922–9. 5 vol. in 6.

Hazlitt, W. Carew. *The coinage of the European continent*. London: Swan Sonnenschein and Co., 1893.

Head, Barclay V. *Historia Numorum: a manual of Greek numismatics*. Oxford: Clarendon Press, 1911.

Hill, Sir George Francis. *A history of Cyprus*. London: Cambridge University Press, 1940–52. 4 vol.

Hill, George Francis. *Catalogue of the Greek coins of Arabia,*

Mesopotamia and Persia. London: British Museum, 1922.
Historia Polski. t. 1, cz. 1. Warszawa: Polska Akademia Nauk, 1957.
Historia Śląska. t. 1. Wrocław: Polska Akademia Nauk, 1960–1.
Hogben, S. J., *and* Kirk-Greene, A. H. M. *The emirates of northern Nigeria: a preliminary survey of their historical traditions*. London: Oxford University Press, 1966.
Hogben, S. J. *The Muhammedan emirates of Nigeria*. London: Oxford University Press, 1930.
Hrvatska enciklopedija. Zagreb, 1941–2. 4 vol. (no more published).
Hulbert, Homer Bezaleel. *Hulbert's history of Korea*. vol. 2. ed. Clarence Norwood Weems. London: Routledge and Kegan Paul, 1962 (1st published 1905).
Hussey, J. M. (ed.) *The Cambridge medieval history*. vol. 4, pt. 1. London: Cambridge University Press, 1966.
Isenburg, Wilhelm Karl, Prinz von, *and* Loringhoven, Baron Freytag von. *Stammtafeln zur Geschichte der europäischen Staaten*. Marburg: Verlag von J. A. Stargardt, 1953–7. 4 vol.
İslâm Ansiklopedisi. İstanbul: Maarif Matbassı, 1940–. 11 vol. to 1970.
Istoriya na Bŭlgariya. t. 1. Sofiya: Bŭlgarska Akademiya na Naukite, 1954.
Iván, Berend T. et al. *Magyarország története*. 2. köt. ed. Erik Molnár et al. Budapest: Gondolat Kiadó, 1967.
Jackson, Kenneth H. 'The Britons in southern Scotland', *Antiquity*, XXIX (1955).
Jireček, Konstantin. *Istorija Srba*. Beograd: Naučna Knjiga, 1952.
Jones, W. Glyn. *Denmark*. London: Benn, 1970.
Katzenstein, H. Jacob. *The history of Tyre from the beginning of the second millenium BCE until the fall of the Neo-Babylonian empire in 538 BCE*. Jerusalem: Schocken Institute for Jewish Research, 1973.
Kenyeres, Agnes (ed.) *Magyar életrajzi leksikon*. Budapest: Akadémiai Kiadó, 1967–9. 2 vol.
Kirby, D. P. 'Bede and Northumbrian chronology', *English Historical Review*, LXXVIII (July 1963).
Kirby, D. P. 'British dynastic history in the pre-Viking period', *Bulletin of the Board of Celtic Studies*, XXVII (November 1976) 1.
Kirby, D. P. 'Problems of early West Saxon history', *English Historical Review*, LXXX (January 1965).
Kirby, D. P. 'Strathclyde and Cumbria: a survey of historical develop-

ment to 1092', *Transactions of the Cumberland and Westmorland Antiquarian and Archaeological Society*, (1962).

Kiwanuka, M. Semakula M. *A history of Buganda, from the foundation of the kingdom to 1900*. London: Longmans Group, 1971.

Kratka bŭlgarska entsiklopediya. Sofiya: Izdatelstvo na Bŭlgarskata Akademiya na Naukite, 1963–9. 5 vol.

Kubijović, Volodymyr. *Ukraine: a concise encyclopaedia*. Toronto: University of Toronto Press for Ukraine National Association, 1963–71. 2 vol.

Labande, Léon Honoré. *Histoire de la principauté de Monaco*. 2nd ed. Monaco: Archives du Palais, 1934.

Labuda, Gerard (ed.) *Pomorze średniowieczne*. Warszawa: Książka i Wiedza, 1958.

Langer, William L. (ed.) *Encyclopedia of world history: ancient, medieval and modern*. 5th ed. London: Harrap, 1972.

Lawlor, John Irving. *The Nabataeans in historical perspective*. Grand Rapids, Michigan: Baker Book House, 1974.

Lietuviškoji tarybinė enciklopedija. vol. 1. Vilnius: Mokslas, 1976.

Lloyd, Sir John Edward. *A history of Wales from the earliest times to the Edwardian conquest*. 3rd ed. London: Longmans, 1939.

McEvedy, C. *Penguin atlas of ancient history*. Harmondsworth: Penguin,

McEvedy, C. *The Penguin atlas of medieval history*. Harmondsworth: Penguin, 1961.

Maina, Mutumba. *Bulozi under the Luyana kings: political evolution and state formation in pre-colonial Zambia*. London: Longman Group, 1973.

Majumdar, R. C. (ed.) *The history and culture of the Indian people*. vol. 1–6.

Mažoji lietuviškoji tarybinė enciklopedija. Vilnius: Mintis, 1966–77. 4 vol.

Meyerowitz, Eva L. R. *The Akan of Ghana: their ancient beliefs*. London: Faber and Faber, 1957.

Meyerowitz, Eva L. R. *Akan traditions of origin*. London: Faber and Faber, 1952.

Minorsky, V. *Studies in Caucasian history*. London: Taylor's Foreign Press, 1953.

Mitkowski, Józef. *Pomorze zachodnie w stosunku do Polski*. Poznań: Wydawnictwo Instytutu Zachodniego, 1946.

Monneret de Villard, Ugo. *Storia della Nubia cristiana*. Roma: Pont. Institutum Orientalium Studiorum, 1938.

Monteil, Charles. *Les Bambara du Ségou et du Kaarta: étude historique, ethnographique et littéraire d'une peuplade du Soudan français*. Paris: Émile Larose, 1924.

Monteil, Charles. *Une cité soudanaise: Djénné, métropole du delta central du Niger*. Paris: Société d'Éditions Géographiques, Maritimes Coloniales, 1932.

Nadel, S. F. *A black Byzantium: the kingdom of Nupe in Nigeria*. London: Oxford University Press (for the International African Institute), 1942.

New Catholic encyclopedia. New York: McGraw-Hill, 1967. 15 vol.

Newell, Edward T. *Royal Greek portrait coins*. Racine, Wisconsin: Whitman Publishing Co., 1970(?) (1st ed. 1930).

Nicholas, C. W., *and* Paranavitana, Senaret. *A concise history of Ceylon*. Colombo: Ceylon University Press, 1961.

Nyakatura, J. W. *Anatomy of an African kingdom: a history of Bunyoro-Kitara*. ed. Godfrey N. Uzoigwe. transl. Teopista Muganwe. New York: Anchor Books, 1973.

O'Callaghan, Joseph F. *A history of medieval Spain*. Ithaca: Cornell University Press, 1975.

Oesterley, W. O. E. *A history of Israel*. vol. 2. Oxford: Clarendon Press, 1932.

O'Fahey, R. S., *and* Spaulding, J. L. *Kingdoms of the Sudan*. London: Methuen and Co., 1974.

Ọlọruntimẹhin, B. O. *The Segu Tukulor empire*. New York: Humanities Press, 1972.

Palau Marti, Montserrat. *Essai sur la notion de roi chez les Yorubas et les Aja-Fon, Nigeria et Dahomey*. Paris: Université de Paris, 1960.

Panikkar, K. Mahdu. *The serpent and the crescent: a history of the Negro kingdoms of western Africa*. Bombay: Asia Publishing House, 1963.

Peake, A. S. *Peake's commentary on the Bible*. ed. Matthew Black. London: Nelson, 1962.

Petech, Luciano. *The medieval history of Nepal*. Roma: Istituto per il Medio ed Estremo Oriente, 1958.

Philips, C. H. (ed.) *Handbook of Oriental history*. London: Royal Historical Society, 1951.

Pirenne, H. *Histoire de Belgique*. vol. 1 and 2. Bruxelles: Henri

Lamertin, 1900–03.
Polski słownik biograficzny. Kraków: nakładem Polskiej Akademji Umiejętnosci, 1935–76. 21 vol.
Popperwell, Ronald G. *Norway*. London: Benn, 1972.
Powicke, Sir F. Maurice, *and* Frye, E. B. (ed.) *Handbook of British chronology*. 2nd ed. London: Royal Historical Society, 1961.
Presnyakov, A. E. *The formation of the great Russian state*. transl. A. E. Moorhouse. Chicago: Quadrangle Books, 1970.
Puri, Baij Nath. *Studies in early history and administration in Assam*. Gauhati: Department of Publication, Gauhati University, 1968.
Rabino, M. 'Les dynasties du Mazandaran de l'an 50 l'avant l'Hégire à l'an 1006 de l'Hégire (572 à 1597/1598) d'après les chroniques locales', *Journal Asiatique*, CCXXVIII (1936).
Regmi, Dilli Raman. *Ancient Nepal*. Calcutta: Mukhopadhyay, 1969.
Regmi, Dilli Raman. *Medieval Nepal*. Calcutta: Mukhopadhyay, 1965–6.
Reischauer, Jean, *and* Robert Karl. *Early Japanese history*. pt. B. London: Princeton University Press, 1937.
Rhode, Gotthold. *Die Ostgrenze Polens*. Köln: Böhlau, 1955.
Richardson, H. E. *Tibet and its history*. London: Oxford University Press, 1962.
Runciman, Steven. *A history of the Crusades*. London: Cambridge University Press, 1951–4. 3 vol.
Russell, P. E. (ed.) *Spain: a companion to Spanish studies*. London: Methuen and Co., 1973.
Russkiĭ biograficheskiĭ slovar'. Moskva, 1897–1914.
Salvatorelli, Luigi. *L'Italia comunale dal secolo XI alla metà del secolo XIV* (*Storia d'Italia*, vol. 4). Milano: A. Mondadori, 1940.
Salvatorelli, Luigi. *L'Italia medioevale dalle invasioni barbariche agli inizi del secolo XI* (*Storia d'Italia*, vol. 3). Milano: A. Mondadori, 1938.
Sansom, George. *A history of Japan*. vol. 1 and 2. London: Cresset Press, 1958–61.
Scobbie, Irene. *Sweden*. London: Benn, 1972.
Šišić, Ferdo. *Pregled povijesti hrvatskoga naroda*. rev. ed. Zagreb: Nakladni Zavod Matice Hrvatske, 1975.
Smith, Robert. *Kingdoms of the Yoruba*. London: Methuen and Co., 1969.
Smith, Vincent A. *The Oxford history of India*. 3rd ed. ed. Perciyal

Spear. Oxford: Clarendon Press, 1958.
Strommenger, Eva. *The art of Mesopotamia*. transl. Christina Haglund. London: Thames and Hudson, 1964.
Strubbe, I., *and* Voet, L. *De chronologie van de middeleeuwen en de moderne tijden in de Nederlanden*. Antwerp: Standaard-Boekhandel, 1960.
Sufi, G. M. D. *Kăshir*. vol. 2. Lahore: University of the Punjab, 1949.
Tamakloe, Emmanuel Forster. *A brief history of the Dagbamba people*. Accra: Government Printing Office, 1931.
Tanner, J. R., Previté-Orton, C. W., *and* Brooke, Z. N. (ed.) *The Cambridge medieval history*. vol. 5. London: Cambridge University Press, 1926.
Tauxier, L. *Le noir du Yatenga*. Paris: Émile Larose, 1917.
Toumanoff, Cyril. *Studies in Christian Caucasian history*. Washington, DC: Georgetown University Press, 1963.
Trimingham, J. Spencer. *A history of Islam in west Africa*. London: Oxford University Press (for the University of Glasgow), 1962.
Urvoy, Y. *Histoire de l'empire du Bornou*. Paris: Librairie Larose, 1949.
Vaccaro, Francesco. *Le monete di Aksum*. Mantova: Casteldario, 1967.
Vaillant, George C. *The Aztecs of Mexico: origin, rise and fall of the Aztec nation*. Harmondsworth: Penguin, 1950.
Valeri, Nino. *L'Italia nell'eta dei principati, dal 1343 al 1516* (*Storia d'Italia*, vol. 5). Milano: A. Mondadori, 1949.
Vansina, Jan. *L'évolution du royaume rwanda des origines à 1900*. Bruxelles: Académie Royale des Sciences d'Outre-Mer, 1962.
Vansina, Jan. *Kingdoms of the savanna*. Madison, Wisconsin: University of Wisconsin Press, 1966.
Vasmer, R. 'Zur Chronologie der Gastaniden und Sallariden', *Islamica*, III (1927).
Verhulpen, Edmond. *Baluba et Balubaïsés du Katanga*. Anvers: L'Avenir Belge, 1936.
Ward, W. E. *A short history of Ghana*. 7th ed. London: Longmans, Green and Co., 1957.
Webster's new geographical dictionary. Springfield, Ma.: G. and C. Merriam, 1972.
Wentz, Gottfried, *and* Schwineköper, Berent. *Das Erzbistum Magdeburg*. vol. 1, pt. 1. *Das Domstift St. Moritz in Magdeburg*. Berlin and New York: de Gruyter, 1972.
Wielka encyklopedia powszechna PWN. Warszawa: Państwowe

Wydawnictwo Naukowe, 1962–70.
Wilks, Ivor. *Asante in the nineteenth century: the structure and evolution of a political order*. London: Cambridge University Press, 1975.
Winstedt, Sir Richard O. *A history of Malaya*. Singapore: Marican and Sons, 1962.
Woodhead, A. G. *The Greeks in the West*. London: Thames and Hudson, 1962.
Wright, John. *Libya*. London: Benn, 1969.
Wroth, Warwick. *Catalogue of the coins of the Vandals, Ostrogoths and Lombards and of the empires of Thessalonica, Nicaea and Trebizond in the British Museum*. London: British Museum, 1911.
Wroth, Warwick. *Catalogue of the Greek coins of Galatia, Cappadocia and Syria*. London: British Museum, 1899.
Wroth, Warwick. *Catalogue of the imperial Byzantine coins in the British Museum*. vol. 2. London: British Museum, 1908.
Yonah, Michael Avi, *and* Shatzman, Israel. *Illustrated encyclopaedia of the classical world*. Jerusalem: Jerusalem Publishing House, 1976.
Zambaur, E. de. *Manuel de généalogie et de chronologie pour l'histoire de l'Islam*. Hanover: Librairie Orientaliste Heinz Lafaire, 1927. 2 vol.

Index of Territories, Dynasties, Sees and Hordes

RULERS AND GOVERNMENTS OF THE WORLD

RULERS AND GOVERNMENTS OF THE WORLD
General Editor: C. G. Allen

Volume 1
Earliest Times to 1491
Compiled by Martha Ross

Volume 2
1492 to 1929
Compiled by Bertold Spuler

Volume 3
1930 to 1975
Compiled by Bertold Spuler (1930 to 1970)
C. G. Allen & Neil Saunders (1971 to 1975)

Forms of Names in Various Languages

The following tables are intended to help the reader to find or recognize names in works in languages other than English. However, the listing of a form does not imply that it is invariably used in that language. Some reference books may prefer, as we do ourselves, to use the form proper to the country concerned. Nor are the correspondences necessarily reversible: while *Basil* appears in Russian as *Vasily*, the Russian grand dukes of that name will most probably be left as *Vasily* in books written in English and not, nowadays, translated into *Basil*.

The tables do not include names which differ only to a minor degree at the end of the name.

In each table the order of the rows of names is determined primarily by the alphabetical order of the English form, but rows are repeated in the appropriate place when they include forms with different initial letters. Thus in each column all names with the same initial letter are grouped together and names that are not in alphabetical order of their initial letter are indented. For this purpose V and W are equated in Latin, Danish, Norwegian and Swedish.

TABLE 1 COMMON EUROPEAN CHRISTIAN NAMES

ENGLISH	BULGARIAN[1]	CZECH	DANISH	DUTCH	FRENCH	GERMAN
Adelaide	Adelaida	Adleta	Adelaide, *or* Adelheid	Adela, *or* Adelheid	Adélaïde	Adelheid
Albert	Albert	Albert, *or* Albrecht	Albert, *or* Albrekt	Albert	Albert	Albrecht, *or* Albert
Alexander	Aleksandŭr	Alexandr	Aleksander	Alexander	Alexandre	Alexander
Elizabeth	Elizabet(a)	Alžběta	Elisabet	Elisabeth	Élisabeth	Elisabeth
Andrew	Andrei	Ondřei	Anders, *or* Andreas	Andreas, *or* Andries	André	Andreas
Antony	Anton	Anton	Anton	Anto(o)n, *or* Ant(h)onie	Antoine	Anton
Ernest	Ern(e)st	Arnošt	Ernst	Ernest	Ernest	Ernst
Baldwin	Baldwin	Balduin	Balduin	Boudewijn	Baudouin	Balduin
Barnabas	Varnava	Barnabaš	Barnabas	Barnabas	Barnabe	Barnabas
Bartholomew	Vartolomei	Bartoloměj	Bartholomæus	Bartholomeüs	Barthélemy, *or* Bartholomée	Bartholomäus
Basil	Vasil	Basilios, *or* Vasil	Basilius	Basilius	Basile	Basilius
Frederick	Frederik	Bedřich	Frederik	Frederik	Frédéric, *or* Ferry	Friedrich
Bernard	Bernard	Bernard	Bernhard, *or* Bernt	Bernhard	Bernard	Bernhard
Carloman	Karloman	Karlman	Karloman	Karloman	Carloman	Karlmann
Casimir	Kazimir	Kazimír	Kasimir	Kasimir	Casimir	Kasimir
Catherine	Ekaterina	Kateřina	Katarina	Catharina	Catherine	Katarina
Charles	Karl	Karel	Carl	Karel	Charles	Karl
Conrad	Konrad	Konrad	Konrad	Coenraad	Conrad	Konrad
Constance	Konstantsa	Konstancie	Constance	Konstanz	Constance	Konstanze

For notes see page lvi

ENGLISH	BULGARIAN[1]	CZECH	DANISH	DUTCH	FRENCH	GERMAN
Constantine	Konstantin	Konstantin	Constantin *or* Konstantin	Constantijn	Constantin	Konstantin
Denis	Dionisi	Diviš, *or* Dionisie	Dionysius, *or* Dines	Dionysius	Denis	Dionysius
Theoderic[2]	Teoderikh	Theoderich	Didrik	Diederik	Théodoric	Theoderich
Theodoric[2]	Teodorikh	Dětřich		Dirk	Thierry	Dietrich
Edward	Eduard, *or* Edvard	Edvard	Edvard	Eduard	Édouard	Eduard
Catherine	Ekaterina	Kateřina	Katarina	Catharina	Catherine	Katarina
Helen	Elena	Helena	Helene	Helena	Hélène	Helena, *or* Helene
Elizabeth	Elizabet(a)	Alžběta	Elisabet	Elisabeth	Élisabeth	Elisabeth
Eric	Erik	Erich	Erik	Erik	Éric	Erich
Ernest	Ern(e)st	Arnošt	Ernst	Ernest	Ernest	Ernst
Stephen	Stefan	Štěpán	Stefan(us), *or* Steffen	Stefanus	Étienne	Stefan
Everard		Eberhard	Ever(har)d	Eberhard	Éverard	Eberhard
Ferdinand	Ferdinand	Ferdinand	Ferdinand	Ferdinand	Fer(di)nand	Ferdinand
Philip	Filip	Filip	Filip, *or* Philip(p)	Filips	Philippe	Philipp
Francis	Frants(isk)	František	Frans	Frans	François	Franz
Frederick	Frederik	Bedřich	Frederik	Frederik	Frédéric, *or* Ferry	Friedrich
Fulke		Fulko	Folke	Fulco	Foulques	Fulco
Theodore	T(e)odor	Fedor	Teodor	Theodor	Théodore	T(h)eodor
Gabriel	Gavrila	Gabriel	Gabriel	Gabriel	Gabriel	Gabriel
Walter	Valter	Valter	Valter	Walter	Gauthier	Walther
Geoffrey[3]			Geoffroi	Geoffroi	Geoffroi	
George	Georgi	Jiří	Georg	Joris	Georges	Georg
Gerard		Gerhard	Gerhard	Gerhard, *or* Gerrit	Gérard	Gerhard
Godfrey[4]	Gotfrid	Gottfried[5]	Godfred	Godfried	Godefroi	Gottfried

For notes see page lvi

ENGLISH	BULGARIAN[1]	CZECH	DANISH	DUTCH	FRENCH	GERMAN
Gregory	Grigori	Řehoř	Gregers, *or* Gregor(ius)	Gregorius	Grégoire	Gregor
Guy	Gi	Vít	Guido	Gwij(de)	Gui	Guido
William	Vilkhelm	Vilém	Vilh(j)elm	Willem	Guillaume	Wilhelm
John	Ioan, *or* Ivan	Jan	Hans	J(oh)an	Jean	Hans, *or* Jo(h)annes
Harold		Harald, *or* Harold	Harald	Harald, *or* Harold	Harald, *or* Harold	Harald, *or* Harold
Helen(a)	Elena	Helena	Helene	Helena	Hélène	Helena, *or* Helene
Henry	Khenrik	Jindřich	Henrik	Hendrik	Henri	Heinrich
Hugh, *or* Hugo	Khugo	Hugo	Hugo	Hugo	Hugues	Hugo
Jane, *or* Joan	Ivana	Johanna	Johanna	Johanna	Jeanne	Johanna
Isabel	Izabela	Isabella	Isabella	Isabella	Isabelle, *or* Isabeau	Isabella
James	Yakov	Jakub	Jakob	Jacob	Jacques	Jakob
Henry	Khenrik	Jindřich	Henrik	Hendrik	Henri	Heinrich
George	Georgi	Jiří	Georg	Joris	Georges	Georg
Jane, *or* Joan	Ivana	Johanna	Johanna	Johanna	Jeanne	Johanna
Jodocus		Jošt	Jost, *or* Just	Joost	Josse	Jobst, *or* Jodokus
John	Ioan, *or* Ivan	Jan	Hans	J(oh)an	Jean	Johann(es), *or* Hans
Charles	Karl	Karel	Karl	Karel	Charles	Karl
Carloman	Karloman	Karlman	Karloman	Karloman	Carloman	Karlmann
Catherine	Ekaterina	Kateřina	Katarina	Catharina	Catherine	Katarina
Casimir	Kazimir	Kazimír	Kasimir	Kasimir	Casimir	Kasimir
Nicholas	Nikola	Mikulaš	Klaus, *or* Niels	Nicolaas	Nicolas	Nikolaus
Conrad	Konrad	Konrad	Konrad	Konrad	Conrad	Konrad

For notes see page lvi

ENGLISH	BULGARIAN[1]	CZECH	DANISH	DUTCH	FRENCH	GERMAN
Constantine	Konstantin	Konstantin	Konstantin, *or* Constantin	Constantijn	Constantin	Konstantin
Constance	Konstantsa	Konstancie	Constance	Konstanz	Constance	Konstanze
Ladislas	Vladislav	Ladislav, *or* Vladislav	Ladislaus	Ladislaus, *or* Vladislav	Ladislas	Ladislaus
Leo	Lev	Lev	Leo	Leo	Léon	Leo(n)
Lothair	Lotar	Lothar	Lothar	Lotharius	Lothaire	Lothar
Louis, *or* Lewis	Lyudovik	Ludvík	Ludvig	Lodewijk	Louis	Ludwig
Matthew, *or* Matthias	Matei	Matěj	Matthæus, *or* Matthias	Mattaeus	Matthieu	Matthäus, *or* Matthias
Michael	Mikhail	Michal	Mikael, *or* Mikkel	Mich(a)el	Michel	Michael
Nicholas	Nikola	Mikulaš	Niels, *or* Klaus	Nicolaas	Nicolas	Nikolaus
Andrew	Andrei	Ondřei	Anders, *or* Andreas	Andreas, *or* Andries	André	Andreas
Paul	Pavel	Pavel	Paul(us), *or* Poul	Paulus	Paul	Paul(us)
Peter	Petŭr	Petr	Peter	Pieter	Pierre	Peter
Philip	Filip	Filip	Filip	Philip(p), *or* Filips	Philippe	Philipp
Pippin	Pipin	Pippin	Pi(p)pin	Pippijn	Pépin	Pippin
Ralph[6]	Raul	(Rudolf)	Ra(du)lf		Raoul	Ralf
Raymond		Raimund	Raimund	Raimond, *or* Raymundus	Raimond	Raimund
Reginald, *or* Ronald			Regnvald	Reinald	Renaud	Reginald
Richard	Richard	Richard	Rikard	Richard	Richard	Richard
Roger		Roger	Roger	Rutger	Roger	Roger
Rudolph	Rudolf	Rudolf	Rolf	Rudolf	Rodolphe	Rudolf

For notes see page lvi

ENGLISH	BULGARIAN[1]	CZECH	DANISH	DUTCH	FRENCH	GERMAN
Gregory	Grigori	Řehoř	Gregers, *or* Gregor(ius)	Gregorius	Grégoire	Gregor
Siegmund, *or* Sigismund	Sigizmund	Sigmund, *or* Zigmunt	Sigmund	Sigismund	Sigismond	Sigismund
Stephen	Stefan	Štěpán	Stefan(us), *or* Steffen	Stefanus	Étienne	Stefan
Theoderic[2]	Teoderikh	Dětřich	Didrik	Diederik	Théodoric	Theoderich
Theodoric[2]	Teodorikh	Theodorich		Dirk	Thierry	Theodorich, *or* Dietrich
Theodore	T(e)odor	Fedor	Teodor	Theodor	Théodore	T(h)eodor
Thomas	Toma	Tomáš	Thomas	Thomas	Thomas	Thomas
Barnabas	Varnava	Barnabaš	Barnabas	Barnabas	Barnabe	Barnabas
Bartholomew	Vartolomei	Bartoloměj	Bartholomæus	Bartholomeüs	Barthélemy, *or* Bartholomée	Bartholomäus
Basil	Vasil	Vasil, *or* Basilios	Basilius	Basilius	Basile	Basilius
Guy	Gi	Vít	Guido	Gwij(de)	Gui	Guido
Vladimir	Vladimer	Vladimír	Vladimir	Vladimir	Vladimir	Wladimir
Ladislas	Vladislav	Vladislav, *or* Ladislav		Vladislav, *or* Ladislaus	Ladislas	Ladislaus
Walter	Valter	Valter	Valter	Walter	Gauthier	Walther
Wenceslas	Vatslav	Václav	Wenzel, *or* Wenzeslaus	Wenceslaus	Venceslas	Wenzel
William	Vilkhelm	Vilém	Vilh(j)elm	Willem	Guillaume	Wilhelm
James	Yakov	Jakub	Jakob	Jacob	Jacques	Jakob
George	Georgi	Jiří	Georg	Joris	Georges	Georg
Siegmund, *or* Sigismund	Sigizmund	Zigmunt, *or* Sigmund	Sigmund	Sigismund	Sigismond	Siegmund, *or* Sigismund

For notes see page lvi

ENGLISH	HUNGARIAN	ITALIAN	LATIN	NORWEGIAN	POLISH	PORTUGUESE
Adelaide	Adelhaid	Adelaide	Adelaida	Adelheid	Adelajda	Adelaide
Albert	Albert	Alberto	Albertus	Albert, *or* Albrecht	Olbracht	Alberto
Alexander	Sándor	Alessandro	Alexander	Alexander	Aleksander	Alexandre
Andrew	András	Andrea	Andreas	Andreas, *or* Anders	Andrzej, *or* Jędrzej	André
Antony	Antal	Antonio	Antonius	Anton	Anton(i)	António
Harold	Harald	Aroldo	Haraldus, *or* Haroldus	Harald	Harald, *or* Harold	Haroldo
Henry	Henrik	Arrigo, *or* Enrico	Henricus	Henrik	Henryk	Enrico
Baldwin	Balduin	Balduino	Balduinus	Balduin	Baldwin	Balduino
Barnabas	Barnabás	Bernabò	Barnaba	Barnabas	Barnaba	Barnabé
Bartholomew	Bertalan	Bartolom(m)eo	Bartholomaeus	Bartlomeus	Bartłomiej	Bartolomeu
Basil	Basilius	Basilio	Basilius	Basilius	Wasily	Basílio
Bernard	Bernát	Bernardo	Bernardus	Bernhard	Bernard	Bernardo
Carloman	Karlman	Carlomanno	Carlomannus	Karloman	Karloman	Carlomano
Casimir	Kázmér	Casimiro	Casimirus	Kasimir	Kazimierz	Casimiro
Catherine	Katalina	Caterina	Catharina	Katarina	Katarzyna	Catarina
Charles	Károly	Carlo	Carolus	Karl	Karel	Carlos
Conrad	Konrád	Corrado	Conradus	Konrad	Konrad	Conrado
Constance	Konstancia	Costanza	Constantia	Konstanse	Konstancja	Constança
Constantine	Konstantin	Costantino	Constantinus	Konstantin	Konstantyn	Constantino
Denis	Dénes	Dionisio	Dionysius	Dionysius	Dionizy	Dinis
Theoderic[2]	Theoderich	Teoderico	Theodericus	Didrik	Dytryk	Teodorico
Theodoric[2]	Theodorik					
Edward	Ede	Eduardo	Eduardus, *or* Edwardus	Edvard	Edward	Eduardo, *or* Duarte
Helen	Ilona	Elena	Helena	Helene	Helena	Helena

For notes see page lvi

ENGLISH	HUNGARIAN	ITALIAN	LATIN	NORWEGIAN	POLISH	PORTUGUESE
Elizabeth	Erzsébet	Elisabetta	Elizabeth(a)	Elisabet	Elżbieta[7]	Isabel
Henry	Henrik	Enrico, *or* Arrigo	Henricus	Henrik	Henryk	Enrico
Eric	Erik	Errico	Ericus	Erik	Eryk	Érico
Ernest	Ernő	Ernesto	Ernestus	Ernst	Ernest	Ernesto
Stephen	István	Stefano	Stephanus	Steffen	Szczepan	Estevão
Everard	Eberhard	Everardo	Eberhardus, *or* Everardus	Eberhard	Eberhard	Everardo
Ferdinand	Ferdinánd, *or* Nándor	Ferdinando	Ferdinandus	Ferdinand	Ferdynand	Fernando
Philip	Fülöp	Filippo	Philippus	Filip	Filip	Filipe
Francis	Ferenc	Francesco	Franciscus	Frans	Franciszek	Francisco
Frederick	Frigyes	Federico, *or* Federigo	Fridericus	Frederik	Fryderyk	Frederico
Fulke	Folkus	Folco	Fulco			
Gabriel	Gábor	Gabriele	Gabriel	Gabriel	Gabriel	Gabriel
Geoffrey[3]			Galfridus, *or* Gaufridus			
George	György	Giorgio	Georgius	Georg	Jerzy	Jorge
Gerard	Gerhard	Gerardo	Gerardus	Gerhard	Gerard	Gerardo
James	Jakab	Giacomo	Jacobus	Jakob	Jakub	Jacó
John	János	Gi(ov)an(ni)	Jo(h)annes	Hans, Jens, *or* Johan(nes)	Jan	João
Jane, *or* Joan	Johanna	Giovanna	Jo(h)anna	Johanne	Joanna	Joana
Godfrey[4]	Gottfried	Goffredo	Godefridus	Godfred, *or* Gotfred	Godfryd	Godofredo
Gregory	Gergely	Gregorio	Gregorius	Gregor	Grzegorz	Gregório
Walter	Valter	Gualtiero	G(u)alterus		Walt(h)er	Gualtiero, *or* Gutierre
Guy	Guido	Guido	Guido	Guido		Guido
William	Vilmos	Guglielmo	Gu(i)lielmus	Vilhelm	Wilhelm	Guilherme

For notes see page lvi

ENGLISH	HUNGARIAN	ITALIAN	LATIN	NORWEGIAN	POLISH	PORTUGUESE
John	János	Gi(ov)an(ni)	Jo(h)annes	Hans, Jens, *or* Johan(nes)	Jan	João
Harold	Harald	Aroldo	Haraldus, *or* Haroldus	Harald	Harald, *or* Harold	Haroldo
Helen(a)	Ilona	Elena	Helena	Helene	Helena	Helena
Henry	Henrik	Enrico, *or* Arrigo	Henricus	Henrik	Henryk	Enrico
Hugh, *or* Hugo	Hugó	Ugo	Hugo	Hugo	Hugo	Hugo
Helen(a)	Ilona	Elena	Helena	Helene	Helena	Helena
Stephen	István	Stefano	Stephanus	Steffen	Szczepan	Estevão
Isabel	Izabella	Isabella	Isabella	Isabella	Izabela, *or* Elżbieta	Isabel[8]
James	Jakab	Giacomo	Jacobus	Jakob	Jakub	Jacó
George	György	Giorgio	Georgius	Georg	Jerzy	Jorge
Andrew	András	Andrea	Andreas	Andreas, *or* Anders	Jędrzej, *or* Andrzej	André
Jane, *or* Joan	Johanna	Giovanna	Jo(h)anna	Johanne	Joanna	Joana
Jodocus	Jodok		Jodocus, *or* Judocus		Jodok, *or* Jost	
John	János	Gi(ov)an(ni)	Jo(h)annes	Jens, Hans *or* Johan(nes)	Jan	João
Charles	Károly	Carlo	Carolus	Karl	Karel	Carlos
Carloman	Karlman	Carlomanno	Carlomannus	Karloman	Karloman	Carlomano
Casimir	Kázmér	Casimiro	Casimirus	Kasimir	Kazimierz	Casimiro
Catherine	Katalina	Caterina	Catharina	Katarina	Katarzyna	Catarina
Nicholas	Miklos	Niccolò	Nicolaus	Klaus, *or* Nils	Mikołaj	Nikolau
Conrad	Konrád	Corrado	Conradus	Konrad	Konrad	Conrado
Constance	Konstancia	Constanza	Constantia	Konstanse	Konstancja	Constança
Constantine	Konstantin	Costantino	Constantinus	Konstantin	Konstantyn	Constantino
Ladislas	László, *or* Ulászló	Ladislao	Ladislaus	Ladislaus	Władysław	Ladislau, *or* Vladislau

For notes see page lvi

ENGLISH	HUNGARIAN	ITALIAN	LATIN	NORWEGIAN	POLISH	PORTUGUESE
Leo	Leo	Leone	Leo	Leo	Lew, *or* Leon	Leão
Lothair	Lothár	Lotario	Lotharius	Lothar	Lotar	Lotário
Louis, *or* Lewis	Lajos	Lodovivo, Luigi *or* Ludovico	Ludovicus	Ludvig	Ludwik	Luís
Matthew, *or* Mathias	Mátyás	Matteo	Matthaeus, *or* Matthias	Mattias	Maciej	Mateus, *or* Matias
Michael	Mihály	Michele	Michael	Mikkel	Michał	Miguel
Nicholas	Miklos	Niccolò	Nicolaus	Nils, *or* Klaus	Mikołaj	Nicolau
Ferdinand	Nándor, *or* Ferdinánd	Ferdinando	Ferdinandus	Ferdinand	Ferdynand	Fernando
Albert	Albert	Alberto	Albertus	Albert, *or* Albrecht	Olbracht	Alberto
Paul	Pál	Paolo	Paulus	Pål, *or* Paul(us)	Paweł	Paulo
Peter	Péter	Pie(t)ro	Petrus	Pe(te)r	Piotr	Pedro
Philip	Fülöp	Filippo	Philippus	Filip	Filip	Filipe
Pippin	Pipin	Pepino	Pippinus	Pip(p)in	Pipin	Pepino
Ralph[6]	Raoul, (Rudolf)	(Rodolfo)	Radulphus			Raul
Raymond	Raimund	Raimondo	Raimundus	Raimond	Rajmund	Raimundo
Reginald, *or* Ronald	Rainald	Rinaldo	Rainaldus, *or* Reginaldus	Ragnvald	Rainald	Re(g)inaldo
Richard	Rikárd	Riccardo	Ricardus	Richard, *or* Rikard	Ryszart	Ricardo
Roger	Roger	Ruggiero	Rogerius	Roger	Roger	Rogério
Rudolph	Rudolf	Rodolfo	Rudolphus	Rodulv	Rudolf	Rodolfo
Alexander	Sándor	Alessandro	Alexander	Alexander	Alexander	Alexandre
Siegmund, *or* Sigismund	Zsigmond	Sigismundo	Sigismundus	Sigmund	Sigismund, *or* Zygmunt	Segismundo
Stephen	István	Stefano	Stephanus	Steffen	Szczepan	Estevão
Theoderic[2]	Theoderich	Teoderico	Theodericus	Didrik	Dytryk	Teodorico
Theodoric[2]	Theodorik	Teodorico	Theodoricus			
Theodore	Tivadar	Teodoro	Theodorus	Theodor	Teodor	Teodoro

For notes see page lvi

ENGLISH	HUNGARIAN	ITALIAN	LATIN	NORWEGIAN	POLISH	PORTUGUESE
Thomas	Tamás	Tommaso	Thomas	Thomas	Tomasz	Tomé
Hugh, *or* Hugo	Hugó	Ugo	Hugo	Hugo	Hugo	Hugo
Ladislas	Ulászló, *or* László	Ladislao	Ladislaus	Ladislaus	Władysław	Ladislau, *or* Vladislau
Wenceslas	Vencel	Venceslao	Venceslaus	Wenzel	Wacław	Venceslau, *or* Wenceslao
Basil	Basilius	Basilio	Basilius	Basilius	Wasily	Basílio
Ladislas	László, *or* Ulászló	Ladislao	Ladislaus	Ladislaus	Władysław	Vladislau, *or* Ladislau
Vladimir	Vladimir	Vladimiro	Ladimirus, Wladimirus, *or* Wlodomerus	Vladimir	Włodzimierz	Vladimiro
Walter	Valter	Gualtiero	G(u)alterius		Walt(h)er	Gualterio, *or* Gutierre
Wenceslas	Vencel	Venceslao	Venceslaus	Wenzel	Wacław	Wenceslao, *or* Venceslao
William	Vilmos	Guglielmo	Gu(i)lielmus	Vilhelm	Wilhelm	Guilherme
Siegmund, *or* Sigismund	Zsigmond	Sigismundo	Sigismundus	Sigmund	Zygmunt, *or* Sigismund	Segismundo

For notes see page lvi

ENGLISH	ROMANIAN	RUSSIAN[1]	SERBO-CROATIAN	SPANISH	SWEDISH
Adelaide	Adelaida	Adelaida	Adelaida	Adelaida	Adelheid
Albert	Albert	Al'bert	Albert	Alberto	Albrekt
Alexander	Alexandru	Aleksandr	Aleksandar	Alejandro	Alexander
Andrew	Andrei	Andrei	Andrija	Andrés	Andreas
Antony	Anton(iu)	Anton(y)	Anton(ije), *or* Antun	Antonio	Anton
Baldwin	Baldovin	Balduin		Balduino	Balduin
Barnabas	Barnabas	Varnava	Varnava	Bernabé	Barnabas
Bartholomew	Bartolomeu	Varfolomei	Vartolomej	Bartolomé	Bartolomeus
Basil	Vasile	Vasily	Vasilije	Basilio	Basilius
Bernard	Bernard	Bern(g)ard	Bernard	Bernardo	Bernhard
Carloman	Carlmann	Karloman	Karlman	Carlomán	Karlman
Casimir	Cazimir	Kazimir	Kazimir	Casimiro	Kasimir
Catherine	Caterina	Ekaterina	Katarina	Catalina	Katarina
Charles	Carol	Karl	Karlo	Carlos	Karl
Conrad	Conrad	Konrad	Konrad	Conrado	Konrad
Constance	Constanţa	Konstantsiya	Konstantia	Constancia	Konstantia
Constantine	Constantin	Konstantin	Konstantin	Constantino	Konstantin
Denis	Dionisie	Denis, *or* Dionisy	Dionizije	Dionisio	Dionysius
George	Gheorghe	Georgy, *or* Yury	Đurađ, *or* Juraj	Jorge	Georg
Theoderic[2]	Teodoric	Teodorikh	Teoderik	Teodorico	Didrik
Edward	Eduard	Éduard	Edvard	Eduardo	Edvard
Catherine	Caterina	Ekaterina	Katarina	Catalina	Katarina
Helen	Elena	Elena	Jelena	Elena	Helena
Elizabeth	Elisabeta	Elizaveta	Jelisav(et)a	Isabel	Elisabet
Henry	Henric	Genrikh	Henrik	Enrique	Henrik

For notes see page lvi

ENGLISH	ROMANIAN	RUSSIAN[1]	SERBO-CROATIAN	SPANISH	SWEDISH
Eric	Erich	Érik	Erih	Erico	Erik
Ernest	Ernest	Ern(e)st	Ernest	Ernesto	Ernst
Stephen	Ştefan	Stepan	Stefan, Stevan, *or* St(j)epan	Estéban	Stefan
Everard	Eberhard	Ébergard	Eberhard	Everardo	
Ferdinand	Ferdinand	Ferdinand	Ferdinand	Fernando, *or* Hernán	Ferdinand
Philip	Filip	Filipp	Filip	Felipe	Filip
Thomas	Toma	Foma	Toma(š)	Tomás	Tomas
Francis	Francisc	Frants	Franjo	Francisco	Frans
Frederick	Frederic	Fridrikh	Fridrik	Federigo	Fred(e)rik
Fulke		Ful'k		Foulque	Folke
Theodore	Teodor, *or* Tudor	Fyodor, *or* Feodor	Teodor	Teodoro	Teodor
Gabriel	Gavril	Gavriil	Gavrilo	Gabriel	Gabriel
Geoffrey[3]				Geofredo	Galfred
Henry	Henric	Genrikh	Henrik	Enrique	Henrik
George	Gheorghe	Georgy, *or* Yury	Đurađ, *or* Juraj	Jorge	Georg
Gerard		Gergard	Gerhard	Gerardo	Gerhard
Godfrey[4]	Gottfried	Gotfrid	Gotfrid	Godofredo	Godfred
Gregory	Grigore	Grigory	Grgur	Gregorio	Gregorius
Walter		Val'ter	Valter	Gualterio	
Hugh, *or* Hugo	Hugo	Gugo	Hugo	Hugo	Hugo
Guy	Guido	Gvido	Guido	Guido	Guido
William	Wilhelm	Vil'gel'm	Viljem	Guillermo	Vilhelm
Harold	Harald	Garal'd, *or* Garol'd	Harald, *or* Harold	Haraldo	Harald
Helen(a)	Elena	Elena	Jelena	Elena	Helena
Henry	Henric	Genrikh	Henrik	Enrique	Henrik

For notes see page lvi

ENGLISH	ROMANIAN	RUSSIAN[1]	SERBO-CROATIAN	SPANISH	SWEDISH
Ferdinand	Ferdinand	Ferdinand	Ferdinand	Hernán, *or* Fernando	Ferdinand
Hugh, *or* Hugo	Hugo	Gugo	Hugo	Hugo	Hugo
Isabel	Izabela	Izabella	Izabel	Isabel[8]	Isabella
John	Io(a)n	Ivan, *or* Ioann	Ivan, *or* Jovan	Juan	Johan(nes)
James	Iacob	Yakov	Jakov	Jaime, *or* Jacobo	Jakob
Helen(a)	Elena	Elena	Jelena	Elena	Helena
Elizabeth	Elisabeta	Elizaveta	Jelisav(et)a	Isabel	Elisabet
George	Gheorghe	Georgy, *or* Yury	Juraj, *or* Đurađ	Jorge	Georg
Jane, *or* Joan	Ioana	Ivanna	Jovanka	Juana	Johanna
Jodocus		Iodok, *or* Io(b)st		Jodoco	Jobst
John	Io(a)n	Ivan, *or* Ioann	Jovan, *or* Ivan	Juan	Johan(nes)
Charles	Carol	Karl	Karlo	Carlos	Karl
Carloman	Carlmann	Karloman	Karlman	Carlomán	Karlman
Catherine	Caterina	Ekaterina	Katarina	Catalina	Katarina
Casimir	Cazimir	Kazimir	Kazimir	Casimiro	Kasimir
Conrad	Conrad	Konrad	Konrad	Conrado	Konrad
Constantine	Constantin	Konstantin	Konstantin	Constantino	Konstantin
Constance	Constanţa	Konstantsiya	Konstantia	Constancia	Konstantia
Ladislas	Ladislau	Vladislav	Ladislav, *or* Vladislav	Ladislao	Vladislav
Leo	Leon	Lev	Leon, *or* Lav	León	Leo
Lothair	Lothar	Lotar'	Lotar	Lotario	Lothar
Louis, *or* Lewis	Ludovic	Lyudvig	Ljudevit, *or* Ludovik	Luis	Ludwig

For notes see page lvi

ENGLISH	ROMANIAN	RUSSIAN[1]	SERBO-CROATIAN	SPANISH	SWEDISH
Matthew, *or* Matthais	Matei	Matvei	Matej, *or* Matija	Mateo	Matteus, *or* Mattias
Michael	Mihai(l)	Mikhail	Mihajlo	Miguel	Mikael
Nicholas	Nicolae	Nikolai	Nikola	Nicolás	Nils
Paul	Paul, *or* Pavel	Pavel	Pavao, *or* Pavle	Pablo	Paul(us)
Peter	Petre, *or* Petru	Pyotr	Petar	Pedro	Per
Philip	Filip	Filipp	Filip	Felipe	Filip
Pippin	Pepin	Pipin	Pipin	Pipino	Pippin
Ralph[6]		Radul'f	Ralf	(Rodolfo)	
Raymond		Raimond	Rajmund	Ramón	Raimund(us)
Reginald, *or* Ronald		Renal'd, *or* Ronal'd	Rainald	Re(g)inaldo	Ragnvald
Richard	Richard	Rikhard	Rikard	Ricardo	Richard, *or* Ri(c)kard
Roger	Roger	Rozher	Ruđer	Rogerio	Roger
Rudolph	Rudolf	Rudol'f	Rudolf	Rodolfo	Rudolf
Siegmund, *or* Sigismund	Sigismund	Zigmund	Sig(is)mund, *or* Zigmund	Segismundo	Sig(is)mund
Stephen	Ştefan	Stepan	Stefan, Stevan, *or* St(j)epan	Estéban	Stefan
Theoderic[2]	Teodoric	Teodorikh	Teoderik	Teodorico	Didrik
Theodoric[2]			Teodorik		Teoderik
Theodore	Teodor, *or* Tudor	Fyodor, *or* Feodor	Teodor	Teodoro	Teodor
Thomas	Toma	Foma	Toma(š)	Tomás	Tomas
Wenceslas	Vaclav, *or* Venceslav	Vyacheslav	Vaclav, *or* Većeslav	Wenceslao	Wenzel
Bartholomew	Bartolomeu	Varfolomei	Vartolomej	Bartolomé	Bartolomeus

For notes see page lvi

ENGLISH	ROMANIAN	RUSSIAN[1]	SERBO-CROATIAN	SPANISH	SWEDISH
Barnabas	Barnabas	Varnava	Varnava	Bernabé	Barnabas
Basil	Vasile	Vasily	Vasilije	Basilio	Basilius
Vladimir	Vladimir	Vladimir	Vladimir	Vladimiro	Vladimir
Ladislas	Ladislau	Vladislav	Vladislav	Ladislao	Vladislav
Walter		Val'ter	Valter	Gualterio	
Wenceslas	Vaclav, *or* Venceslav	Vyacheslav	Vaclav, *or* Većeslav	Wenceslao	Wenzel
William	Wilhelm	Vil'gelm	Viljem	Guillermo	Vilhelm
James	Iacob	Yakov	Jakov	Jaime, *or* Jacobo	Jakob
George	Gheorghe	Yury, *or* Georgy	Đurađ, *or* Juraj	Jorge	Georg
Siegmund, *or* Sigismund	Sigismund	Zigmund	Zigmund, *or* Sig(is)mund	Segismundo	Sig(is)mund

Notes to Table 1

1 Transliterated according to British Standard 2979 : 1958 except that -ii is replaced by -y.

2 The forms Theoderic and Theodoric and their equivalents in other languages are interchangeable.

3 In Czech, German, Hungarian, Italian, Polish, Portuguese and Russian, *Geoffrey* is not recognized as a separate name and is translated in the same way as *Godfrey*. No evidence could be found of usage in Bulgarian, Norwegian, Romanian and Serbo-Croatian.

4 See also note 3.

5 Although *Bohumír* is the Czech equivalent of English *Godfrey* it does not seem to be used to translate foreign names.

6 The forms in parentheses belong properly to the name *Rudolph*.

7 Sometimes used also for English *Isabel* (and its equivalents in other languages).
8 Also represents English *Elizabeth* (and its equivalents in other languages).

Other names

Adalbert: corresponds in form to the English *Æthelberht* (or *Ethelbert*) but oes not appear to be used to represent it. The Hungarian *Béla*, the Czech *Vojtěch* and the Polish *Wojciech* are traditionally equated with *Adalbert*, but it is unlikely that they would be represented by it or similar forms today.
Amalric: similar forms in most languages but *Amaury* in French.
David: *Dafydd* (Welsh), *Da'ud* (Arabic).
Arnulf: *Arnoul* (French).
Hercules: *Ercole* (Italian). The Italian form is commonly retained.
Humphrey: most foreign forms similar, Italian *Umfredo*, corresponds to the medieval French *Onfroi* (*Humfroi*, *Unfroi*), but the French is usually retained.
Lionel: *Leo-* in other languages.
Odo: the French *Eudes* is sometimes so rendered, but is often left unaltered or appears as *Eudo*.

TABLE 2 ARMENIAN, FINNISH AND GEORGIAN

ENGLISH	ARMENIAN	FINNISH	GEORGIAN
Alexander			Aleksandre
Charles		Kaarle	
David			Davit'
Eric		Eerik	
Philip	Filip		
George			Giorgi
Gregory	Grigor		
Henry		Heikki	
Isaac	Sahak		
Isabel	Zabēl		
John	Hovhannes	Juho	Ioane
Charles		Kaarle	
Isaac	Sahak		
Magnus		Maunu	
Theodore	Toros		
Isabel	Zabēl		

TABLE 3 BYZANTINE AND EASTERN ROMAN EMPERORS

The commoner names, which are also those most susceptible to marked variation in different languages, are given in Table 1. Except for the omission of initial H- in some languages, the remaining names differ only in the final syllable, except in Russian. The following Russian forms may cause difficulty.

ENGLISH	RUSSIAN
Alexius	Aleksei
Basiliscus	Vasilisk
Heraclonas	Irakleon
Heraclius	Irakly
Jovian	Iovian
Julian	Yulian
Stauracius	Stavraky
Theo-	Feo-
Zeno	Zinon

TABLE 4 POPES

A number of papal names are borne by other rulers and appear in Table 1. Most of the rest have the same form in English and Latin and vary only slightly in other languages, e.g. *Anacletus*, German *Anaklet*, though an initial H- may be absent in other languages, e.g. *Hippolytus*, Italian *Ippolito*. Those that are different in English and Latin are listed below.

ENGLISH	LATIN	ITALIAN
Adrian	Hadrianus	Adriano
Benedict*	Benedictus	Benedetto
Boniface	Bonifatius	Bonifacio
Celestine†	Coelestinus	Celestino
Christopher	Christophorus	Cristoforo
Clement‡	Clemens	Clemente
Eutychian	Eutychianus	Eutichiano
Fabian	Fabianus	Fabiano
Hilary	Hilarus	Ilaro
Hormisdas	Hormisda	Ormisda
Innocent	Innocentius	Innocenzo
Mark	Marcus	Marco
Martin	Martinus	Martino
Novatian	Novatianus	Novaziano
Paschal	Paschalis	Pasquale
Sabinian	Sabinianus	Sabiniano
Urban	Urbanus	Urbano
Vitalian	Vitalianus	Vitaliano
Zachary	Zacharias	Zaccaria

*French *Benoît*
†German *Coelestin* or *Cölestin*
‡German *Klemens*

TABLE 5 BIBLICAL NAMES

ENGLISH	FRENCH	GERMAN	HEBREW*	ITALIAN	LATIN	RUSSIAN
Abijah	Abiah	Abia	Ăbhīyāh	Abia	Abias	Aviya
Abijam	Abiam	Abiam	Ăbhīyām	Abiam	Abiam	Aviyam
Absalom	Absalon	Absalom	Abhshālōm	Assalonne	Absalom	Avessalom
Ahab	Achab	Ahab	Ah'abh	Acab	Achab	Akhav
Ahaz	Achaz	Ahaz, *or* Ahas	Āḥāz	Achaz	Achaz	Akhaz
Ahaziah	Ochozias, *or* Ochosias	Ahazja, *or* Ahasja	Ăḥazyāh	Achazia, *or* Ocozia	Ochozias	Okhoziya
Amaziah	Amasias	Amazja	Ămaṣyāh	Amasia	Amasias	Amasiya
Amon	Amon	Amon	Āmōn	Amon	Amon	Amon
Omri	Omri	Omri	'Omrī	Amri, *or* Omri	Amri	Amvry
Asa	Asa	Asa	Āsā	Asa	Asa	Asa
Athaliah	Athalie	Athalja	'Ăthalyāh	Atalia	Athalia	Gofoliya
Azariah	Azarias	Asaria	Ăzaryāh	Azaria	Azarias	Azariya
Baasha	Baasa, *or* Baèsa	Baesa	Ba'shā'	Baasa	Baasa	Vaasa
David	David	David	Dāwid	David	David	David
Elah	Ela	Ela	Élāh	Ela	Ela	Ila
Eliakim	Eliaqîm	Eljakim	Elyāqīm		Eliakim	Eliakim
Eshbaal	Isbaal	Eschbaal	Esh-ba'al	Isbaal	Esbaal	Eshbaal
Athaliah	Athalie	Athalja	'Ăthalyāh	Atalia	Athalia	Gofoliya
Hezekiah	Ézéchias	Hiskia	Hizqīyāh	Ezechia	Ezechias	Khizkiya
Hoshea	Osée	Hosea	Hoshé'a	Osea	Osee	Osiya
Pekah	Pékah, *or* Peqah	Pekach	Peqāh	Facea, *or* Pekah	Phacee	Fakei
Pekahiah	Peqahiah	Pekachja	Pĕqahyāh	Faceia, *or* Pekahiah	Phaceia	Fakiya
Jeroboam	Jéroboam	Jerobeam	Yŏrobh'ām	Geroboamo	Jeroboam	Ierovoam
Jehoiachin	Joiakîn, *or* Yeyoakin	Jojachin	Yĕhōyākhīn	Gioacchino	Joachin	Iekhoniya

ENGLISH	FRENCH	GERMAN	HEBREW*	ITALIAN	LATIN	RUSSIAN
Jehoiakim	Joiaqîm	Jojakim	Yĕhōyāqīm	Gioachimo	Joakim	Ioakim
J(eh)oash	Joas	Joas	Y(ĕh)ō'āsh	Gioas, *or* Ioas	Joas	Ioas
Jehoshaphat	Josaphat	Josaphat	Yĕhōshāphāt	Giosafat	Josaphat	Iosafat
Josiah	Josias	Josia	Yō'shīyāh	Giosia	Josias	Iosiya
Eshbaal	Isbaal	Eschbaal	Esh-ba'al	Isbaal	Esbaal	Eshbaal
Elah	Ela	Ela	Élāh	Ela	Ela	Ila
Ishbosheth	Isboseth		Īsh-bōsheth	Isboseth	Isboseth	
Jehoahaz	Joachaz	Joahaz, *or* Joahas	Yĕhō'āḥāz	Ioachaz	Joachaz	Ioakhaz
J(eh)oash	Joas	Joas	Y(ĕh)ō'āsh	Ioas, *or* Gioas	Joas	Ioas
Jehoiachin	Joiakîn, *or* Yeyoakin	Jojachin	Yĕhōyākhīn	Gioacchino	Joachin	Iekhoniya
Jehoiakim	Joiaqîm	Jojakim	Yĕhōyāqīm	Gioachimo	Joakim	Ioakim
J(eh)oram	Joram	Joram	Y(ĕh)ōrām	Ioram	Joram	Ioram
Jehoshaphat	Josaphat	Josaphat	Yĕhōshāphāṭ	Giosafat	Josaphat	Iosafat
Jehu	Jéhu	Jehu	Yéhu	Iehu	Jehu	Iiuĭ
Jeroboam	Jéroboam	Jerobeam	Yŏrobh'ām	Geroboamo	Jeroboam	Ierovoam
Josiah	Josias	Josia	Yō'shīyāh	Giosia	Josias	Iosiya
Jotham	Jotham	Jot(h)am	Yōthām	Iotam, *or* Ioatan	Joatham	Ioafam
Hezekiah	Ézéchias	Hiskia	Hizqīyāh	Ezechia	Ezechias	Khizkiya
Manasseh	Manassé, *or* Manassès	Manasse	Mĕnaśśeh	Manasse	Manasses	Manassiya
Mattaniah	Matthania	Matthanja	Mattanyāh		Mattanias	Matfaniya
Menahem	Menahem	Menahem	Mĕnaḥém	Manahem, *or* Menahem	Manahem	Menaim
Nadab	Nadab	Nadab	Nādhābh	Nadab	Nadab	Navat
Ahaziah	Ochozias, *or* Ochosias	Ahazja, *or* Ahasja	Ăhazyāh	Ocozia, *or* Achazia	Ochozias	Okhoziya
Omri	Omri	Omri	'Omrī	Omri, *or* Amri	Amri	Amvry
Hoshea	Osée	Hosea	Hōshé'a	Osea	Osee	Osiya

ENGLISH	FRENCH	GERMAN	HEBREW*	ITALIAN	LATIN	RUSSIAN
Uzziah	Ozias, *or* Osias	Uzzia	Uzzīyāh	Ozia	Ozias	Oziya
Pekah	Pékah, *or* Peqah	Pekach	Pĕqāh	Pekah, *or* Facea	Phacee	Fakei
Pekahiah	Peqahiah	Pekachja	Pĕqahyāh	Pekahiah, *or* Faceia	Phaceia	Fakiya
Rehoboam	Roboam	Rehabeam	Rĕhabh'ām	Roboamo	Roboam	Rovoam
Zechariah	Zacharie	Sacharja	Zĕkharyāh	Zaccaria	Zacharias	Zakhariya
Saul	Saül	Saul	Shā'ul	Saul	Saul	Saul
Zedekiah	Sédécias	Zedekia	Ṣidhqīyāh	Sedecia	Sedecias	Sedekiya
Shallum	Shallum	Sallum	Ṡhallum	Sallum	Sellum	Sellum
Solomon	Salomon	Salomo	Shĕlōmōh	Salomone	Salomo	Solomon
Uzziah	Ozias, *or* Osias	Uzzia	Uzzīyāh	Ozia	Ozias	Oziya
Baasha	Baasa, *or* Baèsa	Baesa	Ba'shā'	Baasa	Baasa	Vaasa
Jehoahaz	Joachaz	Joahaz, *or* Joahas	Yĕhō'āḫāz	Ioachaz	Joachaz	Ioakhaz
J(eh)oash	Joas	Joas	Y(ĕh)ō'āsh	Ioas, *or* Gioas	Joas	Ioas
J(eh)oram	Joram	Joram	Y(ĕh)ōrām	Ioram	Joram	Ioram
Jehoshaphat	Josaphat	Josaphat	Yĕhōshāphāṭ	Giosafat	Josaphat	Iosafat
Jehoiachin	Yeyoakin, *or* Joiakîn	Jojachin	Yĕhōyākhīn	Gioacchino	Joachin	Iekhoniya
Jehoiakim	Joiaqîm	Jojakim	Yĕhōyāqīm	Gioachimo	Joakim	Ioakim
Jehu	Jéhu	Jehu	Yéhu	Iehu	Jehu	Iiuĭ
Jeroboam	Jéroboam	Jerobeam	Yŏrobh'ām	Geroboamo	Jeroboam	Ierovoam
Josiah	Josias	Josia	Yō'shīyāh	Giosia	Josias	Iosiya
Jotham	Jotham	Jot(h)am	Yōthām	Iotam, *or* Ioatan	Joatham	Ioafam
Zechariah	Zacharie	Sacharja	Zĕkharyāh	Zaccaria	Zacharias	Zakhariya
Zedekiah	Sédécias	Zedekia	Ṣidhqīyāh	Sedecia	Sedecias	Sedekiya
Zimri	Zimri		Zimrī	Zambri, *or* Zimri	Zambri	Zamvry

*Transcription based on column A of the table in *Encyclopaedia Judaica* with the following modifications: h is used in transcribing all variable letters without *dagesh* (hence ph, not f); ī, not iy, is used for *hireq yodh*, é for *ṣere*, and ă, ĕ and ŏ for *ḥaṭeph pathaḥ*, *shewa na'* (sic) and *hateph qames qatan* respectively.

'Abbadids (Banu 'Abbad)

Territory comprised part of present-day south-western Spain and southern Portugal, with the capital at Seville.

Kings

AD 1023/4	*(Abu'l-Qasim) Muhammad I (ibn Isma'il ibn Quraish) ibn 'Abbad (al-Qadi)*, great-grandson of 'Abbad
1042/3	*(Abu 'Amr) 'Abbad al-Mu'tadid (ibn Muhammad)*, son
1068/9 – 1091/2	*(Abu'l-Qasim) Muhammad II al-Mu'tamid (ibn 'Abbad)*, son (d. Aghmat 1095/6)
1091/2	Almoravid conquest

'Abbasids (Banu-l-'Abbas)

At its greatest extent, territory comprised part of present-day Iraq, Egypt, Iran, Syria, Saudi Arabia, Israel, Lebanon, North Africa, Yemen and the southern Iberian peninsula.

Caliphs

In Baghdad

6 Nov AD 749	*Abu'l-'Abbas ('Abdallah) al-Saffah (ibn Muhammad)*, descendant of al-'Abbas
9 Jun 754	*Abu Ja'far 'Abdallah al-Mansur (ibn Muhammad)*, brother
7 Oct 775	*(Abu 'Abdallah Muhammad) al-Mahdi (ibn al-Mansur)*, son
4 Aug 785	*(Abu Muhammad Musa) al-Hadi (ibn al-Mahdi)*, son
15 Sep 786	*(Abu Ja'far) Harun al-Rashid (ibn al-Mahdi)*, brother
24 Mar 809	*(Abu Musa Muhammad) al-Amin (ibn al-Rashid)*, son
26 Sep 813	*(Abu Ja'far 'Abdallah) al-Ma'mun (ibn al-Rashid)*, brother (for 1st time) in rebellion against al-Amin from Oct/Nov 810

24 Jul 817 – 13 Jun 819	*(Ibrahim) al-Mubarak (ibn al-Mahdi)*, uncle, in Baghdad
11 Aug 819	*al-Ma'mun* (for 2nd time) re-entered Baghdad
7 Aug 833	*(Abu Ishaq Muhammad) al-Mu'tasim (ibn al-Rashid)*, brother, governor of Damascus 828/9*
5 Jan 842	*(Abu Ja'far Harun) al-Wathiq (ibn al-Mu'tasim)*, son
10 Aug 847	*(Abu'l-Fadl Ja'far) al-Mutawakkil (ibn al-Mu'tasim)*, brother
11 Dec 861	*(Abu Ja'far Muhammad) al-Muntasir (ibn al-Mutawakkil)*, son; governor of Mecca 847/8 – 851/2; governor of Egypt 849/50 – 856/7, governor of Aleppo, Mosul and Rayy 849/50; governor of Medina 862/3
6 Jun 862 – 3 Jan 866	*(Abu'l-'Abbas Ahmad) al-Musta'in (ibn Muhammad ibn al-Mu'tasim)*, cousin, abdicated
25 Jan 866	*(Abu 'Abdallah Muhammad) al-Mu'tazz (ibn al-Mutawakkil)*, cousin, governor of Fars 849/50, assassinated
11 Jul 869	*(Abu Ishaq Muhammad) al-Muhtadi (ibn al-Wathiq)*, cousin, assassinated
21 Jun 870	*(Abu'l-'Abbas Ahmad) al-Mu'tamid (ibn al-Mutawakkil)*, cousin
16 Oct 892	*(Abu'l-'Abbas Ahmad) al-Mu'tadid (ibn al-Muwaffaq ibn al-Mutawakkil)*, nephew
5 Apr 902	*(Abu Muhammad 'Ali) al-Muktafi (ibn al-Mu'tadid)*, son
13 Aug 908	*(Abu'l-Fadl Ja'far) al-Muqtadir (ibn al-Mu'tadid)*, brother †
31 Oct 932	*(Abu Mansur Muhammad) al-Qahir (ibn al-Mu'tadid)*, brother (d. Oct/Nov 950) deposed
24 Apr 934 – 18 Dec 940	*(Abu'l-'Abbas Ahmad) al-Radi (ibn al-Muqtadir)*, nephew
23 Dec 940	*(Abu Ishaq Ibrahim) al-Muttaqi (ibn al-Muqtadir)*, brother (d. 967/8) deposed
12 Oct 944 – 15 Jan 946	*(Abu'l-Qasim 'Abdallah) al-Mustakfi (ibn al-Muktafi)*, cousin, deposed and put to death

*833/4	*al-'Abbas (ibn al-Ma'mun)*, proclaimed caliph in Damascus, killed in prison 847/8
	Muhammad ibn al-Qasim, pretender, defeated 834/5
†18 Dec 908	*(Abu'l 'Abbas 'Abdallah) al-Murtada (ibn al-Mu'tazz)*, for one day
28 Feb 929	*(Abu Mansur Muhammad) al-Qahir*, for two days

19 Jan 946	*(Abu'l-Qasim al-Fadl) al-Muti' (ibn al-Muqtadir)*, cousin
5 Aug 974	*(Abu'l-Fadl 'Abd al-Karim) al-Ta'i' (ibn al-Muti')*, son (d. 1002/3) deposed by Buyid amir Baha' al-Daula
1 Oct 991	*(Abu'l-'Abbas Ahmad) al-Qadir (ibn Ishaq al-Muqtadir)*, cousin
29 Nov 1031	*(Abu Ja'far 'Abdallah) al-Qa'im (ibn al-Qadir)*, son, revolt of al-Basasiri, in exile Oct/Nov 1058 – Dec 1059/Jan 1060
3 Apr 1075	*(Abu'l-Qasim 'Abdallah 'Uddat al-Din) al-Muqtadi (ibn Muhammad ibn al-Qa'im)*, grandson
4 Feb 1094	*(Abu'l-'Abbas Ahmad) al-Mustazhir (ibn al-Muqtadi)*, son
6 Aug 1118	*(Abu Mansur al-Fadl) al-Mustarshid (ibn al-Mustazhir)*, son
29 Aug 1135	*(Abu Ja'far al-Mansur) al-Rashid (ibn al-Mustarshid)*, son
18 Aug 1136	*(Abu 'Abdallah Muhammad) al-Muqtafi (ibn al-Mustazhir)*, uncle
12 Mar 1160	*(Abu'l-Muzaffar Yusuf) al-Mustanjid (ibn al-Muqtafi)*, son
20 Dec 1170	*(Abu Muhammad al-Hasan) al-Mustadi' (ibn al-Mustanjid)*, son
30 Mar 1180	*(Abu'l-'Abbas Ahmad) al-Nasir (ibn al-Mustadi')*, son
5 Oct 1225	*(Abu Nasr Muhammad) al-Zahir (ibn al-Nasir)*, son
11 Jul 1226	*(Abu Ja'far al-Mansur) al-Mustansir (ibn al-Zahir)*, son
5 Dec 1242 – 20 Feb 1258	*(Abu Ahmad 'Abdallah) al-Musta'sim (ibn al-Mustansir)*, son, put to death by the Mongol khan Hülegü
20 Feb 1258	Mongol sack of Baghdad

Figurehead Caliphs for the Mamluk Sultanate

In Cairo

13 Jun 1261	*(Abul'-Qasim Ahmad) al-Mustansir (ibn al-Zahir)*, son of al-Zahir, 'Abbasid caliph in Baghdad
22 Nov 1262	*(Abu'l-'Abbas Ahmad) al-Hakim I (ibn al-Hasan)*, descendant of al-Rashid, 'Abbasid caliph in Baghdad
Jan 1302 – Feb/Mar 1340	*(Abu Rabi'a Sulaiman) al-Mustakfi I (ibn al-Hakim)*, son
4 May 1340	*(Abu Ishaq Ibrahim) al-Wathiq I (ibn al-Mustamsik ibn al-Hakim)*, nephew

18 Jun 1340	*(Abu'l-'Abbas Ahmad) al-Hakim II (ibn al-Mustakfi)*, cousin
Jul/Aug 1352	*(Abu'l-Fath Abu-Bakr) al-Mu'tadid I (ibn al-Mustakfi)*, brother
Mar 1362	*(Abu 'Abdallah Muhammad) al-Mutawakkil I (ibn al-Mu'tadid)*, son (for 1st time) deposed
Jul 1377	*(Abu Yahya Zakaria) al-Mu'tasim (ibn al-Wathiq)*, cousin (for 1st time) deposed
Aug 1377	*al-Mutawakkil I* (for 2nd time) deposed
Sep 1383	*(Abu Hafs 'Umar) al-Wathiq II (ibn al-Wathiq)*, brother
13 Nov 1386	*al-Mu'tasim* (for 2nd time) deposed
7 May 1389	*al-Mutawakkil I* (for 3rd time)
Dec 1405/Jan 1406	*(Abu'l-Fadl 'Abbas* (or *Ya'qub)) al-Musta'in (ibn al-Mutawakkil)*, ruled as sultan under the name *al-'Adil*, son (d. 1429/30) Mamluk sultan 28 May–6 Nov 1412, deposed
9 Mar 1414	*(Abu'l-Fath Da'ud) al-Mu'tadid II (ibn al-Mutawakkil)*, brother
23 Jul 1441	*(Abu Rabi'a Sulaiman) al-Mustakfi II (ibn al-Mutawakkil)*, brother
Feb 1451	*(Abu Bakr Hamza) al-Qa'im (ibn al-Mutawakkil)*, brother (d. 1457/8) deposed
Jun/Jul 1455	*(Abu'l-Mahasim Yusuf) al-Mustanjid (ibn al-Mutawakkil)*, brother
24 Apr 1479	*(Abu'l-'Azz 'Abd al-'Aziz) al-Mutawakkil II (ibn al-Musta'in)*, nephew
Sep/Oct 1497	*(Abu Sabr Ya'qub) al-Mustamsik (ibn al-Mutawakkil)*, son (for 1st time) (d. 1520/1) deposed
1508/9	*al-Mutawakkil III (ibn al-Mustamsik)*, son (for 1st time)
1516/17	*al-Mustamsik* (for 2nd time) as representative of his son al-Mutawakkil III
1517/18	*al-Mutawakkil III* (for 2nd time) carried off to Istanbul by Ottoman sultan Selim I
1517/18	Ottoman conquest of Egypt

'Abd al-Wadids (Banu Zayyan, Zayyanids)

Territory comprised part of present-day northern Algeria and north-eastern Morocco, with the capital at Tlemcen.

Sultans

Older Branch	
AD 1235/6	*(Abu Yahya) Yaghamrasan ibn Zayyan*, son of Zayyan, Almohad vassal
Mar 1283	*(Abu Sa'id) 'Uthman (ibn Yaghamrasan)*, son
Jun/Jul 1304	*Abu Zayyan I (Muhammad ibn 'Uthman)*, son
14 Apr 1308 – 22 Jul 1318	*Abu Hammu I (Musa ibn 'Uthman)*, brother, assassinated by his son
23 Jul 1318 – May/Jun 1336	*Abu Tashufin I ('Abd al-Rahman ibn Abitlammu)*, son (d. 2 May 1337)
May/Jun 1336 – 1348	Marinid domination, 'Abd al-Wadids sent into exile
May/Jun 1336	*Abu'l-Hasan ('Ali ibn 'Uthman)*, son of Abu Sa'id 'Uthman (b. c. 1297; d. 24 May 1351) Marinid sultan
1336/7	*Abu 'Inan (Faris al-Mutawakkil ibn 'Ali)*, son, Marinid sultan
1348	*Abu Sa'id ('Uthman ibn 'Abd al-Rahman)*, son of Abu Tashufin I (d. Jun/Jul 1352)
(?)	*Abu Thabit (al-Zaim ibn 'Abid al-Rahman)*, brother
Cadet Branch	
Jan 1359	*Abu Hammu II (Musa ibn Abi Ya'qub Yusuf)*, nephew (b. 1323) in exile 1359/60, 1369/70 – 1371/2, 1383/4 – 1384/5 and 1387/8
20 May 1360	*Abu Zayyan II (Muhammad ibn 'Uthman ibn 'Abd al-Rahman)*, grandson of Abu Tashufin I, installed by Marinid sultan Abu Salim Ibrahim ibn 'Ali
20 Nov 1389 – 29 May 1393	*Abu Tashufin II ('Abd al-Rahman ibn Abi Hammu Musa)*, son of Abu Hammu II (b. Apr/May 1351)
May – Jun 1393	*Abu Thabit II (Yusuf ibn 'Abd al-Rahman)*, son, for 40 days
1393	*(Abu'l-Hajjaj) Yusuf (ibn Musa)*, uncle, for ten months
Nov/Dec 1393	*Abu Zayyan III (Muhammad ibn Musa)*, brother,

	Marinid vassal
1397/8	*Abu Muhammad 'Abdallah I (ibn Musa)*, brother
1400/1	*Abu 'Abdallah Muhammad I (al-Wathiq ibn Musa)*, brother
1411/12	*'Abd al-Rahman (ibn Muhammad)*, son, for two months
1411/12	*Sa'id ibn Musa*, uncle
Nov/Dec 1412	*(Abu Malik) 'Abd al-Wahid (ibn Musa)*, brother (for 1st time)
1423/4	*Abu 'Abdallah Muhammad II (ibn 'Abd al-Rahman)*, nephew
1427/8 – 26 Jul 1430	*'Abd al-Wahid* (for 2nd time)
1430	*(Abu'l-'Abbas) Ahmad (al-Mu'tasim ibn Musa)*, brother
1461/2	*Abu 'Abdallah Muhammad III (al-Mutawakkil ibn Muhammad ibn Yusuf)*, grandson of Abu Thabit II
1468	*Abu Tashufin III (ibn Muhammad al-Mutawakkil)*
1468	*Abu 'Abdallah Muhammad IV (al-Thabiti ibn Muhammad)*, son (d. 13 Mar 1508)
1504	*Abu 'Abdallah Muhammad V (al-Thabiti ibn Muhammad)*, son, Spanish vassal 1512/13
1517	*Abu Hammu Musa III (ibn Muhammad)*, brother, Tlemcen captured by Arudj Dec 1517/Jan 1518
1527	*Abu Muhammad 'Abdallah II (ibn Muhammad)*, brother
1540	*Abu Zayyan IV (Ahmad ibn 'Abdallah)*, son (for 1st time) driven out by the Spanish 7 Mar 1543
1543	*Abu 'Abdallah Muhammad VI (ibn 'Abdallah)*, brother
Jun/Jul 1543	*Abu Zayyan IV* (for 2nd time) Ottoman vassal
1550	*al-Hasan (ibn 'Abdallah)*, brother (d. Oran 1555/6)
1554/5	Tlemcen decisively captured by the Ottomans

Achaea

Territory in central and southern Greece.

Princes

AD 1205	*Guillaume I de Champlitte*, grandson of Count

	Hugues of Champagne; conqueror of the Morea
1209	*Geoffroi I de Villehardouin*, co-conqueror of the Morea; acknowledged the suzerainty of Venice Jun 1209 in addition to his prior allegiance to the Latin emperor of Byzantium
c. 1228	*Geoffroi II de Villehardouin*, son; granted suzerainty over the island of Euboea, the duchy of Naxos and the marquisate of Boudonitza by Emperor Baudouin II of Byzantium 1236
1246 – 1 May 1278	*Guillaume II de Villehardouin*, brother; surrendered the principality to Count Charles I of Anjou 24 May 1267 but retained the title of prince until his death
24 May 1267 / 1 May 1278 – 7 Jan 1285	*Charles I*, Count of Anjou and of Provence, King of Sicily, son of King Louis VIII of France (b. Mar 1227; d. Foggia, Italy) claimed kingdom of Jerusalem 1277, deposed in Sicily and founded separate kingdom of Naples 1282
1285	*Charles II*, the Lame, Prince of Salerno, son (b. c. 1254; d. Naples 5 May 1309) at the same time Count of Anjou and of Provence and King of Naples, imprisoned by Aragonese 1285 – 1288, restored Achaea to the Villehardouin family
16 Sep 1289	*Isabelle de Villehardouin*, widowed sister-in-law of Charles II and daughter of Guillaume II; ruled with her second husband, *Florent de Hainaut*, 1289 – 23 Jan 1297; ruled alone 1297 – 1301; ruled with her third husband, *Philippe de Savoie*, 1301 – 1307 after which Philippe relinquished Achaea for concessions in Italy
1307	*Philippe*, Prince of Taranto, son of Charles II
1313	*Mathilde de Hainaut*, daughter of Isabelle (b. Ponticos 30 Nov 1293; d. (in prison) Aversa 1331) ruled until Sep 1316 with her second husband, *Louis de Bourgogne*, brother of Duke Hugues V of Burgundy (d. Sep 1316) then alone; deposed*
Mar 1318	*Jean*, Count of Gravina, brother of King Robert the Wise of Naples; took title after marrying Mathilde; abdicated
1333	*Robert de Tarante*, nephew; titular Latin emperor of Byzantium 1346; ruled with his mother, *Catherine de Valois*, titular Latin empress of Byzantium, Nov 1338 – Jun 1341

*1315 – 1316	*Fernando* of Majorca, pretender

1364	*Marie de Bourbon*, widow; ruled with her second husband, *Hugues de Lusignan*; succession disputed with Philippe II
1370	*Philippe II*, brother-in-law of Marie; named Jacques des Baux as heir
1374	*Jeanne*, Queen (Jeanne I) of Naples, Countess of Provence, great-niece of Jean (b. 1326; d. (murdered) Lucania 22 May 1382) suzerain of Jacques des Baux, overruled his succession in Achaea and styled herself Princess of Achaea; ruled from 1376 with her husband, *Otto*, Duke of Brunswick and Lüneburg (b. 1319 or 1320; d. c. 1399) who styled himself Prince of Taranto; leased Achaea to the Hospitallers
1381 – 1383	*Jacques des Baux*, nephew of Philippe II; recognized as prince by the Navarrese Company
1383 – 1396	Period of anarchy: four or five pretenders claimed the throne
1396	*Pedro Bordo de San Superano*, Commander of the Navarrese Company in the Morea
1404 – 1432	*Centurione II Zaccaria*, usurper
1432	Conquered by the Greek despots of the Morea

Aftasids (Banu-l-Aftas)

Territory comprised part of present-day Portugal andd western Spain, with the capital at Badajoz.

Kings

AD 1022/3 – 30 Dec 1045	*(Abu Muhammad) 'Abdallah al-Mansur (ibn Muhammad ibn Maslama al-Tujibi ibn al-Aftas)*, grandson of al-Aftas
Dec 1045/Jan 1046	*al-Muzaffar (Abu Bakr Muhammad ibn 'Abdallah)*, son, vassal of Fernando I of Castile after 1055/6
1067/8 – 1094	*al-Mutawakkil (Abu Hafs 'Umar ibn Muhammad)*, son, sole ruler* after 1080/1
1094	Almoravid conquest
*1067/8	*al-Mansur (Yahya ibn Muhammad)*, brother of al-Mutawakkil (d. 1080/1) rival for the throne

Aghlabids (Banu al-Aghlab)

Territory comprised a coastal strip of present-day Tunisia, Libya and Algeria and part of Sicily, with the capital at Kairouan.

Amirs

9 Jul AD 800 – 5 Jul 812	*Ibrahim I (ibn al-Aghlab)*, son of al-Aghlab (b. c. 757/8) 'Abbasid governor of Ifriqiya, governor of Zab 795/6
Oct/Nov 812 – 25 Jun 817	*(Abu'l-'Abbas) 'Abdallah I (ibn Ibrahim)*, son
Jun/Jul 817	*(Abu Muhammad) Ziyadat-Allah I (ibn Ibrahim)*, brother (b. c. 788/9) conquered Sicily 827
11 Jun 838	*(Abu 'Iqal) al-Aghlab (ibn Ibrahim, al-Sa'di)*, brother
18 Feb 841	*(Abu'l-'Abbas) Muhammad I (ibn al-Aghlab)*, son (b. 821/2)
11 May 856	*(Abu Ibrahim) Ahmad (ibn Muhammad)*, son
28 Dec 863	*(Abu Muhammad) Ziyadat-Allah II (ibn Muhammad)*, brother
24 Dec 864	*(Abu'l-Gharaniq) Muhammad II (ibn Ahmad)*, nephew
16 Feb 875 – 18 Oct 902	*(Abu Ishaq) Ibrahim II (ibn Ahmad)*, brother (b. 844/5; d. Cosenza, Italy)
Jun/Jul – 28 Jul 903	*(Abu'l-'Abbas) 'Abdallah II (Muhammad ibn Ibrahim)*, son, assassinated
Jul/Aug 903 – 909	*(Abu Mudar) Ziyadat-Allah III (ibn Abdallah)*, son (d. Egypt 911/12(?))
909	Fatimid conquest

Ak Koyunlu (The Horde of the White Sheep)

Territory comprised part of present-day Iraq, eastern Turkey and Iran, with the capital at Tabriz after 1471/2.

Rulers

AD 1378/9	*(Baha' al-Din) Qara Yülük 'Uthman (ibn Fakhr al-Din Qutlu))*
1435/6	*(Nur al-Din) Hamza (ibn Qara Yülük)*, son, in dispute with his brother 'Ali until 1438
1444/5	*(Mu'izz al-Din) Jihangir (ibn 'Ali ibn Qara Yülük)*, nephew
1453/4	*Uzun Hasan (ibn 'Ali)*, brother, conquered Kara Koyunlu 1468/9
1478/9	*Khalil (ibn Uzun Hasan)*, son
1479/80	*Ya'qub (ibn Uzun Hasan)*, brother
1490/1	*Baisonqur (ibn Ya'qub)*, son
1491/2	*Rustam (ibn Maqsud)*, nephew of Khalil
1496/7	*Ahmad Gövde (ibn Muhammad)*, nephew of Khalil
1497/8	*Murad (ibn Ya'qub)*, son of Ya'qub (for 1st time) his rule did not extend beyond Azerbaijan
1499/1500	*Alwand (ibn Yusuf)*, nephew of Ya'qub (d. 1504) ruled initially in Azerbaijan, later ruled in Diyarbakr
1500/1	*Muhammad Mirza (ibn Yusuf)*, brother, ruled in Jibal and Fars until 1499/1500 and thereafter at Isfahan, Alwand and Kirman
1501/2 – 1508	*Murad* (for 2nd time) deposed by the Safavid shah Ismail I
1508	Safavid conquest

Akan (Bron) States

AKWAMU (TWIFO-HEMAN)

Territory comprised part of present-day southern Ghana, with the capital initially at Asaremankese and later at Ayandawaase.

Akwamuhenes

AD c. 1480	*Agyen Kokobo*, founder of the Twifo-Heman State
c. 1500	*Ofusu Kwabi*
c. 1520	*Oduro*
c. 1540	*Ado*
c. 1560	*Otumfo Asare*, founder of the Akwamu State, established capital at Asaremankese
c. 1575	*Akotia*, moved capital to Ayandawaase
c. 1585	*Ansa Saseraku I*
c. 1600	*Ansa Saseraku II*
c. 1620	*Ansa Saseraku III* (d. 1689)
c. 1640	*Abuako Dako*
c. 1660	*Afera Kuma*
c. 1680	*Manukure*
1702	*Akwano Panyini*
1726 – 1734	*Dako Booman*
1734	Conquest by the Akim peoples

ASHANTI (ASANTE)

Territory in present-day southern Ghana, with the capital at Kumasi.

Asantehenes

c. 1570	*Twum*
(?)	*Antwi*
c. 1600	*Kobia Amamfi*
c. 1630	*Oti Akenten*
c. 1660	*Obiri Yeboa*, nephew, founder of Kumasi
c. 1680	*Osei Tutu*, nephew
c. 1720	*Opoku Ware I*, great-nephew (d. 1750)
1750	*Kusi Obodum*, nephew of Osei Tutu
1764	*Osei Kwadwo*, cousin (b. c. 1735)

1777	*Osei Kwame*, great-nephew (b. c. 1764; d. 1803) deposed
1798 – 1799	*Opoku Fofie*, brother
1800 – 1823	*Osei Bonsu* (or *Osei Tutu Kwame*), brother (b. c. 1779)
1824 – 1833	*Osei Yaw Akoito*, brother (b. c. 1800)
1834	*Kwaku Dua I*, nephew (b. c. 1797)
1867	*Kofi Ka(ri)kari*, great-nephew (b. c. 1837; d. 1884) deposed
1874	*Mensa Bonsu*, brother (b. c. 1840; d. 1896) deposed
1884	*Kwaku Dua II*, nephew (b. c. 1860) for 44 days
1884 – 1888	Period of anarchy
1888 – 1900	*Kwaku Dua III* (or (*Agyemen*) *Prempeh I*), brother (for 1st time) (b. c. 1873) exiled to the Seychelles
1 Jan 1902	Formally declared British crown colony, northern provinces incorporated into the Protectorate of the Northern Territories of the Gold Coast
1924	*(Agyemen) Prempeh I* (for 2nd time) restored as figurehead sovereign
1931 – 1970	*Prempeh II*, nephew (b. 1892)
6 Mar 1957	State of Ghana formed by the amalgamation of the Gold Coast colony and the mandated territory of West Togoland
from 1970	*Opoku Ware II* (b. 1919 or 1920)

DENK(Y)ERA

Territory comprised part of present-day south-western Ghana, with the capital established at Abankeseso.

Agona Chiefs and Denkyerahenes

c. 1550	*Ayekeraa* and *Yao Awirri* (or *Yao Awere*)
c. 1570	*Anim Kokobo Boadee*
c. 1590	*Ahaha*
c. 1600	*Ahihi*
c. 1610	*Werempe Ampem*, called *Mumuromfi* in Akyere-kyere tradition, founded the Denk(y)era Kingdom 1620
c. 1650	*Boadu Akafo Berempon*, called *Akafo Biaka* in Adanse tradition
c. 1670	*Boa Amponsem* (or *Boa Siante*)
c. 1690 – 1701	*Ntim Gyakari*, killed by the Ashanti at the battle of

	Feyase
1701	Ashanti conquest

Akkad (Agade)

Territory comprised part of present-day Iraq, northern Syria and eastern Turkey, with the capital at Agade.

Kings

2371 BC	*Sargon*, the Great; conquered Umma 2347 and all of Sumer, Syria, Elam and other areas of present-day south-western Iran
2315	*Rimush*, son, assassinated
2306	*Manishtusu*, brother, assassinated
2291	*Naram-Sin*, son, traditionally reigned 75 years
2254 – 2230	*Shar-kali-sharri*, son, invasions of the Guti
2230 – 2226	Period of anarchy
2226	*Dudu*
2205 – 2191	*Shu-Durul*
2191	Conquest by Gutium

Akshak

Territory comprised part of present-day northern Iraq, with the capital at Akshak.

Kings

(?) BC	*Zuzu*, conquered by Eannatum, the king of Lagash
(?)	*Unzi*, for 30 years(?)
c. 2450	*Undalulu*, for 12 years
(?)	*Ur-ur*, for six years
(?)	*Puzur-Nirakh*, for 20 years
(?)	*Ishu-Il*, for 24 years
c. 2370	*Shu-Sin*, son, for seven years
(?)	Superseded by the kingdom of Akkad

Aleppo and Alalakh

Territory comprised part of present-day northern Syria.

KINGDOM OF YAMKHAD

Capital at Halap (present-day Aleppo).

Kings

(?) BC	*Yarimlim I*
c. 1790	*Hammurabi I*, son(?)
(?)	*Abbael I*, son, ceded Alalakh
before 1700	*Yarimlim II*, son
(?)	*Niqmiepu' I*, son
(?)	*Irkabtum*, son
c. 1650(?)	*Hammurabi II*
(?)	*Yarimlim III*
	Alalakh destroyed by the Hittite king Hattusilis I

KINGDOM OF ALEPPO

Capital at Halap (present-day Aleppo).

Kings

(?) BC	*Sharrael*(?)
(?)	*Abbael II*, son
before 1550	*Ilimilimma I*

KINGDOM OF MUKISH

Capital at Alalakh (present-day Tell Açana)

Kings

before 1500 BC	*Idrimi*, son of Ilimilimma I; vassal of Parattarna, the king of the Mitanni
(?)	*Adad-nirari*(?), son, vassal of the Mitanni

(?)	*Niqmiepu' II* (or *Niqmepa*), brother, vassal of the Mitanni
before 1450	*Ilimilimma II*, son

Almohads (al-Muwahhidun)

Territory comprised part of present-day Morocco, northern Algeria, Tunisia, north-western Libya and the southern Iberian peninsula, with the capital at Marrakesh.

Sultans

AD 1121/2	*Muhammad ibn Tumart (al-Mahdi)*
1129/30	*'Abd al-Mu'min (ibn Ali)* (b. 1094/5) lieutenant of Muhammad, took title of Amir al-Muslimin 1123/4, captured Marrakesh from the Almoravids 1146/7
May/Jun 1163	*(Abu Ya'qub) Yusuf I*, son
1184/5	*(Abu Yusuf) Ya'qub al-Mansur*, son (d. 22 Jan 1199)
1199	*Muhammad al-Nasir*, son (d. 25 Dec 1212)
1214/15	*(Abu Ya'qub) Yusuf II, al-Mustansir*, son (d. 6 Jan 1224)
1223/4	*'Abd al-Wahid I al-Makhlu'*, great-uncle (d. 21 Sep 1224)
1224/5	*(Abu Muhammad) 'Abdallah al-'Adil*, nephew (d. 4 Oct 1227)
11 Oct 1227 – 1230	*(Abu Zakariya') Yahya al-Mu'tasim*, son of Muhammad al-Nasir
Oct 1227 – 17 Oct 1232	*(Abu'l-'Ala') Idris al-Ma'mun (ibn Ya'qub al-Mansur)*, uncle (b. 1185/6) rival of Yahya al-Mu'tasim
Oct/Nov 1232 – 5 Dec 1242	*(Abu Muhammad) 'Abd al-Wahid II al-Rashid (ibn al-Ma'mun)*, son (b. 1218?)
Dec 1242	*(Abu'l-Hasan) 'Ali al-Sa'id (al-Mu'tadid)*, brother (d. 23 Jun 1248)
1248	*(Abu Hafs) 'Umar al-Murtada (ibn Abi Ibrahim Ishaq)*, grandson of Yusuf I
1266/7 – 1269/70	*Abu'l-'Ula al-Wathiq* (or *Abu Dabbus*), great grandson of 'Abd al-Mu'min
1269	Marinid conquest of Marrakesh

Almoravids (al-Murabitun)

Territory comprised part of present-day Morocco and the southern Iberian peninsula, with the capital at Marrakesh.

Sultans

AD (?)	*Yahya ibn Ibrahim*, chief of the Sanhaja Berbers, recognized the spiritual authority of 'Abdallah ibn Yasin
(?)	*Yahya ibn 'Umar*, chief of the Sanhaja Berbers
1056/7	*Abu Bakr (ibn 'Umar) al-Lamtuni*, brother, chief of the Sanhaja Berbers
1061	*Yusuf ibn Tashufin*, cousin (b. 1009/10) assumed title of Amir al-Muslimin, defeated Alfonso VI of León and Castile at Zallaqa (in present-day Spain) 23 Oct 1086
2 Sep 1106	*'Ali ibn Yusuf*, son (b. 1084/5)
1142/3	*Tashufin ibn 'Ali*, son
1145/6	*Ibrahim ibn Tashufin*, son
1145/6 – 1146/7	*Ishaq ibn 'Ali*, uncle
1146/7	Almohad conquest of Marrakesh
1148/9	Death of Yahya ibn Ghaniya, the last Almoravid governor in Spain

'Amirids

Territory comprised part of present-day eastern Spain, with the capital established at Valencia.

Kings

AD 1021/2	*('Abd al-'Aziz) al-Mansur ibn 'Abd al-Rahman ibn Abi 'Amir*, grandson of 'Almanzor', the vizier of the

	Umayyad caliph of Córdoba; captured Almería 1037/8
1061/2	*'Abd al-Malik al-Muzaffar (ibn 'Abd al-'Aziz al-Mansur)*, son
1064/5	*(Abu'l-Hasan Yahya) al-Ma'mun (ibn Isma'il)*, father-in-law, Dhunnunid king
1074/5	*al-Qadir (Yahya ibn Isma'il ibn al-Ma'mun)*, grandson (for 1st time) at the same time Dhunnunid king
1075/6	*Abu Bakr (ibn 'Abd al-'Aziz al-Mansur)*, son of al-Mansur ibn 'Abd al-Rahman
1085/6	*(al-Qadi) 'Uthman ibn Abi Bakr*, son
1085/6	*al-Qadir* (for 2nd time)
1090/1 – 1095/6	*(al-Qadi) Ja'far ibn 'Abdallah (ibn Shahhaf)*
1095/6	Conquest by El Cid (Rodrigo Díaz de Vivar)
1101/2	Almoravid conquest

Amurru (Amorites)

Territory comprised part of present-day western Syria.

Kings

c. 1400 BC	*'Abdi-Ashirta*
c. 1365	*Aziru*, son, Hittite vassal
(?)	*DU-Teshub*,* son, installed by the Hittite king Mursilis II
(?)	*Tuppi-Teshub*, son
(?)	*Bente-shina I*(?), son (for 1st time) deposed by the Hittites c. 1300
(?)	*Shapilis*, placed on the throne by the Hittites
(?)	*Bente-shina I*, (for 2nd time?)

*The ideogram for the first part of the name cannot at present be read and is represented by its standard Sumerian value

c. 1250	*Shaushga-muwash*, son
(?)	Overwhelmed by Indo-European invaders from the north

Anhalt

Territory now part of Magdeburg and Halle districts of German Democratic Republic.

Counts

Ascanian House

AD 1123 – 18 Nov 1170	*Albrecht*, the Bear, son of Otto of Ballenstädt (b. c. 1100) Margrave of the North Mark 1134; Margrave of Brandenburg 1136; Duke of Saxony 1138 – 1142; inherited Anhalt, with Ballenstädt, as part of the Ascanian estates
1170 – 9 Feb 1212	*Bernhard*, son (b. c. 1140) Duke (Bernhard III) of Saxony 1180
1212 – 1251/2	*Heinrich I*, son (b. c. 1170) separated Anhalt from the duchy of Saxony; took the title, Prince of Anhalt, 1218
1251/2	Territory divided between the three sons of Heinrich I, forming the principalities of Anhalt-Aschersleben, Anhalt-Bernburg and Anhalt-Zerbst

ANHALT-ASCHERSLEBEN

Princes

1251/2 – after 12 Jun 1266	*Heinrich II*, son of Heinrich I
1266 – 1304/5	*Otto I*, son; ruled with his brother, *Heinrich III* (d. 9 Nov 1307) Archbishop (Heinrich II) of Magdeburg 1305/6
1305 – 1315	*Otto II*, son of Otto I, died without male heir
1315	Aschersleben lands passed to the Bishops of Halberstadt

ANHALT-BERNBURG

Princes

1251/2 – 1286/7	*Bernhard I*, son of Heinrich I
1287 – 1324	*Bernhard II*, son
1318 – 20 Aug 1348	*Bernhard III*, son
1348	*Bernhard IV*, son
1354	*Heinrich IV*, brother
1374/77 – 1404	*Otto III*, brother
1374/77 – 25 Sep 1410	*Bernhard V*, nephew
1410 – 2 Feb 1468	*Bernhard VI*, son of Otto III, died without heir
2 Feb 1468	Bernburg lands inherited by the Princes of Anhalt-Zerbst

ANHALT-ZERBST

Princes

1251/2 – after 25 Mar 1298	*Siegfried I*, son of Heinrich I (b. 1230)
c. 1298	*Albrecht I*, son
1316 – c. 17 Jul 1362	*Albrecht II*, son (d. c. 17 Jul 1362) ruled with his brother *Waldemar I* (d. 3 Sep 1367)
1362	*Johann I*, son of Albrecht II
c. 1382 – 1391	*Waldemar III*, son
c. 1382 – 1405	*Siegmund I*, brother
c. 1382 – 1396	*Albrecht IV*, brother (d. 24 Nov 1423) became Prince of Anhalt-Köthen following division of lands with Siegmund I
1405 – after 1423	*Waldemar IV*, son of Siegmund I
1405 – 21 Sep 1474	*Georg I*, brother (b. c. 1390)
1405 – 1450	*Siegmund II*, brother
1405 – c. 1469	*Albrecht VI*, brother
1474 – 12 Jul 1516	*Ernst*, son of Georg I
1474 – Nov 1508	*Waldemar VI*, brother (b. 1450)
1474 – 25 Apr 1509	*Georg II*, brother (b. 1456)

Anjou

Territory now Maine-et-Loire department of France.

Counts

AD 879	*Ingelger* (or *Enjeuger*)
899	*Foulques I*, the Red, son
940	*Foulques II*, the Good, son
962	*Geoffroi I Grisegonelle* (i.e. Grey-tunic), son
21 Jul 987	*Foulques III Nerra* (or the Black), son (b. c. 970; d. Metz 21 Jun 1040); took Saumur 1026
1040	*Geoffroi II Martel* (i.e. the Hammer), son (b. 14 Oct 1006; d. Angers 14 Nov 1060); annexed Touraine, 1044, and most of Maine from c. 1048
1060	*Geoffroi III*, the Bearded, nephew; deposed
1069	*Foulques IV le Réchin*, brother
1109	*Foulques V*, the Young, son (b. 1092; d. Acre 10 Nov 1143) inherited the county of Maine 1110, King (Foulques) of Jerusalem 14 Sep 1131, regent of Antioch early 1132 – Apr 1136
1129	*Geoffroi IV Plantagenêt*, son (b. 24 Aug 1113; d. 7 Sep 1151) assumed the government of Anjou, Maine and Touraine with the departure of Foulques V for Jerusalem; Duke of Normandy 1144
1151	*Henri*, son (b. Le Mans 5 Mar 1133; d. Chinon 6 Jul 1189) Duke of Normandy 1151, Duke of Aquitaine May 1152 – 1168, King (Henry II) of England 19 Dec 1154
1189	*Richard* Coeur de Lion (i.e. Lion-heart), Duke of Aquitaine, son (b. Oxford, England, 8 Sep 1157; d. Châlus near Limoges 6 Apr 1199) did homage to King Philippe II Auguste of France for his French possessions 18 Nov 1188; Duke of Normandy 20 Jul 1189, King (Richard I) of England 3 Sep 1189
1199 – 1206	*Jean*, sans Terre (i.e. Lackland) (or *John of England*), brother (b. Oxford, England, 24 Dec 1167; d. Newark, England, 18/19 Oct 1216) Duke of Normandy and King (John) of England, Count of Poitou and Duke of Aquitaine 1199; not recognized as Count of Anjou and Maine by King Philippe II Auguste of France

	until 1200; lost Normandy 1204 and Maine and Anjou 1206
1206	Anjou and Maine annexed to the Crown of France
1232 – 7 Jan 1285	*Charles I*, brother of King Louis IX of France (who invested him with the county as a hereditary apanage) (b. Mar 1227; d. Foggia, Italy) received county of Provence as dowry 31 Jan 1246 and county of Maine as apanage 1246, crowned King of Naples and Sicily 6 Jan 1266, defeated and killed Manfred, Hohenstaufen King of Naples and Sicily, 26 Feb 1266, Prince of Achaea 1267/1278, claimed the kingdom of Jerusalem 1277, defeated by Pedro III of Aragon in struggle for the throne of Sicily Jun 1284
1285	*Charles II*, the Lame, Prince of Salerno, son (b. c. 1254; d. Naples 5 May 1309) Prince of Achaea 1285 – 1289, held prisoner by the Aragonese at his father's death; released in 1288 and was crowned King of Naples 29 May 1289 after renouncing his claim to Sicily
1290 – 16 Dec 1325	*Charles III*, Count of Valois, son-in-law (b. Mar/Apr 1270; d. Le Perray) Count of Alençon 1291, Count of Chartres 1294
	On Charles III's death the county was inherited by his son, Philippe, later King Philippe VI of France who amalgamated the county with crown lands on his accession in 1328

Dukes

1360 – 21 Sep 1384	*Louis I*, son of King Jean II of France who created the hereditary duchy for him (b. Vincennes 23 Jul 1339; d. Bisceglie) received county of Maine as hereditary apanage 1356; Count of Provence 1382; claimed the throne of Naples (crowned May 1382) but never ruled
1384 – 29 Apr 1417	*Louis II*, son (b. Toulouse 7 Oct 1377; d. Angers) Count of Maine and Provence, crowned King of Naples 1389, held Naples 1390 – 1399
1417	*Louis III*, son (b. Anjou 25 Sep 1403; d. Cosenza, Italy, 15 Nov 1434) Duke of Touraine, Count of Maine and Provence, titular King of Naples Sep 1419
Nov 1434 – 1471	*René I*, Duke of Bar, Duke Consort of Lorraine, brother (b. Angers 16 Jan 1409; d. Aix-en-Provence 10 Jul 1480) Duke of Touraine, Count of Maine and

	Provence, gave Maine to his son Charles 1437, King of Naples 1435 – 1442, resigned Duchy of Lorraine 1453; abandoned Anjou to King Louis XI of France 1471
1471	Reunion with the Crown of France

Annam and Tongking

Territory comprised part of present-day Vietnam.

Kings

Hong-Bang (legendary dynasty)

2879 – 258 BC	Kingdom called Van-Tang with the capital at Phong-chau

Thuc

Kingdom called Au-lac with the capital at Loa-thanh.

257 – 208	*Thuc An-Duong Vuong*

Trieu

Kingdom called Nam-viêt with the capital at Phien-ngu (now Fan-yu).

207	*Trieu Vo-Vuong* (or *Trieu Vo-De*)
136	*Trieu Van-Vuong*
124	*Trieu Minh-Vuong*
112	*Trieu Ai-Vuong*
111	*Trieu Vuong Kiên-Duc*
111	Kingdom incorporated into China

Earlier Li

Capital established at Song-biên.

AD 544	*Li Nam-Viêt De Bon* (or *Li Bi*)
549 – 571	*Trieu Viêt-Vuong Quang-Phuc*, usurper
549 – 555	*Li Dao-Lang Vuong Thiên-Bao*
571 – 602	*Li Hau-De Phat-Tu*
602 – 939	Chinese domination

Ngo
Kingdom called Dai-co-viêt with the capital at Co-loa.

939	*Ngo Vuong Quyen*
945	*Duong-Binh Vuong Tam-kha*, usurper
951–965	*Ngo Nam-Tan Vuong Xuong-Van*
951–954	*Ngo Thiên-Sach Vuong Xuong-Ngap*
965–968	Period of anarchy

Dinh

968	*Dinh Tiên-Hoang De*
979–980	*Dinh De-Toan*

Earlier Le

980	*Le Dai-Hanh Hoang-De*
1005–1009	*Le Trung-Ton Hoang-De*, dethroned

Later Li

1009	*Li Thai-To* (or *Li Cong-Uan*)
1028	*Li Thai-To* (or *Li Phat-Ma*)
1054	*Li Thanh-Ton*
1072	*Li Nhon-Ton*
1127	*Li Than-Ton*
1138	*Li Anh-Ton*
1175	*Li Cao-Ton*
1210	*Li Huê-Ton*
1224–1225	*Li Chieu-Hoang*

Tran

1225	*Tran Thai-Ton*
1258	*Tran Thanh-Ton*
1278	*Tran Nhon-Ton*
1293	*Tran Anh-Ton*, conquest of Champa
1314	*Tran Minh-Ton*, Champa regained independence 1326
1329	*Tran Hiên-Ton*
1341	*Tran Du-Ton*
1369	*Duong Nhut-Le*
1370	*Tran Nghe-Ton*
1372	*Tran Duê-Ton*
1377	*Tran De-Hiên* (or *Tran Phe-De*)
1388	*Tran Thuan-Ton*
1398–1400	*Tran Thieu-De*, deposed

Ho	
1400	*Ho Qui-Li*, deposed, Chinese occupation
1400 – 1407	*Ho Han-Thuong*
Restored Tran	
1407	*Tran De-Qui* (or *Tran Gian-Dinh De*)
1409 – 1413	*Tran De Qui-Khoang*
Later Le	
1418	*Le Loi* (or *Binh-Dinh Vuong*), regained independence from China
1420	*Le Nga*, usurper
1426	*Tran Cao*, usurper
1428	*Le Thai-To* (or *Cao Hoang-De*)
1433	*Le Thai-Ton* (or *Van Hoang-De*)
1442	*Le Nhon-Ton* (or *Tuyen Hoang-De*)
1459	*Le Nghi-Dan*, usurper
1460	*Le Thanh-Ton* (or *Thuan Hoang-De*), accomplished the final conquest of Champa 1471
1497	*Le Hiên-Ton* (or *Duê Hoang-De*)
1504	*Le Tuc-Ton* (or *Kham Hoang-De*)
1504	*Le Ui-Muc De*
1509	*Le Tuong-Duc De*
1516	*Tran Cao*
1516	*Tran Thang*, usurper
1518	*Le Bang*, usurper
1518	*Le Du*
1516 – 1526	*Le Chieu-Ton* (or *Than Hoang-De*)
1522 – 1527	*Le Hoang-De-Xuan* (or *Cung Hoang-De*), committed suicide by order of Mac Dang-Dung
1527 – 1533	Overthrown by Mac Dynasty, interregnum
1527	*Mac Dang-Dung*, abdicated
1530 – 1533	*Mac Dang-Doanh*, son
1533	Restoration of Later Le Dynasty, although the Mac Dynasty continued to rule in Tongking until 1592 (see below) and actual power in Annam was wielded by the Nguyen as mayors of the palace (see below) until 1545 when control passed to the Trinh family (see below)
1533*	*Le Trang-Ton* (or *Du Hoang-De*)
1548	*Le Trung-Ton* (or *Vo Hoang-De*)
1556	*Le Anh-Ton* (or *Tuan Hoang-De*)

*From 1533 the kings of the Later Le Dynasty were little more than puppet rulers

1573	*Le The-Ton* (or *Nghi Hoang-De*)
1597	*Nguyen Duong-Minh*, usurper
1597	*Nguyen Minh-Tri*, usurper
1599	*Le Kinh-Ton* (or *Huê Hoang-De*)
1619	*Le Thanh-Ton* (or *Uyen Hoang-De*)
1643	*Le Chan-Ton* (or *Thuan Hoang-De*)
1649	*Le Than-Ton* (or *Ugen Hoang-De*)
1662	*Le Huyen-Ton* (or *Muc Hoang-De*)
1671	*Le Gia-Ton* (or *Mi Hoang-De*)
1671	*Le Hi-Ton* (or *Chuong Hoang-De*)
1705	*Le Du-Ton* (or *Hoa Hoang-De*)
1729	*Le De Duy-Phuong*
1732	*Le Thuan-Ton* (or *Gian Hoang-De*)
1735	*Le I-Ton* (or *Huy Hoang-De*)
1740	*Le Hiên-Ton* (or *Vinh Hoang-De*)
1786 – 1787	*Le Man Hoang-De*, fled to China after Tay-Son invasion
1787	Overthrown by Tay-Son dynasty (see below)

Mac Dynasty

Ruled in Tongking, with their capital at Hanoi.

1533	*Mac Dang-Doanh* (see Later Le Dynasty)
1540	*Mac Phuc-Hai*
1546	*Mac Phuc-Nguyen*
1562	*Mac Mau-Hop*
1592	*Mac Toan*
1592	*Mac Kinh-Chi*
1592	Trinh family (see below) captured Hanoi and obtained control over most of Tongking, the Mac fled to Cao-bang on the Chinese border

Trinh Family

Ruled in Tongking, with their capital initially at Tay-do and from 1593 at Hanoi.

1539	*Trinh Kiêm*, son-in-law of Nguyen Kim of the Nguyen (d. 1570) mayor of the palace for the Later Le dynasty from 1545
1569	*Trinh Coi*
1570	*Trinh Tong*
1623	*Trinh Trang*
1657	*Trinh Tac*
1682	*Trinh Con*
1709	*Trinh Cuong*

1729	*Trinh Giang*
1740	*Trinh Dinh*
1767	*Trinh Sam*, Tay-Son rebellion 1772
1782	*Trinh Can*
1782	*Trinh Khai*
1786 – 1787	*Trinh Phung*
1787	Partition by Tay-Son dynasty (see below)

Tay-Son Dynasty

1778 – 1793	*Nguyen Van-Nhac* (b. c. 1752; d. 16 Dec 1793) captured Annam and most of Tongking by 1778, proclaimed himself emperor
1788	*Nguyen Van-Hué*, brother (b. c. 1752)
1792 – 1793	*Nguyen Quang-Toan*, son, defeated by Nguyen (Phuc-) Anh

Nguyen Dynasty

Ruled in Annam, with their capital initially at Hué and later at Quang-tri.

(?) – 1545	*Nguyen Kim*, helped to restore Later Le dynasty and became mayor of the palace 1533, assassinated
1545 – 1558	Period of rivalry between the sons of Nguyen Kim and the Trinh family
1558	*Nguyen Hoang*, son of Nguyen Kim, from 1570 ruled the southern provinces and moved the capital to Quang-tri
1613	*Nguyen Phuc-Nguyen*
1635	*Nguyen Phuc-Lan*
1648	*Nguyen Phuc-Tan*
1687	*Nguyen Phuc-Tran*
1691	*Nguyen Phuc-Chu*
1725	*Nguyen Phuc-Chu*
1738	*Nguyen Phuc-Khoat*
1765	*Nguyen Phuc-Thuan*, Tay-Son rebellion 1772
1778 – 1802	*Nguyen (Phuc-)Anh*, proclaimed Emperor under the name *Gia Long* 1 Jun 1802 (b. Hué 8 Feb 1762; d. Hué 25 Jan or 3 Feb 1820) recaptured Annam and most of Tongking from Tay-Son dynasty 1793

For continuation, see Vietnam, Volume 2.

Antioch

Territory in southern-central Turkey and western Syria, with capital at Antioch (now Antakya).

Princes

Dec AD 1099 – 7 Mar 1111	*Bohémond I*, Prince of Taranto, son of Duke Robert Guiscard of Apulia and Calabria (b. between 1050 and 1058); *de facto* possessor of Antioch 1098; formally invested by the Patriarch of Jerusalem Dec 1099; captured by the Danishmendid amir Ghazi Gümüshtigin 1100 and imprisoned at Neocaesarea (now Niksar); released 1103; surrendered to Byzantine emperor, Alexius I Comnenus Sep 1108, became a Byzantine vassal and returned to Apulia Regents: Mar 1101* – 1103: *Tancrède de Hauteville*, Prince of Galilee, nephew (for 1st time) (b. 1076(?); d. Antioch 12 Dec 1112) autumn 1104 – 12 Dec 1112: *Tancrède de Hauteville*, Prince of Galilee (for 2nd time) in revolt against the Byzantines 1108/9
1112	*Roger*, nephew, son of Prince Richard of Salerno (d. 28 Jun 1119) recognized King Baudouin I of Jerusalem as feudal overlord; defeated by the Artuqid sultan Ilghazi I and killed in the battle of the Field of Blood
Jun 1119 – Feb 1130	*Bohémond II*, son of Bohémond I (b. 1108 or 1109) killed near Anazarbus by the Danishmendid amir Ghazi Gümüshtigin Regent: Jun 1119 – Oct 1126: King *Baudouin II du Bourg* of Jerusalem (for 1st time) (d. Jerusalem 21 Aug 1131) prisoner of the Artuqid sultan 18 Apr 1123 – Jun 1124

*From 1100 to Mar 1101 the government of Antioch was entrusted to Baudouin II du Bourg, Count of Edessa, later regent for Bohémond II and Constance

Feb 1130	*Constance*,* daughter of Bohémond II (for 1st time) (b. 1128?) Regents: Feb – summer 1130: *Alix*, mother; deposed summer 1130 –21 Aug 1131: King *Baudouin II du Bourg* of Jerusalem (for 2nd time) early 1132 – Apr 1136: King *Foulques* of Jerusalem, son-in-law of Baudouin II (b. 1092; d. Acre 10 Nov 1143)
Apr 1136 – 29 Jun 1149	*Raimond I de Poitiers*, husband of Constance, son of Duke Guillaume IX of Aquitaine (b. c. 1099; d. Fons Murez) Byzantine vassal from 1137; killed in battle against the Zangid atabeg Nur al-Din
29 Jun 1149	*Constance** (for 2nd time) Regent: 29 Jun 1149 – 1153: King *Baudouin III* of Jerusalem, cousin (for 1st time) (b. 1131; d. Beirut 10 Feb 1162)
1153	*Renaud de Châtillon*, second husband of Constance, son of Count Geoffroi of Guienne (d. at the battle of the Horns of Hattin 1187) Byzantine vassal; taken prisoner by the Zangid atabeg Nur al-Din Regent: Nov 1160 – 1163: King *Baudouin III* of Jerusalem (for 2nd time) declared Bohémond III as rightful Prince of Antioch and entrusted administration to the Patriarch Amaury
1163†	*Bohémond III*, the Stammerer, son-in-law of Raimond I de Poitiers (b. 1145) succeeded on attaining majority, exiled Constance
1201	*Bohémond IV*, the One-eyed, Count of Tripoli, son (for 1st time) (d. Mar 1233)
1216	*Raimond Roupên*, nephew (d. in prison in Tarsus 1221) seized control while Bohémond IV was in Tripoli, deposed
1220	*Bohémond IV* (for 2nd time)
Mar 1233	*Bohémond V*, Count of Tripoli, son (b. c. 1198) entrusted government of Antioch to the town council
Jan 1252 – 18 May 1268	*Bohémond VI*, Count of Tripoli, son (b. 1238)

*Constance was never allowed to reign in her own name

†1193 – 1194	*Raimond*, son of Bohémond III (d. 1197) recognized as Prince by Antioch town council during period of capture of Bohémond III by King Leon II of Armenia

	Mongol vassal Regent: 1252: *Lucie* (or *Lucienne*), mother, great-niece of Pope Innocent III, entrusted government of Antioch to her Roman relatives
18 May 1268	Conquest by the Mamluk sultan Baibars I

Apulia

Counts

House of Hauteville	
AD 1042	*Guillaume*, Bras de Fer (i.e. Iron-arm), son of Tancrède de Hauteville, began the expulsion of the Byzantines from Apulia
1046	*Dreu*, brother, assigned the conquest of Calabria to Robert Guiscard, assassinated
1051 – Aug 1057	*Onfroi*, brother

Dukes

Aug 1057 – 17 Jul 1085	*Robert Guiscard*, brother (d. near Cephalonia) Count of Apulia Aug 1057; Duke of Apulia, Calabria and Sicily Aug 1059; granted part of Calabria and of Sicily to his brother, Roger, but retained the suzerainty of all Hauteville possessions in Italy; took Bari from the Byzantines 1071; captured Salerno Dec 1076; took Corfu 1080 and Dyrrachium (now Durazzo) Feb 1082
1085	*Roger Borsa*, son, resigned his rights in Calabria and Sicily to Roger I of Sicily
1111 – 20 Jun 1127	*Guillaume*, son, died childless
1127 – 26 Feb 1154	*Roger II*, Count of Sicily and Duke of Calabria, cousin (b. 22 Dec 1095; d. Palermo) invested 23 Aug 1128, King of Sicily 25 Dec 1130

The title of Duke of Apulia became one of the titles of the King of Sicily

Aquitaine

Charles II the Bald, King of the West Franks, deposed the last independent king of Aquitaine, Pippin II, in 852 (see the Kingdom of the Franks). In 855 the kingdom was assigned to Charles II's son *Charles* (b. 847/8; d. 29 Sep 866). He was succeeded by his brother, *Louis II*, the Stammerer (b. 846; d. Compiègne 10 Apr 879) in 866. With the accession of Louis II to the throne of France in 877, Aquitaine was united to the crown and ceased to exist as a kingdom.

Dukes

AD 845 – 866	*Rainulfe I*, Count of Poitou, grandson of King Pippin II of Aquitaine (d. Brissarthe 5 Jul 866)
880	*Rainulfe II*, Count of Poitou, son (b. c. 855; d. (murdered) 5 Aug 890) refused to recognize King Eudes of France and proclaimed himself King of Aquitaine 887
c. 890	*Guillaume I*, the Pious, Count (Guillaume III) of Auvergne, invested with Aquitaine by King Charles III the Simple of France
918	*Guillaume II*, nephew; Count (Guillaume IV) of Auvergne 918
926	*Alfred*, brother; Count of Auvergne 926
928	*Ebles Manzer*, Count of Poitou, illegitimate son of Rainulfe II; inherited Aquitaine and Auvergne; defeated by King Raoul of France
932	*Raimond Pons*, Count (Raimond III) of Toulouse; invested with Aquitaine and Auvergne by King Raoul of France
951*	*Guillaume III*, Towhead, Count (Guillaume I) of Poitou, son of Ebles Manzer (b. c. 915; d. Abbey of Saint-Maixent 3 Apr 963) Count of Auvergne 951; abdicated
963	*Guillaume IV Fierebrace* (or *Fierabras*), son (b. c. 937; d. Abbey of Saint-Maixent 995/6) abdicated
990	*Guillaume V*, the Great, son (b. c. 969; d. 31 Jan 1030) abdicated
1029 – 15 Dec 1038	*Guillaume VI* the Fat, son (b. 1004)
1038	*Eudes*, brother (b. c. 1012)

*From 951 all dukes of Aquitaine were simultaneously counts of Poitou

1039	*Guillaume VII Aigret*, brother (b. c. 1023)
1058 – 25 Sep 1086	*Guillaume VIII* (originally *Gui Geoffroi*), brother (b. c. 1026)
1086 – 10 Feb 1126	*Guillaume IX*, son (b. c. 22 Oct 1071) usurped power in Toulouse from 1098 to 1100 and from 1114 to 1119
1126 – 9 Apr 1137	*Guillaume X*, son (b. 1099)
1137	*Eléonore* (or *Aliénor*), daughter (b. c. 1122; d. 1 Apr 1204); from 22 Jul 1137 to Mar 1152, ruling with her husband, *Louis*, King (Louis VII) of France (b. 1120; d. 18 Sep 1180) who divorced her
May 1152	*Henri*, Count of Anjou and Duke of Normandy, second husband (b. Le Mans, Maine, 5 Mar 1133; d. Chinon, Touraine, 6 Jul 1189) received Aquitaine and Poitou as Eléonore's dowry, King (Henry II) of England 19 Dec 1154; abdicated in Aquitaine and Poitou in favour of his son, Richard
1168	*Richard*, Coeur de Lion (i.e. Lion-heart), son (b. Oxford, England, 8 Sep 1157; d. Châlus near Limoges, 6 Apr 1199) King of England 3 Sep 1189, Count of Anjou and Maine, and Duke of Normandy, 1189
1196 – 1199	*Otton*, nephew, son of Duke Heinrich III of Saxony (b. 1177; d. Harzburg Castle, Saxony, 9 May 1218) Earl of York 1190, King (Otto IV) of Germany 9 Jun 1198, Holy Roman Emperor 4 Oct 1209; deposed in Aquitaine and Poitou 1199; defeated and deposed in Germany at the Battle of Bouvines 27 Jul 1214

With the deposition of Otton in Aquitaine, the duchy was recovered by King John I of England, brother of Richard Coeur de Lion. The kings of England continued to rule as dukes of Aquitaine (generally called Guyenne from the 13th century) until the reign of Henry VI, when it was surrendered to France. In 1469 King Louis XI of France ceded Aquitaine to his brother, *Charles*, Duke of Berry (d. 12 May 1472). With the death of Charles, Aquitaine was reunited with the French crown.

Aragon

At its greatest extent, territory comprised part of north-eastern Spain, Majorca, the Balearic Islands, Corsica, Sardinia and south-eastern France.

Kings

AD 1035 – 8 May 1063	*Ramiro I*, illegitimate son of King Sancho III of Navarre, was granted the new kingdom of Aragon (previously a county) in his father's will, added the counties of Sobrarbe and Ribagorza
1063 – Jun 1094	*Sancho I*, son (b. 1045; d. Huesca) King (Sancho V) of Navarre 1076, placed his kingdoms under the protection of the papacy 1089
1094	*Pedro I*, son, King of Aragon and Navarre, captured Huesca 1096 and Barbastro 1100
1104	*Alfonso I*, the Battler, brother (b. c. 1073) King of Aragon and Navarre; ruled with his wife, *Urraca*, Queen of Castile and León (b. 1082; d. 8 Mar 1126); abdicated in Castile and León in favour of his stepson 1126; the count of Toulouse became his vassal 1116; conquered Saragossa 1125
1134	*Ramiro II*, the Monk, brother (d. 1147) bishop-elect of Barbastro at the time of his succession, abdicated
1137	*Petronilla*, daughter (b. 1136; d. 13 Oct 1173) with her husband, Count *Ramón Berenguer IV* of Barcelona (b. 1115; d. 1162) who ruled without the title of king
1163 – 25 Apr 1196	*Alfonso II*, son (b. May 1152) Count of Barcelona 1162*
1196 – 13 Sep 1213	*Pedro II*, son (b. 1176) placed the kingdom under the protection of the papacy
1213 – 27 Jul 1276	*Jaime I*, the Conqueror, son (b. Montpellier, France, 2 Feb 1208; d. Valencia) ruled with his uncle, *Sancho*, Count of Rousillon (d. 1236) until 1218; conquered Majorca Dec 1229; took the Balearic Islands by 1235
1276 – 11 Nov 1285	*Pedro III*, the Great, son (b. 1239) King (Pedro I) of Sicily 4 Sep 1282
1285 – 18 Jun 1291	*Alfonso III*, son (b. 1265)

*All the future kings of Aragon were also counts of Barcelona, often referred to as the kings of Aragon and Catalonia

1291 – 5 Nov 1327	*Jaime II*, brother (b. 1262) King (Jaime I) of Sicily 1285 – 1295, after which he exchanged Sicily for Corsica and Sardinia
1327 – 24 Jan 1336	*Alfonso IV*, son (b. 1302)
1336 – 5 Jan 1387	*Pedro IV*, the Ceremonious, son (b. 5 Sep 1319) reincorporated the Balearic Islands and the county of Rousillon into the kingdom 1343 and 1344
1387 – 13 May 1395	*Juan I*, son (b. 27 Dec 1350)
1395 – 31 May 1412	*Martín*, brother; King (Martín II) of Sicily 1409*
1412 – 2 Apr 1416	*Fernando I*, grandson of Pedro IV and son of King Juan I of Castile (b. 27 Nov 1380; d. Igualada) co-regent of Castile for his nephew, Juan II, from 1406
1416 – 27 Jun 1458	*Alfonso V*, the Magnanimous, son (b. 1396; d. Naples) King (Alfonso I) of Naples 2 Jul 1442
1458 – 19 Jan 1479	*Juan II*, King of Navarre, brother (b. Medina del Campo 1398; d. Barcelona)
1479 – 23 Jan 1516	*Fernando II*, the Catholic, son (b. Sos 10 Mar 1452; d. Madrigalejo) ruled as king-consort of Castile (as Fernando V) with his wife *Isabel I* (b. 22 Apr 1451; d. 26 Nov 1504) until his succession as king of Aragon, when Isabel and Fernando became full co-rulers in both kingdoms; conquered the Nasrids of Granada 1492; annexed Navarre 1512; effected the permanent union of Spain

For the continuation of the line of Fernando and Isabel in Volume 2, see Spain.

Armenia

Satraps (Persian Viceroys) and Kings

401 BC	*Orontes I*, satrap under Persia
344	*Orontes II*, satrap, king 331
331 – 317	*Mithranes*
323	*Neoptolemus*, satrap

*Subsequent kings of Aragon were simultaneously kings of Sicily

317	*Orontes I (III)** (or *Erouard*), king
260	*Samus*
243	*Artavaz(anes)*
228	*Xerxes*
c. 212	*Abdissares*
212 – 200	*Orontes II (IV)*

Artaxiad dynasty (Seleucid)

190	*Artashes* (or *Artaxias*) *I*, strategos from 200
159	*Tigran* (or *Tigranes*) *I*, son
123	*Artavazd* (or *Artavasdes*) *I*, son
95†	*Tigran* (or *Tigranes*) *II (I)*, the Great, brother, conquered Great Sophene (in present-day north-eastern Turkey) and parts of Parthia and established capital at Tigranocerta, surrendered to the Roman triumvir Pompey 66 BC and became client king under Rome
56/5	*Artavazd* (or *Artavasdes*) *II (I)* (d. (murdered by Cleopatra) 30) deposed by the Roman triumvir Mark Antony
34	*Alexander*, son of Mark Antony and Cleopatra (b. c. 40) 'King of Armenia, Media and Parthia'
33	*Artashes* (or *Artaxias*) *II*, son of Artavasdes II, deposed
20	*Tigran* (or *Tigranes*) *III (II)*, brother
c. 10	*Tigran* (or *Tigranes*) *IV (III)* and *Erato*, his sister-wife (for 1st time)
5	*Artavazd* (or *Artavasdes*) *III (II)*, son of Artashes II(?), imposed by Rome
4	*Tigran* (or *Tigranes*) *IV* and *Erato* (for 2nd time)

Foreign kings

AD 2(?)	*Ariobarzanes*, son of the Median king Artabazus
4(?)	*Artavazd* (or *Artavasdes*) *IV (III)*, son
6(?)	*Tigran* (or *Tigranes*) *V (IV)*, grandson of King Herod of Judaea
(?)	*Erato* (for 3rd time)
after c. 12	*Vonon* (or *Vonones*), previously king of Parthia (not recognized), assassinated in Syria after 15

*Historians dispute the numeration of the Armenian kings
†Kingdom reckoned from this point by some authorities

15/16	*Orodes*, son of King Artabanus III of Parthia
18	*Artashes* (or *Artaxias*) *III* (or *Zenon* or *Zeno*), son of Polemo, the king of Pontus; with Roman acquiescence
c. 34	*Arshak* (or *Arsaces*) *I*, brother of Orodes, imposed by Parthia
35 – 37	*Mihrdat* (or *Mithridates*), brother of King P'arsman I of Iberia (for 1st time) Roman nominee, summoned to Rome and held in custody by the Roman triumvir Octavian
37	Armenia seized by Parthia
47	*Mihrdat* (for 2nd time) restored by the Roman emperor Claudius, killed by Hrhadamist
51	*Hradamist* (or *Rhadamistus*), nephew, usurper

Arsacid (Parthian) dynasty

52/4	*Trdat* (or *Tiridates*) *I*, brother of King Vologases I of Parthia (for 1st time)
60	*Tigran* (or *Tigranes*) *VI (V)*, kinsman of Tigran V, Roman nominee
62/3 – (?)	*Trdat I* (for 2nd time) recognized by Rome as client king, received crown from the Roman emperor Nero 66
100(?) – 114	*Ashkhadar* (or *Axidares*), son of King Pacorus II of Parthia
113	*Part'amasir* (or *Parthamasiris*), brother, usurper, deposed by the Roman emperor Trajan
114	*L. Catilius Severus*, imperial legate
116(?)	*Sanatruk I*, son of Meherdates; in revolt against Rome
116(?)	*Part'amaspat* (or *Parthamaspates*), cousin, son of King Osroes of Parthia, installed by Trajan, expelled by Osroes and made king of Osroene
117 – 136/7	*Vagharsh* (or *Vologases*) *I*, son of Sanatruk I
c. 140	*Soyemos* (or *Sohaemus*)(?) (for 1st time)
161 – 163	*Pacorus*, installed by King Vologases III of Parthia
163	Armenia invaded by Rome
166	*Soyemos* (for 2nd time?) installed by Statius Priscus
178	*Sanatruk II*
fl. 193	Unknown king
216	*Vagharsh* (or *Vologases*) II
217	*Trdat* (or *Tiridates) II*, the Great, son, or son of King Vologases V of Parthia

(?)	*Khosrov* (or *Chosroes*) *I*, commonly identified with Trdat II
c. 253(?)*	Sasanid invasion, death of Khosrov I and flight of his son Trdat
253 – 272 (262?)	*Hormazd I* (or *Hormizd-Ardashir*), younger son of the Sasanid king Shapur I, viceroy with the title of king of Armenia
272 – 293	*Narses*, brother †
287	*Trdat* (or *Tiridates*) *III*, son of Khosrov I, initially in part of Armenia only, expelled by Narses 295 – 296, restored with extended territory 297
330	*Khosrov* (or *Chosroes*) *II* the Short, son
338	*Tigran* (or *Tigranes*) *VII (VI)*, son, captured by the Persians, abdicated
351	*Arshak* (or *Arsaces*) *II*, son
367 (369?)	*Pap*, son
374	*Varazdat*, cousin, expelled 337 – 378
378 / 380 – 389	*Arshak* (or *Arsaces*) *III*, son of Pap, lost full control of Armenia to the Sasanids 379
378 – 386	*Vagharshak* (or *Valarsaces*), brother, king of Persarmenia
385/6	*Khosrov* (or *Chosroes*) *III* (for 1st time) installed by the Sasanid king Shapur III
387	Formal division of kingdom into Byzantine Armenia and Persarmenia

Kings of Persarmenia

Territory comprised part of present-day south-eastern Turkey and south-western U.S.S.R., with the capital established at Dvin.

387 or 392	*Vrhamshapuh*, brother of Khosrov III
414	*Khosrov III* (for 2nd time)
416 – 420	*Shapur*, son of the Sasanid king Yezdegerd I (d. 421) left to claim throne of Persia
420 – 423	Interregnum

*The death of Khosrov I is assigned to various dates, ranging from 243 to 287, in Armenian tradition, and is placed as early as 238 by some historians. A certain Artavazd V is given the dates 252 – 261, and it is further supposed by some that Armenia was under the control of Palmyra from 261 to 272

†Described as 'Great King of Armenia', i.e. viceroy, in 293. He may have been preceded as viceroy by Bahram I and Bahram II, his predecessors on the Sasanian throne of Persia

423 – 428	*Artashes* (or *Artaxias*) *IV*, son of Vrhamshapuh (b. 404/5)
428	End of kingship

Marzpans (Governors under Persia)

428	*Veh-Mir-Shapur*
442	*Vasak I Siwni*,* deposed
451	*Adhur-Hormizd*
465 – 481	*Adhur-Gushnasp*
482	*Sahak Bagratuni*,* in revolt against the Persians
482 – 483	Persian invasion
483 – 484	*Shapur of Rayy*
484 – 485	Guerrilla warfare
485	*Vahan Mamikonean*,* in revolt, acknowledged as autonomous governor
505 – 509 or 510 – 514	*Vard Mamikonean*,* brother
514 – 524	Persian marzpans
518 – 548	*Mzhezh* (or *Mezezius*) *I Gnuni**
(?)	*Gushnasp Bahram*†
(?)	*Tan-Shapur*†
558/60	*Varazdat**
c. 564	*Suren*, assassinated spring 571 or Feb 572 during revolt of Vardan Mamikonean
572	*Mihran Mihrevandak*
574 – 576	*Filip Siwni**
577	*Tahm-Khusrau*
580	*Varaz-Vzur* (or *Varaz-Buzurg*)
581/2	*Pahlav*
588(?)	*Frahat*
591	*Mushegh Mamikonean*,* gave up post after a short time
(?)	Armenian revolt
(?)	*Smbat Bagratuni*,* the Multivictorious (d. 616/17) marzpan of Hyrcania
613(?)	*Parsayenpet*
616 – 619(?)	*Namder-Gushnasp*
620	*Sharablagan*
624	*Rozbihan*
628 – 635(?)	*Varaz-Tirots Bagratuni*,* son of Smbat Bagratuni (d.

*Armenian princes or nobles
† Relative order uncertain

	643) went over to Byzantium, banished by the Byzantine emperor Heraclius

Presiding Princes

628	*Mzhezh* (or *Mezezius*) *II Gnuni*, Commander-in-chief of the imperial forces, killed by Dawid Saharuni
635	*Dawid Saharuni*, Curopalate
638 – c. 645	*Toros Rshtuni* (for 1st time) High Constable and Patrician
643	*Varaz-Tirots Bagratuni*, Curopalate (see Marzpans)
645 – 653	*Toros Rshtuni* (for 2nd time) High Constable Armenia surrendered to the Arabs by the Byzantine emperor Constans II
653	*Toros Rshtuni* (for 3rd time) governor for the Caliph*
654	*Mushegh Mamikonean*, Master of the Horse for the Byzantine emperor, went over to the Caliph
655 – 658	*Hamazasp Mamikonean*, for the Caliph 655 – 657, Curopalate for the Byzantine emperor 657 – 658
662 – 684/5	*Grigor I Mamikonean*, brother, for the Caliph
686	*Ashot II Bagratuni* (d. 690) for the Caliph
690	*Nerseh Kamsarakan*, Curopalate for the Byzantine emperor
691 – 711	*Smbat VI Bagratuni*, son of Varaz-Tirots Bagratuni; Patrician for the Byzantine emperor 691 – 697, for the Caliph 697 – 700; Curopalate for the Byzantine emperor 700 – 711
732	*Ashot III Bagratuni*, the Blind (d. c. 763) for the Caliph, deposed
748 – 750	*Grigor II Mamikonean*, for the Caliph
c. 750	*Mushegh Mamikonean*, brother (d. 25 Apr 772) head of the insurgent princes
c. 755	*Sahak III Bagratuni*, son of Ashot III Bagratuni (d. 772) High Constable for the Caliph
761 – 772 †	*Smbat VII Bagratuni*, brother (d. 25 Apr 772) High Constable for the Caliph
780 – 782/5	*Tachat Andzewatsi*, for the Caliph

*Until the reign of Hamazasp Mamikonean, the Caliph referred to is the Orthodox caliph; from Grigor I to Ashot III it is the Umayyad caliph; and from Grigor II onwards it is the 'Abbasid caliph

†From 772 to 780 Armenia was directly under Arab governors, viz. *Hasan ibn Qahtaba*, succeeded between 772 and 775 by *Yazid ibn Usain al-Sulami*

806	*Ashot IV Bagratuni*, the Carnivorous, for the Caliph
826 – 855	*Smbat VIII Bagratuni* (or *Abu'l-Abbas*) High Constable for the Caliph
830 – 852	*Bagarat II Bagratuni,* Lord of Tarawn, brother, Prince of Princes for the Caliph
856 – 885	*Ashot V Bagratuni*, son of Smbat VIII Bagratuni, High Constable 856, Prince of Princes for the Caliph c. 862 – 885, became king 885

Kings of Armenia

Territory comprised part of present-day north-eastern Turkey, south-western U.S.S.R. and north-western Iran, with the capital initially at Dvin and later at Ani.

Bagratids

885	*Ashot I (V)*, the Great, recognized by the Caliph and the Byzantine emperor (see Presiding Princes)
890	*Smbat I (IX)*, the Martyr, son
914	*Ashot II (VI)*, the Iron, son, received the title of Shahanshah (King of Kings) from the Caliph 922
928(?)	*Abas I*, brother
952/3	*Ashot III (VII)*, the Merciful, son, moved capital to Ani
977	*Smbat II (X)*, the Conqueror, son
989/90	*Gagik I*, brother
1020 – 1040/41	*Hovhannes-Smbat III (XI)*, son, compelled to make the Byzantine emperor heir to his estates
1021 – 1039/40	*Ashot IV (VIII)*, the Valiant, brother, king of the parts towards Persia
1042 – 1045	*Gagik II*, son (b. c. 1027; d. c. 1079) ceded Armenia to the Byzantine empire
1045 – 1064	Invaded and conquered by the Seljuqs

Princes and King of the Exiled Little (or Cilician) Armenia

Territory comprised part of present-day south-western Turkey, with the capital initially at Bardzrberd and later at Sis (present-day Kozan).

Rubenids

1080	*Ruben I*, lieutenant of Gagik II
1095	*Kostandin I*, son
1100	*Toros I*, son

1129 – 1138	*Leon I*, brother (d. 1141)
1138	Cilicia annexed by the Byzantine emperor John II Comnenus
1145	*Toros II*, son
1169	*Ruben II*, son
1170	*Mleh*, uncle
1175	*Ruben III*, nephew
1186	*Leon II (I)*, the Great, brother, crowned King of Armenia by cardinal Konrad von Wittelsbach 1198/9
1219	*Zabēl*, daughter
1222 – 1225	*Philip of Antioch*, husband, deposed

Hetumids

1226	*Het'um I* of Lambron, married Zabēl (d. 1270)
1269	*Leon III (II)*, son
1289	*Het'um II*, son (for 1st time) (d. 1308)
1293	*Toros III (I)*, brother (d. 1299)
1294	*Het'um II* (for 2nd time)
1296	*Smbat*, brother
1298	*Kostandin II (I)*, brother
1299	*Het'um II* (for 3rd time)
1305	*Leon IV (III)*, nephew
1308	*Oshin*, son of Leon III
1320 – 1341	*Leon V (IV)*, son

Lusignans

1342	*Gui I de Lusignan* (or *Constantine II*), cousin of Leon V; with his brother Jean de Lusignan serving as regent 1342; established capital at Sis; assassinated
1344 – 1363	*Constantine III (II)*, unrelated
1365 – 1373	*Constantine IV (III)*, cousin
1368 – 1369	*Pierre*, King (Pierre I) of Cyprus (b. Nicosia 9 Oct 1329; d. (murdered) Nicosia)
1373 – 1375	*Leon VI (V) de Lusignan*, nephew of Gui I de Lusignan (d. Paris 1393) captured and held to ransom by the Mamluks
1375	Mamluk conquest

Artuqids

Territory comprised part of present-day northern Iraq and eastern Turkey.

Sultans

Hisn Kaifa and Amid Branch

Aug/Sep AD 1102	*(Mu'in al-Din) Sökmen I (ibn Artuq)*, lord of Jerusalem
Oct 1104	*Ibrahim ibn Sökmen*, son
c. 1108/9	*(Rukn al-Daula) Da'ud ibn Sökmen*, brother
1144/5	*(Fakhr al-Din Abu'l-Harith) Qara Arslan ibn Da'ud*, son
1166/7	*(Nur al-Din) Muhammad ibn Qara Arslan*, son, received Amid from Saladin 1183/4
1185/6	*(Qutb al-Din) Sökmen II (ibn Muhammad, al-Malik al-Mas'ud)*, son (for 1st time)
1200/1	*(Nasir al-Din) Mahmud ibn Muhammad (, al-Malik al-Salih)*, brother
1222/3	*(Rukn al-Din) Maudud ibn Mahmud*, son
1231/2	*Sökmen II* (for 2nd time) deposed
1234	Overthrown by the Ayyubids

Mardin and Mayyafariqin Branch

c. 1105 – 3 Nov 1122	*(Najm al-Din) Ilghazi I (ibn Artuq)*, son of Artuq, lord of Jerusalem 1095 – Jul/Aug 1096, governor of Baghdad 1100/1 – 1104/5, lord of Mardin by 1108, lord of Aleppo 1118, lord of Mayyafariqin 1122
1122/3	*(Husam al-Din) Temür Tash ibn Ilghazi*, son; conquest of Aleppo Mar/Apr 1124
1152/3	*(Najm al-Din) Alpı ibn Temür Tash*, son
1176	*(Qutb al-Din) Ilghazi II (ibn Alpı)*, son, lord of Ras el-'Ain from 1173/4
Sep/Oct 1184	*(Husam al-Din) Yülük Arslan ibn Ilghazi*, son; Ayyubid sultan Saladin conquered Mayyafariqin 1185/6
c. 1200/1	*(Nasir al-Din) Artuq Arslan al-Mansur (ibn Ilghazi)*, brother, Ayyubid vassal
1239/40	*(Najm al-Din) Ghazi I (al-Sa'id ibn Artuq Arslan)*, son
1259/60	*Qara Arslan al-Muzaffar (ibn Ghazi)*, son

1291/2	*(Shams al-Din) Da'ud ibn Qara Arslan*, son
1293/4	*(Najm al-Din) Ghazi II (, al-Mansur, ibn Qara Arslan)*, brother
Aug/Sep 1312	*('Imad al-Din) 'Ali Alpı (, al-'Adil)*, son
Sep/Oct 1312	*(Shams al-Din) Salih ibn Ghazi*, brother
1363/4	*Ahmad al-Mansur (ibn Salih)*, son
1367/8	*Mahmud al-Salih (ibn Ahmad)*, son
1367/8	*Da'ud al-Muzaffar (ibn Salih)*, uncle
1376/7	*(Majd al-Din) 'Isa al-Zahir (ibn Da'ud)*, son
1406/7 – 1408/9	*Salih ibn Da'ud*, brother
1408/9	Kara Koyunlu conquest

Assam

Territory comprised at its fullest extent Assam and neighbouring parts of present-day north-eastern India.

Kings of Kamarupa*

c. AD 350	*Pushyavarman*
c. 380	*Samudravarman*, son
c. 400	*Balavarman I*, son
c. 410	*Kalyanavarman*, son
c. 430	*Ganapativarman*, son
c. 450	*Mahendravarman*, son
c. 485	*Narayanavarman*, son
c. 520	*Bhutivarman* (or *Mahabhutavarman*), fl. 554
c. 555	*Chandramukhavarman*, son
c. 570	*Sthitavarman*, son
c. 585 – c. 600	*Susthitavarman*, son
c. 600	Gauda invasion
c. 600	*Suprasthitavarman*, son
c. 605	*Bhaskaravarman*, brother
c. 650	*Avantivarman* (?)
c. 655	*Salastambha*, previously provincial governor, of royal blood
c. 675	*Vigrahastambha* (or *Vijaya*)
c. 685	*Palaka*

*Kamarupa included at times not only Assam but also parts of Bengal and Bihar

c. 700	*Kumara*
c. 715	*Vajradeva*
c. 730 – c. 750	*Harshavarman* (or *Harshadeva*), made conquests in Gauda territory
c. 750	Invasion by Yaśovarman of Kanauj and loss of territory
c. 750	*Balavarman II*, son
c. 765 – c. 800	One or two unknown kings
c. 800	*Pralambha*, son of Aratha (son of Balavarman?)
c. 820	*Harjaravarman*, son, fl. 829
c. 835	*Vanamalavarman*, son, abdicated(?)
c. 860	*Virabahu* (or *Jayamalavarman*?*), son, abdicated
c. 875	*Balavarman III*, son
c. 890 – c. 970	Six(?) unknown kings
c. 970	*Tyaga Singha*
c. 985	*Brahmapala*, possibly a kinsman, abdicated
c. 1000	*Ratnapala*, son
c. 1030	*Indrapala*, grandson
c. 1055	*Gopala*, son
c. 1075	*Harshapala*, son
c. 1090	*Dharmapala*, son
c. 1115	*Jayapala*
c. 1115	Conquest by the King of Gauda Ramapala
c. 1125	*Timgyadeva*, set up by Ramapala, rebelled and was superseded
1131(?)	*Vaidyadeva*, fl. 1142†
1150 – (?)	*Budhadeva* (?), brother
(?)	One unknown king
c. 1200	*Prithu*, killed by Nasir al-Din (son of Bengal sultan Iltutmish)
1228	A son(?) as vassal
(?)	One unknown king

*Some authorities suppose Jayamalavarman to be the real name of Vanamalavarman and not an alternative name of Virabahu

†The following kings, recorded during the 12th century, have no place in the sequence and may have been feudatory chiefs:

Bhaskara
Rayarideva, son
Udayakama, son
Vallabhadeva, fl. 1185

Kings of Kamata

c. 1250	*Sandhya*
c. 1270	*Sindhu*, son
c. 1285	*Rup*, son
c. 1300	*Singhadhvaj*, son, killed by successor
c. 1305	*Pratapadhvaj*, minister of Singhadhvaj
c. 1325	*Dharmanarayan* (or *Dharmapala*), nephew
c. 1330	*Durlabnarayan*, cousin
c. 1350	*Indranarayan*, son
c. 1365	Various usurpers
c. 1365	*Arimatta*, descendant of Dharmanarayan
c. 1385	*Sukaranka*, son
c. 1400	*Sutaranka*, son
c. 1415	*Mriganka*
c. 1440	*Niladhvaj Khan*, a Bhuyan chief(?)
c. 1460	*Chakradhvaj*, son
c. 1480 – 1498	*Nilambar*, son
1498	Muslim conquest

Kings of Ahom Dynasty

1228	*Sukapha*
1268	*Suteupha*, son
1281	*Subinpha*, son
1293	*Sukhangpha*, son
1332	*Sukhrangpha*, son
1364 – 1376	*Sutupha*, brother
1376 – 1380	Interregnum
1380 – 1389	*Tyaokhamti*, brother
1389 – 1397	Interregnum
1397	*Sudangpha*, son
1407	*Sujangpha*
1422	*Suphakpha*
1439	*Susenpha*, son
1488	*Suhenpha*, son
1493	*Supimpha*
1497	*Suhungmung* (or *Dihingia Raja*)
1539	*Suklenmung* (or *Gargayan Raja*), son
1552	*Sukhampha* (or *Khora Raja*)
1603	*Susengpha* (or *Burha Raja* or *Pratap Singh*)
1641	*Surampha* (or *Bhaga Raja*)
1644	*Sutyinpha* (or *Nariya Raja*)

1648	*Sutyinpha* (or *Jayadhvaj Singh*)
1663	*Supungmung* (or *Chakradhvaj Singh*)
1669	*Sunyatpha* (or *Udayaditya Singh*)
1673	*Suklampha* (or *Ramdhvaj*)
1675	*Suhung*
1675	*Gobar*, great-grandson of Suhungmung, for 20 days
1675	*Sujinpha*
1677	*Sudaipha*
1679	*Sulikpha* (or *Lara Raja*)
1681	*Supatpha* (or *Gadadhar Singh*), son of Gobar
1696	*Sukhrungpha* (or *Rudra Singh*), son
1714	*Sutanpha* (or *Sib Singh*), son
1744	*Sunenpha* (or *Pramata Singh*), brother
1751	*Surampha* (or *Rajesvar Singh*), brother
1769	*Sunyeopha* (or *Lakshmi Singh*), brother
1780 – 1794	*Suhitpangpha* (or *Gaurinath Singh*), son
1795	*Suklingpha* (or *Kamalesvar Singh*), great-great-grandson of Supatpha
1810	*Sudinpha* (or *Chandrakant Singh*), brother
1818	*Purandar Singh*, great-great-grandson of Surampha
1819	*Jogesvar Singh*
1819 – 1824	Burmese rule
1824	British conquest

Assyria

Territory based in present-day northern Iraq and eastern Turkey, but at its greatest extent also comprised part of present-day Syria, Lebanon, Israel, Egypt, Saudi Arabia, southern Iraq and Jordan. Capitals established at Ashur (present-day Sharqat), Kalakh (present-day Calah), Nineveh and Dur Sharrukin (present-day Khorsabad).

Kings

c. 2030 BC	*Sulili*(?), 27th king in the traditional list
(?)	*Kikkia*
(?)	*Akkia*
(?)	*Puzur-Ashur I*
before 1940	*Shallim-ahhe*, son
(?)	*Ilushuma*, son

c. 1906	*Erishum I*, son
c. 1866(?)	*Ikunum*, son
(?)	*Sargon I*, son
(?)	*Puzur-Ashur II*, son
before 1830	*Naram-Sin*, probably identical with Naram-Sin, the king of Eshnunna
1818	*Erishum II*, son(?)
1813	*Shamshi-Adad I*
1780	*Ishme-Dagan I*, son
1740(?)	*Mut-Ashkur*, son
(?)	*Rimu(sh?)*
(?)	*Asinum*, grandson of Shamshi-Adad I(?)
(?)	Period of anarchy, eight usurpers beginning with *Puzur-Sin* and ending with *Adasi*
1700	*Belu-bani*, son of Adasi
1690	*Libaia*
1673	*Sharma-Adad I*
1661	*Iptar(?)-Sin*
1649	*Bazaia*
1621	*Lullaia*
1615	*Kidin-Ninua*
1601	*Sharma-Adad II*
1598	*Erishum III*
1585	*Shamshi-Adad II*
1579	*Ishme-Dagan II*
1563	*Shamshi-Adad III*
1547	*Ashur-nirari I*
1521	*Puzur-Ashur III*
1497	*Enlil-nasir I*
1483	*Nur-ili*, kingdom annexed by the Mitanni
(?)	*Ashur-shaduni*, for one month
1472	*Ashur-rabi I*
1452	*Ashur-nadin-ahhe I*
1432	*Enlil-nasir II*
1426	*Ashur-nirari II*
1419	*Ashur-bel-nisheshu*
1410	*Ashur-rim-nisheshu*
1402	*Ashur-nadin-ahhe II*
1392	*Eriba-Adad I*
1365	*Ashur-uballit I*, ended Mitanni overlordship
1329	*Enlil-nirari*, son
1319	*Arik-den-ili*
1307	*Adad-nirari I*, defeated the Mitanni king Wasashatta

	and incorporated his territory into Assyria c. 1275
1274	*Shalmaneser I*, son
1244	*Tukulti-Ninurta I*, son, invaded Hittite territories; conquered Armenia and Babylonia 1235; assassinated
1207	*Ashur-nadin-apli*
1203	*Ashur-nirari III*
1197	*Enlil-kudurri-usur*
1192	*Ninurta-apil-Ekur*
1180	*Ashur-dan I*
(?)	*Ninurta-tukulti-Ashur*
1179	*Mutakkil-Nusku*
1133	*Ashur-resh-ishi I*
1115	*Tiglath-pileser I*, son
1076	*Ninurta-apal-Ekur II*
1074	*Ashur-bel-kala I*, son of Tiglath-pileser I
1056	*Enlil-rabi*, usurper
c.1050	*Ashur-bel-kala II*
(?)	*Eriba-Adad II*
(?)	*Shamshi-Adad IV*, son of Tiglath-pileser I
1038	*Ashur-nasir-pal I*, son
1019	*Shalmaneser II*
1007	*Ashur-nirari IV*
1001	*Ashur-rabi II*
(?)	*Ashur-resh-ishi II*
956	*Tiglath-pileser II*
933	*Ashur-dan II*
911	*Adad-nirari II*, son
889	*Tukulti-Ninurta II*, son
884	*Ashur-nasir-pal II*, son
859	*Shalmaneser III*, son
824	*Shamshi-Adad V*, son
811	*Adad-nirari III*, son Regent: 811 – 808: *Sammu-ramat*, mother
782	*Shalmaneser IV*
772	*Ashur-dan III*
754	*Ashur-nirari V*, deposed
745	*Tiglath-pileser III*, brother; captured Damascus 732, defeated and captured the Babylonian king Ukin-zer 729, king of Babylonia under the name Pulu 729 – 727
727	*Shalmaneser V*, son, king of Babylonia under the name Ululai 727 – 722, conquered Israel, assassinated
722	*Sargon II*, brother(?), king of Babylon 710 – 705,

	assimilated Israel into the empire 722, conquered Urartu
705	*Sennacherib*, son, king of Babylon 705 – 703 and 689 – 681, sacked Babylon 689, assassinated
681	*Esarhaddon*, son, conquered Egypt 671
669	*Ashurbanipal*, son, lost Egypt 656, conquered Elam 640, sacked Susa (present-day Shush) 639
626(?)	*Ashur-etil-ilani* and *Sin-shum-lishir*, brothers and rival kings
621(?) or 619(?) – 612	*Sin-shar-ishkun*, brother(?), lost Ashur 614, lost Nineveh 612
611 – 609	*Ashur-uballit II*
609	Conquest by Media and Babylonia

Asturias and León

Territory comprised part of north-western Spain and northern Portugal, with the capital initially at Cangas de Onis, from c. 780 at Pravia, in the early 9th century at Oviedo and from 925 at León.

Kings

AD 718	*Pelayo*, a Visigoth noble
737 – Jun 739	*Favila*, son
739	*Alfonso I*, Duke of Cantabria, brother-in-law, incorporated Galicia 741
757 – 14 Jan 768	*Fruela I*, son of Favila (b. 732) assassinated
768	*Aurelius*, count of Castile, son
774	*Silo*, brother-in-law of Fruela I, transferred capital to Pravia
783	*Mauregato*, brother-in-law
788	*Bermudo I*, brother of Aurelius (d. 797)
791 – 20 Mar 842	*Alfonso II*, son of Fruela I, transferred capital to Oviedo
842 – 1 Feb 850	*Ramiro I*, son of Bermudo I
850 – 27 May 866	*Ordoño I*, son, established suzerainty over León 855
866 – 20 Dec 910	*Alfonso III*, the Great, son (b. 848)
910	Kingdom divided among Alfonso III's sons
910 – 19 Jan 914	*García I*, King of León
910 – 924	*Ordoño II*, brother, King of Galicia

910 – Mar 925	*Fruela II*, brother, King of Asturias
925	*Alfonso IV*, son of Ordoño II (d. 933) King of Asturias and León,* abdicated
931	*Ramiro II*, brother
950 – Aug 955	*Ordoño III*, son
955	*Sancho I*, the Fat, brother (for 1st time) (d. Dec 966) deposed
958	*Ordoño IV*, son of Alfonso IV
960 – Dec 966	*Sancho I* (for 2nd time)
967	*Ramiro III*, son (b. 961; d. 984) deposed
982	*Bermudo II*, son of Ordoño III
999 – 5 May 1028	*Alfonso V*, son (b. 996)
1028 – 1037	*Bermudo III*, son (d. Tamarón)
1038 – 27 Dec 1065	*Fernando I*, the Great, King of Castile, brother-in-law of Bermudo III, son of Sancho III of Navarre (b. 1016/18; d. León) crowned king of León 1039 although in control of the kingdom a year before, recognized as suzerain in Navarre after 1054
27 Dec 1065	Kingdom divided between Fernando I's sons
1065	*Alfonso VI*, son (for 1st time) (b. 1039; d. Toledo 30 Jun 1109) King of León 1065, defeated and deposed by Sancho II
1070 – 7 Oct 1072	*Sancho II*, King of Castile, brother (b. c. 1038; d. Zamora) killed while trying to pacify León
1072 – 30 Jun 1109	*Alfonso VI* (for 2nd time) restored as King of Castile and León, assumed the title 'Emperor of all Spain' by 1077, conquered the Dhunnunids of Toledo 1085/6
1109 – 8 Mar 1126	*Urraca*, daughter (b. 1082) Queen of Castile and León; ruled with her husband, *Alfonso I*, King of Aragon and Navarre (b. c. 1073; d. 1134), who abdicated in favour of his stepson 1126
1126 – 21 Aug 1157	*Alfonso VII*, son of Urraca (b. 1105; d. Fresnada) King of Galicia 1112, King of Castile and León, acknowledged as emperor by the kings of Aragon and Navarre
1157	Kingdom divided between Alfonso VII's sons
1157 – 21 Jan 1188	*Fernando II*, son (b. 1137; d. Benavente) King of León only, conquered Alcántara 1166 and Badajoz 1169
1188 – 24 Sep 1230	*Alfonso IX*, son (b. 1166; d. Villanueva de Sarria) King of León; King of Castile 1217; captured Cáceres 1227, and Mérida and Badajoz 1230

*Galicia remained independent

1230 – 30 May 1252	*Fernando III*, Saint, King of Castile, son (b. 1200) King of León; conquered Córdoba 1236, Jaén 1246 and Seville 1248; effected the permanent union of Castile and León, canonized 1671

For continuation, see Castile.

Athens

French Dukes

autumn AD 1204	*Otton de la Roche*; granted Athens by Boniface of Montferrat, King of Thessalonica, and ruled with the title of megaskyr ('great lord'); received Argos and Nauplia, 1210/11; abdicated and returned to Burgundy
1225	*Gui I*, nephew; received the title, Duke of Athens, from King Louis IX of France in 1258
1263	*Jean*, son
1280	*Guillaume*, brother; lord of Livadia
1287 – 5 Oct 1308	*Gui II*, son; ruling under the tutelage of his mother, *Helena Comnena Ducaena*, until 1291; from 1291 to 1294, ruling under the tutelage of his uncle, *Hugues*, Count of Brienne and Count of Lecce
1308 – 15 Mar 1311	*Gauthier*, Count of Brienne and Count of Lecce, cousin of Gui II, son of Hugues; defeated and killed at the Battle of Cephissus

Conquered by the Grand Catalan Company who, in 1312, placed themselves under the protection of King Federico III of Sicily. In 1388 Nerio Acciajuoli, lord of Corinth, took the Acropolis and secured recognition as Duke of Athens in 1394. His dynasty lasted until 1458 when Athens was conquered by the Ottomans.

Austria

Margraves of the East Mark

House of Babenberg

AD 976	*Liutpold I*, son of Arnulf of Bavaria
984	*Heinrich I*, son
1018 – 26 May 1053	*Adalbert*, brother
1053 – 9 Jun 1075	*Ernst*, son
1075 – 12 Oct 1102	*Leopold II*, son
1102 – 15 Nov 1136	*Leopold III*, son, canonized 1485
1136 – 18 Oct 1141	*Leopold IV*, son, Duke (Leopold) of Bavaria 1139

Dukes of Austria

1141 – 13 Jan 1177	*Heinrich II Jasomirgott*, brother, Margrave of the East Mark and Duke (Heinrich XI) of Bavaria, deposed in Bavaria 1156 and in compensation created Duke of Austria by the Holy Roman Emperor Friedrich I Barbarossa
1177 – 31 Dec 1194	*Leopold V*, son, Duke of Styria 1192
1195 – 16 Apr 1199	*Friedrich I*, son
1199 – 28 Jul 1230	*Leopold VI*, Duke of Styria, brother
1230 – 15 Jun 1246	*Friedrich II*, the Warlike, son; lost Styria to King Béla IV of Hungary 1237
1246 – 1248	Interregnum
1248 – 4 Oct 1250	*Hermann*, Margrave (Hermann V) of Baden, husband of Gertrude, niece of Friedrich II
Nov 1251 – 1274	*Přemysl Otakar II*, husband of Margarete, niece of Friedrich II (b. c. 1230; d. 26 Aug 1278) King of Bohemia 22 Sep 1253; Duke of Styria 1260; seized Carinthia, Carniola and Istria 1269; lost Austria, Styria and Carinthia to Rudolf I

House of Habsburg

1274	*Rudolf I*, Count of Habsburg, King of Germany, Duke of Swabia, son of Albrecht IV of Habsburg (b. Limburg im Breisgau 1 May 1218; d. Speyer 15 Jul 1291) Duke of Carinthia 1276 – 1286
1282	*Albrecht I*, son (b. Jul 1248; d. (assassinated) Brugg (now in Aargau canton, Switzerland) 1 May 1308)

	Duke of Austria and Styria; King of Germany 27 Jul 1298; with his brother, *Rudolf II* (b. 1271; d. 10 May 1290) Duke of Swabia 1282; Carniola granted to Meinhard II of Tirol 1282; by the Treaty of Rheinfelden, Albrecht I became sole ruler of Austria 1 Jun 1283; Carinthia granted to Meinhard II of Tirol 1286
1 May 1308	*Friedrich III*, the Fair, son of Albrecht I (b. 1286; d. Gutenstein 13 Jan 1330) King of Germany 19 Oct 1314 – 1322; with his brother, *Leopold I* (b. c. 4 Aug 1290; d. 28 Feb 1326)
13 Jan 1330	*Albrecht II*, brother (b. 12 Dec 1298; d. 20 Jul 1358) with his brother, *Otto* (b. 23 Jul 1301; d. 26 Feb 1339); acquired Carinthia and Carniola 1335

Archdukes

20 Jul 1358	*Rudolf IV*, son of Albrecht II (b. 1 Nov 1339) claimed the title Archduke of Austria, acquired Tirol 1363
27 Jul 1365 – 29 Aug 1395	*Albrecht III*, brother (b. 9 Sep 1348; d. 29 Aug 1395) with (until 1379) his brother, *Leopold III* (b. 1 Nov 1351; d. 9 Aug 1386)
1379	Treaty of Neuberg divided the Habsburg territories: Albrecht III received Upper and Lower Austria; Leopold III received Styria, Carinthia, Tirol and central Istria
29 Aug 1395	*Albrecht IV*, son of Albrecht III (b. 21 Sep 1377)
14 Sep 1404 – 27 Oct 1439	*Albrecht V*, son (b. 10 Aug 1397; d. Nezmely, Hungary) King (Albert) of Hungary 1437, King (Albrecht II) of Bohemia 29 Jun 1438, King (Albrecht II) of Germany 18 Mar 1438
1439 – 19 Aug 1493	*Friedrich V*, second cousin, grandson of Leopold III (b. Innsbruck 21 Sep 1415; d. Linz) inherited Styria, Carinthia and Carniola 1439; King (Friedrich III) of Germany 2 Feb 1440; King of the Lombards 1452; Holy Roman Emperor (Friedrich III) 19 Mar 1452; ruled in Austria at first as the guardian of *Ladislaus Posthumus*, son of Albrecht V (b. 22 Feb 1440; d. 23 Nov 1457) King (Vladislav IV) of Bohemia 1440, King (László V) of Hungary 1444

Awan

Territory comprised part of present-day south-western Iran, with the capital at Awan.

Kings

c. 2550 BC	Dynasty of three kings, whose names are unknown
(?)	*Peli*
(?)	*Tata*
(?)	*Ukkutakhash*
before 2450	*Khishur*
(?)	*Shushuntarana*
(?)	*Napilkhush*
(?)	*Kukku-siwe-temti*
fl. c. 2325	*Lukh-ishshan*, vassal of the Akkadian king Sargon
(?)	*Khishep-ratep*, son, vassal of Sargon
(?)	*Khelu*
(?)	*Epir-mupi*
(?)	*Khita*, formed alliance with the Akkadian king Naram-Sin(?)
c. 2240	*Puzur-* (or *Kutik-*) *In-Shushinak*, probably served as governor of Susa (present-day Shush) for Naram-Sin during the reign of Khita, freed from Akkadian overlordship by the time of his accession
(?)	*Tazitta I*
(?)	*Eparti I*
before 2120	*Tazitta II*
(?)	Dynasty ended during the period of Guti invasions

Axum (Aksum)

Territory comprised part of present-day Ethiopia and Sudan, with the capital at Aksum.

Kings

AD c. 250	*Aphilas Bisi-Dimele*

(?)	Unknown number of kings
325	*Ezana (Abreha)*, son of Ella Amida (b. c. 310) and *Shiazana (Asbeha)*, brother, regent, joint ruler from 328
356(?) – c. 370	*Ella Abreha*, *Ella Asfeha* and *Ella Shahel*, sons, jointly
(?)	Unknown number of kings
474(?)	*Agabe* and *Lewi*
475(?)	*Ella Amida (IV?)*
486	*Jacob* and *David*
489	*Armah*
504	*Zitana*
505	*Jacob (II)*, usurper (?)
514	*Caleb (Ella Asbeha)*, son of Zitana
542	*Beta Esrael*, son
c. 550 – 564	*Gabra Masqal*, brother
6th – 10th century	King lists uncertain, many kings of uncertain date are known from coins whose names do not agree with those in the tradition
10th century	Dynasty overthrown by the Agau chieftainess Gudit (Judith), Axum abandoned and the Zagwe dynasty re-established the kingdom at Roha (also called Lalibela) (see Ethiopia)

Ayyubids

Territory comprised part of present-day northern Libya, Egypt, Israel, Jordan, Syria, eastern Turkey, Saudi Arabia, Yemen and western Iraq.

Sultans*

In Egypt	
Mar AD 1169	*(al-Malik) al-Nasir I (Salah al-Din Yusuf ibn Ayyub)* (known in the West as *Saladin*) (b. Takrit 1137/8(?)) recognized Nur al-Din Zangi as suzerain, conquered Amid 1183/4, ruled in Diyarbakr (Mayyafariqin and Jabal Sinjar) 28 Aug 1185 – 1194/5, conquered Jerusalem 4 Oct 1187

*The numeration of rulers takes all lines into consideration

4 Mar 1193 – 29 Nov 1198	*(al-Malik) al-'Aziz I (Imad al-Din Abu'l-Fath 'Uthman)*, son (b. 7 Jan 1172) declared independence 1194/5
3 Dec 1198	*(al-Malik) al-Mansur (Nasir al-Din Muhammad)*, son
1199/1200 – 31 Aug 1218	*(al-Malik) al-'Adil I (Saif al-Din Abu Bakr Ahmad)*, brother of Saladin (b. Jun/Jul 1145; d. 31 Aug 1218) governor of Egypt 1175/6, ruled in Aleppo 1183/4 – Aug/Sep 1186, ruled in Karak 1188/9, ruled in Mesopotamia 1191/2, ruled in Diyarbakr (Mayyafariqin and Jabal Sinjar) 1194/5 – 1199/1200, ruled in Damascus 1195/6 – 1200/1
Sep 1218 – 10 Mar 1238	*(al-Malik) al-Kamil I (Nasir al-Din Abu'l-Ma'ali Muhammad)*, son (b. 18 Aug 1180) ruled in Damascus Dec 1237/Jan 1238 – Feb/Mar 1238
Mar 1238 – 30 Jun 1240	*(al-Malik) al-'Adil II (Saif al-Din Abu Bakr)*, son (b. Jan/Feb 1221; d. in prison 9 Feb 1248) ruled in Damascus Feb/Mar 1238 – 1238/9, deposed
Jun/Jul 1240 – 23 Nov 1249	*(al-Malik) al-Salih (Najm al-Din) Ayyub (ibn Kamil)*, son of al-Kamil I (b. 26 Jan 1207; d. Mansura 23 Nov 1249) ruled in Diyarbakr (Hisn Kaifa and Amid) 1231/2 – 1238/9, ruled at ar-Ruha and Harran 1235/6, ruled at Sinjar and Nisibin 1237/8, ruled in Damascus 1238/9 – 1 Oct 1245
Nov/Dec 1249 – 3 May 1250	*(al-Malik al-Mu'azzam) Turan-Shah IV (ibn Ayyub ibn Kamil)*, son of al-Salih (d. (assassinated) 3 May 1250) ruled in Diyarbakr (Hisn Kaifa and Amid) 1238/9 – 1249/50, ruled in Damascus 1249/50 – 19 Jul 1250
5 May 1250 – 1252/3	*(al-Malik) al-Ashraf II (Muzaffar al-Din Musa ibn Yusuf ibn Muhammad)*, son of Mus'ud Yusuf Salah al-Din of Yemen (b. 1244/5) deposed by Mamluk sultan Aibeg
1252/3	Succeeded by Bahri line of Mamluks

In Damascus

Jul/Aug 1176	*(al-Malik al-Mu'azzam Shams al-Din) Turan-Shah (ibn Ayyub)*, brother of Saladin, ruled in Yemen Feb/Mar 1174 – 26 Jun 1180, lord of Baalbec 1172/3 – 1179/80, government in Damascus conferred on him by Saladin, died in Alexandria
1186/7	*(al-Malik) al-Afdal (Nur al-Din Abu'l-Hasan 'Ali)*, son of Saladin (b. Misr 1169/70; d. Sumaisat

	Feb/Mar 1225) head of the entire dynasty until 1193, deposed and named lord of Sarkhad 1195/6, atabeg in Egypt 1198/9 – 1200/1, lord of Qal'at Najm, Saruj and Samosata 1200/1 – 1202/3
1195/6	*(al-Malik) al-'Adil I (Saif al-Din Abu Bakr Ahmad)* (see In Egypt)
1200/1	*(al-Malik) al-Mu'azzam*, as governor
Aug/Sep 1218 – 12 Nov 1227	*(al-Malik) al-Mu'azzam Sharaf al-Din 'Isa*, nephew of Saladin (b. 1180/1) lord of Karak 1195/6 – 1218/19
Nov/Dec 1227	*(al-Malik) al-Nasir Salah al-Din Da'ud*, son (b. 1205/6) lord of Karak 1228/9, with *Abu-Mansur 'Izz al-Din Aibak al-Mu'azzam*, Lord of Sarkhad, ruling as regent
1228/9 – 27 Aug 1237(?)	*(al-Malik) al-Ashraf I (al-Muzaffar al-Din Abu'l-Fath Musa)*, brother of al-Auhad (b. 1182/3) ruled in Diyarbakr (Mayyafariqin and Jabal Sinjar) 1210/11 – 1220/1
1237	*(al-Malik) al-Salih (Imad al-Din Isma'il)*, brother (for 1st time) (b. 1201/2; d. Cairo 1250/1)
Dec 1237/Jan 1238	*(al-Malik) al-Kamil I (Nasir al-Din Abu'l-Ma'ali Muhammad)* (see In Egypt)
Feb/Mar 1238	*(al-Malik) al-'Adil II (Saif al-Din Abu Bakr)* (see In Egypt)
1238/9	*(al-Malik) al-Salih (Najm al-Din) Ayyub (ibn Kamil)* (for 1st time) (see In Egypt)
28 Sep 1239	*al-Salih* (for 2nd time)
1 Oct 1245	*al-Salih Ayyub* (for 2nd time) recognized the Seljuq Kai-Khusrau II as suzerain
1249/50	*(al-Malik al-Mu'azzam) Turan-Shah IV (ibn Ayyub ibn Kamil)* (see In Egypt)
19 Jul 1250 – Apr/May 1261	*(al-Malik) al-Nasir II (Salah al-Din Yusuf)*, son of al-'Aziz II (b. 1 Aug 1230) Seljuq vassal, ruled in Aleppo 1236/7 – 1 Oct 1260, put to death by the Mongol Khan Hülegü
Apr/May 1261	Mongol conquest

In Aleppo

1183/4	*(al-Malik) al-'Adil I (Saif al-Din Abu Bakr Ahmad)* (see In Egypt)
Aug/Sep 1186 – 7 Oct 1216	*(al-Malik) al-Zahir (Ghiyath al-Din Abu'l-Fath Ghazi I)*, nephew (b. Misr 30 Apr 1173)
Oct 1216 – 5 Nov 1236	*(al-Malik) al-'Aziz II (Ghiyath al-Din Abu'l-Muzaffar Muhammad)*, son (b. 17 Apr 1214)

1236/7 – 1 Oct 1260	*(al-Malik) al-Nasir II (Salah al-Din Yusuf)*, son (see In Damascus)
Oct 1260	Mongol conquest

In Diyarbakr (Mayyafariqin and Jabal Sinjar)

28 Aug 1185	*(al-Malik) al-Nasir I (Salah al-Din Yusuf ibn Ayyub)* (known in the West as *Saladin*) (see In Egypt)
1194/5	*(al-Malik) al-'Adil I (Saif al-Din Abu Bakr Ahmad)* (see In Egypt)
1199/1200	*(al-Malik) al-Auhad (Najm al-Din Ayyub)*, nephew of Saladin
1210/11	*(al-Malik) al-Ashraf I (al-Muzaffar al-Din Abu'l-Fath Musa)* (see In Damascus)
1220/1 – 1230/1	*(al-Malik) al-Muzaffar (Shihab al-Din Ghazi)*, brother
1230/1 – 1244/5	Temporary Mongol conquest
1244/5 – 1259/60	*(al-Malik) al-Kamil II (Nasir al-Din Muhammad)*, son of al-Muzaffar
1259/60	Mongol conquest

In Diyarbakr (Hisn Kaifa and Amid)

1231/2	*(al-Malik) al-Salih (Najm al-Din) Ayyub (ibn Kamil)* (see In Egypt)
1238/9	*(al-Malik al-Mu'azzam) Turan-Shah IV (ibn Ayyub ibn Kamil)* (see In Egypt)
1249/50	*(al-Malik al-Muwahhid) Taqi al-Din ('Abdallah ibn Turan-Shah)*, son
1283/4	*(al-Malik al-Kamil III Abu Bakr) Muhammad ibn 'Abdallah*, son
(?)	*(al-Malik al-'Adil) Mujir al-Din (Muhammad ibn Abu Bakr)*, son
(?)	*(al-Malik al-'Adil) Shihab al-Din (Ghazi ibn Muhammad)*, son
(?)	*(al-Malik al-Salih) Abu Bakr ibn Ghazi*, son
1378/9	*(al-Malik al-'Adil) Fakhr al-Din (Sulaiman ibn Ghazi)*, brother
(?)	*(al-Malik al-Ashraf) Sharaf al-Din (Ahmad ibn Sulaiman)*, son
1432/3	*(al-Malik al-Salih) Salah al-Din (Khalil ibn Ahmad)*, son
1452/3	*(al-Malik al-Kamil IV) Ahmad ibn Khalil*, son
(?)	*(al-Malik al-'Adil) Khalaf ibn Muhammad (ibn Ahmad)*, cousin

1461/2	*Khalil ibn Sulaiman (ibn Ahmad)* (?), cousin
(?)	*Sulaiman ibn Khalil (ibn Sulaiman)*, son
(?)	*al-Husain ibn Khalil (ibn Khalil)*, son
(?)	Ak Koyunlu conquest

In Yemen

Feb/Mar 1174 – 26 Jun 1180	*(al-Malik al-Mu'azzam Shams al-Din) Turan-Shah (ibn Ayyub)* (see In Damascus)
1181/2	*(al-Malik al-'Aziz Saif al-Islam Zahir al-Din Abu'l-Fawaris) Tughtigin ibn Ayyub*, brother, died in Yemen
4 Sep 1197	*Mu'izz al-Din Isma'il (ibn Tughtigin)*, son
1201/2	*(al-Malik) al-Nasir Ayyub (ibn Tughtigin)*, brother
1214/15	*(al-Malik al-Muzaffar) Sulaimán (ibn Sa'd al-Din Shahanshah II)*, grandson of a cousin of al-Nasir Ayyub (d. 1251/2)
1215/16 – 1228/9	*(al-Malik) al-Mas'ud Salah al-Din Yusuf (ibn al-Kamil)*, son of al-Kamil I of Egypt
1228/9	Rasulid conquest

Aztecs

Territory comprised part of present-day Mexico.

Rulers

At Texcoco

AD 1409	*Ixtlilxóchitl*
1418	*Nezahualcóyotl*
1472	*Nezahualpilli*
1516 – 1519	*Cacama*
1519	Spanish conquest

At Tenochtitlan (present-day Mexico City)

1414	*Chimalpopoca*
1428	*Itzcóatl*
1440	*Montezuma I*
1469	*Axayácatl*
1481	*Tizoc*
1486	*Ahuitzotl*

1503	*Montezuma II*, nephew (b. 1466; d. Tenochtitlan c. 30 Jun 1520) believed to have been killed by his subjects because of his submission to the Spanish commander Cortes, who occupied Tenochtitlan 8 Nov 1519
1520	*Cuitlahuac*, brother, rebelled against Spanish occupation and died during the seige of Tenochtitlan after a reign of four months
1520 – 1522	*Cuauhtemoc*, nephew (b. c. 1495; d. 26 Feb 1522) captured by the Spanish 1521 and killed en route to Honduras
1522	Spanish conquest

Babylonia

At its greatest extent, territory comprised part of present-day southern Turkey, Syria, Lebanon, Israel, Jordan, Saudi Arabia and Iraq, with the capital at Babylon.

Kings

First Dynasty (Amorite)

1894 BC	*Sumuabum*
1880	*Sumulael*
1844	*Sabium*
1830	*Apil-Sin*
1812	*Sin-muballit*
1792	*Hammurabi*, son; defeated the Elamite king Siwe-palar-khuppak; conquered Uruk and Isin 1787; defeated Rim-Sin I, the king of Larsa, 1763; conquered Eshnunna c. 1750
1749	*Samsuiluna*, son; defeated Rim-Sin II, the king of Larsa, and conquered his kingdom
1711	*Abieshu'*
1683	*Ammiditana*
1646	*Ammisaduqa*
1625 – 1595	*Samsuditana*
1595	Overthrown by the Hittite king Mursilis I

Kassite Dynasty

(?)	*Gandash*
c. 1700	*Agum I*, son
(?)	*Kashtiliash I*, son, conquered the kingdom of Sealand
before 1650	*Ushshi*, son
(?)	*Abirattash*, brother
(?)	*Kashtiliash II*(?)
(?)	*Urzigurumash*, son
before 1600	*Kharbashikhu*
(?)	*Tiptakzi*
before 1550	*Agum II*, son of Urzigurumash
(?)	*Burnaburiash I*
(?)	Unknown king
(?)	*Kashtiliash III*, son of Burnaburiash I
before 1450	*Ulamburiash*, brother
(?)	*Agum III*, nephew
(?)	Unknown king(?)
(?)	*Kadashmankharbe I*
(?)	*Karaindash*
before 1390	*Kurigalzu I*, son of Kadashmankharbe I
(?)	*Kadashman-Enlil I*, son(?)
c. 1375 – 1347	*Burnaburiash II*
(?)	*Karakhardash*
(?)	*Nazibugash*
1345	*Kurigalzu II*
1323	*Nazimaruttash*
1297	*Kadashman-Turgu*
1279	*Kadashman-Enlil II*
1264	*Kudur-Enlil*
1255	*Shagarakti-Shuriash*
1242 – 1235	*Kashtiliash IV*, Babylon invaded and destroyed by the Assyrian king Tukulti-Ninurta I
1235 – 1227	Period of Assyrian domination
1227	*Enlil-nadin-shumi*
(?)	*Kadashmankharbe II*
1224	*Adad-shuma-iddina*
1218	*Adad-shuma-usur*
1188	*Meli-shikhu*
1173	*Marduk-apla-iddina*
1160	*Zababa-shuma-iddina*
1159 – 1157	*Enlil-nadin-akhi*
1157	Babylon sacked by the Elamites

Second Dynasty of Isin

1156	*Marduk-kabit-ahheshu*
1138	*Itti-Marduk-balatu*
1131	*Ninurta-nadin-shumi*
1125	*Nebuchadrezzar I*, conquered Elam c. 1110
1103	*Enlil-nadin-apli*, son
1099	*Marduk-nadin-ahhe*, brother
1081	*Marduk-shapik-zeri*
1068	*Adad-apal-iddina*
1046	*Marduk-ahhe-eriba*
1045	*Marduk-zer-* . . .
1033 – 1026	*Nabu-shum-libur*

Second Sea Land Dynasty

1025	*Simbar-Shikhu*
1008	*Ea-mukin-shumi* (or *Ea-mukin-zeri*)
1007 – 1005	*Kashshu-nadin-ahhe*

Bazu-Dynasty

1004	*E-ulmash-shakin-shumi*
987	*Ninurta-kudurri-usur I*
985 – 984	*Shiriqti-Shuqamunu*

Dynasty 'G' (Elamite)

984 – 979	*Mar-biti-apal-usur*

Dynasty 'H'

978	*Nabu-mukin-apli*
943	*Ninurta-kudurri-usur II*
942	*Mar-biti-akh-iddin*
(?)	*Shamash-mudammik*, ceded territories to the Assyrian king Adad-nirari II, murdered
(?)	*Nabu-shum-ukin I*
c. 881	*Nabu-apal-iddin I*, son
850	*Marduk-bel-usate*, son
(?)	*Marduk-zakir-shum I*, brother
(?) – 811	*Marduk-balatsu-ikbi*, son
(?)	*Bau-akh-iddin*
(?)	Four unknown kings
(?)	*Adad-shum-ibni*
c. 800	*Marduk-bel-zeri*
(?)	*Marduk-apal-usur*
(?)	*Eriba-Marduk*

c. 760	*Nabu-shum-ukin II*
747	*Nabu-nasir* (or *Nabonasar*)
734	*Nabu-nadin-zer*
732	*Nabu-shum-ukin III*

Dynasty 'J' (Ninth Dynasty)

732	*Ukin-zer* (or *Nabu-mukin-zeri*), defeated and captured by the Assyrian king Tiglath-pileser III 729
729	*Pulu*, king of Assyria under the name of Tiglath-pileser III 745 – 727
727	*Ululai*, king of Assyria under the name of Shalmaneser V 727 – 722, assassinated
722	*Marduk-apal-iddin II* (or *Merodach-Baladan*) an Aramaean prince (for 1st time) deposed
710	*Sargon II*, king of Assyria 722 – 705
705	*Sennacherib* (for 1st time) king of Assyria 705 – 681
703	*Marduk-zakir-shum II*
703	*Marduk-apal-iddin* (for 2nd time) deposed
702	*Bel-ibni*, revolted against Assyrian overlordship 700, defeated
700	*Ashur-nadin-shum*, son of Sennacherib
694	*Nergal-ushezib*, Elamite vassal
693	*Mushezib-Marduk*, Babylon reconquered and destroyed by Assyria
689	*Sennacherib* (for 2nd time) assassinated
681	*Esarhaddon*, king of Assyria 681 – 669; with the title of governor of Babylon
668	*Shamash-shum-ukin*, son, rebelled during the reign of the Assyrian king Ashurbanipal, committed suicide
647 – 626	*Kandalanu*

Chaldaean Dynasty (the New Babylonian Empire)

625	*Nabu-apal-usur* (or *Nabopolassar*), king of the Chaldaeans; with the Median king Cyaxares, destroyed Nineveh 612 and conquered Assyria 609
605	*Nebuchadrezzar II*, son; captured Jerusalem 16 Mar 597 and Jul 586; defeated Baal II, forcing the kingdom of Tyre into vassaldom
562	*Amel-Marduk* (or *Evil-Merodach*), son
560	*Nergal-shar-usur* (or *Neriglissar*), brother-in-law
556	*Labashi-Marduk*, son, murdered
556	*Nabu-na'id* (or *Nabonidus*), usurper, captured by the

	Persians and exiled to Carmania (present-day Kerman)
(?)	*Belshazzar*, son, as regent
12 Oct 539	Persian conquest of Babylon

Bactria

Territory comprised part of present-day Afghanistan, with the capital at Bactra (present-day Balkh).

Kings

c. 256 BC	*Diodotus I*, Seleucid satrap of Bactria, declared himself king c. 256.
235	*Diodotus II*, son, assassinated
235	*Euthydemus I*, brother-in-law, acknowledged Seleucid suzerainty 208 but retained his kingdom
c. 200 – c. 171	*Demetrius I*, son, conquered large territories in northern India
c. 190 – 180	*Antimachus I*, brother, ruled in the absence of Demetrius I
(?)	*Euthydemus II*, nephew, ruled in the absence of Demetrius I
(?)	*Demetrius II*, brother, ruled in the absence of Demetrius I as king of Paropamisadae and Gandhara (present-day Kandahar)
c. 171	*Eucratides I*, grandson of Euthydemus I(?), assassinated
c. 155	*Plato*, son, assassinated
c. 155	*Heliocles I*, brother
c. 140 – (?)	*Eucratides II*, son or brother, killed during Saca invasions
c. 140 – 135	Kingdom overwhelmed by the Sacas (combination of Scythian, Tartar and Chinese tribes)

Bahmanids

Territory comprised part of present-day central India with the capital initially at Ahsanabad (now Gulbarga) and later at Muhammadabad (now Bidar).

Sultans

3 Aug AD 1347 – 11 Feb 1358	*'Ala' al-Din (Hasan) Bahman Shah*
12 Feb 1358	*Muhammad I*, son
Mar/Apr 1375 – 16 Apr 1378	*'Ala' al-Din Mujahid Shah*, son, assassinated
20 May 1378	*Da'ud I*, uncle, assassinated
24 Jun 1378	*Muhammad II*, brother
26 Apr – 14 Jun 1397	*Ghiyath al-Din (Tahamtan)*, son, deposed
Jun 1397	*(Shams al-Din) Dau'd II*, brother
1397/8	*(Taj al-Din) Firuz Shah*, cousin
2 Oct 1422 – 17 Feb 1435	*Ahmad I*, brother
Feb 1435	*('Ala' al-Din) Ahmad II*, nephew
1457/8 – 4 Sep 1461	*('Ala' al-Din) Humayun Zalim*, son
Sep 1461 – 30 Jul 1463	*(Nizam al-Din) Ahmad III*, son (b. 1453/4)
Jul/Aug 1463	*(Shams al-Din) Muhammad III*, brother
Mar/Apr 1482 – 18 Dec 1518	*(Shihab al-Din) Mahmud*, son
Dec 1518	*Ahmad IV*, son
1521	*'Ala' al-Din*, brother, nominal sultan under tutelage of chief minister Amir Barid
1523	*Wali Allah*, brother, nominal sultan under tutelage of Amir Barid
1526	*Kalim Allah*, brother (d. 1527) nominal sultan under tutelage of Amir Barid
1527	Dismemberment into five succession states: Bijapur, Ahmadnagar, Golconda, Berar and Bidar

Bambara States

SEGU

Territory comprised part of present-day southern Mali.

Rulers

AD (?)	*Barama-Ngolo*, brother of Nya Ngolo of Kaarta
(?)	*Soma*, son
(?)	*fa Siné*, son
1660	*Mamari Biton*, son
1710	*Bakari*, son
1711	*Dé-koro*, brother, deposed
1736	*Tonmassa Démbélé*, general of the state, led rebellion against Dé-koro
1740	*Kanou-ba-nyouma Bari*, son
1744 – 1748	*Kafadyougou*, son
1748 – 1750	Period of anarchy
1750	*Ngolo Dyara*
1787	*Man-nson*, son
1808	*Da*, son
1827	*Tyé-folo*, brother
1839 – 1840	*Nyéné-mba*, brother
1840 – 1843	Period of anarchy
1843	*Bén*, brother
1849	*Kon-Maran*, brother
1851	*Démba*, brother
1854	*Touro-koro Mari*, brother
1856 – 1861	*Ali*, brother
1861	Tukulor conquest; dynasty continued in exile until 1890 when Mari, the last ruler, was killed by the French

KAARTA

Territory comprised part of present-day southern Mali and south-eastern Mauritania.

Rulers

(?)	*Nya Ngolo*, brother of Barama-Ngolo of Segu
(?)	*Sounsan*, son
1670	*Massa*, son
1690	*Sé-kolo*, son
1700	*Foro-kolo*, brother
1709	*Séba-Mana*, brother
1760	*Déni-ba Bo*, brother
1780	*Sira Bo*, nephew
1789	*Déssé-koro*, cousin
1802	*Ntin-koro*, cousin
1811	*Sara-ba*, brother
1815	*Moussou-koura Bo . . .*, cousin
1818 – 1833	*Bo-dyan Mori-ba*, cousin
1835	*Nyaralén Gran*, nephew of Moussou-koura Bo . . .
1844 – 1854	*Mamarikan-dyan*, brother
1854	Tukulor conquest

Bamberg

Bishops (and from the 13th century Princes of the Holy Roman Empire)*

1 Nov AD 1007 – 12 or 13 Aug 1040	*Eberhard*
25 Dec 1040 – 24 Dec 1046	*Suidger* (b. Saxony; d. near Pesaro 9 Oct 1047) elevated to Papacy as Clement II 24/25 Dec 1046
Christmas 1047 – 6 Nov 1053	*Hartwig*

*When two dates separated by an oblique stroke are given for the beginning of an episcopate, the first refers to election or nomination and the second to ordination, consecration or investiture

Christmas 1053 – 14 Feb 1057	*Adalbero*
30 Mar 1057 – 23 Jul 1065	*Gunther* (d. Ödenburg)
1065 – 1075	*Hermann I* (d. 1084)
30 Nov 1075 – 11 Jun 1102	*Ruotpert* (or *Rupert*)
25 Dec 1102 – 30 Jun 1139	*Otto I*
before 19 Jul 1139	*Egilbert*
29 May 1146 – 17 Jul 1172	*Eberhard*
1172 – 12 Jun 1177	*Hermann II*
after 12 Aug 1177 – 2 May 1196	*Otto II von Andechs*
before 7 Aug 1196 – 15 Oct 1202	*Thymo*
1202 – 19 Feb 1203	*Konrad*
before Sep 1203 – 5 Jun 1237	*Ekbert von Meran*
1237	*Siegfried von Öttingen*
no later than Sep 1237 – after 22 Jan 1242	*Poppo*, deposed
no earlier than May 1242/2 Oct 1245 – 17 or 18 Sep 1257	*Heinrich I von Catania*
after 17 Sep 1257/11 Jan 1259 – 17 May 1285	*Berthold von Leiningen*
after 17 May 1285 – 1286	*Manegold von Neuenburg*, not confirmed by the Curia
15 May 1286 – 17 Jul 1296	*Arnold*, Count of Solms
c. Oct 1296/21 Mar 1297 – 14 Aug 1303	*Lupold I von Gründlach*
31 Jan 1304 – 14 Mar 1318	*Wulving von Stubenberg*, previously Bishop of Lavant; in disputed election against *Johann von Müchel* and *Gerlach*
1318 – 1322	History not known

16 Jun 1322 – 23 Dec 1323	*Johann I von Güttingen* (d. 25 Apr 1324) previously Bishop of Brixen, in disputed election against *Ulrich von Schlüsselburg* and *Konrad von Giech*, translated to Freising
4 Jul 1324 – 1 Apr 1328	*Heinrich II von Sternberg*
26 Apr 1328 – 18 Apr 1329	*Johann*, Count of Nassau, in rivalry with Werntho, Schenk von Reicheneck (see below), never consecrated
16 Apr 1328 – 8 Apr 1335	*Werntho* (or *Werintho*), *Schenk von Reicheneck*, not recognized by the Curia, in rivalry with Johann, Count of Nassau (see above) until 18 Apr 1329, never consecrated
11 May 1335/24 Apr 1336 – 27 Jun 1343	*Lupold II von Egloffstein*
20 Oct 1344 – 21 Dec 1352	*Friedrich I*, Count of Hohenlohe, in disputed election against *Marquard von Randeck*
12 Jan/15 Apr 1353 – 28 Oct 1363	*Lupold III von Bebenberg*
c. 11 Nov 1363/4 Jan 1364 – 19 May 1366	*Friedrich II*, Count of Truhendingen
6 Jun/30 Aug 1366	*Ludwig von Meissen* (b. 25 Feb 1341; d. Wellmich Castle 21 May 1388) previously Bishop of Halberstadt, translated to Mainz
28 Apr 1374 – before 18 Oct 1398	*Lambert von Burne* (d. 16 Jul 1399) previously Bishop of Strasbourg, resigned
28 Nov 1398/13 Jan 1399 – 19 May 1421	*Albert*, Count of Wertheim
3 Jun/after 4 Sep 1421 – 10 Sep 1431	*Friedrich III von Aufsess*, resigned
before 16 Jan/24 Aug(?) 1432 – 5 May 1459	*Anton von Rotenhan*
18 May/13 Jul 1459 – 4 Feb 1475	*Georg von Schaumberg*
12 Apr 1475 – 26 Jan 1487	*Philipp von Henneberg*
28 Mar 1487 – 27 Mar 1501	*Heinrich III Gross von Trockau*

Barcelona (Catalonia, the Spanish Mark)

The Spanish Mark was formed after the Frankish conquest of Catalonia in 801 and consisted of the counties of Urgel, Gerona, Besalú, Ampurias, Cerdagne, Ausona, Peralada, Conflent and Roselló. The city of Barcelona was the capital of the Mark, and the counts of Barcelona were its premier rulers.

Counts

AD 873	*Wifredo*, the Hairy, Count of Urgel; received the counties of Barcelona and Gerona from King Charles II, the Bald, of France, and became the first hereditary count of Barcelona
898	*Borrell I* (or *Wifredo-Borrell*), son
914	*Sunyer*, brother, abdicated
940	*Borrell II*, son, gained independence from France*
992	*Ramón Borrell*, son (b. 972) conquered Córdoba 1010
1018	*Berenguer Ramón I*, son (b. c. 1006) ruled under the regency of his mother, *Ermesindis* (d. 1058)
1035	*Ramón BerenguerI*, the Old, son (b. 1024) Ampurias became a vassal of Barcelona
1076 – 1082	*Ramón Berenguer II*, son (b. 1054) assassinated
1076	*Berenguer Ramón II*, brother (b. 1054; d. Jerusalem 1097?) ruled alone after the assassination of Ramón Berenguer II, abdicated
1097	*Ramón Berenguer III*, the Great, nephew (b. 1082) Count of Besalú 1111, Count of Provence 1112, Count of Cerdagne 1117
1131 – 1162	*Ramón Berenguer IV*, son (b. 1115) married Petronilla, Queen of Aragon, 1137 and became the effective ruler of Aragon, without the title of king

For continuation, see Aragon.

*940 – 966	*Miro*, brother of Borrell II; Count of Urgel

Bavaria

Dukes

AD 788	Charlemagne deposed *Tassilo III*, last independent Duke of Bavaria of the Agilolfing line; Bavaria was then ruled by the Carolingian kings and their governors
House of Liutpold	
889 – 4 Jul 907	*Liutpold*, governor of Bavaria and Austria, governor of Carinthia from 893
907 – 14 Jul 937	*Arnulf*, the Bad, son, governor of Carinthia 907, refused to accept the suzerainty of the German king until 921
937	*Eberhard*, son; refused to accept the suzerainty of the German king; deposed and exiled by King Otto I of Germany
938 – 23 Nov 947	*Berthold*, uncle, appointed by Otto I; governor of Carinthia 927 – 930
Saxon House (Liudolfings)	
947 – 1 Nov 955	*Heinrich I*, brother of King Otto I of Germany (who invested him with Bavaria) and son-in-law of Arnulf (b. between 919 and 921) Duke of Lorraine for a few months in 940, received the marches of Istria, Verona and Friuli 952
955	*Heinrich II*, the Quarrelsome, son (for 1st time) (b. 951; d. Gandersheim 28 Aug 995) Duke of Carinthia 989, deposed from Bavarian dukedom by Emperor Otto II in 976 for rebellion*
Jul 976 – 31 Oct 982	*Otto I*, Duke of Swabia, nephew of Emperor Otto II (who invested him with Bavaria) (b. 954)
983	*Heinrich III*, the Younger, son of Berthold (b. between 940 and 943; d. 5 Oct 989) Duke of Carinthia 976 – 978 and 985 – 989; appointed by Otto II, deposed
985 – 28 Aug 995	*Heinrich II* (for 2nd time)

*Carinthia, the March of Verona, the Nordgau and East Mark (see Austria) were severed from the Bavarian territories

995 – 1005	*Heinrich IV*, the Saint, son (b. Abbach 6 May 973; d. Göttingen, Saxony, 13 Jul 1024) King (Heinrich II) of Germany 7 Jun 1002, Holy Roman Emperor 14 Feb 1014; appointed his brother-in-law to rule in Bavaria

House of Luxemburg

21 Mar 1004 – 27/28 Feb 1026	*Heinrich V von Luxemburg*, a count in the Ardennes region, brother-in-law of Heinrich IV

Salian House

1027 – 1041	*Heinrich VI*, son of Emperor Konrad II (who invested him with Bavaria) (b. Bodfeld 28 Oct 1017; d. Bodfeld 5 Oct 1056) Duke (Heinrich I) of Swabia 1038, King (Heinrich III) of Germany 4 Jun 1039, Holy Roman Emperor 25 Dec 1046; appointed Heinrich von Luxemburg to rule in Bavaria

House of Luxemburg (restored)

21 Feb 1042 – 14 Oct 1047	*Heinrich VII von Luxemburg*, a count in the Moselle region, nephew of Heinrich V
14 Oct 1047 – 1049	Interregnum
1049 – 1053	*Kuno*, nephew of Archbishop Hermann II of Cologne (d. 1055) deposed

Salian House (restored)

1053 – 10 Apr 1055	*Konrad*, son of Heinrich VI (b. 1052)
1055 – 1061	*Heinrich VIII*, brother (b. Goslar, Saxony, 11 Nov 1050; d. Liège 7 Aug 1106) King (Heinrich IV) of Germany 17 Jul 1054/5 Oct 1056 – 31 Dec 1105, Holy Roman Emperor 31 Mar 1084 – 31 Dec 1105 Regents: 1055 – 1056: *Gebhard*, Bishop of Eichstedt 1056 – 1061: *Agnes*, mother of Heinrich VIII

Supplinburg House

1061 – 1070	*Otto II von Nordheim* (d. 11 Jan 1083) appointed by Empress Agnes, deposed

House of Welf

1070 – 9 Nov 1101	*Welf I*, Duke (Welf IV) of Carinthia, adopted son of Welf III of Carinthia and son-in-law of Otto II von Nordheim (b. 1030/40) invested with Bavaria by King Heinrich IV of Germany

1101 – 24 Sep 1120	*Welf II*, son (b. c. 1073)
1120 – 13 Dec 1126	*Heinrich IX*, the Black, brother (b. c. 1074)
1126 – 20 Oct 1139	*Heinrich X*, the Proud, Margrave of Tuscany, son (b. c. 1100; d. Quedlinburg, Saxony) Duke (Heinrich II) of Saxony 1127 – 1138, deposed in Bavaria and Saxony

House of Liutpold (restored)

1139 – 18 Oct 1141	*Leopold*, Margrave (Leopold IV) of the East Mark
1141 – 1156	*Heinrich XI Jasomirgott*, brother (d. 13 Jan 1177) Margrave (Heinrich II) of the East Mark 1141, deposed in Bavaria and created Duke of Austria by the Holy Roman Emperor Friedrich I Barbarossa

House of Welf (restored)

1156 – Sep 1180	*Heinrich XII*, the Lion, Duke (Heinrich III) of Saxony, son of Heinrich X (b. 1129; d. Brunswick 6 Aug 1195) deposed, restored to his lands in Brunswick 1181

House of Wittelsbach

Sep 1180 – 11 Jul 1183	*Otto I*, son of Otto IV, the Count Palatine of Bavaria (b. c. 1120) appointed by the Holy Roman Emperor Friedrich I Barbarossa
1183 – 15 Sep 1231	*Ludwig I*, son (b. Kelheim 23 Dec 1174; d. (assassinated) Kelheim) Count Palatine of the Rhine 1214 – 1228, regent of Germany 1225 – 1228
1231 – 29 Nov 1253	*Otto II*, Count Palatine of the Rhine (Otto III), son (b. 7 Apr 1206)
1253 – 1255	*Ludwig II*, the Stern, Count Palatine of the Rhine, son (b. 13 Apr 1229; d. 2 Feb 1294) with his brother, *Heinrich I* (b. 19 Nov 1235; d. 3 Feb 1290)
1255	Division of Bavarian territories; Ludwig II became Duke of Upper Bavaria, and Heinrich I became Duke of Lower Bavaria (see below)

Dukes of Upper Bavaria

1255 – 2 Feb 1294	*Ludwig II*, previously Duke of Bavaria
1294 – 11 Oct 1347	*Rudolf I*, son (b. 4 Oct 1274; d. 12 Aug 1319) Count Palatine of the Rhine 1294 – 1317; with his brother, *Ludwig IV*, the Bavarian (b. 1 Apr 1282; d. Munich) King of Germany 20 Oct 1314, King of the Lombards

	31 May 1327, Holy Roman Emperor 17 Jan 1328; divided the Upper Bavarian lands with Rudolf I 1310; compelled Rudolf I to abdicate 1317 and assumed rule over all of Upper Bavaria; granted the Palatinate of the Rhine, the Upper Palatinate and the electoral right to Rudolf I's sons, Rudolf and Ruprecht, 1329; inherited Lower Bavaria 20 Dec 1340

Dukes of Lower Bavaria

1255 – 3 Feb 1290	*Heinrich I*, previously Duke of Bavaria
1290	*Otto III*, son (b. 11 Feb 1261; d. 9 Sep 1312) King (Ottó) of Hungary 1304 – 1307; with his brothers *Ludwig III* (b. 9 Oct 1269; d. 13 May 1296) and *Stefan I* (b. 14 Mar 1271; d. 21 Dec 1310)
21 Dec 1310	*Otto III* (see above) with his nephews (sons of Stefan I), *Heinrich II* (b. 29 Sep 1305; d. 1 Sep 1339) and *Otto IV* (b. 3 Jan 1307; d. 14 Dec 1334)
9 Sep 1312	*Heinrich II* and *Otto IV* (see above) with their cousin (son of Otto III), *Heinrich III* (b. 28 Aug 1312; d. 18 Jun 1333)
14 Dec 1334	*Heinrich II* (see above) alone
1339 – 20 Dec 1340	*Johann I*, son of Heinrich II (b. 29 Nov 1329)
20 Dec 1340	Lower Bavaria inherited by Ludwig IV of Upper Bavaria (see above)

Dukes of Bavaria

1347	Six sons of Ludwig IV succeeded to the duchy
1349	Bavaria divided among the brothers; Bavaria-Landshut and Bavaria-Straubing became the two major lines

Dukes of Bavaria-Straubing

1349	*Albrecht I*, son of Ludwig IV (b. Munich 25 Jun 1336; d. The Hague 13 Dec 1404) Count (Albert) of Hainaut Mar 1389
1392	Partition (see below)

Dukes of Bavaria-Landshut

1349 – 10 May 1375	*Stefan II*, son of Ludwig IV (b. 1317)
1375 – 1392	*Stefan III*, son (b. c. 1337; d. 25 Sep 1413) with his brothers, *Friedrich* (b. c. 1339; d. 4 Dec 1393) and

	Johann II (b. c. 1341; d. 8 Aug 1397)
1392	New partition of Bavaria; Albrecht I retained Bavaria-Straubing, Friedrich retained Bavaria-Landshut, Stefan III became Duke of Bavaria-Ingolstadt and Johann II became Duke of Bavaria-Munich

Dukes of Bavaria-Straubing

1392 – 12 Dec 1404	*Albrecht I* (see above)
1404 – 30 May 1417	*Wilhelm II*, Count (Guillaume IV) of Hainaut, son (b. 5 Apr 1365)
1417 – 6 Jan 1425	*Johann*, brother (b. 1374) Bishop (Joannes VI) of Liège 14 Nov 1389 – 22 May 1418, co-ruler of Holland 13 Feb 1419, Governor of Luxemburg 1419
6 Jan 1425	Territory divided among the three remaining branches of the duchy (see below)

Dukes of Bavaria-Ingolstadt

1392 – 25 Sep 1413	*Stefan III* (see above)
1413	*Ludwig VII*, the Bearded, son (b. 20 Dec 1365; d. (in prison) 1 May 1447) deposed
1443 – 7 Apr 1445	*Ludwig VIII*, the Lame, son (b. 1 Sep 1403)
7 Apr 1445	Passed to Heinrich IV, Duke of Bavaria-Landshut

Dukes of Bavaria-Landshut

1392 – 4 Dec 1393	*Friedrich* (see above)
1393 – 30 Jul 1450	*Heinrich IV*, son (b. 1386) inherited Ingolstadt 7 Apr 1445
1450 – 18 Jan 1479	*Ludwig IX*, the Rich, son (b. 23 Feb 1417)
1479 – 1 Dec 1503	*Georg*, the Rich, son (b. 15 Aug 1455)
1 Dec 1503	Ingolstadt and Landshut claimed by Albrecht IV, Duke of Bavaria-Munich

Dukes of Bavaria-Munich

1392 – 8 Aug 1397	*Johann II* (see above)
1397	*Ernst*, son (b. 1373; d. 2 Jul 1438) and his brother, *Wilhelm III* (b. 1375; d. 12 Sep 1435)
12 Sep 1435	*Ernst* (see above) and his nephew (son of Wilhelm III) *Adolf* (b. 1434; d. 1440)
2 Jul 1438	*Adolf* and his cousin (son of Ernst), *Albrecht III*, the Pious (b. 27 Mar 1401; d. 29 Feb 1460)
1440	*Albrecht III* (see above) alone

1460	*Johann IV*, son (b. 4 Oct 1437; d. 19 Nov 1463) and his brother, *Sigmund* (b. 26 Jul 1439; d. 1 Feb 1501)
19 Nov 1463	*Sigmund* (see above) and his brother, *Albrecht IV*, the Wise (b. 15 Dec 1447); Sigmund abdicated 1467
1467 – 18 Mar 1508	*Albrecht IV* (see above) alone; claimed Ingolstadt and Landshut at the death of Georg the Rich 1503; ruled over almost all of Bavaria by the time of his death

Bawands

Territory comprised part of present-day northern Iran, with the capital initially at Sari and later at Amul.

Ispahbads (Military Leaders) or Muluk al-Jibal (Lords of the Mountains)

Line of Ka'usiya (Tabaristan)

AD 665/6 – 680	*Bau (ibn Shapur)*, assassinated by Walash
680 – 687/8	Interregnum of Walash
687/8	*Surkhab I (ibn Bau)*, son of Bau
717	*Mihr Mardan (ibn Surkhab)*, son
755	*Surkhab II (ibn Mihr Mardan)*, son
771/2	*Sharwin I (ibn Surkhab)*, son, took title Lord of the Mountains
797/8	*Shahriyar I (ibn Qarin ibn Sharwin)*, grandson
825/6	*Shapur* (or *Ja'far*) *(ibn Shahriyar)*, son
836/7	*Qarin I (ibn Shahriyar)*, brother, converted to Islam c. 854
867/8 – Oct/Nov 895	*Rustam I (ibn Surkhab ibn Qarin)*, grandson (d. in prison
895/6	*Sharwin II (ibn Rustam)*, son
930/1	*Shahriyar II (ibn Sharwin)*, son
(?)	*Rustam II (ibn Sharwin)*, brother
965/6	*Dara (ibn Rustam)*, son
968/9	*Shahriyar III (ibn Dara)*, son
1005/6	*Rustam III (ibn Shahriyar)*, son
1057/8 – 1073/4	*Qarin II (ibn Surkhab)*, nephew (d. 1093)

Line of Ispahbadiya (Tabaristan and Gilan)

1073/4	*(Husam al-Daula) Shahriyar ibn Qarin*, son of Qarin II, abdicated
1109/10	*(Najm al-Daula) Qarin ibn Shahriyar*, son
1117/18	*(Shams al-Muluk) Rustam ibn Qarin*, son, poisoned
1117/18	*('Ala' al-Daula) 'Ali ibn Shahriyar*, uncle, abdicated
1139/40 – Apr 1163	*(Nusrat al-Din) Shah Ghazi Rustam I (ibn 'Ali)*, son
1163	*('Ala' al-Daula* or *Sharaf al-Muluk) Hasan (ibn Rustam)*, son, assassinated
1171/2	*(Husam al-Daula) Ardashir (ibn Hasan)*, son
1205/6 – 1 Apr 1210	*(Nasir al-Daula* or *Shams al-Muluk) Shah Ghazi Rustam II (ibn Ardashir)*, son, assassinated
Apr 1210	Conquest of Tabaristan by the Khwarazm-Shah Muhammad

Line of Kinkhwariyya (Il-Khan vassals)

1237/8	*Husam al-Daula (Ardashir ibn Kinkhwar)*, chosen after 30 years of anarchy, moved capital to Amul, first Mongol invasion
1249/50	*Shams al-Muluk (Muhammad ibn Ardashir)*, son, killed by Abaqa
1266/7	*'Ala' al-Daula ('Ali ibn Ardashir)*, brother, second Mongol invasion
1276/7	*Taj al-Daula (Yazdagird ibn Shahriyar)*, nephew
1298/9	*Nasir al-Daula (Shahriyar ibn Yazdagird)*, son
1314/15	*Rukn al-Daula (Kai Khusrau ibn Yazdagird)*, brother
1327/8	*Sharaf al-Muluk (ibn Kai Khusrau)*, son
1333/4 – 1349/50	*Fakhr al-Daula (Hasan ibn Kai Khusrau)*, brother, assassinated
1349/50	Power seized by the Afrasiyab family

Benevento

Dukes

AD 571	*Zottone*
591	*Arechi I*; granted the duchy by Agilulfo, King of the Lombards
641	*Aione*, son

642	*Radoaldo*, son of Duke Gisulfo of Friuli
647	*Grimoaldo I*, brother; King of the Lombards 662; assassinated
671	*Romoaldo I*, son; associated with his father from 662
687	*Grimoaldo II*, son
689	*Gisulfo I*, brother
706	*Romoaldo II*, son
731	*Andelais*, brother; deposed
732	*Gregorio*, nephew of Liutprando, King of the Lombards
739	*Godescalco*; by free election
742	*Gisulfo II*, son of Romoaldo II
751	*Liutprando*, son; deposed by Desiderio, King of the Lombards

Princes

758	*Arechi II*, son-in-law of Desiderio; Duke 758, created Prince of Benevento 774
788	*Grimoaldo III*, son
806	*Gromoaldo IV*, captain of the guard; deposed
817	*Sicone*, gastaldo (steward) of Acerenza
832	*Sicardo*, son; assassinated
839	*Radelchi I*, treasurer of Sicardo
853	*Adelchi*, brother
878	*Gaideri*, son of Radelchi I
881	*Radelchi II*, son (for 1st time)
884–890	*Aione*, brother
	Interregnum
897	*Radelchi II* (for 2nd time); deposed
900	*Atenulfo I*, Count of Capua
910	*Landolfo I*, son
943	*Landolfo II*, son; ruling with his son *Pandolfo I* until 959; from 959 to 961 ruling with his son, *Landolfo III*
961	*Pandolfo I*, son of Landolfo II; until 968 ruling with his brother *Landolfo III*; after 968 ruling with his son *Landolfo IV*
981	*Landolfo IV*, son of Pandolfo I
981	*Pandolfo II*, son of Landolfo III; from 987 ruling with his son *Landolfo V* and from 1013 ruling also with his son *Pandolfo III*
1014–1053	*Pandolfo III* (d. 1059) and *Landolfo V* (d. 1077), sons of Pandolfo II; deposed
1053	Duchy annexed by Pope Leo IX

Bengal Sultanate

Territory comprised part of present-day northern India and Bangladesh, with the capital established at Lakhnawati (later Gaur).

Sultans

In eastern Bengal	
AD 1336/7	*(Fakhr al-Din) Mubarak Shah*
1349/50 – 1352/3	*(Ikhtiyar al-Din) Ghazi Shah*, son
1352/3	Conquest by Ilyas Shah (see below)
In western Bengal and from 1352/3 all Bengal	
1339/40	*('Ala' al-Din) 'Ali Shah*
	Line of Ilyas Shah
1345/6	*(Haji Shams al-Din) Ilyas Shah*, ruled in western Bengal 1345/6 – 1352/3, ruled over all of Bengal after 1352/3
1357/8	*Sikandar Shah I (ibn Ilyas)*, son
1389/90	*(Ghiyath al-Din) A'zam Shah (ibn Sikandar)*, son, in rebellion against Sikandar Shah I 1369/70
1410/11	*(Saif al-Din) Hamza Shah (ibn A'zam)*, son
1412/13	*(Shihab al-Din) Bayazid Shah*, son
1414/15	*('Ala' al-Din) Firuz Shah,* son
	Line of Raja Ganeśa
1414/15	*(Jalal al-Din) Muhammad Shah (ibn Raja Ganeśa)* (or *Jitmal Purbi*), son of Raja Ganeśa
1431/2 – 1436	*(Shams al-Din) Ahmad Shah (ibn Muhammad)*, son
	Line of Ilyas Shah restored:
1437	*(Nasir al-Din) Mahmud Shah*
1459/60	*(Rukn al-Din) Barbak Shah (ibn Mahmud)*, son
1474/5	*(Shams al-Din) Yusuf Shah (ibn Barbak)*, son
1481/2	*Sikandar Shah II (ibn Yusuf)*, son
1481/2	*(Jalal al-Din) Fath Shah (ibn Mahmud)*, son of Mahmud Shah
	Line of Habshis
1486/7	*(Sultan Shahzada) Barbak Shah*
1486/7	*(Saif al-Din) Firuz Shah*, assassinated

1489/90	*(Nasir al-Din) Mahmud Shah ibn Fath Shah*, of doubtful ancestry
1490/1	*(Shams al-Din Abu'l-Nasr) Muzaffar Shah*, Abyssinian usurper, assassinated
	Line of Husain Shah
1494	*(Sayyid 'Ala' al-Din) Husain Shah* (d. Gaur)
1518	*(Nasir al-Din) Nusrat Shah*, son (d. (assassinated) Gaur)
1533	*('Ala' al-Din) Firuz Shah*, son, for three months, murdered
1533–1538	*(Ghiyath al-Din) Mahmud Shah*, son of Husain Shah, pretender since 1525/6
1538	Conquest by the Mughal emperor Humayun and the Afghan chief Shir Shah
	Line of Suri Afghans
1539	*Shir Shah (Sur)* (d. 21 May 1545) defeated Mughal emperor Humayun at Kanauj
1540	*Khidr Khan*, lieutenant of Shir Shah
1545	*Muhammad Khan (Sur)*
1555	*(Khidr Khan) Bahadur Shah*
1561–1564	*(Ghiyath al-Din) Jalal Shah*
	Line of Kararani
1564	*Taj Khan (Kararani)*
1572	*Sulaiman (Kararani)*, brother, ruled in Bengal and Bihar
1572	*Bayazid Khan (Kararani)*, son
1572–1576	*Daud Khan (Kararani)*, brother, defeated and killed by the Mughals
1576	Mughal conquest

Benin

Territory in present-day south-western Nigeria.

Obas (Kings)

c.AD 1170	*Oranmiyan*
c. 1200	*Eweka I*, son
(?)	*Uwakhuahen*, son
(?)	*Ehenmihen*, brother
c. 1255	*Ewedo*, son
c. 1280	*Oguola*, son, usurper
c. 1295	*Edoni*, son
c. 1299	*Udagbedo*, brother
c. 1334	*Ohen*, brother
c. 1370	*Egbeka*, son
(?)	*Orobiru*, brother
(?)	*Uwaifiokun*, brother
c. 1440	*Ewuare*, brother, fl. 1472
c..1473	*Ezoti*, son
(?)	*Olua*, brother
c. 1481	*Ozolua*, brother, fl. 1485
1504	*Esigie*, son
1550	*Orhogbua*, son
1578	*Ehengbuda*, son
c. 1608	*Ohuan* (or *Odogbo*), son
c. 1640	*Ahenzae*, grandson of Orhogbua
c. 1661*	*Akenzae*
c. 1669	*Akengboi*
c. 1675	*Ahenkpaye*
c. 1684	*Akengbedo*
c. 1689	*Oreoghene*
c. 1700	*Ewuakpe*
c. 1712	*Ozuere*, son
c. 1713	*Akenzua I*, brother
c. 1735	*Eresonyen*, son
c. 1750	*Akengbuda*, son
c. 1804	*Obanosa*, son
c. 1816	*Ogbebo*, son

*Several different royal families occupied the throne from c. 1661.

(?)	*Osemwede*, brother
1848	*Adolo*, son
1888 – 1897	*Ovonramven* (or *Overami*), son (d. Calabar 1914), exiled
1897	Benin City stormed by British and kingdom incorporated into British protectorate in Nigeria
20 Apr 1914	*Ebeka II*, son (d. 8 Feb 1933) Oba restored
from 5 Apr 1933	*Akenzua II* (b. Benin City 1899)
1 Oct 1960	Nigeria became independent from Great Britain

Berg

Territory on the Rhine east of Cologne.

Counts (Dukes from 1380)

House of Berg	
AD 1101	*Adolf I*, son of Adolf (d. 12 Oct 1152) Count of Altena 1122
1133	*Adolf II*, son (d. 1161)
1152	*Eberhard I*, son (d. 23 Jan 1180) Count of Altena 1161, territories divided between the senior line of Berg and the junior line of Altena
1166	*Engelbert I*, brother (d. Jun 1189)
1185 – 7 Aug 1218	*Adolf III*, son (b. before 1178; d. near Damietta, Egypt); ruled with his brother, *Adolf (IV)* (d. 1197) 1189 – 1197
1218 – 7 Nov 1225	*Engelbert II*, Archbishop (Engelbert I) of Cologne, brother (b. c. 1185) murdered
House of Limburg	
1225	*Irmgard*, daughter of Adolf III (d. 12 Aug 1248) ruled with her husband, *Heinrich*, Duke of Limburg (d. 25 Feb 1246), who was created Count of Berg 1226 after the death of the last of the male line of Berg, Engelbert, Archbishop of Cologne
1247 – 22 Apr 1259	*Adolf IV*, son (b. c. 1220) Duke of Limburg
1259 – 28 Sep 1296	*Adolf V*, son

1296 – 16 Apr 1308	*Wilhelm I*, brother
1308 – 3 Apr 1348	*Adolf VI*, nephew (b. c. 1290)

House of Jülich

1348 – 18 May 1360	*Gerhard VI von Jülich*, husband of Margarete, the niece of Adolf VI, Count of Ravensburg 1346
1360 – 25 Jun 1408	*Wilhelm II*, son, created Duke of Berg 1380
1408 – 14 Jul 1437	*Adolf VII*, son, Duke of Jülich 1423
1437 – 19 Aug 1475	*Gerhard VII*, nephew, Duke of Jülich and Berg
1475 – 1511	*Wilhelm III*, son (b. 9 Jan 1455) Duke of Jülich and Berg
1511	Territory passed to Johann III, Duke of Cleves

Bithynia

Territory comprised part of north-western Turkey, with the capital at Nicomedia (present-day İzmit)

Kings

327 BC	*Ziboetes*
c. 279	*Nicomedes I*
c. 250	*Ziaelas*
c. 230	*Prusias I*
c. 180	*Prusias II*
149	*Nicomedes II Epiphanes*
c. 94 – 75/4	*Nicomedes III Epiphanes*
91/90 – 75/4	*Nicomedes IV Epiphanes*, brother and pretender; put forward by Mithridates VI Eupator Dionysus, the king of Pontus; willed his kingdom to Rome
74	Roman rule established

Bohemia

Dukes (unless otherwise stated)

House of Přemysl	
AD 845	*Bořivoj I*, vassal of Svatopluk of Moravia
895	*Spytihněv I*, son (d. c. 912)
907(?) – 13 Feb 921	*Vratislav I*, brother
921 – 28 Sep 929	*Václav* (or *Wenceslas*), Saint (b. 911) assassinated Regent: 921 – 924/5: *Drahomíra* (or *Dragomir*), mother
929 – 15 Jul 967	*Boleslav I*, the Cruel, brother; added Moravia, Slovakia and Silesia to the Bohemian territories
967 – 7 Feb 999	*Boleslav II*, the Pious, son
999	*Boleslav III*, the Blind, son (for 1st time) (d. 1035) deposed and banished
1002 – Jan 1003	*Vladivoj*, grandson of Vratislav I
1003	*Boleslav III* (for 2nd time) deposed by Duke Bolesław I of Poland
1003	*Jaromir*, brother (d. 4 Nov 1038)
1012 – 9 Nov 1034	*Oldřich*, brother
1034 – 10 Jan 1055	*Břetislav I*, son; conquered Moravia
1055 – 28 Jan 1061	*Spytihněv II*, son (b. 1031)
1061 – 14 Jan 1092	*Vratislav II*, brother (b. c. 1035) granted the title, King of Bohemia, by the Holy Roman Emperor Heinrich IV 1086
Jan – 6 Sep 1092	*Konrád I*, brother
1092 – 22 Dec 1100	*Břetislav II*, nephew
1100	*Bořivoj II*, brother (b. c. 1065; d. 2 Feb 1124)
1107 – 21 Sep 1109	*Svatopluk*, son of Otto I of Moravia
1109 – 12 Apr 1125	*Vladislav I*, son of Vratislav II
1125 – 14 Feb 1140	*Soběslav I*, brother (b. c. 1075)
1140	*Vladislav II*, nephew (d. 18 Jan 1175) King (Vladislav I) of Bohemia 1158
1173	*Bedřich*, son (for 1st time) (b. c. 1142; d. 25 Mar 1189)
1173	*Soběslav II*, son of Soběslav I (d. 29 Jan 1180)
1179 – 25 Mar 1189	*Bedřich* (for 2nd time)
1189 – 9 Sep 1191	*Konrád Ota*, great-grandson of Konrád I
1191	*Václav* (or *Wenceslas*) *II*, son of Soběslav I

Kings

1192	*Přemysl Otakar I*, son of Vladislav II (b. c. 1155; d. 15 Dec 1230) King of Bohemia 1198; ruling with (from 1193) his cousin, *Břetislav III* (or *Jindřich Břetislav*), Archbishop of Prague (d. 19 Jun 1197); and (from 1197) his cousin, *Vladislav Jindřich* (d. 12 Aug 1222) Margrave of Moravia 1197
15 Dec 1230	*Václav* (or *Wenceslas*) *I*, son of Přemysl Otakar I (b. 1205)
22 Sep 1253	*Přemysl Otakar II*, Duke of Austria, son (b. c. 1230) Duke of Styria 1260; siezed Carinthia, Carniola and Istria 1269; lost Austria, Styria and Carinthia to King Rudolf I of Germany 1274
26 Aug 1278	*Václav* (or *Wenceslas*) *II*, son (b. 1271) King (Wacław I) of Poland Sep 1300, King (Vencel) of Hungary 1301 – 1304 Regent: 1278 – 1283: Elector *Otto IV* of Brandenburg (d. 1308 or 1309)
21 Jun 1305 – 4 Aug 1306	*Václav* (or *Wenceslas*) *III*, nominally King (Wacław II) of Poland, son (b. 6 Oct 1289) assassinated
House of Habsburg	
1306 – 4 Jul 1307	*Rudolf*, Duke (Rudolf III) of Austria and Styria, son of Duke Albrecht I of Austria (b. May 1282)
House of Görz-Tirol	
1307	*Jindřich*, Duke of Carinthia, brother-in-law of Václav III (d. 4 Apr 1335)
House of Luxemburg	
1310	*Jan*, brother-in-law (b. 10 Aug 1296; d. Crécy, France) Count (Johann) of Luxemburg 1310
1346	*Karel* (baptized *Wenzel*), King (Karl IV) of Germany, son (b. Prague 14 May 1316; d. Prague 29 Nov 1378) Margrave of Moravia 1333, Count (Karl) of Luxemburg 1346 – 1353, King of the Lombards 1355, Holy Roman Emperor 5 Apr 1355, Margrave of Brandenburg 1373
1373 – 16 Aug 1419	*Václav IV*, son (b. Nürnberg, Germany, 26 Feb 1361; d. Prague) Elector (Wenzel) of Brandenburg 1373, King (Wenzel) of Germany 10 Jun 1376/29 Nov 1378

	– 20 Aug 1400
1419 – 9 Dec 1437	*Zikmund*, King (Sigismund) of Germany, King (Zsigmond) of Hungary, half-brother (b. Nürnberg, Germany, 14 Feb 1368; d. Znojmo) Duke of Luxemburg 16 Aug 1419, Elector of Brandenburg 1378 – 1397 and 1411 – 18 Apr 1417, King of the Lombards 1431, Holy Roman Emperor 31 May 1433

House of Habsburg (restored)

29 Jun 1438 – 27 Oct 1439	*Albrecht*, Archduke (Albrecht V) of Austria, King (Albert) of Hungary, Duke of Luxemburg, son-in-law (b. 10 Aug 1397; d. Nezmely, Hungary) King (Albrecht II) of Germany 18 Mar 1438
1440 – 23 Nov 1457	*Ladislav Pohrobek* (German: *Ladislaus Posthumus*), posthumous son (b. 22 Feb 1440) at the same time Duke (Ladislaus) of Luxemburg; King (László V) of Hungary 1444

House of Poděbrad

1458 – 22 Mar 1471	*Jiří z Poděbrad* (b. Poděbrady 6 Apr 1420; d. Prague) governor of Bohemia for Ladislaus Posthumus from 1451/1453

Jagiellonians

27 May 1471 – 13 Mar 1516	*Vladislav II* (Polish; *Władysław Jagiełłonczyk*), nephew of Ladislaus Posthumus, son of King Kazimierz IV of Poland (b. 1 Mar 1456) King (Ulászló II) of Hungary 15 Jul 1490

Bosnia

Bans

fl. AD 1154 – 1163	*Borić*
(?)	(?)
1172 – 1204	*Kulin*
(?)	*Stjepan* (d. 1236?)
1232 – c. 1253	*Matej Ninoslav*
1254	*Prijezda I*
1287	*Prijezda II*, son; with his brother, *Stjepan I Kotroman* (d. 1313)
1290	*Stjepan I Kotroman*, sole ruler
1302 – 1304	*Mladen I Šubić*
c. 1305	*Mladen II Šubić*, son
1322	*Stjepan II Kotromanić*, son of Stjepan I
1353 – 1377	(*Stjepan*) *Tvrtko I*, nephew (b. c. 1338; d. 1391)

Kings

1377	*Tvrtko I* (see Bans) acquired the territory between Dubrovnik and Kotor 1378
1391	(*Stjepan*) *Dabiša*, brother
1395	*Jelena*, widow
1398	(*Stjepan*) *Ostoja*, son of Tvrtko I (for 1st time) (d. 1418)
1404	(*Stjepan*) *Tvrtko II*, brother (for 1st time) (d. Nov 1443)
1408	*Ostoja* (for 2nd time)
1418	(*Stjepan*) *Ostojić*, son
1421 – Nov 1443	*Tvrtko II* (for 2nd time)
1444	*Stjepan Tomaš*, son of Ostoja
Jul 1461 – Jun 1463	*Stjepan Tomašević*, son (d. 1463)
Jun 1463	Bosnia occupied by the Turks

Bosporus, Kingdom of the

Territory comprised part of present-day southern Ukraine, with the capital at Panticapaeum (present-day Kerch).

Kings

Archaeanactid Dynasty	
480 – 438 BC	Unknown number of kings
Spartocid Dynasty	
438/7	*Spartocus I*
433/2	*Satyrus I*, ruled with *Seleucus* until 393/2(?)
389/8	*Leucon I*
349/8	*Spartocus II*, and *Pairisades I* (for 1st time)
344/3	*Pairisades I* (for 2nd time) alone
311/10	*Satyrus II*
310/9	*Prytanis*
310/9	*Eumelos*
304/3	*Spartocus III*
284/3	*Pairisades II*
c. 245	*Spartocus IV*
c. 240	*Leucon II*
c. 220	*Hygiainon*
c. 200	*Spartocus V*
c. 180	*Pairisades III*, son-in-law
c. 150	*Pairisades IV Philometor*
c. 125	*Pairisades V*
108	*Saumacus*
107	*Mithridates VI Eupator Dionysus*, king of Pontus 121/20 – 63, annexed Bosporus, committed suicide during a revolt of his troops
63	*Pharnaces II*, son, king of Pontus 63 – 47
47	*Asander*, client king of Rome
17/16	*Dynamis*, Roman vassal
15(?)	*Scribonius*, Roman vassal
14	*Polemo*, Roman vassal
9/8 BC	*Dynamis*, Roman vassal
AD 8/9	Unknown king
10/11	*Aspurgus* (or *Rhescuporis I*), became a Roman citizen 14/15

37/8	*Gepaepyris*, widow (for 1st time)
39/40	*Mithridates*, Roman vassal, ruled jointly for a time with *Gepaepyris* (for 2nd time)
45/6	*Cotys I*, perhaps degraded 62
68	*Rhescuporis II*, Roman vassal
93/4	*Sauromates I*
123/4	*Cotys II*
131/2	*Rhoimetalces*
154/5	*Eupator*
173/4	*Sauromates II*
210/11	*Rhescuporis III*
227/8	*Cotys III*
229/30	*Sauromates III*
233/4	*Rhescuporis IV*
234/5	*Ininthimaios*
239/40 – 275/6	*Rhescuporis V*
253/4	*Pharsanzes*
275/6	*Sauromates IV*
275/6	*Teiranes*
279/80	*Chedosbios*
286/7	*Thothorses*
308/9 – 322(?)	*Rhadamsadios*
318/19 – 332/3 or 336/7	*Rhescuporis VI*
c. 342	Conquest by Ostrogoths

Bourbon

Territory in central France.

Dukes

AD 1327	*Louis I*, Sire of Bourbon, son of Béatrix de Bourbon and Robert Clermont, a son of King Louis IX of France (b. 1279) created Duke of Bourbon 1327
22 Jan 1341	*Pierre I*, son (b. 1311)
19 Sep 1356	*Louis II*, son (b. 4 Aug 1337)
19 Aug 1410	*Jean I*, son (b. Mar 1380)
5 Feb 1434	*Charles I*, son (b. 1401)
4 Dec 1456 – 1 Apr 1488	*Jean II*, son (b. 1426)
23 Apr 1488 – 10 Oct 1503	*Pierre II*, brother (b. 1 Dec 1438) Sire of Beaujeu, with his wife, *Anne*, daughter of King Louis XI of France (b. Belgium 1461; d. 14 Nov 1522); joint regents of France 1483 – 1492

Brabant

Names are given in French with modern Dutch versions in parentheses

Counts of Louvain (Leuven)

before AD 1003	*Lambert* (*Lambert*) *I*, son of Count Régnier III of Hainaut
12 Sep 1015	*Henri* (*Hendrik*) *I*, son (?), son-in-law of Count Baudouin IV of Flanders
1038	*Othon* (*Otto*) son or nephew
before 3 Jun 1041 – after 21 Sep 1062	*Lambert* (*Lambert*) *II* (or *Baldéric* (*Balderik*)), uncle
1062 – 1079	*Henri* (*Hendrik*) *II*, son
1079(?) – Feb or Mar 1095	*Henri* (*Hendrik*) *III*, son

Dukes of Brabant

Feb or Mar 1095	*Godefroi* (*Godfried*) *I*, the Bearded, brother; Duke (Godefroi V) of Lower Lorraine 1106 – 1128
25 Jan 1139	*Godefroi* (*Godfried*) *II*, son
13 Jun 1142	*Godefroi* (*Godfried*) *III*
10 or 21 Aug 1190	*Henri* (*Hendrik*) *I*, son
5 Sep 1235	*Henri* (*Hendrik*) *II*, son
1 Feb 1248	*Henri* (*Hendrik*) *III*, son
28 Feb 1261	*Henri* (*Hendrik*) *IV*, son (b. 1251 or 1252; d. 28 Apr 1272)
1267	*Jean* (*Jan*) *I*, brother (b. 1252 or 1253)
3 May 1294	*Jean* (*Jan*) *II*, son (b. 27 Nov 1275)
27(?) Oct 1312	*Jean* (*Jan*) *III*, son (b. 1300)
5 Dec 1355	*Jeanne de* (*Johanna van*) *Brabant*, daughter (b. 24 Jun 1322; d. 1 Dec 1406) abdicated
7 May 1404	*Marguerite de* (*Margareta van*) *Mâle* (or *Flandres*/*Vlaanderen*), Countess of Flanders, Artois and Franche-Comté, widow of Jeanne's nephew (b. 13 Apr 1350; d. 16 Mar 1405) Regent: 19 May 1404 – 16 Mar 1405: *Antoine de Bourgogne* (*Antoon van Bourgondië*), Count of Rethel, son (d. Agincourt 25 Oct 1415) given title of Duke of Limburg by Jeanne 2 Sep 1404; subsequently Duke of Brabant

House of Burgundy

16 Mar 1405	*Antoine de Bourgogne*, previously regent; ceded Rethel to his brother Philippe 27 Jan 1407; governor of Luxemburg 7 Jan 1412
25 Oct 1415	*Jean* (*Jan*) *IV*, son (b. 11 Jun 1403) co-ruler of Hainaut 8 May 1418
17 Apr 1427	*Philippe de Saint Pol* (*Filips van Sint-Pol*), brother (b. 25 Jul 1404)
4 Aug 1430	Duchy of Brabant inherited by Philippe's cousin, Duke Philippe III of Burgundy and was thenceforth held by the dukes of Burgundy

Brandenburg

Margraves of the North Mark (appointed by the King of Germany)

AD 936	*Siegfried*
938 – 20 May 965	*Gero* (b. c. 890)
965	*Dietrich von Haldensleben*
985 – 25 Jan 1003	*Lothar*, Count of Waldeck
1003	*Werner*, son (d. 11 Nov 1014) abdicated
1009	*Bernhard I*, son of Dietrich von Haldensleben
1018	*Bernhard II*, son (d. 1044/51)
1044 – 10 Sep 1056	*Wilhelm*, son
1056 – 7 Nov 1057	*Lothar Udo I*, Count of Stade (b. after 994)
1057 – 4 May 1082	*Udo II*, son
1082 – 28 Jun 1087	*Heinrich I*, son
1087 – 2 Jun 1106	*Lothar Udo III*, brother
1106	*Rudolf I*, brother (d. 6 Dec 1124) ruled as guardian for Heinrich II
1114 – 4 Dec 1128	*Heinrich II*, nephew
1128 – 15 Mar 1130	*Udo IV*, cousin
1130 – 1133	*Konrad von Plötzkau*

Margraves and Electors of Brandenburg

Ascanian House

1134 – 18 Nov 1170	*Albrecht I*, the Bear, Count of Anhalt and Count of Ballenstädt (b. c. 1100) appointed Margrave of the

	North Mark by the Holy Roman Emperor Lothar II 1134, took the title Margrave of Brandenburg 1136, Duke of Saxony 1138 – 1142
1170 – 7 Mar 1184	*Otto I*, son
1184 – 4 Jul 1205	*Otto II*, son
1205 – 25 Feb 1220	*Albrecht II*, brother (b. c. 1174)
1220	*Otto III*, son (d. 9 Oct 1267) with his brother, *Johann I* (b. c. 1213; d. 4 Apr 1266); Otto III, through his marriage to the daughter of King Václav I of Bohemia 1253, added Upper Lusatia to the Brandenburg possessions*
1266 †	*Otto IV*, son of Johann I (d. 1308 or 1309) with his brothers, *Johann II* (d. 10 Sep 1281) and *Konrad* (d.1304)
1308/9 – 14 Aug 1319	*Waldemar*, son of Konrad (b. c. 1290) conquered Pomerelia and partitioned it with the Teutonic Order 1310, by 1319 ruled over the entire margravate and the Lusatias
14 Aug 1319	Male line extinct, the margravate reverted to the crown and was vacant until 1323
House of Wittelsbach	
1323	*Ludwig I*, son of King Ludwig IV of Germany (b. Jul 1316; d. 18 Sep 1361) ‡
1351	*Ludwig I* (see above) with his brothers, *Ludwig II*, the Roman (b. 12 May 1330; d. 14 May 1365) Margrave 1351, Elector 1355; and *Otto* (b. 1346 or 1347; d. 15 Nov 1379) Margrave 1351, Elector 1366, ruled alone after 14 May 1365, sold the margravate to the Holy Roman Emperor Karl IV 1373
House of Luxemburg	
1373 – 29 Nov 1378	*Karl* (baptized *Wenzel*), Holy Roman Emperor (Karl IV), son of Count Johann of Luxemburg (b. Prague,

*By about this time, the Margraves of Brandenburg were Electors of Germany

†In 1266/7 the Brandenburg possessions were divided between the sons of Otto III and Johann I. The line of Johann I is followed here because, for the most part, they were the most powerful rulers in the fragmented state. But it must be remembered that there were sometimes as many as eight rulers governing the margavate

‡A man claiming to be Waldemar appeared c. 1342; he was invested as Margrave of Brandenburg by King Karl IV of Germany in 1348, but deposed in 1351

	Bohemia, 14 May 1316; d. Prague) Margrave of Moravia 1333, King (Karel) of Bohemia 1346 – 1373; appointed his son Wenzel as Elector of Brandenburg 1373, but administered the margravate until his death
1373	*Wenzel* (or *Wenceslas*), son (b. Nürnberg 26 Feb 1361; d. Prague, Bohemia, 16 Aug 1419) King (Václav IV) of Bohemia 1373, King of Germany 10 Jun 1376/29 Nov 1378 – 20 Aug 1400, Duke of Luxemburg 7/8 Dec 1383
1378	*Sigismund*, brother (for 1st time) (b. Nürnberg 14 Feb 1368; d. Znojmo, Moravia, 9 Dec 1437) King (Zsigmond) of Hungary 31 Mar 1387, King of Germany 20 Sep 1410, Duke of Luxemburg 16 Aug 1419, King (Zikmund) of Bohemia 1419, King of the Lombards 1431, Holy Roman Emperor 31 May 1433; granted Brandenburg to Jodokus
1397 – 18 Jan 1411	*Jodokus* (or *Jobst*), Duke of Luxemburg, cousin (b. 1351; d. Brno, Moravia) King of Germany, in rivalry with Sigismund, 1 Oct 1410
1411 – 18 Apr 1417	*Sigismund* (for 2nd time)

House of Hohenzollern

18 Apr 1417	*Friedrich I*, Burgrave of Nürnberg (b. Nürnberg 1371; d. Cadolzburg 21 Sep 1440) appointed governor of Brandenburg by Sigismund 8 Jul 1411, formally invested as Elector 1417, abdicated
Jan 1426	*Johann*, the Alchemist, son (b. 1406; d. 16 Nov 1464) appointed governor for his father, deposed at the death of Friedrich I
1440	*Friedrich II*, the Iron-tooth, brother (b. 19 Nov 1413; d. Plassenburg, Franconia, 10 Feb 1471) forced to cede the Old Mark and Priegnitz to his brother Friedrich 1447 but when Friedrich died without heir, 1463, these territories reverted to Friedrich II; abdicated
1470 – 11 Mar 1486	*Albrecht III Achilles*, brother (b. Tangermünde 9 Nov 1414; d. Frankfurt am Main, Franconia)
1486 – 9 Jan 1499	*Johann Cicero*, son (b. 2 Aug 1455)

Brittany

Dukes

The earliest dukes were often called Kings of Brittany; while by the French, they were usually referred to as counts.

AD 843	*Noménoë* (d. near Vendôme 7 Mar 851) revolted against Frankish suzerainty and was granted *de facto* independence by King Charles II the Bald of France in 846
851	*Erispoë*, son; assassinated
857–874	*Salomon*, usurper; assassinated
	Period of civil war between *Pascuéten*, Count of Vannes, and *Gurvand*, Count of Rennes
877–907	*Alain I*, the Great, grandson of Erispoë and Count of Vannes
	Interregnum: the Norse invasion
937	*Alain II Barbe-torte*, grandson of Alain I
952	*Dreu*, son; assassinated
980	*Suerech*, brother; Bishop of Nantes; assassinated
985	*Hoël I*, half-brother; assassinated
987	*Conan I le Tours*, Count of Rennes; paramount leader in a period of civil war
992	*Geoffroi I*, son; Count of Rennes and Duke of the Bretons
1008	*Alain III*, son
1040	*Conan II*, son; ruling under the tutelage of his uncle, *Eudes*, Count of Penthièvre
1066	*Havoise*, sister; ruling with her husband, *Hoël II*, Count of Cornouaille
1084	*Alain IV Fergent*, son; abdicated
1112	*Conan III*, the Fat, son
	Period of civil war between the children of Conan III: *Hoël III* and his sister *Berthe*, supported by her husband, *Eudon*, Count of Porhoët. The Count of Nantes, *Geoffroi III*, also laid claim to the duchy at this time
1156	*Conan IV*, the Black; proclaimed duke with the backing of King Henry II of England
1169	*Geoffroi IV Plantagenêt*, son-in-law and son of King Henry II of England (b. 23 Sep 1158; d. 19 Aug 1186)
1186–1203	*Constance*, wife; ruling as regent for her son, *Arthur I*

	(b. Nantes, 29 Mar 1187; d. (in prison) Rouen or Cherbourg, traditionally c. 3 Apr 1203)
1203	*Alix*, half-sister (b. 1196; d. 1221) Regents: 1203 – 1206: *Gui de Thouars*, father 1206 – 1212: King *Philippe II Auguste* of France
1212	*Alix* (see above) and her husband, *Pierre I Mauclerc*, son of Robert II of Dreux (b. 1190; d. 22 Jun 1250) Earl of Richmond 1219; ruled alone from 1221; abdicated 1237, retaining the title, Count of Braine
1237	*Jean I*, the Red, son (b. 1217; d. 8 Oct 1286)
1286	*Jean II*, son (b. 4 Jan 1239; d. 18 Nov 1305)
1305	*Arthur II*, son (b. 25 Jul 1262; d. 27 Aug 1312)
1312	*Jean III*, the Good, son (b. 8 Mar 1286; d. 30 Apr 1341)
1341 – 26 Sep 1345	*Jean de Montfort*, brother (b. 1293); in rivalry with
1341 – 29 Sep 1364	*Charles de Blois*, nephew by marriage (b. c. 1319); defeated and killed at the Battle of Auray; his widow, *Jeanne*, the Lame, of Penthièvre (d. 10 Sep 1384) renounced her claim to the duchy in 1365
1345	*Jeanne*, widow of Jean de Montfort; protected the rights of her son until the death of Charles de Blois and the end of the succession dispute
1365	*Jean IV de Montfort*, son (b. 1339; d. Nantes 1 Nov 1399) Earl of Richmond 1372
1399	*Jean V*, the Valiant, son (b. 24 Dec 1389; d. 28 Aug 1442); ruling under the regency of Duke *Philippe II* of Burgundy, until his coronation on 23 Mar 1402
1442	*François I*, son (b. 11 May 1414; d. 17 Jul 1450)
1450	*Pierre II*, brother (b. 7 Jul 1418; d. 22 Sep 1457)
1457	*Arthur III*, uncle (b. 24 Aug 1393; d. 26 Dec 1458) Earl of Richmond 1399, Constable of France Mar 1425
1458	*François II*, nephew (b. 23 Jun 1435; d. Couëron 9 Sep 1488)
1488 – 9 Jan 1514	*Anne*, daughter (b. Nantes, 25 Jan 1477; d. Blois) ruling from 1491 to 1498 with her husband, King *Charles VIII* of France (b. Amboise 30 Jun 1470; d. Amboise 7 Apr 1498) and from 1498 until her death with her husband, King *Louis XII* of France (b. 27 Jun 1462; d. 1 Jan 1515)

Buganda

Territory comprised part of present-day south-eastern Uganda, with the capital at Kampala.

Bakabaka (Kings)

AD (?)	*Kintu*
(?)	*Cwa I Nabaka*, son
1420	*Kimera*, grandson
1447	*Tembo*, grandson
1474	*Kiggala*, son
1501	*Kiyimba*, son
1528	*Kayima*, nephew
1555	*Nakibinge*, son
1582*	*Mulondo*, son, with his brothers *Jemba* and *Suna I*†
1609	*Sekamanya*, son of Mulondo, with his cousin *Kimbugwe*
1636	*Kateregga*, son of Sekamanya
1663	*Mutebi*, son, with his brothers *Juko* and *Kayemba*
1690	*Tebandeke*, son of Mutebi, with his cousin *Ndawula*
1717	*Kagulu*, son of Ndawula, with his brothers *Kikulwe* and *Mawanda*
1744	*Mwanga I*, nephew of Kagulu, with his brothers *Namugala* and *Kyabaggu*
1771	*Junju*, son of Kyabaggu, with his brother *Semakokiro*
1798	*Kamanya*, son of Semakokiro
1825	*Suna II*, son
1852	*(Mukabya) Mutesa I*, son (d. 1884)
1879 – 9 Aug 1897	*Danieri Mwanga*, son, with his brothers *Mutebi II Kiwewa* and *Kalema*, left Buganda 6 Jul 1897, deposed
1894	British protectorate established over kingdom
14 Aug 1897 – 1939	*Daudi Cwa II*, son of Danieri Mwanga (b. 6 Aug 1896)
1900	Buganda Agreement established native self-government

*All earlier dates are approximate and the first two kings listed are generally thought to be legendary

† Suna may have been the son of Mulondo or Jemba

22 Nov 1939 – 30 Nov 1953	*Mutesa II* (*Sir Edward William Frederick David Walugembe Luwangula Mutebi*) (for 1st time) (b. Makindye, near Kampala, 19 Nov 1924; d. London 22 Nov 1969) deported
30 Nov 1953	Recognition of tribe removed
17 Oct 1955 – May 1966	*Mutesa II* (for 2nd time) recognition restored, fled into exile after defeat during civil war
8 Sep 1967	Monarchy abolished by government of Uganda

Bulgaria

KHANATE

Territory now in southern Romania, Bulgaria, Albania, north-western Greece and Yugoslavia.

Khans

AD 681	*Asparukh* (or *Isperikh*), son of Kubrat, Khan of the Volga Bulgars (b. c. 644)
701/2	*Tervel*, kinsman
718	Unknown khan
725	*Sevar*, kinsman of Tervel
740	*Kormisosh*
756	*Vinekh*
762	*Telets*, installed by the boyars, assassinated
765	*Sabin*, son-in-law of Kormisosh
767	*Umar*, dethroned
767	*Toktu*, installed by the boyars, fled in face of Byzantine invasion, assassinated
772	*Pagan*, assassinated
c. 772	*Telerig*, fled the country
777	*Kardam*
803 – 13 Apr 814	*Krum*
814	*Dukum*
814	*Ditseng* or *Tsok*, usurper(?)
816	*Omurtag*, son of Krum
831	*Malamir*, son

836	*Presiyan*, nephew
852	*Boris I*, son (d. 2 May 907) baptized 864 and took name *Mikhail*, abdicated and retired to a monastery
889 – 893	*Vladimir*, son, deposed by Boris I

FIRST BULGARIAN EMPIRE

Territory now in southern Romania, Bulgaria, Albania, north-western Greece and Yugoslavia.

Tsars

893	*Simeon*, brother of Vladimir (b. 864/5) took title of tsar 925
27 May 927	*Petŭr I*, son
30 Jan 969 – 972	*Boris II*, son (d. 979/80) taken prisoner by Svyatoslav, Grand Duke of Kiev, in alliance with Byzantium; deported to Constantinople
972	Eastern Bulgaria annexed to the Byzantine Empire

Rulers in Western Bulgaria

Territory now in western Bulgaria, Yugoslavia, Albania and north-western Greece.

971	*Samuil*, son of Count Nikola, ruled with his brothers until c. 987, annexed parts of Thrace and Greece 976
6 Oct 1014	*Gavril Radomir*, son, murdered by Ivan Vladislav
1015	*Ivan Vladislav*, cousin, killed in battle
1018	Bulgaria made a Byzantine province

SECOND BULGARIAN EMPIRE

Territory now in Romania, eastern Yugoslavia and northern Bulgaria.

Tsars

1185/6	*Petŭr II Asen* (for 1st time) in revolt, abdicated
1187	*(Ivan) Asen I*, brother, killed by one of his nobles
1196	*Petŭr II* (for 2nd time) assassinated
1197	*Kaloyan* (or *Ioannitsa*), brother
8 Oct 1207	*Boril*, nephew, deposed by Ivan Asen II

1218	*Ivan Asen II*, son of Asen I
1241	*Kaliman* (or *Koloman*) *I*, son (b. c. 1234)
Aug 1246	*Mikhail II Asen*, half-brother, murdered by Kaliman II
	Regent:
	Irina, mother; daughter of Theodore Comnenus, despot of Epirus
1256 – 1257	*Kaliman* (or *Koloman*) *II*, cousin
1257	Civil war
1257 – 1277	*Konstantin Tikh*, installed by the boyars in western Bulgaria, took surname *Asen*, lost parts of Thrace and the Black Sea region, assassinated
1257 – (?)	*Mitso*, son-in-law (brother-in-law?) of Ivan Asen II, proclaimed tsar in southern Bulgaria
1268 – 1275	*Yakov Svetoslav*, autonomous despot in western Bulgaria
1277/8 – autumn(?) 1280	*Ivailo*, nicknamed *Bŭrdokva* or *Lakhana*,* peasant, in revolt, married Konstantin's widow, proclaimed tsar by the boyars 1278, sought help from the Tartars and was murdered by them
1277/9 – Jul 1280	*Ivan Asen III*, son of Mitso, proclaimed tsar by the Byzantines 1277, installed 1279, fled from Ivailo
Jul/Aug 1280 †	*Georgi I Terter*, chosen by his fellow boyars, became Tartar vassal 1285
1290 – 1298	*Smilets*, lord of Sliven, installed by the Tartars
1299	*Chaka*, son of the Tartar khan Nogai, son-in-law of Georgi I, deposed and executed
1300	*Todor Svetoslav*, son of Georgi I, granted land in southern Bessarabia by the Golden Horde
1321	*Georgi II*, son
1323 ‡	Short interregnum
1323 – 28 Jun 1330	*Mikhail Shishman*, son of Shishman, lord of Vidin (see footnote)
1330	*Ivan Stefan*, son, Serbian protégé, expelled
1331	*Ivan Aleksandŭr*, in alliance with Serbia, lost control of Dobruja c. 1350

* *Bŭrdokva* means lettuce or radish or dandelion, and *lakhana* cabbage

†During this reign *Yakov Rostislav* exercised independent authority in the north-west, the brothers *Drŭman* and *Kudelin* in the Branichev district, *Shishman* around Vidin, and *Smilets* (see above) and his brothers *Voisil* and *Radoslav* in Sliven

‡Independent in the region between Sliven and Kopsis: *Voisil* (see previous footnote) as Byzantine vassal

1371* – 1393	*Ivan Shishman*, son, ruling at Trnovo, vassal of the Ottoman sultan, rebelled and was executed
1371* – 1396	*Ivan Stratsimir*, half-brother; at first co-ruler at Vidin, then independent; vassal of the Ottoman sultan 1388
1396	Became a province of the Ottoman empire

Bulozi (Barotseland)

Territory in present-day western Zambia, with the capital at Lealui from 1864.

Litungas (Kings)

Luyana Dynasty	
AD (?)	*Mbuyu*
c. 17th century	*Mboo Muyunda*
(?)	*Inyambo*
(?)	*Ngalama*
(?)	*Yeta Nalute*
(?)	*Ngombala*
(?)	*Yubya Lukama*
(?)	*Mwanawina I*
(?)	*Mwananyanda*
c. 1780	*Mulambwa Santulu*
c. 1830	*Silumelume*, son, assassinated
(?)	*Mubukwanu*, brother
1840	Kololo conquest
1864	*Sipopa Lutangu*, son of Mulambwa Santulu
1876	*Mwanawina II*, nephew
1878	*Lubosi*, later called *Lewanika*, grandson of Mulambwa Santulu (for 1st time) (d. Feb 1916)
1884	*Tatila Akufuna*, cousin
1886 – 13 Mar 1916	*Lewanika* (for 2nd time)
1900	Barotse concession signed with the British South Africa Company accepting British protection in return for a guarantee of the preservation of the chief's constitutional powers

*The formal division took place during the reign of Ivan Aleksandŭr

13 Mar 1916	*Yeta III* (or *Litia*), son, paralysed from 1939, abdicated
Jun 1945	*Imwiko Lewanika*, brother (b. 1885)
Jun 1948 – Nov 1968	*Mwanawina III*, brother (b. c. 1888; d. Nov 1968)
24 Oct 1964	Barotseland became province of the newly independent country of Zambia
from 15 Dec 1968	*Lewanika II* (or *Godwin Mbikusita*), half-brother

Bunyoro

Territory comprised part of present-day western Uganda.

Abakama (Kings)

Babiito Dynasty

AD 14th/15th century	*Isingoma Mpuga Rukidi*; according to Nyoro tradition, brother of Kimera, King of Buganda
(?)	*Ochaki Rwangira*, son, with his brother *Oyo Nyimba*
(?)	*Winyi I*, son of Oyo Nyimba
(?)	*Olimi I*, son
(?)	*Nyabongo I*, son
fl. c. 1550	*Winyi II*, son
fl. 1582	*Olimi II*, son
(?)	*Nyarwa*, son, murdered
(?)	*Cwa I*, brother, killed in battle
(?)	*Mashamba*, sister, ruled as regent, assassinated
(?)	*Kyebambe I*, nephew
(?)	*Winyi III*, son
c. 1710	*Nyaika*, son, with his brother *Kyebambe II*, both murdered
(?)	*Olimi III*, son of Nyaika
c. 1731	*Duhaga I*, son, killed in battle
c. 1782	*Olimi IV*, son, murdered
1786	*Kyebambe III*, brother
1835	*Nyabongo II*, son
1848	*Olimi V*, son, murdered
1852	*Kyebambe IV* (or *Kamurasi*), brother
1870 – 1894	*Cwa II*, *Kabarega*, son (d. 1923), deposed and driven

	out by the British, captured and deported to the Seychelles 1899
1896	Incorporated into British protectorate of Uganda
1924 – (?)	*Sir Tito Gafabusa Winyi IV*, son of Cwa II (b. 1883)
9 Oct 1962	Uganda became independent
8 Sep 1967	Monarchy abolished by government of Uganda

Burgundy, Duchy of

Territory on the west bank of the Rhône north of Lyon.

Dukes

c. AD 888 – 1 Sep 921	*Richard*, le Justicier (i.e. Law-giver), brother of King Boson of Lower Burgundy; created Duke of Burgundy by King Charles III the Simple of France
921 – 923	*Raoul* (or *Rodolphe*), son (d. 14/15 Jan 936); elected King of France 13 Jul 923 in rivalry with Charles III and ruled as king after the imprisonment of Charles III; appointed his brother-in-law, Gislebert, to rule in Burgundy
923	*Gislebert*, Count of Autun, Avalon, Châlon and Beaune, brother-in-law (d. 956)
938	Dukedom divided between *Gislebert* (see above) and Raoul's brother, *Hugues*, the Black (d. 952), and brother-in-law, *Hugues*, the Great (or, the White), Count of Paris and Duke of France (d. 956); Hugues the Black ceded his part to Hugues the Great 943; Gislebert was deposed by King Louis IV d'Outremer of France 943, leaving Hugues the Great as sole Duke
956 – 23 Feb 965	*Otton* (or *Othon*), son of Hugues the Great; confirmed as Duke by King Lothaire of France 960
965 – 15 Oct 1002	*Henri I* (or *Eudes-Henri*), brother, died childless
1003 – 1006	King Robert II of France refused to recognize the succession of Henri I's stepson, Otton-Guillaume, and conquered Burgundy
1015 – 1031	*Henri II*, son of Robert II (b. 1008; d. Vitry-aux-Loges 4 Aug 1060) crowned co-king of France 1026, abdi-

	cated in Burgundy on his succession to the French throne as Henri I
1032 – 21 Mar 1076	*Robert I*, brother (b. c. 1011)
1076	*Hugues I*, grandson (b. c. 1056; d. 29 Aug 1093) abdicated
1079 – 23 Mar 1102	*Eudes I*, brother
1102	*Hugues II*, son (b. c. 1085)
1143 – Sep 1162	*Eudes II*, son (b. c. 1110)
1162 – 25 Aug 1192	*Hugues III*, son (b. c. 1148)
1192 – 6 Jul 1218	*Eudes III*, son (b. 1166)
1218 – Feb 1273	*Hugues IV*, son (b. 9 Mar 1212)
1273 – 9 Oct 1305	*Robert II*, son
1305 – Apr 1315	*Hugues V*, son
1315 – Apr 1349	*Eudes IV*, brother
1349 – 21 Nov 1361	*Philippe I de Rouvres*, grandson (b. Rouvres 1345; d. Rouvres) Count of Auvergne 1360
21 Nov 1361	Burgundy claimed by King Jean II of France

Capetians, of the House of Valois

1363 – 27 Apr 1404	*Philippe II*, the Bold, Count of Touraine, son of King Jean II of France who granted him the duchy (b. Pontoise 17 Jan 1342; d. Hal, Brabant) regent of France 1382 – 1388 and 1392 – 27 Apr 1404; from 1369 ruled with his wife, *Marguerite de Mâle* (b. 13 Apr 1350; d. 16 Mar 1405) Countess of Flanders, Franche-Comté and Artois 30 Jan 1384, Countess of Nevers and Rethel 30 Jan 1384 – 27 Apr 1404, Duchess of Brabant 7 May 1404
1404 – 10 Sep 1419	*Jean*, the Fearless, son (b. Dijon 28 May 1371; d. (assassinated) Montereau) Count of Nevers 27 Apr 1404 – 11 Apr 1405, Count of Artois, Flanders and Franche-Comté* 16 Mar 1405
1419 – 15 Jun 1467	*Philippe III*, the Good, son (b. Dijon 31 Jul 1396; d. Brugge, Flanders) Count of Namur 1 Mar 1429, administered Holland, Zeeland and Hainaut from 1427, inherited Brabant and Limburg 4 Aug 1430, occupied Luxemburg 1443
1467 – 5 Jan 1477	*Charles*, the Bold, son (b. Dijon 10 Nov 1433; d. near Nancy) succeeded in Gelders 1473
1477 – 27 Mar 1482	*Marie*, daughter (b. Brussels 13 Feb 1457; d. Brugge)

*Subsequent dukes of Burgundy were at the same time counts of Artois, Flanders and Franche-Comté

	ruled with her husband, *Maximilian I*, Archduke of Austria and Holy Roman Emperor from 19 Aug 1493 (b. Wiener Neustadt 22 Mar 1459; d. Wels 12 Jan 1519)
1482	By the Treaty of Arras Marie and Maximilian I agreed to retain their Burgundian possessions in the Low Countries, while granting the duchy of Burgundy to their daughter, Margarete of Austria
1482 – 30 Nov 1530	*Margarete* of Austria, daughter (b. 10 Jan 1480)

Burgundy, Kingdoms of

For the Merovingian Kings of Burgundy, see the Kingdom of the Franks.

LOWER BURGUNDY (or CISJURANE BURGUNDY)

Kings

15 Oct AD 879	*Boson*, brother-in-law of King Charles II, the Bald, of the West Franks; proclaimed himself king of an area bounded by the Alps, the Rhône and the Mediterranean, in rebellion against kings Louis III and Carloman of the West Franks who sent Boson's brother Richard (later Duke of Burgundy) to recover the territory
11 Jan 887 – Jun 928	*Louis*, the Blind, son (b. c. 880) under the tutelage (until her death) of his mother, *Ermengarde* (d. 897), who secured recognition for Louis from King Arnulf of the East Franks and Pope Stephen V; King (Ludwig III) of the Lombards Oct 900; Holy Roman Emperor (Ludwig (III)) Feb 901; defeated, deposed and blinded by Berengar I in Italy Jul 905, after which his rule was confined to Burgundy
933	Hugo (French: Hugues), King of the Lombards, Count of Arles, Duke of Provence and Margrave of Vienne surrendered his claims to Lower Burgundy to King Rodolphe II of Upper Burgundy

UPPER BURGUNDY (or TRANSJURANE BURGUNDY) (from 934 BURGUNDY)

Kings

888 – 25 Oct 912	*Rodolphe I*, son of Count Conrad of Auxerre; proclaimed himself king of an area consisting of present-day Switzerland east of the Reuss and an uncertain adjoining area of present-day France
912 – 11 Jul 937	*Rodolphe II*, son; King of the Lombards 923 – 926, King of united Upper and Lower Burgundy 933
937 – 19 Oct 993	*Conrad*, the Peaceful, son
993 – 6 Sep 1032	*Rodolphe III*, son; willed the kingdom to the Holy Roman Emperor Konrad II

After Rodolphe III's death the united kingdom of Burgundy (henceforth usually called the Kingdom of Arles) was held by the Holy Roman Emperors who were either crowned as kings of Arles or appointed imperial vicars. However, they exercised little control over the counts of the area. Arles included the counties of Burgundy (also known as Franche-Comté) (inherited by the dukes of Burgundy 1405), Lyonnais (acquired by the dukes of Bourbon 1371), Mâcon (ceded by its countess to France 1239), Provence (acquired by the counts of Anjou 1246) and Savoy (q.v.) and the dauphiné of Viennois (ceded by its dauphin to France 1349).

Burma

MON KINGDOM OF PEGU (HANTHAWADDY)

Territory comprised part of present-day south-eastern Burma and west central Thailand, with the capital at Pegu.

Kings

AD 825*	*Thamala*, legendary founder of Pegu
837	*Wimala*, brother
854	*Atha*, nephew

*The list before 1287 is traditional

861	*Areindama*
885	A monk
902	*Geinda*
917	*Migadeippagyi*
932	*Geissadiya*
942	*Karawika*
954	*Pyinzala*
967	*Attatha*
982	*Anuyama*
994	*Migadeippange*
1004	*Ekkathamanta*
1016	*Uppala*
1028	*Pontarika*
1043 – 1044	*Tissa*
1044 – 1287	Under the rule of Pagan (see below)
1287	*Wareru*
1306(?)	*Hkun Law*, brother
1310	*Saw O*, nephew
1324	*Saw Zein*, brother
1331	*Zein Pun*, usurper
1331	*Saw E Gan Gaung*, nephew of Saw Zein
1331	*Binnya E Law*, son of Hkun Law
1353	*Binnya U*, son
1385	*Razadarit*, son
1423	*Binnya Dammayaza*, son
1426	*Binnya Ran I*, brother
1446	*Binnya Waru*, nephew
1450	*Binnya Kyan*, cousin
1453	*Mawdaw*, cousin
1453	*Shin Sawbu*, daughter of Razadarit
1472	*Dammazedi*, son-in-law
1492	*Binnya Ran II*, son
1526 – 1539	*Takayutpi*, son, driven out by Burmese
1539 – 1550	First Burmese occupation
1550	*Smim Sawhtut*, minor prince of the old dynasty, leader of revolt against Burmese, eliminated by Smim Htaw
1551	*Smim Htaw*, son of Binnya Ran II, defeated and killed by the Burmese king Bayinnaung
1551 – 1740	Second Burmese occupation
1740	*Smim Htaw Buddhaketi*, son of a Burmese governor of Pagan, leader of revolt against Burmese, exiled
1747 – 1757	*Binnya Dala*, father-in-law and chief minister (d.

	(murdered) Rangoon 1773)
1757	Pegu captured by Burmese and Mon independence finally ended

KINGDOM OF ARAKAN

Territory comprised part of present-day south-western Burma.

Kings

Launggyet Dynasty	
AD 1237	*Alawmahpyu*, son
1243	*Yazathugyi*, son
1246	*Sawlu*, son
1251	*Ossanagyi*, son
1260	*Sawmungyi*, son
1268	*Nankyagyi*, son
1272	*Minbilu*, son
1276	*Sithabin*, usurper
1279	*Minhti*, son of Minbilu*
1374 – 1385	Burmese nominees of the blood
1385	*Ossanange*
1387	*Thiwarit*, brother
1390	*Thinhse*, brother
1394	*Razathu*, son (for 1st time)
1395	*Sithabin*, usurper
1397	*Myinhsainggyi*, usurper
1397	*Razathu* (for 2nd time)
1401 – 1404	*Theinhkathu*, brother
Mrohaung Dynasty	
1404	*Narameikhla* (or *Minsawmun*), son of Razathu
1434	*Ali Khan*, brother
1459	*Basawpyu* (or *Kalima Shah*), son, murdered
1482	*Dawlya*, son
1492	*Basawnyo*, uncle
1494	*Yanaung*, son of Dawlya
1494	*Salingathu*, uncle on mother's side
1501	*Minyaza*, son
1523	*Kasabadi*, son

*Traditionally assigned a reign of 106 years

1525	*Minsaw O*, brother of Salingathu
1525	*Thatasa*, son of Dawlya
1531	*Minbin*, son of Minyaza (d. 1553)
1551	*Dikha*, son
1555	*Sawhla*, son
1564	*Minsetya*, brother
1571	*Minpalaung*, son of Minbin
1593	*Minyazagyi*, son
1612	*Minhkamaung*, son
1622	*Thirithudamma*, son, murdered
1638	*Minsani*, son
1638	*Narapatigyi*, great-grandson of Thatasa, lover of Thirithudamma's chief queen
1645	*Thado*, nephew
1652	*Sandathudamma*, son
1684	*Thirithuriya*, son, murdered
1685	*Waradhammaraza*, brother, placed on throne by the Mughals, deposed
1692	*Munithudhammaraza*, brother, murdered
1694	*Sandathuriyadhamma*, brother
1696	*Nawrahtazaw*, son
1696	*Mayokpiya I*, usurper
1697	*Kalamandat*, usurper
1698	*Naradipati*, son of Sandathuriyadhamma
1700	*Sandawimala*, grandson of Thado
1706	*Sandathuriya*, grandson of Sandathudamma
1710	*Sandawizaya I* (formerly *Maha Danda Bo*) usurper, murdered
1731	*Sandathuriya*, son-in-law
1734	*Naradipati II*, son
1735	*Narapawara*, usurper
1737	*Sandawizaya II*, cousin
1737	*Katya*, usurper
1737	*Madarit*, brother of Sandawizaya II
1742	*Nara-apaya*, uncle
1761	*Thirithu*, son
1761	*Sandapavama*, brother
1764	*Apaya*, brother-in-law
1773	*Sandathumana*, brother-in-law
1777	*Sandawinala*, usurper
1777	*Sandathaditha*
1782 – 1785	*Thamada*, deposed
1785	Burmese conquest

KINGDOM OF PAGAN

Territory comprised part of present-day southern Burma, with the capital at Pagan.

Kings

AD 1044	*Anawrahta*
1077	*Sawlu*, son, murdered
1084	*Kyanzittha*, brother
1113	*Alaungsithu*, grandson
1167	*Narathu*, son, killed
1170	*Naratheinhka*, son
1173	*Narapatisithu*, brother
1210	*Nantonmya* (or *Htilominlo*), son
1234	*Kyaswa*, son
1250	*Uzana*, son
1254	*Narathihapate* (called *Tarokpyemin*, i.e. 'the king who ran away from the Chinese'), son, defeated by the Mongols at the battle of Ngasaunggyan 1277, fled from Pagan during the Mongol invasion of 1283, murdered
1287	*Kyawswa*, son, Mongol vassal, murdered by the Shan chiefs
1298	*Sawhnit*, illegitimate son, placed on throne by the Shan chiefs
1325	*Uzana*, son, ruled at Pinya (see Shan Kingdom of Myinsaing and Pinya)

SHAN KINGDOM OF MYINSAING AND PINYA

Territory comprised part of present-day northern Burma, with the capital initially at Myinsaing and later at Pinya.

Kings

AD 1298	*Athinhkaya*, *Yazathinkyan* and *Thihathu*, the three Shan brothers; the last surviving brother, Thihathu, transferred his capital from Myinsaing to Pinya 1312
1324	*Uzana* (see Kingdom of Pagan)
1343	*Ngashishin*, half-brother
1350	*Kyawswange*, son

1359	*Narathu*, brother
1364	*Uzana Pyaung*, brother
1364	*Thadominbya*, descendant of Thihathu (see also Kingdom of Ava)

KINGDOM OF AVA

Territory comprised part of present-day northern Burma, with the capital at Ava.

Kings

AD 1364	*Thadominbya*, last king of Myinsaing and Pinya, re-established his capital at Ava after the Maw Shan sack of Pinya
1368	*Nga Nu*, usurper
1368	*Minkyiswasawke*, recognized as the governor of Ava by the Chinese
1401	*Tarabya*, son
1401	*Nga Nauk Hsan*, usurper
1401	*Minhkaung*, son of Minkyiswasawke
1422	*Thihathu*, son
1426	*Minhlange*, son
1426	*Kalekyetaungnyo*, son of Tarabya, deposed
1427	*Mohnyinthado*, a Burmese chief
1440	*Minrekyawswa*, son
1443	*Narapati*, brother, Chinese vassal
1469	*Thihathura*, son
1481	*Minhkaung*, son
1502	*Shwenankyawshin*, son, defeated and killed by the Shan ruler
1527	*Thohanbwa*, son of Shan ruler, usurper
1543	*Hkonmaing*, usurper, Shan chief
1546	*Mobye Narapati*, son, Shan chief
1552 – 1555	*Sithukyawhtin*, usurper, Shan chief
1555	Absorbed into the reunited kingdom of Burma created by Bayinnaung (see Volume 2)

Buyids (Buwayhids)

Territory comprised part of present-day Iran and Iraq, with the capital at Baghdad.

Amirs

Line in Fars and Khuzistan

AD 933/4	*'Imad al-Daula (Abu'l-Hasan 'Ali)*, son of Buya, ruled in Jibal 932/3 – 946/7
949/50 – 26 Mar 983	*'Adud al-Daula (Abu Shuja' Fana-Khusrau)*, nephew (b. 24 Sep 936) ruled in Kirman 949/50 – 982/3, ruled in Iraq 30 May 978 – 26 Mar 983
Mar/Apr 983	*Sharaf al-Daula (Abu'l-Fawaris Shirzil)*, son (b. Mar/Apr 962) ruled in Iraq Jan/Feb 987 – Sep/Oct 989
Sep/Oct 989	*Abu 'Ali Sharaf al-Daula*, son, governor of Fars
Aug/Sep 990	*Samsam al-Daula (Abu Kalijar al-Marzuban)*, uncle (b. Jun/Jul 964) ruled in Kirman 982/3 – 998, ruled in Iraq Mar/Apr 983 – Jan/Feb 987, assassinated
998	*Baha' al-Daula (Abu Nasr Firuz)*, brother (b. 967/8) ruled in Kirman 998 – 1012/13, ruled in Iraq Sep/Oct 989 – 1012/13, deposed 'Abassid caliph al-Ta'i' 991/2
1012/13	*Sultan al-Daula (Abu Shuja')*, son (d. Dec 1023/Jan 1024) ruled in Iraq 1012/13 – 1021/2
1021/2	*Musharrif al-Daula (Abu 'Ali al-Hasan)*, brother, ruled in Iraq 1021/2 – 1025/6
1024	*('Imad al-Din) Abu Kalijar al-Marzuban (ibn Sultan al-Daula)*, nephew (b. Basra May/Jun 1009) governor of Ahwaz 1021/2, conquered Basra 1028/9, ruled in Kirman 1028/9 – 1048/9, conquered Wasit 1029/30, ruled in Iraq Mar/Apr 1044 – 15 Oct 1048
1048/9	*al-Malik al-Rahim (Abu Nasr Khusrau Firuz)*, son, ruled in Iraq 1048/9 – 1055, deposed by Seljuq sultan Togrıl I Bey
1055/6 – 1062	*(Abu-Mansur) Fulad-Sutun*, brother, ruled in Fars only
1062	Power in Fars seized by the Kurdish chief Fadluya

Line in Kirman

935/6	*Mu'izz al-Daula (Abu'l-Husain Ahmad)*, son of Buya

	(b. 915/16; d. 1 Apr 967) ruled in Iraq 945/6 – 1 Apr 967
949/50	*'Adud al-Daula (Abu Shuja' Fana-Khusrau)*, nephew (see Line in Fars and Khuzistan)
982/3	*Samsam alDaula (Abu Kalijar al-Marzuban)*, son (see Line in Fars and Khuzistan)
998	*Baha' al-Daula (Abu Nasr Firuz)* (see Line in Fars and Khuzistan)
1012/13	*Qawam al-Daula (Abu'l-Fawaris)*, son (b. 17 Mar 1000)
1028/9 – 1048/9	*('Imad al-Din) Abu Kalijar al-Marzuban (ibn Sultan al-Daula)*, nephew (see Line in Fars and Khuzistan)
1048/9	Superseded by the Seljuq sultan of the Kirman line of Qawurd

Line in Jibal

932/3	*'Imad al-Daula (Abu'l-Hasan 'Ali)* (see Line in Fars and Khuzistan)
946/7 – 16 Sep 976	*Rukn al-Daula (Abu 'Ali al-Hasan)*, brother (b. 897/8)
16 Sep 976	Division of lands

Branch in Hamadan and Isfahan

976/7	*Mu'ayyad al-Daula (Abu Mansur Buya)*, son (d. 987/8)
983/4	*Fakhr al-Daula (Abu'l-Hasan 'Ali)*, brother, ruled in Rayy 976/7 – 997/8, imprisoned by 'Adud al-Daula 979/80 and detained until 983/4
Aug/Sep 997	*Shams al-Daula (Abu Tahir)*, son
1021/2	*Sama' al-Daula (Abu'l-Hasan)*, son, under Kakuyid suzerainty
1023/4	Kakuyids established in Isfahan
1030	Kakuyids established in Hamadan

Branch in Rayy

976/7	*Fakhr al-Daula (Abu'l-Hasan 'Ali)* (see Branch in Hamadan and Isfahan)
997/8 – 1029/30	*Maj al-Daula (Abu Talib Rustam)*, son (b. 989/90)
1029/30	Ghaznavid conquest

Line in Iraq

945/6	*Mu'izz al-Daula (Abu'l-Husain Ahmad)* (see Line in Kirman)

1 Apr 967	*'Izz al-Daula (Abu Mansur Bakhtiyar)*, son (b. 942/3)
30 May 978 – 26 Mar 983	*'Adud al-Daula (Abu Shuja' Fana-Khusrau)*, cousin (see Line in Fars and Khuzistan)
Mar/Apr 983	*Samsam al-Daula (Abu Kalijar al-Marzuban)*, son (see Line in Fars and Khuzistan)
Jan/Feb 987	*Sharaf al-Daula (Abu'l-Fawaris Shirzil)*, brother (see Line in Fars and Khuzistan)
Sep/Oct 989	*Baha' al-Daula (Abu Nasr Firuz)*, brother (see Line in Fars and Khuzistan)
1012/13	*Sultan al-Daula (Abu Shuja')* (see Line in Fars and Khuzistan)
1021/2	*Musharrif al-Daula (Abu 'Ali al-Hasan)* (see Line in Fars and Khuzistan)
1025/6 – 1036/7	*Jalal al-Daula (Abu Tahir Shirzil)*, brother (b. 993/4; d. 9 Mar 1044) governor of Basra 1012/13 – 1025/6
1036/7	Revolt of Baristughan, in favour of Abu Kalijar al-Marzuban
Mar/Apr 1044 – 15 Oct 1048	*('Imad al-Din) Abu Kalijar al-Marzuban*, nephew (see Line in Fars and Khuzistan)
1048/9 – 1055	*al-Malik al-Rahim (Abu Nasr Khusrau Firuz)* (see Line in Fars and Khuzistan)
1055	Seljuq occupation of Baghdad

Byzantine Empire

At its greatest extent, territory comprised part of present-day Turkey, Syria, Jordan, Israel, Lebanon, Egypt, Cyprus, Crete, the coastal strip of North Africa, the southern Iberian peninsula, Italy, Yugoslavia, Bulgaria and Greece, with the capital at Constantinople (present-day Istanbul).

Emperors

For Emperors at Constantinople before the fall of Rome, see the Roman Empire.

11 Apr AD 491	*Anastasius I*, court official (b. Dyrrachium (present-day Durazzo) c. 430) married Ariadne, the widow of Zeno, Roman emperor in the East; defeated the rebel

	Vitalian* 515
1 Jul 518 – 1 Aug 527	*Justin I*, count of the excubitors (b. Bederiana, Macedonia, 450/2) appointed Justinian I as co-emperor
4 Apr 527	*Justinian I*, the Great, nephew (b. Taurisium, Macedonia, 483; d. 14 Nov 565) appointed caesar 525, sole emperor 1 Aug 527, reconquered Africa Mar 534, captured Ravenna 540, recovered nearly all of Italy by 562
15 Nov 565	*Justin II*, nephew (d. 5 Oct 578) parts of Italy lost in the Lombard invasion of 568, became insane 574 Regents: 574 – 578: *Sophia*, wife, and *Tiberius II Constantine* (see below)
26 Sep 578	*Tiberius II Constantine*, a Thracian general (d. 14 Aug 582) appointed caesar Dec 574, served as regent for Justin II (see above)
13 Aug 582 – 22 Nov 602	*Maurice Tiberius*, son-in-law (d. (executed) 26/27 Nov 602) appointed caesar 5 Aug 582
23 Nov 602 – 3 Oct 610	*Phocas*, a Thracian centurion (d. (executed) 4 Oct 610) proclaimed emperor by the army on the Danube, most of Asia Minor lost to the Sasanids by 608, deposed
5 Oct 610	*Heraclius*, son of the exarch of Carthage (b. Cappadocia c. 575) regained, from the Sasanids, most of the territory lost in Asia Minor 611 – 628; lost Byzantine Mesopotamia, Syria and Palestine to the Arabs
11 Feb – 24 May 641	*Heraclius Constantine* (or *Constantine III*), son (b. 3 May 612) co-emperor 22 Jan 613
11 Feb – late Sep 641	*Heraclonas* (or *Heraclius*), brother (b. 625) proclaimed augustus 4 Jul 638, sole ruler 24 May 641, deposed and exiled to Rhodes Sep 641, date of death unknown
Sep 641 – 15 Sep 668	*Constans II* (also called *Constantine Pogonatus*†), son of Heraclius Constantine (b. 630; d. (assassinated) Syracuse) lost Egypt 646, removed to Greece and Italy 662/3

*513 – 515	*Vitalian*, commander-in-chief in Thrace, rebelled 513, came to terms with Anastasius I and was appointed master of the soldiers in Thrace, rebelled again and decisively defeated

† It was formerly supposed that Constantine Pogonatus was Constantine IV

Sep 668	*Constantine IV*, son, co-emperor 654
Sep 685	*Justinian II*, Rhinotmetus, son (for 1st time) (b. 669; d. 711) co-emperor 680, defeated by the Arabs at Sebastopolis and lost the Byzantine possessions in Armenia, deposed and banished to Cherson, escaped to the Khazars
695	*Leontius*, governor of the theme of Hellas (d. (executed) 705) raised to the throne by the party of the Blues, deposed
698	*Tiberius III* (original name *Apsimar*), army commander, raised to the throne by the Greens, deposed and executed
705	*Justinian II* (for 2nd time) restored with Bulgarian help; with his son, *Tiberius* (b. c. 700), as co-emperor, both defeated and killed
Dec 711	*Philippicus* (original name *Bardanes*), son of the patrician Nicephorus of Pergamum, deposed and blinded
Jun 713	*Anastasius II* (original name *Artemius*), chief secretary of Philippicus (d. (executed) 721) deposed by Theodosius III and became a monk in Thessalonica
Jan 716	*Theodosius III*, of Adramytium, a tax collector, proclaimed emperor by the troops of the Opsikion theme, forced to abdicate and became a monk in Ephesus
25 Mar 717	*Leo III*, the Isaurian,* strategus of the Anatolikon theme (b. Germanicia, Commagene, c. 680) proclaimed emperor by his troops
18 Jun 741	*Constantine V Copronymus*, son (b. 718) co-emperor 25 Mar 720, defeated the pretender Artavasdus† 743
14 Sep 775	*Leo IV*, the Khazar, son (b. 25 Jan 749) co-emperor 751
8 Sep 780	*Constantine VI*, son (b. 770; d. after 15 Aug 797) co-emperor 24 Apr 776, deposed and blinded by Irene (see below) Regent: 780 – Oct 790: *Irene*, mother (see below)

*Despite the traditional epithet it is more likely that Leo was a native of Upper Syria

† 27 Jun 742 – end of 743	*Artavasdes*, brother-in-law of Constantine V Copronymus and count of the Opsikion theme, set up as rival emperor with his son *Nicephorus*, defeated

15 Aug 797	*Irene* (b. c. 752; d. Lesbos 803) banished 790 after period as regent for Constantine VI, permitted to return to court with the title of empress 792, deposed and exiled
31 Oct 802	*Nicephorus I*, minister of finance (logothete); recognized Charlemagne as emperor of the Franks and ceded Rome, Ravenna and Pentapolis; killed in battle against the Bulgars
26 Jul 811	*Stauracius*, son (d. 11 Jan 812) co-emperor Dec 803; mortally wounded 26 Jul 811, deposed and removed to a monastery
2 Oct 811	*Michael I Rhangabe*, brother-in-law; with his son, *Theophylactus*, as co-emperor from 25 Dec 811; defeated by the Bulgars at Versinikia 22 Jun 813; deposed and died in a monastery in the Princes (Kızıl) Islands
11 Jul 813	*Leo V*, the Armenian; strategus of the Anatolikon theme; mutinied with his troops at the battle of Versinikia; with his son, *Constantine*, as co-emperor from 25 Dec 813; assassinated
25 Dec 820	*Michael II*, the Amorian, called the Lisper, commander under Leo V, lost Crete to the Arabs
3 Oct 829	*Theophilus*, son (b. c. 805) co-emperor 821, lost Palermo to the Arabs 831, lost Ankara 838
20 Jan 842 – 23 Sep 867	*Michael III*, the Amorian or the Drunkard, son (b. c. 836 or 840) co-emperor 840(?) Regent: 20 Jan 842 – Mar 856: *Theodora*, mother (d. 11 Feb 867)
24 Sep 867	*Basil I*, the Macedonian, chamberlain and favourite (b. 835) co-emperor 26 May 866; with his son, *Constantine* (b. c. 859; d. Sep 879) as co-emperor 6 Jan 869 – Sep 879
29 Aug 886	*Leo VI*, the Wise, son (b. 1 Sep 866) co-emperor 6 Jan 870, lost Sicily 902
11 May 912	*Alexander*, brother (b. 870) co-emperor 886
6 Jun 913 – 9 Nov 959	*Constantine VII*, Porphyrogenitus, son of Leo VI (b. Sep 905) co-emperor 9 Jun 911 – May 912 Regents: 6 Jun 913 – Feb 914: council of regency under *Nicholas I*, Patriarch of Constantinople Feb 914 – May 919: *Zoe Carbounopsina*, mother May 919 – 17 Dec 920: *Romanus Lecapenus*, High

	Admiral (see below)
17 Dec 920 – 16 Dec 944	*Romanus I Lecapenus*, father-in-law (b. c. 872; d. Prote 15 Jun 948) previously regent; co-emperor and in effectual control; deposed and exiled
15(?) Nov 959 – 15 Mar 963	*Romanus II*, son of Constantine VII (b. 938) co-emperor 6 Apr 945
16 Mar 963	*Theophano* (formerly *Anastaso*), widow, as regent for Basil II and Constantine VIII (see below) married Nicephorus II 20 Sep 963
3 Jul/16 Aug 963	*Nicephorus II Phocas*, commander in the East (b. c. 912) proclaimed emperor at Caesarea (present-day Qisarya) 3 Jul 963, crowned co-emperor 16 Aug 963, in effectual control, conquered Cilicia (present-day south-eastern Turkey) and Cyprus 964/6 and most of Syria by 969, assassinated by John I Tsimisces
11 Dec 969	*John I Tsimisces*, commander in the East (b. Çemisgezek 924) usurper, technically guardian of Basil and Constantine, incorporated eastern Bulgaria into the empire
10 Jan 976	*Basil II Bulgaroctonus*, son of Romanus II (b. 957/8) co-emperor Apr 960, achieved the total subjugation of Bulgaria 1014
15 Dec 1025 – 11 Nov 1028	*Constantine VIII*, brother (b. 960/1) co-emperor Apr 961 and nominally fellow ruler with Basil II Bulgaroctonus
18 Nov 1028 – 11 Apr 1034	*Romanus III Argyrus*, son-in-law (b. c. 968)
12 Apr 1034 – 10 Dec 1041	*Michael IV*, the Paphlagonian; husband of Zoe, the widow of Romanus III Argyrus
14 Dec 1041	*Michael V Calaphates*, nephew, adopted son of Zoe, deposed and blinded, date of death unknown
21 Apr 1042	*Zoe*, daughter of Constantine VIII, widow of Romanus III and Michael IV (b. 978; d. 1050); ruled with her sister, *Theodora* (for 1st time) (d. Sep 1056); Zoe was titular empress until her death
11 Jun 1042	*Constantine IX Monomachus*, husband of Zoe (b. c. 980) co-emperor
11 Jan 1055	*Theodora* (for 2nd time)
31 Aug 1056	*Michael VI Stratioticus*, civil servant, appointed by Theodora, deposed
8 Jun/1 Sep 1057	*Isaac I Comnenus*, army commander (b. c. 1005; d. 1061) proclaimed 8 Jun 1057, abdicated
25 Dec 1059	*Constantine X Ducas*, civil servant, lost Armenia

	1064/5
May 1067 – Oct 1071	*Eudocia Macrembolitissa*, widow (b. c. 1021; d. 1096) as regent for her sons (see Michael VII below)
Dec 1067 – 24 Oct 1071	*Romanus IV Diogenes*, second husband (d. summer 1072) army commander, defeated and taken prisoner by the Seljuqs at Manzikert 19 Aug 1071, lost most of southern Italy to the Normans, deposed
Aug 1071	*Michael VII Ducas* (called Parapinaces), son of Constantine X Ducas, titular emperor from May 1067, sole emperor 24 Oct 1071, abdicated and retired to a monastery
24 Mar 1078 – 1 Apr 1081	*Nicephorus III Botaniates*, commander of the Anatolian theme, proclaimed emperor 7 Jan 1078,* deposed Michael VII Ducas and married his wife, abdicated and retired to a monastery
4 Apr 1081	*Alexius I Comnenus*, nephew of Isaac I (b. 1048)
15 Aug 1118	*John II Comnenus*, son (b. 1088) recovered Cilicia 1137, established suzerainty over the Crusader principality of Antioch
8 Apr 1143	*Manuel I Comnenus*, son (b. c. 1122) lost Thebes and Corinth (and Corfu 1147 – 1149); established suzerainty over the kingdom of Jerusalem 1159; incorporated Croatia, Bosnia and Dalmatia into the empire 1167
24 Sep 1180 – Nov 1183	*Alexius II Comnenus*, son (b. 1169) assassinated by Andronicus Comnenus Regents: 24 Sep 1180 – May 1182: *Marie d'Antioche*, mother (d. 1182) May 1182 – Sep/Oct 1183: *Andronicus Comnenus*, later emperor (see below) *de facto* ruler
Oct 1183	*Andronicus I Comnenus*, cousin of Manuel I (b. Constantinople 1118) co-emperor, sole emperor Nov 1183, lost Thessalonica to the Normans Aug 1185, killed by a street mob
12 Sep 1185 †	*Isaac II Angelus*, cousin (for 1st time) (b. c. 1135; d. after 8 Feb 1204) drove the Normans out of Greece

*Besides Nicephorus Botaniates, the Caesar *John Ducas* and *Nicephorus Bryennius*, governor of Dyrrachium, had themselves proclaimed emperor during the reign of Michael VII Ducas. Nicephorus Bryennius renewed his claim under Nicephorus III Botaniates

† 1184 – 1191	*Isaac Ducas Comnenus*, 'Emperor' of Cyprus, refused to recognize the suzerainty of Isaac II Angelus

	1185; recognized the Second Bulgarian Empire 1187; deposed, blinded and imprisoned
8 Apr 1195 – 17 Jul 1203	*Alexius III Angelus* (called *Comnenus*), brother (d. Nicaea 1211) deposed by the Fourth Crusade, escaped to Mosynopolis in Thrace, defeated by Theodore I Lascaris of Nicaea 1210 and entered a monastery
18 Jul 1203 – 28 Jan 1204	*Isaac II Angelus* (for 2nd time) restored by the Fourth Crusade, ruled with *Alexius IV Angelus* (d. (assassinated) Constantinople 8 Feb 1204) both deposed
5 Feb – 12 Apr 1204	*Alexius V Ducas Murtzuphlus*, son-in-law of Alexius III Angelus (d. (executed) Constantinople 1204) fled at the fall of Constantinople, later captured by the Crusaders

Latin Emperors of Constantinople

Controlled the city and surrounding areas only. For the continuation of the Greek line, see the Empire of Nicaea.

9 May 1204	*Baudouin I*, Count (Baudouin IX) of Flanders and Hainaut (b. 1172; d. c. 14 Apr 1205) captured by Tsar Kaloyan of Bulgaria at the battle of Adrianople Mar 1205 and later killed Regent: May 1205 – 20 Aug 1206: *Henri de Hainaut*, brother (b. c. 1174; d. (assassinated) Thessalonica 11 Jun 1216) subsequently emperor
20 Aug 1206*	*Henri de Hainaut*, previously regent
9 Apr 1217*	*Yolande*, sister (d. Sep 1219) and her husband, *Pierre*, Seigneur of Courtenay, Count of Nevers, Marquis of Namur (d. 1219?), who was defeated and imprisoned by Theodore Ducas of Epirus 1217, after which Yolande ruled as regent for her sons, *Philippe*, Marquis of Namur (d. Avignon 1226) who remained in France and *Robert de Courtenay* (d. Morea 1228) subsequently emperor
Sep 1219/25 Mar 1221*	*Robert de Courtenay* (see above) forced to cede most of the Latin Empire's remaining lands in Asia Minor to Emperor John III Vatatzes of Nicaea 1225, lost Thessalonica to Theodore Ducas of Epirus

*Date of coronation

	1224; deposed and killed during a revolt of his barons
1228/1240* – 25 Jul 1261	*Baudouin II de Courtenay*, brother (b. Constantinople 1217; d. Foggia, Italy, Oct 1273) absent in the West 1237 – 1240, fled to the West at the fall of Constantinople Regent: 1228 – 1231: *Jean de Brienne*, father-in-law (b. c. 1148; d. 23 Mar 1237) titular King of Jerusalem 1210 – 1229, subsequently crowned emperor
1231* – 23 Mar 1237	*Jean de Brienne*, previously regent
25 Jul 1261	Greek conquest of Constantinople

Greek Emperors (restored)

15 Aug 1261	*Michael VIII Palaeologus*, son of Andronicus Palaeologus (b. Nicaea c. 1224) regent for John IV, the emperor of Nicaea; recaptured Constantinople and became sole emperor of the restored Byzantine Empire
11 Dec 1282	*Andronicus II Palaeologus*, son (b. Constantinople 1260; d. Constantinople 13 Feb 1332) co-emperor 8 Nov 1272; with his son, *Michael IX* (b. 1277) as co-emperor 21 May 1294 – 13 Oct 1320; ruled with *Andronicus III* from 2 Feb 1325; forced to abdicate and retired to a monastery
24 May 1328	*Andronicus III Palaeologus*, grandson (b. Constantinople 1296) forced to recognize Serbian suzerainty over Macedonia Aug 1334
15 Jun 1341 – 1376	*John V Palaeologus*, son (for 1st time) (b. Nov 1331; d. 16 Feb 1391) crowned Nov 1341, junior emperor with John Cantacuzenus 1347 – 1354 (see below), deposed Regent: 1341 – 1347: *Anne of Savoy*, mother, with *John Cantacuzenus* (see below) until Sep 1341
Sep 1341 – Feb 1347	Civil war
8 Feb 1347 – Dec 1354†	*John VI Cantacuzenus*, chief adviser to Andronicus III Palaeologus (b. 1292; d. Greece 15 Jun

*Date of coronation

† 1353 – 1357 *Matthew Cantacuzenus*, son of John VI Cantacuzenus (d. 1382) proclaimed 1353, renounced claim 1357, later despot of the Morea

	1383) proclaimed emperor 26 Oct 1341, crowned co-emperor Adrianople 21 May 1346, accepted as senior emperor, forced to abdicate and retired to a monastery
12 Aug 1376/18 Oct 1377	*Andronicus IV Palaeologus*, son of John V Palaeologus, crowned 18 Oct 1377, deposed
1 Jul 1379	*John V Palaeologus* (for 2nd time) as Turkish vassal, deposed
14 Apr 1390	*John VII Palaeologus*, grandson (b. 1360; d. Sep 1408) seized Constantinople, deposed, regent for Manuel II Palaeologus 1399 – 1403
17 Sep 1390	*John V Palaeologus* (for 3rd time)
16 Feb 1391	*Manuel II Palaeologus*, son (b. 1350; d. 21 Jul 1425) co-emperor 25 Sep 1373, lost Thessaly and the Morea to the Ottomans 1396, absent in the West 10 Dec 1399 – 9 Jun 1403, lost the Peloponnese 1423, retired to a monastery Regent: 1399 – 1403: *John VII Palaeologus* (see above)
1423	*John VIII Palaeologus*, son (b. 1390; d. 3 Oct 1448) co-emperor 19 Jan 1421, lost Thessalonica Mar 1430
1 Nov 1448 – 29 May 1453	*Constantine XI Palaeologus*, brother, killed in the final defence of Constantinople
29 May 1453	Fall of Constantinople to the Ottomans

Cambodia

KINGDOM OF FUNAN

Territory comprised part of present-day Cambodia and south-western China, with the capital at Vyadhapura.

Kings

late 1st century AD	*Kaundinya* (or *Hun-t'ien*)

(?)	Unknown number of kings
late 2nd century	*Hun P'an-h'uang*
early 3rd century	*P'an-p'an*, son, for three years
c. 205 – c. 225	*Fan Shih-man*, general
(?)	*Fan Chinsheng*, son
(?)	*Fan Chan*, usurper
(?)	*Fan Ch'ang*, son of Fan Shih-man
c. 240	*Fan Hsun*, usurper, fl. 287
(?)	Unknown number of kings
fl. 357	*Chu Chant'an*
(?)	Unknown number of kings
(?)	*Kaundinya II* (or *Kiao-chen-ju*)
fl. 434	*Che-li-pa-mo* (or *Śreshthavarman*?)
(?)	Unknown number of kings
fl. 484	*(Kaundinya) Jayavarman*
514	*Rudravarman* (d. c. 550?) fl. 539

Autonomous existence under the Kingdom of Chenla (see below) until it was incorporated in 627(?).

KINGDOM OF CHENLA

Territory comprised part of present-day Cambodia and Laos, with the capital at Iśanapura.

Kings

c. AD 550	*Bhavavarman I*, grandson of Rudravarman of Funan, conquered Funan
c. 600	*Mahendravarman* (or *Chitrasena*), brother
c. 611	*Iśanavarman I*, son, incorporated Funan, established capital at Iśanapura
635(?)	*Bhavavarman II*, relationship unknown
c. 650	*Jayavarman I*, son(?)
fl. 713	*Jayadevi*, widow

The kingdom was subsequently divided into Upper and Lower Chenla. No dynastic records of Upper Chenla survive. Lower Chenla was initially divided between Aninditapura and Sambhupura. The latter had broken away during the reign of Jayavarman I, but there are no dynastic records before its union with Aninditapura.

Aninditapura
Capital at Angkor Borei.

(?)	*Baladitya*, probably related to the Funan dynasty, conquered by Chenla
7th century	*Nripatindravarman*, grandson, restored independence
(?)	*Pushkaraksha*, son, married heiress of Sambhupura

Aninditapura and Sambhupura (*Lower Chenla*)
Capital at Angkor Borei.

8th century	*Sambhuvarman*, son of Pushkaraksha of Aninditapura, reunited all of Lower Chenla
late 8th century	*Rajendravarman*, son
(?)	*Mahipativarman*, son

KHMER KINGDOM

Territory comprised part of present-day western Vietnam, Laos, Cambodia, Thailand and eastern Burma, with the capital at Angkor until 1432 and thereafter at Phnom Penh.

Kings

AD 802(?)	*Jayavarman II*, probably related to the Chenla dynasty
850	*Jayavarman III*, son
877	*Indravarman I*, cousin
889	*Yaśovarman I*, son, established the first city of Angkor
900	*Harshavarman I*, son
c. 922	*Isanavarman II*, brother
928	*Jayavarman IV*, usurper
942	*Harshavarman II*, son, dethroned
944	*Rajendravarman II*, grandson of Indravarman I
968	*Jayavarman V*, son
1001	*Udayadityavarman I*, nephew
1002(?)	*Jayaviravarman*(?), rival of Suryavarman I, held parts of Cambodia until c. 1011
1002	*Suryavarman I*, usurper
1050	*Udayadityavarman II*, son
1066	*Harshavarman III*, brother, dethroned
1080	*Jayavarman VI*, usurper

1107	*Dharanindravarman I*, brother, deposed
1113	*Suryavarman II*, great-nephew, conquered Champa
1150	*Dharanindravarman II*, cousin
1160	*Yaśovarman II*, son, killed
1166	*Tribhuvanadityavarman*, usurper, killed in the Cham sack of Angkor
1181	*Jayavarman VII*, son of Dharanindravarman II, conquered Champa
c. 1219	*Indravarman II*, son
1243	*Jayavarman VIII*, grandson(?), deposed
1295	*Indravarman III*, son-in-law
1308	*Indrajayavarman*, unknown relative
1327 – 1353(?)	*Jayavarman Paramesvara*, unknown relative
1362(?) – 1369	*Nippean Bat* (or *Nirvanapada*), first Thai conquest of Angkor
1369 – 1375	Thai interregnum in Angkor
1371	*Kalamegha* (or *Huerh-na*), ruled at Basan
(?)	*Kambujadhiraja* (or *Gamkat*), recovered Angkor
(?)	*Dharmasokaraja* (or *Pao-p'i-ya*), died in the second Thai conquest of Angkor
1389	*Ponhea Yat* (or *P'o-p'i-ya*), ruled from Phnom Penh, recovered Angkor
1404	*Narayana Ramadhipati* (or *P'ing-ya*)
1429	*Sodaiya* (or *Srey*), deposed and fled into Ayuthia following final conquest of Angkor
1444	*Dharmarajadhiraja*, ruled at Phnom Penh
1486 – 1512	*Srey Sukonthor*, son

Cappadocia

Territory comprised part of present-day central Turkey, with the capital at Caesarea Mazaca (present-day Kayseri).

Kings

c. 362 BC	*Datames*, Persian satrap
330 – 332	*Ariarathes I*, independent satrap, put to death by the Macedonian rulers Perdiccas and Eumenes

322–301	Macedonian rule
301	*Ariarathes II*, son, Seleucid vassal
280(?)	*Ariaramnes*, son, Seleucid vassal until 260
262/1	*Ariarathes III*, son, began his rule as epistates (governor), then declared himself king
220	*Ariarathes IV Eusebes*, son
163	*Ariarathes V Eusebes Philopator*, son
c. 130	*Nysa*, queen-mother, served as regent, period of disorder
c. 126	*Ariarathes VI Epiphanes Philopator*, son, assassinated
111	*Ariarathes VII Philometor*, son
c. 100	*Ariarathes Eusebes Philopator*, son of Mithridates VI Eupator Dionysus, the king of Pontus, though posing as a son of Ariarathes VII Philometor
96	*Ariarathes VIII*
c. 95	*Ariobarzanes I Philoromaios*, a noble of the court; elected on the death of Ariarathes VIII without heir; until 85, when restored by Sulla, alternated on the throne with his rival *Ariarathes IX*; abdicated
62	*Ariobarzanes II Philopator*, son of Ariobarzanes I
51	*Ariobarzanes III Eusebes Philoromaios*, son, assassinated by Gaius Cassius Longinus
42	*Ariarathes X Eusebes Philadelphos*, brother, executed by the Roman triumvir Mark Antony
36 BC – AD 17	*Archelaus* | *Philopatris, Ktistes*, elected by Mark Antony
AD 17	Kingdom annexed by the Roman empire

Carthage

At its greatest extent, territory comprised part of present-day southern Spain, northern Morocco, northern Algeria, Tunisia, north-western Libya, western Sicily, Sardinia and Corsica, with the capital at Carthage.

Kings

Magonids

c. 550 BC	*Mago*

c. 530	*Hasdrubal*, son
c. 510	*Hamilcar*, nephew
480	*Hanno*, the Navigator or the Sabellian, son
440	*Hannibal*, nephew
406	*Himilco*, cousin, committed suicide
396 – 375	*Mago*
375	Creation of an oligarchy
146	Destruction of Carthage by the Romans

Castile

Kings

AD 1029 – 18 Oct 1035	*Sancho III*, the Great, King of Navarre, son of King García III of Navarre (b. c. 992) accepted as overlord by Gascony and Barcelona, Count of Castile, created the kingdom of Castile for his son
1035 – 27 Dec 1065	*Fernando I*, the Great, son (b. 1016/18; d. León) established his claim to the throne of León by 1038 but not crowned until 1039; recognized as suzerain in Navarre after 1054
27 Dec 1065	Kingdom divided among Fernando I's sons
1066 – 7 Oct 1072	*Sancho II*,* son (b. c. 1038; d. Zamora) deposed King Alfonso VI of León 1070 and King García of Galicia 1071, killed while trying to establish his claim to the throne of León
1072 – 30 Jun 1109	*Alfonso VI*, brother (b. 1039; d. Toledo) King of León 1065 – 1070, restored as King of Castile and León on the death of Sancho II and assumed the title 'Emperor of all Spain' by 1077, conquered the Dhunnunids of Toledo 1085/6
1109 – 8 Mar 1126	*Urraca*, daughter (b. 1082) Queen of Castile and León; ruled with her husband, *Alfonso I*, King of Aragon and Navarre (b. c. 1073; d. 1134), who abdicated in Castile and León in favour of his stepson 1126
1126 – 21 Aug 1157	*Alfonso VII*, son of Urraca (b. 1105; d. Fresnada)

*The numeration follows that of Asturias and León

	King of Castile and León, King of Galicia 1112, assumed the imperial title of Alfonso VI and was acknowledged as emperor by the kings of Aragon and Navarre
1157	Kingdom divided between Alfonso VII's sons
1157 – 31 Aug 1158	*Sancho III*, son (b. 1135) King of Castile only
1158 – 6 Oct 1214	*Alfonso VIII*, son (b. 11 Nov 1155) King of Castile
1214 – 6 Jun 1217	*Enrique I*, son (b. 14 Apr 1204) King of Castile
1217	*Alfonso IX*, King of León, son of King Fernando II of León (b. 1166; d. Villanueva de Sarria 24 Sep 1230) King of Castile

Kings of Castile and León

1217 – 30 May 1252	*Fernando III*, Saint, son (b. 1200) King of Castile; King of León 1230; conquered Córdoba 1236, Jaén 1246 and Seville 1248; effected the permanent union of Castile and León; canonized 1671
1252 – 4 Apr 1284	*Alfonso X*, the Wise, son (b. Burgos 23 Nov 1220; d. Seville) elected King of Germany 1 Apr 1257 but election rejected by Pope Alexander IV; renounced all claims to the German throne 1275
1284 – 26 Apr 1296	*Sancho IV*, son (b. 13 May 1258)
1296 – 7 Sep 1312	*Fernando IV*, son (b. 6 Dec 1285) Regent: *María de Molina*, mother (d. 1 Jun 1322)
1312 – 26 Mar 1350	*Alfonso XI*, son (b. 11 Aug 1311; d. Gibraltar) Regent: 1312–1319: *Pedro*, uncle (b. 1290; d. 25 Jun 1319)
1350	*Pedro I*, the Cruel, son (for 1st time) (b. Burgos 30 Aug 1334; d. (assassinated) Monteil 23 Mar 1369) deposed
1366 – 3 Apr 1367	*Enrique II*, illegitimate son of Alfonso XI (for 1st time) (b. Seville 13 Jan 1334; d. Santo Domingo de la Calzada 29 May 1379) invaded Castile, deposed Pedro I and was crowned king 29 Mar 1366; defeated and deposed at the battle of Nájera
1367 – 23 Mar 1369	*Pedro I* (for 2nd time) defeated and assassinated by Enrique II
1369 – 29 May 1379	*Enrique II* (for 2nd time) founder of the Trastámara dynasty
1379 – 9 Oct 1390	*Juan I*, son (b. Épila 20 Aug 1358; d. Alcalá de Henares) proclaimed himself King of Portugal Jan

	1384, but was defeated at Aljubarrota 14 Aug 1385
1390 – 25 Dec 1406	*Enrique III*, son (b. Burgos 1 Oct 1379)
1406 – 21 Jul 1454	*Juan II*, son (b. Toro 6 Mar 1405; d. Valladolid) Regent: 1406 – 1418: *Catherine of Lancaster*, mother (d. 2 Jun 1418); and until 1416, *Fernando I*, King of Aragon, uncle (b. 27 Nov 1380; d. Igualada 2 Apr 1416)
1454 – 11 Dec 1474	*Enrique IV*, the Impotent, son (b. Valladolid 5 Jan 1425; d. Madrid) last of the Trastámara kings
1474 – 26 Nov 1504	*Isabel I*, sister (b. 22 Apr 1451) ruled with her husband, *Fernando V*, King of Aragon as Fernando II (b. Sos 10 Mar 1452; d. Madrigalejo 23 Jan 1516), who ruled as king-consort of Castile until 1479, when Isabel and Fernando became full co-rulers in both kingdoms; conquered the Nasrids of Granada 1492; annexed Navarre 1512; effected the permanent union of Spain

For the continuation of the line of Fernando and Isabel in Volume 2, see Spain

Ceylon

Kings

Vijaya Dynasty

483 BC*	*Vijaya*
444	*Upatissa*, prime minister, regent
444	*Panduvasudeva*, nephew of Vijaya
414	*Abhaya*
394	*Pandukhabhaya* and *Ganatissa*
307	*Mutasiva*
247	*Devanampiya Tissa*
207	*Uttiya*, brother
197	*Mahasiva*, brother

*The dating is that accepted in the various volumes of *The History and Culture of the Indian People*. Traditional dates before AD 400 are up to 60 years earlier

187	*Suratissa*, brother	
177	*Sena* and *Guttaka*, usurpers	
155	*Asela*	
145	*Elara*	
101	*Dutthagamani*	
77	*Saddhatissa*	
59	*Thulatthana*	
59	*Lañjatissa*	
49	*Khallata Naga*	
43	*Vattagamani Abhaya* (for 1st time)	
43	*Pulahatta*	
(?)	*Bahiya*	
(?)	*Panayamara*	
(?)	*Pilayamara*	
(?)	*Dathika*	
29	*Vattagamani Abhaya* (for 2nd time)	
17	*Mahaculi Mahatissa*	
3 BC	*Coranaga*, poisoned by his wife Anula	
AD 9	*Tissa*	favourites installed and poisoned by Anula
12	*Siva I*	favourites installed and poisoned by Anula
12	*Vatuka*	favourites installed and poisoned by Anula
12	*Darubhatika Tissa*	favourites installed and poisoned by Anula
12	*Niliya*	favourites installed and poisoned by Anula
12	*Anula*, widow of Coranaga	
16	*Kutakanna* (or *Kalakanni*) *Tissa*	
38	*Bhatika Abhaya* (or *Bhatiya Tissa*)	
67	*Mahadathika Mahanaga*	
79	*Amandagamani Abhaya*	
89	*Kanirajanu Tissa*	
92	*Culabhaya*	
93	*Sivali*, sister	
93 and 96 – 102	*Ilanaga*, cousin	
103	*Candamukha Siva*	
112	*Yasalalaka Tissa*	
120 – 127	*Sabha*	

Lambakanna Dynasty

127	*Vasabha*
171	*Vankanasika Tissa*
174	*Gajabahuka-gamani*
196	*Mahallaka Naga*
203	*Bhatika Tissa*
227	*Kanittha Tissa*

246	*Kujjanaga*
248	*Kuñcanaga*
249	*Sirinaga I*
269	*Voharika Tissa*, killed by successor
291	*Abhayanaga*, brother
299	*Sirinaga II*
301	*Vijaya-kumara*
303	*Samghatissa I*
307	*Sisamghabodhi*
309	*Gothabhaya* (or *Meghavanna Abhaya*), son(?) of Sirinaga II
323	*Jetthatissa I*
334	*Mahasena*
362	*Sirimeghavanna*, son
(?)	*Jetthatissa II*, brother or usurper
(?)	*Buddhadasa*, son
(?)	*Upatissa I*, son
409	*Mahanama*, brother
432	*Chattagahaka Jantu*, son-in-law
432–433	*Mittasena*, usurper

Pandyas

433	*Pandu*
438	*Parinda*
441	*Khudda Parinda*
456	*Tiritara*
456	*Dathiya*
459	*Pithiya*

Moriya Dynasty

459	*Dhatusena*
477	*Kaśyapa I*, son, capital established at Sigiriya (now Sigiri)
495	*Moggallana I*, half-brother
512	*Kumara-Dhatusena*, son
520	*Kittisena*, son
521	*Siva II*, uncle
522	*Upatissa II*, brother-in-law of Moggallana I
524	*Silakala*, *Ambasamanera*, son
537	*Dathapabhuti*, son
537	*Moggallana II*, brother
556	*Kittisirimegha*, son
556	*Mahanaga*, commander of the troops, usurper

559	*Aggabodhi I*, nephew
592	*Aggabodhi II*, nephew
602	*Samghatissa II*, brother(?)
602	*Moggallana III*
608	*Silameghavanna*
617	*Aggabodhi III Sirisanghabodhi*, son (for 1st time)
617	*Jetthatissa III*, son of Samghatissa(?)
618	*Aggabodhi III* (for 2nd time)*
632	*Kaśyapa II*, brother
641	*Dappula I*, brother-in-law
641	*Hatthadatha I*, nephew of Dathopatissa I*
650	*Aggabodhi IV*, *Sirisanghabodhi*, brother
666	*Datta*
668 – 684	*Hatthadatha II*

Second Lambakanna Dynasty

684	*Manavamma*, son of Kaśyapa
703	*Aggabodhi V*, son
709	*Kaśyapa III*, brother
716	*Mahinda I*, brother
719	*Aggabodhi VI*, *Silamegha*
759	*Aggabodhi VII*, brother
765	*Mahinda II*, *Silamegha*, son of Aggabodhi VI
785	*Udaya I*, son†
790	*Mahinda III*, son
794	*Aggabodhi VIII*, brother
805	*Dappula II*, brother†
821	*Aggabodhi IX*, son
824	*Sena I*, brother
844	*Sena II*, nephew
879	*Udaya II*, brother†
890	*Kaśyapa IV*, brother
907	*Kaśyapa V*, son of Sena II
917	*Dappula III*, step-brother(?)†
918	*Dappula IV*, brother(?)†
930	*Udaya III*, nephew of Sena II†
933	*Sena III*, brother(?)
942	*Udaya IV* †
950	*Sena IV*

*618 – 632 *Dathopatissa I*, usurper, in conflict with Aggabodhi III

†Some lists have Dappula II instead of Udaya I, the numeration of succeeding Dappulas and Udayas varying accordingly

953	*Mahinda IV*, brother(?)
969	*Sena V*, son
979 – 1015	*Mahinda V*, brother
1015 – 1027	Interregnum, Chola conquest, capital moved to Polonnaruwa
1027	*Kaśyapa VI*, son
1039	*Mahalana-Kitti*
1042	*Vikrama-Pandu*, capital established at Kalutara
1043	*Jagatipala*
1046	*Parakrama-Pandu I*
1048	*Loka*, Sinhalese chief
1054 – 1055	*Kaśyapa VII*, Sinhalese chief, capital established at Kabaragama

Polonnaruva Dynasty

1055	*Vijayabahu I* (or *Kitti*), descendant of royal family, regained independence and moved capital to Polonnaruwa 1070
1110	*Jayabahu I*, brother
1111	*Vikramabahu I*, son of Vijayabahu I
1132	*Gajabahu*, son
1153 – 1186	*Parakramabahu I*

Kalinga Dynasty

1186	*Vijayabahu II*, nephew
1187	*Niśśamkamalla*
1196	*Virabahu*, son, for one night
1196	*Vikramabahu II*, uncle, for three months
1196	*Chodaganga*, nephew of Niśśamkamalla
1197	*Lilavati*, widow of Niśśamkamalla (for 1st time)
1200	*Sahassamalla*, step-brother of Niśśamkamalla
1202	*Kalyanavati*, widow of Niśśamkamalla
1208	*Dharmaśoka*, aged three months
1209	*Anikanga, Mahadipada*, father, for 17 days
1209	*Lilavati* (for 2nd time)
1210	*Lokeśvara*, from southern India
1211	*Lilavati* (for 3rd time)
1212	*Parakrama Pandu II*, of Pandya, deposed
1215 – 1236	*Magha*, local chiefs ruled independently
1232	*Vijayabahu III*, capital moved to Dambadeniya
1236	*Parakramabahu II*
1270	*Vijayabahu IV*
1272 – 1285	*Bhuvanaikabahu I*, capital established at Kurunegala

1285 – 1302	Interregnum
1302	*Parakramabahu III*
1310	*Bhuvanaikabahu II*
1325	*Parakramabahu IV*
1325	*Bhuvanaikabahu III*
1335	*Vijayabahu V*
1341 – 1351	*Bhuvanaikabahu IV*, capital established at Gampola
1344 – 1359	*Parakramabahu V*, son of Vijayabahu V
1357 – 1374	*Vikramabahu III*
1372	*Bhuvanaikabahu V*
1408	*Virabahu II*, brother-in-law
1412	*Parakramabahu VI*, capital established at Kotte
1467	*Jayabahu II*
1470	*Bhuvanaikabahu VI*
1478	*Parakramabahu VII*
1484 – 1508	*Parakramabahu VIII*
1508	Portuguese colonial rule established
1658	Portuguese displaced by the Dutch
1796	British rule established

Chaghatayids

Territory comprised part of Transoxania, Semirechye and eastern Turkestan (present-day Iran, USSR and China), with the capital initially at Tabriz, later at Maragha and after 1307 at Sultaniyya.

Khans

AD 1226/7 – c. Apr/May 1242	*Chaghatay*, son of Chingiz Khan
1242	*Qara Hülegü*, grandson (for 1st time)
1247/8	*Yesü Möngke*, uncle
1252/3	*Qara Hülegü* (for 2nd time)
1252/3	*Orqına Khatun*, widow
1260/1	*Alughu*, grandson of Chaghatay
Mar/Apr 1266	*Mubarak Shah*, son of Qara Hülegü, converted to Islam
Sep/Oct 1266	*Baraq*, cousin, defeated by the Il-Khan Abaqa 22 Jul 1270

c. 1271/2	*Negübey* (or *Nikpay*), grandson of Chaghatay
1271/2	*Buqa Temür*, descendant of Chaghatay
c. 1291	*Duwa*, son of Baraq
1306/7	*Könchek*, son
1308/9	*Taliqu*, brother of Buqa Temür
1309/10	*Kebek* (or *Köpek*), son of Duwa (for 1st time)
1309/10	*Esen Buqa*, brother
c. 1318/19	*Kebek* (for 2nd time)
1325/6	*Eljigidey*, brother
1325/6	*Duwa Temür*, brother
1325/6	*'Ala' al-Din Tarmashirin*, brother, converted to Islam
1333/4	*Changshi*, nephew
c. 1334/5	*Buzan*, cousin
c. 1338/9	*Yesün Temür*, cousin
c. 1342/3	*Muhammad*, grandson of Könchek
1343/4	*Qazan*, nephew of Esen Buqa
1346/7	*Danishmendji*, of the tribe of Ögedey
1348/9	*Bayan Quli*, cousin of Qazan
1358/9	*Shah Temür (ibn 'Abdallah ibn Qarghan)*
1358/9 – 1369/70	*Tughluq Temür*, cousin of Bayan Quli
1369/70	Timurid conquest

Chalukya Kingdom

Territory comprised part of present-day western India, with the capital established at Vatapi (now Badami).

Kings

c. AD 535	*Pulakeshin I*
566	*Kirttivarman I*
c. 597	*Mangalesha*
609	*Pulakeshin II*, grandson of Pulakeshin I, defeated and probably killed by Narasimhavarman I of the Pallava Kingdom
655	*Vikramaditya I*
680	*Vinayaditya*
696	*Vijayaditya*

733	*Vikramaditya II*
746–753	*Kirttivarman II*
753	Overthrown by the Rashtrakutas

Chalukyas of Kalyana

Territory comprised part of present-day northern India.

Kings

AD 973	*Taila II*, dethroned the last of the Rashtrakutas
997	*Satyashraya*, son
1008	*Vikramaditya V*, nephew
1014	*Ayyana II*, cousin
1015	*Jayasimha II* (or *Jagadekamalla*), cousin
1042	*Someshvare I*, son; defeated the Chola king Rajadhiraja I
1068	*Someshvara II*, son
1076	*Vikramaditya VI*, brother
1127	*Someshvara III*, son
1138	*Jagadekamalla II*, son
1151	*Taila III*, brother
1184–1200	*Someshvara IV*, son
1200	Division into smaller states

Champa, Kingdom of

Territory comprised part of present-day south-eastern Vietnam, with the capital initially at Indrapura and later at Vijaya.

Kings

First Dynasty

AD 192	*Sri Mara* (or *K'iu-lien*)

(?)	Unknown son
(?)	Son and unknown grandson
fl. 270	*Fan Hiong*
c. 284 – 336	*Fan Yi*
Second Dynasty	
336	*Fan Wen*, previously chief minister
349	*Fan Fo*, son
fl. 377	*Bhadravarman I*
(?)	*Gangaraja*
(?)	*Manorathavarman*
(?) – 420(?)	*Wen Ti*
Third Dynasty	
420(?)	Seven rulers with the title Fan
fl. 510	*Devararman*
fl. 526/7 – 529(?)	*Vijayavarman*
Fourth Dynasty	
529(?)	*Rudravarman I*
fl. 605	*Sambuvarman*
629(?)	*Kandharpadharma*
(?)	*Bhasadharma*
645	*Bhadresvaravarman*
(?)	Unknown daughter of Kandharpadharma
653	*(Prakasadharma) Vikrantavarman I*
686(?) – 731(?)	*Vikrantavarman II*
fl. 749 – 758(?)	*Rudravarman II*
Fifth Dynasty	
758(?)	*Prithindravarman*
between 774 and 784	*Satyavarman*
between 787 and 801	*Indravarman I*
between 803(?) and 817(?)	*Harivarman I*
fl. 854 – between 875 and 889	*Vikrantavarman III*
Sixth Dynasty	
between 875 and 889	*Indravarman II*
between 898 and 903	*Jaya Sinhavarman I*
(?)	*Jaya Saktivarman*
fl. 910	*Bhadravarman II*

c. 918 – 959	*Indravarman III*
between 960 and 965	*Jaya Indravarman I*
(?)	*Paramesvaravarman I*, killed during invasion of Champa by Annam
982	*Indravarman IV*
986(?) – 989	*Lieou Ki-Tsong*, an Annamite
Seventh Dynasty	
991(?)	*Harivarman II*
between 999 and 1007	*Yan Pu Ku Vijaya*
fl. 1010	*Harivarman III*
fl. 1018	*Paramesvaravarman II*
(?) – 1030	*Vikrantavarman IV*
1044	*Jaya Sinhavarman II*, killed during Annamese conquest of Champa
Eighth Dynasty	
1044	*Jaya Paramesvaravarman I*
fl. 1061	*Bhadravarman III*
1061 – 1074(?)	*Rudravarman III*, captured during Annamese invasion 1069 and later released after ceding the northern provinces of Champa to Annam
Ninth Dynasty	
1074(?)	*Harivarman IV*
1080	*Jaya Indravarman II* (for 1st time)
1081	*Paramabhodisatva*
1086	*Jaya Indravarman II* (for 2nd time)
between 1114 and 1129 – 1139(?)	*Harivarman V*
Tenth Dynasty	
1139(?) – c. 1145	*Jaya Indravarman III*, conquest of Champa by the Khmers
Eleventh Dynasty	
fl. 1145(?)	*Rudravarman IV*
1147	*Jaya Harivarman I*, regained independence from the Khmers
(?)	*Jaya Harivarman II*, son, deposed
1167(?)	*Jaya Indravarman IV*, usurper, conquered by the Khmers and captured, killed while attempting to regain his throne 1192

1190 – 1192	Division into two kingdoms*
1192 – 1203	*Suryavarman*, of Panrang*
1203	Kingdom became a Khmer province
1220	Khmer army evacuated Champa for unknown reasons
1220	*Jaya Paramesvaravarman II*, Annamese invasion of Champa
fl. 1254	*Jaya Indravarman VI*, brother
1265(?)	*Indravarman V*
(?)	*Jaya Sinhavarman III*
1307	*Jaya Sinhavarman IV*, deposed by Annam
1312 – 1318	*Che Nang*, brother, placed on throne by Annam, defeated in rebellion against the Annamese, fled to Java
Twelfth Dynasty	
1318	*Che Anan*, viceroy
1342	*Tra Hoa*
(?) – 1390	*Che Bong Nga*
Thirteenth Dynasty	
1390	*Ko Cheng*
1400	*Jaya Sinhavarman V*
1441	*Maha Vijaya*
1446	*Moho Kouei-lai*
1449 – 1458	*Moho Kouei-yeou*
Fourteenth Dynasty	
1458	*Moho P'an-lo-yue*
1460 – 1471	*P'an-lo T'ou-ts'iuan*
1471	Final conquest of Champa by Annam; a small Cham state continued in the south until 1720

*Kingdom of Vijaya:

1190	*Suryajayavarman*
1191	*Jaya Indravarman V*
Kingdom of Panrang:	
1190	*Suryavarman*

Champagne

Counts

House of Vermandois	
AD 923	*Herbert I*, son-in-law of Robert of France
943	*Robert*, son
968 – 29 Jan 993	*Herbert II*, brother
993	*Étienne I*, son
House of Blois	
1019 – 15 Nov 1037	*Eudes I*, Count (Eudes II) of Blois, cousin (b. c. 990)
1037	*Étienne II*, son (b. c. 1015)
1047/8	*Eudes II*, son (d. after 1096) Count of Aumale c. 1070; deposed
1063	*Thibaut I*, Count (Thibaut III) of Blois, uncle (b. c. 1010)
1089	*Eudes III*, son
c. 1093	*Hugues*, brother (d. Jun 1126) abdicated
1125 – 8/10 Jan 1152	*Thibaut II*, the Great, Count (Thibaut IV) of Blois, nephew (d. Lagny-sur-Marne)
1152 – 16 Mar 1181	*Henri I*, the Liberal, son (b. c. 1126)
1181 – 10 Sep 1197	*Henri II*, the Young, son (b. 29 Jul 1166) King (Henri) of Jerusalem 5 May 1192
1197 – 24 May 1201	*Thibaut III*, brother (b. 1176)
1201 – 8 Jul 1253	*Thibaut IV*, le Chansonnier, son (b. Troyes, 30 May 1201; d. Pamplona) King (Thibaut I) of Navarre 1234 Regent: 1201 – May 1222: *Blanche de Navarre*, mother (d. 1229) under the tutelage of King *Philippe II Auguste* of France
1253 – 4 Dec 1270	*Thibaut V*, son (b. 1237; d. Trapani, Sicily) King (Thibaut II) of Navarre
1270 – 22 Jul 1274	*Henri III*, the Fat, brother; King (Henri I) of Navarre
1274 – 6 Oct 1285	*Jeanne*, daughter (b. 1271; d. 2 Apr 1304) Queen of Navarre; married Philippe, later King Philippe IV the Fair of France, and was crowned Queen of France, 6 Oct 1285

County united with the crown of France. At the death of Jeanne the county passed nominally to her son Louis. At his accession to the French throne as Louis X in 1314, Champagne was permanently united with the crown.

Characene (Mesene)

Territory comprised part of present-day southern Iraq, with the capital at Spasinu Charax.

Kings

c. 125/4 BC	*Hyspaosines*, Iranian governor in Mesene for the Seleucid king Antiochus VII Euergetes
c. 110/9	*Apodakos*
c. 90/89	*Tiraios I Euergetes*
c. 61/60	*Tiraios II Soter Euergetes*
c. 44/43	*Attambelos I Soter Euergetes*
c. 40	*Theonesios I*
c. 30/29	*Attambelos II Soter Euergetes*
c. AD 12/13	*Abinerglos Soter*
c. 21	*Adinnerglos Soter*
c. 51/52	*Theonesios II Soter*
c. 53/4	*Attambelos III Soter Euergetes*
(?)	*Artabazos*
c. 100/101	*Attambelos IV Soter Euergetes*
c. 109/10	*Theonesios III Soter Euergetes*
c. 116	*Attambelos V*, submitted to the Roman emperor Trajan
(?)	Unknown number of kings
c. 228	Fall of kingdom, superseded by the Sasanids

China

Emperors

2674 – 2183 BC*	Era of the Five Emperors

Hsia: First Official Dynasty

Last capital thought to have been Yang-hsia (now T'ai-k'ang hsien).

2183 – 1802*	Legendary dynasty founded by *Ta Yü* (i.e. Yü the Great)

Shang: Second Official Dynasty (latter half also called Yin Dynasty)

1751 – 1111*	Founded by *T'ang*, the Victorious

Chou: Third Official Dynasty

Capitals established at Hao (near present-day Sian), Wang-chêng and Chêng-chou.

1111*	*Wu wang* (or *Fa*), son of Wen wang
1104	*Ch'ěng wang*, son, under regency of his uncle *Chou Kung*
1067	*K'ang wang*, son
1041	*Chao wang*
1023	*Mu wang*, son
982	*Kung wang*, son
966	*I wang*, son
954	*Hsiao wang*, uncle
924	*I wang*, son (not the same character as above)
878	*Li wang*, son (d. 828) exiled to Chin
841	*Kung-ho*, regent†
827	*Hsüan wang*, son of Li wang
781	*Yu wang*, son
770	*P'ing wang*, son
719	*Huan wang*, grandson
696	*Chuang wang*, son

*The dates given are those traditionally accepted. An alternative chronology, based on the Bamboo Books, is preferred by a number of scholars, according to which the Hsia Dynasty runs from 1989 to 1558, the Shang from 1558 to 1051, and the Chou from 1051 to 249.

† It is uncertain whether Kung-ho is the name of the period or the title of the regent (Prince of Kung)

681	*Hsi wang*, son
676	*Hui wang*, son
651	*Hsiang wang*, son
618	*Ch'ing wang*, son
612	*K'uang wang*, son
606	*Ting wang*, brother
585	*Chien wang*, son
571	*Ling wang*, son
544	*Ching wang*, son
519	*Ching wang*, brother-in-law (not the same character as above)
475	*Yüan wang*, son
468	*Chëng-ting wang*, son
440	*K'ao wang*, son
425	*Wei-lieh wang*, son
401	*An wang*, son
375	*Lieh wang*, son
368	*Hsien wang*, brother
320	*Shên-ching wang*, son
314 – 255	*Nan wang*, son

Ch'in (*Ts'in*): *Fourth Official Dynasty*
Capital at Hsien-yang (now Sienyang)

255	*Chao-hsiang wang*, Duke of Ch'in
250	*Hsiao-wên wang*, grandson
249	*Chuang-hsiang wang*, son
246	*Shih-huang Ti* (or *Cheng*), son, proclaimed himself Emperor of all China 221
209 – 207	*Erh-shih*, son
207 – 206	Civil war

Former or Western Han: *Fifth Official Dynasty*
Capital at Ch'ang-an (now Sian).

206	*Kao Tsu*, proclaimed emperor 202
195	*Hui Ti*, son
188	*Kao Hou*, mother and *Lü Shih*
180	*Wên Ti*, son of Kao Tsu
157	*Ching Ti*, son
141	*Wu Ti*, Annam and Tongking incorporated 111
87	*Chao Ti*
74	*Hsüan Ti*
49	*Yüan Ti*, son
33	*Chêng Ti*, son

7	*Ai Ti*, nephew
1 BC – AD 5	*P'ing Ti* (b. 9 BC)
6 – 8	*Ju-tzŭ Ying* (b. AD 5) deposed

Hsin

9	*Wang Mang* (or *Hsin Huang-ti*), usurper, regent from 1 BC
23 – 25	*Huai-yang wang* and *Ti Hsüan*

Later or Eastern Han: continuation of the Fifth Official Dynasty
Capital at Lo-yang (now Honan).

25	*Kuang-wu Ti*
57	*Ming Ti*
75	*Chang Ti*
88	*Ho Ti* (b. 78?)
105	*Shang Ti*, son (b. 105)
106	*An Ti* (b. 92?)
125	*Shao Ti*, nephew
125	*Shun Ti*, cousin (b. 123?)
145	*Ch'ung Ti*, son (b. 143?)
145	*Chih Ti*, son (b. 137?) murdered
146	*Huan Ti* (b. 131?)
168	*Ling Ti*, fifth-generation descendant of Chang Ti (b. 156?)
189	*Shao Ti*, son (b. 172?)
189 – 220	*Hsien Ti* (or *Min Ti*), brother

Shu-Han: Sixth Official Dynasty
Capital at I-chou (now Chengtu).

221	*Chao Lieh Ti*
223 – 263	*Hou Ti* (or *Hou Chu*), son
263	Wei conquest

San Kuo: The Three Kingdoms
Shu-Han (see above) is, by tradition, considered to be the legitimate successor of the Later Han. Its rivals during the period of the Three Kingdoms were Wei and Wu.

Wei

Capital at Lo-yang (now Honan).

220	*Wên Ti*, son of a Han general
226	*Ming Ti*
239	*Fei Ti*, son
254	*Shao Ti*, grandson of Wên Ti

260–265	*Yüan Ti Huan*, grandson of Ming Ti
265	Chin conquest

Wu

Capital at Chien-yeh (now Nanking).

222	*Ta Ti*, a general of the Later Han
252	*Fei Ti*, son
258	*Ching Ti*, brother
264–280	*Mo Ti*, nephew
280	Chin conquest

Chin: *Seventh Official Dynasty*

Capital at Lo-yang (now Honan) until 311, at Ch'ang-an (now Sian) from 311 to 316, and at Chien-yeh (now Nanking) from 317 to 420.

Western Chin

265	*Wu Ti* (or *Ssŭ-ma Yen*)
290	*Hui Ti*, son
306	*Huai Ti*, brother
313–316	*Min Ti*, grandson of Wu Ti

Eastern Chin

317	*Yüan Ti*
322	*Ming Ti*, son
325	*Ch'êng Ti*, son
342	*K'ang Ti*, brother
344	*Mu Ti*, son
361	*Ai Ti*, son of Chêng Ti
365	*Hai Hsi Kung*, brother
371	*Chien Wên Ti*, son of Yüan Ti
372	*Hsiao Wu Ti*, son
396	*An Ti*, son
418–420	*Kung Ti*, brother
420	Overthrown by Sung dynasty

Southern Sung: *Eighth Official Dynasty*

Capital at Chien-k'ang (now Nanking).

420	*Wu Ti*
422	*Shao Ti*, son
424	*Wên Ti*, brother
453	*Hsiao Wu Ti*
464	*(Ch'ien) Fei Ti*, son
465	*Ming Ti*, brother

472	*Fei Ti*, son
477 – 479	*Shun Ti*, brother, abdicated

Shis-liu Kuo: *The Sixteen Kingdoms*

Rival dynasties of the Chin and the Southern Sung (see above).

302 – 347	Chêng or Shu
304 – 329	Former Chao or Northern Han
313 – 376	Former Liang
319 – 352	Later Chao
349 – 370	Former Yen
351 – 394	Former Ch'in
384 – 396	Western Yen, formed one kingdom with Later Yen (see below)
384 – 408	Later Yen, formed one kingdom with Western Yen (see above)
384 – 417	Later Ch'in
385 – 431	Western Ch'in
386 – 403	Later Liang
397 – 414	Southern Liang
397 – 439	Northern Liang
398 – 410	Southern Yen
401 – 421	Western Liang
407 – 431	Hsia
409 – 436	Northern Yen

Southern Ch'i: *Ninth Official Dynasty*

Capital at Chien-k'ang (now Nanking).

479	*Kao Ti*
482	*Wu Ti*, son
493	*Yü-lin wang*, grandson
494	*Hai-ling wang*, brother
494	*Ming Ti*, nephew of Kao Ti
498	*Tung-hun hou*, son
501 – 502	*Hê Ti*

Southern Liang: *Tenth Official Dynasty*

Capital at Chien-k'ang (now Nanking).

502	*Wu Ti*
549	*Chien Wên Ti*
551	*Yü-chang (wang)*
552	*Yüan Ti*
555	*Chên-yang hou*
555 – 557	*Ching Ti*

Southern Chên: *Eleventh Official Dynasty*
Capital at Chien-k'ang (now Nanking).

557	*Wu Ti* (or *Ch'en Pa-hsien*)
559	*Wên Ti*, nephew
566	*Fei Ti*, son
568	*Hsüan Ti*, uncle
582 – 589	*Hou Chu*, son

Sui: *Twelfth Official Dynasty*
Capital at Ch'ang-an (now Sian).

581 (590)	*Wên Ti* (or *Kao Tsu*), reunification of China 589
604	*Yang Ti*, son
617 – 618	*Kung Ti*, grandson

Wei and Succession States
Ruled in northern China from the Chin to the Sui official dynasties (see above).

Wei or Yüan Wei (*House of Toba*)*
Capital at P'ing-chêng from 386 to 494 and at Lo-yang (now Honan) from 495 to 534.

386	*Tao Wu Ti* (or *T'ai-tsu*)
409	*Ming Yüan Ti* (*T'ai-tsung*)
423	*T'ai Wu Ti* (*Shih-tsu*)
452	*Nan-an wang*
452	*Wên ch'êng Ti* (*Kao-tsung*), grandson of Tao Wu Ti
465	*Hsien Wên Ti* (*Hsien-tsu*), son
471	*Hsiao Wên Ti* (*Kao-tsu*), son
499	*Hsüan Wu Ti*
515	*Hsiao Ming Ti* (*Su-tsung*)
528	*Hsiao Chuang Ti* (*Ching-tsung*)
530	*Tung-hai wang* (*Ching-ti*)
531	*Chieh Min Ti*
531	*An-ting wang* (*Ch'u-ti*)
532 – 534	*Hsiao Wu Ti*

Eastern Wei
Capital at Wei-yin.

534 – 550	*Hsiao Ching Ti*

Western Wei
Capital at Ch'ang-an (now Sian).

535	*Wên Ti*
551	*Fei Ti*
554 – 556	*Kung Ti*, son of An-ting wang of the Yüan Wei

*Posthumous names are given in parentheses

Other Rival Kingdoms

550–577	Northern Ch'i
556–581	Northern Chou
555–587	Later Liang

T'ang: Thirteenth Official Dynasty

618	*Kao Tsu* (personal name *Li Yüan*), Duke of T'ang, abdicated
626	*T'ai Tsung* (personal name *Li Shih-min*), son
649	*Kao Tsung*, son
683	*Chung Tsung*, son by Wu Tsê-t'ien (for 1st time)
684	*Jui Tsung*, brother (b. 662) (for 1st time)
690	*Wu Hou* (or *Wu Tsê-t'ien*), concubine of T'ai Tsung and Kao Tsung, usurper
705	*Chung Tsung* (for 2nd time)
710	*Jui Tsung* (for 2nd time)
712	*Hsüan Tsung*
756	*Su Tsung*, son
762	*Tai Tsung*, son
779	*Tê Tsung*, son
805	*Shun Tsung*, son
805	*Hsien Tsung*, son
820	*Mu Tsung*, son
824	*Ching Tsung*, son
826	*Wên Tsung*
840	*Wu Tsung*, brother
846	*Hsüan Tsung*, uncle
859	*I Tsung*, son
873	*Hsi Tsung*, son
888	*Chao Tsung*
904–907	*Chao Hsüan Ti* (or *Ai Ti*), brother

Later Liang: Fourteenth Official Dynasty

Capital at Pien (now Kaifeng).

907	*T'ai Tsu*
912	*Ying wang*, son, usurper
913–923	*Mo Ti*, brother

Later T'ang: Fifteenth Official Dynasty

Capital at Lo-yang (now Honan).

923	*Chuang Tsung*
926	*Ming Tsung*, adopted son
933	*Min Ti*, son

934–936	*Mo Ti* (or *Fei Ti*), brother

Later Chin: *Sixteenth Official Dynasty*
Capital at Lo-yang (now Honan) in 936 and at Pien (now Kaifeng) from 937.

936	*Kao Tsu* (personal name *Shih Ching-t'ang*), son-in-law of Ming Tsung of the Later T'ang
942–946	*Ch'u Ti*

Later Han: *Seventeenth Official Dynasty*
Capital at Pien (now Kaifeng).

947	*Kao Tsu*
948–950	*Yin Ti*, son

Later Chou: *Eighteenth Official Dynasty*
Capital at Pien (now Kaifeng).

951	*T'ai Tsu* (personal name *Kuo Wei*)
954	*Shih Tsung*, son
959–960	*Kung Ti*, son

Sung: *Nineteenth Official Dynasty*

Northern Sung

Capital at Pien-liang (now Kaifeng).

960	*T'ai Tsu* (personal name *Chao K'uang-yin*), began reunification of China
976	*T'ai Tsung*, brother, completed reunification of China
997	*Chên Tsung*, son
1022	*Jên Tsung*, son
1063	*Yin Tsung*, adopted son
1067	*Shên Tsung*, son
1085	*Chê Tsung*, son
1100	*Hui Tsung*
1125–1127	*Ch'in Tsung*

Southern Sung

Capital at Lin-an (now Hangchow).

1127	*Kao Tsung*, son of Hui Tsung of the Northern Sung
1162	*Hsiao Tsung*, adopted son
1189	*Kuang Tsung*, son
1194	*Ning Tsung*, son
1224	*Li Tsung*, adopted son
1264	*Tu Tsung*, adopted son
1274	*Kung Tsung*, son

1276	*Tuan Tsung*, brother
1278 – 1279	*Ti Ping*, brother
1279	Overthrown by Mongol Great Khans (see below)

Ten Minor Kingdoms

In existence from the time of the decline of the T'ang to the period of the Sung.

901 – 925	Former Shu
902 – 937	Wu or Huai-nan
908 – 978	Wu-Yüeh
909 – 944	Min
917 – 971	Southern Han
925 – 963	Nan-p'ing or Ching-nan
927 – 952	Ch'u
934 – 965	Later Shu
937 – 975	Southern T'ang
951 – 979	Eastern or Northern Han

Ch'i-tan Liao

Mongol dynasty which ruled in northern China from the time of the decline of the T'ang to the period of the Sung.

Ch'i-tan Liao

Principal capital at Lin-huang.

907	*T'ai Tsu*
926	*T'ai Tsung*, son
947	*Shih Tsung*, nephew
951	*Mu Tsung*, son
969	*Ching Tsung*, son
982	*Shêng Tsung*, son
1031	*Hsing Tsung*, son
1055	*Tao Tsung*, son
1101 – 1125	*T'ien Tso Ti*, grandson

Western Liao or Kara-khitai

Capital at Balasagun.

1124	*Tê Tsung*
1136	*Kan-t'ien hou*, wife
1142	*Jên Tsung*, son of Tê Tsung
1154	*Ch'êng-t'ien hou*, sister
1168 – 1199	*Mo Chu*, son

Hsia or Western Hsia

Ruled in northern China during the period of Sung, with their capital at Hsing-ch'ing (now Yin-ch'uan).

1032	*Ching Tsung*
1048	*I Tsung*

1069	*Hui Tsung*, son
1086	*Ch'ung Tsung*
1139	*Jên Tsung*, son
1194	*Huan Tsung*
1206	*Hsiang Tsung*
1211	*Shên Tsung*
1223	*Hsien Tsung*, son
1226 – 1227	*Li Hsien*, brother, executed by the Mongols
1227	Mongol conquest

Chin

Ruled in northern China during the period of the Sung, with their capital initially at Hui-ning (now K'ai-yüan) and after 1152 at Ta-hsing (now Peking).

1115	*T'ai Tsu*
1123	*T'ai Tsung*, brother
1135	*Hsi Tsung*, grandson of T'ai Tsu
1149	*Hai-ling wang*
1161	*Shih Tsung*, grandson of T'ai Tsu
1189	*Chang Tsung*, grandson
1208	*Wei-shao wang*, son of Shih Tsung
1213	*Hsüan Tsung*, grandson of Shih Tsung
1223 – 1234	*Ai Tsung*, son
1234	Mongol conquest

Yüan (*Mongol Great Khans*): *Twentieth Official Dynasty**

Capital initially at Karakorum and later at Khanbalik (now Peking).

1206	*T'ai Tsu* (*Chingiz*) (b. 1154/6)
1227	*Tolui*, son, regent
1229	*T'ai Tsung* (*Ögedey*), brother
1241	*Töregene Khatun*, widow, regent
1246 – 22 Jul 1249	*Ting Tsung* (*Güyük*), son
1249	*Oghul Ghaimash*, widow, regent
1251	*Hsien Tsung* (*Möngke*), grandson of Chingiz, moved capital to Khanbalik
1260	*Shih Tsung* (*Qubilai*), brother, Sung dynasty of southern China overthrown 1279
1294	*Ch'êng Tsung* (*Temür Öljeitü*), grandson
1307	*Wu Tsung* (*Qaishan Guluk*), nephew
1311	*Jên Tsung* (*Ayurparibhadra Buyantu*), brother
1320	*Yin Tsung* (*Suddhipala Gege'en*), son
1323	*T'ai Ting Ti* (*Yesün Temür*), nephew of Ch'êng Tsung
1328	*Wên Tsung* (*Arigaba*) (for 1st time)
1329	*Ming Tsung* (*Toq-Temür*), son of Wu Tsung

*Mongol names given in parentheses; see also page 378

1329	*Wên Tsung* (for 2nd time)
1332	*Ning Tsung* (*Rinchendpal*), son
1333 – 1368	*Shun Ti* or *Hui Tsung* (*Toghan Temür*), brother

*Ming: Twenty-first Official Dynasty**

Capital at Chiang-ning (now Nanking) until 1409 and thereafter at Peking.

1368	*T'ai Tsu* (*Hung Wu*)
1398	*Hui Ti* (*Chien Wên*), grandson
1402	*Ch'êng Tsu* (*Yung lo*), uncle
1424	*Jên Tsung* (*Hung Hsi*), son
1425	*Hsüan Tsung* (*Hsüan Tê*), son
1435	*Ying Tsung* (*Chêng T'ung*) (for 1st time)
1449	*Tai Tsung* (or *Ching Ti*) (*Ching T'ai*), brother
1457	*Ying Tsung* (*T'ien Shun*) (for 2nd time)
1464	*Hsien Tsung* (*Ch'êng Hua*), son
1487 – 1505	*Hsiao Tsung* (*Hung Chih*), son

Chola Kingdom

Territory comprised part of present-day south-eastern India.

Kings

c. AD 846	*Vijayalaya*
c. 871	*Aditya I*
907	*Parantaka I*, son
947	*Rajaditya I*
949	*Gandaraditya*
956	*Arinjaya*
956	*Parantaka II* (or *Sundara Chola*)
956	*Aditya II*
969	*Madhurantaka Uttama*
985	*Rajaraja-deva*, the Great
1012	*Rajendra Choladeva I*, son, conquest of Ceylon 1015 – 1027
1044	*Rajadhiraja I*, son, killed in battle against the Chalukyas

*Era names (reign titles) are given in parentheses

1052	*Rajendra Deva II*
1060	*Rajamahendra*
1063	*Virarajendra*
1067	*Adhirajendra*, assassinated
1070	*Rajendra III*
1118	*Vikrama-Chola*
1133	*Kulottunga Chola II*
1146	*Rajaraja II*
1163	*Rajadhiraja II*
1178	*Kulottunga III*
1216	*Rajaraja III*
1246 – 1279	*Rajendra IV*
1279	Defeated during the Muslim invasions and the rise of Vijayanagar

Cologne

Archbishops (and from 13th century Electors)*

AD (?)	*Hildegar*, killed 753
fl. 13 Aug 762	*Berethelm*
fl. c. 780	*Riculf*
(?) – 3 Sep 819	*Hildebold*
819 – 841	*Hadebald* (or *Hadubald*)
842 – c. 845	*Hilduin*
22 Apr 850 – Oct 863	*Günther*, deposed
864 – 866	*Hugo von Welf* (d. 12 May 886)
17 Jan 870 – 11 Sep 889	*Willibert*
890 – 11 Apr 923	*Hermann I*
923 or 924 – 9 Jul 953	*Wicfrid*
Jul/25 Sep 953 – 11 Oct 965	*Brun I*, Duke of Lorraine, brother of King Otto I of Germany (b. c. 925; d. Reims)

*When two dates separated by an oblique stroke are given for the beginning of an episcopate, the first refers to election or nomination and the second to consecration, ordination or investiture

Christmas(?) 965 – 18 Jul 967	*Folcmar* (or *Poppo*)
Easter 969 – 29 Jun 975	*Gero*
975 – 21 Sep 985	*Warin*
985 – 11 Jun 999	*Everger*
Christmas 999 – 16 Mar 1021	*Heribert*
29 Jun 1021 – 24 or 25 Aug 1036	*Piligrim*
1036 – 11 Feb 1056	*Hermann II*
3 Mar 1056 – 4 Dec 1075	*Anno II*
6/13 or 20 Mar 1076 – 21 Jul 1078	*Hildof*
after Christmas 1078 – 31 May 1089	*Sigewin*
25 Jul 1089 – 21 or 22 Nov 1099	*Hermann III*
6 Jan/11 Nov 1100 – 25 Oct 1131	*Friedrich I*
Christmas 1131/before 18 Mar 1132 – 29 May 1137	*Brun II von Berg* (d. Trani, Apulia)
6 Jun – 1 Jul 1137	*Hugo von Sponheim*
4/14 Feb/3(?) Apr 1138 – 3 Apr 1151	*Arnold I*, suspended Mar 1148
7/13 Apr 1151/Jan 1152 – 14 May 1156	*Arnold II von Wied*
before Jul/17 or 18 Sep 1156 – 15 Dec 1158	*Friedrich II von Berg*
May/early Jun 1159 – 14 Aug 1164	*Rainald von Dasseld*
autumn 1167 – 13 Aug 1191	*Philipp von Heinsberg*
1191 – after 28 Jun 1193	*Brun III von Berg* (d. 23 Apr 1196) resigned
before 2 Nov 1193/27 Mar 1194 – 19 Jun 1205	*Adolf I von Berg* (d. 15 Apr 1220) deposed
1205 – 2 Nov 1208	*Brun IV von Sayn*
22 Dec 1208 – 1215	*Dietrich I von Hengebach* (d. 9 May 1224) excom-

	municated 1212, deposed
29 Feb 1216 – 7 Nov 1225	*Engelbert I von Berg*, son of Duke Engelbert I of Berg (b. c. 1185) Count of Berg 1218; murdered
25 Nov 1225 – 26 Mar 1237	*Heinrich I von Mulnarken*
before 30 Apr 1238 – 28 Sep 1261	*Konrad von Hochstaden*
2 Oct 1261/31 Dec 1263 – 20 Oct 1274	*Engelbert II von Falkenburg* (b. c. 1220; d. Bonn)
15 Nov 1274/26 Mar 1275 – 7 Apr 1297	*Sifrid II von Westerburg* (d. Bonn) in disputed election against *Konrad von Berg*
3 May/22 Aug 1297 – 28 Mar 1304	*Wikbold I von Holte*
Apr/May 1304/18 Dec 1305 – 6 Jan 1332	*Heinrich II von Virneburg*
27 Jan 1332 – 14 Aug 1349	*Walram von Jülich*
18 Dec 1349 – 14 Sep 1362	*Wilhelm von Gennep*
21 Jun 1363	*Adolf II von der Mark* (d. 7 Sep 1394) previously Bishop of Münster, in disputed election against *Johann von Virneburg* and *Engelbert von der Mark*, Bishop of Liège (see below), resigned; Count of Cleves 1368, Count of the Mark 1380
15 Apr 1364 – 26 Aug 1369	*Engelbert III von der Mark*, Bishop of Liège 23 Feb 1345 – 15 Apr 1364 Coadjutor: 23 Dec 1366 – 26 Aug 1369: *Kuno von Falkenstein* (see below)
27 Mar 1370 – 2 Jul 1371	*Kuno von Falkenstein*, Administrator (d. Wellmich castle 21 May 1388) Archbishop of Trier 27 May 1362 – 6 Jan 1388
13 Nov 1370/21 Jun 1372 – 9 Apr 1414	*Friedrich III*, Count of Saarwerden, nephew (d. Poppelsdorf)
24 Apr /30 Aug 1414 – 14 Feb 1463	*Dietrich II von Mörs*, in disputed election against *Wilhelm von Jülich-Berg**

*Wilhelm was nominated by a section of the Cologne chapter on 18 Apr 1414 and consecrated by Pope Gregory XII before 12 Jul 1415, but relinquished his claim and left Cologne on 3 Dec 1415

30 Mar/16 Jun 1463 – 16 Jul 1480	*Ruprecht*, son of the Elector Palatine, Ludwig II (b. 27 Feb 1427)
15 Nov 1480 – 27 Sep 1508	*Hermann IV*, son of Ludwig I, the Landgrave of Hesse (b. 1449/50)

Commagene

Territory comprised part of present-day central Turkey, with the capital at Samosata (present-day Samsat).

Kings

c. 163/2 BC	*Ptolemaeus*, ruled initially as dependent epistates (governor) for the Seleucids, independence established c. 163/2
c. 130	*Samus II Theosebes Dikaios*
c. 100	*Mithridates I Callinicus*, son
c. 92	*Mithridates II Philhellen Philoromaios*, son
c. 70 – c. 35	*Antiochus I Theos Dikaios Epiphanes Philoromaios Philhellen*, brother, confirmed by the Roman triumvir Pompey
(?)	Four or five unknown kings, including one *Mithridates*, placed on the throne by the Roman emperor Augustus
(?) – AD 17	*Antiochus III*, son or brother of Mithridates (for 1st time)
17	Annexed by Rome
38	*Antiochus III* (for 2nd time) restored by the Roman emperor Caligula
38 – 72	*Antiochus IV Epiphanes*, son of Antiochus III, deposed for an alleged alliance with the Parthians
72	Reincorporated into the Roman province of Syria

Croatia

Princes

c. AD 810	*Borna*, 'Duke of Dalmatia and Liburnia'
821	*Vladislav*, nephew
c. 835	*Mislav*
c. 845	*Trpimir I*
864	*Domagoj*
876	*Iljko*, son(?), driven out
878	*Zdeslav*, son of Trpimir I, installed with Byzantine help, killed
879	*Branimir*, usurper
892	*Mutimir*, brother of Zdeslav
early 910 – 925	*Tomislav*, son, crowned king (see below)

Kings

925	*Tomislav*, previously prince (see above), extended kingdom to include Pannonian Croats
c. 928	*Trpimir II*, brother
c. 935	*Kresimir I*, son
c. 945	*Miroslav*, son, with his brother, *Mihajlo Kresimir II*
c. 949	*Mihajlo Kresimir II*, sole ruler
c. 969	*Stjepan Držislav*, son
997 – 1000	Civil war between *Svetoslav Suronja* and *Kresimir III*, sons
1000	*Kresimir III Suronja*; with his brother, *Gojslav*, co-ruler 1000 – 1020
after 1030	*Stjepan I*, son of Kresimir III
1058*	*Petar Kresimir IV*, son
1075	*Zvonomir* (or *Demetrius*), descendant of Svetoslav Suronja, killed in uprising
1089† – late 1090	*Stjepan II*, nephew of Petar Kresimir IV
1091 – 1095	*Almos*, nephew of King László I of Hungary (b. c. 1075; d. 1129) appointed by László

*Slavać, formerly dated 1074 – 1075, is now supposed to have been a later local ruler

†Rival factions supported Stjepan II (crowned 1089) and Jelena Lipeja, widow of Zvonomir and sister of King László I of Hungary, who claimed the throne on the ground that no member of the immediate royal family survived. Stjepan II had been a monk for 14 years

1093(?) – Apr/May 1097	*Petar of Knin*, rival supported by Dalmatian nobles, died in battle against the Hungarians
1102 – 1116	*Kálmán*, King of Hungary (b. c. 1074), crowned King of Croatia
1116	Croatia united to the Hungarian crown

Cyprus

Kings and Queens

House of Lusignan

May AD 1192 – May 1194	*Gui de Lusignan*, son of Hugues VIII de Lusignan (b. Lusignan c. 1129; d. Nicosia) King of Jerusalem 1186 – Apr 1192, bought right to rule Cyprus from King Richard I of England
May 1194/Sep 1197 – 1 Apr 1205	*Amaury de Lusignan*, brother (b. c. 1144; d. Acre) not crowned until Sep 1197, King (Amaury II) of Jerusalem Jan 1198, vassal of the Holy Roman Emperor Heinrich VI from Oct 1195
Apr 1205 – 10 Jan 1218	*Hugues I*, son (b. c. 1195; d. Tripoli) vassal of the Holy Roman Emperor Regent: Apr 1205 – 1210: *Gautier de Montbéliard*, brother-in-law
Jan 1218 – 18 Jan 1253	*Henri I*, son of Hugues I (b. Nicosia 3 May 1217; d. Nicosia) renounced allegiance to Holy Roman Emperor Friedrich II Apr 1233, regent of Jerusalem 1246 Regent: Jan 1218 – 1232: *Alix de Champagne*, mother (d. 1246)*

*Alix was prevented from exercising power by the following bailiffs who governed the kingdom:

Jan 1218 – 1227	*Philippe d'Ibelin*, uncle of Alix (d. 1227)
1227 – Aug 1228	*Jean d'Ibelin*, Seigneur of Beirut, brother (d. 1236) Regent of Jerusalem 1205 – 1208

Holy Roman Emperor Friedrich II asserted his right, by marriage, to the throne of

Jan 1253 – Dec 1267	*Hugues II*, son of Henri I (b. Nicosia 1252; d. Nicosia) Regents: Jan 1253 – Sep 1261: *Plaisance*, mother (d. Sep 1261) regent of Jerusalem 18 Jan 1253 Sep 1261 – Dec 1267: *Hugues d'Antioche-Lusignan*, later King Hugues III (see below)

House of Antioche-Lusignan

25 Dec 1267 – 4 Mar 1284	*Hugues III*, cousin of Hugues II (d. Tyre) regent of Jerusalem 1264 – 29 Oct 1268, King of Jerusalem 24 Sep 1269
11 May 1284 – 20 May 1285	*Jean I*, son (b. c. 1267; d. Cyprus) King of Jerusalem May 1284
24 Jun 1285	*Henri II*, brother (for 1st time) (b. 1271; d. Strovilo 30/31 Mar 1324) King of Jerusalem 15 Aug 1286 – 18 May 1292,* deposed by Amaury, exiled to Lambron Feb 1310
26 Apr 1306 – 5 Jun 1310	*Amaury*, brother, usurper, appointed himself Governor, murdered
Jul 1310 – 30/31 Mar 1324	*Henri II* (for 2nd time) restored
15 Apr 1324 – 10 Oct 1359	*Hugues IV*, nephew (b. 1299) crowned his son, Pierre, 24 Nov 1358
24 Nov 1358	*Pierre I*, son (b. Nicosia 9 Oct 1329; d. (murdered) Nicosia) Prince of Little Armenia 1368
17 Jan 1369	*Pierre II*, the Fat, son (b. Nicosia 1354; d. Nicosia) lost Famagusta to Genoa 1372 Regent: 17 Jan 1369 – 6 Jan 1372: *Jean*, uncle

Jerusalem and forced the Cypriots to recognize him as overlord in Aug 1228. To rule in Cyprus he appointed as his bailiffs, *Amaury Barlais*, *Gavin de Chenichy* (d. Kantara summer 1230), *Amaury de Beisan*, *Hugues Embriaco de Jebail* and *Guillaume de Rivet* (d. Cilicia 1230). As soon as Friedrich left the Holy Lands in Jun 1229 civil war began in Cyprus between the Ibelins and Friedrich's bailiffs. By summer 1230 the Ibelins had triumphed and *Jean d'Ibelin* (see above) became head of government again until 1232, when King Henri I came of age. Fighting restarted early in 1232, but Lombard-Imperial resistance was finally ended in Apr 1233 and rule fully restored to Henri I.

*After the fall of Acre in 1292, the Kings of Cyprus continued to style themselves King of Jerusalem

3 Oct 1382/ May 1385* – 9 Sep 1398	*Jacques I*,† uncle of Pierre II (b. 1334; d. Nicosia)
	Regent:
	3 Oct 1382 – May 1385: *Jean de Brie*
11 Nov 1399 – 28 or 29 Jun 1432	*Jannus*, son of Jacques I (b. Genoa 1374; d. Nicosia) captured by the Mamluk sultan 7 Jul 1426, ransomed Apr 1427, vassal of the Mamluk sultan thereafter
	Regent:
	Jul 1426 – 1427: *Hugues*, Archbishop of Nicosia, brother
24 Aug 1432 – 26 Jul 1458	*Jean II*, son (b. Nicosia May 1414; d. Nicosia)
15 Oct 1458 – autumn 1464	*Charlotte*, daughter (d. Rome 16 Jul 1487) deposed by Jacques II
1460 – 1464	Civil war between Charlotte and Jacques II
1460/ 1464 – 6 Jul 1473	*Jacques II*, the Bastard, half-brother (b. Nicosia 1440; d. Nicosia) seized control of most of Cyprus by 1460, defeated final resistance of Charlotte 1464, recaptured Famagusta from Genoa 1464, allied with Venice 1472
late 1473	*Jacques III*, son (b. Nicosia 28 Aug 1473; d. Nicosia) ruled under Venetian protection
	Regent:
	Catarina Cornaro (see below)
26 Aug 1474 – 26 Feb 1489	*Catarina Cornaro*, a Venetian noblewoman, mother (b. 30 Apr 1454; d. Venice 9/ 10 Jul 1510) ruled under Venetian protection, abdicated
26 Feb 1489	Cyprus ruled directly from Venice

*When proclaimed king on the death of Pierre II, Jacques was in prison in Genoa. He was released on 19 Feb 1383 but did not arrive in Nicosia for his coronation until Mar 1385

†From 29 Nov 1393 the Kings of Cyprus also styled themselves King of Armenia

Cyrene

Territory comprised part of present-day north-eastern Libya, with the capital at Cyrene.

Kings

Battiads	
631BC*	*Battus I* (*or Aristocles*), founder of Cyrene
(?)	*Arcesilaus I*, for 16 years
(?)	*Battus II Eudamon*
c. 560	*Arcesilaus II*, the Cruel, murdered
(?)	*Battus III*, the Lame, son
(?)	*Arcesilaus III*, son, murdered
515	*Battus IV*, Persian vassal
470 – 440	*Arcesilaus IV*
440	Establishment of a republic

Dahomey

Territory comprised part of present-day southern Benin, with the capital at Abomey.

Kings

AD c. 1620	*Dakodonu*
c. 1645	*Wégbaja*, son
c. 1685	*Akaba*, son, with his sister *Hangbé*
1708	*Agaja*, brother, conquered Allada 1724 and Whydah 1729
1732	*Tègbésu*, son

*Traditional date

1774	*Kpéngla*, brother
1789	*Agonglo*, son
1797	*Adanzan*, son, deposed
1818	*Gézo*, brother
1856	*Glèlè*, son
1889 – 1892	*Gbéhanzin*, son (d. Blida, Algeria, 1906) deported to Martinique and then to Blida
1892	Abomey captured by French and protectorate established over the city
22 Jun 1894	Incorporated into French colony of Dahomey
1894 – 1898	*Agbo Agoli*, brother
1895	Became part of French West Africa
2 Aug 1960	Dahomey became independent, see Benin in Volume 3

Damascus (Aram or Syria)

Territory comprised part of present-day western Syria, with the capital at Damascus.

Kings

c. 950 BC	*Rezon*, formerly vassal of Hedadezer, the king of Zobah
(?)	*Tab-Rimmon*, son of Hezion
c. 890	*Ben-Hadad I* (or *Adad-idri*),* son, assassinated by Hazael
842/1(?)	*Hazael*, usurper
c. 808	*Ben-Hadad II*, son
fl. c. 742	*Rezin*
732	Coalition of Damascus and Israel defeated by the Assyrians, Damascan territories made Assyrian provinces

*Some have supposed two kings of this name at this point, father and son

Danishmendids

Territory comprised part of present-day central and eastern Turkey, with the capital established initially at Neocaesarea (now Niksar) and later at Caesarea.

Amirs (also with title of Malik, meaning King)

Sivas Branch

c. AD 1071	*Danishmend (Ahmad Ghazi, Shams al-Din)* (d. 1104)
1084/5	*Ghazi Gümüshtigin (ibn Danishmend)*, son
1134	*(Abu'l-Muzaffar) Muhammad Nasir al-Din (ibn Gümüshtigin)*, son
1142/3	*Dhu'l-Nun ('Imad al-Din ibn Muhammad)*, son (for 1st time)
1142/3	*Yaghı-basan (Nizam al-Din ibn Gümüshtigin)*, uncle
1164	*(Abu Muhammad) Isma'il Ghazi (Jamal al-Din ibn Yaghı-basan)*, son
1166/7	*(Abu'l-Qadir) Isma'il Shams al-Din (ibn Ibrahim)*, nephew of Dhu'l-Nun
1168/9 – 1173/4	*Dhu'l-Nun* (for 2nd time) with honorific title of Nasir al-Din
1173/4	Overthrown by Qılıch Arslan II, the Seljuq sultan of Rum

Melitene Branch

c. 1142	*'Ain al-Daula (ibn Gümüshtigin)*, son of Gümüshtigin
1152	*Dhu'l-Qarnain (ibn 'Ain al-Daula)*, son
1162	*Nasr al-Din Muhammad (ibn Dhu'l-Qarnain)*, son (for 1st time)
1170	*Fakhr al-Din Qasim (ibn Dhu'l-Qarnain)*, brother (b. 1155)
1172	*Afridun*, brother
1175 – 1178	*Nasr al-Din Muhammad* (for 2nd time)
1178	Melitene occupied by Seljuqs of Rum

Delhi Sultanate

Territory comprised part of present-day northern India, with the capital established at Delhi.

Sultans

Mu'izzi or Slave Kings

23 Jun AD 1206	*Qutb al-Din Aibak*, son of Mu'izz, conquered Delhi 1193
Nov 1210	*Aram Shah*, son or adopted son
1210/11 – 27 Apr 1236	*Shams al-Din al-Qutbi (Iletmish* or *Iltutmish)*, son-in-law of Qutb al-Din Aibak
Apr/May – 27 Nov 1236	*Rukn al-Din (Firuz Shah)*, son, governor of Badayun from 1227/8, assassinated by Radiyya Begum
Nov 1236	*(Jalalat al-Din) Radiyya Begum*, half-sister (d. 1246/7)
22 Apr 1240 – 15 May 1242	*Mu'izz al-Din Bahram Shah*, brother, assassinated
May/Jun 1242 – 9 Jun 1246	*'Ala' al-Din Mas'ud Shah*, nephew, deposed
Jun 1246	*Nasir al-Din (Mahmud Shah I)*, uncle (b. 1228/9)
17 Feb 1266	*(Ghiyath al-Din Ulugh Khan) Balban*, brother-in-law (b. c. 1203/4)
1287/8	*Mu'izz al-Din (Kai-Qubadh)*, grandson (b. 1269/70) assassinated
Jun 1290	*(Shams al-Din) Kayumarth*, son, assassinated

Khaljis

13 Jun 1290 – 18 Jul 1296	*Jalal al-Din (Firuz Shah)*, assassinated
19 Jul – 3 Oct 1296	*Rukn al-Din (Ibrahim Shah I)*, son, assassinated by 'Ala' al-Din
19 Jul/3 Oct 1296 – 3 Jan 1316	*'Ala' al-Din (Muhammad Shah I)*, brother-in-law (b. c. 1267)
Jan 1316	*Shihab al-Din ('Umar Shah)*, son (b. 1309?) murdered by Qutb al-Din
1 Apr 1316 – 15 Apr 1320	*Qutb al-Din (Mubarak Shah)*, brother (b. 1299?) assassinated
Apr/May 1320	*Nasir al-Din Khusrau Shah*, usurper, vizier of

	Mubarak Shah, assassinated by Tughluq Shah I (see below)
Tughluqids	
Sep/Oct 1320	*(Ghiyath al-Din Ghazi Malik) Tughluq Shah I*
Feb/Mar 1325 – 20 Mar 1351	*(Ghiyath al-Din Ulugh Khan) Muhammad Shah II (ibn Tughluq)* (or *Juna*), son
Mar 1351	*Mahmud ibn Muhammad*, son, for a few days
20 Mar 1351	*Firuz Shah (Tughluq ibn Rajab)*, cousin
21 Sep 1388 – 13 Feb 1389	*(Ghiyath al-Din Salar Shah) Tughluq Shah II*, grandson (b. 6 Jun 1353)
15 Feb – 25 Dec 1389	*Abu Bakr Shah*, cousin, deposed and imprisoned
Dec 1389/Jan 1390	*(Nasir al-Din) Muhammad Shah III*, uncle
1 Mar 1393	*('Ala' al-Din) Sikander Shah I*, son
12 Apr 1393	*(Nasir al-Din) Mahmud Shah II*, brother (for 1st time) (d. 1411/12)
1394/5	*Nusrat Shah*, cousin, in dispute with Mahmud Shah II
1398/9	*Mahmud Shah II* (for 2nd time) defeated by the Timurid khan Temür 17 Dec 1398*
1413/14 – 1414/15	*Daulat Khan Lodi*, interregnum
Sayyids	
19 Jul 1414 – 19 May 1421	*Khidr Khan*
May/Jun 1421 – 27 Jan 1435	*(Mu'izz al-Din) Mubarak Shah II*, son
Jan 1435	*Muhammad Shah IV (ibn Farid)*, nephew
Dec 1445/Jan 1446 – 1451/2	*'Ala' al-Din 'Alam Shah*, son (d. Badayun 1478/9) abdicated
Lodis	
18 Jan 1452	*Bahlul Lodi* (d. Jul 1489) conquered the Sharqi sultans of Jaunpur 1479
1 Jul 1489	*(Nizam Khan) Sikander (ibn Bahlul)*, son (d. 21 Nov 1517)
21 Nov 1517 – 21 Apr 1526	*Ibrahim II*, son (d. 21 Apr 1526) defeated by Mughal emperor Babur at battle of Panipat 1526
Apr 1526 – 1540	Mughal conquest

*1399/1400 *Iqbal Khan (ibn Zafar)*, pretender, defeated 1405/6

Suri Afghans

1540	*Shir Shah (Sur)* (d. 21 May 1545) ruler of Bengal, defeated Mughal emperor Humayun at Kanauj
May/Jun 1545	*Islam Shah*, son (d. Nov 1554)
Nov/Dec 1553	*Muhammad V ('Adil Shah Mubariz)*, nephew (d. Monghyr 1556)
29 Apr – 2 May 1554	*Firuz ibn Islam Shah*, son of Islam Shah (b. 1541/2) assassinated
4 May 1554	*Ibrahim III*, nephew of Shir Shah, killed by Bengal sultan Sulaiman Kararani 1567/8
1554/5	*(Ahmad Khan) Sikander Shah*, nephew of Shir Shah (d. Bengal 1558/9)
23 Jul 1555	Conquest by Mughal emperor Humayun

Denmark

Kings

AD (?)	*Gorm*, the Old
c. 940	*Harald I*, Bluetooth, son (b. c. 910; d. Jumne)
c. 985	*Svend I* (known in England as *Sweyn*), Forkbeard, son (b. 965; d. Gainsborough, England) King of England autumn 1013
3 Feb 1014	*Harald II Svendsen*, son
1019	*Knud I*, the Great (known in England as *Cnut* or *Canute*), King of England, brother (b. c. 995 – 1000; d. Shaftesbury, Dorset, England) King of Norway 1028, lord of the Norse colonies, overlord of the Scots, King of Dublin(?)
12 Nov 1035	*Hardeknud* (known in England as *Harthacnut* or *Hardecanute*), son (b. c. 1018(?)) King of England 12 Nov 1035 – 1037 and Jun 1040 – 8 Jun 1042
8 Jun 1042	*Magnus*, the Good, King (Magnus I Olavsson) of Norway (b. 1024) succeeded in accordance with pact between himself and Hardeknud
25 Oct 1047	*Svend II Estridsen*, grandson of Svend I (b. c. 1020)
28(?) Apr 1074	*Harald III Hen*, illegitimate son
17 Apr 1080	*Knud II*, the Holy, illegitimate son of Svend II (d. (murdered) Odense)
19 Jul 1086	*Oluf I*, the Hungry, illegitimate son of Svend II

18 Aug 1095 – 10 Jun 1103	*Erik I*, the Kind-hearted, illegitimate son of Svend II (b. Slangerup; d. Cyprus)
1104	*Niels*, illegitimate son of Svend II, murdered
1134	*Erik II Emune*, illegitimate son of Erik I (d. (murdered) Tinget, Ribe county)
18 Sep 1137 – 27 Aug 1146	*Erik III*, the Lamb, son of illegitimate daughter of Erik I (d. Odense)
1146	Period of rivalry between *Svend III Grade* (or *Grathe*), son of Erik II (d. Gradehede 23 Oct 1157), *Knud III Magnussen*, grandson of Niels (d. Roskilde 9 Aug 1157) and *Valdemar I*, grandson of Erik I (b. 14 Jan 1131; d. Vordingborg 12 May 1182) after which Valdemar became sole ruler
12 May 1182	*Knud IV Valdemarsen*, son of Valdemar I (b. Begyndelsen 1163)
12 Nov 1202	*Valdemar II*, the Victorious, brother (b. 9 May 1170; d. Vordingborg)
28 Mar 1241	*Erik IV*, Ploughpenny, son (b. 1216; d. Slien) murdered by Abel
10 Aug 1250	*Abel*, brother (b. 1218) died in battle
29 Jun 1252	*Christoffer I*, brother (b. c. 1219; d. Ribe)
29 May 1259	*Erik V Klipping*, son (b. Lolland c. 1249; d. Finderup)
22 Nov 1286 – 13 Nov 1319	*Erik VI Mændved*, son (b. 1274)
1320 – 2 Aug 1332	*Christoffer II*, brother (b. 29 Sep 1276; d. Nykøbing)
1332 – 1340	Interregnum. *Valdemar III*, Duke of Schleswig, great-grandson of Abel (b. 1314; d. 1364) received some support 1326 – 1330
1340 – 24 Oct 1375	*Valdemar IV*, son of Christoffer II (b. c. 1320; d. Gurre Slot)
1376	*Oluf III*, grandson (b. 1370) King (Olav IV) of Norway 1 May 1380 Regent: *Margrete* (or *Margareta*), mother (b. 1353; d. Flensburg 28 Oct 1412) Regent of Norway 1380, Regent of Sweden 1389
3 Aug 1387	*Margrete*, previously Regent
28 Oct 1412	*Erik VII*, King (Erik XIII) of Sweden, King (Erik III) of Norway, Duke (Eryk I) of Pomerania at Stolp, great-nephew of Margrete (b. 1382; d. Jun 1459) driven from office in all three kingdoms
1439	*Christoffer III* (German: *Christoph*), Count of the Upper Palatinate, nephew (b. 26 Feb (?) 1416; d.

	Hälsingborg) King (Kristoffer) of Sweden 1440 and of Norway Jun 1442
House of Oldenburg	
5 or 6 Jan 1448	*Christian* (or *Christiern*) *I*, Duke of Oldenburg and Delmenhorst (b. 1426; d. Copenhagen) King of Norway 1449/50, King of Sweden 1457 – 1464 and 1465 – 1467
21 May 1481 – 20 Feb 1513	*Hans*, son (b. 8 Jul 1455) King of Norway 1483, King (Johan II) of Sweden 1483/97 – 1500

Dhunnunids

Territory comprised part of present-day central Spain, with the capital established at Toledo.

Kings

AD (?)	*'Abd al-Rahman (ibn Dhu'l-Nun)*, son of Dhu'l-Nun
1028	*Isma'il (al-Zafir ibn 'Abd al-Rahman)*, son
1043	*('Abu'l-Hasan Yahya) al-Ma'mun (ibn Isma'il)*, son, Amirid king 1064/5 – 1074/5
1074/5 – 1085/6	*al-Qadir (Yahya ibn Isma'il ibn al-Ma'mun)*, grandson, Amirid king 1074/5 – 1075/6 and 1085/6 – 1090/1
1085/6	Conquest by Alfonso VI of León and Castile

Dienne (Djenne, Jenne)

Territory comprised part of present-day southern Mali.

Djenne-were

AD 1556*	*Abou Bekr I* (or *Ouaïbo Ali*)
1592	*Ismaïl I*, brother, for seven months
1592	*Abdallah I*
1597	*Mohammed I* (or *Bamba*), son of Ismaïl I (for 1st time)
1614	*Abou Bekr II* (or *Sakoura*), son of Abdallah I (for 1st time)
1617 – 13 Sep 1620	*Mohammed I* (for 2nd time)
1620 – Jun 1627	*Abou Bekr II* (for 2nd time)
1627	*Mohammed II* (or *Kounboro*), son of Mohammed I (for 1st time)
1629 – 26 Nov 1632	*Abou Bekr III el Meqtoul*, brother
1632 – 26 Jun 1634	*Mohammed II* (for 2nd time)
27 Jun 1634 – 3 Jan 1642	*Abdallah II*, nephew
4 Jan 1642	*Mohammed II* (for 3rd time)
24 Mar 1643	*Ismaïl II*, brother
1 Jan 1653	*Abou Bekr IV* (or *Ankabala*), brother
31 Oct 1653 – (?)	*Mohammed II* (for 4th time)
(?)	State lapsed into anarchy

*From 1591 the rulers of Dienne recognized the suzerainty of the Moroccan pashas of Timbuktu

Egypt

Kings of the Early Dynastic Period

Territory comprised part of present-day Egypt and southern Israel, with the capital initially at Thinis and later at Memphis.

First Dynasty c. 3100 – 2890 BC

† *Men* (or *Menes*) (*Narmer**), united Upper and Lower Egypt
Iti (or *Athothis*) (*Aha**)
Iti (or *Athothis*) (*Djer**), for 47 years
Iterty (*Djet**)
Khasty (*Den**), for 55 to 60 years
Merpebia (or *Miebis*) (*Anedjib**), for seven years
Irynetjer (*Semerkhet**), for eight years
Qaa, for 25 years

Second Dynasty c. 2890 – 2686

† *Hetep* (*Hetepsekhemwy**)
Nubnefer (*Reneb**)
Nynetjer (*Nynetjer**), for 45 to 47 years
Weneg (or *Wadjnes*), for 19 years
Sened (or *Sethenes*)
Peribsen
Aka (?)
Neferkasokar (?), for eight years
Unknown (*Khasekhem**), for 21 years(?)
Khasekhemwy (*Khasekhemwy**), for 17 years

Kings of the Old Kingdom

Territory comprised part of present-day Egypt, with the capital at Memphis.

Third Dynasty c. 2686 – 2613

† *Nebka* (*Sanakhte**), for 19 years
Djoser (*Netjerykhet**), brother, for 19 years
Djoser Teti (*Sekhemkhet**), for six years
Unknown (*Khaba**), for six years
Huni (or *Nysuteh*?), for 24 years

*Horus name

†Dates of individual kings are unknown

Fourth Dynasty c. 2613 – 2494

† *Sneferu*, for 24 years
Cheops (or *Khufu*), son, builder of the Great Pyramid; for 23 years
Redjedef, son, for eight years
Chephren (or *Khafre*), brother, for 25 years(?)
Baufre(?)
Mycerinus, son of Chephren, for 28 years(?)
Shepseskaf, for four years
Dedefptah(?) (or *'Thamphthis'*), for two years

Fifth Dynasty c. 2494 – 2345

† *Userkaf*, for seven years
Sahure, for 14 years
Neferirkare Kakai, for 10 years
Shepseskare Isi, for seven years
Neferefre, for seven years
Nyuserre, for (3)1 years
Menkauhor Akauhor, for eight years
Djedkare Isesi, for 39 years
Unas, for 30 years

Sixth Dynasty c. 2345 – 2181

† *Teti*, for 12 years
Userkare, usurper, for one year(?)
Meryre Phio(p)s I, son of Teti, for 49 years
Merenre Antyemsaf I, son, for 14 years
Neferkare Phiops II, brother, for 94 years(?)
Merenre Antyemsaf II, for one year
Netjerykare
Menkare(?) *Nitocris*, for two years(?)

Kings of the First Intermediate Period

Territory comprised part of present-day Egypt, with the capital initially at Memphis and later at Heracleopolis.

† Dates of individual kings are unknown

Seventh Dynasty c. 2181 – 2173
Ruled at Memphis.

†	*Neferkare*, the Younger
	Neferkare Neby
	Djedkare Shemay
	Neferkare Khendu
	Meryenhor
	Neferkamin
	Nykare
	Neferkare Tereru
	Neferkahor

Eighth Dynasty c. 2173 – 2160
Ruled at Memphis and controlled part of Upper Egypt.

†	*Wadjkare Pepysonbe* (*Kha-*. . .* (possibly *Khabau*)), for more than four years
	Neferkamin Anu, for two years
	Kakare Ibi, for four years
	Neferkare, for two years
	Neferkauhor Kapuibi (*Netjerybau**), for one year
	Neferirkare (*Demedjibtowy**)

Ninth Dynasty c. 2160 – 2130
Ruled from Heracleopolis.

†	*Meryibre Achthoes I*, ruler of the Heracleopolitan nome
	Unknown king
	Neferkare
	Nebkaure Achthoes II
	Setut
	Unknown king
	Mery- . . .
	Shed- . . .
	H- . . .
	Unknown king
	Unknown king
	Unknown king
	User (?) . . .

*Horus name

† Dates of individual kings are unknown

Tenth Dynasty c. 2130 – 2040
Ruled at Heracleopolis.

†	*Meryhathor*(?)
	Neferkare
	Wahkare Achthoes III
	Merykare
	Unknown king

Kings of the Middle Kingdom

Territory comprised part of present-day Egypt, northern Sudan, Israel, Lebanon and north-western Syria, with the capital initially at Thebes and later at Hj-towy (near present-day al-Lisht).

Eleventh Dynasty
Ruled at Thebes.

2133	*Mentuhotpe(-a) I* (*Tep(y)a**) and *Inyotef I* (*Sehertowy**)
2117	*Inyotef II* (*Wahankh**)
2068	*Inyotef III* (*Nakhtnebtepnefer**)
2060	*Nebhepetre Mentuhotpe II* (*Sankhibtowy, Netjeryhedjet*, *Smatowy**), conquered Heracleopolis and reunited Egypt c. 2039
2009	*Sankhkare Mentuhotpe III (Sankhtowyef*)*, son
1997 – 1991	*Nebtowyre Mentuhotpe IV* (*Nebtowy**) and *The God's Father Sesostris*

Twelfth Dynasty
Ruled from Hj-towy.

1991	*(Sehetepibre) Ammenemes I*, vizier of Mentuhotpe IV, assassinated
1962	*(Kheperkare) Sesostris I*, son, served as co-regent from 1971
1928	*(Nubkaure) Ammenemes II*, son, served as co-regent from 1929
1895	*(Khakheperre) Sesostris II*, served as co-regent from 1897
1878	*(Khakaure) Sesostris III*
1842	*(Nymare) Ammenemes III*, son
1798	*(Makherure) Ammenemes IV*

*Horus name

†Dates of individual kings are unknown

1789 – 1786	*(Sobkkare) Sobkneferu*, queen

Kings of the Second Intermediate Period

*Thirteenth Dynasty 1786 – 1633**

Territory comprised part of present-day eastern Egypt, northern Sudan, Israel, Lebanon and Syria, with the capital at Hj-towy (near present-day al-Lisht).

(?)	*(Sekhemre Khutowy Ammenemes) Sobkhotpe I*, for more than five years
(?)	*(Sekhemkare Ammenemes) Senbuef*, for more than three years
c. 1770 – 1769	*Sehetepibre (II) Ammenemes*, for one year
(?)	*(Sankhibre) Ameny Inyotef Ammenemes*
(?)	*(Hetepibre) Amu Sihornedjheryotef*
(?)	*Sobkhotpe II*, son of Mentuhotpe
(?)	*Renseneb*, for four months
(?)	*(Awibre) Hor*
(?)	*(Sedjefakare) Kay Ammenemes*
(?)	*(Khutowyre) Ugaf*, for two years
(?)	*(Seneferibre) Sesostris IV*
(?)	*(Userkare) Khendjer*, for more than four years
(?)	*Semenkhkare*, the General, for more than three years
(?)	*(Sekhemre Wadjkhau) Sobkemsaf I*, for seven years
(?)	*(Sekhemre Sewadjtowy) Sobkhotpe III*, for three years
c. 1740 – 1730	*(Khasekhemre) Neferhotep I*, for 11 years
(?)	*(Khaneferre) Sobkhotpe IV*, for more than eight years
(?)	*(Khaankhre) Sobkhotpe V*
(?)	*(Mersekhemre) Neferhotep II*
(?)	*(Khahetepre) Sobkhotpe VI*, for four years
(?)	*(Sekhemre Sankhtowy) Neferhotep III*
(?)	*(Wahibre) Yayebi*, for 10 years
(?)	*(Merneferre) Iy*, for 23 years
(?)	*(Merhetepre) Ini*, for two years
c. 1674	*(Djedneferre) Dudimose I* (or *Tutimaios*)
(?)	*(Djedhetepre) Dudimose II*
(?)	*(Sewahenre) Senebmiu*
(?)	*(Meryankhre) Mentuhotpe V*
(?)	*(Djedankhre) Mentuemsaf*

*The traditional list contains the names (many fragmentary) of sixty kings, many of whom are supposed to have been rulers of Upper Egypt only. The choice here follows the *Cambridge Ancient History*

(?) *(Menkhaure) Senaayeb*
(?) *Nehsy*

Fourteenth Dynasty 1786 – c. 1603

According to Julius Africanus's version of Manetho's *History of Egypt*, there were 'seventy-six kings of Xoïs'. They did not rule as kings of Egypt but ruled over part of present-day western Egypt, with their capital at Xoïs.

Fifteenth Dynasty (The Great Hyksos) 1674 – 1567

Territory comprised part of present-day northern Egypt, Israel, Jordan, Lebanon and western Syria, with the capital at Avaris.

* *(Mayebre) Sheshi*, for three (one?) years
(Meruserre) Yakubher, for eight years
(Seuserenre) Khyan
(Auserre) Apophis I, for more than 40 years
(Aqenenre) Apophis II
(Asehre) Khamudy(?)

Sixteenth Dynasty c. 1684 – 1567

Territory comprised part of present-day northern Egypt.

Succession of eight Hyksos, probably contemporary with the Great Hyksos and including some or all of the following:

* *Anather*
Semqen
Khauserre
Seket
Ahetepre
Sekhaenre
Amu
Nebkhepeshre Apophis (III?)

*Dates of individual kings are unknown

Seventeenth Dynasty c. 1650 – 1567
Territory comprised part of present-day southern Egypt and northern Sudan, with the capital at Thebes.

	First Group
*	*(Sekhemre Wahkhau) Rehotpe*
	(Sekhemre Wepmaat) Inyotef V, the Elder, for three years
	(Sekhemre Heruhirmaat) Inyotef VI
	(Sekhemre Shedtowy) Sobkemsaf II, for 16 years
	(Sekhemre Sementowy) Thuty, for one year
	(Sankhenre) Mentuhotpe VI, for one year
	(Sewadjenre) Nebiryerawet I, for six years
	(Neferkare?) Nebiryerawet II
	Semenmedjat(?)re
	Seuserenre (or *Userenre*?), for 12 years
	(Sekhemre) Shedwast
	Second Group
*	*(Nubkheperre) Inyotef VII*, for more than three years
	Senakhtenre
	(Seqenenre) Tao I, the Elder
	(Seqenenre) Tao II, the Brave
	(Wadjkheperre) Kamose, son, for more than three years, began the liberation of Egypt from Hyksos rule

Kings of the New Kingdom

Territory comprised part of present-day Egypt, northern Sudan and Israel, with the capital established initially at Thebes and later at Akhetaton (present-day Tell el-Amarna).

Eighteenth Dynasty

1570	*(Nebpehtyre) Amosis I*, brother, completed the expulsion of the Hyksos and the reunification of Egypt

*Dates of individual kings are unknown

1546	*(Djeserkare) Amenophis I*, son
1525	*(Akheperkare) Tuthmosis* I*, one of Amenophis I's generals
c. 1512	*(Akheperenre) Tuthmosis* II*, son
1503	*(Makare) Hatshepsut*, wife; ruled with her son *(Menkheperre) Tuthmosis* III* (for 1st time)
1482	*Tuthmosis III* (for 2nd time) alone, defeated the Mitanni at the battle of Megiddo 1468 and gained control over Syria-Palestine
1450	*(Akheprure) Amenophis II*, son
1425	*(Menkheprure) Tuthmosis* IV*, son
1417	*(Nebmare) Amenophis III*, son
1379	*(Neferkheprure) Amenophis IV* (or *Akhenaten*), son, established new capital of Akhetaton and instituted the worship of Aton
1362	*(Ankhkheprure) Smenkhkare*, son, ruled as co-regent from 1364
1361	*(Nebkheprure) Tutankhamun*, brother
1352	*Kheperkheprure Ay*, vizier and regent for Tutankhamun
1348 – 1320	*(Djeserkheprure) Horemheb* (or *Haremhab*), one of Tutankhamun's generals
Nineteenth Dynasty	
1320	*(Menpehtyre) Ramesses I*, general and vizier of Horemheb
1318	*(Menmare) Sethos I*, son
1304	*(Usermare) Ramesses II*, the Great, son
1236	*(Baenre) Merneptah*, son
1222(?)	*(Menmare) Amenmesses*,† usurper
1216(?)	*(Userkheprure) Sethos II*, son of Merneptah
1209 – 1200(?)	*(Akhenre-setepenre) Merneptah Siptah* (also named *Sekhaenre Ramesses Siptah*) and *(Sitre-meryetamun) Tewosret*, his queen
Twentieth Dynasty	
1200	*(Userkhaure) Sethnakhte*
1198	*(Usermare-meryamun) Ramesses III*, son

*Also spelt Thutmosis

†Position in dynasty uncertain

1166	*(Usermare-setepenamun*, later named *Hikmare-setepenamun) Ramesses IV*, son
1160	*(Usermare-sekheperenre) Ramesses V*, son(?)
1156	*(Nebmare-meryamun) Ramesses VI*, grandson of Ramesses III(?)
1148	*(Usermare-meryamun-setepenre) Ramesses VII*, son
1147	*(Usermare-akhenamun) Ramesses VIII*
1140	*(Neferkare-setepenre) Ramesses IX*
1121	*(Khepermare-setepenre) Ramesses X*
1113 – 1085	*(Menmare-setepenptah) Ramesses XI*

Kings of the Late Dynastic Period

Twenty-first Dynasty (Tanites) 1085 – 945

Territory comprised part of present-day Egypt, ruled from Tanis (present-day San el Hagar).

†	*(Hedjkheperre-setepenre) Smendes*, governor of Tanis
	(Neferkare-hikwast) Amenemnisu
	(Akheperre-setepenamun) Psusennes I
	(Usermare-setepenamun) Amenemope
	(Nutekheperre-setepenamun) Siamun
	(Titkheperure-setepenamun) Psusennes II

Twenty-second Dynasty (Bubastites)

Territory comprised part of present-day northern Egypt, with the capital at Bubastis (near present-day Zagazig).

c. 947	*Sheshonk I* (or *Shishak*), leader of the Meshwesh Libyans at Bubastis
925	*Osorkon I*, son
889 – 865	*Takeloti I*, son
c. 880	*Osorkon II*, son
c. 850	*Sheshonk II*, son
825	*Iuput*, son
821	*Sheshonk III*, son
769	*Pimai*, son(?)
763 – 725	*Sheshonk IV*, son
750 – 720(?)	*Osorkon IV*, son of Takeloti III of the 23rd dynasty(?)

† Dates of individual kings are unknown

Twenty-third Dynasty (Thebans)
Territory comprised part of present-day southern Egypt, with the capital at Thebes.

860	*Harsiesi*
838	*Pedubaste*
815	*Takeloti II*, son(?)
780 – 750	*Osorkon III*, son
757 – 745(?)	*Takeloti III*, son
750 – 740(?)	*Rudamon*, brother(?), defeated by Piankhi of the 25th dynasty

Twenty-fourth Dynasty (Memphites)
Territory comprised part of present-day northern Egypt, with the capital at Memphis.

726	*Tefnakhte*, a Libyan prince of Saïs
718 – 702	*Bokenranef* (or *Bocchoris*), son, killed by Shabaka of the 25th dynasty
663	*Niku I*

Twenty-fifth Dynasty (Kushites)
Territory comprised part of present-day southern Egypt, Sudan and northern Ethiopia, with the capital at Napata.

c. 745	*Kashta*
742 – 700(?)	*Piankhi*, son(?) ended the 23rd dynasty
715	*Shabaka* (or *Sabaka* or *Seve*(?)), brother
700	*Shabataka* (or *Sebichos*), son
689	*Taharka* (or *Tirhakah* or *Tarakos*), brother, defeated by the Assyrian king Esarhaddon 671
663 – 650	*Tanutamon* (or *Tandamane*), brother

Twenty-sixth Dynasty (Saïtes)
Territory comprised part of present-day Egypt, northern Sudan and north-eastern Libya, with the capital at Saïs.

663	*Psamatik I* (or *Psammetichos*), son of Niku I of the 24th dynasty, expelled the Assyrians, reunited the country and established his capital at Saïs 656
609	*Niku II* (or *Nechao* or *Necho*), son
593	*Psamatik II* (or *Psamatichos*), son
588 – 566	*Uahibre'* (or *Uaphris* or *Apries* or *Hophra*), son, deposed
569	*I'ahmases II* (or *Amasis*), usurper
526 – 525	*Psamatik III* (or *Psammenitos*), son, executed for treason

525 Conquest by the Persian king Cambyses II

Twenty-seventh Dynasty (Achaemenids)

Part of the Persian Empire, comprising present-day Egypt, northern Sudan and north-eastern Libya and centred at Memphis.

525	*Cambyses II*, King of Persia (until 522)
521	*Darius I*, the Great, King of Persia, son of Hystaspes, the satrap of Parthia (b. 550)
486	*Xerxes I*, the Great, son (b. c. 519; d. (assassinated) 465) King of Persia 486 – 465
466	*Artabanus*, minister of Xerxes, for seven months, assassinated
465	*Artaxerxes I*, Macrocheir i.e. Longhand, son of Xerxes I; King of Persia 465 – 425
424	*Xerxes II*, King of Persia, son; for two months
424	*Sogdianus*, half-brother; for seven months, at the same time King of Persia; deposed
424 – 404	*Darius II Ochus*, Nothos i.e. the Bastard, half-brother; King of Persia 423 – 404
404	Persian control of Egypt lost to the Saïtes

Twenty-eighth Dynasty (Saïtes)

Territory comprised part of northern Egypt, with the capital at Saïs.

404 – 399	*Amyrteos of Saïs*, recognized in Upper Egypt, led insurrection against the Achaemenids, regained control of Egypt 404

Twenty-ninth Dynasty

Territory comprised part of present-day Egypt and northern Sudan, with the capital at Mendes.

399	*Nepherites*
393	*Psammuthis*
393	*Achoris*
380	*Nepherites (II)*, son, for four months

Thirtieth Dynasty

Territory comprised part of present-day Egypt and northern Sudan.

380	*Nekhtnebef I*, usurper, successfully opposed Persian attempt at re-conquest
362	*Teos* (or *Takhos*), son
360 – 343	*Nekhtharehbe*, nephew, the last native Egyptian king, defeated by the Persian king Ochus Artaxerxes III
343	Persian re-conquest

Thirty-first Dynasty

Territory comprised part of present-day Egypt and northern Sudan, with the capital at Memphis.

343	King *Ochus Artaxerxes III* of Persia; assassinated by the eunuch Bagoas
338	*Arses*, son, King of Persia Nov 338 – 336, placed on the throne and later assassinated by Bagoas
335 – 332	*Darius III Codommanus*, King of Persia, great-grandson of Darius II Ochus (d. Bactria 330) placed on throne by Bagoas, defeated by Alexander the Great 1 Oct 333, fled to Bactria where he was deposed and killed by the satrap Bessus
332	Egypt became part of the Macedonian empire

Ptolemaic Kings

At its greatest extent, territory comprised part of present-day Egypt, north-eastern Libya, southern Italy, southern Greece, Crete and south-western Israel, with the capital at Alexandria.

323/305	*Ptolemy I Soter I*, son of Lagus, a Macedonian noble (b. Macedonia 367/6 or 364; d. Egypt 283/2) general of Alexander the Great, became satrap of Egypt 323, declared himself king 305
283	*Ptolemy II Philadelphus*, son (b. island of Kos 308) ruled as co-regent from 285
246	*Ptolemy III Euergetes I*, son
221	*Ptolemy IV Philopator*, son
203	*Ptolemy V Epiphanes*, son (b. c. 210)
181/80	*Ptolemy VI Philometor*, son; Egypt occupied by Seleucid king Antiochus IV Epiphanes 169 – 168 but relieved by Rome
145	*Ptolemy VII Euergetes II* (or *Physcon*), brother
116	*Ptolemy VIII Soter II* (or *Lathyrus*), son (for 1st time) deposed
108/7	*Ptolemy IX Alexander I*, brother
88	*Ptolemy VIII Soter II* (for 2nd time) deposed
80	*Ptolemy X Alexander II*, nephew (b. c. 115)
80	*Ptolemy XI Auletes*, cousin (b. c. 112)
51	*Ptolemy XII*, son (b. 63) ruled with his sister, *Cleopatra VII Thea Philopator* (for 1st time)
47	*Ptolemy XIII*, brother, and *Cleopatra VII Thea Philopator* (for 2nd time)

44(?) – 30	*Ptolemy XIV Caesar* (or *Caesarion*), son of Cleopatra VII Thea Philopator, executed by the Roman triumvir Octavian; and *Cleopatra VII Thea Philopator* (for 3rd time) committed suicide
30	Direct Roman rule

Elam

Territory comprised part of present-day south-eastern Iraq and south-western Iran, with the capital at Susa (present-day Shush).

Kings

after 1850 BC	*Eparti III*, king of Anshan (southern Elam) and Susa
(?)	*Shilkhakha*, son, king of Anshan and Susa
before 1830	*Attakhushu*, nephew, Grand Regent
c. 1792	*Sirukdukh I*, brother, king of Elam
(?)	*Shimut-wartash*, brother, Grand Regent
(?)	*Siwe-palar-khuppak*, nephew, defeated by the Babylonian king Hammurabi and took title of Governor of Elam
after 1750	*Kuduzulush I*, brother
c. 1730	*Kutir-Nahhunte I*, nephew(?), Grand Regent
c. 1700	*Lila-ir-tash*, brother, Grand Regent
c. 1698	*Temti-agun I*, nephew, Grand Regent
c. 1685	*Tan-Uli*, cousin, Grand Regent
c. 1655	*Temti-khalki*, nephew(?), Grand Regent
c. 1650	*Kuk-nashur II*, cousin
c. 1635	*Kutir-Shilkhakha I*, brother or cousin
c. 1625	*Temti-raptash*, nephew(?)

before 1600	*Kuduzulush II*
(?)	*Atta-merra-khalki*
(?)	*Pala-ishshan*
after 1550	*Kuk-kirwash*, nephew
(?)	*Kuk-Nahhunte*
c. 1500 – (?)	*Kutir-Nahhunte II*
(?) – c. 1330	Rule by the Kassite dynasty of Babylonia(?)
c. 1330	*Khurpatila*, king of Elam
(?)	*Pakhir-ishshan*
c. 1300	*Attar-kittakh*, brother
c. 1285	*Khumban-numena*, son
c. 1266	*Untash-naprisha*, son
c. 1245	*Unpatar-naprisha*
c. 1242 – 1222	*Kidin-khutran*, brother
1222 – c. 1200	Interregnum, founding of new dynasty
c. 1200	*Khallutush-In-Shushinak*
(?)	*Shutruk-Nahhunte*, son, conquest of Babylonia 1157
before 1150	*Kutir-Nahhunte III*, son
c. 1140	*Shilkhak-In-Shushinak*, brother
c. 1110	*Khutelutush-In-Shushinak*, son, without the title of king
c. 1110	Conquest by the Babylonian king Nebuchadrezzar I
c. 760	*Khumbantakhrah*, re-established dynasty
743	*Khumbanigash I*
717	*Shutur-Nakhkhunte*, deposed
699	*Khallushu*, brother, deposed
693	*Kutir-Nakhkhunte*, assassinated
692	*Umman-Menanu* (or *Khumban-Nimena*)
689	*Khumma-khaldash I* (or *Khumban-Khaldash*)
681	*Khumma-khaldash II* (or *Shilkhak-In-Shushinak II*)
676	*Urtaku*
664	*Teumman*, killed in battle against Assyria
655	*Khumbanigash II* (or *Ummanigash*), son
651	*Tammaritu*
649	*Indabigash*
647 – 640	*Khumma-khaldash III* (or *Umman-aldash* or *Khumban-Khaldash*), Susa sacked by the Assyrian king Ashurbanipal 639
640	Conquest by the Assyrians

Eldigüzids (Ildegizids)

Territory comprised part of present-day northern Iran and southern USSR, centred in Azerbaijan.

Atabegs

AD 1136/7	*(Shams al-Din) Eldigüz*, slave of the Seljuq vizier Simirumi, appointed governor of Arran and part of Azerbaijan, took title Atabeg al-A'zam (Supreme Atabeg), effective master of the Seljuq empire by 1164/5
1174/5 or 1175/6	*(Nusrat al-Din Abu Ja'far Jahan) Pahlawan (Muhammad ibn Eldigüz)*, son; ruled in Arran and much of Azerbaijan, Jibal, Isfahan and Rayy; regent for the Seljuq Sultan Arslan Shah II
1186/7	*(Muzaffar al-Din) Qızıl Arslan ('Uthman ibn Eldigüz)*, brother, ruled at Tabriz until 1186/7, claimed the Seljuq sultanate of Iran, murdered
1191/2	*(Qutlugh Inanch) ibn Pahlawan*, nephew
1195	*(Nusrat al-Din) Abu Bakr (ibn Pahlawan)*, brother, ruled as subordinate in Azerbaijan from 1186
1210/11 – 1225/6	*(Muzaffar al-Din) Özbeg (ibn Pahlawan)*, brother, deposed
1225/6	Khwarazm-Shah conquest

Elymais

Territory comprised part of present-day south-eastern Iraq and south-western Iran, with the capital at Susa (present-day Shush).

Kings (Parthian vassals)

second century BC	*Kamnaskires I Nikephoros*
first century	*Kamnaskires II*, and his wife *Anzaze*
first century	*Kamnaskires III*, son

AD first century	*Orodes I*
first century	*Orodes II*
second century	*Phraates*, son
second century	*Orodes III*
second century	*Orodes IV*
second century	Unknown number of kings
224	Conquest by the Sassanid king Ardashir I

England

BERNICIA

Territory now in south-eastern Scotland and Northumberland, with the capital at Bamburgh.

Kings

AD 558	*Ida*, son of Eoppa
570	*Glappa*
571	*Adda*, son of Ida
579	*Hussa*
586	*Theodric*, son of Ida
593	*Æthelfrith* (or *Ethelfrith*), son, King of Deira from 605
617	*Edwin*, son of King Ælle of Deira (b. 584; d. Hatfield Chase, Doncaster, South Yorkshire) overlord of the southern English, King of Deira ? – 605 and 617 – 12 Oct 634
634	*Eanfrith*, son of Æthelfrith
summer 635 – 5 Aug 643	*Oswald*, Saint, brother (b. 604; d. Maserfeld (probably present-day Oswestry, Shropshire)) at the same time King of Deira
Nov 643 – 655	*Oswiu*, brother (b. 612) King of Northumbria 655 – Feb 671
655	United with Deira to form Northumbria (see below)

DEIRA

Territory now in eastern North Yorkshire and Humberside, with the capital at York.

Kings

c. AD 450	*Soemil*
?	Unknown number of kings
558/560	*Ælle*, son of Yffi
588/590	*Æthelric* (or *Ethelric*), son of King Ida of Bernicia
fl. 597	*Frithuwald*
?	*Edwin*, son of Ælle (for 1st time) (see Bernicia)
605	*Æthelfrith* (or *Ethelfrith*), King of Bernicia (see above)
617	*Edwin*, King of Bernicia (for 2nd time)
12 Oct 634	*Osric*, cousin
summer 635 – 5 Aug 643	*Oswald*, Saint, King of Bernicia (see above)
c. 644 – 20 Aug 652	*Oswine*, son of Osric
652	*Æthelwald* (or *Ethelwald*), son of Oswald, under-king
655	United with Bernicia to form Northumbria (see below)

EAST ANGLIA

Territory comprised part of present-day Norfolk and Suffolk.

Anglian Kings

c. AD 525	*Wehha*
?	*Wuffa*, son
?	*Tyttla*, son
c. 600	*Rædwald* (or *Redwald*), son
c. 620	*Eorpwald*, son
?	One unknown king(?)
c. 632	*Sigeberht*, half-brother of Eorpwald (d. 636?) abdicated
635(?)	*Ecgric*, kinsman, joint king and successor
636(?)	*Anna*, nephew of Rædwald
c. 655 – 15 Nov 656	*Æthelhere*, brother
late 656	*Æthelwold* (or *Ethelwold*), brother

664	*Aldwulf*, nephew of Æthelhere
713(?)	*Ælfwald* (or *Alfwold*), son
749	*Beonna*, with *Hun* and either *Alberht* or *Æthelberht*
?	*Æthelred* (or *Ethelred*)
? – 794	*Æthelberht* (or *Ethelbert*), son
fl. 825	*Athelstan*
fl. 850	*Æthelweard* (or *Ethelweard*)
855 – 866	*Edmund* (b. 841/2; d. Hoxne, Suffolk, 20 Nov 870)
866 – c. 870	Danish occupation
c. 870 – ?	*Oswald*(?)

Danish Kings

880	*Guthrum* (afterwards *Athelstan*)
890/1 – 902	*Eric* (or *Eohric*)
(?)	One king (d. at the battle of Tempsford 917)
917	Submitted to Edward the Elder, King of Wessex

ESSEX (EAST SAXONS)

Territory comprised part of present-day Essex and Greater London, centred on London.

Kings

c. AD 600	*Sæberht*, son of Sledda
616/7	*Seaxred* and *Sæweard*, sons
617(?)	*Sigeberht I*, Parvus, son of Sæweard
c. 652	*Sigeberht II*, Sanctus, son of Sigebald
c. 660	*Swithelm*, son of Seaxbald
c. 664	Essex henceforward subject to Mercia
c. 664	*Sighere*, son of Sigeberht I (d. c. 680?); with *Sebbi*, son of Seaxred or Sæweard(?) (d. c. 694); abdicated
693/4	*Sigeheard* and *Swæbheard* (or *Swæfred*), sons
c. 700	*Offa*, son of Sighere, abdicated
708/9 – 746	*Sælred*, son of Sigeberht II; with (? – 738), *Swæfberht* (or *Swebert*)
746	*Swithred*, descendant of Sebbi
after 758	*Sigeric*, son of Sælred, went to Rome 797/8
797/8(?) – ?	*Sigered*, son
825	Submitted to Egbert, King of Wessex

KENT

Territory comprised part of present-day Kent, with the capital at Canterbury.

Kings

AD 449	*Horsa*, son of Witta
455	*Hengest*, brother
488	*Æsc* (or *Oisc*), son*
512(?)	*Octa*, son*
?	*Eormenric*, son
562/5 – 24 Feb 618	*Æthelberht* (or *Ethelbert*), son
618 – 20 Jan 640	*Eadbald*, son
640 – 14 Jul 664	*Earconberht*, son
664 – 4 Jul 673	*Egbert I*, son
Jul 673 – 6/7 Feb 685†	*Hlothhere*, brother
685 – 31 Aug 686 (687?)†	*Eadric*, nephew, also King of Sussex(?)
688(?)†	*Oswine*, outsider(?) or second cousin; in conflict with Hlothhere from 673
autumn 691 – 23 Apr 725†	*Wihtred*, son of Egbert I, sole king from 694(?)
725 – 762‡	*Æthelberht* (or *Ethelbert*) *II*, son
725 – after 762(?)	*Eadberht I*, brother
c. 747 – c. 765	*Eardwulf*, son
fl. 762	*Sigered*, ruler of part of Kent
fl. c. 762	*Eanmund* (same as Ealhmund below?)
fl. 764, 765	*Heahberht*
c. 765 – c. 780	*Egbert II*
fl. 784	*Ealhmund*, father of Egbert, King of Wessex(?)
796	*Eadberht II Præn*, deposed by King Cenwulf of Mercia
798(?)	*Eadwald*
798 – 807	*Cuthred*, brother of King Cenwulf of Mercia
807(?) – 825	*Baldred*, expelled by King Egbert of Wessex
825	Submitted to Egbert

*Order and filiation reversed in some sources
†Swæfhard (Swæbheard of Essex? q.v.) recorded as king in 676 and 692
‡From c. 730 Kent was under the overlordship of Mercia

MERCIA

Territory comprised part of present-day northern and central England, with the capital at Tamworth.

Kings

AD 585	*Creoda**
c. 597	*Pybba*, son*
c. 600	*Cearl*, kinsman
628/634 – 15 Nov 656	*Penda*, son of Pybba (b. 575 or 582)
? – 641	*Eowa*, brother, under-king(?)
656	Mercia under Northumbria
656	*Peada*, son of Penda; King of South Mercia
659	*Wulfhere*, brother, overlord of the southern English
675 – 704	*Æthelred* (or *Ethelred*), brother (d. 716) abdicated
fl. 685	*Berhtwald* (or *Brihtwold*), nephew (or brother?) under-king
704	*Cenred*, son of Wulfhere (d. c. 709) abdicated
709	*Ceolred*, son of Æthelred
Sep(?) 716	*Æthelbald* (or *Ethelbald*), grandson of Eowa (d. Seckington, near Tamworth) overlord of the southern English
757	*Beonred*, usurper(?)
757 – 26/29 Jul 796	*Offa*, great-great-grandson of Eowa; overlord of the southern English; called himself King of the English 774
Jul – 14/17 Dec 796	*Ecgfrith*, son, for 141 days, under-king from 787
Dec 796 – 821	*Cenwulf*, descendant of Pybba (d. Basingwerk)
821/2	*Ceolwulf*, brother, deposed
823	*Beornwulf*, killed by East Angles
825	*Ludeca*
827 – 829	*Wiglaf* (for 1st time) (d. 840)
829	Mercia overrun by Wessex
830	*Wiglaf* (for 2nd time)
c. 840	*Beorhtwulf*, died or expelled
852	*Burgred* (d. Rome 874/5) driven out by the Danes
874 – 877	*Ceolwulf II*, puppet of the Danes
877	Danes appropriated eastern Mercia
883	*Æthelred* (or *Ethelred*), ealdorman; vassal of King Alfred of Wessex

*It is not certain that these were kings of Mercia

911–918	*Æthelflæd*, daughter of Alfred and widow of Æthelred (d. Tamworth 12 Jun 918) Lady of the Mercians
919	Fully incorporated in Wessex

NORTHUMBRIA

Formed by the union of Bernicia and Deira; for temporary unification before 655 see those kingdoms.

Territory comprised part of southern Scotland and northern England, with the capital at York.

Kings

AD 655	*Oswiu*, King of Bernicia (see above)
Feb 671 – 20 May 685	*Ecgfrith*, son (b. 645; d. near Forfar, Angus)
May 685 – 14 Dec 704	*Aldfrith*, illegitimate son of Oswiu (d. Driffield, North Humberside)
Dec 704	*Eadwulf*, for two months
705	*Osred I*, son of Aldfrith (b. 696/7)
716	*Cenred*, descendant of King Ida of Bernicia
718 – 9 May 729	*Osric*, son of Aldfrith
729	*Ceolwulf*, brother of Cenred (d. 760 or 764) deposed and restored 731, took clerical vows
737	*Eadberht*, cousin (d. 19/20 Aug 768) took clerical vows
757 – 24/25 Jul 759	*Oswulf*, son
5 Aug 759	*Æthelwald* (or *Ethelwald*) *Moll*, expelled
30 Oct 765	*Al(c)hred*, son of Eanwine, a descendant of Ida(?); exiled
Easter 774	*Æthelred* (or *Ethelred*) *I*, son of Æthelwald Moll (for 1st time) (d. 18 Apr 796) exiled
778 – 23 Sep 789	*Ælfwald* (or *Elfwald*) *I*, son of Oswulf
789	*Osred II*, son of Alhred or nephew of Ælfwald (d. 14 Sep 792) expelled
790	*Æthelred I* (for 2nd time)
796	*Osbald* (d. 799) for 27 days
14 May 796	*Eardwulf*, son of Eardwulf (for 1st time) (d. 809?) expelled
807(?)	*Ælfwald II*

809(?)	*Eardwulf* (for 2nd time)
809(?)	*Eanred*, son
841(?)	*Æthelred* (or *Ethelred*) *II*, son (for 1st time) (d. 849?)
844	*Rædwulf*
844	*Æthelred II* (for 2nd time)
849(?)	*Osbert* (for 1st time) (d. 21 Mar 867) expelled
862/3 – 21 Mar 867	*Ælle*, brother(?), son of Hama
867	*Osbert* (for 2nd time) as rival to Ælle
after 21 Mar 867 – 872	*Egbert I*, Danish puppet (d. 873) driven out(?)
873	*Ricsige*, chosen by the Northumbrians
876 – 878(?)	*Egbert II*, ruled in region north of the Tyne; Yorkshire held by the Danes (see York)
(?)	*Eadwulf of Bamburgh**
fl. 923 – 927	*Ealdred of Bamburgh*, son*
fl. 949 – 955	*Oswulf*, later Earl of Northumbria, High-reeve at Bamburgh*
955	Northumbria united with the rest of England

SUSSEX (SOUTH SAXONS)

Territory comprised part of present-day East and West Sussex.

Kings

AD 477	*Ælle*
c. 514(?)	*Cissa*, son(?)
?	Unknown number of kings
c. 660(?) – c. 685	*Æthelwalh*, killed by Cædwalla, later King of Wessex
c. 685	Sussex overrun by Cædwalla
c. 685	*Berhthun* (d. c. 686) and *Andhun*, ealdormen
685 – 686	*Eadric*, King of Kent(?)
c. 686 – 726	Sussex subject to Wessex
fl. 692 – 725	*Nunna* (or *Nothelm*), with *Watt*, under-king(?)
fl. 714	*Æthelstan*
fl. 725 – 750	*Æthelberht* (or *Ethelbert*)
fl. 758 – 772(?)	*Osmund* †
fl. 772	*Oswald*, ealdorman †
fl. 772	*Oslac*, ealdorman †

*Not described as kings in contemporary records
† Under Mercian overlordship

fl. c. 780 – 791	*Aldwulf*, ealdorman*
c. 825	Incorporated in Wessex

WESSEX (WEST SAXONS)

Territory in southern England, with capital at Winchester.

Kings and Queens

AD 519	*Cerdic*, son of Elesa
534	*Cynric*, son †
560	*Ceawlin* (or *Cælin*) ‡ (d. 593) overlord of the southern English, driven out
591	*Ceol* (or *Ceolric*), grandson of Cynric
597	*Ceolwulf*, brother
611 – 643	*Cynegils*, son of Ceol
c. 626	*Cwichelm*, son of Cynegils§
636	*Cuthred*, son (d. 661)
?	*Cenberht*, great-grandson of Ceawlin (d. 661)
643 – 645	*Cenwalh*, son of Cynegils§ (for 1st time) (d. 672 or 675) expelled by King Penda of Mercia
645 – 648	Interregnum
648	*Cenwalh* (for 2nd time)
672/675	*Seaxburh*, widow
673	*Cenfus*, descendant of Cynric ‖
675/676	*Æscwine*, son
678	*Centwine*, son of Cynegils, son of Ceolwulf
686(?) //	*Cædwalla*, son of Cenberht (d. 20 Apr 689) abdicated
688	*Ine*, great-great-great-grandson of Ceawlin (d. 726 or later) abdicated
726	*Æthelheard*, kinsman, subject to Mercia
740	*Cuthred*, kinsman, rebelled 752
756	*Sigeberht*, son of Sigeric (d. 757 or later) deposed

*Under Mercian overlordship
† Son in the earliest annal entries; also said to be the son of Creoda, the son of Cerdic
‡ No relationship stated in the earliest annal entries; made son of Cynric in genealogies
§ It is not certain that the same Cynegils was father of both Cwichelm and Cenwalh or that either is identical with Cynegils, son of Ceol
‖ Not given as king in the Anglo-Saxon Chronicle
// Before the accession of Cædwalla the unity of Wessex seems to have been precarious, and dating is uncertain

757	*Cynewulf*, descendant of Cerdic, subject to Mercia
786	*Beorhtric* (or *Britric*), kinsman
802	*Egbert*, great-great-great-nephew of Ine; defeated the Mercians 825 and acknowledged as overlord by Kent, Surrey, Sussex and East Anglia; conquered Mercia 829; overlord of all English kingdoms 829/830
839	*Æthelwulf* (or *Ethelwulf*), son (d. 13 Jan 858) under-king of Kent, Essex, Surrey and Sussex 825 – 839; went to Rome 855; under-king again 856 – 858
855	*Æthelbald* (or *Ethelbald*), son, hitherto under-king of south-eastern England
860	*Æthelberht* (or *Ethelbert*), brother, under-king from 858
865/6	*Æthelred* (or *Ethelred*), brother
Apr 871	*Alfred*, the Great, brother (b. 849) ruler of Wessex and Mercia, overlord of Bernicia and of Wales
Oct 899	*Edward*, the Elder, son (d. Farndon-on-Dee, Chester); annexed the Danelaw south of the Humber 917 – 918; overlord of York, Bernicia, Strathclyde, of the Scots and of Wales
17 Jul 924/5	*Athelstan*, son, King of Wessex and Mercia, ruler of York from 927
27 Oct 939	*Edmund*, half-brother (b. 921; d. Pucklechurch, Avon) lost York and north-east Midlands to the Danes 940 – 942, from 944 ruler of all England and overlord of the Scots
26 May 946 – 23 Nov 955	*Eadred*, brother (d. Frome, Somerset) lost York 948 – 954, ruler of all England 946 – 948 and from 954

For continuation see below, England.

YORK, SCANDINAVIAN KINGDOM OF

Territory in central, eastern and northern England, with the capital at York.

Kings

AD 875/6	*Halfdene* (or *Halfdan*), son of Ragnar Lothbrok, driven out of Northumbria 877 or 883
883	*Guthred* (or *Guthfrith I*), son of Harthacnut (d. 894 or 24 Aug 896)
?	*Siefred*

?	*Cnut*
c. 899 – 902	*Æthelwold* (or *Ethelwald*), son of King Æthelred of Wessex
902(?)	*Halfdan*, with his brothers, *Eowils* and *Ivar*
912/919	*Rægnald I*, great-grandson, through mother, of Ragnar Lothbrok; invaded Northumbria between 912 and 915; took York 919
921	*Sihtric Caoch* (i.e. the Blind), cousin
927	*Guthfrith* (*II*), brother
927 – 939	Kingdom of York subject to Wessex
after Oct 939	*Olaf Guthfrithson*, son of Guthfrith, conquered the north-east Midlands and regained York, also King of Dublin
941	*Olaf Sihtricson*, second cousin (for 1st time) (d. 952) expelled by Rægnald Guthfrithson
943	*Rægnald Guthfrithson*, brother of Olaf Guthfrithson; in dispute with Olaf 944; killed by King Edmund of Wessex
944 – 948	Subject to Wessex
948	*Eric Bloodaxe*, son of King Harald I Fairhair of Norway (for 1st time) (d. Stainmore, Cumbria, 954) King (Erik I) of Norway c. 940 – 942
949	*Olaf Sihtricson* (for 2nd time)
952 – 954	*Eric Bloodaxe* (for 2nd time)
954	Annexed by Wessex

ENGLAND

Kings

Anglo-Saxon and Danish

23 Nov AD 955 – 1 Oct 959	*Eadwig* (or *Edwy*), son of King Edmund of Wessex (b. before 943) from 957 ruler of Wessex only
957/1 Oct 959	*Edgar*, brother (b. 943) ruler of Mercia, King of England from 1 Oct 959
8 Jul 975	*Edward*, the Martyr, Saint, son (b. c. 962) murdered at Corfe by followers of Æthelred Unræd
18 Mar 978	*Æthelred Unræd* (i.e. No Counsel) (or *Ethelred*, the Unready)(for 1st time) (b. c. 968(?); d. 23 Apr 1016) driven out by Sweyn Forkbeard
autumn 1013 – 3 Feb 1014	*Sweyn Forkbeard*, King (Svend I) of Denmark (b. 965; d. Gainsborough, Lincolnshire)

spring 1014	*Æthelred Unræd* (for 2nd time)
Apr – 30 Nov 1016	*Edmund Ironside*, son (b. c. 990?) ceded all except Wessex to Cnut
summer/30 Nov 1016	*Cnut* (or *Canute* or *Knud*), son of Sweyn Forkbeard (b. c. 995 – 1000; d. Shaftesbury, Dorset) chosen King by the Danish fleet Feb 1014 but repulsed by Æthelred Unræd, initially king of all except Wessex, King of all England 30 Nov 1016, King of Denmark 1019, King of Norway 1028, lord of the Norse colonies, overlord of the Scots, King of Dublin(?)
12 Nov 1035	*Harthacnut* (or *Hardecanute* or *Hardeknud*), son (for 1st time) (b. c. 1018(?); d. 8 Jun 1042) titular king, absent in Denmark
1037 – 1040	*Harold I*, Harefoot, half-brother (d. Oxford 17 Mar 1040) regent from c. Nov 1035, assumed crown
Jun 1040	*Harthacnut* (for 2nd time)
8 Jun 1042 – 5 Jan 1066	*Edward*, the Confessor, Saint, son of Æthelred Unræd (b. Islip, Oxfordshire, between 1002 and 1005; d. London) canonized 1161
6 Jan – 14 Oct 1066	*Harold II*, son of Godwine, Earl of Wessex, and brother-in-law of Edward (b. c. 1020) killed at battle of Hastings
Oct – Dec 1066	*Edgar*, the Atheling, grandson of Edmund Ironside (d. c. 1125) chosen king, submitted to William I
Norman	
25 Dec 1066 – 9 Sep 1087	*William I*, the Conqueror, Duke (Guillaume II) of Normandy and Count of Maine, cousin of Edward (b. Falaise, Normandy, 1027/8; d. Rouen)
26 Sep 1087 – 2 Aug 1100	*William II Rufus*, son (b. between 1056 and 1060; d. Lyndhurst, Hampshire)
5 Aug 1100 – 1 Dec 1135	*Henry I*, brother (b. Selby, North Yorkshire, 1068; d. Lyons-la-Forêt, Normandy) Duke (Henri I) of Normandy from 28 Sep 1106
22 Dec 1135 – 25 Oct 1154*	*Stephen*, grandson (through mother) of William I (b. before 1100; d. Dover, Kent) Duke (Étienne) of Normandy 1135 – 1144

*From 2 Feb to 1 Nov 1141 Stephen was held in captivity by Matilda, daughter of Henry I (b. c. Feb 1102; d. 1167) who was elected queen 8 Apr 1141 but never crowned. Stephen was re-crowned on 25 Dec 1141.

Plantagenet

19 Dec 1154 – 6 Jul 1189*	*Henry II*, Duke (Henri II) of Normandy, Duke (Henri) of Aquitaine, Count of Poitou, Count (Henri) of Anjou, Maine and Touraine, son of Count Geoffroi IV of Anjou and Matilda, daughter of Henry I (b. Le Mans, Maine 5 Mar 1133; d. Chinon, Touraine) abdicated in Aquitaine and Poitou 1168
3 Sep 1189 – 6 Apr 1199	*Richard I*, Coeur de Lion, or the Lion-heart, Duke of Aquitaine and Count of Poitou, Count of Anjou, Maine and Touraine, Duke of Normandy, son (b. Oxford 8 Sep 1157; d. Châlus, near Limoges, Aquitaine) absent from England for most of his reign Regents: 6 Jul – 13 Aug 1189: *Ranulf de Glanville* (b. Stratford St Andrew, near Saxmundham, Suffolk; d. Oct(?) 1190) justiciar 12 Dec 1189 – Jun 1190: *Hugh du Puiset*, Bishop of Durham (b. 1125(?); d. Howden, North Humberside, 3 Mar 1195) justiciar 12 Dec 1189 – Oct 1191: *William Longchamp*, Bishop of Ely (d. Poitiers, Poitou, 31 Jan 1197) chancellor Oct 1191 – 1193: *Walter of Coutances* (French: *Gautier de Coutances*), Archbishop of Rouen (d. 16 Nov 1207) Dec(?) 1193 – 13 Mar 1194 and 12 May 1194 – 11 Jun 1198: *Hubert Walter*, Archbishop of Canterbury (d. Teynham, Kent, 13 Jul 1205) justiciar 11 Jun 1198 – 6 Apr 1199: *Geoffrey FitzPeter, Earl of Essex* (d. 2 Oct 1213) justiciar
27 May 1199 – 18/19 Oct 1216†	*John*, Lackland (or John of England), brother of Richard I (b. Oxford 24 Dec 1167; d. Newark, Nottinghamshire) Duke (Jean) of Aquitaine and Count of Poitou 1199, Count of Anjou, Maine and Touraine 1199, Duke (Jean) of Normandy 1199; French fiefs declared forfeit by King Philippe II of France 1202; lost Normandy Jun 1204, lost Maine and Anjou 1206

* On 14 Jun 1170 Henry, the king's eldest surviving son (b. 28 Feb 1155; d. 11 Jun 1183) was crowned king

†King Louis VIII of France was offered the English crown by some nobles in 1215 and entered London in May 1216, but was defeated at Lincoln May 1217 and renounced all claims to the English throne

28 Oct 1216 – 16 Nov 1272	*Henry III*, son (b. Winchester, Hampshire, 1 Oct 1207; d. London) recognized as Duke of Aquitaine* by King Louis IX of France 1258; abandoned the titles of Duke of Normandy and Count of Anjou 1259 Regent: 29 Oct 1216 – 14 May 1219: *William Marshal, Earl of Pembroke* (b. 1146(?); d. Caversham, Berkshire, 14 May 1219
20 Nov 1272 – 7 Jul 1307	*Edward I*, son (b. Westminster 17/18 Jun 1239; d. Burgh-by-Sands, Cumbria)
8 Jul 1307 – 20 Jan 1327	*Edward II*, son (b. Caernarfon, Gwynedd, 25 Apr 1284; d. Berkeley, Gloucestershire, 21 Sep 1327) deposed
25 Jan 1327 – 21 Jun 1377	*Edward III*, son (b. Windsor, Berkshire, 13 Nov 1312; d. Sheen, Richmond, London) styled himself King of France Oct 1337 – 24 Oct 1360
22 Jun 1377 – 29 Sep 1399	*Richard II*, grandson (b. Bordeaux, Guyenne, 6 Jan 1367; d. Pontefract, West Yorkshire, 14(?) Feb 1400) in captivity from 19 Aug 1399, deposed
30 Sep 1399 – 20 Mar 1413	*Henry IV*, cousin (b. Bolingbroke Castle, Lincolnshire, Apr 1366(?); d. London) previously Duke of Lancaster
21 Mar 1413	*Henry V*, son (b. Monmouth, Gwent, 16 Sep 1387(?); d. Bois de Vincennes, France)
1 Sep 1422	*Henry VI*, son (for 1st time) (b. London 6 Dec 1421; d. London 21 May 1471) deposed Regent: 5 Dec 1422 – 5 Nov 1429: *John, Duke of Bedford*, uncle (b. 20 Jun 1389; d. 14 Sep 1435)
4 Mar 1461	*Edward IV*, third cousin of Henry VI (for 1st time) (b. Rouen, in part of France then occupied by the English, 28 Apr 1422; d. Westminster 9 Apr 1483) previously Duke of York; expelled
3 Oct 1470	*Henry VI* (for 2nd time)
11 Mar 1471	*Edward IV* (for 2nd time)
9 Apr 1483	*Edward V*, son (b. London 2 Nov 1470; d. 1483) deposed
26 Jun 1483 – 22 Aug 1485	*Richard III*, uncle (b. Fotheringhay, Northamptonshire, 2 Oct 1452) Protector of the Realm 30 Apr 1483

*Kings of England continued to be dukes of Aquitaine (usually called Guyenne) until the reign of Henry VI when it was surrendered to France

Tudor

22 Aug 1485 – 21 Apr 1509	*Henry VII*, son of Edmund Tudor, Earl of Richmond,* and Margaret Beaufort, great-great-granddaughter of Edward III (b. Pembroke Castle, Dyfed, 28 Jan 1457; d. Richmond, London)

Epirus, Despotate of

Territory in southern Albania and north-western Greece.

Rulers and Despots

Angeli Dynasty

AD 1204	*Michael I Ducas*, a member of the Byzantine imperial family, ruled without the title of despot, murdered
c. 1215	*Theodore Ducas*, half-brother; probably ruled without the title of despot; conquered Thessalonica 1224 and took the title, Emperor of the Greeks, 1225; defeated and captured by Ivan Asen II, Tsar of Bulgaria, at Klokotnitsa Apr 1230
1225	*Constantine*(?), brother, appointed despot after Theodore Ducas's conquest of Thessalonica
c. 1230	*Michael II*, son of Michael I, recognized the suzerainty of the Byzantine emperor Michael VIII Palaeologus 1264
before 1268(?)	*Nicephorus I*, son
c. 1290 – 1318	*Thomas*, murdered

Orsini Dynasty

1318	*Nicholas Orsini*, of Cephalonia, nephew
1323	*John Orsini*, poisoned
1335 – 1339	*Nicephorus II*, son (for 1st time) Regent: *Anna Palaeologina*, mother
1339	Conquered by the Byzantine emperor Andronicus III and *John Angelus* installed as governor

*Edmund Tudor was a descendant in female line of Rhys ap Gruffydd, Lord of Deheubarth (see Wales)

1348	Conquered by Stefan Dušan, King of Serbia
1349	*Simeon Uroš Palaeologus*, half-brother of Stephen Dušan, Serbian governor of Epirus (b. 1327?) proclaimed himself 'Emperor of the Greeks, Serbs and all Albania' 1356
1356 – 1359	*Nicephorus II* (for 2nd time)
1359 – 1460	Various Serbians, Albanians and Italians ruled in Epirus
1460	Conquered by the Ottoman Turks

Eshnunna

Territory comprised part of present-day eastern Iraq, with the capital at Eshnunna (present-day Tell Asmar).

Kings

after 2030 BC	*Ilshu-ilia*
(?)	*Nur-akhum*
(?)	*Kirikiri*
(?)	*Bilalama*, son
(?)	*Ishar-ramashshu*
before 1940	*Usur-awassu*
(?)	*Azuzum*
(?)	*Ur-Ninmar*
(?)	*Ur-Ningizzidda*
(?)	*Ip(p)iq-Adad I*, son of Ur-Ninmar
before 1895	*Sharria*
(?)	*Belakum*, son
(?)	*Warassa*
(?)	*Ibalpiel I*
before 1860	*Ip(p)iq-Adad II*, son
before 1830	*Naram-Sin*, son, probably identical with the Assyrian king Naram-Sin
(?)	*Dadusha*, brother
c. 1784	*Ibalpiel II*, son
c. 1750	*Silli-sin*, conquered by the Babylonian king Hammurabi
(?)	*Iqish-Tishpak*
(?) – 1727	*Anni* (or *Iluni*)

Ethiopia

For Ethiopia before the 10th century see Axum (Aksum).

Emperors

Zagwe Dynasty	
AD c. 1150 – 1220	*Lalibela*
(?) – 1268	*Nakueto La'ab*
Solomonid Dynasty	
1270	*Tasfa Iyasus* (or *Yekuno Amlak*)
1285	*Solomon I* (or *Yagbe'a S(e)yon*), son
1294 – 1297	*Bahr Asgad* and *Senfa Asgad*, sons
(?)	*Hezba Ar'ed* (or *Hezba Asgad*?), brother
before 1299	*Qedma Asgad*, *Jin Asgad* and *Sab'a Asgad*, brothers
1299	*Wedem Ar'ad*, brother
1314	*'Amda S(e)yon* (or *Gabra Masqal*), son
1344	*Newaya Krestos* (or *Sayfa Ar'ed*), son
1372	*Newaya Maryam* (or *Wedem Asfare*), son
1382	*David I*, brother (d. 6 Oct 1413) abdicated
1411	*Theodore I*, son (d. 23 Jun 1414)
1414	*Isaac* (or *Gabra Masqal*), brother (d. Aug 1429)
1429	*Andrew* (d. Mar 1430)
1430	*Takla Maryam* (or *Hezba Nan*), son of David I (d. Mar 1433)
1433	*Sarwe Iyasus* (or *Mehreka Nan*), brother (d. Sep 1433)
1433	*'Amda Iyasus* (or *Badel Nan*), brother (d. Jun 1434)
1434	*Constantine I* (or *Zar'a Ya'cob*), brother (d. 26 Aug 1468)
1468	*Ba'eda Maryam I*, son (d. 8 Nov 1478)
1478	*Constantine II* (or *Alexander*), son (d. 7 May 1494)
1494	*'Amda Seyon II*, son (b. 1487; d. Nov 1494)
1494 – 1508	*Na'od* (or *'Anbasa Bazar*), brother (d. 31 Jul 1508)

Fatimids

At its greatest extent, territory comprised present-day northern Algeria, Tunisia, northern Libya, Egypt, western Saudi Arabia, Israel, Jordan, Lebanon and southern Syria, with the capital at Cairo from 973.

Caliphs

AD 900/1 – 910/11	Missionary activity by the Da'i (religious leader) Abu 'Abdallah al-Shi'i, assassinated by al-Mahdi
21 Dec 909	*al-Mahdi (Abu Muhammad 'Ubaidallah)* (b. 872/3) conquered Raqqada, conquest of Idrisids 926
4 Mar 934	*(Muhammad Abu'l-Qasim) al-Qa'im* (or *'Abd al-Rahman*), son (b. Mar/Apr 893)
18 May 946 – 19 Mar 953	*al-Mansur (Abu Tahir Isma'il)*, son (b. 914/15)
20 Mar 953 – 10 Dec 975	*al-Mu'izz li Din Allah (Abu Tamim Ma'add)*, son (b. 27 Sep 931) conquered Egypt Jun/Jul 969, entered Cairo Jun/Jul 973
12 Dec 975 – 14 Oct 996	*al-'Aziz bi'llah (Nizar Abu Mansur)*, son (b. 10 May 955)
15 Oct 996 – 13 Feb 1021	*al-Hakim bi-Amr Allah (Abu 'Ali al-Mansur)*, son (b. 13 Aug 985) conquered Hamdanids, disappeared
27 Mar 1021	*al-Zahir (Abu'l-Hasan 'Ali)*, son (b. 20 Jun 1005)
13 Jun 1036 – 29 Dec 1094	*al-Mustansir (Abu Tamim Ma'add)*, son (b. 2 Jul 1029)
Dec 1094/Jan 1095	*al-Musta'li (Abu'l-Qasim Ahmad)*, son (b. 15 Sep 1074)
8 Dec 1101	*al-'Amir (Abu 'Ali al-Mansur)*, son (b. 30 Dec 1096) assassinated
7 Oct 1130 – 10 Oct 1149	*al-Hafiz (Abu'l-Ma'mun 'Abd al-Majid)*, cousin (b. Aug/Sep 1074) ruled as regent until 7 Dec 1131
11 Oct 1149 – 16 Apr 1154	*al-Zafir (Abu'l-Mansur Isma'il)*, son (b. 23 Feb 1133) assassinated
17 Apr 1154 – 23 Jul 1160	*al-Fa'iz (Abu'l-Qasim 'Isa)*, son (b. 31 May 1149)
Jul/Aug 1160 – 6 Sep 1171	*al-'Adid (Abu Muhammad 'Abdallah)*, cousin (b. 9 May 1151; d. 13 Sep 1171) deposed
Sep 1171	Ayyubid conquest

Flanders

Territory now in East and West Flanders provinces, Belgium, and part of Nord department, France. Capital at Lille (Dutch: Rijsel).

Names are given in French with modern Dutch versions in parentheses.

Counts

House of Flanders	
c. AD 864	*Baudouin I Bras de Fer* (*Boudewijn I de IJzere*) (i.e. Iron-arm), son-in-law of King Charles II the Bald of France, who created the county for Baudouin
2 Jan (?) 879	*Baudouin* (*Boudewijn*) *II*, the Bald, son
10 Sep 918	*Arnoul* (*Arnulf*) *I*, the Old, son; ruled with his son, *Baudouin* (*Boudewijn*) *III* 958 – 1 Jan 962
27 Mar 965	*Arnoul* (*Arnulf*) *II*, grandson of Arnoul I
30 Mar 988	*Baudouin* (*Boudewijn*) *IV*, son (b. c. 980) granted fiefs (known as Imperial Flanders) by Holy Roman Emperor Heinrich II
30 May 1035	*Baudouin V de Lille* (*Boudewijn V van Rijsel*), son (b. c. 1012) administered France as guardian for King Philippe I 1060 – 1066
1 Sep 1067	*Baudouin* (*Boudewijn*) *VI*, Count (Baudouin I) of Hainaut, son (b. c. 1030)
17 Jul 1070	*Arnoul* (*Arnulf*) *III*, the Unlucky (b. c. 1055) at the same time Count (Arnoul) of Hainaut; ruled under the guardianship of his mother, *Richilde* (*Richildis*) (d. 18 Mar 1086)
22 Feb 1071	*Robert* (*Robrecht*) *I*, the Frisian, uncle of Arnoul III (d. 12/13 Oct 1093) departed on crusade
1086 – 1 or 2 (?) Oct 1111	*Robert* (*Robrecht*) *II*, son; ruling initially as regent during his father's absence
6 Oct 1111	*Baudouin VII à la Hache* (*Boudewijn VII met het Hapken*) (i.e. with the Axe), son (b. 1093)
17 Jun 1119 – 2 Mar 1127	*Charles* (*Karel*), the Good, cousin, son of King Knud II of Denmark (b. Denmark c. 1083; d. (assassinated) Brugge)
23 Mar 1127 – 1128	*Guillaume* (*Willem*) *Clito*, cousin, son of Duke Robert II of Normandy (d. 27 or 28 Jul 1128) deposed
House of Alsace	
Mar 1128	*Thierry d'Alsace* (*Diederik van de Elzas*), cousin of

	Robert II, son of Duke Thierry II of Upper Lorraine (d. 4 (or 17) Jan 1168); with (from 12 May 1157) his son, *Philippe I d'Alsace* (*Filips I van de Elzas*) (d. 1 Jun 1191) Count of Vermandois 1159, who ruled alone after his father's death
House of Hainaut	
1 Jun 1191	*Marguerite* (*Margareta*), sister of Philippe (d. 15 Nov 1194); with her husband, *Baudouin* (*Boudewijn*) *VIII*, Count (Baudouin V) of Hainaut (b. 1150; d. 18 Dec 1195)
15 Nov 1194	*Baudouin IX de Constantinople* (*Boudewijn IX van Constantinopel*), son (b. 1172) Count (Baudouin VI) of Hainaut 18 Dec 1195, departed on Fourth Crusade Apr 1202, Emperor (Baudouin I) of Constantinople 9 May 1204, captured by Tsar Kaloyan of Bulgaria at the Battle of Adrianople Mar 1205 and later killed
c. 14 Apr 1205	*Jeanne de Constantinople* (*Johanna van Constantinopel*), daughter (b. 1200) at the same time Countess of Hainaut and of Namur; ruled initially under the guardianship of King *Philippe II Auguste* of France, then (from Jan 1212) with her first husband, *Ferrand* (*Ferrand*), son of King Sancho I of Portugal (d. 27 (or 29) Jul 1233), then (from Dec 1237) with her second husband, *Thomas* (*Thomas*), son of Count Thomas I of Savoy (d. 1 Feb 1259)
5 Dec 1244	*Marguerite de Constantinople* (*Margareta van Constantinopel*), sister of Jeanne (b. 1202; d. 10 Feb 1280) at the same time Countess of Hainaut; with (from Oct 1246) her son, *Guillaume de* (*Willem van*) *Dampierre* (b. 1225; d. 5 May 1251); abdicated
*House of Dampierre**	
29 Dec 1278	*Gui de* (*Gwij* (or *Gwijde*) *van*) *Dampierre*, Count of Namur, son of Marguerite (b. 1226 or 1227) taken

*Marguerite married her first husband, Bouchard d'Avesnes (d. 1244), before 23 Jul 1212 and had two sons by him. However, he was an ordained priest and so the marriage was void. The sons were legitimized by Holy Roman Emperor Heinrich II in 1243. Marguerite married Guillaume de Dampierre 1223 and had a son. King Louis IX of France and a papal legate, as arbitrators, decided in 1246 that Hainaut should go to the Avesnes children and Flanders to the Dampierres

	prisoner during French invasion of Flanders and died in prison shortly before French recognition of Flemish independence by Treaty of Athis-sur-Orge
7 Mar 1305	*Robert III de* (*Robrecht III van*) *Bethune*, Count of Nevers, son (b. 1247)
17 Sep 1322	*Louis I de* (*Lodewijk I van*) *Nevers* (or *Crécy*), Count of Nevers, grandson (b. c. 1304; d. Crécy, France) Count of Rethel after 1 Apr 1325
25 Aug 1346	*Louis II de* (*Lodewijk II van*) *Mâle* (b. 29 Nov 1330) at the same time Count of Nevers and Rethel; Count of Artois and of Franche-Comté (the County of Burgundy) 9 May 1382
House of Burgundy	
30 Jan 1384	*Marguerite de* (*Margareta van*) *Mâle* (or *Flandres/ Vlaanderen*), daughter (b. 13 Apr 1350; d. 16 Mar 1405) at the same time Countess of Artois and Franche-Comté, Countess of Nevers and Rethel 30 Jan 1384 – 27 Apr 1404; Duchess of Brabant 7 May 1404; ruled with her second husband, *Philippe* (*Filips*) *II*, the Bold, Duke of Burgundy, son of King Jean II of France (b. Pontoise (now in Val d'Oise department), France, 17 Jan 1342; d. Hal, Brabant, 27 Apr 1404) regent of France 1382 – 1388 and 1392 – 27 Apr 1404
16 Mar 1405	County of Flanders thenceforth held by the dukes of Burgundy

Florence

The Medici

Although the Medici established hereditary power as the heads of Florence, they had no title or constitutional basis for their rule.

AD 1434	*Cosimo*, the Elder, son of Giovanni di Bicci de' Medici (b. 1389; d. Careggi) returned to Florence from exile in 1434, the traditional date for the beginning of the Medici 'principate'; in 1465 the signoria granted him the posthumous title of Pater Patriae
1 Aug 1464	*Piero*, the Gouty, son (b. 1416)
2 Dec 1469 – 9 Apr 1492	*Lorenzo*, the Magnificient, son (b. 1 Jan 1449; d. Careggi)

For the continuation of the Medici in Volume 2, see Tuscany.

Foix

Territory now in Ariège department, France.

Counts

AD 1012	*Bernard Roger*, son of Roger I, Count of Carcassonne; was given the territory of Foix by his father and styled himself Count of Foix
1038	*Roger I*, son
1064	*Pierre*, brother
1070	*Roger II*, son
1125	*Roger III*, son
1149	*Roger Bernard I*, son
1188	*Raimond Roger*, son
1223	*Roger Bernard II*, son
1241	*Roger IV*, son
1265	*Roger Bernard III*, son, Viscount of Castellbò in Catalonia 1284, Seigneur of Béarn 1290
1302	*Gaston I*, son
1315	*Gaston II*, son
1343 – 1 Aug 1391	*Gaston III Phébus*, son (b. 1331; d. Orthez) refused to

	do homage for Béarn to King Jean II of France
1391	*Mathieu de Castelbon*, great-nephew of Gaston II, claimed the Aragonese throne at the death of Juan II 1395
1398	*Isabelle*, sister (d. 1426) ruled with her husband, *Archambault de Grailly* (d. 1412)
1412	*Jean de Grailly*, son
1436	*Gaston IV*, son (d. Jul 1472) peer of France 1458, claimed the throne of Navarre
1470	*François-Phébus*, son, King of Navarre 1479
1483 – 1517	*Catherine*, sister, Queen of Navarre 1483 – 1512; ruled with her husband, *Jean*, Viscount of Tartas

France

For rulers of France before 843, see the Kingdom of the Franks.

Kings

Carolingians

AD 843 – 6 Oct 877	*Charles II*,* the Bald, son of Holy Roman Emperor Ludwig I the Pious (b. Frankfurt am Main 13 Jun 823; d. Brides-les-Bains) received Francia Occidentalis (the Kingdom of the West Franks) by the Treaty of Verdun 843; defeated Pippin (Pépin) II and incorporated Aquitaine into his kingdom Sep 852; annexed Lotharingia (Lorraine) 9 Sep 869, but partitioned it with Ludwig the German, King of the East Franks, by the Treaty of Meerssen 8 Aug 870; Holy Roman Emperor 25 Dec 875; King of the Lombards 876
877 – 10 Apr 879	*Louis II*,† the Stammerer, son (b. 846; d. Compiègne) King of Aquitaine under his father's tutelage 866, King of the West Franks
879 – 5 Aug 882	*Louis III*, son (b. 864) King of the West Franks
879 – 12 Dec 884	*Carloman*, brother, King of the West Franks, ruled alone after 5 Aug 882

*Numeration begins with Karl (Charles) I (i.e. Charlemagne), King of the Franks
†Numeration begins with Ludwig (Louis) I, the Pious, King of the Franks

884 – 887	*Charles (III)*, the Fat, King of Swabia and of the East Franks, son of Ludwig the German, King of the East Franks (b. 839; d. Neidingen, Germany, 13 Jan 888) received the remaining West Frankish portion of Lorraine from Louis III and Carloman 879, King of the Lombards 880, Holy Roman Emperor and King of the West Franks 884; deposed
Capetians	
888 – 1 Jan 898	*Eudes*, son of Robert the Strong, Count of Paris (d. La Fère-sur-Oise) King of the West Franks
Carolingians (restored)	
Jan 893/1 Jan 898 – 923	*Charles III*, the Simple, half-brother of Carloman (b. 17 Sep 879; d. (in prison) Péronne 7 Oct 929) elected king Jan 893 in rivalry with Eudes but not fully recognized until Eudes's death; imprisoned by his rivals, Robert I* and Raoul
Capetians (restored)	
13 Jul 923 – 14/15 Jan 936	*Raoul* (or *Rodolphe*), Duke of Burgundy, son-in-law of Robert I,* elected king in rivalry with Charles III and ruled after Charles III's imprisonment
Carolingians (restored)	
Jun 936 – 10 Sep 954	*Louis IV d'Outremer*, son of Charles III the Simple (b. c. 921; d. Reims) recalled from exile in England by Hugues the Great (son of Robert I) and elected king, accepted the homage of Duke Giselbert of Lorraine 939
954 – 2 Mar 986	*Lothaire*, son (b. 941)
986 – 21/22 May 987	*Louis V*, le Fainéant (i.e. Do-nothing), son (b. 967) crowned co-king with his father 8 Jun 979
Capetians, of the direct line	
987 – 24 Oct 996	*Hugues Capet*, Duke of the Franks and Count of Paris, son of Hugues the Great (b. c. 938; d. Paris) defeated an attempt by Lothaire's brother, Duke Charles of Lower Lorraine, to assert his right to the throne 991

*29 Jun 922 – 15 Jun 923 — *Robert I*, brother of Eudes (b. c. 865; d. near Soissons) elected king in rivalry with Charles III, killed in battle

996 – 20 Jul 1031	*Robert II*, the Pious, son (b. Orléans, c. 970) elected co-king with his father Dec 987; annexed Burgundy 1003 – 1006; ruled with his son, *Hugues* (b. 1007; d. 17 Apr 1025)
1031 – 4 Aug 1060	*Henri I*, son (b. 1008; d. Vitry-aux-Loges) Duke (Henri II) of Burgundy 1015 – 1031, crowned co-king with his father 1026
1060 – 29/30 Jul 1108	*Philippe I*, son (b. 1053) crowned co-king with his father 23 May 1059 Regent: 1060 – 1066: Count *Baudouin V de Lille* of Flanders (b. c. 1012; d. 1 Sep 1067)
1108 – 1 Aug 1137	*Louis VI*, the Fat, son (b. 1081) ruled as co-king with his father from c. 1098
1137 – 18 Sep 1180	*Louis VII*, the Young, son (b. 1120; d. Paris) ruled as co-king with his father from 1131; departed on crusade Jun 1147 and returned Nov 1149; lost Aquitaine to King Henry II of England Regent: Jun 1147 – Nov 1149: *Suger*, abbot of St. Denis
1180 – 14 Jul 1223	*Philippe II Auguste*, son (b. Paris 21 Aug 1165; d. Nantes) ruled as co-king with his father from Nov 1179; received homage for Aquitaine from Richard, son of King Henry II of England, Nov 1188; departed on crusade 1190 and returned to France 1191; declared King John I of England's fiefs forfeit 1202; captured Rouen Jun 1204, took Anjou, Touraine and Poitou 1206; guardian of Brittany 1206 – 1212
1223 – 8 Nov 1226	*Louis VIII*, the Lionheart, son (b. Paris 5 Sep 1187; d. Montpensier) offered the English crown 1215, entered London May 1216, defeated at Lincoln May 1217 and renounced all claims to the English throne
1226 – 25 Aug 1270	*Louis IX*, Saint, son (b. Poissy 25 Apr 1214; d. Tunis) acquired the county of Mâcon 1239, recognized King Henry III of England as Duke of Aquitaine 1258,* on crusade Aug 1248 – Nov 1252 and from 1 Jul 1270; canonized 11 Aug 1297 Regents: 1226 – 1242: *Blanche de Castile*, mother (for 1st time) (b. 1188; d. 27 Nov 1252)

*In return, Henry III renounced English claims to Normandy, Maine, Anjou, Poitou and Touraine

	Aug 1248 – 27 Nov 1252: *Blanche de Castile* (for 2nd time) 1 Jul – 25 Aug 1270: *Mathieu de Vendôme*, abbot of St. Denis
1270 – 5 Oct 1285	*Philippe III*, the Bold, son (b. 30 Apr 1245; d. Perpignan) annexed Poitou and Toulouse Aug 1271, regent in Navarre 1274
1285 – 29 Oct 1314	*Philippe IV*, the Fair, son (b. Fontainebleau 1268; d. Fontainebleau) King (Philippe I) of Navarre with his wife, Jeanne I, 1285 – 1305
1314 – 5 Jun 1316	*Louis X*, the Stubborn, son (b. Paris 4 Oct 1289; d. Vincennes) King (Louis) of Navarre 1305 – 1314
Nov 1316	*Jean I*, son (b. 13/14 Nov 1316; d. 19 Nov 1316)
1316 – 3 Jan 1322	*Philippe V*, the Tall, Count of Poitou, King (Philippe II) of Navarre, uncle (b. c. 1293)
1322 – 1 Feb 1328	*Charles IV*, the Fair, Count of La Marche, brother (b. 1294; d. Vincennes) at the same time King (Charles I) of Navarre

Capetians, of the House of Valois

1328 – 22 Aug 1350	*Philippe VI*, Count of Valois, Anjou and Maine, nephew, son of Charles, Count of Valois (b. 1293) confiscated Guyenne from King Edward III of England* May 1337, lost Calais Aug 1347
1350 – 19 Sep 1356	*Jean II*, the Good, son (b. 26 Apr 1319; d. London 8 Apr 1364) taken prisoner by the English at the battle of Poitiers 19 Sep 1356, released Dec 1360
1356 – 16 Sep 1380	*Charles V*, the Wise, son (b. Vincennes 21 Jan 1338; d. Beauté-sur-Marne) received the dauphiné of Viennois 1349, assumed the government with the title of king's lieutenant on Jean II's imprisonment
1380	*Charles VI*, the Mad, son (b. Paris 3 Dec 1368; d. Paris 21 Oct 1422) became insane 1392 Regents: 1380 – spring 1382: Duke *Louis I* of Anjou, uncle (b. Vincennes 23 Jul 1339; d. Bisceglie 21 Sep 1384) spring 1382 – 1388: Duke *Philippe II* of Burgundy, uncle of Charles VI (for 1st time) (b. 17 Jan 1342; d. Hal, Brabant, 27 Apr 1404) 1392 – 27 Apr 1404: *Philippe II* (for 2nd time)

*Edward III styled himself King of France from Oct 1337 until 24 Oct 1360

14 Jun 1417/Nov 1422 – 22 Jul 1461	*Charles VII*, son of Charles VI (b. Paris 22 Feb 1403; d. Mehun-sur-Yèvre) became dauphin 5 Apr 1417, appointed lieutenant of the realm 14 Jun 1417, assumed the title of regent 1418, crowned king Nov 1422, recovered Normandy 1450 and Guyenne 1453
1461 – 30 Aug 1483	*Louis XI*, son (b. Bourges 3 Jul 1423; d. Plessis-les-Tours) arrested by Duke Charles of Burgundy at Péronne Oct 1468; retained suzerainty over Boulonnais, Picardy and Burgundy, and possession of the Franche-Comté and Artois by the Treaty of Arras 1482; annexed Anjou 1471, inherited Maine and Provence 1481
1483 – 7 Apr 1498	*Charles VIII*, son (b. Amboise 30 Jun 1470; d. Amboise) Duke Consort of Brittany 1491 – 1498, King of Naples 12 May 1495 Regents: 1483 – 1492: *Anne*, *Dame de Beaujeu*, sister (b. 1461; d. 14 Nov 1522) and her husband, Duke *Pierre II* of Bourbon (b. 1 Dec 1438; d. 10 Oct 1503)

Franks, Kingdom of the

In about AD 460 the Franks occupied territory between the Rhine and Somme rivers with a boundary running southwest to northeast from Cambrai to west of Cologne. The kingdom rapidly expanded until Charlemagne (d. 814) ruled over nearly all of continental west and central Europe apart from Iberia beyond the Ebro, southern Italy and Scandinavia.

Names are given in modern German renderings: the French versions are: Bathilda, Bathilde; Berchar, Berthaire; Charibert, Caribert; Childebert, Childebert; Childerich, Childéric; Chilperich, Chilpéric; Chlodomer, Clodomir; Chlodowech, Chlodovech;* Chlothar, Clotaire; Chunibert, Cunibert; Dagobert, Dagobert; Ebroin, Ébroïn or Évroin; Fredegunda, Frédégonde; Grimoald, Grimoald; Gunthchramn, Guntram or Gontran; Himnechilds, Hymnégilde; Karlmann, Carloman; Lothar, Lothaire; Ludwig, Louis; Merowech, Mérovée; Pippin, Pépin; Ragenfrid, Rainfroi; Sigibert, Sigebert; Theudebald, Théodebald; Theudebert, Théodebert or Thibert; Theuderich, Thierri or Théodoric; Wulfoald, Gouffaud.

*However, the name Clovis is usually used in both French and German

Kings

Merovingians

c. AD 457	*Childerich I*, son of Merowech; King of the Salian Franks with his capital at Tournai; extended territory to southwest and northeast to include Cologne, Mainz and Metz
481 or 482 – 27 Nov 511	*Clovis* (or *Chlodowech* or *Chlodwig*) *I*, son (b. 466; d. Paris) conquered the territory of the Roman dux Syagrius and most of the kingdom of the Visigoths, moved capital to Paris
511	Kingdom divided between the four sons of Clovis I: Theuderic I, Chlodomer, Childebert I and Chlothar I

Kings of Metz

511	*Theuderich I*, son of Clovis I
534	*Theudebert I*, son; took part in conquest of Burgundy 535 and ruled over Provence after its surrender by the Ostrogoths 537
548	*Theudebald*, son
555	Theudebald had no sons and on his death his territory was reunited with the rest of the Kingdom of the Franks under his great-uncle, Chlothar I

King of Orléans

511	*Chlodomer*, son of Clovis I (b. 495)
524	On Chlodomer's death, his territory was divided between his brothers, Childebert I and Chlothar I

King of Paris

511 – 23 Dec 558	*Childebert I*, son of Clovis I (b. c. 495) ruled part of the kingdom of Orléans from 524, ruled part of Burgundy after its conquest 535
558	Childebert I had no sons and on his death his territory was taken by his brother, Chlothar I

King of Soissons (later, of the Franks)

511 – Nov or Dec 561	*Chlothar I*, son of Clovis I (b. c. 497; d. Compiègne) conquered the kingdom of the Thuringians 531, ruled

	part of Burgundy after its conquest 535, inherited or annexed the kingdoms of Metz, Orléans and Paris so that he was sole ruler of the Kingdom of the Franks after 558
561	Kingdom divided between the four sons of Chlothar I: Charibert I, Sigibert I, Gunthchramn and Chilperich I

King of Paris

561 – Nov or Dec 567	*Charibert I*, son of Chlothar I (d. Paris)
567	Territory divided between Sigibert I and Chilperich I

Kings of Metz (Austrasia after 575)

561	*Sigibert I*, son of Chlothar I (b. c. 535) ruled part of the kingdom of Paris from 567, assassinated
Dec 575 – Dec 595	*Childebert II*, son (b. 571) King of Burgundy 593
595 or 596	*Theudebert II*, son (b. 586) deposed and killed
612	Austrasia annexed by Theuderich II, King of Burgundy

Kings of Orléans and Burgundy (Burgundy after 593)

561 – 28 Mar 592	*Gunthchramn*, son of Chlothar I (d. Paris)
592 – Dec 595	*Childebert II*, King of Austrasia, nephew and adopted son (b. 571)
595 or 596	*Theuderich II*, son (b. 587) annexed Austrasia 612
613	*Sigibert II*, son, executed by Chlothar II
613	Burgundy and Austrasia annexed by Chlothar II, King of Neustria

Kings of Soissons (Neustria after 584), Kings of the Franks after 613

561 – Sep or Oct 584	*Chilperich I*, son of Chlothar I (b. 539; d. (assassinated) Chelles) ruled part of the kingdom of Paris from 567
584 – 4 Jan 629	*Chlothar II*, son (b. 584; d. Paris) annexed the kingdoms of Austrasia and Burgundy to become sole king of the Franks 613; established the office of *major domus* (head of the household, often called 'mayor of the palace') in Austrasia, Burgundy and Neustria: appointed his son *Dagobert I* to rule in Austrasia 623

	Regent: 584 – 597: *Fredegunda*, mother (d. 597)
629 – Jan 639	*Dagobert I*, son of Chlothar II; King of Austrasia 623, forced the Neustrians to accept him as sole king of the Franks 629, appointed his brother *Charibert II* (d. (assassinated) 631 or 632) as King of Aquitaine and his son *Sigibert III* (b. 630 or 631; d. 1 Feb 656) as King of Austrasia 634
639	Kingdom divided between the sons of Dagobert I: Sigibert III and Clovis II

Kings of Austrasia (eastern dominions)

633/4 – 1 Feb 656	*Sigibert III*, son of Dagobert I (b. 630/1) Regents: 633/4 – 639: *Adalgisile*, a duke, and *Chunibert*, bishop of Cologne
656	*Dagobert II*, son (for 1st time) (b. 652; d. (assassinated) 678) deposed by Grimoald, Carolingian *major domus*
660/1	*Childebert III*, son of Grimoald, for a few months
660/1 – 662	Period of anarchy
662 – 10 Sep/15 Nov 675	*Childerich II*, son of Clovis II (b. 649; d. (assassinated) near Chelles) ruled under the tutelage of *Wulfoald*, *major domus*, and his aunt, *Himnechildis*; King of Neustria and Burgundy 673
675	*Clovis* (or *Chlodowech*), nephew(?); King of Austrasia, Neustria and Burgundy; deposed
676 – 678	*Dagobert II* (for 2nd time)
679 – 691	*Theuderich III*, son of Clovis II; King of Neustria and Burgundy 673, 675 and 676 – 691
691 – 718	Rule by the Carolingian *majores domus*
718 – 719	*Chlothar IV*, son of Theuderich III(?), placed on the throne by the Carolingian *major domus*, Karl Martell
719	Reunited with Neustria under King Chilperich II (see below)

Kings of Neustria and Burgundy (western dominions)

639	*Clovis* (or *Chlodowech*) *II*, son of Dagobert I (b. 634)
657 – 10/11 Mar 673	*Chlothar III*, son (b. 654) Regent: 657 – 664: *Bathilda*, mother

673	*Theuderich III*, brother of Chlothar III (for 1st time) (d. 691) placed on the throne by the *major domus*, Ebroin; King of Austrasia 679 – 691; deposed
673	*Childerich II*, brother (see Kings of Austrasia)
675	*Theuderich III* (for 2nd time) deposed
675	*Clovis* (see Kings of Austrasia)
676	*Theuderich III* (for 3rd time)
691	*Clovis* (or *Chlodowech*) *III*, son
694/5 – 14 Apr 711	*Childebert III*, brother (b. c. 683) placed on the throne by the Carolingian *major domus*, Pippin of Herstal
711	*Dagobert III*, son
715 – 716	*Chilperich II*, son of Childerich II(?) (b. c. 675; d. Soissons 721) placed on the throne by the *major domus*, Ragenfrid; deposed by the Carolingian *major domus* of Austrasia, Karl Martell

Kings of the Franks

719	*Chilperich II* (see Kings of Neustria and Burgundy) restored by Karl Martell (see below)
721 – 737	*Theuderich IV*, son of Dagobert III
737 – 743	Throne vacant
743 – 751/2	*Childerich III*, son of Theuderic IV(?) (d. near Saint Omer 755) placed on the throne by Pippin the Short and Karlmann, sons of Karl Martell (see below), deposed and confined in the monastery of Sithiu at the coronation of Pippin

Carolingian Majores Domus (ruling with the Merovingians as nominal kings)

(?)	*Pippin*, the Old, of Landen, *major domus* for Austrasia under Clotaire II
c. 640 – 662	*Grimoald*, son, *major domus* for Austrasia; deposed Dagobert II and placed Childebert III on the throne of Austrasia 660/1; assassinated
c. 676 – 16 Dec 714	*Pippin (II)*, of Herstal, nephew (b. c. 635) *major domus* for Austrasia; defeated the Neustrian *major domus*, Berchar, 687 and became effective ruler of the whole Frankish kingdom
717 – 22 Oct 741	*Karl Martell* (i.e. the Hammer) (known in English and French as *Charles Martel*) illegitimate son (b. c. 688; d. Quierzy-sur-Oise) defeated the Neustrians to secure

	office as *major domus* for Austrasia; effective ruler of the whole Frankish kingdom by 725
741 – 747	*Karlmann*, son (d. 17 Aug 755) ruled over Austrasia, Swabia and Thuringia; retired to a monastery; ruled with his brother, *Pippin*, the Short (see Carolingian Kings), as *major domus* for Neustria

Carolingian Kings

31 Oct 751/23 Jan 752 – 24 Sep 768	*Pippin (III)*, the Short, son of Karl Martell (b. c. 715; d. Saint-Denis) *major domus* for Neustria 741, *major domus* for the whole kingdom 747, deposed Childerich III 751/2 and was crowned King of the Franks
Sep 768 – 4 Dec 771	*Karlmann*, son; succeeded with his brother, Karl (see below), ruling Burgundy and Austrasia
Sep 768 – 28 Jan 814	*Karl*, the Great (Latin: *Carolus Magnus*; known in English and French as *Charlemagne*), brother (b. 2 Apr 747; d. Aachen) ruled alone as King of the Franks after 771, King of the Lombards Jul 774, Holy Roman Emperor 25 Dec 800
Jan 814 – 20 Jun 840	*Ludwig I*, the Pious, son (b. Chasseneuil, France, Aug 778; d. Petersaue, Germany) ruled in Aquitaine 781 – 814, crowned co-emperor and heir 11 Sep 813, Holy Roman Emperor 28 Oct 816*
840 – 843	Period of continuous warfare between the sons of Ludwig I over the division of the kingdom
843	Dispute resolved by the Treaty of Verdun: Ludwig the German received Francia Orientalis, the kingdom of the East Franks (see Holy Roman Empire); Karl (Charles) II the Bald received Francia Occidentalis, the kingdom of the West Franks (see France);

*Jul 814 – 13 Dec 838	*Pippin I*, son of Ludwig I (b. c. 803) appointed to rule over Aquitaine by his father and crowned as king 817, deposed for rebellion 832, restored 834
839 – Sep 852	*Pippin II*, son (b. c. 825; d. (in prison) Senlis after 864) proclaimed king of Aquitaine by the populace in defiance of Ludwig I's appointment of Karl (Charles) the Bald; defeated Charles in Angoumois 14 Jun 844, was formally granted Aquitaine 845; deposed
Sep 852	Aquitaine incorporated into the Kingdom of the West Franks (see France)

Lothar I received the imperial title and Francia Media, the Middle Kingdom (see below)

King of the Middle Kingdom (Francia Media)

Francia Media extended from the North Sea between the rivers Schelde and Weser to the Mediterranean, including Provence and most of Burgundy

843 – Sep 855 — *Lothar I*, King of the Lombards, son of King Ludwig I the Pious of the Franks (b. 795; d. Prüm 29 Sep 855) King of Bavaria c. 814, crowned co-emperor 817, deposed by his father 830, sole emperor for a short time 833 – 834 but after his father's restoration his rule was limited to Italy; after his father's death he attempted to assert suzerainty over his brothers, Charles II the Bald and Ludwig the German, but was defeated by them at the battle of Fontenoy 25 Jun 841, received Francia Media and the title of Emperor by the treaty of Verdun 843; appointed his eldest son, Ludwig II, to rule in Italy 844; divided Francia Media between his two younger sons Sep 855 and retired to a monastery

Sep 855 — *Lothar II*, son (b. c. 835; d. Piacenza, Italy, 8 Aug 869) King of Lorraine

Karl, brother (b. c. 845; d. 24 Jan 863) King of Provence; kingdom divided between his brothers at his death

Fulani Emirates

For the Fulani emirates of Kano, Katsina and Nupe see Hausa States.

GWANDU

Capital of the western part of the empire, the territory of which is now in north-western Nigeria.

Emirs

AD 1808	*Abdullahi dan Fodio*, brother of Usman, the first Sarkin Musulmi Shehu (b. 1756)
1828	*Muhamman*, son
1833	*Halilu*, brother
1858	*Haliru*, brother
1860	*Aliyu*, brother
1864	*Abdulkadiri*, brother
1868	*Almustafa*, nephew
1875	*Hanufi*, cousin
1876	*Maliki*, cousin
1888	*Umaru Bakatara*, cousin
1897	*Abdullahi Bayero*, cousin
1898	*Bayero Aliyu*, cousin
1903	Came under control of British protectorate of Northern Nigeria
1903	*Muhammadu*, brother
1906	*Haliru*, great nephew of Abdulkadiri
1915	*Muhammadu Bashiru*, son
1918 – 1938	*Usman*, brother
1 Oct 1960	Nigeria became independent, see Volume 3

SOKOTO

Capital of the eastern part of the empire, the territory of which is now in north-western Nigeria.

Sultans

1817	*Muhammadu Bello* (or *Mai Wurno*), son of the first Sarkin Musulmi Shehu Usman
1837	*Abubakar Atiku* (or *Mai Katuru*), brother
1842	*Aliyu Babba* (or *Mai Cinaka*), nephew
1859	*Ahmadu Atiku* or *Zaruka* (or *Mai Cimola*), cousin
1866	*Aliyu Karami*, cousin
1867	*Ahmadu Rufai*, uncle
1873	*Abubakar Atiku na Rabah*, nephew
1877	*Mu'azu Ahmadu*, brother
1881	*Umaru*, nephew
1891 – 9 Oct 1902	*Abdurrahman* (or *Danyen Kasko*), brother of Ahmadu Atiku
12 Oct 1902 – 1903	*Muhammadu Attahiru I*, nephew (d. 27 Jul 1903)
1903	Defeated by British and incorporated into protectorate of Northern Nigeria
1903	*Muhammadu Attahiru II*, brother of Umaru
1915	*Muhammadu* (or *Mai Turare*), brother of Muhammadu Attahiru I
1924	*Muhammadu*, son
1930	*Hassan*, son of Mu'adu Ahmadu
from 1938	*(Alhaji Sir) Abubakar III*, nephew (b. Denge District, Sokoto Division, 15 Mar 1903)
1 Oct 1960	Nigeria became independent, see Volume 3

Fung Kingdom of Sennar

Territory comprised part of present-day eastern Sudan, with the capital at Old Sennar.

Kings or Sultans

AD 1504	*'Amara Dunqas ibn 'Adlan*, converted to Islam
c. 1534	*Nayil*, son
c. 1551	*'Abd al-Qadir I ibn 'Amara*, brother
c. 1558	*'Amara II ibn Nayil*, nephew, deposed
c. 1569	*Dakin ibn Nayil*, brother
c. 1586	*Dawra*, son, deposed
c. 1588	*Tayyib* (or *Tabl*) *ibn 'Abd al-Qadir*, son of Abd al-Qadir I
c. 1592	*Unsa I*, son, deposed
c. 1604	*'Abd al-Qadir II*, son, deposed Dec 1606
1606	*'Adlan ibn Unsa*, brother, deposed
c. 1611	*Badi I ibn 'Abd al-Qadir*, nephew
c. 1616	*Rubat I*
c. 1645	*Badi II* (d. 28 Dec 1680)
1680	*Unsa II ibn Nasir ibn Rubat*, grandson of Rubat I
6 Jun 1692	*Badi III* (b. c. 1680)
13 Apr 1716	*Unsa III*, son, deposed
8 Jun 1720	*Nul* (d. c. May 1723)
8 Jul 1724 – 27 Mar 1762	*Badi IV*, son, deposed
29 Mar 1762 – 26 Dec 1769	*Nasir*, son, deposed
1769 – c. 1772	*Isma'il*, deposed and exiled
1788/9	Increasing usurpation of power by officials, disintegration of kingdom and collapse into anarchy, finally extinguished in 19th century

Galatia

Territory comprised part of present-day central Turkey.

Kings (appointed by the Roman senate)

c. 64 BC	*Deiotarus I*, tetrarch of the Tolistobogii in western Galatia, recognized by the Roman senate
58	*Brogitarus*
36 – 25	*Amyntas*, a Galatian officer under the Roman commanders Brutus and Cassius, appointed by the Roman triumvir Mark Antony and later confirmed by the Roman triumvir Octavian
25	Incorporated into the Roman province of Galatia

Galicia and Volhynia

Dukes of Przemyśl and Halich (Galicia)

AD (?)	*Rostislav Vladimirovich*, grandson of Yaroslav the Wise, Grand Duke of Kiev (b. c. 1045; d. 3 Feb 1067), Duke of Przemyśl; also Duke of Vladimir (Volhynia) 1059 – 1064
?	?
c. 1084 – 1092	*Rurik*, son, Duke of Przemyśl
c. 1084 – 19 Mar 1094	*Volodar*, brother, Duke of Zvenigorod c. 1084, Duke of Przemyśl 1092
c. 1084 – 28 Feb (?) 1124	*Vasilko*, brother (b. c. 1067), Duke of Terebovlya (Polish: Trębowla), Province of Halich
1124 – 1141	*Ivan*, son, Duke of Halich
1124 – 1127	*Yury*, brother, Duke of Terebovlya
1124/5 – 1128	*Rostislav*, son of Volodar, Duke of Przemyśl
1128 – 1144	*Ivan Berladnik*, son (d. 1161), Duke of Zvenigorod
1128 – 1153	*Vladimirko*, uncle, Duke of Przemyśl 1128, Duke of the whole of Halich 1141
1153/4 – 1 Oct 1187	*Yaroslav Osmomysl*, son, Duke of Halich, including Przemyśl

1187 – 1188	*Vladimir*, son (d. c. 1199), Duke of Przemyśl
1187	*Oleg*, illegitimate son of Yaroslav Osmomysl (for 1st time) (d. 1187 or 1189), Duke of Halich, driven out by the boyars
1187	*Vladimir* (for 1st time) (see above), Duke of Halich
1187(?)	*Oleg* (for 2nd time), restored by Kazimierz, King of Poland
1187(?)	*Vladimir* (for 2nd time), expelled by Roman Mstislavich, Duke of Vladimir, Volhynia
1188/9	*Andrei*, son of King Béla III of Hungary who installed him as duke
1189	*Vladimir* (for 3rd time), restored by Kazimierz as agent of the Holy Roman Emperor Friedrich I
1199	Duchies of Halich and Vladimir united

Dukes of Vladimir* (Volhynia)

1059 – 1064	*Rostislav Vladimirovich* (see above)
?	?
1112 – 1118	*Yaroslav*, nephew (d. May 1123)
1125	*Mstislav I*, the Great, son of Vladimir Monomakh (b. 1076) also Grand Duke of Kiev
14 Apr 1132	*Vsevolod*, son (d. 11 Feb 1136 or 1137)
1146 – 13 Nov 1154	*Izyaslav*, brother (b. 1096) Grand Duke of Kiev 1146 – 1149
1147 – 1154	*Svyatopolk*, brother
1154	*Mstislav II*, son of Yaroslav (d. 13 Aug 1172, or 1170?) Grand Duke of Kiev 1167 – 1169
1170	*Roman*, son (for 1st time) (b. after 1160; d. 12 Jun 1205)
1188	*Vsevolod*, brother (d. Apr 1195)
1189	*Roman* (for 2nd time)
1199	Duchy of Vladimir united with Halich

Dukes of Halich-Vladimir

1199	*Roman*, previously Duke of Vladimir (see above)
19 Jun 1205	*Daniil*, son (for 1st time) (b. 1201/2; d. 1264) with his brother *Vasilko* (b. 1203/4; d. 1269) nominal dukes; duchy invaded by Ruthenian princes
	King *András II* of Hungary (b. 1176; d. 21 Sep 1235)

*Ukrainian Volodymyr, Polish Włodzimierz

	guardian and overlord, styled King of Galicia and Lodomeria
1206	*Vladimir*, son of Igor Svyatoslavich, Duke of Kiev (b. 1173; d. after 1211) ruled in Halich; with his brothers *Svyatoslav* (b. 1177; d. Nov 1212, or 1211?) in Przemyśl and *Roman* (d. Nov 1212, or 1211?) in Zvenigorod
1206/7	Daniil and Vasilko expelled from Vladimir by Svyatoslav and took refuge with Leszek the White, Duke of Cracow and Sandomir
1207	Svyatoslav expelled from Vladimir by Leszek
1207	*Alexander*, Duke of Bełz, grandson of Mstislav (for 1st time) (d. before 1234), installed in Vladimir by Leszek
1207(?)	*Ingvar Yaroslavich*, Duke of Lutsk, grandson of Izyaslav, installed by Leszek
c. 1208(?) - 1214	*Alexander* (for 2nd time) in Vladimir
1211	*Daniil* (for 2nd time) reinstated in Halich
1213	*Vladislav Kormilchyts*, usurper
1214	*Mstislav Yaroslavich*, nephew of Mstislav II, Duke of Vladimir (d. 1226/7) in Halich
autumn 1214	*Kálmán* (or *Koloman*), son of András II, King of Hungary (for 1st time) (b. 1207/9; d. 1241) ruled in Halich
1214	*Daniil* (for 3rd time) ruled in Vladimir; expelled by Koloman (?)
1215	*Mstislav Mstislavich*, the Lucky (Udaly), Duke of Novgorod (for 1st time) (d. c. 1228) occupied Vladimir and Halich, joined from 1216 by *Daniil* (for 4th time)
1216(?)	*Kálmán* (for 2nd time) ruled in Halich
c. 1219	*Mstislav Mstislavich* (for 2nd time) and *Daniil* (for 5th time) regained Halich
1226/7	*András*, brother of Kálmán (b. 1210/12; d. before 1245) ruled in Halich
c. 1229 - 1264	*Daniil* (for 6th time) ruled in Halich and Vladimir, ruled in Halich only from 1238, crowned king 1253
1238 - 1264	*Vasilko* (for 2nd time) ruled in Vladimir and Lutsk
1264 - 1269/70	*Shvarno*, son of Daniil, Duke of Eastern Halich and Vladimir
1264 - 1300	*Lev I*, brother (b. c. 1228), Duke of (Western) Halich and Lvov
1264 - 1300	*Mstislav*, brother (d. 1308?) Duke of Eastern Vladimir 1264, Duke of the whole duchy 1288

1269 – 1287	*Vladimir* (or *Ivan*), son of Vasilko (b. after 1248; d. Dec 1288) Duke of Vladimir
1300 – 24 Apr 1308	*Yury I*, son of Lev I (b. 24 Apr 1252) Duke of Halich, Lvov and Vladimir
1308 – spring 1323	*Lev II*, son (d. before 21 May 1323) ruled with his brother *Andrei* (d. (assassinated) 21 May 1323)
1324/5 – 7 Apr 1340	*Yury* (or *Jerzy*) *II* (formerly *Bolesław*), son of Duke Trojden of Mazovia and Maria, daughter of Yury I (b. c. 1310?)
1340/1	Halich and Vladimir subject henceforward to Poland (or Hungary) and Lithuania

Genoa

Doges

23 Sep AD 1339 – 23 Dec 1344	*Simone Boccanegra* (for 1st time) (b. 1301(?); d. Genoa 13 Mar 1363) resigned
1344	*Giovanni di Murta*
1350 – 1352	*Giovanni Valente*
1353 – 1356	Under Milanese rule
15 Nov 1356 – 13 Mar 1363	*Simone Boccanegra* (for 2nd time)
Mar 1363	*Gabriele Adorno* (b. c. 1320; d. 1383)
13 Aug 1370 – 13 Jun 1378	*Domenico Fregoso** (b. Genoa c. 1325; d. Genoa c. 1390)
17 Jun 1378	*Antoniotto I Adorno* (for 1st time) (b. Genoa c. 1340; d. Finale 5 Jun 1398)
Jun 1378	*Nicolò Guarco* (d. Finale)
1383	*Federico da Pagana*
1383	*Leonardo Montaldo*
12 Jun 1384 – 3 Aug 1390	*Antoniotto I Adorno* (for 2nd time)
Aug 1390 – Apr 1391	*Giacomo Fregoso** (b. Genoa 1340; d. 1420)
9 Apr 1391 – 15 May 1392	*Antoniotto I Adorno* (for 3rd time)
16 May 1392 – 5 Jul 1393	*Antonio(tto) Montaldo* (for 1st time) (b. Genoa 1369; d. Genoa 1398)

*The surname is sometimes given as *da Campofregoso*

Jul 1393	*Clemente Promontorio*
Jul/Aug 1393	*Francesco Giustiniani*
Aug 1393 – May 1394	*Antoniotto Montaldo* (for 2nd time)
1394	*Nicolò Zoaglio*
1394	*Antonio Guarco*
3 Sep 1394 – 25 Oct 1396	*Antoniotto I Adorno* (for 4th time)
1396 – 1409	Under French rule
1409 – 1413	Under the rule of Montferrat
27 Mar 1413 – 23 Mar 1415	*Giorgio Adorno* (b. Genoa c. 1350; d. Genoa after 9 Dec 1426)
Mar 1415	*Barnaba Guano*
Jun 1415 – 1421	*Tommas(in)o Fregoso** (for 1st time) (b. Genoa 1402; d. 1485)
1421 – 1435	Under Milanese rule
1435	*Isnardo Guarco*
1436	*Tommaso Fregoso* (for 2nd time)
1437	*Battista I Fregoso**
28 Jan 1443	*Raffaele Adorno* (b. 1375; d. Jul (?) 1458)
4 – 30 Jan 1447	*Barnaba Adorno* (b. Genoa c. 1385; d. 1459)
Jan 1447	*Giano I Fregoso** (b. Genoa 1405; d. 1448)
Dec 1447	*Lodovico Fregoso** (for 1st time) (b. Genoa c. 1406; d. Nice 1489)
1450 – 1458	*Pietro II Fregoso** (b. Genoa 1414; d. Genoa 1459)
1458 – 1461	Under French rule
12 Mar 1461	*Prospero Adorno* (for 1st time) (b. c. 1428; d. 1485)
Jul 1461	*Spinetta Fregoso*
Jul 1461	*Lodovico Fregoso** (for 2nd time)
1462	*Paolo Fregoso*,* cardinal, Archbishop of Genoa (for 1st time) (b. Genoa 1430; d. Rome 19 Mar 1498)
1462	*Lodovico Fregoso** (for 3rd time)
1463	*Paolo Fregoso** (for 2nd time)
1464 – 1478	Under Milanese rule
9 Aug – 25 Nov 1478	*Prospero Adorno* (for 2nd time)
1478	*Battista II* (or *Battistino*) *Fregoso* (b. Genoa 1453; d. Rome 1504)
1483	*Paolo Fregoso** (for 3rd time)
1484 – 16 Jan 1488	*Giano II Fregoso** (for 1st time) (b. Genoa c. 1445; d. after 1527)
1488 – 1499	Under Milanese rule

*The surname is sometimes given as *da Campofregoso*

Georgia

Kings of Iberia (Kartli)

c. 325 BC	*Azon*, variously described as son of the 'king' of Aran-Kartli and as governor of Kartli appointed by Alexander the Great; legendary(?)
Pharnabazid dynasty	
c. 270(?)	*P'arnavaz* (or *Pharnabazes*) *I*, nephew of Samara, the chief of the Iberians at Mtskheta; vassal of the Seleucids
c. 220(?)	*Saurmag* (or *Sauromaces*) *I*, son
Nemrodid (or 2nd Pharnabazid) dynasty	
c. 170(?)	*Mirvan* (or *Mirian*) *I*, Parthian, adopted son of Saurmag I
c. 130(?)	*P'arnajom*, son
Artaxiad dynasty	
c. 100(?)	*Arshak* (or *Arsok*) *I* (or rather *Artaxias*?), son of the king of Armenia (viz. Tigran I(?), 159 – 123)
c. 66	*Artag* (or *Artoces*), son, submitted to the Roman general Pompey
c. 64	*Bartom* (or *Barat'man*) *I* (or *P'arnavaz II*), son
Nemrodid dynasty (restored)	
c. 30(?)	*Mirvan* (or *Mirian*) *II*, son of P'arnajom
c. 20(?)	*Arshak II* (or *Arik*) (or rather *Artaxias*?), son
c. AD 1(?)	*Mihrdat I* (or *Aderki*, *Aderok*),* son of Bartom I, fl. 14/37

*The Georgian, Latin, Greek and Armenian data for the next hundred years are very difficult to reconcile. The king-list in *The life of Georgia* gives the order:

Aderki, son of Bartom
K'art'am, son, and *Bartom II*
P'arsman I, son, and *Kaos*
Azork, son, and *Armazael*
Amazasp I, son, and *Derok*
P'arsman II Kveli, son and *Mihrdat I*

The first of each pair is supposed to have ruled at Armazi, south of the Mtkvari river, the other at Mtskheta on the north side, but this diarchy is now rejected as an anachronism

c. 30(?)	*P'arsman* (*Farsman* or *Pharasmanes*) *I*, son, fl. 35
c. 70(?)	*Mihrdat II* (or *Azork*), son, fl. c. 75
c. 80(?)	*K'art'am* (*Karram* or *Kardzam*), fl. 70/90(?)
c. 100(?)	*Amazasp I* (or *Mihrdat III*), brother of Mihrdat II, fl. 114/15
c. 120(?) (fl. c. 138)	*P'arsman II Kveli* (i.e. the good), son, fl. c. 138
c. 140(?)	*K'sep'arnug* (or *Rok*, garbled from *Farnok*?)
(?)	*Ghadam* (or *Adam*), son of P'arsman, 'reigned [3 years?] and 20 days'
(?)	*P'arsman III*, son, under one year old at accession Regent: *Ghadana*, mother
(?)	*Amazasp II*, son*
(?)	*Rev Mart'ali* (i.e. the truthful), nephew, son of an Armenian king (viz. Pacorus(?), 161 – 163)
(?)	*Vache*, son
(?)	*Bakur I*, son
(?)	*Mihrdat IV*, son
(?) – 289	*Asp'agur I*, son

Chosroid (or Mihranid) dynasty

289	*Mirian* (or *Mirvan, Meribanes*) *III*, Saint, son-in-law, 'son of the Persian king K'asre-Ardashir' †
358	*Bakur II* (or *Bak'ar*), son
364	*T'rdat* (or *Mihrdat V* or *III*), brother(?)
368 – 378(?)	*Saurmag* (or *Sauromaces*) *II* (d. 393?) client of Rome, at Mtskheta
368	*Varaz-Bakur* (or *Asp'agur*, *Asparuces II*), son of T'rdat(?), Sasanid vassal, at Armazi, sole ruler 378(?)
c. 400(?)	*Bakur III*‡
c. 405(?)	*P'arsman IV*, son of Varaz-Bakur

and the extra kings as inventions. The Greek and Latin sources give different names, and Mihrdat I has been identified by some scholars with K'art'am. If K'art'am (AD 55 – 72 in the list) is identical with the Kardzam of Moses of Khoren, he is to be dated in the 70s and 80s, but P'arsman I, traditionally his son, flourished in AD 35. The re-arrangement above, based on Melikishvili, *K istorii drevhei Gruzii*, is not accepted by all.

*An 'Amazasp, king of Iberia' is mentioned in an inscription of the Sasanid king Shapur (241 – 272), but Mirian III, six generations later according to the king-list, flourished early in the third century.

†Hormizd-Ardashir could presumably be meant (Sasanid king 272 – 273), but it is now generally accepted that Mirian came of a noble Persian family, but not the royal house.

‡Omitted from some lists.

c. 410(?)	*Mihrdat VI* (or *IV*), brother
c. 430(?)	*Archil I*, son
c. 440(?)	*Mihrdat VII* (or *V*)
c. 446	*Vakhtang I Gorgasal* (or *Gurgen I*), son (b. c. 439) moved capital to Tiflis 458
519*	*Dachi*, son
531	*Bakur IV* (or *II*), son
544	*P'arsman V*, son
558	*P'arsman VI*, nephew
(?) – 579/80	*Bakur V* (or *III*)
579/80	Monarchy abolished by the Sasanid king Khusrau I or by Hormazd IV

Presiding Princes

Khosroid (or Mihranid) dynasty

588	*Guaram I* (or *Gurgen II*), nephew of Dachi, prince of Cholarzene-Javakheti
c. 595	*Step'anos I*, son (d. at siege of Tiflis)
627	*Adarnase I*, son of Bakur V, prince of Kakheti
639(?)	*Step'anos II*, son, prince of Kakheti, vassal of the Orthodox Caliph 645
c. 650	*Adarnase II*, son, prince of Kakheti, revolted against the Caliph 681/2
c. 684	*Guaram II*, son of Step'anos I (?), prince of Cholarzene-Javakheti
693 (or earlier)	*Guaram III*, son or grandson, prince of Cholarzene-Javakheti
c. 748	*Adarnase III*, duke of Inner Iberia
c. 760	*Nerse*, son (d. before 786) imprisoned in Baghdad 772 – 775, fled to Abasgia
779/80	*Step'anos III*, nephew, grandson of Guaram III, prince of Cholarzene-Javakheti
786 – after 807	*Juansher*, son of Archil II, the Martyr;† prince of Kakheti; de facto presiding prince(?); held in captivity by the Khazars 799/800 – 806/7

*The traditional death date of Vakhtang I, 499, is thought to be due to telescoping in the sources; 503, 510 and 522 have also been proposed.

†Archil II and his brother Mi(h)r, sons of Step'anos II, are described as 'Iberian kings' in the tradition.

Bagratid dynasty

813–830	*Ashot I*, the Great, great-grandson in female line of Guaram III, prince of Cholarzene-Javakheti
842/3	*Bagrat I*, son
876	*Davit' I*, son

Kings of Kartli

Bagratid dynasty

888–923	*Adarnase IV*, son of Davit' I, assumed title of king of the Georgians
912	Kartli controlled by Abasgia
923	*Davit' II*, son, titular king
937	*Bagrat II*, the Sot, nephew, titular king
994	*Gurgen I* (or *III*), son, King of Kings
1008	*Bagrat III*, son, king of Abasgia from 978/9, united Georgia, King of Kings

Kings of Abasgia

Anchabadze dynasty

767/8	*Leon II* (or *I*)
811/12	*T'eodosi II* (or *I*), son
837/8	*Dimitri II* (or *I*)
872/3	*Giorgi I*, brother
878/9	*Ioane Shavliani*
c. 880	*Adarnase Shavliani*, son
887/8	*Bagrat I*, son of Dimitri II
898/9	*Kostantine III*, son
916/17	*Giorgi II*, son, with his brother, *Bagrat II*
960/1	*Leon III* (or *II*), son
969/70	*Dimitri III* (or *II*), brother
976/7	*T'eodosi III* (or *II*), the Blind, brother
978/9	*Bagrat III*, nephew (see Kartli) united Abasgia and Kartli 1008

Kings of Georgia (Abasgia and Kartli only until 1105)

Bagratid dynasty

1008	*Bagrat III* (see Kartli)
1014	*Giorgi I*, son (b. 996) lost Tao, Kola, Ardahan and Javakheti

1027*	*Bagrat IV*, son (b. 1018) at first under the regency of his mother, Mariam Artsruni; absent in Byzantium 1050 – 1053
1072	*Giorgi II*, son*
1089	*Davit' II* (*III* or *IV*), the Builder, son (b. 1073) acquired Kakheti 1105
1125	*Dimitri I*, son (for 1st time) (d. 1156) deposed, became monk
1154	*Davit' III* (or *IV*), son, for six months
1155	*Dimitri I* (for 2nd time)
1156†	*Giorgi III*, brother
1184 – 1212	*Tamar*, daughter (b. c. 1155) co-ruler from 1179
c. 1193 – 1207	*Davit' Soslan*, husband, co-ruler
1212	*Giorgi IV Lasha* (i.e. the Resplendent), son (b. 1194)
Jan 1223 – 1245	*Rusudani*, sister (b. 1195)
1236	Mongol invasion
1239	Mongol occupation of eastern Georgia
1245 – 1250	Interregnum
1250 – 1258	*Davit' IV* (or *V*), son of Rusudani (b. c. 1224) proclaimed king 1234, seceded as king of Imereti (see below)
1250 – 1269	*Davit' V* (or *VI*), illegitimate son of Giorgi IV (b. c. 1220) at first ruled jointly with Davit' IV
1269 – 1273	Interregnum
1273	*Dimitri II*, the Devoted, son (b. c. 1265?) Regent: 1269/73 – 1282: *Sadun Mankaberdeli* (d. 1282)
1289	*Vakhtang II*, brother
1292 – 1310	*Davit' VI* (or *VII*), son of Dimitri II co-ruler 1291 – 1292, fled to the mountains, co-ruler with Vakhtang III and Giorgi V
1301	*Vakhtang III*, brother
1307	*Giorgi V* (or *VI*), the Little, son of Davit' VI
1314	*Giorgi VI* (or *V*), the Illustrious, uncle (b. c. 1290) co-ruler from 1299 and regent for Giorgi V, recovered Imereti 1330

*1039 – 1041	*Dimitri Giorgishvili*, half-brother of Bagrat IV, pretender
1050	*Giorgi* (later Giorgi II) son of Bagrat IV (d. 1059) crowned king in opposition to Bagrat IV, effective power being held by the high constable, Liparit Orbelian
†1174	*Dimitri* (or *Demna*), son of Davit' III; pretender; blinded, castrated and imprisoned by Giorgi III

1346	*Davit' VII*, son
1360	*Bagrat V*, the Great, son, co-ruler from c. 1355, taken prisoner by the Mongols 1387
1395	*Giorgi VII*, son
1405	*Kostantine I*, brother
1412	*Aleksandre I*, the Great, son (d. 1446) co-ruler from c. 1408, abdicated and became a monk
1442	*Vakhtang IV*, son, co-ruler from 1433
1446 – 1453	*Dimitri III*, brother, de jure, co-ruler in Imereti 1433, remained in Imereti
1446 – 1465	*Giorgi VIII*, brother (d. 1476) co-ruler in Kakheti 1433, captured by the atabeg of Samstkhe, restored in Kakheti (see below)
1465	*Bagrat VI*, cousin, lost Kakheti 1466
1478 – 1505	*Kostantine II*, son of Dimitri III, co-ruler from c. 1465, lost Imereti 1484

Kings of Kakheti

*Donauri dynasty**

1010	*Kvirike III*, the Great, proclaimed himself King
1029	*Gagik*, nephew; son of King Davit' Lackland of Lori
1058	*Aghsartan I*, son
1084	*Kvirike IV*, son
1102	*Aghsartan II*, nephew
1105	Kakheti absorbed in Georgia
1466 – 1476	*Giorgi I*, formerly Giorgi VIII of Georgia
1476/90 – 1511	*Aleksandre I*, son, formally recognized 1490

Kings of Imereti

Bagratid dynasty

1258	*Davit' I*, previously King (Davit' IV) of Georgia
1293	*Kostantine*, son
1327	*Michael*, brother
1329	*Bagrat I*, son, captured by Giorgi VI of Georgia
1330	Imereti re-absorbed in Georgia
1484 – 1510	*Aleksandre I*, son of King Bagrat VI of Georgia

*Hereditary *chorepiscopi* from the 8th century

Germany

See Holy Roman Empire

Ghaznavids

Territory comprised part of present-day Afghanistan, north-eastern Iran and northern India, with the capital established at Ghazna.

Amirs or Sultans

AD 977/8	*(Nasir al-Daula Abu Mansur) Sebüktigin* (b. c. 923/4) governor for the Samanids
997/8	*Isma'il (ibn Sebüktigin)*, son
998/9 – 30 Apr 1030	*(Yamin al-Daula Abu'l-Qasim) Mahmud (ibn Sebüktigin)*, brother (b. 970) renounced Samanid vassalage and became nominal vassal of the 'Abbasids, conquered northern India, conquered Khwarazm 1017/18, established in Transoxania (Sogdiana) from Dec 1004/Jan 1005
1030	*(Jalal al-Daula) Muhammad (ibn Mahmud, al-Makhul)*, son (for 1st time) (b. 997) deposed
1030	*(Shibha al-Daula) Mas'ud I (ibn Mahmud)*, brother (b. 997; d. 6 Jan 1042) defeated by the Seljuqs, lost Iranian possessions 23 May 1040, deposed and later murdered
1040/1	*Muhammad* (for 2nd time)
1040/1	*(Shihab al-Daula Abu Sa'd) Maudud (ibn Mas'ud)*, nephew (b. 1021/2)
1049/50	*Mas'ud II (ibn Maudud)*, son (b. c. 1043) for a few days
1049/50	*(Baha' al-Daula Abu'l-Hasan) 'Ali (ibn Mas'ud)*, uncle, deposed
1049/50	*('Izz al-Daula Abu Mansur) 'Abd al-Rashid (ibn Mahmud)*, uncle (b. 1022/3?) murdered by Toghrıl
1052/3	*(Qiwam al-Daula) Toghrıl*, usurper, slave of Mas'ud I, for 40 days, murdered
1052/3 – Mar 1059	*(Jamal al-Daula) Farrukhzad (ibn Mas'ud)*, brother

	of 'Ali (b. 1026)
1059/60 – 25 Aug 1099	*(Zahir al-Daula Abu'l-Muzaffar) Ibrahim (ibn Mas'ud)*, brother (b. 1033) took title of Sultan
1099 – Feb/Mar 1115	*('Ala' al-Daula Abu Sa'd) Mas'ud III (ibn Ibrahim)*, son (b. 1060)
1115	*(Kamal al-Daula) Shirzad (ibn Mas'ud)*, son (b. 1081/2) forced to flee into Tabaristan
1115/16 – Sep/Oct 1118	*(Sultan al-Daula) Arslan Shah (ibn Mas'ud)*, brother (b. 1083/4(?); d. (executed) Sep/Oct 1118) forced to flee into India
1118/19	*(Yamin al-Daula) Bahram Shah (ibn Mas'ud)*, brother, acknowledged suzerainty of Seljuqs
1152/3 – Jul 1160	*(Mu'izz al-Daula) Khusrau Shah (ibn Bahram)*, son
1160 – 1187	*(Taj al-Daula) Khusrau Malik (ibn Khusrau Shah)*, son (d. (executed) 1190(?)) surrendered to the Ghurids Jul/Aug 1187
Jul/Aug 1187	Overthrown by the Ghurids

Ghurids

Territory comprised part of present-day north-western Afghanistan, with the capital initially at Istiya and later at Firuzkuh.

Sultans

Principal Line in Ghur and from 1173 in Ghazna

AD (?)	*Muhammad ibn Suri*, vassal of the Ghaznavid sultan, deposed
1011 – c. 1035	*Abu 'Ali (ibn Muhammad)*, son, deposed
(?)	*Shith* brother
(?)	*'Abbas*, son, deposed
(?)	*Muhammad*, son
(?)	*Qutb al-Din Hasan*, son
1099/1100	*'Izz al-Din Husain (ibn Hasan)*, son
1145/6	*Saif al-Din Suri*, son, executed by the Ghaznavids
1148/9	*Baha' al-Din Sam I*, brother
1149/50	*'Ala' al-Din Husain*, brother
1160/1	*Saif al-Din Muhammad (ibn Husain)*, son, murdered
1162/3	*Shams al-Din* (or *Ghiyath al-Din*) *Muhammad*,

	cousin
1203	*Shihab al-Din* (later *Mu'izz al-Din*) *Muhammad*, brother
1205/6	*Ghiyath al-Din Mahmud*, nephew, assassinated
1212	*Baha' al-Din Sam II (ibn Mahmud)*, son
1213/14	*'Ala' al-Din Atsız (ibn Husain)*, son of 'Ala' al-Din Husain
1214/15 – 1215/16	*'Ala' al-Din* (or *Diya' al-Din*) *Muhammad*, cousin
1215/16	Khwarazm-Shah conquest

Line in Bamiyan and Tukharistan

1145/6	*Fakhr al-Din Mas'ud (ibn Husain)*, son of 'Izz al-Din Husain, dethroned
1162/3	*Shams al-Din Muhammad (ibn Mas'ud)*, son
1192/3	*Baha' al-Din Sam ibn Muhammad*, son
1205/6 – 1215/16	*Jalal al-Din 'Ali (ibn Sam)*, son
1215/16	Khwarazm-Shah conquest

Girai Khanate (Crimean Tartars)

Territory comprised part of present-day Ukraine, with the capital established initially at Kirk-yir and later at Bagche Sarai (now Simferopol).

Khans

c. AD 1427/8	*Hajji (Girai) I (ibn Ghiyath al-Din)*, descended from Togha Temür (for 1st time)
1455/6	*Haidar (Girai)*, son
1455/6	*Hajji I* (for 2nd time)
1466/7	*Nur-Devlet (Girai ibn Hajji)*, son (for 1st time)
1466/7	*Mengli (Girai) I (ibn Hajji)*, brother (for 1st time)
1474/5	*Nur-Devlet* (for 2nd time)
1475/6	*Mengli I* (for 2nd time)
1476/7	*Nur-Devlet* (for 3rd time)
1478/9	*Mengli I* (for 3rd time)
1515/16	*Mehemmed (Girai) I*, son (b. 1466)

1523	*Ghazi (Girai) I (ibn Mehemmed)*, son (b. 1504/5) for six months, assassinated
1523	*Sa'adet (Girai) I (ibn Mengli)*, uncle, abdicated
1532	*Islam (Girai) I (ibn Mehemmed)*, nephew (d. (assassinated) 1537/8) for five months
1532/3	*Sahib (Girai) I (ibn Mengli)*, uncle (d. (executed) 1552) deposed
1551	*Devlet (Girai) I (ibn Mubarek)*, nephew (b. 1511)
25 Jun 1577	*Mehemmed (Girai) II (ibn Devlet)*, son
1584	*Islam (Girai) II (ibn Devlet)*, brother
1587/8	*Ghazi (Girai) II (Bora ibn Devlet)*, brother (for 1st time)
1596	*Feth (Girai) I (ibn Devlet)*, brother, put to death after two months
1596	*Ghazi II* (for 2nd time)
Jan/Feb 1608	*Toqtamısh (Girai ibn Ghazi)*, son, assassinated by Mehemmed III
Jan/Feb 1609	*Selamet (Girai) I (ibn Devlet)*, uncle
May/Jun 1610	*Janbeg (Girai ibn Mubarek)*, nephew (for 1st time) (b. 1555(?); d. 1635) exiled to Rhodes
1623/4 – 1627	*Mehemmed (Girai) III (ibn Sa'adut)*, cousin (d. 1628/9) deposed May/Jun 1627
1624/May/Jun 1627	*Janbeg* (for 2nd time) appointed by the sultan 1624, in exile in Rhodes Oct/Nov 1636
25 Feb 1635	*Inayet (Girai ibn Ghazi)*, cousin, strangled in Istanbul
15 Jun 1636	*Bahadır (Girai) I (ibn Selamet)*, cousin
Oct/Nov 1641	*Mehemmed (Girai) IV (ibn Selamet)*, brother (for 1st time) (b. 1609(?); d. in exile at Daghistan 1674/5) deposed and exiled to Rhodes
Jul 1644	*Islam (Girai) III (ibn Selamet)*, brother
Jun/Jul 1654	*Mehemmed IV* (for 2nd time)
1666	*'Adil (Girai ibn Devlet* or *ibn Choban)*, grandson of Feth I (d. 1672/3) deposed 8 May 1671
May/Jun 1671	*Selim (Girai) I (ibn Bahadır)*, son of Bahadır (for 1st time) (d. Nov/Dec 1704) deposed Jan/Feb 1678
Feb/Mar 1678	*Murad (Girai ibn Mubarek)*, cousin (d. in exile in Yamboli 1695/6)
1683	*Hajji (Girai) II (ibn Qırım)*, cousin (d. Rhodes 1688/9) for nine months
1684	*Selim I* (for 2nd time) renounced khanate 1690/1 and went to Mecca
1691	*Sa'adet (Girai) II (ibn Qırım)*, cousin (d. Rhodes 1704/5) deposed

Dec 1691/Jan 1692	*Safa' (Girai ibn Selamet)*, cousin (b. 1636(?); d. 1703/4) deposed Sep/Oct 1692
6 Nov 1692	*Selim I* (for 3rd time) with the title al-Hajji, abdicated
Mar/Apr 1699	*Devlet (Girai) II (ibn Selim)*, son (for 1st time) deposed
Dec 1702	*Selim I* (for 4th time)
30 Dec 1704	*Ghazi (Girai) III (ibn Selim)*, son (d. 1707/8) deposed
1707	*Qaplan (Girai) I (ibn Selim)*, brother (for 1st time) (d. Chios Nov/Dec 1738) deposed and exiled to Rhodes
1708	*Devlet II* (for 2nd time) deposed and exiled to Rhodes
1713	*Qaplan I* (for 2nd time)
Nov 1716	*Qara-Devlet (Girai ibn 'Adil)*, son of 'Adil, nominally for three months, deposed 6 Feb 1717
Feb 1717	*Sa'adet (Girai) III (ibn Selim)*, son of Selim, abdicated
1724	*Mengli (Girai) II (ibn Selim)*, brother (for 1st time) (d. 30 Dec 1739) deposed
Nov 1730	*Qaplan I* (for 3rd time) deposed
1736	*Feth (Girai) II (ibn Devlet)*, nephew (d. 1746/7) deposed
Jul 1737	*Mengli II* (for 2nd time)
1739/40	*Selamet (Girai) II (ibn Selim)*, brother, deposed
Oct/Nov (20 Dec?) 1743	*Selim (Girai) II (ibn Qaplan)*, nephew (d. 18 May 1748)
May 1748	*Arslan (Girai ibn Devlet)*, cousin (for 1st time) (d. 30 May 1767) deposed and exiled to Chios
Feb/Mar 1756	*Halim (Girai ibn Sa'adet)*, cousin, deposed
21 Oct 1758	*Qırım (Girai ibn Devlet)*, cousin (for 1st time) deposed
Sep 1764	*Selim (Girai) III (ibn Feth)*, nephew (for 1st time) (b. 1708; d. 1781) deposed 14 Mar 1767
Mar 1767	*Arslan* (for 2nd time)
Jun 1767	*Maqsud (Girai ibn Selamet)*, cousin (for 1st time), deposed 1768
19 Oct 1768	*Qırım* (for 2nd time)
1769	*Devlet (Girai) III (ibn Arslan)*, nephew (for 1st time) (d. 1780)
1770(?)	*Qaplan (Girai) II (ibn Selim)*, son of Selim II, deposed Feb 1771(?)
Nov/Dec 1770	*Selim III* (for 2nd time) fled to Istanbul Jul/Aug 1771, formally deposed Mar 1772
14 Nov 1771	*Maqsud* (for 2nd time)
Mar 1772	*Sahib (Girai) II (ibn Ahmed)*, grandson of Devlet II (d. 1804/5) fled to Istanbul
Apr/May 1775	*Devlet III* (for 2nd time) fled to Istanbul

4 Mar 1777 – 1782	*Shahin (Girai ibn Ahmed)*, cousin (for 1st time) (d. (executed) Rhodes Jul 1787)
1782 – 1783	*Bahadır (Girai) II (ibn Ahmed)*
21 Jul 1783	Russian annexation of the Crimea
1784	*Bahadır (Girai) III (ibn Maqsud)*, grandson of Selamet II, Russian vassal
1785	*Shahin* (for 2nd time) Russian vassal
1787	*Shahbaz (Girai)*, khan of the Tartars of Bessarabia as an Ottoman nominee
1789 – 1792	*Bakht (Girai)*, khan of the Tartars of Bessarabia as an Ottoman nominee
1792	Girai khanate finally overthrown

The Golden Horde

Territory comprised part of present-day USSR, with the capital established at Old Sarai (now Sarai-Batu) and then New Sarai (now Sarai-Berke).

Khans

Line of Batu'ids (The Blue Horde) in south Russia and western Kipchak

AD 1226/7	*Batu (ibn Jochi)*, grandson of Chingiz Khan (b. c. 1203/4)
1255/6	*Sartaq (ibn Batu)*, son
1256/7	*Ulaghchi (ibn Batu)*, brother, under the regency of his mother Boruqtshin Khatun
1257/8	*Berke* (or *Baraka*) *(ibn Jochi)*, uncle
1266/7	*Möngke* (or *Mengü*) *Temür*, great nephew
1280/1	*Töde Möngke* (or *Mengü*), brother, abdicated
1287/8	*Töle Buqa*, nephew
1290/1	*(Ghiyath al-Din) Toqtagha*, cousin
1312/13	*(Ghiyath al-Din Muhammad) Özbeg*, nephew
1340/1	*Tini Beg*, son
1340/1	*Jani Beg* (or *Jambek*) *(Jalal al-Din Mahmud)*, brother
1356/7 – 1380/1	Period of rival claimants:
	(Muhammad) Berdi Beg, son
	Qulpa, brother
	Nauruz Beg (Muhammad), brother

Line of Orda (The White Horde) in Siberia and eastern Kipchak, and from 1378 of the Blue and White Hordes united into the Golden Horde of south Russia

1226	*Orda (ibn Jochi)*, brother of Batu
1280/1	*Köchü*, son
1301/2	*Bayan*, son
1309/10	*Sasibuqa* (or *Sarıgh (?) Buqa*), son
c. 1315/16	*Ilbasan*, son
1320/1	*Mubarak Khwaja*, brother
1344/5	*Chimtai*, nephew
1360/1	*Urus*, son
1375/6	*Tuqtaqiya*, son
1375/6	*Temür Malik*, brother
1376/7	*(Ghiyath al-Din) Tokhtamısh*, grandson (d. 1406/7) reunion of the Blue and White Hordes 1378
1394/5	*Temür Qutlugh*, uncle
1400/1	*Shadi Beg*, brother
1407/8	*Pulad*, brother
1410/11	*Temür*, nephew
1412/13	*Jalal al-Din*, great-grandson of Chimtai
1412/13	*Karim Berdi*, brother
1414/15	*Kebek*, brother
1417/18	*Jabbar Berdi*, brother
	Rival khans:
1419/20	*Ulugh Mehmed*, descended from a brother of Orda (for 1st time) in rivalry with Devlat Berdi after 1420/1
1420/1	*Devlat Berdi*, nephew
1421/2	*Baraq*, grandson of Urus
1428/9	*Ulugh Mehmed* (for 2nd time) later ruled in Qazan
1434/5	*Sayyid Ahmed I*
1436/7	*Küchük Mehmed*, grandson of Temür Qutlugh
1466/7	*Ahmad*, son
1481/2	*Shaikh Ahmed* and *Sayyid Ahmed II*, sons
1481/2	*Murtada*, brother
1502	Shaikh Ahmed defeated by the Girai Khans and the remnants of the Golden Horde absorbed into the Crimean Tartar Horde

Gujarat Sultanate

Territory comprised part of present-day western India, with the capital initially at Anahilwara and from 1411 at Ahmadabad.

Sultan

Mar/Apr AD 1391	*(Zafar Khan) Muzaffar I* (b. 29 Jun 1342) initially governor for the Delhi sultan, declaration of independence 1407/8
26 Jul 1411	*Ahmad Shah I (ibn Tatar)*, grandson, capital moved to Ahmadabad
14 Jul 1442	*Muhammad (Karim) I (Shah)*, son, poisoned
11 Feb 1451	*(Qutb al-Din) Ahmad (Shah) II*, son (b. 9 Feb 1432)
13 May 1458	*Da'ud (Shah)*, uncle, for seven days
20 May 1458	*Mahmud (Shah) I (Begŕa)*, nephew (b. 1445/6)
23 Nov 1511	*Muzaffar (Shah) II*, son (d. Apr 1526)
6 Feb 1526	*Sikandar (Shah)*, son, murdered after six weeks
18 May 1526	*(Nasir Khan) Mahmud II*, brother
3 Aug 1526	*Bahadur (Shah)*, brother (d. (murdered by Portuguese) at sea off Diu 13 Feb 1537) conquered Malwa 1531, defeated by Mughal emperor Humayun
Apr – 24 May 1537	*(Miran) Muhammad I (Shah Faruqi)* for six weeks, Sultan of Khandesh 1520 – 24 May 1537
1537	*Mahmud (Shah) III (ibn Latif)*, grandson of Muzaffar II, murdered
Feb 1554	*Ahmad (Shah) III*, son(?) (d. (murdered) 1561)*
1561 – 1572/3	*Muzaffar (Shah) III (Habib)*, brother (for 1st time) (d. (suicide) 1593) renounced sultanate
Apr 1573	Conquest by Mughal emperor Akbar I
1583	*Muzaffar III* (for 2nd time) for five months
1583	Second and definitive Mughal conquest

*1555/6 *Muhammad ibn Muzaffar II*, usurper, brother of Bahadur

Hafsids (Banu Hafs)

Territory comprised part of present-day Tunisia, northern Algeria, northern Morocco and north-western Libya, with the capital at Tunis.

Caliphs

AD 1227/8	*(Abu Zakariya') Yahya I*, grandson of Abu Hafs 'Umar, initially ruled as Almohad governor of Gafsa, then took title of Amir and declared independence
1249/50	*(Abu 'Abdallah) Muhammad I (al-Mustansir)*, son, took title of Caliph and Amir al-Mu'minin 1258
1276/7	*(Abu Zakariya') Yahya II (al-Wathiq)*, son, dethroned and executed by Ibrahim I
Aug 1279 – spring 1283	*(Abu Ishaq) Ibrahim I*, uncle, from Dec 1282 ruled at Bougie, executed c. Jun 1283
spring – Jun 1283	*Abu Faris*, previously governor of Bougie
Dec 1282/Jan 1283	*Ahmad (ibn 'Abi-'Umara)*, usurper, ruled at Tunis
1284/5 – 1294/5	*(Abu Hafs) 'Umar I*, brother of Ibrahim I, ruled at Tunis
1285 – 1301	*(Abu Zakariya') Yahya III (al-Muntakhab ibn Ibrahim)*, nephew (d. 1301) ruled at Bougie
1294/5	*(Abu 'Abdallah* (or *Abu-'Asida)) Muhammad II (al-Muntasir ibn Yahya)*, son of Yahya II, ruled at Tunis
1309/10	*(Abu Yahya) Abu Bakr I (al-Shahid)*, great-grandson of Yahya I, for 17 days
1301	*(Abu'l-Baqa') Khalid I (al-Nasir)*, son of Yahya III, initially ruled at Bougie, ruler of the whole territory 1309 – 1311
1311/12 – 1317/18	*(Abu Yahya) Zakariya' I (al-Lihyani)*, great-nephew of Yahya I, ruled at Tunis
1312	*(Abu Yahya) Abu Bakr II (al-Mutawakkil)*, brother of Khalid I, ruled at Bougie, sole ruler from 1318/19
1317/18	*(Abu Darba) Muhammad III (al-Mustansir)*, son of Zakariya' I, ruled at Tunis
1346/7 – 1348	*(Abu Hafs) 'Umar II*, son of Abu Bakr II
1348	First Marinid occupation of Tunis
1348/9	*(Abu'l-'Abbas) Ahmad I (al-Fadl al-Mutawakkil)*, brother, ruled at Tunis
1350/1 – 1356/7	*(Abu Ishaq) Ibrahim II (al-Mustansir)*, brother (for 1st time) ruled at Tunis

1356/7	Second Marinid occupation of Tunis
1356/7	*Ibrahim II* (for 2nd time) re-established at Tunis
1368/9	*(Abu'l-Baqa') Khalid II (ibn Ibrahim)*, son, ruled at Tunis
1370/1	*(Abu'l-'Abbas) Ahmad II (al-Mustansir)*, cousin, previously ruled at Bougie and Constantine
1393/4	*(Abu Faris) 'Abd al-'Aziz (al-Mutawakkil ibn Ahmad)*, son
Jul/Aug 1434	*(Abu 'Abdallah) Muhammad IV (al-Muntasir ibn Muhammad)*, grandson
Aug/Sep 1435	*(Abu 'Umar) 'Uthman*, brother
1487/8	*(Abu Zakariya') Yahya III (ibn Mas'ud ibn 'Uthman)*, grandson
1488/9	*(Abu Yahya) Zakariya' II*, son
1493/4	*(Abu 'Abdallah) Muhammad V (al-Mutawakkil ibn Hasan)*, cousin
1526 – 1534/5	*(Abu 'Abdallah Muhammad) al-Hasan (ibn Muhammad)*, son (for 1st time)
1534/5	First Ottoman conquest of Tunis
1535/6	*al-Hasan* (for 2nd time) reinstated as vassal of Holy Roman Emperor Charles V
1543 – Aug/Sep 1570	*Ahmad ibn al-Hasan*, son
Aug/Sep 1570	Second Ottoman conquest
1573/4 – 1574/5	*(Abu 'Abdallah) Muhammad VI (ibn al-Hasan)*, brother of Ahmad ibn al-Hasan, Spanish vassal
1574/5	Third and definitive Ottoman conquest

Hainaut

Territory now in Hainaut province, Belgium, and Nord department, France. Names are given in French forms with modern Dutch forms in parentheses. Until about 1139 the counts of Hainaut were vassals of the dukes of Lorraine or Lower Lorraine.

Counts

before 18 Jan AD 908 – after 8 Sep 920	*Sigehard*

before 6 Jan 921 – 923(?)	*Haganon*
before 924 – after 931	*Régnier** (*Reinier*) *II*, son of Reginar I Long-neck of Lorraine
? – 957	*Régnier** (*Reinier*) *III*, Long-neck, son (d. in exile between 971 and 997) captured by Duke Brun of Lorraine and exiled to Bohemia
957	Hainaut divided into counties of Mons (Dutch: Bergen) and Valenciennes (Dutch: Valencijn) by King Otto I of Germany

Counts of Mons

957 – Jul 964	*Godefroi* (*Godfried*)
964 – Feb(?) 973	*Richer* (*Richerus* or *Richizo*) abdicated
Feb(?) – 7 May 973	*Renaud* (*Reinout*), killed in battle with Régnier IV
before 976 – 998	*Godefroi de* (*Godfried van*) *Verdun*

Counts of Valenciennes

957 or 958 (?)	*Amaury* (*Amalricus*) abdicated
Feb(?) – 7 May (?) 973	*Garnier* (*Garnerus* or *Warinharius*), killed in battle with Régnier IV
before 976 – 22 Oct 1011 or 1012	*Arnoul de Cambrai* (*Arnulf van Valencijn*)

Counts of Hainaut

998 – 1013	*Régnier** (*Reinier*) *IV*, son of Régnier III; title restored by Holy Roman Emperor Otto II 977, but the incumbent Counts of Mons and Valenciennes continued in office until their deaths
1013 – after 1039 or 1040	*Régnier** (*Reinier*) *V*, son
?	*Hermann de Mons* (*Herman van Bergen*), son
27 May 1049 or 1050	*Richilde* (*Richildis*), widow (for 1st time) (d. 18 Mar 1086); with (after 31 May 1051) her second husband, *Baudouin* (*Boudewijn*) *I*, son of Count Baudouin V of Flanders (b. c. 1030; d. 17 Jul 1070) Count (Baudouin VI) of Flanders 1067 – 1070

*Also spelt Rainier

17 Jul 1070 – 22 Feb 1071	*Arnoul* (*Arnulf*), the Unlucky (b. c. 1055) at the same time Count (Arnoul III) of Flanders
9 May 1071	*Richilde* (for 2nd time) deposed
1076(?)	*Baudouin* (*Boudewijn*) *II*, son of Baudouin I and Richilde (d. Syria)
c. 8 Jun 1098	*Baudouin* (*Boudewijn*) *III*, son Regent: 1098 – c. 1103: *Ida* (*Ida*), mother (d. c. 1107)
1120	*Baudouin* (*Boudewijn*) *IV*, son of Baudouin III Regent: 1120 – 1125(?): *Yolande de Gueldre* (*Yolande van Gelre*), mother
2 Nov 1171	*Baudouin* (*Boudewijn*) *V*, son-in-law of Count Thierry of Flanders (b. 1150); Count (Baudouin VIII) of Flanders 1 Jun 1191
18 Dec 1195	*Baudouin VI de Constantinople* (*Boudewijn VI van Constantinopel*), Count (Baudouin IX) of Flanders, son (b. 1172) departed on Fourth Crusade Apr 1202, Emperor (Baudouin I) of Constantinople 9 May 1204, captured by Tsar Kaloyan of Bulgaria at the battle of Adrianople Mar 1205 and later killed
c. 14 Apr 1205	*Jeanne de Constantinople* (*Johanna van Constantinopel*), daughter (b. 1200) at the same time Countess of Flanders and of Namur; ruled initially under the guardianship of King *Philippe II Auguste* of France, then (from Jan 1212) with her first husband, *Ferrand* (*Ferrand*), son of King Sancho I of Portugal (d. 27 (or 29) Jul 1233), then (from Dec 1237) with her second husband, *Thomas* (*Thomas*), son of Count Thomas I of Savoy (d. 1 Feb 1259)
5 Dec 1244	*Marguerite de Constantinople* (*Margareta van Constantinopel*), sister of Jeanne (b. 1202) at the same time Countess of Flanders; Count Willem II of Holland, as Antiking of Germany (until 28 Jan 1256), deposed Marguerite in Hainaut 11 Jul 1252; Count Charles I of Anjou invaded Hainaut end 1253 and held it on Marguerite's behalf until 25 Sep 1256

*House of Avesnes**

10 Feb 1280	*Jean* (*Jan*) *I*, grandson; Count (Jan II) of Holland 10

*See footnote on p. 202

	Nov 1299*
11/12(?) Sep 1304	*Guillaume* (*Willem*) *I*, son; entrusted with government of Holland summer 1303
7 Jun 1337	*Guillaume* (*Willem*) *II*, son (b. c. 1307)
26/27 Sep 1345	*Marguerite II d'Avesnes* (*Margareta II van Avesnes*), sister; abdicated in Holland 7 Dec 1354
26 (23?) Jun 1356	*Guillaume* (*Willem*) *III*, son (b. after 1332) Count of Holland 7 Dec 1354; became mentally unfit to rule c. 1357 Regent: early Apr 1358 – 15(?) Mar 1389: *Albert* (*Albrecht*), Duke (Albrecht) of Bavaria-Straubing, brother (b. Munich 25 Jun 1336; d. The Hague 13 Dec 1404) subsequently Count
15(?) Mar 1389	*Albert*, previously Regent Governor: Mar 1389 – 13 Dec 1404: *Guillaume* (*Willem*) *IV*, son (b. 5 Apr 1365) subsequently Count
13 Dec 1404	*Guillaume IV*, previously Governor; at the same time Duke (Wilhelm II) of Bavaria-Straubing
31 May 1417	*Jacqueline de Bavière* (*Jacoba van Beieren*), daughter (for 1st time) (baptized 16 Jul 1401; d. 9 Oct 1436) from Sep 1417 in conflict with her uncle, Duke Johann of Bavaria-Straubing, Bishop (Joannes VI) of Liège (until 22 May 1418) (d. 6 Jan 1425); ruled with her second husband and first cousin, Count *Jean* (*Jan*) *IV* of Brabant (b. 11 Jun 1403; d. 17 Apr 1427), from 8 May 1418 until 11 Apr 1420 when she left him claiming the marriage was void and fled to England; Duke Johann was granted South Holland and made co-ruler of the rest of Holland 13 Feb 1419
11 Apr 1420	Count *Jean IV* of Brabant (see above); pledged Holland to Duke Johann of Bavaria-Straubing 21 Apr 1420 – 6 Jan 1425; ruled with (from summer 1425) his first cousin, *Philippe* (*Filips*), the Good, Duke (Philippe III) of Burgundy, Count of Flanders (b. Dijon, Burgundy, 31 Jul 1396; d. Brugge, Flanders, 15 Jun 1467), who administered Hainaut and Holland alone after Jean IV's death; in conflict with Jacqueline

*From this time counts of Hainaut were simultaneously counts of Holland

	(see above) and Humphrey, Duke of Gloucester,* son of King Henry IV of England (b. 1391; d. 23 Feb 1447)
3 Jul 1428 – 12 Apr 1433	*Jacqueline de Bavière* (for 2nd time) surrendered to Philippe and was allowed to retain the title of countess so long as she did not remarry without permission; forced to abdicate on Philippe's discovery of her secret fourth marriage
12 Apr 1433	Counties of Hainaut and Holland thenceforth held by the dukes of Burgundy

Hamdanids (Banu Hamdan)

Territory comprised part of present-day northern Iraq (al-Jazira) and Syria.

Amirs

Line in Mosul

AD 905	*Abu'l Haija' ('Abdallah)*, governor of Mosul for the 'Abbasid caliph
929/30	*Nasir al-Daula (Abu Muhammad al-Hasan)*, son, died in prison, ruled conjointly with his brother Saif al-Daula of Aleppo 941/2 – 944/5, imprisoned 7 May 967
23 Feb 969 – 979/80	*('Uddat al-Daula) Abu Taghlib (Fadlallah al-Ghadanfar)*, son (b. 19 Aug 940)
979/80	Buyid conquest
981/2 – 990/1	*(Abu Tahir) Ibrahim* and *(Abu 'Abdallah) al-Husain*, brothers of Abu Taghlib, restored as joint rulers by the Buyids
990/1	Mosul conquered by the 'Uqailids and Diyarbakr by the Marwanids

Line in Aleppo

944/5 – 8 Feb 967	*Saif al-Daula (Abu'l-Hasan 'Ali I)*, brother of Nasir al-Daula of Mosul, ruled in Mosul with his brother

*Jacqueline married Humphrey, with permission from Antipope Benedict (XIII), but the marriage was declared invalid by Pope Martin V 9 Jan 1428

	941/2 – 944/5
Feb 967	*Sa'd al-Daula (Abu'l-Ma'ali Sharif I)*, son (b. 952)
991/2	*Sa'id al-Daula (Abu'l-Fada'il Sa'id)*, son, son-in-law of Lu'lu' (a slave of Saif al-Daula), Fatimid vassal
Dec 1001/Jan 1002	*(Abu'l-Hasan) 'Ali II*, son, with *Lu'lu'* (see above) ruling as regent
1003/4	*(Abu'l-Ma'ali) Sharif II*, brother, with *Lu'lu'* (see above) ruling as regent
1003/4	Power seized by *Lu'lu'* under Fatimid suzerainty
1008 – 1015/16	*Murtada al-Daula (Mansur ibn Lu'lu')*, son (d. after 1030)
1015/16	Fatimid conquest

Hammudids

Territory comprised part of present-day southern Spain, with the capital at Málaga.

Governors for the Cordovan Caliphate, Caliphs, and from 1035/6 Kings

AD 1009/10	*'Ali (al-Nasir ibn Hammud)*, son of Hammud; appointed governor of Ceuta by the Umayyad caliph of Córdoba, Sulaiman al-Musta'in; dethroned Sulaiman al-Musta'in and proclaimed himself caliph Jul 1016; murdered
1016/17	*al-Qasim I (al-Ma'mun ibn Hammud)*, brother (for 1st time) appointed governor of Algeciras, Tangier and Arzila, proclaimed caliph on the death of 'Ali, abdicated
5 Aug 1021	*Yahya I (al-Mu'tali ibn 'Ali ibn Hammud)*, nephew (for 1st time) proclaimed caliph
1022/3 – 10 Sep 1023	*al-Qasim I* (for 2nd time) returned as caliph, dethroned
1023	*Yahya I* (for 2nd time) returned as caliph
1035/6	*Idris I (al-Muta'ayyid ibn 'Ali)*, brother, ruled as king of Malaga
1039/40	*Yahya II*
1039/40	*al-Hasan (al-Mustansir ibn Yahya)*, son

1042/3	*Idris II (al-'Ali ibn Yahya)*, brother (for 1st time)
1046/7	*Muhammad I (al-Mahdi ibn Idris)*, cousin
1048/9	*Muhammad II (al-Mu'tasim)*, son of al-Qasim I
1048/9	*al-Qasim II (al-Wathiq)*, son
1054/5	*Idris III (al-Muwaffaq)*, brother of Idris II
1054/5	*Idris II* (for 2nd time)
1055/6 – 1057/8	*Muhammad III (al-Musta'li)*, son
1057/8	Zirid conquest

Hausa States

DAURA

Territory in present-day northern Nigeria.

Habe Queens

The first eight Habe Queens of Daura ruled at Tsofon Birni.

9th – 10th century AD	1. *Kufuru*	10. *Gamata*
	2. *Gino*	11. *Shata*
	3. *Yakumo*	12. *Batatume*
	4. *Yakunya*	13. *Sandamata*
	5. *Walzamu*	14. *Jamata*
	6. *Yanbamu*	15. *Hamata*
	7. *Gizirgizir*	16. *Zama*
	8. *Innagari*	17. *Shawata*
	9. *Daura*	

Habe Kings

from 11th century	1. *Abayajidda**	4. *Gakuma*
	2. *Bawo*	5. *Jaaku*
	3. *Gazaura*	6. *Jaketake*

*According to tradition, Abayajidda was the son of the king of Baghdad. His son, Bawo, succeeded him in Daura, while his remaining six sons founded the other six 'true' Hausa States

7. *Yakama*
8. *Jaka*
9. *Ada Hamta*
10. *Ada Jabu*
11. *Dagamu*
12. *Ada Yaki*
13. *Hamdogu*
14. *Yabau*
15. *Naji*
16. *Gani*
17. *Wake*
18. *Kamutu*
19. *Rigo*
20. *Gaga*
21. *Jabu*
22. *Zamnau*
23. *Shashimi*
24. *Ada Inda*
25. *Doguma*
26. *Ada Gamu*
27. *Ada Sunguma*
28. *Shafau*
29. *Ada Sabau*
30. *Ada Doki*
31. *Nagama I*
32. *Ada Kube*
33. *Hamama*
34. *Dagajirau*
35. *Kamu*
36. *Ada Guguwa*
37. *Hamida*
38. *Abdu Kawo*
39. *Nagama II*
40. *Hanatari*
41. *Rifau*
42. *Hazo*
43. *Dango*
44. *Bawan Allah*
45. *Kalifah*
46. *Tsofo*
47. *Jiro*
48. *Gwari Abdu*, driven from Daura by the Fulani 1805

c.1809	*Lukudi*, brother, first king of Daura ruling in exile at Zango (in present-day northern Nigeria)
1828	*Nuhu*, son
1843	*Muhamman Shah*, cousin
1856	*Haruna*, brother of Nuhu
1862	*Dan Aro*, brother of Muhamman Shah
1868	*Tafida*, son of Nuhu (for 1st time)
1888	*Suleimanu*, son of Dan Aro
1890	*Yusufu*, brother of Haruna
1895 – 1904	*Tafida* (for 2nd time)
1900	Incorporated into British protectorate of Northern Nigeria
1904	*(Malam) Musa*, brother, reinstalled in Daura by the British
from 1911	*Abdurrahman*, son
1 Oct 1960	Nigeria became independent, see Volume 3

GOBIR

Traditionally originating in Arabia and successively established in the Sudan and present-day northern Nigeria.

Kings of Gobir at Gubur (in present-day Saudi Arabia) and Suakin (in present-day eastern Sudan)

7th century AD (?)	1. *Bana Turmi*	7. *Bartadawa*
	2. *Gubur*	8. *Bartakiskia*
	3. *Sanakafo*	9. *Kartaki*
	4. *Majigi*	10. *Sagimma*
	5. *Sarki*	11. *Baran Kwammi*
	6. *Bartuwatuwa*	12. *Masawana Jimri Gaba*

Kings of Gobir at Khartoum

(?)	13. *Ciroma I*	21. *Banizam*
	14. *Dan Goma*	22. *Beyamusi*
	15. *Sakidamma*	23. *Gosi*
	16. *Matsaura*	24. *Jimri Gaba*
	17. *Duguma*	25. *Ciroma II*
	18. *Zaberma*	26. *Majejeri*
	19. *Umi*	27. *Kasimu*
	20. *Gozo*	28. *Cida*

Kings of Gobir in Bornu (in present-day north-eastern Nigeria)

(?)	29. *Gojo*	41. *Dalla Gungumi*
	30. *Dara*	42. *Dalla Kure*
	31. *Jelani*	43. *Hammadmi*
	32. *Bataji*	44. *Humadi*
	33. *Babba I*	45. *Arkal I*
	34. *Munzakka I*	46. *Babba II*
	35. *Munzakka II*	47. *Humdu*
	36. *Munzakka III*	48. *Ubandoma*
	37. *Alazi*	49. *Baciri II*
	38. *Kana Ju'un*	50. *Ubandoma I* (or *Ubandoro I*?)
	39. *Baciri I*	51. *Ubandoma II*
	40. *Hunda*	52. *Baciri III*

Kings of Gobir in Asben (now Air, Niger)

(?)

53. *Ubandoro II*
54. *Abdulla*
55. *Keji*
56. *Dunsumi*
57. *Akwai Allah*
58. *Zamai*
59. *Falali*
60. *Gintsarana*
61. *Dalla*
62. *Baciri IV*
63. *Muhammadu I*
64. *Dara*
65. *Ciroma III*
66. *Mundagas I*
67. *Baran Kwammi*
68. *Ashafa*
69. *Baciri V*
70. *Bustadana Gingama*
71. *Ashafa Dara*
72. *Kawami*
73. *Mundagas II*
74. *Ciroma IV*
75. *Muhamman*
76. *Kazgaba*
77. *Muhammadu II*
78. *Maji*
79. *Ciroma V*
80. *Arkal II*
81. *Usmanu*
82. *Ushuwa*
83. *Makuwa*
84. *Muhammadu dan Ciroma*, c. 1715
85. *Baciri VI*
86. *Muhamman Mai Gici*
87. *Akali*
88. *Arkal III*
89. *Muhammadu*
90. *Soba*
91. *Uban Iche* (or *Ibn Ashe*)

Kings of Gobir at Alkalawa

1742	*Babari dan Ibn Ashe*, son, conquest of Zamfara (in present-day north-western Nigeria) c. 1755 or 1760
1770	*Dan Gudi dan Babari*, son
1777	*Gambai*
1777	*Bawa Jan Gwarzo dan Babari*, brother of Dan Gudi
1795	*Yakuba dan Babari*, brother, killed in battle against Katsina
1801	*Nafata dan Babari*, brother
1803 – 1808	*Yunfa dan Nafata*, son
1808	Defeated by the Fulani, the Gobir kings continued to rule at Tsibiri and then at Sabon Birni (in present-day northern Nigeria)

KANO

Territory in present-day northern Nigeria, with the capital at Kano City.

Habe Kings

AD 999	*Bagauda*, traditionally the grandson of Abayajidda of Daura
1063	*Warisi*, son
1095	*Gajemasu*, son, builder of Kano City
1134	*Nawata* and *Gawata*, twin sons
1136	*Yusa* (or *Sarki*), brother
1194	*Naguji*, son
1247	*Gugwa*, uncle
1290	*Shekarau*, nephew
1307	*Tsamiya*, son, assassinated
1343	*Usman Zamnagawa* (or *Gakingarkuma*), brother
1349	*Yaji*, nephew, probably the first Muslim king
1385	*Bugaya*, brother
1390	*Kanajeji*, nephew, renounced Islam
1410	*Umaru*, son
1421	*Dauda* (or *Bakin Damisa*), brother, vassal of Bornu
1438	*Abdullahi Burja*, brother
1452	*Dakauta*, son
1452	*Atuma*, son
1452	*Yakubu*, uncle
1463	*Mohamman Rumfa*, son, war with Katsina
1499	*Abdullahi*, son, defeated Katsina and Zaria
1509	*Mohamman Kisoki*, son, vassal of Songhay
1565	*Yakufu*, son
1565	*Dauda Abasama*, son
1565	*Abubakar Kado*, brother of Abdullahi, deposed
1573	*Mohamman Shashere*, brother of Dauda Abasama, deposed
1582	*Mohamman Zaki*, uncle
1618	*Mohamman Nazaki*, son
1623	*Kutumbi*, son, killed in battle with Katsina
1648	*Alhaji*, son, killed in battle with Katsina
1649	*Shekarau*, son
1651	*Mohamman Kukuna*, brother (for 1st time)
1652	*Soyaki*, nephew
1652	*Mohamman Kukuna* (for 2nd time)
1660	*Bawa*, son

1670	*Dadi*, son, defeated by Zamfara 1700
1703	*Mohamman Sharefa*, son
1731	*Kumbari*, son, vassal of Bornu
1743	*Alhaji Kabe*, son, vassal of Bornu
1753	*Yaji II*, great-uncle
1768	*Babba Zaki*, son
1776	*Dauda Abasama*, brother
1781 – 1805	*Mohamman Alwali*, brother (d. (killed by Fulani) in exile at Burum Burum 1807)
1805	Fulani conquest

Fulani Emirs

1805	*Sulemanu*, of the Modibawa clan
1819	*Ibrahim Dabo*, of the Sullibawa clan
1846	*Usman*, son
1855	*Abdullahi*, brother
1883	*Muhamman Bello*, brother
1893	*Muhamman Tukur*, son
1894 – 1903	*Aliyu* (or *Abu*) *Babba*, cousin
1903	Incorporated into British protectorate of Northern Nigeria
1903	*Muhammadu Abbas*, brother, installed by the British
1919	*Usman*, brother
1926	*Abdullahi Bayero*, nephew
1953 – Mar 1963	*Muhammadu Sanusi*
1 Oct 1960	Nigeria became independent, see Volume 3
Jun 1963	*Muhammadu Inuwa Abbas*
from 12 Oct 1963	*(Alhaji) Ado Bayero*, son of Abdullahi Bayero (b. Kano 25 Jul 1930)

KATSINA

Territory in present-day northern Nigeria, with the capital at Katsina.

Habe Kings

c. AD 1100	*Kumayo*, traditionally the grandson of Abayajidda of Daura
(?)	*Ramba-Ramba*
(?)	*Bata tare*
(?)	*Jarnanata*

(?)	*Sanau*, last of the Durbawa kings, killed by Korau
c. 1260(?)	*Korau*
(?)	*Ibrahim Yanka Dari*
(?)	*Jida Yaki*, ruled for 40 years
1492/3	*Muhammadu Korau*, first Muslim king, conquest by Songhay 1512
1541/2	*Ibrahim Sura*, probably from Mali, vassal of Songhay
1543/4	*Ali Murabus*, the Marabout or Holy Man, regained independence from Songhay 1554
1568/9	*Muhammadu Toya Rero I*
1572/3	*Aliyu Karya Giwa I*
1585	*Usman Tsagarana*, Eclipser of the Sun
1589/90	*Aliyu Jan Hazo I*, Red like the Harmattan
1595/6	*Muhammadu Mai-sa-maza-gudu*, the Putter of Men to Flight
1612/13	*Aliyu Jan Hazo II*
1614/15	*Maje Ibrahim*
1631/2	*Abdul Karim*
1634/5	*Ashafa*
1634/5	*Ibrahim Gamda*
1644/5	*Muhammad Wari I*, son of Abdul Karim
1655/6	*Sulaiman*
1667/8	*Usman Na yi Nawa*, son of Tsagarana
1684/5	*Muhammadu Toya Rero II*
1701/2	*Muhammadu Wari II*
1704/5	*Uban Yari* (also known as *Muhammadu dan Wari*), defeated Kano
1706/7	*Karya Giwa II*
1715/16	*Jan Hazo III*, son of Muhammadu Wari
1728/9	*Tsagarana Hassan*, son of Toya Rero II
1740/1	*Muhammadu Kabiya*, son of Usman Na yi Nawa
1750/1	*Tsagarana Yahya*
1751/2	*Karya Giwa III*, son of Jan Hazo III
1758/9	*Muhammadu Wari III*
1767/8	*Karya Giwa IV*
1784/5	*Agwaragi*
1801/2	*Tsagarana Gwozo*
1801/2	*Bawa dan Gima*
1804/5	*Mare Mawa Mahmudu*, killed by Umaru Dallaji at Sabon Birni (in present-day northern Nigeria)
1805/6	*Magajin Halidu*, committed suicide after defeat by the Fulani
1806	Fulani conquest, the remaining Habe fled to Maradi

Fulani Emirs

1806	*Umaru Dallaji*
1835	*Sidiku*, son, deposed
1844	*Muhamman Bello*, brother
1869	*Ahmadu Rufai*, brother
1870	*Ibrahim*, nephew
1882	*Musa*, uncle
1887 – 1904	*Abubakar*, great-nephew, defeated the last of the Katsina Habe in exile, pledged allegiance to British 1903, deposed
1904	Treaty with the French and British greatly reduced the size of Katsina, which was made a part of Kano Province
1904	*Yero*, son of Musa, deposed
1906	*Muhammadu Dikko*, son of Gidado, designated by Ibrahim as his successor
from 1944	*(Alhaji Sir) Usman Nagogo*, son (b. Katsina 1905)
1 Oct 1960	Nigeria became independent, see Volume 3

NUPE

Territory in present-day central Nigeria, with the capital initially at Jima, then at Raba and later at Bida.

Etsuzhi Nupe (Kings)

c. AD1531	*Tsoede* (or *Edegi*) (b. c. 1463)
1591	*Shaba*, son
1600	*Zaulla* (or *Zavunla*), brother
1625	*Jiga* (or *Jigba* or *Jia*), brother
1670	*Mamman Wari*, brother
1679	*Abdu Waliyi*, established capital at Jima
1700	*Alyu*
1710	*Ganamace* or *Saci*
1713	*Ibrahim*
1717	*Idrisu*
1721	*Tsado*
1742	*Abubakari Kolo*
1746	*Jibrin* (or *Jibrilu*), probably the first Muslim king, deposed and driven into exile, died in Kutigi (in present-day northern Nigeria)

1759	*Ma'azũ* (for 1st time) abdicated
1767	*Majiya I*
1777	*Ilayasu*
1778	*Ma'azũ* (for 2nd time)
1795	*Alikolo Tankari*, for eight months, deposed
1795	*Mama*, established capital at Raba, division of the kingdom
1796 – 1805	*Jimada*, grandson of Ilayasu, ruled at Jima, war with Majiya II, killed at Jengi (or Ragada?)
1796	*Majiya II*, grandson of Ilayasu (for 1st time) ruled at Raba, defeated by the Fulani and fled to Zuguma (in present-day northern Nigeria)
1810	*Idirisu* (or *Yisa*), son of Jimada, ruled at Adama Lulu as shadow king of Nupe, effective power being in the hands of the Fulani Dendo; killed in rebellion against the Fulani
1830 – 1834	*Majiya II* (for 2nd time) recalled from exile and made shadow king of Nupe in Zugurma
1836	*Tsado*, son, killed in rebellion against the Fulani

Fulani Emirs of Bida*

1832	*Usuman Zaki*, son of Dendo (for 1st time) abdicated after the rebellion of Masaba
1841	*Masaba*, brother (for 1st time) fled to Ilorin (in present-day western Nigeria) during the rebellion of the Hausa general Umar Bahaushe
1856	*Usuman Zaki* (for 2nd time)
1859	*Masaba* (for 2nd time)
1873	*Umaru Majigi*, son of Usuman Zaki
1884	*Maliki*, cousin
1895 – 1901	*Abubakar*, cousin (d. Lokoja 1919) deposed by the British
1901	Incorporated into British protectorate of Northern Nigeria
1901	*Muhammadu*, son of Umaru Majigi (d. Feb 1916)
1916	*Bello*, son of Maliki
1926	*Saïdu*, nephew of Abubakar
19 Mar 1935	*Muhammadu Ndayako*, son of Muhammadu (b. 1883?)
from 29 Oct 1962	*Usman Sarki*

*The emirs also assumed the title of Etsu Nupe

Hesse

Landgraves

AD 1265 – 21 Dec 1308	*Heinrich I*, the Child, son of Duke Henri II of Brabant (b. 24 Jun 1244)
1308 – Feb 1311	*Johann*, son (b. c. 1278) ruled in Lower Hesse
1308 – 17 Jan 1328	*Otto*, brother (b. c. 1272) ruled in Upper Hesse 1308 – 1311, ruled all of Hesse from 1311
1328 – 3 Jun 1376	*Heinrich II*, son (b. c. 1299) with his son, *Otto* (b. 1322; d. 10 Dec 1366), as co-regent 1340 – 10 Dec 1366
1376 – 10 Jun 1413	*Hermann II*, nephew (b. c. 1340) ruled as co-regent with Heinrich II 1367 – 3 Jun 1376
1413 – 17 Jan 1458	*Ludwig I*, son (b. 6 Feb 1402)
17 Jan 1458	Division of Hesse between Ludwig I's sons

Landgraves of Hesse-Marburg

1458 – 13 Jan 1483	*Heinrich III*, son of Ludwig I (b. 15 Oct 1440; d. 13 Jan 1483) with his son, *Ludwig III* (b. c. 15 Nov 1460; d. 1 Jul 1478), ruling as co-regent 1474 – 1 Jul 1478
1483 – 17 Feb 1500	*Wilhelm III*, son (b. 8 Sep 1471)

Landgraves of Hesse-Kassel

1458 – 8 Nov 1471	*Ludwig II*, son of Ludwig I (b. 7 Sep 1438)
1471 – 1493	*Wilhelm I*, son (b. 4 Jul 1466; d. 8 Feb 1515) abdicated
1483 – 11 Jul 1509	*Wilhelm II*, brother (b. 29 Mar 1469) ruled with his brother 1483 – 1493, ruled alone from 1493, Landgrave of Hesse-Marburg 1500

Hildesheim

Bishops (and from 13th century Princes of the Holy Roman Empire)*

AD (?)	*Guntar* (d. 5 Jul (?))
?	*Rembert* (d. 12 Feb (?))
fl. Apr 845 – Oct 847	*Ebo* (d. 20 Mar (?))
3 Oct 852 – 15 Aug 874	*Altfrid*
875	*Ludolf*, died before his consecration
(?) – 2 Feb 880	*Markwart*, killed
880 – 31 Oct or 1 Nov 908(?)	*Wicpert*
(?) – 3 Nov 919	*Walpert*
919 – 10 Oct 928	*Sehard*
928 – 13 Sep 954	*Thiedhart*
954 – 1 Dec 984	*Otwin*
985 – 8 Nov 989	*Osdag*
19 Jun 990 – 7 Dec 992	*Gerdag* (d. Como)
15 Jan 993 – 20 Nov 1022	*Bernward*
2 Dec 1022 – 5 May 1038	*Godehard*
20 Aug 1038 – 14 Nov 1044	*Thietmar*
1044 – 8 Mar 1054	*Azelin*
1054 – 5 Aug 1079	*Hezelo*
1079 – 19 Oct 1114	*Udo*
1115 – 1119	*Bruning*, resigned
after mid-Jun / before mid-Oct 1119 – 14 Mar 1130	*Berthold*
1130	*Bernhard I*, resigned
1153 – 18 Oct 1161	*Brun II*
1161 – 10 Jul 1170	*Hermann I*
1170 – 20 Sep 1190	*Adelog von Dorstadt*
1190 – 28 Oct 1194	*Bern*
1194 – 21 Aug 1198	*Konrad I von Querfurt* (d. (murdered) 6 Dec 1202) translated to Würzburg

*When two dates separated by an oblique stroke are given for the beginning of an episcopate, the first refers to election or nomination and the second to ordination, consecration or investiture

1199 – 21 Mar 1216	*Hartberg von Dalem*
1216 – 26 Jan 1221	*Siegfried I von Lichtenburg*, resigned
after 23 Jun 1221 – 5 Jul 1246	*Konrad II*, resigned
late 1246/early 1247 – 25 May 1257	*Heinrich I von Wernigerode*
Jun 1257 – 14 Jun 1260	*Johann I*
9 Oct 1260 – 4 Jul 1279	*Otto I*, Duke of Brunswick
18 Jul 1279 – 27 Apr 1310	*Siegfried II*
5 Jul 1310 – 13 Jul 1318	*Heinrich II*, Count of Woldenberg (d. Avignon)
23 May 1319 – before 31 Jul 1331	*Otto II*, Count of Woldenberg (d. 22 Aug 1331) resigned
28 Aug 1331/26 May 1354 – 6 Feb 1363	*Heinrich III*, Duke of Brunswick (b.1296/7); in rivalry with *Erich*, Count of Homburg, until Jun 1345*
22 Mar 1363	*Johann II* (d. Koblenz 1 Apr 1378) formerly Bishop of Kulm, translated to Worms 20 Aug 1365
20 Aug 1365 – 15 Nov 1398	*Gerhard vom Berge*, previously Bishop of Verden Coadjutor: 1395 – 15 Nov 1398: *Johann*, Count of Hoya, Bishop of Paderborn
28 Feb 1399 – 12 May 1424	*Johann III*, Count of Hoya, previously Bishop of Paderborn and coadjutor
10 May/30 Dec 1424 – 20 May 1452	*Magnus von Sachsen-Lauenburg* (d. 21 Sep 1452) previously Bishop of Kamin, coadjutor 22 Feb 1424, resigned
20 Oct 1452 – 1458	*Bernhard II*, Duke of Brunswick-Lüneburg (d. 9 Feb 1464) resigned
24 Mar 1458 – 23 Jul 1471	*Ernst von Schaumburg*
15 Jan 1472 – 1480	*Henning von Haus*, resigned
25 Sep 1480 – 4 May 1502	*Barthold von Landesberg*

*Erich was invested by Pope John XXII on 31 Jul 1331 but was defeated by Heinrich III in Jun 1345 and died 21 Oct 1348

Hittites (Hatti)

Territory comprised part of present-day central and western Turkey and northern Syria, with the capital at Hattum or Hattusa (present-day Boğazköy).

Kings

(?) BC	*Pithana of Kussara*, an Assyrian vassal(?)
c. 1792	*Anitta of Kussara*, son, assumed the title of 'Great King'
c. 1740	*Tudhalias I*(?)
c. 1710	*PU-Sharruma*(?),* son
The Old Kingdom	
c. 1680	*Labarnas*, son
c. 1650	*Hattusilis I*, son, invaded the kingdom of Yamkhad and destroyed Alalakh (present-day Tell Açana)
c. 1620	*Mursilis I*, adopted son, conquered the kingdom of Yamkhad, overthrew first (Amorite) dynasty of Babylonia 1595, assassinated
c. 1590	*Hantilis I*, brother-in-law
c. 1560	*Zidantas I*, son-in-law, assassinated
c. 1550	*Ammunas*, son
c. 1530	*Huzziyas I*, son(?), deposed
c. 1525 – c. 1500	*Telepinus*, brother-in-law
The Middle Kingdom	
c. 1500	*Alluwamnas*, son-in-law of Telepinus
c. 1490	*Hantilis II*
c. 1480	*Zidantas II*
c. 1470	*Huzziyas II*
c. 1460	*Tudhalias II*
c. 1440	*Arnuwandas I*, son
c. 1420	*Tudhalias III*, son
c. 1400 – c. 1380	*Hattusilis II*, brother, lost Halap (present-day Aleppo) and Kizzuwadna (part of present-day southern-central Turkey), Hattum captured and burned

*The ideogram representing the first element of the name cannot at present be read and is represented by its standard Sumerian value

The Empire

c. 1380	*Suppiluliumas I*, son; conquered Halap and Alalakh c. 1365; Ugarit, Damascus and Amurru became vassals c. 1360; sacked the Mitanni capital of Wassukkani
c. 1346	*Arnuwandas II*, son
c. 1345	*Mursilis II*, brother
c. 1315	*Muwatallis*, son, regained control of Damascus and Amurru c. 1300
c. 1296	*Urhi-Tesup*, illegitimate son, deposed and exiled to Cyprus
c. 1289	*Hattusilis III*, uncle, signed treaty with the Egyptian king Ramesses II 1284
c. 1265	*Tudhalias IV*, son, invaded Cyprus
c. 1235	*Arnuwandas III*, son, Assyrian invasion of Hittite territories
c. 1215 – c. 1200	*Suppiluliumas II*, brother
c. 1200	Overthrown by the Phrygians and Luvians

Holland

Territory now North and South Holland provinces, Netherlands.

Counts

fl. AD 833 – 839	*Gerulf I* (d. Abbey of Corbie, Kingdom of the Franks) retired to live as a monk 856
fl. 888 – 889	*Gerulf II*
fl. 916 – 928	*Dirk I*, probably son
before 970	*Dirk II*, son
6 May 988	*Arnulf*, son
18 Sep 993	*Dirk III*, son
27 May 1039	*Dirk IV*, son
13/14 Jan 1049	*Floris I*, brother
28 Jun 1061	*Dirk V*, son
	Regent:
	1061 – 1063: *Geertrui*, mother, daughter of Duke Bernhard II of Saxony (d. 4 Aug 1113)

17 Jun or 27 Nov 1091	*Floris II*, son
2 May 1121	*Dirk VI*, son
5/6 Aug 1157	*Floris III*, son (d. Antioch)
1 Aug 1190 – 4 Nov 1203	*Dirk VII*, son
Dec 1203	*Willem I*, Count of Friesland, brother
4 Feb 1222	*Floris IV*, son (b. 24 Jun 1210) Regent: c. 4 Feb 1222 – before 1226: *Boudewijn*, Count of Bentheim (for 1st time)
19 or 28 Jul 1234	*Willem II*, son (b. Leiden 1227; d. Alkmaar, Friesland) Antiking of Germany 3 Oct 1247 – 28 Jan 1256 Regents: 1234 – 1240: Council under leadership of *Boudewijn*, Count of Bentheim (for 2nd time) and Willem's uncles, Bishop *Otto III* of Utrecht (d. 3 Apr 1249) and *Willem* (d. 30 Aug 1238)
28 Jan 1256	*Floris V*, son (b. Jul 1254) murdered Regents: 1256 – 26 Mar 1258: *Floris de Voogd*, uncle (d. 26 Mar 1258) Mar 1258 – 1263: *Aleydis*, sister of Floris de Voogd (d. 1284) and her nephew, Duke *Henri III* of Brabant (d. 28 Feb 1261) 1263 – 1266(?): *Otto II van Gelre* and Bishop *Henricus III* of Liège
27 Jun 1296 – 10 Nov 1299	*Jan I*, son (b. 1284) Regent: *Jan II*, Count (Jean I) of Hainaut, son of Jan I's great-aunt Aleydis; governor from 27 Oct 1299 and subsequently Count
10 Nov 1299	County of Holland thenceforth held by counts of Hainaut

Holy Roman Empire

'Holy Roman Emperor' is a term used by modern historians to refer to Charlemagne and those of his successors who received a papal coronation. The first list given here is a summary listing of all the Carolingian Emperors; their biographical details will be found in their entries under the kingdoms they ruled.

Holy Roman Emperors

Carolingians

25 Dec AD 800 – 28 Jan 814	*Charlemagne* (or *Karl I*, the Great), King of the Franks; crowned by Pope Leo III with the title Romanorum Gubernans Imperium
28 Oct 816 – 20 Jun 840	*Ludwig I*, the Pious, King of the Franks, son; crowned co-emperor and heir 11 Sep 813
843 – Sep 855	*Lothar I*, King of the Lombards, son; crowned co-emperor 817
855 – 12 Aug 875	*Ludwig II*, King of the Lombards, son
25 Dec 875 – 6 Oct 877	*Karl* (French: *Charles*) *II*, the Bald, King of the West Franks (see France), son
884 – 887	*Karl III*, the Fat, King of the East Franks (see below) and of the West Franks (see France), nephew; deposed
896 – 8 Dec 899	*Arnulf*, King of the East Franks (see below), nephew
Feb 901 – Jul 905	*Ludwig (III)*, the Blind, King (Ludwig III) of the Lombards and (Louis) of Lower Burgundy; deposed
915 – 7 Apr 924	*Berengar*, King of the Lombards, grandson of Ludwig I; exercised no real power outside Italy

After Berengar the title of Holy Roman Emperor is always associated with kings of Germany, who were successors, territorially, to the kings of the East Franks, who are listed next.

Kings of the East Franks

By the treaty of Verdun 843, Ludwig the German received territory roughly corresponding to part of the present-day Federal Republic of Germany east of the rivers Rhine and Ems and excluding Friesland.

Carolingians

843 – 28 Aug 876	*Ludwig II*,* the German, son of King Ludwig I of the

*Numeration begins with Ludwig I, the Pious, King of the Franks

	Franks (b. c. 806) annexed Alsatia, received eastern part of Lorraine, including Aachen and Friesland, by Treaty of Meerssen 8 Aug 870
876	Kingdom divided among Ludwig II's three sons: Karlmann (b. c. 829; d. 29 Sep 880) received Bavaria and the southeastern marks; Ludwig III, the Younger (b. c. 830; d. 20 Jan 882) received Franconia, Thuringia and Saxony; Karl III the Fat (see below) received Swabia and the title King of the East Franks
876	*Karl III*,* the Fat, son (b. 839; d. Neidingen 13 Jan 888) received the remainder of Lorraine 879, King of the Lombards 880, sole ruler after death of brothers, Holy Roman Emperor 884; gained control over the Kingdom of the West Franks (apart from Lower Burgundy) 884; deposed
887 – 8 Dec 899	*Arnulf*, nephew (b. c. 850; d. Regensburg) Duke of Bavaria and governor of Carinthia 880; chosen by leaders of tribal groups as King of the East Franks 887; Holy Roman Emperor 896
900 – 24 Nov 911	*Ludwig*, the Child, son (b. Sep or Oct 893) reigned during period of internal feuds leading to the establishment of 'tribal duchies' (including Bavaria, Saxony, Swabia and Thuringia), the leaders of which regarded the German King chosen by them as their feudal overlord

Kings of Germany

Date in the left-hand column is the date of accession to the German kingship.

Franconian House

8 Nov 911 – 23 Dec 918	*Konrad I*, Duke of Franconia; chosen by an assembly of nobles at Forchheim, Franconia

Saxon House (Liudolfings)

12 May 919 – 2 Jul 936	*Heinrich I*, the Fowler, Duke of Saxony, son of Duke Otto I of Saxony (b. c. 876; d. Memleben)
8 Aug 936 – 7 May 973	*Otto I*, the Great, Duke (Otto II) of Saxony, son (b. 23 Nov 912; d. Memleben 7 May 973) King of the

*Karl I the Great (Charlemagne), King of the Franks and Holy Roman Emperor, and Karl (Charles) II the Bald, King of the West Franks and Holy Roman Emperor, are included in the numeration

	Lombards 951, Holy Roman Emperor (styled himsel Romanorum Imperator Augustus) 2 Feb 962
26 May 961 – 7 Dec 983	*Otto II*, son (b. early 955; d. Rome) crowned co-king o Germany and Italy 961, crowned co-emperor 25 De 967
24 Dec 983 – 21 Jan 1002	*Otto III*, son (b. Jul 980; d. near Viterbo, Italy) King o the Lombards 996, Holy Roman Emperor 21 May 99 Regents: 24 Dec 983 – 991: *Theophano*, mother (b. 956) 991 – 994: *Adelheid*, grandmother (d. Dec 999)
7 Jun 1002 – 13 Jul 1024	*Heinrich II*, the Saint, Duke (Heinrich IV) o Bavaria, cousin (b. Abbach, Bavaria, 6 May 973; d. Göttingen), Holy Roman Emperor 14 Feb 1014
Salians	
8 Sep 1024	*Konrad II*, son of Heinrich von Speyer (b. 990; d. Utrecht) King of the Lombards 1026, Holy Roman Emperor 26 Mar 1027, crowned King of Burgundy 2 Feb 1033*
4 Jun 1039	*Heinrich III*, Duke (Heinrich I) of Swabia, son (b. Bodfeld 28 Oct 1017; d. Bodfeld) crowned king of Germany 14 Apr 1028; Duke (Heinrich VI) of Bavaria 1027 – 1041, Holy Roman Emperor 25 Dec 1046
5 Oct 1056†	*Heinrich IV*, son (b. Goslar, Saxony, 11 Nov 1050; d. Liège 7 Aug 1106) crowned king of Germany 17 Jul 1054; Duke (Heinrich VIII) of Bavaria 1055 – 1061; took Rome Mar 1084; Holy Roman Emperor 31 Mar 1084; deposed; ruled 1090 – 1093 with his son, *Konrad* (b. 12 Feb 1074; d. 27 Jul 1101) Duke of Lower Lorraine 1076 – 1089, crowned King of Germany 30 May 1087, deposed after rebellion Regents: 1056 – 1062: *Agnes*, mother 1062 – 1065: Archbishop *Anno II* of Cologne

*Konrad II inherited the Kingdom of Burgundy (from this time usually called the Kingdom of Arles) from Rodolphe III, of the House of Welf. The Kings of Germany and Holy Roman Emperors were titular kings of Arles until 1378, when Karl IV ceded Arles to the dauphin, later King Charles VI of France

† 15 Mar 1077 – 15 Oct 1080 *Rudolf von Rheinfelden*, Duke of Swabia (d. Merseburg) elected in opposition to Heinrich IV as antiking, deposed in Swabia May 1077

31 Dec 1105 – 23 May 1125	*Heinrich V*, son of Heinrich IV (b. 8 Jan 1081) crowned king of Germany 6 Jan 1099, deposed Heinrich IV, Holy Roman Emperor 13 Apr 1111

Supplinburg House

30 Aug 1125 – 4 Dec 1137	*Lothar II*, Duke (Lothar) of Saxony, son of Gebhard von Supplinburg (b. Jun 1075; d. Breitenwang, Austria) resigned in Saxony 1127; Holy Roman Emperor 4 Jun 1133

House of Hohenstaufen

7 Mar 1138 – 15 Feb 1152	*Konrad III*, son of Duke Friedrich I of Swabia (b. 1093; d. Bamberg) Duke of Franconia 1115, German antiking 18 Dec 1127 – 1135, King of the Lombards Jun 1128
4 Mar 1152	*Friedrich I Barbarossa*, Duke (Friedrich III) of Swabia, nephew (b. 1122; d. Cilicia, Turkey) Holy Roman Emperor 18 Jun 1155
10 Jun 1190 – 28 Sep 1197	*Heinrich VI*, son (b. Nijmegen Nov 1165; d. Messina, Sicily) elected king of Germany 24 Jun 1169, Holy Roman Emperor 15 Apr 1191, King (Heinrich) of Sicily 25 Dec 1194
8 Mar 1198 – 21 Jun 1208	*Philipp*, Duke of Swabia, brother (b. 1178; d. (murdered) Bamberg) Bishop of Würzburg 1190 – Jan 1192; Duke of Spoleto 1195; in conflict with *Otto IV* (see below)

Welfs

9 Jun 1198 – 27 Jul 1214	*Otto IV*, Duke (Otton) of Aquitaine, son of Duke Heinrich III of Saxony (b. 1177; d. Harzburg Castle, Saxony, 9 May 1218) Earl of York 1190; deposed in Aquitaine 1199; civil war with Philipp until 1208; Holy Roman Emperor 4 Oct 1209, but deposed and defeated at the Battle of Bouvines 27 Jul 1214

House of Hohenstaufen (restored)

5 Dec 1212	*Friedrich II*, King of Sicily, Duke (Friedrich VI) of Swabia, son of Heinrich VI (b. Iesi, Mark of Ancona, Italy, 26 Dec 1194; d. Castel Fiorentino, Apulia, Kingdom of Sicily, 30 Dec 1250) Holy Roman Emperor 22 Nov 1220, resigned in Swabia 1235, King of Jerusalem Aug 1225/18 Mar 1229 – 5 Apr 1243; ruled Apr 1220 – Jul 1235 with his son *Heinrich (VII)*

	(b. Sicily 1211; d. in prison, Martirano, Calabria, Kingdom of Sicily, 10 Feb 1248) King of Germany 23 Apr 1220, rebelled 1234, defeated 1237 Regent: 1225 – 1228: Elector Palatine *Ludwig I* (b. Kelheim, Bavaria, 23 Dec 1174; d. (assassinated) Kelheim 15 Sep 1231)
30 Dec 1250 – 21 May 1254*	*Konrad IV*, Duke (Konrad III) of Swabia, son of Friedrich II (b. Andrea, Italy, 25 Apr 1228; d. Lavello, Kingdom of Sicily) elected king of Germany Feb 1237; pretender to the throne of Sicily 1251; defeated by Heinrich Raspe* and forced to flee to Sicily

The Great Interregnum

13 Jan 1257	*Richard*, Earl of Cornwall (b. Winchester, England, 5 Jan 1209; d. Berkhamsted Castle, Hertfordshire, England, 2 Apr 1272) elected King of Germany but unable to enforce his claim
1 Apr 1257	King *Alfonso X*, the Wise, of Castile and León (b. Burgos, Castile, 23 Nov 1220; d. Seville, Castile, 4 Apr 1284) election rejected by the Pope, abandoned his claim to the throne in 1275

House of Habsburg

29 Sep 1273 – 15 Jul 1291	*Rudolf I*, Count of Habsburg, Duke of Swabia, son of Count Albrecht IV of Habsburg (b. Limburg im Breisgau 1 May 1218; d. Speyer) Duke of Austria 1274 – 1282, Duke of Carinthia 1276 – 1286

House of Nassau

5 May 1292 – 23 Jun 1298	*Adolf*, Count of Nassau, son of Count Walram II of Nassau (b. c. 1248; d. Göllheim 2 Jul 1298) deposed

House of Habsburg (restored)

27 Jul 1298 – 1 May 1308	*Albrecht I*, Duke of Austria and Styria, son of Rudolf I (b. Jul 1248; d. (assassinated) Brugg (now in Aargau canton, Switzerland))

*22 May 1246 – 16 Feb 1247	*Heinrich Raspe*, Landgrave of Thuringia, son of Hermann I (b. c. 1202; d. Wartburg Castle, Thuringia) antiking
3 Oct 1247 – 28 Jan 1256	Count *Willem II* of Holland (b. Leiden, Holland, 1227; d. Alkmaar, Friesland, 28 Jan 1256) antiking

House of Luxemburg

27 Nov 1308 – 24 Aug 1313	*Heinrich VII*, Count (Heinrich V) of Luxemburg (b. Valenciennes c. 1274; d. Buonconvento, near Siena, Italy) King of the Lombards 6 Jan 1311, Holy Roman Emperor 29 Jun 1312

House of Habsburg (restored)

19 Oct 1314 – 1326	*Friedrich*, the Fair, Duke of Austria, son of Albrecht I (b. 1286; d. Gutenstein 13 Jan 1330) civil war with Ludwig IV, defeated 28 Sep 1322, made joint-king with Ludwig IV 1325, retired to Austria after 1326

House of Wittelsbach

20 Oct 1314	*Ludwig IV*, the Bavarian, son of Duke Ludwig II of Bavaria (b. 1 Apr 1282; d. Munich 11 Oct 1347) ruled in Upper Bavaria from 1294, defeated Friedrich III 1322, King of the Lombards 31 May 1327, Holy Roman Emperor 17 Jan 1328; in conflict with Karl IV 1346 – 1347

House of Luxemburg (restored)

11 Jul 1346	*Karl IV* (baptized *Wenzel*) grandson of Heinrich VII (b. Prague, Bohemia, 14 May 1316; d. Prague) Margrave of Moravia 1333, King (Karel) of Bohemia 1346 – 1373, Count (Karl) of Luxemburg 1346 – 1353, King of the Lombards 1355, Holy Roman Emperor 5 Apr 1355, Margrave of Brandenburg 1373 – 1378*
29 Nov 1378 – 20 Aug 1400	*Wenzel*, King (Václav IV) of Bohemia, son (b. Nürnberg 26 Feb 1361; d. Prague, Bohemia, 16 Aug 1419) elected king of Germany 10 Jun 1376; Elector of Brandenburg 1373 – 1378, Duke of Luxemburg 7/8 Dec 1383; deposed

House of Wittelsbach (restored)

21 Aug 1400 – 18 May 1410	*Ruprecht I*, Elector Palatine (Ruprecht III) of the Rhine (b. Amberg, Rhenish Palatinate, 5 May 1352; d. near Oppeinheim)

*30 Jan – 14 Jun 1349	*Günther*, son of Count Heinrich VII of Schwarzburg (b. Blankenburg 1304; d. Frankfurt am Main) Count of Schwarzburg – Blankenburg 1330; elected king in opposition to Karl IV, defeated and relinquished all claim to the throne

House of Luxemburg (restored)

1 Oct 1410 – 18 Jan 1411	*Jodokus* (or *Jobst*), Margrave of Brandenburg and Moravia, cousin of Wenzel (b. 1351; d. Brno, Moravia) granted Lusatia 1397, Duke of Luxemburg 1388 – 1402 and 1407 – 1411; in rivalry with Sigismund
20 Sep 1410 – 9 Dec 1437	*Sigismund*, King (Zsigmond) of Hungary, son of Karl IV and cousin of Jodokus (b. Nürnberg 14 Feb 1368; d. Znojmo, Moravia) Elector of Brandenburg 1378 – 1397 and 1411 – 18 Apr 1417, King (Zikmund) of Bohemia 1419; undisputed king after the death of Jodokus, King of the Lombards 1431, Holy Roman Emperor 31 May 1433

House of Habsburg (restored)

18 Mar 1438 – 27 Oct 1439	*Albrecht II*, Archduke (Albrecht V) of Austria, King (Albrecht) of Bohemia, Duke (Albrecht) of Luxemburg, King (Albert) of Hungary, son-in-law of Sigismund (b. 10 Aug 1397; d. Nezmely, Hungary)
2 Feb 1440 – 19 Aug 1493	*Friedrich III*, Archduke (Friedrich V) of Austria, second cousin, grandson of Archduke Leopold III of Austria (b. Innsbruck 21 Sep 1415; d. Linz) inherited Styria, Carinthia and Carniola 1439; King of the Lombards 1452, Holy Roman Emperor 19 Mar 1452

Hungary

Chiefs or Princes, later Kings

AD 895/6(?)	*Árpád*, son of Álmos, led the Magyars over the Carpathians to take possession of the Great Hungarian Plain
905(?) – 946	*Zsolt* (or *Zoltán*), son (b. c. 896; d. 949) abdicated in favour of his son Taksony (*sic*)
947(?)	*Vál* (or *Fajsz*), son of Jutas, the elder brother of Zsolt
952(?)	*Taksony*, son of Zsolt (b. 931)*
972 – 1 Feb 997	*Géza*, son

*Sometimes given as direct successor of Zsolt c. 947

997 – 15 Aug 1038	*István I** (known in English as *Saint Stephen*, original name *Vajk*), son (b. 969(?)†), crowned king 25 Dec 1000
1038	*Péter*, nephew, son of Ottone Orseolo, the doge of Venice (for 1st time) (b. 1011; d. 1058) driven out
1041 – after 5 Jul 1044	*Sámuel Aba*, brother-in-law of István I (b. c. 990) murdered
15 Aug 1044	*Péter* (for 2nd time) restored by King Heinrich III of Germany, again driven out
1046 – 1060	*András I*, great-grandson of Taksony
6 Dec 1060 – Jul/Aug 1063	*Béla I*, brother (b. c. 1016)
1063	*Salamon*, son of András I (b. 1051/2; d. 1087/8) driven out
14 Mar 1074	*Géza I*, son of Béla I
25 Apr 1077	*László I*, Saint, brother (b. 1040)
25 Jul 1095	*Kálmán*, son of Géza I (b. c. 1074) conquered Croatia 1102
3 Feb 1116 – 1 Mar 1131	*István II*, son (b. 1101)
28 Apr 1131 – 13 Feb 1141	*Béla II*, cousin (b. 1108)
1141 – 31 Mar 1162	*Géza II*, son (b. 1130)
1162	*István III*, son (for 1st time) (b. 1147; d. 4 Mar 1172)
1162 – 14 Jan 1163	*László II*, uncle
1163 – 1165	*István IV*, brother (b. 1132 or 1133; d. 11 Apr 1165) in rivalry with István III
19 Jun 1163 – 4 Mar 1172	*István III* (for 2nd time)
4 Mar 1172/18 Jan 1173	*Béla III*, brother (b. 1148)
23 Apr 1196 – 30 Nov 1204	*Imre*, son (b. 1174)
26 Aug 1204‡ - 7 May 1205	*László III*, son (b. 1199)
1205 – 21 Sep 1235	*András II*, uncle (b. 1176)
14 Oct 1235 – 3 May 1270	*Béla IV*, son (b. Nov 1206)

* Throne also claimed by his elder kinsman Koppány (d. 998)

† Birth put at 962 by some sources; according to others he was 'still a child' in 997

‡ Crowned to ensure succession

17 May 1270 – 6 Aug 1272	*István V*, son (b. 1239)
3 Sep 1272 – 10 Jul 1290	*László IV*, son (b. 1262) murdered Regents: *Erzsébet*, mother (b. 1240; d. between 1290 and 1295) and *Joakim Pektari*
23 Jul 1290* – 14 Jan 1301	*András III*, grandson of András II (b. c. 1265)
Aug 1301	*Vencel*,† King (Václav II) of Bohemia and (Wacław I) of Poland, great-great-nephew of Béla IV (b. 1271; d. 21 Jun 1305)
1304	*Ottó (von Wittelsbach)*,† Duke (Otto III) of Lower Bavaria, nephew of István V (b. 11 Feb 1261; d. 9 Sep 1312)
1307/20 Aug 1310 – 26 Jul 1342	*Károly I* (or *II*) (or *Charles Robert*, *Caroberto*),† son of Charles Martel (b. 1288)
1342 – 10 Sep 1382	*Lajos* (or *Louis*) *I*, the Great, son (b. 5 Mar 1326) King (Ludwik) of Poland 5 Nov 1370
17 Sep 1382	*María*, daughter (for 1st time) (b. 1370) driven out by Károly II Regent: *Erzsébet*, mother (b. 1339; d. Jan 1387)
31 Dec 1385	*Károly II* (or *III*), King (Charles III) of Naples, nephew of Lajos I (b. Naples 1345; d. (assassinated) Pest)
24 Feb 1386‡	*María* (for 2nd time); until Jan 1387 under the regency of her mother, *Erzsébet* (see above); from 31 Mar 1387 with her husband, *Zsigmond*, Elector (Sigismund) of Brandenburg (b. Nürnberg, Germany, 14 Feb 1368; d. Znojmo, Bohemia, 9 Dec 1437) King of Germany 20 Sep 1410, King (Zikmund) of Bohemia 1419, Duke of Luxemburg 16 Aug 1419, Holy Roman Emperor 31

*At the death of László IV, who was without direct heir, András III was in prison in Vienna. The throne was claimed by László IV's nephew Charles Martel of Anjou (sometimes referred to as King Károly I of Hungary), Otto von Wittelsbach (king 1304 – 1307) and King Václav II of Bohemia (king 1301 – 1304)

†All these three claimed the throne on the death of András III. Károly I (or II for those who include Charles Martel) had already been crowned at Zagreb in Aug 1300, but was not crowned with St. Stephen's crown until 1310.

‡24 Feb 1386/May 1390 – 6 Aug 1414	*László*, Nápolyi, son of Károly II (b. Naples 11 Feb 1377; d. Naples) King (Ladislas) of Naples Feb 1386 – Aug 1390 and 9 Jul 1399 – 6 Aug 1414, Prince of Taranto 1406; pretender

	May 1433; Zsigmond ruled alone after María's death
1437 – 27 Oct 1439	*Albert* (or *Albrecht*), Archduke (Albrecht V) of Austria, son-in-law (b. 10 Aug 1397; d. Nezmely) at the same time Duke of Luxemburg; King (Albrecht II) of Bohemia and of Germany 1438
8 Mar 1440 – 10 Nov 1444	*Ulászló I*, King (Władysław III) of Poland, nephew of María (b. Cracow 21 Oct 1424; d. Varna)
1444 / 1453 – 23 Nov 1457	*László V* (German: *Ladislaus Posthumus*), King (Ladislav) of Bohemia, Duke (Ladislaus) of Luxemburg, posthumous son of Albert (b. 22 Feb 1440) Regent: 1444 – 1453: *János Hunyadi* (b. between 1407 and 1409; d. Zimony 11 Aug 1456)
24 Jan 1458 – 6 Apr 1490	*Mátyás I*, Corvinus, son of János Hunyadi (b. Cluj 23 Feb 1443) elected by the nobles
15 Jul 1490 – 13 Mar 1516	*Ulászló II* (Polish: Władysław Jagiełłonczyk), King (Vladislav II) of Bohemia, nephew of Ulászló I (b. 1 Mar 1456)

Idrisids

Territory comprised part of present-day Morocco and north-western Algeria, with the capital initially at Walila and after 807/8 at Fez.

Imams

5 Feb AD 789 – 16 Jul 793	*Idris I (ibn 'Abdallah ibn Hasan II)*, poisoned
13 Sep 793	*Idris II (ibn Idris)*, surnamed *al-Saghir*, son (b. 13 Sep 793) his mother Kanza ruled during his minority
May / Jun 828	*Muhammad (ibn Idris al-Mustansir)*, son
Mar / Apr 836	*'Ali I (ibn Muhammad)*, son
Jan / Feb 849	*Yahya I (ibn Muhammad)*, brother
(?)	*Yahya II (ibn Yahya)*, son
(?)	*'Ali II (ibn 'Umar ibn Idris)*, grandson of Idris II
(?)	*Yahya III (al-Miqdam ibn al-Qasim ibn Idris)*, cousin
904 / 5	*Yahya IV (ibn Idris ibn 'Umar)*, great-grandson of

	Idris II
922/3–926	*al-Hasan (ibn Muhammad ibn al-Qasim, al-Hajjam)*, great-grandson of Idris II
926	Fatimid conquest

Ikhshidids

Territory comprised part of present-day Egypt and Syria, with the capital at al-Fustat (Old Cairo).

Ikhshids (Princes)

AD 935	*(Abu Bakr) Muhammad al-Ikhshid (ibn Tughj)* (b. 8 Feb 882) initially as ‘Abbasid governor of Egypt
24 Jul 946 – 29 Dec 960	*(Abu'l-Qasim) Unujur (ibn al-Ikhshid)*, son (b. Dec 931/Jan 932)
11 Jan 961	*(Abu'l-Hasan) ‘Ali (ibn al-Ikhshid)*, brother (b. 2 Jan 938)
7 Jan 966 – 22 Apr 968	*(Abu'l-Misk) Kafur*, the eunuch of Muhammad al-Ikhshid, vizier from 946
Apr/May 968 – 6 Jul 969	*(Abu'l-Fawaris) Ahmad (ibn ‘Ali)*, son of ‘Ali (b. 957/8)
6 Jul 969	Conquest of Egypt by the Fatimid general Jauhar

Il-Khans

Territory comprised part of present-day Iran, Iraq and Syria, with the capital initially at Tabriz, then at Maragha and after 1307 at Sultaniyya.

Il-Khans (later Khans)

AD 1256/7 – 8 Feb 1265	*Hülegü*, grandson of Chingiz (b. c. 1217/18) conquered Baghdad 4 Feb 1258

Feb 1265 – 1 Apr 1282	*Abaqa*, son (b. Mar/Apr 1234)
Apr 1282 – 10 Aug 1284	*Ahmad Tegüder* (or *Takudar*), brother, assassinated by Arghun
11 Aug 1284 – 10 Mar 1291	*Arghun*, nephew
Mar/Apr 1291	*Gaikhatu*, brother
Apr/May – 4 Oct 1295	*Baidu*, cousin, killed by Ghazan
Oct/Nov 1295	*(Mahmud) Ghazan*, son of Arghun (b. 1271/2) ended the Il-Khans' allegiance to the Mongol Great Khans and took the title of Khan
May/Jun 1304	*(Muhammad Khudabanda) Öljeitü*, brother (d. 17 Dec 1316)
8 Sep 1316 – 30 Nov 1335	*Abu Sa'id*, son
1335/6	*Arpa*, descended from a brother of Hülegü
1335/6	*Musa*, grandson of Baidu
1336 – 1353	Period of rival khans; power largely in the hands of the vizier, Taj al-Din Hasan Buzurg ibn Husain (see Jalayirids)
1335/6 – 1337/8	*Muhammad*, descended from a son of Hülegü
1337/8 – 1351/2	*Tughai Temür*, descended from Chingiz's brother, Otchigin (d. 1353/4) lord of Khurasan after 1336/7
1338/9 – 1340/1	*Jehan Temür*, grandson of Gaikhatu
1338/9 – 1339/40	*Sati Beg Khatun*, daughter of Öljeitü
1339/40 – 1343/4	*Sulaiman*, descended from a son of Hülegü
1344/5 – 1353/4	*Nushirwan al-'Adil*
1355	Kingdom divided among the Jalayirids, Muzaffarids and Sarbadarids of Khurasan

Incas

Territory comprised part of present-day Peru, Ecuador, Bolivia and Chile, with the capital at Cuzco.

Rulers

AD (?)	*Manqo Qhapaq* (*Manco Capac*)*
(?)	*Zinchi Roq'a* (*Sinchi Roca*), son
(?)	*Lloq'e Yupanki* (*Lloque Yupanqui*), son
(?)	*Mayta Qhapaq* (*Mayta Capac*), son
(?)	*Qhapaq Yupanki* (*Capac Yupanqui*), son
(?)	*'Inka Roq'a 'Inka* (*Inca Roca*), son
(?)	*Yawar Waqaq* (*Yahuar Huacac*), son
(?)	*Wiraqocha 'Inka* (*Viracocha Inca*), son, began Inca wars of expansion
1438	*Pachakuti 'Inka Yupanki* (*Pachacuti Inca Yupanqui*), son, abdicated
1471	*Thupa 'Inka Yupanki* (*Topa Inca Yupanqui*), son
1493	*Wayna Qhapaq* (*Huayna Capac*), son
1525	*Washkar 'Inka* (*Huascar*), son, defeated and captured by the Spaniards under Pizarro Apr 1532 near Cuzco
1532	*'Ataw Wallpa 'Inka* (*Atahuallpa*), brother, in revolt against Huascar from 1525, kidnapped by Pizarro in Cajamarca 16 Nov 1532 and later executed
1533	*Thupa Wallpa* (*Topa Huallpa*), brother, placed on throne by the Spaniards, poisoned
1533	*Manqo 'Inka Yupanki* (*Manco Inca Yupanqui*), brother, placed on throne by the Spaniards, rebelled and established small independent Inca state
1545 – 1572	*Thupa 'Amaru* (*Topa Amaru*), executed by the Spaniards at Cuzco
1572	Final Spanish conquest

*Names in parentheses are the Spanish spellings of Inca names

Ireland (Eire)

High-Kings (ard-rithe) of Tara

The high-kings of Tara were not kings of all Ireland. The five Fifths of Ireland — Ulster (Ulaid), Meath (Mide), Leinster (Laigin), Munster (Muma) and Connaught (Connacht) — were each ruled by a line of kings. The great prestige of the high-kings (who were normally associated with the kingship of Meath) arose from the sacred character of the early kingship and later from the power of the Uí Néill dynasties.

The high-kingship alternated between different branches and collaterals of the Uí Néill. These divisions are indicated in the following list by numbers following the names: [1]The Connachta; [2]Uí Néill; [3]Southern Uí Néill; [4]Northern Uí Néill; [5]Síl nÁedo Sláine, a division of the Southern Uí Néill; [6]Cenél nEógain, a division of the Northern Uí Néill; [7]Clann Cholmáin, a division of the Southern Uí Néill.

	Niall Noígiallach (*Neil of the Nine Hostages*) *mac Echach Mugmedóin*, a descendant of Conn Cétchathach (Con of the Hundred Battles), a semi-legendary King of Tara; ended the hegemony of the Fifth of Ulster; founder of the Uí Néill
	Nath Í mac Fiachrach,[1] nephew; sometimes omitted from the list of high-kings
	Lóeguire mac Néill,[2] son of Niall
c. AD 463	*Ailill Molt mac Nath Í*,[1] son of Nath Í
c. 487	*Lugaid mac Lóeguiri*,[3] son of Lóeguire
c. 507	*Muirchertach mac Ercae maic Eógain*,[4] great nephew of Lóeguire; King of Ailech
c. 536	*Tuathal Máelgarb mac Cormaic Caích maic Coirpri*,[3] great nephew of Lóeguire
c. 544	*Diarmait mac Cerbaill*,[3] great nephew of Lóeguire; King of Meath and founder of the Síl nÁedo Sláine and Clann Cholmáin branches of the Southern Uí Néill; defeated by the king of Connaught and Colum Cille (St. Columba) at Cúl Dreimne (near Sligo), 561
c. 565	*Forggus mac Muirchertaig*[4] and *Domnall mac Muirchertaig*,[4] sons of Muirchertach and co-kings of Ailech
c. 566	*Ainmuire mac Sétnai*,[4] descended from Niall through Conall Gulban
c. 569	*Báetán mac Muirchertaig*,[4] brother of Forggus and Domnall; ruling with *Eochaid mac Domnaill*,[4] son of

	Domnall; co-kings of Ailech
c. 572	*Báetán mac Ninnedo*,[4] descended from Niall through Conall Gulban
c. 586	*Áed mac Ainmuirech*,[4] son of Ainmuire
c. 598	*Áed Sláine mac Diarmato*,[5] son of Diarmait; King of Brega; ruling with *Colmán Rímid mac Báetáin*,[4] son of Báetán mac Muirchertaig; King of Ailech
604	*Áed Allán* (or *Áed Uaridnach*) *mac Domnaill*,[4] son of Domnall; King of Ailech
c. 612	*Máel Cobo mac Áedo*,[4] son of Áed mac Ainmuirech
614	*Suibne Menn mac Fiachnai*,[4] great nephew of Muirchertach mac Ercae; King of Ailech
628	*Domnall mac Áedo*,[4] brother of Máel Cobo; defeated Congal Cáech, King of Ulster, at Mag Roth (County Down), 637
642	*Cellach mac Máele Cobo*[4] and *Conall Cáel mac Máele Cobo*,[4] sons of Máel Cobo
658	*Diarmait mac Áedo Sláine*[5] and *Blathmac mac Áedo Sláine*,[5] sons of Áed Sláine and co-kings of Brega
665	*Sechnussach mac Blathmaic*,[5] son of Blathmac; King of Brega
671	*Cenn Fáelad mac Blathmaic*,[5] brother; King of Brega
674	*Fínsnechta Fledach mac Dúnchado*,[5] cousin; King of Brega
695	*Loingsech mac Óengusso*,[4] grandson of Domnall mac Áedo
704	*Congal Cennmagair*,[4] cousin
710	*Fergal mac Máele Dúin*,[4] great grandson of Áed Allán; King of Ailech
722	*Fogartach mac Néill*,[5] great grandson of Diarmait mac Áedo Sláine; King of Brega
724	*Cináed mac Írgalaig*,[5] King of Brega
728	*Flaithbertach mac Loingsig*,[4] son of Loingsech (d. 765); abdicated
734	*Áed Allán mac Fergaile*,[6] son of Fergal mac Máele Dúin; King of Ailech; defeated Ulster, 735, and Leinster, 738
743	*Domnall Midi mac Murchado*,[7] descended from Diarmait mac Cerbaill through Colmán Már; King of Meath
763	*Niall Frossach mac Fergaile*,[6] brother of Áed Allán; King of Ailech
770	*Donnchad Midi mac Domnaill*,[7] son of Domnall

	Midi; King of Meath
797	*Áed Oirdnide (the Ordained) mac Néill*,[6] son of Niall Frossach; King of Ailech; perhaps the first Christian high-king
819	*Conchobar mac Donnchada*,[7] son of Donnchad Midi; King of Meath
833	*Niall Caille mac Áeda*,[6] son of Áed Oirdnide; King of Ailech
846	*Máelsechnaill mac Máele Ruanaid*,[7] nephew of Conchobar (d. 27 Nov 862); King of Meath; defeated the Vikings and plundered Dublin, 848; established suzerainty over nearly all of Ireland
862	*Áed Findliath mac Néill*,[6] son of Niall Caille; King of Ailech
879	*Flann Sinna mac Máelsechnaill*,[7] son of Máelsechnaill; King of Meath
916	*Niall Glúndub mac Áeda*,[6] son of Áed Findliath; King of Ailech
919	*Donnchad Donn mac Flainn*,[7] son of Flann Sinna; King of Meath
944	*Congalach Cnogba mac Máelmithig*,[5] King of Brega
956	*Domnall ua Néill*,[6] grandson of Niall Glúndub; King of Ailech
980	*Máelsechnaill mac Domnaill*,[7] grandson of Donnchad Donn (d. 1022); King of Meath; deposed
1002 – 1014	*Brian Bóruma (Brian Boru) mac Cennétig*, brother of Mathgamain, King of Munster; King of Munster; defeated the King of Dublin at the Battle of Clontarf, 1014
	Period of anarchy
1072	*Tairrdelbach Ua Briain*, grandson of Brian Bóruma; King of Munster
1086 – 1119	*Muirchertach Ua Briain*, son of Tairrdelbach; King of Munster
1086	*Domnall Ua Lochlainn*
1121	*Tairrdelbach Ua Conchobair*; King of Connaught
1156	*Muirchertach Mac Lochlainn*
1166 – 1186	*Ruaidrí Ua Conchobair (Rory O'Connor)*, son of Tairrdelbach Ua Conchobair (d. 1198); King of Connaught; accepted King Henry II of England as overlord by the Treaty of Windsor 1175; deposed
	English conquest and rule of Ireland

Isin

Territory comprised part of present-day southern Iraq, with the capital at Isin (near present-day ad-Diwaniyah).

Kings

2017 BC	*Ishbi-Erra*, a chief of Mari
1984	*Shu-ilishu*
1974	*Iddin-Dagan*
1953	*Ishme-Dagan*
1934	*Lipit-Ishtar*
1923	*Ur-Ninurta*
1895	*BurSin*
1874	*Lipit-Enlil*
1869	*Erra-imitti*
1861	*Enlil-bani*
1837	*Zambia*
1834	*Iter-pisha*
1830	*Ur-dukuga*
1827	*Sin-magir*
1816 – 1794	*Damiq-ilishu*
1794	Conquered by Larsa

For the Second Dynasty of Isin, see Babylonia.

Isma'ilis (Assassins)

Territory comprised part of present-day northern Iran, centred at Alamut.

Grand Masters

AD 1090/1	*al-Hasan I (ibn al-Sabbah)* (b. Rayy) seized Alamut
12 Jun 1124 – 9 Feb 1138	*(Kiya) Buzurg-Ummid (al-Rudbari)*, son, ruled at Qal'at Lamsar (now Lambasar) after 5 Sep 1102

Feb/Mar 1138 – 20 Feb 1162	*Muhammad I (ibn Buzurg-Ummid)*, son
Feb/Mar 1162 – 9 Jan 1166	*al-Hasan II (ibn Muhammad)*, son
Jan/Feb 1166	*(Nur al-Din) Muhammad II (ibn al-Hasan)*, son, poisoned
Sep/Oct 1210	*(Jalal al-Din) al-Hasan III (ibn Muhammad)*, son, returned to Sunni orthodoxy 1211/12, poisoned
Nov/Dec 1221 – 31 Dec 1255	*('Ala' al-Din) Muhammad III (ibn al-Hasan)*, son (b. 1212/13) assassinated
Dec 1255 – 19 Nov 1256	*(Rukn al-Din) Khurshah*, son, killed by the Il-Khan Hülegü
1256	Alamut captured by Mongols

Israel

Territory comprised part of present-day Israel and western Jordan, with the capital initially at Gibeah and then at Hebron, Jerusalem, Shechem (present-day Nablus), Tirzah (near present-day Nablus) and Samaria (present-day Sabastiyah).

Kings

c. 1025 BC*	*Saul*, son of Kish, capital at Gibeah, killed by the Philistines at the battle of Mount Gilboa
c. 1010 – 1008	*Eshbaal* (or *Ishbosheth*), son (b. c. 1050), fled to Mahanaim (in present-day north-eastern Israel), nominal ruler of the northern districts
c. 1010 †	*David*, son-in-law of Saul (b. c. 1040) ruler initially in

*No length is given for the reign of Saul in the Bible; David and Solomon are each credited with forty years. Figures are given for the kings of the divided territory, and their accession is fixed with reference to their fellow kings; but the data are inconsistent. The reconstruction given above, one of many in which dates for the death of Solomon range from 937 to 922 BC, is that given by J. Gray in *Peake's Commentary*

†c. 980(?)	*Absalom*, son of David (b. c. 1005?) stirred up revolt in the north, anointed at Hebron, took Jerusalem, pursued David over the Jordan, defeated, killed by Joab

	Judah only with capital at Hebron; took Jerusalem and made it his capital; conquered Edom (part of present-day southern Israel and western Jordan); overlord of Damascus, Ammon and Moab (part of present-day southern Syria)
c. 970	*Solomon*, son
c. 930	Division of the kingdom into Israel and Judah
c. 930	*Jeroboam I*, chosen by the northern tribes as king of Israel in opposition to Solomon's son Rehoboam, established capital at Shechem and later at Tirzah, lost external territories
910/9	*Nadab*, son, killed by Baasha
909/8	*Baasha*, son of Ahijah, usurper
886/5	*Elah*, son, killed by Zimri
885/4	*Zimri*, usurper, for seven days
885/4	*Omri*, made king by his soldiers, in rivalry with Tibni until c. 880, built new capital at Samaria 880, recovered Moab
874/3	*Ahab*, son
853	*Ahaziah*, son
852	*Jehoram*, brother, revolt of Moab
842/1	*Jehu*, son of (Jehoshaphat, son of) Nimshi, acclaimed as king by his troops
814/13	*Jehoahaz*, son
798/7	*Jehoash*, son
782/1	*Jeroboam II*, son, co-regent from 793/2
753/2	*Zechariah*, son, for six months, murdered
752	*Shallum*, son of Jabesh, usurper, for one month, murdered
752	*Menahem*, usurper
742/1	*Pekahiah*, son, murdered
740/39	*Pekah*, son of Remaliah, usurper, autonomous ruler in Gilead from 752(?), killed by Hoshea
732 – 722	*Hoshea*, son of Elah, accepted as king by the Assyrian king Tiglath-Pileser III
722	Revolt and fall of Samaria, Israel became an Assyrian province

Jahwarids

Territory comprised part of present-day southern Spain, with the capital established at Córdoba.

Heads of a republican government, refusing to take the title of Sultan

AD 1030/1	*(Abu'l-Hazm) Jahwar (ibn Muhammad ibn Jahwar)*, vizier of Hisham III, the last Umayyad caliph
1043/4 – 1068/9	*(Abu'l-Walid) Muhammad (ibn Jahwar)*, son, exiled
1058/9 – 1068/9	*'Abd al-Malik (ibn Muhammad)*, son, regent, exiled
1068/9	'Abbadid conquest

Jalayirids

Territory comprised part of present-day northern Syria, Iraq and western Iran, with the capital at Baghdad.

Sultans

AD 1335/6	*(Taj al-Din) Hasan (Buzurg ibn Husain)*, governor of Rum under Abu Sa'id
1356 – 8 Nov 1374	*Uwais I (ibn Hasan)*, son, assumed sovereignty 1358
Nov/Dec 1374	*(Jalal al-Din) Husain I (ibn Uwais)*, son, assassinated by Ahmad
1382/3 – 1383/4	*Bayazid (ibn Uwais)*, brother, ruled in Kurdistan
1382/3 – 1 Sep 1410	*(Ghiyath al-Din) Ahmad (ibn Uwais)*, brother, governor of Basra after 1374/5, killed by Qara Yusuf of the Kara Koyunlu
Sep 1410	*(Shah) Walad*, nephew, assassinated
1411/12	*Mahmud (ibn Walad)*, son (for 1st time) under the tutelage of the Queen-Mother Tandu
1415/16	*Uwais II (ibn Walad)*, brother
1421	*Muhammad (ibn Walad)*, brother

1421/2	*Mahmud* (for 2nd time)
1423/4 – 11 Oct 1431	*Husain II (ibn 'Ala' al-Daula)*, grandson of Ahmad, put to death by Iskander of the Kara Koyunlu
1431	Kara Koyunlu conquest

Japan

HEADS OF STATE

Emperors

c. 40 BC	*Jimmu**
c. 10	*Suizei*, son
c. AD 20	*Annei*, son
c. 50	*Itoku*, son
c. 80	*Kosho*, son
c. 110	*Koan*, son
c. 140	*Korei*, son
c. 170	*Kogen*, son
c. 200	*Kaika*, son
c. 230	*Sujin*, son
259	*Suinin*, son
291	*Keiko*, son
323	*Seimu*, son
356	*Chuai*, brother
363	*Jingo-Kogo*, wife, regent
380	*Ojin*, son
395	*Nintoku*, son
428	*Richu*, son
433	*Hansho*, brother
438	*Ingyo*, brother
455	*Anko*, son
457	*Yuryaku*, brother
490	*Seinei*, son
495	*Kenso*, grandson of Richu

*In official style *Jimmu-Tennō*, but in accordance with the practice of most historians *Tennō* has been omitted from the titles of all the emperors

498	*Ninken*, brother
504	*Buretsu*, son
510	*Keitai*, brother-in-law
534	*Ankan*, son
536	*Senka*, brother
540	*Kimmei*, son-in-law
572	*Bidatsu*, son
586	*Yomei*, brother
588	*Sushun*, brother
593	*Suiko*, sister
629	*Jomei*, grandson
642	*Kokyoku*, wife, abdicated
645	*Kotoku*, brother
655	*Saimei*
662	*Tenchi*, son of Kokyoku
672	*Kobun*, son
673	*Temmu*, brother-in-law
686	*Jito*, wife
697	*Mommu*, son of Gemmyo
708	*Gemmyo*, mother
715	*Gensho*, daughter
724	*Shomu*, nephew, abdicated
749	*Koken* (later named *Shotoku*), daughter (for 1st time) abdicated
759	*Junnin*, descendant of Temmu, deposed
765	*Shotoku* (for 2nd time) originally named Koken
770	*Konin*, descended from a brother of Kobun
782	*Kammu*, son
806	*Heijo*, son (d. 824) abdicated
810	*Saga*, brother (d. 842) abdicated
824	*Junna*, brother (d. 840) abdicated
834	*Nimmyo*, nephew
851	*Montoku*, son
859	*Seiwa*, son (d. 880) abdicated
877	*Yozei*, son (d. 949) abdicated
885	*Koko*, brother of Montoku
889	*Uda*, nephew (d. 937) abdicated
898	*Daigo*, son
931	*Suzaku*, son (d. 952) abdicated
947	*Murakami*, brother
968	*Reizei*, son (d. 1011) abdicated
970	*En'yu*, brother (d. 991) abdicated
985	*Kazan*, nephew (d. 1008) abdicated

987	*Ichijo*, cousin
1012	*Sanjo*, cousin (d. 1017) abdicated
1017	*Go-ichijo*, son of Ichijo
1037	*Gosuzaku*, brother
1046	*Goreizei*, son
1069	*Gosanjo*, brother (d. 1073) abdicated
1073	*Shirakawa*, son (d. 1129) abdicated
1087	*Horikawa*, son
1108	*Toba*, son (d. 1156) abdicated
1124	*Sutoku*, son (d. 1164) abdicated
1142	*Konoe*, brother
1156	*Goshirakawa*, brother (d. 1192) abdicated
1159	*Nijo*, son
1166	*Rokujo*, son (d. 1176) abdicated
1169	*Takakura*, uncle (d. 1181) abdicated
1181	*Antoku*, son (d. 1185) deposed
1184	*Gotoba*, brother (d. 1239) abdicated
1199	*Tsuchimikado*, son (d. 1231) abdicated
1211	*Juntoku*, brother (d. 1242) abdicated
1221	*Chukyo*, son, for 70 days, deposed
1222	*Gohorikawa*, grandson of Takakura (d. 1234) abdicated
1233	*Shijo*, son, abdicated
1243	*Gosaga*, son of Tsuchimikado, abdicated
1247	*Gofukakusa*, son (d. 1304) abdicated
1260	*Kameyama*, brother (d. 1305) abdicated
1275	*Go-uda*, son (d. 1324) abdicated
1288	*Fushimi*, son of Gofukakusa (d. 1317) abdicated
1299	*Gofushimi*, son (d. 1336) abdicated
1302	*Gonijo*, son of Go-uda
1309 – 1319	*Hanazono*, brother of Gofushimi (d. 1348) abdicated

*The Southern Court**

1319	*Godaigo*, brother of Gonijo
1339	*Gomurakami*, son

**The Northern Court*:

1331	*Kogon*, son of Gofushimi, abdicated
1336	*Komyo*, brother, abdicated
1349	*Suko*, abdicated
1352	*Gokogon*
1372	*Go-en'yu*, abdicated
1382	*Gokomatsu*, later became emperor of reunited Japan

1368	*Chokei*, son, abdicated
1373 – 1384	*Gokameyama*, brother, abdicated

Reunification of North and South

1384	*Gokomatsu*, formerly holder of the northern throne,* abdicated
1413	*Shoko*, son
1429	*Gohanazono*, grandson of Suko of the northern court*
1465 – 1500	*Gotsuchimikado*, son (b. 1442)

SHOGUNATE

Minamoto Family

AD 1192	*Yoritomo*
1199	*Yoriiye*, son
1203 – 1219	*Sanetomo*, brother

Huziwara Family

1226	*Yoritsune*, deposed
1244 – 1251	*Yoritsugu*, son

Imperial Princes

1251	*Munetaka*, brother of emperor Gofukakusa
1266	*Koreyasu*, son
1289	*Hisaakira*, son of emperor Gofukakusa
1308 – 1336	*Morikuni*, son

Ashikaga Family

1336	*Takauji*
1358	*Yoshiakira*, son
1368	*Yoshimitsu*, son, abdicated
1394	*Yoshimochi*, son, abdicated
1423	*Yoshikazu*, son
1429	*Yoshinori*, uncle
1441	*Yoshikatsu*, son
1443	*Yoshimasa*, brother (d. 1490) abdicated
1473	*Yoshihisa*, son
1490	*Yoshitane*, cousin (for 1st time) abdicated
1493	*Yoshizumi*, abdicated

*See footnote on page 282

1508	*Yoshitane* (for 2nd time) restored
1521	*Yoshiharu*, abdicated
1545	*Yoshiteru*, murdered
1565	*Yoshihide*
1568 – 1573	*Yoshiaki* (d. 1597) deposed
1573 – 1603	Shogunate eclipsed by civil war following disintegration of the Ashikaga house

Jaunpur, Sharqi Sultans of (Sharqids)

Territory comprised part of present-day northern India.

Sultans

AD 1393/4	*Khwaja Jahan* (original name *Malik Sarwar*, granted title of Malik al-Sharq, i.e. King of the East), vizier of the Delhi sultan Mahmud Shah II
1399/1400	*Mubarak Shah* (or *Malik Wasil*), adopted son
1400/1	*(Shams al-Din) Ibrahim Shah (Sharqi ibn Mubarak)*, son
1440/1	*Mahmud Shah (ibn Ibrahim)*, son
1456/7	*Muhammad Shah*, son, deposed
1458/9 – 1479	*Husain Shah (ibn Mahmud)*, brother (d. 1499/1500)
1479	Conquest by the Lodi sultans of Delhi

Java, Kingdoms of

TARUMA

Territory comprised part of western Java.

Kings

fl. AD 132	*Devavarman*(?)
(?)	Unknown number of kings
fl. c. 400	*Purnavarman*
fl. 424	*P'o-to-kia*
fl. 435	*Dvaravarman*(?)
(?)	Unknown number of kings
fl. 1030	*Jayabhupati*
(?)	Unknown number of kings
(?)	*Niskalavastu*
(?)	*Deva Niskala*
1333 – 1357	*Ratu Devata*

EARLY MATARAM

Territory comprised part of central Java.

Kings

fl. AD 674	*Simo*(?), Queen
fl. 732	*Sanjaya, Raka of Mataram*
fl. 778	*Pancapana, Raka of Panangkaran*
(?)	*The Raka of Panunggalan*
(?)	*The Raka of Varak*
fl. 829 or 839	*The Raka of Garung*
fl. 864(?)	*The Raka of Pikatan*
fl. 879 – 882	*The Raka of Kayuvangi*
fl. 886	*Humalang, Raka of Vatu*
fl. 898 – 910	*Balitung Uttungadeva, Raka of Vatukura*
fl. 915	*Daksa, Raka of Hino*
fl. 919 – 921	*Tulodong, Raka of Layang*
fl. 924 – 928	*Vava, Raka of Pangkaya*

EAST JAVA

Territory comprised part of eastern Java.

Kings

AD (?)	*Devasimha*
fl. 760	*Gajayana*
(?)	Unknown number of kings
fl. 929 – 947	*Sindok, Raka of Hino*, probably came from Mataram to found new dynasty in eastern Java
fl. 947(?)	*Sri Iśanatunggavijaya*, daughter
(?)	*Makutavamsavardhana*, son
fl. 991 – 1007	*Dharmavamsa Anantavikrama*, invaded Sumatra and was killed in later counter-attack
fl. 1019 – 1049	*Airlangga*, son-in-law
fl. 1060	*Juru* (or *Janggala*?)
fl. 1104	*Jayavarsa of Kediri*
fl. 1115 – 1130	*Kamesvara I*
fl. 1135 – 1157	*Jayabhaya*
fl. 1160	*Sarvvesvara*
fl. 1171	*Aryyesvara*
fl. 1181	*Kroñcaryyadipa, Gandra*
fl. 1185	*Kamesvara II*
fl. 1190 – 1200	*Sarvvesvara II, Srngga*
fl. 1216 – 1222	*Kertajaya*, dethroned by Rajasa of Singosari (see below)

SINGOSARI AND MAJAPAHIT

Territory comprised part of eastern Java.

Kings

AD 1222	*Rajasa* (or *Ken Angrok*), murdered
1227	*Anusapati*, stepson, murdered
1248	*Tohjaya*, son of Rajasa
1248	*Vishnuvardhana*, son of Anusapati
1268	*Kertanagara*, son, last king of Singosari, murdered
1292	*Jayakatwang of Kediri*, usurper, deposed
1293	*Kertarajasa Jayavardhana* (or *Vijaya*), nephew and son-in-law of Kertanagara, founded kingdom at Majapahit

1309	*Jayanagara*, son, murdered
1329	*Tribhuvana*, sister
1350	*Rajasanagara* (or *Hayam Wuruk*), son
1389	*Vikramavardhana*, nephew and son-in-law
1429	*Suhita*, daughter
1447	*Kertavijaya* (personal name *Bhre Tumapel*), brother
1451 – 1453	*Rajasavardhana* (personal name *Bhre Pamotan*)
1453 – 1456	Interregnum
1456	*Hyang Purvavisesa* (personal name *Bhre Vengker*)
1466 – 1478(?)	*Singhavikramavardhana* (personal name *Bhre Pandan Solar*)
fl. 1486	*Ranavijaya*
fl. 1516	*Pateudra*
early 16th century	Superseded by Muslim state of Demak (see below)

DEMAK

Territory comprised part of eastern Java.

Rulers

c. AD 1500	*Raden Patah Senapati Jimbun*, son of the last king of Majapahit
1518	*Pangeran Sabrang Lor* (or *Pati Eunus*), son
1521	*Tranggana*, brother, assumed the title of sultan, killed in battle
1546	*Prawata*, son, sultan
(?)	*Aria Pangiri* (or *Adipati*?), son
(?)	*Pangeran Mas*, son
(?)	Disintegration of state

BANTAM

Territory comprised part of western Java.

Rulers

AD 1526	*Sunan Gunung Jati*, called *Falatehan* by the Portuguese (d. c. 1570) founder of the Bantam state
c. 1550	*Maulana Hasanuddin* (or *Pangeran Sebakinking*), son

1570	*Maulana Yusup* (or *Pangeran Paserean*), son
1580	*Maulana Muhamjad* (or *Pangeran Sedangrana*), so
1596	*Sultan Abdul Kadir*, son
1651	*Abdul Fatah, Sultan Agung*, son
1682 – 1687	*Abdul Kahar, Sultan Haji*, son
1687	Disintegration of state

MATARAM

Territory comprised a large part of Java, with the capital initially at Kartasur and later at Surakarta.

Rulers

AD 1582	(*Panembahan*) *Senapati Ingalaga*, founder o Mataram state
1601	*Panembahan Krapyak*, son
1613	*Rangsang* (later known as *Sultan Agung*)
1645	*Amangkurat I* (personal name *Sunan Tegalwangi*) son
1677	*Amangkurat II* (personal name *Adipati Anom*)
1703	*Amangkurat III* (personal name *Sunan Mas*), son driven out by the Dutch 1705, went into exile i Ceylon
1705	*Pakubuwono I* (personal name *Sunan Puger*), Dutch vassal
1719	*Amangkurat IV*, son
1725	*Pakubuwono II*, moved capital to Surakarta
1749 – 1755	*Pakubuwono III* (see also Surakarta)
1755	Division by the Dutch into Surakarta and Jogjakart (see below)

SURAKARTA

Territory comprised the eastern half of Java.

Rulers

AD 1755	*Pakubuwono III* (see also Mataram)
1788	*Pakubuwono IV*
1820	*Pakubuwono V*

1823	*Pakubuwono VI*
1830	*Pakubuwono VII*
1858	*Pakubuwono VIII*
1861	*Pakubuwono IX*
1893	*Pakubuwono X*
1939	*Pakubuwono XI*
1944 – 1949	*Pakubuwono XII*
1949	Incorporated into the republic of the United States of Indonesia

JOGJAKARTA

Territory comprised the western half of Java.

Sultans

AD 1755	*Abdurrahman Amangkubuwono I, Mangkubumi*
1792	*Abdurrahman Amangkubuwono II, Sultan Sepuh*
1810	*Abdurrahman Amangkubuwono III, Raja*
1814	*Abdurrahman Amangkubuwono IV, Seda Pesijar*
1822	*Abdurrahman Amangkubuwono V, Menol*
1855	*Abdurrahman Amangkubuwono VI, Mangkubumi*
1877	*Abdurrahman Amangkubuwono VII*
1921	*Abdurrahman Amangkubuwono VIII*
from 1939	*Abdurrahman Amangkubuwono IX, Sultan Dorodjatun* (b. 12 Apr 1912)

Jerusalem

Crusader kingdom in the Holy Land.

Kings

17 Jul AD1099* – 18 Jul 1100	*Godefroi de Bouillon*, Duke (Godefroi IV) of Lower Lorraine, son of Count Eustache II of Boulogne (b. c.

*Date of coronation

	1060; d. Jerusalem) accepted the crown but refused the title of king, preferring to be called 'Defender of the Holy Sepulchre'
11 Nov 1100 – 2 Apr 1118	*Baudouin I de Boulogne*, brother (b. 1058(?); d. al-'Arish) Count of Edessa 10 Mar 1098 – Sep 1100
14 Apr 1118* – 21 Aug 1131	*Baudouin II du Bourg*, cousin (d. Jerusalem) Count of Edessa Sep 1100 – 14 Apr 1118, Regent of Antioch Jun 1119 – Oct 1126 and summer 1130 – 21 Aug 1131, Regent of Edessa 13 Sep 1122 – 18 Apr 1123; captured by the Artuqid sultan 18 Apr 1123 and imprisoned at Harpurt, released Jun 1124 †
14 Sep 1131* – 10 Nov 1143	*Foulques*, Count (Foulques V) of Anjou and Maine, son-in-law (b. 1092; d. Acre) Regent of Antioch early 1132 – Apr 1136
25 Dec 1143*	*Mélisende*, wife, daughter of Baudouin II (d. Jerusalem 1161); crowned jointly with her son, *Baudouin III* (b. 1131; d. Beirut 10 Feb 1162) Regent of Antioch 29 Jun 1149 – 1153 and Nov 1160 – 1163, who deposed her 2 Apr 1152 and thereafter ruled alone
Feb 1162 – 11 Jul 1174	*Amaury I*, brother (b. 1136) Regent of Tripoli 1164 – 1171; Byzantine vassal
15 Jul 1174*	*Baudouin IV*, the Leper, son (b. 1161; d. Jerusalem) Regents: 1174 – 1177: Count *Raimond III* of Tripoli (for 1st time) (b. 1140) 1182 – Nov 1183: *Gui de Lusignan*, brother-in-law of Baudouin IV, son of Hugues VIII de Lusignan (b. 1129; d. Cyprus May 1194) later King (see below), King of Cyprus May 1192; deposed Nov 1183 – Mar 1185: Count *Raimond III* of Tripoli (for 2nd time)
Mar 1185	*Baudouin V*, nephew of Baudouin IV (b. Jerusalem 1177; d. Acre) crowned as king by Baudouin IV during final illness Nov 1183 Regent: Mar 1185 – Aug 1186: Count *Raimond III* of Tripoli (for 3rd time)
Aug 1186	*Sibylle*, mother of Baudouin V (by first husband),

*Date of coronation

†During Baudouin II's captivity, *Eustache I Garnier*, Seigneur of Caesarea and Sidon, was elected as constable and bailiff of Jerusalem

sister of Baudouin IV (b. 1162; d. autumn 1190); ruled with her second husband, *Gui de Lusignan*, previously Regent (see above); Jerusalem capitulated to the Ayyubid sultan Saladin 2 Oct 1187;* deposed Apr 1192†

Apr 1192 *Isabelle* (or *Isabeau*) *I*, sister of Sibylle (b. 1172; d. 1205); with (from 5 May 1192) her third husband, *Henri de Troyes*, Count (Henri II) of Champagne (b. 29 Jul 1166; d. 10 Sep 1197); and (from Jan 1198) with her fourth husband, *Amaury II*, King (Amaury) of Cyprus (b. c. 1144; d. Acre 1 Apr 1205), vassal of the Holy Roman Emperor Heinrich VI

1205 *Marie de Montferrat*, 'La Marquise', daughter of Isabelle I and Corrado (b. 1191; d. 1212); initially under the regency of her uncle, *Jean d'Ibelin*, Seigneur of Beirut (d. 1236) bailiff of Cyprus 1227 – 1232; from 3 Oct 1210‡ with her husband, *Jean de Brienne* (b. c. 1148; d. Constantinople 23 Mar 1237) Regent and Latin Emperor of Constantinople 1228

1212 *Isabelle II* (or *Yolande de Brienne*), daughter of Jean de Brienne and Marie de Montferrat (b. 1212; d. Palermo, Sicily, 1 May 1228); Jean continued to style himself King and left for the West autumn 1222, appointing *Eudes de Montbéliard*, grandson of Amaury II, as Regent; Isabelle was married to Holy Roman Emperor *Friedrich II*, King of Sicily (b. Iesi, Mark of Ancona, 26 Dec 1194; d. Castel Fiorentino, Apulia, Kingdom of Sicily, 30 Dec 1250) and was crowned Empress and Queen of Jerusalem Aug 1225 in Rome; Friedrich promised Jean that he could retain the title of King of Jerusalem but on 18 Feb 1229 Friedrich recaptured Jerusalem and was crowned King there 18 Mar 1229; Friedrich returned to the West May 1229 leaving Eudes de Montbéliard as Regent jointly with *Balian I Garnier*, Seigneur of

*Gui de Lusignan recaptured the city of Acre 12 Jul 1191 and the kingdom was henceforth based there. Jerusalem was recovered 18 Feb 1229 but finally lost in 1244

†King Richard I of England convened a council of knights which deposed Gui de Lusignan and chose Baudouin V's uncle, Margrave Corrado of Montferrat, as successor, but Corrado was murdered on 28 Apr 1192 and the throne passed to his wife, Isabelle I (her marriage to him was possibly bigamous)

‡Date of coronation

	Sidon, and *Garnier* the German
5 Apr 1243 – 21 May 1254	King *Konrad IV* of Germany, son of Friedrich II and Isabelle II (b. Andrea, Italy, 25 Apr 1228; d. Lavello, Kingdom of Sicily) refused to take up his inheritance in the Holy Land Regents: Jun 1243 – 1246: *Alix de Champagne*,* great-aunt, daughter of Isabelle I and Henri de Troyes (d. 1246) Regent of Cyprus 1218 – 1233; lost Jerusalem to a band of Khwarazmians fleeing from the Mongols 1244 1246† – 18 Jan 1253: King *Henri I* of Cyprus, son (b. 1217; d. 18 Jan 1253) 18 Jan 1253 – 21 May 1254: *Plaisance*, wife (d. Sep 1261) at the same time Regent of Cyprus
May 1254 – 29 Oct 1268	*Konradin* (also known as *Konrad V*), Duke of Swabia, son of Konrad IV (b. Wolfstein 25 Mar 1252; d. (beheaded) Naples) titular king Regents: May 1254 – Sep 1262: *Plaisance* (see above) 1263 – 1264: *Isabelle*, of Cyprus, sister of King Henri I of Cyprus

*Alix was originally joint regent with her husband Raoul de Soissons, but on learning that he was not to be granted the fief of Tyre he returned to France

†From 1246 the regents were mainly absentees and appointed the following bailiffs:

1246 – 1247	*Balian I Garnier* (d. 1247)
1247 – 24 Apr 1254	*Jean d'Ibelin*, Seigneur of Arsuf, brother (for 1st time) (d. 1259)
mid 1250 – 24 Apr 1254	King *Louis IX* of France, Saint (b. Poissy 25 Apr 1214; d. Tunis 25 Aug 1270) given supreme authority during his stay in the kingdom, not appointed bailiff; canonized 1297
24 Apr 1254 – 1256	*Jean d'Ibelin-Jaffa*, Count of Jaffa (b.c. 1200; d. spring 1266)
1256 – 1259	*Jean d'Ibelin* (for 2nd time)
1259 – 1263	*Geoffroi de Sargines* (d. spring 1269)
1263 – 1264	*Henri*, of Antioch, husband of Isabelle of Cyprus (the Regent at the time)
1264 – 1276	Direct rule by Hugues d'Antioche-Lusignan: no bailiff appointed
1276 – 1277	*Balian d'Ibelin*, Seigneur of Arsuf
1277 – 1282	*Roger de San Severino*, appointed by King Charles I of Sicily
1282 – Jun 1286	*Eudes Poilechien*, finally renounced Angevin claim to kingdom
Sep 1286 – Sep 1289	*Baudouin d'Ibelin*
Sep 1289 – May 1291	*Amaury*, of Cyprus, Seigneur of Tyre

1264 – 29 Oct 1268: *Hugues d'Antioche-Lusignan*, Regent of Cyprus, son (d. Tyre) King (Hugues III) of Cyprus 25 Dec 1267; crowned King of Jerusalem 24 Sep 1269, returned to Cyprus 1276

The crown of Jerusalem was thenceforth held (nominally) by the kings of Cyprus. After beheading Konradin, King Charles I of Sicily, Count of Anjou and of Provence, claimed the kingdom of Jerusalem and, with papal support, appointed a bailiff after Hugues' return to Cyprus (see footnote on p. 292) but his claim became ineffective after his defeat in Sicily. He and his successors continued to style themselves King of Jerusalem. The Mamluk sultan Khalil conquered Acre 19 May 1291, and captured Tyre on 14 Jul and Beirut on 31 Jul, thus ending the Crusader kingdom.

Judaea

Territory comprised part of present-day Israel and western Jordan, with the capital at Jerusalem.

Hasmonaean Kings and High-priests

166/5 BC	*Judas Maccabaeus*, son of Mattathias, killed at the battle of Elasa
160/59	*Jonathan*, brother, High-priest, appointed by the Seleucid king Alexander Balas, murdered by Tryphon
142/1	*Simon*, brother, High-priest, murdered
134/3	*John Hyrcanus I*, son, High-priest and King, Seleucid capture of Jerusalem 135/4, vassal of the Seleucid king Antiochus VII Euergetes, declared independence after Antiochus's death and assumed the kingship with the support of Rome
103/2	*Aristobulus I*, son, High-priest and King
102/1	*Alexander Jannaeus*, brother, High-priest and King
75/4	*Alexandra*, wife, and her son *Hyrcanus II* (for 1st time) High-priest
67/6	*Hyrcanus II* (for 2nd time) alone, High-priest, defeated and deposed by Aristobulus II
66/5 – 63	*Aristobulus II*, brother, High-priest and King, deposed by Hyrcanus II with the help of the Roman triumvir Pompey

63	Judaea incorporated into the Roman province of Syria
63	*Hyrcanus II* (for 3rd time) High-priest, under the authority of the proconsuls of Syria
40	*Antigonus*, son of Aristobulus II, High-priest and King
37–4	*Herod*, the Great, son of Antipater, King*
4	Kingdom divided among Herod's sons †

Judah

Territory comprised part of present-day southern Israel, with the capital at Jerusalem.

Kings

c. 930 BC ‡	Division of kingdom of Israel into Israel and Judah
c. 930	*Rehoboam*, son of King Solomon of Israel
913	*Abijah* (or *Abijam*), son
911/10	*Asa*, son
870/69	*Jehoshaphat*, son, co-regent from 873/2
848	*Joram* (or *Jehoram*), son (b. 880/79) co-regent from 853, lost Edom (part of present-day southern Israel and western Jordan)
841	*Ahaziah*, son (b. 863/2)
841	*Athaliah*, mother, daughter of King Ahab of Israel
835	*Joash* (or *Jehoash*), grandson (b. 842/1)

*High-priesthood permanently separated from the kingship

†The sons of Herod the Great:

4 BC – AD 6	*Herod Archelaus* (b. 22 BC; d. AD 18) Ethnarch of Judaea; deposed and exiled; Judaea became a Roman province
4 BC – AD 39	*Herod Antipas* (b. c. 21 BC; d. AD 39) Tetrach of Galilee and Peraea; established his capital at Tiberias; deposed and exiled
4 BC – AD 34	*Philip* (b. c. 20 BC) Tetrarch of Ituraea and Trachonitis

‡ For the dating see the footnote to Israel, p. 277

796	*Amaziah*, son (b. 821/20)
767	*Azariah* (or *Uzziah*), son (b. c. 805) co-regent from 791, recovered Edom
740	*Jotham*, son (b. 775?) co-regent from 750
732/1	*Ahaz*, son (b. 755?) co-regent from 735, lost Edom, became a vassal of Assyria from 722
716/15	*Hezekiah*, son (b. 740)
687/6	*Manasseh*, son (b. 707) co-regent from 696/5
642/1	*Amon*, son (b. 683)
640/39	*Josiah*, son (b. 647) regained independence
608	*Jehoahaz*, son (b. 631/30) for a few months, deposed by the Egyptian king Niku II
608/7	*Jehoiakim* (originally *Eliakim*), half-brother (b. 633/2) vassal of Babylon, revolted c. 598, deported to Babylonia, beginning of the Babylonian captivity
Jan 597	*Jehoiachin*, son (b. 615/14; d. after 562) for three months, siege and capture of Jerusalem by the Babylonian king Nebuchadrezzar II 16 Mar 597, deported to Babylon
Mar/Apr 597 – Jul 586	*Zedekiah* (originally *Mattaniah*), uncle (b. c. 618) installed by Babylon, led unsuccessful rebellion and deported to Babylon
Jul 586	Second Babylonian conquest of Jerusalem

Kakuyids (Kakwaihids)

Territory comprised part of present-day Iran, centred at Isfahan and Hamadan.

Ispahbads (Military Leaders)

AD 1007/8	*'Ala' al-Daula (Abu Ja'far Muhammad ibn Dushmanziyar, ibn Kakuya)*, governor of Isfahan, seized Hamadan 1023/4
1041/2 – 1051	*Zahir al-Din (Abu Mansur Faramurz)*, son, ruled at Isfahan, Seljuq vassal after 1046/7
1041/2 – c. 1048	*('Ala' al-Daula Abu Kalijar) Garshasp I*, brother (d. 1051/2) ruled in Hamadan and Nihavand
(?)	*(Abu Mansur) 'Ali (ibn Faramurz)*, nephew, ruled in

	Yazd
1095 – c. 1119/20	*('Ala' al-Daula Abu Kalijar) Garshasp II*, son, ruled in Yazd
1119/20	Seljuq annexation

Kanem-Bornu

At its fullest extent, territory comprised part of present-day southern Chad, northern Cameroon, north-eastern Nigeria and eastern Niger.

Rulers

Dougouwa Dynasty

c. AD 784	*Dougou*
835(?)	*Founé*, son
893(?)	*Aritso*, son
942(?)	*Katouri*, son
961(?)	*Ayoma*, son
1019(?)	*Boulou*, son
1035(?)	*Arki*, son
1077(?)	*Shou* or *Houwa*, son
1081(?)	*Abd al-Jelil*, son
1085 – 1097	*Houmé*, son, first Muslim ruler and first sultan

Mais or Sultans

Saifawa (Maghumi) Dynasty

1098	*Dounama*, son of Houmé
1150	*Biri I*, son
1176	*Bikorou*, son
1193	*Abd al-Jelil Selma*, the Black, son
1210	*Dounama Dibbalém*, son
1224	*Kadé*, son, assassinated
1242	*Kachim Biri*, brother
1262	*Djil*, brother (?)
1262	*Dari of Kalinwa*
1281	*Ibrahim Nikalé*, son of Kachim Biri
1301	*Abdoullahi*, cousin

1320	*Selma*, son
1323	*Kouré Gana*, the Small, brother
1325	*Kouré Koura*, the Great, brother
1327	*Mohammad*, brother
1329	*Idriss*, son of Ibrahim Nikalé
1353	*Daoud*, brother
1356	*Othman ibn Daoud*, son
1369	*Othman ibn Idriss*, cousin
1371	*Abou-Bekr Lagatou*, cousin
1372	*Idriss ibn Haritso, Dounama III*
1380	*Omar ibn Idriss*, cousin
1388	*Sa'id*, brother
1388	*Kadé Alounou ibn Idriss*, brother
1389	*Biri (Othman)*, brother
1421	*Othman Kalinouwama*, son of Daoud, deposed
1422	*Dounama IV*, son of Omar
1424	*Abdallah*, brother, deposed
1432	*Ibrahim ibn Othman*, assassinated by Kadaï
1440	*Kadaï*, son of Othman Kalinouwama, assassinated
1446	*Dounama V ibn Biri*, son of Biri
1450	*Mohammed ibn Matala*, relationship to Saifawa line unknown, deposed
1451	*Amarma ibn Othman*, son of Biri(?)
1453	*Mohammad ibn Kadaï*, son of Kadaï
1458	*Ghazi ibn Amarma*, son of Amarma
1463	*Othman ibn Kadaï*, brother of Mohammad
1473	*Omar ibn Abdallah*, grandson of Idriss
1474	*Mohammad ibn Mohammad*, of the Matala line
1479 – 29 Mar 1507	*Ali Gazi*, son of Dounama V
30 Mar 1507	*Idriss Katakarmabé ibn Ali Gazi*, son
1529	*Mohammad ibn Idriss*, son
1544	*Ali ibn Idriss*, brother
1548	*Dounama ibn Mohammad*, nephew
1566	*Dala* (or *Abdallah*) *ibn Dounama*, son
1573	*Aïssa Kili N'guirmamaramama*, sister
1580	*Idriss Alaoma ibn Ali*, son of Ali
1617	*Mohammad Boukalmarami*, son
1632	*Ibrahim*, brother
1639	*Hadj Omar*, brother
1657	*Ali*, son
1694	*Idriss*, son
1711	*Dounama*, brother
1726	*Hadj-Hamdoun*, son

1738	*Mohammad*, son
1751	*Dounama Gana*, son
1753	*Ali ibn al-Hadj-Dounama*
1793	*Ahmed*, son, expelled by the Fulani
1808	*Dounama Lefiami* (for 1st time)
1811	*Mohammad Ngileruma*
1814	*Dounama Lefiami* (for 2nd time) returned to power by Mohammad el Amin al-Kanemi of Bornu, ruled as shadow king
1817	*Ibrahim*
1846	*Ali Dalatumi*
1846	Dynasty extinguished

Sheikhs or Shehus

The Kuburi (Al-Kanemi) Dynasty of Bornu

1814	*Mohammad el Amin al-Kanemi*, retained the Saifawa Dynasty as titular sultans
1835	*Umar*, son (for 1st time) dethroned
1853	*Abdu Rahman*, brother, usurper
1854	*Umar* (for 2nd time)
1880	*Bukar Kura*, son
1884	*Ibrahim*, brother
1885	*Hashimi*, brother
1893	*Mohammed el Amin (Kiari)*, nephew
1893	*Sanda Limananbe Wuduroma*, brother, executed by Rabeh
1893	*Rabeh*, conquest of Bornu (in present-day north-eastern Nigeria)
1900	*Fad el-Allah*, son; conquered by the French, who reinstated the Kaburi dynasty in Dikwa (in present-day north-eastern Nigeria), while the British installed a counterpart shehu in Bornu*
1900	*Umar Sanda Kura*, son of Ibrahim, ruled at Dikwa, ruled at Bornu 1922 – 1937
1901	*Bukar Garbai*, brother, ruled at Dikwa, ruled at Bornu 1902 – 1922
1902	*Sanda Mandarama (Umar)*, nephew (for 1st time) ruled at Dikwa

*Shehus in Bornu:

1902	*Bukar Garbai*, son of Ibrahim, ruled in Dikwa 1901 – 1902
1922 – 1937	*Umar Sanda Kura*, brother, ruled in Dikwa 1900 – 1901

1905	*Ibrahim*, brother, ruled at Dikwa
1906	*Sanda Mandarama* (for 2nd time) ruled at Dikwa
from 1917	*Umar Sanda Kiarimi*, nephew, ruled at Dikwa, succeeded in Bornu 1937

Kara Koyunlu (The Horde of the Black Sheep)

Territory comprised part of present-day Iran, eastern Turkey and Iraq, with the capital at Tabriz.

Rulers

AD 1378/9	*Qara Muhammad (Turmush ibn Bairam Khwaja)*
c. 1388 – 1399/1400	*(Abu Nasr) Qara Yusuf (Nuyan ibn Muhammad)*, son (for 1st time) (b. 1354/5; d. Dec 1419/Jan 1420)
1399/1400 – 1405/6	Timurid invasion
1405/6	*Qara Yusuf* (for 2nd time)
1420/1	*Iskander (ibn Yusuf)*, son
1437/8 – 10 Nov 1467	*(Muzaffar al-Din) Jahan Shah (ibn Yusuf)*, brother, conquest of the whole of Iran 1457/8, killed by Uzun Hasan of the Ak Koyunlu
Nov 1467 – 1468/9	*Hasan 'Ali*, son, executed by Uzun Hasan (see above)
1468/9	Ak Koyunlu conquest

Karamanids (Karaman-Oghlu)

Territory comprised part of present-day central Turkey, with the capital at Karaman (now Laranda).

Begs

c. AD 1256/7	*(Qarim al-Din) Qaraman* (or *Karaman*) *(ibn Nura Sufi)* (d. 1279/80?)
1261/2	*Muhammad I (ibn Qaraman)*, son
1278/9	*(Badr al-Din) Mahmud (ibn Qaraman)*, brother
(?)	*(Burhan al-Din) Musa (ibn Mahmud)*, son
(?)	*(Fakhr al-Din) Ahmad (ibn Ibrahim)*, nephew
1349/50	*Shams al-Din (ibn Ibrahim)*, brother
1352/3	*('Ala' al-Din) Khalil (ibn Mahmud)*, uncle (d. 1390/1)
1381/2 – 1390/1	*'Ala' al-Din ('Ali ibn Khalil)*, son
1390/1 – 1402/3	Ottoman occupation
1402/3 – 1419/20	*Muhammad II (ibn 'Ala' al-Din)*, son (for 1st time) deposed by the Mamluks
1419/20 – 1421	Mamluk occupation
1421	*Muhammad II* (for 2nd time)
1423/4	*('Ala' al-Din) 'Ali (ibn 'Ala' al-Din)*, brother
1423/4	*(Taj al-Din) Ibrahim (ibn Muhammad II)*, nephew
1464	*Pir Ahmad (ibn Ibrahim)*, brother (d. Tarsus 1475/6) in dispute with his elder half-brother, *Ishaq*, whom he defeated 1465, ruled with his brother, *Qasim*, after 1469/70
1475/6 – 1483/4	*Qasim*, sole ruler (see above)
1483/4	Ottoman conquest

Kars

Territory in north-eastern Turkey, with the capital at Ani.

Kings

Bagratid Dynasty	
AD 962	*Mushel*, son of King Abas I of Armenia; territory ceded to him by his brother King Ashot III of Armenia
984	*Abas I*, son
1029 – 1064	*Gagik-Abas II*, son (d.1080)
1064	Kingdom ceded to the Byzantine Empire

Kashmir

Territory comprised the valley of Kashmir and neighbouring parts of north-western India.

Kings

Karkota Dynasty	
AD 627	*Prajñaditya* (or *Durlabhavardhana*), son-in-law of Baladitya of previous dynasty
632	*Pratapaditya II* (or *Durlabhaka*), son
682	*Chandrapida*, son
691	*Tarapida*, brother
695	*Lalitaditya I* (or *Muktapida*), son of Pratapaditya II
732	*Kuvalayapida*, son
740	*Prithivyapida*, son
744	*Sangramapida*, brother
751	*Jayapida*, brother
782	*Jajja*, brother-in-law, usurper
785	*Lalitapida*, son
797	*Prithivyapida II* (or *Sangramapida II*), brother
804	*Chippatajayapida* (or *Brihaspati*), son of Lalitapida by a concubine
816	*Ajitapida*, nephew, deposed

(?)	*Anangapida*, son of Prithivyapida II
(?) – 857	*Utpalapida*, son of Ajitapida

Utpala Dynasty

857	*Avantivarman*, grandson of Chippatajayapida's mother's brother
884	*Shamkaravarman*, son
903	*Gopalavarman*, son
905	*Samkatavarman*, brother, for 10 days
905	*Sugandha*, widow of Shamkaravarman
907	*Nirjitavarman* (or *Pangu*), great-nephew of Avantivarman (for 1st time) for a few days
907	*Partha*, son (for 1st time) (b. 897)
923	*Nirjitavarman* (for 2nd time)
924	*Chakravarman*, brother of Partha (for 1st time)
935	*Suravarman I*, brother
936	*Partha* (for 2nd time)
936	*Chakravarman* (for 2nd time)
938	*Umattavanti*, son of Partha
(?) – 940	*Suravarman II*

Yaçaskara Dynasty

940	*Yaçaskara*
948	*Vanata*, for a few days before Yaçaskara's death
949 – 950	*Samgramadeva*, son of Yaçaskara

Parvagupta Dynasty

950	*Parvagupta*
951	*Kshemagupta*, son
960	*Abhimanyu*, son, under regency of his mother *Didda*
973	*Nandigupta*, son, under regency of *Didda*
975	*Tribhuvana*, brother, under regency of *Didda*
976	*Bhimagupta*, brother
981 – 1004	*Didda*, previously regent

First Lohara Dynasty

1004	*Samgramaraja*, nephew
1029	*Hariraja*, son, for 22 days
1029	*Ananta*, brother, abdicated
1064	*Kalaça*, son
1090	*Utkarça*, son, for 22 days
1090 – 1102	*Harsha*, brother

Second Lohara Dynasty

1102	*Uchchala*, nephew
1113	*Radda*, son, for a few days
1113	*Salhana*, half-brother of Uchchala
1113	*Sussala*, brother of Uchchala (for 1st time)
1120	*Bhikshachara*
1120	*Sussala* (for 2nd time)
1127	*Jayasimha* (or *Simhadeva*), son
1154	*Pramanuka*, son
1164 – 1171	*Varttideva*, son

Vopyadeva Dynasty

1171	*Vopyadeva*
1180	*Jassaka*, brother
1198	*Jagadeva*, son
1213	*Rajadeva*, son
1236	*Samgramadeva*, son
1252	*Ramadeva*, son
1273 – 1286	*Lakshmanadeva*, son

Simhadeva Dynasty

1286	*Simhadeva*
1301 – 1320	*Sahadeva* (or *Ramachandra*), brother
1320	Throne seized by rival dynasty who converted to Islam (see below)

Sultans

Capital at Jayapidapura.

1320	*Sadr al-Din* (originally *Riñchana*), seized throne, converted to Islam
25 Nov 1323	*Haidar Khan*, son, under the regency of his mother *Kota Rani*
Dec 1323	*Udayanadeva*, brother of the former king Sahadeva, second husband of Kota Rani
end of 1338	*Kota Rani*, wife, mother of Haidar Khan, previously regent
mid 1339	*Shams al-Din (Shah Mir Swati)* (b. 1262) former minister of Kota Rani, whom he married and deposed
1342	*Jamshid* (d. 1345)
1343	*'Ala' al-Din ('Ali Shir)*, brother
1354	*Shihab al-Din (Shirashamak)*, son
1373	*Qutb al-Din Hindal*, brother

1389	*Sikandar (ibn Hindal)* (called *Butshikan*, i.e. the Iconoclast), son (b. 1380(?); d. 24 Apr 1413)
1413	*'Ali Shah (Mir Khan)*, son
Jun 1420	*Zain al-'Abidin (Shahi Khan)* (or *Bad Shah*), brother (b. 1401)
Nov/Dec 1470	*Haidar Shah (Hajji Khan)*, son
Jan 1472	*Hasan Shah (ibn Haidar)*, son
19 Apr 1484	*Muhammad Shah (ibn Hasan)*, son (for 1st time) (b. 1477; d.1537)
1484 – 1485	*Sayyid Hasan*, maternal grandfather (d. 1485?) regent
14 Oct 1486	*Fath Shah (ibn Adam)*, nephew of Haidar Shah (for 1st time) (d. Aug 1519)
1493	*Muhammad Shah* (for 2nd time)
1505	*Fath Shah* (for 2nd time)
1514	*Muhammad Shah* (for 3rd time) for nine months
1515	*Fath Shah* (for 3rd time) nominal sultan while country was divided and partly ruled by nobles
Aug 1516	*Muhammad Shah* (for 4th time) dethroned and imprisoned by his vizier Kaji Chak
1528(?)	*Ibrahim Shah I*, son, nominal sultan
1529	*Nazuk Shah*, son of Fath Shah (for 1st time)
summer 1530	*Muhammad Shah* (for 5th time) nominal sultan
mid 1537	*Shams al-Din II*, son
1538	*Isma'il Shah I*, brother
1539	*Ibrahim Shah II*, son, for four months
Nov/Dec 1540*	*Nazuk Shah* (for 2nd time) nominal ruler, deposed
1552	*Ibrahim Shah III*, son
1555	*Isma'il Shah II*, son of Ibrahim Shah I
1557 – 1561	*Habib Shah*, son (d. 1573?) deposed
Chak Dynasty	
1561	*Ghazi Shah (ibn Hasan Chak)*, nephew of Muhammad Shah's vizier Kaji Chak (b. 1509/10; d. 1566/7) deposed
1563	*(Nasr al-Din) Husain Shah I*, half-brother, son of Kaji Chak (d. 1571/2) abdicated
1570	*(Zahir al-Din Muhammad) Ali Shah*, brother
May(?) 1579	*(Nasr al-Din Muhammad) Yusuf Shah*, son (for 1st time) (d. 22 Sep 1592)

*1541 – 1551 *Mirza Muhammad Haidar Dughlat* (b. Tashkent 1500; d. 1551) Mughal general, in effective control

Jul(?) 1579	*Sayyid Mubarak Khan Baihaqi*, vizier of Ali Shah (d. 1589) usurper
Oct(?) 1579	*Lohar Shah* (or *Bahi' al-Din Gauhar Shah*), cousin
Nov 1580	*Yusuf Shah* (for 2nd time) fled Feb 1586, imprisoned 28 Mar 1586
Feb 1586	*Ya'qub Shah*, son (for 1st time) (d. Oct 1593)
Sep(?) 1586	*Husain Shah II*, grandson of Ghazi Shah, for four days
Oct 1586 – Jul 1588	*Ya'qub Shah* (for 2nd time)
Jul 1588	Mughal conquest

Khandesh, Faruqi Sultans of

Territory comprised part of present-day western India, with the capital at Burhanpur (now Asirgahr).

Sultans

AD 1370/1	*(Malik) Raja Ahmad Faruqi*, initially as governor for the Delhi sultan
17 Apr 1399	*Nasir Khan*, son
18 Sep 1437 – 30 Apr 1441	*(Miran Ghani) 'Adil Khan I*, son; assassinated
Apr/May 1441 – 5 Jun 1457	*(Miran) Mubarak Khan I*, son (d. 5 Jun 1457)
Jun 1457	*'Adil Khan II (Humayun)*, son
28 Sep 1501	*Daud Khan*, brother
28 Aug 1508	*Ghazni Khan*, son, poisoned ten days after his accession
1508	*Hasan Khan*, uncle
1508	*Alam Khan*, usurper
1509	*Adil Khan III*, son of Gujarat sultan Muzaffar II (d. 25 Aug 1520)
1520 – 24 May 1537	*(Miran) Muhammad (Shah) I*, son, incorporated Gujarat Sultanate 1537
1537	*Ahmad Shah*
1537 – 19 Dec 1566	*(Miran) Mubarak (Shah) II*, son
Dec 1566	*(Miran) Muhammad (Shah) II*, son

1576/7	*Hasan Khan*
1577/8	*Raja 'Ali Khan* (or *'Adil Shah IV*)
1597 – 1601	*Bahadur Shah*, son, deposed
1601	Conquest by Mughal emperor Akbar I

Khwarazm-Shahs

Territory comprised part of present-day Iran, eastern Turkey and USSR, with the capital at Hazarasp.

Shahs

Afrigids of Kath

AD (?) – 995/6	*Abu 'Abdallah Muhammad (ibn Ahmad)*
995/6	Ma'munid conquest

Ma'munids of Gurganj

c. 992/3	*(Abu 'Ali) Ma'mun I (ibn Muhammad)*, son
997/8	*(Abu'l-Hasan) 'Ali (ibn Ma'mun)*, son
1008/9	*(Abu'l-'Abbas) Ma'mun II (ibn Ma'mun)*, brother
1016/17 – 1017/18	*(Abu'l-Harith) Muhammad ibn 'Ali (ibn Ma'mun)*, nephew
1017/18	Ghaznavid conquest

Ghaznavid Governors

1017/18	*(Abu Sa'id) Altuntash (al-Hajib)*
1031/2	*Harun (ibn Altuntash)*, son, lieutenant of the nominal Khwarazm-Shah, Sa'id ibn Mas'ud of Ghazna, later independent
1033/4 – 1040/1	*Isma'il Khandan (ibn Altuntash)*, brother, independent of Ghazna
1040/1	The Oghuz Yabghu, Shah Malik of Jand, conquered Khwarazm

Line of Anushtigin (ruling initially as Seljuq governors and later as independent rulers in central Asia and Iran)

c. 1077/8	*Anushtigin (Gharcha'i)*, slave of the Seljuq amir, Bilga-tagin, nominal governor

1096/7	*Ekinchi (ibn Qochqar)*, governor, assassinated
1096/7	*Qutb al-Din (Muhammad ibn Anushtigin)*, son of Anushtigin, Seljuq vassal
1127/8 – 30 Jul 1156	*('Ala' al-Din) Atsız (ibn Muhammad)*, son (b. 1098/9) Seljuq vassal
22 Aug 1156 – Mar 1172	*(Abu'l-Fath) Il-Arslan (ibn Atsız)*, son
1172	*(Sultan-Shah), Abu'l-Qasim Mahmud (ibn Il-Arslan)*, son (d. 29 Sep 1193) deposed by Tekish
11 Dec 1172* – 3 Jul 1200	*('Ala' al-Din) Tekish*, brother, overthrew the Seljuqs in Iraq and western Persia 1194
3 Aug 1200	*('Ala' al-Din) Muhammad (ibn Tekish)*, son
1220/1 – Aug 1231	*(Jalal al-Din) Mingburnu (ibn Muhammad)*, son (d. 16 Aug 1231)
Aug 1231	Mongol conquest

Kilwa

Territory comprised part of present-day western Tanzania, with the capital at Zanzibar.

Sultans

AD 957	*'Ali ibn al-Husain ibn 'Ali*
996	*'Ali ibn Bashat*, grandson
999	*Da'ud ibn 'Ali*, uncle
1003	*Khalid ibn Bakr*, usurper
1005	*al-Hasan ibn Sulaiman I*, grandson of 'Ali
1042	*'Ali ibn Da'ud I*, son of Da'ud
1100	*'Ali ibn Da'ud I*, brother
1106	*al-Hasan ibn Da'ud*, brother
1129	*Sulaiman*, descent unknown
1131	*Da'ud ibn Sulaiman I*, son
1170	*Sulaiman al-Hasan ibn Da'ud*, son

*1172 *Sultan-Shah* (see above) rival ruler in northern Khurasan

1188	*Da'ud ibn Sulaiman II*, son
1190	*Talut ibn Sulaiman*, brother
1191	*al-Hasan ibn Sulaiman*, brother
1215	*Khalid ibn Sulaiman*, brother
1225	brother, name unkown
1263	*'Ali ibn Da'ud*, nephew
1277	*al-Hasan ibn Talut*, grandson
1294	*Sulaiman ibn al-Hasan*, son
1308	*Da'ud ibn Sulaiman III*, son (for 1st time)
1310	*al-Hasan ibn Sulaiman*, brother
1333	*Da'ud ibn Sulaiman III* (for 2nd time)
1356	*Sulaiman ibn Da'ud*, son
1356	*al-Husain ibn Sulaiman*, uncle
1362	*Talut ibn al-Husain*, son
1364	*Sulaiman ibn al-Husain*, brother
1366	*Sulaiman*, uncle
1389	*al-Husain ibn Sulaiman*, son
1412	*Muhammad ibn Sulaiman*, brother
1421	*Sulaiman ibn Muhammad*, son
1442	*Isma'il ibn al-Husain*, son of al-Husain ibn Sulaiman
1454	*Muhammad Yarik ibn Sulaiman (al-Madhlum)*, of the House of the Amirs, usurper
1455	*Ahmad ibn Sulaiman*, son of Sulaiman ibn Muhammad of the Royal House
1456	*al-Hasan ibn Isma'il (al-Khatib)*, son of Isma'il
1466	*Sa'id ibn al-Hasan*, son
1476	*Sulaiman ibn Muhammad*, son of Muhammad Yarik of the House of the Amirs, usurper
1477	*'Abdullah ibn al-Hasan*, brother of Sa'id of the Royal House
1478	*'Ali ibn al-Hasan*, brother
1479	*al-Hasan ibn Sulaiman*, son of Sulaiman of the House of the Amirs (for 1st time) usurper
1485	*Sabhat ibn Muhammad*, son of Muhammad ibn Sulaiman of the Royal House
1486	*al-Hasan ibn Sulaiman* (for 2nd time) usurper
1490	*Ibrahim ibn Muhammad*, brother of Sabhat of the Royal House
1495	*al-Fudail ibn Sulaiman*, nephew
1499	*Ibrahim ibn Sulaiman*, brother of al-Hasan of the House of the Amirs (for 1st time) usurper
(?)	Unknown number of kings
(?)	*Muhammad Mikatu ibn Muhammad*, cousin, of the

	House of the Amirs, usurper
(?)	*Ibrahim ibn Sulaiman* (for 2nd time)
(?)	*Sa'id ibn Sulaiman*, brother
c. 1513	*Muhammad ibn al-Husain*, nephew of al-Fudail of the Royal House, still alive in 1520
(?)	Unknown number of kings
(?)	*'Ali* (or *Alawi*)
(?)	*Muhammad ibn 'Ali*, son, under the regency of his sister *Fatima binti 'Ali* (fl. 1710 – 1711)
(?)	*Yusuf ibn Muhammad*, son, under the regency of *Fatima binti 'Ali*
fl. 1720	*Ibrahim ibn Yusuf*, son
fl. 1776	son, name unknown
fl. 1776	*Yusuf ibn Ibrahim*, brother
fl. 1777(?)	*Hasan ibn Ibrahim*, brother
fl. 1797	*Abu Bakr ibn Hasan ibn Ibrahim*, son
fl. 1813	*Yusuf ibn Hasan*, brother
fl. 1819	*Muhammad*, brother
fl. 1819	*Sulaiman*, brother
fl. 1830	*Hasan*, son, deported by Sultan Sa'id of Oman and Zanzibar c. 1842/3
c. 1842/3	Control assumed by the Sultan of Oman and Zanzibar

Kish

Territory comprised part of central Iraq, with the capital at Kish (present-day Tall al-Uhaimer).

Kings

c. 2700 BC	*Enmebaragisi*, traditionally ruled for 900 years
(?)	*Agga*, son, traditionally ruled for 625 years
before 2550	*Su- . . .*
(?)	*Dadasig*
(?)	*Mamagalla*
(?)	*Galbum*, son

(?)	*TÚG-e**
(?)	*Mennunna*
c. 2450	*I-bí-(Ishtar)*(?)
(?)	*En-bi-Ishtar*, perhaps the same as above
(?)	*Lugalmu*
(?)	*Ku-Baba*, queen
(?)	*Puzur-Sin*, son, for 25 years
before 2370	*Ur-Zababa*
(?)	*Simudar*, for 30 years(?)
(?)	*Usi-watar*, for seven years(?)
(?)	*Ishtar-muti*, for 11 years(?)
(?)	*Ishme-Shamash*, for 11 years(?)
before 2230	*Nannia*, for seven years(?)

Kizzuwadna

Territory comprised part of present-day southern-central Turkey.

Kings†

(?) BC	*Pelliya I*
(?)	*Pariyawatri*
c. 1500	*Ishputakhshu*
(?)	*Shunashshura I*
before 1450	*Pelliya II*
(?)	*Paddatishshu*
(?)	*Talzush*
c. 1400	*Shunashshura II*
(?)	Vassal of the Mitanni(?)

*The ideogram representing the name cannot at present be read and is represented by the standard Sumerian value

† Tentative chronology

Kongo Kingdom

Territory comprised part of present-day north-western Angola, western Zambia and south-western Zaïre, with the capital at Mbanzakongo (now São Salvador).

Mani Kongo (Kings)

c. AD 1482	*Nzinga Nkuwu*, later called *João I*, first contact with the Portuguese 1482
1506	*Afonso I Mvemba-Nzinga*, son (b. c. 1455)
c. 1543	*Dom Pedro I Nkanga Mvemba*, son, deposed
c. 1545	*Dom Diogo I*, grandson of Afonso I
1561	*Afonso II*, son, killed by Bernardo I
1561	*Bernardo I*, brother
1567 or 1568	*Henrique I*
1568	*Alvare I*, stepson
1587	*Alvare II Mpanzu a Nimi*, son
1614	*Bernardo II*, half-brother, defeated and deposed by the Duke of Mbamba
1615	*Alvare III*, son-in-law of the Duke of Mbamba
1622	*Pedro II Afonso*, uncle
1624	*Garcia I Afonso, Duke of Mbamba* (d. in exile Jun 1626) deposed
1626	*Ambrosio I*
1631	*Alvare IV*, son of Alvare III
1636	*Alvare V*, for six months
1636	*Alvare VI Afonso, Duke of Mbamba*
1641	*Garcia II Afonso*
1661 – Oct 1665	*Antonio I*, son, killed at the battle of Ulanga
Oct 1665	Portuguese victory at Ulanga led to the disintegration of the kingdom, dynasty continued as local rulers

Korea

KINGDOM OF KOGURYŎ

Territory comprised part of present-day North Korea.

Kings*

37 BC	*Tongmyŏng (Chumong)*
18 BC	*Yuri*
AD 19	*Taemusin (Muhyŏl)*
45	*Minjung (Haeŭpchu)*
49	*Mobon (Haeu)*
54	*T'aejo (Kung)*
147	*Ch'adae (Susŏng)*
166	*Sindae (Paekko)*
180	*Kogukch'ŏn (Nammo)*
197	*Sansang (Yŏn-u)*
228	*Tongch'on (Uwikŏ)*
250	*Chungch'ŏn (Yŏnbul)*
271	*Sŏch'ŏn (Yangno)*
292	*Pongsang (Sangbu)*
300	*Mich'ŏn (Ŭlbul)*
331	*Kogukwŏn (So-e)*
372	*Sosuyim (Kubu)*
384	*Koguk-yang (Yiyŏn)*
392	*Kwanggaet'o (Tamdŏk)*
414	*Changsu (Kŏyŏn)*
491	*Munja (Naon)*
520	*Anjang (Hŭng-an)*
532	*Anwŏn (Poyŏn)*
546	*Yangwŏn (Pyŏngsŏng)*
560	*P'yŏngwŏn (Yangsŏng)*
591	*Yŏngyang (Wŏn)*
619	*Yŏngyu (Kŏnmu)*
643 – 668	*Pojang (Chang)*
668	Defeated by Silla (see below)

*Posthumous titles are given in parentheses

KINGDOM OF PAEKCHE

Territory comprised part of present-day western South Korea.

Kings*

18 BC	*Onjo*, son of King Tongmyŏng of Koguryŏ
AD 29	*Taru*
78	*Kiru*
128	*Kaeru*
168	*Ch'ogo*
215	*Kusu*
(?)	*Saban*
235	*Koi*
287	*Ch'aege*
299	*Punso*
305	*Piryu*
344	*Sŏl* or *Kye*
347	*Konch'ogo*
376	*Kongusu*
385	*Ch'imyu*
385	*Chinsa*
392	*Asin*
406	*Chŏnji*
421	*Kuisin*
427	*Piyu*
455	*Kaero*
476	*Munju*
478	*Samkŭn*
480	*Tongsŏng (Modae)*
501	*Muryŏng (Sama)*
524	*Sŏng (Myŏngnong)*
555	*Widok (Ch'ang)*
599	*He (Kyemyŏng)*
600	*Pŏp (Sŏn)*
601	*Mu (Chang)*
642 – 660	*Ŭija*
660	Conquered by Silla (see below)

*Posthumous titles are given in parentheses

KINGDOM OF SILLA

Territory comprised part of present-day eastern South Korea.

Kings*

57 BC	*Hyŏkkŏse*
AD 4	*Namhae*
25	*Yuri*
58	*T'alhae*
81	*P'asa* or *Sapa*
113	*Jima*
135	*Ilsŏng*
154	*Atalla*
185	*Pŏlhyu*
196	*Naehae*
231	*Chobun*
248	*Ch'ŏmhae*
262	*Mich'u*
285	*Yurye*
299	*Kiyim*
310	*Kŭlhae*
356	*Naemul*
402	*Silsŏng*
417	*Nulji*
458	*Chabi*
479	*Soji*
500	*Chijŭng (Chidaero)*
514	*Pobhŭng (Wŏnjong)*
541	*Chinhŭng (Maekchong)*
576	*Chinji (Kŭmyun)*
579	*Chinp'yŏng (Paekchŏng)*
632	*Sŏndŏk (Tŏngman)*, Queen
647	*Chindŏk (Sŭngman)*, Queen
654	*Muryŏl (Ch'unch'u)*, conquered Paekche 660
661	*Munmu (Pŏbmin)*, conquered Koguryŏ 668
681	*Sinmun (Chŏngmyŏng)*
692	*Hyoso (Yihong)*
702	*Sŏngdŏk (Hŭnggwang)*
738	*Hyosŏng (Sŭnggyŏng)*
742	*Kyŏngdŏk (Hŏng-yŏng)*

*Posthumous titles are given in parentheses

765	*Hegong (Kŏn-un)*
780	*Sŏndŏk (Yangsung)*
785	*Wŏnsŏng (Kyŏngsin)*
799	*Sosŏng (Chung-ong)*
800	*Aejang (Chunghi)*
809	*Hŏndŏk (Ŏnsŭng)*
826	*Hŭngdŏk (Sojong)*
836	*Hŭigang (Cheyung)*
(?)	*Minae*
839	*Sinmu (Ujing)*
840	*Munsŏng (Kyŏngong)*
858	*Hŏn-an (Ŭijŏng)*
862	*Kyŏngmun (Ongyŏm)*
876	*Hŏngang (Chŏng)*
887	*Chŏnggang (Hwang)*
888	*Chinsŏng (Man)*, Queen
898	*Hyogong (Yo)*
913	*Sindŏk (Kyŏnghwi)*
918	*Kyŏngmyŏng (Sŭngyŏng)*
925	*Kyŏng-ae (Wiong)*
928 – 935	*Kyŏngsun (Pu)*
935	Conquered by Koryŏ (see below)

KINGDOM OF KORYŎ

Territory comprised part of present-day North and South Korea.

Kings*

AD 918	*T'aejo (Wang Kŏn)* (b. 14 Jan 877)
943 – 15 Sep 945	*Hejong (Wang Mu)*, son (b. 912)
946 – 13 Mar 949	*Chŏngjong*† *(Wang Yo)*, brother (b. 923)
953	*Kwangjong (Wang So)*, brother (b. 925; d. 23 May 975)
975	*Kyŏngjong (Wang Chu)*, son (b. 22 Sep 965; d. 11 Jul 981)
981 – 27 Oct 997	*Sŏngjong (Wang Ch'i)*, cousin (b. Dec 960)
998	*Mokchong (Wang Song)*, son of Kyŏngjong (b. 20 May 980; d. 3 Feb 1009)

*Posthumous titles are given in parentheses
†The names of the kings who acceded in 946 and 1034 are represented by different ideograms

1009	*Hyŏnjong (Wang Sun)*,cousin of Sŏngjong (b. 7 Jan 992; d. 25 May 1031)
1031	*Tokchong (Wang Hŭm)*, son (b. 5 Feb 1016; d. 17 Sep 1034)
1034	*Chŏngjong* (Wang Hyŏng)*, brother (b. 17 Jul 1018; d. 18 May 1046)
1046	*Munjong (Wang Hwi)*, brother (b. 12 Jan 1019; d. 18 Jul 1083)
Jul – Oct 1083	*Sunjong (Wang Hun)*, son (b. 15 Jan 1048; d. 23 Oct 1083)
1084	*Sŏnjong (Wang Un)*, brother (b. 10 Sep 1049; d. 2 May 1094)
1094	*Hŏnjong (Wang Uk)*, son (b. 27 Jun 1084; d. 19 Feb 1097)
1095	*Sukchong (Wang Ong)*, son of Munjong (b. 28 Jul 1054; d. 2 Oct 1105)
1105	*Yejong (Wang O)*, son (b. 7 Jan 1078; d. 9 Apr 1122)
1122	*Injong (Wang Hae)*, son
1146	*Ŭijong (Wang Hyŏn)*, son (b. 11 Apr 1127; d. 1 Oct 1173)
1171 – 1197	*Myŏngjong (Wang Ho)*, brother (b. 17 Oct 1131; d. 18 Nov 1202)
1198	*Sinjong (Wang T'ak)*, brother (b. 11 Jul 1144; d. 13 Jan 1204)
1204	*Hijong (Wang Yŏng)*, son (b. May 1181; d. 10 Aug 1237) deposed
1211 – 9 Aug 1213	*Kangjong (Wang O)*, son of Myŏngjong (b. Apr 1152)
1216 – 30 Jun 1259	*Kojong (Wang Ch'ŏl)*, son (b. 18 Jan 1192)
1260 – 18 Jan 1274	*Wŏnjong (Wang Sik)*, son (b. 19 Mar 1119)
1275	*Ch'ungyŏl wang (Wang Chun)*, son (b. 26 Feb 1225; d. 13 Jul 1308)
1308	*Ch'ungsŏn wang (Wang Won)*, son (b. 30 Sep 1275; d. 13 May 1325)
1314 – 1330	*Ch'ungsuk wang (Wang To)*, son (for 1st time) (b. 7 Jul 1294; d. 25 Mar 1339)
1331	*Ch'unghe wang (Wang Chŏng)*, son (for 1st time) (b. 18 Mar 1315; d. 15 Jan 1344)
1332 – 1339	*Ch'ungsuk wang* (for 2nd time)
1340 – 1344	*Ch'unghe wang* (for 2nd time)

*The names of the kings who acceded in 946 and 1034 are represented by different ideograms

1345 – 5 Dec 1348	*Ch'ungmok wang (Wang Hun)*, son (b. 15 Apr 1336)
1349	*Ch'ungjŏng wang (Wang Chŏ)*, brother (b. 1338; d. 7 Mar 1352)
1351 – 22 Sep 1374	*Kongmin wang (Wang Chŏn)*, son of Ch'ungsuk wang (b. May 1330) assassinated
1375	*(Sin) U*, son, abdicated
1389 – 1392	*Kongyang wang (Wang Yo)*, descendant of Sinjong (b. 5 Feb 1345; d. 1395)
1392	Overthrown by Yi Dynasty (see below)

KINGDOM OF KOREA

Territory comprised part of present-day North and South Korea, with the capital at Hanyang (now Seoul).

Kings*

Yi Dynasty	
AD1392 – 1398	*T'aejo (Yi Sŏng-gye)*, abdicated
1399 – 1400	*Chŏngjong (Yi Kyong)*, son (d. 1419) abdicated
1401	*T'aejong (Yi Pang-wŏn)*, brother
1419	*Sejong (Yi To)*, son
1451	*Munjong (Yi Hyang)*, son
1453	*Tanjong (Yi Hong-wi)*, son (d. 1457) abdicated
1456	*Sejo (Yi Yu)*, uncle
1469	*Yejong (Yi Kwang)*, son
1470 – 1494	*Sŏngjong*, nephew
1495	*Yŏnsan-gun (Yi Yung)*, son, deposed
1506 – 1544	*Chungjong (Yi Tu)*, brother
1545	*Injong (Yi Ho)*, son
1546 – 1567	*Myŏngjong (Yi Hang)*, brother
1568 – 1608	*Sŏnjo (Yi Kweng)*, nephew
1609	*Kwanghae-gun (Yi Hon)*, son (d. 1642) deposed
1623 – 1649	*Injo (Yi Chong)*, nephew
1650 – 1659	*Hyojong (Yi Ho)*, son
1660 – 1674	*Hyŏnjong (Yi Yun)*, son
1675 – 1720	*Sukchong (Yi Sun)*, son
1721 – 1724	*Kyŏngjong (Yi Kyun)*, son
1725 – 1776	*Yŏngjo (Yi Eum)*, brother

*Posthumous titles are given in parentheses

1777 – 1800	*Chŏngjo (Yi Sun)*, grandson
1801 – 1834	*Sunjo (Yi Kwang)*, son
1835 – 1849	*Hŏnjong (Yi Whan)*, grandson
1850 – 1863	*Ch'ŏlchong (Yi Chung)*, descendant of Yŏngjo
1864	*Kojong (Yi Hyong)*, descendant of Yŏngjo (d. 1919) created Emperor 1897, abdicated
1907 – 1910	*Sunjong (Yi Wang)*, son (d. 1926) Emperor, abdicated
1910	Japanese invasion and annexation

Kush

Territory comprised part of present-day southern Egypt, Sudan and northern Ethiopia.

Kings

At Napata (in present-day northern Sudan)

745 BC*	*Kashta*
742 – 700	*Piankhi*, son, ended 23rd Dynasty in Egypt
715	*Shabaka* (or *Sabaka* or *Seve*(?)), brother
700	*Shabataka*
689	*Taharka* (or *Tirhakah* or *Tarakos*), brother; defeated by the Assyrians 671, lost Upper Egypt
663	*Tanutamon* (or *Tandamane*), brother
650	*Atlenersa*
643	*Senkamenseken*
623	*Anlamen*
593	*Aspelta*
568	*Amtleq*
553	*Malneqen*
538	*Analma'aye*
533	*Amani-natake-lebte*
513	*Karkamani*
503	*Amani-astabarqa*
478	*Si'aspiqa*
458	*Nasakhma*

*All dates are approximate

453	*Malewiebamani*, son(?)
423	*Talakhamani*, brother(?)
418	*Aman-nete-yerike*, nephew(?)
398	*Baskakeren*, brother
397	*Harsiotef*, nephew(?)
362	Unknown king, son
342	*Akhratan*, son
328	*Nastasen*, brother

At Meroe (in present-day central Sudan)

308(?)	*Arakakaman*
280	*Amanislo*
265	*Bartare*
255	*Aman . . tekha*
242	*Hinayka*
225	*Arqamani* (or *Ergamenes*)
200	*Adikhalamani*(?)
180	*Naqyrinsan*
160	Queen *Nahirqa*
150	*Shanak-dakhete*(?)
125	Unknown king
100	*Tañyidamani*(?)
80	*Teriteqas*(?)
60	Queen *Amanirenas*
(?)	*Akinidad*, uncertain
45	Queen *Amanishakhete*
(?)	Queen *Naldamak*
25	*Amanikhabale*(?)
15 BC – AD 15	*Natakamani*
15 BC – AD 15	Queen *Amanitere*
AD 15	*Sherakarer*
20	Unknown king
40	*Akhyesbekhe*
50	*Amanitenmemide*
75	*Amanikhatashan*
100	Unknown king
105	*Aritanyesbekhe*
130	*Teqerideamani I*(?)
150	Unknown king
160	*Takizemani*
180	Unknown king
200	*Tarikenidal*
220	Unknown king

225	Unknown king
235	Unknown king
250	*Teqerideamani II*
270 – 355	Six unknown kings
355	Conquest by Axum

Lagash

Territory comprised part of present-day south-eastern Iraq, with the capital at Lagash (present-day Telloh).

Kings

(?) BC	*Enkhegal*
c. 2600	*Lugalshagengur*
after 2550	*Ur-Nanshe*
(?)	*Akurgal*, son
(?)	*Eannatum*, son
(?)	*Enannatum I*, brother
c. 2450	*Entemena*, son
(?)	*Enannatum II*, son
(?)	*Enetarzi*
2384	*Lugalanda*
2378 – 2371	*Urukagina*
2371	Conquered by Lugalzaggisi, the king of Umma; period of domination by Akkad, then the Guti
c. 2230	*Lugalushumgal*
(?)	*Puzur-Mama*
(?)	Some or all of the following: *Ur-Utu*, *Ur-Mama*, *Lu-Baba*, *Lugula*, *Kakug*
(?)	*Ur-Baba*, for more than 14 years
(?)	*Gudea*, son-in-law, for more than 16 years
(?)	*Ur-Ningirsu*, son, for more than five years
(?)	*Ugme*, son, for more than two years
c. 2120	*Urgar*, son-in-law of Ur-Baba
before 2000	*Nammakhni*, son-in-law of Ur-Baba
c. 2000	Conquered by Ur-Nammu of the third dynasty of Ur

Lang Chang (later Luang Prabang)

Territory comprised part of present-day northern Laos.

Kings*

Muong Swa (predecessor of Lang Chang)

†	*Phaya Nan Tha*, of Ceylon(?)
	Phaya Inthapatha, of Cambodia, married the widow of Phaya Nan Tha
	Thao Phu Tha Saine, son
	Phaya Ngu Lueum, son
	Thao Phe Si, son
	Ay Saleukheuk, son
	Ay Tiet Hai, son
	Thao Tiantha Phanit, a betel-nut merchant from Vientiane
	Khun Swa, a Kha chief
	Khun Ngiba, son
	Khun Viligna, son
	Khun Kan Hang, son
	Khun Lo, son of Khun Borom Rajathiraj (or Kolofeng), a Thai prince; ruler of Nanchao, founded Muong Swa AD 757
	Khun Swa Lao, son
	Khun Sung
	Khun Khet
	Khun Khum
	Khun Khip (or *Khun Khim*)
	Khun Khap
	Khun Khoa
	Khun Khane
	Khun Phèng

*The names and numbers of the kings are variously given in the traditions

† A few events that can be related to reigns and have ascertainable dates are noted in the right-hand column; otherwise the dates of reigns are unknown

	Khun Phéng
	Khun Pheung
	Khun Phi
	Khun Kham
	Khun Hung
	Thao Thene, son
	Thao Nhung
	Thao Nheuk
	Thao Pinh
	Thao Phat
	Thao Vang (d. 1271?)
	Phaya Lang Thirat (d. 1316)
	Phaya Suvanna Kham Phong, son, grandfather of Fa Ngum (see below)

Lang Chang

AD 1353	*Fa Ngum* (b. 1316) founder of Lang Chang
1373	*Sam Sene Thai*, son
1416	*Lan Kham Deng*, son
1428	*Phommathat*, son
1429	*Pak Huei Luong*, uncle
1430	*Thao Sai*, brother
1430	*Phaya Khai*, son of Lan Kham Deng
1433	*Chieng Sai*, son of Sam Sene Thai
1434	Unknown son of Lan Kham Deng
1435	*Kam Kheut*, son of a palace slave
1438	*Sai Tiakaphat*, son of Sam Sene Thai
1479	*Thene Kham*, son
1486 – 1496	*La Sene Thai*, brother (b. 1463)

For continuation, see Laos, Volume 2.

Larsa

Territory comprised part of present-day south-eastern Iraq, with the capital at Larsa (present-day Tall Sankarah).

Kings

2025 BC	*Naplanum*
2004	*Emisum*
1976	*Samium*
1941	*Zabaia*
1932	*Gungunum*, successfully invaded Elam, acquired suzerainty over Ur from Isin
1905	*Abisare*
1894	*Sumuel*
1865	*Nur-Adad*
1849	*Sin-iddinam*, son
1842	*Sin-eribam*
1840	*Sin-iqisham*
1835	*Silli-Adad*
1834	*Warad-Sin*
1822 – 1763	*Rim-Sin I*, brother, captured Isin 1794, defeated by the Babylonian king Hammurabi
1763	Became a vassal state of Babylonia
c. 1750	*Rim-Sin II*, nephew, declared himself king of Larsa and led revolt against Babylonia, defeated by the Babylonian king Samsuiluna
c. 1750	Babylonian conquest

Liège

Bishops (and from 972 Princes of the Holy Roman Empire)*

fl. AD735	*Florebert*, Saint
fl. 748 – 769(?)	*Fulchar* (or *Folchrich*)
769(?) – 787	*Agilfrid*
787(?) – 810	*Gärbald*
810 – 8 Apr(?) 831	*Waltcaud* (or *Waldgoz*)
831 – 840	*Erard*
before Aug 840 – 852/855	*Hartgar*
852/856 – 9 Jan 901/904	*Franko*
fl. 904 – 920	*Stephan*
920/922 – 945	*Richar*, in rivalry with Hilduin
920 – 922	*Hilduin*, antibishop, deposed
945 – 26 Jan 947	*Ougo*
947 – 28 Aug 953	*Farabert*
25 Sep 953 – 955	*Rather*, expelled
955 – 959	*Baldrich I*
959 – 27 Oct 971	*Evraker*
23 Apr(?) 972 – 10 Apr 1008	*Notker*
before 12 Sep 1008 – 29 Jul 1018	*Baldrich II*
before 26 Nov 1018 – 21 Apr 1021	*Walbod* (or *Fulmod*), Saint
1021 – 14 or 23 Jan 1025	*Durand*
1025 – 5 Dec 1037	*Reginard*, Saint
1037 – 16 Aug 1042	*Nithard*
1042 – 8 Jul 1048	*Wazo*
1048 – 23 Jun 1075	*Dietwin*
summer 1075 – 31 May 1091	*Henricus I*, of Verdun †

*When two dates separated by an oblique stroke are given for the beginning of an episcopate the first refers to election or papal confirmation and the second to ordination, consecration or investiture

† From this point in the list baptismal names are given in Latin forms and the descriptions of territorial or family origin are translated into English

winter 1091/1 Feb 1092 – 31 Jan 1119	*Otbertus*
1119	*Alexander I*, of Jülich (for 1st time) (d. 9 Mar 1135) for less than 3 months, resigned
23 Apr/26 Oct 1119 – 27 or 28 May 1121	*Fredericus*, of Namur, Saint
? – 2 or 4 Sep 1121	*Alexander I* (for 2nd time) resigned
? – 1 Jan 1128	*Adalbero* (or *Albero*) *I*, of Louvain, Saint
18 Mar/15 Jun 1128 – 9 Mar 1135	*Alexander I* (for 3rd time)
1135 – 23 Mar 1145	*Adalbero* (or *Albero*) *II*, of Chiny
13 May/24 Jun 1145 – Aug 1164	*Henricus II*, of Leyen
1164 – 9 or 10 Aug 1167	*Alexander II*
1167 – 1191	*Radulphus*
8 Sep 1191 – 24 Nov 1192	*Albertus*, of Louvain, or of Brabant, Saint; murdered
15 Jan* – c. 24 May 1192	*Lotharius*, of Hochstaden; deposed
Oct 1193 – 1 Aug 1195	*Simon*, of Limburg, rejected by the Curia
mid-Nov 1194/6 Jan 1196 – 2 Feb 1200	*Albertus II*, of Cuyk; elected antibishop during civil war, confirmed by Pope Celestine III on death of Simon
3 Mar 1200/21 Apr 1202 – 12 Apr 1229	*Hugo II*, of Pierrepont
24 May 1229/9 (24?) Mar 1230 – 30 Apr or 2 May 1238	*Joannes II*, of Eppes
25 Jun 1238/29 May 1239 – Oct or Nov 1239	*Guilielmus*, of Savoy; previously Bishop of Valencia
summer 1240 – 16 Oct 1246	*Robertus I*, of Thourotte, or of Langres; previously Bishop of Langres
26 Sep 1247 – 3 Jul 1274	*Henricus III*, of Gelder; resigned
28 Jul 1274 – 24 Aug 1281	*Joannes III*, of Enghien; previously Bishop of Tournai
9 Jun 1282 – 14 Oct 1291	*Joannes IV*, of Flanders; previously Bishop of Metz; in disputed election with *Burchard*, of Avesnes, and *Guilielmus*, of Auvergne

*Date of appointment

1292 – 1295	See vacant
12 Dec 1295 / before 2 Jan 1296 – before 1 Sep 1301	*Hugo III*, of Châlons, summoned to Rome and deposed, translated to Besançon 11 Dec 1301
1 Sep 1301 – 12/13 Dec 1302	*Adolphus I*, of Waldeck
16 Apr / 10 Jun 1313 – 3 Nov 1344	*Adolphus II*, of Mark
25 Feb / 12 Apr 1345 – 15 Apr 1364	*Engelbertus*, of Mark (d. 26 Aug 1369) translated to Cologne
15 Apr / 30 Jul 1364 – 1 Jul 1378	*Joannes V*, of Arkel; previously Bishop of Utrecht
5 Jul / 8 Nov 1378 – 1379	*Eustachius Persand*, of Rochefort (d. Avignon 1395) expelled
1378 – 8 Mar 1389	*Arnoldus*, of Horn
5 Jun – ? 1389	*Theodericus*, of Mark; resigned
14 Nov 1389 / 13 Mar 1390 – 22 May 1418	*Joannes VI*, of Bavaria-Straubing (b. 1374; d. 6 Jan 1425) Duke (Johann) of Bavaria-Straubing 1417, co-ruler of Holland 1419, governor of Luxembourg 1419; in rivalry with Theodericus of Horn and Perwez (see below) from 18 Mar 1407; resigned
18 Mar 1407 – 23 Sep 1408	*Theodericus*, of Horn and Perwez; killed by Joannes VI at Battle of Othée
30 May / 4 Jul 1418 – 28 May 1419	*Joannes VII*, of Wallenrode, previously Archbishop of Riga
Jun / 20 Sep 1419 – 22 Nov 1455	*Joannes VIII*, of Heinsburg (d. 18 Oct 1459) resigned
7 Apr 1455 – 30 Aug 1482	*Ludovicus*, of the House of Bourbon
17 Dec 1483 – 19 Dec 1505	*Joannes IX*, of Horn

Lithuania

Grand Dukes

The names are given in their Lithuanian forms, except for Władysław and Kazimierz, with the Polish or Russian equivalents in parentheses.

AD 1240	*Mindaugas* (*Mendog*, *Mindowe*), son of Ringaudas(?), unified Lithuania, king 1253, killed by Treniota
1263	*Treniota* (*Trojnat*) *of Samogitia*, nephew, killed by Vaišvilkas
1264	*Vaišvilkas* (*Wojsiełk*), son of Mindaugas, abdicated and returned to monastery
1267	*Švarnas* (*Shvarno*), Duke of Volhynia, brother-in-law (d. c. 1269)
1270 – 1281/2	*Traidenis* (*Trojden*)
c. 1283 – 1294	*Pukuveras* (*Pukuwer*) (or *Putaviras*?)
1295	*Vytenis* (*Witen*), son
1316	*Gediminas* (*Gedymin*), brother (b. c. 1275)
1341/2	*Jaunutis* (*Jewnut Iwan*), son (d. after 1366)
1345	*Algirdas* (*Olgierd*), brother (b. 1296; d. May 1377)
1377	*Iogaila* (*Jagiełło*), son (for 1st time) (b. c. 1351; d. 1 Jun 1434)
summer 1381	*Kęstutis* (*Kiejstut*), brother (b. c. 1300; d. 14 Aug 1382) co-ruler from 1345
12 Jun 1382	*Iogaila* (for 2nd time) Supreme Duke 1401, King (Władysław II) of Poland 1386
1401 – 27 Oct 1430	*Vytautas* (*Witowd Alexander*), son of Kęstutis (b. 1352) Grand Duke, formerly governor
1430 – 10 Feb 1432	*Švitrigaila* (*Świdrygiełło Bolesław*), brother of Iogaila (b. c. 1370) Grand Duke
1432 – 1440	*Žygimantas* (*Sigismund*), brother of Vytautas (b. c. 1365) Grand Duke
1434 – 1440	*Władysław*, King (Władysław III) of Poland, son of Iogaila (b. Cracow 21 Oct 1424; d. Varna 10 Nov 1444) Supreme Duke, King (Ulászló I) of Hungary 1440
1440 – 7 Jun 1492	*Kazimierz*, brother (b. 30 Nov 1427) sent as viceroy, acclaimed as Grand Duke, crowned King (Kazimierz IV) of Poland 25 Jun 1447

Livonia

Territory in Latvia and Estonia. The government of Livonia was shared, in varying fashion and not always peaceably, between the Livonian Knights,* the bishops and archbishops of Riga, the bishops of Semigallia, Courland, Leal-Dorpat, Ösel-Wiek and Reval, and the city of Riga. During the periods 1225 – 1226 and 1232 – 1233 parts of Livonia were directly governed by papal legates, William of Savoy, Bishop of Modena, and Balduin of Aulne (see Bishops of Selonia, later Semigallia). Livonia was annexed by Poland on 28 Nov 1561.

Masters of the Livonian Order

c. AD 1204 – summer 1209	*Wenno* (or *Vinno*), murdered at Riga
1209 – 22 Sep 1236	*Volkwin* (or *Folkwin, Volquin*) (d. Saule, i.e. Šiauliai(?), Lithuania)
Jun 1237 – 5 Mar 1239(?)	*Hermann Balke*, absent for most of the period
1238 – 1251(?)	*Dietrich von Groningen* (b. c. 1210; d. 3 Sep (1259?)) frequently absent
1240 – spring 1241 (or 1243?)	*Andreas de Velven*, acting(?)
c. 1245 – c. 1246	*Heinrich von Heimburg*
1248 †	*Andreas von Stirland* (or *Stîre*), resigned
1253 – Jul 1256	*Anno von Sangerhausen* (d. 8 Jul 1273/4) became Grand Master
1256 – 13 Jul 1260	*Burchard von Hornhusen* (d. at the battle of the Durbe)
1261/autumn 1262 – Feb 1263 ‡	*Werner*, resigned
1263 – 1266	*Konrad von Mandern* (or *von Medem*) (d. before 1298?)
1266/7 – 16 Feb 1270	*Otto von Lutterberg* (or *von Rodenstein*) (d. Karuse)

*Originally a separate order, called the Brothers of the Sword (Fratres Militiae Christi), reconstituted in 1237 as part of the Teutonic Knights under the name Order of the Teutonic Knights of Livonia (Fratres de domo sanctae Mariae Theutonicorum Jerusalemitana per Livoniam)

†Jul 1252 – Apr 1254	*Eberhard von Seyne*, Vice Grand Master in Livonia
‡1262	*Helmerich von Würzburg* (*von Rechenberg*) (d. 12 Jul 1263) Vice Grand Master in Livonia

1270 – 1273	*Walter von Nortecken* (or *Nordeck*), returned to Germany in consequence of illness
1274 – 5 Mar 1279	*Ernst von Rassburg* (or *von Ratzeburg*) (d. Aizkraukle)
1279	*Konrad von Feuchtwangen* (d. 1296) Grand Master 1291
1281 – 26 Mar 1287	*Willekin von Endorp* (d. Grösen) acting until 1283
1288	*Kuno von Hazzigenstein* (or *von Herzogenstein*)
1290 – 1293	*Halt (von Hohenbach?)*
1295 – 28 Oct 1296	*Heinrich von Dinkelaghe*
1296 – 1 Jun 1298	*Bruno* (d. Toraida on the Gauja) at first Vice Master
1298 – 1305/7	*Gottfried von Rogge*
1307/9 – 19 Jul 1322	*Gerhard von Jorke* (or *York*), resigned
1322 – 1324	*Konrad Ketelhoed*, Vice Master
6 Jul 1324 – 25 May 1328	*Reimer Hane*, resigned
1328 – 24 Jun 1340	*Eberhard von Monheim* (or *Munheim*) (d. c. 1380?) resigned
1340 – 14 Dec 1345	*Burchard von Dreileben*, resigned
1345 – 10 Sep 1359	*Goswin von Herike* (d. c. 1390?)
Feb 1360 – 11 Jul 1364	*Arnold von Vietinghof*
29 Sep 1364 – 1385	*Wilhelm von Vrimersheim* (or *von Freimersheim*) (d. in or before Mar 1385)
1385 – 26 Mar 1389	*Robin von Eltz*
1389 – 17 Aug 1415	*Dietrich York*
Sep 1415 – 3 Apr (27 Mar?) 1424	*Siegfried Lander von Spanheim*
May 1424 – Oct(?) 1432	*Cisse von Rutenberg*
1433/4 – 1 Sep 1435	*Franke Kerskorff* (d. in the battle of the Swienta)
1438 – 29 Jun 1450	*Heidenreich Vinke von Overberg* (d. Riga?)
Sep 1450 – 15 Aug 1469	*Johann von Mengede*, called *Osthof*
Mar 1470 – Sep 1471	*Johann Wolthus von Herse* (d. in prison at Wenden (now Cēsis) 1472/3) deposed
Jan 1472 – 18 Nov 1483	*Bernd von der Borch*, resigned
1483 – 26 May 1494	*Johann Freitag von Lorighofe*, acting until Jan 1485
7 Jul/9 Oct 1494 – 28 Feb 1535	*Wolter von Plettenberg* (d. Wenden (now Cēsis))
1535 – 5 Feb 1549	*Hermann von Brüggenei*, called *Hasenkamp*

Feb 1549 – 18 May 1551	*Johann von der Recke* (b. Heren c. 1480; d. Viljandi)
Jun 1551 – 30 May 1557	*Heinrich von Galen* (d. Tarvastu)
Jun 1557 – Sep 1559	*(Johann) Wilhelm (von) Fürstenberg* (b. c. 1500; d. Lyubim spring 1568)
Sep 1559 – 5 Mar 1562	*Gotthard Kettler* (b. Eggeringhausen 1517; d. Mitau 17 May 1587) did homage to the Polish king and became Duke of Courland and Semigallia 5 Mar 1562

Bishops and Archbishops of Riga

Mar/Apr 1199 – 17 Jan 1229	*Albert (von Buxhoevden)* (b. Bremen c. 1165; d. Riga)
1229/8 Apr 1231* – 1253	*Nikolaus (von Nauen?)*
1253 – 1272/3	*Albert Suerbeer* (b. c. 1200) Archbishop of Livonia, Estonia and Prussia 1245; confirmed as Archbishop of Riga 1255
1273/5 Nov 1274 – 1284	*Johann von Lune*
1285/10 Jan 1286 – 1294	*Johann von Vechten*
1294/18 Apr 1295 – 1300	*Johann*, Count Schwerin (d. Rome)
19 Dec 1300	*Isarnus Takkon* (d. 18 Sep 1310) translated to Lund
30 Mar 1302 – 1304	*Jens Grand*, previously Archbishop of Lund (b. c. 1255; d. 30 May 1327) resigned
21 Mar 1304 – 1341	*Friedrich von Pernstein* (d. Avignon)
18 Oct 1341 – 9 Sep 1347	*Engelbert von Dolen* (d. Avignon) Bishop of Leal 26 Nov 1323 – 18 Oct 1341
17 Mar 1348 – 28 Dec 1369	*Bromhold von Vyffhusen* (d. Rome)
11 Feb 1370 – 30 Jun 1374	*Siegfried Blomberg* (d. Avignon)
23 Oct 1374 – 24 Sep 1393	*Johann von Sinten* (d. after 8 Sep 1397)
27 Sep 1393 – 30 May 1418	*Johann von Wallenrode* (b. Wasserknoden c. 1370; d. Alken 28 May 1419)

*The Archbishop of Bremen nominated Albert Suerbeer (see next entry), but the dispute was eventually settled in favour of Nikolaus

11 Jul 1418 – 16 Jun 1424	*Johann Ambundii* (or *Habundi*) (b. Schwaan; d. Rauna)
13 Oct 1424 – 5 Apr 1448	*Henning Scharpenberg* (d. Rauna)
9 Oct 1448 – 12 Jul 1479	*Silvester Schodewescher* (d. Kokenhusen)
12 Mar 1480 – 20 Dec 1483	*Stephan Grube* (d. Riga)
4 Jun 1484 – 6 Feb 1509	*Michael Hildebrand* (d. Rauna)
18 Feb/23 May 1509	*Jasper* (or *Caspar*) *Linde* (b. Kamen c. 1460(?); d. Rauna)
29 Jun 1524 – 9 Sep 1527	*Johann Blankenfelde* (b. Berlin c. 1481; d. Torquemada, Spain) coadjutor from 29 Nov 1523, Bishop of Reval 30 Oct 1514 – Jan 1525, Bishop of Dorpat 14 Jun 1518 – 9 Sep 1527
6 Feb 1528/6 Mar 1531 – 11 Aug 1539	*Thomas Schöning* (d. Kokenhusen?)
Aug 1539 – 4 Feb 1563	*Wilhelm*, Margrave of Brandenburg (b. 30 Jun 1498; d. Riga) coadjutor from 15 Sep 1529
Nov 1555 – 4 Aug 1563/1569	*Christoph*, Duke of Mecklenburg (b. Augsburg 30 Jun 1537; d. Tempzin 4 Mar 1592) temporalities seized by King Sigismund II of Poland 1563; imprisoned; resigned 1569

Bishops of Selonia (later of Semigallia)

1217 – 30 Apr 1224	*Bernhard zur Lippe* (b. c. 1140; d. Mežotne(?))
Aug 1225 – 1231	*Lambert* (d. 1234 or earlier)
28 Jan 1232 – 1236	*Balduin of Aulne* (d. 1243) papal vice-legate 1230; legate of Gottland, Finland, Estonia, Courland and Semigallia 1232
c. 1246 – 1247	*Arnold* (d. after 1261)
5 Dec 1247 – Mar 1251	*Heinrich von Lützelburg* (d. 3 Oct 1273) translated to Courland
Mar 1251	See abolished

Bishops of Courland

c. Sep 1234(?) – winter 1236/7	*Engelbert*, killed by the Kurs at Degerhovede
1237 – 1245(?)	See vacant

*	*Guarnerus* (or *Werner*?) (d. 1291) expelled
3 Mar 1251	*Heinrich von Lützelburg*, Bishop of Semigallia 5 Dec 1247 – Mar 1251 (see above)
5 Mar 1263 – 1299(?)	*Emund von Werd*
(?)	*Johann*
1300 – (?)	*Burchard* (d. before 24 Jul 1317)
1317/5 Mar 1322 – 1326	*Paul*, elected before 24 Jul 1317
1326/11 Oct 1328	*Johann*
1330	*Bernard*
1332 – after Oct 1353	*Johann Jodis*
14 Mar 1354 – c. 1359	*Ludolf*, previously provost of Courland
25 Jan 1360 – 1370/1	*Jakob*, previously canon of Courland
8 Jun 1371 – 1398	*Otto*, previously custos of Courland
12 Jun 1399 – 1404	*Rutger von Brüggenei*
12 Jan 1405 – 17 Nov 1424	*Gotschalk Schutte*
19 Jan 1425 – 28 Nov 1456	*Johann Tiergart*
20 Jun 1457	*Paul Einwald*, coadjutor since 1456, resigned
9 Jul 1473 – 31 Jan 1500	*Martin Lewitz*
4 May – 4 Nov 1500	*Michael Sculteti* (d. Rome)
12 Feb 1501 – 1523	*Heinrich Basedow* (d. Hasenpoth)
2 Mar 1524 – 1540	*Hermann Ronneberg*
1540 – Apr 1560	*Johann von Münchhausen* (d. c. 1583) also administrator of the see of Ösel
1560 – 18 Mar 1583	*Magnus*, Duke of Holstein (b. 1540; d. Pilten)

Bishops of Leal (later of Dorpat)

spring 1211 – 15 Jun 1219	*Theoderich* (or *Dietrich*) *von Treiden* (b. c. 1160?) Bishop of Estonia, killed by the Estonians at Lyndanise
1219	*Hermann von Buxhoevden*, brother of Albert, Bishop of Riga (d. Falkenau(?) c. 1250) Bishop of Leal, resigned

*Faculty for consecration was granted for Guarnerus 8 Nov 1245, but there is no record of consecration. The see was no longer vacant in 1246 and 1248, but the name of the then bishop is not known. Guarnerus may be identical with the Werner, Bishop of Courland, who was acting as suffragan in Germany in 1276

1245 – 1254	*Bernhard*
fl. 1254	Unnamed bishop
fl. 1259	Unnamed bishop
1263 – 18 Feb 1268	*Alexander* (d. at the battle of the Kähhola)
May 1268 – 4 Dec (1285?)	*Friedrich von Haseldorf* (b. c. 1220)
1286(?) – 1299(?)	*Bernhard* (d. 1302)
1302/3 (1304) – 1312	*Dietrich von Fischhausen* (or *Vyshusen*) (d. Avignon)
14 Jan 1313 – 1323	*Nikolaus*
26 Nov 1323 – 18 Oct 1341	*Engelbert von Dolen*, translated to Riga (see above)
25 Sep 1342 – 1344	*Wescelus* (or *Wesselus*)
1344 – 1346	See vacant
23 Sep 1346 – 1373	*Johann von Vifhusen*
5 Sep 1373 – 1378	*Heinrich von Velde*
21 Dec 1378 – 2 Jul 1400*	*Dietrich Damerow* (d. after Jul 1408) resigned
15 Dec 1400 – 1410	*Heinrich Wrangel*
Dec 1410/7 Jan 1411 – 1413	*Bernhard Bulowe* (d. before 28 Feb 1413)
14 Apr 1413 – Mar 1441	*Dietrich Resler*
27 Mar 1441/17 Mar (1442?)	*Bartholomäus Savijerwe* (d. before 29 May 1461) resigned
10 Dec 1459 – 23 Mar 1468	*Helmich von Mallinckrodt* (d. after Mar 1485) resigned
5 Dec 1468 – Feb 1473	*Andreas Peper*
Mar/6 Jun 1473 – c. 24 Feb 1485	*Johann Bertkow*
18 Jul 1485 – Dec 1498	*Dietrich Hake*
20 Mar 1499 – c. 26 Mar 1505	*Johann von der Rope*
Jul 1505 – c. 9 Nov 1513	*Gerhard Schrove*
30 Oct 1514† – 15 Apr 1518	*Christian Bomhower*

*24 Jan 1379 – 1386 *Albrecht Hecht*, provost of Dorpat, nominated bishop by the anti-pope Clement (VII), resigned

†The bishop elected in 1513 resigned before consecration

14 Jun 1518 – 9 Sep 1527	*Johann Blankenfelde*, Bishop of Reval 30 Oct 1514 – Jan 1525, Archbishop of Riga 29 Jun 1524 – 9 Sep 1527 (see above)
Feb 1528/3 Aug 1532 – c. Apr 1543	*Johann Bey*
21 May 1543 – 18 Apr 1551	*Jodocus von der Recke*, finally resigned 22 Oct 1553
17 Oct 1552/22 Oct 1553 – 18 Jul 1558	*Hermann Wesel* (d. Moscow or Lyubim Jun 1563) surrendered to the Russians

Bishops of Ösel

summer 1227/1228 – 1229	*Godefridus* (or *Gottfried*), consecrated in Germany 1227, returned to Livonia 1228, abandoned the see
1229 – 1234	Ösel administered from Riga
10 Sep 1234 – 10 Mar 1260	*Heinrich I*
1262 – 1285	*Hermann von Buxhoevden*
1290 – 1294	*Heinrich II*
1297 – 1307 or 1310	*Konrad*
1310 – 1321	*Hartung*
8 Mar 1322 – 1337	*Jakob* (d. Lübeck)
23 Feb 1338 – 1362	*Hermann Osenbrugge*
24 Jul 1363 – 1374	*Konrad*
23 Oct 1374 – 1381	*Heinrich* (d. (murdered) Arensburg)
1383/Mar 1385* – 5/6 Nov 1419	*Winrich von Kniprode* (d. Arensburg)
8 Jan 1420 – 10 Aug 1423	*Kaspar Schuwenflug* (d. Montefiascone)
5 Sep 1423 – 21 Jul 1432	*Christian Kuband* (d. Rome)
22 Oct 1432 – 12 Sep 1438	*Johann Schutte* (d. Hapsal)
20 Mar 1439	*Johann Creul* (d. Hapsal 1457) nominated by the pope
1454	*Ludolf Grove* (d. Arensburg 11 Mar 1458) elected by the chapter
12 Jul 1458 – 17 Jan 1471	*Jodocus Ho(g)enstein* (b. Danzig c. 1115; d. Hapsal)

*The chapter's candidate did not receive papal confirmation. *Johann Sluter de Hex* was nominated by the anti-pope Clement (VII) on 16 Dec 1383

10 Feb/17 Jun 1471 – 1491	*Petrus Wetberch*
26 Mar 1492 – 19 Mar 1515	*Johann Orgies* (d. Hapsal)
23 Mar 1515 – 22 Apr 1527	*Johann Kyvel* (d. Hapsal) coadjutor from 3 Oct 1513
4 May 1527 – 2 Oct 1530	*Georg von Tiesenhausen* (d. Arensburg) Bishop of Reval c. Mar 1525 – 2 Oct 1530
18 Oct 1530/3 Aug 1532 – 1541	*Reinhold von Buxhoevden* (d. Lode 2 May 1552) resigned
13 Jul 1541 – 1578	See administered by the Bishop of Courland

Bishops of Reval

1219 – 1226	*Wesselin*, previously chaplain to Bishop Theoderich of Estonia(?), journeyed to Germany and did not return
1227 – 1240	See vacant
1240 – 14 Oct 1260	*Thorkill*
13 Sep 1263 – 2 Jul 1279	*Thrugot*
1280 – 1293/4	*Johann*
1294 – 1298	The elected or nominated candidates did not become bishop
23 Dec 1323 – 7 Mar 1350	*Olaf*
15/16 Jul 1352 – 1 Apr 1389	*Ludwig von Münster*, resigned and died soon after
10 Mar 1390 – 7 Jan(?) 1403	*Johann Rekelink*
2 Jul 1403 – 1405	*Dietrich Tholke*
3 Aug 1405 – c. 20 Feb 1418	*Johann von Aken* (or *Achmann*)
18 Apr 1418 – 1419	*Arnold Stoltevoet*
20 Nov 1419 – 13 Apr 1456	*Heinrich Üxküll* (b. c. 1400)
26 Jan 1457 – 13 Mar 1475	*Everhard Kalle*
5 Jul 1475 – early 1477	*Iwanus Stoltevoet*
16 Jun 1477 – 22 Oct 1492	*Simon von der Borch*

6 Mar 1493 – Jan/Feb 1509	*Nikolaus Roddendorp*
4 May 1509 – 1513	*Gotschalk Hagen*
Oct 1513/6 Feb 1514 – Mar/Apr 1514	*Christian Czernikow*
30 Oct 1514 – Jan 1525	*Johann Blankenfelde*, Bishop of Dorpat 14 Jun 1518 – 9 Sep 1527, Archbishop of Riga 29 Jun 1524 – 9 Sep 1527 (see above)
c. Mar 1525 – 2 Oct 1530	*Georg von Tiesenhausen* (d. Arensburg) Bishop of Ösel 4 May 1527 – 2 Oct 1530
30 Aug 1531 – 1536	*Johann Roterd* (d. before 27 Jun 1536)
1536 – 19 Jan 1551	*Arnold Annebat*
1551 – 1557	*Friedrich von Ampten*, coadjutor 1546, 1550 – 1551, resigned(?)
1558 – 1560	*Mauritius Wrangel*, resigned
1560 – 1578	See administered by the Bishop of Courland

Lombards, Kingdom of the

Lombard Kings

AD 568 – 28 Jun 572	*Alboin*, son of Audoin, the king of the Lombards in Pannonia and Noricum (d. (assassinated) Verona) succeeded his father c. 565; invaded Italy 568 and took Pavia 572
572 – 574	*Klef*; assassinated
	Interregnum
584 – 5 Sep 590	*Autari*, son (d. Pavia)
Nov 590	*Agilulfo*, Duke of Turin, with his wife, *Teodolinda*, widow of Autari (d. 628); captured Perugia 593 and Padua 602
615	*Adaloaldo*, son (b. Monza 602; d. c. 626) ruled under the regency of his mother, *Teodolinda*; deposed
624	*Arioaldo*, Duke of Turin, brother-in-law, first husband of Adaloaldo's sister Gundeberga
636	*Rotari*, Duke of Brescia, second husband of Gundeberga; captured Genoa 652

652	*Rodoaldo*, son; for about five months
653	*Ariperto I*, nephew of Teodolinda
661	*Pertarito* (for 1st time) and *Godeperto*, sons; deposed
662	*Grimoaldo*, Duke of Benevento, brother-in-law; conquered most of Calabria, with Taranto and Brindisi; assassinated
672	*Pertarito* (for 2nd time)
688	*Cunimperto*, son; ruled with his father from 680
700	*Luitperto*, son; for eight months
700	*Ragimperto*, son of Godeperto
701	*Ariperto II*, son
712	*Ansprando* (d. 13 Jun 712) for three months
712	*Liutprando*, son; captured Bologna 728 and besieged Rome 739
Jan 744	*Ildeprando*, son; ruled with his father fron 735
Sep 744	*Ratchis* (for 1st time)
Jul 749	*Astolfo*, brother; captured Ravenna 751; defeated by Pippin III the Short, King of the Franks, at Pavia 755 and was forced to recognize Frankish suzerainty
Dec 756	*Ratchis* (for 2nd time)
757 – Jun 774	*Desiderio*, Duke of Tuscany; surrendered Pavia and taken as a prisoner to France
774	Kingdom of the Lombards conquered by Charlemagne, King of the Franks

Frankish Kings

Names are given in modern German renderings. The Italian versions are: Adalbert, Adalberto; Adalhard, Adalardo; Berengar, Berengario; Bernhard, Bernardo; Hugo, Ugo; Karl, Carlo; Karlmann, Carlomano; Lambert, Lamberto; Lothar, Lotario; Ludwig, Ludovico; Pippin, Pipino; Rudolf, Rodolfo; Wido, Guido.

Jul 774 – 28 Jan 814	*Karl I*, the Great (Italian: *Carlomagno*; known in English and French as *Charlemagne*), King of the Franks (b. 2 Apr 747; d. Aachen) invaded Italy at the invitation of Pope Adrian I, defeated and deposed Desiderio Jun 774; crowned Holy Roman Emperor 25 Dec 800
781 – 8 Jul 810	*Pippin*, son (b. Apr 773) appointed King of Italy by his father (Charlemagne retained the title King of the Lombards), ruled at first with Frankish deputies; conquered Venetia 810 leading to treaty of 814 with

	the Byzantines whereby the Franks received Istria and northern Croatia
810 – 813	*Adalhard*, Abbot of Corbie (b. 750; d. 2 Jan 826) and his brother, *Wala* (d. 836), grandsons of Charlemagne for whom they ruled as regents
Sep 813	*Bernhard*, illegitimate son of Pippin (b. c. 797; d. 17 Apr 818) recognized as King of Italy by Charlemagne; deposed by Holy Roman Emperor Ludwig I the Pious
817	*Lothar I*, son of Holy Roman Emperor Ludwig I the Pious (b. 795; d. Prüm 29 Sep 855) King of Bavaria c. 814, crowned co-emperor 817, Holy Roman Emperor 843; abdicated
15 Jun 844 – 12 Aug 875	*Ludwig II*, son (b. c. 825; d. near Brescia) appointed King of the Lombards by his father; recaptured Benevento from the Muslims 847; Holy Roman Emperor 855; inherited area around Lyon and Vienne from his brother Karl 863; died without male heir
876 – 6 Oct 877	*Karl II*, the Bald, Holy Roman Emperor, King (Charles) of the West Franks (b. 13 Jun 823; d. Brides-les-Bains) appointed *Berengar* of Friuli as his deputy
877 – 29 Sep 880	*Karlmann*, nephew (b. c. 829) King of Bavaria 876; ruled in Italy with *Berengar* of Friuli (see below) as deputy; area around Lyon and Vienne incorporated in independent kingdom of Burgundy 879
880 – 13 Jan 888	*Karl III*, the Fat, King of the East Franks, brother (b. 839; d. Neidingen, Germany) King (Charles) of the West Franks 884, Holy Roman Emperor 884; with *Berengar* of Friuli (see below) as deputy
888	*Berengar I*, Margrave of Friuli, cousin, grandson of Holy Roman Emperor Ludwig I the Pious (b. between 850 and 860; d. (assassinated) Verona 7 Apr 924); held only a small part of Italy against his rivals;* crowned

*889	*Wido*, Duke of Spoleto; defeated Berengar I at Trebbia River 889; crowned Holy Roman Emperor by Pope Stephen V 21 Feb 891 but exercised no real power
autumn 894 – Oct 898	*Lambert*, son; crowned co-emperor by Pope Formosus 30 Apr 892; inherited Spoleto and his father's claim to the Italian throne, exercised no real power
12 Oct 900 – Jul 905	*Ludwig III*, the Blind, King (Louis) of Lower Burgundy (b. c. 880; d. Jun 928) Holy Roman Emperor Feb 901; defeated, deposed and blinded by Berengar I and rule then confined to Burgundy

	Holy Roman Emperor Nov or Dec 915 but exercised no power outside Italy; defeated by Rudolf at Fiorenzuola 17 Jul 923
921/17 Jul 923	*Rudolf*, King (Rodolphe II) of Upper Burgundy (d. 11 Jul 937) proclaimed King of Italy 921, defeated Berengar I 17 Jul 923; abandoned Italy in favour of Hugo in exchange for rule over the whole of Burgundy
spring 926	*Hugo*, Count of Arles, Duke of Provence and Margrave of Vienne; crowned at Pavia July 926; forced to abdicate by Berengar II
10 Apr 947 – 22 Nov 950	*Lothar II*, son (d. Turin); ruled at first with his father
15 Dec 950 – 963	*Berengar II*, Margrave of Ivrea, grandson of Berengar I (b. c. 900; d. 6 Aug 966); with his son, *Adalbert* (b. c. 936; d. c. Jul 968); Berengar II did homage to King Otto I of Germany Aug 952; defeated and deposed by Otto I

King Otto I the Great of Germany assumed the title of King of the Lombards during his first invasion of Italy 951. With Otto I the titles of King of the Lombards (or of Italy) and Holy Roman Emperor were permanently attached to the German crown. King of the Lombards became a ceremonial title indicating the claim of the German kings and emperors to Italy.

Lori (Tashir)

Kings

Bagratid Dynasty

AD 982	*Gurgen I*, son of King Ashot III of Armenia
989	*Davit' Lackland*, son
1046/8 – 1081/9	*Gurgen II Kvirike*, son
1081/9	Annexed by the Seljuqs

Lorraine

On the division of Francia Media in Sep 855, *Lothar II* (see Kingdom of the Franks) received the portion north of the sources of the Oise, Aisne and Marne, which became known as Regnum Lotharii, or Lotharingia (Lorraine in English and French). King Charles II the Bald of France annexed Lorraine after the death of Lothar II but ceded eastern parts of it to his brother, King Ludwig II the German, King of the East Franks. In 879 Kings Louis III and Carloman of France ceded the rest of Lorraine to King Karl III the Fat of the East Franks.

In May 895, Karl III's successor, King Arnulf of the East Franks, appointed his illegitimate son, *Zwentibold* (b. c. 870; d. 13 Aug 900), as King of Lorraine. After Zwentibold's death, the title was adopted by his half-brother, *Ludwig*, the Child, King of the East Franks (b. Sep or Oct 893; d. 24 Nov 911), who in 904 nominated *Gebhard*, uncle of Duke Konrad of Franconia (subsequently King Konrad I of Germany) (d. 22 Jun 910), as Duke of Lorraine.

The East Franks exercised little control over Lorraine: the most important count in the area at the time was *Reginar I*, Long-neck, grandson of Lothar I (b. c. 850; d. Aug or Nov 915), whose allegiance lay with King Charles III the Simple of France. Reginar was succeeded by his son, *Giselbert*, who accepted German overlordship in 925 and was granted the title Duke of Lorraine by King Heinrich I of Germany.

Dukes of Lorraine

AD 925 – 2 Oct 939	*Giselbert* (b. c. 890)
939	*Heinrich*, son (b. c. 931; d. c. 944) deposed immediately after accession for rebellion against King Otto I of Germany
Saxon House (Liudolfings)	
940	*Heinrich*, brother of King Otto I of Germany who appointed him to the dukedom (b. 919 or 921; d. 1 Nov 955) deposed after a few months for rebellion; Duke of Bavaria 947
House of Verdun	
940 – 944	*Otto*, son of Richwin, Count of Verdun; appointed by King Otto I of Germany
Salian House	
944	*Konrad*, the Red, son-in-law of King Otto I of Germany (d. at the Lechfeld, near Augsburg, Bavaria,

	10 Aug 955) deposed after rebelling against Otto I

Saxon House (restored)

953	*Brun*, Archbishop (Brun I) of Cologne, brother of King Otto I of Germany (b. 925; d. 11 Oct 965) divided the duchy for administrative purposes into Upper and Lower Lorraine 959

Dukes of Lower Lorraine

Carolingians

976	*Charles*, disaffected brother of King Lothaire of France (b. 953; d. Orléans, France, 22 Jun (?) 995) appointed to the dukedom by his uncle, Holy Roman Emperor Otto II; captured and imprisoned by King Hugues Capet of France 29 Mar 991 after attempting to assert his right to the French throne
991	*Otton*, son (b. c. 985)

House of Ardennes

1005 or 1012 – 26 Sep 1023	*Godefroi I*, son of Count Godefroi of Verdun; appointed to the dukedom by King Heinrich II of Germany
1023 – 19 Apr 1044	*Gothelon* (or *Gozelon*) *I*, the Great, brother; Duke of Upper Lorraine 1033; duchy redivided between his sons at his death by King Heinrich III of Germany
1044 – 18 May 1046	*Gothelon II*. the Coward, son (d. c. 22 May 1046); deposed shortly before his death

House of Luxemburg

1046 – 28 Aug 1065	*Friedrich von Luxemburg*; appointed by Holy Roman Emperor Heinrich III

House of Ardennes (restored)

Oct or Nov 1065 – 24 Dec 1069	*Godefroi II*, the Bearded, son of Gothelon I (d. Verdun) Duke of Upper Lorraine 1044 and May 1046 – 1047
1069 – 26 Feb 1076	*Godefroi III*, the Hunchback, son (d. (assassinated) Utrecht)

Salian House (restored)

1076 – 1089	*Konrad*, son of King Heinrich IV of Germany (b. 12 Feb 1074; d. 27 Jul 1101) renounced the dukedom in

	favour of Godefroi IV; King of Germany 1090 – 1093

House of Ardennes (*restored*)

1089 – 18 Jul 1100	*Godefroi IV de Bouillon*, nephew of Godefroi III (b. c. 1060; d. Jerusalem) departed on the First Crusade 1096, elected 'Defender of the Holy Sepulchre' 17 Jul 1099

House of Limburg

25 Dec 1101	*Henri*, Count of Limburg and of Arlon (d. 1119?) appointed by Holy Roman Emperor Heinrich IV, deposed by King Heinrich V of Germany
13 May 1106	*Godefroi V*, the Bearded, Duke (Godefroi I) of Brabant (d. 25 Jan 1139) deposed by King Lothar II of Germany
before 13 Jun 1128 – 16 Jul(?) 1139	*Walram*, Count (Walram II) of Limburg and of Arlon, son of Henri (b. c. 1085)

No further dukes of Lower Lorraine were appointed. The most important rulers in the area thereafter were the bishops of Liège and Utrecht, the dukes of Brabant, and the counts of Hainaut and Holland.

Dukes of Upper Lorraine (Mosellane)

House of Bar

959	*Friedrich I*, Count of Bar, nephew of Duke Brun of Lorraine who appointed him to the dukedom (b. c. 912; d. between 978 and 984)
978	*Dietrich* (or *Thierry*) *I*, son
1027 (probably) – 18 or 20 May 1033	*Friedrich II*, son

House of Ardennes

1033 – 19 Apr 1044	*Gothelon* (or *Gozelon*) *I*, the Great, Duke of Lower Lorraine; duchy redivided at his death between his two sons by King Heinrich III of Germany
1044	*Godefroi*, the Bearded, son (d. Verdun 24 Dec 1069) deposed Sep 1044 for rebellion against Heinrich III, restored May 1046 but deposed again; Duke (Godefroi II) of Lower Lorraine 1065

House of Metz

1047	*Adalbert*, a count in Alsace; appointed by King Heinrich III of Germany
1048 – 6 Mar 1070	*Gerard*, nephew
1070 – 23 Jan 1115	*Thierry II*, son
1115 – 14 Jan 1138	*Simon I*, son
1138* – 13 May 1176	*Mathieu I*, son
1176	*Simon II*, son (b. c. 1152; d. 14 Jan 1207) retired to the Abbey of Sturzelbronn and named his nephew, Ferry II, as successor
1205	*Ferry I*, brother (b. c. 1152; d. 1207) with his son, *Ferry II* (d. 10 Oct 1213) who ruled alone after his father's death
1213 – 17 Feb 1220	*Thiébaut I*, son
1220 – 24 Jun 1251	*Mathieu II*, brother
1251 – 31 Dec 1303	*Ferry III*, son (b. 1238)
1304 – 13 May 1312	*Thiébaut II*, son
1312 – 23 Aug 1328	*Ferry IV*, son (b. Gondreville 15 Apr 1282)
1328 – 26 Aug 1346	*Raoul*, son (b. 1318)
1346 – 27 Sep 1390	*Jean I*, son (b. 1346)
1391 – 25 Jan 1431	*Charles II*, son (b. 1364)
1431	*Isabelle*, daughter (d. 27 Feb 1453); with her husband, *René I*, Duke of Bar (b. Angers, Anjou, 16 Jan 1409; d. Aachen 10 Jul 1480) Duke Consort; Duke of Anjou Nov 1434 – 1471, King of Naples 1435 – 1442; resigned in Lorraine at or possibly before the death of Isabelle
1453 – 13 Dec 1470	*Jean II*, son (b. 2 Aug 1425)
1470	*Yolande*, sister (b. 2 Nov 1428; d. c. 23 Feb 1483) with her husband, *Ferry VI*, Count of Vaudemont (b. 1428; d. 31 Aug 1470)
1473 – 10 Dec 1508	*René II*, Count of Vaudemont, son (b. 2 May 1451) Duke of Bar 1480

*Soon after this time, with the end of the duchy of Lower Lorraine, the dukes of Upper Lorraine became known simply as dukes of Lorraine

Luba/Lunda and Lunda/Kazembe States

THE 'SECOND' LUBA EMPIRE

Territory now in southern Zaïre, with the capital at Munza.

Balopwe (Kings)

AD 1620*	*Ilunga waLwefu*, brother of Cibinda Ilunga of Lunda
(?)	*Kasongo Mwine Kibanza*
(?)	*Ngoi Sanza*
(?)	*Kasongo Kabundulu*
(?)	*Kumwimba Mputu*
(?)	*Kasongo Bonswe*
(?)	*Mwine Kombe Dai*, son
c. 1740	*Kadilo*, son
(?)	*Kekenya*, son
(?)	*Kaumbo*, nephew
(?)	*Miketo*, son
(?)	*Ilunga Sungu*, son of Kekenya
c. 1835	*Kumwimba Ngombe*, son (d. c. 1835?)
(?)	*Ndai aMujinga*, son, assassinated by Ilunga Kabale
c. 1850	*Ilunga Kabale*, brother
(?)	*Muloba*, son
(?)	*Kitamba*, brother
c. 1860	*Kasongo Kalombo*, brother
c. 1885	*Dai Mande*, brother(?), killed by Kasongo Niembo
(?)	*Kasongo Niembo*, brother; in conflict with his brother, *Kabongo Kumwimba Shimbu*
1905	Kingdom divided equally between Kasongo Niembo and Kabongo Kumwimba Shimbu following the intervention of the Congo Independent State in the civil war

*All dates are tentative

LUNDA

Territory now in north-eastern Angola and south-western Zaïre, with the capital at Musumba.

Aata Yamvo (Kings)

AD 1600*	*Cibinda Ilunga*, brother of Ilunga waLwefu of Luba
1630	*Mwaant Luseeng*, son
1660	(*Mwaant Yeev*) *Naweej I*, son
1690	*Muteba*
(?)	Two brothers of Muteba(?)
1720	*Mukanza*, brother of Muteba
1740	*Mulaji*, brother
1750	*Mbala I*, brother
1760	*Yaav yaMbany*
1810	*Cikombe Yaav*, for two months, abdicated
1810	*Naweej II*
1852	*Mulaji II* (*a Mbala*), owing to his infirmity appointed Mbumba (see below) as governor
1857	*Cakasekene*
(?)	*Muteba II* (*ya Cikombe*), son of Cikombe Yaav, usurper
1874	*Mbala II*, killed by Mbumba
1874	*Mbumba*, formerly governor of Lunda under Mulaji II
1883	*Cimbindu*, son of Naweej II, usurper, for five months
1884	*Kangapu*, usurper, killed by Mudiba
1885	*Mudiba*, usurper, killed in battle against the Cokwe tribe
1886	*Mukanza*, fled following the Cokwe invasion, deposed
May 1887	*Mbala III*, killed by Mushiri
1887	*Mushiri*, cousin (d. 1909) usurper, fled following Cokwe invasion to a reduced area of Lunda territory and continued to fight a guerrilla war against the Cokwe and the Congo Independent State
1898	*Muteba III*, of the Congo Independent State
(?)	Disintegration of the kingdom, superseded by the Cokwe tribe

*All dates are tentative

KAZEMBE OF THE LUAPULA

Territory now in southern Zaïre and northern Zambia.

Abamwata (Kings)

AD 1650*	*Mwin Tibaraka*
1680	*Cinyanta*, nephew, Lunda vassal
1710	*Kazembe I* (*Nganda Bilonda*), son, Lunda vassal
1740	*Kazembe II* (*Kaniembo*), son, Lunda vassal
1760	*Kazembe III* (*Ilunga* or *Lukwesa*)
Oct 1805	*Kazembe IV* (or *Kibangu Keleka*), son
1850	*Kazembe V* (*Kapumb*) (or *Mwonga Mfwama*)
1854	*Makao*, sister of Kazembe VI, regent while her brother travelled to the kingdom to take up his title
1855	*Kazembe VI* (or *Cinyanta Munona*), brother, former rival of Kazembe V
1862	*Lukwesa Mpanga* (for 1st time) isolated in the bush for circumcision rite
1862	*Kazembe VII* (or *Mwonga Nsemba* or *Sunkutu*), usurper in the absence of Lukwesa Mpanga, kingdom degenerated into civil war
1870	*Kazembe VIII* (or *Cinkonkole Kafuti*) (d. 1872)
1870	*Kazembe IX* (or *Lukwesa Mpanga*) (for 2nd time) killed Kazembe VIII 1872, civil war
c. 1883	*Kazembe X* (or *Kaniembo Ntemena*), brother, civil war
1899	Kazembe obliged to accept colonial rule by the British South Africa Company

Luxemburg

Counts

before AD 1059 – after 6 Jul 1083	*Konrad I*

*All dates are tentative

before 1089 – 1095 or 1096	*Heinrich I*
1096 – 23 Jan 1130 (or 1131)	*Wilhelm*, brother
before 23 Apr 1131 – 1136(?)	*Konrad II*
before Apr 1138 – 14 Aug 1196	*Heinrich II*, the Blind, son-in-law of Konrad I (b. after 1112)
1196	*Otto*, Count of Burgundy (Franche-Comté) invested with county by Holy Roman Emperor Heinrich VI; deposed
before 5 Apr 1198	*Ermesinde*, daughter of Heinrich II (b. Jul 1186) Regent: 18 Nov 1235: *Heinrich III*, the Fair, son; subsequently count
13 (or 17) Feb 1247	*Heinrich III*, the Fair; previously regent
24 Dec 1281	*Heinrich IV*, son
5 Jun 1288	*Heinrich V*, son (b. Valenciennes c. 1274; d. Buonconvento, near Siena, Italy, 24 Aug 1313) King (Heinrich VII) of Germany 27 Nov 1308, King of the Lombards 6 Jan 1311, Holy Roman Emperor 29 Jun 1312; appointed his son to rule in Luxemburg
25 Jun/3 Jul 1310	*Johann*, son (b. 10 Aug 1296; d. Crécy, France) King (Jan) of Bohemia 1310
26 Aug 1346	*Karl* (baptized *Wenzel*), King (Karl IV) of Germany, son (b. Prague, Bohemia, 14 May 1316; d. Prague 29 Nov 1378) King (Karel) of Bohemia 1346–1373; Margrave of Moravia 1333, King of the Lombards 1355, Holy Roman Emperor 5 Apr 1355, Margrave of Brandenburg 1373
between 15 Nov and 19 Dec 1353	*Wenzel I*, half-brother; created Duke of Luxemburg 13 Mar 1354

Dukes

7/8 Dec 1383	*Wenzel II*, King (Wenzel) of Germany and (Václav IV) of Bohemia, Elector (Wenzel) of Brandenburg (b. Nürnberg, Germany, 26 Feb 1361; d. Prague, Bohemia, 16 Aug 1419) pledged Luxemburg to his cousin Jodokus; deposed in Germany 20 Aug 1400
26 Feb 1388	*Jodokus* (or *Jobst*), Margrave of Brandenburg and Moravia, cousin (for 1st time) (b. 1351; d. Brno, Moravia, 18 Jan 1419) King of Germany 1 Oct 1410;

	transferred his interest to Duke Louis I of Orléans
18 Aug 1402	*Louis I*, Duke of Orléans, brother of King Charles VI of France (b. Paris 13 Mar 1372; d. (assassinated) Paris)
23 Nov 1407	*Jodokus* (for 2nd time) seized Luxemburg on the death of Louis
18 Jan 1411	*Wenzel II* (for 2nd time)
7 Jan 1412	*Elisabeth von Görlitz*, niece; granted Luxemburg during her lifetime by Wenzel (in lieu of dowry) on condition that Wenzel could recover it on payment of 120,000 Rhenish florins*
	Governors:
	7 Jan 1412 – 25 Oct 1415: *Antoine de Bourgogne*, Duke of Brabant, husband (d. Agincourt 25 Oct 1415)
	end May 1419 – 6 Jan 1425: Duke *Johann* of Bavaria-Straubing, co-ruler of Holland, husband (d. 6 Jan 1425) Bishop (Joannes VI) of Liège 14 Nov 1389 – 22 May 1418
	10 Jan 1442 – 3 Aug 1451: Duke *Philippe III*, the Good, of Burgundy, nephew of Antoine de Bourgogne (b. Dijon, Burgundy, 31 Jul 1396; d. Brugge, Flanders, 15 Jun 1467) occupied Luxemburg 1443; made heir by Elisabeth
3 Aug 1451	Luxemburg held by the dukes of Burgundy, the hereditary dukes having abandoned their claims

*Hereditary dukes:

16 Aug 1419	*Sigismund*, King of Germany, King (Zsigmond) of Hungary half-brother of Wenzel II (b. Nürnberg, Germany, 26 Fe 1361; d. Znojmo, Bohemia) at the same time King (Zikmund of Bohemia; Elector of Brandenburg 1378 – 1397 and 1411 18 Apr 1417, King of the Lombards 1431, Holy Roma Emperor 31 May 1433
9 Dec 1437	*Albrecht*, Archduke (Albrecht V) of Austria, son-in-law (b 10 Aug 1397; d. Nezmely, Hungary) at the same time Kin (Albert) of Hungary; King (Albrecht) of Bohemia 29 Ju 1438, King (Albrecht II) of Germany 18 Mar 1438
27 Oct 1439	*Elisabeth*, widow (b. 27 Nov 1409; d. 25 Dec 1442); grante the right to recover Luxemburg to her daughter's fiancé Wilhelm, Duke of Saxony, 23 Dec 1439 on condition that her unborn child should be a son then he would have the righ to recover Luxemburg from Wilhelm
22 Feb 1440 – 23 Nov 1457	*Ladislaus Posthumus*, son; at the same time King (Ladislav of Bohemia; King (László V) of Hungary 1444; died withou issue

Lydia

Territory comprised part of present-day western Turkey, with the capital at Sardis.

Kings

Mermnads	
c. 685 BC	*Gyges* (or *Gugu*), assassinated Candaules, last of the Heraclid kings of Lydia*
c. 657	*Ardys*
(?)	*Sadyattes*
c. 600	*Alyattes*, son
c. 560 – 546	*Croesus*, son, completed the conquest of mainland Ionia begun by Alyattes, fate after the conquest of Sardis unknown
546	Conquest and destruction of Sardis by the Persian king Cyrus II

Magadha

Territory comprised part of present-day north-eastern India (Bihar), with the capital at Pataliputra (now Patna).

Kings

c. 544 BC	*Bimbisara*
c. 493	*Ajatasatru*
c. 462	*Udayabhadra*, son
c. 447	*Anurrudha*, son
(?)	*Munda*, son
(?)	*Nagadasaka*
c. 430	*Sisunaga*
c. 413	*Kalasoka*
c. 385 – 364	Ten sons of Kalasoka

*The chronology and historicity of the Heraclid dynasty have not been established

Nanda Dynasty

c. 364	*Mahapadma*
c. 336 – 324	Sons of Mahapadma

Mauryas

c. 324	*Chandragupta*, overthrew the Nanda dynasty
c. 302	*Bindusara* (or *Amitraghata*), son
c. 273 – 232	*Asoka* (or *Ashokavardhana*), son
c. 232	Empire divided between the grandsons of Asoka
c. 185 BC	Last Maurya killed

Guptas

AD 320	*Chandra Gupta I*
c. 330	*Samudra Gupta*, son
c. 380	*Chandra Gupta II* (or *Vikramaditya*), son
c. 415	*Kumara Gupta I* (or *Mahendraditya),* son
c. 455 – 467	*Skanda Gupta* (or *Vikramaditya*), son
c. 467	Invasions of the Hunas or Huns, resulting in the division and decay of the Gupta empire

Magdeburg

Archbishops*

AD 968 – 20 Jun 981	*Adalbert*
10 Sep 981 – 25 Jan 1004	*Gisiler*
30 Jan/2 Feb 1004 – 9 Jun 1012	*Tagino*
22 Jun – 12 Aug 1012	*Walthard*
22 Sep 1012 – 22 Oct 1023	*Gero*
1023 – 28 Feb 1051	*Hunfrid*
1051 – 30 or 31 Aug 1063	*Engelhard*

*When two dates separated by an oblique stroke are given for the beginning of an episcopate, the first refers to election or nomination and the second to ordination, consecration or investiture

Sep(?) 1063	*Werinhar* (or *Wezel*), killed
7 or 8 Aug 1079 – 17 Jun 1102*	*Hartwig*
11 Jun 1105 – 15 Apr 1107	*Heinrich I von Asloe*
2 Jun 1107 – 12 Jun 1119	*Adelgoz*
Jun 1119 – 19 or 20 Dec 1125	*Rotger* (or *Rüdiger*)
summer 1126 – 6 Jun 1134	*Norbert von Gennepp*
29 Jun 1134 – 2 May 1142	*Konrad I von Querfurt* (b. c. 1100)
May 1142 – 14 or 15 Jan 1152	*Friedrich von Wettin*
May 1152 – 24 or 25 Aug 1192	*Wichmann von Seeburg*
21 Oct 1192 – 16 or 17 Aug 1205	*Ludolf von Kroppenstädt*
Aug 1205/26 Feb 1206 – 15 Oct 1232	*Albert von Kevernburg*
late 1232 – 3 Apr(?) 1235	*Burchard von Woldenberg*
31 May/Jul 1235 – 5 Apr 1253	*Wilbrand von Kevernburg*
before 3 May/ before 25 Oct 1253 – 26 Feb 1260	*Rudolf von Dingelstädt*
before 25 Apr/before 26 Nov 1260 – 19 Dec 1266	*Ruprecht von Querfurt*
26 Dec 1266/before 18 Mar 1267 – 5 Jan 1277	*Konrad II von Sternburg*
before 24 Jan 1277 – after 27 Apr 1279	*Günther von Schwalenberg* (d. 25 May after 1310) resigned, subsequently Bishop of Paderborn
Mar/Jul 1279 – 6 Dec 1282/Mar 1283	*Bernhard von Wölpe*, resigned
14 May/10 Sep 1283 – 21 Dec 1295	*Erich von Brandenburg*

* 13 Jul 1085 – 1102 *Hartwig*, anti-archbishop

before 5 Feb/12 Jul 1296 – 13 May 1305	*Burchard von Blankenburg*
before 8 Jul 1305/22 Jan 1306 – 9 Nov 1307	*Heinrich II,* Count (Heinrich III) of Anhalt 1266 – 1305
25 Nov 1307/18 Mar 1308 – 20/21 Sep 1325	*Burchard von Schraplau* (d. (murdered) Magdeburg)
before 3 Jan 1326 – 28 Jan 1327	*Heidenreich von Erpiz* (d. Eisenach) attacked while travelling to his confirmation and imprisoned at Brandenfels
Mar 1327 – 30 Apr 1361	*Otto von Hessen* (b. 1301), in rivalry against *Heinrich von Stolberg*
18 Jun/16 Nov 1361 – 17 or 18 Dec 1367	*Dietrich aus Stendal*, previously Bishop of Minden
9 Jun/3 Dec 1368 – 1371	*Albrecht von Sternburg* (d. 14 Jan 1380) previously Bishop of Leitomischl, resigned, translated again to Leitomischl 13 Oct 1371
13 Oct 1371/22 Feb 1372 – May 1381	*Peter Gelyto* (d. Landskron 13 Feb 1387) previously Bishop of Leitomischl, translated to Olmütz
May/10 Aug 1381 – 17 Feb 1382	*Ludwig von Meissen* (b. 25 Feb 1341) previously Archbishop of Mainz
23 Feb – 8 or 9 Nov 1382	*Friedrich von Hoym*, previously Bishop of Merseburg
Nov 1382/29 Jun 1383 – 12 Jun 1403	*Albrecht von Querfurt*
25 Jun/12 Oct 1403 – 23 Mar 1445	*Günther von Schwarzburg* (b. 1382) coadjutor from 27 Mar 1403
19 Apr 1445 – 11 Nov 1464	*Friedrich von Beichlingen*
20 May 1465 – 13 Dec 1475	*Johann von Simmern-Zweibrücken-Veldenz* (b. 1429)
19 Mar 1479 – 3 Aug 1513	*Ernst von Sachsen* (b. 26 Jun 1464)

Mainz

Archbishops (and from 14th century Chancellors and Electors of the Holy Roman Empire)*

AD (?) – 5 Jun 754	*Boniface*
752(?) – 16 Oct 786	*Lul*
4 Mar 787 – 9 Aug 813	*Riculf*
? – 826	*Heistolf*
? – 21 Apr 847	*Otgar*
26 Jun 847 – 4 Feb 856	*Hraban*
12 Mar 856 – 4 Jun 863	*Karl*
30 Nov 863 – 17 Feb 889	*Liutbert*
before 6 Jul 889 – 26 Jun 891	*Sundarold*
891 – 15 May 913	*Hatto I*
913 – 1 Dec 927	*Heriger*
Dec 927 – 31 May 937	*Hildibert*
Jun/9 Jul 937 – 954	*Friedrich*
17/24 Dec 954 – 2 Mar 968	*Wilhelm*
summer/23 Nov 968 – 18 Jan 970	*Hatto II*
8 or 15 Mar 970 – 13 Jan 975	*Ruodbert*
25 Jan/18 Aug 975 – 23 Feb 1011	*Willigis*
1 Apr 1011 – 17 Aug 1021	*Erchenbald*
1 Oct 1021 – 6 Apr 1031	*Aribo* (d. Como)
30 May/29 Jun 1031 – 10 Jun 1051	*Bardo*

*When two dates separated by an oblique stroke are given for the beginning of an episcopate, the first refers to election or nomination and the second to ordination, consecration or investiture

before 31 Jul 1051 – 7 Dec 1059	*Liutpold*
7 Jan 1060 – 16 Feb 1084	*Siegfried I*
Sep or early Oct 1084 – 6 Aug 1088	*Wernher* (or *Wezelin*) *I*
25 Jul 1089 – 2 May 1109	*Ruthard*
1109/15 Aug 1111 – 23 Jun 1137	*Adalbert I*
17/23 Apr/29 May 1138 – 17 Jul 1141	*Adalbert II von Saarbrücken*
before 1 Sep 1141 – 9 Jun 1142	*Markolf*
27 Sep 1142 – Whitsun 1153	*Heinrich I*, deposed
after 14 Jun/before 12 Jul 1153 – 24 Jun 1160	*Arnold*, murdered
19 Jun 1161 – summer 1165	*Konrad I von Wittelsbach* (for 1st time) deposed
19/24 Sep 1165/5 Mar 1167 – 25 Aug 1183	*Christian I*
Nov 1183 – 20 Oct 1200	*Konrad I von Wittelsbach* (for 2nd time), consecrated in Rome 18 Dec 1165
late 1200 – 1208	*Lupold von Scheinfeld*, imperial appointment, banished
late 1200/30 Sep 1201 – 9 Sep 1230	*Siegfried II von Eppenstein*, until 1208 in rivalry with Lupold von Scheinfeld
1230/19 Jan(?) 1231 – 9 Mar 1249	*Siegfried III von Eppenstein*, nephew
after 4 May/before 5 Aug 1249 – Jul 1251	*Christian II von Weissenau* (d. 21 Nov 1251) resigned
c. Jul 1251/24 Mar 1252 – 25 Sep 1259	*Gerhard I*, Count of Daun and Kirberg (d. Erfurt)
late Sep or early Oct 1259/ Oct or Nov 1260 – 2 Apr 1284	*Wernher II von Eppenstein* (d. Aschaffenburg)
15 May 1286 – 17/18 Mar 1288	*Heinrich II von Isny*, Bishop of Basel; in disputed election against *Peter Reich von Reichenstein* and

	Gerhard von Eppenstein (see below)
after 18 Mar 1288/ before 30 Mar 1289 – 25 Feb 1305	*Gerhard II von Eppenstein*, in rivalry with *Emmerich von Schöneck* until 6 Mar 1289
10 Nov 1306 – 5 Jun 1320	*Peter Aspelt*, Bishop of Basel, in disputed election against *Emmerich von Schöneck* and *Emmerich von Sponheim*
4 Sep 1321/3 Jul 1323 – 9 Sep 1328	*Mathias*, Count of Buchek, in disputed election against *Balduin von Trier*
1 Oct 1328	*Heinrich III von Virneburg* (d. 21 Dec 1353) in rivalry with *Balduin von Trier* until 10 Jan 1337, deposed
7 Apr 1346 – 12 Feb 1371	*Gerlach*, Count of Nassau (b. c. 1322)
28 Apr 1371 – 4 Apr 1373	*Johann I*, Count of Luxemburg-Ligny, previously bishop of Strasbourg
28 Apr 1374 – 1379	*Ludwig von Meissen* (b. 25 Feb 1341; d. 17 Feb 1382) previously Bishop of Halberstadt and then of Bamberg; in disputed election against *Adolf*, Bishop of Speyer, and *Kuno II von Falkenstein*, Archbishop of Trier (d. Wellmich castle 21 May 1388); resigned; translated to Magdeburg May 1381
18 Apr 1379 – 6 Feb 1390	*Adolf I von Nassau* (b. 1353)
27 Feb 1390/10 Apr 1391 – 19 Oct 1396	*Konrad II von Weinsberg*
17 Nov 1396/26 Jan 1397 – 13 Sep 1419	*Johann II*, Count of Nassau (b. 1360) in rivalry with Joffrid von Leiningen (see below) until 6 Nov 1397
17 Nov 1396/16 Jan 1397 – 6 Nov 1397	*Joffrid* (or *Schaffrüde*) *von Leiningen*, exiled
10 Oct/14 Dec 1419 – 10 Jun 1434	*Konrad III, Wild- und Rheingraf zum Stein*
Jul 1434 – 4 May 1459	*Dietrich I*
Jan 1460 – 1461	*Dieter von Isenburg* (for 1st time) (d. 6 May 1482) deposed
21 Aug 1461 – 6 Sep 1475	*Adolf II von Nassau* (b. c. 1422)

5 Apr 1476 – 6 May 1482	*Dieter von Isenburg* (for 2nd time)
12 Jan 1481 – 1 May 1484	*Albert II* (b. 1467)
20 May 1484 – 21 Dec 1504	*Bertold von Henneberg-Römhild* (b. 1442)

Malacca Sultanate

Territory comprised part of present-day Malaya.

Sultans

c. AD 1403	*Parameswara* (from 1414(?): *Megat Iskandar Shah*) founded the Malacca Sultanate after fleeing from Singapore
1424	*Sri Maharaja Muhammad* (or *Ahmad*?) *Shah*, son
1444	*Sri Parameswara Deva Shah*, son, murdered
c. 1446	*Muzaffar Shah*, brother, took title of sultan 1456(?
c. 1456	*Mansur Shah*, son
1477	*Alaedin Riayat Shah*, son
1488 – 1511	*Mahmud*, son; ruled in Malacca, Johore, Riau and Kampar
1511	Conquest by Alfonso d'Albuquerque, viceroy of th Portuguese Indies

Mali

At its greatest extent, territory comprised part of present-day Mali, eastern Mauritania and Upper Volta, with capitals at Jeriba, Narena and Nyini (all in present-day southern Mali).

Mansa (Kings)

Keyta Dynasty

AD 1200	*Nare fa Maghan*
1218 – 1228	*Dangaran Tuma*, son
1230	*Sun (Mari) Dyata I*, brother
1255	*Wali* (or *Ule*), son
1270	*Wati*, brother
1274	*Khalifa*, brother
1275	*Abu Bakr I*, nephew
1285	*Sabakura* (or *Sakura*), usurper, freed slave of the royal family, killed
1300	*Gaw*, uncle of Abu Bakr I
1305	*Muhammad*, son
1310	*Abu Bakr II*, descended from a daughter of Nare fa Maghan
1312	*Musa I*, son
1337	*Maghan I*, son
1341	*Sulaiman*, uncle
1360	*Qasa*, son, assassinated
1360	*Mari Dyata II*, son of Maghan I
1374	*Musa II*, son
1387	*Maghan II*, brother
1388	*Sandigi*, official of the court, assassinated
1390 – (?)	*Maghan III Mahmud*, descended from Wali, pretender
c. 1390	Conquest by Songhay, dynasty continued to rule a small area of present-day Mali until the 16th century

Malwa Sultanate (Malava)

Territory comprised part of present-day central India, with the capital established at Mandu.

Sultans

Line of Ghuris

AD 1401/2	*Dilavar Khan (Husain Ghuri)*, initially as governor for the Delhi sultan
1405/6 – 5 Jul 1435	*Alp Khan (Hushang ibn Dilavar)*, son
Jul 1435	*Muhammad I (Ghazni Khan)*, son, poisoned
1436	*Mas'ud Khan*

Line of Khaljis

Jul/Aug 1436	*Mahmud (Shah) I (Khalji)*, the Great (d. Mandu 1 Jun 1469)
3 Jun 1469	*Ghiyath Shah (ibn Mahmud)*, son (d. 28 Feb 1501)
22 Oct 1500	*Nasir al-Din (Shah ibn Ghiyath)*, son (d. 1511)
2 May 1511 – 1531	*Mahmud (Shah) II (ibn Nasir)*, son, killed by Gujarat sultan Bahadur*
1531	Conquest by the Bahadur
1536/7 – 1542	*Qadir Shah* (or *Mallu Khan*), formerly governor of Sarangpur in the service of the Gujarat sultan Mahmud II, deposed by the Afghan chief Sher Shah
1542	Sher Shah invaded Malwa
1542	*Shujat Khan*, governor, installed by Sher Shah (d. 1555)
1555 – 1561	*Baz Bahadur (ibn Shujat)*, son, governor
1601	Conquest by Mughal emperor Akbar I

*1511/12 – 1515/16 *Muhammad II (, Sahib Khan)*, brother of Mahmud II, in rebellion

Mamluks

Territory comprised part of present-day north-eastern Libya, Egypt, western Saudi Arabia, Israel, Lebanon and western Syria, with the capital established at Cairo.

Sultans (with 'Abbasids as Figurehead Caliphs)

Bahri Line

AD 1250/1	*Shajar (al-Durr)*, slave of the Ayyubid sultan al-Salih Ayyub (d. 15 Apr 1257)
31 Jul 1250	*(al-Mu'izz 'Izz al-Din) Aibeg*, husband (d. 12 Apr 1257) named sultan two months after the death of the Ayyubid sultan Turan-Shah IV
Apr 1257	*(al-Mansur Nur al-Din) 'Ali*, son, deposed
12 Nov 1259 – 23 Oct 1260	*(al-Muzaffar Saif al-Din) Qutuz* (d. 23 Oct 1260)
24 Oct 1260 – 2 Jul 1277	*(al-Zahir Rukn al-Din) Baibars I (al-Bunduqdari)* (b. Kipchak 1223/4) conquered the principality of Antioch 1268
Jul 1277	*(al-Sa'id Nasir al-Din) Baraka Khan* (or *(al-Sa'id Nasir al-Din) Berke Khan*), son (d. 18 Mar 1280) deposed
Aug 1279	*(al-'Adil Badr al-Din) Salamish*, brother (b. 1273) deposed; *Qalawun* (see below) ruled as atabeg and regent
Nov 1279	*(al-Mansur Saif al-Din) Qalawun (, Abu'l-Ma'ali al-Alfi)*, brother-in-law
10 Nov 1290	*(al-Ashraf Salah al-Din) Khalil*, son; conquered Acre 19 May 1291
12 Dec 1293	*(al-Nasir Nasir al-Din) Muhammad (ibn Qalawun)*, brother (for 1st time) (b. 1284?)
Dec 1294	*(al-'Adil Zain al-Din) Kitbugha*
7 Dec 1296	*(al-Mansur Husam al-Din) Lajin (al-Mansuri)*
16 Jan 1299	*Muhammad* (for 2nd time)
5 Apr 1309 – 17 Feb 1310	*(al-Muzaffar Rukn al-Din) Baibars II (al-Jashankir)* (d. 16 Apr 1310) abdicated
5 Mar 1310	*Muhammad* (for 3rd time)
6 Jun 1341	*(al-Mansur Saif al-Din) Abu Bakr (ibn al-Nasir)*, son
1341	*(al-Ashraf 'Ala' al-Din) Kujuk (ibn al-Nasir)*, brother
1342	*(al-Nasir Shihab al-Din) Ahmad (ibn al-Nasir)*,

	brother
1342/3	*(al-Salih 'Imad al-Din) Isma'il (ibn al-Nasir)*, brother
1345/6	*(al-Kamil Saif al-Din) Sha'ban I (ibn al-Nasir)*, brother
1346/7	*(al-Muzaffar Saif al-Din) Hajji I (ibn al-Nasir)*, brother
Dec 1347	*(al-Nasir Nasir al-Din) al-Hasan (ibn al-Nasir)*, brother (for 1st time)
1351	*(al-Salih Salah al-Din) Salih (ibn al-Nasir)*, brother (b. 1337/8)
1354	*al-Hasan* (for 2nd time)
1361	*(al-Mansur Salah al-Din) Muhammad II*, nephew
1362/3	*(al-Ashraf Nasir al-Din) Sha'ban II*, cousin
1376/7	*(al-Mansur 'Ala' al-Din) 'Ali*, son (b. 1370?)
1381/2	*(al-Salih Salah al-Din) Hajji II*, brother (for 1st time) (b. 1375/6; d. in prison 1411/12) also ruled as Burji Mamluk 1 Jun 1389 – Feb 1390
26 Nov 1382	*(al-Zahir Saif al-Din) Barquq (ibn Anas al-'Uthman al-Yalbughawi)* (b. 1336(?); d. 20 Jun 1399) also ruled as Burji Mamluk 1382/3 – 1 Jun 1389
1 Jun 1389 – 1 Feb 1390	*Hajji II*, with the title al-Malik al-Muzaffar (for 2nd time) deposed

Burji Line (no hereditary succession)

1382/3	*(al-Zahir Saif al-Din) Barquq (ibn Anas al-'Uthman al-Yalbughawi)* (for 1st time) (see Bahri Line)
1 Jun 1389	*(al-Salih Salah al-Din) Hajji II* (see Bahri Line) reinstated
Feb 1390	*Barquq* (for 2nd time)
20 Jun 1399	*(al-Nasir Nasir al-Din) Faraj (ibn Barquq)*, son (for 1st time) assassinated at Damascus
20 Sep 1405	*(al-Mansur 'Izz al-Din) 'Abd al-'Aziz (ibn Barquq)* (d. 20 Sep 1406)
20 Nov 1405	*Faraj* (for 2nd time)
28 May 1412	*(al-'Adil Abu'l-Fadl 'Abbas* (or *Ya'qub*) *) al-Musta'in (ibn al-Mutawakkil)*, son (d. 1429/30) 'Abbasid caliph proclaimed sultan
6 Nov 1412	*al-Mu'aiyad (Saif al-Din) Shaikh (al-Mahmudi)*
13 Jan 1421	*al-Muzaffar Ahmad*, son
29 Aug 1421	*(al-Zahir Saif al-Din) Tatar*
30 Nov 1421	*(al-Salih Nasir al-Din) Muhammad (ibn Tatar)*
1 Apr 1422	*(al-Ashraf Saif al-Din) Barsbai*

Mar 1438	*(al-'Aziz Jamal al-Din) Yusuf (ibn Barsbai)*, for 94 days
7 Jun 1438	*(al-Zahir Saif al-Din) Jaqmaq*
13 Feb 1453	*(al-Mansur Fakhr al-Din) 'Uthman (ibn Jaqmaq)*
19 Mar 1453	*(al-Ashraf Saif al-Din) Inal al-'Ala'i (al-Zahir al-Ajrud)*
26 Feb 1461	*(al-Mu'ayyad Shihab al-Din) Ahmad (ibn Inal)*, for four months
28 Jun 1461	*(al-Zahir Saif al-Din) Khushqadam*
9 Oct 1467	*(al-Zahir Saif al-Din) Bilbai*
3 Dec 1467	*(al-Zahir) Timurbugha*
31 Jan 1468 – 7 Aug 1496	*(al-Ashraf Saif al-Din) Qa'it Bai* (d. 9 Aug 1496)
Aug/Sep 1496	*(al-Nasir) Muhammad (ibn Qa'it Bai)*
2 Nov 1498	*(al-Zahir) Qansuh*, escaped 24 Jun 1500
28 Jun 1500	*(al-Ashraf) Janbalat*, assassinated
Dec 1500/Jan 1501	*(al-'Adil Saif al-Din) Tuman Bai*
Apr 1501	*(al-Ashraf) Qansuh al-Ghawri*
1516/17	*al-Ashraf Tuman Bai*, executed
1517	Conquest by Ottoman sultan Selim I

Man, Isle of

The list of British kings, the earlier of whom are thought to have ruled in Galloway, is derived from a genealogy. It is not certain, therefore, that every member of the dynasty reigned, nor that there were not other kings whose names have not been recorded, because they did not belong to the direct line. The Norse rulers held the Hebrides (Sudreys) as well as Man, but these never passed to England.

British Kings

c. AD 400	***Anthun*** (or ***Annun***)
?	***Eidniuet*** (or ***Ednyfed***), son
?	***Tutagual*** (or ***Tudwal***), son
?	***Dinacat*** (or ***Dingad***), son
?	***Senill*** (or ***Senyllt***), son
?	***Neithon***, son
?	***Run*** (or ***Rhun***), son

?	*Tutagual* (or *Tudwal*) *II*, son
?	*Anthec* (or *Anllech*), son
?	*Cynfyn*, son
?–682	*Mermin* (or *Merfyn Mawr*), son
7th century	Galloway conquered by the Angles
?	*Anaraut* (or *Anarawd Gwalchcrwn* or *Gallcrwn*), so
?	*Tutagual* (or *Tudwal*) *III*, son, ancestor, through hi daughter, of Rhodri Mawr, King of Gwynedd
?	*Iudgual* (or *Idwal*), son
9th century	Man taken by the Norsemen

Norse Rulers (from 1079 Kings)

mid 9th century(?)	*Ketil Flatnef*, status uncertain
c. 870	*Tryggvi*, earl under King Harald Fairhair of Norwa
?	*Asbjörn Skerjablesi*, earl
c. 913	*Ragnall*
921–940	*Mac Ragnall*, son(?), vassal of Olaf Guthfrithson King of Dublin and of York
?	—— *Mac Harold*
977	*Godred*, son of Harold, brother(?), under Norwegia suzerainty from 985(?)
989	*Sigurd, Earl of Orkney*(?)*
1014	*Thorfinn, Earl of Orkney*, son(?)*
c. 1060	*Godred(?) Mac Ragnall*, tributary to the Kingdom o Dublin
?	*Godred*, son of Sytric, of the royal house of Dublin(?
1070	*Fingal*, son, expelled(?)
1079	*Godred I Crovan*, grandson of Godred (son o Harold)(?) (d. 1095) also King of Dublin(?)
1095 (1089?)	*Lagman*, son (d. Jerusalem 1096/7)
1096	*Olaf*, brother (for 1st time)
1096	*Donald*, son of Teige, regent, seized throne
1098	*Magnus*, King (Magnus III) of Norway (b. 1073; d Ulster 24 Aug 1103)
1099 or 1102	*Sigurd*, son
1103	*Olaf I* (for 2nd time)
1153	*Godred II*, son (for 1st time) (d. 10 Nov 1187)
1158	*Somerled*, Lord of Argyll, brother-in-law, usurper
1164	*Reginald*, illegitimate son of Olaf I, usurper, for fou days

*Possibly in the Sudreys only, Man being subject to Dublin

1164	*Godred II* (for 2nd time)
1187	*Reginald I*, illegitimate son (for 1st time) (d. Feb 1229)
1226	*Olaf II*, son of Godred II (for 1st time) (d. 21 May 1237)
1228	*Reginald I* (for 2nd time)
1228 – 21 May 1237	*Olaf II* (for 2nd time)
1230	*Godred Don*, son of Reginald I, co-ruler for a short time (d. 1230)
21 May 1237 – Oct/ Nov 1248	*Harold I*, son of Olaf II (b. 1222/3)
6 – 30 May 1249	*Reginald II*, brother
1249 – 1250	*Harold II*, son of Godred II, usurper, deprived
1250 – 1252	Interregnum
1252 – 24 Nov 1265	*Magnus*, son of Olaf II; became vassal of Alexander III, King of Scots, c. 1264

Scottish Rulers

2 Jul 1266	Sudreys and Man ceded to Scotland by King Magnus VI of Norway
2 Jul 1266	*Alexander III*, King of Scots (b. 4 Sep 1241) ruling through lieutenants
19 Mar 1286 – 1289/90	*Margaret*, Queen of Scots, granddaughter (b. before 9 Apr 1283)

English Grantees

late 1289 or early 1290	Man annexed by King Edward I of England
1290	*Richard de Burgh, Earl of Ulster* (b. c. 1259; d. Jun 1326)
4 Jun 1290	*Walter de Huntrecombe*, custodian
1293 – 10 Jul 1296	*John Balliol*, King of Scots (b. c. 1250; d. Apr 1313) under English suzerainty, deposed
(?) – 3 Mar 1311(?)	*Anthony Bek*, Bishop of Durham (d. Eltham 3 Mar 1311)
[illegible] May – (?) 1310	*Henry de Beaumont* (for 1st time)
1310	*Gilbert Makaskyl* (for 1st time) and *Robert de Leiburn*, custodians
1311	*Piers Gaveston, Earl of Cornwall* (d. Warwick 19 Jun 1312)
1312	*Henry de Beaumont* (for 2nd time)
1312	*Gilbert Makaskyl* (for 2nd time) custodian

Scottish Grantee

Dec 1313 – ? *	*Thomas Randolph, 1st Earl of Moray* (b. before 1280(?); d. 20 Jul 1332)
c. 1332(?)	Scottish claim abandoned

Lords of Man

8 Jun/9 Aug 1333	*William de Montague* (from 1337: *1st Earl of Salisbury*) (b. Feb 1302; d. 30 Jan 1344)
30 Jan 1344	*William de Montague, 2nd Earl of Salisbury* (b. 19 Jun 1328; d. 3 Jun 1397)
1393 – 30 Jul 1399	*William le Scrope* (from 1397: *1st Earl of Wiltshire*) (b. c. 1350; d. 30 Jul 1399)
19 Oct 1399	*Henry de Percy, 1st Earl of Northumberland* (b. 10 Nov 1341; d. 19 Feb 1408)
4 Oct 1405	*Sir John Stanley I* (b. 1350(?); d. 1414)
1414	*Sir John Stanley II* (d. 1437)
1437	*Thomas Stanley, Lord Stanley* (b. 1406; d. 20 Feb 1459)
1459 – 29 Jul 1504	*Thomas Stanley* (from 1485; *1st Earl of Derby*) (b. c. 1435; d. 29 Jul 1504)

The Lordship continued to be held, with occasional gaps, by the Earls of Derby until 1736, when it passed to the Dukes of Atholl. On 21 Jun 1765 it was resumed by the crown.

Mantua

Seigneurs

House of Bonacolsi	
AD 1276	*Pinamonte*, son of Martino Bonacolsi; abdicated
29 Sep 1291	*Bardellone*, son; abdicated
2 Jul 1299	*Guido*, known as *Botesella*, nephew
18 Nov 1309	*Rinaldo*, known as *Passerino*, brother; imperial vicar of Mantua 1311; deposed

*The island changed hands several times during the wars between England and Scotland

Captains General

House of Gonzaga	
16 Aug 1328 – 18 Jan 1360	*Luigi Gonzaga* (b. 1267)
1360 – 22 Sep 1369	*Guido*, son (b. 1291)
1369 – 4 Oct 1382	*Ludovico II*, son (b. 1334)
1382 – 8 Mar 1407	*Francesco I*, son (b. 1363)

Margraves

1407 – 25 Sep 1444	*Gianfrancesco*, son (b. 1395) Captain general 1407, Margrave 1433
1444 – 12 Jun 1478	*Ludovico III*, son (b. 5 Jun 1414)
1478 – 14 Jul 1484	*Federico*, son (b. 25 Jun 1441)
1484 – 29 Mar 1519	*Francesco II*, son (b. 10 Aug 1466)

Marinids (Banu Marin)

Territory comprised part of present-day Morocco and western Algeria, with the capital established at Fez.

Sultans

AD 1195/6	*Abu Muhammad 'Abd al-Haqq I (ibn Abi Khalid Hahyu'l-Marini)*
28 Sep 1217	*Abu Sa'id 'Uthman (ibn 'Abd al-Haqq)*, son
Jul 1240	*Abu Marraf Muhammad I (ibn 'Abd al-Haqq)*, brother
Nov 1244	*Abu Yahya Abu Bakr (ibn 'Abd al-Haqq)*, brother
1258 – 28 Mar 1286	*Abu Yusuf Ya'qub (ibn 'Abd al-Haqq)*, brother
Mar/Apr 1286	*Abu Ya'qub Yusuf (ibn Ya'qub, al-Nasir)*, son
13 May 1307	*Abu Thabit 'Amir (ibn Abi-'Amir)*, grandson
28 Jul 1308	*Abu'l-Rabi' Sulaiman (ibn Abi-'Amir)*, brother
28 Nov 1310	*Abu Sa'id 'Uthman (ibn Ya'qub)*, great-uncle
30 Aug 1331	*Abu'l-Hasan 'Ali (ibn 'Uthman)*, son (b. c. 1297; d. 24 May 1351) domination over Abd al-Wadids May/Jun 1336 – 1348

28 Jun 1348	*Abu 'Inan (Faris al-Mutawakkil ibn 'Ali)*, son, initially in rebellion
27 Nov 1358	*Abu Zayyan Muhammad II (ibn Faris ibn Abi 'Inan)*, son, proclaimed, deposed and murdered
28 Nov 1358	*Abu Yahya Abu Bakr (al-Sa'id ibn Abi 'Inan)*, brother (b. 1353(?); d. 1363(?))
Jul/Aug 1359 – 23 Sep 1361	*Abu Salim (Ibrahim ibn 'Ali)*, uncle (b. 1333/4)
30 Sep 1361	*Abu 'Umar Tashfin (ibn 'Ali)*, brother, deposed
Oct/Nov 1361	*'Abd al-Halim (ibn Abi 'Ali-'Umar)*, cousin, ruled at Sijilmassa (now Tafilalt) only after Dec 1361/Jan 1362
20 Dec 1361	*Abu Zayyan Muhammad III (al-Mutawakkil ibn Abi 'Abd al-Rahman)*, nephew of Abu 'Umar Tashfin (b. 1348/9)
30 Aug 1366	*Abu'l-Faris 'Abd al-'Aziz I (al-Mustansir ibn 'Ali)*, uncle (b. 1349/50)
21 Oct 1372	*Abu Zayyan Muhammad IV (al-Sa'id ibn 'Abd al-'Aziz)*, son (b. 1367/8) deposed
17 Jun 1374	*Abu'l-Abbas Ahmad (al-Muntasir ibn Ibrahim)*, son of Abu Salim (for 1st time) (b. 1356)
Jun/Jul 1374	*'Abd al-Rahman (ibn Abi Ifallusin)*, nephew of 'Abd al-Halim, ruled concurrently with *Abu'l-'Abbas Ahmad* (for 2nd time) until Sep/Oct 1382 and then solely
13 May 1384	*Abu Faris Musa (ibn Abi 'Inan)*, cousin of Abu Zayyan Muhammad IV (b. 1356)
28 Sep 1386	*Abu Zayyan Muhammad V (al-Muntasir ibn Ahmad)*, nephew, son of Abu'l-'Abbas Ahmad, for 45 days
9 Nov 1386	*Abu Zayyan Muhammad VI (al-Wathiq ibn Abi'l Fadl)*, grandson of Abu'l-Hasan 'Ali (b. 1359/60)
19 Sep 1387 – 12 Nov 1393	*Abu'l-'Abbas Ahmad* (for 3rd time)
14 Nov 1393/Jan 1394	*Abu Faris ('Abd al-'Aziz ibn Ahmad)*, son (b. 1375/6)
11 Nov 1396	*Abu Amir 'Abdallah (ibn Ahmad)*, brother (b. 1378/9)
19 Mar 1398	*Abu Sa'id 'Uthman III (ibn Ahmad)*, brother (b. 1382/3)
1420/1 – 1427/8	Interregnum of *(Abu Malik) 'Abd al-Wahid (ibn Musa)*, 'Abd al-Wadid sultan Nov/Dec 1412 – 1423/4 and 1427/8 – 26 Jul 1430
1427/8	*Abu Muhammad 'Abd al-Haqq II (ibn Abi Sa'id*

	'Uthman), son of Abu Sa'id 'Uthman III
Apr/May 1465 – 1470/1	Interregnum of the Imam *Abu 'Abdallah Muhammad (ibn 'Ali ibn 'Imran al-Juti)*
1470/1	Succeeded by the Wattasids

Marwanids

Territory comprised part of present-day northern Iraq, with the capital at Amid (now Diyarbakır).

Amirs

AD (?)	*Badh*
990/1	*Abu 'Ali (al-Hasan ibn Marwan)*, son of Marwan
996/7	*(Mumahhid al-Daula) Abu'l-Mansur (Sa'id ibn Marwan)*, brother
1010/11	*Abu Shuja' (Parwiz ibn Muhammad)*
1010/11 – 16 Nov 1061	*(Nasr al-Daula) Abu Nasr (Ahmad ibn Marwan)*, brother of Sa'id (b. 986/7)
Nov/Dec 1061	*(Niẓam al-Din Abu'l-Qasim) Nasr (ibn Ahmad)*, son, ruled at Mayyafariqin until 1063 and thereafter at Mayyafariqin and Amid
1061/2	*Sa'id*, brother, ruled at Amid until 1063
1079/80 – 1085/6	*(Abu'l-Muzaffar) Mansur*, son of Nasr
1085/6	Seljuq conquest

Massina

Territory comprised part of present-day southern Mali, with the capital at Kébey.

Ardos or Fõdokos (Kings)

AD 1400	*Maghan*
1404	*Birahim I*, son
1424	*Ali I*, brother
1433	*Kanta*, nephew
1466	*Ali II*, brother
1480	*Nguia*, nephew, conquered by Songhay
1510	*Saouadi*, nephew
1539	*Ilo*, son
1540	*Amadi Siré*, son of Nguia
1543	*Hamadi I*, *Foulani*, brother of Ilo
1544	*Boubou I*, nephew
1551	*Ibrahim*, cousin
1559	*Boubou II*, brother
1583	*Hamadi II*, son of Boubou I
1603	*Boubou III*, *Nyamé*, son
1613	*Birahim II*, brother
1625	*Silamaran*, brother
1627	*Hamadi III*, nephew
1663	*Hamadi IV*, cousin
1663	*Ali III*, brother
1673	*Gallo*, brother
1675	*Gourori I*, son
1696	*Guéladjo*, brother
1706	*Guidado*, nephew
1761	*Hamadi V*, son
1780	*Ia*, cousin
1801 – 1810	*Gourori II*, son

Amirs

1810	*Bokr Amma Sala Dja*
1843	*Ahmadou Bari*, *Sissé*, son of Cheikou Amdou
1844	*Abdoullahi Bari*, *Sissé*, brother
1852	*Abdoullahi Bari*, *Sissé*, nephew, conquered by 'Umar

	al-Hajj of the Tukulor Empire
1862	*Abdoullahi Dja*, son of Bokar Amma Sala Dja
1863	*Sidi El Bekkay*, the Young, died at Tenenkou
1864	*Abbidine El Bekkay*, for eight months
1864	*Badi Tali*
1871	*Badi Sidi*
1872	*Ahmadou*, son of Ba Lobbo
1873	*Abbidine*, of the family of the Bekkays
1874 – 1885	*Amma Sala Dja, Sissé*, nephew of Bokar Amma Sala Dja
1885	Conquest by Tidjani, Massina evacuated
1895	*Abdoullahi*, son of Amma Sala Dja, re-established by the French
1899	Agreement between British and French recognized Mali area as being in the French sphere of influence
24 Nov 1958	Mali became autonomous member of French Community

Mauritania

Territory now in Morocco and north-western Algeria.

Kings

111 – 80 BC	*Bocchus I*, father-in-law of King Jugurtha of Numidia; signed a treaty of friendship with Rome c. 105
(?)	Unknown king
c. 50 – 31	*Bocchus II*
(?)	Unknown king
25	*Juba II*, son of King Juba I of Numidia; installed by the Roman emperor Augustus; ruled with his wife, *Cleopatra Selene*, daughter of the Roman triumvir Mark Antony and Queen Cleopatra VII of Egypt
AD 23 – 40	*Ptolemy*, son, murdered
40	Annexed by Rome and formed into the provinces of Mauritania Caesariensis and Mauritania Tingitana

Mazyadids (Banu Mazyad)

Territory comprised part of present-day central Iraq, with the capital at Hilla.

Amirs

c. AD 961	*(Sana' al-Daula Abu'l-Hasan) 'Ali I (ibn Mazyad)*, son of Mazyad
1017/18	*(Nur al-Daula Abu'l-A'azz) Dubais I*, son
1081/2	*(Baha' al-Daula Abu-Kamil) Mansur*, son
1086/7	*(Saif al-Daula) Sadaqa I (Abu'l-Hasan)*, son
1107/8 – 25 Sep 1135	*(Nur al-Daula) Dubais II (Abu'l-A'azz)*, son, murdered
Sep/Oct 1135	*(Saif al-Daula) Sadaqa II*, son
1137/8	*Muhammad*, brother
1145/6 – 1150/1	*'Ali II*, brother
1150/1	Conquest by Seljuq troops

Media

Territory comprised part of present-day north-western Iran, with the capital at Ecbatana (present-day Hamadan).

Kings

c. 708 BC	*Deioces* (or *Dayoukku*)
c. 655	*Phraortes* (or *Fravartish*), son
c. 630(?)	*Cyaxares* (or *Huvakshatara*), unified the Median tribes; with the Babylonian king Nabu-apul-usur, destroyed Nineveh 612 and conquered Assyria 609
584(?) – 550	*Astyages* (or *Ishtuvegu*), son, defeated by the Persian king Cyrus II
550	Persian conquest

Meissen (Misnia)

Separated from the territories of the East Mark on the death of Gero, Margrave of the North Mark (Brandenburg) in 965.

Margraves

AD 980	*Rikdag*
985 – 30 Apr 1002	*Ekkehard I*, Margrave of Merseburg (d. (assassinated) Pöhlde) appointed Margrave of Meissen by the Holy Roman Empress Theophano
1002	*Gunzelin*, brother; abdicated
1010	*Hermann I*, nephew
1032 – 24 Jan 1046	*Ekkehard II*, brother
1046	*Wilhelm*, son of Wilhelm III of Weimar
1062	*Otto I*, brother, Count of Orlamünde
1067 – 11 Jan 1068	*Ekbert I*, Count of Brunswick
1068 – 1086	*Ekbert II*, son (d. (assassinated) 1090) deposed and condemned after an unsuccessful attempt to gain the German throne
1086 – 1089	Margravate held by the Holy Roman Emperor Heinrich IV
1089	*Heinrich I von Ellenburg*, Count of Wettin, appointed by Holy Roman Emperor Heinrich IV
1103	*Heinrich II*, son (b. 1103)
1123 – 22 May 1124	*Wiprecht von Groitzsch*, son-in-law of Otto I, Margrave of Lusatia 1117
1124	*Hermann II*, son of Hermann I of Winzenburg (d. (assassinated) 29/30 Jan 1152) deposed by King Lothar II of Germany, on a charge of high treason
1130	*Konrad*, the Great, Count of Wettin (b. 1098; d. 5 Feb 1157) abdicated
1156 – 18 Feb 1190	*Otto II*, the Rich, son (b. 1125)
1190 – 24 Jun 1195	*Albrecht I*, the Proud, son (b. 1158)
24 Jun 1195 – 1197	Margravate held by the Holy Roman Emperor Heinrich VI
1197 – 17 Feb 1221	*Dietrich*, the Oppressed, brother of Albrecht I (b. 1162) seized the margravate on the death of Heinrich VI
1221 – c. 8 Feb 1288	*Heinrich III*, the Illustrious, son (b. 1215/16) Landgrave of Thuringia 1249 – 1265
1288 – 16 Aug 1291	*Friedrich Tuta*, grandson (b. 1269)

1291	*Diezmann*, cousin (b. 1260; d. (assassinated) 10 Dec 1307) and his brother, *Friedrich I*, the Dauntless (b. 1257; d. 16 Nov 1323) formally invested as Margrave of Meissen and Landgrave of Thuringia by King Heinrich VII of Germany, 1310
1324 – 18 Nov 1349	*Friedrich II*, the Grave, son (b. 1310) Landgrave of Thuringia
1349	*Friedrich III*, the Stern, son (b. 14 Oct 1332; d. 25 May 1381) ruled Meissen and Thuringia with his brothers *Balthasar* (b. 21 Dec 1336; d. 18 May 1406) and *Wilhelm I* (b. 19 Dec 1343; d. 10 Feb 1407)
1382	By the agreement of Chemnitz, following the death of Friedrich III, the surviving brothers divided the Wettin domains: Balthasar took Thuringia and Wilhelm I became sole ruler of Meissen
1382 – 10 Feb 1407	*Wilhelm I* (see above)
1407 – 4 Jan 1428	*Friedrich IV*, the Warlike, nephew (b. 11 Apr 1370) Duke (Friedrich I) of Saxony 6 Jan 1423
4 Jan 1428	Incorporated into the Duchy of Saxony

Milan

Seigneurs

Visconti

AD 1295	*Matteo I* the Great, grandnephew of Archbishop Ottone Visconti of Milan (b. Invorio 1250; d. Milan 24 Jun 1322) captain of the people 1287, imperial vicar 1294, seigneur 1295; exiled from Milan 1302 – 1310 during the return to power of the Della Torre; renounced the title of imperial vicar 1317; abdicated
May 1322 – 6 Aug 1328	*Galeazzo I*, son (b. 21 Jan 1277)
1328 – 16 Aug 1339	*Azzo*, son (b. 7 Dec 1302)
1339	*Luchino*, uncle (b. 1287; d. (assassinated) 24 Jan 1349); with his brother, *Giovanni* (b. 1290; d. 5 Oct 1354) Archbishop of Milan 1342, ruled alone as seigneur of Milan after 1349
1354	*Matteo II*, nephew (d. 29 Sep 1355)
1355 – 1385	*Bernabò*, brother (b. 1319; d. (in prison) 19 Dec 1385)

	ruled the eastern portion of the Visconti domains; deposed by Gian Galeazzo shortly before his death
1355 – 4 Aug 1378	*Galeazzo II*, brother (b. c. 1320; d. 4 Aug 1378) ruled the western portion of the Visconti domains, with capital at Pavia

Dukes

1378	*Gian Galeazzo*, son (b. Milan 1351; d. Melegnano, 3 Sep 1402) ruled the western portion of the Visconti domains until 1385 when he deposed Bernabò and reunited the seigneury; created Duke of Milan 1395 and Count of Pavia 1396; overlord of Pisa and Siena 1399, of Perugia 1400; annexed Bologna 1402
1402 – 16 May 1412	*Giovanni Maria*, son (b. 1389) assassinated
1412 – 13 Aug 1447	*Filippo Maria*, brother (b. 23 Sep 1392)
	Succession disputed between Francesco Sforza and Alfonso V of Aragon

Sforza

26 Feb 1450 – 8 Mar 1466	*Francesco Sforza*, son-in-law (b. San Miniato, 23 Jul 1401; d. Milan)
1466 – 26 Dec 1476	*Galeazzo Maria*, son (b. 24 Jan 1444) assassinated
1476 – 22 Oct 1494	*Gian Galeazzo II Maria*, son (b. 10 Jun 1469) exercised no real power Regents: 1476 – 1480: *Bona*, of Savoy, mother (d. 1485) deposed by Ludovico il Moro and exiled 1480 – 22 Oct 1494: *Ludovico il Moro*, brother-in-law (b. Vigevano, Pavia, 27 Jul 1452; d. (in prison) Loches (now in Indre-et-Loire department, France) 27 May 1508) Duke of Milan 1494

Mirdasids

Territory comprised part of present-day northern Syria, with the capital at Aleppo.

Amirs

AD 1024/5 – May/Jun 1029	*(Asad al-Daula Abu 'Ali) Salih ibn Mirdas (al-Kilabi)*
1029/30 Jun/Jul 1038	*(Shibl al-Daula Abu Kamil) Nasr I ibn Salih*, son
Jun/Jul 1038	Aleppo seized by the Fatimid general Anushtigin
1038	Thimal ibn Salih (see below) recaptured Aleppo for a short time
Nov/Dec 1041	*(Mu'izz al-Daula Abu 'Ulwan) Thimal ibn Salih*, brother of Nasr I ibn Salih (for 1st time) proclaimed on the death of Anushtigin, recaptured the Citadel Sep/Oct 1042
1057/8 – 1058/9	*(Makin al-Daula Abu 'Ali) al-Hasan (ibn 'Ali ibn Mulham)*, governor after the second Fatimid conquest
1060/1	*(Rashid al-Daula Taj al-Muluk) Mahmud ibn Nasr*, son of Nasr I ibn Salih (for 1st time) (d. Constantinople (now Istanbul) 1072/3)
1061/2	*Thimal ibn Salih (for 2nd time)*
1062/3	*(Abu Duaba) 'Atiyya ibn Salih*, brother
1064/5 – 1072/3	*Mahmud ibn Nasr* (for 2nd time)
1073/4	*(Jalal al-Daula Abu'l-Muzaffar) Nasr II ibn Mahmud*, son, killed
1075/6 – 1079/80	*Abu'l-Fadail Sabiq (ibn Mahmud)*, brother*
1079/80	Town surrendered to the 'Uqailid amir Muslim ibn Quraish

*1075/6 *Waththab*, in rebellion against his brother Sabiq

Mitanni

Territory comprised part of present-day south-eastern Turkey and northern Iraq, with the capital at Wassukkani.

Kings

(?) BC	*Kirta*(?)
before 1550	*Shuttarna I*, son
(?)	*Parattarna*
before 1500	*Parsatatar*(?)
c. 1480	*Saustatar*, son, annexed Assyria
c. 1450	*Artatama*, son
(?)	*Shuttarna II*, son
before 1390	*Artashshumara*, son
(?)	*Tushratta*, brother (d. c. 1360) Wassukkani sacked by the Hittite king Suppiluliumas I, lost Assyria, assassinated
before 1350	*Kurtiwaza*, Hittite vassal
before 1300	*Shattuara*, Hittite vassal
(?)	*Wasashatta*, Hittite vassal, defeated by the Assyrian king Adad-nirari I
c. 1275	Became Assyrian province

Modena, Reggio and Ferrara

Margraves of Este

House of Este

AD (?)	*Alberto Azzo II*, son of Alberto Azzo I (b. c. 996)
1097 – 15 Dec 1128	*Folco*, son
1128 – 25 Dec 1193	*Obizzo I*, son
1193 – 18 Nov 1212	*Azzo VI*, grandson; podesta of Ferrara 1196, siegneur 1208*

*With the death of Azzo VI the House of Este lost most of its power in Ferrara to Salinguerra, head of the Ghibellines

1212 – 10 Oct 1215	*Aldobrandino I*, son
1215 – 16 Feb 1264	*Azzo VII*, brother (b. c. 1205)

Seigneurs of Modena, Reggio, and Ferrara

1264 – 13 Feb 1293	*Obizzo II*, illegitimate grandson (b. 1247) Seigneur of Ferrara 1264, of Modena 1288, of Reggio 1289
1293 – 31 Jan 1308	*Azzo VIII*, son
1308	*Fresco*, illegitimate son
1309 – 26 Jul 1326	*Aldobrandino II*, uncle
1326	*Rinaldo II*, son (d. 31 Dec 1335); with his brother, *Nicolò I* (d. 1 May 1344)
1344 – 20 Mar 1352	*Obizzo III*, brother (b. 14 Jul 1294)
1352 – 3 Nov 1361	*Aldobrandino III*, son (b. 14 Sep 1335)
1361 – 26 Mar 1388	*Nicolò II*, the Lame, brother (b. 17 May 1338)
1388 – 30 Jul 1393	*Alberto V*, brother (b. 27 Feb 1347)
1393 – 26 Dec 1441	*Nicolò III*, son
1441 – 1 Oct 1450	*Leonello*, illegitimate son (b. 21 Sep 1407)

Dukes of Modena, Reggio, and Ferrara

1450 – 20 Aug 1471	*Borso*, brother (b. 24 Aug 1413) created Duke of Modena and Reggio by Holy Roman Emperor Friedrich III 18 May 1452, created Duke of Ferrara by Pope Paul II 15 Apr 1471
1471 – 25 Jan 1505	*Ercole I*, half-brother (b. 26 Oct 1431)

Monaco

Seigneurs

House of Grimaldi
The connection of the Grimaldi family with Monaco, a Genoese possession since the 12th century, began in 1295, when the Guelfs were expelled from Genoa. Rainier I settled in Provence. On 8 Jan 1297 François, nicknamed Malizia, seized the fortress and held it until 1301, when it passed to Nicolas Spinola. Between 1317 and 1327 Gaspar Grimaldi was in power at Genoa and indirectly at Monaco, but then lost Monaco again to the Spinola faction

AD 1341 – Aug 1357	*Charles I*, son of Rainier I, with his distant cousins, *Antoine** and *Gabriel*,* sons of Gaspar; Monaco held by Charles in the name of the Republic of Genoa 12 Sep 1331 – Feb 1335 and thereafter against it
1357	Monaco handed over to Genoa; Rainier II, son of Charles I, for a short time seigneur of Cagnes, Castillon, Menton and Roquebrune (at a later date part of the territory of the state of Monaco)
Jan – Dec 1395	*Jean* and *Louis*, co-seigneurs of Beuil, collateral relatives, held Monaco; captured in attack on Vintimille
Dec 1395	*Pierre* held Monaco, joined 11 May 1397 by *Jean* and *Louis*
1402	Monaco recovered for Genoa by *Jean le Maingre*, called Boucicault, French governor of Genoa
5 Jun 1419	*Ambroise*, *Antoine* and *Jean I*, sons of Rainier II; co-seigneurs
1427 or earlier	*Jean I*, alone; prisoner of the Duke of Milan Dec 1438 – Sep 1440
8 May 1454	*Catalan*, son (b. 1415)
Jul 1457 – Mar 1494	*Claudine*, daughter (d. 1514) Regent: Jul 1457 – 16 Mar 1458: *Pomelline*, grandmother
16 Mar 1458 – Mar 1494	*Lambert*, husband of Claudine, son of Nicolas Grimaldi, seigneur of Antibes, and descendant of Antoine (co-seigneur 1341 – 1357), co-regent from Oct 1347, co-ruler in his own right

*By 1352 Charles and Antoine each held half

Mongol Great Khans (Yüan Dynasty of China)

Territory based on part of present-day Mongolia, Tibet and northern China (from 1368 Mongolia only) and at its greatest extent stretched from eastern Europe to China, with the capital initially at Karakorum and later at Khanbalik (now Peking).

For Chinese names see page 150.

Great Khans

AD 1206	*Chingiz* (or *Ghenghis*) *(Khan)* (b. 1154/6)
Aug/Sep 1227 – 11 Dec 1241	*Ögedei*, son, completed conquest of northern China and Korea, conquered Khwarazm-Shahs 1231
1241	*Töregene Khatun*, widow, regent
1246 – 22 Jul 1249	*Güyük*, son of Ögedei
1249	*Oghul Ghaimish*, widow, regent
1251	*Möngke* (or *Mengü*), cousin of Güyük, moved capital to Khanbalik
4 Jun 1260	*Qubilai*, brother, Sung dynasty of southern China overthrown 1279
1294	*Temür Öljeitü* (or *Uljaitu*), grandson
1307	*Qaishan Gülük*, nephew, overthrew the Seljuqs of Rum 1307/8
1311	*(Ayurparibhadra) Buyantu*, brother
1320	*Suddhipala Gege'en* (or *Gegen*), son
1323	*Yesün Temür*, nephew of Temür
1328	*Arigaba* (or *Asikipa*)
1328	*(Jijaghatu) Toq-Temür*, son of Qaishan
1328/9	*Qushila Qutuqtu*, brother
1332	*Rinchendpal* (or *Irinjipal*), son
1332 – c. 1370	*Toghan Temür*, brother
1368	Power in China seized by the Ming dynasty, Tibet regained independence
c. 1370	*Biliktu*, son (b. 1338?)
1379	*Ussakhal*, brother (b. 1342)
1389	*Engke Sosiktu*, son or nephew
1392	*Elbek*, brother (b. 1361)
1400	*Gun-Temür*, son (b. 1377; d. 1402)
1402	*Ugechi* (for 1st time) usurper

1403	*Uljei-Temür*, brother of Gun-Temür, assassinated
1411 – 1415	*Delbek* (b. 1395) son, according to some authorities
1418	*Ugechi* (for 2nd time) usurper
1422	*Usseku*, son, usurper
c. 1425 – 1438	*Ad(s)ai*, son of Elbek (b. 1389)*
1439	*Taissong*, son (b. 1422)
1452	*Akbarji*, brother
1452	*Ukektu*, son of Taissong (b. 1445?)
1453 – 1454	*Molon*, brother (b. 1436?)
1454 – 1463	Interregnum
1463 – 1467	*Mandaghol*, son of Ad(s)ai
1470 – (?)	*Dayan*, great-grandson of Akbarji (b. 1465; d. 1543(?))
?)	Kingdom divided

Monomotapa (Mwene Mutapa), Empire of

Territory comprised part of present-day Rhodesia.

Monomotapa or Mwene Mutapa (Kings)

. AD 1420	*Nyatsimba Mutota*
. 1450	*Matope Nyanhehwe 'Mutavara' 'NeBedza'*, son
. 1480	*Mavura Maobwe*, son
. 1480	*Mukombero Nyahuma*, brother
. 1490	*Changamire I*, usurper and founder of the Changamire Kingdom
. 1494	*Kakuyo Komunyaka* (or *Chikuyo Chisamarengu*?), son of Mukombero Nyahuma
. 1530	*Neshangwe Munembire*, grandson of Mavura Maobwe
. 1550	*Chivere Nyasoro*, son of Kakuyo Komunyaka
. 1560	*Chisamharu Negomo Mupunzagutu*, son

Some authorities distinguish between *Adai* (c. 1425 – 1433/4) and *Adsai*, unrelated, ominal Khan 1433/4 – 1437(?)

c. 1589	*Gatsi Rusere*, grandson of Neshangwe Munembire
c. 1623	*Nyambo Kapararidze*, son, deposed by the Portuguese
c. 1629 – 1719	Portuguese put their own nominees on the throne
1719	Dynasty extinguished

Montenegro (Zeta)

Territory now in Albania and south-western Yugoslavia.
Earlier rulers of Zeta are listed under Serbia: Dioclea.

Princes

Balšić dynasty	
AD 1360	*Đurađ*, lord of Zeta, became independent c. 1371 after death of Serbian Emperor Stefan Uroš V
Jan 1378	*Balša II*, brother; lord of Valona, Berat and Himara from 1372
15 Sep 1383	*Đurađ Stracimirović*, nephew, 'lord of all Zeta and the coast', with capitals at Scutari and Ulcinj
1403 – 28 Apr 1421	*Balša III*, son
Crnojević dynasty	
1421	*Stefan* (or *Stefanica*)
1465	*Ivan*, son (b. c. 1430?)
1490 – 1496	*Đurađ*, son (d. Anatolia 1503)

Montferrat

Margraves

House of Aleramo	
23 Mar AD 967	*Aleramo*, son of Guglielmo

?	*Oddone I*, son
990	*Guglielmo I*, son
1017 – 20 Nov 1084	*Oddone II*, son
1084	*Guglielmo II*, son
c. 1101	*Ranieri*, son
c. 1136	*Guglielmo III*, son (b. c. 1110)
1191 – 28 Apr 1192	*Corrado*, son (b. c. 1146) chosen King of Jerusalem but assassinated before coronation
1192 – Sep 1207	*Bonifacio I*, brother (b. c. 1150; d. near Mosynopolis) King of Thessalonica Sep 1204
1207 – 17 Sep 1225	*Guglielmo IV*, son (b. c. 1180)
1225	*Bonifacio II*, son (b. c. 1202)
1253/55	*Guglielmo V*, son (b. 1243; d. 1292) abdicated
1290 – 9 Mar 1305	*Giovanni I*, son (b. 1276)

House of Palaeologus

1305 – 21 Apr 1338	*Teodoro I*, grandson of Guglielmo V and son of the Byzantine emperor Andronicus II (b. 1292)
1338 – 20 Mar 1372	*Giovanni II*, son
1372 – 16 Dec 1378	*Secondotto*, son (b. 1361)
1378	*Giovanni III*, brother
1381 – 2 Dec 1418	*Teodoro II*, brother (b. 1364)
1418 – 13 Mar 1445	*Giangiacomo*, son (b. 23 Mar 1395)
1445 – 29 Jan 1464	*Giovanni IV*, son
1464 – 28 Feb 1483	*Guglielmo VI*, brother
1483 – 31 Jan 1494	*Bonifacio III*, brother

Moravia

Princes or Dukes

c. AD 833 – Aug (?) 846	*Mojmír I*, deposed
846	*Rastislav* (or *Rostislav*), nephew, driven out by Svatopluk, condemned by the imperial diet Nov 870 and imprisoned for life
spring (?) 870	*Svatopluk*, nephew
894 – 906	*Mojmír II*, son; Bohemia became independent 894
906	Completion of Hungarian conquest begun c. 896

Morea (Mistra)

Territory in southern Greece, with the capital at Mistra.

Byzantine Despots

AD 1348	*Manuel Cantacuzenus*, son of the Byzantine emperor John VI
1380	*Matthew Cantacuzenus*, brother
1383	*Demetrius Cantacuzenus*, son
1383	*Theodore I Palaeologus*, son of the Byzantine emperor John V, recognized suzerainty of the Ottomans
1407 – 1443	*Theodore II Palaeologus*, son of the Byzantine emperor Manuel II, conquered Achaea 1432
1428 – 1449	*Constantine Palaeologus*, brother, (d. Constantinople 29 May 1453) became Byzantine emperor Constantine XI 1449
1428 – 1460	*Thomas Palaeologus*, brother; ruled with his brother, *Demetrius Palaeologus*, from 1449
1460	Conquered by the Ottomans

Mossi/Dagomba States

DAGOMBA (DAGBON)

Territory comprised part of present-day northern Ghana and southern Upper Volta.

Kings

AD 1416	*Nyagse*
1432	*Zulande*, son
1442	*Beriguwiemda*, son
1454	*Beriguwiemda*
1469	*Zolgo*, nephew
1486	*Zongman*, son
1506	*Nengmitoni*, brother

1514	*Dimani*, brother
1527	*Yanzo*, brother
1543	*Dariziogo*, brother
1554	*Luro*, brother
1570	*Tutugri*, son
1589	*Zagale*, brother
1609	*Zokuli*, brother
1627	*Gungoble*, brother
1648	*Zangina*, nephew
1677	*Andani Sigili*, cousin
1687	*Jimli*, son of Zangina
1700	*Gariba*, brother
1720	*Zibirim Na-Sa*, son of Andani Sigili
1735	*Zibirim*, son of Gariba
1749	*Mahame*, son
1765	*Sumani*, son
1783	*Andani I*, brother of Zibirim
1806	*Zibirim Kulunku*, son
1824	*Yakuba*, brother
1849 – 1876	*Abdulai*, son
1874	British established crown colony of the Gold Coast
1876	*Andani II*, brother
1899 – 16 Jan 1917	*Alasan*, nephew

WAGADUGU (OUAGADOUGOU)

Territory comprised part of present-day Upper Volta, with the capital at Wagadugu.

Mogho Naba (Kings)

c. AD 1233*	*Nédéga*, king of Dagomba
1253	*Riàlé*, son, ruled with *Yennenga*, daughter of Nédéga
1273	*Ouidiraogo*, son
1293	*Zoungourana*, son
1313	*Oubri*, son
1320	*Sorba* or *Narimtoré*
1335	*Nassikiemdé*
1350	*Koundoumié*, grandson of Oubri
1380	*Kouda*

*All dates are tentative

1400	*Dawoéma*
1425	*Zettembousma*
1450	*Niandeffo*
1475	*Nattia*
1500	*Namoéro*
1520	*Kida*
1540	*Kimba*
1560	*Kobra*
1580	*Sana*
1600	*Guiliga*
1620	*Oubia*
1640	*Mottaba*
1660	*Ouarga*
1680	*Zombéré*
1700	*Kom I*
1720	*Sagha I*
1740	*Boulougou*
1760	*Savadoro*
1780	*Karfo*
1800	*Baoro*
1830	*Koutou*
1850	*Sanom*
1890	*Boukari Koutou*
1896 – 1897	*Mazi*
1897	French protectorate established
1897	*Kouka*
1906	*Kom II*
1942	*Sagha II*, son
1957 – 1971	*Kougi Naba*
1960	Upper Volta achieved independence from France and President Yaméogo stripped the mogho naba of much of his power
1971	Line of Mossi sovereigns ended

Musafirids (Sallarids or Kangarids)

Territory comprised part of present-day north-western Iran, with the capital at Ardabil.

Lords of Dailam

before AD 916	*Muhammad (ibn Musafir)*, son of Musafir; lord of Tarom in Dailam
941/2	*al-Marzuban I (ibn Muhammad)*, son, ruled in Azerbaijan and Arran
941/2	*Wahsudan (ibn Muhammad)*, brother, ruled in Tarom
957/8	*Justan I (ibn al-Marzuban)*, nephew, ruled in Azerbaijan
960/1 – 983	*Ibrahim I (ibn al-Marzuban)*, brother, ruled in Azerbaijan
965/6 – 984	*al-Marzuban II (ibn Isma'il ibn Wahsudan)*, cousin, ruled in Tarom
997/8	*Ibrahim II (ibn al-Marzuban)*, son, re-established at Tarom, still alive 1029/30
fl. 1045	*(Abu-Salih) Justan II (ibn Ibrahim)*, son
fl. 1062	*Musafir (ibn Ibrahim)*, brother .
(?)	Dynasty ended by the Rawwadids

Muzaffarids

Territory comprised part of present-day southern Iran, with the capital at Shiraz.

Amirs

Feb/Mar AD 1314 – 25 Aug 1358	*(Mubariz al-Din) Muhammad ibn al-Muzaffar*, son of al-Muzaffar (b. 25 Feb 1301; d. Bam Dec

	1363/Jan 1364) received Yazd from the Il-Kha Nov/Dec 1318 and Kirman Jun/Jul 1340, deposed
Aug/Sep 1358	*Qutb al-Din Shah Mahmud*, son (d. 13 Mar 1375 ruled in Isfahan and Abarqu until 1375
Aug/Sep 1358/6 Jan 1364 – 9 Oct 1384	*(Jalal al-Din) Shah Shuja'*, brother (b. 1332/3 in dispute with his father and brother, ruled i Fars and Kirman and also in Isfahan after 1375
Oct 1384 – 1387	*(Mujahid al-Din) Zain al-'Abidin 'Ali*, son, dethrone by the Timurid khan Temür
1384/5 – 1392/3	*('Imad al-Din) Ahmad*, uncle, ruled in Kirman
1387/8 – 1392/3	*(Nusrat al-Din) Yahya*, nephew, ruled in Yazd
1387/8 – 1392/3	*Mansur*, brother; ruled in Isfahan, Fars and Iraq
1392/3	Timurid conquest

Nabathea

Territory comprised part of present-day southern Israel, north-western Saud Arabia, southern Syria and Jordan, with the capital at Petra.

Kings

fl. 169 BC	*Aretas I*
(?)	*Malichus I*
110 – 100	*Erotimus*
(?)	*Aretas II*
(?)	*Obodas I*, son
(?)	*Rabbel I*
87	*Aretas III Philhellen*, acquired Damascus 85, killed the Seleucid king Antiochus XII 64, recognized by Rome 62
c. 47	*Malichus II*, vassal of the Judaean king Herod the Great and of Rome

fl. 25	*Obodas II*, son, Roman vassal
9 BC	*Aretas IV Philopatris*, brother, with his queens *Chuldu* and *Shaqilath*
AD 40	*Malichus III*, son, with his queen *Shaqilath*
70/71 – 106	*Rabbel II Soter*, son, with his queen *Gamilath*
106	Annexed by the Roman emperor Trajan and formed into the Roman province of Arabia

Naples

Kings

House of Anjou

AD 1282 – 7 Jan 1285	*Charles I*, Count of Anjou and of Provence, son of King Louis VIII of France (b. Mar 1227; d. Foggia) King of Sicily 6 Jan 1266; defeated and killed Manfred, Hohenstaufen King of Sicily, 26 Feb 1266; Prince of Achaea 1267/1278, King of Jerusalem 1277; expelled from Sicily during the Sicilian Vespers Mar 1282, but retained the Neapolitan portion of the kingdom; defeated by Pedro III of Aragon Jun 1284
1285 – 5 May 1309	*Charles II*, the Lame, Prince of Salerno, son (b. c. 1254; d. Naples) at the same time Count of Anjou and of Provence and Prince of Achaea; held prisoner by the Aragonese until 1288 and crowned King of Naples 29 May 1289 after renouncing his claim to Sicily; abdicated in Achaea 16 Sep 1289
1309 – 16 Jan 1343	*Robert*, the Wise, Duke of Calabria, son (b. 1277; d. Naples)
1343	*Jeanne I*, granddaughter (b. 1326; d. (assassinated) Lucania 22 May 1382) Countess of Provence; Princess of Achaea 1374; deposed and imprisoned
1/2 Jun 1381 – 24 Feb 1386	*Charles III*, of Durazzo, nephew by marriage, nephew of King Lajos of Hungary (b. Naples 1345; d. (assassinated) Pest) named heir by Jeanne I 1369; crowned king by Pope Urban VI 2 Jun 1381; took Naples and expelled Jeanne I Jun – Aug 1381; ruled in

	opposition to Louis I of Anjou;* King (Károly II) of Hungary 31 Dec 1385
Feb 1386 – Aug 1390	*Ladislas*, son (for 1st time) (b. Naples 11 Feb 1377; d. Naples 6 Aug 1414) crowned May 1390; expelled by Louis II; pretender to the throne of Hungary Regent: 24 Feb 1386 – May 1390: *Marguerite*, mother (b. Jul 1347; d. 6 Aug 1412)
1389/Aug 1390	*Louis II*, Duke of Anjou, Count of Provence, son of Louis I* (b. Toulouse 7 Oct 1377; d. Angers 29 Apr 1417) crowned 1389; entered Naples Aug 1390; expelled by Ladislas
9 Jul 1399 – 6 Aug 1414	*Ladislas* (for 2nd time) Prince of Taranto 1406
1414 – 2 Feb 1435	*Jeanne II*, sister (b. Naples 25 Jun 1373; d. Naples) crowned 28 Oct 1419; recognized both Alfonso of Aragon and Louis III of Anjou as heirs
1435 – 2 Jun 1442	*René I*, Duke of Bar, Duke Consort of Lorraine, Duke of Anjou and Touraine, Count of Maine and Provence, brother (b. Angers, Anjou, 16 Jan 1409; d. Aix-en-Provence 10 Jul 1480) made heir by Jeanne II; prisoner of the Duke of Burgundy until 1437; lost Naples to Alfonso I Regent: 1435–1438: *Isabelle*, wife
House of Aragon	
1435/2 Jun 1442 – 27 Jun 1458	*Alfonso I*, the Magnanimous, King (Alfonso V) of Aragon, King of Sicily (b. 1396; d. Naples) took Naples from René I 2 Jul 1442
1458 – 25 Jan 1494	*Ferdinand I* (or *Ferrante*), illegitimate son (b. Valencia, 1423)

*May 1382 – 21 Sep 1384	*Louis I*, Duke of Anjou, Count of Provence, son of King Jean II of France (b. Vincennes, 23 Jul 1339; d. Bisceglie) adopted as heir by Jeanne I 1380; crowned May 1382; unable to uphold his claims
Sep 1419 – 15 Nov 1434	*Louis III*, Duke of Anjou and Touraine, Count of Provence, son of Louis II (b. Anjou 25 Sep 1403; d. Cosenza) crowned Sep 1419; made unsuccessful attempt on Naples 1421; named as heir by Jeanne II but did not rule

Nasrids of Granada (Banu-l-Ahmar)

Territory comprised part of present-day southern Spain, with the capital at Granada.

Sultans

AD 1231/2	*(Abu 'Abdallah) Muhammad I (al-Ghalib ibn Yusuf ibn Nasr)*, grandson of Nasr
1272/3	*(Abu 'Abdallah) Muhammad II (al-Faqih ibn Muhammad)*, son
1301/2	*(Abu 'Abdallah) Muhammad III (al-Makhlu' ibn Muhammad)*, son
1308/9	*(Abu'l-Juyush) Nasr (ibn Muhammad)*, brother
1313/14	*(Abu'l-Walid) Isma'il I (ibn Faraj)*, cousin
1324/5	*Muhammad IV (ibn Isma'il)*, son
1332/3	*(Abu'l-Hajjaj) Yusuf I (al-Niar ibn Isma'il)*, brother
1354/5	*Muhammad V (al-Ghani ibn Yusuf)*, son (for 1st time)
1358/9	*(Abu'l-Walid) Isma'il II (ibn Yusuf)*, brother
1359/60	*(Abu Sa'id) Muhammad VI (ibn Isma'il)*, cousin
1361/2	*Muhammad V* (for 2nd time)
1390/1	*(Abu'l-Hajjaj) Yusuf II (ibn Muhammad)*, son
1394/5	*Muhammad VII (al-Musta'in ibn Yusuf)*, son
1407/8	*(Abu'l-Hajjaj) Yusuf III (, al-Nasir ibn Yusuf)*, brother
1417/8	*Muhammad VIII (al-Mutamassik ibn Yusuf)*, son (for 1st time)
1427/8	*Muhammad IX (al-Saghir ibn Nasr)*, grandson of Muhammad V
1429/30	*Muhammad VIII* (for 2nd time)
1431/2	*(Abu'l-Hajjaj) Yusuf IV (ibn Muhammad)*, son of Muhammad VI
1431/2	*Muhammad VIII* (for 3rd time)
1444/5	*Muhammad X (al-Ahnaf ibn 'Uthman)*, nephew (for 1st time)
1445/6	*Sa'd (al-Musta'in ibn 'Ali)*, grandson of Yusuf II (for 1st time)
1446/7	*Muhammad X* (for 2nd time)
1453/4	*Sa'd* (for 2nd time)

1461/2	*(Abu'l-Hasan) 'Ali (ibn Sa'd)*, son (for 1st time)
1482/3	*(Abu 'Abdallah) Muhammad XI (ibn 'Ali)* (or *Boabdil*), son (for 1st time)
1483/4	*'Ali* (for 2nd time)
1485/6	*Muhammad XII (ibn Sa'd al-Zaghall)*, brother
1486/7 – 1491/2	*Muhammad XI* (for 2nd time)
1491/2	Conquest of Granada by Fernando V (II) and Isabel of Castile and Aragon

Navarre (Pamplona)

Territory now Navarra province, Spain, and western part of Pyrénées-Atlantiques department, France. The capital was at Pamplona.

Kings

AD 905	*Sancho I*, son of García I, Prince of Navarre
926	*García II*, son
970	*Sancho II*, son, Count of Aragon, vassal of the Umayyad caliph of Córdoba
992	*García III*, son
1000 – 18 Oct 1035	*Sancho III*, the Great, son (b. c. 992) accepted as overlord by Barcelona and Gascony, Count of Castile 1029
1035 – 1 Sep 1054	*García IV*, son
1054 – 4 Jun 1076	*Sancho IV*, son (b. c. 1039; d. (assassinated) Peñalén) recognized the suzerainty of King Fernando I of Castile and León
1076 – Jun 1094	*Sancho V*, King (Sancho I) of Aragon, son of King Ramiro I of Aragon (b. 1045; d. Huesca) placed his kingdoms under the protection of the papacy 1089
1094	*Pedro I*, son, King of Aragon and Navarre, captured Huesca 1096 and Barbastro 1100
1104	*Alfonso I*, the Battler, brother (b. c. 1073) King of Aragon and Navarre; ruled with his wife *Urraca*, Queen of Castile and León (b. 1082; d. 8 Mar 1126); abdicated in Castile and León in favour of his stepson 1126; the count of Toulouse became his vassal 1116; conquered Saragossa 1125

1134 – 21 Nov 1150	*García V*, the Restorer, great-grandson of García IV; restored the independence of Navarre
1150 – 27 Jun 1194	*Sancho VI*, the Wise, son (b. c. 1132) accepted King Alfonso VII of Castile as suzerain
1194 – 7 Apr 1234	*Sancho VII*, the Strong, son (b. 1154; d. Tudela) received the homage of Gascony 1196, lost the provinces of Álava and Guipúzcoa to Castile 1200
1234 – 8 Jul 1253	*Thibaut I*, le Chansonnier, Count (Thibaut IV) of Champagne, nephew (b. Troyes, France, 30 May 1201; d. Pamplona)
1253 – 4 Dec 1270	*Thibaut II*, son (b. 1237; d. Trapani, Sicily) Count (Thibaut V) of Champagne
1270 – 22 Jul 1274	*Henri I*, brother; Count (Henri III) of Champagne
1274 – 2 Apr 1304	*Jeanne I*, daughter (b. 1271) Countess of Champagne and Queen of Navarre; ruled with her husband, *Philippe I*, the Fair (b. Fontainebleau, France, 1268; d. Fontainebleau 29 Oct 1314) King (Philippe IV) of France 1285 Regent: King *Philippe III* of France (b. 30 Apr 1245; d. Perpignan 5 Oct 1285)
1305	*Louis*, the Stubborn, son (b. Paris, France, 4 Oct 1289; d. Vincennes, France, 5 Jun 1316) resigned in Navarre on his succession to the French throne as Louis X
1314 – 3 Jan 1322	*Philippe II*, the Tall, Count of Poitou, brother (b. c. 1293) King (Philippe V) of France 1316
1322 – 1 Feb 1328	*Charles I*, Count of La Marche, brother (b. 1294; d. Vincennes, France) King (Charles IV) of France 1322
1328 – 6 Oct 1349	*Jeanne II*, daughter of Louis (b. 28 Jan 1311) ruled until 16 Sep 1343 with her husband, *Philippe III*, Count of Évreux (b. 1301; d. 16 Sep 1343)
1349 – 1 Jan 1387	*Charles II*, the Bad, son (b. Oct 1332) vassal of Castile
1387 – 8 Sep 1425	*Charles III*, the Noble, son (b. 1361)
1425 – 1 Apr 1441	*Blanche*, daughter
1425 – 19 Jan 1479*	*Juan*, husband (b. Medina del Campo, Castile, 1398; d. Barcelona, Aragon) King (Juan II) of Aragon 1458
1479	*François-Phébus*, Count of Foix, grandson

*1441 – 1461	*Carlos*, Prince of Viana, son of Blanche and Juan (b. Oct 1421; d. 23 Sep 1461) inherited kingdom on the death of his mother on condition that he did not use the title of king without his father's permission; in prison or exile from 1452

1483 – 1512	*Catherine*, sister (d. 1517) Queen of Navarre and Countess of Foix; ruled with her husband, *Jean* Viscount of Tartas
1512	Southern Navarre annexed by Fernando V, King of Aragon and Castile
1589	Northern Navarre inherited by King Henri IV of France

Nepal

Rulers

*Thakuri Dynasty**

AD 881 – 943	*Raghavadeva*, from 923 in part of the country only
923 – 933	*Jayadeva*
933 – 943	*Vikramadeva I*
942 – 1008	*Gunakamadeva I*
943 – 962	*Śankaradeva I*
962 – 996	*Sahadeva*
996 – 997	*Vikramadeva II*
997 – 999	*Narendrdeva I*, ruled jointly with his successor
998 – 1004	*Udayadeva*
1004 – 1009	*Nirbhayadeva*
c. 1005 – 1018	*Rudradeva I*
1008 – 1041	*Lakshmikamadeva I*, sole ruler from c. 1020
1009 – 1020	*Bhojadeva*
c. 1041 – 1061	*Jaya(kama)deva*, son of Lakshmikamadeva I
1043 – 1050	*Bhaskaradeva*, elected by the Thakuris of Nuwakot
c. 1050 – 1062	*Bala(nta)deva*
c. 1061 – 1067	*Pradyumnakamadeva* (or *Padmadeva*)
c. 1062 – 1065	*Nagarjunadeva*
c. 1065 – 1082	*Śankaradeva II*, overthrown by the Thakuris of Patan
1082 – 1085	*Vamadeva*, son of King Yaśodeva

*Owing to discrepancies in the traditional and epigraphical records and the frequent overlapping of rulers, whether as associates, sub-kings or rivals, the dating and order are somewhat conjectural. In the case of the Lichchhavi dynasty (c. 150 – 750) and the earlier Thakuris the difficulties are so great that no attempt has been made to give a list here.

1085 – 1098	*Harshadeva*, already ruling jointly with his predecessor from 1082(?)
1098 – 1126	*Śivadeva III*, son of Śankaradeva II (b. 19 Jun 1057)
c. 1110 – 1125	*Si(m)hadeva*
c. 1124 – 1136	*Indradeva*, usurper
c. 1136 – 1140	*Manadeva*
1140 – 1147	*Narendradeva II*, son, already local or associate ruler by 1134
11 Jan 1147	*Anandadeva*, son of Si(m)hadeva (b. 11 May 1099)
5 Jan 1167	*Rudradeva II*, brother (b. 26 Feb 1108) abdicated
1175	*Amritadeva*, brother (b. 15 Sep 1112; d. 15 Sep 1180) abdicated
3 Nov 1178 – 1182	*Someśvaradeva*, grandson of Si(m)hadeva or Śivadeva III (b. 25 Feb 1119)
1182 – 1184	Interregnum
1183 – 1184	*Ratnadeva*, a nobleman, usurper
11 Dec 1184 – 1196(?)	*Gunakamadeva II*
c. 1192 – 1198	*Lakshmikamadeva II*, rival
c. 1192 – 1200	*Vijayakamadeva*, rival

Malla Dynasty

1200	*Arimalla* (or *Arideva*), son of Jayaśimalla (b. Nov/Dec 1153)
Sep/Oct 1216	*Abhayamalla*, son (b. Dec 1182; d. 13 Jun 1255)
7 Jun 1255	*Jayadeva(malla)*, son (b. 1 Nov 1203; d. 11 Jan 1258)
Jan(?) 1258 – Mar/Apr 1271	*Jayabhimadeva*, already ruling locally from 1256
1271 – 1274	*Jayasimhamalla* (or *Jayasthamalladeva*), son of Jayadanekamalla (b. 19 Apr 1229; d. 8 Nov 1287) underking from 1258, deposed(?)
c. 1274 – 23 Aug 1310(?)	*Anantamalla*, nephew (b. 21 Apr 1246)
(?) – 1293	*Jayadityadeva*, son of Jayabhimadeva (b. 1238; d. 1293) underking
c. 1310	Khasiya and Tirhutiya invasions
c. 1310 – 1330	*Jayanandadeva*, half-brother, nominal ruler
c. 1310 – 1326	*Jayarudramalla*, son of Jayatungamalla (b. 20 Dec 1295; d. 16 Jun 1326) ruled at Bhatgaon 1311, *de facto* ruler of the whole territory from c. 1320
5 Apr 1320 – 14 Sep 1344	*Jayarimalla*, son of Anantamalla, initially associate king
c. 1326 – 1332	*Padmalladevi*, mother of Jayarudramalla, regent in the name of her granddaughter *Nayakadevi* (d. 1347)

1344 – 1347	Interregnum at Patan, foreign invasion
Jan 1347	*Jagatsimha, Prince of Tirhut*, husband of Nayakadevi (d. Jan 1347) for a few days
6/7 Jan 1347 – 1385	*Rajalladevi*, daughter (b. 1347; d. 5 Oct 1385) under the regency of her grandmother *Devaladevi* (d. 1366) and later of her husband *Jayasthitimalla* (see below)
Jan 1347	*Paśumipatimalla*, son(?) of Jayarimalla (d. Dec 1348) pretender
1347	Invasion by Haji Shams al-Din Ilyas Shah of the Bengal sultanate
27 Jul 1347 – 1361	*Jayarajadeva*, son of Jayanandadeva (b. 9 Mar 1317)
18 Apr 1360/1361	*Jayarjunadeva* (or *Jayarjunamalla*), son (b. 2 Feb 1338; d. 3 Feb 1382) in conflict with Jayasthitimalla (see below)
3 Feb 1382	*Jayasimha Rama*, lord protector
15 Sep 1382 – 1395/6	*Jayasthitimalla*,* husband of Rajalladevi, king at Patan (*de facto* from 1372), prince-consort at Bhatgaon from 1354, regent 1366
c. 1392	*Ratnajyotirdeva*, local ruler
1396 – c. 1408	*Jayadharmamalla*,* son of Jayasthitimalla (b. 1367) jointly with his two successors
1396 – c. 1405	*Jayakirttimalla*,* brother (b. 1377)
1396 – 1428	*Jayajyotirmalla*,* brother (b. 1373; d. 28 Oct 1428)
1428 – 1480	*Jayayakshamalla*,* son, associate king from 1424
c. 1440 – (?)	*Jayajivamalla*,* brother, associate king
c. 1457 – 1467	*Rayamalla*, son of Jayayakshamalla, usurper(?)
1480	Kingdom divided between Rayamalla, Ranamalla and Ratnamalla, sons of Jayayakshamalla, and their heirs

*In all these names the initial Jaya- is sometimes omitted

Nicaea

Territory comprised part of present-day western Turkey, with the capital established at Nicaea.

Emperors

Successors of the Byzantine emperors and rivals of the Latin emperors of Constantinople.

12 Apr AD 1204 – 1205(?)	*Constantine Lascaris*, brother of Theodore I, proclaimed emperor at the fall of Constantinople and fled to Nicaea
1205(?)/1208	*Theodore I Lascaris*, son-in-law of the Byzantine emperor Alexius III Angelus (b. c. 1175) leader of the Byzantine refugees in Nicaea, took the title of emperor 1208
1222	*John III Ducas Vatatzes*, son-in-law, forced the despotate of Thessalonica to acknowledge his suzerainty by 1242, deposed the last despot of Thessalonica 1246
Nov 1254	*Theodore II Lascaris*, son (b. 1222)
Aug 1258 – 15 Aug 1261	*John IV Lascaris*, son (b. 1250; d. (in prison) Bithynia 1261(?)) blinded and imprisoned; ruled under the regency of *Michael VIII Palaeologus* (b. Nicaea c. 1224; d. Thrace 11 Dec 1282) crowned co-emperor 1259, retook Constantinople 25 Jul 1261, crowned sole emperor of the restored Byzantine Empire 15 Aug 1261
15 Aug 1261	Reincorporated into restored Byzantine Empire

Normandy

Dukes

AD 911	*Rollon*, son of Rognewald, Jarl of Mörle (b. 846); invaded France by 890; by Treaty of St-Clair-sur-Epte accepted the French king as overlord 911; created Duke of Normandy by King Charles III the Simple of France 912

931 – 17 Dec 942	*Guillaume I*, Long-Sword, illegitimate son; associated with his father from 927; assassinated
942 – 20 Nov 996	*Richard I*, son (b. 932)
996 – 28 Aug 1026	*Richard II*, son (d. Fécamp)
1026 – 3 Feb 1027	*Richard III*, son (d. Rouen)
1027 – 22 Jul 1035	*Robert I* the Devil, brother (d. Nicaea)
1035 – 9 Sep 1087	*Guillaume II*, the Bastard or the Conqueror, illegitimate son (b. Falaise 1027/8; d. Rouen) Count of Maine 1062, King (William I) of England 25 Dec 1066
1087	*Robert II*, *Curthose*, son (d. (in prison) Cardiff 3 Feb 1134?) yielded the counties of Eu and Aumale to his brother, King William II of England 1091; defeated by his brother, King Henry I of England at battle of Tinchebray Sep 1106
28 Sep 1106 – 1 Dec 1135	*Henri I*, King (Henry I) of England, brother (b. Selby, England, 1068; d. Lyons-la-Forêt)
1135	*Étienne*, grandson (through mother) of Guillaume II (b. before 1100; d. Dover, England, 25 Oct 1154) King (Stephen) of England 22 Dec 1135
1144 – 7 Sep 1151	*Geoffroi Plantagenêt*, Count (Geoffroi IV) of Anjou, Maine and Touraine, son-in-law of Henri I (b. 24 Aug 1113)
1151 – 6 Jul 1189	*Henri II*, son (b. Le Mans, Maine, 5 Mar 1133; d. Chinon, Touraine) at the same time Count (Henri) of Anjou, Maine and Touraine; Duke (Henri) of Aquitaine May 1152, King (Henry II) of England 19 Dec 1154; abdicated in Aquitaine 1168
20 Jul 1189 – 6 Apr 1199	*Richard*, Coeur de Lion (i.e. Lion-heart), Duke of Aquitaine, son (b. Oxford, England, 8 Sep 1157; d. Châlus, near Limoges) at the same time Count of Anjou, Maine and Touraine; King (Richard I) of England 3 Sep 1189; deposed in Aquitaine 1196
1199 – 1204	*Jean*, sans Terre (i.e. Lackland) (or *John of England*) brother (b. Oxford, England, 24 Dec 1167; d. Newark, England, 18/19 Oct 1216) at the same time Count of Anjou, Maine and Touraine; King (John) of England 27 May 1199; lost Normandy to King Philippe II Auguste of France 1204 and Maine and Anjou 1206
1204	Normandy became French crown land

Norway

Kings

c. AD 900	*Harald I*, Fairhair (b. c. 853) established Kingdom of Norway
c. 940	*Erik I*, Bloodaxe, son (d. Stainmore, England, 954) in continuous strife with illegitimate sons of Harald I, fled to England, King of York 948 – 949 and 952 – 954
c. 942	*Håkon I*, Adalsteinsfostre (i.e. fostered by Athelstan (King of Wessex, Mercia and York)), or the Good, illegitimate son of Harald I (b. c. 927) returned from England and overcame rivals
c. 956	*Harald II Eriksson*, Greyfell, son of Erik I
c. 970	*Håkon Sigurdsson*, a Lade earl from Trondheim
c. 995 – 1000	*Olav I Tryggvason*, probably a great-grandson of Harald I, defeated at Battle of Øresund by King Svend I of Denmark and King Olof of Sweden, who divided Norway between them
1015/16	*Olav II Haraldsson*, probably a great-great-grandson of Harald I (b. 995; d. Stiklestad 29 Jul 1030) established himself as King of Norway, fled to Kiev when threatened by Danish forces
1028	*Knud* (known in England as *Cnut* or *Canute*), King of Denmark, King of England (b. c. 995 – 1000; d. Shaftesbury, England, 12 Nov 1035) appointed as governors: 1028 – 1029: *Håkon Eriksson*, a Lade earl 1029 – 1035: *Svein*, son of Knud (d. 1036), and his mother, *Ælfgive*; fled on arrival of Magnus I
1035	*Magnus I Olavsson*, son of Olav II Haraldsson (b. 1024) King (Magnus) of Denmark 8 Jun 1042
25 Oct 1047	*Harald III Sigurdsson*, Hardråde, half-brother of Olav II Haraldsson (b. 1015) co-ruler from 1046, killed at Battle of Stamford Bridge
10 Sep 1066	*Magnus II*, son (b. 1049; d. 28 Apr 1069) and his brother, *Olav III*, the Peaceful (b. 1050; d. 22 Sep 1093)
22 Sep 1093	*Magnus III*, Bareleg, son of Olav III (b. 1073; d. Ulster 24 Aug 1103) King of the Isle of Man 1098 – 1099 or 1102; and *Håkon*, son of Magnus II (b. 1069; d. Feb 1095)

24 Aug 1103	*Øystein I*, son of Magnus III (b. 1088 or 1089; d. 29 Aug 1122) and his brothers, *Sigurd I*, the Crusader (b. c. 1090; d. 26 Mar 1130) and *Olav (IV)* (b. 1099; d. 22 Dec 1115)
26 Mar 1130	*Magnus IV*, the Blind, son of Sigurd I (b. c. 1115; d. 1139) in conflict with *Harald IV*, Gille, who claimed to be an illegitimate son of Magnus III (d. (murdered) 1136)
	Harald fled to Denmark 1134, returned 1135, captured Magnus, blinded him and confined him to a monastery. *Sigurd Slembe*, who claimed to be an illegitimate son of Magnus III (d. 1139), murdered Harald 1136 and released Magnus IV with whom he made joint attempts to claim the throne until their deaths
1136 – 4 Feb 1161	*Inge I*, son of Harald IV (d. 4 Feb 1161) and his (illegitimate) half-brother *Sigurd II* (b. 1133; d. (in battle with Inge) 10 Jun 1155) in conflict with:
1142 – 21 Aug 1157	*Øystein II*, illegitimate son of Harald IV, proclaimed king by people of Trøndelag
1157 – 1162	*Håkon II Sigurdsson*, illegitimate son of Sigurd II (b. 1147) defeated Inge I at Oslo, was defeated by supporters of Magnus V
1162	*Magnus V Erlingsson*, grandson of Sigurd I (b. 1156) proclaimed king by Inge's faction, defeated and killed in battle of Fimreite by Sverre
Jul 1184	*Sverre*, claimed to be illegitimate son of Sigurd II
9 Mar 1202 – 1 Jan 1204	*Håkon III*, son
1205	*Inge II Bårdsson* (b. 1185; d. 23 Apr 1217) in conflict with *Filippus* (d. 1217)
1217	*Håkon IV*, claimed to be illegitimate son of Håkon III (b. 1204)
15/16 Dec 1263	*Magnus VI*, Lagabøter (i.e. improver of laws), son (b. 1238)
9 May 1280	*Erik II*, son (b. 1268)
15 Jun 1299	*Håkon V Magnusson*, brother (b. 10 Apr 1270)
8 May 1319	*Magnus VII*, grandson, nephew of King Birger of Sweden (b. 1316; d. 1 Dec 1374) King (Magnus II) of Sweden 1319, abdicated when son attained majority
1355	*Håkon VI*, son (b. 1338)

1 May 1380 – 3 Aug 1387	*Olav IV*, King (Oluf III) of Denmark, son (b. 1370) Regent: *Margrete* (or *Margareta*), Regent of Denmark, mother (b. 1353; d. Flensburg, 28 Oct 1412) Regent of Sweden 1389
1389	*Erik III*, grandnephew of Margrete and son of Warcisław VII, the Duke of Pomerania at Stolp (b. 1382; d. Jun 1459) Duke (Eryk I) of Pomerania at Stolp 1394, King (Erik XIII) of Sweden 1397, King (Erik VII) of Denmark 28 Oct 1412, deposed in all Scandinavian kingdoms
Jun 1442 – 5 or 6 Jan 1448	*Kristoffer* (or *Cristoffer*) (German: *Christoph*), King (Christoffer III) of Denmark, King (Kristoffer) of Sweden, nephew (b. 26 Feb (?) 1416; d. Hälsingborg)
Jun 1449/1450* – 21 May 1481	*Christian I*, King of Denmark (b. 1426; d. Copenhagen) King of Sweden 1457 – 1464 and 1465 – 1467
1483 – 20 Feb 1513	*Hans* (or *Johannes*), King of Denmark, son (b. 8 Jul 1455) King (Johan II) of Sweden 1483/97 – 1500

Nubia (Nobatia)

Territory comprised part of present-day Sudan and southern Egypt, with the capital at Faras (now Begrash, Sudan).

Kings

c. AD 536	*Silko*, first Christian king
559 or 574	*Eirpanome*
651 – 652	*Qalidurut* (or *Qalidurun*)
645 – 655	*Zakarya*, doubtful
697 – c. 710	*Mercurius*

*1449 *Karl Knutsson Bonde*, King (Karl VIII Knutsson Bonde) of Sweden, crowned king of Norway at Nidaros after Christian's election at Oslo; withdrew claim to crown; Christian crowned at Nidaros 1450

744 – 768	*Simon*
744 – 768	*Abraham*
744 – 768	*Mark*
744 – 768	*Cyriacus*
end of 8th century	*Michael*
(?)	*John*
822 – (?)	*Zakarya Israel*, son
872 – 892	*George I*, son
(?)	*Zakarya III*, son
943	*Kubra ibn Surur*
979	*George II*
1002 – 1006	*Raphael*
1080	*Solomon*
1089	*Basil*, son
1130 – 1158	*George III*
1272 – 1273	*David I*
1274 – 1277	*David II*, son
1275 – 1276	*Shakanda*, nephew
(?)	*Meškedet*(?)
1279 – 1290	*Berek*
1286	*Shamamun* (for 1st time)
1288	Unknown son of one Sorella
(?)	*Shamamun* (for 2nd time)
1290	Unknown nephew of David II(?)
1290 – 1293	*Shamamun* (for 3rd time)
(?)	*Any*
(?)	*Budeminah*
1304 – 1305	*Amai*
1312	*Kerembes* (for 1st time)
(?)	*'Abdallah*
(?)	*Kanz al-Dawla* (for 1st time)
(?)	*Abraham*, brother of Kerembes, reign of three days
1323	*Kerembes* (for 2nd time)
1323	*Kanz al-Dawla* (for 2nd time)
14th century	Conquered by the Mamluks, disintegrated into many petty states

Numidia

Territory comprised part of present-day northern Algeria, southern Tunisia and north-western Libya, with the capital at Cirta (present-day Constantine).

Kings

202 BC	*Massinissa*, son of Gula
148	*Micipsa*, son, divided his kingdom between his three sons
118 – 112	*Adherbal*, son
118	*Hiempsal I*, brother
118	*Jugurtha*, adopted son of Micipsa, ruled over the entire kingdom by 112, defeated by the Romans and taken to Rome as a prisoner 106
106	*Hiempsal II*, ruled small area of Numidia, driven from his kingdom 81 but reinstated by the Roman triumvir Pompey
60 – 46	*Juba I*, son, defeated at the battle of Thapsus 46, committed suicide
46	Incorporated into the Roman province of Africa

Orléans

Dukes, of the Royal House

AD 1344 – 1 Sep 1375	*Philippe*, son of King Philippe VI of France (b. 1 Jul 1336) died without heir leaving the duchy vacant
1392 – 23 Nov 1407	*Louis I*, Count of Valois and of Asti, son of King Charles V of France (b. Paris 13 Mar 1372; d. (assassinated) Paris) Duke of Touraine 1386 – 1392; Duke of Luxemburg 18 Aug 1402
1407 – 4 Jan 1465	*Charles*, son (b. Paris, 24 Nov 1394; d. Amboise)
1465	*Louis II*, son (b. Blois, 27 Jun 1462; d. Paris 1 Jan 1515) King (Louis XII) of France 7 Apr 1498
1498	Duchy united with the French crown

Orthodox Caliphs (Rightly Guided Caliphs, al-Khulafa' al-Rashidun)

At its greatest extent, territory comprised part of present-day Libya, Egypt, Israel, Jordan, Lebanon, Saudi Arabia, Syria, Iran and Iraq, with the capital at Medina and Kufa.

Caliphs

7 Jun AD 632	*(Abu-Bakr) 'Abdallah ('Atiq al-Siddiq)*, father-in-law of Muhammad
23 Aug 634	*'Umar (ibn al-Khattab, al-Faruq)*, father-in-law of Muhammad, took the title Amir al-Mu'minin (Commander of the Faithful), conquered Egypt 640/2
6 Nov 644	*'Uthman (ibn 'Affan, Dhu'l-Nurayn)*, son-in-law of Muhammad, assassinated, conquered the Sasanids 637–649
16 Jun 656 – 661	*'Ali (ibn Abi Talib al-Murtada)*, cousin, son-in-law and foster brother of Muhammad, murdered
661	Umayyad caliphs gained control

Osnabrück

Bishops*

AD (?)	*Wiho*
?	*Meingaz*(?)
fl. 829 – 866(?)	*Gefwin*
after 845 – 874(?)	*Gozbert*
before 864 – 1 Feb 885	*Egilbert*

*When two dates separated by an oblique stroke are given for the beginning of an episcopate the first refers to election or nomination and the second to ordination, consecration or investiture

before 11 Sep 889 – 11 May 918(?)	*Egilmar*
before 7 Nov 921 – 14 May or 14 Jun 949	*Doddo I*
Jun 949 / Apr 950 – 7 Nov 967	*Drogo*
late 967 – 978	*Liudolf*
978(?) – 14 May or 14 Jun 996	*Doddo II*
996 – 24 or 27 Nov 998	*Gunther*
998(?) – 17 Feb 1003	*Othilulf*
1003 – 18 Jun 1023	*Thiedmar*
before 27 Jul 1023 – 1027	*Meginher*
1027 or 1028 – 10 Dec 1036 or 1037	*Gozmar*
1036 or 1037 – 3 Dec 1052	*Alberich*
1052(?) – 19 or 20 Sep 1068	*Benno I*
23 Nov 1068 / 1 Feb 1069 – 27 or 28 Jul 1088	*Benno II*
1088 – 1093	*Marcward* (d. 18 Dec 1107) deposed
1093 – 11 Nov 1101	*Wido*
1101 – 13 Jul 1110	*Johann I*
1110 – 31 Dec 1118 or 1 Jan 1119	*Godescalk*
1119 / 11 Apr 1120 – 11 Feb 1137	*Diethard*
1137 – 28 or 29 Jun 1141	*Udo*
1141 – 15 Jul 1173	*Philipp*
1173(?) – 15 Dec 1190(?)	*Arnold*
no later than 1193 – no later than 1216	*Gerhard von Oldenburg*, previously Archbishop of Hamburg-Bremen, resigned
no later than 1216 – 30 Jun 1224	*Adolf von Teklenburg*
before 9 Oct 1224 – before 31 May 1226	*Engelbert von Isenburg* (for 1st time) (d. 30 Oct 1250) suspended 3 Feb 1226, resigned

autumn 1226 – 6 Apr 1227	*Otto I*
autumn 1227 – 16 Apr 1239	*Konrad I von Velber*
before 17 May 1239 – 30 Oct 1250	*Engelbert von Isenburg* (for 2nd time)
before 5 Feb 1251 – 20 Dec 1258	*Bruno*, Count of Altena-Isenberg
before 19 Feb 1259 – 13 Feb 1264	*Baldewin von Rüssel*
before 27 Nov 1264 – 1265	*Engelbert von der Mark*, rejected by Pope Clement IV 11 Jun 1265
7 May 1265 – before 18 Nov 1269	*Widekind*, Count of Waldeck
18 Jan 1270 – 16 Apr 1297	*Konrad II*, Count of Rietberg
before 20 Jun 1297 – 5 Nov 1308	*Ludwig*, Count of Ravensberg
after 20 Dec 1308/before 30 Oct 1309 – after 1 Nov 1320	*Engelbert II von Weihe*
13 Apr/14 May 1321 – 13 Jun 1348	*Gottfried*, Count of Arnsberg, translated to Bremen
27 Jul 1349 – 17 Aug 1366	*Johann II*
1368 – 17 Oct 1375	*Melchior*, Duke of Brunswick-Grubenhagen (b. c. 1341; d. 6 Jun 1381) translated to Schwerin
4 Mar 1377 – 19 Jan 1402	*Dietrich von Horne*
18 Aug 1402 – c. 15 Jul 1410	*Heinrich II*, Count of Holstein, from Oct 1404 under guardianship of *Otto von Hoya* (see below), resigned
15 Jul 1410 – 4 Oct 1424	*Otto II von Hoya*, Bishop of Münster 11 Apr 1392 – 4 Oct 1424
18 Oct 1424/3 Aug 1425 – 29 Mar 1437	*Johann III von Diepholz*
4 Nov 1437	*Erik von Hoya*
24 Jan 1442	*Heinrich III von Mörs*
30 Aug 1454	*Rudolf von Diepholz*
15 Dec 1455	*Konrad III von Diepholz*
11 Nov 1482	*Konrad IV*, Count of Rietberg

Ostrogoths, Kingdom of the

Kings

c. AD 455	*Valamer*, settled in Pannonia (now in Hungary and Yugoslavia)
?	*Theodemir*
471 – 26 Aug 526	*Theodoric*, the Great, son; adopted as son by Zeno, the Roman Emperor in the East, and appointed consul 484; appointed by Zeno to conquer Italy, took Ravenna 5 Mar 493 and killed Odoaker, the first barbarian king in Italy
31 Aug 526 – 2 Oct 534	*Athalaric*, grandson Regent: *Amalasuntha*, mother; subsequently Queen
3 Oct 534	*Amalasuntha*, previously Regent; ruled (until 30 Apr 535) with her cousin and husband, *Theodahad*; deposed, banished and murdered
30 Apr 535	*Theodahad* (see above) alone; lost Naples to the Byzantine general Belisarius 536; deposed
536 – spring 540	*Witigis*, a general and husband of Matasuntha, granddaughter of Theodoric (d. 542); lost Rome to Belisarius, 537, and was deposed and imprisoned at the capture of Ravenna
	First Byzantine conquest of Italy. A line of Ostrogoth kings continued in exile.
spring 540	*Hildibad*
spring 541	*Eraric*
autumn 541	*Totila*; captured Rome 546 and by 550 had retaken most of Ostrogothic Italy; defeated and killed by the Byzantine general Narses near Ancona
summer 552 – 553	*Teia* (or *Theia*); defeated and killed in the battle of Mons Lactarius, near Naples
	Second Byzantine conquest: territories incorporated into the Byzantine Empire

Ottomans (Osmanlis)

Territory comprised part of present-day Turkey, the Balkans and the Arab lands, with the capital initially at Bursa and after 1366 at Edirne (or Adrianople).

Sultans

AD 1281	*'Othman* (or *Osman) I (ibn Ertoghril)* (b. Söğüt(?) 1258; d. Söğüt 1324) abdicated
c. 1324	*Orkhan (Ghazi ibn 'Othman)*, son (b. 1288; d. Apr 1360) abdicated
1360	*Murad I (Khudawandikiar ibn Orkhan)*, son (b. Bursa(?) 1326; d. (assassinated) Kosova)
Jun 1389 – 28 Jul 1402	*Bayezid I (Yıldırım ibn Murad)*, son (b. Edirne(?) 1360; d. Akşehir 10 Mar 1403) deposed by the Timurid khan Temür
Jul – Aug 1402	Timurid invasion, the Great Interregnum
Aug 1402 – 5 Jul 1413	*Mehmed I (Chelibi ibn Bayezid)*, son (for 1st time) (b. Edirne(?) 1389) ruled at Amasya in Anatolia 1402 – 1404, at Bursa and Amasya 1404 – 1413
Aug 1402	*Süleiman I (ibn Bayezid)*, brother, ruled in Rumelia (Ottoman possessions in Balkan peninsula)
17 Feb 1411 – 5 Jul 1413	*Musa Chelebi (ibn Bayezid)*, brother, ruled in Rumelia and also in Bursa 1403 – 1404
5 Jul 1413	*Mehmed I* (for 2nd time) re-united Anatolia and Rumelia
26 May 1421	*Murad II (Qoja ibn Muhammad)*, son (for 1st time) (b. Amasya 1404; d. Edirne 3 Feb 1451) abdicated
1 Dec 1444	*Mehmed II (Fathih ibn Murad II)*, son (for 1st time) (b. Edirne 30 Mar 1432; d. Maltepe 3 May 1481) deposed
Sep 1446	*Murad II* (for 2nd time)
3 Feb 1451	*Mehmed II* (for 2nd time) captured Constantinople 29 May 1453
3 May 1481 – 24 Apr 1512	*Bayezid II (Wali ibn Mehmed)*, son (b. Dimetoka Jan 1448; d. Dimetoka 26 May 1512) deposed

For continuation, see Turkey, Volume 2.

Oyo (Yoruba State)

Territory in present-day south-western Nigeria, with the capital initially at Old Oyo (or Oyo-Ile) and later at New Oyo (or Katunga).

Alafin (Kings)

AD (?)	*Oranyan* (or *Oranmiyan*), founder of Old Oyo
(?)	*Ajaka*, son (for 1st time) dethroned
(?)	*Sango*, brother, committed suicide
(?)	*Ajaka* (for 2nd time)
(?)	*Aganju*, son
(?)	*Kori*, grandson, committed suicide
(?)	*Oluaso*
c. 1530	*Onigbogi*, son, evacuation of Old Oyo during Nupe attack
c. 1542	*Ofiran* (or *Ofinran*), son
c. 1554	*Eguguojo* (or *Egunoju*), son, founder of Oyo-Igboho
c. 1560	*Orompoto*, possibly a woman
c. 1580	*Ajiboyede* (or *Sopasan*)
c. 1590	*Abipa*, son, re-occupied Old Oyo
c. 1614	*Obalokun*
(?)	*Ajagbo*
(?)	*Odarawu*
(?)	*Kanran*
(?)	*Jayin*, son
(?)	Interregnum
(?)	*Ayibi*, grandson of Jayin, committed suicide
(?)	*Osiyago*
(?)	*Ojigi*, committed suicide
c. 1735	*Gberu*
(?)	*Amuniwaiye*
1746	*Onisile*
1754*	*Labisi*, for less than a year
1754*	*Agboluaje*
1754*	*Majeogbe*
c. 1770*	*Abiodun*

*During the period, 1754 – 1774, effective power was in the hands of the Basorun Gaha, head of the council of notabilities

c. 1789	*Awole Arongangan*, cousin, committed suicide
(?)	*Adebo*, for a few months
(?)	*Maku*, for three months, committed suicide
(?)	Interregnum
(?)	*Majotu*
c. 1830	*Amodo*
c. 1833	*Oluewa*
c. 1837	*Atiba*, son of Abiodun, founder of New Oyo
1859	*Adelu*
1876	*Adeyemi*, placed all of Yorubaland under British protection 1888
1905	*Lawani*
1911	*Ladigbolu I*
1944 – 1970	Unknown alafin
1 Oct 1960	Nigeria became independent
from 19 Nov 1970	*(Oba) Lamadi Olayiwola Adeyemi* (b. Oyo 1939)

Paderborn

Bishops (from c. 1100 Princes of the Holy Roman Empire)*

c. AD 800 – after Jul 815	*Hathumar*
(?) – 17 Sep 859 or 860	*Badurad*
860 – 2 May 886 or 887	*Liuthard*
886 – 9 Sep 908	*Biso*
908 – 8 Dec 917	*Dietrich*
25 Jan 917 – 20 Jul 935	*Unwan*

*When two dates separated by an oblique stroke are given for the beginning of an episcopate the first refers to election or nomination and the second to ordination, consecration or investiture

935 – 26 Jul 960	*Dudo*
961 – 17 Feb 983	*Folcmar*
983 – 6 Mar 1009	*Rethar*
13 Mar 1009 – 5 or 6 Jun 1036	*Meginwerk*
1036 – 6 Nov 1051	*Rudolf*
25 Dec 1051 – 3 Feb 1076	*Imad*
1076 – 28 Nov 1083	*Poppo*
1083 – 1102	*Heinrich* (d. 15 Apr 1107) in rivalry with Heinrich von Werle, translated to Magdeburg
1084 – 14 Oct 1127	*Heinrich von Werle*, Imperial anti-bishop, supported by the Papacy from 1105
1127 – 16 Jul 1160	*Bernhard I*
1160 – 28 Sep 1178	*Evergis*
1178 – 10 Feb 1188	*Siegfried*
1188 – 23 Apr 1203	*Bernhard II von Ibbenbüren*
1203 – 28 Mar 1223	*Bernhard III von Oesede*
1223/7 Apr 1225 – 27 Sep 1225	*Oliver* (d. 1227) appointed cardinal
autumn 1225 – 1227	*Wilbrand von Oldenburg* (d. 26 Jul 1233) translated to Utrecht
1228 – 14 Apr 1247	*Bernhard IV von Lippe*
1247 – 26 or 27 Dec 1276	*Simon I von Lippe*
14/18 Aug 1277 – 23 Oct 1307	*Otto*, Count of Rietberg, in rivalry with *Heinrich von Schwalenberg*(?) until 7 Jul 1278, renominated and confirmed 24 Oct 1278, in rivalry with *Dietrich von Beilstein* 13 Mar 1285 – 28 Apr 1287, consecrated 28 Apr 1287
1307/before 9 Dec 1308 – between 1 Aug and 7 Sep 1310	*Günther von Schwalenberg*, in disputed election against Dietrich von Itter (see below), resigned
3 Dec 1310 – 20 Sep 1321	*Dietrich von Itter*
after 20 Sep 1321 – 13 Jan 1340	*Bernhard V von Lippe*
before 23 Mar/before 13 Dec 1341 – before 17 Mar 1361	*Baldwin von Steinfurt* (d. 31 Mar 1361) resigned
17 Mar 1361 – 27 Mar 1380	*Heinrich von Spiegel*, coadjutor from 1360

before 15 Jul 1380 – 25 Jan 1389	*Simon II von Steinberg* (b. c. 1331 – 2)
15 Mar/9 Nov 1389 – 25 Jun 1394	*Rupert von Jülich-Berg*, previously Bishop of Passau
1394 – 28 Feb 1399	*Johann*, Count of Hoya (d. 12 May 1424) translated to Hildesheim
4 Mar 1399 – 14 Mar 1401	*Bertrand de Arvazano*, fled from Paderborn 24 Nov 1399, forced to resign and discharged from arrest
5 Nov 1400/14 Mar 1401 – 19 Feb 1416	*Wilhelm von Jülich-Berg*, admitted to Paderborn 14 Mar 1401, resigned
13 Apr 1415/19 Feb 1416 –	*Dietrich von Moers*, appointed administrator 13 Apr 1415
18 May 1463 – 7 Mar 1498	*Simon III von Lippe* (b. c. 1430)

Palas of Bengal

Territory comprised part of present-day northern India, with the capital at Pataliputra (now Patna).

Kings

mid 8th century AD	*Gopala I*
c. 770 – 810	*Dharmapala*, son, conquered most of northern India
c. 810 – 850	*Devapala*, son
(?)	*Vigrahapala I*, nephew
c. 875	*Narayanapala*, son
(?)	*Rajyapala*, son
(?)	*Gopala II*
(?)	*Vigrahapala II*, son
c. 988 – 1038	*Mahipala I*, son
(?)	*Nayapala*, son
c. 1074	*Vigrahapala III*, son

(?)	*Mahipala II*, son
(?)	*Shurapala II*, brother
c. 1077 – 1120	*Ramapala*, brother
c. 1142	*Kumarapala*, son
(?)	*Gopala III*, son
(?)	*Madanapala*, uncle
1199	Muslim conquest

The Palatinate

Counts Palatine of Lorraine (Lotharingia)*

AD 989	*Hermann I*
1020 – 21 May 1034	*Ezzo*, son (b. 955)
1035	*Otto I*, son (d. 1047) Duke (Otto II) of Swabia 1045
1045	*Heinrich I*, cousin
1061	*Hermann II*, brother(?)
1085 – 12 Apr 1095	*Heinrich II von Laach*, nephew(?), Count Palatine of the Rhine
1095 – 9 Mar 1113	*Siegfried von Ballenstadt*, grandson(?) (b. c. 1075) Count of Orlamünde, Count Palatine of Lorraine
1113	*Gottfried*, Count of Calw (d. 1131/2)
1129 – 13 Feb 1140	*Wilhelm*, son of Siegfried von Ballenstadt
1140	*Otto II*, Count of Salm (d. 1150) Count Palatine of Rheineck
1140	*Heinrich III*, son of Margrave Leopold IV of the East Mark
1142	*Hermann III von Stahleck*

Counts and Electors Palatine of the Rhine

House of Hohenstaufen

1156 – 8 Nov 1195	*Konrad*, brother of the Holy Roman Emperor Friedrich I, united the office of count palatine with

*Appointed by the Holy Roman Emperor

	possession of the Rhine lands owned by the German king
House of Welf	
1195	*Heinrich IV*, son-in-law, son of Duke Heinrich III of Saxony (b. c. 1173; d. 28 Apr 1227) first Elector Palatine
1214	*Heinrich V*, son (b. c. 1195; d. 1 May 1214)
House of Wittelsbach	
1214	*Ludwig I*, Duke of Bavaria, son of Duke Otto I of Bavaria (b. Kelheim, Bavaria, 23 Dec 1174; d. (assassinated) Kelheim 15 Sep 1231) regent of Germany 1225 – 1228
1228 – 29 Nov 1253	*Otto III*, son (b. 7 Apr 1206) Duke (Otto II) of Bavaria 1231
1253 – 2 Feb 1294	*Ludwig II*, the Stern, son (b. 13 Apr 1229) Duke of Bavaria 1253, Duke of Upper Bavaria 1255
1294	*Rudolf I*, son (b. 4 Oct 1274; d. 12 Aug 1319) Duke of Upper Bavaria 1294; forced to abdicate
1317 – 29 Jan 1327	*Adolf*, son (b. 27 Sep 1300)
1327 – 4 Oct 1353	*Rudolf II*, brother (b. 8 Aug 1306) Elector 1329*
1353– 16 Feb 1390	*Ruprecht I*, brother (b. 9 Jun 1309)
1390 – 6 Jan 1398	*Ruprecht II*, nephew (b. 12 May 1325)
1398 – 18 May 1410	*Ruprecht III*, son (b. Amberg, Rhenish Palatinate, 5 May 1352; d. near Oppeinheim) King (Ruprecht I) of Germany 21 Aug 1400
18 May 1410	Lands of the Palatinate divided among Ruprecht III's four sons: Ludwig III received the Electoral Palatinate; Johann received the Upper Palatinate; Stefan received Simmern-Zweibrücken; and Otto I received Mosbach
1410 – 30 Dec 1436	*Ludwig III*, son of Ruprecht III (b. 1378)
1436 – 13 Aug 1449	*Ludwig IV*, son (b. 1 Jan 1424)
1449 – 12 Dec 1476	*Friedrich I*, the Victorious, brother (b. 1 Aug 1425)
1476 – 28 Feb 1508	*Philipp*, the Sincere, nephew (b. 14 Jul 1448)

*By the Treaty of Pavia 1329, the descendants of Rudolf I received the Palatinate of the Rhine, the Upper Palatinate and the electoral right while the descendants of Rudolf's brother, Holy Roman Emperor Ludwig IV the Bavarian, received the duchy of Bavaria

Pallava Kingdom

Territory comprised part of present-day southern India, with the capital at Kanchi (now Conjeevaram).

Kings

c. AD 436	*Simhavarman IV*
c. 450	*Vishnugopa*
(?)	*Simhavishnu*
(?)	*Mahendravarman I*, son, defeated by the Chalukya king Pulakeshin II
c. 642 – 668	*Narasimhavarman I*, conquered the Chalukya capital of Vatapi (now Badami)
(?)	*Mahendravarman II*
c. 674	*Parameshvaravarman I*
(?)	*Narasimhavarman II*
(?)	*Parameshvaravarman II*
(?)	*Mahendravarman III*
c. 717 – 782	*Nandivarman II*
late 9th century	Kingdom overthrown by the Chola king Aditya I

Papacy

Popes (Bishops of Rome)

The bishops of Rome asserted their primacy over other bishops of the Christian Church at an early stage and, from Stephen I onwards, based their claim to primacy on their succession to Peter, held to have been appointed by Jesus to lead the Church. To emphasize this primacy they were regularly addressed as *papa* (i.e. father) by other bishops from about the 6th century and in 1073 Gregory VII prohibited the use of this term of address for any but the bishop of Rome.

From Gregory XV onwards, each pope (with two exceptions in the 16th century) has chosen on election to be known by a name differing from his baptismal name (always choosing the name of a predecessor). In the list baptismal and family names are given in parentheses. Because of their familiarity, the names of the popes are given in conventional English forms; for the Latin equivalents see the table on p. lvix (the language of the early church was probably Greek, however).

When two dates separated by an oblique stroke are given for the beginning of a pontificate the first is of election, the second of coronation (episcopal consecration before the 10th century).

At its greatest extent the temporal domain of the popes (the States of the Church) covered central Italy and the Comtat Venaissin in southern France.

AD ? – 64 or 65 or 67*	*Peter*, Saint (originally *Shim'on* (Hebrew)/*Simon* (Greek); named *Kefa* (i.e. 'rock', Greek form *Kephas*) by Jesus, which was later translated into Greek as *Petros*) (b. Bethsaida of Galilee (site uncertain); d. (martyred(?)) Rome(?))
67(?)	*Linus*, Saint
76(?)	*Anacletus* (or *Cletus*), Saint
88	*Clement I*, Saint (b. Rome(?); d. Rome)
97 or 99	*Evaristus*, Saint (b. Greece(?); d. Rome)
105 or 107 or 109	*Alexander I*, Saint (d. Rome(?))
115 or 116 or 119	*Sixtus* (or *Xystus*) *I*, Saint
125(?)	*Telesphorus*, Saint
136 or 138	*Hyginus*, Saint
140 or 142	*Pius I*, Saint (b. Aquilea; d. Rome)
155	*Anicetus*, Saint (b. Syria(?); d. Rome)
166(?)	*Soter*, Saint (b. Fondi; d. Rome)
175 (or 174?)	*Eleutherius*, Saint (b. Nicopolis, Epirus; d. Rome)
189(?)	*Victor I*, Saint (b. Africa; d. Rome)
199 (or 198)	*Zephyrinus*, Saint (b. Rome(?); d. Rome)
217(?)†	*Calixtus* (or *Callistus*) *I*, Saint (b. Rome; d. Rome)
222 (or 223) – 230	*Urban I*, Saint (b. Rome(?); d. Rome)
21 Jul 230 – 28 Sep 235	*Pontianus*, Saint (b. Rome; d. Sardinia Oct 235) resigned and exiled to Sardinia with 'antipope' Hippolytus† by Emperor Maximin
21 Nov 235 – 3 Jan 236	*Anterus*, Saint (b. Greece; d. Rome)

*Traditions about the first 17 bishops of Rome listed here are unreliable

†217(?) – 235	*Hippolytus*, Saint (b. c. 170; d. Sardinia 235 or 236) consecrated as rival bishop because of doctrinal differences, abandoned claim and exiled with Pontianus to Sardinia by Roman emperor Maximin

10 Jan 236 – 20 Jan 250	*Fabian*, Saint (b. Rome; d. (martyred) Rome)
Mar 251 – Jun 253*	*Cornelius*, Saint (b. Rome; d. Centum Cellae (now Civitavecchia)) banished to Centum Cellae Jun 252 during persecution of Christians by Emperor Gallus
25 Jun 253 – 5 Mar 254	*Lucius I*, Saint (b. Rome; d. Rome)
12 May 254 – 2 Aug 257	*Stephen I*, Saint (b. Rome; d. Rome)
30 Aug 257 – 6 Aug 258	*Sixtus* (or *Xystus*) *II* (b. Greece(?); d. (martyred) Rome)
22 Jul 259 – 26 Dec 268	*Dionysius*, Saint (d. Rome)
5 Jan 269 – 30 Dec 274	*Felix I*, Saint (b. Rome(?); d. Rome)
4 Jan 275 – 7 Dec 283	*Eutychian*, Saint (d. Rome)
17 Dec 283 – 22 Apr 296	*Gaius*, Saint (b. Dalmatia; d. Rome)
30 Jun 296 – 25 Oct 304	*Marcellinus*, Saint (b. Rome; d. Rome)
304 – 308	See vacant
27 May (or 26 Jun) 308 – 16 Jan 309	*Marcellus I*, Saint (b. Rome) banished from Rome by Emperor Maxentius and died shortly after
18 Apr – 17 Aug 309 (or 310)	*Eusebius*, Saint (b. Greece; d. Sicily) for four months; exiled to Sicily by Emperor Maxentius
2 Jul 311 – 11 Jan 314	*Miltiades* (or *Melchiades*), Saint (b. Africa(?); d. Rome)
31 Jan 314 – 31 Dec 335	*Sylvester I*, Saint (b. Rome; d. Rome)
18 Jan – 7 Oct 336	*Mark*, Saint (b. Rome; d. Rome)
6 Feb 337 – 12 Apr 352	*Julius I*, Saint (b. Rome; d. Rome)
17 May 352 – 24 Sep 366†	*Liberius* (b. Rome; d. Rome) exiled to Beroea, Thrace, Nov or Dec 355 by Emperor Constantius II

*251	*Novatian* (d. (martyred) 258) consecrated as rival bishop because of doctrinal differences, excommunicated by Cornelius 251, fled Rome during persecution by Gallus, had following among clergy throughout Christian world
†Nov or Dec 355 – 22 Nov 365	*Felix (II)* (d. Porto, near Rome) put in place of Liberius during exile, fled when Liberius returned to popular acclaim, asked by council of bishops to exercise power jointly with Liberius but never returned

	for supporting Athanasius; allowed to return 358
1 Oct 366 – 11 Dec 384*	*Damasus I*, Saint (b. Rome c. 305; d. Rome)
15 or 22 or 29 Dec 384 – 26 Nov 399	*Siricius*, Saint (b. Rome; d. Rome)
27 Nov 399 – 19 Dec 401	*Anastasius I*, Saint (b. Rome(?); d. Rome)
22 Dec 401 – 12 Mar 417	*Innocent I*, Saint (b. Rome(?); d. Rome)
18 Mar 417 – 26 Dec 418	*Zosimus*, Saint (b. Greece; d. Rome)
28 or 29 Dec 418 – 4 Sep 422 †	*Boniface I*, Saint (b. Rome; d. Rome) elected by *presbyterium*
10 Sep 422 – 27 Jul 432	*Celestine I*, Saint (b. Roman Campagna; d. Rome)
31 Jul 432 – 19 Aug 440	*Sixtus* (or *Xystus*) *III*, Saint (b. Rome; d. Rome)
29 Sep 440 – 10 Nov 461	*Leo I*, the Great, Saint, Doctor of the Church (b. Tuscany c. 400; d. Rome)
19 Nov 461 – 29 Feb 468	*Hilary*, Saint (b. Sardinia; d. Rome)
3 Mar 468 – 10 Mar 483	*Simplicius*, Saint (b. Tivoli; d. Rome)
13 Mar 483	*Felix II (III)*, ‡ Saint (b. Rome; d. Rome)
1 Mar 492 – 21 Nov 496	*Gelasius I*, Saint (b. Africa; d. Rome)
24 Nov 496 – 19 Nov 498	*Anastasius II* (b. Rome; d. Rome)
22 Nov 498 – 19 Jul 514 §	*Symmachus*, Saint (b. Sardinia; d. Rome)

*between 24 Sep and 1 Oct 366 – 367	*Ursinus*, consecrated by followers of Felix (see preceding footnote) and immediately exiled by prefect of Rome, returned Sep 367 and exiled at end of 367 to Gaul, active in Milan 370 – 2
†27 or 29 Dec 418 – 419	*Eulalius*, acclaimed by people of Rome but soon lost support

‡ The higher number is used if Felix (II) (see footnote on p. 415) is counted as a Pope

§Nov 498	*Laurentius*, elected by minority faction, gave up claim when Symmachus received support of the Ostrogothic king Theodoric, became bishop of Nocera, returned late 501 and received popular support as rival to Symmachus for about four years

20 Jul 514 – 6 Aug 523	*Hormisdas*, Saint (d. Rome)
13 Aug 523 – 18 May 526	*John I*, Saint (b. Tuscany; d. (martyred) Ravenna) imprisoned by the Ostrogothic king Theodoric the Great 526
12 Jul 526	*Felix III (IV)*,* Saint (b. Rome; d. Rome)
22 Sep 530 – 17 Oct 532 †	*Boniface II* (b. Rome; d. Rome)
2 Jan 533 – 8 May 535	*John II* (before election: *Mercurius*) (b. Rome; d. Rome)
13 May 535 – 22 Apr 536	*Agapetus* (or *Agapitus*) *I*, Saint (b. Rome; d. Constantinople)
1 Jun 536 – 11 Nov 537	*Silverius*, Saint, son of Hormisdas (d. Ponza 2 Dec 537) taken to Patara, Lycia, Mar 537 at instigation of Empress Theodora; then taken to Ponza and forced to resign
29 Mar 537 – 7 Jun 555	*Vigilius* (b. Rome before 500; d. Syracuse) elected during absence of Silverius and subsequently recognized as legitimate
16 Apr 556 – 4 Mar 561	*Pelagius I* (b. Rome; d. Rome)
17 Jul 561 – 13 Jul 574	*John III* (before election: *Catelinus*) (d. Rome)
2 Jun 575 – 30 Jul 579	*Benedict I* (d. Rome)
26 Nov 579 – 7 Feb 590	*Pelagius II* (d. Rome)
3 Sep 590 – 12 Mar 604	*Gregory I*, the Great, Saint, Doctor of the Church (b. Rome c. 540; d. Rome)
13 Sep 604 – 22 Feb 606	*Sabinian*
19 Feb – 12 Nov 607	*Boniface III* (b. Rome)
25 Aug 608 – 8 May 615	*Boniface IV*, Saint
19 Oct 615 – 8 Nov 618	*Deusdedit* (or *Adeodatus*) *I*, Saint (b. Rome; d. Rome)
23 Dec 619 – 25 Oct 625	*Boniface V* (b. Naples)
27 Oct or 3(?) Nov 625 – 12 Oct 638	*Honorius I* (b. Roman Campagna)

*The higher number is used if Felix (II) (see footnote on p. 415) is counted as a Pope

† 22 Sep – 14 Oct 530 *Dioscorus*, elected by majority faction but died suddenly

28 May – 2 Aug 640	*Severinus* (b. Rome; d. Rome)
24 Dec 640 – 12 Oct 642	*John IV* (b. Dalmatia; d. Rome)
24 Nov 642 – 14 May 649	*Theodore I* (b. Jerusalem)
Jul 649 – 16 Sep 655	*Martin I*, Saint (d. Kherson, Ukraine) captured by troops of the Byzantine emperor 17 Jun 653, taken to Constantinople and condemned to exile for treason
10 Aug 654 – 2 Jun 657	*Eugenius I*, Saint (b. Rome; d. Rome) elected during absence of Martin I
30 Jul 657 – 27 Jan 672	*Vitalian*, Saint (b. Segni, near Rome; d. Rome)
11 Apr 672 – 17 Jun 676	*Deusdedit* (or *Adeodatus*) *II* (b. Rome)
2 Nov 676 – 11 Apr 678	*Donus* (b. Rome; d. Rome)
27 Jun 678 – 10 Jan 681	*Agatho*, Saint
17 Aug 682 – 3 Jul 683	*Leo II*, Saint (b. Sicily; d. Rome)
26 Jun 684 – 8 May 685	*Benedict II*, Saint (b. Rome)
23 Jul 685 – 2 Aug 686	*John V* (b. Syria(?); d. Rome)
21 Oct 686 – 21 Sep 687	*Conon* (d. Rome)
15 Dec 687 – 8 Sep 701*	*Sergius I*, Saint (b. Palermo; d. Rome)
30 Oct 701 – 11 Jan 705	*John VI* (b. Greece(?); d. Rome)
1 Mar 705 – 18 Oct 707	*John VII* (b. Greece(?); d. Rome)
15 Jan – 4 Feb 708	*Sisinnius* (b. Syria; d. Rome)
25 Mar 708 – 9 Apr 715	*Constantine* (b. Syria; d. Rome)
19 May 715 – 11 Feb 731	*Gregory II*, Saint (b. Rome c. 669; d. Rome)
18 Mar 731 – Nov 741	*Gregory III*, Saint (d. Rome)

*At first, *Theodore* and *Paschal* (d. 692) were elected as well as Sergius. A fresh election in Dec 687 decided in favour of Sergius. Theodore acquiesced but Paschal continued to claim to be bishop of Rome and was imprisoned

0 Dec 741 – 22 Mar 752*	*Zachary*, Saint
6 Mar 752 – 26 Apr 757	*Stephen II* (b. Rome; d. Rome) granted by Pippin, the Short, King of the Franks, territory in central Italy that he conquered from Astolfo, King of the Lombards, 754
ıpr/29 May 757 – 28 Jun 767	*Paul I*, Saint, brother (b. Rome; d. Rome)
/7 Aug 768 – 24 Jan 772 †	*Stephen III* (b. Sicily c. 720; d. Rome)
/9 Feb 772 – 25 Dec 795	*Adrian I* (b. Rome)
6/27 Dec 795 – 12 Jun 816	*Leo III*, Saint (b. Rome; d. Rome)
2 Jun 816 – 24 Jan 817	*Stephen IV* (b. Rome; d. Rome)
5 Jan 817 – 11 Feb 824	*Paschal I*, Saint (b. Rome; d. Rome)
etween Feb and May 824 – 27(?) Aug 827	*Eugenius II* (b. Rome; d. Rome)
ug – Sep 827	*Valentinus* (or *Valentine*) (b. Rome; d. Rome)
ate 827	*Gregory IV* (b. Rome; d. Rome)
an 844 – 27 Jan 847 ‡	*Sergius II* (b. Rome; d. Rome)
an/10 Apr 847 – 17 Jul 855	*Leo IV*, Saint (b. Rome; d. Rome)
ul/29 Sep 855 – 17 Apr 858§	*Benedict III*
4 Apr 858 – 13 Nov 867	*Nicholas I*, Saint (b. c. 819 – 22; d. Rome)

22 (23?) – 26 (25?) Mar 752	*Stephen* (b. Rome; d. Rome) died before episcopal consecration
28 Jun/5 Jul 767 – 769	*Constantine (II)*, election secured by his brother, Duke Toto of Nepi; opposed by Lombard king Desiderio; Lateran Council of Apr 769 annulled all acts of Constantine and sentenced him to imprisonment
31 Jul 768	*Philip*, appointed by Desiderio but immediately resigned in favour of Stephen
Jan 844	*John*, a deacon, acclaimed by people of Rome
Aug – Sep 855	*Anastasius*, the Librarian (b. c. 800; d. 879) supported by faction of Holy Roman Emperor Ludwig II

14 Dec 867 – Nov or 14(?) Dec 872	*Adrian II* (b. Rome 792)
14 Dec 872	*John VIII* (b. Rome 820; d. (assassinated) Rome)
16 Dec 882 – 15 May 884	*Marinus I* (or *Martin II*) (b. Gallese, near Rom
17 May 884 – c. Sep 885	*Adrian III*, Saint (b. Rome; d. near Moden canonized 2 Jun 1891
Sep 885 – 14 Sep 891	*Stephen V* (b. Rome; d. Rome)
6 Oct 891 – 4 Apr 896	*Formosus* (b. Rome(?) c. 816)
Apr 896	*Boniface VI* (b. Rome; d. Rome) for 15 days
May 896	*Stephen VI*, imprisoned and strangled duri popular revolt
Aug – Nov 897	*Romanus*
Dec 897	*Theodore II* (b. Rome; d. Rome) for 20 days
Jan 898 – Jan 900	*John IX* (b. Tivoli 840; d. Rome)
Jan or Feb 900	*Benedict IV* (b. Rome)
Jul – Sep 903*	*Leo V* (b. Ardea; d. Rome) imprisoned and killed antipope Christopher
29 Jan 904 – 14 Apr 911	*Sergius III* (b. Rome; d. Rome)
Apr or Jun 911 – Jun or Aug 913	*Anastasius III* (b. Rome; d. Rome)
Jul(?) 913 – Feb(?) 914	*Lando* (b. Rome; d. Rome)
Mar 914	*John X* (b. Tossignano 860; d. Rome)
May 928	*Leo VI* (b. Rome; d. Rome)
Dec 928 – Feb 931	*Stephen VII* (b. Rome; d. Rome)
Feb or Mar 931 – Dec 935	*John XI* (b. Rome 906; d. Rome)
3 Jan 936 – 13 Jul 939	*Leo VII* (b. Rome; d. Rome)
14 Jul 939 – Oct 942	*Stephen VIII* (b. Rome; d. Rome)
30 Oct 942 – Apr or May 946	*Marinus II* (or *Martin III*) (d. Rome)
10 May 946 – Dec 955	*Agapetus* (or *Agapitus*) *II* (b. Rome; d. Rome)
16 Dec 955 – 14 May 964	*John XII* (before election: *Ottaviano*) (b. Ro c. 936; d. Rome) deposed at instigation of H Roman Emperor Otto I 4 Dec 963

*Jul or Sep 903 – Jan 904 *Christopher*, deposed and executed by Sergius III

/6 Dec 963 – 1 Mar 965	*Leo VIII** (b. Rome; d. Rome) nominated by Otto I, deposed and excommunicated by John XII 26 Feb 964, reinstated by Otto 23 Jun 964
2 May 964 – 4 Jul 966(?)	*Benedict V** (d. Hamburg) elected by people of Rome, exiled by Otto I Jun 964
Oct 965 – 6 Sep 972	*John XIII* (b. Rome; d. Rome) supported by Otto I
9 Jan 973 – Jun 974 †	*Benedict VI* (b. Rome; d. in prison Rome Jul 974) imprisoned by the Crescentii
)ct 974 – 10 Jul 983	*Benedict VII* (b. Rome) supported by Emperor Otto II
)ec 983 – 20 Aug 984 ‡	*John XIV* (*Pietro Canepanova*) (b. Pavia; d. Rome) supported by Holy Roman Emperor Otto II, imprisoned in the Castel Sant' Angelo by the Crescentii
ug 985 – Mar 996	*John XV* (b. Rome; d. Rome) supported initially by the Crescentii
May 996 – 18 Feb 999§	*Gregory V* (*Brun von Kärnten*), son of Duke Otto of Carinthia (b. 972; d. Rome) forced into exile by the Crescentii autumn 996 – Mar 998
Apr 999 – 12 May 1003	*Sylvester II* (*Gerbert d'Aurillac*) (b. Auvergne c. 945; d. Rome)
un – Dec 1003	*John XVII* (*Giovanni Sicco*) (b. Rome; d. Rome)
an 1004 – Jul 1009	*John XVIII* (*Giovanni Fasano*) (b. Rome; d. Abbey of St Paul-outside-the-Walls, Rome) retired to Abbey to live as a monk shortly before his death
1 Jul 1009 – 12 May 1012 ‖	*Sergius IV* (*Pietro Buccaporci*) (b. Luna; d. Rome) supported by the Crescentii
8 May 1012 – 9 Apr 1024	*Benedict VIII* (*Teofilatto*), supported by the Tusculani and approved by Holy Roman Emperor Heinrich II

Either Leo VIII or Benedict V may be considered to be an antipope

Jun – Jul 974	*Boniface VII* (before election: *Franco*) (for 1st time) (b. Rome; d. Rome Jul 985) supported by Crescentii, expelled by forces of Holy Roman Emperor Otto II and fled to Constantinople
Aug 984 – Jul 985	*Boniface VII* (for 2nd time) murdered by Roman mob
Apr 997 – Feb 998	*John XVI* (*Giovanni Filagato*) (b. Rossano; d. Fulda 1013?) supported by Crescentii, blinded and sent to monastery by Holy Roman Emperor Otto III
1012	*Gregory (VI)* supported by the Crescentii, abandoned claim when Holy Roman Emperor Heinrich III approved Benedict VIII

Apr or May 1024 – between Oct 1032 and Jan 1033	*John XIX* (*Romano*), brother (d. Rome)
8 Aug or 3(?) Sep 1032 – 1044	*Benedict IX* (*Teofilatto*), nephew (for 1st time (d. Monastery of Grottaferrata(?) end of 1055(?) obtained pontificacy by simony, fled from Rome
20 Jan – 10 Feb 1045	*Sylvester III* (*Giovanni*) elected by people of Rome driven out by supporters of Benedict IX
10 Apr – 1 May 1045	*Benedict IX* (for 2nd time) sold pontificacy
5 May 1045 – 20 Dec 1046	*Gregory VI* (*Giovanni de' Graziani*), godfathe (b. Rome; d. Cologne(?) c. Nov 1047) deposed b Synod of Sutri under influence of Holy Roma Emperor Heinrich III and exiled to Germany
24/25 Dec 1046 – 9 Oct 1047	*Clement II* (*Suidger*) (b. Saxony; d. near Pesaro Bishop of Bamberg 1040 – 1046; supported b Heinrich III
8 Nov 1047	*Benedict IX* (for 3rd time) driven from Rome o orders of Heinrich III
17 Jul – 9 Aug 1048	*Damasus II* (*Poppo*) (b. Bavaria; d. Palestrina)
12 Feb 1049 – 19 Apr 1054	*Leo IX*, Saint (*Bruno*) (b. Eguisheim, nea Colmar, 21 Jun 1002; d. Rome)
16 Apr 1055 – 28 Jul 1057	*Victor II* (*Gebhard*, Count of Dollnstein Hirschberg) (d. Arezzo)
3 Aug 1057 – 29 Mar 1058	*Stephen IX* (*Frédéric*), cousin of Leo IX son of Duke Gothelon I of Lower Lorraine (b Lorraine c. 1000)
24 Jan 1059 – 27 Jul 1061*	*Nicholas II* (*Gérard de Bourgogne*) (b. Chevron en-Bourgogne, Savoy, (now in Isère department France) c. 980; d. Florence) elected at Siena b cardinals who did not recognize antipope Benedict X
1 Oct 1061 – 21 Apr 1073 †	*Alexander II* (*Anselmo*) (b. Baggio, near Milan)
22 Apr/30 Jun 1073 – 25 May 1085 ‡	*Gregory VII*, Saint (*Ildebrando*) (b. Soana(?) Tuscany, c. 1020 – 5; d. Salerno) 'deposed' 1084 b

*5 Apr 1058 – 24 Jan 1059	*Benedict X* (*Giovanni*), proclaimed by the Tusculani, fled o election of Nicholas II
†28 Oct 1061 – 1071	*Honorius (II)* (*Cadalo*) (b. Verona(?) 1009 or 1010; Parma(?)) elected by Roman civilians and dissident clerg supported by German court but abandoned by them afte condemnation by Council of Mantua 1064
‡25 Jun 1080/24 Mar 1084 – 8 Sep 1100	*Clement (III)* (*Ghiberto* or *Wiberto*), elected at Synod o Brixen, supported by Heinrich IV

	Holy Roman Emperor Heinrich IV and fled to Castel Sant' Angelo and then to Salerno, canonized 1606
24 May 1086 – 16 Sep 1087	*Victor III*, Blessed (*Daufari*; adopted name of *Desiderius* on entering monastery) (b. Benevento 1027; d. Monte Cassino) beatified 23 Jul 1887
12 Mar 1088 – 29 Jul 1099	*Urban II*, Blessed (*Odon de Lagny* or *Eudes de Châtillon*) (b. Châtillon-sur-Marne c. 1042; d. Rome) beatified 14 Jul 1881
13/14 Aug 1099 – 21 Jan 1118*	*Paschal II* (*Rainieri*) (b. Bieda)
24 Jan/10 Mar 1118 – 28 Jan 1119+	*Gelasius II* (*Giovanni*) (b. Gaeta; d. Abbey of Cluny) fled to France Sep 1118
2/9 Feb 1119 – 13 Dec 1124	*Calixtus* (or *Callistus*) *II* (*Guido*) (d. Rome)
15/21 Dec 1124 – 13 Feb 1130 ‡	*Honorius II* (*Lamberto Scannabecchi*) (b. Fagnano, near Imola; d. Rome) supported by Frangipani family
14/23 Feb 1130 – 24 Sep 1143 §	*Innocent II* (*Gregorio Papareschi*) (b. Rome) elected by small committee of cardinals, forced by antipope Anacletus II to flee to France
26 Sep/3 Oct 1143 – 8 Mar 1144	*Celestine II* (*Guido*) (b. Macerata(?))
12 Mar 1144 – 15 Feb 1145	*Lucius II* (*Gerard Caccianemici*) (b. Bologna)
15/18 Feb 1145 – 8 Jul 1153	*Eugenius III*, Blessed (*Bernardo*) (b. near Pisa; d. Tivoli) beatified 3 Oct 1872
12 Jul 1153 – 3 Dec 1154	*Anastasius IV* (*Corrado de Suburra*) (b. Rome)

*Antipopes supported by the Holy Roman Emperor's faction:

1100	*Theodoric* (d. near Cava de' Tirreni 1102) confined in monastery by Paschal II 1101
1102	*Albert* (or *Aleric*), captured by Paschal's supporters, blinded and sent to monastery
18 Nov 1105 – 1111	*Sylvester IV* (*Maginolfo*) (b. Rome)
8 Mar 1118 – 1121	*Gregory (VIII)* (*Maurice* or *Mauritius* 'Burdinus' (i.e. 'little mule')) (d. 1137) supported by Emperor Heinrich V, driven out of Rome 1119
Dec 1124	*Celestine (II)* (*Tebaldo Buccapeco*), supported by Pierleoni family, submitted almost immediately to Honorius II
§14/23 Feb 1130 – 25 Jan 1138	*Anacletus II* (*Pietro Pierleoni*) elected by majority of cardinals, supported by King Roger II of Sicily
Mar – 29 May 1138	*Victor (IV)* (*Gregorio*), supported by Roger II, submitted to Innocent II

4/5 Dec 1154 – 1 Sep 1159	*Adrian IV* (*Nicholas Breakspear*) (b. Abbots Langley, England, 1100(?); d. Anagni)
7/20 Sep 1159 – 30 Aug 1181*	*Alexander III* (*Rolando Bandinelli*) (b. Siena c. 1105; d. Rome) in exile in France Apr 1162 – 22 Nov 1165 and in Benevento 1167 – Aug 1177
1/6 Sep 1181 – 25 Sep 1185	*Lucius III* (*Ubaldo Allucingoli*) (b. Lucca 1097(?); d. Verona)
25 Nov/1 Dec 1185 – 20 Oct 1187	*Urban III* (*Uberto Crivelli*) (b. Milan c. 1120; d. Ferrara)
21/25 Oct – 17 Dec 1187	*Gregory VIII* (*Albert de Morra*) (b. Benevento; d. Pisa)
19/20 Dec 1187 – Mar 1191	*Clement III* (*Paolo Scolari*) (b. Rome)
30 Mar(?)/14 Apr 1191 – 8 Jan 1198	*Celestine III* (*Giacinto Bobo* or *Giacinto di Pietro di Bobone*) (b. Rome c. 1106; d. Rome)
8 Jan/22 Feb 1198 – 16 Jul 1216	*Innocent III* (*Lotario dei conti di Segni*) (b. 1160 or 1161; d. Perugia)
18/24 Jul 1216 – 18 Mar 1227	*Honorius III* (*Cencio Savelli*) (b. Rome; d. Rome)
19/21 Mar 1227 – 22 Aug 1241	*Gregory IX* (*Ugolino dei conti di Segni*) (b. Anagni c. 1170; d. Rome)
25/28 Oct – 10 Nov 1241	*Celestine IV* (*Goffredo Castiglioni*), nephew of Urban III (b. Milan)
25/28 Jun 1243 – 7 Dec 1254	*Innocent IV* (*Sinibaldo Fieschi*) (b. Genoa c. 1200; d. Naples)
12/20 Dec 1254 – 25 May 1261	*Alexander IV* (*Rainaldo dei signori di Ienne*), nephew of Gregory IX
29 Aug/4 Sep 1261 – 2 Oct 1264	*Urban IV* (*Jacques Pantaléon*) (b. Troyes, Champagne c. 1200; d. Perugia)
5/15 Feb 1265 – 29 Nov 1268	*Clement IV* (*Gui Foulques*) (b. Saint-Gilles (now in Gard department, France); d. Viterbo)
1 Sep 1271/27 Mar 1272 – 10 Jan 1276	*Gregory X*, Blessed (*Teobaldo* (or *Tebaldo*) *Visconti*) (b. Piacenza 1210; d. Arezzo)
21 Jan/22 Feb	*Innocent V*, Blessed (*Pierre de Tarentaise*)

*Antipopes supported by Holy Roman Emperor Friedrich I Barbarossa:

7 Sep/4 Oct 1159 – 20 Apr 1164	*Victor (IV)* (*Ottaviano de Monticello*) (d. Lucca) (ignored the antipope of 1138 when adopting his name)
22/26 Apr 1164 – 20 Sep 1168	*Paschal III* (*Guido*) (d. Rome)
Sep 1168 – 29 Aug 1178	*Calixtus* (or *Callistus*) *(III)* (*Giovanni*), submitted to Alexander III
29 Sep 1179 – 1180	*Innocent (III)* (*Lando*), sent to monastery

–22 Jun 1276	(b. Champagny, near Albertville (now in Savoie department, France) c. 1224; d. Rome) beatified 13 Mar 1898
1 Jul – 18 Aug 1276	*Adrian V* (*Ottobono Fieschi*), nephew of Innocent IV (b. Genoa early 13th century; d. Viterbo) layman, died before he was ordained or episcopally consecrated
/20 Sep 1276 –20 May 1277	*John XXI** (*Pedro Julião*, also known as *Petrus Hispanus*) (b. Lisbon between c. 1210 and 1215; d. Viterbo)
5 Nov/26 Dec 1277 –22 Aug 1280	*Nicholas III* (*Giovanni Gaetano Orsini*) (b. Rome between 1210 and 1225; d. Soriano nel Cimino, near Viterbo)
2 Feb/23 Mar 1281 –28 Mar 1285	*Martin IV (II)* † (*Simon de Brion* or *Simon de Brie*) (b. near Angers, Anjou; d. Orvieto)
Apr/20 May 1285 –3 Apr 1287	*Honorius IV* (*Giacomo Savelli*), great-nephew of Honorius III (b. Rome 1210; d. Rome)
2 Feb 1288 – 4 Apr 1292	*Nicholas IV* (*Girolamo Masci*) (b. Lisciano, near Ascoli, 30 Sep 1227; d. Rome)
Jul/29 Aug –13 Dec 1294	*Celestine V*, Saint (*Pietro Angeleri* or *Pietro del Morrone*) (b. Isernia 1215; d. Castello di Fumone 19 May 1296) resigned, canonized 5 May 1313
4 Dec 1294/23 Jan 1295 – 11 Oct 1303	*Boniface VIII* (*Benedetto Caetani*) (b. Anagni c. 1235; d. Rome)
2/27 Oct 1303 –7 Jul 1304	*Benedict XI*, Blessed (*Niccolò Boccasini*) (b. Treviso 1240; d. Perugia) beatified 24 Apr 1736
vignon Papacy	
Jun/14 Nov 1305 –20 Apr 1314	*Clement V* (*Bertrand de Got*) (b. Villandraut c. 1260; d. Roquemaure, Comtat Venaissin) crowned at Lyon, settled at Avignon 1309
Aug/5 Sep 1316 –4 Dec 1334 ‡	*John XXII* (*Jacques Duèse* or *Jacques d'Euze*) (b. Cahors c. 1245; d. Avignon)

11th-century historians mistakenly believed there was a pope called John between ntipope Boniface VII and John XV. They therefore numbered John XV to XIX as XVI to X and the next John himself adopted the number XXI.

Martin II and III are now usually known as Marinus I and II

12/22 May 1328 – 25 Aug 1330	*Nicholas (V)* (*Pietro Rainalducci* or *Rainallucci*) (b. Corvaro (now in Rieti province, Italy); d. Avignon 16 Oct 1333) elected by people of Rome at instigation of Holy Roman Emperor Ludwig IV, submitted to John XXII

20 Dec 1334/8 Jan 1335 – 25 Apr 1342	*Benedict XII* (*Jacques Fournier*) (b. Saverdu (now in Ariège department, France); d. Avignon)
7/19 May 1342 – 6 Dec 1352	*Clement VI* (*Pierre Roger*) (b. Maumont (now i Corrèze department, France) c. 1291; d. Avignon)
18/30 Dec 1352 – 12 Sep 1362	*Innocent VI* (*Étienne Aubert*) (b. Beyssac-e Corrèze; d. Avignon)
28 Sep/6 Nov 1362 – 19 Dec 1370	*Urban V*, Blessed (*Guillaume de Grimoar* (b. Grisac castle, Gévaudan, c. 1310; d. Avigno beatified 10 Mar 1870
30 Dec 1370/5 Jan 1371 – 26 Mar 1378	*Gregory XI* (*Pierre-Roger de Beaufort*), nephe of Clement VI (b. Limoges 1329; d. Rome) returne Papal court to Rome 17 Jan 1377

Popes in Rome during Western Schism

8/18 Apr 1378 – 15 Oct 1389	*Urban VI* (*Bartolomeo Prignano*) (b. Napl c. 1318; d. Rome)
2/9 Nov 1389 – 1 Oct 1404	*Boniface IX* (*Pietro Tomacelli*) (b. Napl c. 1355; d. Rome)
17 Oct/11 Nov 1404 – 6 Nov 1406	*Innocent VII* (*Cosimo de' Migliorati*) (b. Sulmon c. 1336; d. Rome)
30 Nov/19 Dec 1406 – 4 Jul 1415	*Gregory XII* (*Angelo Correr*) (b. Venice c. 132 d. Porto, near Rome, 18 Oct 1417) resigned

Antipopes in Avignon during Western Schism

20 Sep/31 Oct 1378 – 16 Sep 1394	*Clement (VII)* (*Robert*) (b. Geneva 1342; Avignon) elected by cardinals who refused t recognize Urban VI, settled in Avignon after failing t expel Urban from Rome
28 Sep/11 Oct 1394 – 23 May 1423	*Benedict (XIII)* (*Pedro de Luna*) (b. Illueca Spain, c. 1328; d. Peñíscola, near Valencia) too refuge in castle at Peñíscola 1415, refused to accep election of Martin V

Antipopes residing in Bologna, appointed by Council of Pisa during Wester Schism

26 Jun/7 Jul 1409 – 3 May 1410	*Alexander V* (*Petros Philargos*) (b. Candi Crete, c. 1339; d. Bologna)
17/25 May 1410 – 29 May 1415	*John (XXIII)* (*Baldassare Cossa*) (b. Naple d. Florence 22 Nov 1419) deposed by Council c Constance

'opes in Rome after resolution of Western Schism

1/21 Nov 1417 – 20 Feb 1431	*Martin V* (*Ottone* (or *Oddone*) *Colonna*) (b. Genazzano; d. Rome) elected by Council of Constance
/11 Mar 1431 – 23 Feb 1447*	*Eugenius IV* (*Gabriele Condulmer*) (b. Venice c. 1383; d. Rome)
/19 Mar 1447 – 24 Mar 1455	*Nicholas V* (*Tommaso Parentucelli*) (b. Sarzana 15 Nov 1397; d. Rome)
/20 Apr 1455 – 6 Aug 1458	*Calixtus* (or *Callistus*) *III* (*Alfonso de Borgia* or *Alfonso de Borja*) (b. near Játiva, Spain, 31 Dec 1378; d. Rome)
9 Aug/3 Sep 1458 – 15 Aug 1464	*Pius II* (*Enea Silvio Piccolomini*) (b. Corsignano (now Pienza), near Siena, 18 Oct 1405; d. Ancona)
0 Aug/16 Sep 1464 – 26 Jul 1471	*Paul II* (*Pietro Barbo*) (b. Venice 23 Feb 1417; d. Rome)
/25 Aug 1471 – 12 Aug 1484	*Sixtus IV* (*Francesco della Rovere*) (b. Celle, near Savona, 21 Jul 1414; d. Rome)
9 Aug/12 Sep 1484 – 25 Jul 1492	*Innocent VIII* (*Giovanni Battista Cibo*) (b. Genoa 1432; d. Rome)

Parthia

At its greatest extent, territory comprised part of present-day south-eastern Turkey, north-eastern Syria, northern Iraq, Iran and southern U.S.S.R., with the capital initially at Dara (present-day Abivard) and then at Hecatompylos (probably near present-day Damghan), Ctesiphon and Susa (present-day Shush).

Kings

Arsacid dynasty

249(?) BC	*Arsaces I*

*5 Nov 1439/24 Jul 1440 – 7 Apr 1449 — *Felix V* (*Amédée*) (b. Chambéry, Savoy, 4 Dec 1383; d. Thonon, near Geneva, Savoy, 7 Jan 1451) Duke (Amédée VIII) of Savoy 1416 – 1434, elected by Council of Basel, received little support, resigned (last antipope)

247(?)	*Tiridates I*, brother*
c. 211	*Artabanus I* (or *Arsaces II* or *III*), Seleucid vassal
c. 191	*P(h)riapatius*, son
c. 176	*Phraates I*, son
c. 171	*Mithridates*† *I* (or *Arsaces IV*), brother
138	*Phraates II*, son
c. 128	*Artabanus II*, son of Priapatius
124/3 – 87	*Mithridates*† *II*, son
c. 91 – 78(?)	*Gotarzes I*, in dispute with Mithridates II and Orodes I
(?) – 78(?)	*Orodes I*
78/7	*Sanatruces* (or *Sinatruces*), brother of Phraates II (b. c. 140)
70	*Phraates III*, son
58/7 – 55	*Mithridates* † *III*, deposed 57 but continued the succession
57	*Orodes II*, brother
37	*Phraates IV*, son (for 1st time) (d. 2 BC)
c. 30	*Tiridates II* (for 1st time) pretender, with Roman support
c. 29	*Phraates IV* (for 2nd time)
c. 28	*Tiridates II* (for 2nd time)
c. 26	*Phraates IV* (for 3rd time) sent elder sons to Rome c. 10 BC ‡, poisoned by Phraataces
2 BC	*Phraataces* (or *Phraates V*), youngest son, assassinated
AD 4	*Orodes III*, assassinated
6/7	*Vonones I*, eldest son of Phraates IV, sent from Rome, defeated by Artabanus III, fled to and ruled in Armenia, assassinated in Syria after 15
11/12 §	*Artabanus III*, son of viceroy of Hyrcania and of Arsacid descent in female line, King of Media Atropatene, seized Armenia 37
38 – 51	*Gotarzes II*, ruling in the north only c. 40 – 47
c. 39 – 47(?) ‖	*Vardanes*, brother, ruling in the south, murdered
51	*Vonones II*, for a few months

*Sometimes identified with *Arsaces I*, sometimes called *Arsaces II*

† Also spelt Mithradates

‡ At this time Parthia was threatened by a pretender named *Meherdates*

§ Throne disputed by *Phraates* c. 35 and by *Tiridates III*, grandson of Phraates IV, c. 36

‖ After Vardanes's death the throne was disputed by *Meherdates*, grandson of Phraates IV

51 – 80(?)	*Vologases I*, son
78	*Pacorus II* (for 1st time) (d. 115)
79	*Artabanus IV*
81 – 115 *	*Pacorus II* (for 2nd time)
105/6 – 147(?) *	*Vologases II*
109/110(?)*	*Osroes* (or *Chosroes*), brother or brother-in-law of Pacorus II (for 1st time) (d. 128?)
116	*Parthamaspates*, son, installed as vassal-king of Parthia and Armenia by the Roman emperor Trajan, expelled by Osroes and made king of Osroene (part of present-day south-eastern Turkey and north-western Syria)
117 – 128(?)	*Osroes* (for 2nd time)
128 – 147(?)	*Mithridates*† *IV*, usurper, ruled in present-day Iran
148 – 192	*Vologases III*
191	*Vologases IV*, initially in rebellion against Vologases III
207 – (?)	*Vologases V*, son, ruled at Ctesiphon, at Seleucia 228/9
213 – 224 (226?)	*Artabanus V*, brother, ruled at Susa, killed in battle against the Sasanid king Ardashir
226 – 227(?)	*Artavasdes*, son
224 – c. 229	Sasanid conquest

Passau

Bishops (and Princes of the Holy Roman Empire from 1217)‡

AD (?)	*Vivilo*
(?)	*Beatus*

*Coins struck by a certain Vologases are dated 89/90. If he is included as Vologases II, the numeration of the kings of this name will require adjustment. Coins are struck by Osroes as early as c. 89/90. It is uncertain to what extent the rival kings overlap and to what extent they alternate.

†Also spelt Mithradates

‡When two dates separated by an oblique stroke are given for the beginning of an episcopate, the first refers to election or nomination and the second to ordination, consecration or investiture

fl. 754	*Sidonius*
(?)	*Anthelm*
(?) – between 26 Sep 770 and 14 Aug 774	*Wisurich*
(?) – 22 Aug 804 or 805	*Waldrich*
(?) – 14 Aug 806	*Urolf*
806 – 8 Dec 817(?)	*Hatto*
817 – 837 or 838	*Reginhar*
838(?) – 864 or 865	*Hartwich*
late 865/early 866 – 26 Dec 874	*Ermanrich*
(?) – 899	*Engilmar*
899	*Wiching*, deposed
899 – 16 Sep 902	*Richar*
903 – 10 Oct 915(?)	*Purchard*
914 – 12 May 930(?)	*Gundbolt*
(?) – 3 Jan 946(?)	*Gerhard*
946(?) – 15 Jun 971	*Adalbert*
971 – 20 May 991	*Piligrim*
991(?) – 20 or 21 Sep 1013	*Christian*
1013 – 14 Jul 1045	*Beringer*
1045(?) – 17 May 1065	*Engilbert*
midsummer(?) 1065 – 8 Aug 1091*	*Altmann*
16 May 1092 – 6 Aug 1121	*Udalrich*
1121 – 30 Sep 1138	*Reginmar*
1138 – 10 Nov 1147	*Reginbert* (d. on expedition to Jerusalem)
1147 – 1164	*Konrad I* (d. 28 Sep 1168) translated to Salzburg
Jul 1164 – 5 Nov 1165	*Rupert*
11 Nov 1165 – 1169	*Albo*, deposed
4 Aug 1169 – 1171	*Heinrich I von Berg*, resigned
Feb or Mar 1172 – 3 Nov 1190	*Dietbald von Berg*
11 Mar/9 Jun 1191 – 1204	*Wolfger von Ellenbrechtskirchen* (d. 1218) became patriarch of Aquileia
before 15 Oct 1204 – 17 Feb 1206(?)	*Poppo*

*1085 – 1087	*Hermann*, Imperial anti-bishop
1087 – c. 1092	*Thiemo*, Imperial anti-bishop

206 – 9 or 10 Jun 1215	*Manegold*
215/1216 – 31 Oct 1221	*Ulrich II*
222 – 10 Oct 1232	*Gebhard von Plain*, resigned
?7 Jun 1233 – 1249	*Rudiger von Radeck* (d. Passau 1257) deposed by Berthold
?8 Jan 1249 – 1250	*Konrad II*, son of Duke Henryk II of Silesia (d. 6 Aug 1273 or 1274); resigned; Duke of Silesia-Glogau 1251
5 Feb 1249/1 Jul 1250 – 10 Apr 1254	*Berthold*, Count of Petinkeu and Sigmaringen, appointed temporal administrator in opposition to Rudiger von Radeck 15 Feb 1249, in disputed election against *Bernhard* (or *Marquard*) *von Morsbach*, invested 1 Jul 1250, seized Passau 11 Sep 1250
after 10 Apr/26 Jul 1254 – 9 Apr 1265	*Otto von Lonsdorf*
after 10 Apr – 10 Nov 1265	*Władysław*, Duke of Breslau (d. 27 Apr 1270) translated to Salzburg
?4 Nov 1265/before 11 Jun 1267 – 1 May 1280	*Peter*
c. Mar/5 May 1280 – 18 Dec 1282	*Weichard von Polheim* (d. Vienna)
10 Feb/7 Mar 1283 – 26 Apr 1285	*Gottfried I*
May 1285 – 28 Jul 1313	*Bernhard* (or *Werenhard*) *von Prambach*
after 28 Jul 1313 – 12 Jun 1315(?)	*Gebhard von Wallsee* (d. Avignon) in disputed election against the Austrian prince, *Albert*; never consecrated
3 Jun 1317 – 1319	*Henri de Viennois*, under age, translated to Metz
14 Jun 1320/14 Jun 1321 – 19 May 1342	*Albert* (or *Albrecht*) *von Sachsen*, son of Duke Albrecht II of Saxony (b. c. 1285)
3 Jun/6 Aug 1342 – 16 Sep 1362	*Gottfried II von Weisseneck*
after 25 May 1363/29 Jan 1364 – Apr 1380	*Albert III von Winkel* (or *Winkler*)
before 29 Mar 1381 – 3 Feb 1387	*Johann I von Scharffenberg*, nephew of Gottfried II
after 3 Feb 1387/Jan 1388 – 1388	*Hermann Digni*, in rivalry with Rupert von Jülich-Berg, resigned, supported candidature of Georg von Hohenlohe
11 May 1387 – 15 Mar 1389	*Rupert von Jülich-Berg* (d. 25 Jun 1394) Papal candidate, translated to Paderborn

18 Jun 1389 – 8 Aug 1423	*Georg von Hohenlohe* (d. Gran) Austrian candidat
10 Jan 1424 – 24 Jun 1451	*Leonhard von Laymingen*, in disputed electio against *Heinrich Flöchl*
4 Nov 1454 – 2 Sep 1479	*Udalric Nussdorfer*
28 Jan 1480 – 1482	*Georg Hesler*
4 Nov 1482 – 22 Nov 1485	*Friedrich I Mauerkirchner*
15 Feb 1486 – 3 Mar 1490	*Friedrich II*, Count of Oettingen
26 Jun 1490 – 3 Jan 1500	*Christof von Schachner*

Pergamum

Territory comprised part of present-day western Turkey, with the capital a Pergamum (present-day Bergama).

Kings

Attalids

282 BC	*Philetaerus*, a eunuch, lord of Pergamum as the vassa of Lysimachus of Thrace and then of the Seleuci kings Seleucus I Nicator and Antiochus I Soter
263	*Eumenes I*, nephew, declared independence fror Antiochus I Soter
241	*Attalus I Soter*, nephew, defeated the Galatian declared himself king 241
197	*Eumenes II Soter*, son, allied with Rome
160/59	*Attalus II Philadelphus*, brother
139/8 – 133	*Attalus III Philometor Euergetes*, nephew, willed hi kingdom to Rome
129	Incorporated into the Roman province of Asia

Persian Empire

At its greatest extent, territory comprised part of present-day Turkey, north-eastern Greece, Cyprus, south-western U.S.S.R., Iran, Afghanistan, northern Iraq, Syria, Lebanon, Israel, Egypt, northern Sudan and north-eastern Libya, with capitals at Ecbatana (present-day Hamadan), Pasargadae, Babylon and Susa (present-day Shush).

Kings

Achaemenids

(?) BC	*Cyrus I*, son of Teispes, ruled Anshan (present-day south-western Iran), Assyrian vassal
c. 600	*Cambyses I*, son, ruled Anshan, vassal of the Median king Astyages
c. 559	*Cyrus II*, the Great, son (b. Media or Persis between 590 and 580) overthrew Astyages and conquered the Median empire 550; conquered kingdom of Lydia 546; conquered Babylonian empire 12 Oct 539; established capitals at Ecbatana, Pasargadae and Babylon
529	*Cambyses II*, son, appointed regent in Babylon 530, conquered 26th dynasty of Egypt 525, King of Egypt 525 - 521
522	*Darius I*, the Great; son of Hystaspes, the satrap of Parthia (b. 550) member of the bodyguard of Cambyses II; deposed the usurper Bardiya (or Gaumata the Magician); King of Egypt 521 - 486; expanded the empire as far east as the Indus valley; conquered Thrace and Macedonia c. 513, defeated by the Athenians at the battle of Marathon Sep 490; established capital at Susa and founded new royal residence at Persepolis
486	*Xerxes I*, son (b. c. 519) before 486 governor of Babylon, King of Egypt 486 - 466, defeated by the Athenians at the battle of Salamis 29 Sep 480, assassinated
465	*Artaxerxes I*, Macrocheir i.e. Longhand, son, King of Egypt 465 - 424
425	*Xerxes II*, son, King of Egypt 424
424	*Sogdianos*, half-brother, for seven months, deposed

	and executed by Darius II Ochus
423	*Darius II Ochus*, Nothos i.e. the Bastard, half-brother, King of Egypt 424 – 404
404	*Artaxerxes II*, Mnemon i.e. the Mindful, son, lost Egypt 404, defeated and killed the rebel Cyrus the Younger* at Cunaxa 401
359/8	*Ochus Artaxerxes III*, son, conquered Egypt 343, King of Egypt 343 – 338, assassinated by the eunuch Bagoas
Nov 338	*Arses*, son, King of Egypt 338 – 335, placed on throne and later assassinated by Bagoas
336 – 330	*Darius III Codommanus*, great-grandson of Darius II Ochus (d. Bactria 330) King of Egypt 335 – 332, placed on throne by Bagoas, defeated by Alexander the Great 1 Oct 333, fled to Bactria where he was deposed and killed by the satrap Bessus
330	Conquest by Alexander the Great, Persia became part of the Macedonian Empire

Poland

There is no consensus on the treatment of the names of Polish rulers, some writers using the original Polish in all cases, others anglicizing some or all of the names. English forms will be found on p. xlvii. As with other states, epithets are translated, but in view of the frequency with which in the literature the Polish epithets are used untranslated, even to the exclusion of the name, the original Polish is added in parentheses. This will mean, for instance, that those who meet with plain Łokietek will be able to equate it with Władysław, the Short.

Dukes and Grand Dukes

AD 861	*Siemowit*, 'son of Piast', Duke of Polanie
892	*Leszek* (or *Lestek* or *Lestko*), son (d. 921) Duke of Polanie

**Cyrus the Younger*, brother of Ochus Artaxerxes II; satrap of Lydia and Phrygia and Cappadocia (all in present-day western Turkey); commander-in-chief of forces in Asia Minor from 407; rebelled 401

913	*Ziemomysł*, son (b. c. 900) Duke of Polanie, conquered Mazovia
c. 960	*Mieszko I*, son (b. c. 922) Duke of Poland, conquered Western Pomerania 967 – 972, conquered Silesia and Cracow 989 – 992
25 May 992	*Bolesław I*, the Brave (Chrobry), son (b. c. 967) annexed Lusatia and Milzenland and Moravia 1018, crowned king 1025
17 Jul 1025	*Mieszko II Lambert*, son (for 1st time) (b. 990; d. 10 May 1034) King, expelled by Bezprym
1031	*Bezprym*, brother (b. 986/7; d. c. 1032) Duke, gave up Lusatia and Moravia
1032	*Mieszko II* (for 2nd time) Duke; ruled with his brother, *Otto* (d. 1033) and his cousin, *Dytryk*, supposedly Duke of Pomerania (d. after 7 Jul 1032)
25 Apr 1034 – 1037(?)	*Kazimierz I*, the Restorer (Odnowiciel), son (for 1st time) (b. 25 Jul 1016; d. 28 Nov 1058) expelled
1034 – 1039	Period of anarchy, Western Pomerania and Silesia lost*
1039	*Kazimierz I* (for 2nd time) Silesia regained, Cracow made capital
1058 – 11 Apr 1079	*Bolesław II*, the Bold (Śmiały) or the Generous (Szczodry), son (b. c. 1042; d. 1081) Duke, crowned King 25 Dec 1076, expelled, fled to Hungary
1079 – 4 Jun 1102	*Władysław Herman*, brother (b. c. 1043), Duke
1097	Country divided, Władysław retaining his old dukedom of Mazovia and the principal towns
1097 – 1107	*Zbigniew*, son (b. before 1080; d. after 1112) Duke of Great Poland and Cujavia (and of Mazovia from 1102)
1099	*Bolesław III*, the Wrymouth (Krzywousty), brother (b. 20 Aug 1085) Duke of Little Poland and Silesia 1099 – 1107, Duke of Poland 1107 – 1138
1138	Statute passed providing for division of country among the sons of the reigning duke, with the eldest member of the dynasty as Grand Duke (the several duchies were later further subdivided)
28 Oct 1138	*Władysław II*, the Exile (Wygnaniec), son (b. 1105; d. 30 May 1159) Duke of Silesia and of Cracow and Grand Duke, expelled by Bolesław IV

*Of the lords who ruled various parts of Poland only *Miecław* (or *Majsław* or *Masław*), Duke of Mazovia 1037 – 1047, is known by name.

1146	*Bolesław IV*, the Curly (Kędzierzawy), brother (b. 1125) Duke of Mazovia and part of Cujavia from 28 Oct 1138, Duke of Silesia and of Cracow and Grand Duke 1146, Duke of Sandomir 1166, vassal of the Holy Roman Emperor Friedrich I 1157
3 Nov 1173	*Mieszko III*, the Old (Stary), brother (for 1st time) (b. 1126/7; d. 13 Mar 1202) Duke of Greater Poland, Poznań and part of Cujavia from 28 Oct 1138; Grand Duke 1173; expelled from Cracow and Greater Poland, regained part of Greater Poland 1181
1177 – 1190/1	*Kazimierz II*, the Just (Sprawiedliwy), brother (for 1st time) (b. 1138; d. 5 May 1194) Duke of Cracow and Sandomir and Grand Duke 1177, Duke of Mazovia and Cujavia 1186
1180	Principle of seniorate abolished and hereditary dukedom of Cracow created
1190/1	*Mieszko III* (for 2nd time)
1190/1 – 5 May 1194	*Kazimierz II* (for 2nd time)
1194 – 1211*	Intermittent civil war between Mieszko III, Mieszko Plątonogi, Duke of Ratibor and Oppeln, and Leszek I
1194	*Leszek I*, the White (Biały), son of Kazimierz II (for 1st time) (b. c. 1186; d. 23 Nov 1227) Duke of Cracow and Sandomir
1194	*Mieszko III* (for 3rd time) *de facto* Grand Duke
1195 – 1198/9, 1201 and 1202 – 1210	*Leszek I* (for 2nd time) Regent: 1198/9 – 13 Mar 1202: *Mieszko III* (see above)
end of 1210(?)	*Mieszko Plątonogi*, Duke of Ratibor and Oppeln, *de facto* Grand Duke
16 May 1211 – 23 Nov 1227	*Leszek I* (for 3rd time)

*During the period 1194 – 1227 two ideas of central authority, that of the senior duke, as established by the testament of Bolesław III in 1138, and that of the hereditary dukedom of Cracow set up by Kazimierz II in 1180, were at odds. After the death of Leszek I the central authority for a time was only fitfully exercised, but the dukes of the former grand-ducal territory of Cracow, including those who reigned during the minority of Bolesław the Chaste, are frequently listed among the grand dukes and kings.

THE POLAND OF THE SEPARATE DUCHIES

CRACOW AND SANDOMIR (LITTLE POLAND)*

1227/43 – 7 Dec 1279	*Bolesław (V)*, the Chaste (Wstidliwy), son of Grand Duke Leszek (b. 21 Jun 1226) *De facto* dukes during minority: 1227 – 1228: *Władysław*, called Spindleshanks (Laskonogi), Duke of Greater Poland (see below) 1228 – 1232: Dukedom of Cracow contested by Duke Henryk I of Silesia, later also by Duke Konrad I of Mazovia and Cujavia 1232 – 19 Mar 1238: *Henryk I*, the Bearded (Brodaty), Duke of Silesia (b. c. 1163) 1238 – 9 Apr 1241: *Henryk II*, the Pious (Pobozny), Duke of Silesia (b. c. 1191) 1241 – 1243: *Konrad I*, Duke of Mazovia and Cujavia (see below)
1279 – 30 Sep 1288	*Leszek II*, the Black; grandson of Duke Konrad I of Mazovia and Cujavia (b. c. 1240) Duke of Leczyca and Sieradz 1260
1289 – 23 Jun 1290	*Henryk*, Probus, Duke (Henryk IV) of Breslau (b. c. 1257) bequeathed dukedom to Przemysł
1290	*Przemysł II*, Duke of Greater Poland (see below)
1290 – 21 Jun 1305	*Wacław I*, King (Václav II) of Bohemia (b. 17 Sep 1271) invaded Little Poland 1290, expelled the Duke of Greater Poland early 1300 and assumed title, crowned King of Poland Sep 1300, King (Vencel) of Hungary 1301 – 1304, lost Sandomir Feb(?) 1305
Jun 1305	*Wacław II*, King (Václav III) of Bohemia, son (b. 6 Oct 1289; d. (assassinated) 4 Aug 1306) nominally King of Poland, lost Cracow to Władysław I
spring 1306 – 2 Mar 1333	*Władysław*, the Short (Łokietek) (see Mazovia and Cujavia) King of Poland 20 Jan 1320

GREATER POLAND

1202	*Władysław*, called Spindleshanks (Laskonogi), son of Grand Duke Mieszko III (b. 1161/7; d. 3 Nov 1231)
1229	*Władysław Odonic*, nephew (b. c. 1190; d. 5 Jun 1239)

*See footnote on p. 436

1239	*Przemysł I* and *Bolesław*, sons (see below)
1247 – 1257	Duchy divided between Przemysł I and Bolesław
1247 – 4 May 1257	*Przemysł* (or *Przemysław*) *I* (b. 1220/1; d. 4 May 1257) Duke of Poznań, Duke of Kalisz 1249 – 1253, Duke of Gniezno from 1250
1247	*Bolesław*, the Pious (Pobożny), brother (b. after 1221; d. 13 Apr 1279) Duke of Kalisz 1247 – 1249 and 1253 – 1257, Duke of Gniezno 1249 – 1250, Duke of Greater Poland 4 May 1257
12 Apr 1279 – 8 Feb 1296	*Przemysł II*, son of Przemysł I (b. 14 Oct 1257) Duke of Cracow 1290, Duke of Pomerelia and King of Poland 1295
Feb/Mar 1296	*Władysław*, the Short, Duke of Brest (for 1st time) (see Mazovia and Cujavia) vassal of Bohemia Aug 1299, expelled by Wacław
1300 – 21 Jun 1305	*Wacław I*, King (Václav II) of Bohemia, King (Vencel) of Hungary 1301 – 1304 (see Cracow and Sandomir)
1306 – 9 Dec 1309	*Henryk*, Duke of Glogau, styled from 1305 'heir to the kingdom of Poland'
1309	The five sons of Henryk, local nobility in revolt
1314	*Władysław*, the Short (for 2nd time) King of Poland 20 Jan 1320

MAZOVIA AND CUJAVIA

1202 – 31 Aug 1247	*Konrad I*, son of Grand Duke Kazimierz II (b. 1187/8)
1248	Duchy divided*
1248 – 1262	*Siemowit I*, son (b. 1224) Duke of Mazovia
1248 – 14(?) Dec 1267	*Kazimierz I*, brother (b. c. 1211) Duke of Cujavia, Łęczyca and Sieradz
1262 – 23 Jun 1294	*Konrad II*, son of Siemowit I (b. c. 1252) Duke of Mazovia
1262 – 1294	*Bolesław II*, brother (b. c. 1260; d. 20 Apr 1313) Duke of Plock, later of Czersk; from 1294 Duke of Mazovia (see below)
Dec 1267 – 1287	*Siemomysł*, son of Kazimierz I (b. 1241/5) Duke of (northern) Cujavia, driven out during 1268 by Duke Bolesław of Greater Poland
1260 – 10 Sep 1288	*Leszek*, the Black (Czarny), brother (b. c. 1240) Duke

*Division agreed 1233

	of Sieradz and Łęczyca
1275	*Władysław*, the Short (Łokietek), brother (b. 1260; d. 2 Mar 1333) Duke of Łęczyca and Cujavia and from Jun 1294 of Sieradz; Duke of Greater Poland Feb/Mar 1296 – 1300 and 1314; Duke of Cracow spring 1306; expelled 1300 – 1306 by King Václav II of Bohemia (King Wacław I of Poland); King of Poland 20 Jan 1320
1287/1294	*Leszek*, son of Siemomysł (b. 1276/7; d. c. 1340) Duke of Inowrocław, at first under the guardianship of his mother and brothers
30 Sep 1288	*Kazimierz II*, son of Kazimierz I; Duke of Łęczyca and Sieradz
1306	Cujavia, Sieradz and Łęczyca reintegrated in the kingdom of Poland (see below); Mazovia (see below) remained independent, became vassal 1355 and was reintegrated 1526

MAZOVIA ONLY

1294	*Bolesław II*, formerly Duke of Plock (see Mazovia and Cujavia)
20 Apr 1313	Duchy divided*
20 Apr 1313 – Nov/Dec 1343	*Siemowit II*, son (b. 1283) Duke of Wiżna, Rawa and Sochaczew
20 Apr 1313 – 13 Mar 1341	*Trojden*, brother (b. c. 1285) Duke of Czersk, Warsaw, Łomża, Ciechanów, Rożan, Nursk and Liw
20 Apr 1313 – 23 May 1336	*Wacław* (or *Wańko*), brother (b. c. 1293) Duke of Płock, Gostynin, Wyszogród and Zakroczym
1338 – 20 Aug 1351	*Bolesław III*, son (b. 1322 or later) Duke of Płock, Gostynin, Wyszogród and Zakroczym, and (after 18 Feb 1345) of Sochaczew and Wiżna
1341 – 18 Feb 1345	*Siemowit III*, son of Siemowit II, Duke of Wiżna, Rawa and Sochaczew
1341 – 26 Nov 1355	*Kazimierz I*, son of Trojden (b. before 1329) Duke of Czersk, Warsaw, Łomża, Ciechanów, Rożan, Nursk and Liw 1341, of Rawa 1345, of Sochaczew 1351
1341 – 16 Jun 1381	*Siemowit III* (or *IV*), the Elder (Starszy), brother (b.

*As the allocation of the duchies into which Mazovia was divided and sub-divided varied from time to time, it seemed better in this case to list the dukes in one chronological sequence and not by duchy.

	before 1326) Duke of Czersk, Rawa and Sochaczew with Kazimierz I, Duke of Wiżna and Mazovia 1370; became vassal of Poland 1355
1374	Duchy again divided
1374/1381 – 8 Dec 1429	*Janusz I*, the Elder (Starszy), son (b. c. 1340) Duke of Wyszogród, Ciechanów, Zakroczym, Liw, Wiżna and Warsaw, and (from 1379) of Czersk
1374/1381 – 1425/6	*Siemowit IV* (or *V*), brother (b. before 1352) Duke of Czersk until 1379; Duke of Sochaczew, Rawa, Płock, Gostynin, Płoń, Wiżna, Cujavia and Bełz
1426	Duchy further divided
1426 – 17 Feb 1442	*Siemowit V* (or *VI*), son (b. c. 1389) Duke of Rawa, Sochaczew and Gostynin
1426 – 15 Sep 1442	*Kazimierz II*, brother (b. c. 1400) Duke of Bełz
1426 – 24 Jul 1427	*Trojden II*, brother (b. c. 1400) Duke of Płock
1426 – 11/12 Dec 1455	*Władysław I*, brother (b. 1398/1411) Duke of Płock, Wiżna, Zawkrze, and (from 1442(?)) of Sochaczew, Gostynin and Bełz
8 Dec 1429 – 10 Sep 1454	*Bolesław IV*, grandson of Janusz I (b. 1421) Duke of Warsaw, Czersk, Zakroczym, Ciechanów, Łomża and Płock
1454/1462 – 28 Oct 1503	*Konrad III*, the Red (Rudy), son (b. c. 1448) Duke of Czersk and Liw 1454/62, of Płock 1462, of Wyszogród 1474, of Warsaw, Zakroczym and Nur 1488; lands declared forfeit 1496; reinstated in Czersk by Jan Olbracht, King of Poland, who assumed title of Lord of Mazovia; granted the remaining territories for life, with Płock, Wiżna, Ciechanów and Łomża
1454 – 1475	*Kazimierz III*, son of Bolesław IV (b. c. 1449; d. 9 Jun 1480) Duke of Wyszogród and Zakroczym, and (from 1462) of Płock, Płoń and Wiżna
1455/2 Jan 1459 – 1462	*Siemowit VI* (or *VII*), son of Władysław I (b. 1444/6; d. 1 Jan 1462) and *Władysław II*, brother (b. 1445/7; d. 26/27 Feb 1462) Dukes of Płock, Wiżna, Zawkrze, Płoń, Rawa, Sochaczew, Gostynin and Bełz
1471 – 27 Apr 1488	*Bolesław V*, son of Bolesław IV (b. before 10 Sep 1454) Duke of Warsaw and Nur, and from 1475 of Zakroczym, Płock and Wiżna
1471 – 14 Feb 1495	*Janusz II*, brother (b. 1455) Duke of Łomża and Ciechanów, and from 1475 of Płock, Wiżna, Wyszogród and Warsaw
1503 – 1524/1526	*Stanisław*, son of Konrad III (b. Jun 1501; d. 1524) and *Janusz III*, brother (b. winter 1502/3; d. 9 Mar

	1526) granted duchies of Czersk, Warsaw, Zakroczym, Ciechanów, Łomża, Wyszogród and Nowogród
1526	Mazovia incorporated in Poland

KINGDOM OF POLAND*

26 Jun 1295 – 8 Feb 1296	*Przemysł II*, Duke of Greater Poland (see Greater Poland) King of Greater Poland and Pomerelia(?)
Sep 1300 – 21 Jun 1305	*Wacław I*, King (Václav II) of Bohemia (see Cracow and Sandomir)
1306/20 Jan 1320	*Władysław I*, the Short (Łokietek) (see Mazovia and Cujavia) lost Cujavia 1329/32
2 Mar 1333	*Kazimierz III*, the Great (Wielki), son (b. 30 Apr 1310) recovered Cujavia 1343
5 Nov 1370 – 10/11 Sep 1382	*Ludwik*, King (Lajos) of Hungary, nephew (b. 3 Mar 1326 Regents: 1370 – 1377: *Elżbieta*, mother, sister of Kazimierz III (for 1st time) (b. 1300; d. 29 Dec 1381) 1378 – 1379: *Władysław*, Duke of Oppeln (d. 1401) 1379 – 1380: *Elżbieta* (for 2nd time) 1380 – 1382: Five regents under the leadership of *Zawisza of Kurozwęki*, Bishop of Cracow (d. 12 Jan 1382)
1382 – 1384	The Council of Regency continued to act
1384	*Jadwiga*, daughter of Ludwik (b. c. 1374; d. 17 Jul 1399)
1386	*Władysław II Jagiełło* (or *Jogaila*), husband (b. c. 1351) Grand Duke (Iogaila) of Lithuania 1377 – summer 1381 and 1382 – 1401, Supreme Duke of Lithuania 1401 – 1434
1 Jun 1434	*Władysław III*, Warneńczyk, son (b. Cracow 21 Oct 1424; d. Varna 10 Nov 1444) Supreme Duke (Władysław) of Lithuania 1434 – 1440, King (Ulászló I) of Hungary 1440 Regent: *Zbigniew of Oels*, Bishop of Cracow (b. 1389; d. 1455)

*As the re-establishment of the kingdom was a somewhat lengthy and spasmodic process, there is some overlap with the divided duchies above.

31 Oct 1444 – 25 Jun 1447	Interregnum
25 Jun 1447* – 7 Jun 1492	*Kazimierz IV*, Jagiełłończyk, Grand Duke (Kazimierz) of Lithuania, brother (b. 30 Nov 1427)

Pomerania

The region known as Pomerania extended along the Baltic Sea coast of Germany and Poland from Stralsund to the River Vistula and included the island of Rügen (q.v.). The eastern part of the region became known as Pomerelia (q.v.) but its separate identity was not clearly established before the late 12th century and it is not always certain what territory was held by the earlier dukes.

All rulers in the following list are dukes of Pomerania, the official style being, for example, Duke of Pomerania at Stettin.

German forms of place names are used. The Polish equivalents are: Barth, Bardo; Rügenwalde, Darłówo; Demmin, Dynin; Schlawe, Sławno; Steinborg, Kamien; Stettin, Szczecin; Stolp, Słupsk; Wolgast, Wołogoszcz. Of these towns, Barth, Demmin and Wolgast are now in the German Democratic Republic and the others are now in Poland.

Dukes

AD 967 – 972†	Conquered by Mieszko I, Duke of Poland
972 – c. 1050	Directly governed(?)
c. 1050†	*Siemomysł* (or *Ziemomysł*), restored by Kazimierz I, Duke of Poland; possibly only in eastern Pomerania
fl. c. 1100†	*Świętobor*, son(?)
c. 1106 – 1121†	*Świętopełk*, son(?), on the Oder (odrzanski)

* Date of coronation. Kazimierz was invited to accept the throne as King of Poland and Lithuania in spring 1445 and accepted in Sep 1446, but without agreeing to more than a personal union of the territories.

† Both Świętobor and Świętopełk are described in *Kronika Galla* as kinsman of Bolesław III, Duke of Poland. A modern conjectural pedigree makes Siemomysł the son of Dytryk (co-ruler of Poland with Mieszko II and supposedly Duke of Pomerania), and Dytryk the son of Świętopełk alias Mieszko, the son of Mieszko I, making the Swiętopełk of the list the fourth cousin of Bolesław. The prevalence of Bogusław, the Polish equivalent of Dytryk, among the names of the Pomeranian dukes may be significant in this context, but it should be noted that Swiętopełk and Mieszko, sons of Mieszko I, are not usually identified.

1121(?) – 1147/8	*Warcisław I*, son(?), vassal of Poland
(?) – 7 May 1156	*Racibor I*, brother, at first at Schlawe
1156 – 18 May 1187	*Bogusław I*, son of Warcisław I (b. c. 1130) at first jointly with *Kazimierz I* (see below), then at Stettin; at Stettin and Demmin from 1180; vassal of the Holy Roman Emperor 1184
1156 – 1180	*Kazimierz I*, brother, at Demmin
1156 – 1194(?)	*Bogusław*, son of Racibor I (b. 1138) with his brothers, *Świętopełk* (fl. 1175) and *Warcisław* (fl. 1186) (?) at Schlawe
1187 – 23/24 Jan 1220	*Bogusław II*, son of Bogusław I (b. c. 1178) at Stettin, at first under the guardianship of Warcisław of Schlawe (?) (see above)
1187 – 1219/20	*Kazimierz II*, brother (b. c. 1180) at Demmin
1194(?)	*Bogusław III*, son of Bogusław (or of Warcisław?), at Schlawe
c. 1200 – 1238	*Racibor II*, son (or brother?), at Schlawe, lost Schlawe to Denmark 1205 – 1225(?), line extinct with his death
1219/20 – 17 May 1264	*Warcisław II*, son of Kazimierz II (b. c. 1210) at Demmin
1220	*Barnim I*, son of Bogusław II (b. c. 1210) at Stettin until 1264; lost Schlawe to Wisław II, Prince of Rügen c. 1260; with Bogusław IV from 1276
13/14 Dec 1278	*Bogusław IV*, son (b. c. 1252; d. 13 Feb 1309) with his brothers, *Barnim II* (b. c. 1275; d. 26 Jun 1295) and *Otto I* (b. 1279; d. 30/31 Dec 1344)
1295	Duchy divided

At Wolgast

1295	*Bogusław IV* (see above)
19 Feb 1309	*Warcisław IV*, son (b. c. 1290) Duke at Rügen from 8 Nov 1325
1 Aug 1326 – 1368	*Bogusław V*, son (b. 1318/9; d. 7 Dec 1373) with his brothers, *Barnim IV* (b. c. 1325(?); d. 22 Aug 1365) and *Warcisław V* (b. Nov(?) 1326; d. 1390) Guardian: 1326 – 1332: *Barnim III*, Duke at Stettin 1320 (see below)
1368	Stolp (see below), under *Bogusław V*, separated from Wolgast
1368 – 7 Mar 1393	*Warcisław V* (see above) ruled until 1390 with *Warcisław VI* (b. c. 1345; d. 13 Jun 1394) and

	Bogusław VI (b. c. 1350; d. 7 Mar 1393), sons of Barnim IV
1372	Barth and Rügen (see below), under *Warcisław VI*, separated from Wolgast
7 Mar 1393	Wolgast, Barth and Rügen re-united under *Warcisław VI*
13 Jun 1394	Barth and Rügen again separated
13 Jun 1394	*Warcisław VIII*, son of Warcisław VI (b. 1373) incorporated Barth and Rügen 1405(?)
22/23 Aug(?) 1415	*Warcisław IX*, son (b. c. 1400); with his brother, *Barnim VII* (b. c. 1404; d. 21 Jun 1451); confirmed by King Sigismund of Germany; reunited Rügen and Wolgast c. 15 Dec 1451
17 Apr 1457	*Eryk II*, son of Warcisław IX (b. 1425; d. 5 Jul 1474) Duke at Stolp Jun 1459 – 1464, Duke at Stettin 1464 (see below)
1459(?)	*Warcisław X*, brother (b. c. 1435) Duke at Barth 17 Apr 1457, reunited Barth and Rügen with Wolgast
17 Dec 1478	*Bogusław X*, son of Eryk II (b. 3 Jun 1454) Duke at Stettin 5 Jul 1474, Duke of re-united (western) Pomerania
5 Dec 1523	*Jerzy I*, son (b. 11 Apr 1493) with his brother, *Barnim IX* (b. 2 Dec 1501; d. 2 Nov 1573) Dukes of (western) Pomerania
9/10 May 1531	*Barnim IX* (see above) and *Filip I*, son of Jerzy I (b. 14 Jul 1415; d. 14 Feb 1560) Dukes of (western) Pomerania
1532	Stettin, under Barnim IX, separated once more from Wolgast
1532	*Filip I*, Duke at Wolgast
14 Feb 1560	*Ernest Ludwik*, son (b. 2 Nov 1545) under the guardianship of *Barnim IX* of Stettin until 1569(?)
17 Jun 1592	*Filip Juliusz*, son (b. 27 Dec 1584) under the guardianship of *Bogusław XIII*, Duke at Barth (see below) until 1606(?)
6 Feb 1625 – 10 Mar 1637	*Bogusław XIV*, son of Bogusław XIII of Barth and Stettin, Duke at Stettin 27 Nov 1620, Duke of the re-united duchy (see below)
10 Mar 1637	Western Pomerania escheated to Brandenburg on the death of Bogusław XIV

At Stettin

1295	*Otto I*, son of Barnim I

30/31 Dec 1344	*Barnim III*, son (b. c. 1298) ruling jointly since 1320, guardian at Wolgast 1326 – 1332
24 Aug 1368	*Kazimierz III*, son (b. before 12 Jun 1348)
1372	*Świętobor I*, brother (b. 1351) until 1404 with his brother, *Bogusław VII* (b. c. 1355; d. 1404)
21 Jun 1413	*Otto II*, son (b. c. 1380; d. 27 May 1428) with his brother *Kazimierz V* (b. after 1380; d. 13 Apr 1435)
1434	*Joachim*, the Younger, son of Kazimierz V (b. after 1424; d. (after 29 Sep) 1451)
1451 – 10 Nov 1464	*Otto III*, son (b. 29 May 1444)
1464	*Eryk II*, distant cousin (see Wolgast)
5 Jul 1474	*Bogusław X*, son (see Wolgast) re-united Stettin and Wolgast 17 Dec 1478
1478 – 1531	See Wolgast
1532	Stettin separated from Wolgast
1532	*Barnim IX*, son (see Wolgast) abdicated
1569	*Jan Fryderyk*, son of Filip I, Duke at Wolgast (b. 27 Aug 1542)
9 Feb 1600	*Barnim X*, brother (b. 15 Feb 1549) Duke at Rügenwalde from 1569
1 Nov 1603	*Bogusław XIII*, brother (b. 9 Aug 1544) Duke at Barth from 1569
7 Mar 1606	*Filip II*, son (b. 28 Jul 1573)
3 Feb 1618	*Franciszek*, brother (b. 24 Mar 1577)
27 Nov 1620 – 1625	*Bogusław XIV*, brother (b. 31 Mar 1580; d. 13 Mar 1637)
1625	Stettin re-united with Wolgast

At Stolp

1368 – 7 Dec 1373	*Bogusław V*, Duke at Wolgast 1 Aug 1326 (see below)
1374	*Kazimierz IV* (or *Kaźko*), son (b. 1351)
2 Jan 1377	*Warcisław VII*, brother (d. after 29 Nov 1394)
1394 – Jun 1459	*Eryk I*, son, King of Norway (as Erik III) (b. 1382) King of Sweden (as Erik XIII) 1397 – 1435, King of Denmark (as Erik VII) 1412 – 1439
1397/8	*Barnim IV*, uncle (b. 1369; d. after 13 May 1403) co-ruler
1403	*Bogusław VIII*, son of Bogusław V (b. 1363/4) co-ruler
11 Feb 1418	*Bogusław IX*, son (b. c. 1407/10) co-ruler
Jun 1459 – 1464	*Eryk II*, distant cousin (see Wolgast)
1464	Stolp re-united with Stettin

At Barth and Rügen

1372 – 13 Jun 1394	*Warcisław VI* (see Wolgast)
7 Mar 1393	Barth and Rügen re-united with Wolgast under *Warcisław VI*
13 Jun 1394	Barth and Rügen separated
13 Jun 1394	*Barnim VI*, son (b. c. 1365)
22 Sep 1405	United with Wolgast(?) under *Warcisław VIII*, brother (see Wolgast)
Aug 1415	Rügen separated again
Aug 1415 – c. 15 Dec 1451	*Barnim VIII*, son (b. 1405/7) Duke at Rügen 1440
Aug 1415 – 1432/6	*Świętobor*, brother (b. c. 1408/10) Duke at Rügen
c. 15 Dec 1451	Re-united with Wolgast under *Warcisław IX*, cousin (see Wolgast)
17 Apr 1457	*Warcisław X*, son (see Wolgast)
1459(?)	Barth and Rügen re-united with Wolgast

Pomerelia

Territory now in Polish provinces of Gdańsk and Bydgoszcz.

For earlier dukes who may have reigned wholly or partly in eastern Pomerania see Pomerania.

Dukes

AD (?)	*Subisław* (or *Sobiesław*)
c. 1180	*Sambor*, son
before 24 Apr 1209	*Mściwoj* (or *Mszczuj*) *I*, brother
1/2 May 1220 – 10/11 Jan 1266	*Świętopełk*, son (b. c. 1200) at first at Gdańsk only*
1/2 May 1220 – c. 1230	*Warcisław I*, brother (b. c. 1202) at Świecie and Gniew
10/11 Jan 1266 – 1271	*Warcisław II*, son of Świętopełk (b. after 1226) at Danzig
10/11 Jan 1266 – 25 Dec 1294	*Mściwoj* (or *Mszczuj*) *II*, brother (b. before 17 Jun 1231) at first at Świecie only

*The younger brothers, *Sambor II* (b. 1204; d. 13 Nov 1278) and *Racibor* (d. 1275?), had subordinate holdings at Lubieszów and Białgard nad Lebą respectively.

1294	Duchy inherited by Przemysł II, Duke of Greater Poland; subsequently lost to the Teutonic Knights

Pontus

Territory comprised part of present-day northern Turkey and southern Ukraine, with the capital initially at Arnasia (present-day Amasya) and later at Sinope (present-day Sinop).

Kings

Mithridatids

337/6 BC	*Mithridates I*, dynast of Cius
302/1	*Mithridates II*, son, established independence from the Seleucids
266/5	*Ariobarzanes*, son
c. 250	*Mithridates III*
c. 185	*Pharnaces I*, son, moved capital to Sinope
c. 170	*Mithridates IV Philopator Philadelphus*, brother
c. 150	*Mithridates V Euergetes*, nephew, assassinated
121/20	*Mithridates VI Eupator Dionysus*, son; ruled with *Laodice*(?), the queen-mother, until 115; annexed kingdom of the Bosporus and became king c. 100; committed suicide during a revolt of his troops
63–47	*Pharnaces II*, son, at the same time King of the Bosporus, confirmed by the Roman triumvir Pompey
39–37(?)	*Darius*, son, deposed
37(?)	Territory divided and ruled directly by Rome

Portugal

Kings

House of Burgundy

AD 1095 – 1 Nov 1112	*Henri*, grandson of Duke Robert I of Burgundy (b 1069/70) appointed Count of Portugal by Kin Alfonso VI of Castile and León, in response to th Almoravid invasion of Spain
1112 – 6 Dec 1185	*Afonso I Henriques*, son (b. Guimarães c. 1109 defeated the Muslims at Ourique 25 Jul 1139 and the began to use the title of king; autonomy recognized b King Alfonso VII of Castile and León at Zamora Oc 1143; captured Lisbon 1147 Regent: 1112 – 1128: *Tarasia*, mother, illegitimate daughter o King Alfonso VI of Castile and León (b. 1070; d. Nov 1130) deposed and exiled
1185 – 27 Mar 1211	*Sancho I*, son (b. 11 Nov 1154)
1211 – 25 Mar 1223	*Afonso II*, the Fat, son (b. Coimbra 23 Apr 1185 captured Alcácer do Sal 1217
1223	*Sancho II*, son (b. 8 Sep 1207; d. Toledo 3 Jan 1248 excommunicated and deposed
1245/1248 – 16 Feb 1279	*Afonso III*, brother (b. Coimbra 5 May 1210) Coun of Boulogne 1238, entered Lisbon and appointe regent 1245, named king 1248, transferred capita from Coimbra to Lisbon
1279 – 7 Jan 1325	*Dinis*, son (b. 9 Oct 1261)
1325 – 28 May 1357	*Afonso IV*, son (b. Lisbon 8 Feb 1291; d. Lisbon)
1357 – 18 Jan 1367	*Pedro I*, son (b. 18 Apr 1320)
1367 – 29 Oct 1383	*Fernando I*, son (b. 31 Oct 1345)
1383 – 1385	*Leonor Teles*, widow (d. 27 Apr. 1386) ruled as regen

House of Aviz

Mar/Apr 1385 – 14 Aug 1433	*João I*, illegitimate son of Pedro I and master of Avi (b. Lisbon 11 Apr 1357; d. Lisbon) ended Castilia claims to the Portuguese throne at the Battle o Aljubarrota 14 Aug 1385, conquered Ceuta 1415
1433 – 9 Sep 1438	*Duarte*, son (b. Viseu 31 Oct 1391; d. Tomar)
1438 – 28 Aug 1481	*Afonso V*, nephew of Pedro (b. Sintra 15 Jan 1432; d Sintra)

	Regents: 1438 – 1440: *Leonor*, widow of Duarte and daughter of King Fernando I of Aragon (d. 18 Feb 1445) deposed 1440 – 1449: *Pedro*, Duke of Coimbra, brother of Duarte (b. 9 Dec 1392; d. Alfarrobeira 20 May 1449) deposed
1481 – 25 Oct 1495	*João II*, son (b. Lisbon 3 May 1455; d. Alvor)

Pratiharas of Kanauj

Territory comprised part of present-day northern India, with the capital at Kanauj.

Kings

c. AD 750	*Nagabhata I*
(?)	*Devaraja*, nephew
c. 783	*Vatsaraja*, son
c. 815	*Nagabhata II*, son, conquest of Kanauj
c. 833	*Ramabhadra*, son
c. 836	*Bhoja I* (or *Mihira Pratihara*), son
c. 893	*Mahendrapala I*, son; drove the Palas out of Magadha
c. 914	*Mahipala*, son; Kanauj taken by the Rashtrakuta king Indra III
(?)	*Bhoja II*, brother(?)
(?)	*Vinayakapala*, brother(?)
c. 946	*Mahendrapala II*, son(?)
c. 948	*Devapala*, son of Mahipala
c. 960	*Vijayapala*, brother
(?) – 1018	*Rajyapala*
1018	Conquest by the Ghaznavid sultan Mahmud

Pushyabhuti of Kanauj

Territory comprised part of present-day northern India, with the capital initially at Thanesar and later at Kanauj.

Kings

AD (?)	*Prabhakaravardhana*, Raja of Thanesar
c. 605	*Rajyavardhana II*, son, assassinated
606 – c. 647	*Harshavardhana*, brother; moved capital to Kanauj defeated by the Chalukya king Pulakeshin II leading to the dissolution of the empire

Qarakhanids (Kara-Hanlılar, Ilek or Ilig Khans, House of Afrasiyab)

Territory comprised part of present-day northern Iran, southern USSR and western China.

Qaghans

Great Khans of the united kingdom
Centred at Balasaghun (also called Kara Ordu).

AD (?)	*(Abu'l-Hasan) 'Ali (ibn Musa)*
998	*(Abu Nasr) Ahmad I* (or *Toghan Khan*), son (d. 1017/18) established in Khurasan from Dec 1004/Jan 1005
1015/16	*Mansur (Arslan Khan)*, brother
1024/5	*Ahmad II (Toghan Khan)*, son of a cousin of 'Ali (d. after 1056/7)
1026/7 – 1032	*Yusuf I (Qadır Khan)*, brother

Great Khans of the western kingdom: Transoxania (Sogdiana), including Bukhara, Samarkand and western Transoxania

Capital established at Bukhara.

1041/2	*Muhammad I ibn Nasr ('Ain al-Daula)*, nephew of Ahmad I
1052/3	*Ibrahim I* (or *Böritigin*) *(Tamghach Khan)*, brother
1068	*(Shams al-Mulk) Nasr I*, acknowledged Seljuq suzerainty 1073/4
1080	*al-Khidr*, brother
1080/1(?)	*Ahmad I*, son (d. 1095) Seljuq vassal, deposed and executed
1089	*Ya'qub*, son of Sulaiman of the eastern khanate, Seljuq vassal
1095	*Mas'ud I*, cousin of Ahmad I, Seljuq vassal
1097	*Sulaiman*, cousin, Seljuq vassal
1097	*(Abu'l-Qasim) Mahmud I*, grandson of Mansur of the united khanate, Seljuq vassal
1099	*Jibra'il*, great-grandson of Yusuf I of the united khanate
1102–1130*	*Muhammad II*, son of Sulaiman (d. 1132) Seljuq vassal
1130	*(Abu'l-Ma'ali) al-Hasan (ibn 'Ali)*, descended from a brother of Yusuf I of the united khanate, Seljuq vassal
1132	*(Abu'l Muzaffar) Ibrahim II (ibn Sulaiman)*, brother of Muhammad II, Seljuq vassal
1132	*Mahmud II (ibn Muhammad)*, nephew (d. 1163) later ruled in Khurasan, Seljuq vassal
1141	*Ibrahim III (ibn Muhammad)*, brother, Qara Khitai vassal
1156	*'Ali (ibn al-Hasan)*, Qara Khitai vassal
1160	*(Abu'l-Muzaffar) Mas'ud II (ibn al-Hasan)*, brother
1178	*Ibrahim IV (ibn al-Husain)*, nephew, Qara Khitai vassal, ruled in Farghana 1164/5 – 1178, ruled in Samarkand from 1178
1203/4–1212	*'Uthman*, son, Qara Khitai vassal, killed by the Khwarazm-Shah Muhammad
1212	Overthrown by the Khwarazm-Shahs

*1128/9(?)	*Nasr II*, son (d. 1129?) Seljuq vassal, rival
1128/9(?)	*Ahmad II*, brother (d. 1132?) Seljuq vassal, rival

Great Khans of the eastern kingdom: Talas, Isfijab, Shash, Semirechye Kashghar and eastern Farghana

1031/2	*Sulaiman (ibn Yusuf)*, son of Yusuf I of the unite khanate (d. 1057/8)
1057	*Muhammad I (ibn Yusuf)*, brother
1058	*Ibrahim I (ibn Muhammad)*, son
1059	*Mahmud (ibn Yusuf)*, uncle
1074/5	*'Umar (ibn Mahmud)*, son, for two months
1074/5	*(Abu 'Ali) al-Hasan (ibn Sulaiman)* (or *Harun*), son o Sulaiman
1102/3	*Ahmad (ibn al-Hasan)* (or *Harun*), son
after 1128	*Ibrahim II (ibn Ahmad)*, son
after 1158	*Muhammad II (ibn Ibrahim)*, son, detained by th Qara Khitai
(?)	*(Abu'l Muzaffar) Yusuf II (ibn Muhammad)*, son
1205 – 1210/11	*(Abu'l-Fath) Muhammad III (ibn Yusuf)*, son
1210/11	Occupation by the Mongol Küchlüg

Rashtrakutas

Territory comprised part of present-day northern and central India, with the capital at Manyakheta or Malkhed.

Kings

AD (?)	*Dantivarman I*
(?)	*Indra I*, son
(?)	*Govinda I*, son
(?)	*Karka I*, son
(?)	*Indra II*, son
754	*Dantivarman II* (or *Dantidurga*), son, overthrew the Chalukya kingdom 753
768	*Krishna I*, son of Karka I
783	*Govinda II*, son
(?)	*Dhruva*, brother
793	*Govinda III*, son
814	*Amoghavarsha I*, son
877	*Krishna II*, son

915	*Indra III*, grandson, captured Kanauj
917	*Amoghavarsha II*, son
918	*Govinda IV*, brother
c. 934	*Amoghavarsha III* (or *Vaddiga*), grandson of Krishna II
939	*Krishna III*, son
968	*Khottiga*, brother
972	*Karka II* (or *Amoghavarsha IV*), grandson of Amoghavarsha III
973 – 982	*Indra IV*
982	Overthrown by the Chalukyas of Kalyana

Rasulids

Territory comprised part of present-day Yemen, with the capital at Zabid.

Sultans

AD 1228/9	*(al-Mansur Nur al-Din) 'Umar I (ibn 'Ali)*, grandson of Rasul, governor of Mecca 1222/3 – 1223/4
Feb/Mar 1250	*(al-Muzaffar Shams al-Din) Yusuf I (ibn 'Umar)*, son
Jul/Aug 1295	*(al-Ashraf Mumahhid al-Din Abu'l-Fath) 'Umar II (ibn Yusuf)*, son
Nov/Dec 1296	*(al-Mu'ayyad Hizabr al-Din) Da'ud (ibn Yusuf)*, brother
Dec 1321/Jan 1322	*(al-Mujahid Saif al-Din) 'Ali (ibn Da'ud)*, son
Mar/Apr 1363	*(al-Afdal Dirgham al-Din) al-'Abbas (ibn 'Ali)*, son
Jan/Feb 1377	*(al-Ashraf Mumahhid al-Din) Isma'il I (ibn al-'Abbas)*, son
Nov/Dec 1400	*(al-Nasir Salah al-Din) Ahmad (ibn Isma'il)*, son
Apr 1424	*(al-Mansur) 'Abdallah (ibn Ahmad)*, son
Feb/Mar 1427	*(al-Ashraf) Isma'il II (ibn Ahmad)*, brother
Mar/Apr 1428	*(al-Zahir) Yahya (ibn Isma'il)*, uncle
Jan/Feb 1439	*(al-Ashraf) Isma'il III (ibn Yahya)*, son
Feb/Mar 1442 – 1442/3	*(al-Muzaffar) Yusuf II (ibn 'Umar ibn Isma'il)*, cousin Rival claimants:
1442/3	*(al-Mufaddal) Muhammad*
1442/3	*(al-Nasir) 'Abdallah*

1450/1 – 1454	*al-Mas'ud*
1451/2 – 1454	*(al-Mu'ayyad) al-Husain*
1454	Conquest by the Sunni Tahirids of Lahij and Aden

Rawwadids

Territory comprised part of present-day north-western Iran, with the capital established at Tabriz in 961.

Amirs

AD (?)	*Muhammad (ibn al-Husain al-Rawwadi)*, conquered portions of Azerbaijan
c. 951	*Husain I (ibn Muhammad)*, son, occupation of Tabriz 956
(?)	*(Abu'l-Haija') Mamlan I (ibn Husain)* (or *(Abu'l-Haija') Muhammad I (ibn Husain)*), son, ruled over all of Azerbaijan, his brother Marzuban in revolt until 996
1000/1	*(Abu Nasr) Husain II (ibn Mamlan)*, son
1025/6	*(Abu Mansur) Wahsudan (ibn Mamlan)*, brother, Seljuq vassal
Mar 1059 – 1070/1	*Mamlan II (ibn Wahsudan)*, son, Seljuq vassal
1070/1	Seljuq occupation

Roman Empire

At its greatest extent, territory comprised most of present-day Europe (with the exception of Ireland, Scandinavia, northern Netherlands, northern Germany, Poland, Czechoslovakia, Hungary, Romania and U.S.S.R.), the coastal strip of North Africa, Turkey, Syria, Lebanon, Israel and Jordan, with the capital at Rome until the division between East and West.

Kings*

754 – 717 BC	*Romulus*
747 – 742	*Titus Tatius*, King of the Sabines
715	*Numa Pompilius*, son-in-law
672	*Tullus Hostilius*
641	*Ancus Martius*, grandson of Numa Pompilius
616	*Tarquinius Priscus*, assassinated
579	*Servius Tullius*, assassinated
(?) – 509	*Tarquinius Superbus*, son of Tarquinius Priscus, deposed and exiled
509	Revolt of Lucius Junius Brutus and the foundation of the Republic

The Republic

509 – 44	Power was initially divided between the Senate, the popular assemblies and the magistrates; sovereign executive power resting with a magistrate called the *praetor maximus*. This was superseded by the election of two consuls, who shared the *imperium* for a single year. The power of the consuls was later limited by the appointment of tribunes. During times of emergency a dictator was appointed.

The Triumvirates

First Triumvirate †

61 – 53	*Pompey* (*Gnaeus Pompeius Magnus*), son of Pompeius Strabo (b. Rome 29 Sep 106; d.

*Traditional list and dating

† Unofficial

	(assassinated) Pelusium, Egypt, 28 Sep 48) defeated by Julius Caesar at Pharsalus 48
	Crassus (*Marcus Licinius Crassus Dives*) (b. c. 115; d. Carrhae (present-day Haran), Anatolia, 53) governor of Syria 54
	(Gaius) Julius Caesar, son of Gaius Caesar (b. 12/13 Jul 100*; d. (assassinated) Rome 15 Mar 44) governor of Farther Spain 61 – 60, consul 59, commander in Gaul 58 – 50, entered Italy in revolt 10/11 Jan 49, dictator 49 – 44

Second Triumvirate (*Tresviri rei publicae constituendae*)

Nov 43 – 32	*Marcus Aemilius Lepidus*, son of Marcus Aemilius Lepidus (d. 13/12) influence in the triumvirate ended c. 37
	Marcus Antonius (known in English as *Mark Antony*), son of Marcus Antonius (b. 82/1; d. Egypt Aug 30) administrator of the eastern provinces 41, defeated by Octavian at Actium 2 Sep 31
	Octavian (*Gaius Octavius*, later *Gaius Julius Caesar*), great nephew and adopted son of Julius Caesar (b. 23 Sep 63; d. Rome 19 Aug AD 14) governed Italy and the West, defeated Mark Antony at Actium 2 Sep 31, emperor as *Augustus* 27 (see Emperors)

Emperors†

27	*Augustus* (*Imperator Caesar Augustus*) (see Second Triumvirate: *Octavian*) appointed tribune for life 23
17 Sep AD 14	*Tiberius* (*Tiberius Caesar Augustus*; *Tiberius Claudius Nero*), stepson (b. 16 Nov 42 BC; d. (assassinated) Capreae (present-day Capri) 16 Mar AD 37)
Mar 37	*Caligula* (or *Gaius*) (*Imperator Gaius Caesar Augustus Germanicus*; *Gaius Caesar*) great-grandson of Augustus (b. Antium (present-day Anzio) 31 Aug 12; d. (assassinated) Rome 24 Jan 41)

*Traditional date

†In view of the notorious variation in the rendering of the names of the earlier emperors in the literary tradition they are given here in three forms (so far as these are ascertainable from *Prosopographia imperii romani* and *The prosopography of the later Roman empire*): the conventional English form, the official style, and the original name

25 Jan 41	*Claudius* (*Imperator Tiberius Claudius Caesar Augustus Germanicus*; *Tiberius Claudius Nero Germanicus*), nephew of Tiberius (b. Lugdunum (present-day Lyon) 1 Aug 10 BC; d. (assassinated) 13 Oct 54)
Oct 54	*Nero* (*Imperator Nero Claudius Caesar Augustus Germanicus*; *Lucius Domitius Ahenobarbus*), stepson (b. 15 Dec 37; d. Rome 9 Jun 68) adopted as heir 50, committed suicide during Galba's revolt
Jun 68	*Galba* (*Servius Galba Imperator Caesar Augustus*; *Servius Sulpicius Galba*), son of Gaius Sulpicius Galba (b. c. 5 BC) governor of Nearer Spain from 60, led revolt against Nero, assassinated in Rome
15 Jan 69	*Otho* (*Imperator Marcus Otho Caesar Augustus*; *Marcus Salvius Otho*) (b. 32; d. 16 Apr 69) governor of Lusitania from 58, proclaimed emperor on the death of Galba, defeated by Vitellius near Cremona and committed suicide
Apr 69	*Vitellius* (*Aulus Vitellius Imperator Germanicus*), son of Lucius Vitellius (b. 15) commander of the army of Lower Germany 68, acclaimed emperor 2 Jan 69, defeated Otho Apr 69, entered Rome Jul 69, assassinated
1 Jul 69	*Vespasian* (*Imperator Caesar Vespasianus Augustus*; *Titus Flavius Vespasianus*) (b. Reate (present-day Rieti) 9; d. 23 Jun 79) special commander to quell the Jewish revolt Feb 67, acclaimed emperor by his troops 1 Jul 69, took Rome by Dec 69
Jun 79	*Titus* (*Imperator Titus Vespasianus Augustus*; *Titus Flavius Vespasianus*), son (b. 30 Dec 39; d. 13 Sep 81)
Sep 81	*Domitian* (*Imperator Caesar Domitianus Augustus*; *Titus Flavius Domitianus*), brother (b. 24 Oct 51) assassinated
18 Sep 96	*Nerva* (*Imperator Nerva Caesar Augustus*; *Marcus Cocceius Nerva*) (b. c. 30; d. Rome 27/28 Jan 98)
Jan 98	*Trajan* (*Imperator Caesar Nerva Traianus Augustus*; *Marcus Ulpius Traianus*) (b. Italica, Spain, 53; d. Selinus, Cilicia, c. 8 Aug 117) adopted as heir c. 27 Oct 97
11 Aug 117	*Hadrian* (*Imperator Caesar Traianus Hadrianus Augustus*; *Publius Aelius Hadrianus*), a distant relation of Trajan (b. Italica, Spain, 24 Jan 76; d. Baiae (present-day Baia) 10 Jul 138)

Jul 138	*Antoninus Pius* (*Imperator Caesar Titus Aelius Hadrianus Antoninus Augustus Pius*; *Titus Aurelius Fulvus Boionius Arrius Antoninus*) (b. 19 Sep 86; d. Lorium, near Rome, 7 Mar 161) adopted as heir 138
Mar 161 – 17 Mar 180	*Marcus Aurelius* (*Marcus Aurelius Antoninus*; *Marcus Annius Verus*),* nephew by marriage (b. 26 Apr 121) adopted as heir 138
Mar 161 – 169	*Lucius Verus* (*Lucius Aurelius Verus*; *Lucius Ceionius Commodus*, afterwards *Lucius Aelius Aurelius Commodus*), co-emperor (b. 15 Dec 130) adopted by Antoninus Pius 138
176 – 31 Dec192	*Commodus* (176 – 180: *Lucius Aelius Aurelius Commodus*; 180 – 192: *Marcus Aurelius Commodus Antoninus*), son of Marcus Aurelius (b. Lanuvium (present-day Lanuvio) 31 Aug 161; d. (assassinated) Rome) co-emperor 176 – Mar 180
Jan 193	*Pertinax* (*Publius Helvius Pertinax*), prefect of the city of Rome from 191 (b. Liguria 1 Aug 126) assassinated
28 Mar – 2 Jun 193	*Didius Julianus* (*Marcus Didius Severus Julianus*), senator (b. 30 Jan 133 or 2 Feb 137; d. Rome) killed by the legions of Septimius Severus
Jun 193 – Feb 211	*Septimius Severus* (*Lucius Septimius Severus Pertinax*), legate of Upper Pannonia (b. Leptis Magna (present-day Lebda), Tripolitania, 146) overthrew Didius Julianus
198 – 8 Apr 217	*Caracalla* (*Marcus Aurelius Severus Antoninus*; *Septimius Bassianus*), son (b. Lugdunum (present-day Lyon) 4 Apr 186; d. (assassinated) Carrhae (present-day Haran), Anatolia), received the title of Caesar 197, co-emperor with his father 198 – 211
209 – Feb 212	*Geta* (*Publius Septimius Geta*), brother (b. Milan 189; d. (assassinated) Rome) received the title of Caesar 198, joint emperor with his father and brother, killed by Caracalla
11 Apr 217	*Macrinus* (*Marcus Opellius Severus Macrinus*), praetorian prefect (b. Caesarea, Mauretania, c. 164) proclaimed emperor by the army, killed in Bithynia during the revolt of Elagabalus
Jun 218	*Elagabalus* (*Sacerdos dei invicti solis Elagabali*

*From this point on the imperial style invariably begins with *Imperator Caesar* and ends with *Augustus*. For the sake of economy these titles are omitted here

	Marcus Aurelius Antoninus; *Varius Avitus Bassianus*), cousin of Caracalla (b. Emesa (present-day Homs), Syria, 204) proclaimed emperor in Syria in rivalry with Macrinus, confirmed by the Senate after his defeat of Macrinus, assassinated
Mar 222	*Alexander Severus* (*Marcus Aurelius Severus Alexander*; *Marcus Julius Gessius Bassianus* (?)), cousin (b. Phoenecia, Syria, 208) adopted as heir 221, assassinated
Mar 235	*Maximin* (*Gaius Julius Verus Maximinus*) (b. 172?) proclaimed emperor by the Rhine army, deposed by the Senate 238 and killed by his troops
Mar – Apr 238	*Gordian I* (*Marcus Antonius Gordianus Sempronianus Romanus Africanus*), proconsul of Africa, proclaimed emperor by local landowners and committed suicide a few weeks later
Mar – Apr 238	*Gordian II* (*Marcus Antonius Gordianus Sempronianus Romanus Africanus*), son, co-emperor with his father for three weeks before being killed in battle
spring 238	*Maximus* (*Marcus Clodius Pupienus Maximus*), appointed by the Senate, killed by the praetorian guard 90 days later
spring 238	*Balbinus* (*Decius Caelius Calvinus Balbinus*), consul and proconsul of Asia under Septimius Severus, appointed co-emperor with Maximus by the Senate, killed by the praetorian guard 90 days later
Aug 238	*Gordian III* (*Marcus Antonius Gordianus*), nephew of Gordian II, associated initially with Maximus and Balbinus, killed by his troops
spring 244	*Philip* (*Marcus Julius Philippus*), the Arab, praetorian prefect, killed in the revolt of Decius
autumn 249	*Decius* (*Gaius Messius Quintus Traianus Decius*), commander in the Danube (b. Budalia (in present-day Yugoslavia) c. 201; d. Dobrogea (now Dobraja)) proclaimed emperor by his troops and killed Philip
Jun 251	*Hostilian* (*Gaius Valens Hostilianus Messius Quintus*), son, received the title of Caesar 250, adopted by Gallus and made co-emperor 251 but died within a few weeks
Jun 251	*Gallus* (*Gaius Vibius Trebonianus Gallus*), legate of Moesia (d. Interamna (present-day Narni), summer 253) killed by his troops during the revolt of Aemilian

Jul/Aug – Sep/Oct 253	*Aemilian* (*Marcus Aemilius Aemilianus*), commander of the army of Moesia, defeated Gallus and confirmed as emperor by the Senate, killed near Spoletium (present-day Spoleto) by his troops during the revolt of Valerian
autumn 253 – Jun 260	*Valerian* (*Publius Licinius Valerianus*), commander on the upper Rhine under Gallus, defeated and captured by the Sasanid king Shapur I, died in captivity
autumn 253	*Gallienus* (*Publius Licinius Egnatius Gallienus*), son (b. c. 218) ruled in the West as co-emperor 253 – 260, murdered near Mediolanum (present-day Milan) during the revolt of Aureolus
268	*Claudius Gothicus* (*Marcus Aurelius Valerius Claudius*), cavalry commander under Gallienus (b. Dardania, Moesia Superior, 10 May 214(?))
Sep 269 or Apr/May 270	*Quintillus* (*Marcus Aurelius Claudius Quintillus*), brother, for a few weeks or months only
Nov 269 or May 270 – 23 Mar 275	*Aurelian* (*Lucius Domitius Aurelianus*), cavalry commander under Claudius Gothicus (b. 9 Sep 214?) assassinated
23 Mar – Sep 275	Interregnum; the government continued under *Ulpia Severina*, widow of Aurelian
Sep 275	*Tacitus* (*Marcus Claudius Tacitus*) (b. 200) appointed by the Senate
7 Jun – 9 Sep 276	*Florian* (*Marcus Annius Florianus*), half-brother(?) (b. 19 Aug 232) killed by his troops
Jun 276 – Sep(?) 282	*Probus* (*Marcus Aurelius Probus*), praetorian prefect in the East, proclaimed emperor by his troops, killed by his troops
Sep 282 – Jul 283	*Carus* (*Marcus Aurelius Carus*), prefect of the guard to Probus
summer 283 – Jul 285	*Carinus* (*Marcus Aurelius Carinus*), son, named Caesar and sent to the army of the Rhine 282, killed by his troops during a battle atMargus (present-day Morava in Yugoslavia) against Diocletian
May 283 – Nov 284	*Numerian* (*Marcus Aurelius Numerius Numerianus*), brother (d. 284) co-emperor, murdered
20 Nov 284 – 1 May 305	*Diocletian* (*Gaius Aurelius Valerius Diocletianus**), commander of the household guards

*Originally Diocles

of Numerian (b. 236/7(?); d. Salonae, Dalmatia, 313 or 316) proclaimed emperor at Nicomedia (present-day Izmit), defeated and killed Carinus 285, divided the empire for administrative purposes and appointed Maximian as Caesar to rule in the West 285

Emperors in the East before Constantine I

285	*Diocletian* (see above) abdicated and resumed the name of Diocles
1 May 305	*Galerius* (*Gaius Galerius Valerius Maximianus*) (d. May 311) proclaimed Caesar 1 Mar 293; on the abdication of Diocletian assumed the title Augustus and the rule of Moesia, Thrace, Asiana and Pontica
Spring 311 – 313	*Maximinus Daia* (*Galerius Valerius Maximinus Daia*), nephew, proclaimed Caesar 1 May 305 and ruled in Syria and Egypt under Galerius, proclaimed himself Augustus 309/10 and ruled Asia Minor, invaded the territories of Licinius in Thrace 313, defeated at Tzurulum, died at Tarsus
11 Nov 308 – 324 *	*Licinius* (*Valerius Licinianus Licinius*), fellow-soldier of Galerius (b. c. 265(?); d. (executed) Thessalonica 325) proclaimed Augustus 11 Nov 308 by Galerius to rule in the West, but confined to Pannonia (comprised part of present-day Hungary and Yugoslavia); occupied the European territories at the death of Galerius 311; sole emperor in the East 313; lost Pannonia and Moesia to Constantine I 314; defeated by Constantine I 324; deposed and exiled

Emperors in the West before Constantine I

1 Mar 286	*Maximian* (*Marcus Aurelius Valerius Maximianus Heraclius*) (for 1st time) (d. 310) created Caesar to rule Gaul by Diocletian 285; limited to Italy, Spain and Africa 293; forced to abdicate with Diocletian
1 May 305	*Constantius I Chlorus* (*Flavius Valerius Constantius*), governor of Dalmatia, appointed Caesar to rule Gaul and Britain 1 Mar 293, died at Eboracum (present-day York)

* 316	*Aurelius Valerius Valens*, made Caesar 316, styled Augustus on coins, deposed by Constantine I and executed

25 Jul 306 – 307	*Severus* (*Flavius Valerius Severus*), a Pannonian officer, appointed Caesar to rule Pannonia 1 May 305, captured and executed by Maxentius 307
28 Oct 306 – 28 Oct 312	*Maxentius* (*Marcus Aurelius Valerius Maxentius*), son of Maximian, proclaimed emperor in Rome and recalled Maximian to the throne, defeated and executed Severus 307, lost Spain to Constantine I 310, defeated by Constantine I and killed at the battle of Milvian Bridge
306 – 308	*Maximian*, father (for 2nd time) attempted to depose Maxentius and forced to flee to Constantine I, persuaded to abdicate by Diocletian 308, rebelled and captured by Constantine I at Massilia (present-day Marseille) 310

Emperors of East and West

25 Jul 306 – 22 May 337	*Constantine I* (*Flavius Valerius Constantinus*), the Great, son of Constantius I Chlorus (b. Naissus (present-day Niš), Moesia, 27 Feb 272(?)) proclaimed Augustus by the troops of Constantius I Chlorus at York, ruled over Gaul, defeated Maxentius and confirmed by the Senate as sole emperor in the West 312, conquered Pannonia and Moesia 314/15, defeated Licinius and became sole emperor 324, dedicated Constantinople as new capital 11 May 330, on his death empire divided between his three sons
9 Sep 337 – 340	*Constantine II* (*Flavius Claudius* (or *Julius*) *Constantinus*), illegitimate son (b. Arelate (present-day Arles), Gaul, Feb 317) proclaimed Caesar 1 Mar 317; ruled Britain, Gaul and Spain; invaded the Italian territories of Constans I; defeated and killed at Aquileia
9 Sep 337 – Jan 350	*Constans I* (*Flavius Julius Constans*), half-brother (b. 320 or 323) proclaimed Caesar 333; ruled Italy, Africa and Illyricum (comprised part of present-day western Yugoslavia); sole emperor in the West 340; defeated and killed by Magnentius in Gaul
9 Sep 337 – 3 Nov 361	*Constantius II* (*Flavius Julius* (or *Valerius*) *Constantius*), brother (b. Illyricum 7 Aug 317; d. Mopsuestia (now Misis, Turkey)) proclaimed Caesar 8 Nov 324; ruled Thrace, Macedonia, Greece, Asia and Egypt; sole emperor on defeat of Magnentius 351

18 Jan 350 – 351	*Magnentius* (*Flavius Magnus Magnentius*) (b. c. 303(?); d. (suicide) 10 Aug 353) usurper, defeated by Constantius II
360 – 26 Jun 363	*Julian* (*Flavius Claudius Julianus*), the Apostate, cousin of Constantius II (b. Constantinople May/Jun 332) created Caesar to rule Gaul 6 Nov 355, proclaimed emperor by his troops, sole emperor 361, invaded Persia 5 Mar 363 and killed during the retreat
27 Jun 363 – 17 Feb 364	*Jovian* (*Flavius Jovianus*), son of Varronianus, count of the domestics (b. Singidunum (present-day Belgrade) c. 331) proclaimed emperor by the troops on the death of Julian, died at Dadastana

Emperors in the East until the fall of Rome

28 Mar 364 – 9 Aug 378	*Valens* (*Flavius Valens*), brother of Valentinian I (b. c. 328) killed in the battle of Adrianople
28 Sep 365 – 27 May 366	*Procopius* (b. c. 326) promised succession by Julian, yielded claim to Jovian, executed by Valens
19 Jan 379	*Theodosius I* (*Flavius Theodosius*), the Great; son of Theodosius, a commander under Valentinian I (b. Cauca, Gallaecia, c. 346; d. Mediolanum (now Milan)) appointed emperor in the East by Gratian, sole emperor May 392 (see also Emperors in the West until the fall of Rome)
17 Jan 395	*Arcadius* (*Flavius Arcadius*), son (b. c. 377) proclaimed Augustus 19 Jan 383
1 May 408 – 28 Jul 450	*Theodosius II*, son (b. Constantinople 10 Apr 401) crowned Augustus 10 Jan 402 Regents: 408 – 414: *Anthemius*, praetorian prefect of the East 4 Jul 414 – 416(?): *Pulcheria*, sister of Theodosius II (d. 453)
25 Aug 450 – Jan/Feb 457	*Marcian* (*Marcianus*), husband of Pulcheria (b. Thrace 396)
7 Feb 457	*Leo I* (*Leo Thrax Magnus*), a Thracian soldier, recognized Majorian as emperor in the West 457, refused similar recognition to Libius Severus 461, sent Anthemius to the West as emperor 25 Mar 467, defeated by the Vandals 468
3 Feb 374	*Leo II*, grandson, proclaimed Augustus Oct 473

17 Nov 474 – 9 Apr 491	*Zeno* (originally named *Tarasicodissa*), father, co-emperor 9 Feb 474, briefly ousted by Basiliscus*

For the continuation of the empire in the East, see Byzantine Empire.

Emperors in the West until the fall of Rome

26 Feb 364	*Valentinian I* (*Flavius Valentinianus*), brother of Valens (d. Brigetio (now Szöny, Hungary)) a tribune in the army of Julian; proclaimed emperor by the army on the death of Jovian; appointed Valens emperor in the East 28 Mar 364
17 Nov 375 – 25 Aug 383	*Gratian* (*Flavius Gratianus Augustus*), son (b. Sirmium, Pannonia, 359; d. (assassinated) Lugdunum (now Lyon)) received the title Augustus 24 Aug 367, appointed Theodosius I as emperor in the East 19 Jan 379, assassinated during the revolt of Maximus†
22 Nov 375	*Valentinian II* (*Flavius Valentinianus*), brother (b. Augusta Treverorum (present-day Trier) 371; d. (assassinated?) Vindobona (now Vienna)) proclaimed emperor by the troops at Aquincum (present-day Buda) and accepted as co-emperor by Gratian; ruled in Italy, Africa and Illyricum; fled to Thessalonica during the invasion of Maximus,† restored in the West 388
15 May 392	*Theodosius I* (see Emperors in the East until the fall of Rome) defeated the usurper Eugenius‡ 6 Sep 394
17 Jan 395 – 15 Aug 423	*Honorius* (*Flavius Honorius*), son (b. 9 Sep 384) proclaimed Augustus 23 Jan 393, removed capital to Ravenna after sack of Rome by the Visigoths Aug 410
8 Feb – 2 Sep 421	*Constantius III*, brother-in-law, co-emperor

*9 Jan 475 – Aug 476	*Basiliscus*, uncle of Zeno's wife, executed
†spring 383 – 388	*Maximus* (*Magnus Clemens Maximus*), commander of the troops in Britain (d. (executed) 28 Aug 388) proclaimed emperor by his troops; after the death of Gratian ruled Britain, Gaul and Spain; invaded Italy 387; defeated by Theodosius I at Poetovio 388
‡22 Aug 392 – 6 Sep 394	*Eugenius*, a professor of rhetoric; proclaimed emperor by Arbogast, a Frankish general; invaded Italy 393; defeated and executed

15 Aug 423	*Valentinian III* (*Flavius Placidius Valentinianus*), son (b. Ravenna 2 Jul 419; d. (assassinated) Rome 16 Mar 455) Regent: 15 Aug 423 – 435: *Galla Placidia*, mother (b. 388/9(?); d. Rome 27 Nov 450)
17 Mar 455	*Petronius Maximus* (*Flavius Ancius Petronius Maximus*), prefect of the city of Rome, killed by a Roman mob
May 455 – 17 Oct 456	*Avitus* (*Flavius Maccilius Eparchus Avitus*), a military commander (d. 456) forced to abdicate by Ricimer, a Roman general; became Bishop of Placentia (now Piacenza)
1 Apr 457 – 2 Aug 461	*Majorian* (*Julius Valerius Maioranus*), master of the soldiers (d. (executed) Tortona 7 Aug 461) defeated by the Vandals at Lucentum (present-day Alicante) May 460, forced to abdicate by Ricimer
461	*Libius Severus* (*Libius Severianus Severus*) appointed emperor by Ricimer, refused recognition by Leo I, deposed
12 Apr 467	*Anthemius* (*Procopius Anthemius*), son-in-law of Marcian (d. (executed) Rome 11 Jul 472) sent to Italy by Leo I 25 Mar 467 and recognized by him as emperor, defeated by Ricimer
Apr – 2 Nov 472	*Olybrius* (*Anicius Olybrius*), son-in-law of Valentinian III, refused recognition by Leo I
5 Mar 473	*Glycerius*, appointed emperor by Ricimer's nephew Gundobad, refused recognition by Leo I, surrendered and became Bishop of Salona
Jun 474 – 9 May 480	*Julius Nepos* (d. (assassinated) Salona) commander under Leo I, defeated and deposed Glycerius, recognized independence of the Visigoth kingdom in Spain 475, fled to Dalmatia during the revolt of the patrician Orestes Aug 475, recognized as emperor by Gaul and the East until his death
31 Oct 475 – 28 Aug 476	*Romulus Augustus* (nicknamed *Augustulus*) (*Flavius Momyllus Romulus Augustus*), son of the patrician Orestes, proclaimed emperor by his father (who retained actual power) at Ravenna, exiled to Campania (southern Italy), date of death unknown
28 Aug 476	End of Roman Empire when *Odoaker*, a Germanic warrior (b. 433; d. Ravenna 15 Mar 493) killed Orestes and deposed Romulus

Romania

Hospodars of Moldavia

Territory now in north-west Romania and the Moldavian SSR.

c. AD 1352 – 1353	*Dragoş*
c. 1354 – 1358	*Sas*
1359	*Balc*, son
c. 1359	*Bogdan I*, at Maramureş
c. 1365	*Laţcu*, son
c. 1377	*Ştefan*, connection by marriage
c. 1378	*Petru I Muşat*, son
c. 1393	*Roman I*, brother, vassal of Poland
c. 1394 – 12 Aug(?) 1399	*Ştefan I*, brother
1399 – 1400	*Iuga*, son
11 Feb 1400	*Alexandru*, the Kind, brother
1 Jan 1432	*Iliaş*, son (for 1st time) (d. Poland)
Nov 1433 (1434?) – 13 Jul 1447	*Ştefan II*, brother, killed by Roman II
27 Aug 1435 – 29 May 1443	*Iliaş* (for 2nd time) co-ruler
26 Apr 1444 – Apr 1445	*Petru II*, brother (for 1st time) co-ruler or pretender, expelled
13 Jul – Sep 1447	*Petru II* (for 2nd time)
13 Jul 1447 – 23 Feb 1448	*Roman II*, son of Iliaş (d. (poisoned) 2 Jul 1448) with Polish support, at first co-ruler
Feb 1448 – Mar 1449*	*Petru II* (for 3rd time)
Feb 1449	*Alexăndrel* (*Alexandru* or *Olechno*), brother of Roman II (for 1st time) (b. c. 1432; d. spring 1455)
12 Oct 1449	*Bogdan II*, son of Alexandru the Kind, killed by Petru Aron
16 Oct 1451	*Petru Aron*, brother (for 1st time)
Feb 1452	*Alexăndrel* (for 2nd time)
1454	*Petru Aron* (for 2nd time)
Jan/Feb 1455	*Alexăndrel* (for 3rd time)
25 May 1455	*Petru Aron* (for 3rd time)

*1448 – 1449 *Ciubăr*, pretender

14 Apr 1457 – 2 Jul 1504	*Ştefan*, the Great, son of Bogdan II, vassal of Poland

Voivodes and Hospodars of Wallachia

Territory now in southern Romania.

before 1247 – c. 1273	*Litovoi*
fl. 1247	*Seneslav*, voivode at Argeş
c. 1273	*Barbat*
c. 1290	*Tihomir* (or *Tugomir*)
c. 1310	*(Ivanco* or *Ioan) Basarab*, son
1352	*Nicolae-Alexandru*, son
16 Nov 1364 – c. 1377	*Vladislav I* (or *Vlaicu*), son
1372	*Radu I*, brother (or son?), at first co-ruler
c. 1383 – Sep 1386	*Dan I*, son
c. 1383 – 31 Jan 1418*	*Mircea*, the Old, brother, at first co-ruler, vassal of the Turks 1393
1408 – Aug 1420	*Mihail*, son, at first co-ruler
Aug 1420	*Dan II*, the Brave, brother (for 1st time)
May 1421	*Radu II Prasnaglava*, the Simple or the Bald, brother (for 1st time)
Nov 1421	*Dan II* (for 2nd time)
spring 1423	*Radu II* (for 2nd time)
1423	*Dan II* (for 3rd time)
Nov(?) 1424	*Radu II* (for 3rd time)
(?)	*Dan II* (for 4th time)
May – (?) 1426	*Radu II* (for 4th time)
1426	*Dan II* (for 5th time)
Jan 1427	*Radu II* (for 5th time)
Mar(?) 1427	*Dan II* (for 6th time)
Feb/Mar 1431	*Alexandru I* (or *Aldea*), brother
Dec 1436	*Vlad*, the Devil, brother (for 1st time) (d. Dec 1446)
autumn 1442	*Mircea*, son (d. Dec 1446)
Dec 1442	*Basarab II*, army commander in Hungary
spring 1443	*Vlad*, the Devil (for 2nd time)
Dec 1446 – 1456	*Vladislav II* (or *Dan III*), son of Dan II(?) (d. 3 Jul 1456)
Apr/Jun 1456	*Vlad*, the Impaler, son of Vlad the Devil (for 1st time) (d. Dec 1476)
Nov 1462	*Radu*, the Handsome, brother (for 1st time)

*Nov 1394 – Jan 1397 *Vlad I*, rival

Nov 1473	*Basarab Laiotă*, the Old, son of Dan II (for 1st time)
Dec 1473/Jan 1474	*Radu* (for 2nd time)
spring 1474	*Basarab Laiotă* (for 2nd time)
1474	*Radu* (for 3rd time)
Oct 1474	*Basarab Laiotă* (for 3rd time)
Oct/Nov 1474	*Radu* (for 4th time)
Jan 1475	*Basarab Laiotă* (for 4th time)
Nov(?) 1476	*Vlad*, the Impaler (for 2nd time)
Dec 1476	*Basarab Laiotă* (for 5th time)
Nov 1477	*Basarab*, the Young, surnamed *Ţepeluş*, son of Basarab II (for 1st time) (d. Mar/Apr 1482)
Sep 1481	*Mircea*, supported by Ştefan the Great, Hospodar of Moldavia
Sep 1481	*Vlad*, the Monk, brother of Vlad the Impaler (for 1st time) (d. Sep 1495)
Nov 1481 – Mar/Apr 1482	*Basarab* (for 2nd time)
Apr 1482 – Sep 1495	*Vlad*, the Monk (for 2nd time)

Rügen

Princes

AD 1168	*Jaromar* (or *Jaromir*) *I*
1218	*Wisław I*, son (b. 1193)
7 Jun 1249	*Jaromar II*, son (b. 1231)
1260/1	*Wisław II*, son, established himself at Schlawe and assumed title of Prince of Rügen and Duke of Pomerania
29 Dec 1302	*Wisław III*, son (b. 1286)
8 Nov 1325	*Warcisław IV*, Duke of Pomerania at Wolgast, nephew (b. c. 1290; d. 1 Aug 1326) inherited Rügen

For later dukes at Rügen see Pomerania – Barth and Rügen.

Russia

The principal series of grand duchies (or grand principalities), ultimately producing the Grand Dukes (later Tsars) of All Russia, is that of Kiev-Vladimir-Moscow. Subordinate to this were a varying number of duchies, of which those of Nizhegorod, Ryazan and Tver succeeded at different times in establishing overlordship over neighbouring duchies and thus becoming grand duchies. All three were absorbed in the end by the grand duchy of Vladimir-Moscow.

Dukes of Novgorod (later Grand Dukes of Kiev)

AD 862(?)	*Rurik* (or *Ryurik*), Scandinavian warrior, made Duke of Novgorod
880(?) – 912	*Oleg*, the Seer, kinsman, captured Kiev 882
912(?)	*Igor* (or *Ingvarr*), son of Rurik (b. 877)
945 – 972	*Svyatoslav I*, son Regent: 945 – 964: *Olga*, mother (b. c. 890; d. 969)
972/3	*Yaropolk I*, son of Svyatoslav I, murdered
c. 980 – 15 Jul 1015	*Vladimir I*, brother
1015	*Svyatopolk I*, the Damned, son (for 1st time) (d. 1019)
1016(?)	*Yaroslav (I)*, the Wise, brother (for 1st time) (b. 978; d. 1054)
1017	*Svyatopolk I* (for 2nd time)
1019	*Yaroslav* (for 2nd time)
1054	*Izyaslav I*, son (for 1st time) (b. 1024; d. 3 Oct 1078)
1068	*Vseslav Bryachislavich*, Duke of Polotsk (d. 1101) usurper, for seven months
1069	*Izyaslav I* (for 2nd time)
1073 – 27 Dec 1076	*Svyatoslav II*, brother (b. 1027)
1076 – 3 Oct 1078	*Izyaslav I* (for 3rd time)
1078 – 1093	*Vsevolod I*, brother (b. 1030)
1093/4 – 16 Apr 1113	*Svyatopolk II*, son of Izyaslav I
1113 – 19 May 1125	*Vladimir II Monomakh*, son of Vsevolod I (b. 1053)
1125 – 14 Apr 1132	*Mstislav I*, the Great, son (b. 1 Jun 1076)
1132	*Yaropolk II*, brother (b. 1082)
1139	*Vyacheslav*, brother (for 1st time) (b. 1083; d. 1154)
1139 – 1 Aug 1146	*Vsevolod II Olgovich*, Duke of Chernigov, second cousin
1146	*Igor II*, brother (d. 19 Sep 1147) abdicated and took monastic vows
1146	*Izyaslav II*, son of Mstislav I (b. 1096; d. 13 Nov 1154)

1149	*Yury I Dolgoruky*, Duke of Suzdal, uncle (for 1st time) (b. c. 1090; d. 1157)
1150	*Vyacheslav* (for 2nd time) titular ruler for Izyaslav II
1150	*Yury I* (for 2nd time)
1154	*Rostislav I*, Duke of Smolensk, brother of Izyaslav II (for 1st time) (d. 14 Mar 1158)
1155	*Yury I* (for 3rd time)
1157	*Izyaslav III Davidovich*, second cousin (for 1st time) (d. 6 Mar 1161)
1159	*Rostislav I* (for 2nd time)
1161	*Izyaslav III* (for 2nd time)
1161	*Rostislav I* (for 3rd time)
1167	*Mstislav II*, son of Izyaslav II (d. 1170) driven out by Andrei I Bogolyubsky, Duke of Vladimir (see below)
Mar 1169 – 1170	*Gleb*, son of Yury I, deputy for Andrei I
1170	Kiev ceased to be seat of Grand Duke

Grand Dukes of Vladimir and Novgorod (later of Moscow (and Vladimir))

1169 – 29 Jun 1174	*Andrei I Bogolyubsky*, son of Yury I (b. 1110) Duke of Vladimir from 1157
1174 – 1176	Civil war
1176	*Vsevolod III*, called Bignest, brother (b. 1154)
1212	*Yury II*, son (for 1st time) (b. 26 Nov 1187; d. 4 Mar 1238)
1217 – 1218	*Konstantin*, brother (b. 1186)
1219	*Yury II* (for 2nd time) Duke of Suzdal 1217 – 1219, Tartar invasions
1238 – 30 Sep 1246	*Yaroslav II* (*I*), Duke of Tver, brother (b. 8 Feb 1191)
1246	*Svyatoslav III*, brother (b. 27 Mar 1196) rule challenged by his nephews, Andrei and Aleksandr (see below)
1248	*Mikhail Khorobrit*, Duke of Moscow, son of Yaroslav II (d. 1248)
1249 – 1252	Rule divided between Mikhail Khorobrit's brothers, *Andrei II* (d. 1264), Duke of Pereyaslavl, and *Aleksandr Nevsky* (b. 1220; d. 14 Nov 1263), Duke of Novgorod
1252 – 14 Nov 1263	*Aleksandr Nevsky* (previously Duke of Novgorod) Grand Duke
27 Jan 1264 – 1271	*Yaroslav III* (*II*), Duke of Tver, brother
1272	*Vasily*, Duke of Kostroma, brother, Tartar vassal
1276	*Dmitry*, Duke of Pereyaslavl, son of Aleksandr

	Nevsky (for 1st time) (b. 1246; d. 1294)
after 1280	*Andrei III*, Duke of Gorodets, brother (for 1st time) (b. 1255; d. 27 Jul 1304) in revolt, Tartar vassal
(?)	*Dmitry* (for 2nd time) expelled by Andrei III
1293 – 27 Jul 1304	*Andrei III* (for 2nd time) Tartar vassal
1304 – 22 Nov 1318	*Mikhail I*, Duke of Tver, son of Yaroslav III (b. 1271) executed by Tartar envoys
1319	*Yury III*, nephew of Andrei III (b. 1281; d. 21 Nov 1325) Tartar vassal, murdered by Dmitry
before Nov 1325	*Dmitry*, son of Mikhail
1326 – 1327	*Aleksandr*, Duke of Tver, brother (b. 1300; d. 1330)
1328 – 31 Mar 1341	*Ivan I Kalita* (i.e. Moneybag), Duke of Moscow, brother of Yury III (b. 1304?)
1 Oct 1341 – 26 Apr 1353	*Simeon*, the Proud, son (b. 7 Sep 1316) Grand Duke of Moscow and Vladimir
Mar 1354 – Nov 1359	*Ivan II*, brother (b. 30 Mar 1326)
1359	*Dmitry (II) Donskoi*, son (for 1st time) (b. 12 Oct 1350) in dispute with Dmitry, Duke of Suzdal
22 Jun 1360	*Dmitry*, the Elder, Duke of Suzdal, great-grandson of Andrei II (b. 1323/4; d. 5 Jul 1383) confirmed by the Khan of the Golden Horde
1362	*Dmitry Donskoi* (for 2nd time)
1363(?)	*Dmitry*, Duke of Suzdal (for 2nd time) for two weeks
1363(?) – 9 May 1389	*Dmitry Donskoi* (for 3rd time) confirmed by the Khan of the Golden Horde 1364
1389	*Vasily I (II)*, son (b. 30 Dec 1371)
Feb 1425	*Vasily II (III)*, the Blind, son (for 1st time) (b. 10 Mar 1415) rule challenged by his uncle, Yury (see below) 1425; at war 1431; confirmed by the Khan of the Golden Horde Sep 1432; taken prisoner in renewed civil war
late 1432	*Yury IV*, son of Dmitry Donskoi (for 1st time) (d. 5 Jun 1434) deserted by nobility
1433(?)	*Vasily II* (for 2nd time)
Mar 1434	*Yury IV* (for 2nd time)
5 Jun 1434	*Vasily II* (for 3rd time) rule challenged by *Vasily Kosoi* (i.e. the Cross-Eyed) (b. 1421; d. 1448) and *Dmitry Shemyaka* (b. 1420; d. 1453), sons of Yury IV
27 Mar 1462 – 27 Oct 1505	*Ivan III*, the Great, son of Vasily II (b. 22 Jan 1440)

Grand Dukes of Nizhegorod (Suzdal, Nizhny Novgorod and Gorodets)

1341 (1350?)	*Konstantin*, Duke of Suzdal, Grand Duke of Vladimir, grandson of Andrei II (d. 21 Nov 1354 (1355?))
1354	*Andrei*, son (d. 2 Jun 1365) entered monastery
1365	*Boris*, brother (for 1st time) (b. before 1340; d. 12 May 1394 (1393?))
1365(?)	*Dmitry*, the Elder, brother (b. 1323/4; d. 5 Jul 1385) formerly Grand Duke of Vladimir
1385	*Boris* (for 2nd time)
c. 1388	*Vasily Kirdiapa*, son of Dmitry (d. 1403) and his brother, *Simeon* (d. 21 Dec 1402)
1389	*Boris* (for 3rd time) retired to Suzdal
1390(?)	*Vasily I*, Grand Duke of Moscow (see above) transferred Nizhny Novgorod and Gorodets to the Grand Duchy of Moscow; war between Simeon and Vasily I
	Oct 1395 – 1401; Nizhny Novgorod captured and devastated by Simeon with Tartar aid Oct 1395, recaptured by Vasily I
1408 – 1410	*Daniil*, son of Boris (d. after 1417) in revolt
1412 – 1414	*Ivan Borisovich*, called Tugoi Luk (i.e. Strongbow), brother (b. 1370; d. 1418)
1414	*Aleksandr*, the Potbellied (Puzaty), son, installed by Vasily I
1418	*Aleksandr*, cousin
	Nizhegorod thenceforth ruled by Muscovite deputies

Grand Dukes of Ryazan

1258	*Roman*, son of Oleg; descendant of Yaroslav, the younger son of Svyatoslav II, Grand Duke of Kiev, killed by the Tartars
1270	*Fyodor*, son
1293	*Yaroslav*, brother
1299	*Ivan*, son, killed by the Tartars
1327	*Ivan Korotopol*, son
1343	*Yaroslav-Dmitry*, for less than a year
1343(?)	*Ivan II*, brother
1350	*Oleg*, son (for 1st time) (d. 1402) driven out by Dmitry Donskoi, Grand Duke of Moscow and Vladimir
Dec 1371	*Vladimir*, Duke of Pronsk, cousin (d. 1372)

1372	*Oleg* (for 2nd time)
1402	*Fyodor II*, son
c. 1430(?) – 1456	*Ivan III*, son
1464	*Vasily*, son, vassal of Moscow
1483	*Ivan IV*, son
1500 – 1503	*Fyodor III*, brother; willed Ryazan to Ivan III, Grand Duke of Moscow

Grand Dukes of Tver

1327	*Konstantin*, son of Mikhail I, Duke of Tver and Grand Duke of Vladimir (b. 1306) asserted authority over other dukes of the Tver land 1339
c. 1348	*Vsevolod*, nephew; son of Aleksandr, Grand Duke of Vladimir (b. 1328; d. 1365) for one year
1349	*Vasily*, uncle (b. 1304; d. 1367/8)
autumn 1366 – 26 Aug 1399	*Mikhail II*, brother of Vsevolod (b. 1333)
1399	*Ivan I*, son (b. 1357)
22 May 1425	*Aleksandr*, son (b. 1378)
25 Oct 1425	*Yury*, son (b. after 1398; d. 22 Apr 1426) for four weeks
Nov 1425	*Boris*, brother (b. 1422)
10 Feb 1461 – 12 Sep 1485	*Mikhail III*, son (b. 1453; d. after 1505) attacked by Ivan III, Grand Duke of Moscow; fled to Lithuania
12 Sep 1485	Tver became an apanage of Moscow

Rustamids

Territory comprised part of present-day western Algeria, with the capital at Tahart.

Imams

AD 776/7	*'Abd al-Rahman (ibn Rustam)*, Berber governor of Kairouan, expelled by the Arabs, made imam, founded Tahart 761/2
784/5	*'Abd al-Wahhab* (or *'Abd al-Warith*) *(ibn 'Abd al-Rahman)*, son

823/4	*Abu Sa'id al-Aflah (ibn 'Abd al-Wahhab)*, son
871/2	*Abu Bakr (ibn alAflah)*, son
(?)	*Abu'l-Yaqzan Muhammad (ibn al-Aflah)*, brother
894/5	*Abu Hatim Yusuf (ibn Muhammad)*, son (for 1st time)
897	*Ya'qub (ibn al-Aflah)*, uncle
901	*Abu Hatim Yusuf* (for 2nd time)
906/7 – 908/9	*Yaqzan (ibn Muhammad)*, brother
908/9	Capture of Tahart by *Abu 'Abdullah al-Shi'i*, the Fatimid Da'i (religious leader)

Rwanda

Territory comprised part of present-day Rwanda.

Abami (Kings)

AD 1386*	*Ndahiro Ruyange*
1410	*Ndoba*, son
1434	*Samembe*, son
1458	*Nsoro Samukondo*, son
1482	*Ruganzu I Bwimba*, son
1506	*Cyilima I Rugwe*, brother
1528	*Kigeri I Mukobanya*, defeated the son of Cyilima I Rugwe to succeed to throne
1552	*Mibambwe I Mutabaazi*, brother
1576	*Yuhi II Gahima*, son
1600	*Ndahiro Cyaamatare*, son, abdicated
1624	*Ruganzu II Ndoori*
1648	*Mutara I Seemugeshi* (or *Mutara I Muyenzi*), son
1672	*Kigeri II Nyamuheshera*, son
1696	*Mibambwe II Gisanura*, son
1720	*Yuhi III Mazimpaka*, son
1744	*Karemeera Rwaaka*, son
1768	*Cyilima II Rujugira*, brother

*All dates before 1895 are approximate

1792	*Kigeri III Ndabarasa*, son
1797	*Mibambwe III Seentaabyo*, son
1830	*Yuhi IV Gahindiro*, son
1860	*Mutara II Rwoogera*, son
c. 1865	*Kigeri IV Rwaabugiri*, son
1895	*Mibambwe IV Rutarindwa*, son
1896 – 1931	*Yuhi V Musinga*, deposed
1899 – 1917	Became part of German East Africa
1923	Belgium given League of Nations mandate, ruling through the traditional kings
1931 – 25 Jul 1959	*(Charles) Mutara III Rudahigwa*, son
28 Jul 1959	*(Jean Baptiste) Kigieri Ndahindurwa*, forced into exile and deposed following civil war 1959
Jan 1961	Establishment of republic
2 Oct 1961	Abolition of the monarchy

Saffarids

Territory comprised part of present-day eastern Iran, centred in Sistan.

Amirs

AD 867 – 14 Jun 879	*(Abu Yusuf) Ya'qub al-Saffar (ibn Laith)*
879	*'Amr (ibn Laith)*, brother; recognized as 'Abbasid governor in Sistan, Khurasan and Fars, assassinated in Baghdad
901/2	*Tahir (ibn Muhammad ibn 'Amr)*, grandson
908/9	*Laith (ibn 'Ali ibn Laith)*, grandson of Laith
910/11	*Muhammad (ibn 'Ali)*, brother, imprisoned by the Samanid governor Ahmad II
910/11 – 912/13	First Samanid occupation, usurpations of Kuthayyir ibn Ahmad and Ahmad ibn Qudam
912/13	*'Amr ibn Ya'qub (ibn Muhammad ibn 'Amr)*, great-grandson of 'Amr
912/13 – 922/3	Second Samanid occupation
922/3	*(Abu Ja'far) Ahmad ibn Muhammad (ibn Khalaf)*, descendant of Laith, appointed governor for the Samanids

963/4 – 1002/3	*(Wali al-Daula) Khalaf (ibn Ahmad)*, son (b. 937/8) Samanid vassal
1002/3	Ghaznavid occupation
(?)	*Tahir ibn Khalaf*, son, governor for the Ghaznavid amir Mahmud
1029/30	*Nasr (ibn Ahmad)*, uncle, Ghaznavid vassal until 1048, thereafter Seljuq vassal
1072/3	*(Baha' al-Daula) Tahir ibn Nasr*, son
1089/90	*(Baha' al-Daula) Khalaf ibn Nasr*, brother
after 1102/3	*(Taj al-Din) Nasr* ——, grandson
1163/4	*(Shams al-Din) Ahmad ibn Nasr* (or *(Shams al-Din) Muhammad ibn Nasr*), son
1166/7	*(Taj al-Din) Harb (ibn Muhammad)*, son
1215/16	*(Shams al-Din) Bahram Shah (ibn 'Uthman)*, grandson
1221/2	*(Taj al-Din) Nasr ibn Bahram Shah*, son
1221/2	Mongol invasion, the Saffarids became Mongol vassals
1221/2	*Rukn al-Din (Abu-Mansur ibn Bahram Shah)*, brother
1222/3	*Shihab al-Din (Mahmud ibn 'Uthman)*, uncle
1225/6	*'Ali (ibn 'Uthman)*, brother
1228/9	*Shams al-Din 'Ali (ibn Mas'ud ibn Khalaf)*, descendant of Tahir ibn Nasr
1254/5	*Nasr al-Din (ibn Abi'l-Fath ibn Mas'ud)*, nephew
1327/8	*Nusrat al-Din (ibn Nasr al-Din)*, son
Dec 1330/Jan 1331	*Qutb al-Din Muhammad (ibn Rukn al-Din Mahmud)*, nephew
1346/7	*Taj al-Din I (ibn Muhammad)*, son
1350/1	*Sultan Mahmud (ibn Shah 'Ali)*, grandson of Nasr al-Din
1362/3	*'Izz al-Din (ibn Rukn al-Din Mahmud)*, cousin
1382/3	*Qutb al-Din I (ibn 'Izz al-Din)*, son
1386/7	*Taj al-Din II (ibn Qutb al-Din)*, son
1402/3	*Qutb al-Din II (ibn Taj al-Din)*, son
1419/20	*Shams al-Din (ibn Qutb al-Din)*, uncle
1438/9	*Nizam al-Din Yahya (ibn Shams al-Din)*, son
1480/1 – (?)	*Shams al-Din Muhammad (ibn Yahya)*, son

Salghurids

Territory comprised part of present-day south-western Iran, centred in Fars.

Atabegs

AD 1148/9	*(Muzaffar al-Din) Sonqur (ibn Maudud)*, great-grandson of Salghur
1160/1	*(Muzaffar al-Din) Zangi (ibn Maudud)*, brother, Seljuq vassal
1174/5	*Dakla (ibn Zangi)*, son
1193/4	*Toghrıl (ibn Sonqur ibn Maudud)*, cousin
1202/3	*Sa'd I (ibn Zangi)*, cousin, Khwarazm-Shah vassal
1230/1 – 18 May 1260	*Abu Bakr (Qutlugh Khan ibn Sa'd)*, son, surrendered to the Mongol great khan Ögedei
May 1260	*Sa'd II (ibn Qutlugh)*, son, died twelve days after his father
1260	*Muhammad (ibn Sa'd)*, son, as infant under the regency of his mother *Turkan Khatun*
Oct/Nov 1262	*Muhammad Shah (ibn Salghur Shah)*, cousin
18 Jul 1263	*Seljuq Shah (ibn Salghur Shah)*, brother, assassinated
Nov/Dec 1264 – 1270	*Abish Khatun (bint Sa'd)*, daughter of Sa'd II; married Mengü Temür, son of the Il-khan Hülegü, nominal regent
1270	Direct Mongol rule

Salzburg

Archbishops (and from 1278 Princes of the Holy Roman Empire)*

AD (?)	*Johannes*
15 Jun 767 – 27 Nov 784	*Virgil*

*When two dates separated by an oblique stroke are given for the beginning of an episcopate the first refers to nomination or election and the second to ordination, consecration or investiture

11 Jun 785 – 24 Jan 821	*Arn*
821 – 4 Jan 836	*Adalram*
836 – 14 Oct 859	*Liutpram*
(?) – 14 May 873	*Adalwin*
13 Sep 873 – Jul 907	*Theotmar*, killed
(?) – 24 Sep 923	*Piligrim*
923 – 14 Nov 935	*Udalbert*
935 – 22 Aug 939	*Egilolf*
before 29 May 940 – 958	*Herold*, resigned
18 Apr 958 – 1 May 991	*Friedrich I*
8 Nov 991 – 5 or 6 Dec 1023	*Hartwich*
26 Jan 1024 – 1 Nov 1025	*Gunther*
21 Dec 1025 – 28 Jul 1041	*Dietmar II*
25 Oct 1041 – 8 Apr 1060	*Baldewin*
11 Jun/30 Jul 1060 – 15 Jun 1088*	*Geberhard*
25 Mar/7 Apr 1090 – Sep(?) 1101*	*Thiemo*, murdered
7 Jan/21 Oct 1106 – 8 or 9 Apr 1147	*Konrad I*
Apr/11 May 1147 – 21 or 22 Jun 1164	*Eberhard I*
1164 – 28 Sep 1168	*Konrad II*, Bishop (Konrad I) of Passau 1147 – 1164
Oct 1168/16 Mar 1169 – 26 May 1174	*Adalbert I* (for 1st time) (d. 7 or 8 Apr 1200), deposed
27 May 1174 – 1177	*Heinrich*, resigned
1177 – Nov 1183	*Konrad III von Wittelsbach*, previously and subsequently Archbishop of Mainz
19 Nov 1183 – 7 or 8 Apr 1200	*Adalbert I* (for 2nd time)
before 28 May 1200 – 30 Nov 1246	*Eberhard II*
25 Feb – before 7 Oct 1247	*Burchard von Ziegenhagen*
7 Oct 1247 – 5 Sep 1257	*Philipp von Ortenburg*, initially as administrator, deposed
May/5 Sep 1257 – 1 Sep 1265	*Ulrich* (d. 6 Jul 1268) previously Bishop of Seckau; resigned, translated again to Seckau
10 Nov 1265/11 Jun 1267 – 27 Apr 1270	*Władysław*, Duke of Breslau, previously Bishop of Passau

*May 1085 – 1106 *Perhtold*, Imperial anti-archbishop, expelled

between 28 Apr and 20 Oct 1270/7 May 1273 – 7 Apr 1284	*Friedrich II von Walchen*
21 Apr(?)/1 Dec 1284 – 3 Aug 1290	*Rudolf von Hohenegg*
13 Jan 1291 – 29 Jun 1312	*Konrad IV von Fohnsdorf von Praitenfurt*, previously Bishop of Lavant; in disputed election against *Stefan I*, Duke of Lower Bavaria (b. 14 Mar 1271; d. 21 Dec 1310)
31 Mar/12 Aug 1312 – 6 Oct 1315	*Weichard von Polheim*
24 Oct 1315 – 30 Mar 1338	*Friedrich III von Leibnitz*
after 30 Mar/31 Aug 1338 – 29 Jul 1343	*Heinrich von Pirnbaum*
after 29 Oct/1 Dec 1343 – 11/13 Aug 1365	*Ortolf von Weisseneck*
after 11 Sep 1365/7 Jan 1366 – 5 Apr 1396	*Pilgrim* (or *Peregrin*) *II von Puchheim*, in disputed election against *Ortolf von Ovenstetten*
10 Apr/2 Jun 1396 – 9 May 1403	*Gregor*
22 May 1403/13 Jan 1406 – 18 Jan 1427*	*Eberhard III von Neuhaus*, in rivalry with Berthold von Wächingen until 13 Jan 1406
after 18 Jan/11 Apr 1427 – 9 Feb 1429	*Eberhard IV von Starhemberg*
after 9 Feb/22 Apr 1429 – 30 Sep 1441	*Johann II von Reisberg*
1441 – 4 Apr 1452	*Friedrich IV von Emmerberg*
9 Jun 1452 – 3 Nov 1461	*Sigismund von Volkerstorf*
23 Jan 1462 –	*Burghard von Weissbriach*
21 Apr 1466 –	*Bernard von Rohr* (d. 31 Mar 1487) resigned
20 Dec 1484 – 15 Dec 1489	*Johann Peckenschlager*
3 Mar 1490 – 4 Oct 1494	*Friedrich V*, Count of Schaumberg

*6 Feb 1404 – 13 Jan 1406 *Berthold von Wächingen* (d. Freising 7 Sep 1410) previously Bishop of Freising; appointment cancelled by Pope Innocent III

Samanids

Territory comprised part of present-day southern USSR and Iran, with the capital at Bukhara.

Governors of Transoxania and Khurasan for the 'Abbasids

AD 819/20	*Ahmad I (ibn Asad)*, grandson of Saman, governor of Farghana
864/5	*Nasr I (ibn Ahmad)*, son, appointed 'Abbasid governor of Transoxania 875
Aug/Sep 892 – 24 Nov 907	*(Abu Ibrahim) Isma'il (ibn Ahmad)*, brother (b. Farghana Apr/May 849) governor of Bukhara 873/4 – 892/3
Nov/Dec 907 – 24 Jan 914	*(Abu Nasr) Ahmad II (ibn Isma'il)*, son, appointed 'Abbasid governor of Khurasan, assassinated
Jan 914 – Mar/Apr 943	*(al-Amir al-Sa'id) Nasr II (ibn Ahmad)*, son*
Apr/May 943	*(al-Amir al-Hamid) Nuh I (ibn Nasr)*, son
954/5	*(al-Amir al-Mu'ayyad Abu'l-Fawaris) 'Abd al-Malik I (ibn Nuh)*, son
961/2	*Nasr (ibn 'Abd al-Malik)*, son, for one day
961/2	*(al-Amir al-Sadid Abu Salih) Mansur I (ibn Nuh)*, uncle
976/7 – 22 Jul 997	*(al-Amir al-Rida) Nuh II (ibn Mansur)*, son
Jul/Aug 997 – 1 Feb 999	*(Abu'l-Harith) Mansur II (ibn Nuh)*, son, dethroned
Feb 999	*(Abu'l-Fawaris) 'Abd al-Malik II (ibn Nuh)*, brother
999/1000 – Dec 1004/Jan 1005	*(Abu Ibrahim) Isma'il II (al-Muntasir ibn Nuh)*, brother, killed
Dec 1004/Jan 1005	Qarakhanids established in Transoxania
Dec 1004/Jan 1005	Ghaznavids established in Khurasan

*913/14	*Ishaq (ibn Ahmad)*, in rebellion against his brother Nasr II
918/19	*Mikail (ibn Ja'far)*, in rebellion until 920/1

Sasanids

At its greatest extent, territory comprised part of present-day eastern Turkey, south-western U.S.S.R., Iran, Iraq, Syria, Lebanon, Israel, Jordan, Egypt and north-eastern Libya, with the capital at Ctesiphon.

Kings

AD (?)	*Papak*, son of Sasan, King of Persis
211/12	*Shapur*, son, King of Persis
211/12	*Ardashir I*, brother; King of Persis; took the title 'King of Kings' 28 Apr 224 after conquest of the Parthians; conquered Kerman, Persian Gulf area and present-day western Iran
241	*Shapur I*, son, crowned 20 Mar 242, conquered parts of Syria and Turkey, invaded Armenia c. 253(?), defeated and captured the Roman emperor Valerian Jun 260
272	*Hormazd I* (or *Hormizd-Ardashir*) son, viceroy of Armenia with title King of Armenia 253 – 272 (262?)
273	*Bahram I*, brother, governor of Gilan before 273
276	*Bahram II*, son, invasion by the Roman emperor Carus 283
293	*Bahram III*, cousin
293	*Narses*, uncle, viceroy of Armenia 272 – 293
303	*Hormazd II*, son
310	*Adarnarseh*, son, assassinated
310	*Shapur II*, brother, invaded Armenia and Mesopotamia 337, gained full control of Armenia 379
379	*Ardashir II*, brother, king of Adiabene (part of present-day northern Iraq) before 379, deposed
383	*Shapur III*, nephew
388	*Bahram IV*, brother, governor of Kerman before 388
399	*Yezdegerd I*, nephew, assassinated
420	*Khusrau*, usurper
420	*Bahram V*, the Wild Ass, son of Yezdegerd I, extended kingdom into central Asia
438	*Yezdegerd II*, son
457	*Hormazd III*, son
457	*Firoz I*, brother
484	*Balash*, brother, deposed

488	*Kobad I*, nephew (for 1st time) deposed and imprisoned in Susiana (part of present-day south-eastern Iraq and south-western Iran)
497	*Jamasp*, brother
499	*Kobad I* (for 2nd time)
13 Sep 531	*Khusrau I*, the Just, son, held Antioch (present-day Antakya) for a short time
Feb 579	*Hormazd IV*, son, deposed and killed
590	*Khusrau II*, the Victorious; son; gained throne with the aid of the Byzantine emperor Maurice;* conquered Armenia and large areas of Asia Minor c. 604, Damascus 613, Jerusalem 614, Alexandria 616, Chalcedon (present-day Kaldıköy) 617; expansion ended by the Byzantine emperor Heraclius 622 – 627; deposed and killed
25 Feb 628	*Kobad II*, son
Sep 628	*Ardashir III*, son
27 Apr 630 – 9 Jun 630	*Shahrbaraz*, usurper
(?)	*Khusrau III*, cousin of Kobad II
(?)	*Juvansher*, brother of Kobad II
May 630 – Oct 631	*Boran* (or *Puran-Dukht*), sister
(?)	*Gushnasbandeh*, brother of Khusrau III
(?)	*Azarmidukht*, sister of Boran
631 – 632	*Hormazd V*, nephew
(?)	*Khusrau IV*, grand-nephew of Hormazd IV
(?)	*Firoz II*, brother
632	*Khusrau V*, brother of Hormazd V
632 or 633 – Sep 651	*Yezdegerd III*, nephew, at war with the Orthodox caliphate 637 – 649, fled to Media and killed at Merv (present-day Mary)
649	Rule by the Orthodox caliphs

*590	*Bahram VI* or (*Bahram Chubin*) (the Javelin?), usurper, supreme commander in Khorasan, led revolt against Hormazd IV and took the throne, deposed and fled to Turkistan, where he was assassinated
591/2 – 595/6	*Bistam*, usurper

Savoy

Originally part of the kingdom of Arles (see Kingdoms of Burgundy). Territory now in Savoie and Haute-Savoie departments of France. Chief town Chambéry.

Counts

AD 1027	*Humbert I*, the Whitehanded, traditionally, a son of Bérold of Saxony (d. 1 Jul 1042/51) acquired Chablais 1035
c. 1047	*Amédée I*, son (b. 1016)
c. 1051	*Odon*, brother (d. 19 Jan 1057/60)
c. 1057 – 9 Aug 1078	*Pierre I*, son
1078 – 26 Jan 1080	*Amédée II*, brother
1080 – 18 Sep 1103	*Humbert II*, the Strong, son
1103 – 30 Aug 1148	*Amédée III*, son (b. c. 1092) Regents: 1103 – 1109: *Gisèle de Bourgogne*, mother, and *Aimon*, Count of Genevois
1148 – 4 Mar 1189	*Humbert III*, the Holy, son (b. 1 Aug 1136)
1189 – 6 Mar 1233	*Thomas I*, son (b. 20 May 1177)
1233 – 24 Jun 1253	*Amédée IV*, son (b. 1197) created Duke of Chablais and Aosta by Holy Roman Emperor Friedrich II 1238
1253 – c. 7 Jun 1263	*Boniface*, son (b. 1 Dec 1244)
1263 – 14/15 May 1268	*Pierre II*, the Little Charlemagne, uncle (b. Susa, 1203; d. Pierre-Châtel) Count of Vaud and Bugey c. 1234
1268 – 17 Nov 1285	*Philippe I*, brother (b. 1207) Archbishop of Lyon 1245 – 1267
1285 – 16 Oct 1323	*Amédée V*, the Great, nephew (b. c. 1253)
1323 – 4 Nov 1329	*Édouard*, the Liberal, son (b. 8 Feb 1284)
1329 – 22 Jun 1343	*Aimon*, the Peaceful, brother (b. 15 Dec 1291)
1343 – 1 Mar 1383	*Amédée VI*, the Green Count, son (b. Chambéry 4 Jan 1334; d. Castropignano) imperial vicar 1365
1383 – 1 Nov 1391	*Amédée VII*, the Red Count, son (b. Chambéry 24 Feb 1360; d. Thonon, near Geneva)

Dukes

1391	*Amédée VIII*, the Peaceful, son (b. Chambéry 4 Dec 1383; d. Thonon, near Geneva, 7 Jan 1451) created

	Duke of Savoy, 1416, abdicated 1434; elected antipope (Felix V) 5 Nov 1439, resigned 1449 and appointed cardinal
1434 – 29 Jan 1465	*Louis*, son (b. 24 Feb 1402)
1465 – 30 Mar 1472	*Amédée IX*, the Blessed, son (b. 1 Feb 1435)
1472 – 22 Apr 1482	*Philibert I*, the Hunter, son (b. 7 Aug 1465)
1482 – 13 Mar 1490	*Charles I*, the Warrior, brother (b. 29 Mar 1468)
1490 – 16 Apr 1496	*Charles II*, son (b. 24 Jun 1489) Regent: 1490 – 1496: *Blanche de Montferrat*, mother

Saxony

Territory comprised part of present-day northern West Germany.

Dukes

Liudolfings (*Saxon House*)

AD 880 – 30 Nov 912	*Otto I*, the Illustrious, son of Liudolf (b. c. 836)
912 – 2 Jul 936	*Heinrich I*, the Fowler, son (b. c. 876; d. Memleben, near Merseburg) King of Germany 919
936 – 961	*Otto II*, son (b. 23 Nov 912; d. Memleben, near Merseburg, 7 May 973) King (Otto I) of Germany 8 Aug 936, King of the Lombards 951, Holy Roman Emperor 2 Feb 962

Billungs

961 – 27 Mar 973	*Hermann Billung*, son of Count Billung; Margrave 953
973 – 9 Feb 1011	*Bernhard I*, son
1011 – 29 Jun 1059	*Bernhard II*, son
1059 – 28 Mar 1072	*Ordulf*, son
1072 – 23 Aug 1106	*Magnus*, son (b. c. 1045)

Supplinburg House

1106 – 1127	*Lothar*, son of Gebhard von Supplinburg (b. Jun 1075; d. Breitenwang, Austria, 4 Dec 1137) King (Lothar II) of Germany 30 Aug 1125, Holy Roman Emperor 4 Jun 1133

House of Welf

1127 – 1138	*Heinrich II*, the Proud, Duke (Heinrich X) of Bavaria, Margrave of Tuscany, son-in-law (b. c. 1100; d. Quedlinburg 20 Oct 1139) deposed

Ascanian House

1138	*Albrecht*, the Bear, Count of Anhalt, Margrave of Brandenburg, son of Otto of Ballenstädt (b. c. 1100; d. 18 Nov 1170)

House of Welf (restored)

1142 – 1180	*Heinrich III*, the Lion, son of Heinrich II (b. 1129; d. Brunswick 6 Aug 1195) Duke (Heinrich XII) of Bavaria 1156, deposed and exiled; restored to his lands in Brunswick, 1181
1180	Large areas of the duchy lost

Ascanian House (restored)

1180 – 9 Feb 1212	*Bernhard III*, Count of Anhalt, son of Albrecht (b. c. 1140)
1212 – 1260	*Albrecht I*, son (d. 8 Nov 1261)
1260	Duchy divided into Saxe-Lauenburg and Saxe-Wittenberg

Dukes and Electors of Saxe-Wittenberg

1260 – 25 Aug 1298	*Albrecht II*, son of Albrecht I, Duke of Saxony
1298 – 11 Mar 1356	*Rudolf I*, son, Duke
1356 – 6 Dec 1370	*Rudolf II*, son, Elector
1370 – 15 May 1388	*Wenzel*, brother
1388 – 9 Jun 1419	*Rudolf III*, son
1419 – 27 Nov 1422	*Albrecht III*, brother

House of Wettin

6 Jan 1423 – 4 Jan 1428	*Friedrich I*, the Warlike, Margrave (Friedrich IV) of Meissen, son of Friedrich III of Meissen and Thuringia (b. 11 Apr 1370)
1428 – 7 Sep 1464	*Friedrich II*, the Mild, son (b. 22 Aug 1412) inherited Thuringia 1440 but forced to grant it to his brother, Wilhelm, 1445
1464	Division of the Wettin domains between the Ernestine and Albertine Lines

Electors of the Ernestine Line

1464 – 26 Aug 1486	*Ernst*, son of Friedrich II (b. 24 Mar 1441)
1486 – 5 May 1525	*Friedrich III*, the Wise, son (b. 17 Jan 1463)

Dukes of the Albertine Line

1464 – 12 Sep 1500	*Albrecht*, the Courageous, son of Friedrich II (b. 31 Jul 1443) governor of the Netherlands 1488 – 1493, governor of Friesland 1498

Scotland

Kings of the Picts*

c. AD 400	*Uuradach Uetla* (or *Feradach Finlegh*)
c. 402	*Gartnait II Diuperr*
?	*Talorc I mac Achiuir*
413(?)	*Drust*, son of Erp (d. c. 450)
451(?)	*Talorc II*, son of Aniel
455(?)	*Nechtan I Morbet* (or *Celchamoch*), son of Erp
c. 465	*Drust II Gurthinmoch*
c. 495	*Galam I*
c. 510	*Drust III*, son of Gigurum; and until c. 525 *Drust*, son of Hudrossig (or Uudrost)
c. 530	*Gartnait III*, brother of Drust III
c. 537	*Cailtram* (or *Caltarni*), brother
c. 539	*Talorc III*, son of Murtholoic
c. 550	*Drust V*, son of Munait (or Moneth)
c. 551 – 556	*Galam II Cennalath* (d. c. 580)
c. 555	*Brude*, son of Maelchon (i.e. Maelgwn Gwynedd, King of Gwynedd?)
586/7(?)	*Gartnait IV* (or *Garnard*), son of Domelch (or Donath)

*Although the fathers of most kings are given in the traditional lists, the succession was matrilineal, and the relation of a king to his predecessor (uterine brother, nephew, cousin) is seldom known. The names appear in some lists in Gaelicized forms, in others in forms which are Pictish but often corrupt. The best known forms are used here, with alternatives in parentheses. Brude, Drust and Nechtan are Gaelic forms, the Pictish being Bred or Bredei, Drest and Naiton.

597(?)	*Nechtan II*, grandson of Uerb (d. 621?)
617(?)	*Cinioch*, son of Lutrin
631	*Gartnait V* (or *Nechtan III*), son of Uuid (or Fothe)
635	*Brude II*, brother
641	*Talorc IV*, brother
653	*Talorcen* (or *Talargan*), son of Eanfrith, King of Bernicia
657	*Gartnait VI*, son of Donuel (i.e. Domnall Brecc, King of Dalriada?)
664	*Drust V*, brother, expelled
672	*Brude III*, son of Bile (perhaps Beli ap Neithon, King of Strathclyde) and nephew(?) of Talorcen
693	*Tara(i)n*, son of Entifidich (or Ainftech?), expelled
697	*Brude IV*, son of Derile (or Derelei)
706	*Nechtan IV*, brother (for 1st time) retired to monastery
724	*Drust VI* (d. 729)
726	*Alpin* (or *Elpin*), King of Dalriada 733 – 736 (?)
728	*Oengus* (or *Onuist*) *I*, son of Fergus (or Urguist) (for 1st time)
728	*Nechtan IV* (for 2nd time)
729	*Oengus I* (for 2nd time)
761	*Brude V*, brother
763	*Ciniod*, son of Uuredech (i.e. Feradoch of Lorne?)
775	*Alpin* (or *Elpin*) *II*
780(?)	*Drust VII*, son of Talorcen
781(?)	*Talorcen II* (or *Talorgan*), son of Drostan
785(?) – 787 (?)	*Talorcen III* (or *Talorgen*), son of Oengus
785(?) – 789	*Conall* (or *Canaul*), son of Tadg (or Tang) (d. 807) ousted by Constantine
before 789	*Constantine*, son of Fergus, at first jointly with Conall
820 – 834	*Oengus* (or *Unuist*) *II*, son of Fergus (or Urguist)
832	Brief occupation by *Alpin*, father of Kenneth mac Alpin
834	*Drust VIII*, son of Constantine; and *Talorc V* (or *Talorgen*), son of Uuthal (or Fethal)
837(?)	*Eoganan* (or *Uuen*), son of Oengus II; King of Dalriada 836(?) – 839
839	*Ferat* (or *Uurad*), son of Bargot
842(?)	*Brude VI*, son of Ferat
842/3 – 848	*Kenneth mac Alpin*, son of Alpin (d. 858) King of Dalriada 840 and of part of Pictavia 842/3
? – 843	*Kenneth* (or *Cinaed*), son of Ferat

843(?)	*Brude VII*, son of Fethal
845(?)	*Drust IX*, son of Ferat
848(?)	Kenneth mac Alpin united the kingdoms of Dalriada and Pictavia

For continuation, see Kings of (the Picts and) Scots.

Kings of Strathclyde (Dumbarton)*

Territory comprised part of present-day south-western Scotland and north-western England.

fl. c. AD 450(?)	*Ceretic* (*Coroticus*, *Ceredig*)
?	*Cinuit* (*Cynwyd*), son
?	*Dumngual* (*Dyfnwal*) *Hen*, son
?	*Clinoch* (*Clynog*), son
?	*Guithno* (*Gwyddno*), brother
?	*Tutagual Tutclyt* (*Tudwal Tudclyd*), son of Clinoch
?	*Neithon*, son of Guithno
?	*Riderch* (*Rhydderch ap Tudwal*), son of Tutagual
fl. c. 600(?)	*Beli*, son of Neithon (d. 627?)
fl. c. 645	*Eugein* (*Owain ap Beli*), son
?	*Gwriad*
c. 660	*'Domnall'* (*Dyfnwal*), son of 'Auin' (Owain ap Beli) (d. c. 694)
c. 660	Strathclyde subject for a time to Northumbria
c. 694	*Beli*, son of Elfin, nephew
?	*Teuduber* (*Tewdwr*), son

*As both the British of Strathclyde and those of Cumberland and Westmorland, like the Welsh, are called Cymry, it is not always certain whether the terms Cumbria and Cumbrians refer to Strathclyde proper, to Cumberland and Westmorland, or to the whole region. They have therefore been left uninterpreted.

Up to 872 the list is based on a genealogy, occasionally supported by entries in annals, and it cannot be assumed that all members of the direct line reigned, nor that no others did whose names have not survived. The names are given as they appear in the manuscript, with the modern Welsh equivalents in parentheses. From about 900 the list depends on entries in annals and chronicles — Irish, Latin, Welsh and Anglo-Saxon. They are difficult to reconcile, and one cannot be certain whether the original form of some names was British or Gaelic, nor whether the bearers of similar names are identical: the names are given as they appear in the source. In interpreting these names it should be remembered that the *m* in Domnall sounds like a *v* or *w* in English (or a Welsh *f*) and that the *g* in *Eogan* is practically silent. In view of the uncertainties the data for the later period are presented merely as isolated facts. *Floruit* entries refer to events other than accession or death.

752	*Dumnagual* (*Dyfnwal ap Tewdwr*), son (d. 760)
?	*Eugein* (*Owain ap Dyfnwal*), son*
?	*Riderch* (*Rhydderch ab Owain*), son*
?	*Dumnagual* (*Dyfnwal ap Rhydderch*), son*
?	*Arthgal*, son*
872	*Run* (*Rhun ab Arthgal*), son
?	*Eochaid*, son, King of Scots 878 – 889
c. 900	Eastern parts of Cumberland and Westmorland annexed
after 908(?)	*Donevaldus* (*Dyfnwal? Donald?*), died
after 908(?)	*Duvenaldus* (*Domnall? Donald?*), son of Aed,† succeeded
915/16	*Eugenius* (*Eogan*, *Owen*), son of Domnall II, King of Scots; made Lord of Cumbria by Constantine II, King of Scots
fl. 927, 934	*Eugenius* (*Owinus*), King of the Cumbrians (the same, or a member of the original dynasty?)
fl. 945	*Dunmail* (*Dumngual? Domnall?*), King of Cumbria
945	Cumbria handed by Edmund, King of Wessex, to Malcolm I, King of Scots
945 – 954	*Indulf*, son of Constantine II; Lord of Cumbria ‡; King of Scots 954 – 962
950	*Dwnwallawn*§, killed by the Vikings
954 – 962	*Dub*, son of Malcolm I; Lord of Cumbria; King of Scots 962 – 966
c. 971	*Malcolm*, son of Dub, made under-king of Cumbria (d. 991)
fl. 973	*Malcolm*, King of the Cumbrians (the same?; but see 997)
fl. 973	*Dufnal*, kingdom unspecified (the same as Dunmail?)
974	*Dunguallaun*§, King of Strathclyde, went to Rome (the same?)
975	*Domnall*, son of Eogan (Eugenius 927?), King of the Britons of the North, died on pilgrimage (the same?)
after 991	*Malcolm*, son of Kenneth II, King of Scots (b. c. 954) under-king of Cumbria; King of Scots as Malcolm II

*Accession conjectural

†Conjectured to be the brother of Constantine II, King of Scots

‡According to John of Fordun. The accession of Eugenius and that of Indulf are recorded in remarkably similar terms, and the first may be a mistake

§The names Dumnguallaun and Dumnagual (Dyfnwal) are sometimes confused

	25 Mar 1005 – 25 Nov 1034
997	*Malcolm*, son of Domnall; King of the Britons of the North; died
c. 1016	*Owen*, the Bald, son of Dumnagual*; King of Strathclyde; died
c. 1016	*Duncan*, grandson of Malcolm II; King of Strathclyde; King of Scots 25 Nov 1034 – 14 Aug 1040
1034	Strathclyde absorbed into the Scottish kingdom on the accession of Duncan

Kings of Dalriada (Dál Riata)†

AD 474(?) or 498(?)	*Fergus Mor mac Erca*, of the Dál Riata of Ireland
501(?)	*Domangort*, son, retired to monastery
506(?)	*Comgall*, son
538(?)	*Gabran*, brother
560(?)	*Conall*, son of Comgall
574	*Aedan*, son of Gabran
608(?)	*Eochaid Buide*, son
629	*Connad Cerr*, son of Conall, for three months
629 – 13(?) Dec 642	*Domnall Brecc*, son of Eochaid
637	*Ferchar*, son of Connad Cerr
650	*Conall Crandomna*, brother of Domnall Brecc (d. 660) and *Dunchad*, son of Duban, descendant of Eoganan, brother of Aedan(?) (d. 680?)
660	*Domangort II*, son of Domnall Brecc
673 – 689	*Maelduin*, son of Conall
677 – 697	*Ferchar Fota* (the Tall), descendant of Loarn, brother of Fergus Mor
689	*Domnall Donn*, brother of Maelduin
696	*Eochaid* (or *Eochu*) *Crooked-Nose*, grandson of Domnall Brecc
697	*Ainbcellach*, son of Ferchar Fota
698 – 711/714	*Eogan* (or *Ewen*), brother‡
698 – 700	*Fiannamail*(?), son of Dunchad(?)
700	*Selbach*, brother of Ainbcellach (d. 730)
723	*Dungal*, son, driven out

*The names Dumnguallaun and Dumnagual (Dyfnwal) are sometimes confused
†Comprising at its fullest extent Lorne, Argyll, Cowal and Kintyre, Islay, Mull(?), and until about 640 the original territory in Ireland, north of Larne. The kingship of the whole region seems at times to have been in dispute among the kings of the districts
‡Not in the more reliable lists

726	*Eochaid* (or *Eochu*) *the Venomous* (angbaid, i.e. ruthless), son of Eochaid Crooked-Nose
733	*Alpin*, brother, King of the Picts 726 – 728 (?); and *Muiredach*, son of Ainbcellach; ruled in different parts(?)
736 – 739(?)	*Eogan*, son of Muiredach*
739(?) – 748	Interregnum under Pictish domination
748	*Aed Finn*, son of Eochaid the Venomous (d. 780?)
778	*Fergus*, brother
781 – 805(?)	*Domnall*†
fl. 792	*Donndorci*, in part of the region(?)
805(?)	*Conall*, son of Tadg (d. 807) King of the Picts 785(?) – 789
807(?)	*Conall*, son of Aedan
811(?)	*Constantine*, son of Fergus; King of the Picts before 789 – 820
820	*Oengus*, brother (Oengus II, King of the Picts 820 – 834)
834	*Aed*, son of Boanta (d. 839)
836(?)	*Eoganan*, son of King Oengus II, of the Picts; King of the Picts 837(?) – 839
839	*Alpin*, grandson of Aed Finn
840	*Eoganan*, of unknown parentage
840	*Kenneth mac Alpin*, son of Alpin (d. 858)
848	Dalriada united with Pictavia under Kenneth mac Alpin

For continuation see Kings of (the Picts and) Scots

Kings of (the Picts and) Scots

848	*Kenneth mac Alpin*, King of Dalriada from 840; King of part of Pictavia from 842/3
858	*Domnall* (or *Donald*) *I mac Alpin*, brother
862	*Constantine I*, son of Kenneth
877	*Aed*, brother
878	*Eochaid*, son of Rhun, nephew (see Strathclyde); with *Giric*, regent or usurper
889	*Domnall* (or *Donald*) *II*, son of Constantine I
900	*Constantine II*, son of Aed

*Not in the more reliable lists

†Described (mistakenly?) as son of Constantine, King of Dalriada in 811(?)

943	*Malcolm I*, son of Domnall, acquired Cumbria 945
954	*Indulf*, son of Constantine II; Lord of Cumbria 945 – 954
962	*Dub*, son of Malcolm I; Lord of Cumbria 954 – 962
966	*Culen*, son of Indulf
971	*Kenneth II*, brother of Dub; King of Scots
995	*Constantine III*, son of Culen, killed by Kenneth III
997	*Kenneth III*, son of Dub, acquired Lothian from England, killed by Malcolm II
25 Mar 1005	*Malcolm II*, son of Kenneth II (b. c. 954) under-king of Cumbria after 991 – 997
25 Nov 1034	*Duncan I*, grandson, through mother; from c. 1016 King of Strathclyde; killed by Macbeth
14 Aug 1040	*Macbeth*, grandson, through mother, of Kenneth II or Malcolm II (b. c. 1005) killed by Malcolm III
15 Aug 1057	*Lulach*, great-grandson, through mother, of Kenneth II or Kenneth III; stepson of Macbeth (b. c. 1032) killed by Malcolm III
17 Mar 1058	*Malcolm III*, son of Duncan I (b. c. 1031)
3 Nov 1093	*Donald Bane*, brother (for 1st time) (b. c. 1033)
May 1094	*Duncan II*, son of Malcolm III (b. c. 1060) killed by Donald Bane(?)
12 Nov 1094	*Donald Bane* (for 2nd time) with his nephew *Edmund*(?); deposed
Oct 1097	*Edgar*, son of Malcolm III (b. c. 1074)
8 Jan 1107(?)	*Alexander I*, brother (b. c. 1077)
25 Apr 1124(?)	*David I*, brother (b. c. 1085?)
24 May 1153	*Malcolm IV*, grandson (b. 1141?)
9 Dec 1165	*William (I)*, brother (b. 1142?)
4 Dec 1214	*Alexander II*, son (b. 24 Aug 1198)
8 Jul 1249	*Alexander III*, son (b. 4 Sep 1241)
19 Mar 1286	*Margaret*, granddaughter; daughter of King Erik II of Norway (b. before 9 Apr 1283) Regents (Guardians): 29 Mar 1286 – Nov 1292: *William Fraser*, Bishop of St Andrews (d. Artuyl 20 Aug 1297) 29 Mar 1286 – 25 Sep 1288(?); *Duncan, 9th Earl of Fife* (b. c. 1262; d. 25 Sep 1288 or 7 Apr (1289?)) 29 Mar 1286 – Mar 1289: *Alexander Comyn, Earl of Buchan* (b. c. 1242; d. shortly before 12 Mar 1289) 29 Mar 1286 – Nov 1292: *Robert Wishart*, Bishop of Glasgow (d. after 30 Apr 1316) 29 Mar 1286 – Nov 1292: *James*, the High Steward (d

	16 Jul 1309)
	29 Mar 1286 – Nov 1292: *Sir John Comyn*, the Black Comyn, of Badenoch (d. 1304)
	Jun 1291 – Nov 1292: *Brian FitzAlan, Lord of Bedale* (d. May/Jun 1306)
26 Sep 1290 – 17 Nov 1292	Throne in dispute between 13 claimants
17 Nov 1292	*John Balliol*, great-great-great-grandson, through mother, of David I (b. c. 1250; d. Apr 1313) awarded throne by King Edward I of England, deposed by Edward I
10 Jul 1296 – 25 Mar 1306*	Interregnum and intermittent war with England; government of Scotland entrusted to: *John de Warenne, Earl of Surrey* (b. Aug 1231(?); d. c. 29 Sep 1304) *Hugh Cressingham* (d. 11 Sep 1297) Scottish Guardians: autumn 1296 – 11 Sep 1297: *Sir Andrew Moray of Bothwell*, the Elder (d. Nov(?) 1297) autumn 1298 – after 13 Nov 1299: *Robert Bruce, Earl of Carrick* (later *Robert I*) autumn 1298 – early 1301 and (see below) Nov(?) 1302 – 9 Feb 1304: *John Comyn, Lord of Badenoch*, the Red Comyn, nephew of John Balliol (d. Dumfries 10 Feb 1306) 12 Aug 1299 – early 1301(?): *William de Lamberton*, Bishop of St Andrews (d. St Andrews 20 May 1328) Principal Guardian 10 May 1300 – early 1301(?): *Sir Ingram de Umfraville* before May 1301 – Nov(?) 1302: *Sir John de Soulis* (d. Dundalk 14 Oct 1318) English Lieutenants: 15 Sep 1305 – 1306 and Sep 1307 – (?): *John of Brittany* (from 15 Oct 1306: *Earl of Richmond*) (b. c. 1266; d. 17 Jan 1334) before 5 Apr 1306 – Sep 1307: *Aymer de Valence, Earl of Pembroke* (b. c. 1270; d. France 23 Jun 1324)
27 Mar 1306	*Robert I (Bruce)*, great-grandson of Isabella, great-granddaughter of David I (b. 11 Jul 1274) at war with Edward I and Edward II, Kings of England

*1297 – 22 Jul 1298 — Insurrection of *Sir William Wallace* (b. Elderslie(?) 1272(?); d. London Aug 1305)

7 Jun 1329 – 22 Feb 1371*	*David II*, son (b. 5 Mar 1324) imprisoned by the English 13 Oct 1346 – 7 Oct 1357 Regents (Guardians): 7 Jun 1329 – 20 Jul 1332: *Thomas Randolph, 1st Earl of Moray* (b. before 1280(?); d. 20 Jul 1332) 2 – 12 Aug 1332: *Donald, 8th Earl of Mar* (b. c. 1300; d. 12 Aug 1332) Aug 1332 – 19 Jul 1333: *Sir Archibald Douglas* (b. 1296(?); d. Halidon 19 Jul 1333) 1334 – Aug 1335: *Robert*, the High Steward (later *Robert II*) (for 1st time) (see below) 1334 – Aug 1335: *John Randolph, 3rd Earl of Moray* (d. Neville's Cross 17 Oct 1346) late 1335 – spring 1338: *Sir Andrew Moray of Bothwell*, the Younger (b. 1298; d. Avoch Jun/Jul(?) 1338) spring 1338 – 2 Jun 1341: *Robert*, the High Steward (for 2nd time) Regent (Lieutenant): 13 Oct 1346 – 7 Oct 1357: *Robert*, the High Steward (for 3rd time)
House of Stewart	
22 Feb 1371	*Robert II*, nephew of Robert I (b. 2 Mar 1316) previously High Steward (see above)
13 Apr 1390	*Robert III*, son (b. c. 1337)
4 Apr 1406	*James I*, son (b. Jul 1394) in captivity in England until 31 Mar 1424, assassinated Regents: Apr 1406 – 3 Sep 1420: *Robert Stewart, 1st Duke of Albany*, uncle (b. c. 1340; d. 3 Sep 1420) 3 Sep 1420(?) – 31 Mar 1424: *Murdoch Stewart, 2nd Duke of Albany*, son of Robert Stewart (b. 1362(?); d. 25 May 1425)
21 Feb 1437	*James II*, son of James I (b. 16 Oct 1430) Regents: 21 Feb 1437 – 4 Sep 1439: *Joan (Beaufort)*, widow of James I (d. Dunbar 15 Jul 1445) Mar/Apr 1437 – 26 Jan 1439: *Archibald Douglas, 5th*

*6 Aug – 16 Dec 1332 and 1333 – 1341	*Edward Balliol*, son of John Balliol (d. Jan 1364) invaded Scotland, crowned 24 Sep 1332, abandoned claim to throne 1356

	Earl of Douglas (b. c. 1390; d. 26 Jun 1439) Lieutenant-General of the Kingdom
3 Aug 1460	*James III*, son of James II (b. May 1452) Regents: 3 Aug 1460 – Dec 1463: *Mary of Gueldres*, widow of James II (d. 1 Dec 1463) 3 Aug 1460 – 24 May 1465: *James Kennedy*, Bishop of St Andrews (b. 1406(?); d. 24 May 1465) Oct 1466 – Nov 1469: *Robert Boyd, 1st Lord Boyd* (b. 1439; d. Dec(?) 1469)
11 Jun 1488 – 9 Sep 1513	*James IV*, son of James III (b. 17 Mar 1473)

Sealand (Sea Country)

Territory comprised part of present-day southern Iraq and the Gulf.

Kings

(?) BC	*Ilima-ilu*, traditionally for 60 years, warred against Babylon
c. 1700	*Itti-ili-nibi*
(?)	*Damiq-ilishu*, for 26 years
before 1650	*Ishkibal*, for 15 years
(?)	*Shushshi*, brother, for 24 years
(?)	*Gulkishar*, for 55 years
before 1550	*Peshgaldaramash*, for 50 years
(?)	*Adarakalamma*, for 28 years
c. 1500	*Ekurduanna*, for 26 years
(?)	*Melamkurkurra*, for seven years
before 1450	*Ea-gamil*, for nine years
(?)	Conquered by Kashtiliash I, the Kassite king of Babylon

Seleucids

At its greatest extent, territory comprised part of present-day Turkey, south-western U.S.S.R., Iran, Iraq, Syria, Lebanon and northern Israel, with the capital initially at Seleucia and then at Antioch (present-day Antakya).

Kings

312 BC	*Seleucus I Nicator*, a general of Alexander the Great (b. Europus, Macedonia, between 358 and 354) granted the satrapy of Babylon 321, defeated by the Macedonian king Antigonus 316, recovered Babylon Aug 312, took the title of king 305, defeated Antigonus at the battle of Ipsus 301 and was granted present-day Syria, transferred capital from Seleucia to Antioch 301/300, murdered in Thrace by Ptolemy Ceraunus
280	*Antiochus I Soter*, son, appointed king east of the Thraco-Macedonian border c. 292
261/60	*Antiochus II Theos*, son, appointed king east of the Thraco-Macedonian border 280
246/5	*Seleucus II Callinicus*, son, compelled to cede territory in Asia Minor to his brother Antiochus Hierax
225/4	*Seleucus III Ceraunos*, son, assassinated
223	*Antiochus III*, the Great, brother (b. 242) defeated by the Romans at the battle of Magnesia 190; kingdom reduced to present-day Syria, Mesopotamia and western Iran
187	*Seleucus IV Philopator*, son
175	*Antiochus IV Epiphanes*, brother (b. c. 215) occupied Egypt 169 – 168, but forced by Rome to withdraw
163	*Antiochus V Eupator*, son, with three Roman commissioners as administrators
162	*Demetrius I Soter*, cousin, usurper
150	*Alexander Balas*, pretended son of Antiochus IV Epiphanes
145*	*Demetrius II Nicator*, son of Demetrius I (for 1st time), captured by the Parthians
139/8	*Antiochus VII Euergetes* (or *Sidetes*), brother;

*145 – 142/1 *Antiochus VI Epiphanes Dionysus*, son of Alexander Balas
142/1 – 138 *Tryphon*, usurper, deposed by Antiochus VII

	deposed the usurper Tryphon* and married Cleopatra Thea, the queen of Demetrius II Nicator; captured Jerusalem 135/4 and made King John Hyrcanus I of Judaea his vassal, killed during Parthian war
129	*Demetrius II Nicator* (for 2nd time)
126/5	*Seleucus V*, son, assassinated
125–96	*Antiochus VIII Philometor* (or *Grypus*), brother
115–95	*Antiochus IX Cyzicenus*, son of Antiochus VII Euergetes, rival
	Period of rival claimants, including:
(?)	*Seleucus VI Epiphanes Nicator*, son of Antiochus VIII Philometor
(?)	*Antiochus X Eusebes Philopator*, son of Antiochus IX Cyzicenus
(?)	*Antiochus XI Epiphanes Philadelphus*, son of Antiochus VIII Philometor
(?)	*Philip I Epiphanes Philadelphus*, brother
(?)	*Demetrius III Theos Philopator Soter* (or *Eukairos*), brother
69–64	*Antiochus XII Dionysus Epiphanes Philopator Callinicus*, brother, killed by King Aretas III Philhellen of Nabathea
73–64	*Antiochus XIII Asiaticus*, son of Antiochus X, ruled in Antioch, defeated by the Roman triumvir Pompey
64	Roman rule†

Seljuqs

At its greatest extent, territory comprised part of present-day Iraq, Iran, Turkey, Saudi Arabia, Israel, Lebanon, Jordan and Syria, centred at Isfahan.

Sultans

Great Seljuqs in Iraq and Iran

AD 1037/8	*(Rukn al-Din Abu Talib Muhammad) Toghrıl I Beg (ibn Mikail)*, grandson of Seljuq (b. 995/6)
4 Sep 1063	*('Adud al-Daula Abu Shuja' Muhammad) Alp-Arslan (ibn Da'ud)*, nephew (b. 20 Jan 1029) governor of

*See footnote on page 496

†In 56 *Philip II*, son of Philip I, claimed the kingship but disappeared almost immediately

	Khurasan after 1059/60, occupied Baghdad 1055, officially installed by the Caliph at Baghdad 27 Apr 1064, assassinated
24 Nov 1072	*(Jalal al-Daula Abu'l-Fath) Malik-Shah I (ibn Alp-Arslan)*, son (b. 6 Aug 1055) overthrew main line of Shaddadids 1073/4
18 Nov 1092	*(Nasir al-Din) Mahmud I (ibn Malik-Shah)*, son (b. 1088; d. 1095) under the regency of his mother *Tarkhan-Khatun,* civil war
1095 – 21 Dec 1104	*(Rukn al-Din Abu'l-Muzaffar) Berk-yaruq (ibn Malik-Shah)*, brother (b. 1079/80)
22 Dec 1104	*(Jalal al-Daula Mu'izz al-Din) Malik-Shah II (ibn Berk-yaruq)*, son (b. 1099/1100) deposed
9 Feb 1105	*(Ghiyath al-Din Abu Shuja') Muhammad I (ibn Malik-Shah)*, uncle (b. 21 Jan 1082) governor of Baghdad after 1098/9
18 Apr 1118 – 1157/8	*(Nasir al-Din* (then *Mu'izz al-Din*) *Abu'l-Harith Ahmad) Sanjar (ibn Malik-Shah)*, brother
1157/8	Uprising of the Oghuz tribesmen

Seljuqs in Iraq and western Persia only

18 Apr 1118 – 10 Sep 1131	*(Mughith al-Din Abu'l-Qasim) Mahmud II (ibn Muhammad)*, son of the Great Seljuq Muhammad I (b. 1103/4)
Sep 1131	*(Ghiyath al-Din Abu'l-Fath) Da'ud (ibn Mahmud)*, son, ruled in Jabal and Azerbaijan only
1131/2	*Toghrıl II (ibn Muhammad)*, uncle
1132/3 – 13 Sep 1152	*(Ghiyath al-Din) Mas'ud (ibn Muhammad)*, brother (b. 4 Jun 1109)
Sep/Oct 1152	*(Mu'in al-Din) Malik-Shah III (ibn Mahmud)*, nephew
1153/4 – Dec 1159/ Jan 1160	*Muhammad II (ibn Mahmud)*, brother (b. Apr/May 1128) besieged Baghdad 1157/8
Mar/Apr – Oct/Nov 1160	*Sulaiman Shah (ibn Muhammad)*, uncle (d. Mar/Apr 1161) imprisoned
1160/1	*Arslan-Shah (ibn Toghrıl, Abu'l-Muzaffar)*, nephew, poisoned
1177/8 – 1194	*Toghrıl III (ibn Arslan-Shah)*, son
1194	Overthrown by the Khwarazm-Shahs

Seljuqs of Syria

1078/9	*(Taj al-Daula Abu Sa'id) Tutush (ibn Alp-Arslan)*, son of the Great Seljuq Alp-Arslan, conquered Aleppo 1084/5

1095 – 11 Nov 1113	*Ridwan (ibn Tutush)*, son, ruled at Aleppo
1095 – 14 Jun 1104	*Duqaq (ibn Tutush)*, brother, ruled at Damascus
1113/14	*(Taj al-Daula) Alp-Arslan al-Akhras (ibn Ridwan)*, nephew (b. Jul/Aug 1066) ruled at Aleppo
1114/15 – 1117/18	*Sultan Shah (ibn Ridwan)*, brother, ruled at Aleppo
1117/18	Succeeded by the line of Tughtigin of the Borids (or Burids) in Damascus and the Artuqid sultan Ilghazi in Aleppo

Seljuqs of Kirman

1041/2	*('Imad al-Din Qara-Arslan) Qawurd (ibn Da'ud)*, brother of the Great Seljuq Alp-Arslan
1073/4	*Kirman Shah (ibn Qawurd)*, son
1074/5	*(Rukn al-Daula) Sultan Shah ibn Qawurd*, brother
1074/5	*Husain 'Umar*, pretender
1084/5	*(Muhyi'l-Din 'Imad al-Daula) Turan Shah I (ibn Qawurd)*, brother of Sultan Shah
1096/7	*(Baha' al-Din) Iran Shah (ibn Turan Shah)*, son
1101/2	*(Muhyi'l-Din) Arslan Shah I (ibn Kirman Shah)*, cousin
1142/3	*(Mughith al-Din) Muhammad I Malik Shah (ibn Arslan-Shah)*, son
1156/7	*(Muhyi'l-Din) Toghrıl Shah (ibn Malik Shah)*, son
1169/70	*Bahram-Shah (ibn Toghrıl Shah)*, son*
1174/5	*Arslan Shah II (ibn Toghrıl Shah)*, brother
1176/7	*Turan Shah (ibn Toghrıl Shah)*, brother
1183/4 – 1186/7	*Muhammad II (ibn Bahram Shah)*, nephew
1186/7	Ghuzz occupation

Seljuqs of Rum

Capital established initially at Nicaea (now İznik) and from 1099 at Iconium (now Konya).

1077/8	*Sulaiman (ibn Qutalmısh)*, great-grandson of Seljuq
1086/7 – 1092/3	Interregnum
1092/3	*Qılıch Arslan I (Da'ud ibn Sulaiman)*, son
1106/7	*Malik-Shah I (ibn Qılıch Arslan)*, son
1116/17	*(Rukn al-Din) Mas'ud I (ibn Qılıch Arslan)*, brother
1156/7 – 26 Aug 1192	*('Izz al-Din) Qılıch Arslan II (ibn Mas'ud)*, son, division of territory among his sons during latter part of his reign: *Rukn al-Din Sulaiman-Shah*, ruled at Tukat *(Nasir al-Din) Berk-yaruq-Shah*, ruled at Neocaesarea

*1169/70 *Arslan Shah ibn Toghrıl Shah*, pretender

	(now Niksar)
	(Mughith al-Din) Toghrıl-Shah (d. ar-Ruha 1225/6) ruled at Ablustain, Erzurum and Baiburt, deposed 1200/1
	(Nur al-Din) Sultan-Shah, ruled at Caesarea
	(Qutb al-Din) Malik-Shah II, ruled at Sivas and Aksaray
	(Mu'izz al-Din) Qaisar-Shah, ruled at Melitene
	(——) Sanjar-Shah, ruled at Ereğli
	(——) Arslan-Shah, ruled at Niğde
	(Nizam al-Din) Arghun-Shah, ruled at Amasya
	(Muhi al-Din) Mas'ud-Shah, ruled at Ankara
	(Ghiyath al-Din) Kai-Khusrau I, ruled at Iconium and Borğlu, later ruled over entire sultanate (see below)
	(Ismet al-Din) Gauhar Khatun, ruled at Caesarea succeeding Sultan-Shah (see above)
1192/3	*(Ghiyath al-Din) Kai-Khusrau I*, son of Qılıch Arslan II (for 1st time) earlier ruled at Iconium and Borğlu (see above)
1195/6	*(Rukn al-Din) Sulaiman-Shah II (ibn Qılıch Arslan)*, brother
6 Jul 1204	*('Izz al-Din) Qılıch Arslan III (ibn Sulaiman-Shah)*, son
Nov 1204	*Kai-Khusrau I* (for 2nd time) killed at battle of Khonas
Jul 1210	*('Izz al-Din) Kai-Ka'us I (ibn Kai-Khusrau)*, son
1219/20	*('Ala' al-Din) Kai-Qubadh I (ibn Kai-Khusrau)*, brother, poisoned
1236/7	*(Ghiyath al-Din) Kai-Khusrau II (ibn Kai-Qubadh)*, son
1246/7	*('Izz al-Din) Kai-Ka'us II*, son (for 1st time) (d. 1279/80) ruled alone
1248/9	*Kai-Ka'us II* (for 2nd time) with his brother *Qılıch Arslan IV* (for 1st time)
1249/50 – 1257/8	*Kai-Ka'us II* (for 3rd time) with his brothers *Qılıch Arslan IV* (for 2nd time) and *('Ala' al-Din) Kai-Qubadh II*
1257/8	Flight of Kai-Ka'us II into Kipchak
1257/8	*Qılıch Arslan IV* (for 3rd time) ruled alone, assassinated
1264/5	*(Ghiyath al-Din) Kai-Khusrau III*, son, aged 2½ at his succession, Iconium captured by the Egyptians*

*1277/8 *Siawush (ibn Kai-Ka'us)*, pretender, assassinated 1283/4

1282/3	*(Ghiyath al-Din) Mas'ud II (ibn Kai-Ka'us)*, cousin (for 1st time) (d. 1304/5)
1284/5	*('Ala' al-Din) Kai Qubadh III*, nephew (for 1st time)
1284/5	*Mas'ud II* (for 2nd time)
1292/3	*Kai-Qubadh III* (for 2nd time)
1293/4	*Mas'ud II* (for 3rd time)
1300/1	*Kai-Qubadh III* (for 3rd time)
1302/3	*Mas'ud II* (for 4th time)
1305	*Kai-Qubadh III* (for 4th time)
1307/8	*(Ghiyath al-Din) Mas'ud III (ibn Kai-Qubadh)*, son
1307/8	Mongol occupation

Senas of Bengal

Territory comprised part of present-day north-eastern India, with the capital at Vijayapura.

Kings

AD (?)	*Hemanta Sena*
c. 1095	*Vijaya Sena*
c. 1159	*Ballala Sena*, son
c. 1178	*Lakshmana Sena*, son
c. 1210	*Vishvarupa Sena*, son
c. 1225	*Keshava Sena*, brother
c. 1225	Political power passed to the Muslims

Serbia

The various principalities and kingdoms that arose on Serbian territory are listed in chronological order. Their geographical distribution is as follows:

Rascia (or Raška): the Serbian heartland, the mountainous region between the Morava and the Drin

Dioclea (or Duklja): the southern portion of present-day Montenegro, later known as Zeta, extending to Lake Scutari and the mountains of northern Albania

Zachlumia (Zahumlja or Hum): extending northwards from Cetinje to the Neretva (=Herzegovina)

Tribunia (or Travunja): south of Dubrovnik

Princes of the Serbians (in Rascia?)

fl. c. AD 780	*Višeslav*
after 800	*Radoslav*, son
before 835	*Prosigoj*, son
c. 835	*Vlastimir*, son
c. 870	*Mutimir*, son
891	*Prvoslav*, son, expelled by Petar
892	*Petar Gojniković*, cousin (d. in prison in Bulgaria)*
917	*Pavle Branović*, nephew of Prvoslav (for 1st time) as Bulgarian vassal
920(?)	*Zaharije Prvoslavljević*, son of Prvoslav (for 1st time) as Byzantine pretender, captured and sent to Bulgaria by Pavle
920(?)	*Pavle* (for 2nd time) went over to Byzantium
923	*Zaharije* (for 2nd time) as Bulgarian candidate, returned to Byzantine allegiance, driven out by the Bulgarians
924 – 927	Rascia devastated by the Bulgarians
after May 927 – after 950	*Časlav Klonimirović*, second cousin (d. c. 960)
after 950	Successors not known; Rascia remained under Bulgarian and later Byzantine domination, with local župans, until it was annexed by Dioclea (Zeta) (for the revived realm, later the Serbian Empire, see after Dioclea)

DIOCLEA (later called ZETA) †

Princes, later kings

c. AD 900	*Petar*
?	Unknown ruler or rulers
before 1000 – 1016	*Jovan Vladimir*, Saint, murdered by Ivan Vladislav, Tsar of Bulgaria
c. 1018	*Dragomir*, cousin or brother, 'Prince of Zachlumia

*Pretenders: *Bran*, brother of Prvoslav, apprehended and blinded 894
Klonimir, cousin, son of Strojimir (d. in battle 896)

†Later included also the principalities of Tribunia and Zachlumia. Among the rulers of these were: *Krajina*, župan of Tribunia (fl. c. 850) made prince by Vlastimir, Prince of Rascia; his descendants, *Hvalimir* and *Cucimir*, vassals of Rascia; and *Mihajlo*, Prince of Zachlumia 912 – after 949.

	and Tribunia', murdered by the citizens of Kotor
before 1040	*Stefan Vojislav*, descendant of Mihajlo, Prince of Zachlumia (?);* Prince of Dioclea, Tribunia and Zachlumia
c. 1050	*Mihajlo*, son, took title of king 1077
1081/2	*(Konstantin) Bodin*, son; proclaimed Tsar of the Bulgarians 1073 but suppressed by the Byzantines; annexed Rascia and Bosnia; defeated and imprisoned by the Byzantines 1091, losing control of Rascia
c. 1101 – ?|†	*Dobroslav*, brother; overthrown and taken prisoner by Vukan, grand župan of Rascia
?	*Kočapar*, cousin, fled before Vukan to Bosnia
?	*Vladimir II*, son-in-law of a Rascian župan; poisoned by Jaquinta, widow of Bodin
1113 – 1116 or 1114 – 1118	*Đurađ*, son of Bodin (for 1st time) banished to Rascia by the Byzantine emperor John II Comnenus
1116 – 1123 or 1118 – 1125	*Grubeša*, second cousin; installed by John II Comnenus; overthrown by Uroš I, grand župan of Rascia
1125	*Đurađ* (for 2nd time) sent to Constantinople and imprisoned
1135 – 1146(?)	*Gradihna*, brother of Grubeša
?	*Radoslav*, son, described as 'prince'
?	Unknown ruler or rulers
?	*Mihajlo*, prince
c. 1190	Zeta incorporated in Serbia by grand župan Stefan Nemanja

RASCIA (later SERBIAN EMPIRE)

Grand Župans

c. AD 1083 – c. 1114	*Vukan* (or *Vlkan*), made župan by Bodin, King of Dioclea; asserted independence
fl. 1130	*Uroš I*, nephew (b. c. 1080)
fl. 1150	*Uroš II*, son(?) (for 1st time) thrown out
?	*Desa*, brother or son (for 1st time)
1155	*Uroš II* (for 2nd time) restored by the Byzantine emperor Manuel I Comnenus

*See preceding footnote
† The list from this point depends on one original authority and is of doubtful validity.

c. 1155	*Prvoslav*, sometimes identified with Uroš II, overthrown by the Byzantines
1158(?)	*Beluš* (?), commonly identified with *Beloš*, son of Uroš I (d. after 1198) Ban of Croatia 1142 – 1157
c. 1161	*Desa* (for 2nd time) taken captive to Constantinople
1162 – c. 1165	Interregnum
c. 1165	*Desa* (for 3rd time) overran Dioclea
1168 (?)	*Tihomir*, son of Zavida
c. 1170	*Stefan Nemanja*, brother (d. 1200) took rule by force, annexed part of Dalmatian coast 1180, recognized by Byzantium as ruler of autonomous Serbia 1190, made sebastocrator 119–, abdicated and became a monk
1196	*Stefan*, the First-Crowned, son (for 1st time) (b. c. 1165; d. 24 Sep 1228(?)) driven out by King Imre of Hungary and Vukan, brother of Stefan the First-Crowned
1202	*Imre*, King of Hungary, took title of King of Serbia
Apr 1203	*Vukan*, brother of Stefan the First-Crowned (b. c. 1160; d. after 1209) proclaimed himself grand župan
summer 1203	*Stefan*, the First-Crowned (for 2nd time) grand župan, made king 1217 (see below)

Kings and Emperors

1217	*Stefan*, the First-Crowned, formerly grand župan (see above)
1228(?)	*(Stefan) Radoslav*, son, expelled and became a monk
before Feb 1234	*(Stefan) Vladislav*, brother (d. after 1264) abdicated, but remained king of part of the coast region, with his seat at Scutari
spring 1243	*(Stefan) Uroš I*, brother (d. 1 May 1277(?)) dethroned by Dragutin and became a monk
autumn 1276 – Mar 1316	*(Stefan) Dragutin*, son, handed over power to Stefan Uroš II 1282 but retained certain districts in the north and the title of king
early 1282 – 29 Oct 1321	*Stefan Uroš II Milutin*, brother, conquered northern Macedonia, 'King of Albania' 1318
1321 – 1324	Civil war between *Konstantin*, son (b. c. 1275(?); d. 1322) proclaimed king in Zeta, killed in flight; and *Vladislav*, son of Dragutin, pretender in the north, retired to Hungary 1324
1321	*Stefan Uroš III Dečanski*, son of Stefan Uroš II, crowned 6 Jan 1322, with his son Stephen Dušan (see

	below) as king of Zeta
8 Sep 1331	*Stefan (Uroš IV) Dušan*, son (b. c. 1308) annexed Macedonia, Albania, Epirus and Thessaly; proclaimed emperor 1345; crowned 16 Apr 1346
20 Dec 1355 – 4 Dec 1371	*Stefan Uroš V*, son (b. 1336(?)) Emperor, King from 1346
1356 – c. 1370	*Simeon Uroš Palaeologus*, half-brother of Stefan Dušan (b. 1327(?))) governor of Epirus, proclaimed himself 'Emperor of the Greeks, Serbs and all Albania'
1358	Empire divided between Stefan Uroš V and Simeon
before Nov 1366 – 26 Sep 1371	*Vukašin Mrnjačević*, župan of Prilep 1350, subsequently named despot, made king by Stefan Uroš V, 'lord of the Serbian land and of the Greeks and the southern parts', killed at the battle of the Maritsa
1366 – 26 Sep 1371	*(Jovan) Uglješa Mrnjačević*, brother, despot of Serres, called himself also king and emperor, killed at the battle of the Maritsa
26 Sep 1371	Province of Serres, Macedonia, lost to the Ottoman Turks

After the death of Stefan Uroš V in December 1371 there was no emperor, and Serbia became a conglomerate of aristocratic territories. The widow of Stefan Dušan and his sister, widow of the sebastocrator Dejan, despot of Kumanovo, claimed the title of empress, and the sons of Dejan, Jovan Dragaš and Konstantine (see below) speak of 'our empire'. The title of king was borne by Marko (Kraljević), son of Vukašin (see below) and was assumed by Tvrtko, hitherto Ban of Bosnia (q.v.).
The list continues with the princes, from 1402 despots, of northern Serbia, followed by the numerous lords, despots and župans of such parts of the west and south as had not fallen to the Turks.

Princes and Despots of Northern Serbia

1372	*Lazar I Hrebeljanović*, son of Pribac (b. 1329) chancellor of Stefan Dušan; lord of Rudnik 1370 – 1371; called himself 'Stefan Lazar, prince and autonomous lord of Serbia and the Danube valley', holding the country from the Morava valley to the Sava and the Danube, with the capital at Kruševac; executed on the field after the battle of Kosovo Polje
15(?) Jun 1389 – 19 Jul 1427	*Lazar II* (or *Stefan Lazarević*), son (b. c. 1370) vassal of the Turks, created despot by the Byzantine

	emperor 1402
1427	*Đurađ Branković* (or *Đurađ Vuković*), nephew; son of Vuk Branković, lord of Skoplje (b. c. 1375) lost Belgrade to the emperor Sigismund, King of Hungary, by whom he was recognized as 'duke and despot of the whole state of Rascia and Albania'; made Smederevo his capital
24 Dec 1456 – 20 Jan 1458	*Lazar III Branković*, son (b. c. 1421)
3 Feb 1458	Regency: *Jelena Paleologa*, widow (d. as nun 1473) *Stefan*, the Blind, brother (b. 1420; d. 9 Oct 1476) *Mihajlo Anđelović*, collateral(?) descendant of Manojlo Anđelović Filantropen, 14th-century ruler of Thessaly; imprisoned 31 Mar – autumn 1458
Apr 1458	*Stefan*, the Blind (see above) with his brother, *Grgur*, the Blind (b. c. 1416; d. 16 Oct 1459) pretender
21 Mar – 20 Jun 1459	*Stefan Tomašević*, Prince of Bosnia (d. 1463) King of Bosnia Jul 1461 – Jun 1463
20 Jun 1459	Fall of Smederevo to the Ottoman Turks*

Independent rulers in the western and southern portions of the former Serbian Empire after 1371 (from northwest to southeast)

1463 – 1466	*Stefan Vukčić Kosača* (b. 1435; d. 22 May 1466) Duke of St Sava from 1448, ruled the territory in the neighbourhood of Split
1466 – c. 1470(?)	*Vladislav Hercegović*, son (d. Croatia 1489/90 ruled north of the Neretva

*The despotate was revived in name in southern Hungary, when Vuk II Grgurović Branković was made 'despot of Rascia' by the King of Hungary. The principal function of the despots, who were individually appointed by the king, was to command the Serbian exiles in Hungary and to guard the southern frontier. The successive despots were:

Sep 1471 – 16 Apr 1485	*Vuk II Grgurović Branković*, son of the pretender Grgur (b. c. 1438)
1486 – 1496	*Đurađ II Stefanović Branković*, son of Stefan the Blind (b. 1465; d. 18 Jan 1516) abdicated and became a monk
1492 – 10 Dec 1502	*Jovan Branković*, brother (b. 1462) ruled with Đurađ until 1496
1504 – 1514	*Jovan* (or *Ivaniš*) *Berislavić*, Croatian nobleman
1515 – 1535	*Stefan Berislavić*, son
20 Sep 1537 – late 1537 or early 1538	*Pavle Bakić* (d. in battle)

1466 – c. 1470(?)	*Vlatko Hercegović*, brother (d. Rab 1489, or after 1510(?)) ruled south of the Neretva

For Bosnia see p. 85

1368 – 1374	*Nikola Altomanović* (d. after 1395) župan of the mountain region east of Kotor; defeated by Lazar I, Prince of Serbia, and Tvrtko I, Ban of Bosnia, territory divided

For Montenegro (Zeta) see p. 380.

c. 1371 – 1398(?)	*Vuk Branković*, son of Branko Mladenović, sebastocrator of Ohrid under Stefan Uroš V (b. Prilečac c. 1329; d. 6 Oct 1398) lord of Priština, Trepča, Vučitran, Zvečan, Skoplje and Prizren; ceded Skoplje to the Turks 6 Jan 1392, driven out of remaining possessions 1398(?)

c. 1365(?) – (?)	*(Jovan) Dragaš (Dejanović)*, despot of Kumanovo, Kočani and Strumica; Turkish vassal
c. 1378 – 7 May 1395	*Konstantin Dejanović* (or *Konstantin Dragaš*), brother

(1359)	*Charles Thopia*, 'Albanian prince' (for 1st time) (d. 1388) ruled from Durazzo southwards
1372	*Louis*, count of Évreux, husband of Jeanne, Duchess of Durazzo (d. 1373) captured Durazzo
Mar 1374 or earlier	*Charles Thopia* (for 2nd time)
1379 or earlier	*Robert*, Count of Artois, second husband of Jeanne (d. 20 Jul 1387) in possession of Durazzo
c. 1383	*Charles Thopia* (for 3rd time) possession disputed by Balša II, Prince of Montenegro 1385
1388	*George Thopia*
1392	Durazzo handed over to the Venetians

1371(?) – 1385(?)	*Andrei Gropa*, grand župan of Ohrid 1377, overcome by the Turks

1371 – 17 May 1395	*Marko Kraljević*, son of Vukašin (b. c. 1335) called himself king, holding territory round Prilep as Turkish vassal; died in battle and territory lost to the Turks

1372	*Balša II Balšić*, Prince of Montenegro; lord of Valona, Berat and Himara
18 Sep 1385	*Komnina*, widow, as Venetian vassal
1396 – 1414	*Mrksa Zarković*, son-in-law, nephew of Dragaš of Kumanovo; lord of Berat, Valona and Kanina
1367(?)	*Toma Preljubović*, son-in-law of the Serbian emperor Simeon, lord of Yannina, assassinated
1385 – 1403	*Esaù Buondelmonte* (b. Florence 1345/50) second husband of Toma's widow
(1371) – 1379(?)	*Gino Spata*, despot of Arta, driven out, but still calling himself Despot of Arta in 1395
fl. 1384	*Stefan Hlapenić*, lord of Pharsala

Shaddadids (Banu Shaddad)

Territory comprised part of present-day north-western Iran and southern USSR, with the capital initially at Dvin and later at Ganja (now Kirovabad).

Amirs

Main Line in Ganja and Dvin

c. AD 951/2	*Muhammad (ibn Shaddad)*, ruled in Dvin
970/1	*(Abu'l-Hasan) 'Ali Lashkari I (ibn Muhammad)*, son, ruled in Ganja
978/9	*Marzuban (ibn Muhammad)*, brother, murdered by al-Fadl I
985/6	*(al-Mansur) al-Fadl I (ibn Muhammad)*, brother
1030/1	*(Abu'l-Fath) Musa (ibn al-Fadl)*, son
1033/4	*'Ali Lashkari II (ibn Musa)*, son
1048/9	*Anushirvan (ibn Lashkari)*, son
1049/50	*(Abu'l-Aswar) Shawur I (ibn al-Fadl)*, great uncle, ruled in Dvin 1022/3 – 1049/50, ruled in Ganja after 1049/50, appointed governor of Armenia by Seljuq sultan Alp-Arslan 1064/5
1066/7	*al-Fadl II (Manuchihr ibn Shawur)*, son, Seljuq vassal
1073/4	*(Abu'l-Muzaffar) Fadl III* (or *(Abu'l-Muzaffar)*

	Fadlun III) *(ibn al-Fadl)*, son
1073/4	Seljuq occupation

Ani Branch

c. 1072/3	*Manuchihr ibn Shawur*, son of Shawur I of Ganja and Dvin; Seljuq vassal
c. 1118/19 – 1124/5	*(Abu'l-Aswar) Shawur II (ibn Manuchihr)*, son
1124/5 – c. 1125/6	First Georgian occupation
c. 1125/6	*Fadl* (or *Fadlun*) *IV (ibn Shawur)*, son of Shawur II
(?)	*Mahmud (ibn Shawur)*, brother
c. 1130/1	*Khushchihr*
(?)	*Shaddad (ibn Mahmud)*, son of Mahmud
1155/6 – 1160/1	*Fadl V (ibn Mahmud)*, brother
1160/1 – 1163/4	Second Georgian occupation
1163/4 – 1175/6	*Shahanshah (ibn Mahmud)*, brother of Fadl V
1175/6	Third and final Georgian occupation

Sicily

Kings

House of Hauteville

AD 1072 – 22 Jun 1101	*Roger I*, son of Tancrède de Hauteville (b. Normandy, 1031; d. Mileto) invested as Count of Calabria and Sicily in 1072 following the capture of Palermo; conquest of Sicily completed, 1091
1101 – 26 Feb 1154	*Roger II*, son (b. 22 Dec 1095; d. Palermo) Count of Sicily and Duke of Calabria 1101; until 1112 ruling under the regency of his mother, *Adelheid* (d. 1118); Duke of Apulia, 1127; formally invested as Duke of Apulia, Calabria and Sicily 23 Aug 1128, King of Sicily 25 Dec 1130
4 Apr 1154 – 7 May 1166	*Guillaume I* the Bad, son (b. 1120; d. Palermo) ruled with his father from 1151
1166 – 18 Nov 1189	*Guillaume II* the Good, son (b. 1154; d. Palermo) until 1171 ruling under the regency of his mother, *Margaret of Navarre* (d. 1183); died without heir
	Succession dispute between the remaining members

	of the House of Hauteville* and the House of Hohenstaufen

House of Hohenstaufen

25 Dec 1194	*Heinrich*, Holy Roman Emperor (Heinrich VI), son-in-law of Roger II and son of Holy Roman Emperor Friedrich I Barbarossa (b. Nijmegen Nov 1165; d. Messina 28 Sep 1197) claimed Sicily at the death of Guillaume II but was unable to take the island until 1194
1197 – 30 Dec 1250	*Friedrich II*,† son (b. Iesi, Mark of Ancona, 26 Dec 1194; d. Castel Fiorentino, Apulia); ruling until 1198 under the regency of his mother, *Constance* (b. 1154; d. 27 Nov 1198), and then under the guardianship of Pope *Innocent III* (b. 1160/1; d. 16 Jul 1216); Duke (Friedrich VI) of Swabia 1208; King of Germany 5 Dec 1212; Holy Roman Emperor 22 Nov 1220; King of Jerusalem Aug 1225/18 Mar 1229 – 5 Apr 1243
	Period of civil war and succession disputes between the heirs of Friedrich II‡ and the Angevins

House of Anjou

28 Jun 1265/26 Feb 1266 – Mar 1282	*Charles I*, Count of Anjou and of Provence, son of King Louis VIII of France (b. Mar 1227; d. Foggia 7 Jan 1285) invested with the Kingdom of Sicily 28 Jun 1265 and crowned 6 Jan 1266; defeated Manfred‡ at

*1189	*Tancrède*, illegitimate nephew of Guillaume I (d. 20 Feb 1194) Count of Lecce; claimed the throne at the death of Guillaume II
1194	*Guillaume III*, son; inherited his father's claim to the throne but was defeated by Heinrich

†Usually, Friedrich I Barbarossa is tacitly included when numbering the kings of Sicily; some sources, however, list Friedrich II as Friedrich I, and so on

‡1251	*Konrad*, King (Konrad IV) of Germany, Duke (Konrad III) of Swabia, son of Friedrich II (b. Andrea 25 Apr 1228; d. Lavello 21 May 1254) claimed the throne of Sicily 1251
1254	*Manfred*, half-brother (b. 1232; d. 26 Feb 1266) effective king of Sicily from 1258; killed by Charles I of Anjou in the Battle of Benevento
1266 – 23 Aug 1268	*Konradin*, or *Konrad V*, Duke of Swabia, nephew (b. Wolfstein, 25 Mar 1252; d. (executed) Naples, 29 Oct 1268) invaded Italy Sep 1267; defeated by Charles I of Anjou at the Battle of Tagliacozza 23 Aug 1268

	Benevento 26 Feb 1266; Prince of Achaea 1267/1278, King of Jerusalem 1277; expelled from Sicily during the Sicilian Vespers Mar 1282, but retained the Neapolitan portion of the kingdom (see Naples); defeated by Pedro III of Aragon Jun 1284

House of Aragon

4 Sep 1282 – 11 Nov 1285	*Pedro I* the Great, King (Pedro III) of Aragon, son-in-law of Manfred (b. 1239) defeated Charles I Jun 1284
1285	*Jaime I*, son (b. 1262; d. 5 Nov 1327) King (Jaime II) of Aragon 1291; exchanged Sicily for Corsica and Sardinia
11 Dec 1295	*Federico III* (or *II*), brother (b. 1271; d. Paterno, 25 Jun 1337); regent of Sicily for his brother from 1291; from 1302 to 1310 used the title, 'King of Trinacria' (in accordance with the terms of the Peace of Caltabellotta)
Sep 1337 – 15 Aug 1341	*Pedro II*, son (d. Calascibetta)
1341	*Luis*, son (b. 1338; d. Aci); ruled under the regency of his mother, *Elizabeth of Tirol*
1355 – 27 Jul 1377	*Federico IV* (or *III*), brother (b. 1342)
1377 – 25 May 1402	*Maria*, daughter (b. Catania, 1367; d. Lentini); ruling under the regency of *Artale d'Alagona*, who divided Sicily into four quarters, each ruled by a nearly autonomous vicar
1391 – 25 Jul 1409	*Martín I*, husband (b. 1374; d. Sanluri) overthrew the rule of the vicars
1409 – 31 May 1412	*Martín II*, King (Martín) of Aragon, father
1412	Kingdom of Sicily held by the Kings of Aragon

Silesia

Soon after the beginning of its independent existence the duchy of Silesia was divided into two, and during the following centuries the component parts were further divided and subdivided. The more important individual duchies are listed separately in chronological order of their independent existence; others are grouped. The lists are in the following order (Polish place names in parentheses):

Silesia (Ślansk) 1138
Ratibor and Oppeln (Racibórz and Opole) 1163
Breslau (Wrocław) 1248
Glogau (Głogów) 1249
Liegnitz (Legnica) 1249
Sagan (Żagań) 1273
Steinau (Ścinawa) 1273
Jauer (Jawór), Schweidnitz (Świdnica) and Münsterberg (Ziembice) 1274
Beuthen (Bytom), Gleiwitz (Gliwice), Kosel (Koźle) and Tost (Toszek) 1281
Oppeln (Opole), Falkenberg (Niemodlin) and Gross-Strelitz (Strzelce) 1281
Ratibor (Racibórz) 1281
Teschen (Cieszyń) and Auschwitz (Oświęcim) 1281
Oels (Oleśnica) 1312

Some of the duchies, still further fragmented, continued into the 17th century but in the first half of the 14th century the Silesian dukes became vassals of the Bohemian crown, which issued general orders and privileges applying to the whole of Silesia. The lists have not been continued beyond this point.

The Silesian dukes recognized the overlordship of the senior Polish duke (see Poland) in theory until 1201 and in practice until 1163.*

SILESIA

Dukes

28 Oct AD 1138	*Władysław II*, the Exile (Wygnaniec), son of Bolesław III, Duke of Poland (b. 1105; d. 30 May 1159) Grand Duke of Poland, expelled by Bolesław IV
1146	*Bolesław IV*, the Curly (Kędzierzawy), Duke of Mazovia and Cujavia, brother (b. 1125; d. 3 Nov 1173) Grand Duke of Poland
1163†	Restoration of the sons of Władysław II and division of the duchy; Ratibor, with Kosel and Tost, and later Oppeln, became a separate duchy
1163 – 7 Dec 1201	*Bolesław I*, the Tall (Wysoki), son of Władysław II (b after 1129) Duke of Silesia, including Oppeln and Leubus

*As with other states, epithets are translated, but in view of the frequency with which in the literature the Polish epithets are used untranslated, even to the exclusion of the name, the original Polish is added in parentheses

†The division may not have taken place until 1177, in which case Mieszko Plątonogi (see Ratibor and Oppeln) will have been subordinate or co-ruler from 1163 to 1177. After the division the senior duchy, though comprising only Lower and Central Silesia, was still officially called Silesia, but its holders are often referred to as Dukes of Breslau

1163 – 19 Feb 1203	*Konrad*, brother (b. c. 1139) Duke of Glogau
8 Dec 1201	*Henryk I*, the Bearded (Brodaty), son of Bolesław I (b. c. 1163) Duke of Silesia, Duke of Cracow (see Poland) 1232 – 1238, absorbed Duchy of Glogau Feb 1203
19 Mar 1238	*Henryk II*, the Pious (Pobożny), son (b. c. 1191) Duke of Cracow (see Poland)
9 Apr 1241	*Anna*, widow; daughter of Přemysl Otakar I, King of Bohemia, (b. 1204; d. 23 Jun 1265) regent
before Mar 1242 – 1249	*Bolesław II Rogatka*, the Bald (Lysy), son (b. c. 1225(?); d. 25 Dec(?) 1278)
1247/8	*Henryk III*, the White (Biały), brother (b. c. 1229; d. 3 Dec 1266) co-ruler
1248 – 1248/9	*Konrad I*, brother (d. 6 Aug 1273/4) co-ruler
1248/9	Duchy divided into Breslau, Glogau and Liegnitz*

RATIBOR AND OPPELN

AD 1163 – 16 May 1211	*Mieszko I Plątonogi*, son of Władysław II, Duke of Silesia, Duke of Ratibor; Duke of Oppeln 1201 – 1202; Duke of Cracow 1210/11 – 16 May 1211
1211	*Kazimierz I*, son (b. 1178/9) Duke of Oppeln (and Ratibor)
13 May 1229	*Mieszko II*, the Fat (Otyły), son (b. 1225/6; d. 22 Oct 1246) ruled with his brother, *Władysław* (for 1st time) (d. 13 Nov (or 27 Aug?) 1281), minors Guardians: 1229: *Viola*, daughter of Asen I, Tsar of Bulgaria; widow of Kazimierz I (d. 7 Sep 1251) 1229(?) – 1238: *Henryk I*, Duke of Silesia (see above)
1238/40	*Mieszko II* (see above) independent Duke of Oppeln
22 Oct 1246 – 1281	*Władysław*, brother (for 2nd time) Duke of Oppeln
1281	Duchy divided into Beuthen, Oppeln, Ratibor and Teschen

BRESLAU

Dukes

AD 1248 – 3 Dec 1266	*Henryk III*, previously co-ruler of Silesia (see above) lost Leubus 1249
1250 – 1265(?)	*Władysław*, brother (d. 27 Apr 1270) co-ruler,

*Mieszko, the remaining son of Henryk II, held territory at Krossen (Leubus) on the Lusatian frontier until his death c. 1249

	consecrated bishop of Passau 1265, continued to hold part of Breslau; Archbishop of Salzburg 1265/1267 – 1270
3 Dec 1266	*Henryk IV*, Probus, son of Henryk III (b. c. 1257)
23 Jun 1290	*Henryk V*, the Stout (Gruby), Duke of Liegnitz; son of Bolesław II, Duke of Silesia (b. 1248/9) Duke of Jauer 1274 – 1278
22 Feb 1296	*Bolesław III*, son (b. 23 Sep 1291) Duke of Brieg and Liegnitz 1311 – 1342; ruled with his brothers, *Henryk VI* (see below) and *Władysław* (see Liegnitz) Guardians: 1296 – 9 Nov 1301: *Bolesław* (or *Bolko*) *I*, Duke of Jauer and Schweidnitz (see below) 1301 – 1302: *Henryk z Wierzbna*, Bishop of Breslau from 19 Apr 1302 Governor (Starosta): before 8 Jan 1303 – Jun 1305: *Beneš*, appointed by Václav II, King of Bohemia, the father-in-law of Bolesław III
1311 – 24 Nov 1335	*Henryk VI*, brother of Bolesław III (b. 18 Mar 1294)
24 Nov 1355	Duchy passed to Bohemia

GLOGAU

Dukes

AD 1249	Duchy held by *Bolesław II Rogatka*, Duke of Liegnitz, Duke of Silesia before Mar 1242 – 1249 (see above)
1251 – 6 Aug 1273/4	*Konrad I*, son of Duke Henryk II of Silesia; previously Bishop of Passau
6 Aug 1273/4	Sagan and Steinau became separate duchies
6 Aug 1273/4	*Henryk III* (or *I*), son, Duke of Steinau 26 Feb 1289 – 1297, Duke of Sagan 11 Oct 1304 – 9 Dec 1309, Duke of Greater Poland 1306 – 1309
9 Dec 1309	*Henryk IV* (or *II*), son (b. after 1291; d. 22 Jan 1342) with his four brothers
1312 – 1318	*Henryk IV*, with his brothers, *Jan* (d. 1361/5) and *Przemko* (d. 11 Jan 1331), Duke of Glogau and Poznań
1318 – 1323	*Henryk IV* – with *Przemko* – Duke of Glogau and Poznań; Henryk became Duke of Sagan and Jan became Duke of Steinau in 1323
c. 1323	*Przemko*, Duke of Glogau

Jan – 1 Oct 1331	*Konstancja*, widow of Przemko; daughter of Bernard, Duke of Schweidnitz (d. 1360/3) held Glogau itself, remainder of inheritance divided between *Jan*, Duke of Steinau (see below), and *Henryk IV*, Duke of Sagan
	Regent:
	Bolesław II, Duke of Schweidnitz (see Jauer and Schweidnitz)
1 Oct 1331	*Jan*, Duke of Steinau, resigned claim
2 Oct 1331	Glogau directly annexed to the Bohemian crown

LIEGNITZ

Dukes

AD 1249 – 25 Dec(?) 1278	*Bolesław II Rogatka*, Duke of Silesia before Mar 1242 – 1249 (see above), Duke of Glogau 1249 – 1251
1274	Jauer became a separate duchy
25 Dec(?) 1278	*Henryk V*, the Stout (Gruby), son, Duke of Breslau 23 Jun 1290 – 22 Feb 1296 (see above), Duke of Jauer 1274 – 1278
22 Feb 1296 – 1311	Duchy held by Duke of Breslau (see above)
1311 – 1342	*Bolesław III*, Duke of Breslau 22 Feb 1296 – 1311 (see above), also Duke of Brieg; Bohemian vassal Nov 1331
1311 – 1312	*Władysław*, brother (b. 6 Jan 1296; d. after 1352) co-ruler, Duke of Breslau 22 Feb 1296 – 1311, took holy orders
1342 – 1345	*Wacław I*, son of Bolesław III (b. before 1310)
1342 – 1346	*Ludwik I*, brother (b. c. 1311; d. 6/23 Dec 1398) at first co-ruler

SAGAN

Dukes

6 Aug AD 1273/4	*Konrad II*, the Hunchback (Garbaty); son of Konrad I, Duke of Glogau (b. c. 1260)
11 Oct 1304	*Henryk III*, Duke of Glogau (see above), brother, Duke of Steinau 26 Feb 1289 – 1297
9 Dec 1309 – 1323	Duchy held by Duke of Glogau (see above)
1323	*Henryk IV*, son of Henryk III, Duke of Glogau 9 Dec 1309 – c. 1323 (see above)
22 Jan 1342 – Apr 1369	*Henryk V*, the Iron (Żelazny), son, Bohemian vassal 23 Nov 1344

STEINAU

Dukes

6 Aug AD 1273/4	*Przemko*, son of Conrad I, Duke of Glogau
26 Feb 1289 – 1297	*Henryk III*, brother Duke of Glogau 6 Aug 1273/4 – 9 Dec 1309 (see above), Duke of Sagan 11 Oct 1304 – 9 Dec 1309
1297 – 1309	History uncertain
1309 – 1323	Duchy held by Duke of Glogau (see above)
1323	*Jan*, son (d. 1361/5) co-ruler of Glogau Jan – 1 Oct 1331; Bohemian vassal 29 Apr 1329

JAUER AND SCHWEIDNITZ (and MÜNSTERBERG)

Dukes

AD 1274	*Henryk V*, Duke of Breslau 23 Jun 1290 – 22 Feb 1296 (see above), Duke of Liegnitz 25 Dec(?) 1278 – 22 Feb 1296
1278	*Bolesław* (or *Bolko*) *I*, brother; ruled with his brother, *Bernard* (d. 25 Apr 1286)*
1301 – 1312	Minority of the sons of Bolko I; guardianship claimed by *Hermann II*, Margrave of Brandenburg (d. Jan 1308) brother-in-law of Bolesław I
1312	Duchy divided into Jauer, Münsterberg and Schweidnitz
1312 – Mar/May 1346	*Henryk I*, son of Bolesław I (b. c. 1294) Duke of Jauer
1312 – 6 May 1326	*Bernard*, brother (b. c. 1290) Duke of Schweidnitz
1312 – 1321	*Bolesław* (or *Bolko*) *II*, brother (b. 1298; d. 11 Jun 1341) co-ruler of Schweidnitz
1321 – 11 Jun 1341	*Bolesław II* (see above) Duke of Münsterberg; Bohemian vassal 29 Aug 1336
6 May 1326 – 14 Aug 1343	*Henryk II*, son of Bernard; Duke of Schweidnitz
6 May 1326 – 28 Jul 1368	*Bolesław* (or *Bolko*) *II*, the Younger (b. 1312?) Duke of Schweidnitz, Duke of Jauer from 1346
11 Jun 1341 – 23 Apr 1358	*Mikołaj*, son of the previous duke of Münsterberg, Bolesław II; Duke of Münsterberg; Bohemian vassal 24 Aug 1341

*Some authorities suggest that Bolesław was Duke of Schweidnitz and Bernard Duke of Jauer

BEUTEN, GLEIWITZ, KOSEL and TOST

Dukes

13 Nov AD 1281 – 10 Mar 1312	*Kazimierz II*, son of Władysław, the Duke of (Ratibor and) Oppeln
1306 – 1328	*Bolesław*, son (b. before 1289; d. 13 Jan 1329) Duke of Tost, Archbishop of Gran fron 1321
1328	Tost re-integrated
c. 1311 – 1342	*Ziemowit*, brother, Duke of Beuten c. 1311 – 1327, Duke of Gleiwitz c. 1337
10 Mar 1312 – 1351/5	*Władysław*, brother, Duke of Kosel 1312 – 1337, Duke of Beuten c. 1327, Duke of Tost 1328
c. 1337 – 1349	*Kazimierz*, son, Duke of Kosel

OPPELN, FALKENBERG and GROSS-STRELITZ

Dukes

AD 1281 – 14 May 1313	*Bolesław* (or *Bolko*) *I*, son of Władysław, the Duke of (Ratibor and) Oppeln (b. c. 1260)
14 May 1313	Duchy divided
14 May 1313 – 21 Jun 1356	*Bolesław* (or *Bolko*) *II*, son (b. after 1293) Duke of Oppeln; Bohemian vassal 5 Apr 1327
14 May 1313 – 1362/5	*Bolesław I*, brother (b. before 1293) Duke of Falkenberg
14 May 1313 – after 22 Jan 1366	*Olbracht*, brother, Duke of Gross-Strelitz

RATIBOR

Dukes

AD 1281	*Przemysł* (or *Przemko*), son of Władysław, the Duke of (Ratibor and) Oppeln; and his brother, *Mieszko*; Dukes of Ratibor and Teschen
1291	*Przemysł* (see above) Duke of Ratibor
7 May 1306 – 1336	*Leszek*, son (b. before 1285) Bohemian vassal 18/19 Feb 1327
14 Jan 1337	Ratibor annexed by Bohemia and united with Troppau

TESCHEN and AUSCHWITZ

Dukes

AD 1281	Duchy held by Duke of Ratibor (see above)
1291	*Mieszko I*, son of Władysław, the Duke of (Ratibor and) Oppeln
1313/17	Duchy divided
1313/17 – Nov/Dec 1358	*Kazimierz I*, son (b. before 31 Jan 1278) Duke of Teschen, Bohemian vassal 18/19 Feb 1327
1313/17 – 1321	*Władysław*, brother (b. before 1278) Duke of Auschwitz
1322/6 – 1370/2	*Jan* (or *Jaśko*) *I*, son, Duke of Auschwitz, Bohemian vassal 24 Feb 1327

OELS

Dukes

AD 1312 – 1313	*Konrad I*, son of Duke Henryk III of Glogau (for 1st time) (b. after 1292; d. 22 Dec 1366) Duke of Oels. Gniezno* and Kalisz*; Duke of Namslau 1313 – 1323
1312	*Bolesław*, brother (b. c. 1295; d. early 1321) Duke of Kalisz* until 1313 and Oels
1321 – 22 Dec 1366	*Konrad I* (for 2nd time) Duke of Oels; Bohemian vassal 9 May 1329

Siunia

Kings

Line of Siunia

AD 963	*Smbat II*, proclaimed himself king 970
c. 998	*Vasak VI*, son
1019	*Smbat III*, cousin
(?) – c. 1091	*Grigor V*, brother

*In Greater Poland

Line of Gardman-Albania

c. 1091	*Hovhannes-Sennacherib*, adopted son of Grigor V
? – 1166	*Grigor VI*, son
1166	Annexed by the princes of Khachen

Songhay

Territory comprised part of present-day Mali, western Niger and north-western Nigeria, with the capital established at Kukiya (later Gao).

Za or Dya

AD 860(?)	*Alayaman* (or *Aliamen*)
(?)	*Zakoi*
(?)	*Takoi*
(?)	*Akoi*
(?)	*Ku*
(?)	*'Ali Fai*
(?)	*Biyai Komai*
(?)	*Biyai*
(?)	*Karai*
(?)	*Yama Karawai*
(?)	*Yama*
(?)	*Yama Danka Kiba'o*
(?)	*Ku-korai*
(?)	*Kenken*
fl. 1009	*Kosoi Muslim Dam*, traditional date for conversion to Islam 1009
(?)	*Kosoi* (or *Kosor*) *Dariya*
(?)	*Henkon Wan Kodam*
(?)	*Biyai-Koi Kimi*
(?)	*Nintasanai*
(?)	*Biyai Kaina Kimba*
(?)	*Kaina Shinyumbo*
(?)	*Tib*
(?)	*Yama Da'o*
(?)	*Fadazu*
(?)	*'Ali Koro*

(?)	*Bir Foloko*
c. 1260	*Yasi Boi* (or *Assibai*)
(?)	*Duro*
(?)	*Zenko Baro*
(?)	*Bisi Baro*
(?)	*Bada*

Sis or Sonnis

c. 1275	*'Ali Kolon* (or *Golom*), son of Yasi Boi(?)
(?)	*Salman Nari*
(?)	*Ibrahim Kabay*
(?)	*'Uthman Kanafa*
(?)	*Bar-Kaina Ankabi*
(?)	*Musa*
(?)	*Bokar Zonko*
(?)	*Bokar Dala Boyonbo*
(?)	*Mari* (or *Muhammad*) *Kiray*
c. 1420	*Muhammad Da'o*
(?)	*Muhammad Kukiya*
(?)	*Muhammad Fari*
(?)	*Karbifo*
(?)	*Mari Fay Koli Jimo*
(?)	*Mari Arkona*
(?)	*Mari Arandan*
(?)	*Salman Dama* (or *Sulaiman Dandi*)
1464	*'Ali* (or *Ber*), son of Muhammad Da'o, founder of the Songhay empire, conquered Timbuktu 1469 and Dienne 1470
Nov 1492	*Baru*, *Bokar Da'o* (or *Abu Bakr Da'o*), son, for a few months, deposed

Askiyas

12 Apr 1493	*Muhammad I Ture*, nephew (?) and general of 'Ali (d. 1538) deposed
1528	*Musa*, son
1531	*Muhammad II Bengan* (or *Burkan*), nephew of Muhammad I
1537	*Isma'il*, son of Muhammad I
1539	*Ishaq I*, brother
1549	*Da'ud*, brother
1582	*Muhammad II*, son

1586	*Muhammad III Bani*
1588	*Ishaq II*, Kukiya captured by the Moroccans 1591, deposed
1591 – 1592	*Muhammad Gao*, killed by the Moroccans
1592	Moroccan conquest (see Timbuktu)

Sulaihids

Territory comprised part of present-day Yemen, with the capital established initially at San'a and Dhu-Jibla.

Kings

AD 1047/8	*(Abu Kamil) 'Ali (ibn Muhammad al-Da'i)*, captured San'a 1063, murdered by the followers of Sa'id ibn al-Najjah of Tihama
25 Apr 1081	*al-Mukarram Ahmad (ibn 'Ali)*, son
1091/2	*al-Mansur Abu Himyar Saba' (ibn Ahmad ibn al-Muzaffar)*, second cousin
1098/9	*al-Mufazzal (ibn Abi'l-Barakat ibn al-Walid al-Himyari)*
1111	*al-Saiyida Arwa*, widow of al-Mukarram Ahmad (b. 1051/2?) exercised effective power from c. 1085 until her death
1137/8 – 1168	*al-Mansur (ibn alMufazzal)*, son of al-Mufazzal
1168	Power seized by the Zurai'ids of Aden

Swabia

Dukes

Franconian House

AD 927 – 10 Dec 949	*Hermann I*, brother of King Konrad I of Germany; Duke of Swabia and Alemannia

Saxon House (Liudolfings)

949 – 6 Sep 957	*Liudolf*, son of King Otto I of Germany (b. 930)
957 – 11/12 Nov 973	*Burkhard (II)*, son-in-law of Duke Heinrich I of Bavaria
973 – 31 Oct 982	*Otto I*, son of Liudolf (b. 954) Duke of Bavaria Jul 976

Franconian House (restored)

982 – 20 Aug 997	*Konrad I*, nephew of Hermann I
997 – 4 Apr 1003	*Hermann II*, son
1004 – 1 Apr 1012	*Hermann III*, son

House of Liutpold

1012 – 31 May 1015	*Ernst I*, son of Liutpold, the Margrave of the East Mark
1015 – 17 Aug 1030	*Ernst II*, son
1030 – 28 Jul 1038	*Hermann IV*, brother

Salian House

1038	*Heinrich I*, Duke (Heinrich VI) of Bavaria, son of Holy Roman Emperor Konrad II (b. Bodfeld 28 Oct 1017; d. Bodfeld 5 Oct 1056) King (Heinrich III) of Germany 4 Jun 1039, Holy Roman Emperor 25 Dec 1046

Saxon House (restored)

1045 – 1047	*Otto II*, son of Ezzo, Count Palatine (Otto I) of Lorraine 1035 – 1045

House of Liutpold (restored)

1048 – 28 Sep 1057	*Otto III*, grandnephew of Liutpold, the Margrave of the East Mark; Margrave of Schweinfurt

House of Rheinfelden

1057 – May 1077	*Rudolf von Rheinfelden*, son of Kuno (d. Merseburg 15 Oct 1080) elected German king 15 Mar 1077 in opposition to Heinrich IV; deposed; defeated and killed at Elster River

House of Hohenstaufen

1079 – 6 Apr 1105	*Friedrich I*, son-in-law of King Heinrich IV of Germany (b. 1050)
1105 – 4/6 Apr 1147	*Friedrich II*, son
1147	*Friedrich III*, son (b. 1122; d. Cilicia, Turkey, 10 Jun

	1190) King (Friedrich I) of Germany 4 Mar 1152 – 15 Aug 1169, Holy Roman Emperor 18 Jun 1155
1152 – 19 Aug 1167	*Friedrich IV*, cousin; Duke of Rothenburg and Swabia
1167 – 20 Jan 1191	*Friedrich V*, son of Friedrich III (b. 16 Jul 1164)
1191 – 15 Aug 1196	*Konrad II*, brother; Duke of Rothenburg 1188
1196 – 21 Jun 1208	*Philipp*, Duke of Spoleto, brother (b. 1178; d. (murdered) Bamberg) Bishop of Würzburg 1190 – Jan 1192, King of Germany 8 Mar 1198
1208	*Friedrich VI*, King (Friedrich II) of Sicily, nephew (b. Iesi, Mark of Ancona, 26 Dec 1194; d. Castel Fiorentino, Apulia, Kingdom of Sicily, 30 Dec 1250) King (Friedrich II) of Germany 5 Dec 1212, Holy Roman Emperor 22 Nov 1220, King of Jerusalem Aug 1225/18 Mar 1229 – 5 Apr 1243
1235 – 21 May 1254	*Konrad III*, son (b. Andrea, Italy, 25 Apr 1228; d. Lavello, Kingdom of Sicily) King (Konrad IV) of Germany Feb 1237/30 Dec 1250, pretender to the throne of Sicily 1251
1254	*Konradin*, also known as *Konrad V*, son (b. Wolfstein 25 Mar 1252; d. (beheaded) Naples 29 Oct 1268) pretender to the throne of Sicily 1267; lost large areas of the duchy to the Counts of Württemberg
House of Habsburg	
1273	*Rudolf I*, Count of Habsburg, son of Albrecht IV of Habsburg (b. Limburg im Breisgau 1 May 1218; d. Speyer 15 Jul 1291) King of Germany 29 Sep 1273, Duke of Austria 1274, Duke of Carinthia 1276 – 1286, took over the vacant duchy and tried unsuccessfully to regain the territories lost under Konradin
1282 – 10 May 1290	*Rudolf II*, son (b. 1271) at the same time Duke of Austria and Styria (until 1 Jun 1283) with his brother *Albrecht I*
1290 – 13 Dec 1313	*Johann*, son (b. 1290) titular duke only
13 Dec 1313	Title discontinued

Sweden

Kings

AD?	*Erik*, the Victorious
c. 994	*Olof*, son
c. 1022	*Anund Jakob*, son
c. 1050	*Emund*, half-brother
c. 1060	*Stenkil*, son-in-law
c. 1080*	*Inge I*, son, and his brother, *Halsten*
c. 1110*	*Filip*, son of Halsten
c. 1118*	*Inge II*, brother
c. 1130	*Sverker I*, a magnate from Östergötland
c. 1156 – c. 1160	*Erik (IX)† Jedvardsson*, Saint, cousin (d. Uppsala)
1161	*Karl (VII)† Sverkersson*, son of Sverker I, defeated by Knut Eriksson
1167	*Knut Eriksson*, son of Erik IX Jedvardsson
1196	*Sverker II Karlsson*, son of Karl VII Sverkersson (d. 17 Jul 1210)
1208 – 10 Apr 1216	*Erik (X) Eriksson*, son of Knut Eriksson
1216	*Johan I Sverkersson*, son of Sverker II Karlsson
1222 – 2 Feb 1250	*Erik (XI) Eriksson*, son of Erik X Knutsson (b. 1216) died childless
1250	*Birger*, son-in-law of Erik X Knutsson (d. 1 Oct 1266) Jarl of Sweden under Erik XI Eriksson and Regent after his death
1250	*Valdemar*, son (b. 1243; d. 26 Dec 1302) until 1266 under direction of Birger; deposed
1275	*Magnus I*, Ladulås (i.e. Barn-lock), brother
1290 – 1318	*Birger Magnusson*, son (b. 1280; d. 31 May 1321) exiled by magnates Regent: 1290 – 1298: *Torgils Knutsson* (d. (executed) 1306), Marsk (i.e. Marshal) of Sweden
1319	*Magnus II Eriksson*, King (Magnus VII) of Norway, nephew of Birger Magnusson and grandson of King

*Between 1060 and 1130, the nation was not united and the periods and territorial extents of the reigns of Inge I, Halsten, Filip and Inge II are uncertain

†Earlier rulers named Erik and Karl led single tribes only before the establishment of the Swedish nation or are legendary. The ordinal numbers are often omitted when referring to Erik IX – XIII and Karl VII and VIII

	Håkon V of Norway (b. 1316; d. 1 Dec 1374) deposed and imprisoned by magnates
1363	*Albrekt* (German: *Albrecht*), nephew, son of Duke Albrecht of Mecklenburg (d. 31 Mar 1412)
1389	*Margareta* (or *Margreta*), Queen of Denmark, Regent of Norway, daughter-in-law of Magnus II (b. 1353; d. Flensburg, 28 Oct 1412) acknowledged as queen in Sweden everywhere except Stockholm
1397	*Erik (XIII)* (or *Erik av Pommern*), King (Erik III) of Norway, Duke (Eryk I) of Pomerania at Stolp, great-nephew of Margareta (b. 1382; d. Jun 1459) crowned 1397 at Kalmar as King of the North (i.e. Denmark, Norway and Sweden), King (Erik VII) of Denmark 28 Oct 1412 – 1439; deposed in all Scandinavian kingdoms
1435	*Engelbrekt Engelbrektsson* (d. (murdered) 1436) elected regent by a national assembly at Arboga after leading a popular revolt against Erik XIII
1435/6 – 1440	*Karl Knutsson Bonde* (b. 1408; d. 1470) appointed regent by Swedish magnates in opposition to Engelbrekt
1440 – 6 Jan 1448	*Kristoffer* (German: *Christoph*), King (Christoffer III) of Denmark, nephew of Erik XIII (b. 26 Feb (?) 1416; d. Hälsingborg) King (Kristoffer) of Norway Jun 1442
1448	*Karl (VIII) Knutsson Bonde* (for 1st time) previously regent
1457	*Christian I* (for 1st time), King of Denmark and of Norway (b. 1426; d. 21 May 1481)
1464	*Karl (VIII) Knutsson Bonde* (for 2nd time)
1465	*Christian I* (for 2nd time)
1467	*Karl (VIII) Knutsson Bonde* (for 3rd time)
1470 – 1503	*Sten Sture I*, the Elder, nephew, regent
	(*Johan II*, King (Hans) of Denmark and of Norway, son of Christian I, was elected King of Sweden 1483 but was not crowned until 1497; Sten Sture continued as regent until his death)

Syracuse

Territory comprised part of present-day southern Italy and Sicily, with the capital in Syracuse.

Tyrants

491 BC	*Gelon*
478	*Hieron I*, brother
466 – 465	*Thrasybulus*, for less than a year, deposed
465 – 405	Democracy
405	*Dionysius I*, the Elder, a general
367	*Dionysius II*, the Younger, son (for 1st time) period of anarchy
356	*Dion*, anarchy
347 – 344	*Dionysius II* (for 2nd time) anarchy
345 – 337	*Timoleon*, a Corinthian, re-established order, defeated Carthage, instituted an oligarchy
337 – 317	Rule by the oligarchy
317 – 289	*Agathocles*, the Tyrant, declared himself king
289 – 265	Internal disorder
270	*Hieron II*
215 – 214	*Hieronymus*, son, assassinated
211	Roman conquest

Tahirids

Territory comprised part of present-day north-eastern Iran.

Governors of Khurasan for the 'Abbasid Caliphate (virtually independent)

AD 820/1 – 14 Nov 822	*(Abu Tayyib) Tahir I (Dhu'l-Yaminain ibn al-Husain)* (b. 775/6) governor of Syria 813/14
Nov 822	*Talha (ibn Tahir)*, son
Sep/Oct 828 – 26 Nov 844	*(Abu'l-'Abbas) 'Abdallah (ibn Tahir)*, brother (b. 798/9) governor of Syria 821/2, governor of Egypt 825/6

844/5	*Tahir II (ibn 'Abdallah)*, son
862/3 – 872/3	*Muhammad (ibn Tahir)*, son (b. 851/2; d. 882/3)
872/3	Territory captured by the Saffarids and Samanids

Thailand

KINGDOM OF SUKHOTHAI

Territory comprised part of western Thailand.

Kings

AD 1238	*Sri Intharathitya* (or *Sri Indraditya*)
(?)	*Ban Muang*, son
1283	*Rama Khamheng*, brother
c. 1317	*Lo Thai*, son, gradual decline of power
1347	*Thammaraja Lu Thai*, son, abdicated
1361	*Thammaraja II*, son, defeated by Ayuthia and became its vassal
1406	*Thammaraja III*, son
1419	*Thammaraja IV*, brother, governor under Ayuthia
(?)	Succeeding rulers acting as governors under Ayuthia
1438	Officially incorporated into Ayuthia (see below)

KINGDOM OF AYUTHIA

Territory comprised part of southern and central Thailand

Kings

AD 1350	*Rama Thibodi*, first conquest of Angkor 1362
1369	*Ramesuen*, son (for 1st time) abdicated
1370	*Boromoraja I*, uncle, conquest of Sukhothai
1388	*Thon Lan*, son, deposed and executed
1388	*Ramesuen* (for 2nd time) second conquest of Angkor
1395	*Ram Raja*, son, deposed

1408	*Intharaja*, nephew of Boromoraja I
1424	*Boromoraja II*, son, final conquest of Angkor
1448	*Boromo Trailokanat*, son
1488	*Boromoraja III*, son
1491 – 1529	*Rama Thibodi II*, brother

Thessalonica

Territory in northern Greece.

Latin Kings

Sep AD 1204 – Sep 1207	*Boniface*, Margrave (Bonifacio I) of Montferrat (b. c. 1150; d. near Mosynopolis) conquered most of Greece during the Fourth Crusade
1207 – 1221	*Demetrius*, infant son; ruled under the regency of his mother, *Maria*; fled to Italy at the invasion of Theodore Ducas
1224	Final conquest of Thessalonica by Theodore Ducas of Epirus

Greek Emperors and Despots

1225 – Apr 1230	*Theodore Ducas*, half-brother of Michael I of Epirus; ruler of Epirus c. 1215 – 1225; conquered Thessalonica 1224 and crowned Emperor* 1225; defeated and captured by Ivan Asen II, Tsar of Bulgaria, at Klokotnica Apr 1230, returned to Thessalonica 1237 and became virtual ruler during the reign of John (see below); captured and imprisoned by John III Ducas Vatatzes, Emperor of Nicaea, 1241
1230	*Manuel*, brother; lost most of Thessalonica to Ivan Asen II but was able to retain his rule of the city, with the title of despot; deposed by Theodore Ducas
1237	*John*, nephew, installed by Theodore with the title of

*i.e. he claimed to be the Emperor of the Greeks. This placed him in a position of rivalry with the Latin Emperors of Constantinople (see Byzantine Empire) and with the Greek Emperors of Nicaea

	Emperor, invaded by John III Ducas Vatatzes 1242 and forced to acknowledge the suzerainty of Nicaea, took title of Despot
1244 – 1246	*Demetrius*, brother, ruled with the title of Despot, defeated and imprisoned by John III Ducas Vatatzes
1246	Incorporated into the Empire of Nicaea

Thuringia

Landgraves

Ludovingians

c. AD 1039	*Ludwig*, the Bearded (d. 1055/1080) Count in Thuringia
1055/1080 – 6/8 May 1123	*Ludwig*, son, Count in Thuringia
1123 – 12 Jan 1140	*Ludwig I*, son (b. c. 1090) appointed Landgrave of Thuringia by King Lothar II of Germany 1131
1140 – 14 Oct 1172	*Ludwig II*, son (b. c. 1128)
1172 – 16 Oct 1190	*Ludwig III*, son (b. c. 1152) Count Palatine of Saxony 1180/1
1190 – 25 Apr 1217	*Hermann I*, brother, Count Palatine of Saxony 1181
1217 – 11 Sep 1227	*Ludwig IV*, son (b. 28 Oct 1200)
1227 – 2/3 Jan 1241	*Hermann II*, son (b. 28 Mar 1223) ruled under the guardianship of Heinrich Raspe
1241 – 16 Feb 1247	*Heinrich Raspe*, uncle (b. c. 1202; d. Wartburg Castle, Thuringia) German antiking 22 May 1246
1247 – 1249	Period of dispute over succession

House of Wettin

1249	*Heinrich*, the Illustrious, Margrave (Heinrich III) of Meissen, nephew of Heinrich Raspe (b. 1215/16; d. c. 8 Feb 1288) abdicated
1265	*Albrecht*, son (b. 1240; d. 13 Nov 1314) sold the landgravate to King Adolf of Germany 1293
1310 – 16 Nov 1323	*Friedrich I*, the Dauntless, son (b. 1257) invested with Thuringia and Meissen by King Heinrich VII of Germany

1324 – 18 Nov 1349	*Friedrich II*, the Grave, son (b. 1310) Margrave of Meissen
1349	*Friedrich III*, the Stern, son (b. 14 Oct 1332; d. 25 May 1381) ruled Meissen and Thuringia with his brothers, *Balthasar* (b. 21 Dec 1336; d. 18 May 1406) and *Wilhelm I* (b. 19 Dec 1343; d. 10 Feb 1407)
1382	By the agreement of Chemnitz, following the death of Friedrich III, the surviving brothers divided the Wettin domains; Wilhelm I took Meissen, while Balthasar became sole ruler of Thuringia
1406 – 7 May 1440	*Friedrich IV*, son of Balthasar (b. c. 30 Nov 1384)
1440	*Friedrich*, the Mild, Elector (Friedrich II) of Saxony, grandson of Friedrich III (b. 22 Aug 1412; d. 7 Sep 1464) forced to grant Thuringia to his brother Wilhelm
1445 – 17 Sep 1482	*Wilhelm*, brother (b. 30 Apr 1425)
17 Sep 1482	Thuringia passed permanently to the Electors of Saxony and was divided between Albrecht and Ernst in the partition of 1485

Tibet

Chö-Gye (Religious Kings)

First Kingdom

c. AD 618	*Song-tsen Gam-po* (b. c. 605) founder of Lhasa
649	*Mang-song Mang-tsen* (b. c. 626)
676	*Dü-song Mang-po-je*
704	*Tri-de Tsug-ten*
754	*Tri-song De-tsen* (b. 742)
c. 797	*Mu-ne Tsen-po*
c. 800	*Tri-de Song-tsen* (or *Se-na-lek*)
815	*Tri-tsung De-tsen* (or *Ral-pa-chen*)
c. 838 – 842	*Lang Darma*
c. 842	Kingdom divided into various lay and monastic principalities

Viceroys

Period of Mongol Rule

1207	Mongols became the overlords of Tibet
1244	*Sakya Pandita*, a Tibetan Lama, appointed first Mongol viceroy
1253	*Phagpa*, given the title *Tisri* 1260
1280	*Rinchen Tisri*, a Lama of Sakya
1282	*Dharmapalarakshita Tisri*
1286	*Yishe Rinchen Tisri*
1295	*Tragpa Öser Tisri*
1303	*Rinchen Gyantsen Tisri*
1304	*Dorje Pal Tisri*
1313	*Sangye Pal Tisri*
1316	*Kunga Lotro Tisri*
1327	*Kunga Lekpa Chungne Tisri*
1330 – 1358	*Kunga Gyantsne Tisri*

Kings

Second Kingdom

c. 1350	*Chang-chub Gyantsen of Pagmotru*, regained independence from the Mongols 1368
1372	*Sakya Gyantsen*
1386	*Trakpa Chang-chub*
1388	*Sonam Trakpa Gyantsen*
1440	*Trakpa Chungne*
c. 1465	*Sangye Gyantsen Pal Zangpo*
1481 – 1522	*Dön-yö Dorje*

Dalai Lamas*

1391	*Gedün Truppa*
1475 – 1542	*Gedün Gyatso*

*The lamas of the Gelugpa sect, on whom the title of Dalai Lama was conferred by the Mongol Altan Khan in 1578, had no political authority before the 17th century but are included for the sake of completeness.

Timbuktu

Territory comprised part of present-day Mali, centred at Timbuktu.

Moroccan Pashas (appointed by the Sa'adi Sharifs of Morocco)

AD 1589	*Judar*
1590/1	*Mahmud ibn 'Ali (ibn Zarghun)*
1594/5	*al-Mansur ibn 'Abd al-Rahman*
1597/8	*Mahmud Taba'*
1598/9	*'Ammar al-Fita*
1599/1600	*Sulaiman*
1603/4	*Mahmud Longo*
1611/12	*'Ali ibn 'Abdallah*
1617	*Ahmad ibn Yusuf (al-'Ilji)*
1617/18	*Haddu ibn Yusuf (al-Ajnasi)*
1618/19	*Muhammad ibn Ahmad (al-Massi)*
1621/2	*Yusuf ibn 'Umar (al-Qasri)*
1626/7	*Ibrahim ibn 'Abd (al-Qarim al-Jarrari)*
1627/8	*'Ali ibn 'Abd (al-Qadir)*
1631/2	*'Ali ibn al-Mubarak (al-Massi)*
1631/2	*Sa'ud ibn Ahmad ('Ajrud al-Sharqi)*
1633/4	*'Abd al-Rahman ibn Qa'id-Hammadi (ibn Sa'dun)*
1634/5	*Sa'id ibn 'Ali (al-Mahmudi)*
1636/7	*Mas'ud ibn Mansur (al-Za'ari)*
1642/3	*Muhammad ibn Muhammad (ibn 'Uthman)*
1646/7	*Ahmad ibn 'Ali (al-Tilimsani)*
1647/8	*Hamid ibn 'Abd al-Rahman (al-Haiyuni)*
1648/9	*Yahya ibn Muhammad (al-Gharnati)*
1650/1	*Hammadi ibn Haddu (al-Ajnasi)*
1653/4	*Muhammad ibn Musa*
1654/5	*Muhammad ibn Ahmad (Sa'dun al-Shiadami)*
1656/7	*Muhammad (ibn al-Haj al-Shatuki) Qa'id Buya* (for 1st time)
Aug/Sep 1660	*'Allal ibn Sa'id (al-Harusi)*, for one day
1660/1	*al-Haj al-Mukhtar ibn Biyukhaf (al-Sharqi)*
1660/1	*Hammu ibn 'Abdallah (al-'Ilji)*
1660/1	*'Ali ibn 'Abd al-'Aziz (al-Faraji)*
1661/2	*'Ali ibn Bashud-Muhammad (al-Tazarkini)*
1662/3	*'Ammar ibn Ahmad-'Ajrud (al-Sharqi)*
1665/6	*Muhammad Qa'id Buya* (for 2nd time)

1666/7	*Nasir ibn 'Abdallah (al-A'mashi al-Dar'i)*
1666/7	*'Abd al-Rahman ibn Sa'id (al-Andalusi)*
1667/8	*Nasir ibn 'Ali (al-Tilimsani)*
1670/1	*Muhammad ibn Ahmad (al-Kuihil al-Sharqi)*
1671/2	*Muhammad ibn 'Ali (al-Mubarak al-Dar'i)* (for 1st time)
1672/3	*'Ali ibn Ibrahim (al-Dar'i)*
1675/6	*Sa'id ibn 'Umar (al-Fasi)*
1678/9	*'Abdallah ibn Muhammad (ibn al-Qa'id-Hassun al-Dar'i)*
1679/80	*Dhu'l-Nun ibn al-Haj (al-Mukhtar al-Sharqi)* (for 1st time)
1680/1	*Muhammad ibn Ba-Ridwan (al-'Ilji)* (for 1st time)
1680/1	*Yahya ibn 'Ali (al-Mubarak al-Dar'i)*
1681/2	*Dhu'l-Nun ibn al-Haj* (for 2nd time)
1682	*Muhammad ibn 'Ali* (for 2nd time)
1682/3	*Ba-Haddu Salim al-Hassani*
1682/3	*al-Fa' Benkano (al-Sharqi ibn Muhammad al-Mudasani)*, for three days
1682/3	*Zenka 'Abd al-Rahman (ibn Bu-Zanad al-Fasi)*
1683/4	*Muhammad ibn Ba-Ridwan* (for 2nd time)
1683/4	*'Ali ibn Humayd (al-'Amri)*
1684/5	*al-Mubarak ibn Mansur (al-Za'ari)* (for 1st time)
1685/6	*Sa'ud Bokarna (ibn Muhammad ibn 'Uthman)* (for 1st time)
1685/6	*al-Hasan ibn Mansur al-Munabbih*
1686/7	*'Abdallah ibn Muhammad ibn al-Qa'id Hasan al-Dar'i*
1687/8	*al-'Abbas ibn Sa'id al-'Amri*
1687/8	*al-Mansur ibn Mas'ud (al-Za'ari) Sanibar* (for 1st time)
1688/9	*Ahmad ibn 'Ali al-Tazarkini*
1689/90	*Sa'ud Bokarna* (for 2nd time)
1690/1	*Sanibar ibn Muhammad Buya* (for 1st time)
1690/1	*Ibrahim ibn Hassun (al-Dar'i)* (for 1st time)
1692/3	*Baba Sayyid ibn Talib (Hammadi al-Sharqi)*
1692/3	*al-Mubarak ibn Mansur* (for 2nd time)
1693/4	*Ibrahim ibn Hassun* (for 2nd time)
1693/4	*Dhu'l-Nun ibn al-Haj* (for 3rd time)
1693/4	*Ahmad al-Khalifa (al-Tilimsani)*
1694/5	*Sanibar ibn Muhammad Buya* (for 2nd time)
1695/6	*'Abdallah ibn Nasir (al-A'mashi al-Dar'i)*
1695/6	*Hammadi ibn 'Ali (al-Tazarkini)* (for 1st time)

1696/7	*al-Mubarak ibn Hammadi (al-Dar'i)*
1696/7	*Muhammad ibn Muhammad al-Sayyidi (al-Sharqi al-Sana'uni)* (for 1st time) for one day
1696/7	*'Ali ibn Muhammad (ibn Shaikh 'Ali al-Dar'i)*
1697/8	*Yahya ibn Muhammad Zankana (al-Fishtani)* (for 1st time)
1697/8	*'Abdallah ibn Nasir (al-Tilimsani)* (for 1st time)
1697/8	*al-Mansur ibn Mas'ud Sanibar* (for 2nd time)
1699/1700	*Hammadi ibn 'Ali* (for 2nd time)
1700/1	*'Abdallah ibn Nasir* (for 2nd time)
1700/1	*Yusuf ibn 'Abdallah (al-Dar'i)* (for 1st time)
1701/2	*Muhammad ibn Sa'id (ibn 'Umar al-Fasi)*
1702/3	*Ahmad ibn Mansur (al-Sharqi)*
1702/3	*'Ali ibn Mubarak (ibn 'Ali al-Dar'i)*
1702/3	*Santa'a ibn Faris (al-Fasi)*
1703/4	*Mami ibn 'Ali (al-Tazarkini)* (for 1st time)
1703/4	*Muhammad ibn Sa'id (ibn 'Umar)*
1703/4	*Muhammad ibn Muhammad al-Sayyidi* (for 2nd time)
1704/5	*Yahya ibn Muhammad Zankana* (for 2nd time)
1704/5	*'Abdallah ibn Nasir* (for 3rd time)
1704/5	*Sa'id ibn Buzi'an (al-Khabbazi)*
1704/5	*Mami ibn 'Ali* (for 2nd time)
1706/7	*al-Mubarak ibn Muhammad (al-Gharnati)*
1706/7	*Nasir ibn 'Abdallah (al-A'mashi al-Dar'i)*
1707/8	*'Abdallah ibn Nasir* (for 4th time)
1707/8	*'Ali ibn Rahmun (al-Munabbih)* (for 1st time)
1708/9	*Muhammad ibn Hammadi al-Tazarkani*
1708/9	*Hammadi Zenko*
1709/10	*Yahya ibn Muhammad Zankana* (for 3rd time)
1709/10	*Yahya ibn Muhammad (ibn Shaikh 'Ali al-Dar'i)*
1710/11	*Ba-Bakr ibn Muhammad Sayyidi*
1711/12	*Yusuf ibn 'Abdallah* (for 2nd time)
1711/12	*'Abd al-Qadir ibn 'Ali (al-Tazarkini)*
1712/13	*'Abdallah ibn Nasir* (for 5th time)
1712/13	*'Ali ibn al-Mubarak (al-Dar'i)*
1712/13	*al-Mansur ibn Mas'ud Sanibar* (for 3rd time)
1713/14	*Mami ibn 'Ali* (for 3rd time)
1713/14	*'Ali ibn Rahmun* (for 2nd time)
1713/14	*'Abdallah ibn al-Haj (ibn Sa'id al-'Imrani)* (for 1st time)
1714/15	*'Ammar ibn Sa'ud Bokarna*
1714/15	*Ba-Haddu ibn Yahya (ibn al-Mubarak al-Dar'i)* (for

	1st time)
1714/15	*'Abdallah ibn al-Haj* (for 2nd time)
1715	*Ba-Haddu ibn Yahya* (for 2nd time)
1715	*Muhammad ibn Hammadi (al-Tazarkini)*
1715/16	*'Ali ibn Muhammad (al-Dar'i)*
1715/16	*'Abdallah ibn al-Haj* (for 3rd time)
1715/16	*al-Mansur ibn Mas'ud Sanibar* (for 4th time)
1718/19	*Ba-Haddu ibn Yahya* (for 3rd time)
1720/1	*'Abd al-Ghaffar ibn 'Ali (al-Tazarkani)*
1721/2	*'Abdallah ibn al-Haj* (for 4th time)
1725/6	*Mahmud ibn al-Qa'id (Muhammad Buya)*
1725/6	*'Abd al-Rahman ibn Hammadi (al-Tazarkani)*
1726/7	*'Abdallah ibn al-Haj* (for 5th time)
1726/7	*Ba-Haddu ibn Yahya* (for 4th time)
1728/9	*Yusuf ibn 'Abdallah* (for 3rd time)
1729/30	*'Abdallah ibn al-Haj* (for 6th time)
1731/2	*Muhammad Bohhu ibn Sanibar (al-Za'ari)*
1732/3	*al-Hasani ibn Hammadi al-Tazarkani*
1733/4	*Muhammad ibn Hammadi al-Tazarkani*, brother (for 1st time)
1734/5	*Sa'id ibn 'Ali*, uncle (for 1st time)
1735/6	*Hammadi ibn Sanibar (ibn Mansur al-Za'ari)* (for 1st time)
1736/7	*Sa'id ibn 'Ali* (for 2nd time)
1737/8	*Hammadi ibn Sanibar* (for 2nd time)
1737/8	*Muhammad ibn Hammadi al-Tazarkani* (for 2nd time)
1737/8	*al-Fa' Ibrahim ibn Mansur (al-Dar'i)*
1738/9	*Hammadi ibn Mansur*, brother
1738/9	*al-Fa' Ibrahim ibn Hammadi (al-Tazarkini)*
1738/9	*Sa'id ibn Sanibar (al-Za'ari)* (for 1st time)
1739/40	*Yahya ibn Hammadi (al-Tazarkini)*
1740/1	*Bàba-Sayyid ibn Hammadi (Zenko)* (for 1st time)
1741/2	*al-Hasan ibn Muhammad (al-'Amri)*
1741/2	*Sa'id ibn Sanibar* (for 2nd time)
1742/3	*Sa'id ibn Hammadi (al-Tazarkani)* (for 1st time)
1743/4	*Sa'id ibn Sanibar* (for 3rd time)
1745/6	*Baba-Sayyid ibn Hammadi* (for 2nd time)
1746/7	*al-Fa' Mahmud ibn Sanibar (ibn Muhammad-Buya al-Shatuki)*
1748	*'Abd al-Ghaffar ibn Usama (al-Tazarkani)*
1748	*Ba-Bakr ibn al-Fa' Mansur (al-Dar'i)*
(?)	*Sa'id ibn Hammadi* (for 2nd time)

(?)	*'Ali ibn 'Abd (al-Rauf al-Dar'i)*
(?)	*'Ali ibn 'Ammar (ibn Sa'ud Bokarna)*
(?)	*Ba-Haddu ibn Ba-Bakr (ibn al-Fa' Mansur al-Dar'i)*
(?)	*Baba-'Ali ibn Mansur (al-Tazarkini)*
1787	Tuareg conquest

Timurids

Territory comprised part of present-day USSR, Iraq, eastern Turkey and Iran.

Khans

Supreme Rulers in Samarkand

9 Apr AD 1370 – 18 Feb 1405	*Temür* (or *Timur*) *(Lang)* (or *Tamerlane*) (b. 10 Apr 1336)
1405 – 1409/10	*Khalil (ibn Miranshah)*, grandson (b. 1384)
1405	*Shah Rukh*, uncle (b. 1377/8) ruled initially in Khurasan only, from 1415/16 ruled entire khanate
1446/7	*('Ala' al-Daula) Ulugh Beg (ibn Shah Rukh)*, son, assassinated by 'Abd al-Latif
Oct/Nov 1449 – 9 May 1450	*(Rukn al-Din) 'Abd al-Latif (ibn Ulugh Beg)*, son, assassinated
May 1450	*'Abdallah ibn Ibrahim (ibn Shah Rukh)*, cousin
1451/2	*Abu Sa'id ibn Muhammad (ibn Miranshah)*, grandson of Temür (b. 1426/7; d. 8 Feb 1469)
1467/8	*Ahmad (ibn Abu Sa'id)*, son
1493/4 – 1500	*Mahmud (ibn Abu Sa'id)*, brother
1500	Shaibanid conquest

Rulers in Khurasan after Ulugh Beg's death

1449/50	*(Abu'l-Qasim) Babur ibn Baisonqor (ibn Shah Rukh)*, grandson of Shah Rukh
1456/7	*(Shah) Mahmud ibn Babur*, son
1458/9 – 8 Feb 1469	*Abu Sa'id ibn Muhammad* (see Supreme Rulers in Samarkand)
1469	*Yadigar Muhammad (ibn Muhammad ibn Baisonqor)*, nephew of Babur ibn Baisonqor
1470/1 – May/Jun 1506	*Abu'l-Ghazi (Husain Baiqara)*, descended from Temür's son 'Umar Shaikh (b. Jun/Jul 1438)

1506	*Badi' al-Zaman*
1506	Shaibanid conquest

Rulers in western Persia and Iraq after Temür's death

1404/5 – 21 Apr 1408	*(Jalal al-Din) Miranshah (ibn Timur)*, son of Temür (b. 1366/7)
1409/10	*Khalil*, son (see Supreme Rulers in Samarkand)
1414/15	*'Ayyal (ibn Miranshah)*, brother
1414/15 – 1415/16	*Ailankar (ibn Abu Bakr)*, nephew, ruled under Shah Rukh
1415/16	Territories united with Shah Rukh's possessions (see above)

Toltecs

Territory comprised part of present-day central Mexico, with the capital at Tollán (present-day Tula).

Rulers of the first Nahuatl Empire*

AD 869	*Huetzin*
(?)	*Totepeuh* (or *Mixcóatl*), led his people to Culhuacan, assassinated
877	*Ihuitimal*, brother, killed
923	*Topiltzin*, nephew, founder of the Toltec empire at Tollán, abdicated
947	*Matlacxóchitl*
983	*Nauhyotzin I*
997	*Matlaccoatzin*
1025	*Tlilcoatzin*
1047 – 1122	*Huemac*
1122	Tula destroyed by an invasion of the nomadic Chichimec (among which were the Aztecs)

*According to Anales de Cuauhtitlán

Toulouse

Counts

AD 849	*Frédelon*, granted the county of Toulouse by King Charles II, the Bald, of the West Franks
852 – c. 862	*Raimond I*, brother, gained Limousin
c. 862 – 865	County occupied by Humfrid of Gothia
865	*Bernard*, son of Raimond I, assassinated by Bernard Plantevelue
872 – (?)	*Bernard Plantevelue*, ruled the county until his death
886	*Eudes*, brother of Bernard
918/19	*Raimond II*, son
923	*Raimond III Pons*, son, Count of Auvergne and Duke of Aquitaine 932
950 – Sep 1037	*Guillaume III Taillefer*,* son (b. c. 947)
1037	*Pons*, son (b. c. 990)
1060	*Guillaume IV*, son (b. c. 1040; d. 1093) abdicated
1088 – 28 Feb 1105†	*Raimond IV de Saint-Gilles*, brother (d. near Tripoli) departed on the First Crusade Oct 1096
1105 – 21 Apr 1112	*Bertrand*, illegitimate(?) son, Count of Tripoli Jul 1109 – Jan/Feb 1112
1112 – Apr 1148†	*Alphonse I Jourdain*, brother (b. 1103)
1148	*Raimond V*, son (b. 1134) ruled for a short time with his brother, *Alphonse II*
1194	*Raimond VI*, son of Raimond V (for 1st time) (b. 27 Oct 1156; d. 2 Aug 1222) defeated by Simon de Montfort at the Battle of Muret Jun 1211, deprived of his lands by the Lateran Council
1215 – 25 Jun 1218	*Simon de Montfort*, leader of the Albigensian Crusade (d. Toulouse) Count of Béziers and Carcassonne 1209, died while besieging Toulouse
1218	*Raimond VI* (for 2nd time)
1222 – 27 Sep 1249	*Raimond VII*, son (b. Beaucaire Jul 1197; d. Millau) excommunicated and deprived of his lands by the Council of Bourges Jan 1226, did public penance at

*Guillaume I and II were counts or dukes of Toulouse appointed by the Merovingian kings of the Franks

†Guillaume IX of Aquitaine, son-in-law of Guillaume IV, usurped power in the county 1098 – 1100 and 1114 – 1119

	Notre Dame and formally reinvested with his lands 1229
1249 – 25 Aug 1271	*Jeanne*, daughter (b. 1220) ruled with her husband, *Alphonse III*, Count of Poitou (b. 11 Nov 1220; d. 21 Aug 1271)
Aug 1271	Toulouse and Poitou annexed to the crown by Philippe III, King of France

Trier

Archbishops (and from 13th century Electors of the Holy Roman Empire)*

AD (?)	*Milo* (d. 753 or 757)
?	*Hartham*(?)
? – 791	*Weomad*
791 or 792 – 1 Oct 804	*Richbod*
?	*Wazo*
fl. 813	*Amalar*
fl. 27 Aug 816 – 847	*Hetti*
847 – Oct 863	*Thietgaut* (d. 869) deposed
869 – 10 Feb 883	*Bertulf*
8 Apr 883 – 30 Mar 915	*Ratbod*
? – 27 Jan 930 or 931	*Ruotger*, appointed to duties of Lord High Chancellor 27 Dec 929
931 – 18 or 19 May 956	*Ruotbert*
956 – 3 Jul 964	*Heinrich I*
before 2 Jun 965 – 5 Jun 977	*Dietrich*
between 30 Jul and 8 Sep 977 – 8 or 9 Dec 993	*Ekbert*
994 – 7 Apr 1008	*Liudolf*

*When two dates separated by an oblique stroke are given for the beginning of an episcopate, the first refers to election or nomination and the second to ordination, consecration or investiture

spring 1008 – 24 Dec 1015	*Megingoz*
1 Jan 1016 – 16 Jun 1047	*Poppo*
28 Jun 1047 – 15 Apr 1066	*Eberhard*
before 18 May – 1 Jun 1066	*Konrad*, murdered
1066 – 11 Nov 1078	*Uoto*
6 Jan 1079/Oct 1084 – 3 or 5 Sep 1101	*Egilbert*
Christmas 1101/6 Jan 1102 – 25 Apr 1124	*Brun*
2 Jul 1124 – 17 May 1127	*Gottfrid*, resigned
Jun 1127/Apr 1128 – 1 Oct 1130	*Meginher*
Easter 1131/between 27 Feb and 7 Mar 1132 – 18 Jan 1152	*Adelbero von Münsterol*
31 Jan 1152 – 23 Oct 1169	*Hillin von Fallemanien*
1169 – 25 May 1183	*Arnold I*
May 1183/1 Jul 1186 – 26 Jun 1189	*Folmar*, deposed
autumn 1189 – 14 Jul 1212	*Johann I*
1212 – 27 Mar 1242	*Dietrich von Wied*
1242 – 5 Nov 1259	*Arnold II von Isenburg*
Aug 1260 – 26 Apr 1286	*Heinrich II von Finstingen* (d. Boulogne) after rejection of alternative candidates, *Heinrich von Bollanden* and *Arnold von Sleida*
after 26 Apr 1286/6 Mar 1289 – 9 Dec 1299	*Bohemund I von Warnesberg*, in disputed election against *Ebert* and *Johann von Sierk**
18 Jan 1300 – 22 Nov 1307	*Diether von Nassau*, in rivalry with Heinrich von Virneburg
26 Jan 1300 – 26 Jan 1306	*Heinrich III von Virneburg* (d. 6 Jan 1332) translated to Cologne
7 Dec 1307/12 Feb 1308 – 21 Jan 1354	*Baldwin von Luxemburg*, in rivalry with *Emicho*, Count of Sponheim-Kreuznach, until 12 Feb 1308

*By 1289 Johann had renounced his claim and Ebert had died

3 Feb/8 Mar 1354 – late 1361	*Bohemund II von Saarbrücken* (d. Saarburg 10 Feb 1367) resigned
27 May 1362 – 6 Jan 1388	*Kuno II von Falkenstein* (d. Wellmich castle 21 May 1388) coadjutor from 4 Apr 1360, coadjutor for Cologne archbishopric 23 Dec 1366 – 26 Aug 1369, administrator for Cologne archbishopric 27 Mar 1370 – 2 Jul 1371, resigned
3 Apr/after 9 Sep 1388 – 4 Oct 1418	*Werner von Falkenstein*, coadjutor from 6 Jan 1388
13 Oct/22 Dec 1418 – 13 Feb 1430	*Otto von Ziegenhain* (d. Koblenz)
22 May 1430 – 27 Jun 1438	*Raban von Helmstatt* (d. Speyer 4 Nov 1439) previously Bishop of Speyer; resigned
19 May/30 Aug 1439 – 28 May 1456	*Jakob von Sierk*, coadjutor from 10 Apr 1439
25 Oct 1456 – 9 Feb 1503	*Johann II von Baden* (b. 9 Feb 1430) Coadjutor: 11 Sep 1500 – 9 Feb 1503: *Jakob von Baden*

Tujibids and Hudids

Territory comprised part of present-day north-eastern Spain, with the capital at Saragossa.

Kings

Tujibids

AD 1019/20	*Mundhir I (al-Mansur ibn Yahya al-Tujibi)*
1023/4	*Yahya (al-Muzaffar ibn Mundhir)*, son
1029/30 – 1039/40	*Mundhir II (ibn Yahya)*, son, murdered

Hudids

1039/40	*(Abu Ayyub) Sulaiman (al-Musta'in ibn Hud)*, son of Hud
1046/7	*Ahmad I (Saif al-Daula al-Muqtadir ibn Sulaiman)*, son
1081/2	*Yusuf (al-Mu'tamin ibn Ahmad)*, son
1085/6	*Ahmad II (al-Musta'in ibn Yusuf)*, son

1109/10	*'Abd al-Malik ('Imad al-Daula ibn Ahmad)*, son, conquered by the Almoravids
1119/20 – 1141/2	*Ahmad III (Saif al-Daula al-Mustansir ibn 'Abd al-Malik)*, son
1141/2	Conquest by Aragon

Tukulor Empire

Territory comprised part of present-day Mali and eastern Senegal, with the capital at Timbuktu.

Rulers

Mar AD 1854 – 12 Feb 1864	*'Umar (ibn Sa'id Tall) al-Hajj* (b. Aloar, Futa Toro (in present-day Senegal), c. 1794; d. Hamdalahi 1864) appointed caliph for black Africa by the head of the Tijaniya brotherhood, began the jihad Mar 1854, defeated the Bambara States
1864 – 1893	*Ahmadu (ibn 'Umar ibn Sa'id Tall)*, son (d. Sokoto 1898) put to flight by the French
Dec 1893	Timbuktu captured by French

Tulunids

Territory comprised part of present-day north-eastern Libya, Egypt, Saudi Arabia, Israel, Jordan, Lebanon and western Syria, with the capital at al-Fustat (Old Cairo).

Rulers

15 Sep AD 868 – 20 May 884	*Ahmad (ibn Tulun)* (b. Samarra 20 Sep 835) appointed 'Abbasid governor of Egypt 868, declaration of independence 879/80

May 884	*(Abu'l-Jaish) Khumarawaih (ibn Ahmad)*, son, assassinated near Damascus
Jan/Feb 896 – 25 Jul 896	*(Abu'l-'Asakir) Jaish (ibn Khumarawaih)*, son (b. 881/2) deposed and later killed
Jul/Aug 896	*(Abu Musa) Harun (ibn Khumarawaih)*, brother (b. 882/3) Syria lost 902/3
30 Dec 904 – 10 Jan 905	*(Abu'l-Manaqib) Shaiban (ibn Ahmad)*, uncle
Jan 905	Conquest by the 'Abbasid general Muhammad ibn Sulaiman

Tyre

Territory comprised part of present-day Lebanon, with the capital established at Tyre (present-day Sur).

Kings

c. 990 BC	*Abibaal*
c. 978	*Hiram I*, the Great, son (b. c. 997)
c. 944	*Baal-eser I*, son
c. 927	*Abdastratus*, son (b. c. 957) deposed
c. 918	*Methusastartus*, foster-brother(?) (b. c. 960)
c. 906	*Astarymus*, brother (b. c. 955) killed by Phelles
c. 897	*Phelles*, brother (b. c. 947) for eight months, assassinated
c. 896	*Ethbaal I* (b. c. 920) usurper, traditionally a priest of Astarte
c. 863	*Baal-azor II*, son, traditionally for six years
fl. 841	*Ba'li-ma-AN-zeri**
c. 829	*Mattan I*, son, traditionally for 29 years
c. 820	*Pygmalion*, son

*Mentioned in Assyrian records but not by Josephus, the sole authority for the king-list. Usually identified with Baal-azor II. The ideogram for the third element of the Assyrian name cannot at present be read in the original language and is represented by its standard Sumerian value

c. 774	One unknown king(?)
c. 750	*Ethbaal II*
c. 739	*Hiram II*, perhaps king of Sidon and Tyre
c. 730/29	*Mattan II*
c. 729 – c. 694	*Eloulaios*
c. 694 – c. 680	Unknown number of kings
c. 680 – c. 660	*Baal I*
c. 660 – c. 591/90	Unknown number of kings
c. 591/90	*Ethbaal III*
c. 573/2	*Baal II*, defeated by the Babylonian king Nebuchadrezzar II, Tyre became a Babylonian vassal
c. 564	*Iakinbaal*, Babylonian vassal
c. 564/3	*Chelbes*, Babylonian vassal
c. 563	*Abbar*, Babylonian vassal
c. 562	*Mattan III* and *Ger-asthart*, Babylonian vassals
c. 556	*Baal-eser III*, Babylonian vassal
c. 555	*Mahar-baal*, Babylonian vassal
c. 551 – c. 532	*Hiram III*, Babylonian vassal
539	Passed under Persian rule with Cyrus II's conquest of Babylon

Ugarit

Territory comprised part of present-day north-western Syria, with the capital at Ugarit (present-day Ras Shamra).

Kings

c. 1400 BC	*Ammishtamru I*, Egyptian vassal
(?)	*Niqmaddu II*, son, Hittite vassal
(?)	*Ar-Khalba*, son, led rebellion against the Hittites, deposed
before 1300	*Niqmepa*, brother, placed on the throne by the Hittites
c. 1265	*Ammishtamru II*, son, Hittite vassal
(?)	*Ibiranu*, son, Hittite vassal
(?)	*Niqmaddu III*, son, Hittite vassal
before 1200	*'Ammurapi*, Hittite vassal
c. 1200	Destroyed by the Luvians (or Sea Peoples)

Umayyad Caliphate

At its greatest extent, territory comprised part of present-day Syria, Israel, Lebanon, Iran, Iraq, USSR, Saudi Arabia, Yemen, Egypt, North Africa, Portugal and Spain, with the capital established at Damascus.

Caliphs

Sufianids	
Jul/Aug AD 661	*Mu'awiya I (ibn Abu-Sufyan)*, great-grandson of Umayya; governor of Mosul 645/6 – 656/7
Apr/May 680	*Yazid I (ibn Mu'awiya)*, son
11 Nov 683 – 22 Jun 684	*Mu'awiya II (ibn Yazid)*, son
Marwanids	
22 Jun 684	*Marwan I (ibn al-Hakam)*, great-grandson of Umayya, governor of Mecca 668/9 – 672/3, governor of Medina 661/2 – 668/9 and 675/6 – 676/7
7 May 685	*'Abd al-Malik (ibn Marwan)*, son (b. 646/7)
8 Oct 705	*al-Walid I (ibn 'Abd al-Malik)*, son
25 Feb 715	*Sulaiman (ibn 'Abd al-Malik)*, brother
22 Sep 717	*'Umar (ibn 'Abd al-'Aziz)*, cousin, governor of Mecca and Medina 705 – 711/12
5 Feb 720	*Yazid II (ibn 'Abd al-Malik)*, cousin
28 Jan 724	*Hisham (ibn 'Abd al-Malik)*, brother
6 Feb 743	*al-Walid II (ibn Yazid)*, nephew, killed
16 Apr 744	*Yazid III (ibn al-Walid)*, cousin
20 Sep 744	*Ibrahim (ibn al-Walid)*, brother
25 Nov 744 – 750	*Marwan II (ibn Muhammad, al-Himar)*, nephew of 'Abd al-Malik; governor of Mosul 732/3 – 738/9
750	Overthrown by the 'Abbasid caliphate

Umayyads of Spain (Caliphate of Córdoba)

Territory comprised part of present-day Spain and Portugal.

Amirs (from 929 Caliphs)

Jul AD 755	*(Abu'l-Mutarrif) 'Abd al-Rahman I (ibn Mu'awiya, al-Dakhil)*, grandson of the Umayyad caliph Hisham
15 Nov 788	*(Abu'l-Walid al-Radi* (or *al-'Adil)) Hisham I (ibn 'Abd al-Rahman)*, son
17 Apr 796	*(Abu'l-'Asi) al-Hakam I (al-Muntasir ibn Hisham)*, son
23 May 822	*(Abu'l-Mutarrif) 'Abd al-Rahman II (ibn al-Hakam)*, son
22 Sep 852	*(Abu 'Abdallah) Muhammad I (ibn 'Abd al-Rahman)*, son
4 Aug 886	*(Abu'l-Hakam) al-Mundhir (ibn Muhammad)*, son
29 Jun 888 – 16 Oct 912	*(Abu Muhammad) 'Abdallah (ibn Muhammad)*, brother
19 Oct 912	*(Abu'l-Mutarrif) 'Abd al-Rahman III (al-Nasir al-Umawi ibn Muhammad ibn 'Abdallah)*, grandson
15 Oct 961	*(Abu'l-Mutarrif) al-Hakam II (al-Mustansir ibn 'Abd al-Rahman)*, son
1 Oct 976	*(Abu'l-Walid) Hisham II (al-Mu'ayyad ibn al-Hakam)*, son (for 1st time) actual power exercised by his vizier, Muhammad ibn Abi 'Amir al-Mansur (called Almanzor in Latin and Spanish texts of the time)
22 Feb 1009	*Muhammad II (al-Mahdi ibn Hisham ibn 'Abd al-Jabbar)*, great-grandson of 'Abd al-Rahman III (for 1st time)
5 Nov 1009	*Sulaiman (al-Musta'in ibn al-Hakam ibn Sulaiman)*, great-grandson of 'Abd al-Rahman III (for 1st time)
May/Jun 1010	*Muhammad II* (for 2nd time)
Jul/Aug 1010	*Hisham II* (for 2nd time)
Apr/May 1013	*Sulaiman* (for 2nd time)
28 Jun 1016	*'Ali (al-Nasir ibn Hammud)*, Hammudid pretender (see Hammudids)
22 Mar 1018	*'Abd al-Rahman IV (al-Murtada ibn Muhammad)*,

	great-grandson of 'Abd al-Rahman III
1019	*al-Qasim (al-Ma'mun ibn Hammud)* (for 1st time) Hammudid pretender (see Hammudids)
1021/2	*Yahya (al-Mu'tali ibn 'Ali ibn Hammud)*, nephew (for 1st time) Hammudid pretender (see Hammudids)
1022/3	*al-Qasim* (for 2nd time)
26 Dec 1023	*'Abd al-Rahman V (al-Mustazhir ibn Hisham)*, great-grandson of 'Abd al-Rahman III
9 Feb 1024	*Muhammad III (al-Mustakfi ibn 'Abd al-Rahman)*, great-grandson of 'Abd al-Rahman III
17 Jun 1025	*Yahya* (for 2nd time)
1 Mar 1026 – 30 Nov 1031	*Hisham III (al-Mu'tadd ibn 'Abd al-Rahman)*, son of 'Abd al-Rahman IV
Nov 1031	Dominions of the caliph divided into numerous petty kingdoms, which are entered separately under their dynastic names

Umma

Territory comprised part of present-day central Iraq, with the capital established at Umma.

Kings

(?) BC	*Ush* (or *Gish*)
(?)	*Enakalli*, son(?)
(?)	*Urlumma*, son, deposed
c. 2450	*Il*, nephew; placed in power by Entemena, the king of Lagash
(?)	*Gishakkidu*, son
(?)	*Bubu*
before 2370 – 2347	*Lugalzaggisi*, son, King of Uruk c. 2371 – 2347, captured by the Akkadian king Sargon
2347	Akkadian conquest

'Uqailids

Territory comprised part of present-day northern Iraq (al-Jazira) and northern Syria.

Amirs

Line in Jazirat ibn 'Umar, Nisibin and Balad

c. AD 990/1	*(Abu'l-Dawwad) Muhammad ibn al-Musayyib*
996/7	*(Janah al-Daula Abu'l-Hasan) 'Ali ibn al-Musayyib*, brother
999/1000	*(Sinan al-Daula Abu 'Amir) al-Hasan ibn al-Musayyib*, brother
1002/3	*(Nur al-Daula Abu Marakh) Mus'ab ibn al-Musayyib*, brother

Line in Mosul (later in Jazirat ibn 'Umar, Nisibin and Balad)

c. 992	*(Abu'l-Dawwad) Muhammad ibn al-Musayyib* (see above)
996/7	*(Husam al-Daula Abu Hasan) al-Muqallad ibn al-Musayyib*, brother
1000/1	*(Mu'tamid al-Daula Abu'l-Muni') Qirwash ibn al-Muqallad*, son (d. Oct/Nov 1052)
1050/1	*(Za'im al-Daula Abu Kamil) Baraka ibn al-Muqallad*, brother
Apr/May 1052	*('Alam al-Din Abu'l-Ma'ali) Quraish ibn Badran*, nephew, Mosul lost to Basasiri 1056/7
Jan/Feb 1061 – 12 Jun 1085	*(Sharaf al-Daula Abu'l-Makarim) Muslim ibn Quraish*, son (b. 29 Mar 1041) ruled at Aleppo 1079/80
1085/6	*Ibrahim ibn Quraish*, brother, killed by Seljuq sultan Tutush of Syria
1093/4 – 1095/6	*'Ali ibn Muslim*, nephew, deposed by Tutush
1095/6	Seljuq conquest

Banu-Ma'n at Takrit

(?)	*(Abu'l-Musayyib) Rafi' ibn al-Husain (ibn Ma'n)*
1035/6	*(Abu'l-Man'a) Khamis ibn Taghlib (ibn al-Husain)*, nephew
1043/4	*Abu Ghashsham ibn Khamis*, son
1052/3	*'Isa ibn Khamis*, brother

056	*Nasr ibn Khamis*, brother
057 – (?)	*Abu'l-Ghana'im*, governor on behalf of 'Isa ibn Khamis's widow

Ur

Territory comprised part of present-day south-eastern Iraq, with the capital at Ur (present-day Tall al-Muqayyar).

Kings

First Dynasty	
(?) BC	*Meskalamdug*
c. 2600	*Akalamdug*
(?)	*Mesannipada*
(?)	*A'annipada*, son
c. 2550	*Meskiagnunna*, brother
(?)	*Annanne* (or *A'annipada*?)
(?)	*Meskiag-Nanna*, son, for 36 years(?)
(?)	*Elulu*, for 25 years
(?)	*Balulu*, for 36 years(?)
(?)	Overthrown by Eannatum, the king of Lagash(?)
Second Dynasty	
c. 2450	Four unknown kings
(?)	*Kaku*
c. 2230	*Elili II*
(?)	Probably ended by the Akkadians
Third Dynasty	
2113	*Ur-Nammu*, conquered kingdoms of Lagash and Uruk
2095	*Shulgi*
2047	*Amar-Sin*, son
2038	*Shu-Sin*, brother
2029 – 2006	*Ibbi-Sin*, son
2006	Conquered by the Elamites, Subarians and the Guti

Urartu (Kingdom of Van, Ararat)

Territory comprised part of present-day north-eastern Turkey, south-westerr U.S.S.R. and north-western Iran, with the capital at Tushpa (present-day Van)

Kings

(?) BC	*Amme-baal of Nairi*
(?)	*Arame* (or *Arramu*)
c. 840	*Sarduris I*
820	*Ishpuinis*, son, from c. 810 ruling with his son *Menuas* as co-regent
805	*Menuas*, alone
785	*Argistis I*, son
760	*Sarduris II*, son, defeated by the Assyrian king Tiglath-pileser III 743
733	*Uedipris-Rusas I*, son, committed suicide after defeat by the Assyrian king Sargon II
714	*Argistis II*, son
(?)	*Mita of Mushki* (or *Midas?*)
c. 680	*Rusas II*, son
645	*Sarduris III*, son(?)
640	*Sarduris IV*, son
625	*Erimenas*
605 – c. 595	*Rusas III*, son
c. 595	Destroyed by the Medes and Scythians

Urbino

Counts

House of Montefeltro

AD 1234	*Buonconte*, grandson of Antonio di Montefeltro, the imperial vicar of Urbino; Count of Montefeltro and Urbino
1255	*Montefeltrano*, son; podesta

1292	*Guido*, grandson
1298	*Federico I*, son
1322	*Nolfo*, son
1359	*Federico II*, son; expelled from Urbino by the papal party and never ruled there
1375	*Antonio*, son; recovered Urbino, 1377
1404	*Guidantonio*, son
1443	*Oddantonio*, son

Dukes

1444 – 10 Sep 1482	*Federico III*, illegitimate brother (b. Gubbio, 1422; d. Ferrara) created Duke of Urbino 23 Mar 1474
1482 – 23 Apr 1508	*Guidobaldo*, son (b. 24 Jun 1472; d. Fossombrone); from Jun to Nov 1502 Urbino was occupied by Cesare Borgia

Uruk (Erech)

Territory comprised part of present-day southern Iraq, with the capital at Uruk (present-day Warka).

Kings

c. 2700(?) BC	*Gilgamesh*
(?)	*Urlugal I*, son, for 30 years
(?)	*Utulkalamma*, son, for 15 years
(?)	*La-ba-'-(š)um*, for nine years
(?)	*En-nun-dàra-an-na*, for eight years
c. 2600	*Mes-hé*, for 36 years(?)
(?)	*Melamanna*, for six years
(?)	*Lugal-ki-tùn*, for 36 years(?)
(?)	*En-pirig-du-an-na*
(?)	*Ur-lugal II*
(?)	*Ar-ga-an-de-a*, for seven years
(?)	*Enshakushanna*
c. 2450	*Lugalkinishedudu*
(?)	*Lugalkisalsi*, son

(?)	*Lugal-TAR*,* perhaps the same as Lugaltarsi, the titular king of Kish
c. 2371 – 2347	*Lugalzaggisi*, King of Umma from before 2370 to 2347, captured by the Akkadian king Sargon
2347 – c. 2230	Akkadian conquest
c. 2230	*Urnigin*
(?)	*Urgigir*, son
(?)	*Lugalmelam*(?), son(?)
(?)	*Kuda*
(?)	*Puzur-ili*
(?)	*Urutu*
2120 – 2114	*Utu-khegal*, defeated the Guti
2114	Conquered by the third dynasty of Ur

Utrecht

Bishops†

21 Nov AD 695‡ – 7 Nov 739	*Willibrord*
?	See vacant
? – 25 Aug 775 or 780	*Gregor*, Saint
? – 784	*Albrich I*
?	*Thiaderd*
?	*Ermaker*
fl. 18 Mar 815	*Ryxfrid* (or *Hrikfred*)
before 7 Feb 828 – after 26 Dec 834	*Friedrich I*, Saint
fl. 23 Mar 838	*Albrich II*

*The ideogram for the second element of the name cannot at present be read in the original language and is represented by its standard Sumerian value

†When two dates separated by an oblique stroke are given for the beginning of an episcopate, the first refers to election or nomination and the second to ordination, consecration or investiture

‡Date of consecration

fl. 21 Mar 845	*Hegihard*
fl. 12 Aug 850(?)	*Luidger*
before 18 May 854 – after 863	*Hungar*, Saint
before 7 Jan 870 – 25 Sep (?) 899	*Odebald*
before 13 Jun 900 – 917	*Radbold*, Saint
1 Mar 918(?)* – 27 Dec 975	*Balderich*
after 18 Jun 976 – 10/11 Dec 990	*Volcmar*
990 or 991 – 10 May 995	*Baldewin I*
late Apr/early May 995 – 3 May 1010	*Ansfrid*, Saint
1010 – 27 Nov 1026(?)	*Adalbold*
1026 or 1027 – 19 Jul 1054	*Bernulf*, Saint
1054(?) – 27 Apr 1076	*Guilielmus I*†
before 23 May 1076 – 13/14 Apr 1099	*Conradus*; murdered
30 May 1100* – 16 May 1112	*Burchardus*
1114 – 12/13 Nov 1127	*Godebaldus*
before 13 Jun 1128 – – 23 Jun 1139	*Andreas*, of Cuyk?
1139 – 11 Nov 1150	*Hartbertus*
1150 – 27 Mar 1156	*Hermannus*, of Horn?
1156 – 27 May 1178	*Godefridus*, of Rhenen
before 14 Sep 1178 – 30 Apr (or 27 Apr or 4 Jun?) 1196	*Balduinus II*, of Holland
1196	*Arnoldus I*, of Isenburg (d. 6 Apr or Jun 1197); in conflict with *Theodericus I*, of Holland (d. 5 Nov(?) 1197)

*Date of consecration

†From this point in the list baptismal names are given in Latin forms and the descriptions of territorial or family origins are translated into English

1198 – 5 or 6 Dec 1212	*Theodericus II*, of Are
1212/1213 – 27 Mar 1215	*Otto I*, of Geldern
1215 – 28 Jul 1227	*Otto II*, of Lippe
1227 – 26 Jul 1233	*Wilbrandus*, of Oldenburg; previously Bishop of Paderborn
before 6 Feb 1234 – 3 Apr 1249	*Otto III*, of Holland
between 3 Apr and 4 Jul 1249 – 4 Jun 1267	*Henricus I*, of Vianden; in rivalry with *Gosewinus*, of Randenrath, until 2 Dec 1249
after Jun 1267 – 1288	*Joannes I*, of Nassau (d. after 1295); never formally elected, resigned
10 Jan/before 8 May 1291 – 3 Feb 1296	*Joannes II*, of Sierck (d. Bordeaux 1305) translated to Toul
4 Feb 1296 – 4 Jul 1301	*Guilielmus II Berthout*, of Mechelen; killed in battle against the nobles
Jul/before 15 Mar 1301 – 29 May 1317	*Guido*, of Avesnes; in disputed election against *Adolphus*, of Waldeck, Bishop (Adolphus I) of Liège 1 Sep 1301 – 12/13 Dec 1302
c. Jun/21 Nov 1317 – 19 Jul 1322	*Fredericus II*, of Sierck; in disputed election against *Heinrich*, Count of Sponheim-Starkenburg
25 Jul – 22 Sep 1322	*Jacobus*, of Oudshoorn; in disputed election against Jakob von Denemarken and Florenz von Juthaas; died before consecration
8 Nov 1322 – 1 Jul(?) 1340	*Joannes III*, of Diest; in disputed election against *Joannes*, of Bronkhorst
10 Jan 1341 – before 20 Nov 1342	*Nicolaus de Caputio*; in rivalry with *Joannes*, of Bronkhorst, and *Joannes IV*, of Arkel (see below), from 5 Jul 1340; never went to Utrecht, resigned
20 Nov 1342/8 May 1343 – 15 Apr 1364	*Joannes IV*, of Arkel (d. 1 Jul 1378) translated to Liège
24 Apr 1364 – 23 Jun 1371	*Joannes V*, of Virneburg; previously Bishop of Münster
30 Jun/9 Jul 1371 – after 26 Aug 1378	*Arnoldus II*, of Horn (d. 8 Mar 1389); in disputed election against *Suederus*, of Uterloe; translated to Liège
26 Aug 1378/7 Nov 1379 – 3 Apr 1393	*Florentius* (or *Floris*), of Wevelinchoven; previously Bishop of Münster; in rivalry with *Reinaldus*, of Vianen

28 Apr/7 Jul 1393 – 9 Oct 1423	*Fredericus III*, of Blankenheim (b. Kasselburg c. 1355; d. Burg Ter Horst) Bishop of Strasbourg until 21 Jul 1393; in disputed election against *Roger*, of Bronkhorst
10 Nov 1423/6 Feb 1425 – Feb 1426	*Suederus*, of Culemborg (d. Basel 21 Sep 1433); in disputed election against *Rudolphus*, of Diepholt (see below) and *Walraven*, of Mörs; deposed*
6 Oct 1426/10 Dec 1432 – 24 Mar 1455	*Rudolphus*, of Diepholt; in disputed election against *Walraven*, of Mörs
7 Apr 1455 – 1457	*Gisbertus*, of Brederode (d. 1474) resigned
12 Sep 1457 – 16 Apr 1494	*David*, of Burgundy

Vandals, Kingdom of the

Kings

AD 428	*Gaiseric* (*Genseric*), brother of Gunderic, the King of the Asdingi Vandals in Spain; invaded North Africa May 428; settlement recognized by the Roman Emperor Valentinian III in 435; rebelled against Roman overlordship and captured Carthage 19 Oct 439 (traditional date for the founding of the Vandal Kingdom); sack of Rome Jun 455; annexed Sicily, Corsica, Sardinia and the Balearic Islands
25 Jan 477	*Huneric*, son
484	*Gunthamund*, brother
496	*Thrasamund*, brother
523	*Hilderic*, nephew; deposed and imprisoned
531 – Mar 534	*Gelimer*, cousin; defeated by the Byzantine general Belisarius at Ad Decimum, near Carthage, 13 Sep 533; surrendered in Mar 534 and was granted an estate in Galatia by the Byzantine Emperor Justinian I
534	Territories incorporated into the Byzantine Empire

*Pope Martin V put up Raban of Speyer in 1424 as a compromise appointment but revoked the appointment very soon after

Vaspurakan

Territory now in south-eastern Turkey and north-western Iran.

Kings

Preceded by a line of princes, who were vassals of the King of Armenia.

Arcruni Dynasty

AD 908	*Khachik-Gagik*, proclaimed King of Vaspurakan by the Sajid emir Yusuf
936/7	*Derenik-Ashot*, son
953	*Abusahl-Hamazasp*, brother
972	*Ashot-Sahak*, son
983	*Gurgen-Khachik*, brother
1003 – 1021	*Sennacherib-Hovhannes*, brother (d. Cappadocia 1027) ceded the kingdom to the Byzantine emperor Basil II and received lands in Cappadocia in compensation
1021	Vaspurakan became the Byzantine province of Basparacania

Venice

Doges

The *magister militum* was a Byzantine official appointed from Ravenna; the *dux* was a rebel leader chosen by the Venetians. Once the autonomy of Venice was established, the position of the *dux* evolved into that of the elected doge.

AD 723 – 727	*Paulicius patricius*, exarch of Ravenna; assassinated
? – 727	*Marcellus* (or *Marcello Tagalliano*), magister militum
727	*Ursus* (or *Orso I Partecipazio*), dux
739	*Domenicus*, magister militum
744	*Deusdedit*
756	*Galla Gaulo*
756	*Domenico Monegario*
765	*Maurizio I*

787	*Giovanni* and *Maurizio II*
802	*Antenoreo Obelerio* (d. 832?); with his brother, *Beato*
811	*Agnello Partecipazio*
827	*Giustiniano Partecipazio*, son
829	*Giovanni I Partecipazio*, brother
836 – 15 Mar 864	*Pietro Tradònico*
864	*Orso II Partecipazio*
881	*Giovanni II Partecipazio* (for 1st time)
17 Apr – 18 Sep 887	*Pietro I Candiano*
Sep 887 – 8 Apr 888	*Giovanni II Partecipazio* (for 2nd time)
Apr 888	*Pietro Tribuno*
May 912 – 931	*Orso III Partecipazio Paureta*; retired to a monastery
932	*Pietro II Candiano*
939	*Pietro Partecipazio* (sometimes called *Pietro Badoer*)
942	*Pietro III Candiano*
959 – 11 Jun 976	*Pietro IV Candiano*, son (d. 11 Aug 976)
Jul 976 – Aug 978	*Pietro I Orseolo* (d. 987); abdicated
Sep 978 – Oct 979	*Vitale Candiano*
Dec 979	*Tribuno Memmo*; deposed
991 – Sep 1008	*Pietro II Orseolo*, son of Pietro I
1008	*Ottone Orseolo*, son
1026	*Domenico Barbolano Centranico*; deposed
1030	*Orso Orseolo*, son of Ottone; Patriarch of Grado
1032	*Domenico Orseolo*, brother; for one day
1032	*Domenico Flabanico*
1043	*Domenico Contarini*
1070	*Domenico Selvo*
1084	*Vitale Falier*
1096	*Vitale I Michiel*
1101	*Ordelaffo Falier*
1118	*Domenico Michiel* (d. Venice 1130)
1129	*Pietro Polani*
Jul 1148	*Domenico Morosini* (d. 1156)
Feb 1155	*Vitale II Michiel*
27 May 1172 – 12 Apr 1178	*Sebastiano Ziani* (d. 1178) abdicated
14 Apr 1178	*Orio Malipiero*
21 Jun 1192 – 1 Jun 1205	*Enrico Dandalo* (b. 1107; d. Constantinople)
5 Aug 1205 – 26 Feb 1229	*Pietro Ziani*, son of Sebastiano (d. 13 Mar 1230); abdicated
6 Mar 1229 – May/Jun 1249	*Giacomo Tiepolo* (d. 19 Jul 1249); abdicated

13 Jun 1249 – 1 Jan 1253	*Marino Morosini*
1253	*Ranieri Zen* (or *Zeno*)
23 Jul 1268 – 16 Aug 1275	*Lorenzo Tiepolo*, son of Giacomo
5 Sep 1275 – 6 Mar 1280	*Giacomo Contarini*
1280	*Giovanni Dandolo*, great nephew of Enrico
1289 – 13 Aug 1311	*Pietro Gradenigo* (b. 1251)
22 Aug 1311 – 2 Jun 1312	*Marino Zorzi*
13 Jun 1312 – 13 Dec 1328	*Giovanni Soranzo*
1329	*Francesco Dandolo*
1339	*Bartolomeo Gradenigo* (b. 1263)
4 Jan 1343	*Andrea Dandolo* (b. Venice 1307) podesta of Trieste 1333
11 Sep 1354	*Marino Falier* (b. 1274; d. (executed) 17 Apr 1355)
1355	*Giovanni Gradenigo* (b.1285)
1356	*Giovanni Dolfin* (b. Venice 1280)
1361	*Lorenzo Celsi*
1365	*Marco Corner*
20 Jan 1368 – 5 Jun 1382	*Andrea Contarini*
1382 – 15 Oct 1382	*Michele Morosini*
21 Oct 1382	*Antonio Venier* (d. 23 Nov 1400)
7 Jan 1400 – 26 Dec 1413	*Michele Steno* (b. c. 1331)
7 Jan 1414 – 4 Apr 1423	*Tommaso Mocenigo* (b. 1343)
1423 – 31 Oct 1457	*Francesco Foscari* (b. 1373) abdicated
1457	*Pasquale Malipiero*
1462 – 2 Nov 1471	*Cristoforo Moro*
23 Nov 1471 – 28 Jul 1473	*Nicolò Tron*
13 Aug 1473	*Nicolò Marcello* (b. Venice c. 1398)
1474	*Pietro Mocenigo* (b. 1406)
6 Mar 1476 – 6 May 1478	*Andrea Vendramin* (b. 1393)
1478 – 14 Nov 1485	*Giovanni Mocenigo*, brother of Pietro (b. 1408)
19 Nov 1485 – 14 Aug 1486	*Marco Barbarigo*

28 Aug 1486 – 20 Sep 1501	*Agostino Barbarigo*

Verona

Podestas and Seigneurs

House of Della Scala	
AD 1260 – 26 Oct 1277	*Mastino I*, son of Jacobino della Scala (d. (assassinated) Verona) elected podesta 1260, captain of the people 1262
1277 – 3 Sep 1301	*Alberto I*, brother; podesta of Mantua
1301 – 7 Mar 1304	*Bartolomeo I*, son; podesta
1304	*Alboino*, brother (d. 28 Oct 1311) podesta and imperial vicar; with his brother, *Cangrande I* (b. 9 Mar 1291; d. Treviso 22 Jul 1329) podesta and imperial vicar, who ruled alone after 1311; captain general of the Ghibelline League 1318, imperial vicar of Mantua 1328
1329	*Mastino II*, nephew (b. 1308; d. Verona 3 Jun 1351) and his brother, *Alberto II* (b. 1306; d. 13 Sep 1352)
1351/2 – 14 Dec 1359	*Cangrande II*, nephew (b. 8 Jun 1332) Seigneur; assassinated
1359 – 16 Oct 1375	*Paolo Alboino II*, brother (b. 1343) Seigneur
1365 – 18 Oct 1375	*Cansignorio*, brother (b. c. 1334) Seigneur
1375	*Bartolomeo II*, illegitimate son
12 Jul 1381 – 19 Oct 1387	*Antonio*, brother
1387	Occupation of Verona by Gian Galeazzo, Duke of Milan

Vijayanagar, Yadavas of

Territory comprised part of present-day southern India.

Kings

Sangama Dynasty	
AD 1336	*Harihara I*, son of Sangama
1356	*Bukka I*, brother
1377	*Harihara II*, son
1404	*Virupaksha I*, son
1405	*Bukka II*, brother, deposed
1406	*Devaraya I*, brother
1422	*Ramachandra*, son
1422 – 1430	*Vijaya-Bukka* (or *Vira Vijaya*), son
1422 – 1446	*Devaraya II*, son
1446 – 1447	*Vijaya II*, brother
1446 – 1465	*Mallikarjuna*, son of Devaraya II
1465 – 1485	*Virupaksha II*, cousin, murdered
Saluva Dynasty	
1485	*Narasimha*, son of Gunda
1490	*Timma*, son
1491	*Immadi Narasimha*, brother, deposed by the Vijayanagar general Narasa
1505	*Vira Narasimha*, son of Narasa, abdicated
May/Nov 1509	*Krishnadevaraya*, brother
1530	*Achyuta*, brother
1542	*Venkata*, son, for a few days
1542 – 1565	*Sadashivaraya*, nephew of Achyuta, executed at Talikota
1565	Muslim conquest

Visigoths

Successively in the Balkans, Italy, Gaul and Spain, with capital finally at Toledo; a kingdom from the time of Theodoric I.

Chiefs, later Kings

fl. AD376	*Fritigern*, in Thrace, and *Athanaric*, in Moldavia
395 – autumn 410	*Alaric I* (b. Peuce Island, Danube delta, c. 370; d. Cosenza) in the Balkans; moved to Italy 401; sacked Rome 24 Aug 410
410 – Aug 415	*Ataulf*, brother-in-law (d. (assassinated) Barcelona) entered Gaul spring 412, seized Narbonne, Toulouse and Bordeaux;* invaded Spain
415	*Sigeric*
415	*Wallia*, settled once more in Aquitaine
418	*Theodoric I*, took title of king
451	*Thorismund*, son; assassinated
453	*Theodoric II*, brother
466	*Euric*, brother, established capitals at Toulouse and Arles; formally received Spain and southern Gaul from Julius Nepos, the Roman emperor in the West, 475
28 Dec 484	*Alaric II*, son; defeated and killed by Clovis, King of the Franks, at the battle of Vouillé; Toulouse, Bordeaux, Angoulême and Tours lost to the Franks
506	*Amalaric*, son (b. 502); ruled under the protection of Theodoric the Great, King of the Ostrogoths, with Count Theudis as regent until 526; capital established at Narbonne; lost Narbonne to Childebert I, King of Paris, 531; assassinated
531	*Theudis*, former regent; established capital at Barcelona
548	*Theudesgesil*; assassinated
549	*Agila*; established capital at Merida
554	*Athanagild*; established capital at Toledo
568 – 572	*Leova I*, brother
568	*Leovigild*, brother (d. May 586); ruled alone after 572; annexed the Kingdom of the Sueves 585
586	*Recared I*, son; professed Catholicism 589

*Until the time of Euric the capital varied between Toulouse and Bordeaux

601	*Leova II*, son; deposed and executed
603	*Witterich*; assassinated
610	*Gundemar*
612	*Sisebut*
621	*Ricared II*, son; deposed
621	*Swinthila*; expelled the remaining Byzantines from Spain; deposed
631	*Sisenand*, governor of Septimania; the kingship was made elective in 631
636	*Chintila*
640	*Tulga*, son; deposed
642	*Chindaswinth*
653	*Receswinth*, son (d. Valladolid, Sep 672)
672	*Wamba*; deposed
680	*Erwig*, son
687	*Egica*, a distant relative
701	*Witiza*, son
709 – 19 Jul 711	*Roderick*, Duke of Baetica (d. Sep 713?); defeated by Tariq ibn Ziyad, 19 Jul 711, at Lake Janda; retreated to Galicia and was again defeated, Sep 713; probably killed in battle

Muslim conquest

Wales

DEHEUBARTH

Consisting of Ceredigion and Ystrad Tywi (together known as Seisyllwg, acquired about 871 by Rhodri Mawr of Gwynedd, brother-in-law of the last king), Brycheiniog (acquired in the 10th century) and Dyfed (acquired 904?).

Kings and Princes

AD 871	*Cadell ap Rhodri Mawr*, King of Seisyllwg
909	*Hywel Dda*, King of Dyfed; son; joint ruler of Seisyllwg with his brother, *Clydog* (d. 920); acquired Brycheiniog; annexed Gwynedd and(?) Powys 942, assumed title of King of Wales

949/50	*Owain ap Hywel Dda*, son (d. 988) ruled initially with his brothers, *Rhodri* (d. 953) and *Edwin* (d. 954); King of Deheubarth; abdicated
986	*Maredudd ab Owain ap Hywel Dda*, son, annexed Gwynedd
999	Succession uncertain
1018	*Llywelyn ap Seisyll*, son-in-law of Maredudd ab Owain
1023	*Rhydderch ap Iestyn*, usurper
1033 – 1035	*Maredudd ab Edwin*, great-nephew of Maredudd ab Owain
1033 – 1042/1044	*Hywel ab Edwin*, brother (d. 1044)
1042/1044	*Gruffydd ap Llywelyn*, son of Llywelyn ap Seisyll (for 1st time) (d. 5 Aug 1063) drove out Hywel 1042(?) and defeated and killed him on his return 1044, King of Gwynedd and Powys from 1039
1046	*Gruffydd ap Rhydderch*, son of Rhydderch ap Iestyn, usurper
1055 – 1063	*Gruffydd ap Llywelyn* (for 2nd time)
c. 1064	*Maredudd ab Owain ab Edwin*, nephew of Hywel ab Edwin, restored by King Harold of England
1072	*Rhys ab Owain*, brother
1078	*Rhys ap Tewdwr*, cousin
Apr 1093	Deheubarth invaded at various points by Gwynedd and by the Normans
1135	*Gruffydd ap Rhys*, son of Rhys ap Tewdwr; lord of Cantref Mawr in Ystrad Tywi
1137 – 1143	*Anarawd ap Gruffydd*, son
1137 – 1151(?)	*Cadell ap Gruffydd*, brother (d. 1175) recovered Ceredigion 1151, retired owing to wounds 1151 or soon after
1151(?) – 1155	*Maredudd ap Gruffydd*, brother (b. c. 1130) in Cantref Mawr
1151(?) – 1197	*Rhys ap Gruffydd (Yr Arglwydd Rhys)*,* brother (b. c. 1132) did homage to King Henry II of England 1158; territory confined to Cantref Mawr; recovered remainder of Ystrad Tywi, Ceredigion and parts of Dyfed 1165 – 1166, confirmed by Henry II 1171; Justice of All Deheubarth, including Morgannwg, May 1172
28 Apr 1197 – 1282	Deheubarth fragmented by the rivalry of the sons and

*Ancestor, through his daughter Gwenllian, of Henry Tudor

descendants of Rhys ap Gruffydd, who eventually surrendered or did homage to Edward I

DYFED

Kings

Modern forms of the names are used, the medieval form, if different, following in parentheses.

AD (?)	*Tryffin* (*Triphun*, *Trestin*), son of Aed Brosc, son of Corath, son of Eochaid Allmuir mac Artchuirp, from Ireland(?)*
(?)	*Aergul Lawhir* (*Aircol*, *Agricola*), son
fl. 544	*Gwerthefyr* (*Guortepir*, *Voteporix*, *Votecorix*), son
(?)	*Cyngar* (Cincar), son
(?)	*Pedr* (*Petr*), brother(?)†
547(?)	*Arthur*, brother(?)†
c. 585	*Nowy* (*Nougoy*) *ab Arthur*, son
(?)	*Gwlyddien* (*Cloten*), son
(?)	*Cathen*, son
(?)	*Cadwgon Trydelig* (*Catgocaun*), son
(?)	*Rhain* (*Regin*) *ap Cadwgon*, son
(?)	*Tewdws* (*Teudos*), son
(?)	*Maredudd* (*Margetiud*), son
796	*Rhain* (*Regin*) *ap Maredudd*, son
808	*Tryffin* (*Triphun*) *ap Rhain*, son
814	One or two unknown kings
fl. c. 870(?)	*Hyfaidd* (*Himeid*) *ap Bleddri*, great-grandson, through female line, of Maredudd
893	*Llywarch* (*Loumarc*) *ap Hyfaidd*, son
904	*Rhodri ap Hyfaidd*, brother, killed in Arwystli
906	Throne passed to *Hywel Dda*, King of Deheubarth 909 – 949/50 (see above), son-in-law of Llywarch ap Hyfaidd

*Welsh sources give different ancestors for Tryffin. Irish sources give the descent from Eochaid Allmuir, which is generally accepted.

†Both the Welsh and Irish sources make Arthur the son of Pedr the son of Cyngar, giving impossible chronology. The conjecture that they are brothers comes from J. W. James (*Bulletin of the Board of Celtic Studies*, Vol. 23)

GWYNEDD

Kings and Princes

AD 534(?)	*Maelgwn Gwynedd* (or *Mailcun* or *Maglocunus*), descendant of Cunedda (or Cunedag) of Manaw Gododdin in south-eastern Scotland
547 (549?)	*Cynlas* (or *Cunoglasus*) *ab Owain*, cousin
(?)	*Rhun ap Maelgwyn Gwynedd*, son of Maelgwn Gwynedd
(?)	*Cangan ap Maig*(?), grandson of Cynlas, or *Cadwal*(?), son of Cangan
(?)	*Idgwyn ap Cadwal*(?)
(?)	*Beli ap Rhun*, son of Rhun
(?)	*Iago ap Beli*, son (d. 616?) abdicated and retired to a monastery(?)
c. 615	*Cadfan* (or *Catamanus*) *ab Iago*, son
c. 625	*Cadwallon ap Cadfan*, son (d. 635)
fl. 656	*Cadafael (ap Cynfeddw?)*, collateral(?)
(?)	*Cadwaladr ap Cadafael*(?), son (d. 664)
(?)	*Cadwaladr Fendigaid ap Cadwallon*, son of Cadwallon (d. 682)
682(?)	*Idwal ap Cadwaladr*, son
(?)	*Rhodri Molwynog*, son (d. 754)
754(?)	*Caradog ap Meirion*, great-great-grandson of Idgwyn (d. 798)
798(?)	*Hywel Farf-fehinog ap Caradog*, son; until 816 ruled with *Cynan Dindaethwy*, son of Rhodri Molwynog
825	*Merfyn Frych ap Gwriad*, son (or husband?) of Esyllt, daughter of Cynan (d. 844)
844 or later – 878	*Rhodri Mawr*, son; acquired Powys 855 and became king 856; occupied Seisyllwg c. 872 and parts of South Wales
878	Territories divided among the six sons of Rhodri
878	*Anarawd ap Rhodri*, ruled over Gwynedd
916 – 942	*Idwal Foel*, son
942	Gwynedd and(?) Powys annexed by Hwel Dda, King of Deheubarth
950	*Iago ab Idwal Foel*, son of Idwal Foel, captured and dispossessed 979; until 969 ruled with his brother, *Idwal Ieuaf* (d. 985)
979	*Hywel ap Ieuaf*, son of Idwal Ieuaf
985	*Cadwallon ap Ieuaf*, brother, killed by Maredudd ab

	Owain ap Hywel Dda of Deheubarth
986	Maredudd ab Owain ap Hywel Dda annexed Gwynedd
999	*Cynan ap Hywel*, son of Hywel
1005*	*Llywelyn ap Seisyll*, son-in-law of Maredudd ab Owain (d. 1023)
1023 or 1033† – 1039	*Iago ab Idwal ap Meurig*, great-grandson of Idwal Foel
1039	Gwynedd and Powys annexed by Gruffydd ap Llywelyn, King of Deheubarth
1063	*Bleddyn ap Cynfyn ap Gwerstan*, King of Powys, half-brother of Gruffydd ap Llywelyn, installed by Harold, Earl of Wessex (later King of England)
1075	*Trahaearn ap Caradog*, cousin, King of Arwystli (for 1st time) (d. 1081)
1075	*Gruffydd ap Cynan ap Iago*, grandson of Iago ab Idwal (for 1st time) (b. c. 1055; d. 1137)
1075	*Trahaearn* (for 2nd time)
1081	*Gruffydd* (for 2nd time) for a short time; imprisoned by Hugh, Earl of Chester
	Interregnum; 'North Wales' granted to *Robert of Rhuddlan* (d. 3 Jul 1088) and then to *Hugh, Earl of Chester*
c. 1094	*Gruffydd* (for 3rd time) at first only in Anglesey and Arfon
1137 – 1170	*Owain Gwynedd*, son (b. c. 1108; d. 28 Nov 1170)
1170 – 1200	Gwynedd divided between *Cadwaladr ap Gruffydd* (d. 29 Feb 1172), brother; and his sons, *Iorwerth Drwyndwn* (d. c. 1174), *Maelgwn*, *Dafydd* (d. 1203) dispossessed 1195, *Rhodri* (d. 1195), and *Cynan* (d. 1173), who engaged in frequent disputes among themselves
1173	*Grufydd ap Cynan ab Owain* (d. 1200) and *Maredudd ap Cynan* (d. 1212) succeeded to their fathers inheritance
1200	*Llywelyn ap Iorwerth*, the Great, son of Iorwerth Drwyndwn (b. 1173) Prince of Gwynedd east of the Conway from 1195, King of all Gwynedd except Lleyn (acquired 1202), annexed Powys 1208 – 1210,

*Some date Llywelyn's accession 1018, when he killed the usurper Aeddan ap Blegywryd

†If Iago acceded in 1033, the gap is presumably filled by Rhydderch ap Iestyn of Deheubarth

	overlord of Glamorgan 1216
11 Apr 1240 – 25 Feb 1246	*David ap Llywelyn*, son (b. 1208)
1247 – 1255	*Owain Goch ap Gruffydd*, nephew (d. c. 1280?)
1247 – 1277	*Llywelyn ap Gruffydd*, known as *Llywelyn y Llyw Olaf* (i.e. the last leader), brother (b. c. 1225; d. 11 Dec 1282) assumed the title of 'Prince of Wales' 1258
1277	Llywelyn defeated by King Edward I of England; lost conquests in South and Mid Wales; surrendered Gwynedd between Conway and Dee to the English crown; gave up Lleyn to his brother, *Owain*, and Rhufionog and Dyffryn Clwyd to his brother, *David ap Gruffydd* (d. (executed) 3 Oct 1283); and rendered homage to Edward I
Mar 1282	Rebellion and later death without male issue of Llywelyn
1282 – 1283	*David ap Gruffydd*, brother, assumed title of Prince of Wales
1283	End of the Kingdom of Gwynedd

MORGANNWG

Embracing Glywysing (i.e. Glamorgan east of the Tawe) and Gwent, but later often confined to Glywysing.

Glywysing

AD (?)	*Glywys Cernyw ap Solor*
(?)	*Gwynllyw ap Glywys*, son, King of Gwynllwg (between the Rhymney and the Usk) and his brother
(?)	One or two unknown kings
fl. c. 630	*Meurig ap Tewdrig*, King of Glywysing and Gwent
(?) – 665	*Morgan ab Arthrwys*, grandson
fl. c. 720(?)	*Ithel ap Morgan*, son, King of Morgannwg
(?)	*Rhys ab Ithel*, *Rhodri ab Ithel* and *Morgan ab Ithel*, sons, Kings of Glywysing
(?)	Unknown kings
c. 870	*Hywel ap Rhys ap Arthfael*, supposedly great-great-great-grandson of Rhys ab Ithel
fl. 926	*Owain ap Hywel*, son, King of Glywysing and(?) overlord of Gwent (see below)
c. 930	*Morgan Mawr* (or *Morgan Hen*) *ab Owain*, son, gave name Morgannwg to the territory(?)

974	*Owain ap Morgan*, son
(?)	*Rhys ab Owain ap Morgan*, son
(?)	*Hywel ab Owain ap Morgan*, brother (d. 1043)
c. 1040	*Meurig ap Hywel*, son, seized Gwent
(?) – 1055	*Cadwgan ap Meurig*, son (for 1st time) lord of Gwent under his father from c. 1040
1055	Morgannwg seized by Llywelyn ap Iorwerth, King of Gwynedd
1063	*Cadwgan* (for 2nd time) restored in Morgannwg with the loss of Gwynllwg and Gwent
c. 1073	*Caradog ap Gruffydd ap Rhydderch*, son of Gruffydd ap Rhydderch of Deheubarth, since 1063 King of Gwynllwg and Upper Gwent
1081 – c. 1093	*Iestyn ap Gwrgant*, usurper, claiming descent from Morgan Mawr ab Owain; dispossessed by King William Rufus of England; retired to the priory of Llangennydd, Gower

Gwent

(?) – 775	*Ffernfael ab Ithel ap Morgan*, son of King Ithel ap Morgan of Morgannwg (see Glywysing)
(?)	*Arthrwys ap Ffernfael*, son
(?) – 848	*Ithel ab Arthrwys*, son
848 – c. 870	Held by King of Glywysing(?)
c. 870	*Meurig ab Arthfael*, grandson of King Rhys ab Ithel of Glywysing
874	*Ffernfael ap Meurig*, son
c. 880	*Brochwel ap Meurig*, brother
926	*Owain ap Hywel*, King of Glywysing, and his son, *Cadwgan*, who was described as King of Gwent
fl. 927	*Arthfael ap Hywel*, son
(?) – 942	*Cadell ab Arthfael*, son
fl. 955	*Noe ap Gwriad*, of a new dynasty
fl. 982	*Arthfael ap Noe*, son
(?)	*Rhodri ab Elise*, nephew
(?)	*Gruffydd ab Elise*, brother
c. 1020	*Edwin ap Gwriad*, of unknown origin
c. 1040	Conquered by Meurig ap Hywel, King of Glywysing

POWYS

Kings or Princes

later 5th century AD	*Cadell Ddyrnllug* (or *Catel Durnluc*)
(?)	*Cyngen* (or *Cincen*) *ap Cadell Ddyrnllug*, son
(?)	*Brochwel* (or *Brocmail*) *Ysgithrog*, son
(?)	*Cynan* (or *Cinan*) *Garwyn*, son
(?)	*Selyf* (or *Selim*) *Sarffgadau*, son (d. c. 616)
c. 616	One or two unknown kings
fl c. 640 – c. 660(?)	*Cynddylan Wyn ap Cyndrwyn*, descendant of Cadell Ddyrnllug
(?)	*Gwyllog* (or *Guoillauc*) *ap Beli*, descendant of Gwrtheyrn Gwrtheneu (or Vortigern)*
mid 8th century	*Elise* (or *Elized* or *Eliseg*) *ap Gwylog*, son
(?)	*Brochwel* (or *Brocmail*) *ab Elise*, son
(?)	*Cadell* (or *Catell*) *ap Brochwel*, son
808	*Cyngen* (or *Concenn*) *ap Cadell*, son (d. Rome)
856	*Rhodri Mawr*, King of Gwynedd, nephew
878	A son(?)
942	Powys acquired by Hywel Dda, King of Deheubarth(?)
c. 950	Passed to Gwynedd(?)
1039 – 1063	Held by Gruffydd ap Llywelyn, King of Deheubarth
1063	*Bleddyn ap Cynfyn ap Gwerstan*, King of Gwynedd, and his brother, *Rhiwallon ap Cynfyn* (d. 1070)
1075	Territory frequently divided
1075 – 1088	*Madog ap Bleddyn*, son
1075 – 1088	*Rhirid ap Bleddyn*, brother
1075 – 1109	*Cadwgan ap Bleddyn*, half-brother (for 1st time) (d. 1111)
(?) – 1103	*Iorwerth ap Bleddyn*, brother (for 1st time) (d. 1111)
(?) – 1103	*Maredudd ap Bleddyn*, half-brother (for 1st time) (d. 1132)
1109 – 1110	*Madog ap Rhirid*, nephew (for 1st time) and his brother, *Ithel ap Rhirid* (d. 1124)

*Vortigern, from whom the eighth-century rulers of Powys claim descent, is not himself described as King of Powys but is numbered among the 'Kings of Britain'. The name is interpreted by some as a title, meaning 'overlord', and it is likely that for a time at any rate he was supreme leader of a confederacy. His own domain seems to have been located in south-central Wales and the marches. Traditional genealogies link Cadell Ddyrnllug with Vortigern, but in inconsistent ways. Details before Rhodri Mawr are somewhat uncertain.

1110 – 1111	*Cadwgan* (for 2nd time)
1110 – 1111	*Iorwerth* (for 2nd time)
1111 – 1114	*Madog* (for 2nd time)
1111 – 1116	*Owain ap Cadwgan*, cousin
c. 1111 – 1132	*Maredudd* (for 2nd time)
1116 – 1123	*Einon ap Cadwgan*, nephew
1116 – 1124	*Maredudd ap Cadwgan*, half-brother
1116 – 1128	*Morgan ap Cadwgan*, half-brother
1132 – Feb 1160	*Madog ap Maredudd ap Bleddyn*, cousin
Feb 1160	Territory permanently divided

Northern Powys (*Powys Fadog*)

Feb 1160 – (?)	*Iorwerth Goch*, brother
Feb 1160 – 1187	*Owain Fychan ap Madog*, nephew
Feb 1160 – (?)	*Owain Brogyntyn*, brother (d. after 1188)
Feb 1160 – 1191	*Gruffydd Maelor I ap Madog*, brother
1191 – 1197	*Owain ap Gruffydd Maelor*, son
1191 – 1236	*Madog ap Gruffydd Maelor*, brother, vassal of King Llywelyn ap Iorwerth of Gwynedd from 1218(?)
1236 – 1238	*Gruffydd Ial ap Madog*, son
1236 – 1238	*Maredudd ap Madog*, brother (for 1st time) (d. 1256)
1236 – 1269	*Gruffydd Maelor II ap Madog*, brother
(?) – 1256	*Maredudd* (for 2nd time)
1269	Northern Powys divided among the sons of Gruffydd Maelor II: *Madog* (d. 1277); *Gruffydd* (d. 1289) ancestor of Owain Glyndwr; *Llywelyn* (d. 1282); and *Owain* (d. 1282)
1282	Conquest of Wales by King Edward I of England

Southern Powys (*Powys Wenwynwyn*)

Feb 1160	*Owain Cyfeiliog ap Gruffydd ap Maredudd*, nephew of Iorwerth Goch (b. c. 1125; d. 1197) retired to a monastery
1195 – 8 Oct 1208	*Gwenwynwyn ab Owain Cyfeiliog*, son (for 1st time) (d. 1216) dispossessed by King John
8 Oct 1208	Powys invaded by King Llywelyn ap Iorwerth of Gwynedd
Nov 1210	*Gwenwynwyn* (for 2nd time) expelled by Llywelyn
after spring 1216 – 1241	Southern Powys under Gwynedd
Oct(?) 1241	*Gruffydd ap Gwenwynwyn*, son (for 1st time) (d. 1286/7)
Oct(?) 1257	Southern Powys again under Gwynedd

12 Dec 1263 – summer 1274	*Gruffydd* (for 2nd time) as vassal of King Llywelyn ap Gruffydd of Gwynedd, revolted and fled to Shrewsbury
summer 1274	Southern Powys occupied by Llywelyn
1277 –	*Gruffydd* (for 3rd time)
1282	Gruffydd surrendered his princely rights
1286 – 1287	Conquest of Wales by King Edward I of England

Wattasids (Banu-Wattas)

Collateral branch of the Marinids. Territory comprised part of present-day Morocco, with the capital at Fez.

Regents for the Marinid Sultans (and from 1472 Sultans)

AD 1427/8	*Abu Zakariya' Yahya I (ibn Zayyan al-Wattasi)*, son of al-Wattasi, regent for the Marinid sultan 'Abd al-Haqq II
1448/9	*'Ali ibn Abi'l-Hajjaj Yusuf (ibn Mansur ibn Zayyan)*, great-nephew of al-Wattasi, regent
1458/9	*Abu Zakariya' Yahya II (ibn Yahya ibn Zayyan)*, son of Abu Zakariya' Yahya I, for two months
1458/9	*Muhammad I al-Shaikh (ibn Yahya ibn Zayyan)*, brother, initially ruled at Asila, in conflict with Marinid sultan Abu 'Abdallah Muhammad 1465 – 1472, proclaimed sultan 1472
1504	*Muhammad II al-Burtukali (ibn Muhammad)*, son, seizure of Marrakesh by the Sa'adi Sharifs 1523
1526	*(Abu'l 'Abbas) Ahmad (ibn Muhammad)*, son (for 1st time)
1545	*Muhammad III al-Kasri (ibn Ahmad)*, son
1547	*Ahmad* (for 2nd time)
1549	*'Ali Abu Hassan*, brother of Muhammad al-Burtukali, pretender; occupation of Fez by the Sa'adi Sharifs 1550
1554	Fez briefly regained but then finally taken by the Sa'adi Sharifs

Württemberg

Counts

AD 1236	*Eberhard I*
1241	*Ulrich I*, brother (b. c. 1226) gained large parts of the duchy of Swabia
25 Feb 1265	*Ulrich II*, son (b. 1253/4)
18 Sep 1279	*Eberhard II*, the Illustrious, brother (b. 13 Mar 1265)
5 Jun 1325	*Ulrich III*, son
11 Jul 1344	*Ulrich IV*, son (d. 24 Jul 1366); with his brother, *Eberhard III* (b. 1315; d. 15 Mar 1392) who ruled alone after Ulrich IV's death
15 Mar 1392	*Eberhard IV*, the Mild, grandson (b. 1364)
16 May 1417	*Eberhard V*, son (b. 23 Aug 1388)
2 Jul 1419	*Ulrich V*, son (b. c. 1413; d. 1 Sep 1480); with his brother, *Ludwig I* (b. 1412; d. 24 Sep 1450)
1441	Division of county: Ulrich V ruled at Stuttgart, Ludwig I at Urach
24 Sep 1450	*Ludwig II*, son of Ludwig I (b. 3 Apr 1439; d. 3 Nov 1457) ruled at Urach with his brother, *Eberhard VI* (b. 11 Dec 1445; d. 24 Feb 1496)
1482	Reunification of county under Eberhard VI, who was created Duke of Württemberg 21 Jul 1495

Würzburg

Bishops*

AD 741 – ?	*Burchard* (d. between 749 and 5 Jun 754)
before 5 Jun 754 – ?	*Megingoz*
794 – 26 Sep 800	*Berenwelf*
800 – 27 Feb 803	*Liuderich*
803 – 24 Apr 810	*Agilward*

*When two dates separated by an oblique stroke are given for the beginning of an episcopate, the first refers to election or nomination and the second to ordination, consecration or investment

810 – 12 Nov 832	*Wolfger*
832 – 9 Mar 842	*Humbert*
2 Apr(?) 842 – 20 Sep 855	*Gozbald*
1 Dec(?) 855 – 14 Jul 892	*Arn*, killed
892 – 3 Aug 908	*Rudolf*, killed
908 – 15 Nov 931	*Thiedo*
1 or 2 Dec 931 – 24 or 25 Mar 941	*Burchard II*
summer(?) / before 13 Dec 941 – 14 or 15 Feb 961	*Poppo I*
961 – 15 or 21 or 22 Jul 983	*Poppo II*
983 / 1 Jan 984 – 29 Aug 990	*Huc*
990(?) – 20 Sep 995	*Brunward*
995 or 996 – 14 Nov 1018	*Heinrich I*
1 Jan 1019 – 22 Mar 1034	*Meginhard*
14 Apr 1034 – 26 or 27 May 1045	*Brun*
29 Jun 1045 – 6 Oct 1090	*Adalbero*, in rivalry with Meginhard*
25 Jul 1089 / 27 Mar 1093 – 27 Feb 1105	*Emehard*
1105 – 28 Dec 1121	*Erlung*
1122 – 1127	*Gebhard von Henneberg*, in rivalry with *Rugger* until 1125
25 Dec 1127 – 10 Nov 1146	*Embrich*
1146 / 15 Jun 1147 – 16 Sep 1150	*Siegfried von Truhendingen*
1150 – 17 Mar 1159	*Gebhard von Henneberg*
1160 – 14 Apr 1165	*Heinrich II*
1165 – 3 Aug 1171	*Herold*
1171 – 15 Jun 1186	*Reinhard von Abensberg*
1186 – 8 Jul 1190	*Gottfried I von Helfenstein*

*25 May 1085 – 20 Jun 1088 *Meginhard*, Imperial anti-Bishop

1190	*Philipp von Hohenstaufen* (b. 1178; d. (murdered) Bamberg 21 Jun 1208) Duke of Spoleto 1195, Duke of Swabia 1196, King of Germany 8 Mar 1198
Jan 1192 – Jun 1197	*Heinrich III*
(?) – 24 Aug 1197	*Gottfried II*, never consecrated
21 Aug 1198 – 6 Dec 1202	*Konrad I von Querfurt*, Bishop of Hildesheim 1194 – 21 Aug 1198, murdered
1202 or early 1203 – 13 Jul 1207	*Heinrich IV Caseus*
before 8 Aug 1207 – 4 Dec 1223	*Otto von Lobdeburg*
between late 1223 and early 1224 – between 14 Dec 1224 and 25 Feb 1225	*Dietrich von Hohenburg*
before 25 Feb 1225 – 13 Feb/18 Mar 1254	*Hermann I von Lobdeburg*
after 3 Mar/12 Apr 1254 – 22 Nov 1265	*Iring von Hohenburg*, in rivalry with *Heinrich von Leiningen* until 30 Jan 1255
after 22 Nov 1265/24 May 1268 – 19 Sep 1270	*Poppo von Trimberg*, in disputed election against *Berthold*, Count of Henneberg, who was defeated in the battle of Kitzingen 8 Aug 1266
after 17 Jun 1270/23 Oct 1274 – 13 Nov 1287	*Berthold II von Sternberg*
after 8 Dec 1287 – 29 Jul 1303	*Manegold von Neuenburg*
before 29 Aug 1303 – 14 Dec 1313	*Andries von Gundelfingen*
after 6 Feb 1314/20 Jun 1317 – 4 Sep 1322	*Gottfried III von Hohenlohe*, in rivalry with *Friedrich von Stahelberg* until the latter's death 20 Apr 1314
16 Nov 1322/26 Aug 1323 – 6 Jul 1333	*Wolfram von Grumbach*
30 Jul 1333 – 21 Mar 1335	*Hermann II von Lichtenberg*, in rivalry with Otto II von Wolfstal; never formally consecrated, maintaining his position after Otto's consecration
2 Dec 1333/21 Jul 1334 – 23 Aug 1345	*Otto II von Wolfstal*
19 Oct 1345 – 6 Oct 1349	*Albert I*, Count of Hohenberg (d. 25 Apr 1359) in disputed election against Albert von Hohenlohe,

	translated to Freising
8 Feb 1350 – 27 Jun 1372	*Albert II von Hohenlohe*
6 Oct 1372 – 9 Nov 1400	*Gerhard*, Count of Schwarzburg, Bishop of Naumburg after 12 Jan/13 May 1359 – 6 Oct 1372, in disputed election against *Wittig* and *Albrecht II von Hessberg**
19 Nov 1400/9 May 1402 – 22 Nov 1411	*Johann I von Egloffstein*
8 Dec 1411/18 Mar 1412 – 9 Jan 1440	*Johann II von Brunn*
20 Jan 1440/2 Nov 1444 –	*Sigismund von Sachsen* (b. 3 Mar 1416; d. 24 Dec 1471) deposed(?)
16 Oct 1443 – 1 Apr 1455	*Gottfried Styrum von Limpurg*
14 Apr/16 Jun 1455 – 11 Apr 1466	*Johann III von Grumbach*
30 Apr/20 Jun 1466 –	*Rudolf von Scherenberg*

Zaidi Imams (Rassids)

Territory comprised part of present-day Yemen, with the capital initially at Sa'da and later at San'a.

Imams

AD 893/4	*(Yahya) al-Hadi ila'l-Haqq I (ibn al-Husain)*, son
Jul/Aug 911	*(Muhammad) al-Murtada (Abu'l-Qasim ibn Yahya)*, son (d. 922/3) abdicated
913/14	*(Ahmad) al-Nasir (ibn Yahya)*, brother (d. 936/7)
(?)	*(al-Husain) al-Muntakhad (ibn Ahmad)*, son
935/6	*(al-Qasim) al-Mukhtar (Abu Muhammad ibn Ahmad)*, brother
(?)	*(Yusuf) al-Mansur al-Da'i (ibn Yahya)*, nephew
(?)	*(al-Qasim) al-Mansur (ibn 'Ali al-Iliani)*

*Wittig became Bishop of Naumburg from 6 Oct 1372 and Albrecht had been subjugated by Albert II by 1376

1002/3	*(al-Husain) al-Mahdi (ibn al-Qasim)*, son (d. 1013/14)
(?)	*Ja'far (ibn al-Qasim)*, brother
1034/5	*(Abu Hashim) al-Hasan (ibn 'Abd al-Rahman)*
1038/9 – c. 1055	*(Abu'l-Fath) al-Nasir al-Dailami (ibn al-Husain ibn Muhammad)* (d. c. 1055)
1063	San'a captured by the Sulaihids
1087/8	*'Imran (ibn al-Fadl)*, Sulaihid governor
(?)	*Saba' (ibn Ahmad)*, Sulaihid governor
1098/9	*Hatim (ibn al-Rashim al-Hamdani)*, of the Hamdanid line
1108/9	*'Abdallah (ibn Hatim)*, son, of the Hamdanid line
1110/11	*Ma'n (ibn Hatim)*, brother, of the Hamdanid line
1137/8	*Hamid al-Daula (Hatim ibn Ahmad)*, of the Hamdanid line
1150/1	*(Ahmad) al-Mutawakkil (ibn Sulaiman ibn Muhammad)* (d. 1170/1) in a brief restoration of the Rassid line
1160/1	*'Ali al-Wahid (ibn Hatim)*, son of Hatim, of the Hamdanid line, defeated by Ayyubid sultan Turan Shah of Damascus 1173/4
1197/8	*'Abdallah al-Mansur (ibn Hamza)*, of the Rassid line (b. 1165/6) recaptured San'a 1197/8
1217/18	*(Yahya) al-Hadi ila'l-Haqq II (ibn Hamza)*, brother, ruled in Sa'da
1217/18	*Muhammad al-Nasir (ibn 'Abdallah)*, nephew, ruled the southern districts until 1226
1248/9	*(Ahmad) al-Mahdi (al-Muti' ibn al-Husain ibn Ahmad)*, murdered
1258	*Shams al-Din Ahmad al-Mutawakkil (ibn 'Abdallah)*, son of 'Abdallah al-Mansur
c. 1281/2	*Da'ud al-Muntasir*

Imamate resumed at the end of the 16th century. For continuation, see Yemen, Volume 2.

Zangids

Territory comprised part of present-day northern Iraq (al-Jazira) and Syria.

Atabegs

Principal Line in Mosul and Aleppo

AD 1127 – 14 Sep 1146	*('Imad al-Din) Zangi (ibn Aq Sonqur)*, appointed governor of Mosul and Aleppo by the Seljuq sultan Mahmud II 17 Jan 1127, assassinated*
Sep/Oct 1146 – 3 Nov 1149	*(Saif al-Din) Ghazi I (ibn Zangi)*, son
Nov 1149	*(Qutb al-Din) Maudud (ibn Zangi, al-A'raj)*, brother
1168/9	*(Saif al-Din) Ghazi II (ibn Maudud)*, son
11 Aug 1176 – 28 Aug 1193	*('Izz al-Din) Mas'ud I (ibn Maudud)*, brother, Ayyubid vassal after 1185/6
Aug 1193	*(Nur al-Din) Arslan Shah I (ibn Mas'ud, Abu'l-Harith al-'Adil)*, son
15 Jan 1211 – 22 Jul 1218	*('Izz al-Din) Mas'ud II (ibn Arslan Shah, al-Malik al-Qahir)*, son (b. 1193/4)
Jul 1218	*(Nur al-Din) Arslan Shah II (ibn Mas'ud)*, son
1219/20 – 1222	*(Nasir al-Din) Mahmud (, al-Malik al-Qahir)*, brother
1222	Power seized by the vizier Badrai-Din Lu'lu'

Line in Damascus, later Aleppo

Sep/Oct 1146 – 15 May 1174	*(al-Malik al-'Adil) Nur al-Din (Abu'l-Qasim Mahmud ibn Zangi)*, son of Zangi (b. 11 Feb 1118)
May/Jun 1174 – 1181/2	*(al-Salih Nur al-Din) Isma'il ibn Mahmud*, son (b. 1162/3)
1181/2	Reunited with Mosul

*1146/7 *Alp Arslan ibn Mahmud (Seljuqi)*, pretender

Zirids (Banu Ziri)

Territory comprised part of present-day Tunisia and eastern Algeria, with th capital initially at Kairouan and later at al-Mahdiyya.

Amirs

Oct/Nov AD 972	*(Abu'l-Futuh Yusuf) Buluggin (ibn Ziri)*, initiall ruled as Fatimid governor
25 May 984	*al-Mansur (ibn Buluggin, 'Uddat al-'Aziz)*, son
26 Mar 996 – 9 May 1016	*(Abu Mannad) Badis ibn Mansur (Nasir al-Daula)* son (b. 14 Aug 984)
10 May 1016	*al-Mu'izz (ibn Badis, Sharaf al-Daula)*, son (b. 19 Ja 1008) declared independence from Fatimid suzeraint 1026/7, fled from Kairouan and moved capital t al-Mahdiyya
19 Oct 1061 – 29 Feb 1108	*(Abu Tahir) Tamim ibn Mu'izz*, son (b. al Mansuriya 6 Jul 1031)
1087/8	al-Mahdiyya taken by the Franks
29 Feb 1108	*(Abu Tahir) Yahya ibn Tamim*, son (b. al-Mahdiyy 1064/5) assassinated
25 Apr 1116 – 10 Jul 1121	*'Ali ibn Yahya*, son (b. al-Mahdiyya 1 Jun 1086
Jul 1121 – 1148/9	*(Abu Yahya) al-Hasan ibn 'Ali*, son (b. Feb/Ma 1109; d. 1167/8) governor of al-Mahdiyya under the name of *'Abd al-Mu'min* after 1160
1148/9	Conquest by Roger II of Sicily
21 Jan 1160	Almohad conquest

Hammadids Branch (Banu Hammad)

Capital established initially at Qal'at Bani-Hammad and after 1090/1 at Bougie

AD 1015	*Hammad (ibn Buluggin ibn Ziri)*, son of Buluggin (see above) 'Abbasid vassal
1028/9	*al-Qa'id (ibn Hammad)*, son, Fatimid vassal
1054/5	*al-Muhsin (ibn al-Qa'id)*, son
1055/6	*Buluggin (ibn Muhammad)*, cousin, assassinated by al-Nasir
1062/3	*al-Nasir (ibn 'Alanas)*, cousin
1088/9	*al-Mansur (ibn al-Nasir)*, son
1104/5	*Badis (ibn al-Mansur)*, son
1106/7	*al-'Aziz (ibn al-Mansur)*, brother

1121/2–1152/3	*Yahya (ibn al-'Aziz)*, son (d. 1192/3)
1152/3	Almohad conquest

Ziyarids

Territory comprised part of present-day northern Iran, centred in Tabaristan and Gurgan.

Amirs

AD 927/8	*Mardawij (ibn Ziyar)*, assassinated at Isfahan
934/5	*(Zahir al-Daula Abu Mansur) Vushmagir (ibn Ziyar)*, brother, Samanid vassal
966/7	*(Zahir al-Daula Abu Mansur) Bisutun (ibn Vushmagir)*, son
977/8	*(Shams al-Ma'ali Abu'l-Hasan) Qabus (ibn Vushmagir)*, brother, in exile 981/2 – 998
1012/13	*(Falak al-Ma'ali) Manuchihr (ibn Qabus)*, son
1029/30	*(Abu Kalijar) Anushirvan (ibn Manuchihr)*, son
1049/50	*('Unsur al-Ma'ali) Kai Ka'us (ibn Iskandar ibn Qabus)*, cousin
(?) – c. 1090/1	*Gilan (Shah)*, son
1090/1	Overthrown by the Isma'ilis (?)

Index of Persons

This index includes everyone listed in Volume 1 of *Rulers and Governments of the World.*

Entries are made under the first word of each name. However, if a name begins with words that are often omitted (in the text such words are enclosed in parentheses) then those words are put at the end of the name after a comma and entry is under the first word of the commonly used part of the name. Thus, for example, 'Abdallah, the first Orthodox Caliph, will be found under that name and not under Abu-Bakr.

The Arabic article *al-* is ignored when it is the first word of a name.

Entries follow the order of the English alphabet. Accents and other modifications of letters are ignored, as are apostrophes (') and turned commas ('). Ligatured æ is regarded as two separate letters, as is the Dutch ij.

The entries are arranged word by word – that is, all entries beginning with the same word are grouped together and then arranged according to the alphabetical order of their second words (and so on).

Parts of a name joined by a hyphen are regarded as separate words.

Parts of a name separated by an apostrophe (without a space or hyphen) are regarded as forming one word.

Numerals are put in numerical order and come before letters of the alphabet.

Parts of a name (including numerals) enclosed in parentheses are ignored when putting the index entries into order except when it is necessary to use them to put in order otherwise identical entries.

After each name there is an indication of the territory, dynasty, etc., under which the name is listed in the text. These notes are ignored when putting the index entries into order except when it is necessary to use them to put in order otherwise identical entries.

INDEX OF PERSONS

The index notes all appearances of a person in the list noted after his or her name. In the person's first entry in the text in that list will be found details of his or her entries in other lists in the book.

If the name of a ruler (especially in Europe) is not found in the index it may be because he or she has been listed under a different form of the name. The lists of forms of names in various languages on pages xli to lxiii should be consulted for guidance.

When the same person is mentioned more than once on the same page in the text then the number of mentions is given in square brackets.

PETER NORTON'S

Introduction to Computers

PETER NORTON'S

Introduction to Computers

Sixth Edition

McGraw Hill Technology Education

Boston Burr Ridge, IL Dubuque, IA Madison, WI New York San Francisco St. Louis
Bangkok Bogotá Caracas Kuala Lumpur Lisbon London Madrid Mexico City
Milan Montreal New Delhi Santiago Seoul Singapore Sydney Taipei Toronto

Technology Education

PETER NORTON'S® INTRODUCTION TO COMPUTERS
Published by McGraw-Hill Technology Education, a business unit of The McGraw-Hill Companies, Inc., 1221 Avenue of the Americas, New York, NY, 10020.

This book is printed on acid-free paper.

1 2 3 4 5 6 7 8 9 0 QPD/QPD 0 9 8 7 6 5 4

ISBN 0-07-297890-2

Editor in chief: *Bob Woodbury*
Senior sponsoring editor: *Christopher Johnson*
Developmental editor: *Pamela Woolf*
Marketing manager: *Sankha Basu*
Director, Sales and Marketing: *Paul Murphy*
Lead producer, Media technology: *Ed Przyzycki*
Senior project manager: *Lori Koetters*
Lead production supervisor: *Michael R. McCormick*
Senior designer: *Mary E. Kazak*
Senior photo research coordinator: *Jeremy Cheshareck*
Photo researcher: *Teri Stratford*
Supplement producer: *Lynn M. Bluhm*
Senior digital content specialist: *Brian Nacik*
Cover design: *Melissa Welch/Studio Montage*
Cover images: © *Corbis*; © *Getty*
Peter Norton photos: *Kelly Barrie*
Interior design: *Amanda Kavanagh/Ark Design Studio*
Typeface: *10/12 Sabon*
Compositor: *Cenveo*
Printer: *Quebecor World Dubuque Inc.*

Library of Congress Cataloging-in-Publication Data

Norton, Peter, 1943–
[Introduction to computers]
Peter Norton's introduction to computers.
p. cm.
Includes index.
ISBN 0-07-297890-2 (alk. paper)
1. Computers. 2. Computer software. I. Title.
QA76.5.N6818 2005
004—dc22

2004055992

www.mhhe.com

About Peter Norton

Acclaimed computer software entrepreneur Peter Norton is active in civic and philanthropic affairs. He serves on the boards of several scholastic and cultural institutions and currently devotes much of his time to philanthropy.

Raised in Seattle, Washington, Mr. Norton made his mark in the computer industry as a programmer and businessman. *Norton Utilities*™, *Norton AntiVirus*™, and other utility programs are installed on millions of computers worldwide. He is also the best-selling author of computer books.

Mr. Norton sold his PC-software business to Symantec Corporation in 1990 but continues to write and speak about computers, helping millions of people better understand information technology. He and his family currently reside in Santa Monica, California.

Editorial Consultant

Tim Huddleston

Academic Reviewers

Michael Anderson
ECPI College of Technology, VA

Lee Cottrell
Bradford School, PA

Lynn Dee Eason
Sault College of Applied Arts & Technology, Ontario

Terry Ann Felke
William Rainey Harper College, IL

Timothy Gottleber
North Lake College, TX

Captain Jim Jackson
West Point Academy, NY

Yvonne Ng Ling
Temasek Polytechnic, Singapore

Keith Samsell
Florida Metropolitan University

Cherie Ann Sherman
Ramapo College, NJ

Erik Sorensen
College of Redwoods, CA

Karen Stanton
Los Medanos College, CA

Umesh Varma
Campbell University, NC

ACKNOWLEDGEMENTS

Special thanks go to others who contributed to the content and development of this project: Kenny Atkins, Brian Carroll, Scott Clark, Lee Cottrell, Timothy Gottleber, Jane and Chuck Holcombe, Richard Mansfield, Bridget McCrea, Dan Shoemaker, Corey Schou, Natalie Walker Whitlock, and Teri Stratford.

FOREWORD TO STUDENTS

Why Study Computer Technology?

The computer is a truly amazing machine. Few tools can help you perform so many different tasks. Whether you want to track an investment, publish a newsletter, design a building, or practice landing an F14 on the deck of an aircraft carrier, you can use a computer to do it. Equally amazing is the fact that the computer has taken on a role in nearly every aspect of our lives. Consider the following examples:

- Tiny embedded computers control our alarm clocks, entertainment centers, and home appliances.
- Today's automobiles could not even start—let alone run efficiently—without embedded computer systems.
- In the United States, more than half of all homes now have at least one personal computer, and the majority of those computers are connected to the Internet.
- An estimated 10 million people now work from home instead of commuting to a traditional workplace, thanks to PCs and networking technologies.
- People use e-mail for personal communications nearly 10 times as often as ordinary mail, and nearly five times more often than the telephone.
- Routine, daily tasks such as banking, using the telephone, and buying groceries are affected by computer technologies.

Here are just a few personal benefits you can enjoy by developing a mastery of computer technology:

- **Improved Employment Prospects.** Computer-related skills are essential in many careers. Whether you plan a career in automotive mechanics, nursing, journalism, or archaeology, having computer skills will make you more marketable to prospective employers.
- **Skills That Span Different Aspects of Life.** Many people find their computer skills valuable regardless of the setting—at home, work, school, or play. Your knowledge of computers will be useful in many places other than your work.
- **Greater Self-Sufficiency.** Those people who truly understand computers know that computers are tools—nothing more or less. We do not give up control of our lives to computer systems; rather, we use computer systems to suit our needs. By knowing how to use computers, you can actually be more self-sufficient, whether you use computers for research, communications, or time-management.
- **A Foundation of Knowledge for a Lifetime of Learning.** Basic computing principles have not changed over the past few years, and they will be valid well into the future. By mastering fundamental concepts and terminology, you will develop a strong base that will support your learning for years to come.

Regardless of your reasons for taking this course, you have made a wise decision. The knowledge and skills you gain should pay dividends in the future, as computers become even more common at home and at work.

CONTENTS AT A GLANCE

FEATURE ARTICLES

At Issue

Norton Notebook

Productivity Tip

Computers In Your Career

Computing Keynotes

CONTENTS

STUDENT AND INSTRUCTOR RESOURCES

This textbook is supplemented by a variety of resources for students and teachers.

SimNet™ XPert

SimNet XPert is a complete learning and assessment program of Microsoft Office applications and computer concepts.

The **Learning Component** is a computer-based program that teaches skills and tasks using a variety of methods.

- **Teach Me** mode introduces the skill using text, graphics, and interactivity.
- **Show Me** mode employs narration and animation to illustrate how the skill is used.
- **Let Me Try** mode enables you to practice and improve your proficiency in SimNet XPert's non-threatening simulated environment.

The **Assessment Component** allows you to take practice exams and assessment tests assigned by your instructor in SimNet XPert's robust simulated environment. This means your proficiency in any of these applications can finally be tested as you perform a task, rather than based on how well you can answer true/false and multiple choice questions.

Peter Norton Web Site (www.mhhe.com/peternorton)

The Peter Norton Web site includes a variety of resources for students and teachers. For students, the Web site offers a variety of learning resources, including:

- Web link database
- Internet labs and activities
- Course outlines and slides
- Online quizzes
- Ezine articles that offer news about technology trends
- Information about IT careers

For instructors, the Web site provides additional materials that help teach the course using the textbook:

- Course outlines
- Classroom presentations
- Teaching tips and discussion topics
- Extra projects

Instructor Resource Kit

In addition to the Web site, an instructor's resource kit is available on CD-ROM. The CD-ROM includes:

- An Instructor's Manual and Answer Key
- ExamView Pro test bank software with hundreds of questions
- Instructor Classroom Presentations
- SCANs Correlations
- PageOut™, an online instructor tool
- WebCT and Blackboard Distance Learning Platforms

PREREQUISITES

What You Should Know Before Using This Book

This book assumes that you have never used a computer before or that your computer experience has been very brief. If so, you may need to learn some basic computer skills before proceeding with this course. This Prerequisites section introduces basic skills, using illustrations to help you recognize and remember the hardware or software involved in each skill. Some of these skills are covered in greater detail in other units of this book. In such cases, you will find references that point you to more information.

Equipment Required for This Book's Exercises

- IBM-compatible personal computer
- Keyboard
- Two-button mouse
- Windows 98 or higher
- Internet connection
- Web browser

Turning the Computer On and Off

Turning the Computer On

As simple as it may sound, there is a right way to turn a computer's power on and off. If you perform either of these tasks incorrectly, you may damage the computer's components or cause problems for the operating system, programs, or data files.

1. Before turning on your computer, make sure that all the necessary cables (such as the mouse, keyboard, printer, modem, etc.) are connected to the system unit. Also make sure that the system's power cords are connected to an appropriate power source.
2. Make sure that there are no diskettes in the computer's diskette drive, unless you must boot the system from a diskette. (The term *booting* means starting the computer.) If you must boot the system from a diskette, ask your instructor for specific directions.
3. Find the On/Off switch on each attached device (the monitor, printer, etc.) and place it in the ON position. A device's power switch may not be on the front panel. Check the sides and back to find the On/Off switch if the switch is not located on the front panel.

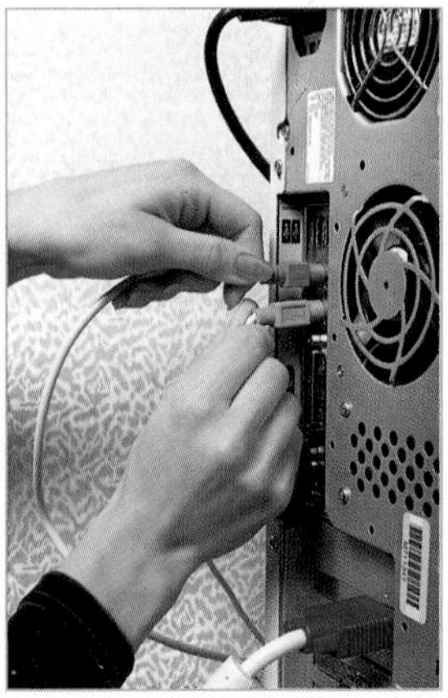

4. Find the On/Off switch on the computer's system unit—its main box into which all other components are plugged—and place it in the ON position.

Most computers take a minute or two to start. Your computer may display messages during the start-up process. If one of these messages prompts you to perform an action (such as providing a network user ID and password), ask your instructor for directions. After the computer has started, the Windows desktop will appear on your screen.

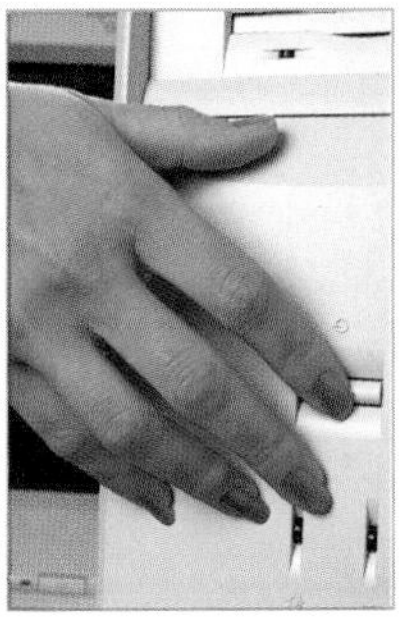

Turning the Computer Off

In Windows-based systems, it is critical that you shut down properly, as described here. Windows creates many temporary files on your computer's hard disk when running. By shutting down properly, you give Windows the chance to erase those temporary files and do other "housekeeping" tasks. If you simply turn off your computer while Windows or other programs are running, you can cause harm to your system.

Note: The illustration shows the shut-down process in Windows 98. The process, menus, and dialog boxes are the same in all versions of Windows except Windows XP, as noted in the following instructions.

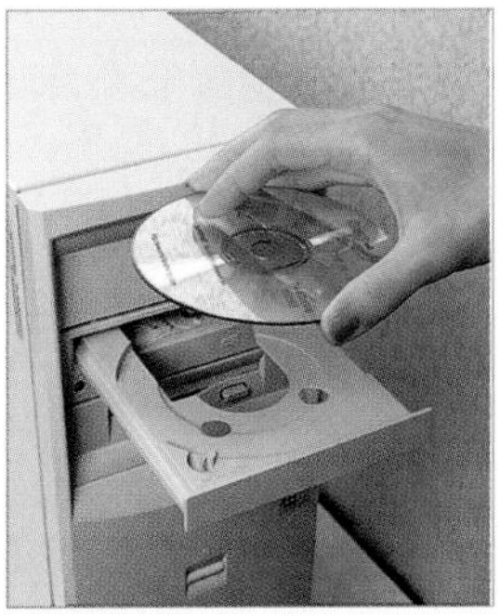

For more information on Windows and other operating systems, see Chapter 7, "Using Operating Systems."

1. Remove any disks from the diskette and CD-ROM drives and make sure that all data is saved and all running programs are closed. (For help with saving data and closing programs, ask your instructor.)
2. Using your mouse pointer, click the Start button, which is located on the taskbar. The Start menu will appear. On the Start menu, click Shut Down. (If you use Windows XP, click the Turn Off Computer option.) The Shut Down Windows dialog box will appear. (In Windows XP, the Turn Off Computer dialog box will appear.)

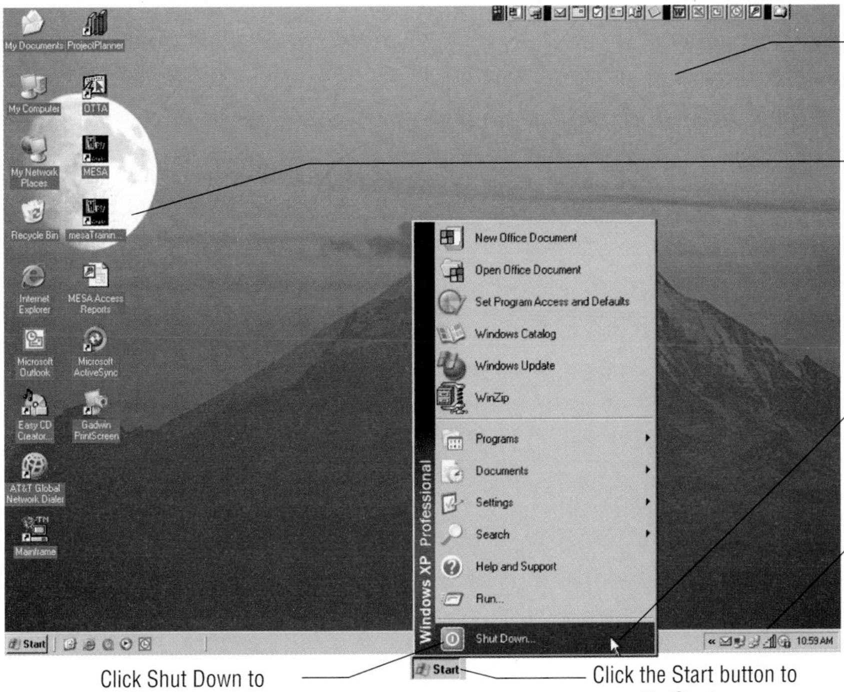

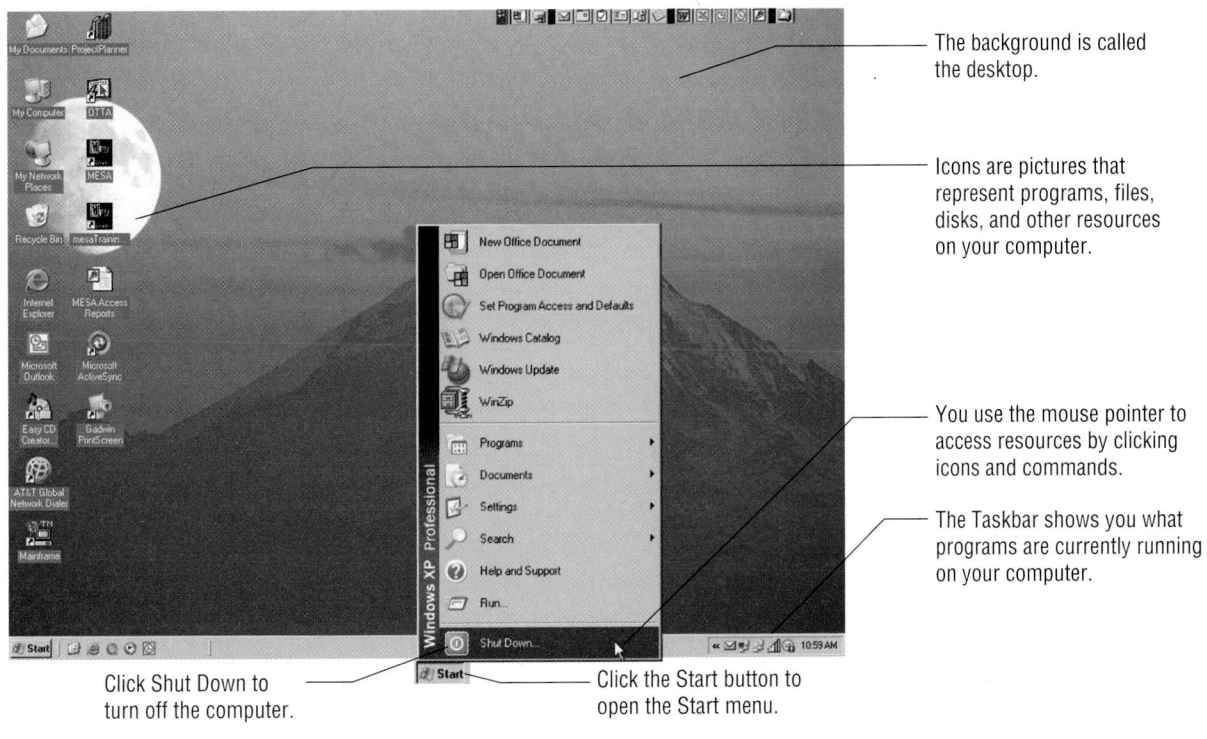

The background is called the desktop.

Icons are pictures that represent programs, files, disks, and other resources on your computer.

You use the mouse pointer to access resources by clicking icons and commands.

The Taskbar shows you what programs are currently running on your computer.

Click Shut Down to turn off the computer.

Click the Start button to open the Start menu.

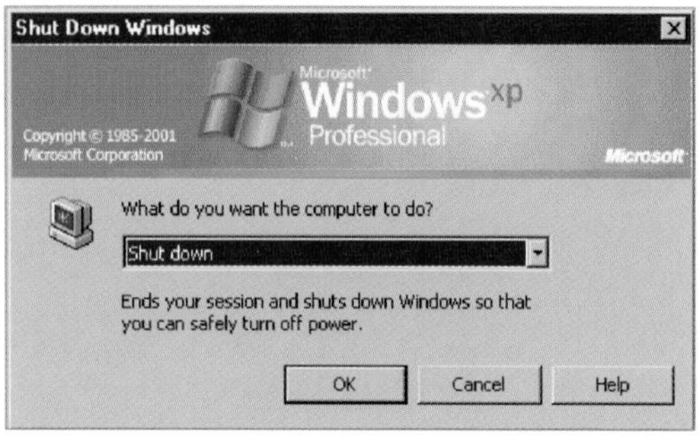

Windows will begin the shut-down process. Windows may display a message telling you that it is shutting down. Then it may display the message "It is now safe to turn off your computer." When this message appears, turn off the power to your system unit, monitor, and printer.

In some newer computers, the system unit will power down automatically after Windows shuts down. If your computer provides this feature, you need to turn off only your monitor and other devices.

The keyboard is covered in detail in Lesson 3A, "Using the Keyboard and Mouse."

Using the Keyboard

If you know how to type, then you can easily use a computer keyboard. The keyboard contains all the alphanumeric keys found on a typewriter, plus some keys that perform special functions.

1. In Windows, the ENTER key performs two primary functions. First, it lets you create paragraph ("hard") returns in application programs such as word processors. Second, when a dialog box is open, pressing ENTER is like clicking the OK button. This accepts your input and closes the dialog box.
2. The SHIFT, CTRL (control), and ALT (alternate) keys are called modifier keys. You use them in combination with other keys to issue commands. In many programs, for example, pressing CTRL+S (hold the CTRL key down while pressing the S key) saves the open document to disk. Used with all the alphanumeric and function keys, the modifier keys let you issue hundreds of commands.
3. In Windows programs, the ESC (escape) key performs one universal function. That is, you can use it to cancel a command before it executes. When a dialog box is open, pressing ESC is like clicking the CANCEL button. This action closes the dialog box and ignores any changes you made in the dialog box.
4. Depending on the program you are using, the function keys may serve a variety of purposes or none at all. Function keys generally provide shortcuts to program features or commands. In many Windows programs, for example, you can press F1 to launch the online help system.
5. In any Windows application, a blinking bar—called the cursor or the insertion point—shows you where the next character will appear as you type. You can use the cursor-movement keys to move the cursor to different positions. As

1.

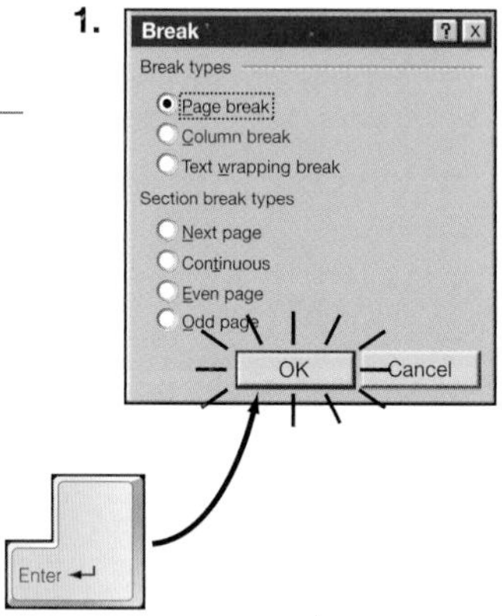

2.

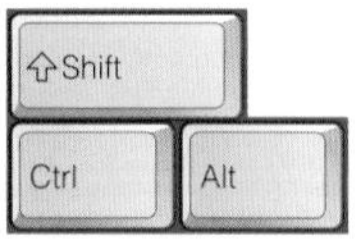

3.

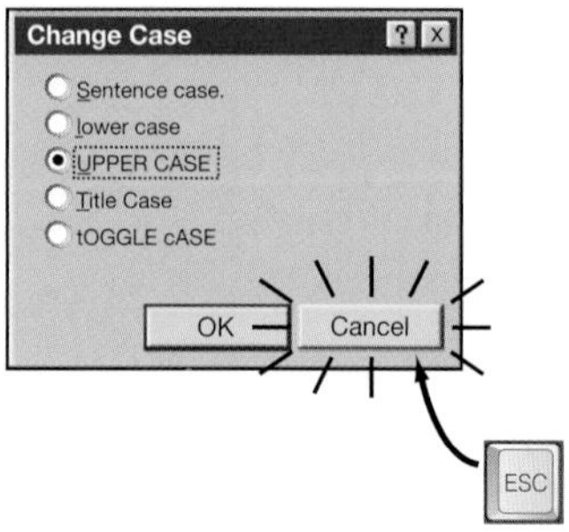

4.

their arrows indicate, these keys let you move the cursor up, down, left, and right.

6. The DELETE key erases characters to the right of the cursor. The BACKSPACE key erases characters to the left of the cursor. In many applications, the HOME and END keys let you move the cursor to the beginning or end of a line, or farther when used with a modifier key. PAGE UP and PAGE DOWN let you scroll quickly through a document, moving back or ahead one screen at a time.

5.

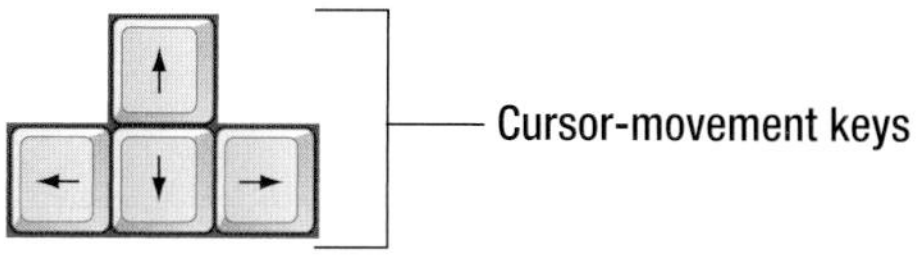

6.

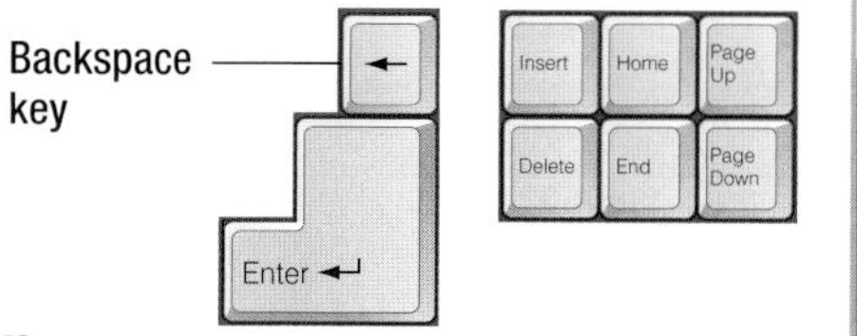

Using the Mouse

The mouse makes your computer easy to use. In fact, Windows and Windows-based programs are mouse-oriented, meaning their features and commands are designed for use with a mouse.

1. This book assumes that you are using a standard two-button mouse. Usually, the mouse's left button is the primary button. You click it to select commands and perform other tasks. The right button opens special "shortcut menus," whose contents vary according to the program you are using.
2. You use the mouse to move a graphical pointer around on the screen. This process is called pointing.
3. The pointer is controlled by the mouse's motions across your desktop's surface. When you push the mouse forward (away from you), the pointer moves up on the screen. When you pull the mouse backward (toward you), the pointer moves down. When you move the mouse to the left or right, or diagonally, the pointer moves to the left, right, or diagonally on the screen.

1.

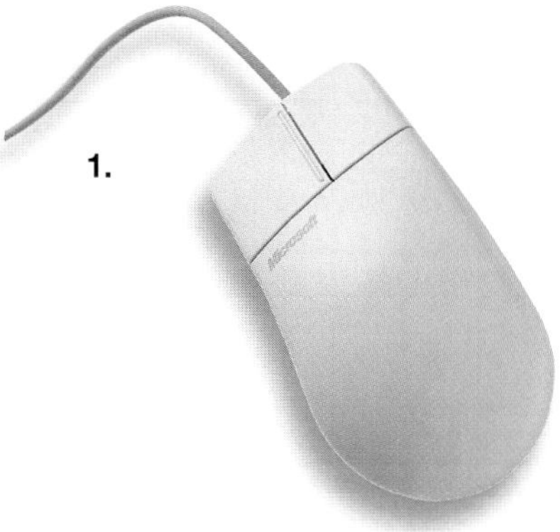

The mouse is covered in greater detail in Lesson 3A, "Using the Keyboard and Mouse."

2.

3.

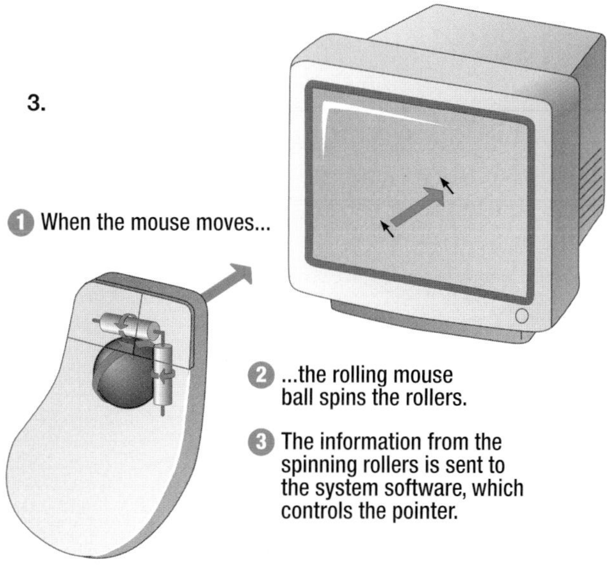

1 When the mouse moves...
2 ...the rolling mouse ball spins the rollers.
3 The information from the spinning rollers is sent to the system software, which controls the pointer.

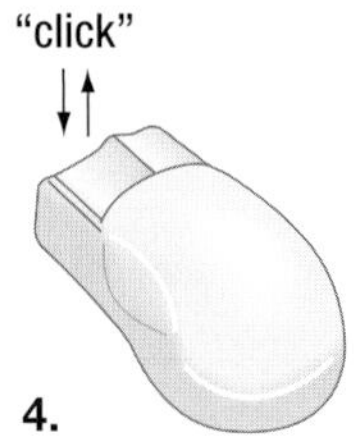

4.

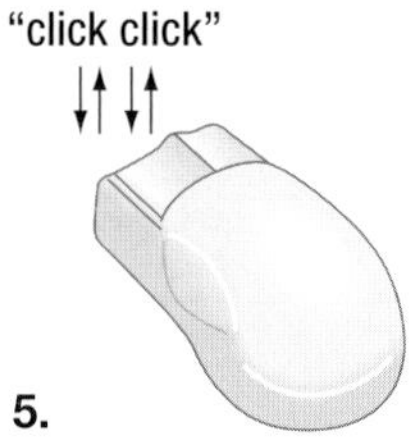

5.

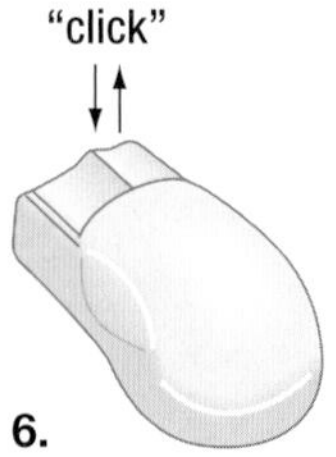

6.

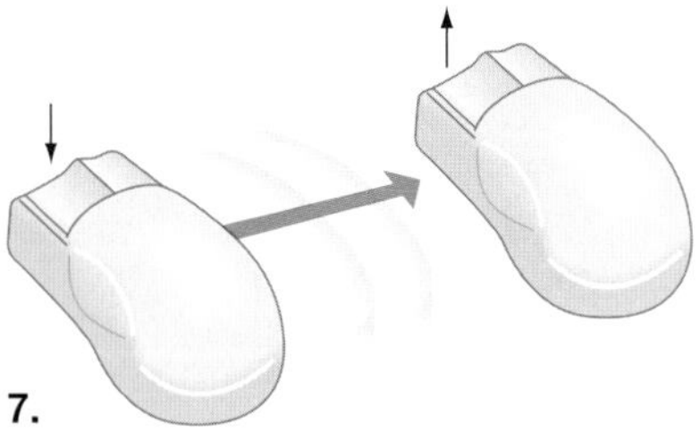

7.

4. To click an object, such as an icon, point to it on the screen, then quickly press and release the left mouse button one time. Generally, clicking an object selects it, or tells Windows that you want to do something with the object.
5. To double-click an object, point to it on the screen, then quickly press and release the left mouse button twice. Generally, double-clicking an object selects and activates the object. For example, when you double-click a program's icon on the desktop, the program launches so you can use it.
6. To right-click an object, point to it on the screen, then quickly press and release the right mouse button one time. Generally, right-clicking an object opens a shortcut menu that provides options for working with the object.
7. You can use the mouse to move objects around on the screen. For example, you can move an icon to a different location on the Windows desktop. This procedure is often called drag-and-drop editing. To drag an object, point to it, press and hold down the left mouse button, drag the object to the desired location, then release the mouse button.

ABOUT THIS BOOK

Effective Learning Tools

This pedagogically rich book is designed to make learning easy and enjoyable. It will help you develop the skills and critical thinking abilities that will enable you to understand computers and computer technology, troubleshoot problems, and possibly lead you into an IT career.

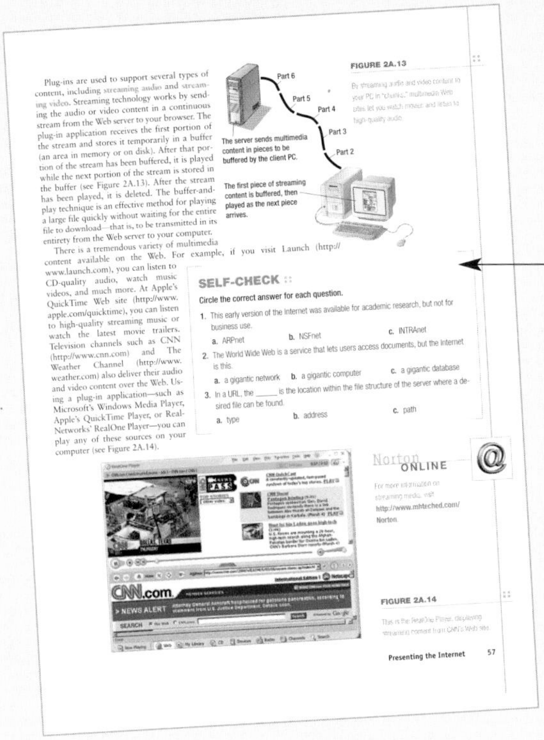

Self-check quizzes keep the students engaged and test their understanding of the lesson topics.

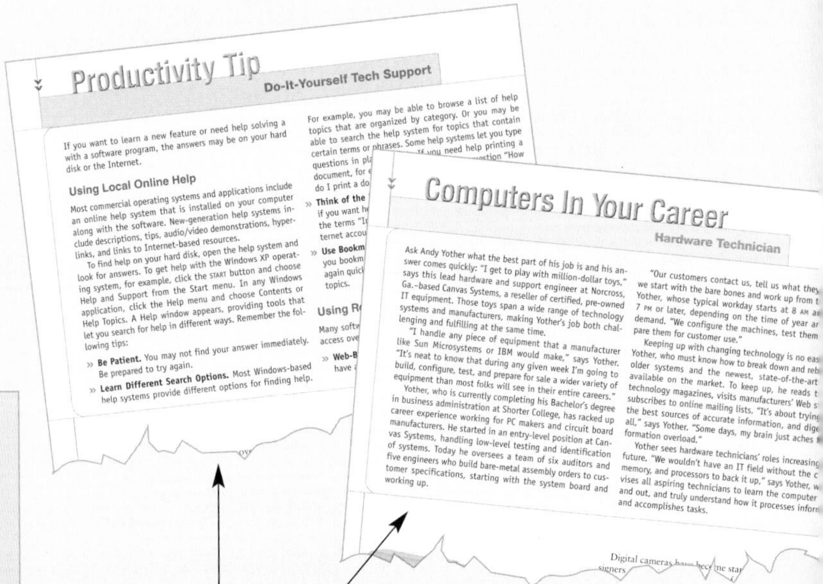

Each chapter includes . . .

- **Learning objectives** that set measurable goals for lesson-by-lesson progress
- **Four-color illustrations** that give you a clear picture of the technologies
- **More review materials at the end of each chapter *and* lesson:** Key terms quiz, multiple choice questions, short answer review questions, lab activities, discussion questions, research and report assignments, and ethical issue discussions

Productivity Tips, Computers In Your Career, and other feature articles offer students a more in-depth discussion of today's technology and how it affects their everyday lives.

Important Technology Concepts

Information technology (IT) offers many career paths leading to occupations in such fields as PC repair network administration, telecommunications, Web development, graphic design, and desktop support. To become competent in any IT field you need certain basic computer skills. *Peter Norton's Introduction to Computers,* 6e, builds a foundation for success in the IT field by introducing you to fundamental technology concepts and giving you essential computer skills.

Your IT career starts here!

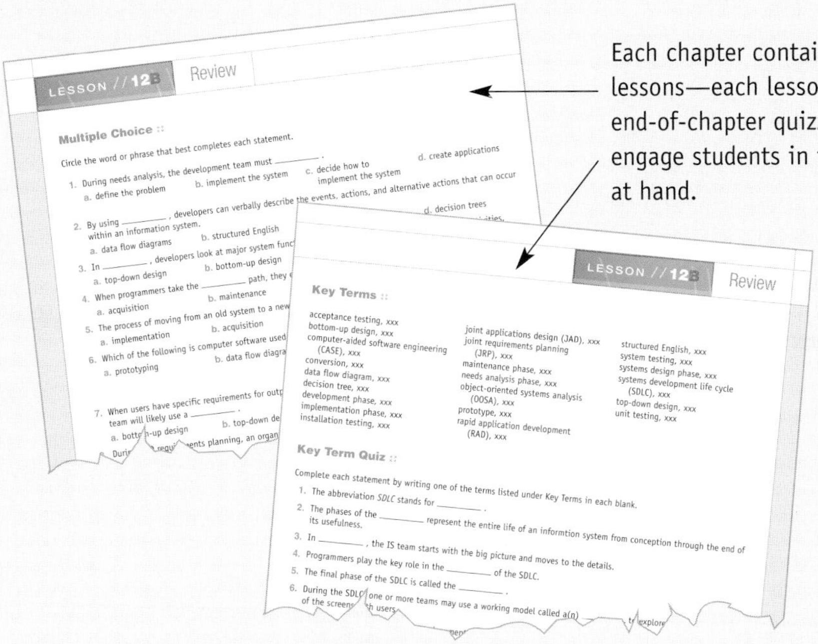
LESSON // 12B Review

Multiple Choice ::

Circle the word or phrase that best completes each statement.

1. During needs analysis, the development team must ________.
a. define the problem b. implement the system c. decide how to implement the system d. create applications

2. By using ________, developers can verbally describe the events, actions, and alternative actions that can occur within an information system.
a. data flow diagrams b. structured English d. decision trees

3. In ________, developers look at major system func...
a. top-down design b. bottom-up design

4. When programmers take the ________ path, they ...
a. acquisition b. maintenance

5. The process of moving from an old system to a new ...
a. implementation b. acquisition

6. Which of the following is computer software used ...
a. prototyping b. data flow diagra...

7. When users have specific requirements for outp... team will likely use a ________.
a. bottom-up design b. top-down de...

LESSON // 12B Review

Key Terms ::

acceptance testing, xxx
bottom-up design, xxx
computer-aided software engineering (CASE), xxx
conversion, xxx
data flow diagram, xxx
decision tree, xxx
development phase, xxx
implementation phase, xxx
installation testing, xxx
joint applications design (JAD), xxx
joint requirements planning (JRP), xxx
maintenance phase, xxx
needs analysis phase, xxx
object-oriented systems analysis (OOSA), xxx
prototype, xxx
rapid application development (RAD), xxx
structured English, xxx
system testing, xxx
systems design phase, xxx
systems development life cycle (SDLC), xxx
top-down design, xxx
unit testing, xxx

Key Term Quiz ::

Complete each statement by writing one of the terms listed under Key Terms in each blank.

1. The abbreviation *SDLC* stands for ________.
2. The phases of the ________ represent the entire life of an informtion system from conception through the end of its usefulness.
3. In ________, the IS team starts with the big picture and moves to the details.
4. Programmers play the key role in the ________ of the SDLC.
5. The final phase of the SDLC is called the ________.
6. During the SDLC, one or more teams may use a working model called a(n) ________ to explore ...

Each chapter contains two lessons—each lesson offers end-of-chapter quizzes that engage students in the topics at hand.

This book is full of detailed IT concepts and current photographs of the latest technologies. Norton Online sidebars point students to the new Norton web site accompanying this textbook where students can find more information on IT-specific topics.

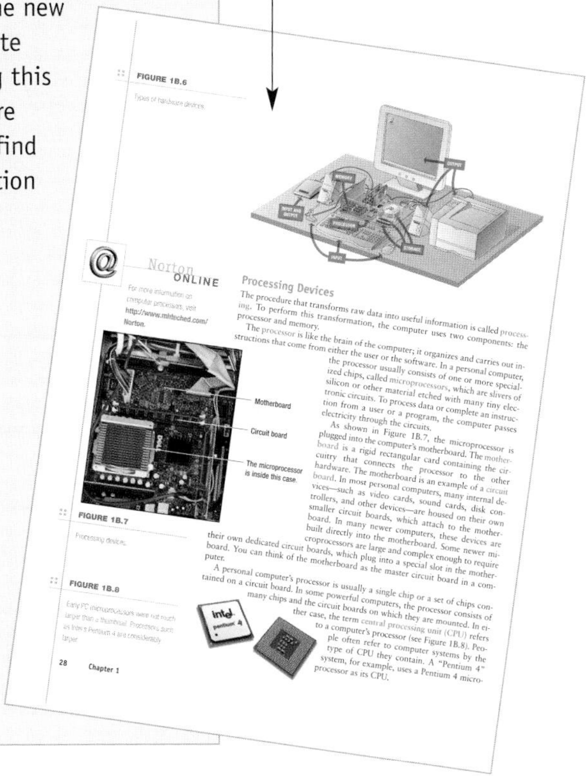
FIGURE 1B.6

Types of hardware devices.

Norton ONLINE

For more information on computer processors, visit http://www.mhhe.com/Norton.

Processing Devices

The procedure that transforms raw data into useful information is called processing. To perform this transformation, the computer uses two components: the processor and memory.

The processor is like the brain of the computer; it organizes and carries out instructions that come from either the user or the software. In a personal computer, the processor usually consists of one or more specialized chips, called microprocessors, which are slivers of silicon or other material etched with many tiny electronic circuits. To process data or complete an instruction from a user or a program, the computer passes electricity through the circuits.

As shown in Figure 1B.7, the microprocessor is plugged into the computer's motherboard. The motherboard is a rigid rectangular card containing the circuitry that connects the processor to the other hardware. The motherboard is an example of a circuit board. In most personal computers, many internal devices—such as video cards, sound cards, disk controllers, and other devices—are housed on their own smaller circuit boards, which attach to the motherboard. In many newer computers, these devices are built directly into the motherboard. Some newer microprocessors are large and complex enough to require their own dedicated circuit boards, which plug into a special slot in the motherboard. You can think of the motherboard as the master circuit board in a computer.

A personal computer's processor is usually a single chip or a set of chips contained on a circuit board. In some powerful computers, the processor consists of many chips and the circuit boards on which they are mounted. In either case, the term central processing unit (CPU) refers to a computer's processor (see Figure 1B.8). People often refer to computer systems by the type of CPU they contain. A "Pentium 4" system, for example, uses a Pentium 4 microprocessor as its CPU.

Motherboard

Circuit board

The microprocessor is inside this case.

FIGURE 1B.7

Processing devices.

FIGURE 1B.8

Early PC microprocessors were not much larger than a thumbnail. Processors such as Intel's Pentium 4 are considerably larger.

28 Chapter 1

- **Self-check quizzes** in each lesson (two per chapter) help students apply their knowledge as they work through the lesson

Feature articles

- **Norton Notebooks** offer insightful thoughts about emerging technologies and computers in our society.
- **At Issue** articles spotlight trends in information technology and offer a compelling look at how technology is used to help people enhance their lives.
- **Computers In Your Career** offer students a "human face" into IT professions by providing IT interviews and ideas for where an IT career might take today's students.
- **Productivity Tips** cover topics such as adding RAM, printer maintenance, and sharing Internet connections.

PETER NORTON'S

Introduction to Computers

CHAPTER 1

Introducing Computer Systems

CHAPTER CONTENTS ::

This chapter contains the following lessons:

LESSON // 1A

Exploring Computers and Their Uses

Overview: Computers in Our World

Consider this sentence: "Computers are everywhere." Does it sound like an overstatement? A cliché? No matter how you perceive the impact of computers, the statement is true. Computers *are* everywhere. In fact, you can find them in some pretty unlikely places, including your family car, your home appliances, and even your alarm clock!

In the past two decades, computers have reshaped our lives at home, work, and school. The vast majority of businesses now use computerized equipment in some way, and most companies are networked both internally and externally. More than half of all homes in the United States have at least one computer, and most of them are connected to the Internet. Workers who once had little use for technology now interact with computers almost every minute of the workday.

This lesson examines the many types of computers that are in common use today. Although this class will focus on personal computers (the ones that seem to sit on every desktop), you will first learn about the wide variety of computers that people use, and the reasons they use them. As your knowledge of computers grows, you will understand that all computers—regardless of their size or purpose—are basically similar. That is, they all operate on the same fundamental principles, are made from the same basic components, and need instructions to make them run.

OBJECTIVES ::

- In basic terms, define the word *computer*.
- Discuss various ways computers can be categorized.
- Identify six types of computers designed for individual use.
- Identify four types of computers used primarily by organizations.
- Explain the importance of computers in today's society.
- Describe how computers are used in various sectors of our society.

The Computer Defined

@ Norton ONLINE

For more information on digital computers, analog computers, and the history of computers, visit **http://www.mhhe.com/peternorton.**

simnet™

In basic terms, a computer is an electronic device that processes data, converting it into information that is useful to people. Any computer—regardless of its type—is controlled by programmed instructions, which give the machine a purpose and tell it what to do.

The computers discussed in this book—and which are everywhere around you—are digital computers (see Figure 1A.1). As you will learn in Chapter 5, "Processing Data," digital computers are so called because they work "by the numbers." That is, they break all types of information into tiny units, and use numbers to represent those pieces of information. Digital computers also work in very strict sequences of steps, processing each unit of information individually, according to the highly organized instructions they must follow.

A lesser-known type of computer is the analog computer, which works in a very different way from digital computers. The earliest computers were analog systems, and today's digital systems owe a great deal to their analog ancestors. Analog and digital computers differ in many respects, but the most important distinction is the way they represent data. Digital systems represent data as having one distinct value or another, with no other possibilities. Analog systems, however, represent data as variable points along a continuous spectrum of values. This makes analog computers somewhat more flexible than digital ones, but not necessarily more precise or reliable. Early analog computers were mechanical devices, weighing several tons and using motors and gears to perform calculations (see Figure 1A.2). A more manageable type of analog computer is the old-fashioned slide rule (see Figure 1A.3).

Computers can be categorized in several ways. For example, some computers are designed for use by one person, some are meant to be used by groups of people, and some are not used by people at all. They also can be categorized by their power, which means the speed at which they operate and the types of tasks they can handle. Within a single category, computers may be subcategorized by price, the types of hardware they contain, the kinds of software they can run, and so on.

FIGURE 1A.1

The personal computer is an example of a digital computer.

FIGURE 1A.2

This early analog computer, created by Vannevar Bush in the late 1920s, was called a "differential analyzer." It used electric motors, gears, and other moving parts to solve equations.

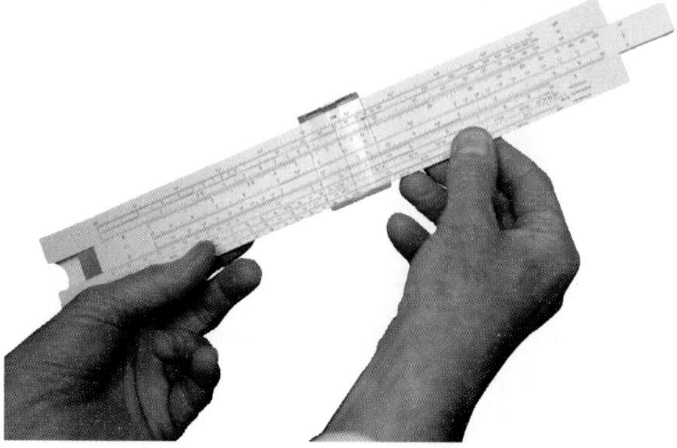

FIGURE 1A.3

Although analog computers have largely been forgotten, many of today's computer scientists grew up using slide rules—a simple kind of analog computer.

Computers for Individual Users

simnet™

Most computers are meant to be used by only one person at a time. Such computers are often shared by several people (such as those in your school's computer lab), but only one user can work with the machine at any given moment (see Figure 1A.4).

The six primary types of computers in this category are

- Desktop computers
- Workstations
- Notebook computers
- Tablet computers
- Handheld computers
- Smart phones

FIGURE 1A.4

Many kinds of computers can be shared by multiple users but can be used by only one person at a time.

These systems are all examples of personal computers (PCs)—a term that refers to any computer system that is designed for use by a single person. Personal computers are also called microcomputers, because they are among the smallest computers created for people to use. Note, however, that the term *personal computer* or *PC* is most often used to describe desktop computers, which you will learn about in the following section.

Although personal computers are used by individuals, they also can be connected together to create networks (see Figure 1A.5). In fact, networking has become one of the most important jobs of personal computers, and even tiny handheld computers can now be connected to networks. You will learn about computer networks in Chapter 9, "Networks."

FIGURE 1A.5

Networking is a key task for today's computers, especially portable systems that allow users to connect to their home or office even when they are traveling.

Desktop Computers

The most common type of personal computer is the desktop computer—a PC that is designed to sit on (or under) a desk or table. These are the systems you see all around you, in schools, homes, and offices, and they are the main focus of this book.

Today's desktop computers are far more powerful than those of just a few years ago, and are used for an amazing array of tasks. Not only do these machines enable people to do their jobs with greater ease and efficiency, but they can be used to communicate, produce music, edit photographs and videos, play sophisticated games, and much more. Used by everyone from preschoolers to nuclear physicists, desktop computers are indispensable for learning, work, and play (see Figure 1A.6).

Norton ONLINE

For more information on desktop computers, visit **http://www.mhhe.com/peternorton.**

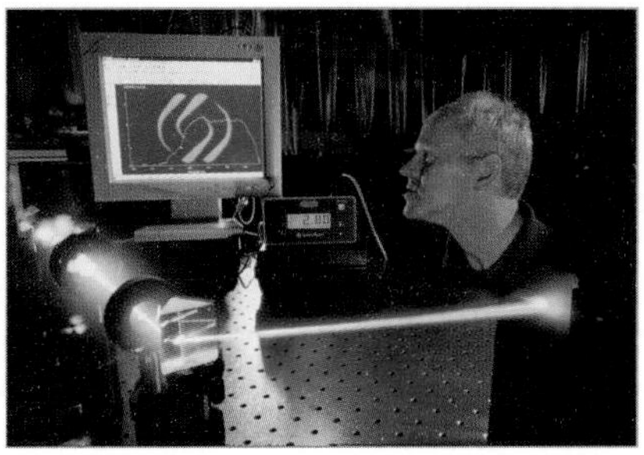

FIGURE 1A.6

Desktop PCs are a familiar item in homes, schools, and workplaces.

FIGURE 1A.7

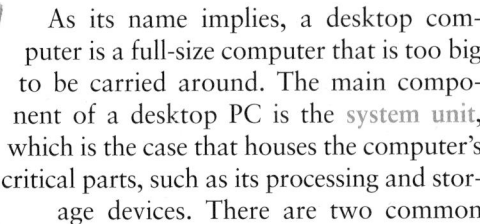

This desktop PC follows the traditional design, with the monitor stacked on top of the system unit.

As its name implies, a desktop computer is a full-size computer that is too big to be carried around. The main component of a desktop PC is the **system unit**, which is the case that houses the computer's critical parts, such as its processing and storage devices. There are two common designs for desktop computers. The more traditional desktop model features a horizontally oriented system unit, which usually lies flat on the top of the user's desk. Many users place their monitor on top of the system unit (see Figure 1A.7).

Vertically oriented tower models have become the more popular style of desktop system (see Figure 1A.8). This design allows the user to place the system unit next to or under the desk, if desired.

FIGURE 1A.8

This desktop PC has a "tower" design, with a system unit that sits upright and can be placed on either the desk or the floor.

Workstations

A **workstation** is a specialized, single-user computer that typically has more power and features than a standard desktop PC (see Figure 1A.9). These machines are popular among scientists, engineers, and animators who need a system with greater-than-average speed and the power to perform sophisticated tasks. Workstations often have large, high-resolution monitors and accelerated graphics–handling capabilities, making them suitable for advanced architectural or engineering design, modeling, animation, and video editing.

Norton ONLINE

For more information on workstations, visit **http://www.mhhe.com/peternorton.**

FIGURE 1A.9

Workstation computers are favored by engineers and designers who need a high-performance system.

Notebook Computers

Notebook computers, as their name implies, approximate the shape of an 8.5-by-11-inch notebook and easily fit inside a briefcase. Because people frequently set these devices on their lap, they are also called **laptop computers**. Notebook computers can operate on alternating current or special batteries. These amazing devices generally weigh less than eight pounds, and some even weigh less than three pounds! During use, the computer's lid is raised to reveal a thin monitor and a keyboard. When not in use, the device folds up for easy storage. Notebooks are fully functional microcomputers; the people who use them need the power of a full-size desktop computer wherever they go (see Figure 1A.10). Because of their portability, notebook PCs fall into a category of devices

Norton ONLINE

For more information on notebook computers, visit **http://www.mhhe.com/peternorton.**

called mobile computers—systems small enough to be carried by their user.

Some notebook systems are designed to be plugged into a docking station, which may include a large monitor, a full-size keyboard and mouse, or other devices (see Figure 1A.11). Docking stations also provide additional ports that enable the notebook computer to be connected to different devices or a network in the same manner as a desktop system.

FIGURE 1A.10

Notebook computers have the power and features of desktop PCs but are light and portable.

Tablet PCs

The tablet PC is the newest development in portable, full-featured computers (see Figure 1A.12). Tablet PCs offer all the functionality of a notebook PC, but they are lighter and can accept input from a special pen—called a stylus or a digital pen—that is used to tap or write directly on the screen. Many tablet PCs also have a built-in microphone and special software that accepts input from the user's voice. A few models even have a fold-out keyboard, so they can be transformed into a standard notebook PC. Tablet PCs run specialized versions of standard programs and can be connected to a network. Some models also can be connected to a keyboard and a full-size monitor.

Norton ONLINE

For more information on tablet PCs, visit **http://www.mhhe.com/peternorton**.

FIGURE 1A.11

A docking station can make a notebook computer feel like a desktop system, by adding a full-size monitor, keyboard, and other features.

Handheld PCs

Handheld personal computers are computing devices small enough to fit in your hand (see Figure 1A.13). A popular type of handheld computer is the personal digital assistant (PDA). A PDA is no larger than a small appointment book and is normally used for special applications, such as taking notes, displaying telephone numbers and addresses, and keeping track of dates or agendas. Many PDAs can be connected to larger computers to exchange data. Most PDAs come with a pen that lets the user write on the screen. Some handheld computers feature tiny built-in keyboards or microphones that allow voice input.

Many PDAs let the user access the Internet through a wireless connection, and several models offer features such as cellular telephones, cameras, music players, and global positioning systems.

Norton ONLINE

For more information on handheld PCs, visit **http://www.mhhe.com/peternorton.**

Smart Phones

Some cellular phones double as miniature PCs (see Figure 1A.14). Because these phones offer advanced features not typically found in cellular phones, they are sometimes

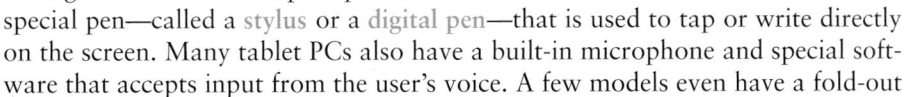

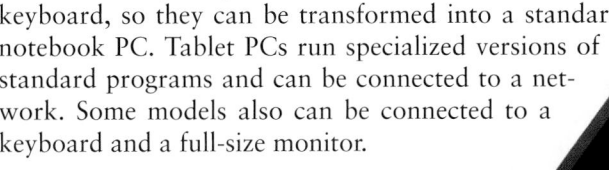

Norton ONLINE

For more information on smart phones, visit **http://www.mhhe.com/peternorton.**

FIGURE 1A.12

Tablet PCs are gaining in popularity among professionals who need to take lots of notes and deal with hand-drawn documents, such as architects.

FIGURE 1A.13

Devices such as PDAs put a computer in your pocket and can be used in many different ways.

called smart phones. These features can include Web and e-mail access, special software such as personal organizers, or special hardware such as digital cameras or music players. Some models even break in half to reveal a miniature keyboard.

simnet™

Computers for Organizations

Some computers handle the needs of many users at the same time. These powerful systems are most often used by organizations, such as businesses or schools, and are commonly found at the heart of the organization's network.

Generally, each user interacts with the computer through his or her own device, freeing people from having to wait their turn at a single keyboard and monitor (see Figure 1A.15). The largest organizational computers support thousands of individual users at the same time, from thousands of miles away. While some of these large-scale systems are devoted to a special purpose, enabling users to perform only a few specific tasks, many organizational computers are general-purpose systems that support a wide variety of tasks.

Norton ONLINE

For more information on network servers, visit **http://www.mhhe.com/peternorton**.

Network Servers

Today, most organizations' networks are based on personal computers. Individual users have their own desktop computers, which are connected to one or more centralized computers, called network servers. A network server is usually a powerful personal computer with special software and equipment that enable it to function as the primary computer in the network.

PC-based networks and servers offer companies a great deal of flexibility. For example, large organizations may have dozens or hundreds of individual servers working together at the heart of their network (see Figure 1A.16). When set up in such groups—sometimes called *clusters* or *server farms*—network servers may not even resemble standard PCs. For example, they may be mounted in large racks or reduced to small units called "blades," which can be slid in and out of a case. In these large networks, different groups of servers may have different purposes, such as supporting a certain set of users, handling printing tasks, enabling Internet communications, and so on.

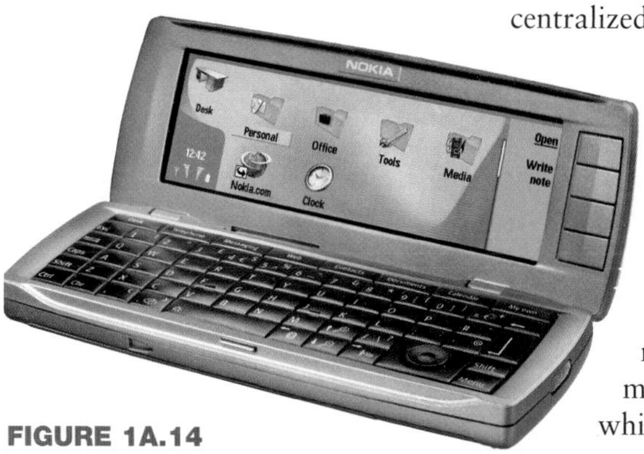

FIGURE 1A.14

New cellular phones, like the Nokia 9500 Communicator, double as tiny computers, offering many of the features of PDAs.

A PC-based server gives users flexibility to do different kinds of tasks (see Figure 1A.17). This is because PCs are general-purpose machines, designed to be used in many ways. For example, some users may rely on the server for e-mail access, some may use it to perform accounting tasks, and others may use it to perform word-processing or database-management jobs. The server can support these processes, and many others, while storing information and programs for many people to use.

FIGURE 1A.15

In many companies, workers use their desktop systems to access a central, shared computer.

Depending on how the network is set up, users may be able to access the server in multiple ways. Of course, most users have a standard desktop PC on their desk that is permanently connected to the network. Mobile users, however, may be able to connect a notebook PC or a handheld device to the network by wireless means. When they are away from the office, users may be able to use the Internet as a means of connecting to the company's network servers (see Figure 1A.18).

FIGURE 1A.16

Large corporate networks can use hundreds of servers.

Mainframe Computers

Mainframe computers are used in large organizations such as insurance companies and banks, where many people frequently need to use the same data. In a traditional mainframe environment, each user accesses the mainframe's resources through a device called a terminal (see Figure 1A.19). There are two kinds of terminals. A *dumb terminal* does not process or store data; it is simply an input/output (I/O) device that functions as a window into a computer located somewhere else. An *intelligent terminal* can perform some processing operations, but it usually does not have any storage. In some mainframe environments, however, workers can use a standard personal computer to access the mainframe.

Norton ONLINE

For more information on mainframe computers, visit **http://www.mhhe.com/peternorton.**

FIGURE 1A.17

These workers may be connected to the same network server, yet using it for very different tasks.

Mainframes are large, powerful systems (see Figure 1A.20). The largest mainframes can handle the processing needs of thousands of users at any given moment. But what these systems offer in power, they lack in flexibility. Most mainframe systems are designed to handle only a specific set of tasks. In your state's Department of Motor Vehicles, for example, a mainframe system is probably devoted to storing information about drivers, vehicles, and driver's licenses, but little or nothing else. By limiting the number of tasks the system must perform, administrators preserve as much power as possible for required operations.

You may have interacted with a mainframe system without even knowing it. For example, if you have ever visited an airline's Web site to reserve a seat on a flight, you probably conducted a transaction with a mainframe computer.

FIGURE 1A.18

Many users can access their organization's network no matter where they go.

FIGURE 1A.19

Hundreds, even thousands, of mainframe users may use terminals to work with the central computer.

FIGURE 1A.20

Mainframe computers are often housed alone in special rooms, away from their users.

Norton **ONLINE**

For more information on minicomputers, visit **http://www.mhhe.com/peternorton.**

Minicomputers

First released in the 1960s, minicomputers got their name because of their small size compared to other computers of the day. The capabilities of a minicomputer are somewhere between those of mainframes and personal computers. For this reason, minicomputers are often called midrange computers.

Like mainframes, minicomputers can handle much more input and output than personal computers can. Although some "minis" are designed for a single user, the most powerful minicomputers can serve the input and output needs of hundreds of users at a time. Users can access a central minicomputer through a terminal or a standard PC.

Supercomputers

Supercomputers are the most powerful computers made, and physically they are some of the largest (see Figure 1A.21). These systems can process huge

SELF-CHECK ::

Circle the correct answer for each question.

1. Any computer is controlled by ______________ .
   a. hardware b. information c. instructions
2. Which of these is a powerful type of personal computer, favored by professionals such as engineers?
   a. workstation b. notebook c. mainframe
3. Which type of computer will you most likely encounter at the Department of Motor Vehicles?
   a. smart phone b. mainframe c. supercomputer

amounts of data, and the fastest supercomputers can perform more than one trillion calculations per second. Some supercomputers can house thousands of processors. Supercomputers are ideal for handling large and highly complex problems that require extreme calculating power. For example, supercomputers have long been used in the mapping of the human genome, forecasting weather, and modeling complex processes like nuclear fission.

FIGURE 1A.21

Supercomputers are most common in university and research settings, but a few government agencies and very large businesses use them as well.

Norton **ONLINE**

For more information on supercomputers, visit **http://www.mhhe.com/peternorton.**

Computers in Society

How important are computers to our society? People often talk in fantastic terms about computers and their impact on our lives. You probably have heard or read expressions such as "computers have changed our world" or "computers have changed the way we do everything" many times. Such statements may strike you as exaggerations, and sometimes they are. But if you stop and really think about the effect computers have had on our daily lives, you still may be astonished.

One way to gauge the impact of computers is to consider the impact of other inventions. Can you imagine, for instance, the many ways in which American life changed after the introduction of the automobile (see Figure 1A.22)? Consider a few examples:

- Because of the car, people were able to travel farther and cheaper than ever before, and this created huge opportunities for businesses to meet the needs of the traveling public.
- Because vehicles could be mass-produced, the nature of manufacturing and industry changed and throngs of people began working on assembly lines.
- Because of road development, suburbs became a feasible way for people to live close to a city without actually living in one.
- Because of car travel, motels, restaurants, and shopping centers sprang up in places where there had previously been nothing.

FIGURE 1A.22

At the beginning of the 20th century, few could envision how the automobile would change the world. Today, the same holds true for computers and other forms of technology.

Productivity Tip

Choosing the Right Tool for the Job

Buying a computer is a lot like buying a car because there are so many models and options from which to choose! Before deciding which model is best for you, identify the type of work for which you want to use the computer.

Depending on your job, you may need to use a computer on a limited basis. A handheld system is great if you want to

- » **Manage Your Schedule on a Daily or Hourly Basis.** Handheld computers are popular for their calendar and schedule-management capabilities, which enable you to set appointments, track projects, and record special events.
- » **Manage a List of Contacts.** If you need to stay in touch with many people and travel frequently, personal digital assistants provide contact-management features.
- » **Make Notes on the Fly.** Some PDAs feature small keyboards, which are handy for tapping out quick notes. Others feature pens, which enable the user to "write" directly on the display screen. Many newer handheld systems also provide a built-in microphone, so you can record notes digitally.
- » **Send Faxes and E-Mail.** Most popular handheld PCs have fax and e-mail capabilities and a port that lets them exchange data with a PC.

If your job requires you to travel, but you still need a full-featured computer, you may consider using a laptop or notebook computer. This option is the best choice if you want to

- » **Carry Your Data with You.** If you need to make presentations on the road or keep up with daily work while traveling, portable PCs are ideal. Laptop systems offer as much RAM and storage capacity as desktop models. Many portables have built-in CD-ROM or DVD drives; others accept plug-in CD-ROM, DVD, and hard drives, which can greatly increase their capacity.
- » **Be Able to Work Anywhere.** Portable PCs run on either rechargeable batteries or standard current.
- » **Communicate and Share Data from Any Location.** Most portable computers have built-in modems or slots for plugging in a modem.

Think of other great inventions and discoveries, such as electricity, the telephone, or the airplane. Each, in its own way, brought significant changes to the world, and to the ways people lived and spent their time. Today, still relatively soon after its creation, the computer is only beginning to make its mark on society.

Why Are Computers So Important?

People can list countless reasons for the importance of computers (see Figure 1A.23). For someone with a disability, for example, a computer may offer freedom to communicate, learn, or work without leaving home. For a sales professional, a PC may mean the ability to communicate whenever necessary, to track leads, and to manage an ever-changing schedule. For a researcher, a computer may be the workhorse that does painstaking and time-consuming calculations.

But if you took all the benefits that people derive from computers, mixed them together, and distilled them down into a single element, what would you have? The answer is simple: *information.*

Computers are important because information is so essential to our lives. And information is more than the stuff you see and hear on television. Facts in a textbook or an encyclopedia are information, but only one kind. Mathematical formulas and their results are information, too, as are the plans for a building or the recipe for a cake. Pictures, songs, addresses, games, menus, shopping lists, resumes—the list goes on and on. All these things and many others can be thought of as information, and they can all be stored and processed by computers. (Actually,

If you work in one place and need to perform various tasks, a desktop computer is the best choice. Choose a desktop computer if you want to

- **Work with Graphics-Intensive or Desktop Publishing Applications.** Complex graphics and page-layout programs require a great deal of system resources, and a desktop system's large monitor reduces eye fatigue.
- **Design or Use Multimedia Products.** Even though many portable computers have multimedia features, you can get the most for your money with a desktop system. Large screens make multimedia programs easier to see, and stereo-style speakers optimize sound quality.
- **Set Up Complex Hardware Configurations.** A desktop computer can support multiple peripherals—including printers, sound and video sources, and various external devices—at the same time. If you want to swap components, or perform other configuration tasks, a desktop system will provide many options.

Portable computers enable you to work almost anywhere.

PRODUCTIVITY TIP

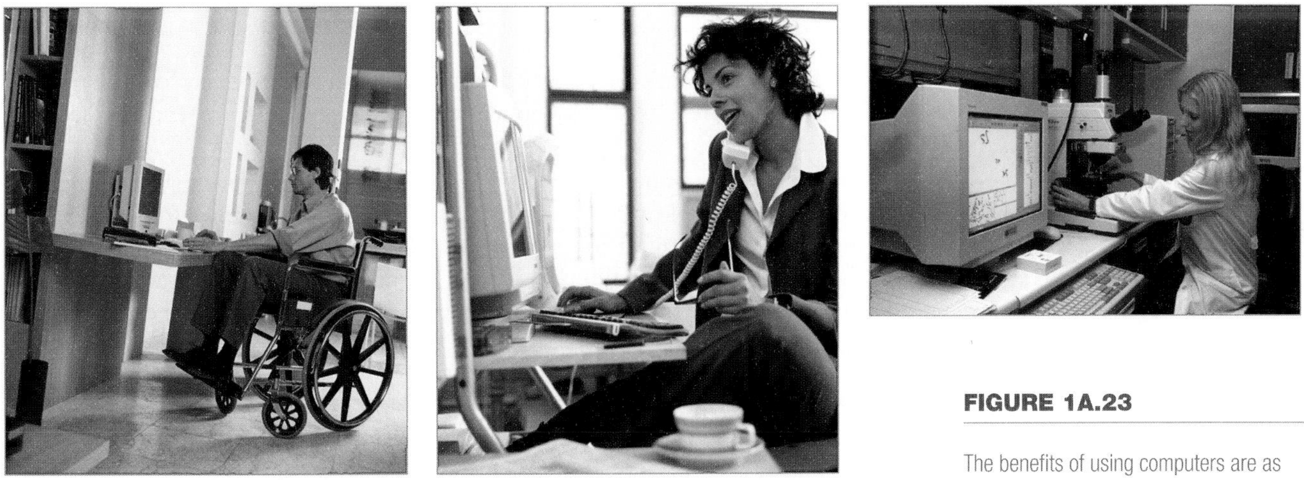

FIGURE 1A.23

The benefits of using computers are as varied as the people who use them.

computers store these things as *data*, not as information, but you'll learn the difference between the two later in this book.) So, when you consider the importance of computers in our society, think instead about the importance of information. As tools for working with information, and for creating new information, computers may be one of humanity's most important creations.

FIGURE 1A.24

E-mail software and Internet connections make it easy for people to keep in touch.

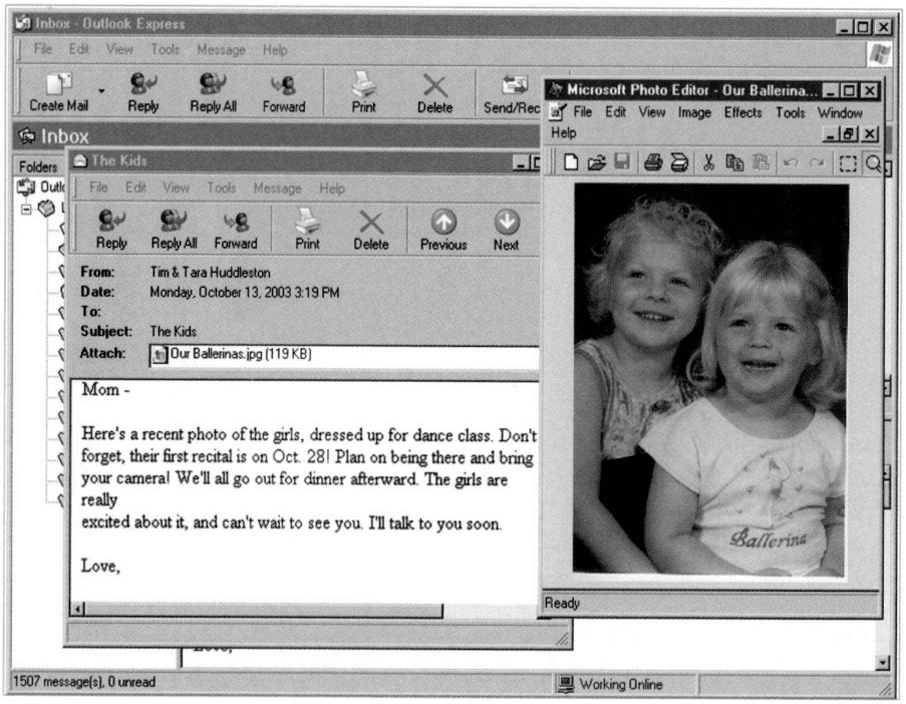

Norton ONLINE

For more information on computers in the home, visit **http://www.mhhe.com/peternorton**.

Home

In many American homes, the family computer is nearly as important as the refrigerator or the washing machine. People cannot imagine living without it. In fact, a growing number of families have multiple PCs in their homes; in most cases, at least one of those computers has an Internet connection. Why do home users need their computers?

- **Communications.** Electronic mail (e-mail) continues to be the most popular use for home computers, because it allows family members to communicate with one another, and to stay in contact with friends and coworkers (see Figure 1A.24).
- **Business Work Done at Home.** Thanks to computers and Internet connections, more people are working from home than ever before. It is possible for many users to connect to their employer's network from home and do work that could not be done during regular business hours. Computers also are making it easier for people to start their own home-based businesses.
- **Schoolwork.** Today's students are increasingly reliant on computers, and not just as a replacement for typewriters. The Internet is replacing printed books as a reference tool (see Figure 1A.25), and easy-to-use software makes it possible for even young users to create polished documents.
- **Entertainment.** If you have ever played a computer game, you know how enjoyable they can be. For this reason, the computer has replaced the television as the entertainment medium of choice for many people. As computer, audio, video, and broadcast technologies converge, the computer will someday be an essential component of any home entertainment center.
- **Finances.** Computers and personal finance software can make balancing your checkbook an enjoyable experience. Well, almost. At any rate, they certainly make it easier, and home users rely on their PCs for bill paying, shopping, investing, and other financial chores (see Figure 1A.26).

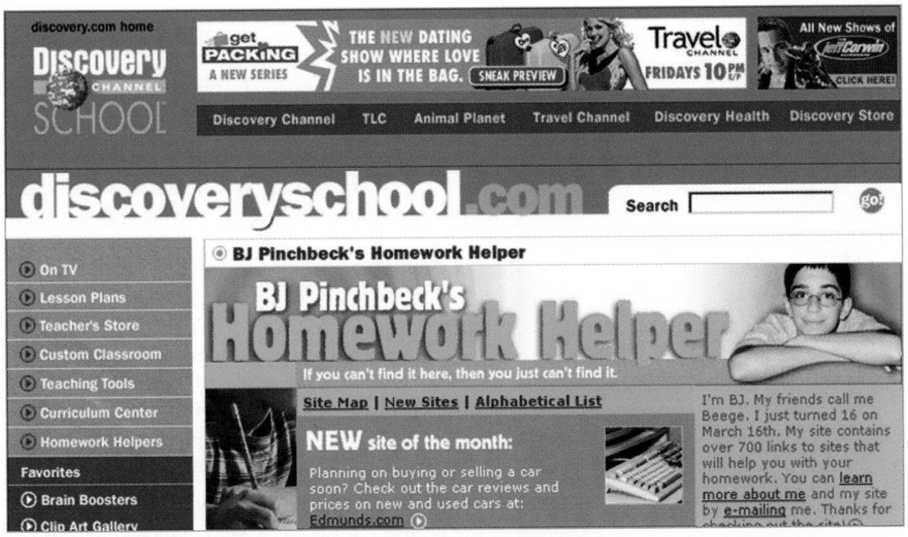

FIGURE 1A.25

The Internet is a tremendous resource for study, offering thousands of authoritative Web sites where students can find information and help on all kinds of subjects.

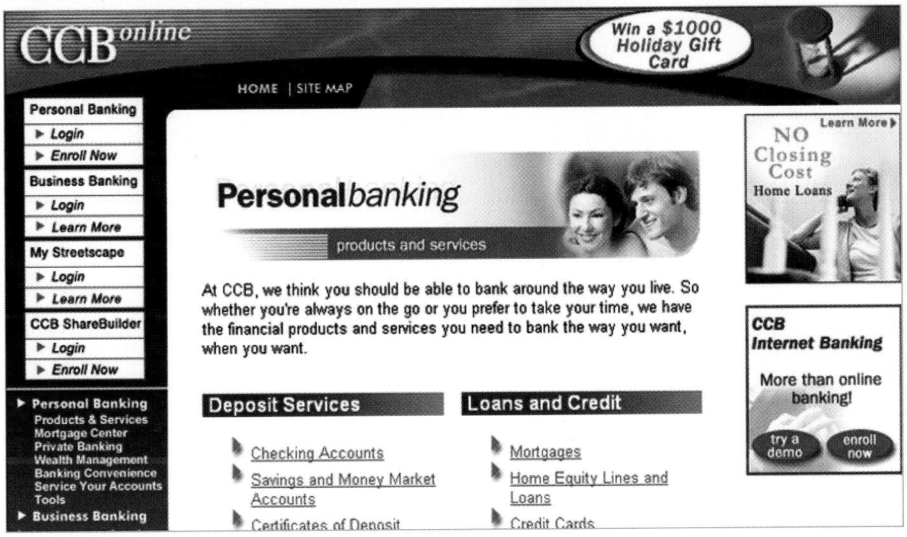

FIGURE 1A.26

Many banks now offer their services online. If you have an account with such a bank, you can access your accounts, pay bills, and conduct other transactions online.

Education

More and more schools are adding computer technology to their curricula, not only teaching pure computer skills, but incorporating those skills into other classes. Students may be required to use a drawing program, for example, to draw a plan of the Alamo for a history class, or use spreadsheet software to analyze voter turnouts during the last century's presidential elections.

Educators see computer technology as an essential learning requirement for all students, starting as early as preschool. Even now, basic computing skills such as keyboarding are being taught in elementary school classes (see Figure 1A.27). In the near future, high school graduates will enter college not only with a general diploma, but with a certification that proves their skills in some area of computing, such as networking or programming.

Norton ONLINE

For more information on computers in education, visit **http://www.mhhe.com/peternorton**.

Small Business

Many of today's successful small companies simply could not exist without computer technology. Each year, hundreds of thousands of individuals launch businesses based from their homes or in small-office locations. They rely on inexpensive computers and software not only to perform basic work functions, but to manage and grow their companies.

Norton ONLINE

For more information on computers in small business, visit **http://www.mhhe.com/peternorton**.

Norton ONLINE

For more information on computers in industry, visit **http://www.mhhe.com/peternorton**.

FIGURE 1A.27

Basic computer skills are now being taught to early learners, who quickly pick up mouse and keyboard use.

These tools enable business owners to handle tasks—such as daily accounting chores, inventory management, marketing, payroll, and many others—that once required the hiring of outside specialists (see Figure 1A.28). As a result, small businesses become more self-sufficient and reduce their operating expenses.

Industry

Today, enterprises use different kinds of computers in many combinations. A corporate headquarters may have a standard PC-based network, for example, but its production facilities may use computer-controlled robotics to manufacture products.

Here are just a few ways computers are applied to industry:

- **Design.** Nearly any company that designs and makes products can use a computer-aided design or computer-aided manufacturing system in their creation (see Figure 1A.29).
- **Shipping.** Freight companies need computers to manage the thousands of ships, planes, trains, and trucks that are moving goods at any given moment. In addition to tracking vehicle locations and contents, computers can manage maintenance, driver schedules, invoices and billing, and many other activities.
- **Process Control.** Modern assembly lines can be massive, complex systems, and a breakdown at one point can cause chaos throughout a company. Sophisticated process-control systems can oversee output, check the speed at which a machine runs, manage conveyance systems, and look at parts inventories, with very little human interaction.

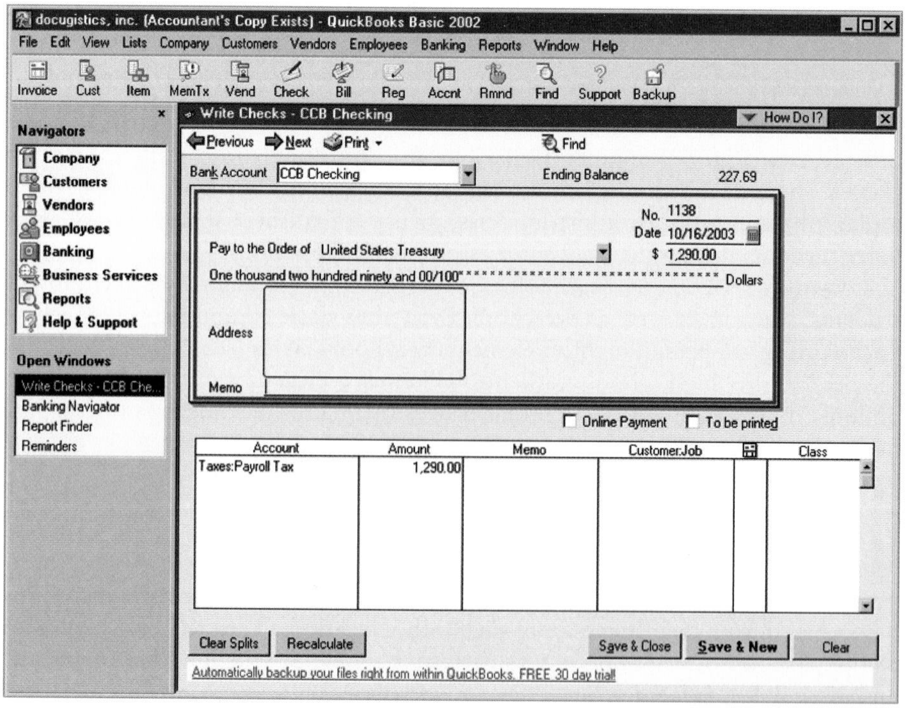

FIGURE 1A.28

Easy-to-use accounting programs such as QuickBooks allow business owners to manage their finances, even if they do not have any accounting expertise.

Government

Not only are governments big consumers of technology, but they help to develop it as well. As you will learn in Chapter 2, "Presenting the Internet," the U.S. government played a key role in developing the Internet. Similarly, NASA has been involved in the development of computer technologies of all sorts. Today, computers play a crucial part in nearly every government agency:

- **Population.** The U.S. Census Bureau was one of the first organizations to use computer technology, recruiting mechanical computers known as "difference engines" to assist in tallying the American population in the early 20th century.
- **Taxes.** Can you imagine trying to calculate Americans' tax bills without the help of computers? Neither could the Internal Revenue Service. In fact, the IRS now encourages taxpayers to file their tax returns online, via the Internet.
- **Military.** Some of the world's most sophisticated computer technology has been developed primarily for use by the military. In fact, some of the earliest digital computers were created for such purposes as calculating the trajectory of missiles. Today, from payroll management to weapons control, the armed forces use the widest array of computer hardware and software imaginable.
- **Police.** When it comes to stocking their crime-fighting arsenals, many police forces consider computers to be just as important as guns and ammunition (see Figure 1A.30). Today's police cruisers are equipped with laptop computers and wireless Internet connections that enable officers to search for information on criminals, crime scenes, procedures, and other kinds of information.

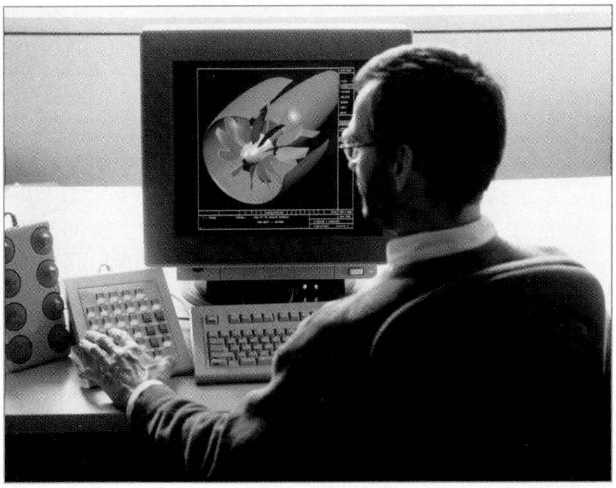

FIGURE 1A.29

Computer-aided design programs allow engineers to design and test new products, and even to control the machines that manufacture them.

Norton **ONLINE**

For more information on computers in government, visit **http://www.mhhe.com/peternorton**.

FIGURE 1A.30

Portable computers are now among police officers' weapons of choice.

Norton Notebook

The Merging of Media and Meaning

I imagine that you have been aware of personal computers for some time. Even if you or your family has never owned a PC—and even if this course is your first opportunity to use one—you're probably at least peripherally aware of the prominent place we've given to PCs in our lives. As a matter of fact, it's only been over the course of our lives, yours and mine, that PCs have earned their place on desks in homes and places of business, if *earned* is the right word. Personal computers' slow start has accelerated to a staggering pace as we humans have done what we always do: Take a new tool and exploit its every possible use.

For many of us, the 30-year evolution of uses for the PC has been no less *revolutionary* than was the introduction of electricity to the home a century ago. What began as a simple, if seemingly miraculous, light to read by has become the center of most everything we do at home. Why, even many fireplaces—yesterday's reading light—ignite today by electric power. Personal computers started life similarly, as humble things, miraculous for their multipurpose ability to work with words *and* numbers, yet able to display virtually nothing but text in response to typed commands, barely able to print anything usefully, and closed—unable to communicate "outside of the box," as it were.

A huge industry developed to support personal computers and expand their potential use as a tool. And for roughly the first five years of the PC's existence, the greatest innovations came from within the world of computing—people researching specifically to improve video performance, to reduce the cost of increasingly massive data storage, to connect computers together over world-shrinking distances. The creativity of these folks was staggering. When faced with the question, "I can talk around the world on the telephone; why can't my computer?" for example, they literally gave the computer a voice. That's what a modem does: it turns a computer's digital signals into audible sound that the plain old telephone system can handle. If you like, you can think of this as being somewhat analogous to the early years of electricity when pioneers such as Thomas Edison and George Westinghouse worked tirelessly to improve the potential of their original innovation and make an arguably honest buck. Other industries—automotive, electronics, and entertainment, to name a prominent few—adopted the technology developed for and made economically feasible by computing's growing popularity.

Gradually, this relationship became more symbiotic, and the PC started to benefit from technology originally developed for other purposes. Consider the compact disc. Introduced in 1980, by 1983 it was just beginning to gain a foothold in the music world. Six years later, CD-ROMs appeared on personal computers and ushered in a second

Norton ONLINE

For more information on computers in health care, visit **http://www.mhhe.com/peternorton**.

Health Care

Pay a visit to your family doctor or the local hospital, and you'll find yourself surrounded by computerized equipment of all kinds. Computers, in fact, are making health care more efficient and accurate while helping providers bring down costs. Many different health care procedures now involve computers, from ultrasound and magnetic resonance imaging, to laser eye surgery and fetal monitoring (see Figure 1A.31).

Surgeons now can use robotic surgical devices to perform delicate operations, and even to conduct surgeries remotely. New virtual-reality technologies are being used to train new surgeons in cutting-edge techniques, without cutting an actual patient.

But not all medical computers are so high-tech. Clinics and hospitals use standard computers to manage schedules, maintain patient records, and perform billings. Many transactions between physicians, insurance companies, and pharmacies are conducted by computers, saving health care workers time to devote to more important tasks.

generation of PC possibilities. PCs by then had evolved sophisticated graphical user interfaces and detailed displays. Combining the CD's digital sound with these visual technologies went a long way toward making computer experiences *interactive*—something that previously only people and unpopular toys had been. The PC world increasingly became a place where many other worlds met, particularly the varied worlds of information and entertainment—an interactive, *multimedia* world.

This is today's world. It's a world in which we expect our computers to toot, whistle, plunk, and boom; to speak to us and to listen when we dictate; to remember what we forget and to distract us so we will forget. Having spent much of the late 1990s forgetting that a technology company must actually *produce* something useful in order to realize a profit, the computing world turned back to substance with a renewed focus on the PC as the center of media. As I write this, a new generation of media PCs is appearing on the market. These systems can blend virtually every media technology in existence into a seamless, single experience. The traditional capabilities of PCs, CD and DVD players, DVD recorders, televisions, VCRs, surround-sound music systems can all be provided by one device—or two, if you add the possibilities of printing and film. What's really new about these systems is their power—practical video editing has been the private world of a wealthy few until the latest advances in processor, memory, and massive storage all came together in affordable systems that put these capabilities into homes and small offices.

This means that you can produce your own DVD movies with just a consumer video camera and a media PC (fast-talking agents are now entirely optional). In a band? Record and distribute albums of your music directly or through a Web site that software almost automatically designs for you. Paint? Create your own online gallery. Write? Self-publish on demand while promoting your creations through an existing online bookseller. Walt Disney said, "If you can dream it, you can do it." Technology has helped prove him right. Today the "you" who can "do it" means more people from more cultures and backgrounds than ever before.

NORTON NOTEBOOK

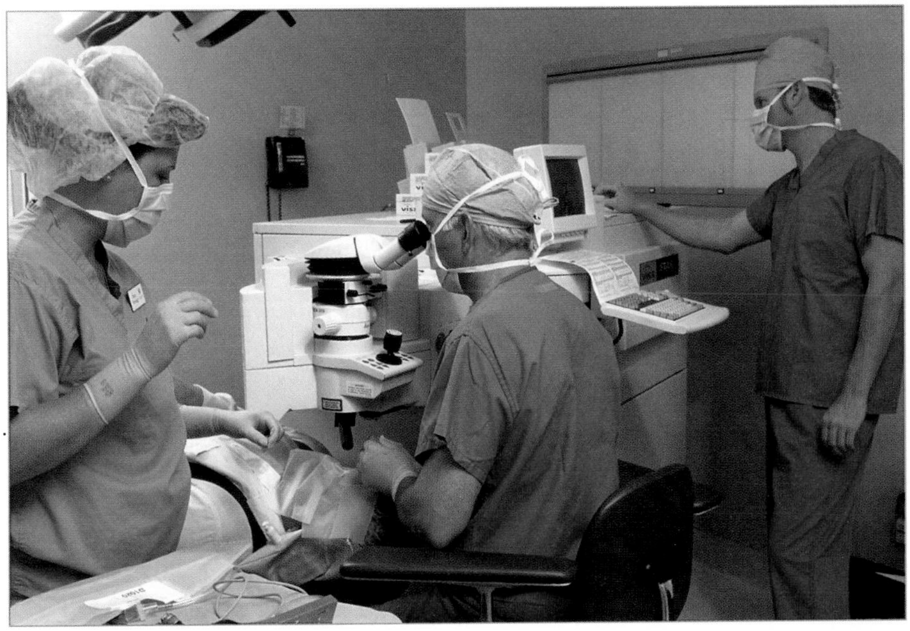

FIGURE 1A.31

Computers make many health care procedures more accurate and more comfortable for patients.

LESSON // 1A Review

Summary ::

- A computer is an electronic device that processes data, converting it into information that is useful to people.
- There are two basic types of computers: analog and digital. The computers commonly used today are all digital computers.
- Computers can be categorized by the number of people who can use them simultaneously, by their power, or by other criteria.
- Computers designed for use by a single person include desktop computers, workstations, notebook computers, tablet computers, handheld computers, and smart phones.
- The terms personal computer (PC) and microcomputer can be used when referring to any computer meant for use by a single person.
- The desktop computer is the most common type of personal computer. This computer is designed to sit on top of a desk or table, and comes in two basic styles.
- A workstation is a specialized, single-user computer that typically has more power and features than a standard desktop PC.
- Notebook computers are full-featured PCs that can easily be carried around.
- A tablet PC is another type of portable PC, but it can accept handwritten input when the user touches the screen with a special pen.
- Handheld personal computers are computing devices that fit in your hand; the personal digital assistant (PDA) is an example of a handheld computer.
- Smart phones are digital cellular phones that have features found in personal computers, such as Web browsers, e-mail capability, and more.
- Some types of computers—such as network servers, mainframes, minicomputers, and supercomputers—are commonly used by organizations and support the computing needs of many users.
- A network server is a powerful personal computer that is used as the central computer in an organization's network.
- Mainframes are powerful, special-purpose computers that can support the needs of hundreds or thousands of users.
- Minicomputers support dozens or hundreds of users at one time.
- Supercomputers are the largest and most powerful computers made.
- Many families have at least one computer and an Internet connection in their home and use their PC for tasks such as communication, work, schoolwork, and personal finances.
- Computer technology is playing an ever-growing role in schools, where students are being taught computer skills at younger ages and asked to incorporate computers into their daily work assignments.
- Computers enable small businesses to operate more efficiently by allowing workers to do a wider variety of tasks.
- In industries of all kinds, computers play vital roles in everything from personnel management, to product design and manufacturing, to shipping.
- Governments not only use a great deal of computer technology, but also contribute to its development.
- Computers are involved in nearly every aspect of the health care field, from managing schedules and handling billing, to making patient diagnoses and performing complex surgery.

Key Terms ::

computer, 4
desktop computer, 5
digital pen, 7
docking station, 7
handheld personal computer, 7
input/output (I/O) device, 9
laptop computer, 6
mainframe, 9
microcomputer, 5
midrange computer, 10
minicomputer, 10
mobile computer, 7
network server, 8
notebook computer, 6
personal computer (PC), 5
personal digital assistant (PDA), 7
smart phone, 8
stylus, 7
supercomputer, 10
system unit, 6
tablet PC, 7
terminal, 9
workstation, 6

Key Term Quiz ::

Complete each statement by writing one of the terms listed under Key Terms in each blank.

1. The ______________ is the case that holds the computer's critical components.
2. A(n) ______________ is a specialized, single-user computer that typically has more power than a standard PC.
3. When not in use, a(n) ______________ computer folds up for easy storage.
4. A tablet PC lets you use a(n) ______________ to tap or write directly on the screen.
5. A popular type of handheld computer is the ______________ .
6. A(n) ______________ is usually a powerful personal computer that functions as the primary computer in a network.
7. In a traditional mainframe environment, each user accesses the mainframe through a device called a(n) ______________ .
8. A terminal is an example of a(n) ______________ device.
9. The capabilities of a(n) ______________ are somewhere between mainframes and personal computers.
10. ______________ are the most powerful computers made.

LESSON // 1A Review

Multiple Choice ::

Circle the word or phrase that best completes each statement.

1. A computer converts data into this.
   a. information b. charts c. software d. input/output
2. The earliest computers were ______________ systems.
   a. digital b. paper c. analog d. slide rule
3. Most computers are meant to be used by only one ______________ at a time.
   a. company b. program c. organization d. person
4. Personal computers are also called ______________ .
   a. minicomputers b. microcomputers c. maxicomputers d. supercomputers
5. Many scientists, engineers, and animators use specialized computers, called ______________.
   a. personal digital assistants b. minicomputers c. workstations d. networks
6. Notebook PCs fall into a category of devices called ______________ .
   a. mobile computers b. small computers c. handheld computers d. minicomputers
7. Some notebook systems can be plugged into one of these devices, which give the computer additional features.
   a. port station b. network station c. workstation d. docking station
8. Some tablet PCs can be connected to a keyboard and a full-size ______________ .
   a. computer b. monitor c. PDA d. workstation
9. Network servers are sometimes set up in groups that may be called ______________ or server farms.
   a. units b. workgroups c. clusters d. racks
10. A(n) ______________ terminal can perform some processing operations.
   a. system b. input/output c. computing d. intelligent

Review Questions ::

In your own words, briefly answer the following questions.

1. What is a computer?
2. Explain a few of the different ways in which computers can be categorized.
3. List six types of computers that are designed for use by a single person.
4. Describe the two common designs for desktop computers.
5. How much do notebook computers typically weigh?
6. List four types of computers that are designed for use by organizations, and are commonly used by multiple people at the same time.
7. Why are mainframe systems usually limited in the number of tasks they perform?
8. What is the most popular use for home computers?
9. How are computer technologies used by the military?
10. How are computer technologies being used to train surgeons?

Lesson Labs ::

Complete the following exercises as directed by your instructor.

1. During the course of a normal day, keep a list of your encounters with computers of various kinds. Your list should show the place and time of the encounter, the type of interaction you had with the technology, and the results of that interaction. (Remember, computers can take many sizes and forms, so be alert to more than just PCs.) Share your list with the class.
2. Pay a visit to any business or government office in your town, and observe the people working there. Are they using computers? Simply by watching, can you tell what kinds of computers they are using and what types of work they are performing? In a single paragraph, list your findings and explain the reasoning behind them. Be prepared to share your findings with the class.

LESSON // 1B

Looking Inside the Computer System

OBJECTIVES ::

- List the four parts of a complete computer system.
- Name the four phases of the information processing cycle.
- Identify four categories of computer hardware.
- List four units of measure for computer memory and storage.
- Name the two most common input and output devices.
- Name and differentiate the two main categories of storage devices.
- Name and differentiate the two main categories of computer software.
- Explain the difference between data, information, and programs.
- Describe the role of the user, when working with a personal computer.

Overview: Dissecting the Ultimate Machine

Most people believe that computers must be extremely complicated devices, because they perform such amazing tasks. To an extent, this is true. As you will learn later in this book, the closer you look at a computer's operation, the more complex the system becomes.

But like any machine, a computer is a collection of parts, which are categorized according to the kinds of work they do. Although there are many, many variations on the parts themselves, there are only a few major categories. If you learn about those families of computer components and their basic functions, you will have mastered some of the most important concepts in computing. As you will see, the concepts are simple and easy to understand.

This lesson gives you a glimpse inside a standard desktop computer and introduces you to its most important parts. You will learn how these components work together and allow you to interact with the system. You also will discover the importance of software, without which a computer could do nothing. Finally, you will see that the user is (in most cases, at least) an essential part of a complete computer system.

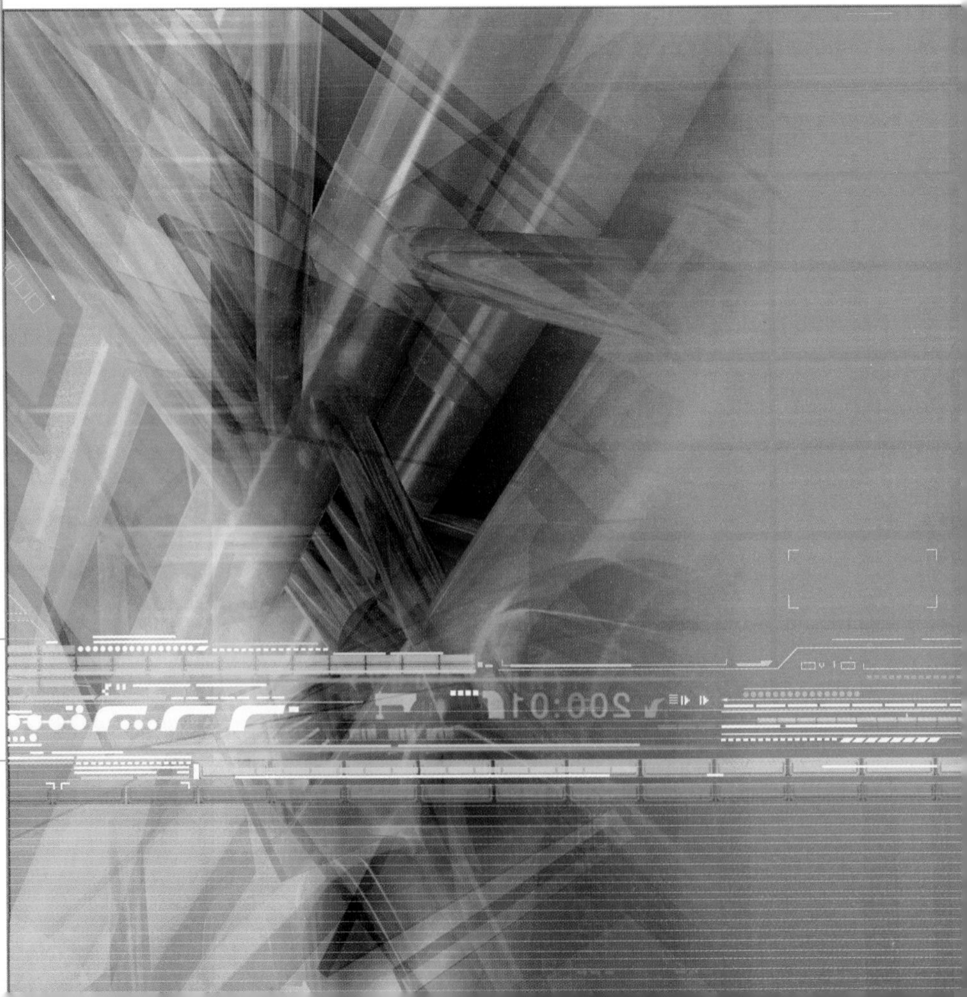

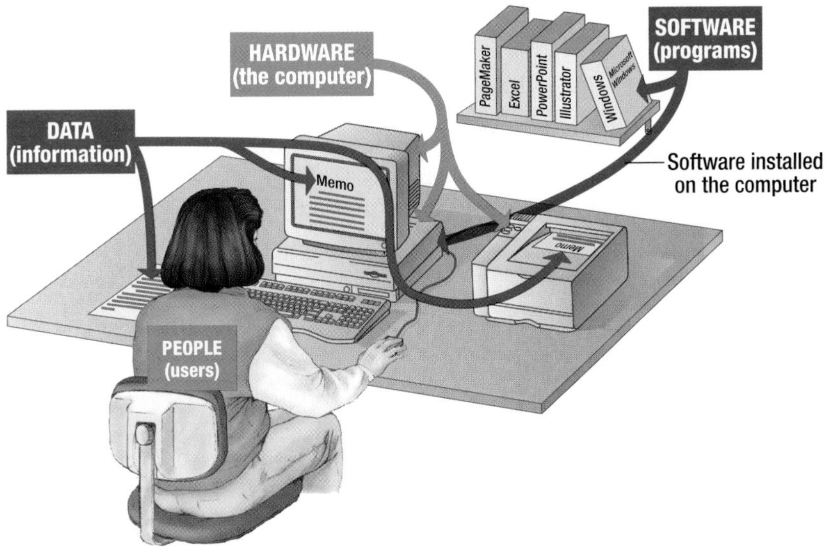

FIGURE 1B.1

A complete computer system.

The Parts of a Computer System

simnet™

As you saw in Lesson 1A, computers come in many varieties, from the tiny computers built into household appliances, to the astounding supercomputers that have helped scientists map the human genome. But no matter how big it is or how it is used, every computer is part of a system. A complete computer system consists of four parts (see Figure 1B.1):

- Hardware
- Software
- Data
- User

Hardware

The mechanical devices that make up the computer are called hardware. Hardware is any part of the computer you can touch (see Figure 1B.2). A computer's hardware consists of interconnected electronic devices that you can use to control the computer's operation, input, and output. (The generic term device refers to any piece of hardware.)

FIGURE 1B.2

Whether it's a keyboard, a printer, or a PDA, if you can touch it, it is hardware.

Software

Software is a set of instructions that makes the computer perform tasks. In other words, software tells the computer what to do. (The term program refers to any piece of software.) Some programs exist primarily for the computer's use to help it perform tasks and manage its own resources. Other types of programs exist for the user, enabling him or her to perform tasks such as creating documents. Thousands of different software programs are available for use on personal computers (see Figure 1B.3).

Data

Data consist of individual facts or pieces of information that by themselves may not make much sense to a person. A computer's primary job is to process these tiny pieces of data in various ways, converting them into useful information. For

FIGURE 1B.3

A visit to any software store reveals a dizzying variety of products.

example, if you saw the average highway mileages of six different cars, all the different pieces of data might not mean much to you. However, if someone created a chart from the data that visually compared and ranked the vehicles' mileages, you could probably make sense of it at a glance (see Figure 1B.4). This is one example of data being processed into useful information.

Users

People are the computer operators, also known as users. It can be argued that some computer systems are complete without a person's involvement; however, no computer is totally autonomous. Even if a computer can do its job without a person sitting in front of it, people still design, build, program, and repair computer systems. This lack of autonomy is especially true of personal computer systems, which are the focus of this book and are designed specifically for use by people.

Norton **ONLINE**

For more information on the information processing cycle, visit **http://www.mhhe.com/peternorton.**

simnet™

The Information Processing Cycle

Using all its parts together, a computer converts data into information by performing various actions on the data. For example, a computer might perform a mathematical operation on two numbers, then display the result. Or the computer might perform a logical operation such as comparing two numbers, then display that result. These operations are part of a process called the information processing cycle, which is a set of steps the computer follows to receive data, process the data according to instructions from a program, display the resulting information to the user, and store the results (see Figure 1B.5).

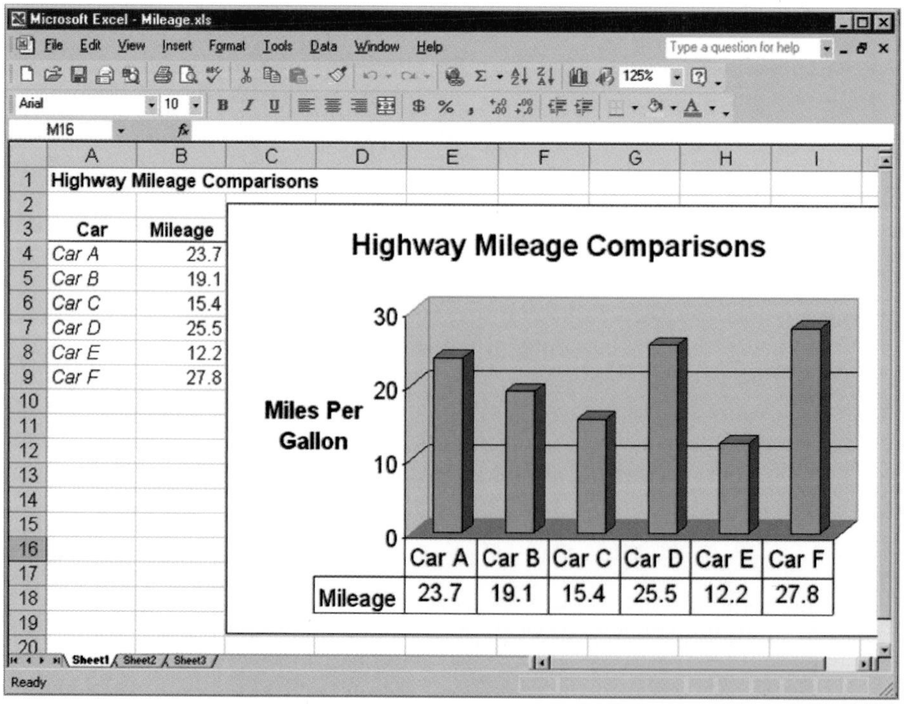

FIGURE 1B.4

Converting pieces of data into useful information is a key task of computers.

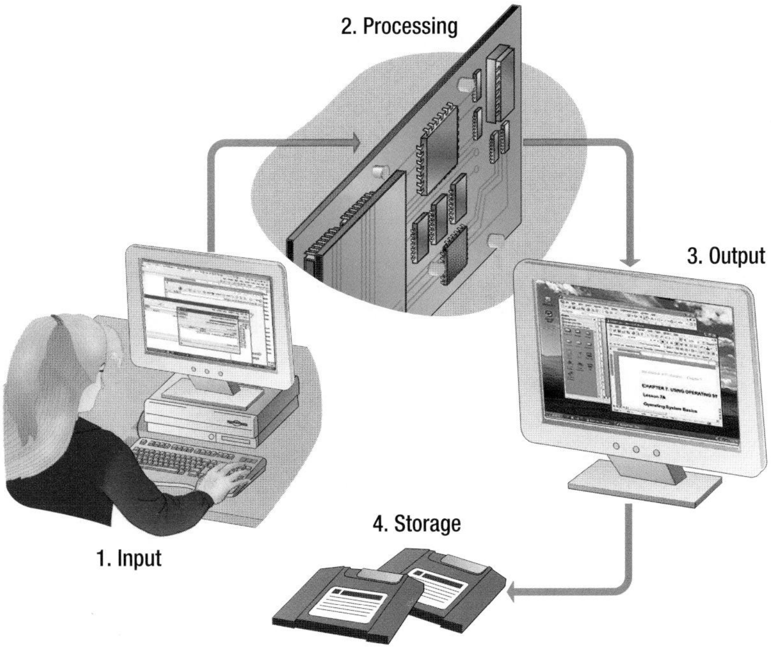

FIGURE 1B.5

The information processing cycle.

The information processing cycle has four parts, and each part involves one or more specific components of the computer:

» **Input.** During this part of the cycle, the computer accepts data from some source, such as the user or a program, for processing.
» **Processing.** During this part of the cycle, the computer's processing components perform actions on the data, based on instructions from the user or a program.
» **Output.** Here, the computer may be required to display the results of its processing. For example, the results may appear as text, numbers, or a graphic on the computer's screen or as sounds from its speaker. The computer also can send output to a printer or transfer the output to another computer through a network or the Internet. Output is an optional step in the information processing cycle but may be ordered by the user or program.
» **Storage.** In this step, the computer permanently stores the results of its processing on a disk, tape, or some other kind of storage medium. As with output, storage is optional and may not always be required by the user or program.

Essential Computer Hardware

simnet™

A computer's hardware devices fall into one of four categories (see Figure 1B.6):

1. Processor
2. Memory
3. Input and output
4. Storage

While any type of computer system contains these four types of hardware, this book focuses on them as they relate to the personal computer, or PC.

FIGURE 1B.6

Types of hardware devices.

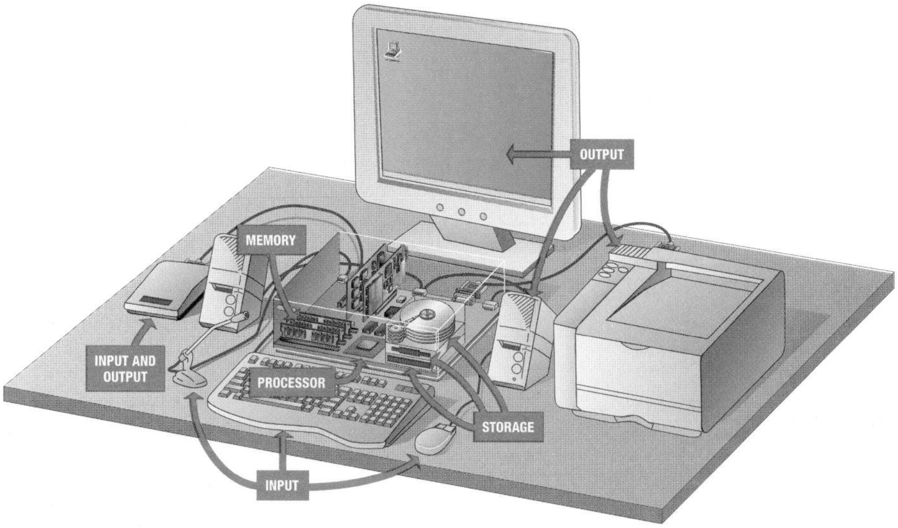

Norton ONLINE

For more information on computer processors, visit **http://www.mhhe.com/peternorton.**

Processing Devices

The procedure that transforms raw data into useful information is called processing. To perform this transformation, the computer uses two components: the processor and memory.

The processor is like the brain of the computer; it organizes and carries out instructions that come from either the user or the software. In a personal computer, the processor usually consists of one or more specialized chips, called microprocessors, which are slivers of silicon or other material etched with many tiny electronic circuits. To process data or complete an instruction from a user or a program, the computer passes electricity through the circuits.

FIGURE 1B.7

Processing devices.

As shown in Figure 1B.7, the microprocessor is plugged into the computer's motherboard. The motherboard is a rigid rectangular card containing the circuitry that connects the processor to the other hardware. The motherboard is an example of a circuit board. In most personal computers, many internal devices—such as video cards, sound cards, disk controllers, and other devices—are housed on their own smaller circuit boards, which attach to the motherboard. In many newer computers, these devices are built directly into the motherboard. Some newer microprocessors are large and complex enough to require their own dedicated circuit boards, which plug into a special slot in the motherboard. You can think of the motherboard as the master circuit board in a computer.

A personal computer's processor is usually a single chip or a set of chips contained on a circuit board. In some powerful computers, the processor consists of many chips and the circuit boards on which they are mounted. In either case, the term central processing unit (CPU) refers to a computer's processor (see Figure 1B.8). People often refer to computer systems by the type of CPU they contain. A "Pentium 4" system, for example, uses a Pentium 4 microprocessor as its CPU.

FIGURE 1B.8

Early PC microprocessors were not much larger than a thumbnail. Processors such as Intel's Pentium 4 are considerably larger.

Memory Devices

In a computer, memory is one or more sets of chips that store data and/or program instructions, either temporarily or permanently. Memory is a critical processing component in any computer. Personal computers use several different types of memory, but the two most important are called random access memory (RAM) and read-only memory (ROM). These two types of memory work in very different ways and perform distinct functions.

Norton ONLINE

For more information on computer memory, visit **http://www.mhhe.com/peternorton**.

Random Access Memory

The most common type of memory is called random access memory (RAM). As a result, the term *memory* is typically used to mean RAM. RAM is like an electronic scratch pad inside the computer. RAM holds data and program instructions while the CPU works with them. When a program is launched, it is loaded into and run from memory. As the program needs data, it is loaded into memory for fast access. As new data is entered into the computer, it is also stored in memory—but only temporarily. Data is both written to and read from this memory. (Because of this, RAM is also sometimes called *read/write memory*.)

Like many computer components, RAM is made up of a set of chips mounted on a small circuit board (see Figure 1B.9).

FIGURE 1B.9

Random access memory (RAM).

RAM is volatile, meaning that it loses its contents when the computer is shut off or if there is a power failure. Therefore, RAM needs a constant supply of power to hold its data. For this reason, you should save your data files to a storage device frequently, to avoid losing them in a power failure. (You will learn more about storage later in this chapter.)

RAM has a tremendous impact on the speed and power of a computer. Generally, the more RAM a computer has, the more it can do and the faster it can perform certain tasks. The most common measurement unit for describing a computer's memory is the byte—the amount of memory it takes to store a single character, such as a letter of the alphabet or a numeral. When referring to a computer's memory, the numbers are often so large that it is helpful to use terms such as kilobyte (KB), megabyte (MB), gigabyte (GB), and terabyte (TB) to describe the values (see Table 1B.1).

Today's personal computers generally have at least 256 million bytes (256 MB) of random access memory. Many newer systems feature 512 MB or more.

TABLE 1B.1

Units of Measure for Computer Memory and Storage

Unit	Abbreviation	Pronounced	Approximate Value (bytes)	Actual Value (bytes)
Kilobyte	KB	KILL-uh-bite	1,000	1,024
Megabyte	MB	MEHG-uh-bite	1,000,000 (1 million)	1,048,576
Gigabyte	GB	GIG-uh-bite	1,000,000,000 (1 billion)	1,073,741,824
Terabyte	TB	TERR-uh-bite	1,000,000,000,000 (1 trillion)	1,099,511,627,776

Read-Only Memory

Unlike RAM, read-only memory (ROM) permanently stores its data, even when the computer is shut off. ROM is called nonvolatile memory because it never loses its contents. ROM holds instructions that the computer needs to operate. Whenever the computer's power is turned on, it checks ROM for directions that help it start up, and for information about its hardware devices.

Norton ONLINE

For more information on input and output devices, visit **http://www.mhhe.com/peternorton.**

Input and Output Devices

A personal computer would be useless if you could not interact with it because the machine could not receive instructions or deliver the results of its work. Input devices accept data and instructions from the user or from another computer system (such as a computer on the Internet). Output devices return processed data to the user or to another computer system.

The most common input device is the keyboard, which accepts letters, numbers, and commands from the user. Another important type of input device is the mouse, which lets you select options from on-screen menus. You use a mouse by moving it across a flat surface and pressing its buttons. Figure 1B.10 shows a personal computer with a keyboard, mouse, and microphone.

A variety of other input devices work with personal computers, too:

- The trackball and touchpad are variations of the mouse and enable you to draw or point on the screen.
- The joystick is a swiveling lever mounted on a stationary base that is well suited for playing video games.
- A scanner can copy a printed page of text or a graphic into the computer's memory, freeing you from creating the data from scratch.
- A digital camera can record still images, which you can view and edit on the computer.
- A microphone enables you to input your voice or music as data.

FIGURE 1B.10

The keyboard, mouse, and microphone are common input devices.

The function of an output device is to present processed data to the user. The most common output devices are the monitor and the printer. The computer sends output to the monitor (the display screen) when the user needs only to see the output. It sends output to the printer when the user requests a paper copy—also called a *hard copy*—of a document.

Just as computers can accept sound as input, they can use stereo speakers or headphones as output devices to produce sound. Figure 1B.11 shows a PC with a monitor, printer, and speakers.

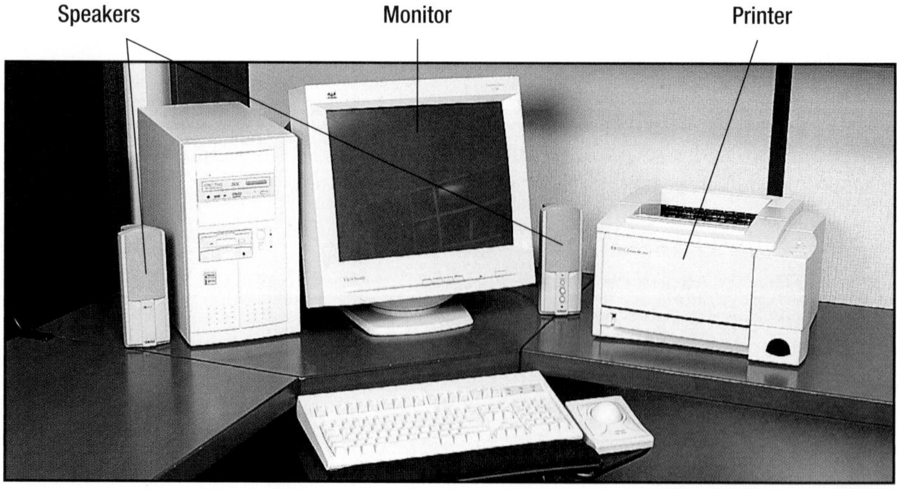

FIGURE 1B.11

The monitor, printer, and speakers are common output devices.

Some types of hardware can act as both input and output devices. A touch screen, for example, is a type of monitor that displays text or icons you can touch. When you touch the screen, special sensors detect the touch and the computer calculates the point on the screen where you placed your finger. Depending on the location of the touch, the computer determines what information to display or what action to take next.

Communications devices are the most common types of devices that can perform both input and output. These devices connect one computer to another—a process known as networking. The most common kinds of communications devices are modems, which enable computers to communicate through telephone lines or cable television systems, and network interface cards (NICs), which let users connect a group of computers to share data and devices.

Storage Devices

A computer can function with only processing, memory, input, and output devices. To be really useful, however, a computer also needs a place to keep program files and related data when they are not in use. The purpose of storage is to hold data permanently, even when the computer is turned off.

You may think of storage as an electronic file cabinet and RAM as an electronic worktable. When you need to work with a program or a set of data, the computer locates it in the file cabinet and puts a copy on the table. After you have finished working with the program or data, you put it back into the file cabinet. The changes you make to data while working on it replace the original data in the file cabinet (unless you store it in a different place).

Novice computer users often confuse storage with memory. Although the functions of storage and memory are similar, they work in different ways. There are three major distinctions between storage and memory:

- There is more room in storage than in memory, just as there is more room in a file cabinet than there is on a tabletop.
- Contents are retained in storage when the computer is turned off, whereas programs or the data in memory disappear when you shut down the computer.
- Storage devices operate much slower than memory chips, but storage is much cheaper than memory.

There are two main types of computer storage: magnetic and optical. Both are covered in the following sections.

Norton ONLINE

For more information on storage devices, visit **http://www.mhhe.com/peternorton**.

Magnetic Storage

There are many types of computer storage, but the most common is the magnetic disk. A disk is a round, flat object that spins around its center. (Magnetic disks are almost always housed inside a case of some kind, so you can't see the disk itself unless you open the case.) Read/write heads, which work in much the same way as the heads of a tape recorder or VCR, are used to read data from the disk or write data onto the disk.

The device that holds a disk is called a disk drive. Some disks are built into the drive and are not meant to be removed; other kinds of drives enable you to remove and replace disks (see Figure 1B.12). Most personal computers have at least one nonremovable hard disk (or hard drive). In addition, there is also a diskette drive, which allows you to use removable diskettes (or floppy disks). The hard disk serves as the computer's primary filing cabinet because it can store far more data than a diskette can contain. Diskettes are used to load data onto the hard disk, to trade data with other users, and to make backup copies of the data on the hard disk.

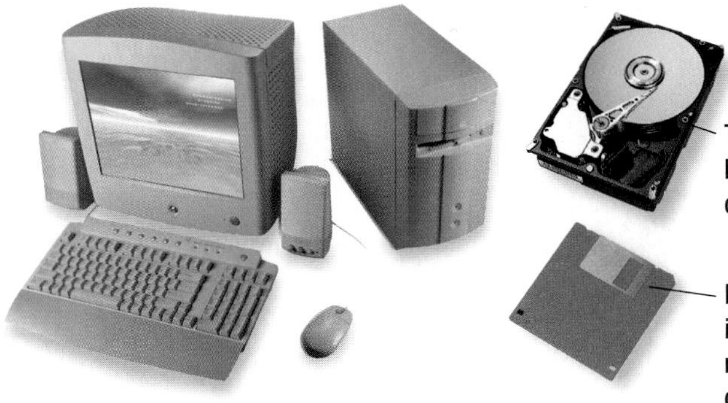
The hard disk is built into the computer's case.
Diskettes can be inserted into and removed from the diskette drive.

FIGURE 1B.12

Standard PCs have a built-in hard disk and a diskette drive.

Optical Storage

In addition to magnetic storage, nearly every computer sold today includes at least one form of optical storage—devices that use lasers to read data from or write data to the reflective surface of an optical disc.

The CD-ROM drive is the most common type of optical storage device. Compact discs (CDs) are a type of optical storage, identical to audio CDs. Until recently, a standard CD could store about 74 minutes of audio or 650 MB of data. A newer breed of CDs can hold 80 minutes of audio or 700 MB of data (see Figure 1B.13). The type used in computers is called Compact Disc Read-Only Memory (CD-ROM). As the name implies, you cannot change the information on the disc, just as you cannot record over an audio CD.

Microsoft
Office
Professional Edition 2003
Microsoft

FIGURE 1B.13

Software makers commonly sell their products on CD because of the disc's high storage capacity.

If you purchase a CD-Recordable (CD-R) drive, you have the option of creating your own CDs. A CD-R drive can write data to and read data from a compact disc. To record data with a CD-R drive, you must use a special CD-R disc, which can be written on only once, or a CD-ReWritable (CD-RW) disc, which can be written to multiple times, like a floppy disk.

An increasingly popular data storage technology is the Digital Video Disc (DVD), which is revolutionizing home entertainment. Using sophisticated compression technologies, a single DVD (which is the same size as a standard compact disc) can store an entire full-length movie. DVDs can hold a minimum of 4.7 GB of data and as much as 17 GB. Future DVD technologies promise much higher storage capacities on a single disc. DVD drives also can locate data on the disc much faster than standard CD-ROM drives.

DVDs require a special player (see Figure 1B.14). Many DVD players, however, can play audio, data, and DVD discs, freeing the user from purchasing different players for each type of disc. DVD drives are now standard equipment on many new personal computers. Users not only can install programs and data from their standard CDs, but they also can watch movies on their personal computers by using a DVD.

simnet™

Software Brings the Machine to Life

The ingredient that enables a computer to perform a specific task is software, which consists of instructions. A set of instructions that drive a computer to perform specific tasks is called a program. These instructions tell the machine's physical components what to do; without the instructions, a computer could not do anything at all. When a computer uses a particular program, it is said to be running or executing that program.

Although the array of available programs is vast and varied, most software falls into two major categories: system software and application software.

@ Norton ONLINE

For more information on computer software, visit **http://www.mhhe.com/peternorton**.

System Software

System software is any program that controls the computer's hardware or that can be used to maintain the computer in some way so that it runs more efficiently. There are three basic types of system software:

- An operating system tells the computer how to use its own components. Examples of operating systems include Windows, the Macintosh Operating System, and Linux (see Figure 1B.15). An operating system is essential for any computer, because it acts as an interpreter between the hardware, application programs, and the user.

  When a program wants the hardware to do something, it communicates through the operating system. Similarly, when you want the hardware to do something (such as copying or printing a file), your request is handled by the operating system.
- A network operating system allows computers to communicate and share data across a network while controlling network operations and overseeing the network's security.
- A utility is a program that makes the computer system easier to use or performs highly specialized functions (see Figure 1B.16). Utilities are used to manage disks, troubleshoot hardware problems, and perform other tasks that the operating system itself may not be able to do.

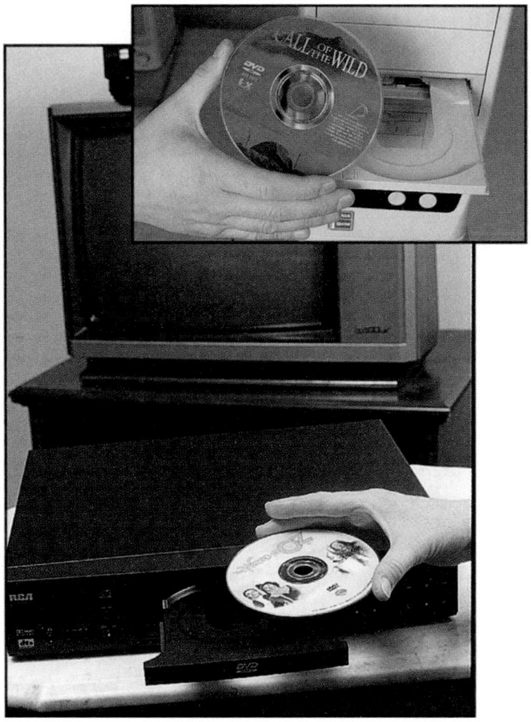

FIGURE 1B.14

DVD players are now standard on many PCs and are found in many home entertainment centers.

Application Software

Application software tells the computer how to accomplish specific tasks, such as word processing or drawing, for the user. Thousands of applications are available for many purposes and for people of all ages. Some of the major categories of these applications include

- Word processing software for creating text-based documents such as newsletters or brochures (see Figure 1B.17).
- Spreadsheets for creating numeric-based documents such as budgets or balance sheets.

FIGURE 1B.15

Windows is the most popular of all PC operating systems, running on about 90 percent of all personal computers.

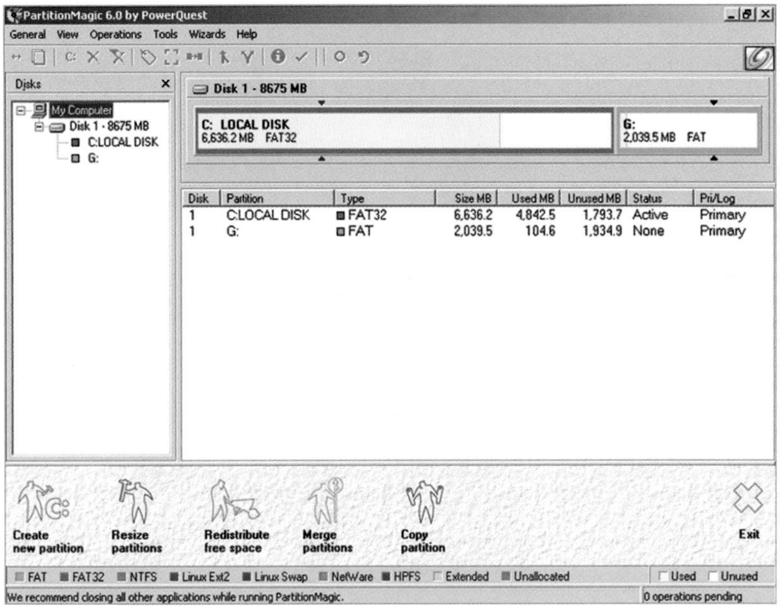

FIGURE 1B.16

There are hundreds of utility programs available for personal computers. This one, called PartitionMagic, helps you manage your hard disk to get the most from it.

simnet™

- Database management software for building and manipulating large sets of data, such as the names, addresses, and phone numbers in a telephone directory.
- Presentation programs for creating and presenting electronic slide shows (see Figure 1B.18).
- Graphics programs for designing illustrations or manipulating photographs, movies, or animation.
- Multimedia authoring applications for building digital movies that incorporate sound, video, animation, and interactive features.
- Entertainment and education software, many of which are interactive multimedia events.
- Web design tools and Web browsers, and other Internet applications such as newsreaders and e-mail programs.
- Games, some of which are for a single player and many of which can be played by several people over a network or the Internet.

Computer Data

You have already seen that, to a computer, data is any piece of information or fact that, taken by itself, may not make sense to a person. For example, you might think of the letters of the alphabet as data. Taken individually, they do not mean a lot. But when grouped into words and sentences, they make sense; that is, they become information (see Figure 1B.19). Similarly, basic geometric shapes may not have much meaning by themselves, but when they are grouped into a blueprint or a chart, they become useful information.

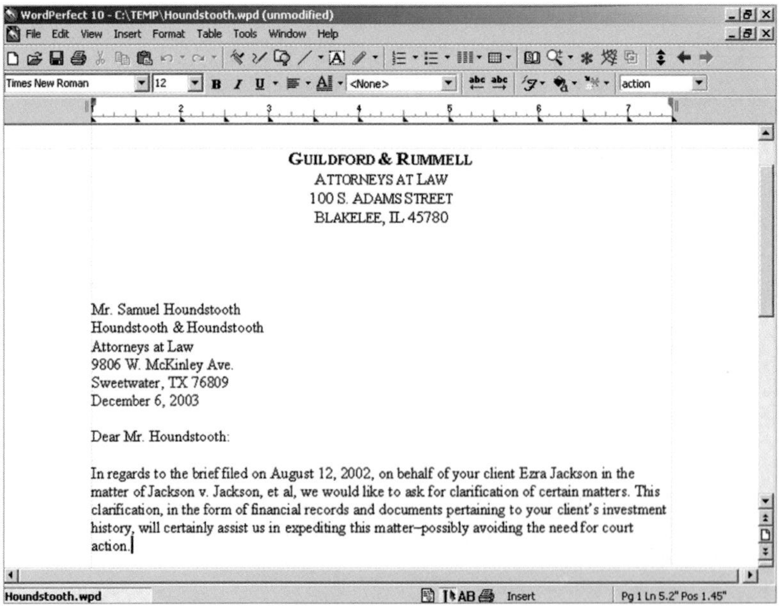

FIGURE 1B.17

Word processing software is designed for creating documents that consist primarily of text, but also lets you add graphics and sounds to your documents. It also provides layout features that let you create brochures, newsletters, Web pages, and more.

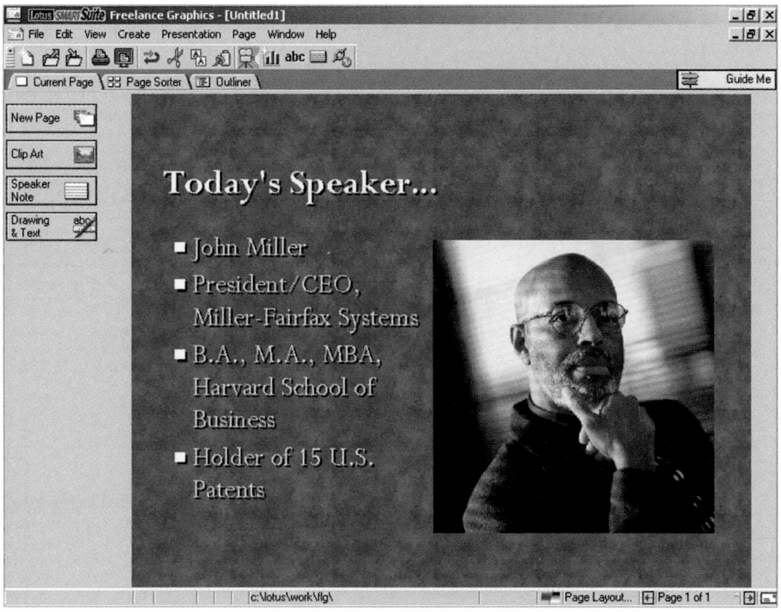

FIGURE 1B.18

Presentation software is most often used for creating sales presentations, although it can be effective for any type of electronic slide show.

A	B	C	D
E	F	G	H
I	J	K	L
M	N	O	P
Q	R	S	T
U	V	W	X
Y	Z		

Data = Piece of information without context

RESUME

Johnathon Smith — 704-555-5555
1512 N. Main Street — smith@try.net
Troy, NC 28265 — www.jon.com

Objective

A career as a sales associate with a leading grocery chain

Education

- Ph.D, Nuclear Phsyics, *Massachussetts Institute of Technology*, 1998.
- M.S., Physics, *Duke University*, 1996
- B.S., Chemistry/Physics, *Center College*, 1994

Maintained average GPA of 3.8 during collegiate career.

Experience

2000 – Present. Head Bag Boy, *Tom's QuickShop*, Cambriage City, IN
1999 – 2000. Bag Boy, *The Village Pantry*, Nitro, W.V.
1998 – 1999. Assistant Janitor, *McCreary County Jail*, Whitley City, KY

Special Skills

- Expert in the programming of differential analysers
- Proficient at operation of particle accelerators
- Developed method for creating anti-matter in standard household bathroom

References

Available on request.

Information = Data placed in context

FIGURE 1B.19

A piece of data, like a letter of the alphabet, has little meaning by itself. When pieces of data are combined and placed in some sort of context, such as a resume, they become meaningful information.

At Issue

Computerized Disease Management

Despite the abundance of widely recognized, evidence-based standards, health care is notoriously inconsistent from one doctor to the next, one hospital to the next, and one region to the next. So much so, that the experts at the National Academies Institute of Medicine have proclaimed it to be a health system quality chasm.

Through the use of global information technology, new technology-driven disease management systems are offering the health care industry a solution to the high variability of practice. Interactive computerized disease management programs promise to close this "quality chasm."

The goal of interactive computerized disease management (DM) programs is to monitor patients with chronic diseases such as heart disease or diabetes, track their progress, and encourage compliance with medical best practices. Through wireless telephony or Web interfaces, patients report vital signs, symptoms, and other medical information to their caregivers. In some cases, patients are hooked up to remote monitoring devices that automatically transmit information to a physician or medical database. Case managers then monitor patient data, looking for early problems and intervening before costly emergencies arise.

Computerized DM systems have been shown to facilitate communication between patients and health care providers, cut health care costs, and improve quality of care.

One leading provider of these systems is LifeMasters Supported SelfCare, Inc. LifeMasters offers high-tech DM programs that create cooperative health partnerships among patients, physicians, and payors.

With the LifeMasters program, computers monitor disease across large patient groups; report patient status to doctors and their clinical teams; send reminders when patients are due for testing, evaluation, and treatment; and track the outcomes to support improvement and continuity of care. LifeMasters claims their computerized information technology system improves quality of life for individuals with chronic illnesses, supports physicians with improved disease management tools, and reduces chronic-disease costs for payors.

Headquartered in Irvine, California, LifeMasters currently provides disease management services for more than 275,000 patients with diabetes, congestive heart failure, coronary artery disease, chronic obstructive pulmonary disease, hypertension, and asthma in all 50 states, the District of Columbia, and Puerto Rico.

Taking the computerized disease management model one step further, LifeMasters also maintains the LifeMasters Online Web site, the first fully interactive health monitoring and management service for individual use.

SELF-CHECK ::

Circle the correct answer for each question.

1. There is more room in storage than in ____________ in a computer.
   a. the processor **b.** memory **c.** the workspace
2. A device that holds a disk is called a ____________ .
   a. drive **b.** ROM **c.** memory
3. ____________ software is used for tasks such as managing disks and troubleshooting hardware problems.
   a. Application **b.** Operating system **c.** Utility

The computer reads and stores data of all kinds—whether words, numbers, images, or sounds—in the form of numbers. Consequently, computerized data is **digital**, meaning that it has been reduced to digits, or numbers. This is because the computer can work only with strings of numbers (see Figure 1B.20). Just as people represent their own language by using strings of letters to make up words and sentences, computers use strings of numbers to represent every type of data they must handle. (You will learn more about this in Chapter 5, "Processing Data.") Following instructions from the software and the user, the computer manipulates data by performing calculations, doing comparisons, or arranging the bits of information so they make sense to the user.

Just as computer data is different from information, it also differs from programs. Recall that a software program is a set of instructions that tells the

LifeMasters Online offers health management tools and content similar to those offered through LifeMasters' caregiver-supervised model, but it is available free to the general public. Here, users enter their own vital-sign and symptom information via the Web site or through a Touch-Tone phone. The information goes into a database and, when the data indicate that medical intervention is required, the patient's physician is notified.

Patients have access to support groups and medical information on a 24 × 7 basis. LifeMasters Online also provides self-directed health education and behavior modification modules addressing health concerns such as diet, exercise, and smoking cessation.

"We built this for the future," says Christobel Selecky, LifeMasters CEO. "As the Baby Boom generation ages and develops chronic diseases, we're going to need to use technology tools to help physicians and their patients manage their health care more effectively and efficiently than in traditional ways."

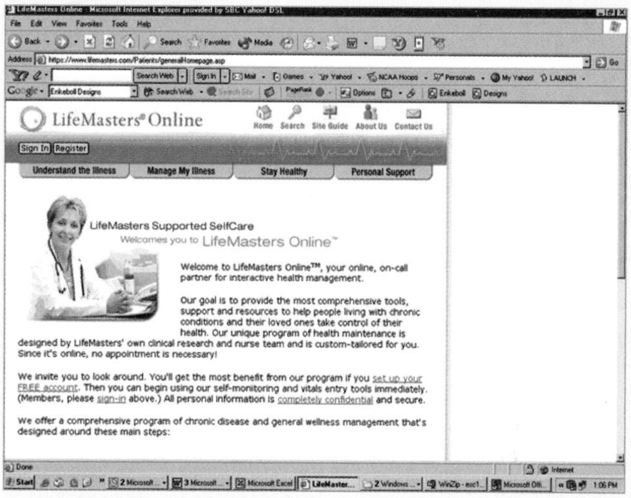

AT ISSUE

computer how to perform tasks. Like data, these instructions exist as strings of numbers so the computer can use them. But the resemblance ends there. You can think of the difference between data and programs this way: data is for people to use, but programs are for computers to use.

Within the computer, data is organized into files. A file is simply a set of data that has been given a name. A file that the user can open and use is often called a document. Although many people think of documents simply as text, a computer document can include many kinds of data (see Figure 1B.21). For example, a computer document can be a text file (such as a letter), a group of numbers (such as a budget), a video clip (which includes images and sounds), or any combination of these items. Programs are organized into files as well; these files contain the instructions and data that a program needs in order to run and perform tasks.

0001010010110101010101010111
1110110101010101010110110001
00110101100010101011100010
10101000011011011100101101
01010100110011001001011010
01010100101010100010110010
10110010101010001010111010
11010011110000101010111010
01001011010010110100110110

FIGURE 1B.20

If you could see data as the computer does, it would look something like this.

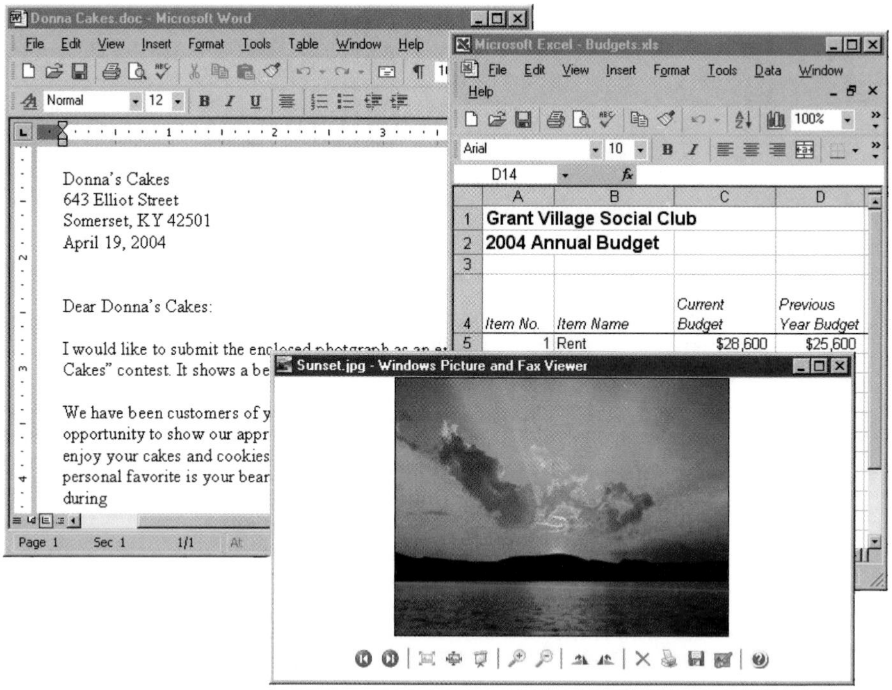

FIGURE 1B.21

A letter, a budget, a picture—each one is an example of a document that a person can use.

FIGURE 1B.22

Even the most powerful computers require human interaction to perform their tasks.

Computer Users

Personal computers, which are the focus of this book, are designed to work with a human user. In fact, the user is a critical part of a complete computer system, especially when a personal computer is involved.

This may seem surprising, since we tend to think of computers as intelligent devices, capable of performing amazing tasks. People also sometimes believe that computers can think and make decisions, just like humans do. But this is not the case. Even the most powerful supercomputers require human interaction—if for no other reason than to get them started and tell them which problems to solve (see Figure 1B.22).

The User's Role

When working with a personal computer, the user can take on several roles, depending on what he or she wants to accomplish:

- **Setting up the System.** Have you ever bought a new PC? When you got it home, you probably had to unpack it, set it up, and make sure it worked as expected (see Figure 1B.23). If you want to change something about the system (a process called configuration), you will likely do it yourself, whether you want to add a new hardware device, change the way programs look on your screen, or customize the way a program functions.
- **Installing Software.** Although your new computer probably came with an operating system and some applications installed, you need to install any other programs you want to use. This may involve loading software from a disk or downloading it from a Web site. Either way, it is usually the user's responsibility to install programs, unless the computer is used at a school or business. In that case, a system administrator or technician may be available to do the job.

- **Running Programs.** Whenever your computer is on, there are several programs running in the background, such as the software that runs your mouse and printer. Such programs do not need any user input; in fact, you may not even be aware of them. But for the most part, if you want to use your computer to perform a task, you need to launch and run the software that is designed for the task. This means installing the program, learning its tools, and working with it to make sure it gives you the results you want.

FIGURE 1B.23

Setting up a new computer is usually the user's job.

- **Managing Files.** As you have already learned, a computer saves data in files. If you write a letter to a friend, you can save it as a file, making it available to open and use again later. Pictures, songs, and other kinds of data are stored as files. But it is the user's job to manage these files, and this means setting up a logical system for storing them on the computer. It also means knowing when to delete or move files, or copy them to a disk for safekeeping.
- **Maintaining the System.** System maintenance does not necessarily mean opening the PC and fixing broken parts, as you would repair a car's engine. But it could! In that case, you might call a qualified technician to do the job, or roll up your sleeves and tackle it yourself. PC maintenance, however, generally means running utilities that keep the disks free of clutter and ensure that the computer is making the best use of its resources.

"Userless" Computers

Of course, there are many kinds of computers that require no human interaction, once they have been programmed, installed, and started up. For example, if you own a car that was built within the last decade, it almost certainly has an on-board computer that controls and monitors engine functions (see Figure 1B.24). Many new home appliances, such as washers and dryers, have built-in computers that monitor water usage, drying times, balance, and other operations. Sophisticated userless computers operate security systems, navigation systems, communications systems, and many others.

Userless computers are typically controlled by their operating systems. In these devices, the operating system may be installed on special memory chips rather than a disk. The operating system is programmed to perform a specific set of tasks, such as monitoring a function or checking for a failure, and little else. These systems are not set up for human interaction, except as needed for system configuration or maintenance.

FIGURE 1B.24

A car's on-board computer not only controls some engine functions, but communicates with diagnostic systems to help technicians identify and repair problems with the vehicle.

Computers In Your Career

Using Computers Outside of the IT Industry

Few hardwood products manufacturers can boast an e-commerce-enabled Web site where customers view catalogs, place orders, track orders, and review their account history 24 hours a day, seven days a week. Even fewer can offer customers a solution that uses computer modeling and simulation techniques to recreate "real world" projects in a virtual environment.

Thanks to the efforts of Richard Enriquez, Enkeboll Designs of Carson, California, can boast that and more in an industry where manufacturing and related processes remain largely manual and labor-intensive. "No one else offers e-commerce capabilities in our category," said Richard Enriquez, director of marketing, who envisions a time when the firm's woodcarvers will be able to use a computer to go from concept to finished product without ever having to touch a piece of wood or a chisel.

Having worked in the software development industry for 15 years, Enriquez aspires to use technology to bring more value to the customers while also making Enkeboll Designs' architectural woodcarving manufacturing process more efficient and productive. In 2003, for example, he spearheaded the conversion of the entire product line into three-dimensional formats that can be used in conjunction with commercial and residential previsualization applications to minimize specification errors.

Enriquez, who earned a Bachelor of Science degree from DeVry University, handles myriad tasks at Enkeboll Designs, including managing internal and external staff associated with marketing and new product development, evaluating technologies, reviewing strategic relationships, and overseeing the development of the company's Web site. He works 50 to 55 hours a week and enjoys the challenge of incorporating technology into a company that has traditionally conducted business utilizing traditional methods.

"When the company wanted to start leveraging technology, they hired me," says Enriquez. "Before I came on board, the company was very traditional and didn't believe, for example, in putting e-commerce capabilities on the Web site." One year later, Enriquez says the naysayers wouldn't have it any other way. "It all boils down to results."

Enriquez says opportunities for IT professionals in the non-IT space are plentiful. One need only look around the business world to see how technology is making an impact in the most unlikely occupations, such as

- **Restaurant and Grocery Store Managers.** Restaurants, grocery stores, and retail outlet managers use computer systems of all kinds—from handheld units to mainframes—to monitor inventories, track transactions, and manage product pricing.

- » **Courier Dispatchers.** Courier services of all types use computerized terminals to help dispatchers schedule deliveries, locate pickup and drop-off points, generate invoices, and track the location of packages.
- » **Construction Managers.** Construction managers and estimators use specialized software to analyze construction documents and to calculate the amount of materials and time required to complete a job.
- » **Automotive Mechanics.** Automotive mechanics and technicians use computer systems to measure vehicle performance, diagnose mechanical problems, and determine maintenance or repair strategies.

Each of the following chapters in this textbook features a discussion of computers in the professional world. Each discussion focuses on the type of technology introduced in that unit and is designed to help you understand how that particular technology is used in one or more professions.

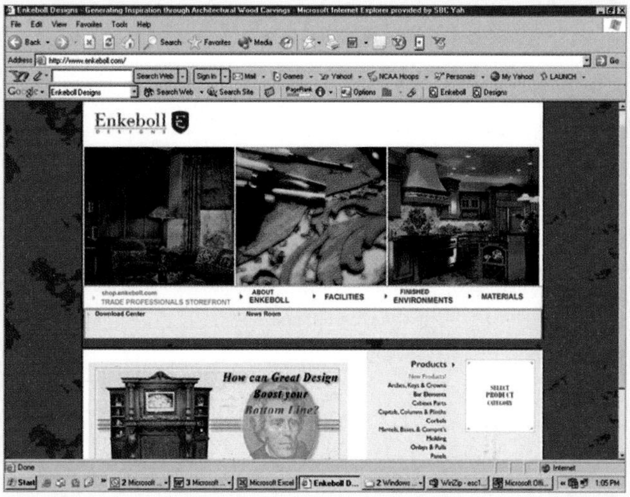

LESSON // 1B Review

Summary ::

- A complete computer system includes hardware, software, data, and users.
- Hardware consists of electronic devices, the parts you can touch.
- Software (programs) consists of instructions that control the computer.
- Data can be text, numbers, sounds, and images that the computer manipulates.
- People who operate computers are called users.
- To manipulate data, the computer follows a process called the information processing cycle, which includes data input, processing, output, and storage.
- A computer's hardware devices fall into four categories: processing, memory, input and output (I/O), and storage.
- The processing function is divided between the processor and memory.
- The processor, or CPU, carries out instructions from the user and software.
- Random access memory (RAM) holds data and program instructions as the CPU works with them.
- The most common units of measure for memory are the byte, kilobyte, megabyte, gigabyte, and terabyte.
- Read-only memory (ROM) is another important type of memory, which holds instructions that help the computer start up and information about its hardware.
- The role of input devices is to accept instructions and data from the user or another computer.
- Output devices present processed data to the user or to another computer.
- Communications devices perform both input and output functions, allowing computers to share information.
- Storage devices hold data and programs permanently, even when the computer is turned off.
- The two primary categories of storage devices are magnetic storage and optical storage.
- The two primary categories of software are system software and application software.
- The operating system tells the computer how to interact with the user and how to use the hardware devices attached to the computer.
- Application software tells the computer how to accomplish tasks the user requires.
- In a computer, data consists of small pieces of information that, by themselves, may not make sense to a person. The computer manipulates data into useful information.
- Program instructions are different from data, in that they are used only by the computer and not by people.
- A user is an essential part of a complete personal computer system. Generally, the user must perform a wide range of tasks, such as setting up the system, installing software, managing files, and other operations that the computer cannot do by itself.
- Some computers are designed to function independently, without a user, but these systems are not personal computers.

Key Terms ::

application software, 33
byte, 29
CD-Recordable (CD-R), 32
CD-ReWritable (CD-RW), 32
CD-ROM drive, 32
central processing unit (CPU), 28
circuit board, 28
communications device, 31
compact disc (CD), 32
Compact Disc Read-Only Memory (CD-ROM), 32
computer system, 25
data, 25
device, 25
digital, 36
digital camera, 30
Digital Video Disc (DVD), 32
disk drive, 31
diskette, 31
diskette drive, 31
document, 37
execute, 32
file, 37
floppy disk, 31
gigabyte (GB), 29
hard disk, 31
hard drive, 31
hardware, 25
information processing cycle, 26
input device, 30
joystick, 30
keyboard, 30
kilobyte (KB), 29
magnetic disk, 31
megabyte (MB), 29
memory, 29
microphone, 30
microprocessor, 28
monitor, 30
motherboard, 28
mouse, 30
network operating system, 33
nonvolatile, 29
operating system, 33
optical storage, 32
output device, 30
printer, 30
processing, 28
processor, 28
program, 25
random access memory (RAM), 29
read/write head, 31
read-only memory (ROM), 29
run, 32
scanner, 30
software, 25
storage, 31
system software, 33
terabyte (TB), 29
touch screen, 31
touchpad, 30
trackball, 30
user, 26
utility, 33
volatile, 29

Key Term Quiz ::

Complete each statement by writing one of the terms listed under Key Terms in each blank.

1. A complete ______________ refers to the combination of hardware, software, data, and people.
2. A(n) ______________ is a set of data or program instructions that has been given a name.
3. A(n) ______________ is a device that holds a disk.
4. Electronic instructions that tell the computer's hardware what to do are known as ______________ .
5. The generic term ______________ refers to a piece of hardware.
6. Data and program instructions are temporarily held in ______________ while the processor is using them.
7. The ______________ includes four stages: input, processing, output, and storage.
8. One ______________ is roughly equivalent to one million bytes of data.
9. Operating systems fall into the category of ______________ software.
10. In a magnetic disk drive, a special device called the ______________ reads data from and writes data to a disk's surface.

LESSON // 1B Review

Multiple Choice ::

Circle the word or phrase that best completes each statement.

1. Which of the following devices stores instructions that help the computer start up?
   a. joystick b. RAM c. ROM d. monitor
2. A __________ can perform both input and output functions.
   a. trackball b. microphone c. communications device d. CPU
3. Which type of software would you use to make the computer perform a specific task, such as writing a letter or drawing a picture?
   a. application software b. utility software c. operating system software d. system software
4. Which of the following units represents the largest amount of data?
   a. kilobyte b. terabyte c. gigabyte d. megabyte
5. You can use this output device when you need only to see information.
   a. printer b. speaker c. monitor d. communications
6. Generally, a __________ cannot be removed from the computer.
   a. mouse b. keyboard c. diskette d. hard disk
7. A file that the user can open and use is called a(n) __________.
   a. application b. document c. program d. data
8. Because computer data has been reduced to numbers, it is described as being __________.
   a. digital b. numeric c. information d. processed
9. Which type of disk can store up to 17 gigabytes of data?
   a. floppy disk b. compact disc c. optical disc d. digital video disc
10. Which type of software is used for creating slide shows?
    a. Web design software b. presentation software c. word-processing software d. spreadsheet software

Review Questions ::

In your own words, briefly answer the following questions.

1. List the four parts of a complete computer system.
2. What are the four phases of the information processing cycle?
3. Identify four categories of computer hardware.
4. List four units of measure for computer memory and storage, not including the byte.
5. What are the two most common input and output devices?
6. Name and differentiate the two main categories of storage devices.
7. Name and differentiate the two main categories of computer software.
8. What is the difference between data and information?
9. What is a fundamental difference between data and programs?
10. List five tasks a user may be responsible for, when working with a personal computer.

Lesson Labs ::

Complete the following exercises as directed by your instructor.

1. What type of computer system do you use in class or in the lab? How much can you tell about the system by looking at it? List as much information as you can about the computer. Is it a desktop or tower model? What brand is it? What type of processor does it have? What are the model and serial numbers? What external devices does it have? Is it connected to a network or printer?
2. What kind of software is installed on your computer? To find out, all you have to do is turn on your computer. After it starts, you should see a collection of icons—small pictures that represent the programs and other resources on your computer. List the icons that appear on your screen and the names of the software programs they represent.

Chapter Labs

Complete the following exercises using a computer in your classroom, lab, or home.

1. Get some help. If you do not know how to perform a task on your computer, turn to its online help system for answers and assistance. Browse your operating system's help system to learn more about your computer. (This activity assumes you use Windows XP. If you use a different operating system, ask your instructor for assistance.)
   a. Click the Start button on the Windows taskbar to open the Start menu.
   b. On the Start menu, click Help and Support. The Help and Support Center window opens.
   c. Under Pick a Help Topic, click the Windows Basics link. When the list of Windows basics topics appears in the next window, click any two of the topics and read the information that appears on your screen.
   d. Close the Help window by clicking the Close button (with an X on it) in the upper-right corner of the window.
2. Explore your disk. Once you are familiar with your computer's hardware, it is time to see the folders and files that reside on its hard disk. To see what is on your disk, take these steps:
   a. Minimize or close all running program windows, so you can see the Windows desktop.
   b. On the desktop, double-click the My Computer icon. The My Computer window opens, listing all the disks on your computer.
   c. Double-click the icon labeled LOCAL DISK (C:) to open a window displaying that disk's contents.
   d. Double-click at least five of the folders and review the contents of each one. Can you tell which files are data files and which are program files?
   e. When you finish exploring your disk, close all open windows.
3. Learn more about browsers. There are many different Web browsers available, and you may decide you like one of the lesser-known browsers better than the most popular ones. The following Web sites can provide information about browsers:
   - **Microsoft.** Visit http://www.microsoft.com/windows/ie/default.asp for information about Microsoft Internet Explorer.
   - **Netscape.** Visit http://channels.netscape.com/ns/browsers/default.jsp for information about Netscape Navigator.
   - **Opera Software.** Visit http://www.opera.com for information about Opera.
   - **Ubvision.** Visit http://www.ultrabrowser.com for information about UltraBrowser.

Discussion Questions

As directed by your instructor, discuss the following questions in class or in groups.

1. Home computers are used more extensively than ever for tasks such as banking, investing, shopping, and communicating. Do you see this trend as having a positive or a negative impact on our society and economy? Do you plan to use a computer in these ways? Why or why not?
2. Describe your experience with computers so far. Have you worked with (or played with) computers before? If so, why? Has your past experience with computers influenced your decision to study them?

Research and Report

Using your own choice of resources (such as the Internet, books, magazines, and newspaper articles), research and write a short paper discussing one of the following topics:

- The world's smallest computer.
- The use of supercomputers in mapping the human genome.
- The history of computer operating systems.

When you are finished, proofread and print your paper, and give it to your instructor.

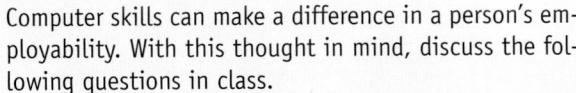

ETHICAL ISSUES

Computer skills can make a difference in a person's employability. With this thought in mind, discuss the following questions in class.

1. A factory is buying computerized systems and robots to handle many tasks, meaning fewer laborers will be needed. The company needs people to run the new equipment but wants to hire new workers who already have computer skills. Is the company obligated to keep the workers with no computer skills and train them to use the equipment? Are workers obligated to learn these new skills if they want to keep their jobs?
2. You are a skilled drafter with 15 years of experience. You have always done your drafting work using traditional methods (using pen and paper). Now you want to move to a different city and have sent resumes to several drafting firms there. You learn, however, that none of those firms will consider you for employment because you have no experience drafting on a computer. Is this fair? Why or why not? What would you do?

CHAPTER

2 Presenting the Internet

CHAPTER CONTENTS ::

This chapter contains the following lessons:

Lesson **2A:**
The Internet and the World Wide Web

- The Internet's History
- The Internet's Major Services
- Understanding the World Wide Web
- Using Your Browser and the World Wide Web
- Searching the Web

Lesson **2B:**
E-Mail and Other Internet Services

- Using E-Mail
- More Features of the Internet

LESSON // 2A

The Internet and the World Wide Web

Overview: What Is the Internet?

Even if you have not had a lot of experience with computers, it wouldn't be surprising to learn that you have been on the Internet.

In the past few years, millions of people have gone online—and some of them probably thought they would never have a use for a computer. Indeed, many Internet enthusiasts buy computers just so they can go online, and for no other reason.

But what is the Internet? Simply put, the Internet is a network of networks—a global communications system that links together thousands of individual networks. As a result, virtually any computer on any network can communicate with any other computer on any other network. These connections allow users to exchange messages, to communicate in real time (seeing messages and responses immediately), to share data and programs, and to access limitless stores of information.

The Internet has become so important that its use is considered an essential part of computer use. In other words, mastering the Internet is one of the first things you should do, if you want to get the most from your computing experience. In this lesson, you will get an overview of the Internet by reviewing its history, the basics of the World Wide Web, and browser use.

OBJECTIVES ::

- List two reasons for the Internet's creation.
- Identify six major services you can access through the Internet.
- Name three ways in which people commonly use the Internet.
- Use a Web browser to navigate the World Wide Web.
- Find content on the Web, using standard search tools.

The Internet's History

Norton ONLINE

For more information on the history of the Internet, visit **http://www.mhhe.com/peternorton**.

No introduction to the Internet is complete without a short review of its history. Even though today's Internet bears little resemblance to its forebear of 30-plus years ago, it still functions in basically the same way.

The Beginning: A "Network of Networks"

The seeds of the Internet were planted in 1969, when the Advanced Research Projects Agency (ARPA) of the U.S. Department of Defense began connecting computers at different universities and defense contractors (see Figure 2A.1). The resulting network was called ARPANET. The goal of this early project was to create a large computer network with multiple paths—in the form of telephone lines—that could survive a nuclear attack or a natural disaster such as an earthquake. If one part of the network were destroyed, other parts of the network would remain functional and data could continue to flow through the surviving lines.

FIGURE 2A.1

Before it became known as the Internet, ARPA's network served universities, defense contractors, and a few government agencies.

ARPA had a second important reason for creating such a network. That is, it would allow people in remote locations to share scarce computing resources. By being part of the network, these users could access faraway systems—such as governmental mainframes or university-owned supercomputers—and conduct research or communicate with other users.

At first, ARPANET was basically a large network serving only a handful of users, but it expanded rapidly. Initially, the network included four primary host computers. A host is like a network server, providing services to other computers that connect to it. ARPANET's host computers (like those on today's Internet) provided file transfer and communications services and gave connected systems access to the network's high-speed data lines. The system grew quickly and spread widely as the number of hosts grew (see Figure 2A.2).

The network jumped across the Atlantic to Europe in 1973, and it never stopped growing. In the mid-1980s, another federal agency, the National Science Foundation (NSF), joined the project after the Defense Department stopped funding the network. NSF established five "supercomputing centers" that were available to anyone who wanted to use them for academic research purposes.

FIGURE 2A.2

This map shows the extent of the ARPANET in September 1971.

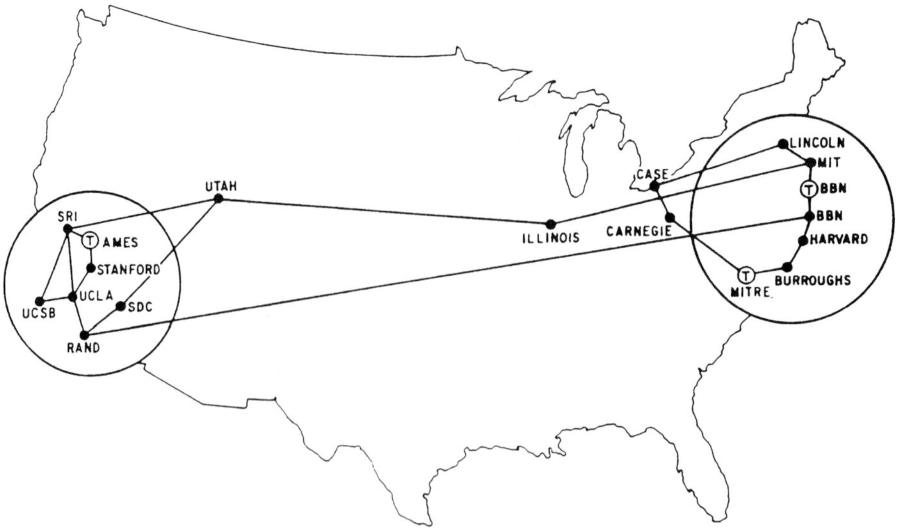

The NSF expected the supercomputers' users to use ARPANET to obtain access, but the agency quickly discovered that the existing network could not handle the load. In response, the NSF created a new, higher-capacity network, called NSFnet, to complement the older, and by then overloaded, ARPANET. The link between ARPANET, NSFnet, and other networks was called the Internet. (The process of connecting separate networks is called internetworking. A collection of "networked networks" is described as being internetworked, which is where the Internet—a worldwide network of networks—gets its name.)

NSFnet made Internet connections widely available for academic research, but the NSF did not permit users to conduct private business over the system. Therefore, several private telecommunications companies built their own network backbones that used the same set of networking protocols as NSFnet. Like a tree's trunk or an animal's spine, a network backbone is the central structure that connects other elements of the network (see Figure 2A.3). These private portions of the Internet were not limited by NSFnet's "appropriate use" restrictions, so it became possible to use the Internet to distribute business and commercial information.

The original ARPANET was shut down in 1990, and government funding for NSFnet was discontinued in 1995, but the commercial Internet backbone services replaced them. By the early 1990s, interest in the Internet began to expand dramatically. The system that had been created as a tool for surviving a nuclear war found its way into businesses and homes. Now, advertisements for movies are far more common online than collaborations on physics research.

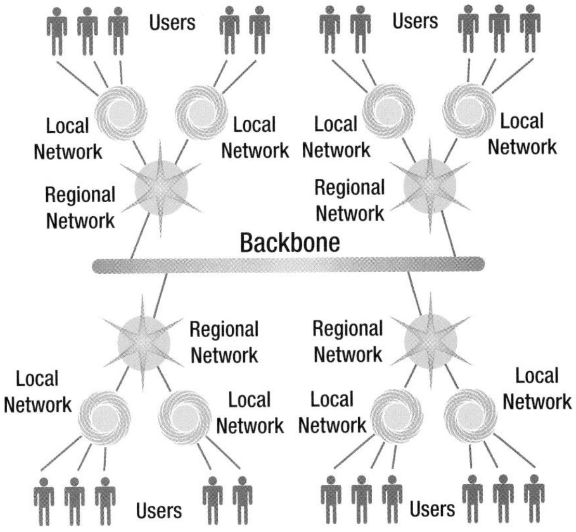

FIGURE 2A.3

At its heart, the Internet uses high-speed data lines, called backbones, to carry huge volumes of traffic. Regional and local networks connect to these backbones, enabling any user on any network to exchange data with any other user on any other network.

Today: Still Growing

Today, the Internet connects thousands of networks and hundreds of millions of users around the world. It is a huge, cooperative community with no central ownership. This lack of ownership is an important feature of the Internet, because it means that no single person or group controls the network. Although there are several organizations (such as The Internet Society and the World Wide Web Consortium) that propose standards for Internet-related technologies and guidelines for its appropriate use, these organizations almost universally support the Internet's openness and lack of centralized control.

As a result, the Internet is open to anyone who can access it. If you can use a computer and if the computer is connected to the Internet, you are free not only to use the resources posted by others, but to create resources of your own; that is, you can publish documents on the World Wide Web, exchange e-mail messages, and perform many other tasks.

This openness has attracted millions of users to the Internet. Internet access was available to nearly one-half billion people worldwide in 2001. The number of actual users continues to climb dramatically, as shown in Figure 2A.4.

FIGURE 2A.4

The number of Internet users is expected to continue its dramatic increase for the foreseeable future.

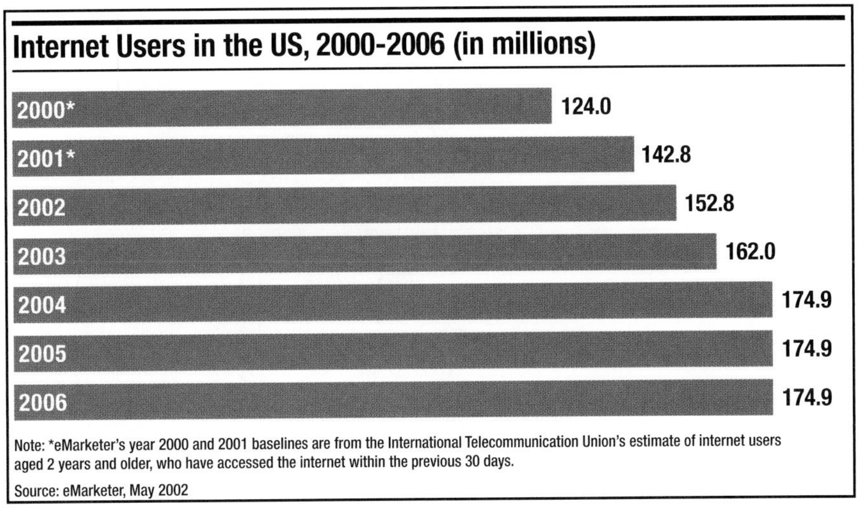

Norton ONLINE

For more information on the Internet's services, visit **http://www.mhhe.com/peternorton.**

simnet™

The Internet's Major Services

The Internet acts as a carrier for several different services, each with its own distinct features and purposes (see Figure 2A.5). The most commonly used Internet services are

- The World Wide Web
- Electronic mail
- News
- File Transfer Protocol
- Chat
- Instant messaging
- Online services
- Peer-to-peer services

To use any of these services, you need a computer that is connected to the Internet in some way. Most individual users connect their computer's modem to a telephone line (or use a high-speed connection such as DSL or a cable modem) and set up an account with an **Internet service provider (ISP)**, a company that provides local or regional access to the Internet backbone. Many other users connect to the Internet through a school or business network. To use a specific service, you also need the right type of software. Some programs enable you to use multiple Internet services, so you do not necessarily need separate applications for each service.

Norton ONLINE

For more information on the World Wide Web, visit **http://www.mhhe.com/peternorton.**

simnet™

Understanding the World Wide Web

The **World Wide Web** (also known as the **Web** or **WWW**) was created in 1989 at the European Particle Physics Laboratory in Geneva, Switzerland, as a method for incorporating footnotes, figures, and cross-references into online documents. The Web's creators wanted to create a simple way to access any document that was stored on a network, without having to search through indexes or directories of files, and without having to manually copy documents from one computer to another before viewing them. To do this, they established a way to "link" documents that were stored in different locations on a single computer, or on different computers on a network.

If you imagine a collection of billions of documents, all stored in different places, but all linked together in some manner, you might imagine them creating a

FIGURE 2A.5

The Internet's services differ in the way they look and function, but each one has a unique set of uses and its own special appeal to different users.

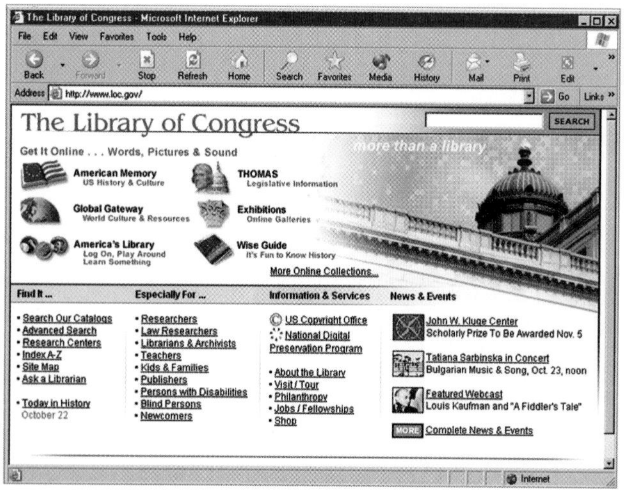

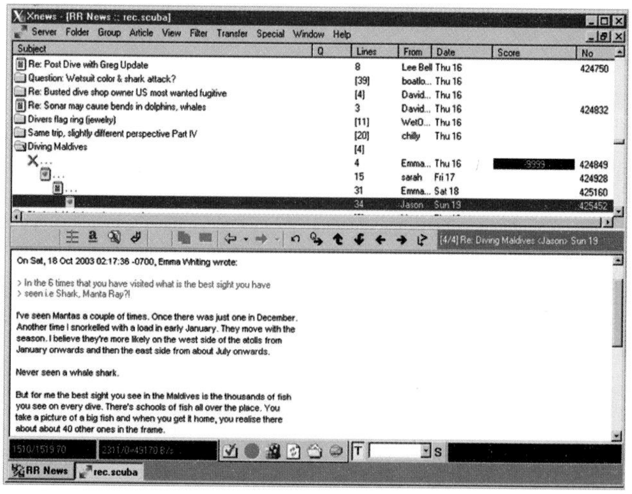

"web" of interconnected information (see Figure 2A.6). If you extend that collection of documents and their links to cover the entire globe, you have a "world-wide web" of information. This concept is where the Web gets its name.

Many people believe that the Web and the Internet are the same thing, but this is not correct. In fact, they are two different things. The Web is a service (a system for accessing documents) that is supported by the Internet (a gigantic network).

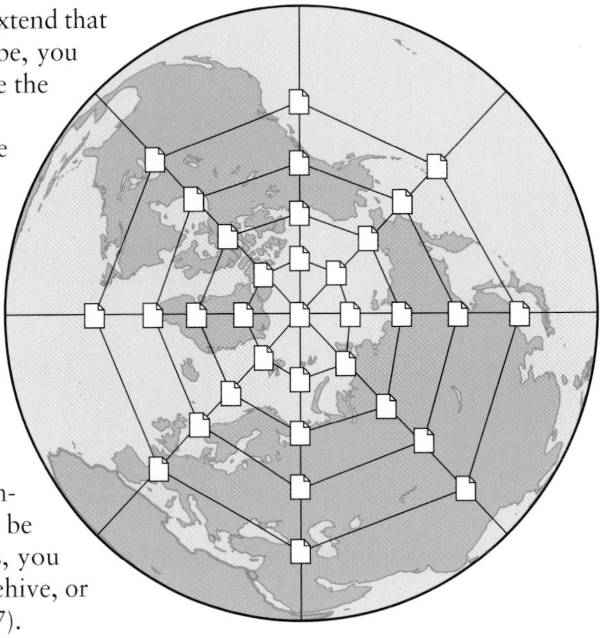

FIGURE 2A.6

Billions of documents and their links create a web of information that reaches around the world.

How the Web Works

Web documents can be linked together because they are created in a format known as hypertext. Hypertext systems provide an easy way to manage large collections of data, which can include text files, pictures, sounds, movies, and more. In a hypertext system, when you view a document on your computer's screen, you also can access all the data that might be linked to it. So, if the document is a discussion of honey bees, you might be able to click a hypertext link and see a photo of a beehive, or a movie of bees gathering pollen from flowers (see Figure 2A.7).

To support hypertext documents, the Web uses a special protocol, called the hypertext transfer protocol, or HTTP. (You will learn more about protocols in Chapter 9, "Networks.") A hypertext document is a specially encoded file that uses the hypertext markup language, or HTML. This language allows a document's author to embed hypertext links—also called hyperlinks or just links—in the document. HTTP and hypertext links are the foundations of the World Wide Web.

As you read a hypertext document—more commonly called a Web page—on screen, you can click a word or picture encoded as a hypertext link and immediately jump to another location within the same document or to a different Web page (see Figure 2A.8). The second page may be located on the same computer as the original page, or anywhere else on the Internet. Because you do not have to learn separate commands and addresses to jump to a new location, the World Wide Web organizes widely scattered resources into a seamless whole.

A collection of related Web pages is called a Web site. Web sites are housed on Web servers, Internet host computers that often store thousands of individual

Norton ONLINE

For more information on hypertext and HTML, visit **http://www.mhhe.com/peternorton.**

simnet™

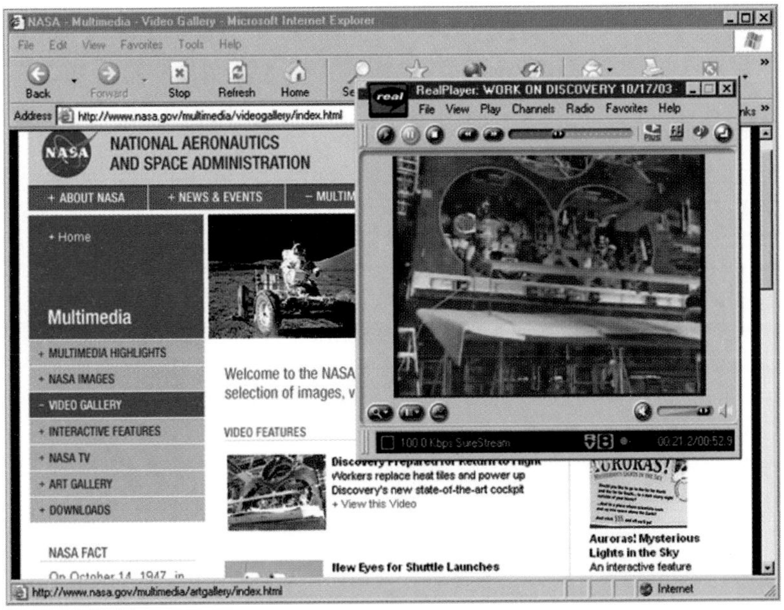

FIGURE 2A.7

Hypertext systems, such as the Web, let you view a document and other data that might be linked to that document. Here, a Web page is being viewed in a browser and a video is being viewed in a media player. The video started playing automatically when the user clicked a link on the Web page.

FIGURE 2A.8

This an example of a typical Web site. The user can click one of the hyperlinked text lines or images to jump to a different location in the same site, or to a different site.

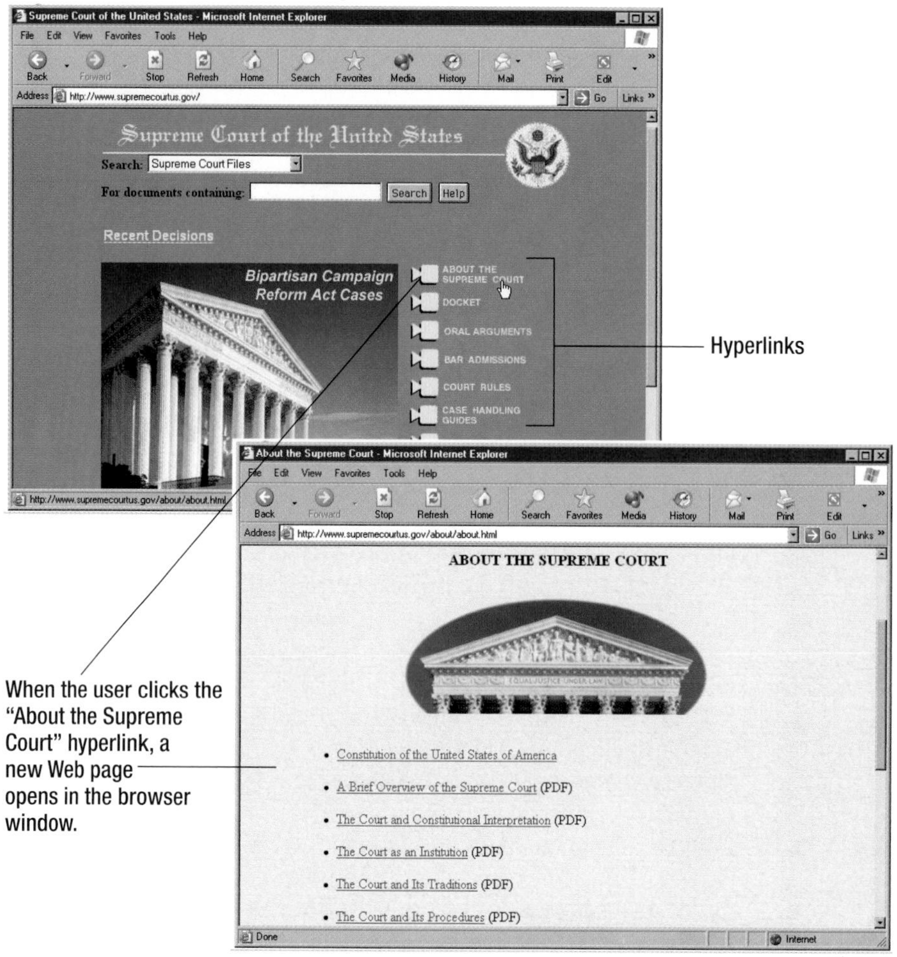

pages. Copying a page onto a server is called publishing the page, but the process also is called posting or uploading.

Web pages are used to distribute news, interactive educational services, product information, catalogs, highway traffic reports, and live audio and video, and other kinds of information. Web pages permit readers to consult databases, order products and information, and submit payment with a credit card or an account number.

Norton ONLINE

For more information on Web browsers, visit **http://www.mhhe.com/peternorton**.

simnet™

Web Browsers and HTML Tags

For several years, the Web remained an interesting but not particularly exciting tool used by scientific researchers. But in 1993, developers at the National Center for Supercomputing Applications (NCSA) created Mosaic, a point-and-click Web browser. A Web browser (or browser) is a software application designed to find hypertext documents on the Web and then open the documents on the user's computer. A point-and-click browser provides a graphical user interface that enables the user to click hyperlinked text and images to jump to other documents or view other data. Several text-based Web browsers are also available and are used in nongraphical operating systems, such as certain versions of UNIX. Mosaic and Web browsers that evolved from it have changed the way people use the Internet. Today, the most popular graphical Web browsers are Microsoft's Internet Explorer (see Figure 2A.9) and Netscape Navigator (see Figure 2A.10).

Later in this chapter, you will learn about using a browser to navigate the Web and find content.

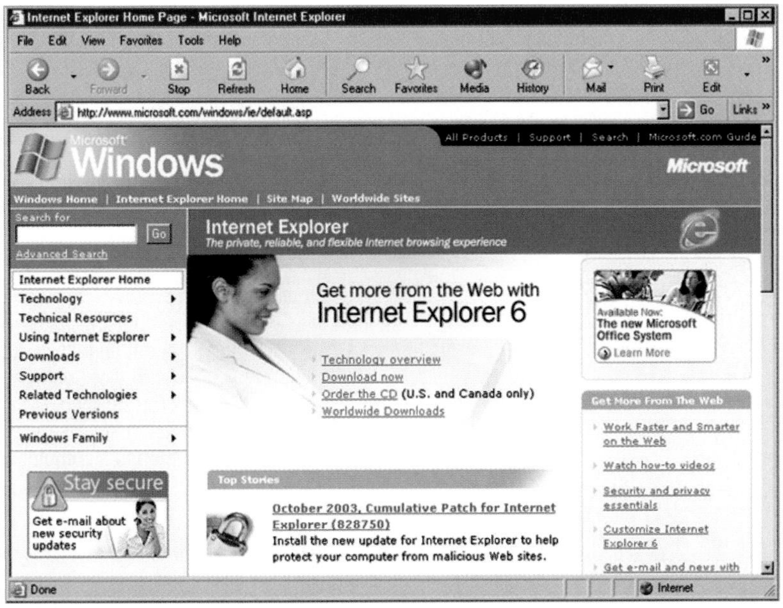

FIGURE 2A.9

This is Microsoft Internet Explorer version 6, the most popular of all available Web browsers. It is available at no cost from Microsoft Corporation and is included with the Windows operating system.

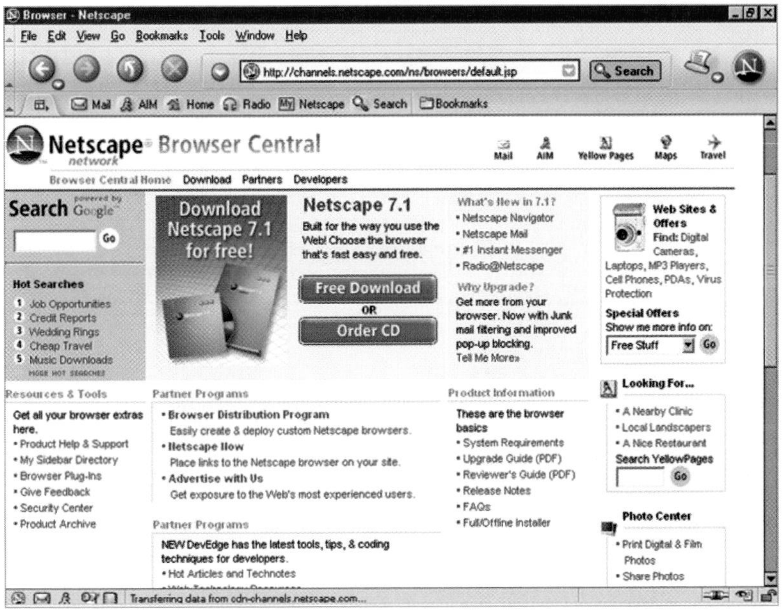

FIGURE 2A.10

This is Netscape Navigator version 7, which is available for free from Netscape Corporation and many other sources.

URLs

The hypertext transfer protocol uses Internet addresses in a special format, called a uniform resource locator, or URL. (The acronym is usually pronounced by spelling its letters out, as in "U-R-L.") URLs look like this:

type://address/path

In a URL, *type* specifies the type of server in which the file is located, *address* is the address of the server, and *path* is the location within the file structure of the server. The path includes the list of folders where the desired file (the Web page itself or some other piece of data) is located. Consider the URL for a page at the Library of Congress Web site, which contains information about the Library's collection of permanent exhibits (see Figure 2A.11).

FIGURE 2A.11

The parts of a typical URL.

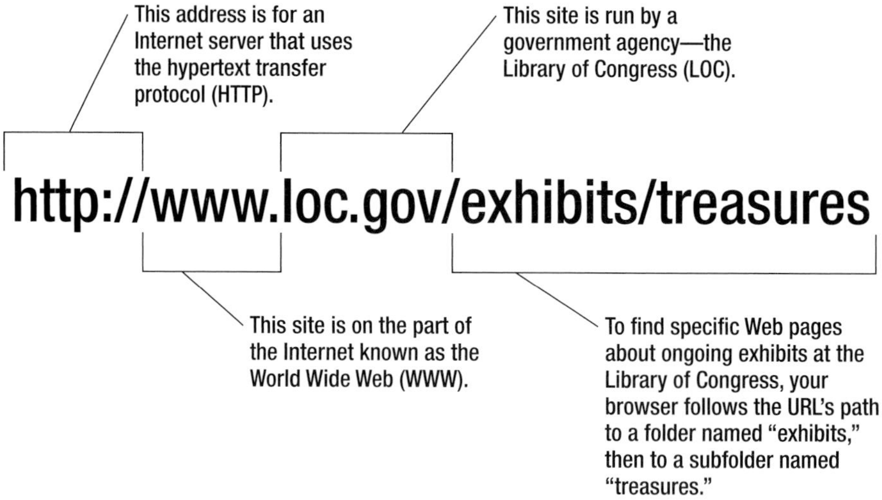
This address is for an Internet server that uses the hypertext transfer protocol (HTTP).
This site is run by a government agency—the Library of Congress (LOC).
http://www.loc.gov/exhibits/treasures
This site is on the part of the Internet known as the World Wide Web (WWW).
To find specific Web pages about ongoing exhibits at the Library of Congress, your browser follows the URL's path to a folder named "exhibits," then to a subfolder named "treasures."

FIGURE 2A.12

This is an example of a typical Web site. The user can click one of the hyperlinked text lines or images to jump to a different location in the same site, or to a different site.

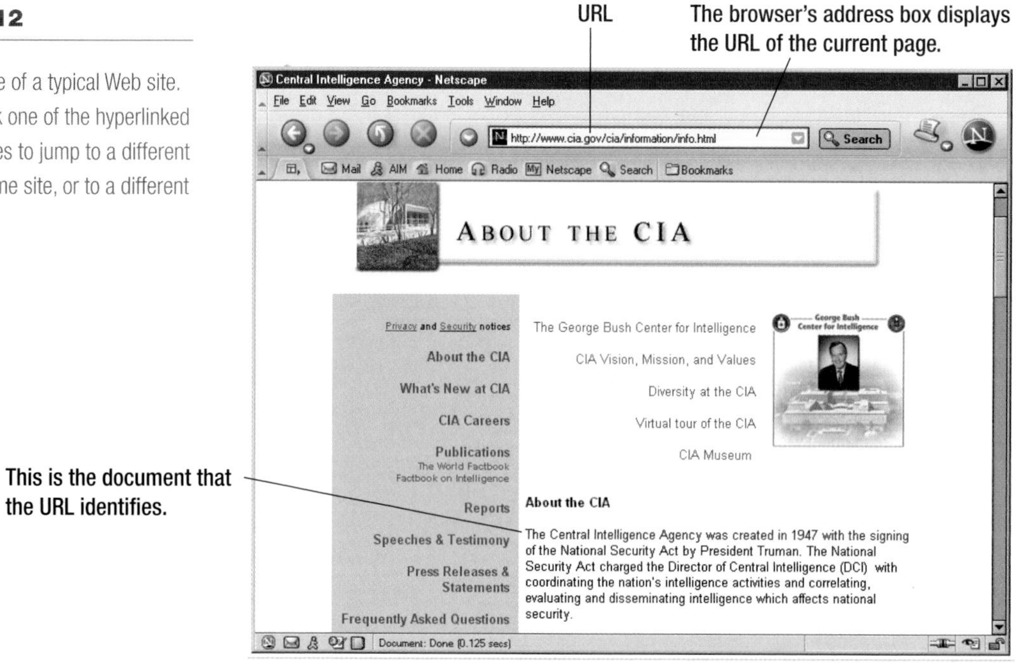
URL
The browser's address box displays the URL of the current page.
This is the document that the URL identifies.
About the CIA

If you were looking for an HTML document (that is, a Web page) named "Exhibition Overview" at this Web site, its URL would look like this:

http://www.loc.gov/exhibits/treasures/tr66.html

Because URLs lead to specific documents on a server's disk, they can be extremely long; however, every single document on the World Wide Web has its own unique URL (see Figure 2A.12).

Norton ONLINE

For more information on helper applications for browsers, visit **http://www.mhhe.com/peternorton**.

simnet™

Helper Applications and Multimedia Content

As versatile as they are, Web browsers alone cannot display every type of content—especially multimedia content—now available on the Web. Many Web sites feature audio and video content, including full-motion animation and movies. These large files require special applications in order to be played in real time across the Web. Because these applications help the browser by being "plugged in" at the right moment, they are called helper applications or plug-in applications.

Plug-ins are used to support several types of content, including streaming audio and streaming video. Streaming technology works by sending the audio or video content in a continuous stream from the Web server to your browser. The plug-in application receives the first portion of the stream and stores it temporarily in a buffer (an area in memory or on disk). After that portion of the stream has been buffered, it is played while the next portion of the stream is stored in the buffer (see Figure 2A.13). After the stream has been played, it is deleted. The buffer-and-play technique is an effective method for playing a large file quickly without waiting for the entire file to download—that is, to be transmitted in its entirety from the Web server to your computer.

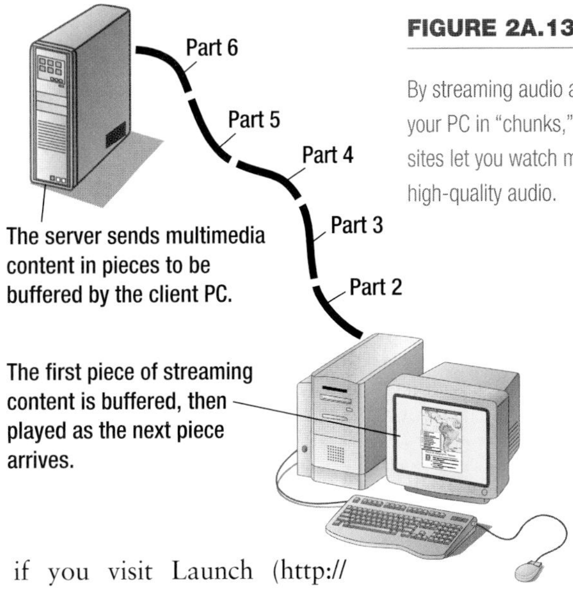

FIGURE 2A.13

By streaming audio and video content to your PC in "chunks," multimedia Web sites let you watch movies and listen to high-quality audio.

There is a tremendous variety of multimedia content available on the Web. For example, if you visit Launch (http://www.launch.com), you can listen to CD-quality audio, watch music videos, and much more. At Apple's QuickTime Web site (http://www.apple.com/quicktime), you can listen to high-quality streaming music or watch the latest movie trailers. Television channels such as CNN (http://www.cnn.com) and The Weather Channel (http://www.weather.com) also deliver their audio and video content over the Web. Using a plug-in application—such as Microsoft's Windows Media Player, Apple's QuickTime Player, or RealNetworks' RealOne Player—you can play any of these sources on your computer (see Figure 2A.14).

SELF-CHECK ::

Circle the correct answer for each question.

1. This early version of the Internet was available for academic research, but not for business use.

   a. ARPAnet **b.** NSFnet **c.** INTRAnet

2. The World Wide Web is a service that lets users access documents, but the Internet is this.

   a. a gigantic network **b.** a gigantic computer **c.** a gigantic database

3. In a URL, the _____ is the location within the file structure of the server where a desired file can be found.

   a. type **b.** address **c.** path

Norton ONLINE

For more information on streaming media, visit **http://www.mhhe.com/peternorton**.

FIGURE 2A.14

This is the RealOne Player, displaying streaming content from CNN's Web site.

Norton Notebook

Internet Time Travel: The Wayback Machine

For roughly four millennia, if you were a scholar and needed—or simply wanted—access to some piece of your culture's knowledge, heritage, or history, you could enter a library and obtain what you needed. At least, that's how it worked in theory. Certainly there have always been private, religious, and royal libraries with limited access to materials. (Thousands of these still exist today—probably millions, if you include private corporate archives.) And, naturally, if you were a scholar in Tibet around 245 B.C.E. and the document you required was in Alexandria, access to materials once you were *in* the library was the least of your worries.

It would be, frankly, a gross overstatement to say that the Internet "has changed all of that," by making the world a smaller place, collapsing distances, providing ubiquitous access to everything ever known . . . and all of those other wonderful things the Internet was supposed to do. Even for those of us fortunate enough to *have* access to the Internet, finding useful resources can seem a monumental task. Sometimes the difficulty lies in the act of searching and the tools we use to find materials online. In many cases, however—and the more specialized the information you need, the more often this happens—even the most skilled searching simply produces one of the many Web browser error messages that mean "what you want is no longer available." To understand why this happens, it's useful to reconsider briefly both the history and nature of the Internet itself.

As you have already seen in this chapter, what we now call the Internet is actually a vast collection of computer networks that interoperate through the use of common standards and protocols. Originally, a much smaller collection of these networks allowed researchers and scientists to share documents (by which I mean text) across distances by file transfer and e-mail. Which documents were shared—what information was *available online*, as we say now—depended entirely on the individual people who were using the networks. This was information-on-demand in the strictest possible sense: Until someone knew that another person needed a particular document, it just wasn't available. Given that storage used to be phenomenally expensive, and data communications comparably slow, this was a need-driven environment, and often when a document was no longer needed, it was removed. New documents appeared, and so forth. From the start, we should think of the early Internet not as a library so much as a magazine rack.

As economy and technology began to cooperate, more people shared documents and kept them around. In 1990–1991, Tim Berners-Lee and others invented the World Wide Web, and the Internet, collectively, went through a real qualitative change. The Web made it possible to combine text documents, images, hypertext, and other media; store and share them practically across the growing Internet; and access them by using one of a number of different browser tools. This multimedia quality dramatically increased both the appeal and practical usefulness of the Internet to average computer users. As in the economics of supply and demand, more people online made it reasonable (indeed, necessary, as each person had his or her own interests) for ever-increasing amounts of information to be available online. In time, scholars, researchers, and traditional librarians and archivists began to store what we might call "traditional" documents online. One of the oldest and most significant of these efforts is The Gutenberg Project (http://www.gutenberg.net), the point of which is to provide free online access to significant and historical texts. While The Gutenberg Project is not aligned with a particular subject or field, unnumbered specialty sites, usually called "archives," have sprouted that provide similar access to more finely tuned collections, like the Confucian Etext Project, hosted at Wesleyan University (http://sangle.web.wesleyan.edu/etext), and the Classics Archive, hosted by

One of the most commonly used multimedia design tools is made by Macromedia, Inc. This tool—called Flash—enables Web page designers to create high-quality animation or video, complete with audio, that plays directly within the browser window. These types of animation do not require the browser to spawn (launch) an external application for viewing. In fact, many Web sites use this approach with all their multimedia content. For example, if you go to the Apple QuickTime Web site to watch movie trailers, they will run directly within your browser window instead of appearing in a separate QuickTime Player window—as long as you have the QuickTime plug-in installed.

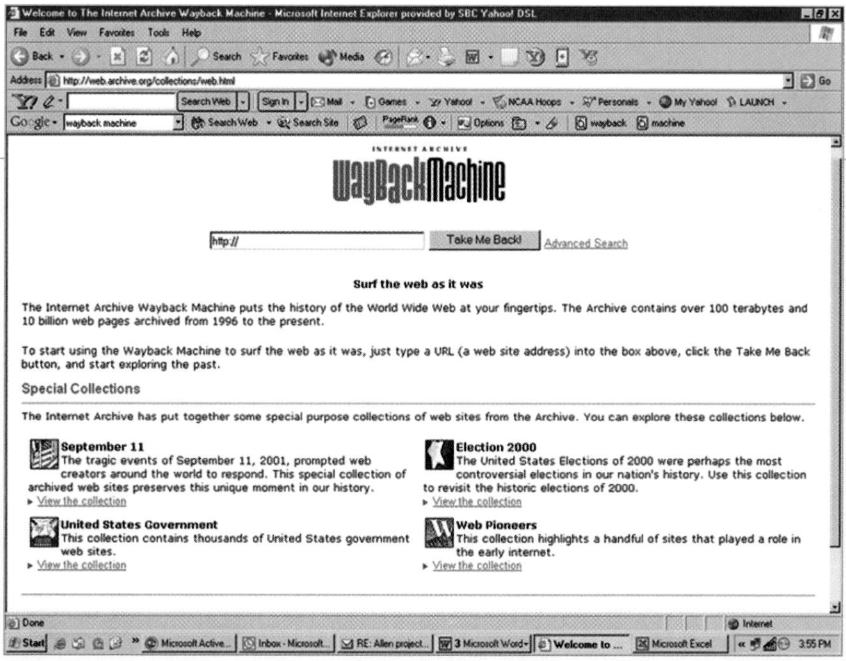

MIT (http://classics.mit.edu). Established institutions and museums, like the Louvre, are also increasingly providing multimedia access to their collections (http://www.louvre.fr). These large, institutional resources aren't in much danger of suddenly disappearing, either. It now costs only pennies to store gargantuan amounts of data, and user demand for these famous and "significant" media continues to grow.

So much for *significant* and historical resources. (As in the past, what qualifies today as *significant* media continues to be determined by the individuals—or institutions—that create and manage these resources.) But the Internet gathers a lot more than just Shakespeare, Michelangelo, and the Smithsonian Institution. Millions of individuals have spent as many hours making their own collections and interests available. These aren't collections of "significant" or "traditional" documents; they're personal expressions put forth for the joy of sharing interests with others. Still others are professional sites, either created specifically to earn money or to promote products that are for sale. These online resources are more transient. Individuals stop paying for online space to host their creations; companies update their sites at least daily to showcase the latest products. Thus, bookmarks and indexed Web page links "break" and fail. A wealth of information seems in just as much danger of disappearing now as it was before our online world evolved.

In an attempt to prevent this from happening, the Internet Archive (www.waybackmachine.org) was formed in 1996. Its purpose: to permanently collect and make available *everything* on the World Wide Web, starting from its 1996 inception. To date, the Internet Archive has saved over 10 billion Web pages, using over 100 terabytes of storage. (A terabyte is roughly 1,000 gigabytes.) All these pages have been catalogued and are searchable; many of them have been culled together into specific collections of their own, such as a September 11, 2001, collection. You can go back and see what was on the Web back in 1998 exactly as it was. Both personal and corporate sites are archived and search capabilities are impressive. The Internet Archive is a surprisingly unknown resource, but I've found it invaluable. The next time you use a search engine and think you've found the perfect resource—only to discover that it's no longer online—switch over to the Internet Archive and take a look. With so much effort being made to share and preserve knowledge by means of the Internet, the Internet Archive's Wayback Machine satisfies a tremendous need: the Internet sharing and preserving *itself*.

Using Your Browser and the World Wide Web

Throughout this book, you will find many Internet-related discussions, as well as exercises and review questions that require you to use the Web. As you learned earlier, the Web enables users to view specially formatted documents, called Web pages, which can contain text, graphics, and multimedia objects such as video, audio, or animations. (Remember that a collection of related Web pages is called a Web site.) Web pages also can display navigational tools to help you move around within a Web page, from one page to another within a Web site, or among different sites.

Norton ONLINE

For more information on using a browser, visit **http://www.mhhe.com/peternorton**.

simnet™

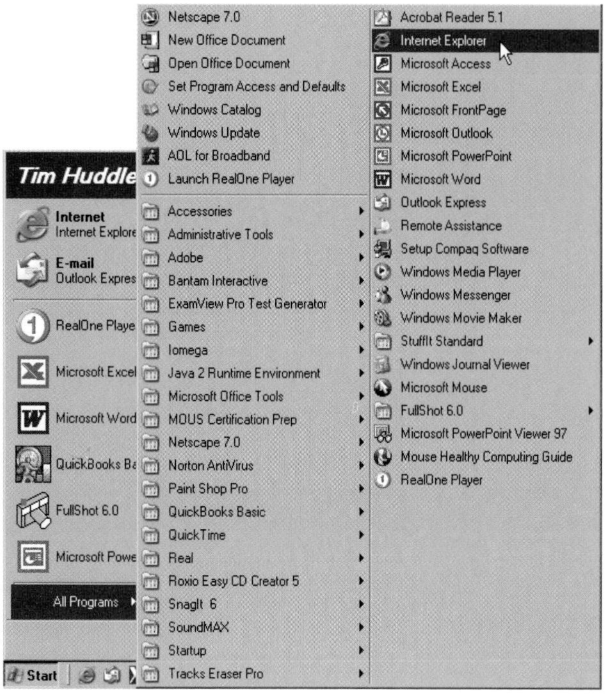

FIGURE 2A.15

Launching a Web browser from the Windows Start menu.

To access the Web, you need a special software program called a Web browser. This section shows you the basic steps required for using a browser and navigating the Web. You should complete the following steps and become familiar with your browser before going any further in this book.

Note that the following discussions assume that you are using a personal computer running Windows XP Professional. If you use a different version of Windows, the actual steps you take may differ slightly from those discussed in the following sections. Ask your instructor for help, if necessary.

Launching Your Browser

Your browser is an application stored on your computer's disk. You must launch the program before you can view any Web pages. You may need to connect to the Internet before launching the browser. (If so, ask your instructor for directions on connecting to the Internet.) Once you have established a connection, launch your browser by following these steps:

1. Click the Start button on the Windows taskbar. The Start menu opens.
2. Point to All Programs to open the Programs submenu. When the Programs submenu opens, find the name of your browser and click it, as shown in Figure 2A.15.

Your browser will open on your screen, as shown in Figure 2A.16. The browser shown here is Microsoft Internet Explorer version 6.0. If you are using a different browser (or a different version of Internet Explorer), you will notice that your screen looks different.

Depending on how your browser is configured, a Web page may open in the browser window as soon as you launch the program. This page is called the start page. You can set the browser to open any page (either from a Web site or from your computer's disk) when it launches. In Figure 2A.16, the Excite home page is the start page.

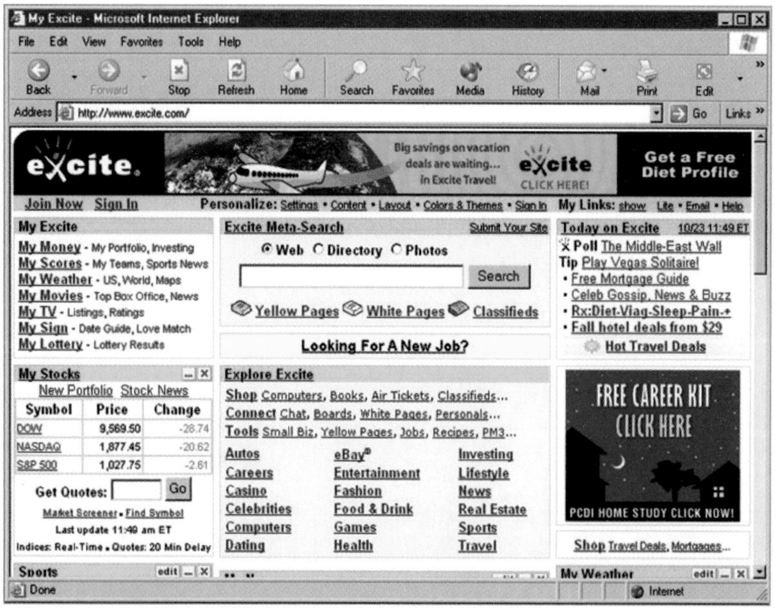

FIGURE 2A.16

The Internet Explorer browser.

Navigating the Web

Navigating the Web means moving from one Web page to another or from one Web site to another. Your browser provides several different ways to navigate the Web. Once you are familiar with your browser's interface, you can select the navigational tools and techniques that work best for you.

Using URLs

As you learned previously, every Web page has a unique address, called a uniform resource locator, or URL. URLs are the key to navigating the Web. When you provide a URL for the browser, the browser finds that URL's page and then transfers the page to your PC. The page's content then appears on your screen, in the browser window.

You can specify a URL in several ways, but three methods are most commonly used:

- Type the URL in the browser's Address box.
- Click a hyperlink that is linked to that URL.
- Store the URL in your browser's Favorites list, then select the URL from the list. (If you use Netscape Navigator, this list is called Bookmarks.)

For example, suppose you want to visit the Web site of the National Football League (NFL). To do this, you can click in the Address box, type **http://www.nfl.com,** and then press ENTER. The home page of the NFL Web site appears in the browser window (see Figure 2A.17).

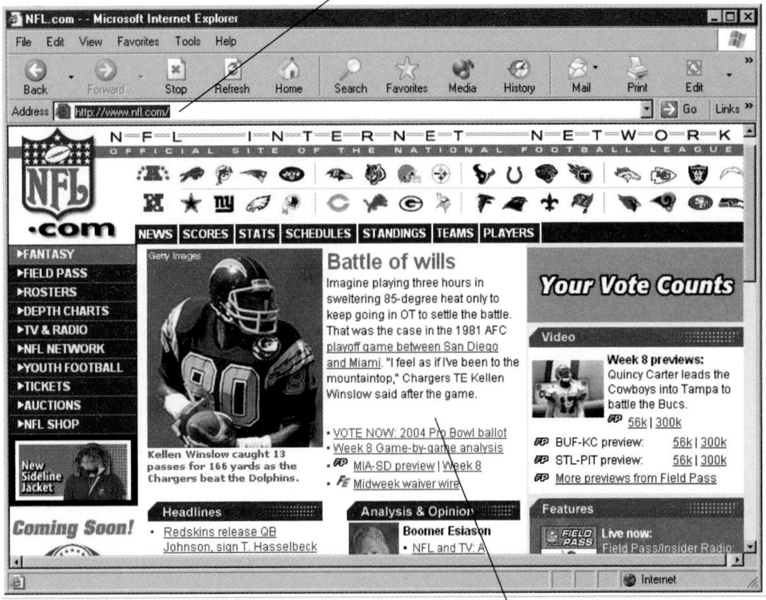

FIGURE 2A.17

Navigating the Web by typing a URL.

Using Hyperlinks

A hyperlink is simply a part of the Web page that is linked to a URL. A hyperlink can appear as text, an image, or a navigational tool such as a button or an arrow. You can click a hyperlink and "jump" from your present location to the URL specified by the hyperlink. Hyperlinked text usually looks different from normal text in a Web page: it is often underlined, but can be formatted in any number of ways (see Figure 2A.18). When your mouse pointer touches hyperlinked text, the hyperlink's URL appears in the browser's status bar, and the pointer changes shape to resemble a hand with a pointing index finger.

Many Web pages also provide hyperlinked pictures or graphical buttons—called navigation tools—that direct you to different pages, making it easier to find

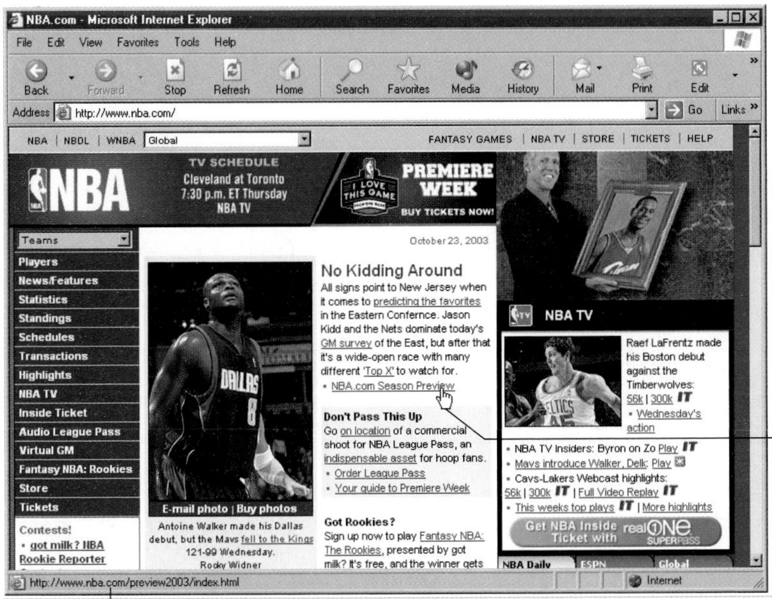

FIGURE 2A.18

Using hyperlinked text on a Web page.

FIGURE 2A.19

Using hyperlinked graphics on a Web page.

the information you need (see Figure 2A.19). Another common navigation tool is the image map, a single image that provides multiple hyperlinks. You can click on different parts of the image map to jump to different pages. When your mouse pointer touches a navigation tool or image map, it turns into a hand pointer, and the hyperlink's URL appears in your browser's status bar.

FIGURE 2A.20

The Back and Forward buttons in Internet Explorer.

Using the Browser's Navigation Tools

Web browsers offer a variety of tools to help you move around the Web. These tools can save you the trouble of typing URLs or searching for links, and they allow you to quickly go back to pages that you have already visited.

The Back and Forward buttons return you to recently viewed pages, similar to flipping through a magazine (see Figure 2A.20). The Back button returns you to the previously opened Web page. After using the Back button, you can click Forward to move forward again, returning to the last page you opened before you clicked the Back button.

Most browsers allow you to "bookmark" Web pages that you visit frequently. Instead of typing the page's URL, you simply select the page's title from your list of bookmarks. Depending on the browser you use, your bookmarks may be stored in a list called Bookmarks, Favorites, or something similar (see Figure 2A.21). Simply select a bookmark from that list, and the browser returns to that page.

When you type URLs into the Address bar, your browser saves them, creating a history list for the current session (see Figure 2A.22). You can choose a URL from this list and return to a previously opened page without having to use the Back button or any other tools.

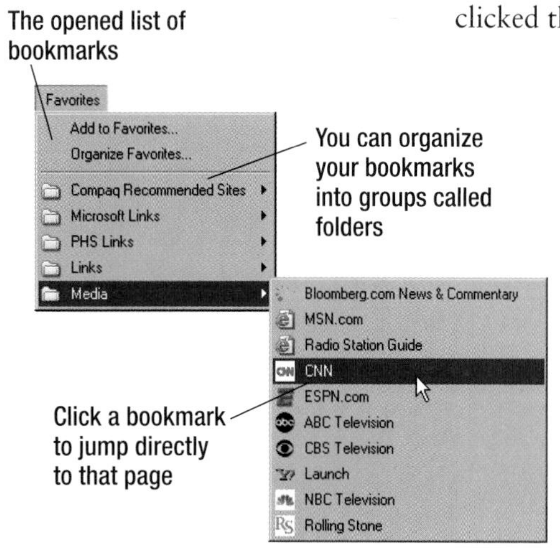

FIGURE 2A.21

Selecting a bookmark from Internet Explorer's Favorites list.

Closing Your Browser

To close your browser, open the File menu and choose Close. You also can close the browser by clicking the Close button on the title bar. It may be necessary to close your Internet connection, too.

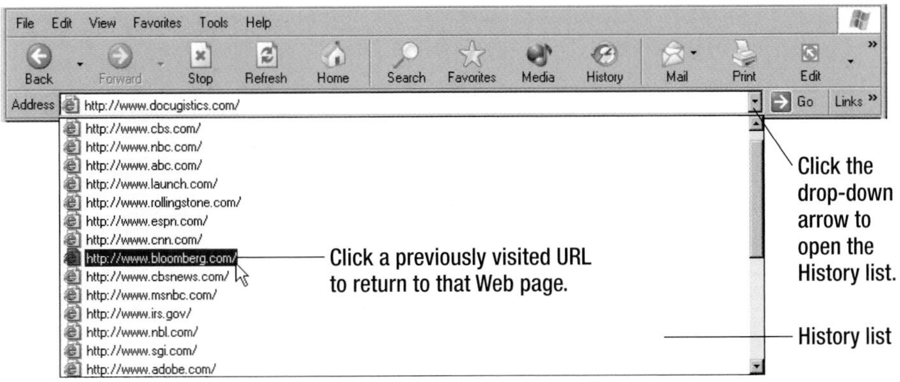

FIGURE 2A.22

Selecting a Web page's URL from the History list.

Getting Help with Your Browser

Although most browsers are easy to use, you may need help at some point. Browsers provide comprehensive Help systems, which can answer many of your questions about browsing and the World Wide Web.

Open the browser's Help menu, and then choose Contents and Index. (Depending on your browser, this option may be called Contents, Help Contents, or something similar.)

A Help window appears, listing all the topics for which help or information is available (see Figure 2A.23). Look through the list of topics and choose the one that matches your interest. When you are done, click the Close button on the window's title bar.

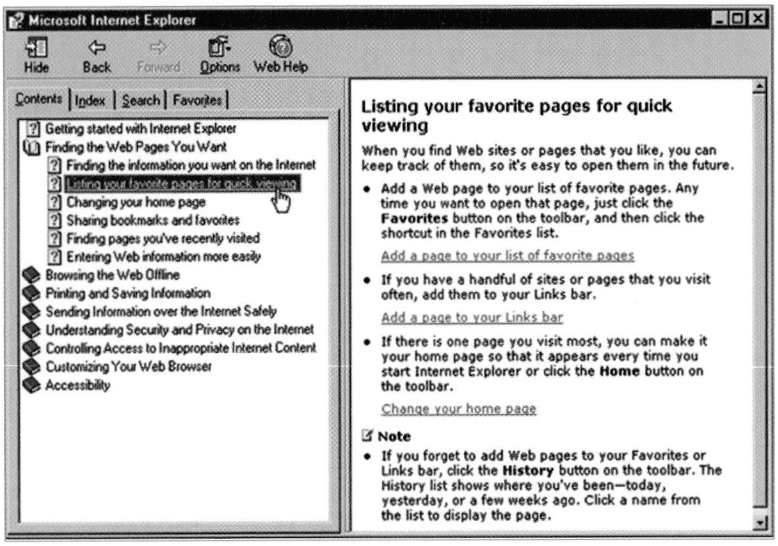

FIGURE 2A.23

Internet Explorer's Help window.

To get help from your browser maker's Web site, open your browser's Help menu and look for an option that leads you to the product's Web site. The resulting Web page will provide access to lists of frequently asked questions, links to help topics, and methods for getting in-depth technical support.

Searching the Web

It is not always easy to find what you want on the Web. That is because there are tens of millions of unique Web sites, which include billions of unique pages! This section explains the basics of Web search tools and their use. However, there are many more specific search tools available than can be listed here. To search the Web successfully, you should use this section as a starting point; then spend some time experimenting with a variety of search tools.

The two most basic and commonly used Web-based search tools are

- **Directories.** A directory enables you to search for information by selecting categories of subject matter. The directory separates subjects into general categories (such as "companies"), which are broken into increasingly specific subcategories (such as "companies—construction—contractors—builders and designers"). After you select a category or subcategory, the directory displays a list of Web sites that provide content related to that subject. The LookSmart directory at http://www.looksmart.com is shown in Figure 2A.24.
- **Search Engines.** A search engine lets you search for information by typing one or more words. The engine then displays a list of Web pages that contain

Norton ONLINE

For more information on searching the Web, visit **http://www.mhhe.com/peternorton**.

simnet™

FIGURE 2A.24

The LookSmart home page. You can use the site's directory to search for Web sites relating to many topics.

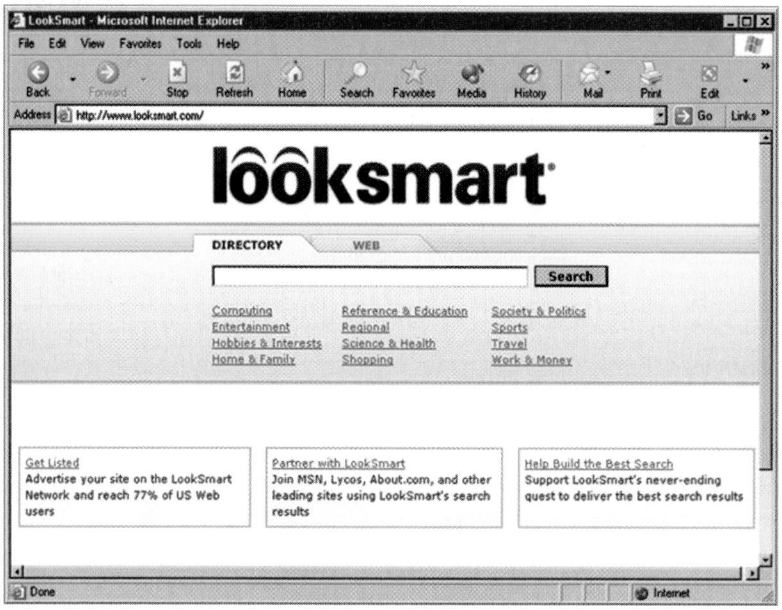

information related to your words. (This type of look-up is called a keyword search.) Any search engine lets you conduct a search based on a single word. Most also let you search for multiple words, such as "scanner AND printer." Many search engines accept "plain English" phrases or questions as the basis for your search, such as "movies starring Cary Grant" or "How do cells divide?" The Google search engine at http://www.google.com is shown in Figure 2A.25.

FIGURE 2A.25

Google has become one of the Web's most popular search engines.

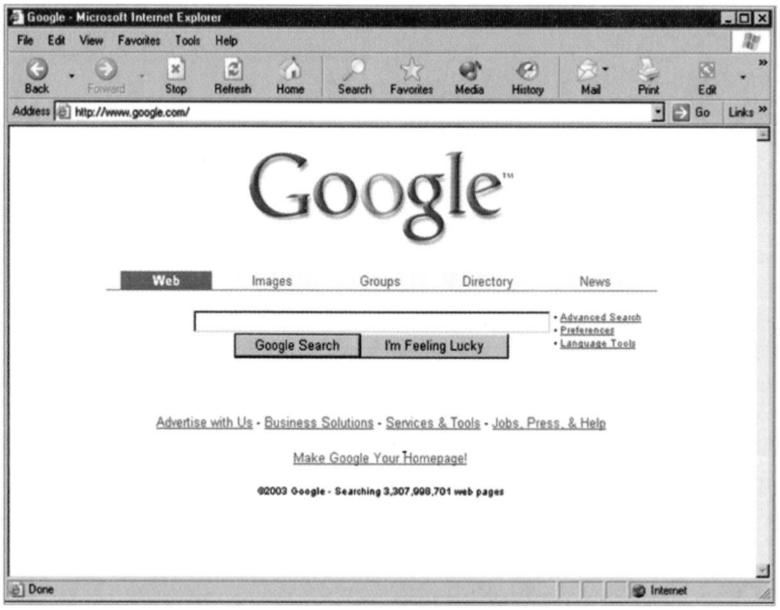

Note that both types of search tools are commonly called search engines. While this terminology is not technically correct, the differences between the two types are blurring; most Web-based search tools provide both directories and keyword search engines. In fact, if you look back at Figure 2A.24, you will see that LookSmart provides a box for performing keyword searches as well as its list of categories for performing directory-style searches.

Using a Directory

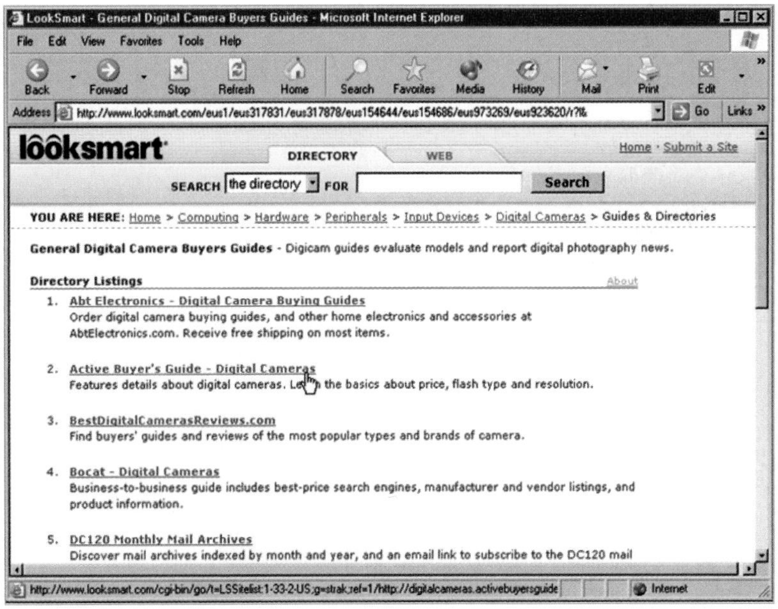

FIGURE 2A.26

After you select the final subcategory, LookSmart displays a list of Web sites that provide information related to your topic.

Suppose you want to find some Web sites that provide information about the latest digital cameras. Perhaps you want to buy a camera, or you just want to read about the technology before deciding whether to buy one. In the following exercise, you will use the LookSmart directory to find Web sites that provide "buyers guide" information.

1. Launch your Web browser.
2. In the Address box, type **http://www.looksmart.com** and press ENTER. The LookSmart home page opens in your browser window.
3. On the LookSmart home page, click the Computing category. A new page opens, displaying a list of subcategories under Computing.
4. Click the Hardware subcategory. A third page appears, displaying a list of subcategories under Hardware.
5. Choose Peripherals | Input Devices | Digital Cameras | Guides & Directories. A new page appears listing sites that provide information about buying digital cameras (see Figure 2A.26).
6. Browse through the list of Web sites and click one. The new site opens in your browser window. After reviewing it, you can use your browser's Back button to navigate back to the list of buyers' guides to choose another Web site.

Using a Search Engine

Suppose you want to find some information about ink jet printers. You know there are many different types of printers that are available at a wide range of prices. You also know that you want a printer that prints in color rather than in black and white only. In the following exercise, you will use a search engine to help you find the information you need.

1. Launch your Web browser.
2. In the Location/Address bar, type **http://www.lycos.com** and press ENTER. The Lycos home page opens in your browser window, as shown in Figure 2A.27. (Lycos is just one example of a Web search engine.)
3. In the Search text box, type **"ink jet printer"** (include the quotation marks) and click the Search button. A new page appears, listing Web pages that contain information relating to ink jet printers. Note, however, that the list includes hundreds of thousands of pages (see Figure 2A.28). This happens because a search engine assumes that a Web site is relevant to your needs if it contains terms that match the keywords you provide.
4. To narrow the search results, you must provide more specific search criteria. Click in the Search text box and type **"ink jet printer" "color"** (again, including the quotation marks); then click the Search button. Another page appears, listing a new selection of Web sites that match your keywords. Note that this list is shorter than the original one, by thousands of matches.

FIGURE 2A.27

The Lycos home page.

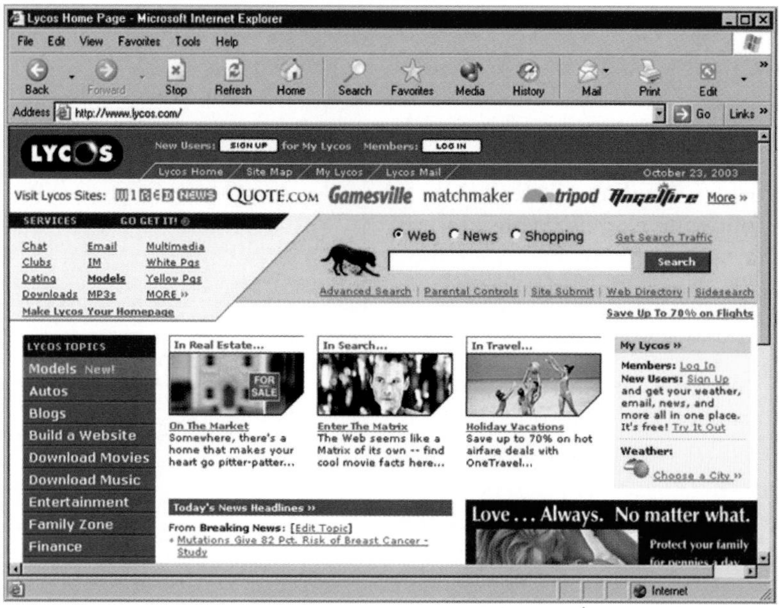

This search produced more than 240,000 matches.
WEB RESULTS: Showing Results 1 thru 10 of 242,913 (info)
1. Bulk ink jet printer ink refill kit 24 hour super store - Refill your... Sidesearch »
For your Inkjet Printer Cartridge Refill needs...<P>. More on Inkjet Printer Cartridge Refill ...
www.printerfillingstation.com September 22, 2003 - 22 KB
2. InkCartridge.com - InkJet Cartridges and Ink Jet Printer Supplies Sidesearch »
Source for inkjet cartridges and printer supplies.
www.inkcartridge.com January 8, 2003 - 5 KB
3. Printer Cartridges Onn-Line - Original and Compatible Ink Jet Printer... Sidesearch »
<b>I-shops' ORIGINAL PRINTER CARTRIDGE store</b>
Accept no imitations. Suppliers of Original and Compatible Printer Ink Jet Cartridges
www.printercartridges-onnline.co.uk October 16, 2003 - 25 KB

FIGURE 2A.28

Search engines commonly produce thousands (even hundreds of thousands) of matches, depending on your search criteria. To narrow your list of results, you need to provide more specific keywords.

5. Scroll through the list and notice if it contains any duplicate entries. How many of the suggested pages actually seem irrelevant to your search criteria? Duplicate and useless entries are two significant problems users encounter when working with search engines.

The preceding examples showed quotation marks (" ") surrounding some keywords. Many search engines require you to place quotation marks around multiple-word phrases. The marks tell the engine to treat the words as a phrase ("ink jet printer"), rather than as individual words ("ink," "jet," "printer"). You can use quotation marks to separate parts of a multiple-part keyword ("ink jet printer" "color"). Here, the marks tell the engine that the word "color" is separate from the phrase "ink jet printer."

Fortunately, most search engines provide other tools to help you search more accurately and find Web pages that are more relevant to your interests. These include Boolean operators and advanced search tools, which are discussed in the following sections.

Using Boolean Operators in Your Searches

Many—but not all—search engines accept special words, called Boolean operators, to modify your search criteria. Boolean operators are named after George Boole, a 19th century British mathematician.

Three basic Boolean operators are sometimes used in Web searches: AND, OR, and NOT. To use an operator, simply include it in the text box where you type your keywords. The following table shows simple examples of keyword searches that include the operators, and it explains how the operator affects each search.

A few search engines also support a fourth operator, NEAR. This operator determines the proximity, or closeness, of your specified keywords. For example, you may specify "printer NEAR color," with a closeness of 10 words. This tells the search engine to look for pages that include both terms, where the terms are no more than 10 words apart.

A good way to determine whether you need to use operators is to phrase your interest in the form of a sentence, and then use the important parts of the sentence as your keywords along with the appropriate operators.

A few (but not all) search engines will let you use multiple operators and set the order in which they are used. Suppose, for example, that you want to want to find information about cancer in dogs. You might set up your search criteria like this:

(dog OR canine) AND cancer

This tells the engine to look for pages that include either "dog," "canine," or both, and then to search those pages for ones that also include "cancer."

A few search engines accept symbols to represent operators. For example, you may be able to use a plus sign (+) to represent the AND operator, and a minus sign (–) to represent NOT.

Many search engines use implied Boolean logic by default, meaning you may not need to include an operator in some searches. For example, if you type the following search criteria:

dog canine

some search engines will assume that you want to find pages that include either term (using the OR operator by default). Others will assume you want pages that include both terms (using the AND operator by default), as was the case in your Lycos searches.

When dealing with implied logic, remember that each search engine operates in a slightly different way. For example, in some engines, you should use quotation marks when searching for a phrase or when you want all words to be included, as in

"ink jet printer"

Without the quotation marks, some engines will return pages that include the word "ink," others that include "jet," and others that include "printer," as well as pages that include all three.

The best way to determine how any search engine works is to study its Help-related pages (see Figure 2A.29). The Help section will tell you whether or how you can use operators with that particular engine.

Note, however, that all search engines do not support Boolean searches and multiple-word searches in the same way. Some engines will not even accept Boolean operators. In these cases, a better approach is to use the engine's advanced search tools, which are explored next.

Operator	Search Criteria	Effect
AND	printer AND color	The search engine looks only for pages that include both terms and ignores pages that include only one of them.
OR	printer OR color	The search engine looks for pages that include either or both of the terms.
NOT	printer NOT color	The search engine looks for pages that include the term *printer,* but do not also include the term *color.* The engine ignores any pages that include both terms.

Interest	Search
I need information about cancer in children.	cancer AND children
I need information about dogs, which are sometimes called canines.	dog OR canine
I need information about acoustic guitars, but not electric guitars.	guitar NOT electric

Using Advanced Search Options

To overcome the problems of duplicate and irrelevant results, many search engines provide a set of advanced search options, sometimes called advanced tools.

Productivity Tip

Evaluating the Reliability of Search Results and Web Sites

Once you master the science of searching the Web, you need to determine whether the information you find is accurate and useable. This may sound strange, but remember: the Web is not like a magazine that is published by a single group that takes responsibility for its accuracy and honesty.

By contrast, *anyone* can publish documents on the Web, and millions of people do. While many Web publishers work hard to post accurate, authoritative information, many others do not. In fact, lots of people use the Internet as a way to distribute misinformation or try to mislead others.

The Web is also rife with plagiarism, which is the act of copying someone else's work and using it as your own. This practice enables unscrupulous Webmasters to appear authoritative on a subject when they really know little about it.

These are important points when you are conducting serious research online—whether you are looking for movie reviews, shopping for a computer, or gathering data for a term paper. Relying on the wrong information source can lead to mistakes, or even land you in trouble.

How do you evaluate a Web site to make sure that the information it offers is accurate, honest, and useful? Here are some tips:

- Try to identify the author of the information, and remember that the writer may not be the same person as the Web site's owner or manager. Check the site for information about the author and see if it is possible to contact that person directly. If you cannot find out anything about the author, then there is a chance that the site's material is not original or the author wishes to remain anonymous.
- Look for copyright information on the site. If someone has gone to the trouble of researching, writing, and publishing information on a serious topic, then that person will probably try to protect it by posting a copyright notice. If the site is posting material authored by someone else, then there should be a notice stating that the material has been used with permission from the original

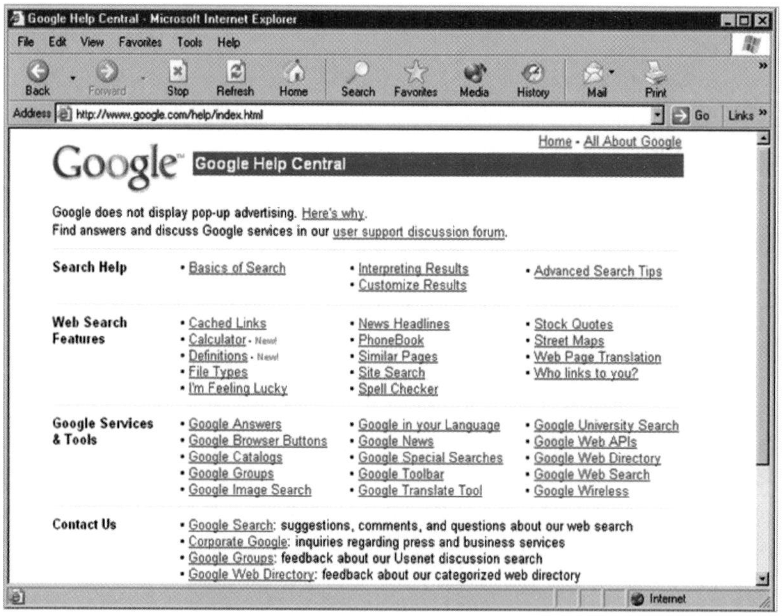

FIGURE 2A.29

The Help links at the Google search engine site. This Help section provides a basic overview of Google and how it conducts searches. You also can find information about Google's support for Boolean operators, basic and advanced search techniques, and more. The Help section is the best place to start when working with a search engine for the first time.

It is important to remember that each engine's advanced tool set is somewhat different from the tool set of another, but they all have the same goal of helping you refine your search criteria to get the best results.

In some engines, advanced search options include support for phrase-based searching or Boolean operators, as already discussed. In other engines, an advanced search provides you with customized tools. At Yahoo!, for example, if you

Unlike the printed resources you can find at your library, many Web sites cannot be trusted to provide accurate information.

PRODUCTIVITY TIP

author or publisher. If you cannot find such a notice, then the site's owner or writer may not hold a copyright and may have failed to acknowledge the material's source. In other words, it may have been plagiarized.

» Look for signs of bias in the information. Authoritative information is normally written in an objective, unbiased manner, but this is not necessarily the case. Still, if you find a document that reflects an obvious bias, then it probably is not trustworthy. Ask yourself if the author seems to be promoting a certain viewpoint, theory, practice, or product over others. If so, look at the material skeptically.

» Make sure the material is current. Credible Web designers place a date on each page of their site, noting when it was last updated. Authoritative articles are often dated. Otherwise, look for signs that the information is old or outdated by reading it closely. If the page contains non-working hyperlinks, the publisher has probably neglected it, and this may indicate that the information has been lying around for some time.

select the Advanced link, you can work in a special form to structure your search criteria (see Figure 2A.30). The form lets you use multiple words and phrases and specify whether any or all of the terms should be included in or omitted from the results. The form also provides tools that let you filter adult-oriented content (such as pornographic Web sites) from your results and search for information in a different language or from a given country.

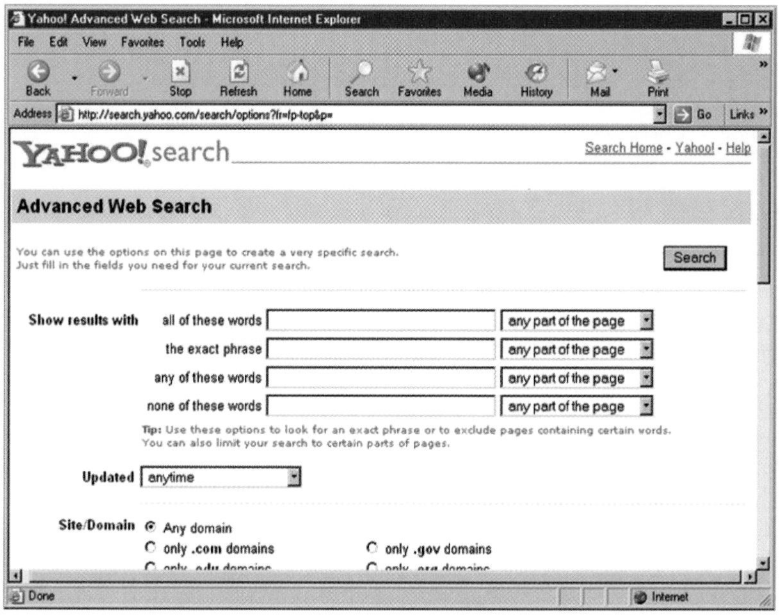

FIGURE 2A.30

The advanced search form at Yahoo!.

While some advanced tool sets allow you to use Boolean operators in their search forms, some do not. This is because some advanced search forms are based on Boolean logic and are designed to help you create complex Boolean-based searches without deciding which operators to use or where to use them.

Using a Metasearch Engine

In addition to the tools described in the preceding sections, another type of Web-based search engine is also popular. These sites, called metasearch engines, use multiple search engines simultaneously to look up sites that match your keywords, phrase, or question.

Examples of metasearch engines include Mamma (http://www.mamma.com) and Dogpile (http://www.dogpile.com), as shown in Figure 2A.31. Metasearch engines are helpful if you are not certain which keywords to use or if you want to get a very long list of Web sites that meet your search criteria.

Norton ONLINE

For more information on metasearch engines, visit **http://www.mhhe.com/peternorton**.

Sponsored versus Nonsponsored Links

A growing number of Web search engines allow Web sites to pay for preferential listings. In other words, a Web site's owner can pay a search engine to place the site at the top of the list of search results. These purchased listings are called sponsored links, and they have become the subject of some controversy.

Suppose, for example, that you need information about a specific kind of printer, so you use a search engine and conduct a search on the term "printer." The search engine displays a list of Web sites that match the term, but you notice that the first dozen sites in the list are all retailers—not printer manufacturers, reviewers, or technical experts. In this case, it's a good bet that some or all of these retailers paid the search engine to place their sites at the top of the list.

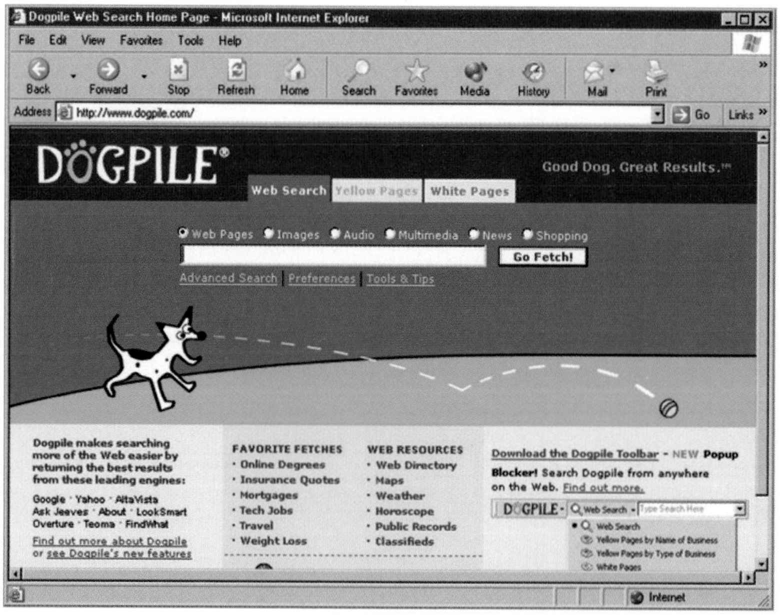

FIGURE 2A.31

Metasearch engines, such as Dogpile, use multiple search engines at one time to give you exhaustive results.

Sponsored links have become controversial because they are not always most relevant to the user's needs. Instead, they are a way for search engines to generate revenues. Some search engines display sponsored links in a special way—putting them in boxes or separate lists—so users can identify them.

Should you avoid sponsored links? No, especially if they are relevant and helpful to you. Be aware, however, that some search engine results may be sponsored; take care to look through search results carefully to find the sites that are most useful. If your favorite search engine does not highlight sponsored links in some way, consider using an engine that does.

Using Site-Specific Search Tools

Many high-volume Web sites feature built-in search tools of their own, enabling you to look for information on the Web site you are currently visiting. Sites such as Microsoft Corporation (http://www.microsoft.com), CNN (http://www.cnn.com), Netscape Communications (http://www.netscape.com), and many others feature such tools.

Suppose, for example, you are visiting the Microsoft Web site and want to find information about Flight Simulator, which is a popular Microsoft game. Instead of jumping from one page to another looking for information, you can click in the Search box, type the words **Flight Simulator**, and click the Go button. The site's search engine displays a list of pages on the Microsoft site that are related to Flight Simulator.

Some site-specific search tools also let you search outside that particular site. At ZDNet's site (http://www.zdnet.com), for example, you can type one or more keywords in the Search box and then decide whether you want to search only the ZDNet site or the entire Web for related information before clicking the Search button (see Figure 2A.32).

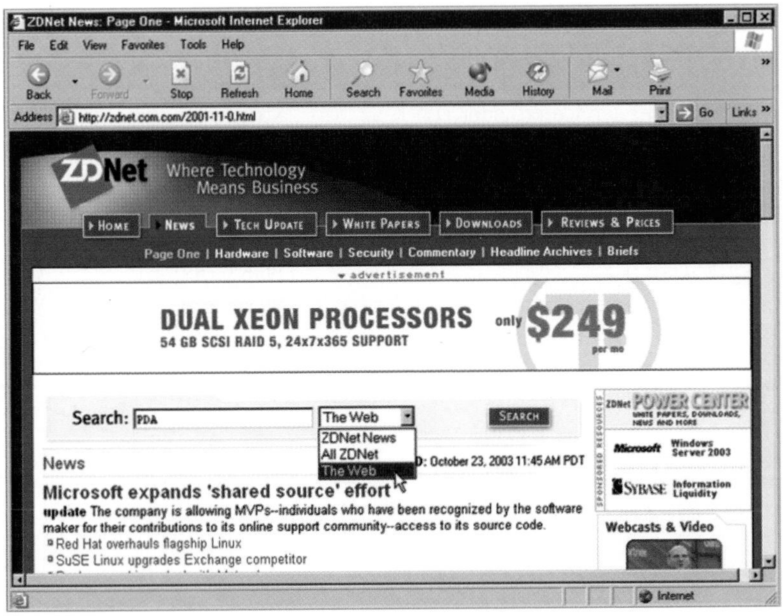

FIGURE 2A.32

You can search only the ZDNet site or the entire Web.

LESSON // 2A Review

Summary ::

- The Internet was created for the U.S. Department of Defense as a tool for communications. Today the Internet is a global network of interconnected networks.
- The Internet carries messages, documents, programs, and data files that contain every imaginable kind of information for businesses, educational institutions, government agencies, and individuals.
- One of the services available through the Internet is the World Wide Web (or Web). To access the Web, you need an Internet connection and a Web browser.
- Navigating the Web means moving from one Web page or Web site to another.
- Web pages can contain navigational tools, in the form of hyperlinks, which help the user move from page to page.
- Most Web browsers allow the user to navigate the Web in various ways by using toolbar buttons, hyperlinks, bookmarks, and a history list.
- Web browsers, like other application programs, feature online Help systems.
- To search for content on the Web, you can use a directory, a search engine, or a metasearch engine.
- A directory is a categorized list of links. Users can find the information they need by selecting categories and subcategories of topics.
- A search engine lets users search for content by using keywords. The engine lists any Web sites it finds that match the keywords.
- Users can refine their Web searches by using tools such as Boolean operators or advanced search tools.
- Metasearch engines use multiple search engines simultaneously to look up sites that match your keywords, phrase, or question.

Key Terms ::

ARPANET, 50
backbone, 51
Boolean operator, 66
browser, 54
directory, 63
helper application, 56
host, 50
hyperlink, 53
hypertext, 53
hypertext link, 53
hypertext markup language (HTML), 53
hypertext transfer protocol (HTTP), 53
Internet, 49
Internet service provider (ISP), 52
internetworking, 51
keyword, 64
link, 53
metasearch engine, 70
NSFnet, 51
plug-in application, 56
publish, 54
search engine, 63
spawn, 58
sponsored link, 70
start page, 60
streaming audio, 57
streaming video, 57
uniform resource locator (URL), 55
Web browser, 54
Web page, 53
Web site, 53
World Wide Web (Web, WWW), 52

Key Term Quiz ::

Complete each statement by writing one of the terms listed under Key Terms in each blank.

1. On the Internet, a(n) ____________ computer works like a network server computer.
2. To access the Internet, you need the right software and an account with a(n) ____________ .
3. A Web page is a document formatted with the ____________ language.
4. A(n) ____________ is software you can use to navigate the World Wide Web.
5. AND, OR, and NOT are examples of ____________ .
6. To allow you to view some kinds of content, your Web browser may need to spawn a(n) ____________ application.
7. A(n) ____________ uses multiple search engines simultaneously to look up sites that match your keywords, phrase, or question.
8. The process of connecting separate networks together is called ____________ .
9. A(n) ____________ helps you find content on the Web by allowing you to choose categories and subcategories of topics.
10. A(n) ____________ is the Web page that appears in your browser window as soon as you launch the program.

Review

Multiple Choice ::

Circle the word or phrase that best completes each statement.

1. Construction of the network now known as the Internet began in ____________ .
   a. 1949 b. 1959 c. 1969 d. 1979
2. The Internet is open to ____________ .
   a. members b. government agencies c. university researchers d. anyone who can access it
3. A collection of related Web pages is called a ____________ .
   a. Web book b. Web site c. Web directory d. Web engine
4. Every Web page has a unique address, called a ____________ .
   a. hyperlink b. uniform resource locator c. HTTP d. map
5. When you use a search engine, you specify one or more ____________ .
   a. keywords b. Web pages c. sites d. URLs
6. The Internet acts as a(n) ____________ for services such as the World Wide Web and e-mail.
   a. provider b. host c. carrier d. server
7. Because it uses HTTP, the Web supports ____________ documents.
   a. electronic b. hypertext c. colorful d. overlapping
8. The first point-and-click Web browser was named ____________ .
   a. Mosaic b. Moselle c. Moseying d. Mostly
9. After streaming content is played in your browser, it is ____________ .
   a. returned b. saved c. copied d. deleted
10. Before you launch your browser and view a Web page, you may need to ____________ .
    a. get permission b. connect to the Internet c. call your ISP d. launch a helper application

Review Questions ::

In your own words, briefly answer the following questions.

1. How was ARPANET created, and what was its goal?
2. Why is the Internet sometimes described as a "network of networks"?
3. What is a backbone?
4. List eight of the Internet's major services.
5. What happens when you provide a URL for your Web browser?
6. List three ways you can specify a URL in your Web browser.
7. What is a bookmark in a Web browser and what do bookmarks allow you to do?
8. How does a search engine let you search for information on the Web?
9. List four Boolean operators that are sometimes used in Web searches.
10. The advanced tools of some search engines do not allow you to use Boolean operators. Why?

Lesson Labs ::

Complete the following exercises as directed by your instructor.

1. Practice using your browser. Launch your browser and practice navigating the Web. Try using URLs based on the names of people or companies you want to learn more about. For example, if you type **http://www.cheerios.com** in your Address box, what happens? Make up five different URLs from company, product, or individual names and see where they lead your browser. As you visit different sites, look for hyperlinked text and graphics; click them, and see where they lead.
2. Search, search, search. Pick a topic and search the Web for information about it. Pick a keyword to use in your search, then visit three search engines and use each of them to conduct a search using your chosen keyword. Use Yahoo! (http://www.yahoo.com), AltaVista (http://www.altavista.com), and Google (http://www.google.com) for your searches. Do the results differ from one search engine to another?

LESSON // 2B

E-Mail and Other Internet Services

Overview: Communicating through the Internet

With its graphics-rich pages and streaming multimedia content, the World Wide Web belies the Internet's original purpose—to serve as a means of communication. As you have already seen, millions of people use the Internet to exchange e-mail. In fact, e-mail is now a more common means of communication than telephone calls.

The Internet's other services, though lesser known and used, provide users with other unique and interesting ways to communicate. While e-mail and news enable people to exchange "delayed" messages, services such as chat and instant messaging allow users to send and respond to message in real time. Other services, such as FTP and peer-to-peer systems, are used mainly for exchanging different types of files through the Internet—a practice that is now an essential part of electronic communications.

This lesson introduces you to each of these important Internet-based services. You will learn how each one is used and the types of software you will need to communicate or send information through them.

OBJECTIVES ::

- Explain how e-mail technologies allow users to exchange messages.
- Describe the parts of a typical e-mail address.
- Explain how Internet newsgroups function.
- Describe the process of transferring a file via FTP.
- Differentiate between Internet relay chat and instant messaging.
- Identify two ways in which Internet-based peer-to-peer services are used.

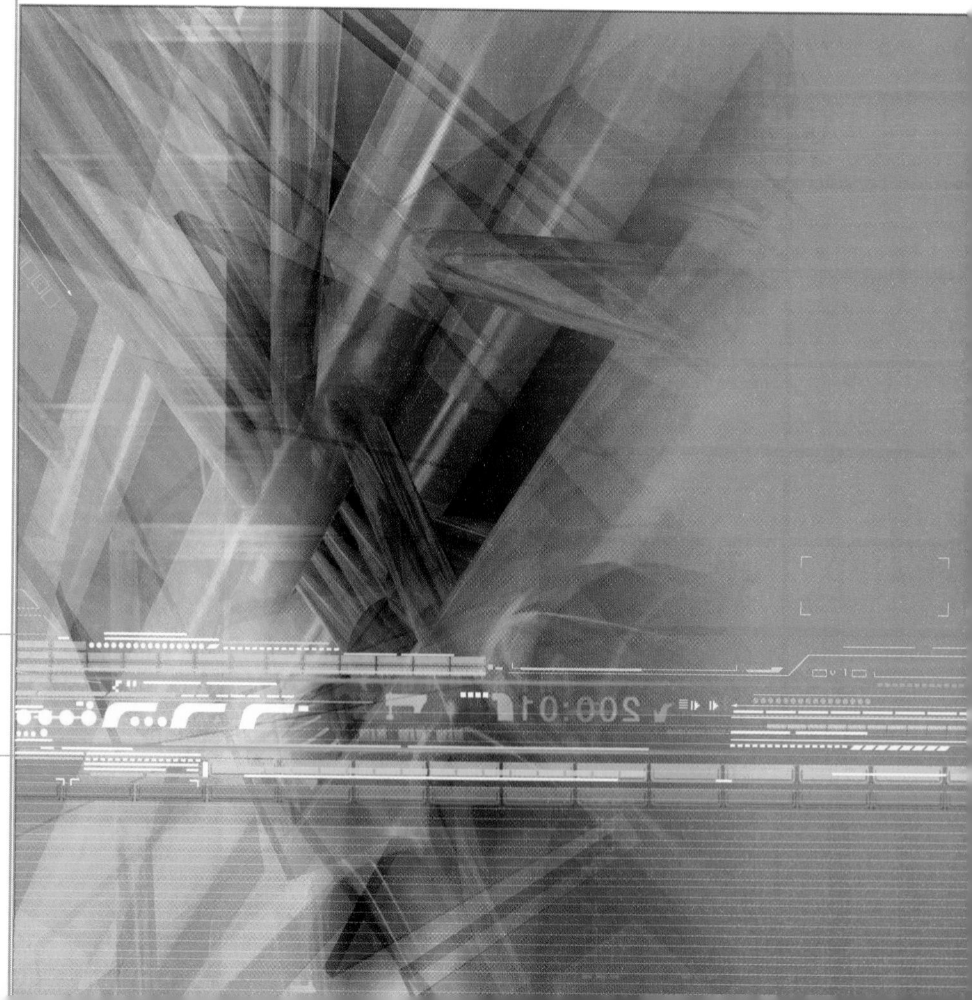

Using E-Mail

The only Internet service that is more frequently used than the Web is electronic mail. Electronic mail, or e-mail, is a system for exchanging messages through a computer network. People most commonly use e-mail to send and receive text messages, but depending on the software you use, you may be able to exchange audio or video messages with someone else.

E-mail was one of the first uses of the Internet, and quickly became a popular feature because it lets users exchange messages from anywhere in the world. Further, e-mail is less expensive than using the telephone because there is no charge for using it, beyond the regular fees you pay your ISP. E-mail is also a faster way to communicate than postal mail because e-mail messages typically reach their destination in seconds rather than days.

E-mail services are very easy to access, and this is another reason for e-mail's popularity. You can manage e-mail through a typical ISP account and a desktop computer, or use a Web-based e-mail service, which lets you check your messages wherever you have Web access. Many cellular telephones and pagers provide e-mail features, too (see Figure 2B.1). Some e-mail systems can even interact with any telephone and actually "read" your messages to you.

Another advantage of e-mail is the ability to attach data files and program files to messages. For example, you can send a message to a friend and attach a digital photograph or some other file to the message. The recipient then can open and use the document on his or her computer.

E-mail, however, is not a real-time communications system. This means that once you send a message to someone, you must wait until he or she reads it and sends you a reply. This delay, however, doesn't stop people from exchanging billions of messages each year.

Understanding E-Mail

The most common way to create, send, and receive e-mail is by using an e-mail program (also called an e-mail client) and an Internet connection through an ISP or LAN. Popular Internet e-mail programs include Eudora, Microsoft Outlook, Microsoft Outlook Express, Netscape Messenger, and others.

(There are many Web-based e-mail services that allow you to send and receive e-mail by using your Web browser. Those services will be discussed later in this lesson.)

E-Mail Addresses

If you have an account with an ISP or if you are a user on a corporate or school LAN, then you can establish an e-mail address. This unique address enables other users to send messages to you and enables you to send messages to others.

You can set up an e-mail account by creating a unique user name for yourself, which identifies your postal mailbox on the Internet. If your name is John Smith, for example, your user name might be "jsmith" or "john_smith." In an e-mail address, the user name usually appears before the ISP host computer's name. The user name and the host computer's name are separated by the @ symbol (commonly called the "at" symbol). So, if your ISP is America Online (AOL), your e-mail address might look like this:

jsmith@aol.com

You read this address as "J Smith at a-o-l dot com." Figure 2B.2 shows an e-mail address being used in a message.

Norton ONLINE

For more information on Internet e-mail, visit **http://www.mhhe.com/peternorton**.

simnet™

FIGURE 2B.1

Portable devices, such as this BlackBerry® Wireless Handheld™ handheld system, let you send and receive e-mail messages wirelessly, from virtually any location.

FIGURE 2B.2

E-mail addresses enable people to send and receive e-mail messages over the Internet.

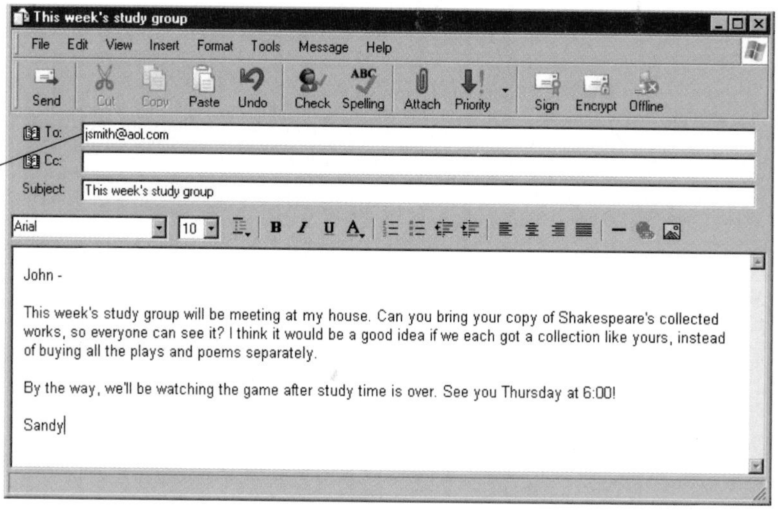

When you send an e-mail message, the message is stored on a server until the recipient can retrieve it. This type of server is called a mail server. Many mail servers use the post office protocol (POP) and are called POP servers. Nearly all ISPs and corporate networks maintain one or more mail servers for storing and forwarding e-mail messages.

Listserv Systems

The most common use for e-mail is when one person sends a message to someone else, or to a small group. However, e-mail systems can be used to distribute messages to thousands of people at the same time. These electronic, automated mailing lists are commonly used to distribute electronic newsletters or bulletin board–style messages to a group. For example, you might join a mailing list for people who are interested in antiques or a particular type of music and receive the group's bulletin with your regular e-mail. Members can contribute messages to the group, too.

One type of mailing list is the automated list server, or listserv. Listserv systems allow users on the list to post their own messages, so the result is an ongoing discussion that the entire group can see and join. Hundreds of mailing-list discussions are in progress all the time, on a huge variety of topics.

Norton ONLINE

For more information on e-mail programs, visit **http://www.mhhe.com/peternorton**.

Using an E-Mail Program

Standard e-mail programs are free and easy to use. If you have purchased a computer in the last few years, it probably came with an e-mail program already installed. Microsoft Outlook Express is commonly installed on Windows-based computers.

The following sections briefly show you how to create and send an e-mail message using Outlook Express running under Windows XP. If you use a different e-mail program or operating system, the steps will be similar, but your screen will look different and the tools may have different names.

Creating a Message

To create a new e-mail message in Outlook Express, follow these steps:

1. Launch the program by choosing Start | All Programs | Outlook Express.
2. When the Outlook Express window appears, click the Create Mail button. A new window appears, where you can compose the message (see Figure 2B.3).
3. Click in the To: box and type the recipient's e-mail address. You can specify more than one recipient. (If the recipients' addresses are already stored in the

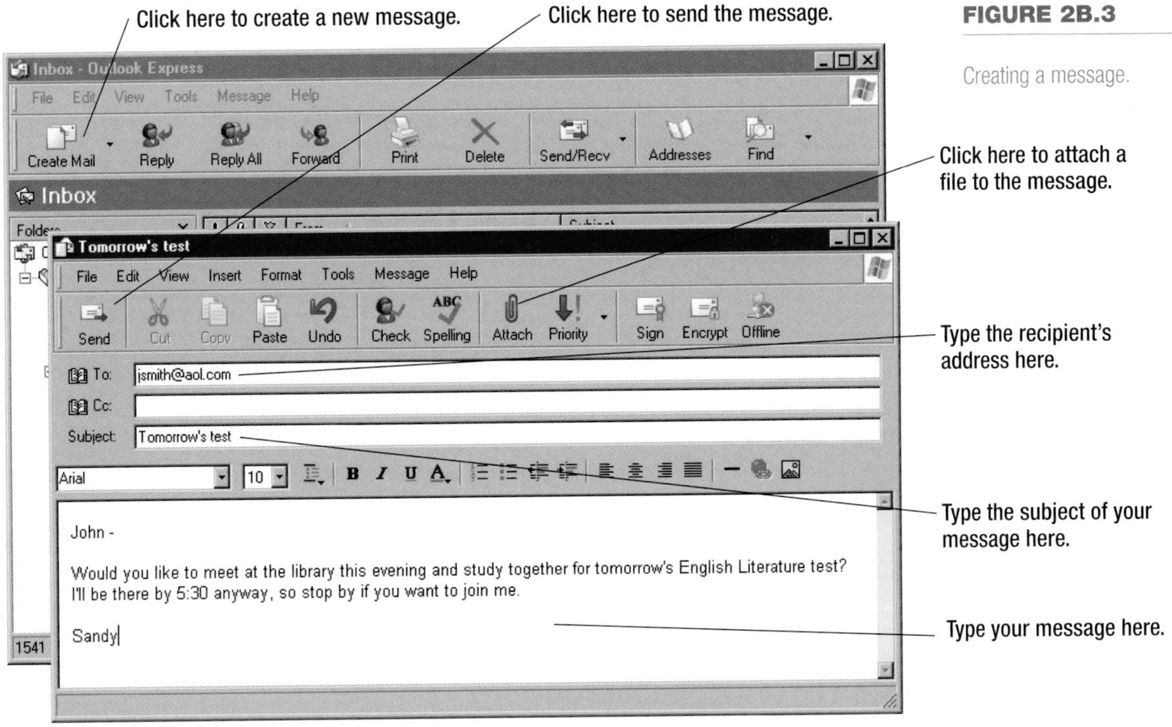

FIGURE 2B.3

Creating a message.

program's address book, you can open it by clicking the To: button and selecting the addresses there.)

4. Click in the Subject: box and type the message's subject. This will let the recipient know what your message is about.
5. Click in the big text box at the bottom of the window and type your message.
6. When the message is ready, click the Send button to deliver the message.

Receiving and Reading a Message

When someone sends you a message, it will appear in your Inbox folder in Outlook Express (see Figure 2B.4), unless you have set the program to receive messages in a different folder. If you select the Inbox folder in the Folders list (in the left-hand pane of the Outlook Express window), a list of messages you have received will appear in the right side of the window. Double-click any message in the list to open and read it.

Once you receive a message, you can do several things with it:

- **Reply.** This means sending a response back to the person who sent you the message.
- **Print.** This creates a paper copy of the message.
- **Forward.** This means sending the message on to someone else—someone other than you or the person who sent it.
- **Delete.** By deleting old or unneeded messages, you keep your Inbox and other folders from getting too full.

SELF-CHECK ::

Circle the correct answer for each question.

1. Your _____ is unique to you.
   a. ISP   b. e-mail address   c. e-mail software
2. A _____ is a computer that stores and forwards e-mail messages.
   a. mail server   b. mail center   c. mail system
3. Standard e-mail programs are _____.
   a. hard to use   b. Web-based   c. free

At Issue

Stomping Out Spam

In a society almost as dependent on e-mail as the U.S. Postal Service, junk e-mail—better known as "spam"—has become more than a mere annoyance. For Internet-connected individuals, it's an increasingly time-consuming and offensive aggravation. In the business world, it's a growing crisis, draining resources and bandwidth and laying networks vulnerable to numerous security hazards.

In the last several years, unsolicited e-mail has quadrupled. Today, spam makes up an estimated 20 percent of corporate e-mail traffic, and the Aberdeen Group predicts spam will soon double, accounting for up to 50 percent of all corporate e-mail.

For personal users, the forecast is even grimmer: More than half of all e-mail traffic is now junk, say experts, up from only 8 percent just two years ago. That's 15 billion spam messages crisscrossing the Internet daily, or 25 spam e-mails a day for every person online in the world. Even worse, spam could make up the majority of message traffic on the Internet by the end of 2002, according to data from the three largest e-mail service providers.

Among the many problems caused by unsolicited e-mail, spam consumes significant time and resources. For example, in one year alone, unwanted commercial e-mail cost U.S. corporations almost $10 billion. Loss was measured in terms of lost worker productivity (workers waste an average of 4.5 seconds on each spam message); use of technical support time; and consumption of bandwidth and other tech resources used to fight spam.

E-mail is the lifeblood of the Internet—hands down it's the most popular application. But thanks to spam, many are losing faith in this modern-day marvel. Because of spam, about three-fourths of e-mail users now avoid giving out their e-mail addresses, more than half say they trust it less, and one in four uses it less, according to a recent study by the Pew Internet and American Life Project. Some are even

FIGURE 2B.4

Reading a message.

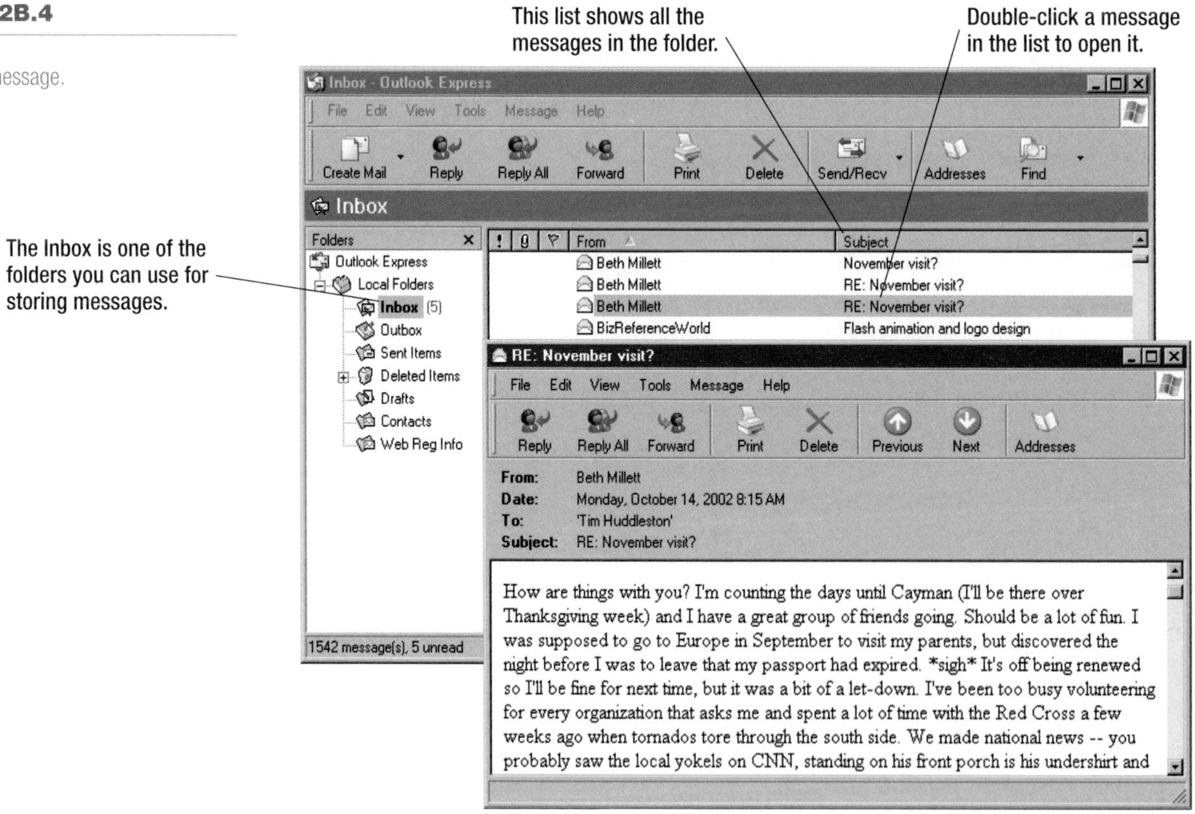

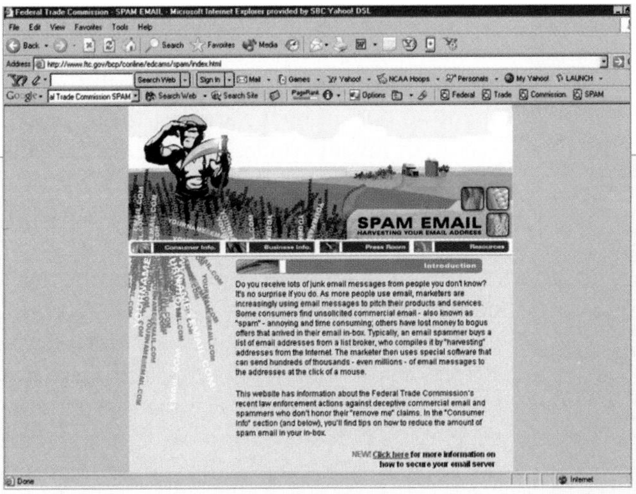

turning to more traditional forms of communication: the telephone and U.S. Postal Service.

So, what will it take to stem the tide? Many fork out big bucks for software blocking and filtering tools. Internet service providers spend hundreds of millions of dollars to improve their spam-blocking technology. Others are taking spammers to court, so far with limited success.

The Federal Trade Commission (FCC) has repeatedly warned that it will go after spammers in court, but the commission's threats have yet to be manifested in legal action (although the FTC does file complaints against spammers who run scams such as pyramid schemes and chain letters soliciting money).

Some feel only comprehensive federal legislation can effectively combat spam. In 2003, the U.S. House of Representatives gave final approval to the first federal anti-spam legislation, authorizing the creation of a Do Not Spam registry and imposing tough penalties for fraudulent e-mail.

Yet, most Internet experts agree. Spam will probably never be entirely eradicated. Ultimately, a consensus approach that coordinates legal and high-tech responses is likely to provide the best defense against the unrelenting flood of junk e-mail.

AT ISSUE

Using Web-Based E-Mail Services

You don't need to have a stand-alone e-mail program to send and receive messages. You can easily manage e-mail by using one of the many Web-based e-mail services. These services offer several advantages over standard e-mail programs:

- **Cost.** Web-based e-mail services such as Hotmail and Mail.com offer free e-mail accounts, although storage space can be limited.
- **Ease of Use.** Web-based e-mail services offer the same tools as standard e-mail programs, all within the familiar confines of your browser, so they are easy to use (see Figure 2B.5).
- **Accessibility.** You can access a Web-based e-mail account from any computer that has Web access. You do not need to log into your ISP's account, which may be impossible if you are traveling.

Norton ONLINE

For more information on Web-based e-mail services, visit **http://www.mhhe.com/peternorton**.

More Features of the Internet

simnet™

Because the Internet is a gigantic network, it can support many different types of services besides the Web and e-mail. In fact, some Internet services have been available for decades and are still widely used.

News

In addition to the messages distributed to mailing lists by e-mail, the Internet also supports a form of public bulletin board called news. There are tens of thousands of active Internet newsgroups, each devoted to discussion of a particular topic. Many of the most widely distributed newsgroups are part of a system called Usenet, but others are targeted to a particular region or to users connected to a specific network or institution, such as a university or a large corporation.

Norton ONLINE

For more information on Internet news, visit **http://www.mhhe.com/peternorton**.

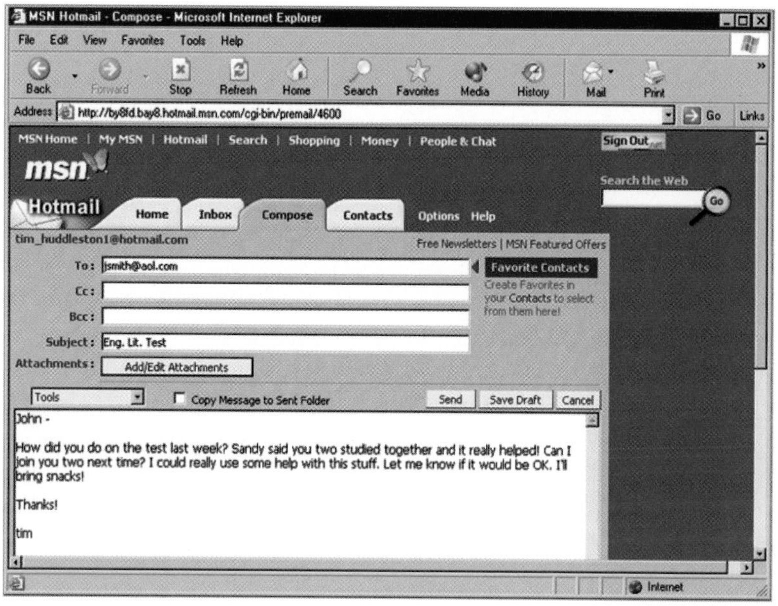

FIGURE 2B.5

Composing a message in Hotmail, a popular Web-based e-mail service.

To participate in a newsgroup, users post articles (short messages) about the newsgroup's main topic. As users read and respond to one another's articles, they create a thread of linked articles. By reading the articles in a thread, you can see the message that initiated the discussion and all the messages that have been posted in response to it.

The most popular way to participate in newsgroups is by using a newsreader program. Popular newsreaders include News Rover, Xnews, and NewsPro, and there are many others. Some free e-mail programs, such as Microsoft Outlook Express and Netscape's Messenger, also have built-in newsreaders. A newsreader program obtains articles from a news server, a host computer that exchanges articles with other servers through the Internet. Because these servers use the network news transfer protocol (NNTP) , they are sometimes called NNTP servers. To participate in newsgroups, you can run a newsreader program to log on to a server. Most ISPs provide access to a news server as part of an Internet account. You also can use a Web browser to participate in newsgroups, by visiting a Web site—such as Google (http://groups.google.com) or Newsfeeds.com (http://www.newsfeeds.com)—that publishes newsgroup content.

To see articles that have been posted about a specific topic, you can subscribe to the newsgroup that addresses that topic. Newsgroups are organized into major categories, called domains, and categorized by individual topics within each domain. There are several major domains within the Usenet structure and many more alternative domains. Table 2B.1 lists the major Usenet domains.

The name of a newsgroup begins with the domain, followed by one or more words that describe the group's topic, such as alt.food. Some topics include separate newsgroups for related subtopics, such as alt.food.chocolate. Newsgroup names can be quite long. As Figure 2B.6 shows, subscribing to a newsgroup is a three-step process. Figure 2B.7 shows a series of articles and responses that make up a thread.

To subscribe, you must download a list of available newsgroups from the server, choose the groups that interest you, and select articles. In most newsreaders, you can choose to reply to an article by posting another article to the newsgroup or by sending a private e-mail message to the person who wrote the original article.

Newsgroups are a relatively fast way to distribute information to potentially interested readers, and they allow people to discuss topics of common interest. They also can be a convenient channel for finding answers to questions. Many questions are asked again and again, so it is always a good idea to read the articles that other people have posted before you jump in with your own questions. Members of many newsgroups post lists of frequently asked questions (FAQ) and their answers every month or two.

TABLE 2B.1

Common Usenet Domains

Domain	Description
comp	Computer-related topics
sci	Science and technology (except computers)
soc	Social issues and politics
news	Topics related to Usenet
rec	Hobbies, arts, and recreational activities
misc	Topics that do not fit into one of the other domains
The most important alternative topics include the following:	
alt	Alternative newsgroups
bionet	Biological sciences
biz	Business topics, including advertisements
clari	News from the Associated Press and Reuters, supplied through a service called Clarinet
K12	Newsgroups for primary and secondary schools

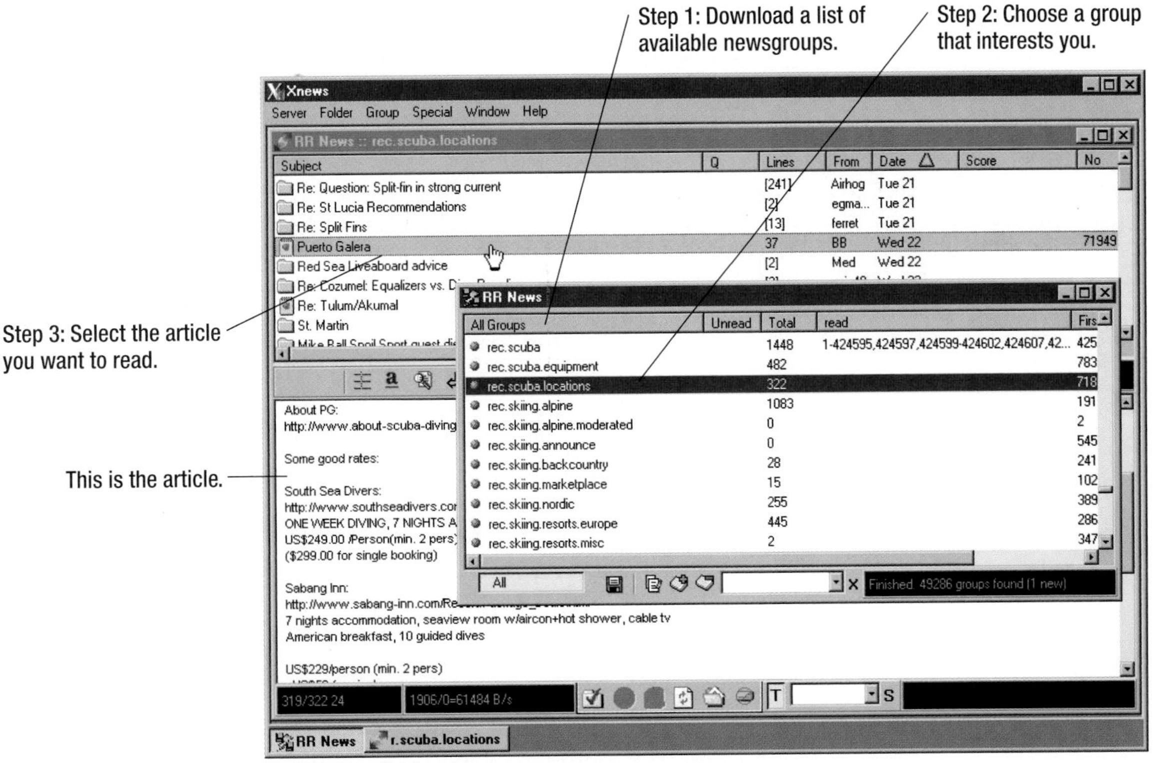

FIGURE 2B.6

Subscribing to a newsgroup.

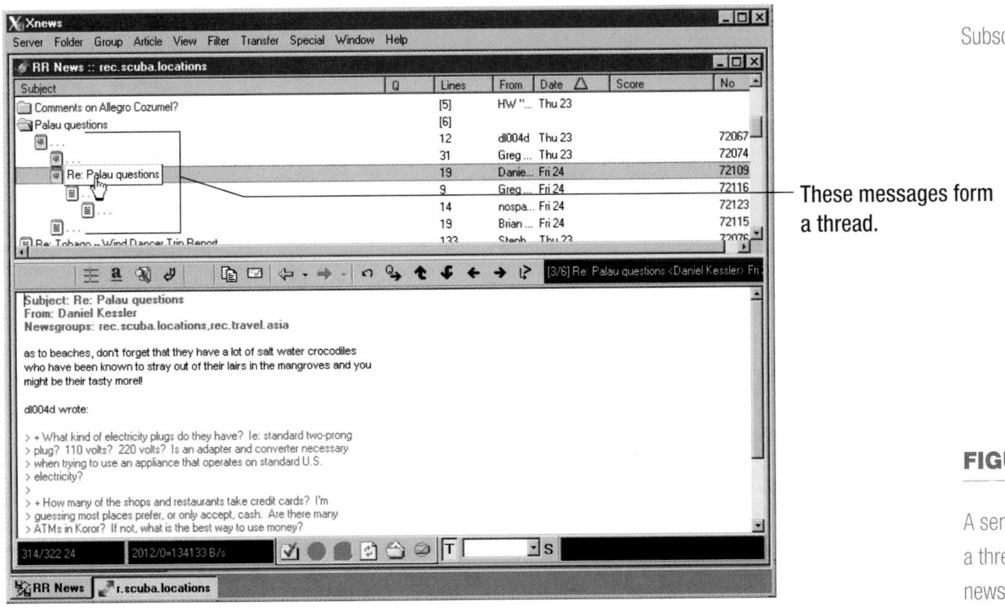

FIGURE 2B.7

A series of articles and responses create a thread, or ongoing discussion, in a newsgroup.

FTP

File transfer protocol (FTP) is the Internet tool used to copy files from one computer to another.

An FTP site is a collection of files, including data files and/or programs, that are housed on an FTP server. FTP sites, which are often called *archives*, may contain thousands of individual programs and files. Public FTP archives permit anyone to make copies of their files by using special FTP client software (see Figure 2B.8). Because these public archives usually require visitors to use the word "anonymous" as an account name, they are known as anonymous FTP archives.

Norton ONLINE

For more information on FTP, visit **http://www.mhhe.com/peternorton**.

It is not always necessary to use an FTP client to download files from an FTP site. Web browsers also support FTP. In fact, if you visit a Web site such as Microsoft (http://www.microsoft.com) or Macromedia (http://www.macromedia. com), you can download programs and data files directly onto your computer through your Web browser. This type of file transfer usually is an FTP operation and is available through many different Web sites.

FTP sites provide access to many different types of files. You can find information of all kinds, from weather maps to magazine articles, housed on these systems. Computer hardware and software companies frequently host their own FTP sites, where you can copy program updates, bug solutions, and other types of software.

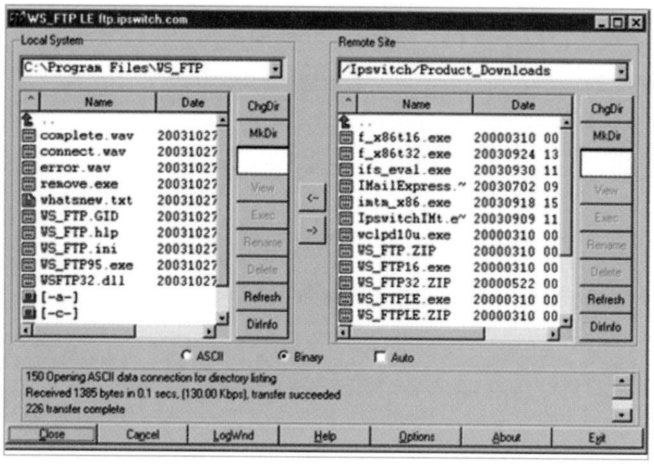

FIGURE 2B.8

Here is a popular FTP client program named WS_FTP LE, which is used to transfer files from an FTP site (the remote site) to the user's computer (the local system).

Although FTP is easy to use, it can be hard to find a file that you want to download. One way to find files is to use Archie, the searchable index of FTP archives maintained by McGill University in Montreal. (Archie is a nickname for archives.) The main Archie server at McGill gathers copies of the directories from more than 1,000 other public FTP archives every month and distributes copies of those directories to dozens of other servers around the world. When a server receives a request for a keyword search, it returns a list of files that match the search criteria and the location of each file. Many FTP client programs provide Archie search tools, and some Web sites enable you to conduct Archie searches through your Web browser (see Figure 2B.9).

Norton ONLINE

For more information on Internet chat, visit **http://www.mhhe.com/peternorton**.

simnet™

Internet Relay Chat (IRC) and Web-Based Chat

Internet relay chat (IRC), or just chat, is a popular way for Internet users to communicate in real time with other users. Real-time communication means communicating with other users in the immediate present. Unlike e-mail, chat does not require a waiting period between the time you send a message and the time the other person or group of people receives the message. IRC is often referred to as the "CB radio" of the Internet because it enables a few or many people to join a discussion.

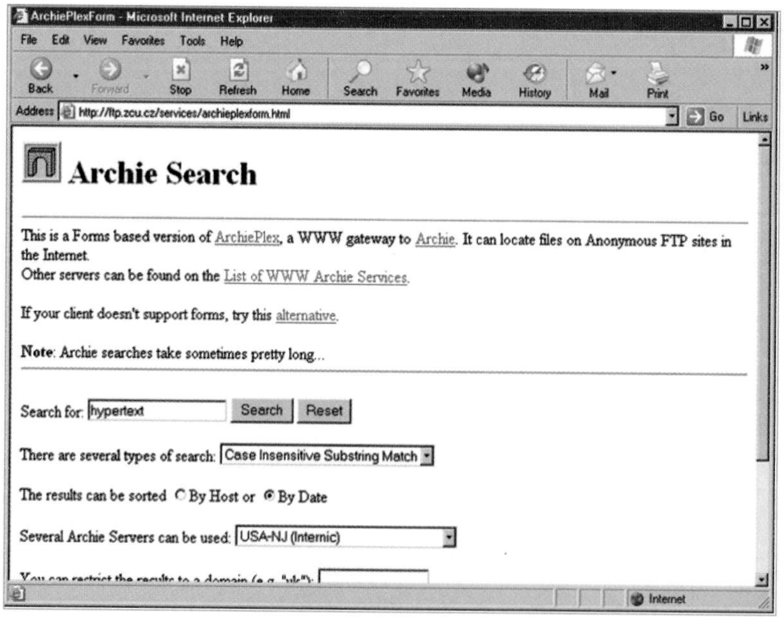

FIGURE 2B.9

Web sites like this one enable you to use Archie to search for files on the Internet. Here, the user is searching for files related to the keyword *hypertext*.

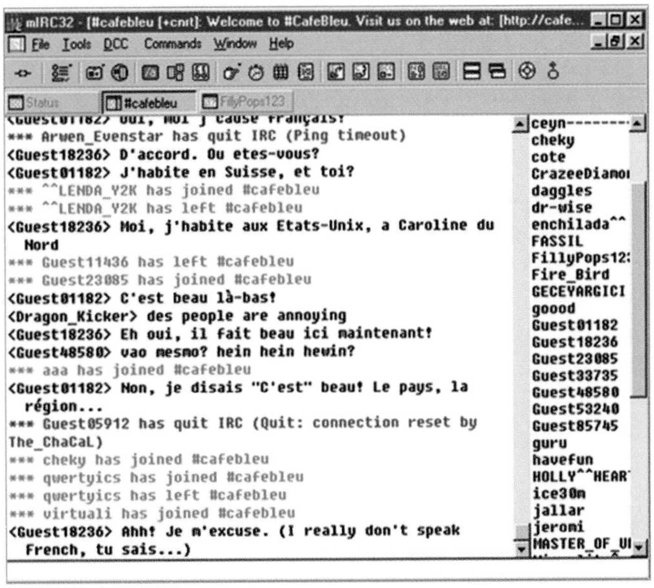

FIGURE 2B.10

A chat in progress.

IRC is a multi-user system where people join channels to exchange these real-time messages. Channels are discussion groups where chat users convene to discuss a topic. Chat messages are typed on a user's computer and sent to the IRC channel, where all users who have joined that channel receive the message. Users can then read, reply to, or ignore that message or create their own message (see Figure 2B.10).

Chat rooms are also a popular addition to Web sites. Users can participate in chat sessions directly within a Web browser window without installing or running special chat software (see Figure 2B.11).

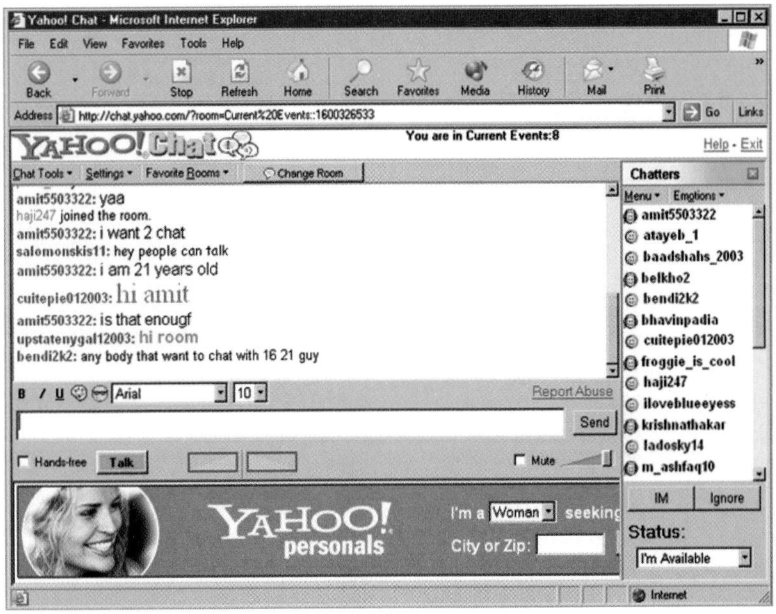

FIGURE 2B.11

Many Web sites, including Yahoo!, MSN, and others, provide chat rooms for visitors. At these sites, you can chat without navigating channels or using special chat software.

Instant Messaging

The popularity of public chat rooms created a huge demand for a way to chat privately, so that a limited number of invited people could exchange real-time messages on their screens without being seen or interrupted by anyone else online.

This demand led to the development of instant messaging (IM), a type of chat software that restricts participation to specific users. There are several popular IM services available, such as Windows Messenger, AOL Instant Messenger, and others (see Figure 2B.12).

Using one of these programs, you can create a buddy list—a list of other users with whom you would like to chat. Whenever your IM program is running and you are online, the software lets you know when your "buddies" are also online, so you can chat with them.

Norton ONLINE

For more information on instant messaging, visit **http://www.mhhe.com/peternorton**.

Online Services

An online service is a company that offers access, generally on a subscription basis, to e-mail, discussion groups, databases on various subjects (such as weather information, stock quotes, newspaper articles, and so on), and other services

Computers In Your Career

Documentation and Online Help System Designer

Five years ago, most of Mark Jensen's help documents were produced and distributed to customers as paper-based manuals. A technical writer with Epicor Software's Vista Development division in Minneapolis, Jensen says the process has changed dramatically since then, and that most of those documents are now published online. The trend has driven Jensen to learn new applications like HTML and XML, both of which help him design and update Vista Development's online help system.

A developer of software enterprise solutions for small manufacturers, Vista Development relies on tech-savvy professionals like Jensen to produce materials that the company's customers use for help with their applications. An English major, Jensen earned his Bachelor's degree from Concordia College and a Master's in Fine Arts from the University of Nevada, Las Vegas.

When he's not cramming to finish up a large project, Jensen works a 40-hour week and populates his agenda with tasks that need "immediate" attention (documenting the changes that users can expect from a new version of Epicor's software, for example); tasks that are "ongoing" (updating and adding new features to the firm's online help system); and creating and distributing a monthly technical newsletter for customers.

Jensen says he likes the variety that his job provides, particularly when it comes to learning new things and helping customers make better use of their technology investments. "It's very gratifying to know that the customers really need the help, and that I can provide it," says Jensen. "There's a good feeling that comes from creating something that can be useful to others."

Calling job opportunities for documentation and online help designers "stable," Jensen says both the Internet and technology have created a steady demand for technically oriented individuals who can create help systems and populate them with content that users rely on to help them maximize their own technology infrastructures.

Online documentation isn't limited to the IT space. Whether it's a new toaster or the latest PC operating system, and whether the documentation is in a brochure or on a compact disk, all product documentation has one thing in common: Someone has to research, write, edit, design, and

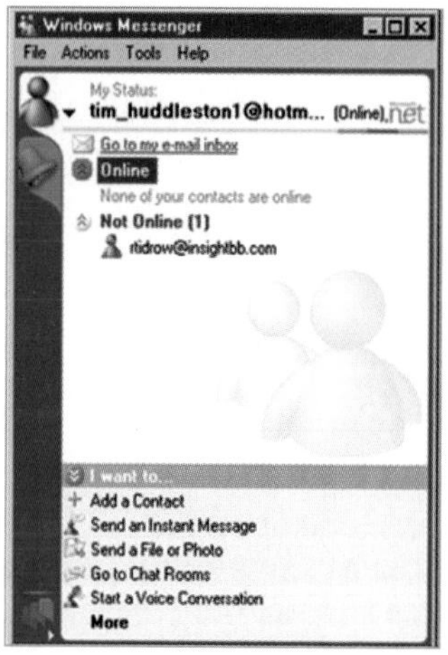

FIGURE 2B.12

Microsoft Messenger, a popular instant messaging program.

ranging from electronic banking and investing to online games. Online services also offer access to the Internet, functioning as an ISP to their subscribers. The most popular online services are America Online (see Figure 2B.13), CompuServe, and Prodigy.

In addition to Internet access, online services offer other features that typical ISPs do not. For example, America Online has become famous for its casual chat rooms, and CompuServe is probably best known for its discussion forums geared to technically oriented users. These activities do not take place on the Internet, where everyone can access them. Rather, these services are provided only for the subscribers of the online services. Discussion groups hosted by online services are often monitored by a system operator, or sysop, who ensures that participants follow the rules. Users typically pay by the month for a subscription that allows them to use the service for a limited number of hours per month; they may pay by the hour for additional time, if needed. Subscriptions with unlimited hours are also available.

Norton ONLINE

For more information on online services, visit **http://www.mhhe.com/peternorton**.

Norton ONLINE

For more information on peer-to-peer services on the Internet, visit **http://www.mhhe.com/peternorton**.

Peer-to-Peer Services

Peer-to-peer (P2P) services are distributed networks (individual computers, which may be miles apart, that are connected by a network) that do not require a central

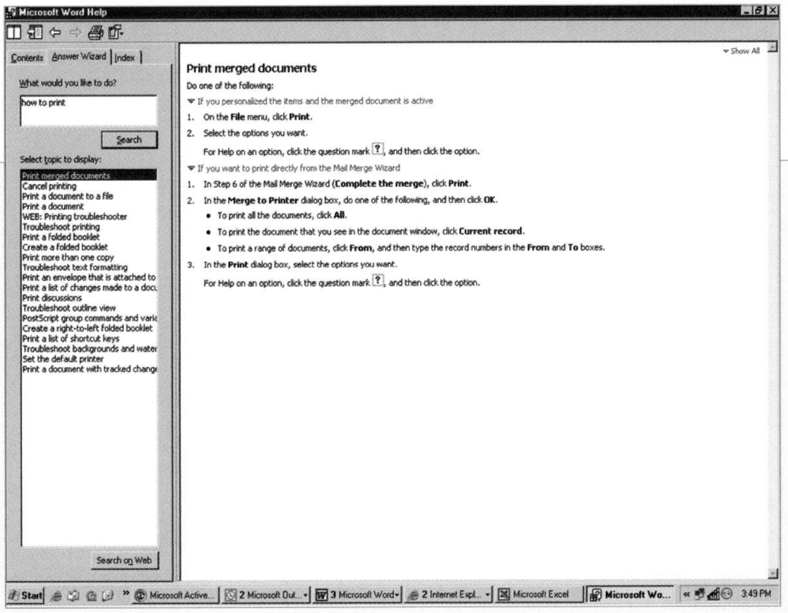

COMPUTERS IN YOUR CAREER

publish it. These tasks are usually handled by professionals who have special skills and who use a variety of tools in their work.

Technical writers like Jensen create the documentation team's backbone, which is rounded out by technical illustrators who create the graphic components and page layout technicians who take the manuscript and illustrations and use desktop publishing software to prepare a professional-looking document. Online help architects use software tools to compile hundreds or thousands of individual documents (each one dealing with a specific topic) and link them together into a seamless online help system.

Many products include printed documentation to help users master its features and troubleshoot problems, but today nearly all software products provide online help, and often in lieu of printed documentation. This is simply documentation in electronic format and must be researched and written just like printed documentation. The Bureau of Labor Statistics reports median annual earnings for salaried technical writers at $47,790 in 2000, with the middle 50 percent earning between $37,280 and $60,000.

server, such as a Web server, to manage files. Instead, specialty software is created, allowing an individual's computer to communicate directly with another individual's computer and even have access to files or information on that computer. Instant messaging, which you read about earlier, is an example of a P2P service.

File-sharing services are another type of P2P service that you may know about already. Services such as gnutella, Kazaa, and others allow users to search for files on each others' computers via the Internet. These file-sharing systems are most commonly used by people who want to share or trade music files online.

Peer-to-peer services are popular because they allow people to share files of all types directly from the peer connections available via the peer software. Corporations have adopted P2P technology as a quick means of transporting information without having to have all the information stored in a centralized location.

FIGURE 2B.13

Users of online services can exchange e-mail messages not only with one another, but with anyone else who has an e-mail account on the Internet. This screen shows the mailbox of an AOL user.

LESSON //2B Review

Summary ::

- Even though it is not a real-time communications medium, e-mail is more commonly used than the Web.
- To send and receive e-mail messages, you need an e-mail account with an ISP or some other resource (such as your school or business) and an e-mail program. Otherwise, you can exchange e-mail through a Web-based mail service.
- An e-mail address is a unique identifier that enables someone to send and receive e-mail messages. It includes a user name, the @ symbol, and the host computer's name, such as jsmith@aol.com.
- A listserv system allows many people to exchange messages with one another, so that everyone in the group can see and respond to them.
- Internet news consists of thousands of newsgroups, each devoted to a topic. Users can post messages and responses in the group, creating discussions.
- File transfer protocol (FTP) is the Internet tool used to copy files from one computer to another.
- Internet relay chat (IRC) enables users to communicate in real time, in special groups called channels. Web-based chatrooms are an alternative to the more traditional IRC.
- Instant messaging (IM) is like chat, but is private. Users can create their own chatrooms, where invited guests (called buddies) can participate.
- Online services provide Internet access in addition to other features, which are available only to their subscribers.
- Peer-to-peer (P2P) services allow users to access one another's computers via the Internet. P2P services form the basis for popular file-sharing systems such as Kazaa.

Key Terms ::

anonymous FTP archive, 83
article, 82
buddy list, 85
channel, 85
chat, 84
electronic mail (e-mail), 77
e-mail address, 77
e-mail client, 77
e-mail program, 77
file transfer protocol (FTP), 83
frequently asked questions (FAQ), 82
FTP client software, 83
FTP server, 83
FTP site, 83
instant messaging (IM), 85
Internet relay chat (IRC), 84
listserv, 78
mail server, 78
network news transfer protocol (NNTP), 82
news, 81
news server, 82
newsgroup, 81
newsreader, 82
NNTP server, 82
online service, 85
peer-to-peer (P2P) service, 86
POP server, 78
post office protocol (POP), 78
subscribe, 82
system operator (sysop), 86
thread, 82
user name, 77

Key Term Quiz ::

Complete each statement by writing one of the terms listed under Key Terms in each blank.

1. ____________ is more commonly used than the World Wide Web.
2. Outlook Express is an example of a(n) ____________ .
3. An e-mail address typically includes a(n) ____________ , followed by the @ symbol and the ISP's domain name.
4. Mail servers generally use the ____________ protocol.
5. The ____________ system is like a public message board that is based on e-mail.
6. alt.food.chocolate could be an example of an Internet ____________ .
7. In a newsgroup, a string of related messages and responses is called a(n) ____________ .
8. If you want to get a specific file via the Internet, you might use the ____________ protocol.
9. IRC users hold discussions in special areas called ____________ .
10. CompuServe is an example of a(n) ____________ .

LESSON //2B Review

Multiple Choice ::

Circle the word or phrase that best completes each statement.

1. E-mail is a system for exchanging messages through a ________ .
   a. client b. program c. network d. backbone
2. A disadvantage of e-mail is that it does not operate in ________ .
   a. real time b. time lines c. time outs d. time zones
3. The @ character is typically called the ________ symbol.
   a. approximate b. at c. address d. about
4. When you send an e-mail message, it is stored on a ________ until the recipient can retrieve it.
   a. protocol b. backbone c. mailbox d. server
5. A ________ system lets you participate in discussion groups by using your regular e-mail software.
   a. groupserv b. mailserv c. softserv d. listserv
6. When you receive an e-mail message, you can ________ it to someone else.
   a. serve b. forward c. store d. copy
7. Many of the widely distributed Internet newsgroups are part of a system called ________ .
   a. NNTPnet b. Newsnet c. Usenet d. Topicnet
8. To see newsgroup articles that have been posted about a specific topic, you can ________ to a newsgroup that addresses the topic.
   a. subscribe b. transfer c. submit d. publish
9. FTP sites are often called ________ .
   a. channels b. archives c. groups d. domains
10. ________ is a type of chat software that restricts participation to specific users.
    a. IRC b. Usenet c. Newsreader d. Instant messaging

Review Questions ::

In your own words, briefly answer the following questions.

1. What is e-mail most commonly used for?
2. E-mail is not a real-time communications system. What does this mean?
3. What is the purpose of a user name, in an e-mail address?
4. What is a POP server?
5. In Outlook Express, what happens when you click the Create Mail button?
6. List four things you can do with an e-mail message, once you receive it.
7. How are Internet newsgroups organized?
8. What is a public FTP archive?
9. What is Archie?
10. What is a "buddy list"?

Lesson Labs ::

Complete the following exercises as directed by your instructor.

1. Identify your e-mail program. If you haven't already done so, check your computer to see what e-mail programs have been installed. Click the Start menu, then click All Programs. When the Programs submenu appears, search for the names of any programs that look like e-mail clients. With your instructor's permission, launch each of the programs to see if you were right.
2. Send a message. Once you locate and launch your e-mail program, send a message to a classmate. First, exchange e-mail addresses with a classmate. Then, use your e-mail software to compose and send a short message. (If you need guidance, follow the instructions given earlier in this lesson, or ask your instructor for assistance.) Then wait for your classmate to respond to the message. How long does the process take? When you are finished, close the e-mail program.

Chapter Labs

Complete the following exercises using a computer in your classroom, lab, or home.

1. Learn more about the Internet. One of the best places to learn about the Internet is on the Internet. Dozens of authoritative Web sites provide information on the history of the Internet and technical issues, as well as tutorials for using the Web, Internet software, and more. To find more basic information about the Internet, visit these Web sites:

   » **Webmonkey Guides.** http://www.hotwired.lycos.com/webmonkey/guides
   » **Newbie.** http://www.newbie.org
   » **Internet 101.** http://www.internet101.org

2. Master your browser. Following the directions given earlier in this chapter, launch your Web browser and open its Help window. Search for help on each of the following topics and then read the information you find. Your instructor may ask you to demonstrate one or more of these tasks after you learn about it:

   » Changing your browser's start page.
   » Printing a Web page.
   » Saving information from a Web page.
   » Customizing your browser's toolbar.
   » Turning Web page graphics off and on.

3. Set up a free e-mail account. Even if you don't have an ISP account, you can still send and receive e-mail if you can use a computer with access to the World Wide Web. Visit the following sites to learn more about free e-mail accounts. Pick a provider and then follow the directions on that site to set up an account. Remember to write down your user name and password, and then exchange an e-mail message with someone in your class.

   » **Hotmail.** http://www.hotmail.com
   » **Mail.com.** http://www.mail.com
   » **E-Mail.com.** http://www.email.com
   » **Yahoo!** http://mail.yahoo.com

Discussion Questions

As directed by your instructor, discuss the following questions in class or in groups.

1. Despite the promise that the Internet will someday be as universal as radio and television, how do you feel about the growing "commercialization" of the Internet? Do you think the motive to use the Internet as a vehicle for profit will have a negative or positive effect on it as a source of information?
2. What is your view of the Internet's value to individual people? How important do you think the Internet is in the daily life of average people? For example, could you live without Internet access and enjoy the same quality of life you enjoy today?

Research and Report

Using your own choice of resources (such as the Internet, books, magazines, and newspaper articles), research and write a short paper discussing one of the following topics:

- The Internet's growth.
- A survey of the costs of ISP accounts in your area.
- The dangers of using Internet chatrooms and instant messaging.

When you are finished, proofread and print your paper and give it to your instructor.

ETHICAL ISSUES

Despite all the conveniences it offers, the Internet is filled with pitfalls. With this thought in mind, discuss the following questions in class.

1. People can do many things online, and Web designers, Internet marketers, ISPs, and other companies encourage us to use the Internet as much as possible, for any reason. But can Internet use be bad? At what point do we become too dependent on the Internet? At what point does Internet use interfere with our normal routines, instead of enhancing them?
2. Imagine that a large company, such as a bank, discovers that several of its employees are using the company network to view pornography on the Web. These workers also are using the company's e-mail system to exchange images with one another and with people outside the company. In your view, what should the company do about such behavior? Is firing the employees too harsh a punishment? Support your position.

If you have put off creating a Web page because you think it's a long or difficult process, think again. Web design can be very easy, especially if you just want to build a simple personal Web page or a basic noncommerce Web site. Creating and publishing Web content is straightforward and does not have to be any more difficult than creating any other kind of digital document. You just need to understand the process.

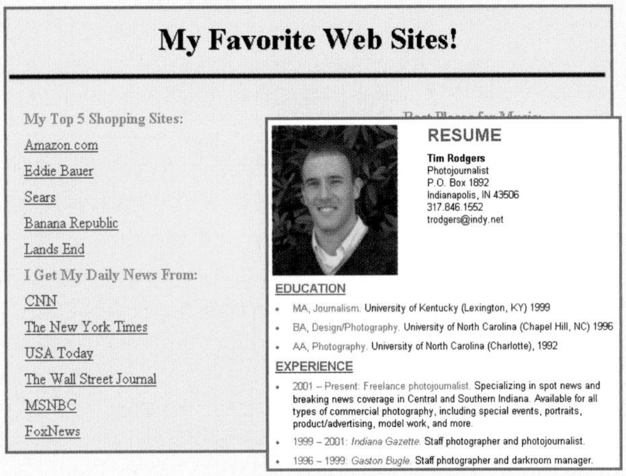

With the right tools, you can create simple Web pages—such as a list of your favorite links or a basic resume—in a snap.

Choosing Your Design Tools

When you set out to create a Web site, your first challenge is deciding which tools to use. Luckily, there are many Web design programs that let you create a site without mastering HTML or learning a scripting language. This means that you can design and lay out your pages as if you were using a word processing program; the software handles all the coding and formatting chores "behind the scenes," so you don't have to do it yourself. If you are enthusiastic about creating Web content but prefer to avoid a steep learning curve, these programs offer the easiest route to follow.

To that end, this *Computing Keynote* feature shows you how to create a Web page using Microsoft FrontPage—a popular Web page design program. Because FrontPage is intuitive and easy to use, it is a good choice for the first-time Web designer. What is more, it comes with templates that simplify the page-creation process. If you have Microsoft Office, then you may already have a copy of FrontPage installed on your PC. If not, you can get a trial copy of FrontPage by visiting Microsoft's Web site at http://www.microsoft.com/frontpage.

Of course, there are many other popular and easy-to-use Web design programs. The most popular programs for novice

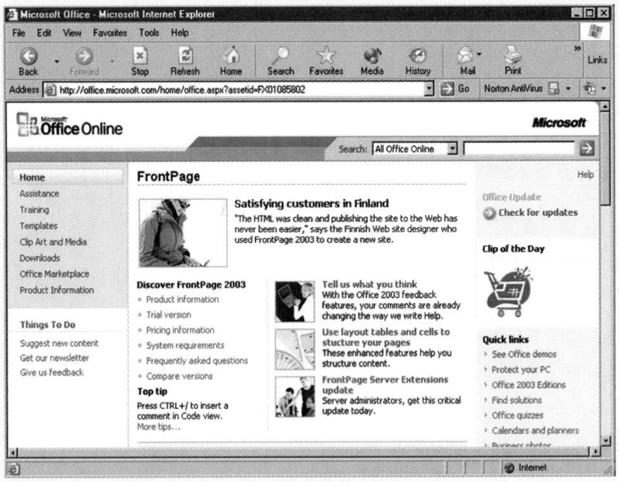

Visit http://www.microsoft.com/frontpage/ for more information about FrontPage or to download a trial copy.

designers work in much the same manner as FrontPage, by doing the "grunt work" of HTML coding automatically. You work in a graphical user interface, which lets you create text, import graphics, and format pages by clicking icons and menus. All of these programs, like FrontPage, also let you view and edit the HTML codes yourself, if you want to, and some offer detailed tutorials on the basics of HTML and Web-page design.

Some other popular Web design programs are

- **NetObjects Fusion,** from Website Pros, Inc. For more information, visit http://www.netobjects.com.
- **Dreamweaver MX,** from Macromedia, Inc. For more information, visit http://www.macromedia.com.
- **GoLive CS,** from Adobe Systems, Inc. For more information, visit http://www.adobe.com.

If you want to add graphics to your Web page, you will need a graphics-editing program. A professional tool such as Adobe Photoshop can be used, or you can choose from a variety of affordable yet feature-rich graphics programs. Four low-cost favorites include the following:

- **Paint Shop Pro,** from Jasc, Inc. For more information, visit http://www.jasc.com.
- **Fireworks MX,** from Macromedia, Inc. For more information, visit http://www.macromedia.com.
- **LView Pro,** from MMedia Research Corp. For more information, visit http://www.lview.com.
- **The GIMP,** from The Free Software Foundation. For more information, visit http://www.gimp.org.

Graphics products like Paint Shop Pro offer professional imaging tools that are simple enough for beginners to master quickly.

Planning Your Page or Site

Before you design anything, you need to determine what your Web page (or site, if you want to publish several pages) is going to be about. For example, you may want to publish information about yourself or your family. Or you might want to create a page or small site for an organization, such as a synagogue, club, neighborhood association, or community center.

It is important to know each page's main topic before you start. The topic will help you decide what kind of information to prepare, and it will also help you keep the contents focused. Otherwise, visitors will quickly lose interest and leave your site. You need to engage your visitors right away and let them know why they should stay on your site, reading your content and visiting any other pages within the site.

Organizing Text The next step in planning is to arrange your site's information into sensible categories. Whether you are designing a single page or a site with many pages, you should organize your thoughts in order to help the site's visitors understand what you are trying to do. Get out a piece of paper and start organizing your ideas.

Some common topics for a personal page or site include the following:

- About You (or your organization)
- Photo Album
- Friends and Family
- Poems and Stories
- Favorite Links
- Resume

Be careful here, because many pages suffer from the "Too Much Stuff" syndrome. Clutter can turn visitors off. The best way to avoid this problem is to look carefully at the way you have organized the information you would like to have on your page. Keep written content short and to the point. If you have a lot of written content, such as information about your organization, break up the information by using headers and lists. This makes the information easier to read and more interesting.

Planning for Graphical Appeal Of course, a Web page can have much more than just words on it! You will want to create your own graphics or find suitable graphics for your Web site from popular graphic repositories.

Importing Graphics Graphics—such as scanned drawings or digital photos—can add a touch of your own personality and talent to your pages. To import graphics, you will need a graphics program, as mentioned earlier, as well

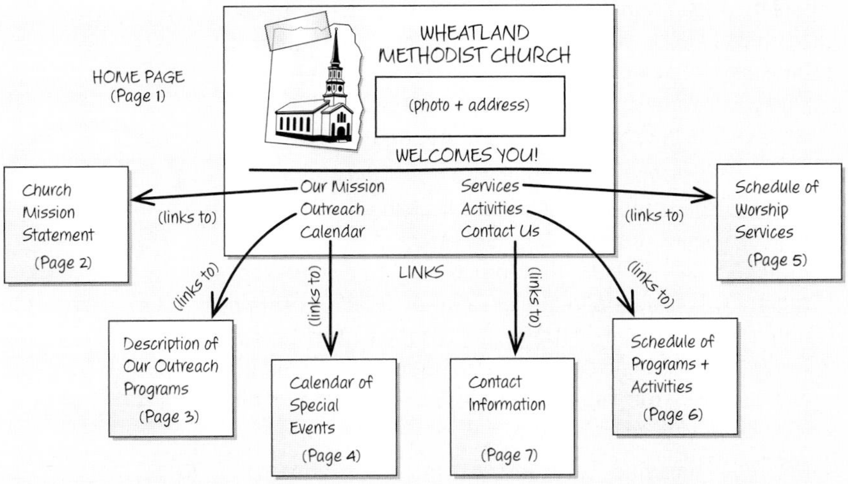

If your site is small, you can draw a basic layout on paper, as shown here. At this stage of the process you do not need too much detail; you just need an idea of the major topic or topics you want to include. And remember—limit your site to one topic per page.

CONTINUED

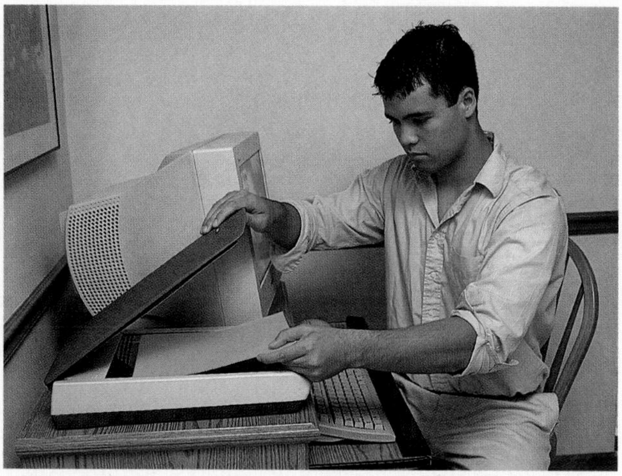

If you have a scanner, you can use it to digitize your own snapshots or illustrations. However, you should not scan published images (such as photographs from a magazine), because they are protected by copyright law.

as the software that came with your scanner and/or digital camera.

If you want to import photos from your digital camera into your imaging software, you may need to resize them or touch them up to make them more suitable for Web use. Read the documentation that came with your digital camera and your image-editing program to learn about resizing, cropping, changing colors, and dealing with imperfections (such as "red eye" or poor lighting).

Scanning images demands a little more attention. If you scan your work improperly, the results will be disappointing. Follow these tips for successful scanning:

- Clean your scanner's surface and the items to be scanned. Check your scanner's documentation for the best way to clean your scanner. To clean photos and art work, use canned air—available at most office and art supply stores—to blast away smudges and dust.
- Scan and save your image files at 72 DPI (dots per inch), which is the standard resolution for images on the Web. If your images are fairly detailed or colorful, save them in JPEG (JPG) format; this format works best for photographs. If images do not have a lot of detail or contain only a few colors, save them in GIF format; this format works best for drawings and items such as backgrounds and buttons. You can find resolution settings and file formats in your imaging software.
- Use your imaging software to crop and refine the scanned image.

Web graphics should be attractive, but it's just as important that they download quickly to the visitor's browser. This means keeping your graphics at a reasonable size and resolution. What's reasonable? That depends on a lot of factors, but if an image is too large to fit on a single screen at 800 × 600 resolution without scrolling, or if it takes more than three or four seconds to download, then it's too large. There are no hard-and-fast rules for setting image sizes or resolutions, and you can find images of all sizes and quality on the Web. Generally speaking, however, smaller is better. Size your images so they look attractive on the page and work in harmony with other elements. Also, if you use an up-to-date version of an HTML editor such as FrontPage, the program can tell you how long your page will take to download over a standard modem connection. Pay attention to this information and use it as a guide to make sure that your pages aren't too big to download quickly. If you do not know how to work with Web graphics, you can learn from many helpful tutorials available online. One good place to start is Internet Eye's Paint Shop Pro Resources page, at http://the-internet-eye.com/resources/psp.htm. It provides articles and links to many other graphics-related sites.

Finding Graphics Online If you want to use clip art, photos, and animations—but you are not an artist—you may find free or inexpensive resources to use for your page by visiting these Web sites:

- Barry's Clipart Server (http://www.barrysclipart.com) serves up a great big helping of clip art, animated GIFs, related links, and helpful software.
- Jupiterimages (http://www.jupiterimages.com) is a clearinghouse of art, design samples and galleries, tuto-

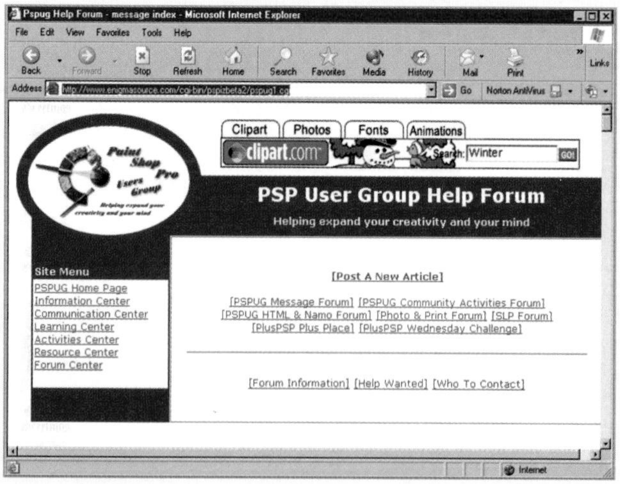

Web sites like the Paint Shop Pro User Group Help Forum (at http://www.enigmasource.com/cgi-bin/pspizbeta2/pspug1.cgi) can help you learn how to add graphics to your Web site.

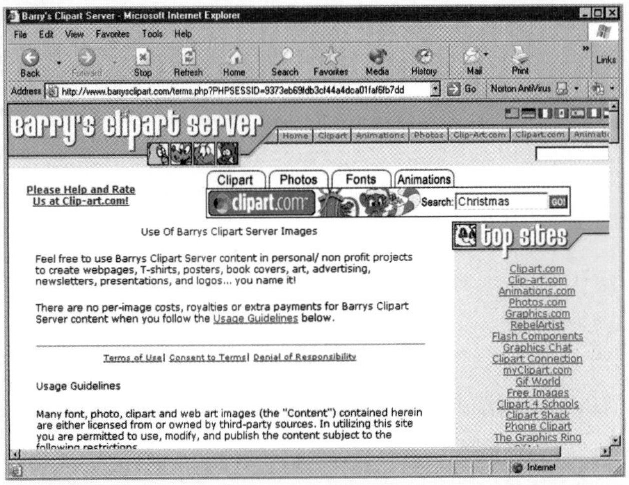

Look for license or usage agreements before you download an image from a clip-art service. This agreement appears on Barry's Clipart Server.

rials, and services for designers of all types and ability levels. The site features links to many other sites, where you can find graphics resources for your Web site. Some are free, others require a membership.

Before you download any kind of image from a Web site (or any other online source), however, be sure to read the licensing or usage agreement that governs its use. Reputable online clip-art services post these agreements on their Web sites, so you cannot miss them. Even free images can have some usage restrictions; for example, the image's owner may require you to acknowledge the owner or artist on your site or get written permission before you use the graphic.

You will find more information about borrowing images, text, and HTML code from other Web sites in the section titled "Web Content and Intellectual Property Rights," at the end of this *Computing Keynote*.

Building Your Site

So you have gathered your tools, organized your ideas, and gotten up to speed with Web graphics. Now it is time to roll up your sleeves and start building your Web site.

Start by launching FrontPage. To do this, open the Start menu, and then open the Programs menu (or the All Programs menu, if you use Windows XP). When you launch FrontPage, it creates a folder on your PC called My Webs. This folder contains a subfolder called Images. Before going any further, open Windows Explorer or My Computer and move all your images into the Images subfolder.

Now it is time to actually create a site, step by step.

Selecting a Template Since your goal is to create a site right away, you will work with a template and modify it to suit your needs. Follow these steps to select the template in FrontPage:

1. Open the File menu, click New | Page or Web. The New Page or Web task pane appears.
2. On the task pane, click Page Templates. The Page Templates dialog box opens.
3. In the dialog box, click the General tab, if necessary. Click the One-Column Body with Two Sidebars icon, and then click OK. The layout appears in FrontPage.
4. Open the File menu and click Save As. The Save As dialog box appears. Here, you need to do three things:
   a. Click the Change Title button next to the Page title. When the Set Page Title dialog box appears, give the page a suitable title, such as Tiny Dancers' Home Page. Click OK to return to the Save As dialog box.
   b. Give the file a name, and then click Save. (If this is the site's first page, name it INDEX or HOME. The word *Index* is often used for a site's opening page because this page usually contains a list—or index—of links to other pages in the site.) The dialog box closes and FrontPage saves the file in the My Webs folder.
   c. Because this layout includes a picture, FrontPage displays the Save Embedded Files dialog box. For now, click Ok. You'll replace the sample picture later.

Adding an Image Next, replace the placeholder image (on the right side of the page) with one of your own images:

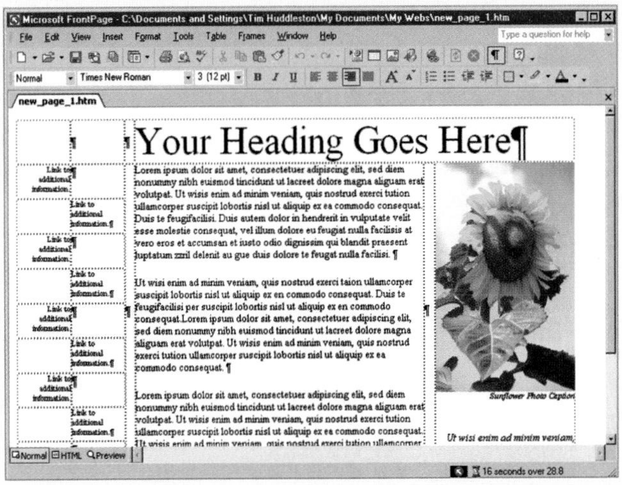

Using a FrontPage template to create an attractive home page.

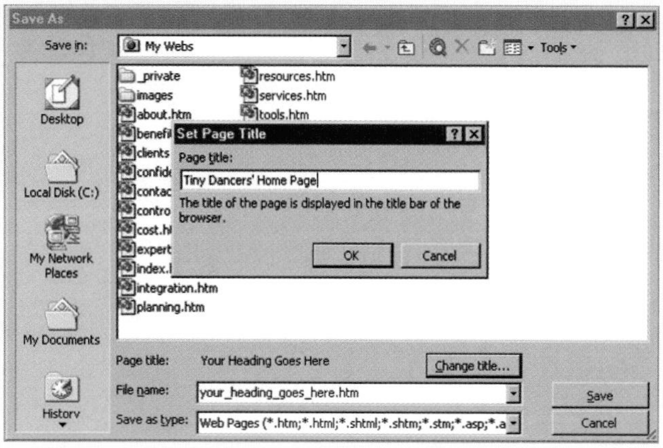

Saving your first Web page, with a file name and a title.

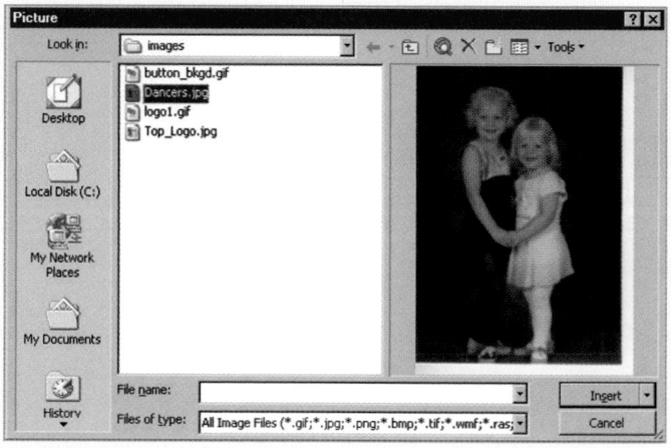

Adding an image to a Web page.

1. Click the existing image and then right-click it. When the shortcut menu opens, click Cut. The image disappears from the template. Leave the cursor where it is.
2. Open the Insert menu, click Picture, and then click From File. The Picture dialog box appears. Navigate to the Images subfolder, if necessary, and then open the subfolder by double-clicking it.
3. When the Images subfolder opens, click the image you want to use. Click INSERT. The picture is now inserted into your design.
4. To change the picture caption, select the old text (by dragging across it with the mouse pointer) and type your own caption in its place.

Modifying a Heading and Adding Content Now you are ready to fill in all the template's text areas with your custom information:

1. To modify the heading, select it and type your new heading.
2. To add content to the main section, find the text you would like to use, and then copy and paste it right over the placeholder text. Or you can delete the placeholder text and type your own text in its place.
3. Continue replacing the placeholder text until you're happy with the results. You can modify font styles and sizes by using FrontPage's tools. Be careful to use these features lightly because using too many fonts and sizes can make reading difficult.

Adding Pages and Linking to Them Links are the most important part of a Web page. Luckily, the template you are using allows for a number of links. If you want to add other pages to your site—and the page you created earlier is the site's index page—then you will probably want to add lines of text to this page and format them as hyperlinks that lead to the other pages. Here's how to do that:

1. To add new pages, follow the same steps you used earlier for working with the template. Be sure to name your files (they will be empty until you wish to edit them later) and save them in the My Web folder.
2. In the index page, highlight the placeholder text where you would like to add the link and rename the link as is appropriate for your needs. Then select the text.
3. Open the Insert menu and then click Hyperlink. The Insert Hyperlink dialog appears.
4. Select the page to which you want to link by clicking its name. Click Ok.

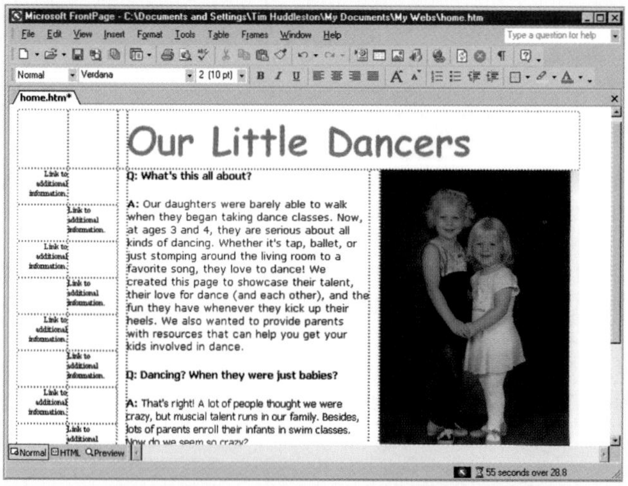

The template with a new image, heading, and content in place. Here, notice that the text is formatted differently than in the template.

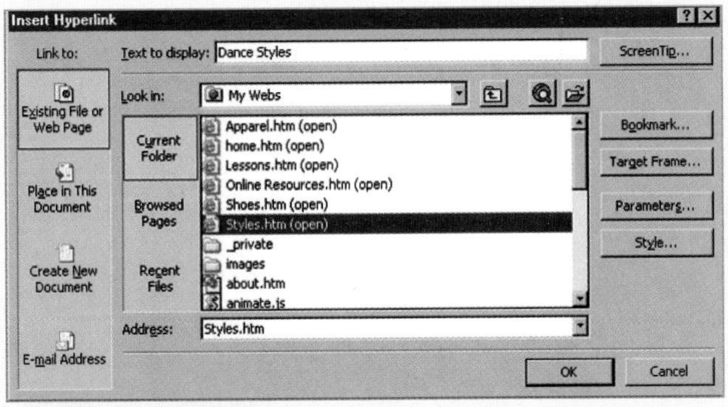

Creating a hyperlink to another page on your site.

Continue adding links until you have added all the links you require. Save the page so your changes are updated. When you have finished (or whenever you want to see how your page will look online), you can click the Preview tab. Alternatively, if you prefer to see your page in an actual Web browser, open the File menu, and then click Preview in Browser.

Of course, there are many other modifications and additions you can make to this document, but you are off to a great start.

Web Design Tips

No matter what kind of content your Web page or site contains, you want it to look great. Just as important, you want your site's visitors to find your content easy to read and navigate. You can accomplish these goals and avoid common Web design pitfalls by following these tips:

- Use bold and italic sparingly. Bold and italic effects actually make text harder to read. Use bold and italic for emphasis only.
- Be sure to properly align body text. Centered body text (that is, paragraphs of body text centered between the margins, usually with "ragged" left and right edges) can be hard to read. It is better to adjust your margins than to center body text. You can center headers, footers, and accent text.
- Use a plain background that will not interfere with your text. Don't use complicated backgrounds (such as patterns or textures). Plain backgrounds are almost always best with any text.
- Use contrasting colors for backgrounds, text, and links. The higher the contrast, the better the readability. White text on a yellow background is just annoying.
- Keep body text at its default size.
- Look carefully at your page. Is there anything on it that is unnecessary? If so, get rid of it!
- Unless you update your pages regularly, do not post the date on which the page was last updated, and do not put time-sensitive information on it. If you are offering Christmas greetings to your visitors in July, for example, they will think your whole site is stale!
- Never put your home address or home phone number on a Web page, and always think carefully before putting very personal information on a page.

Finding a Host for Your Web Site

Once your page or site is ready to go, you will want to publish it online. This means finding a "host"—a person or company with a server computer that stores Web pages. A wide range of Web hosting options are available.

If you already have an account with an Internet service provider (ISP), you may have some free Web space available as part of your account. Check with your provider to see if this is true, and ask how to access your area on the ISP's Web server.

If your ISP does not provide Web space, there are plenty of other hosting options. The most popular options for enthusiasts are free hosting services and low-cost services.

Free Hosting Services Free services can be a terrific option if you are just starting out. The big problem with using a free service, however, is that you may have no control over the advertisements that the service uses. This means your site might display pop-up advertisements (which "pop

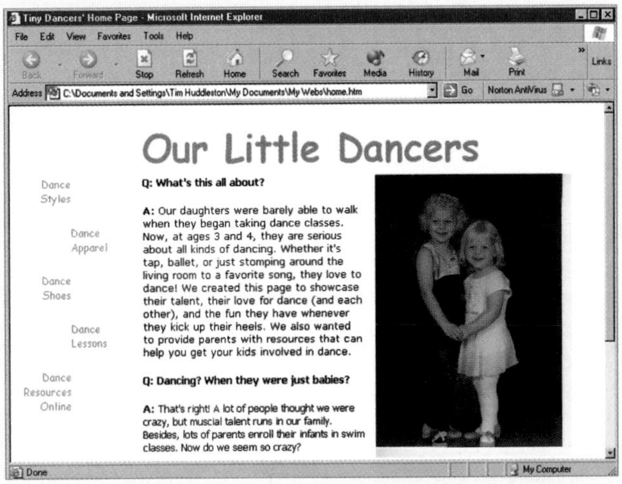

The final results: a simple but attractive home page, shown here in Microsoft Internet Explorer.

CONTINUED

Complex backgrounds and poorly contrasting color schemes can make your Web pages hard to read.

up" in a small browser window) or banner ads (which appear as part of your page, in the form of a banner). This is the price you pay for the free hosting.

Some free hosting services include

- **Free Servers.** This service offers ad-supported free Web hosting. If you upgrade to Free Servers' premium pay service, you can get rid of the advertising. For information, visit http://www.freeservers.com.
- **FortuneCity.** Another service with ad-supported free home page publishing. There are low-cost and flex options as well, should you decide to upgrade. Visit http://www.fortunecity.com for information.
- **AngelFire.** Particularly popular among young Web designers, AngelFire offers a variety of services including ways to connect to other home pages with similar interests. The service is free if you accept the display of advertisements on your page, and low-cost options are also available. To learn more, visit http://www.angelfire.lycos.com.

Fee-Based Hosting Services When you pay for hosting services, you can expect to receive other services along with storage for your Web site. Some fee-based hosts provide e-mail accounts, or even the ability to host your own domain name (such as www.yourname.com). Your choice of service depends on what you want to do and how much you can afford. Some pay services include the following:

- **Hosting.Com.** This company offers a wide range of services to meet all kinds of needs from beginning to high-end professional. For information, visit http://www.hosting.com.
- **Cedant Web Hosting.** Cedant provides a variety of services, ranging from low to medium cost. To learn more, visit http://www.cedant.com.
- **TopHosts.com.** This portal site can help you find the best hosting service for you. Visit http://www.tophosts.com.

When you set up an account with a Web host, the service will set aside server space for your Web pages, and you will create a user name and password that allow you to access that space and store your content there. The next step is to publish your site.

Publishing Your Site

With your logon information to your Web host at the ready, you are prepared to publish.

Publishing your pages to a Web server requires you to have some form of file transfer software. If you create your site in FrontPage, open the File menu, then click Publish Web. A set of steps will appear, telling you how to publish your Web content to your host's server.

If you decide not to use FrontPage, or if you want to use a different means of transferring files, you need to use FTP client software. This type of program uses the File Transfer Protocol (FTP) to transfer your files over the Internet to the host's computer. Two very popular FTP client programs are WS_FTP (http://www.wsftp.com) and CuteFTP (http://www.cuteftp.com).

Additional Resources on Web Design

Building professional Web sites is quite different than creating personal sites. The reasons are many, but usually have to do with the amount of technology that must be learned

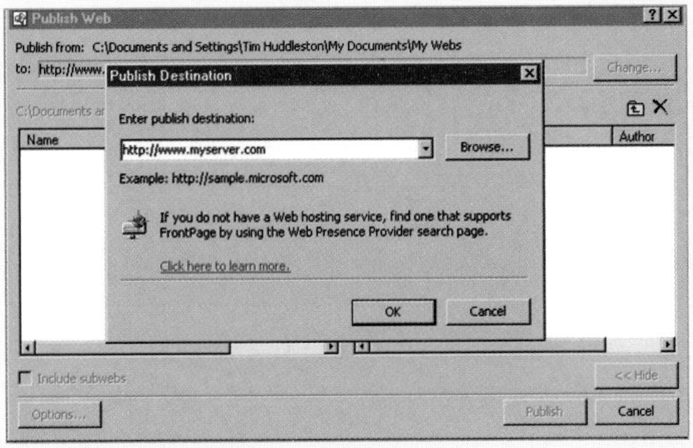

Publishing Web content with FrontPage.

in order to effectively create the many layers of complexity that today's professional sites entail.

There are many technologies and standards emerging, and as a result, the way professionals are working today is much different than the way an enthusiast will work. Still, the idea is essentially the same: create content and publish it on the Web.

If the process of creating a Web page excites you, and if you would like to learn more about professional Web design and development, consider a visit to these sites to see what a variety of resources are available to you.

- **World Wide Web Consortium (W3C).** http://www.w3.org
- **HTML Writers Guild.** http://www.hwg.org
- **WebReference.com.** http://www.webreference.com
- **Webmonkey.com.** http://hotwired.lycos.com/webmonkey
- **List Apart.** http://www.alistapart.com
- **Digital Web Magazine.** http://www.digital-web.com
- **Web Developer's Virtual Library.** http://www.wdvl.com
- **Builder.com.** http://www.builder.com

Web Content and Intellectual Property Rights

A lot of information sharing happens on the Web, but it is not always OK to use an item you happen to find online; you could be breaking the law. If you are not sure whether you should use a graphic, text, or code you find on a Web site, check the following list of questions and answers:

1. Can I swipe HTML code from a Web site I like?

   While many people use their browser's View Source feature to look at the way code is written, it is not necessarily helpful to simply swipe it! Be inspired by it, use it as an example to learn from, but do not just take it. Even though HTML code itself cannot be copyrighted, you should either learn how to work with it or use software that generates it for you.

2. Is it okay to "borrow" a graphic from someone else's page?

   Without express permission from the image's owner, you should not put other people's work on your Web site. Learn to create your own graphics, or use graphics that are royalty-free, such as those available from the Web sites mentioned earlier in this article.

3. Can I put quotes from articles, books, movies, and other sources on my page?

   If you use one paragraph or less, place it in quotes, and clearly state the source, you are following the general rules of what is known as "fair use." Be cautious and fair, however. Anything more than a paragraph can be considered infringement of copyright, and if you use someone else's work without referencing the source, you are guilty of plagiarism! Stay safe and honest—always ask for permission before using materials that are likely to be copyrighted.

It is also a good idea to protect your own work. If you have original art, writing, and music on your pages, it is a good idea to copyright it. You can learn more about copyright with a visit to these sites:

- **United States Copyright Office.** http://www.copyright.gov
- **Canadian Intellectual Property Office.** http://cipo.gc.ca
- **Ten Big Myths About Copyright Explained.** http://www.templetons.com/brad/copymyths.html
- **Intellectual Property Law Primer for Multimedia and Web Developers.** http://www.eff.org/pub/CAF/law/ip-primer

CHAPTER

3 Interacting with Your Computer

CHAPTER CONTENTS ::

This chapter contains the following lessons:

LESSON // 3A

Using the Keyboard and Mouse

Overview: The Keyboard and Mouse

If you think of the CPU as a computer's brain, then you might think of the input devices as its sensory organs—the eyes, ears, and fingers. From the user's point of view, input devices are just as important as the CPU, perhaps even more important. After you buy and set up the computer, you may take the CPU for granted because you interact directly with input devices and only indirectly with the CPU. But your ability to use input devices is critical to your overall success with the whole system.

An input device does exactly what its name suggests: it enables you to enter information and commands into the computer. The most commonly used input devices are the keyboard and the mouse. If you buy a new personal computer today, it will include a keyboard and mouse unless you specify otherwise. Other types of input devices are available as well, such as variations of the mouse and specialized "alternative" input devices such as microphones and scanners.

This lesson introduces you to the keyboard and the mouse. You will learn the importance of these devices, the way the computer accepts input from them, and the many tasks they enable you to perform on your PC.

OBJECTIVES ::

- Identify the five key groups on a standard computer keyboard.
- Name six special-purpose keys found on all standard computer keyboards.
- List the steps a computer follows when accepting input from a keyboard.
- Describe the purpose of a mouse and the role it plays in computing.
- Identify the five essential techniques for using a mouse.
- Identify three common variants of the mouse.
- Describe five steps you can take to avoid repetitive stress injuries from computer use.

The Keyboard

The keyboard was one of the first peripherals to be used with computers, and it is still the primary input device for entering text and numbers. A standard keyboard includes about 100 keys; each key sends a different signal to the CPU.

If you have not used a computer keyboard or a typewriter, you will learn quickly that you can use a computer much more effectively if you know how to type. The skill of typing, or keyboarding, is the ability to enter text and numbers with skill and accuracy. Certainly, you can use a computer without having good typing skills. Some people claim that when computers can interpret handwriting and speech with 100 percent accuracy, typing will become unnecessary. But for now and the foreseeable future, keyboarding remains the most common way to enter text and other data into a computer.

Norton ONLINE

For more information on computer-based keyboard tutorials, visit **http://www.mhhe.com/peternorton**.

simnet™

The Standard Keyboard Layout

Keyboards come in many styles. The various models differ in size, shape, and feel; except for a few special-purpose keys, most keyboards are laid out almost identically. Among IBM-compatible computers, the most common keyboard layout is the IBM Enhanced Keyboard. It has about 100 keys arranged in five groups, as shown in Figure 3A.1. (The term IBM-compatible computer refers to any PC based on the first personal computers, which were made by IBM. Today, an IBM-compatible PC is any PC other than a Macintosh computer.)

Norton ONLINE

For more information on computer keyboards and keyboard manufacturers, visit **http://www.mhhe.com/peternorton**.

The Alphanumeric Keys

The alphanumeric keys—the area of the keyboard that looks like a typewriter's keys—are arranged the same way on almost every keyboard. Sometimes this common arrangement is called the QWERTY (pronounced KWER-tee) layout because the first six keys on the top row of letters are Q, W, E, R, T, and Y.

Along with the keys that produce letters and numbers, the alphanumeric key group includes four keys having specific functions. The TAB, CAPS LOCK, BACKSPACE, and ENTER keys are described in Figure 3A.2.

The Modifier Keys

The SHIFT, ALT (Alternate), and CTRL (Control) keys are called modifier keys because they modify the input of other keys. In other words, if you hold down a modifier key while pressing another key, then you are changing the second key's

FIGURE 3A.1

Most IBM-compatible PCs use a keyboard like this one. Many keyboards feature a number of specialized keys, and keyboards can vary in size and shape. But nearly all standard PC keyboards include the keys shown here.

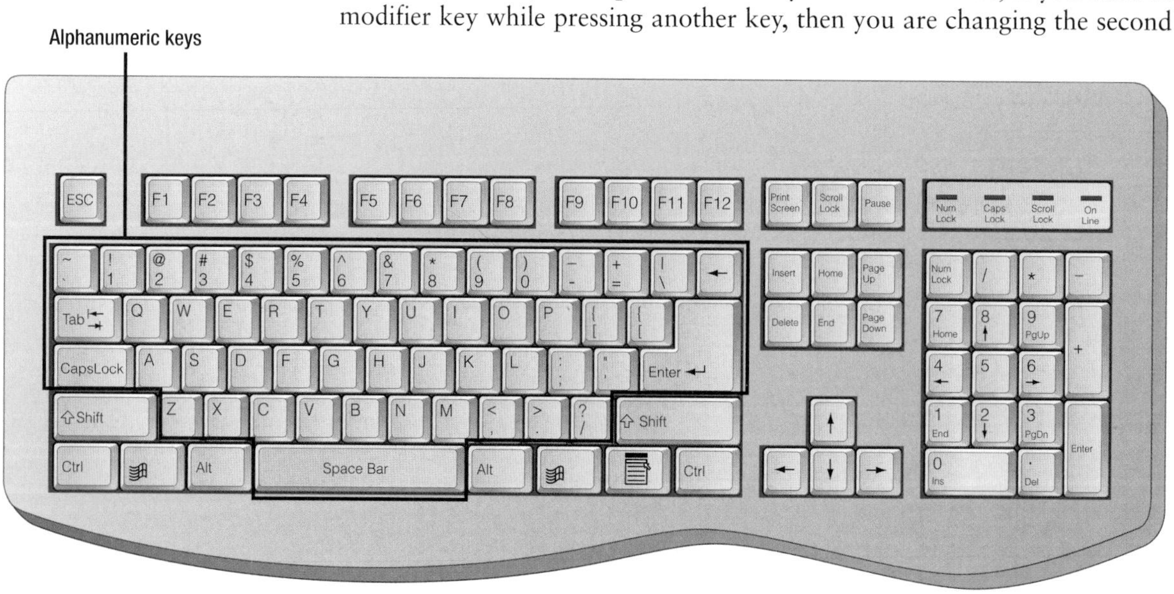

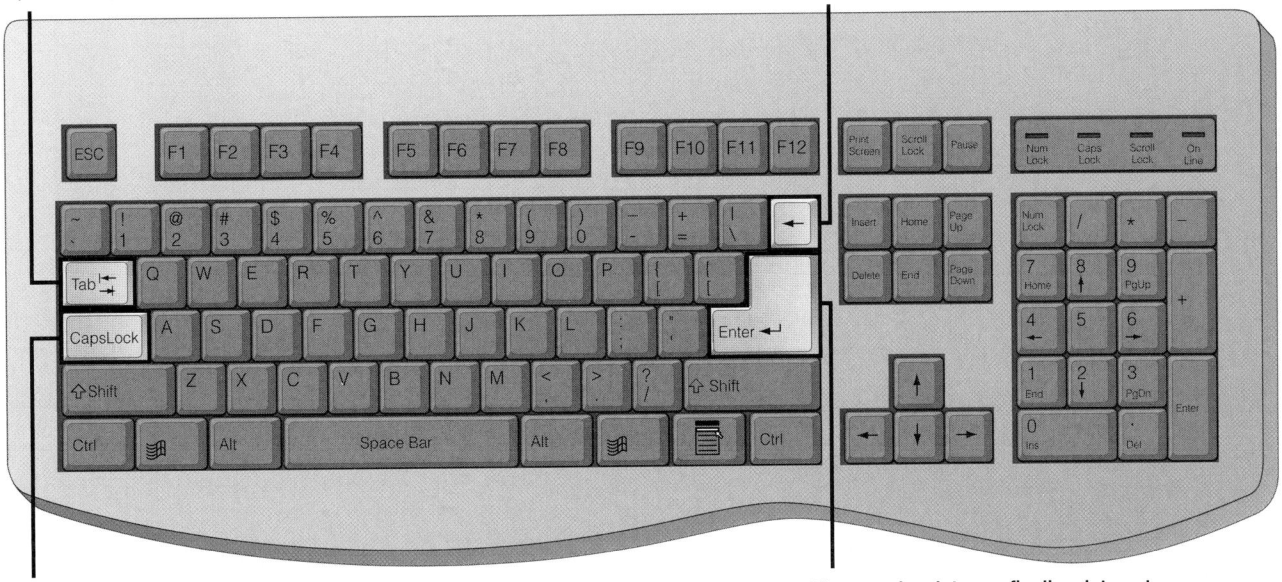
The TAB key moves you to predefined tab stops in many application programs (such as word processors).
The BACKSPACE key erases characters you have just typed. For example, in a word processing program you can press BACKSPACE to "back over" an incorrect character and delete it.
The CAPS LOCK key lets you "lock" the alphabet keys so they produce only capital letters.
The ENTER key lets you finalize data entry in many types of application programs. You also can use ENTER to choose commands and options in many programs and at various places in an operating system's interface.

FIGURE 3A.2

Functions of the TAB, CAPS LOCK, BACKSPACE, and ENTER keys.

input in some way. For example, if you press the J key, you input a small letter *j*. But if you hold down the SHIFT key while pressing the J key, you input a capital *J*. Modifier keys are extremely useful because they give all other keys multiple capabilities. Figure 3A.3 describes the modifier keys and their uses.

The Numeric Keypad

The numeric keypad is usually located on the right side of the keyboard, as shown in Figure 3A.1. The numeric keypad looks like a calculator's keypad, with its 10 digits and mathematical operators (+, -, *, and /). The numeric keypad also features a NUM LOCK key, which forces the numeric keys to input numbers. When NUM LOCK is deactivated, the numeric keypad's keys perform cursor-movement control and other functions.

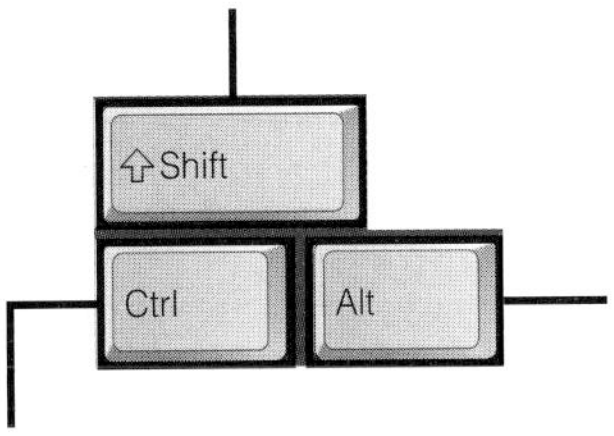
When pressed along with an alphanumeric key, SHIFT forces the computer to output a capital letter or symbol. SHIFT is also a modifier key in some programs; for example, you can press SHIFT along with cursor-movement keys to select text for editing.
Shift
Ctrl
Alt
The ALT (ALTERNATE) key operates like the CTRL key, but produces a different set of results. In Windows programs, ALT-key combinations enable you to navigate menus and dialog boxes without using the mouse.
The CTRL (CONTROL) key produces different results depending on the program you are using. In many Windows-based programs, CTRL-key combinations provide shortcuts for menu commands. For example, the combination CTRL+O enables you to open a new file.

FIGURE 3A.3

Functions of the SHIFT, CTRL, and ALT keys.

The Function Keys

The function keys, which are labeled F1, F2, and so on (as shown in Figure 3A.1), are usually arranged in a row along the top of the keyboard. They allow you to input commands without typing long strings of characters or navigating menus or dialog boxes. Each function key's purpose depends on the program you are using. For example, in most programs, F1 is the help key. When you press it, a special window appears to display information about the program you are using. Most IBM-compatible keyboards have 12 function keys. Many programs use function keys along with modifier keys to give the function keys more capabilities.

The Cursor-Movement Keys

Most standard keyboards also include a set of cursor-movement keys, which let you move around the screen without using a mouse. In many programs and operating systems, a mark on the screen indicates where the characters you type will be entered. This mark, called the cursor or insertion point, appears on the screen as a blinking vertical line, a small box, or some other symbol to show your place in a document or command line. Figure 3A.4 describes the cursor-movement keys and Figure 3A.5 shows an insertion point in a document window.

Special-Purpose Keys

In addition to the five groups of keys described earlier, all IBM-compatible keyboards feature six special-purpose keys, each of which performs a unique function. Figure 3A.6 describes these special-purpose keys.

Since 1996, nearly all IBM-compatible keyboards have included two additional special-purpose keys designed to work with the Windows operating systems (see Figure 3A.7):

- START. This key, which features the Windows logo (and is sometimes called the Windows logo key), opens the Windows Start menu on most computers. Pressing this key is the same as clicking the Start button on the Windows taskbar.
- SHORTCUT. This key, which features an image of a menu, opens an on-screen shortcut menu in Windows-based application programs.

One of the latest trends in keyboard technology is the addition of Internet and multimedia controls. Microsoft's Internet Keyboard and MultiMedia Keyboard, for example, feature buttons that you can program to perform any number of tasks. For example, you can use the buttons to launch a Web browser, check e-mail,

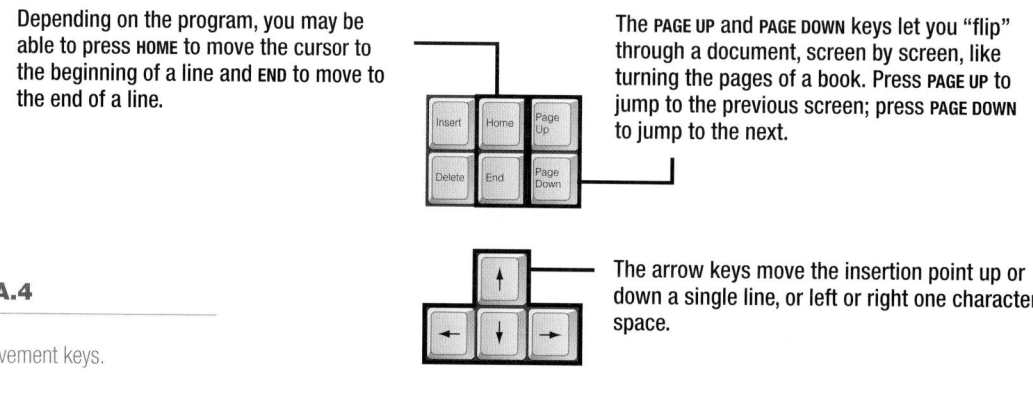

Depending on the program, you may be able to press **HOME** to move the cursor to the beginning of a line and **END** to move to the end of a line.

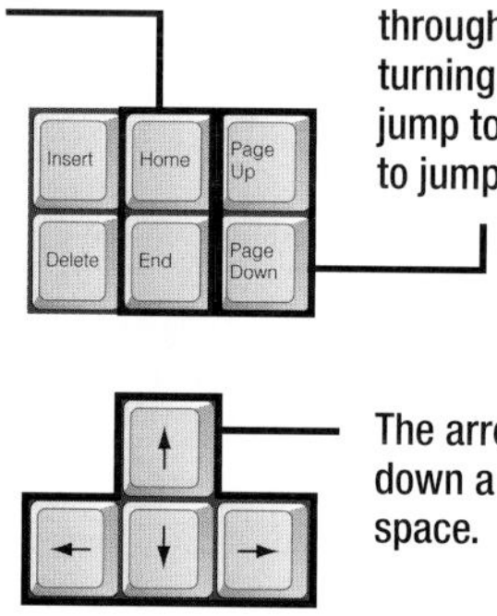

The **PAGE UP** and **PAGE DOWN** keys let you "flip" through a document, screen by screen, like turning the pages of a book. Press **PAGE UP** to jump to the previous screen; press **PAGE DOWN** to jump to the next.

The arrow keys move the insertion point up or down a single line, or left or right one character space.

FIGURE 3A.4

The cursor-movement keys.

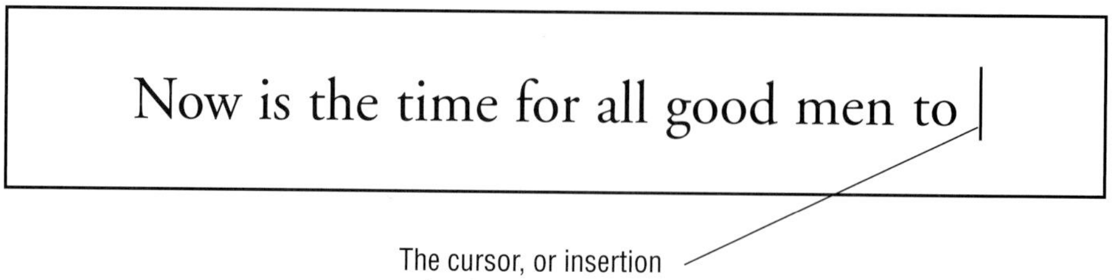

Now is the time for all good men to

The cursor, or insertion point, in a document

FIGURE 3A.5

The cursor, or insertion point, shows where the next letter typed will appear.

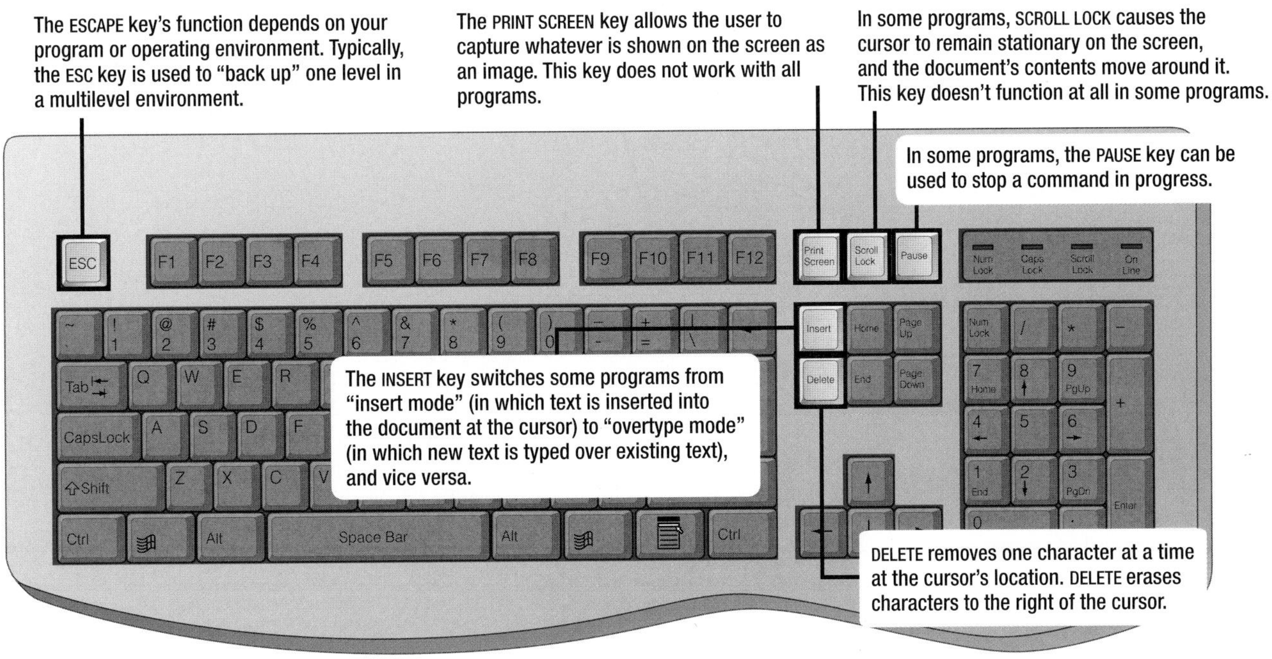
The ESCAPE key's function depends on your program or operating environment. Typically, the ESC key is used to "back up" one level in a multilevel environment.
The PRINT SCREEN key allows the user to capture whatever is shown on the screen as an image. This key does not work with all programs.
In some programs, SCROLL LOCK causes the cursor to remain stationary on the screen, and the document's contents move around it. This key doesn't function at all in some programs.
In some programs, the PAUSE key can be used to stop a command in progress.
The INSERT key switches some programs from "insert mode" (in which text is inserted into the document at the cursor) to "overtype mode" (in which new text is typed over existing text), and vice versa.
DELETE removes one character at a time at the cursor's location. DELETE erases characters to the right of the cursor.

FIGURE 3A.6

Special-purpose keys on most standard keyboards.

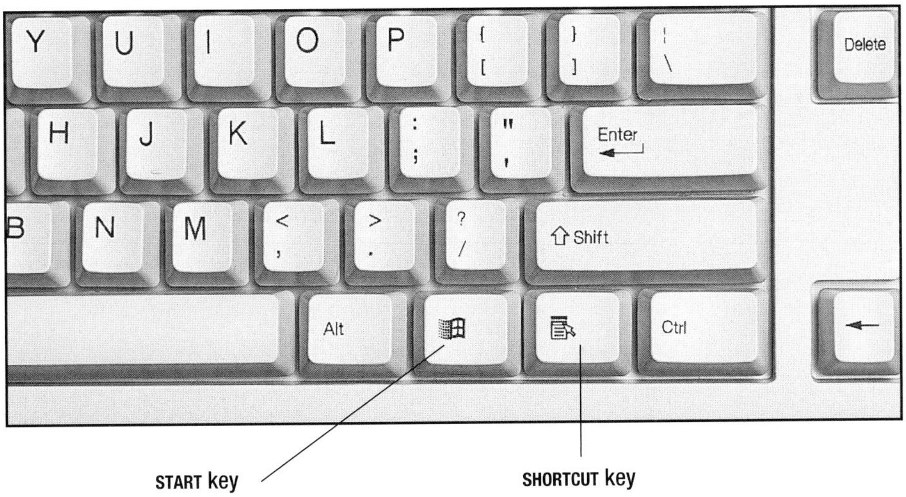
START key
SHORTCUT key

FIGURE 3A.7

The START key and the SHORTCUT key appear frequently on the newer keyboards that are sold with Windows-based computers.

and start your most frequently used programs. Multimedia buttons let you control the computer's CD-ROM or DVD drive and adjust the speaker volume. Many keyboard makers offer such features on newer models (see Figure 3A.8).

How the Computer Accepts Input from the Keyboard

You might think the keyboard simply sends the letter of a pressed key to the computer—after all, that is what appears to happen. Actually, the process of accepting input from the keyboard is more complex, as shown in Figure 3A.9.

When you press a key, a tiny chip called the keyboard controller notes that a key has been pressed. The keyboard controller places a code into part of its memory,

FIGURE 3A.8

Internet and multimedia features are commonplace on newer keyboards.

called the keyboard buffer, to indicate which key was pressed. (A buffer is a temporary storage area that holds data until it can be processed.) The keyboard controller then sends a signal to the computer's system software, notifying it that something has happened at the keyboard.

When the system software receives the signal, it determines the appropriate response. When a keystroke has occurred, the system reads the memory location in the keyboard buffer that contains the code of the key that was pressed. The system software then passes that code to the CPU.

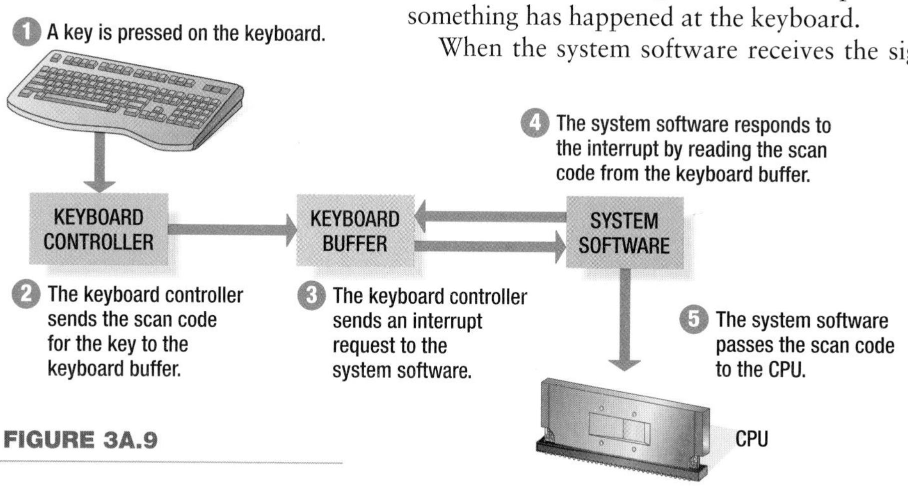

1 A key is pressed on the keyboard.
KEYBOARD CONTROLLER
2 The keyboard controller sends the scan code for the key to the keyboard buffer.
KEYBOARD BUFFER
3 The keyboard controller sends an interrupt request to the system software.
4 The system software responds to the interrupt by reading the scan code from the keyboard buffer.
SYSTEM SOFTWARE
5 The system software passes the scan code to the CPU.
CPU

FIGURE 3A.9

How input is received from the keyboard.

The keyboard buffer can store many keystrokes at one time. This capability is necessary because some time elapses between the pressing of a key and the computer's reading of that key from the keyboard buffer. With the keystrokes stored in a buffer, the program can react to them when it is convenient. Of course, this all happens very quickly. Unless the computer is very busy handling multiple tasks, you notice no delay between pressing keys and seeing the letters on your screen.

In some computers, the keyboard controller handles input from the computer's keyboard and mouse and stores the settings for both devices. One keyboard setting, the repeat rate, determines how long you must hold down an alphanumeric key before the keyboard will repeat the character and how rapidly the character is retyped while you press the key. You can set the repeat rate to suit your typing speed. (You will learn how to check your keyboard's repeat rate in the lab exercises at the end of this chapter.)

The Mouse

A personal computer that was purchased in the early 1980s probably included a keyboard as the only input device. Today, every new PC includes a pointing device as standard equipment, as shown in Figure 3A.10. Full-size PCs usually include a mouse as the pointing device. A mouse is an input device that you can move around on a flat surface (usually on a desk or keyboard tray) and controls the pointer. The pointer (also called the *mouse pointer*) is an on-screen object, usually an arrow, that is used to select text; access menus; and interact with programs, files, or data that appear on the screen. Figure 3A.11 shows an example of a pointer in a program window.

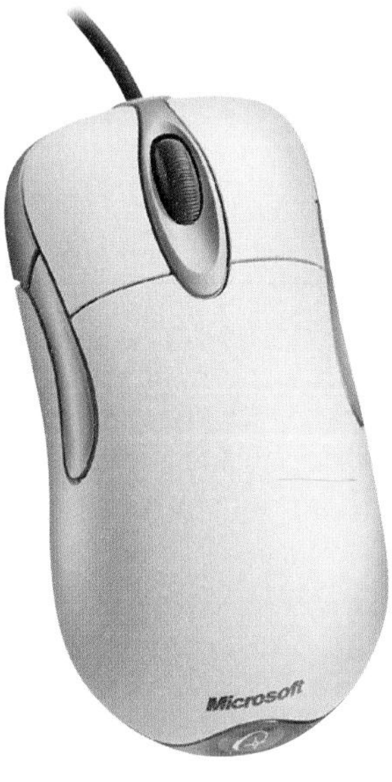

Microsoft

FIGURE 3A.10

Most modern personal computers are equipped with a mouse.

The mechanical mouse is the most common type of pointing device. A mechanical mouse contains a small rubber ball that protrudes through a hole in the bottom of the mouse's case (see Figure 3A.12). The ball rolls inside the case when you move the mouse around on a flat surface. Inside the mouse, rollers and sensors send signals to the computer, telling it the distance, direction, and speed of the ball's motions (see Figure 3A.13). The computer uses this data to position the mouse pointer on the screen.

Another popular type of mouse, the optical mouse, is nonmechanical. This type of mouse emits a beam of light from its underside; it uses the light's reflection to judge the distance, direction, and speed of its travel (see Figure 3A.14).

The mouse offers two main benefits. First, the mouse lets you position the cursor anywhere on the screen quickly without using the cursor-movement keys. You simply move the pointer to the on-screen position you want and press the mouse button; the cursor appears at that location.

Second, instead of forcing you to type or issue commands from the keyboard, the mouse and mouse-based operating systems let you choose commands from easy-to-use menus and dialog boxes (see Figure 3A.15). The result is a much more intuitive way to use computers. Instead of remembering obscure command names, users can figure out rather easily where commands and options are located.

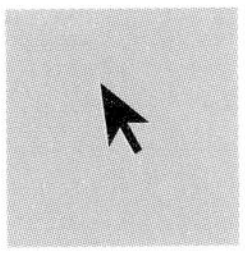

FIGURE 3A.11

An example of a pointer as it might appear on a computer screen.

Norton ONLINE

For more information on mice and mouse manufacturers, visit **http://www.mhhe.com/peternorton**.

simnet™

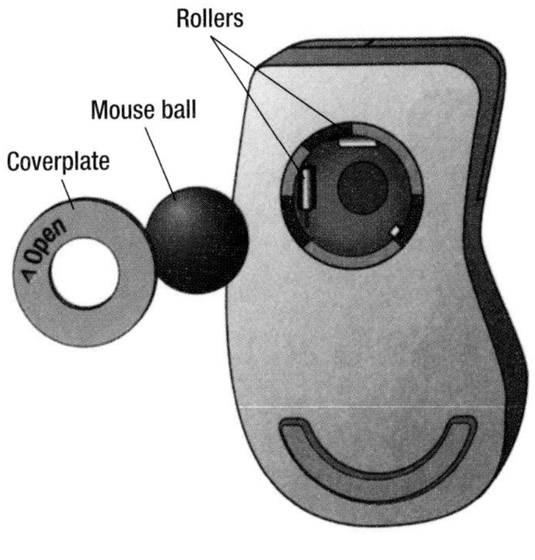

FIGURE 3A.12

The parts of a mechanical mouse, seen from the bottom.

Norton ONLINE

For more information on optical mice, visit **http://www.mhhe.com/peternorton**.

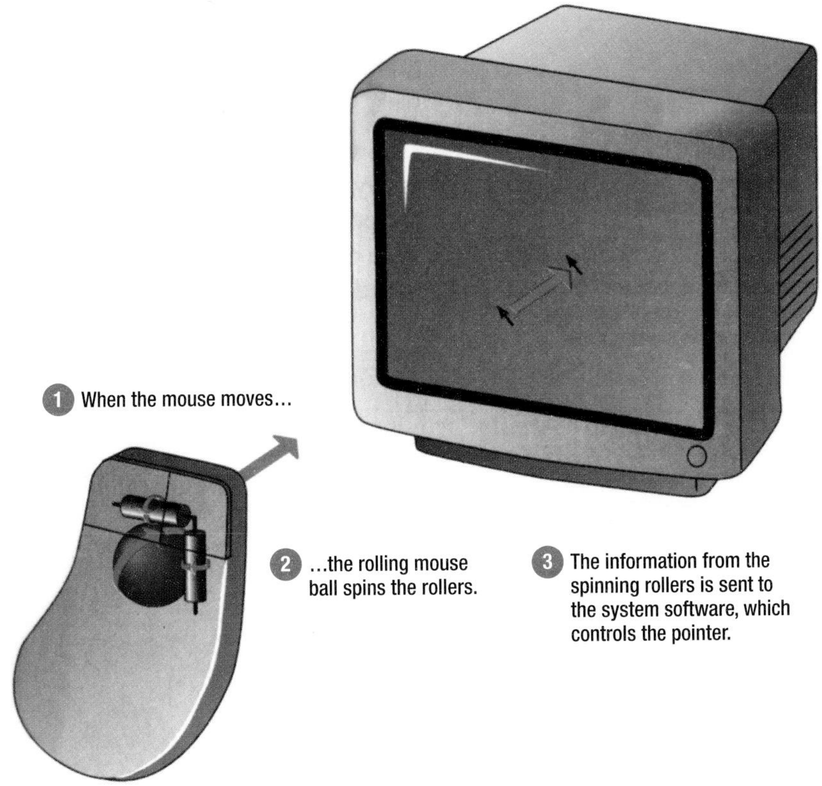

1 When the mouse moves...
2 ...the rolling mouse ball spins the rollers.
3 The information from the spinning rollers is sent to the system software, which controls the pointer.

FIGURE 3A.13

How the mouse controls the pointer.

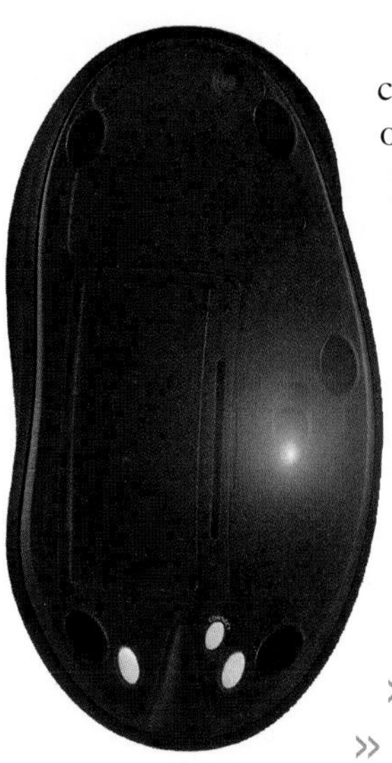

FIGURE 3A.14

The underside of an optical mouse.

Norton ONLINE

For more information on mouse techniques, visit **http://www.mhhe.com/peternorton**.

If you use a drawing program, you can use the mouse to create graphics such as lines, curves, and freehand shapes on the screen. The mouse has helped establish the computer as a versatile tool for graphic designers, starting what has since become a revolution in the graphic design field.

Using the Mouse

You use a mouse to move the pointer to a location on the screen, a process called *pointing*. Everything you do with a mouse is accomplished by combining pointing with these techniques:

- Clicking
- Double-clicking
- Dragging
- Right-clicking

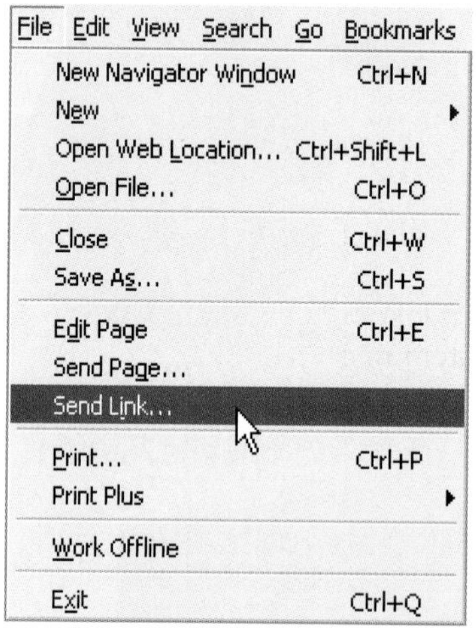

FIGURE 3A.15

Using the mouse to choose a command from a menu.

Pointing means pushing the mouse across your desk. On the screen, the pointer moves in relation to the mouse (see Figure 3A.16). Push the mouse forward, and the pointer moves up. Push the mouse to the left, and the pointer moves to the left. To point to an object or location on the screen, you simply use the mouse to place the pointer on top of the object or location.

The mice that come with IBM-compatible computers usually have two buttons, but techniques such as clicking, double-clicking, and dragging are usually carried out with the left mouse button (see Figure 3A.17). In multi-button mice, one button must be designated

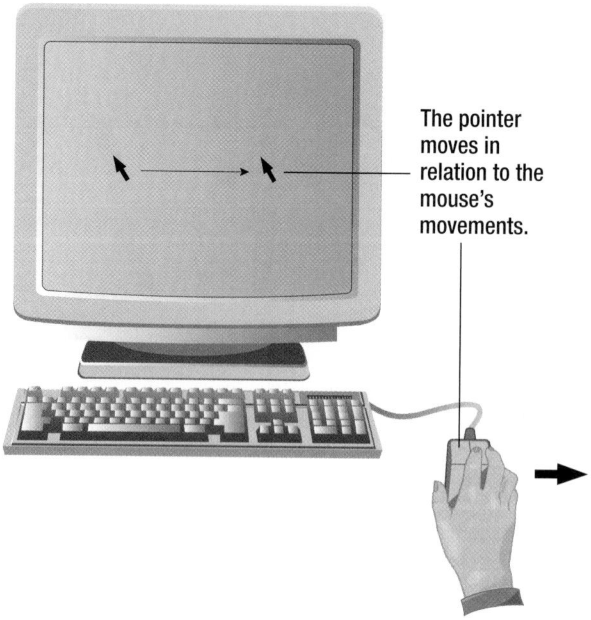

FIGURE 3A.16

Using the mouse to control the on-screen pointer.

as the "primary" button, referred to as the mouse button. Some mice can have three or more buttons. The buttons' uses are determined by the computer's operating system, application software, and mouse-control software.

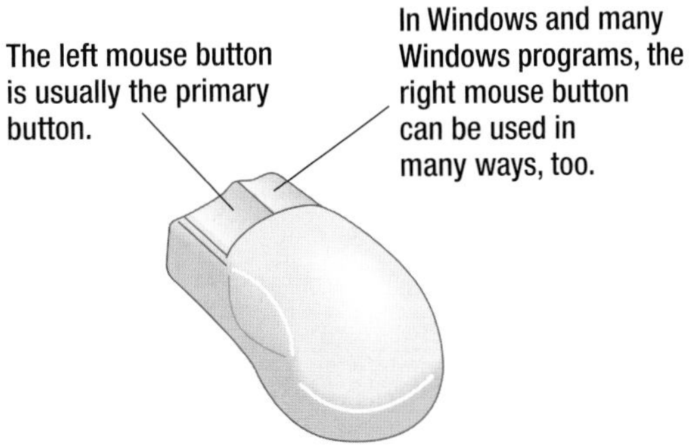
The left mouse button is usually the primary button.
In Windows and many Windows programs, the right mouse button can be used in many ways, too.

FIGURE 3A.17

Standard button configuration on a two-button mouse.

To click an item with the mouse, you move the pointer to the item on the screen. When the pointer touches the object, quickly press and release the primary mouse button once (see Figure 3A.18). Clicking—or *single-clicking*, as it is also called—is the most important mouse action. To select any object on the screen, such as a menu, command, or button, you click it.

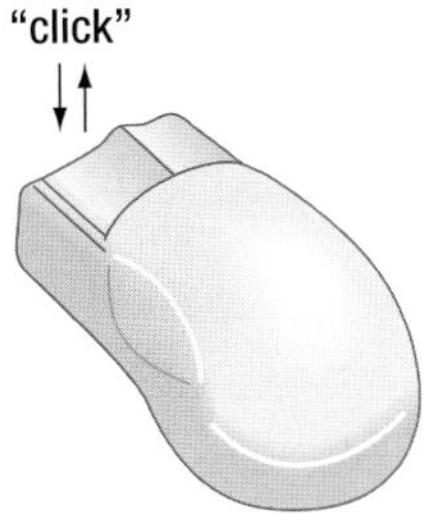
"click"

FIGURE 3A.18

Clicking a mouse.

Double-clicking an item means pointing to the item with the mouse pointer and then pressing and releasing the mouse button twice in rapid succession (see Figure 3A.19). Double-clicking is primarily used with desktop objects such as icons. For example, you can double-click a program's icon to launch the program.

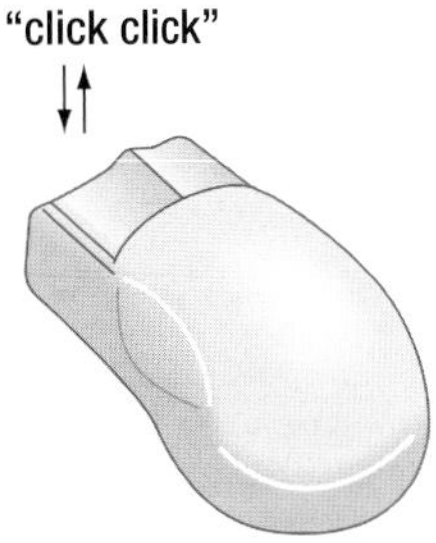
"click click"

FIGURE 3A.19

Double-clicking a mouse.

Dragging an item means positioning the mouse pointer over the item, pressing the primary mouse button, and holding it down as you move the mouse. As you move the pointer, the item is "dragged" along with it across the screen (see Figure 3A.20). You can then drop the item in a new position on the screen. This technique is also called drag-and-drop editing, or just drag and drop. Dragging is a very handy tool. In a word-processing program, for example, you can drag text from one location to another in a document. In a file-management program, you can drag a document's icon and drop it onto a printer's icon to print the document.

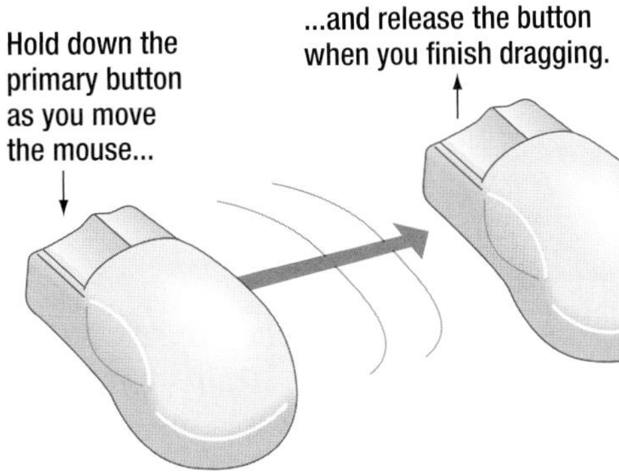
Hold down the primary button as you move the mouse...
...and release the button when you finish dragging.

FIGURE 3A.20

Dragging with a mouse.

Windows and many Windows programs support right-clicking, which means pointing to an item on the screen, then pressing and releasing the right mouse button (see Figure 3A.21). Right-clicking usually opens a shortcut menu that contains commands and options that pertain to the item to which you are pointing.

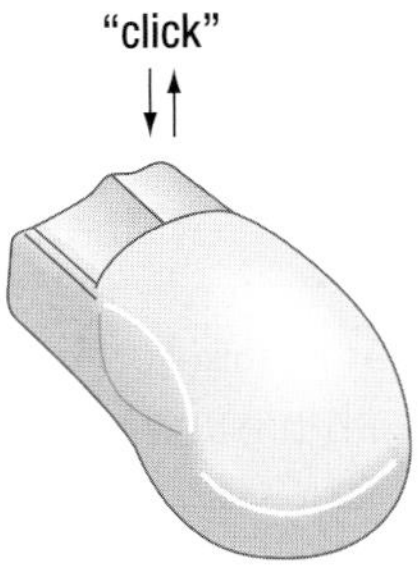
"click"

FIGURE 3A.21

Right-clicking a mouse.

A wheel mouse has a small wheel nestled among its buttons (see Figure 3A.22). You can use the wheel for various purposes, one of which is scrolling through long documents. Not all applications and operating systems support the use of the wheel.

Norton ONLINE

For more information on the care and usage of mice, visit **http://www.mhhe.com/peternorton**.

Mouse Button Configurations

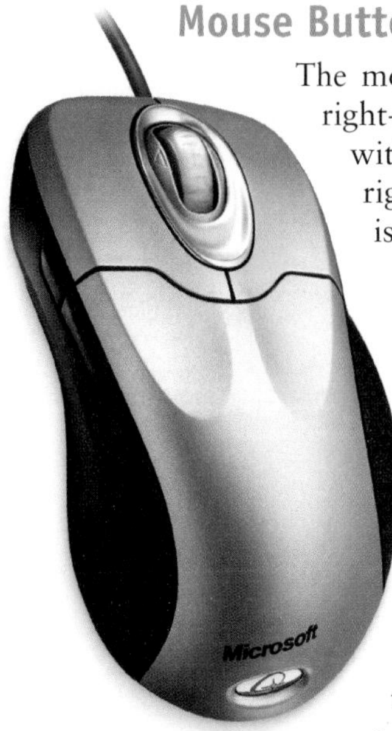

FIGURE 3A.22

A wheel mouse.

The mouse usually sits to the right of the keyboard (for right-handed people), and the user maneuvers the mouse with the right hand, pressing the left button with the right forefinger. For this reason, the left mouse button is sometimes called the primary mouse button.

If you are left-handed, you can configure the right mouse button as the primary button (as shown in Figure 3A.23). This configuration lets you place the mouse to the left of the keyboard, control the mouse with your left hand, and use your left forefinger for most mouse actions.

Newer mice enable you to configure buttons to perform different tasks than clicking. You might configure a button to delete selected text, for example, or to open a program that lets you search for files. Such settings may limit the usefulness of the mouse but can be helpful if you need to perform a certain task many times.

simnet™

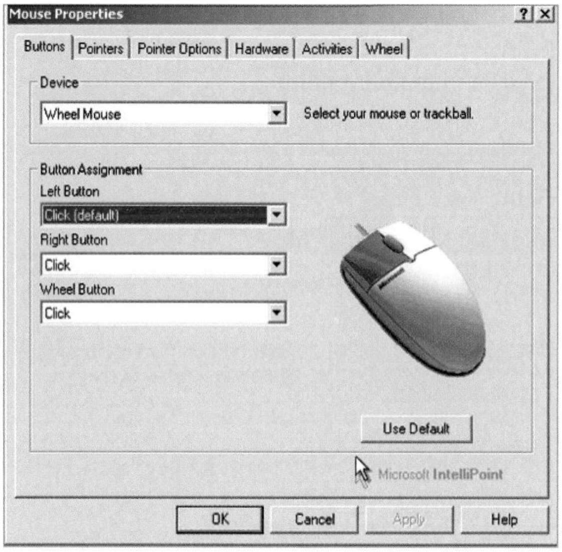

FIGURE 3A.23

Most operating systems provide tools for configuring mouse buttons.

Variants of the Mouse

Although the mouse is a handy tool, some people do not like using a mouse or have difficulty maneuvering one. For others, a mouse requires too much desktop space—a real problem when you are not working at a desk!

For these reasons and others, hardware makers have developed devices that duplicate the mouse's functionality but interact with the user in different ways. The primary goals of these "mouse variants" are to provide ease of use while taking up less space than a mouse. They all remain stationary and can even be built into the keyboard.

Norton ONLINE

For more information on trackballs, visit **http://www.mhhe.com/peternorton**.

Trackballs

A trackball is a pointing device that works like an upside-down mouse. You rest your index finger or thumb on an exposed ball, then place your other fingers on the buttons. To move the pointer around the screen, you roll the ball with your index finger or thumb. Because you do not move the whole device, a trackball requires less space than a mouse. Trackballs gained popularity with the advent of laptop computers, which typically are used on laps or on small work surfaces that have no room for a mouse.

Trackballs come in different models, as shown in Figure 3A.24. Some trackballs are large and heavy with a ball about the same size as a cue ball. Others are much smaller. Most trackballs feature two buttons, although three-button models

SELF-CHECK ::

Circle the correct answer for each question.

1. The most common keyboard layout has about this many keys.
   a. 10 b. 100 c. 110
2. Which special keyboard key has a picture of the Windows logo on it?
   a. START key b. SHORTCUT key c. ALTERNATE key
3. Most full-size PCs feature one of these as the pointing device.
   a. Keyboard b. Mouse c. Scanner

are also available. Trackball units also are available in right- and left-handed models.

FIGURE 3A.24

Trackballs come in many shapes and sizes.

Trackpads

The trackpad (also called a touchpad) is a stationary pointing device that many people find less tiring to use than a mouse or trackball. The movement of a finger across a small touch-sensitive surface is translated into pointer movement on the computer screen. The touch-sensitive surface may be only 1.5 or 2 inches square, so the finger never has to move far. The trackpad's size also makes it suitable for a notebook computer. Some notebook models feature a built-in trackpad rather than a mouse or trackball (see Figure 3A.25).

Like mice, trackpads usually are separate from the keyboard in desktop computers and are attached to the computer through a cord. Some special keyboards feature built-in trackpads. This feature keeps the pad handy and frees a port that would otherwise be used by the trackpad.

Trackpads include two or three buttons that perform the same functions as mouse buttons. Some trackpads are also "strike sensitive," meaning you can tap the pad with your fingertip instead of using its buttons.

Norton ONLINE

For more information on trackpads and integrated pointing devices, visit **http://www.mhhe.com/peternorton**.

Pointers in the Keyboard

Many portable computers now feature a small joystick positioned near the middle of the keyboard, typically between the G and H keys. The joystick is controlled with either forefinger, and it controls the movement of the pointer on screen. Because users do not have to take their hands off the keyboard to use this device, they can save a great deal of time and effort. Two buttons that perform the same function as mouse buttons are just beneath the spacebar and are pressed with the thumb.

Several generic terms have emerged for this device; many manufacturers refer to it as an integrated

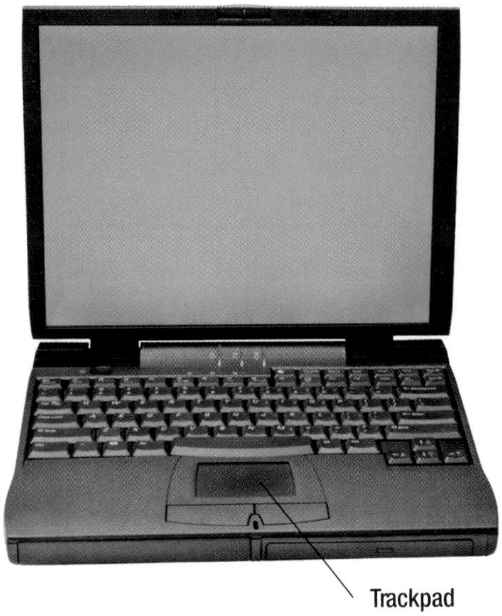

FIGURE 3A.25

Some notebook computers and desktop keyboards feature a built-in trackpad.

Productivity Tip

Saving Time With Keyboard Shortcuts

In the 1980s, as programmers began packing more features into PC software, they also developed ways for users to issue an ever-increasing number of commands. Software packages came with long lists of commands, all of which had to be entered at the keyboard. (This was before the mouse came into common use.) As a result, the computer keyboard rapidly became a valuable tool.

Programmers began devising keyboard shortcuts that allow users to issue commands quickly by typing a short combination of keystrokes. Keyboard shortcuts involve using a modifier key (such as ALT or CTRL) along with one or more alphanumeric or function keys. To print a document in many applications, for example, the user can press CTRL+P.

Function keys also became important. The F1 key, for example, became the universal way to access online help. IBM-compatible computer keyboards originally had 10 function keys; eventually the number of function keys was expanded to 12.

Another common type of keyboard shortcut involves pressing the ALT key to access a program's menu system. When running any Windows program, you can press ALT to activate the menu bar, and then press a highlighted letter in a menu's name to open that menu.

Still, a keyboard can hold only so many keys, and the lists of keyboard shortcuts became unmanageable. A single program could use dozens of "hotkeys," as these shortcuts were called. If you used several programs, you had to learn different shortcuts for each program. Finally, the Common User Access (CUA) standard led to the standardization of many commonly used hotkeys across different programs and environments. With this standard for commonly used hotkeys, users have fewer hotkeys to remember.

Despite such standards, pointing devices (such as the mouse) came along none too soon for hotkey-weary computer users. Microsoft Windows and the Macintosh operating system gained popularity because of their easy-to-use, mouse-oriented graphical interfaces. By operating the mouse, users could make selections visually from menus and dialog boxes. Emphasis rapidly began shifting away from the keyboard to the screen; today, many users do not know the purpose of their function keys!

TrackPoint

FIGURE 3A.26

IBM's ThinkPad computers feature the TrackPoint pointing device, and similar devices are found in many other portable PCs.

pointing device, while others call it a 3-D point stick. On the IBM ThinkPad line of notebook computers, the pointing device is called the TrackPoint (see Figure 3A.26).

Ergonomics and Input Devices

Any office worker will tell you that working at a desk all day can be extremely uncomfortable (see Figure 3A.27). Sitting all day and using a computer can be even worse. Not only does the user's body ache from being in a chair too long, but hand and wrist injuries can result from using a keyboard and mouse for long periods. Eyes can become strained from staring at a monitor for hours. Such injuries can be extreme, threatening the user's general health and ability to work.

Much is being done to make computers easier, safer, and more comfortable to use. Ergonomics, which is the study of the physical relationship between people and their tools—such as computers—addresses these issues. Now more than ever before, people recognize the importance of having ergonomically correct computer furniture and using proper posture and techniques while working with computers. (The term *ergonomically correct* means that a tool or a workplace is designed to work properly with the human body, and thus reduces the risk of strain and injuries.)

Pointing, however, can slow you down. As menus and dialog boxes become increasingly crowded, commands can be hard to find and their locations can be as difficult to remember as keyboard shortcuts. Many computer users overcome these problems by using a combination of keyboard shortcuts and a pointing device. You use one hand to issue many basic shortcuts (such as CTRL+P and CTRL+S) or to launch macros. A macro is a series of commands that a program memorizes for you. Macros enable you to issue an entire set of commands in just a few keystrokes. Using these techniques minimizes keystrokes and leaves a hand free to use a pointing device.

The following table lists some of the shortcut keys available in Microsoft Word.

Press	To
CTRL+B	Toggle bold character formatting on or off for the selected or inserted text; make letters bold or unbold
CTRL+I	Toggle italic character formatting on or off for the selected or inserted text; make letters italic
CTRL+U	Toggle underline character formatting on or off for the selected or inserted text; underline letters
CTRL+SHIFT+<	Decrease font size for the selected or inserted text
CTRL+SHIFT+>	Increase font size for the selected or inserted text
CTRL+Q	Remove paragraph formatting for the selected paragraph or paragraphs
CTRL+SPACEBAR	Remove character formatting for the selected text
CTRL+C	Copy the selected text or object
CTRL+X	Cut the selected text or object
CTRL+V	Paste text or an object
CTRL+Z	Undo the last action
CTRL+Y	Redo the last action

PRODUCTIVITY TIP

Repetitive Stress Injuries

The field of ergonomics did not receive much attention until a certain class of injuries began appearing among clerical workers who spend most of their time entering data on computer keyboards. These ailments are called **repetitive stress injuries (RSIs)** or *repetitive strain injuries* and result from continuously using the body in ways it was not designed to work. One type of RSI that is especially well documented among computer users is **carpal tunnel syndrome**, a wrist or hand injury caused by using a keyboard for long periods of time.

Norton ONLINE

For more information on ergonomics and avoiding computer-related injuries, visit **http://www.mhhe.com/peternorton**.

simnet™

FIGURE 3A.27

Experience shows that office work can pose specific health risks.

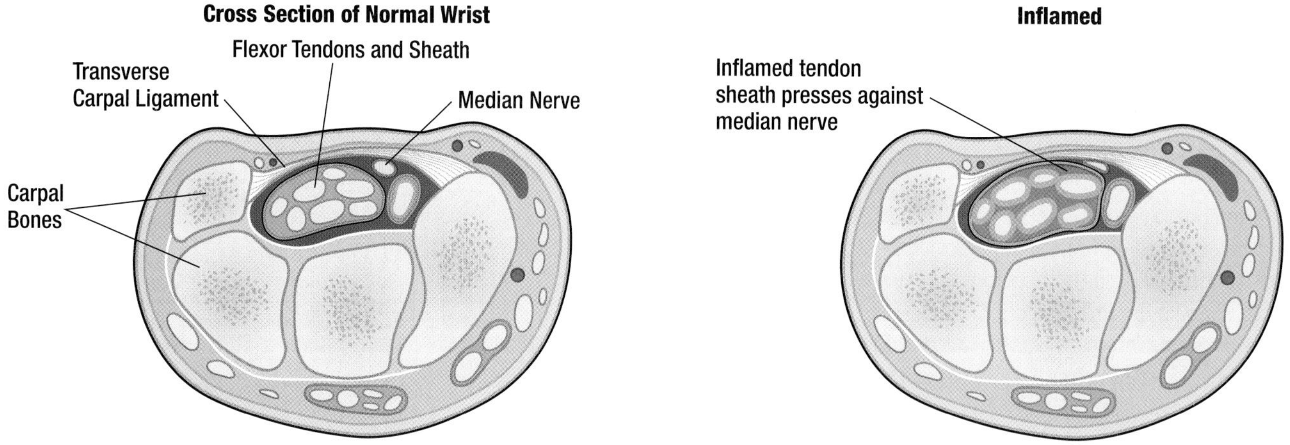

FIGURE 3A.28

Carpal tunnel syndrome affects the nerves running through the carpal tunnel of the wrist.

The carpal tunnel is a passageway in the wrist through which nerves pass (see Figure 3A.28). In carpal tunnel syndrome, tendons in the tunnel become inflamed because the victim has held his or her wrists stiffly for long periods, as people tend to do at a keyboard. When the tendons become inflamed, they press against the nerves, causing tingling, numbness, pain, or the inability to use the hands. Carpal tunnel syndrome is the best-known repetitive stress injury. It can become so debilitating that victims can miss weeks or months of work. In extreme cases, surgery is required.

Avoiding Keyboard-Related Injuries

If you use a computer frequently, you can avoid RSIs by adopting a few good work habits, and by making sure that your hardware and workspace are set up in an ergonomically friendly way.

At Issue

Computer Voting—Is It a Good Thing?

The dispute over electronic voting is as heated as a debate between presidential candidates. The risks versus the benefits are discussed, investigated, and argued. But what are the facts that lie beneath the fuss?

The key function of an electronic voting system is to obtain voter preferences and report them—reliably and accurately. Some assert that electronic systems are safer than other methods of voting because they implement security checks and audit trails, and are tougher to tamper with than paper ballots.

One of the most widely used electronic voting systems, Diebold Election Systems (http://www.diebold.com/dieboldes/accuvote_ts.htm), boasts some 33,000 voting stations in locations across the United States. Diebold's AccuVote-TS system is a voter-activated interactive touch-screen system using an intelligent Voter Card as the voter interface. The interface allows voters to view and cast their votes by touching target areas on an electronically generated ballot pad.

Each unit provides a direct-entry computerized voting station that automatically records and stores ballot information and results. While classified as a direct record entry (DRE) device, the AccuVote-TS system has additional capabilities. The tabulator is a multifunctional interface that counts and tabulates the ballots at precincts on election day and communicates with the host computer at Election Central for accurate and timely jurisdictionwide results.

However, electronic voting systems have generated concern because their work is not readily accessible for inspection; what goes on behind the screen is a mystery to the general public and therefore causes uneasiness. With computer voting, voter records are intangibly stored on a hard drive, with voting results recorded in electronic memory.

Indeed, a July 2003 analysis of the Diebold touch screen by computer researchers from Johns Hopkins and Rice universities (found at http://www.newscientist.com) showed that the software was riddled with errors and open to fraud. However, even with the possibility of fraud, electronic

When setting up your computing workspace, make it a priority to choose a comfortable, ergonomically designed chair (see Figure 3A.29). Your office chair should

- Allow you to adjust its height.
- Provide good lower-back support.
- Have adjustable armrests.

Your desk also should be well-suited to computer use, like the one shown in Figure 3A.30. The desk should hold your keyboard and mouse at the proper height, so that your hands are at the same height as your elbows (or a few inches lower) when you hold them over the keyboard.

Here are some other tips that can help you avoid RSIs while working with your keyboard and mouse:

- **Use an Ergonomic Keyboard.** Traditional, flat keyboards are not well-suited to the shape of human hands. An ergonomic keyboard allows you to hold your hands in a more natural position (with wrists straight, rather than angled outward) while typing (see Figure 3A.31).
- **Use a Padded Wrist Support.** If you type a lot, a wrist support can be helpful by allowing you to rest your hands comfortably when you are not actually typing. Remember, however, that

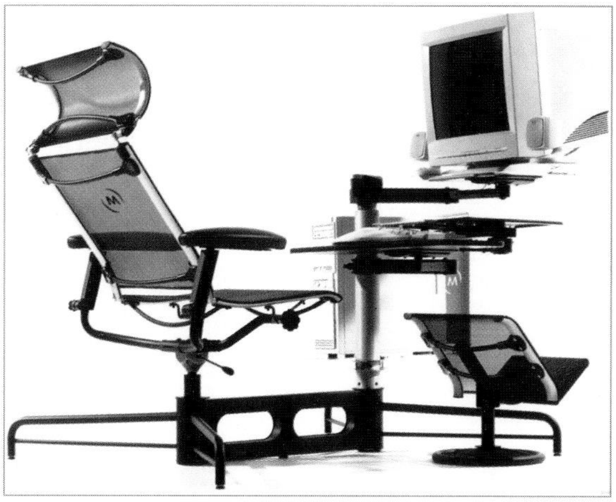

FIGURE 3A.29

An ergonomically designed computer chair and desk.

FIGURE 3A.30

A properly designed computer desk features a built-in shelf or tray to hold the keyboard and mouse.

AT ISSUE

systems may still be safer than prior methods of voting because they implement redundant security checks and audits and may be more difficult to tamper with because of the size and nature of their tabulating components.

Another argument in favor of paper ballots, or at least paper receipts, is that in order to verify an election, all you need to do is gather up the ballots and tabulate them a second (or third, as the case may be) time. However, auditing paper ballot systems is not always as easy as it sounds. Ballots, particularly punch-cards, sometimes provide ambiguous results, as seen in a recent presidential election. They are easily forged and they must be physically handled and transported, which provides the opportunity for substitution or loss.

Whether computerized or traditional, no election system is infallible, and in truth, perhaps it doesn't need to be. As some have said, every safe has the capability to be cracked. The same is true for voting systems. The issue is not whether they are 100 percent secure, but whether they present adequate safeguards to give us faith in the integrity of our elections.

you should never rest your wrists on anything—even a comfortable wrist support—while you type. Use the support only when your fingers are not moving over the keyboard.

» **Keep Your Wrists Straight.** When typing, your hands should be in a straight line with your forearms, when viewed either from above or from the side (see Figure 3A.32). Keeping the wrists bent in either direction can cause muscle fatigue.

» **Sit Up Straight.** Avoid slouching as you type, and keep your feet flat on the floor in front of you. Avoid crossing your legs in front of you or under your chair for long periods.

» **Learn to Type.** You will use the keyboard more efficiently and naturally if you know how to type. If you "hunt and peck," you are more likely to slouch and keep your head down while looking at the keyboard. This technique not only slows you down, but it leads to fatigue and stiffness.

» **Take Frequent Breaks.** Get up and move around for a few minutes each hour, and stretch occasionally throughout the day.

FIGURE 3A.31

An example of an ergonomic keyboard.

FIGURE 3A.32

When typing, your hands should be in line with your forearms at all times and when viewed from any angle.

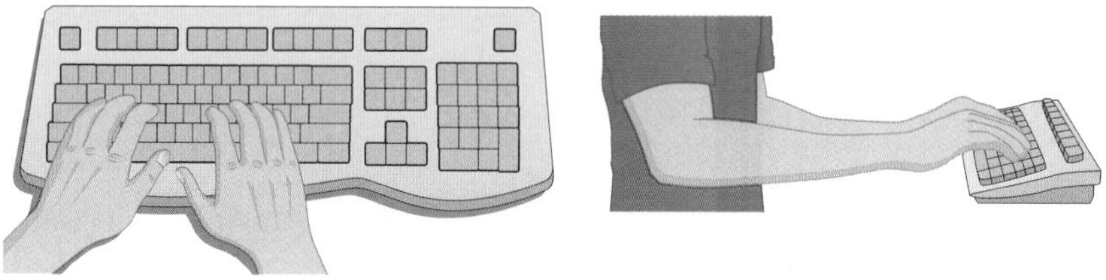

Summary ::

- A standard computer keyboard has about 100 keys.
- Most keyboards follow a similar layout, with their keys arranged in five groups. Those groups include the alphanumeric keys, numeric keypad, function keys, modifier keys, and cursor-movement keys.
- When you press a key, the keyboard controller places a code in the keyboard buffer to indicate which key was pressed. The keyboard sends the computer a signal, which tells the CPU to accept the keystroke.
- The mouse is a pointing device that lets you control the position of a graphical pointer on the screen without using the keyboard.
- Using the mouse involves five techniques: pointing, clicking, double-clicking, dragging, and right-clicking.
- A trackball is like a mouse turned upside-down. It provides the functionality of a mouse but takes less space on the desktop.
- A trackpad is a touch-sensitive pad that provides the same functionality as a mouse. To use a trackpad, you glide your finger across its surface.
- Many notebook computers provide a joystick-like pointing device built into the keyboard. You control the pointer by moving the joystick. On IBM systems, this device is called a TrackPoint. Generically, it is called an integrated pointing device.
- Continuous use of a keyboard and pointing device can lead to repetitive stress injuries.
- The field of ergonomics studies the way people use tools. This study leads to better product designs and techniques that help people avoid injuries at work.
- Ergonomically designed keyboards are available to help users prevent repetitive stress injuries to the wrists and hands.

Key Terms ::

alphanumeric key, 104
buffer, 108
carpal tunnel syndrome, 115
click, 111
cursor, 106
cursor-movement key, 106
double-clicking, 111
drag and drop, 111
drag-and-drop editing, 111
dragging, 111
ergonomics, 114
function key, 105
insertion point, 106
integrated pointing device, 113
keyboard buffer, 108
keyboard controller, 107
keyboarding, 104
mechanical mouse, 109
modifier key, 104
numeric keypad, 105
optical mouse, 109
pointer, 108
pointing, 110
pointing device, 108
repeat rate, 108
repetitive stress injury (RSI), 115
right-clicking, 111
trackpad, 113
TrackPoint, 114
wheel mouse, 111

LESSON //3A Review

Key Term Quiz ::

Complete each statement by writing one of the terms listed under Key Terms in each blank.

1. In computer use, the skill of typing is often referred to as ____________ .
2. IBM-compatible PCs have 10 or 12 ____________ keys.
3. In many programs, an on-screen symbol called a(n) ____________ or a(n) ____________ shows you where you are in a document.
4. A(n) ________ is a temporary storage area that holds data until the CPU is ready for it.
5. In addition to pointing, the four primary mouse techniques are ____________ , ____________ , ____________ , and ____________ .
6. You use a mouse (or one of its variants) to position a(n) ____________ on the screen.
7. In many Windows applications, you can open a shortcut menu by ____________ the mouse.
8. Many laptop computers feature a small joystick between the G and H keys, which is called a(n) ____________ or a(n) ____________ .
9. ____________ is the study of the way people work with tools.
10. ____________ is a common type of repetitive stress injury among computer users.

Multiple Choice ::

Circle the word or phrase that best completes each statement.

1. Some people claim that when computers can interpret handwriting and speech with 100 percent accuracy, this will become unnecessary.
   a. mice b. typing c. pointing device d. special-purpose keys
2. These keys make up the part of the keyboard that looks like a typewriter's keys.
   a. special-purpose keys b. function keys c. typing keys d. alphanumeric keys
3. The common keyboard arrangement is called the ____________ layout.
   a. QWERTY b. QEWTYR c. QYWERT d. QWERYT
4. Which of the following is *not* a modifier key?
   a. SHIFT b. CTRL c. ALT d. BACKSPACE
5. In most programs, you can press this key to get help.
   a. ESC b. F1 c. ALT d. F10
6. When you press a key, this device notifies the system software.
   a. keyboard b. keyboard buffer c. keyboard controller d. keyboard CPU
7. In many Windows applications, you can use this key as an alternative to the right mouse button.
   a. ESC b. F1 c. SPACEBAR d. SHORTCUT

8. This type of mouse uses reflected light to measure its movements.
   a. optical b. laser c. mechanical d. wheel
9. In a multi-button mouse, one button must be designated as the ________ button.
   a. first b. left c. primary d. user
10. You can ________ a program's icon to launch the program.
   a. point to b. double-click c. right-click d. drag

Review Questions ::

In your own words, briefly answer the following questions.

1. Most standard keyboards include five major groups of keys. List them.
2. Why are most standard keyboards called "QWERTY" keyboards?
3. What does the CTRL key do?
4. What is the purpose of the START key, which appears on many IBM-compatible keyboards?
5. What happens when you press a key on the computer's keyboard?
6. What is the purpose of the mouse pointer?
7. How does a mechanical mouse work?
8. Describe two benefits of using a mouse.
9. What does the term *dragging* mean and how do you do it?
10. Describe the cause and effect of carpal tunnel syndrome.

Lesson Labs ::

Complete the following exercises as directed by your instructor.

1. Test your typing skills in Notepad. Click the START button, point to All Programs, click Accessories, and then click Notepad to open the Notepad text-editing program. Notepad opens in a window. Have a classmate time you as you type a paragraph of text. The paragraph should be at least five lines long and should make sense. (For example, you could type a paragraph of text from any page in this book.) Do not stop to correct mistakes; keep typing until you are finished typing the selection.
2. Inspect your system's mouse settings. (Do not change any settings without your instructor's permission.) Use the following steps:
   a. Click the START button to open the Start menu; then click Control Panel. The Control Panel window opens.
   b. Double-click the Mouse icon to open the Mouse Properties dialog box. Click the tabs in this dialog box and inspect your settings.
   c. Experiment with the Pointer Speed and Show Pointer Trails tools. How do they affect your mouse's performance. When you are finished, click Cancel.

LESSON // 3B

Inputting Data in Other Ways

OBJECTIVES ::

- List two reasons why some people prefer alternative methods of input over a standard keyboard or mouse.
- List three categories of alternative input devices.
- List two types of optical input devices and describe their uses.
- Describe the uses for speech-recognition systems.
- Identify two types of video input devices and their uses.

Overview: Options for Every Need and Preference

Although the keyboard and the mouse are the input devices that people use most often, there are many other ways to input data into a computer. Sometimes the tool is simply a matter of choice. Some users just prefer the feel of a trackball over a mouse. In many cases, however, an ordinary input device may not be the best choice. In a dusty factory or warehouse, for example, a standard keyboard or mouse can be damaged if it becomes clogged with dirt. Grocery checkout lines would slow down dramatically if cashiers had to manually input product codes and prices. In these environments, specialized input devices tolerate extreme conditions and reduce the risk of input errors.

Alternative input devices are important parts of some special-purpose computers. Tapping a handheld computer's screen with a pen is a much faster way to input commands than typing on a miniature keyboard. On the other hand, a specialized device can give new purpose to a standard system. If you want to play action-packed games on your home PC, for example, you will have more fun if you use a joystick or game controller than a standard keyboard or mouse.

This lesson examines several categories of alternative input devices and discusses the special uses of each. You may be surprised at how often you see these devices, and you may decide that an alternative device will be your primary means of interacting with your computer.

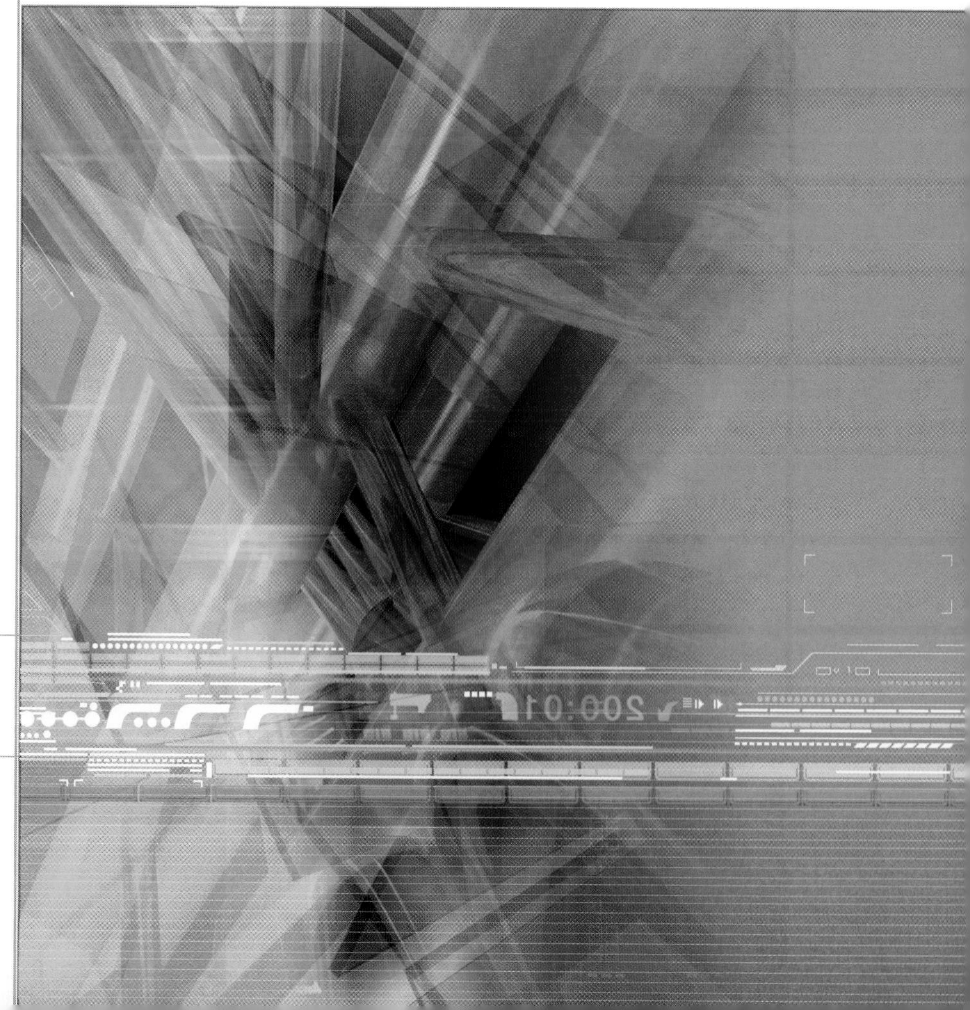

Devices for the Hand

Most input devices are designed to be used by hand. Even specialized devices like touch screens enable the user to interact with the system by using his or her fingertips. Unlike keyboards and mice, many of these input devices are highly intuitive and easy to use without special skills or training.

Pens

Pen-based systems—including many tablet PCs, personal digital assistants, and other types of handheld computers—use a pen for data input (see Figure 3B.1). This device is sometimes called a stylus. You hold the pen in your hand and write on a special pad or directly on the screen. You also can use the pen as a pointing device, like a mouse, to select commands by tapping the screen.

You might think that pen-based systems would be a handy way to enter text into the computer for word processing. In reality, developers have had a great deal of trouble perfecting the technology so that it deciphers people's handwriting with 100 percent reliability. Because handwriting recognition is so complex, pen-based computers are not used generally to enter large amounts of text, although they are used frequently for taking notes, creating short messages, and writing annotations on electronic documents (see Figure 3B.2). PDAs and tablet PCs are popular for these kinds of tasks, which do not require keyboarding.

Pen-based computers are commonly used for data collection, where the touch of a pen might place a check in a box to indicate a part that must be ordered or a service that has been requested. Another common use is for inputting signatures or messages that are stored and transmitted as a graphic image, such as a fax. When delivery-service drivers make deliveries, they often have recipients sign their names on such a computer-based pad (see Figure 3B.3). As handwriting-recognition technology becomes increasingly reliable, pen-based systems will undoubtedly become more common.

Norton ONLINE

For more information on pen-based computing systems, visit **http://www.mhhe.com/peternorton**.

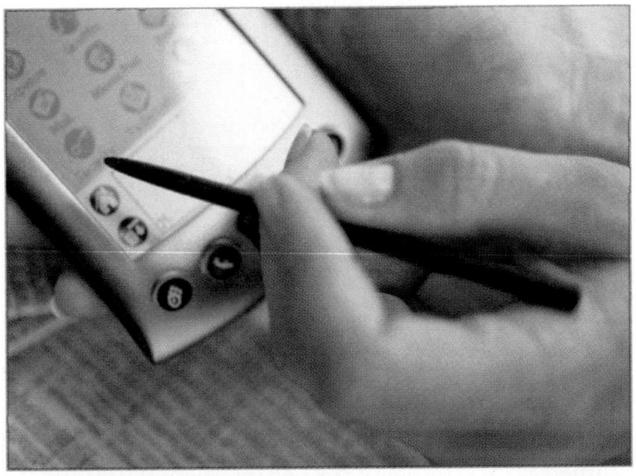

FIGURE 3B.1

To interact with a pen-based computer, you can use the pen to point, tap, drag, draw, and even write on the device's screen.

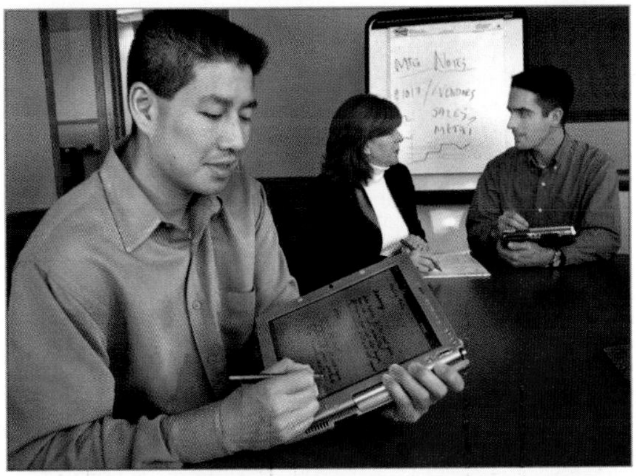

FIGURE 3B.2

Tablet PCs allow the user to input data (such as notes, appointments, or phone numbers) by writing directly on the screen with the unit's pen.

FIGURE 3B.3

When you receive a package via UPS, you may be asked to sign your name on a pen-based computer system.

Norton ONLINE

For more information on touch screens, visit **http://www.mhhe.com/peternorton**.

simnet™

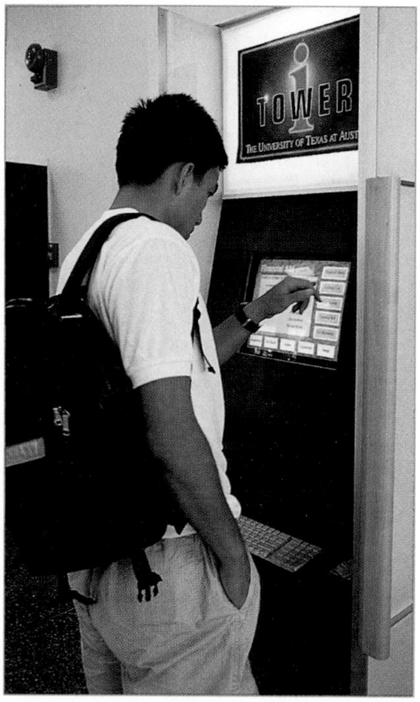

FIGURE 3B.4

This student is using a touch-screen system to get information at a public-information kiosk.

Touch Screens

Touch screens accept input by allowing the user to place a fingertip directly on the computer screen, usually to make a selection from a menu of choices. Most touch-screen computers use sensors on the screen's surface to detect the touch of a finger, but other touch screen technologies are in use, as well.

Touch screens work well in environments where dirt or weather would render keyboards and pointing devices useless, and where a simple, intuitive interface is important. They are well-suited for simple applications, such as automated teller machines or public information kiosks (see Figure 3B.4). Touch screens have become common in fast-food restaurants, department stores, drugstores, and supermarkets, where they are used for all kinds of purposes, from creating personalized greeting cards to selling lottery tickets.

Norton ONLINE

For more information on gaming devices, visit **http://www.mhhe.com/peternorton**.

Game Controllers

You may not think of a game controller as an input device, but it is. Personal computers are widely used as gaming platforms, challenging dedicated video game units like the Sony PlayStation and others (see Figure 3B.5). Because PCs offer higher graphics resolution than standard televisions, many gamers believe a well-equipped PC provides a better game-playing experience. If your computer is connected to the Internet, you can play games with people around the world.

A game controller can be considered an input device because a computer game is a program, much like a word processor. A game accepts input from the user, processes data, and produces output in the form of graphics and sound. As computer games become more detailed and elaborate, more specialized game controllers are being developed to take advantage of their features.

FIGURE 3B.5

With their fast processors and high-quality graphics, PCs are great for playing games.

Game controllers generally fall into two broad categories: game pads and joysticks (see Figure 3B.6). Joysticks have been around for a long time and can be used with applications other than games. (Some joystick users actually prefer using a joystick rather than a mouse with some business applications.) Joysticks enable the user to "fly" or "drive" through a game, directing a vehicle or character. They are popular in racing and flying games. A variant of the joystick is the racing game controller, which includes an actual steering wheel; some racing game controllers even include foot pedals and gearshifts.

If you have ever used a video gaming system, you are familiar with game pads.

A game pad is a small, flat device that usually provides two sets of controls—one for each hand. These devices are extremely flexible and are used to control many kinds of games. If you do not have a joystick, you can use a game pad to control most racing and flying games. (Many computer games still provide support for a mouse or keyboard, so a dedicated game controller is not always required.)

FIGURE 3B.6

Several kinds of game control devices are available, some of which are quite sophisticated. Some controllers even provide tactile feedback, such as vibrations or pulses, to help players "feel" the action in the game.

Optical Input Devices

For a long time, futurists and computer scientists have had the goal of enabling computers to "see." Computers may never see in the same way that humans do, but optical technologies allow computers to use light as a source of input. These tools fall into the category of optical input devices.

Norton ONLINE

For more information on bar codes and bar code readers, visit **http://www.mhhe.com/peternorton**.

Bar Code Readers

Bar code readers are one of the most widely used input devices. The most common type of bar code reader is the flatbed model, which is commonly found in supermarkets and department stores (see Figure 3B.7). Workers for delivery services, such as FedEx, also use handheld bar code readers in the field to identify packages (see Figure 3B.8).

These devices read bar codes, which are patterns of printed bars that appear on product packages. The bar codes identify the product. The bar code reader emits a beam of light—frequently a laser beam—that is reflected by the bar code image. A light-sensitive detector identifies the bar code image by recognizing special bars at both ends of the image. These special bars are different, so the reader can tell whether the bar code has been read right-side up or upside down.

After the detector has identified the bar code, it converts the individual bar patterns into numeric digits—code the computer can understand (see Figure 3B.9). The reader then feeds the data into the computer, as though the number had been typed on a keyboard.

FIGURE 3B.7

To enter prices and product information into a cash register, a cashier passes groceries over a flatbed bar code reader. The reader projects a web of laser beams onto the package's bar code and measures the pattern of the reflected light.

FIGURE 3B.8

Courier services, like FedEx, use handheld bar code readers to track packages all the way to their destination.

FIGURE 3B.9

Manufacturers use bar codes to identify millions of unique products.

Image Scanners and Optical Character Recognition (OCR)

The bar code reader is a special type of image scanner. Image scanners (also called *scanners*) convert any printed image into electronic form by shining light onto the image and sensing the intensity of the light's reflection at every point. Figure 3B.10 illustrates the scanning process.

Color scanners use filters to separate the components of color into the primary additive colors (red, green, and blue) at each point. Red, green, and blue are known as primary additive colors because they can be combined to create any other color. Processes that describe color in this manner are said to use RGB color.

The image scanner is useful because it translates printed images into an electronic format that can be stored in a computer's memory. Then you can use software to organize or manipulate the electronic image. For example, if you scan a photo, you can use a graphics program such as Adobe Photoshop to increase the contrast or adjust the colors. If you have scanned a text document, you might want to use optical character recognition (OCR) software to translate the image into text that you can edit. When a scanner first creates an image from a page, the image is stored in the computer's memory as a bitmap. A bitmap is a grid of dots, each dot represented by one or more bits. The job of OCR software is to translate that array of dots into text that the computer can interpret as letters and numbers.

To translate bitmaps into text, the OCR software looks at each character and tries to match the character with its own assumptions about how the letters should look. Because it is difficult to make a computer recognize an unlimited number of typefaces and fonts, OCR software is extremely complex and not always 100 percent reliable. Figure 3B.11 shows a few of the many ways the letter *g* can appear on a printed page.

Despite the complexity of the task, OCR software has become quite advanced. Today, many programs can decipher a page of text received by a fax machine. In fact, computers with fax modems can use OCR software to convert faxes directly into text that can be edited with a word processor.

Scanners come in a range of sizes from handheld models to flatbed scanners that sit on a desktop (see Figure 3B.12). Handheld scanners are more portable but

Norton ONLINE

For more information on image scanners and OCR software, visit **http://www.mhhe.com/peternorton**.

simnet™

FIGURE 3B.10

How an image is scanned.

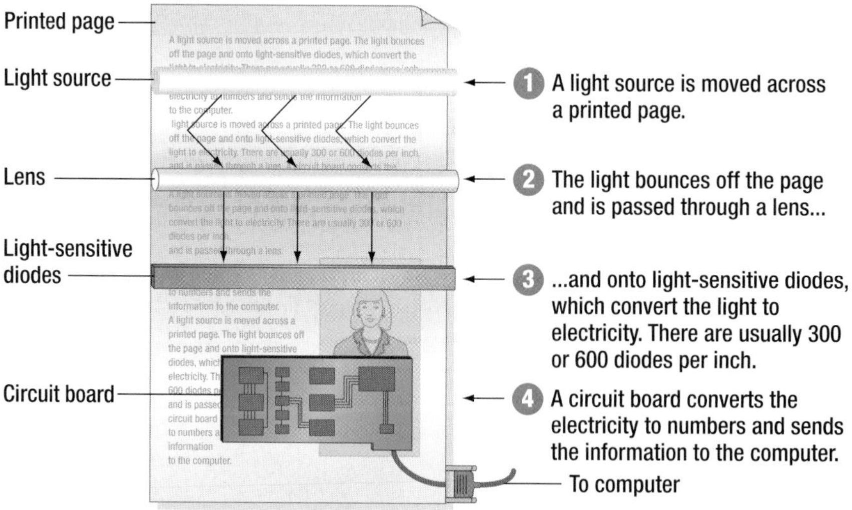
Printed page
Light source
Lens
Light-sensitive diodes
Circuit board
1 A light source is moved across a printed page.
2 The light bounces off the page and is passed through a lens...
3 ...and onto light-sensitive diodes, which convert the light to electricity. There are usually 300 or 600 diodes per inch.
4 A circuit board converts the electricity to numbers and sends the information to the computer.
To computer

typically require multiple passes to scan a single page because they are not as wide as letter-size paper. Flatbed scanners offer higher-quality reproduction than do handheld scanners and can scan a page in a single pass. (Multiple scans are sometimes required for color images, however.) To use a flatbed scanner, you place the printed image on a piece of glass similar to the way you place a page on a photocopier. In some medium-sized scanners, you feed the sheet to be scanned through the scanner, similar to the way you feed a page through a fax machine.

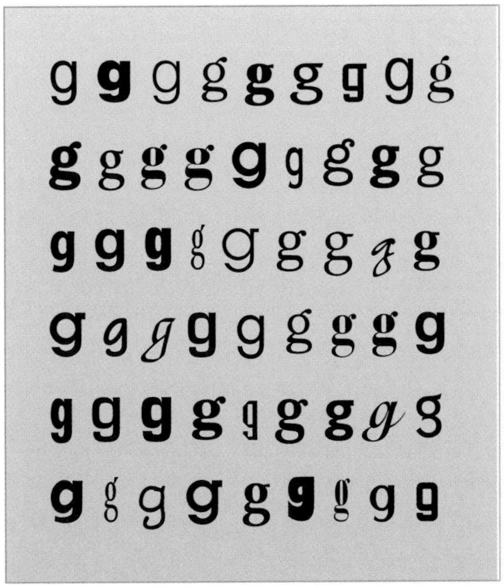

FIGURE 3B.11

A few of the ways that a lowercase *g* can appear in print.

FIGURE 3B.12

Large-format flatbed scanners produce high-resolution, digitized versions of documents. Graphic artists prefer this type of scanner because it yields the highest-quality scans of photographs and other images.

SELF-CHECK ::

Circle the correct answer for each question.

1. These are often used for taking notes, but not for entering large amounts of text.
   a. touch screens b. pen-based computers c. optical scanners
2. The racing game controller is a variation of this.
   a. joystick b. mouse c. scanner
3. A bar code reader emits this.
   a. sound b. light c. commands

Norton Notebook

Speech Recognition

The youngest daughter of an associate recently entered graduate studies at MIT. She's already received a BS in Engineering and an MA in Mathematics. So what has drawn her to Cambridge? "The speech-recognition railroad," she says. When I asked her how long she plans to stay on that train—"All the way to retirement!"

That answer speaks about more than just her smart sense of humor and the lucrative prospects of an MIT doctorate. It also reveals the nearly glacial pace of movement toward achieving that "holy grail" of human interface. Science has explored this idea—talk to machines and they do what we tell them—for nearly a century, and simulations of success have been in the public eye for almost as long. A popular sight at the 1939–1940 New York World's Fair was Westinghouse's "Elektro," a 10-foot-tall "robot" (the word was coined just 18 years prior) that could walk, dance, speak, and smoke a cigarette, all in apparent obedience to spoken commands. Of course, Elektro had a lot of human help, and there wasn't much progress in the world of speech recognition during the subsequent 50 years. Meanwhile Gene Roddenberry's *Star Trek* and George Lucas's *Star Wars* made commonplace the fantasy of machines that could, at the least, understand anything spoken by anyone and, at best, carry on conversations that expressed their own personalities. But, in the words of some forgotten sage, our own real future isn't what it used to be.

It's not for want of trying. Serious research has been done on the subject of voice recognition and control since the earliest days of computing. It turns out that what is such an innate skill for us humans is far from easy for computers. And this was something of a surprise, because of how we humans hierarchically rate our own five senses. When we have thought about those senses in the past—sight, hearing, taste, smell, and touch—we've tended to order them with our precious and delicate binocular, full-color sight at the pinnacle. The eye and our entire vision mechanism are so complex—as I'm writing this, it remains one of very few organs of the body that we cannot transplant with impressive success. This complexity led many to assume that we would have computers listening to our voices long before they could see us. Wrong, again.

Computers can recognize individual human faces, machine parts, and components with accuracy and a precision far greater than our organic vision. Computers do this by using very sophisticated software to compare live video images with massive databases of, say, faces and facial features. Just like people, then, a computer needs to be taught what you look like before it can recognize you. Once the software records certain characteristics of your face, it can still recognize you even if you change your hair, grow a beard, even pretend to be of the opposite sex.

Voice recognition isn't nearly as successful. Part of the problem resides in the nature of sound. There are recognizable edges to your face, a line to the angle of your nose, and so forth, but there are no obvious "lines" to separate the sound waves of your voice from the background noise of, say, a loud party. As human beings, we rely tremendously on the context of a conversation to help understand what is

Audiovisual Input Devices

Today, many new PCs are equipped with complete multimedia capabilities. New computers have features that enable them to record audio and video input and play it back.

Norton ONLINE

For more information on microphones, sound cards, and speech recognition, visit **http://www.mhhe.com/peternorton**.

simnet™

Microphones

Now that sound capabilities are standard in computers, microphones are becoming increasingly important as input devices to record speech. Spoken input is used often in multimedia, especially when the presentation can benefit from narration. Most PCs now have phone-dialing capabilities. If you have a microphone and speakers (or a headset microphone with an earphone), you can use your PC to make telephone calls.

Microphones also make the PC useful for audio and videoconferencing over the Internet. For this type of sound input, you need a microphone and a sound card. A sound card is a special device inside the computer, which translates analog

said to us in a noisy environment. Computers can be programmed to work with context, but they have to be able to distinguish our voices *first*. So, while facial recognition systems can pick out an individual walking along a busy street, speech recognition requires a carefully controlled environment from the start.Good voice recognition systems can be trained to recognize and associate certain sounds with human words. Training usually involves spending several hours reading passages of text into a microphone while the computer "listens" and learns how the speaker pronounces certain sounds. Once the computer recognizes these phonemes, it can combine them together—usually in conjunction with a dictionary—to make whole words from the sounds.

But what happens when those sounds don't sound like those sounds? When I say, "Print a letter," it sounds like me—not like you, or like someone with a different regional accent. In fact, when I say, "Print a letter," with a bad sinus infection, even *I* no longer sound like myself. How is a computer to know that "pibbta lebrah" means anything at all? Given today's technology, it can't. Each voice recognition system needs to be trained to recognize the voice of each user, and if a user's voice changes significantly—or if the noise environment of the speaker changes—the computer must be retrained. Most of the best trained systems provide better than 99 percent accuracy, which sounds excellent, until you consider that means that the computer makes as many as one recognition mistake for every 100 sounds—not words, *sounds*—it hears. (A few "no-training" systems are beginning to appear, but these have had limited applications, such as speaking numbers to choose from a telephone menu of options.)

Thousands of human hours have gone into the research and development of computer speech recognition to bring us to where we are today. Has it been worth it? Absolutely! Speech recognition holds untold promise for millions of people with different abilities, some of which have limited their freedom of creativity with modern technology. As personal computers continue to benefit from advances in processor power, it will be increasingly possible to make ever-more complex analyses of sound. This, in turn, will push recognition capabilities closer and closer to a level of perfection that has remained so elusive. It's also possible, even likely, that a new group of thinkers will conceive of an entirely new way to look at the problem. It may be *you* who finally unlocks speech recognition for generations to come.

audio signals (that is, sound waves) from the microphone into digital codes the computer can store and process. This process is called digitizing. Sound cards also can translate digital sounds back into analog signals that can then be sent to the speakers.

FIGURE 3B.13

Your PC may enable you to record spoken messages with a microphone and sound card.

Using simple audio recording software that is built into your computer's operating system, you can use a microphone to record your voice and create files on disk (see Figure 3B.13). You can embed these files in documents, use them in Web pages, or e-mail them to other people.

There is also a demand for translating spoken words into text, much as there is a demand for translating handwriting into text. Translating voice to text is a capability known as speech recognition (or voice recognition). With it, you can dictate to the computer instead of typing, and you can control the computer with simple commands, such as Open or Cancel.

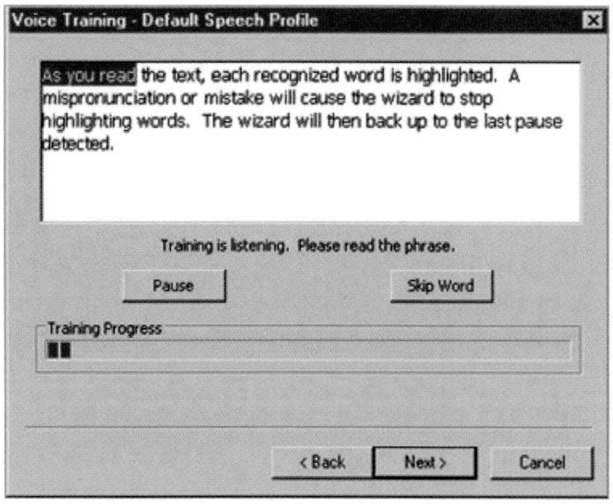

FIGURE 3B.14

This dialog box helps the user "train" speech-recognition software to achieve higher accuracy in dictation.

Speech-recognition software takes the smallest individual sounds in a language, called *phonemes*, and translates them into text or commands. Although the English language uses only about 40 phonemes, reliable translation is difficult. For example, some words in English have the same sound but have different meanings (*two* versus *too*, for example). The challenge for speech-recognition software is to deduce a sound's meaning correctly from its context and to distinguish meaningful sounds from background noise.

Speech-recognition software has been used in commercial applications for years, but traditionally it has been extremely costly, as well as difficult to develop and use. Low-cost commercial versions of speech-recognition software are now available, and they promise to be a real benefit to users who cannot type or have difficulty using a keyboard.

Newer-generation speech-recognition programs are much more reliable than the packages that were available a few years ago. Some packages can recognize accurately 80 to 90 percent of spoken words by using large stored vocabularies, or words they can recognize. The user may need to "train" the software to recognize speech patterns or the pronunciation of some words, but this procedure is relatively simple (see Figure 3B.14). Another enhancement to speech-recognition programs is their ability to recognize continuous speech. Older systems required the user to pause between words, which improved accuracy but greatly slowed the data-entry process.

Speech-recognition programs usually require the use of a noise-canceling microphone (a microphone that filters out background noise). Most commercial packages come with a microphone (see Figure 3B.15).

FIGURE 3B.15

Microphones are becoming increasingly popular input devices.

Other Types of Audio Input

Computers can accept many kinds of audio input. If your computer has a sound card with the appropriate plugs, you may be able to input music from a compact disc, a tape player, a radio, or even a record player.

If the audio source outputs sounds in the form of analog waves (as is the case when you speak into a microphone), the computer's sound card must convert the analog signals into digital code so the computer can store and use it. This is not necessary when recording audio from a compact disc or a digital video disc, but conversion is required for analog sources such as phonograph records and cassette tapes.

If your sound card has a built-in Musical Instrument Digital Interface (MIDI) port, or if you have a dedicated MIDI adapter, you can connect many kinds of electronic musical instruments to your computer. MIDI-based instruments can communicate with and control one another, and any PC can be used to control MIDI instruments and to record their output (see Figure 3B.16). MIDI is extremely popular among musicians of all stripes, who use it to write, record, and edit music, and even to control instruments and effects during performances.

FIGURE 3B.16

Keyboards, drum machines, sequencers, and other types of electronic instruments can be connected together—and to a computer—by using MIDI technology.

Video Input

With the growth of multimedia and the Internet, computer users are adding video input capabilities to their systems in great numbers. Applications such as videoconferencing enable people to use full-motion video images, which are captured by a PC video camera, and transmit them to a limited number of recipients on a network or to the world on the Internet. Videos are commonly used in presentations and on Web pages where the viewer can start, stop, and control various aspects of the playback.

The video cameras used with computers digitize images by breaking them into individual pixels. (A pixel is one or more dots that express a portion of an image.) Each pixel's color and other characteristics are stored as digital code. This code is then compressed (video images can be very large) so that it can be stored on disk or transmitted over a network.

A popular and inexpensive type of PC video camera—called a Webcam—can sit on top of a PC monitor or be placed on a stand, so the user can "capture" images of himself or herself while working at the computer (see Figure 3B.17). This arrangement is handy for videoconferencing, where multiple users see and talk to one another in real time over a network or Internet connection (see Figure 3B.18).

Using a video capture card, the user also can connect other video devices, such as VCRs and camcorders, to the PC. This enables the user to transfer images from the video equipment to the PC, and vice versa. Affordable video capture cards enable home users to edit their videotapes like professionals.

Norton ONLINE

For more information on different types of video input, visit **http://www.mhhe.com/peternorton**.

FIGURE 3B.17

Using a PC video camera or Webcam system, you can conduct online videoconferences and include full-motion video in your documents or e-mail messages.

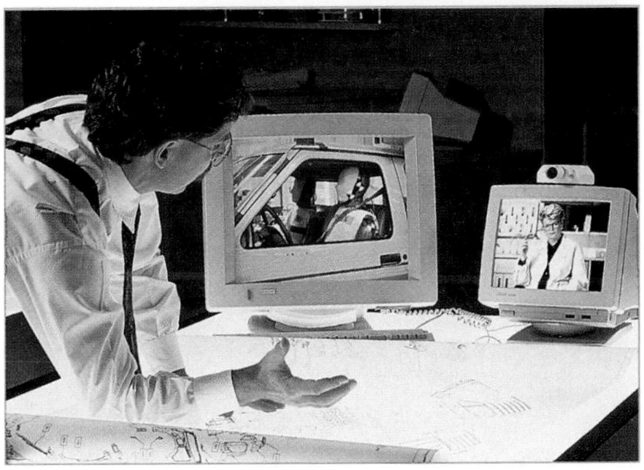

FIGURE 3B.18

PC video cameras enable you to conduct video phone calls. Many PCs feature built-in software that transforms a conventional telephone call into a two-way video phone call.

Digital Cameras

Digital cameras work much like PC video cameras, except that digital cameras are portable, handheld devices that capture still images (see Figure 3B.19). Whereas normal film cameras capture images on a specially coated film, digital cameras capture images electronically. The digital camera digitizes the image, compresses it, and stores it on a special memory card. The user can then copy the information to a PC, where the image can be edited, copied, printed, embedded in a document, or transmitted to another user.

Most digital cameras can store dozens of high-resolution images at a time, and most cameras accept additional memory that increases their capacity even further. Moving digital images from a digital camera to a computer is a simple process that uses standard cables, disks, or even infrared networking capabilities. A wide range of digital cameras are available, from inexpensive home-use models (with prices starting at just over $100) to professional versions costing several thousand dollars.

Norton ONLINE

For more information on digital cameras, visit **http://www.mhhe.com/peternorton**.

simnet™

Computers In Your Career

Hardware Technician

Ask Andy Yother what the best part of his job is and his answer comes quickly: "I get to play with million-dollar toys," says this lead hardware and support engineer at Norcross, Ga.–based Canvas Systems, a reseller of certified, pre-owned IT equipment. Those toys span a wide range of technology systems and manufacturers, making Yother's job both challenging and fulfilling at the same time.

"I handle any piece of equipment that a manufacturer like Sun Microsystems or IBM would make," says Yother. "It's neat to know that during any given week I'm going to build, configure, test, and prepare for sale a wider variety of equipment than most folks will see in their entire careers."

Yother, who is currently completing his Bachelor's degree in business administration at Shorter College, has racked up career experience working for PC makers and circuit board manufacturers. He started in an entry-level position at Canvas Systems, handling low-level testing and identification of systems. Today he oversees a team of six auditors and five engineers who build bare-metal assembly orders to customer specifications, starting with the system board and working up.

"Our customers contact us, tell us what they need, and we start with the bare bones and work up from there," says Yother, whose typical workday starts at 8 AM and ends at 7 PM or later, depending on the time of year and level of demand. "We configure the machines, test them, and prepare them for customer use."

Keeping up with changing technology is no easy task for Yother, who must know how to break down and rebuild both older systems and the newest, state-of-the-art systems available on the market. To keep up, he reads trade and technology magazines, visits manufacturers' Web sites, and subscribes to online mailing lists. "It's about trying to find the best sources of accurate information, and digesting it all," says Yother. "Some days, my brain just aches from information overload."

Yother sees hardware technicians' roles increasing in the future. "We wouldn't have an IT field without the circuits, memory, and processors to back it up," says Yother, who advises all aspiring technicians to learn the computer inside and out, and truly understand how it processes information and accomplishes tasks.

FIGURE 3B.19

Although most digital cameras look like traditional film cameras, they work in a very different way.

Digital cameras have become standard equipment for designers of all kinds. In the field of Web page design, for example, digital cameras enable designers to shoot a subject and quickly load the images onto their computers. This process saves the step of acquiring existing photographs or developing and printing film-based photos—which must be scanned into the computer. Designers can update a Web site's illustrations quickly and regularly using digital cameras.

Graphic designers can edit and enhance digital photographs in innumerable ways, using photo-editing software (see Figure 3B.20). For example, a landscape designer can use a digital camera to take a picture of a house, and then use landscape design software to modify the image to show how the house might appear with different landscaping.

Whether they're working for a company like Canvas Systems or within a firm's IT department, hardware maintenance technicians are responsible for the following kinds of tasks:

- Installing and configuring new computer hardware.
- Installing peripherals.
- Upgrading computers (installing updated cards, memory, drives, etc.).
- Dealing with network-related hardware issues (installing network interface cards, working with cabling, installing hubs or routers, etc.).
- Troubleshooting and repairing hardware of all types.

Many companies rely on their hardware maintenance technicians for input when planning for new system development, expansion, or acquisitions. Their input is important because technicians are in daily contact with end users and develop a good understanding of their needs. A significant advantage of the hardware technician's job is that it is a great springboard to other, more advanced careers in technology. Entry-level technicians typically earn $20,000 to $25,000, with pay scales increasing quickly with experience to levels of $50,000 a year or more.

FIGURE 3B.20

Using photo-editing software, a photographer can edit a digital photograph in many different ways.

LESSON // 3B Review

Summary ::

- With a pen-based system, you use a pen (also called a stylus) to write on a special pad or directly on the screen.
- Pen-based computers are handy for writing notes or selecting options from menus, but they are not well-suited for inputting long text documents.
- Touch-screen systems accept input directly through the monitor. Touch-screen systems are useful for selecting options from menus, but they are not useful for inputting text or other types of data in large quantities.
- A game controller is a special input device that accepts the user's input for playing a game. The two primary types of game controllers are joysticks and game pads.
- Bar code readers, such as those used in grocery stores, can read bar codes, translate them into numbers, and input the numbers into a computer system.
- Image scanners convert printed images into digitized formats that can be stored and manipulated in computers.
- An image scanner equipped with OCR software can translate a page of text into a string of character codes in the computer's memory.
- Microphones can accept auditory input. Using speech-recognition software, you can use your microphone as an input device for dictating text, navigating programs, and choosing commands.
- To use a microphone or other audio devices for input, you must install a sound card on your computer.
- A sound card takes analog sound signals and digitizes them. A sound card also can convert digital sound signals to analog form.
- PC video cameras and digital cameras can digitize full-motion and still images, which can be stored and edited on the PC or transmitted over a LAN or the Internet.

Key Terms ::

bar code, 125
bar code reader, 125
digital camera, 131
digitizing, 129
game controller, 124
game pad, 125
image scanner, 126
joystick, 124
optical character recognition (OCR) software, 126
PC video camera, 131
pen, 123
sound card, 128
speech recognition, 129
stylus, 123
video capture card, 131
voice recognition, 129
Webcam, 131

Key Term Quiz ::

Complete each statement by writing one of the terms listed under Key Terms in each blank.

1. The pen used with a computer—such as a tablet PC—is also called a(n) ____________.
2. You might not think of a(n) ____________ as a true input device, but it is.
3. You can find ____________ being used as input devices in supermarkets and department stores everywhere.
4. A bar code reader is a special type of ____________.
5. In a computer, a(n) ____________ translates analog audio signals into digital codes the computer can use.
6. The process of translating voice into text or commands the computer can understand is called ____________.
7. Using a special ____________ camera, you can participate in online videoconferences.
8. A(n) ____________ is a popular and inexpensive type of PC video camera.
9. Using a(n) ____________, you can connect video devices such as a VCR or camcorder to your PC.
10. A(n) ____________ stores still images on a special memory card, rather than on film.

LESSON //3B Review

Multiple Choice ::

Circle the word or phrase that best completes each statement.

1. With a pen-based system, you can use the pen as a(n) ____________, to select commands.
   a. keyboard b. pointing device c. antenna d. microphone
2. Pen-based computers are commonly used for this type of work.
   a. writing lots of text b. taking pictures c. data collection d. recording sounds
3. ____________ are well-suited for use as input devices at automated teller machines or public information kiosks.
   a. Touch screens b. Pens c. Microphones d. Monitors
4. A game controller can be considered an input device because a computer game is one of these.
   a. a joystick b. a part of a computer c. a fun pastime d. a program
5. Game pads usually have two sets of these, one for each hand.
   a. controls b. joysticks c. games d. microphones
6. This type of technology lets computers use light as a source of input.
   a. optative b. optical c. optimal d. optional
7. A(n) ____________ is used to identify a product and provide information about it, such as its price.
   a. price check b. bar code c. numeric digit d. light-sensitive detector
8. Which type of software can translate scanned text into text that you can edit?
   a. OCS b. ORC c. OCR d. ORS
9. The process of converting analog sounds into code a computer can use is called ____________.
   a. sound recognition b. optical character recognition c. scanning d. digitizing
10. This type of connection lets a computer communicate with, control, and record electronic musical instruments.
    a. DIMI b. MIDI c. DIIM d. MDII

Review Questions ::

In your own words, briefly answer the following questions.

1. In what ways can you use the pen in a pen-based computing system?
2. How do most touch-screen systems work?
3. List one reason why many people believe a PC provides a better game-playing experience than dedicated video game units do.
4. Explain how a bar code reader reads a bar code and what it does with the information from a bar code.
5. What does an image scanner do?
6. How does OCR software translate scanned text into text that you can edit?
7. List three things you can do with the files you create by recording your voice on your computer.
8. What two capabilities does speech-recognition software give you?
9. List four audio sources you can use to record music on your computer.
10. What can you do with a video capture card?

Lesson Labs ::

Complete the following exercise as directed by your instructor.

1. If your computer has a microphone and sound card, complete the following steps to record a message and play it back:
   a. Click the START button to open the Start menu; then click All Programs | Accessories | Entertainment | Sound Recorder.
   b. When the Sound Recorder program opens, click the RECORD button and speak into your computer's microphone; then click the STOP button.
   c. Click PLAY to hear your message.
   d. Close the program by clicking the CLOSE button (with an X on it) in the upper-right corner of the window. If Windows prompts you to save the file, click No.

Chapter Labs

Complete the following exercises using a computer in your classroom, lab, or home.

1. Check your keyboard's repeat rate. You can control the length of time your keyboard "waits" as you hold down an alphanumeric key before it starts repeating the character. You also can set the repeat speed. In this exercise, check the repeat settings but do not change any settings without your instructor's permission.
   a. Click the START button on the Windows taskbar to open the Start menu.
   b. Click Control Panel. Double-click the Keyboard icon in the Control Panel window.
   c. Click the tabs at the top of the Keyboard Properties dialog box and inspect the current settings.
   d. Click the Speed tab. Drag the Repeat delay and Repeat rate indicators all the way to the right, then to the left, and in different combinations. Test the repeat rate at each setting by clicking in the test box and then holding down an alphanumeric key.
   e. Drag the Cursor blink rate indicator to the right and left. How fast do you want your cursor to blink?
   f. Click Cancel to close the dialog box without making changes.
2. Mouse practice. Take the following steps:
   a. Click the START button on the Windows taskbar to open the Start menu.
   b. Point to All Programs, click Accessories, and then click WordPad. The WordPad program will open in its own window. (WordPad is a "lightweight" word-processing application.) Notice the blinking insertion point in the window.
   c. Type: **Now is the time for all good men to come to the aid of their country.**
   d. Using your mouse, click in different parts of the sentence. The insertion point moves wherever you click.
   e. Double-click the word *good*. The word becomes selected: the letters change from black to white, and the background behind the word changes color.
   f. Right-click the selected word. A shortcut menu appears.
   g. Choose the Cut option. The highlighted word disappears from your screen.
   h. Click in front of the word *country* to place the insertion point; right-click again. When the shortcut menu appears, choose Paste. The word *good* reappears.
   i. Double-click the word *good* again to select it. Now click on the selected word and drag it to the left while holding down the mouse button. (A little mark appears on the mouse pointer, indicating that you are dragging something.) When the mouse pointer arrives in front of the word *men*, release the mouse button. The word *good* is returned to its original place.
   j. Continue practicing your mouse techniques. When you are finished, close the WordPad program by clicking the CLOSE button (the button marked with an X) in the upper-right corner of the window. The program will ask if you want to save the changes to your document; choose No.
3. Pick your favorite pointing device. Visit these commercial Web sites for information on various types of pointing devices.

- **AVB Products.** http://www.avbusa.com
- **Cirque.** http://www.cirque.com
- **Hunter Digital.** http://www.footmouse.com
- **Logitech.** http://www.logitech.com
- **Razer.** http://www.razerzone.com
- **Pegasus Technologies.** http://www.pegatech.com

When you are finished, decide which device would work best for you. Be prepared to tell your classmates about the device and explain why you selected it.

Discussion Questions

As directed by your instructor, discuss the following questions in class or in groups.

1. Despite the rapid advancements being made with handwriting-recognition software, do you think that the keyboard will continue to be the preferred input device for generating text? Which alternative—speech recognition or handwriting recognition—do you think has a better chance of ultimately replacing the keyboard as the primary means of input?
2. Suppose that you are responsible for computerizing a gourmet restaurant's order-entry system. What type of input devices do you think would work best for waiters to input orders to the kitchen?

Research and Report

Using your own choice of resources (such as the Internet, books, magazines, and newspaper articles), research and write a short paper discussing one of the following topics:

- The availability and use of screen-reading technologies for computer users who are sight impaired.
- The kind of information stored in a product's bar code.
- The DVORAK keyboard (an alternative to the standard QWERTY keyboard).

When you are finished, proofread and print your paper, and give it to your instructor.

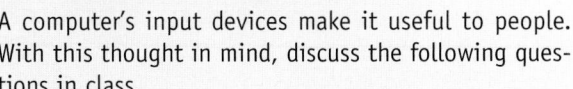

ETHICAL ISSUES

A computer's input devices make it useful to people. With this thought in mind, discuss the following questions in class.

1. Currently, commercially available PCs are configured for use by persons who do not suffer from physical impairments or disabilities that would prohibit using a computer. If a person with a physical impairment wants to use a computer, he or she may need to purchase special equipment or software. Do you think this is fair? Should every PC be accessible to everyone, whether they have physical impairments or not? If you believe this should be the case, how would you make computers accessible to everyone?
2. You have applied for a job as a reporter for a newspaper. Your journalistic skills are excellent. You are not a touch typist, however, and your typing speed is very slow. For this reason, the managing editor is reluctant to hire you at the position's advertised salary. How would you react to this situation? Is the editor right? Should keyboarding skills be a requirement for such a job? Would you be willing to learn to type or accept the job at a lower salary? Be prepared to defend your position.

CHAPTER 4

Seeing, Hearing, and Printing Data

CHAPTER CONTENTS ::

This chapter contains the following lessons:

LESSON // 4A

Video and Sound

Overview: Reaching Our Senses with Sight and Sound

In the beginning, computing was anything but a feast for the senses. The earliest computers were little more than gigantic calculators controlled by large panels of switches, dials, and buttons. Today, nearly every computer features some kind of visual display, but display screens were uncommon until the 1960s.

Now, computers can communicate information to you in several ways, but the most exciting types of output are those that appeal to the senses. It is one thing to read text on a printed page, but it is very different to see a document take shape before your eyes. It can be very exciting to watch moving, three-dimensional images on a large, colorful screen while listening to sounds in stereo.

Modern display and sound systems make the computing experience a more inviting one. Because of these sophisticated output technologies, computers are easier to use, data is easier to manage, and information is easier to access. These technologies enable us to play games and watch movies, experience multimedia events, and use the PC as a communications tool.

This lesson introduces you to monitors and sound systems. You will learn about the different types of monitors commonly used with computers and how they work. You also will learn some important criteria for judging a monitor's performance. This lesson also shows you how computers can output sounds.

OBJECTIVES ::

- List the two most commonly used types of computer monitors.
- Explain how a CRT monitor displays images.
- Identify two types of flat-panel monitors and explain their differences.
- List four characteristics you should consider when comparing monitors.
- Describe how data projectors are used.
- Explain how a computer outputs sound.

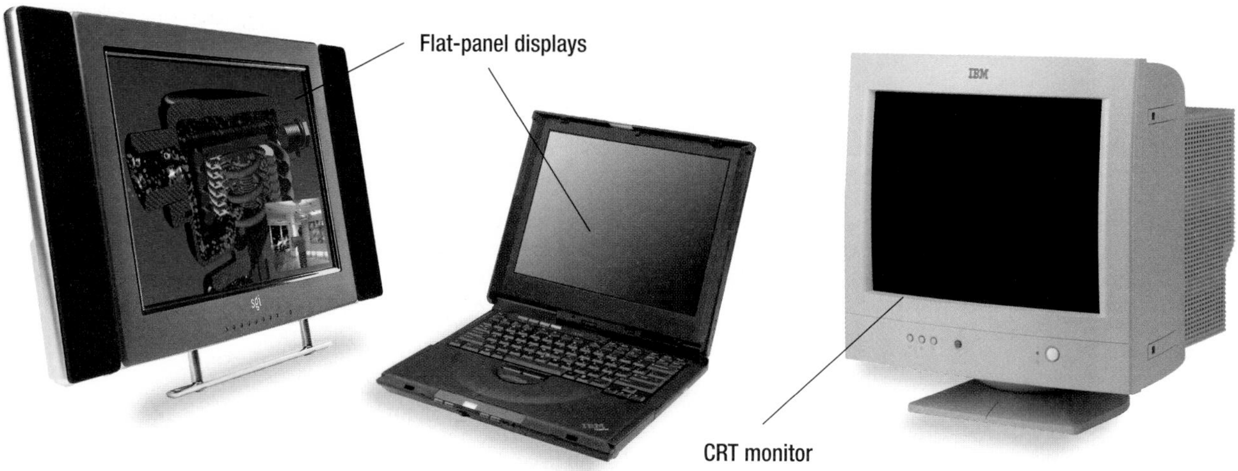

FIGURE 4A.1

The most common types of monitors used with personal computers.

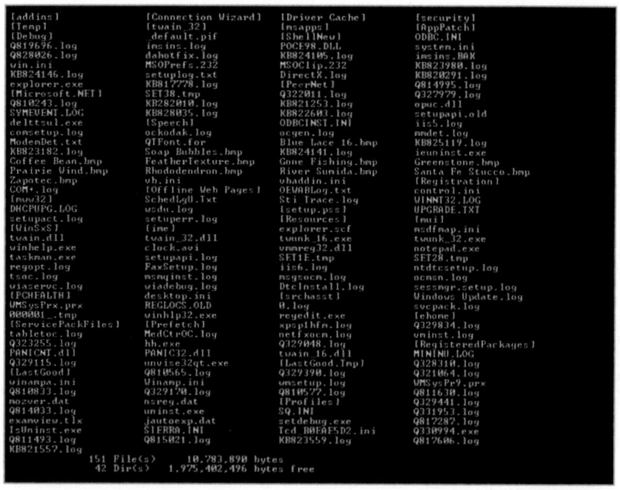

FIGURE 4A.2

Monochrome monitors are usually used for text-only displays.

simnet™

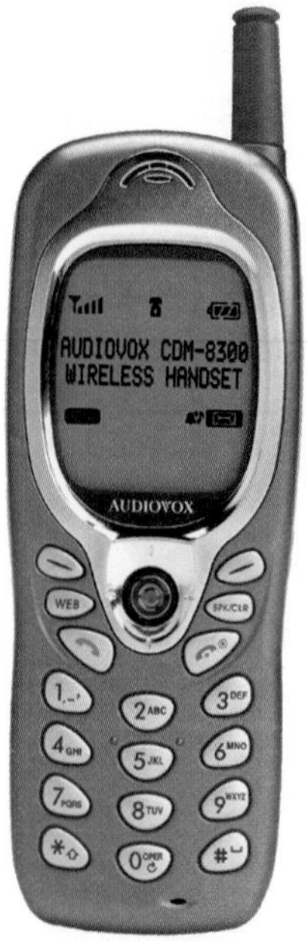

FIGURE 4A.3

Grayscale displays are often used in lower-cost models of handheld computers because they are cheaper than color displays.

Monitors

The keyboard is the most commonly used input device and the monitor is the most commonly used output device on most personal computer systems. As you use your computer—whether you are typing a letter, copying files, or surfing the Internet—hardly a moment goes by when you are not looking at your monitor. In fact, people often form an opinion about a computer just by looking at the monitor. They want to see whether the image is crisp and clear and how well graphics are displayed on the monitor.

Two important hardware devices determine the quality of the image you see on any monitor: the monitor itself and the video controller. In the following sections, you will learn about both of these devices in detail and find out how they work together to display text and graphics.

In general, two types of monitors are used with PCs (see Figure 4A.1). The first is the typical monitor that comes with most desktop computers; it looks a lot like a television screen and works in much the same way. This type of monitor uses a large vacuum tube, called a cathode ray tube (CRT). The second type, known as a flat-panel display, was used primarily with portable computers in the past. Today, flat-panel monitors are a popular feature with desktop computers.

All monitors can be categorized by the way they display colors:

- » Monochrome monitors display only one color (such as green, amber, or white) against a contrasting background, which is usually black. These monitors are used for text-only displays where the user does not need to see color graphics (see Figure 4A.2).
- » Grayscale monitors display varying intensities of gray (from a very light gray to black) against a white or off-white background and are essentially a type of monochrome monitor. Grayscale flat-panel displays are used in low-end portable systems—especially handheld computers—to keep costs down (see Figure 4A.3).

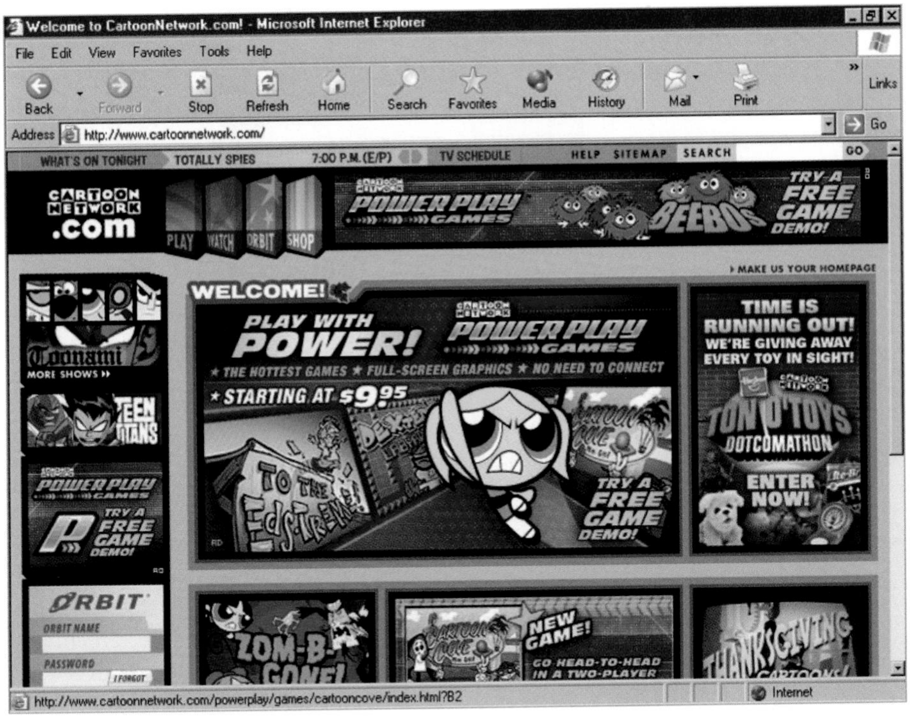

FIGURE 4A.4

Color monitors are almost always included with new computers. This screen is set to display more than 16 million colors, making it a good choice for multimedia content and browsing the World Wide Web.

Norton ONLINE

For more information on computer monitors, visit **http://www.mhhe.com/peternorton**.

» Color monitors can display between 16 colors and 16 million colors (see Figure 4A.4). Today, most new monitors display in color. Many color monitors can be set to work in monochrome or grayscale mode.

CRT Monitors

Figure 4A.5 shows how a typical CRT monitor works. Near the back of a monitor's housing is an electron gun. The gun shoots a beam of electrons through a magnetic coil (sometimes called a yoke), which aims the beam at the front of the monitor. The back of the monitor's screen is coated with phosphors, chemicals that glow when they are struck by the electron beam. The screen's phosphor coating is organized into a grid of dots. The smallest number of phosphor dots that the gun can focus on is called a pixel, a contraction of the term *pic*ture *el*ement. Each pixel has a unique address, which the computer uses to locate the pixel and control its appearance. Some electron guns can focus on pixels as small as a single phosphor dot.

FIGURE 4A.5

How a CRT monitor creates an image.

Actually, the electron gun does not just focus on a spot and shoot electrons at it. It systematically aims at every pixel on the screen, starting at the top left corner and scanning to the right edge. Then it drops down a tiny distance and scans another line, as shown in Figure 4A.6.

Like human eyes reading the letters on a page, the electron beam follows each line of pixels across the screen until it reaches the bottom of the screen. Then it starts over. As the electron gun scans, the circuitry driving the monitor adjusts the intensity of each beam. In a monochrome monitor, the beam's intensity determines whether a pixel is on (white) or off (black). In the case of a grayscale monitor, the beam's intensity determines how brightly each pixel glows.

FIGURE 4A.6

The scanning pattern of the CRT's electron gun.

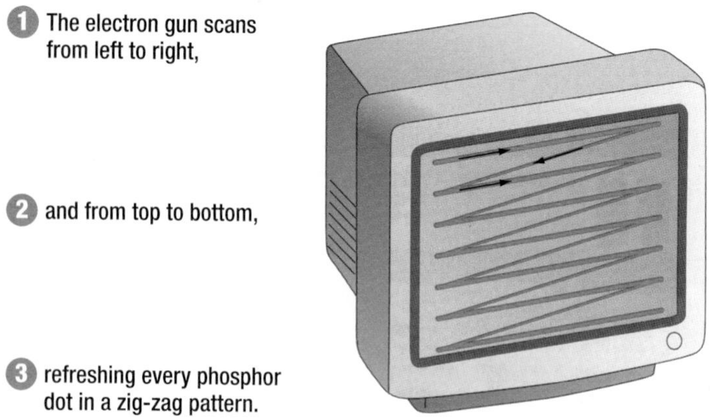

1 The electron gun scans from left to right,
2 and from top to bottom,
3 refreshing every phosphor dot in a zig-zag pattern.

Norton ONLINE

For more information on CRT monitors, visit **http://www.mhhe.com/peternorton**.

FIGURE 4A.7

In color monitors, each pixel is made of three dots—red, green, and blue—arranged in a triangle.

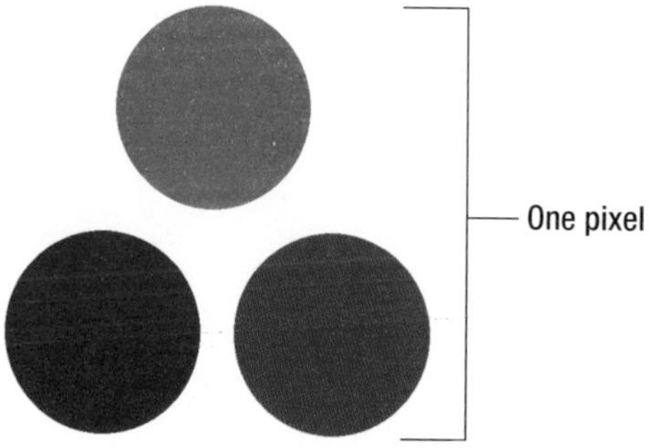

A color monitor works like a monochrome one, except that there are three electron beams instead of one. The three guns represent the primary additive colors (red, green, and blue), although the beams they emit are colorless. In a color monitor, each pixel includes three phosphors—red, green, and blue—arranged in a triangle (see Figure 4A.7). When the beams of each of these guns are combined and focused on a pixel, the phosphors light up. The monitor can display different colors by combining various intensities of the three beams.

A CRT monitor contains a shadow mask, which is a fine mesh made of metal, fitted to the shape and size of the screen. The holes in the shadow mask's mesh are used to align the electron beams, to ensure that they strike precisely the correct phosphor dot. In most shadow masks, these holes are arranged in triangles.

CRT monitors have long been the standard for use with desktop computers because they provide a bright, clear picture at a relatively low cost. There are two major disadvantages, however, associated with CRT monitors:

- Because CRT monitors are big, they take up desktop space and can be difficult to move. A standard CRT monitor may be more than 16 inches deep and weigh about 30 pounds. (A new breed of "thin" CRTs is significantly thinner and lighter than old-fashioned CRT monitors, but they are still relatively deep and heavy.) By contrast, flat-panel monitors are gaining popularity because they are only a few inches deep and usually weigh less than 10 pounds (see Figure 4A.8).
- CRT monitors require a lot of power to run; therefore, they are not practical for use with notebook computers. Instead, notebook computers use flat-panel monitors that are less than one-half-inch thick and can run on battery power that is built into the computer.

Flat-Panel Monitors

Although flat-panel monitors have been used primarily on portable computers, a new generation of large, high-resolution, flat-panel displays is gaining popularity among users of desktop systems. These new monitors provide the same viewable area as CRT monitors, but they take up less desk space and run cooler than traditional CRT monitors.

FIGURE 4A.8

Comparing the size of a standard CRT monitor and a flat-panel monitor.

There are several types of flat-panel monitors, but the most common is the liquid crystal display (LCD) monitor (see Figure 4A.9). The LCD monitor creates images with a special kind of liquid crystal that is normally transparent but becomes opaque when charged with electricity.

One disadvantage of LCD monitors is that their images can be difficult to see in bright light. For this reason, laptop computer users often look for shady places to sit when working outdoors or near windows. A bigger disadvantage of LCD monitors, however, is their limited viewing angle—that is, the angle from which the display's image can be viewed clearly (see Figure 4A.10). With most CRT monitors, you can see the image clearly even when standing at an angle to the screen. In LCD monitors, however, the viewing angle shrinks; as you increase your angle to the screen, the image becomes fuzzy quickly. In many older flat-panel systems, the user must face the screen nearly straight on to see the

Norton ONLINE

For more information on flat-panel monitors, visit **http://www.mhhe.com/peternorton**.

FIGURE 4A.9

Today, most portable computers and handheld computing devices feature a color LCD monitor. Even very small devices can deliver crisp, sharply detailed images by using the latest advances in LCD technology.

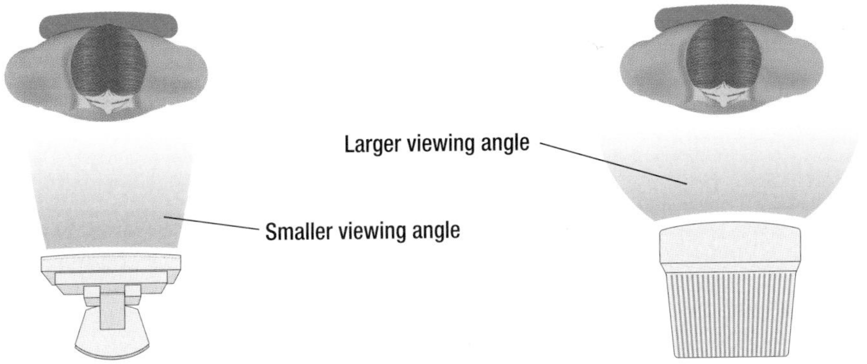

FIGURE 4A.10

Flat-panel displays typically have a smaller viewing angle than CRT monitors.

image clearly. Technological improvements have extended the viewing angles of flat-panel monitors.

There are two main categories of liquid crystal displays:

Norton **ONLINE**

For more information on monitor manufacturers, visit **http://www.mhhe.com/peternorton**.

» The passive matrix LCD relies on transistors for each row and each column of pixels, thus creating a grid that defines the location of each pixel. The color displayed by a pixel is determined by the electricity coming from the transistors at the end of the row and the top of the column. Although passive matrix monitors are inexpensive to manufacture, they have a narrow viewing angle. Another disadvantage is that they don't "refresh" the pixels very quickly. (Refresh rate is described in more detail later in this lesson.) If you move the pointer too quickly, it seems to disappear, an effect known as submarining. Animated graphics can appear blurry on a passive matrix monitor.

  Most passive matrix screens now use dual-scan LCD technology, which scans the pixels twice as often. Submarining and blurry graphics are less troublesome than they were before the dual-scan technique was developed.

» The active matrix LCD technology assigns a transistor to each pixel, and each pixel is turned on and off individually. This enhancement allows the pixels to be refreshed much more rapidly, so submarining is not a problem. Active matrix screens have a wider viewing angle than passive matrix screens. Active matrix displays use thin-film transistor (TFT) technology, which employs as many as four transistors per pixel. Today, most notebook computers feature TFT displays (see Figure 4A.11).

FIGURE 4A.11

As the cost of high-quality TFT displays has come down, they have become the most commonly used type of display on notebook computers.

Other Types of Monitors

While CRT and flat-panel monitors are the most frequently used types of displays in PC systems, there are other kinds of monitors. These displays use specialized technologies and have specific uses:

» Paper-white displays are sometimes used by document designers such as desktop publishing specialists, newspaper or magazine compositors, and other persons who create high-quality printed documents. A paper-white display produces a very high contrast between the monitor's white background and displayed text or graphics, which usually appear in black. An LCD version of the paper-white display is called a page-white display. Page-white displays utilize a special technology, called supertwist, to create higher contrasts.

» Electroluminescent displays (ELDs) are similar to LCD monitors but use a phosphorescent film held between two sheets of glass. A grid of wires sends current through the film to create an image.

» Plasma displays are created by sandwiching a special gas (such as neon or xenon) between two sheets of glass. When the gas is electrified via a grid of small electrodes, it glows. By controlling the amount of voltage applied at various points on the grid, each point acts as a pixel to display an image.

Comparing Monitors

If you need to buy a monitor, go comparison shopping before making a purchase (see Figure 4A.12). Look for a monitor that displays graphics nicely and is easy on your eyes, allowing you to work longer and more comfortably. A poor monitor can reduce your productivity and may even contribute to eyestrain.

When shopping for a monitor, first look at a screen full of text and examine the crispness of the letters, especially near the corners of the screen. In standard CRT monitors, the surface of the screen is curved, causing some distortion around the edges and especially in the corners (see Figure 4A.13). In some low-cost monitors, this distortion can be bothersome. Thin CRT displays have flat screens so, like flat-panel LCD monitors, they eliminate this problem.

Next, display a picture with which you are familiar and see whether the colors look accurate. If possible, spend some time surfing the World Wide Web to display different types of pages.

Even if the monitor looks good (or if you are buying it through the mail), you need to check several specifications. The following are the most important:

- Size
- Resolution
- Refresh rate
- Dot pitch

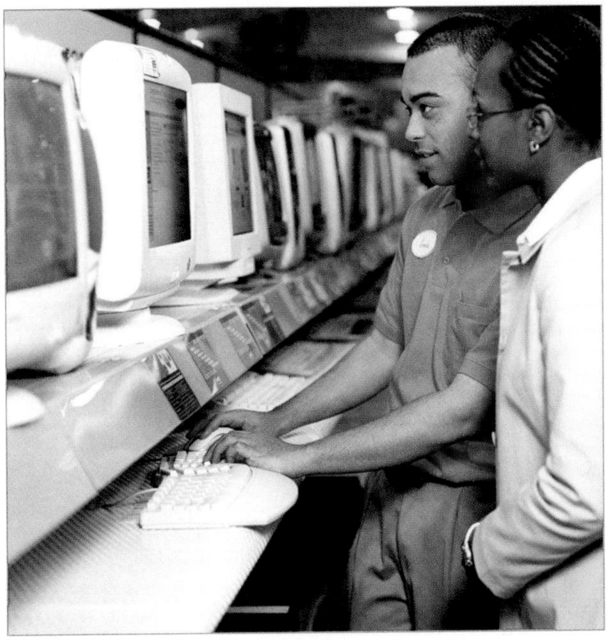

FIGURE 4A.12

It's a good idea to compare monitors before buying one, to find one that is right for you.

FIGURE 4A.13

In a standard CRT monitor, the screen's surface is curved. This can cause some distortion of images.

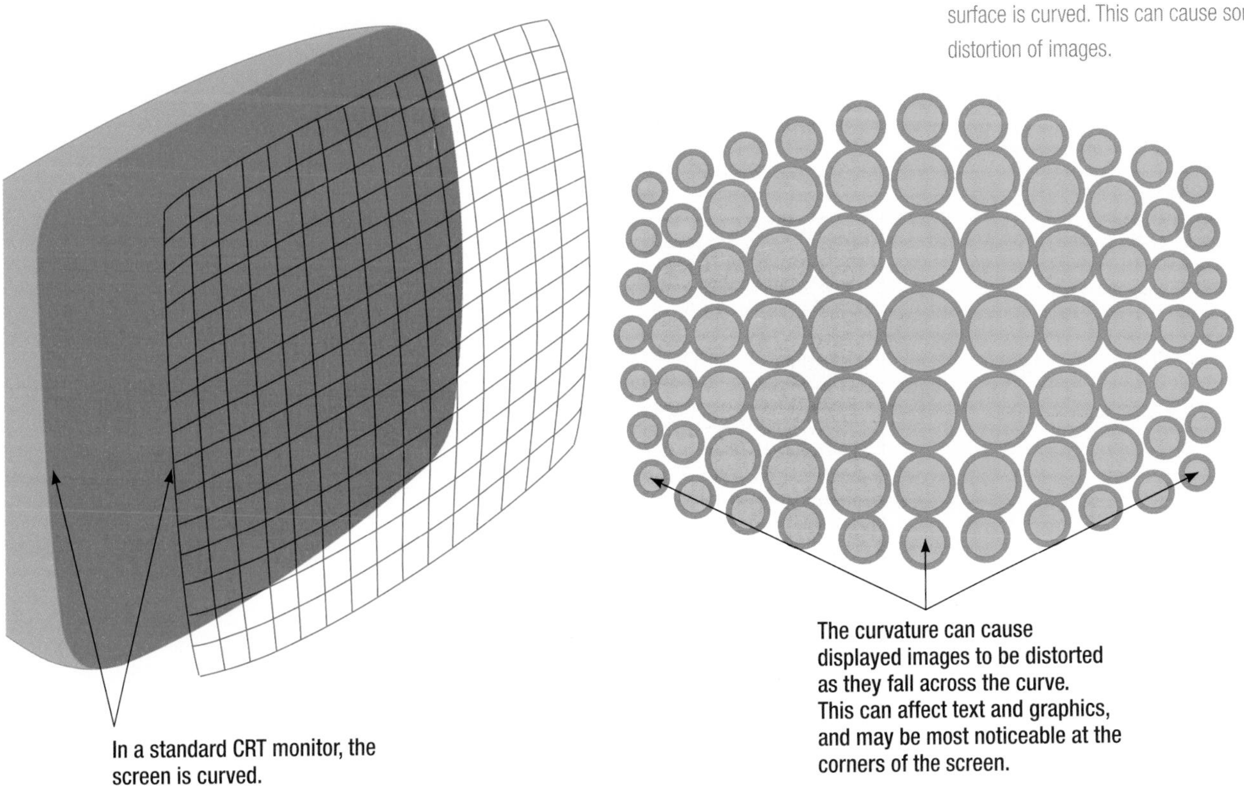

In a standard CRT monitor, the screen is curved.
The curvature can cause displayed images to be distorted as they fall across the curve. This can affect text and graphics, and may be most noticeable at the corners of the screen.

Size

A monitor's size affects how well you can see images. With a larger monitor, you can make the objects on the screen appear bigger, or you can fit more of them on the screen (see Figure 4A.14). Monitors are measured diagonally, in inches, across the front of the screen. A 17-inch monitor measures 17 inches from the lower left to the upper right corner. However, a CRT monitor's actual viewing area—that is, the portion of the monitor that actually displays images—is smaller than the monitor's overall size. The viewing area of a flat-panel display will be somewhat larger than the viewing area of a comparably sized CRT monitor. As a rule of thumb, buy the largest monitor you can afford.

Resolution

The term resolution refers to the sharpness or clarity of an image. A monitor's resolution is determined by the number of pixels on the screen, expressed as a matrix. The more pixels a monitor can display, the higher its resolution and the clearer its images appear. For example, a resolution of 640 × 480 means that there are 640 pixels horizontally across the screen and 480 pixels vertically down the screen. Because the actual resolution is determined by the video controller—not by the monitor itself—most monitors can operate at several different resolutions. Figure 4A.15 shows five commonly used resolution settings: (a) 640 × 480,

FIGURE 4A.14

The larger your monitor, the more easily you can see text and graphics.

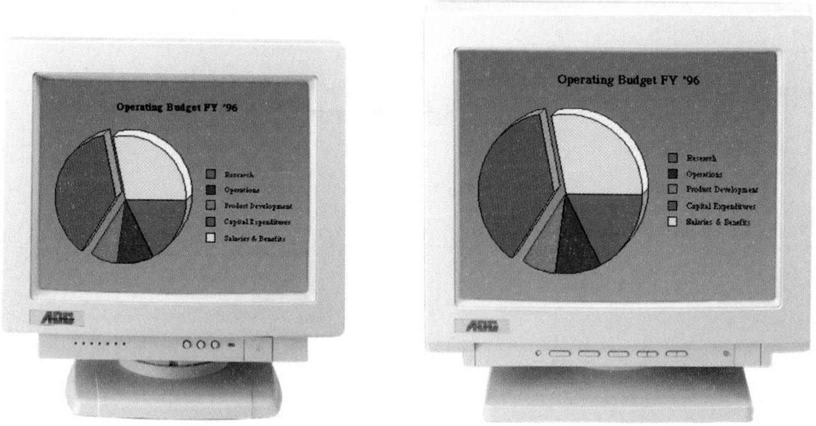

FIGURE 4A.15

Most monitors can operate at different resolutions, as shown here.

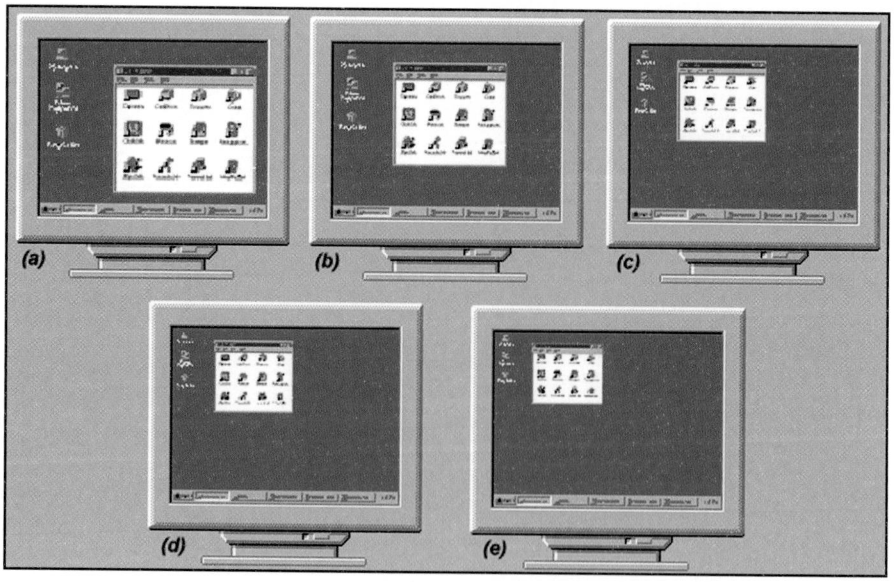

(b) 800 × 600, (c) 1024 × 768, (d) 1152 × 864, and (e) 1280 × 1024. Note that, as the resolution increases, the image on the screen gets smaller.

There are various standards for monitor resolution. The Video Graphics Array (VGA) standard is 640 × 480 pixels. The Super VGA (SVGA) standard expanded the resolutions to 800 × 600 and 1024 × 768. Today, nearly any color monitor can be set to even higher resolutions. Higher settings are not always better, however, because they can cause objects on the screen to appear too small, resulting in eyestrain and squinting. Compare the two screens shown in Figure 4A.16. Both were taken from the same 17-inch monitor. The first image is displayed at 640 × 480 resolution; the second image shows the same screen at 1280 × 1024.

Refresh Rate

A monitor's refresh rate is the number of times per second that the electron guns scan every pixel on the screen (see Figure 4A.17). Refresh rate is important because phosphor dots fade quickly after the electron gun charges them with electrons. If the screen is not refreshed often enough, it appears to flicker, and flicker is one of the main causes of eyestrain. Refresh rate is measured in Hertz (Hz), or in cycles

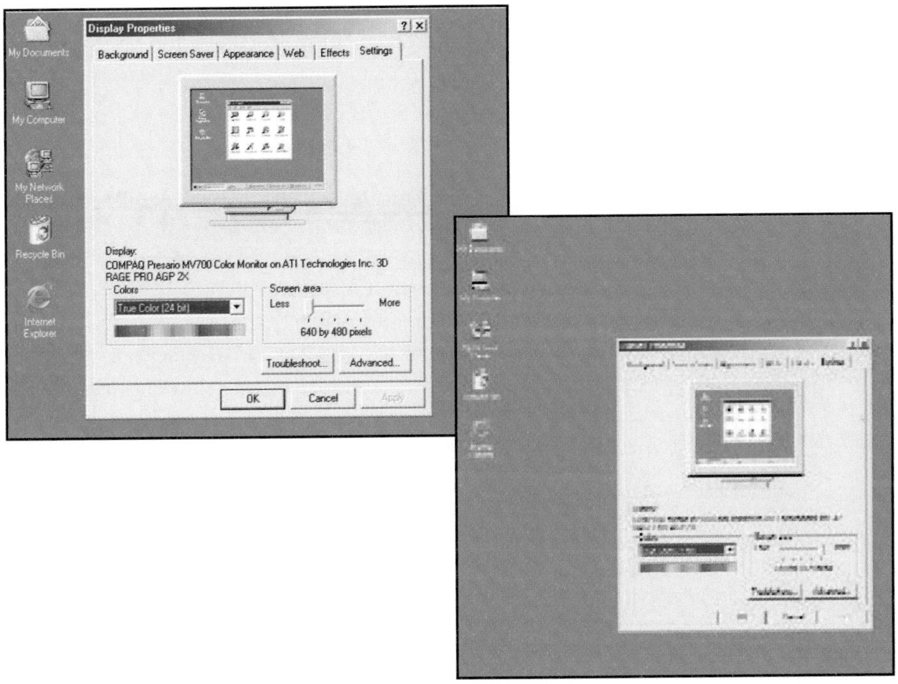

FIGURE 4A.16

VGA and Super VGA.

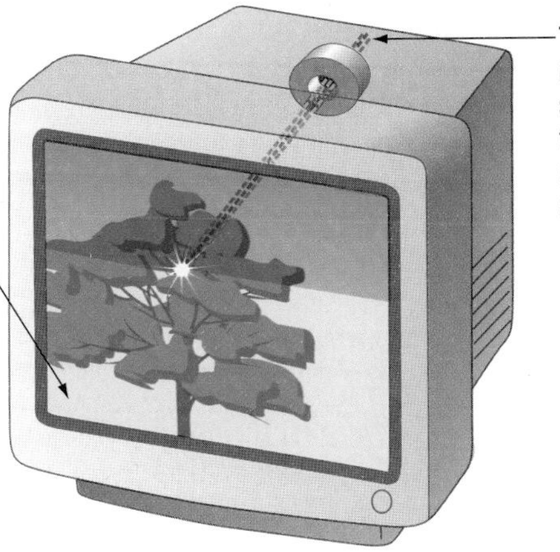

FIGURE 4A.17

This illustration shows how a monitor refreshes its pixels.

per second. This means that if a monitor's refresh rate is 100 Hz, it refreshes its pixels 100 times every second.

When purchasing a monitor, look for one with a refresh rate of 72 Hz or higher. The high refresh rate can help you avoid eyestrain. Note that some monitors have different refresh rates for different resolutions. Make sure the refresh rate is adequate for the resolution you will be using.

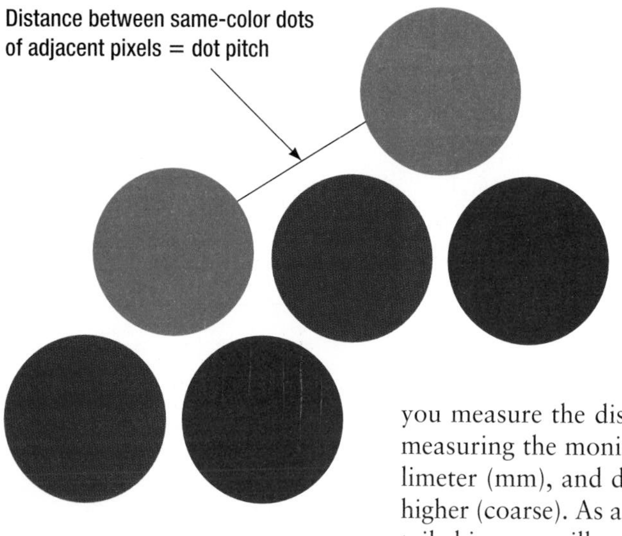

Distance between same-color dots of adjacent pixels = dot pitch

FIGURE 4A.18

Measuring dot pitch in a color monitor.

Dot Pitch

The last critical specification of a color monitor is the dot pitch, the distance between the like-colored phosphor dots of adjacent pixels (see Figure 4A.18). In other words, if you measure the distance between the red dots of two adjacent pixels, you are measuring the monitor's dot pitch. Dot pitch is measured as a fraction of a millimeter (mm), and dot pitches can range from .15 mm (very fine) to .40 mm or higher (coarse). As a general rule, the smaller the dot pitch, the finer and more detailed images will appear on the monitor.

Most experts agree that, when shopping for a color monitor, you should look for a dot pitch no greater than 0.28 millimeter (.28 mm). That number generally applies to 15-inch monitors. If you want a larger monitor, look for an even finer dot pitch, such as .22 mm or less.

Video Cards

The quality of the images that a monitor can display is defined as much by the video card (also called the *video controller* or the *video adapter*) as by the monitor itself. As shown in Figure 4A.19, the video controller is an intermediary device between the CPU and the monitor. It contains the video-dedicated memory and other circuitry necessary to send information to the monitor for display on the screen. In most computers, the video card is a separate device that is plugged into the motherboard. In many newer computers, the video circuitry is built directly into the motherboard, eliminating the need for a separate card.

In the early days of personal computing, PC screens displayed only text characters and usually only in one color. These displays took little processing power because there were only 256 possible characters and 2,000 text positions on the screen. Rendering each screen required only 4,000 bytes of data. Today, however, computers are required to display high-quality color graphics as well as full-motion animations and video. These displays require the CPU to send information to the video controller about every pixel on the screen. At a minimum resolution of 640 × 480, there are 307,200 pixels to control. If you run your monitor at 256 colors, each pixel requires one byte of information. Thus, the computer must send 307,200 bytes to the monitor for each screen. The screen changes constantly as you work—the screen is updated many times each second, whether anything on the screen actually changes or not.

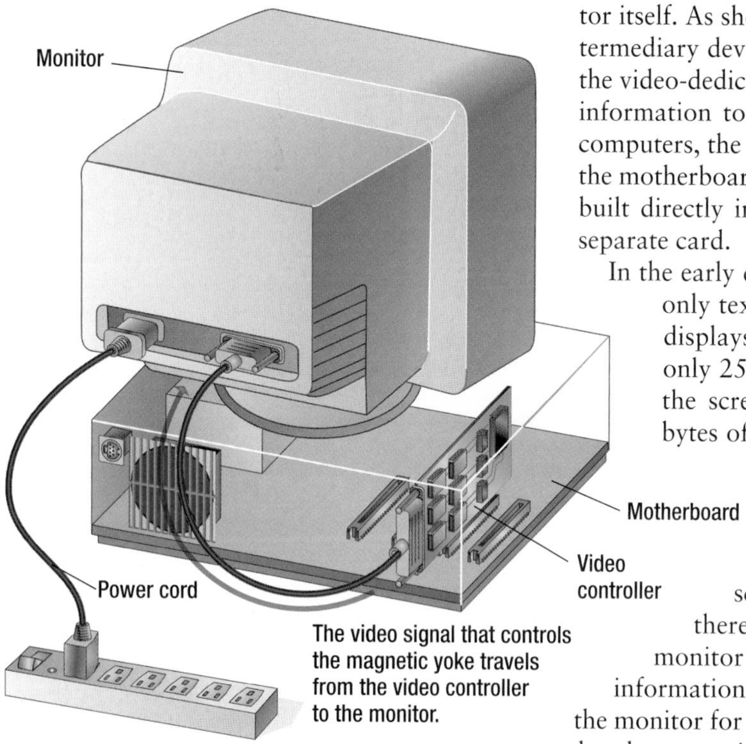

Monitor
Motherboard
Video controller
Power cord
The video signal that controls the magnetic yoke travels from the video controller to the monitor.

FIGURE 4A.19

The video controller connects the CPU, via the data bus on the motherboard, to the monitor.

If the user wants more colors or a higher resolution, the amount of data can be much higher. For example, for "high color" (24 bits, or 3 bytes, per pixel will render millions of colors) at a resolution of 1024 × 768, the computer must send 2,359,296 bytes to the monitor for each screen.

The result of these processing demands is that video controllers have increased dramatically in power and importance. Today's video controllers feature their own built-in microprocessors (see Figure 4A.20), which frees the CPU from the burden of making the millions of calculations required for displaying graphics. The speed of the video controller's chip determines the speed at which the monitor can be refreshed.

Video controllers also feature their own built-in video RAM, or VRAM (which is separate from the RAM that is connected to the CPU). VRAM is dual-ported, meaning that it can send a screen full of data to the monitor and at the same time receive the next screen full of data from the CPU. Today's most sophisticated video controllers, which are fine-tuned for multimedia, video, and 3-D graphics, may have as much as 256 MB or more of video RAM.

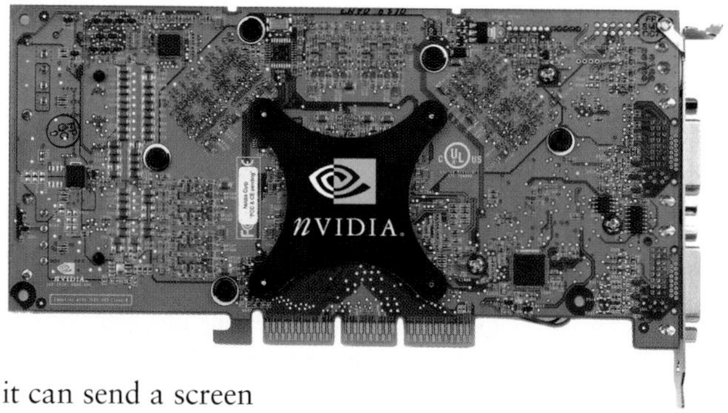

FIGURE 4A.20

Today's video controllers feature sophisticated circuitry to meet the demands of animation, 3-D graphics, and full-motion video.

Ergonomics and Monitors

As you saw in Chapter 3, a number of health-related issues have been associated with computer use. Just as too much keyboarding or improper typing technique can lead to hand or wrist injuries, too much time at a monitor can endanger your eyesight. Protecting your eyesight means choosing the right kind of monitor and using it correctly.

Norton ONLINE

For more information on video controllers, visit **http://www.mhhe.com/peternorton**.

simnet™

Eyestrain

Eyestrain is one of the most frequently reported health problems associated with computers, but is also one of the most easily avoided. Eyestrain is basically fatigue of the eyes, caused by focusing on the same point for too long. When you look at the same object (such as a monitor) for too long, the eye's muscles become strained.

Think of how your arms would feel if you held them straight out for several minutes. Your shoulders and upper arms would soon begin to ache and feel weak; eventually you would have to rest your arms, or at least change their position. The same kind of thing occurs in eyestrain.

Experts say that eyestrain does not pose any long-term risks to eyesight, but it can lead to headaches. It also can reduce your productivity by making it harder to concentrate on your work.

Luckily, you can take several steps to reduce eyestrain when using a computer:

- Choose a monitor that holds a steady image without flickering. The dot pitch should be no greater than .28 mm and the refresh rate should be at least 72 Hz.
- Position your monitor so it is 2–2½ feet away from your eyes, so that the screen's center is a little below your eye level. Then tilt the screen's face upward about 10 degrees, as shown in Figure 4A.21. This angle will enable you to view the monitor comfortably without bending your neck. If you have vision problems that require corrective lenses, however, ask your optometrist about the best way to position your monitor.
- Place your monitor where no light reflects off the screen. If you cannot avoid reflections,

Norton ONLINE

For more information on monitors and your vision, visit **http://www.mhhe.com/peternorton**.

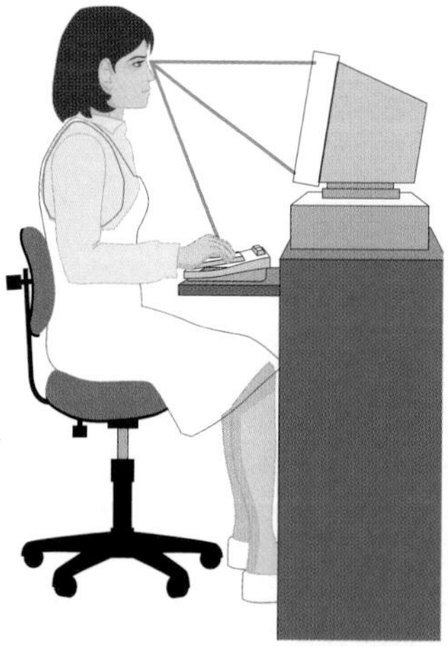

FIGURE 4A.21

By positioning your monitor as shown here, you can avoid eyestrain and neck fatigue.

Norton Notebook

Flat Video Is Anything But

You may find it hard to believe, but it wasn't too long ago that a full 50 percent of my usable desk space was monopolized by my PC's monitor. And it wasn't just me. Since the first days of the PC, computer users have turned to video displays to see their work. Unfortunately, video displays are large, and big ones are *huge*. A video display with a 21-inch diagonal view was commonly in a case that was about two feet square! You lose desk real estate pretty quickly with hardware like that, but video monitors had one undeniable advantage: They were the only game in town. If you needed to use a PC and see what you were doing—always helpful—there was no alternative but to place what amounted to an overpriced television set smack in the middle of your workspace. (In fact, early models of Apple brand personal computers actually *did* use television sets as their displays.) Early relocatable PCs weighed in at about 25 pounds, so the success of portable computing relied entirely on the success of making components lighter and smaller. Video displays were quickly replaced with a variety of panel-type screens. Batteries weigh more than most anything else, but small batteries were drained powerless in as little as 30 minutes by early flat panels. Flat panel screens are also delicate to manufacture, and yields—the number of usable products a factory makes (as opposed to the total number of a product that it *tries* to make that aren't useable for whatever reason)—were originally very low. This kept costs very high, which suppressed demand, which discouraged investment in cheaper methods, and on and on.

It was around this time that the first freestanding flat panel displays for desktop PCs were marketed. For a variety of reasons—they were generally larger than notebook flat panel displays, and so were more expensive and difficult to manufacture, and they required a different type of video interface than was standard on every desktop PC at the time—desktop flat panels were priced well out of the reach of the average user. It was not at all uncommon for a desktop flat panel to retail for twice what the entire desktop PC cost. They were, however, sharp and colorful and produced clear, vibrant images. Desktop flat panels definitely possessed the marketing "Wow!" factor (and they gave you your desk back). Demand increased and production technology improved. Slowly, prices began to fall.

Now, roughly half way through the first decade of the twenty-first century, flat panels are everywhere. They remain a bit more expensive than comparably-sized CRT video monitors, but that gap continues to shrink, and the so-called average PC system usually now includes a flat panel instead of a CRT. As flat-panel displays for television and home theatre increase in popularity, technology will continue to improve and prices will continue to drop. Already, what was once a $2,000 desktop flat panel now costs less than one-third of that.

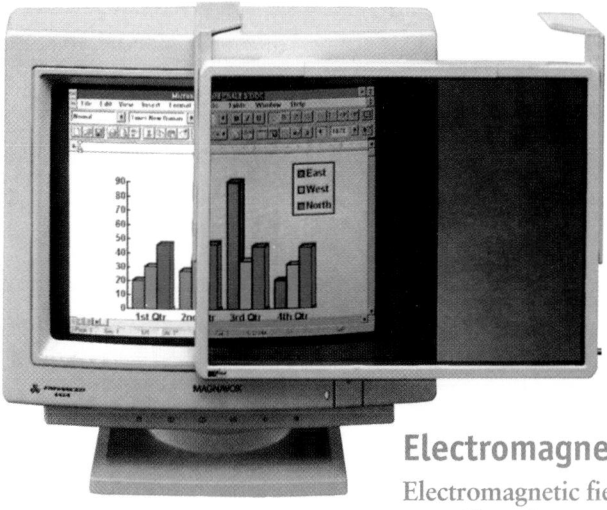

FIGURE 4A.22

An antiglare screen cuts down the reflections on a monitor's surface.

use an antiglare screen to reduce the reflections on the screen (see Figure 4A.22).

- Keep your screen clean.
- Avoid looking at the monitor for more than 30 minutes without taking a break. When taking a break from the monitor, focus on objects at several different distances. It is a good idea to simply close your eyes for a few minutes, to give them some rest.
- Do not let your eyes become dry. If dryness is a problem, ask your optometrist for advice.

Electromagnetic Fields

Electromagnetic fields (EMFs) are created during the generation, transmission, and use of low-frequency electrical power. These fields exist near power lines, electrical appliances, and any piece of equipment that has an electric motor. A debate has continued for years whether EMFs can be linked to cancer. Conclusions vary depending on the study and criteria used, but many people remain convinced that EMFs pose a health threat of some kind.

NORTON NOTEBOOK

But flat panels are in no danger of becoming boring technology. Already, people are transitioning from CRT-based home televisions to flat-panel screens. A number of technologies are sparring for preeminence, and it's likely that several types of flat panel will continue to co-exist to meet the tastes and price-points of the world market. One of the newest developments in the flat-panel world might even herald the most significant change in home entertainment since the introduction of color television. Sharp Corporation recently introduced the world's first notebook computer with a true 3D display. (By "true 3D" I mean a display that shows images in three dimensions *without* special glasses.) An innovative way of producing the flat panel itself (a matter of *parallax*, if you're curious) makes it possible for Sharp to send a slightly different image to a user's left eye than to his or her right eye. When the brain combines the images, it's tricked into perceiving depth. What this technology could mean for medical diagnostics, for pharmaceutical and genetic research, and for education is staggering. What it could mean for entertainment—think "3D TV"—is astounding. For years, researchers have tried to develop practical three-dimensional television, most of which was based on dubious holographic processes or required cumbersome wired goggles or glasses. Displaying 3D content on this new screen simply requires the user press a button labeled "3D."

Already, at least one producer of the very successful IMAX3D movies has released their films on DVD. A number of major game manufacturers, including the ubiquitous Electronic Arts, also have agreed to develop 3D games for this new way of seeing. Sharp itself has created a 3D slide creator/viewer that allows any user to create 3D images of family, friends, and places with an existing digital camera.

Of course, there is no guarantee that any particular innovation or technology will be the one that gets adopted universally and changes major aspects of our lives. There's also no publicly available evidence at the time of this writing that this system will work on the "living room" scale, as a three-dimensional entertainment system for whole families. But Sharp has the distinction of having the first three-dimensional video system that is practical, convenient, and affordable. We may all need to come up with a replacement name for "flat panels." That old name just may not seem appropriate for long.

EMFs have an electrical component and a magnetic component. Of the two, the magnetic fields raise the health concern because they can penetrate many kinds of materials. These fields, however, lose strength rapidly with distance. To reduce your exposure to EMFs, take the following steps:

- Take frequent breaks away from the computer.
- Sit at arm's length away from the system unit, monitor, and other equipment.
- If possible, use a flat-panel display, which does not radiate EMFs.

SELF-CHECK ::

Circle the correct answer for each question.

1. A monitor is an example of this kind of device.
   a. processing   b. input   c. output
2. The back of a CRT monitor's screen is coated with these.
   a. phosphors   b. electrons   c. elements
3. In a plasma display, gas is electrified by a grid of these.
   a. electronics   b. electrodes   c. electrons

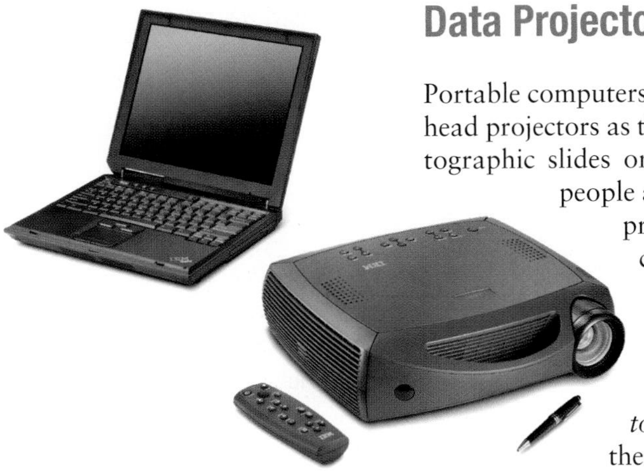

FIGURE 4A.23

Data projectors make it easy to deliver a presentation directly from a computer, so it can be viewed by a group of people.

Data Projectors

Portable computers have all but replaced old-fashioned slide projectors and overhead projectors as the source of presentations. Instead of using 35-millimeter photographic slides or 8.5- by 11-inch overhead transparencies, more and more people are using software to create colorful slide shows and animated presentations. These images can be shown directly from the computer's disk and displayed on the PC's screen or projected on a wall or large screen.

To get these presentations onto the "big screen," data projectors are becoming increasingly common. (Data projectors also are called *digital light projectors* and *video projectors*.) A data projector plugs into one of the computer's ports and then projects the video output onto an external surface (see Figure 4A.23). These small devices weigh only a few pounds and can display over 16 million colors at high resolution. Many projectors can work in either still-video (slide) mode or full-video (animation) mode, and can display output from a VCR or DVD drive as well as from a computer disk.

Most projectors use LCD technology to create images. (For this reason, these devices are sometimes called *LCD projectors*.) Like traditional light projectors, LCD projectors require the room to be darkened. They display blurry images in less-than-optimal lighting conditions.

Newer models use digital light processing (DLP) technology to project brighter, crisper images. DLP devices use a special microchip called a digital micromirror device, which actually uses mirrors to control the image display. Unlike LCD-based projectors, DLP units can display clear images in normal lighting conditions.

Norton ONLINE

For more information on computer data projectors, visit **http://www.mhhe.com/peternorton**.

Sound Systems

Microphones are now important input devices, and speakers and their associated technologies are key output systems (see Figure 4A.24). Today, nearly any new multimedia-capable PC includes a complete sound system, with a microphone, speakers, a sound card, and a CD-ROM or DVD drive. Sound systems are especially useful to people who use their computer to create or use multimedia products, watch videos or listen to music, or participate in online activities such as videoconferences or distance learning.

The speakers attached to these systems are similar to those you connect to a stereo. The only difference is that they are usually smaller and may contain their own amplifiers. Otherwise, they do the same thing any speaker does: They transfer a constantly changing electric current to a magnet, which pushes the speaker cone back and forth. The moving speaker cone creates pressure vibrations in the air—in other words, sound (see Figure 4A.25).

FIGURE 4A.24

Speakers are common features on today's multimedia PCs. Top-of-the-line PC audio systems include premium sound cards and tweeters, midrange speakers, and subwoofers for sound quality that rivals home stereo systems.

Sound Cards

The most complicated part of a computer's sound system is the sound card. A computer's sound card is a circuit board that converts sound from analog to digital form, and vice versa, for recording or playback. A sound card actually has both input and output functions (see Figure 4A.26). If you want to use your computer's microphone to record your voice, for instance, you connect the microphone to the sound card's input jack. Other audio input devices connect to the sound card as well, such as the computer's CD-ROM or DVD drive. You may be able to attach other kinds of audio devices to your sound card, such as tape players, record players, and others.

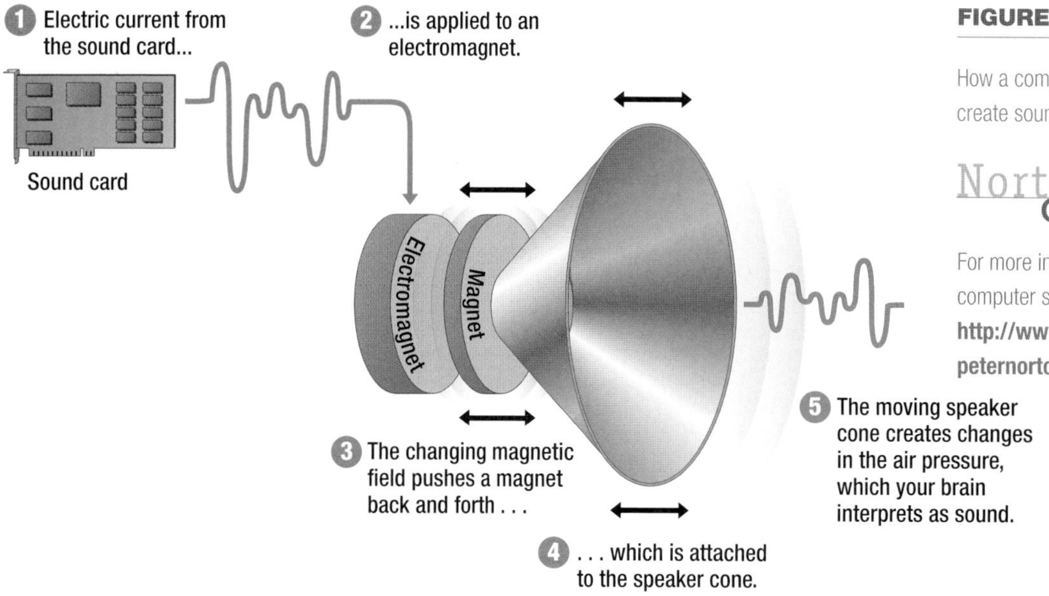

1 Electric current from the sound card...
2 ...is applied to an electromagnet.
Sound card
Electromagnet
Magnet
3 The changing magnetic field pushes a magnet back and forth . . .
4 . . . which is attached to the speaker cone.
5 The moving speaker cone creates changes in the air pressure, which your brain interprets as sound.

FIGURE 4A.25

How a computer uses a speaker to create sound.

Norton ONLINE

For more information on computer sound systems, visit **http://www.mhhe.com/peternorton**.

As you learned in Chapter 3, the sound card accepts sound input (from a microphone or other device) in the form of analog sound waves. You can think of analog signals as fluctuations in the intensity of an electrical current. The sound card measures those signals and converts them into a digital format, which the computer can use.

To play back audio, the sound card reverses the process. That is, it translates digital sounds into the electric current that is sent to the speakers, which are connected to the card's output jacks.

With the appropriate software, you can do much more than simply record and play back digitized sound (see Figure 4A.27). Sound editing programs provide a miniature sound studio, allowing you to view the

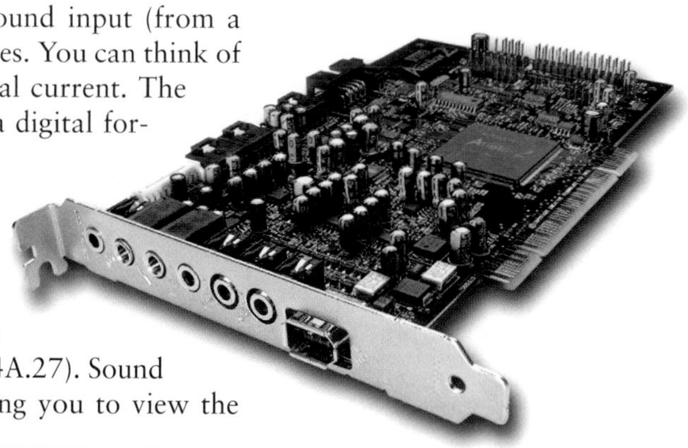

FIGURE 4A.26

High-end sound cards support all sorts of devices, and allow you to record, play, and edit all kinds of audio.

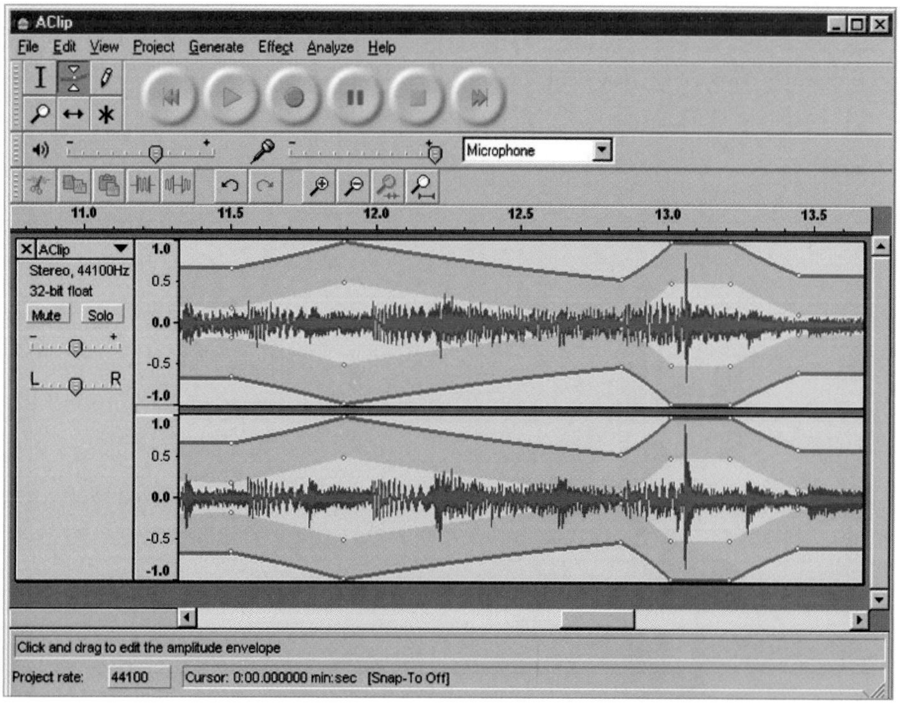

FIGURE 4A.27

Editing an audio file with Audacity, a free, open-source audio editing program.

At Issue

Call of the Wild: Bioacoustic Research

Using high-tech hardware and software to "bug" the Earth's wild places from the African savannah to the ocean floor, scientists are gaining a better understanding of the secret lives of animals. Bioacoustics Research gives scientists and researchers new insight into animal biodiversity by recording animal vocalization. This valuable statistical information yields a wealth of data about the health and behavior of indigenous animal populations.

Those listening to the calls of the wild hear sounds ranging from clicks and rumbles to squawks and whines, as they try to interpret and analyze the sounds the creatures they study make. These Bioacoustics Researchers use sound to understand everything from the spawning habits of fish to the migratory path of herons to the social behaviors of humpback whales.

The Bioacoustics Research Program (BRP) at Cornell University is one of the world's leading Bioacoustics programs. The computer software, techniques, and equipment developed at BRP for recording and analyzing sounds are used by scientists both at Cornell and around the world to study animal communication.

One of the key tools used by the Cornell team is an ARU—an autonomous acoustic recording device—which consists of a microphone (or hydrophone), amplifier, frequency filter, programmable computer, and specially developed software that schedules, records, and stores the acoustic data. The crucial features of the ARU are its small size, low power consumption, and large storage capacity (an ARU can collect up to 60 gigabytes of digital recordings).

One exciting application of the technology is the ongoing study of whale communication. BRP has several projects underway recording ocean sounds in locations ranging from Southern California to the North Atlantic to the southern ocean. Subjects include the study of Blue, Finback, Bowhead, Minke, Humpback, and the highly endangered North Atlantic Right whale.

For the collection of whale sounds, researchers use a special ARU device, called a "pop-up," for undersea deployment. The pop-up is carried out to sea by ship or small boat and released, sinking to the ocean floor, where it hovers like a balloon tied to a brick. It contains a computer microprocessor, enough hard disks for up to six months of data

sound wave and edit it. In the editing, you can cut bits of sound, copy them, and amplify the parts you want to hear more loudly; cut out static; and create many exotic audio effects.

Headphones and Headsets

Many computer users prefer listening to audio through headphones or a headset, rather than using speakers. These devices are helpful when using portable computers, which do not have very high-quality speakers, or when playing audio might disturb other people.

FIGURE 4A.28

Listening to audio through headphones.

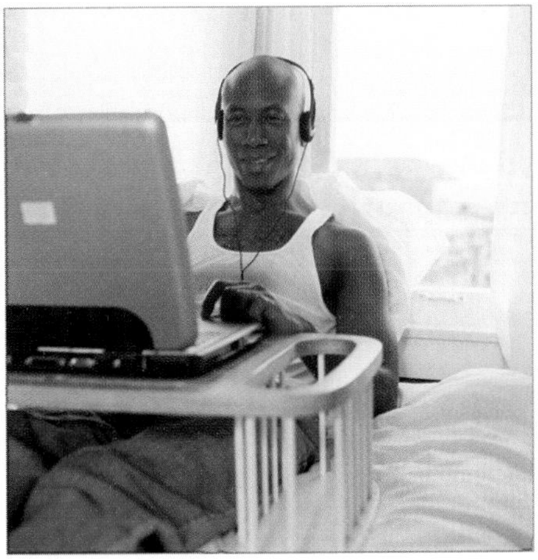

Headphones include a pair of speakers, which are attached to an adjustable strap that can be custom-fitted to the wearer's head (see Figure 4A.28). Today, even inexpensive headphones (such as those that come with portable CD players) have reasonably high-quality speakers, are lightweight, and are comfortable to wear. Nearly any set of standard headphones can be plugged into the output jack of a computer's sound card, as long as they have a "mini" stereo plug. For headphones equipped with larger plugs, adapters are available.

storage, acoustic communications circuitry, and batteries, all sealed in a single 17-inch glass sphere. An external hydrophone is connected to the internal electronics through a waterproof connector. At the conclusion of a mission, the sphere separates itself from its anchor and "pops up" to the surface where it is recovered. Scientists then extract the data and process it to quantify ocean noises, detect endangered species, and describe the densities and distributions of different whale species.

Back on land, the computer workstation used by Cornell is powered by RAVEN, a software application for the digital acquisition, visualization, measurement, manipulation, and analysis of sound. RAVEN was developed by BRP with support from the National Science Foundation to provide a low-cost, user-friendly research and teaching environment tailored to the needs of biologists working with acoustic signals.

Together, this combination of technologies have given scientists some of "the best profiles of any endangered species yet," according to BRP.

AT ISSUE

A headset includes one or two speakers and a microphone, all mounted to an adjustable headstrap. The headset's microphone plugs into the sound card's microphone input, and the speakers connect to the sound card's speaker jack. Headsets replace both remote microphones and speakers and are useful for speech-recognition applications, or when using the computer to make phone calls or participate in videoconferences.

LESSON // 4A Review

Summary ::

- Computer monitors are roughly divided into two categories: CRT and flat-panel displays.
- Monitors also can be categorized by the number of colors they display. Monitors are usually monochrome, grayscale, or color.
- A CRT monitor uses an electron gun that systematically aims a beam of electrons at every pixel on the screen.
- Most LCD displays are either active matrix or passive matrix.
- When purchasing a monitor, you should consider its size, resolution, refresh rate, and dot pitch.
- The video controller is an interface between the monitor and the CPU. The video controller determines many aspects of a monitor's performance; for example, the video controller lets you select a resolution or set the number of colors to display.
- The video controller contains its own on-board processor and memory, called video RAM.
- A digital light projector is a portable light projector that connects to a PC. This type of projector is rapidly replacing traditional slide projectors and overhead projectors as a means for displaying presentations.
- Many digital light projectors provide the same resolutions and color levels as high-quality monitors, but they project the image on a large screen.
- The newest projectors use digital light processing to project bright, crisp images. A DLP projector uses a special microchip that contains tiny mirrors to produce images.
- Multimedia PCs generally come with sound systems, which include a sound card and speakers.
- The sound card translates digital signals into analog signals that drive the speakers.
- Many people prefer to listen to audio output through headphones or a headset, instead of using speakers.

Key Terms ::

active matrix LCD, 146
antiglare screen, 152
cathode ray tube (CRT), 142
color monitor, 143
data projector, 154
digital light processing (DLP), 154
dot pitch, 150
dual-scan LCD, 146
electroluminescent display (ELD), 146
electromagnetic field (EMF), 152
eyestrain, 151
flat-panel display, 142
grayscale monitor, 142
headphones, 156
headset, 157
Hertz (Hz), 149
liquid crystal display (LCD), 145
monochrome monitor, 142
page-white display, 146
paper-white display, 146
passive matrix LCD, 146
pixel, 143
plasma display, 146
refresh rate, 149
resolution, 148
shadow mask, 144
sound card, 154
submarining, 146
Super VGA (SVGA), 149
thin-film transistor (TFT), 146
video card, 150
Video Graphics Array (VGA), 149
video RAM (VRAM), 151
viewing angle, 145
viewing area, 148

Key Term Quiz ::

Complete each statement by writing one of the terms listed under Key Terms in each blank.

1. Standard computer monitors work by using a large vacuum tube, which is called a(n) __________ .
2. In a CRT monitor, the electron gun can focus on __________ as small as a single phosphor dot.
3. In a CRT monitor, the holes in the __________ align the electron beams so they precisely strike the phosphor dots.
4. The most common type of flat-panel monitor is the __________ monitor.
5. One disadvantage of __________ LCD monitors is that they don't refresh very quickly.
6. In active matrix displays that use __________ technology, each pixel has multiple transistors.
7. The portion of a monitor that actually displays images is called the __________ .
8. VGA and SVGA are standards for monitor __________ .
9. In most computers, a device called the __________ sends information to the monitor for display on the screen.
10. A(n) __________ lets you display data on a big screen, directly from the computer's disk.

Multiple Choice ::

Circle the word or phrase that best completes each statement.

1. Which type of monitor is most commonly used with portable computers?
   a. cathode ray tube b. monochrome c. flat-panel display d. data projector
2. This type of monitor can display only one color, such as white, against a black background.
   a. grayscale b. monochrome c. color d. SVGA
3. In a CRT monitor, this component helps the electron gun aim its beam at the screen's phosphor dots.
   a. magnetic coil b. magnetic field c. magnetic switch d. magnetic tube
4. An LCD monitor uses crystals that become opaque when __________ is applied.
   a. pressure b. force c. phosphor d. electricity
5. Most passive matrix LCD monitors now use __________ technology.
   a. thin-film b. active matrix c. dual-scan d. flat-panel
6. Document designers sometimes use a special type of monitor called a __________ display.
   a. CRT b. paper-white c. TFT d. electroluminescent
7. Resolution is determined by the computer's __________ .
   a. monitor b. video controller c. CPU d. system unit
8. A monitor's __________ is measured in Hertz (Hz).
   a. refresh rate b. speed c. resolution d. viewable area
9. The Video Graphics Array (VGA) resolution standard is __________ pixels.
   a. 640×480 b. 800×600 c. 1024×768 d. 1280×1024
10. When you choose a monitor, look for one with a dot pitch that is no greater than __________ .
    a. .18 mm b. .28 mm c. .38 mm d. .08 mm

LESSON //4A Review

Review Questions ::

In your own words, briefly answer the following questions.

1. There are two basic types of monitors used with PCs. List them.
2. How does a color CRT monitor produce images on the screen?
3. What are two disadvantages of CRT monitors, compared to flat-panel displays?
4. What are two disadvantages of LCD monitors, compared to CRT monitors?
5. How does a plasma display monitor work?
6. List the four factors you should consider when comparing monitors.
7. As it relates to monitors, what does the term "resolution" refer to?
8. What is dot pitch?
9. How should you position your monitor, if you want to avoid eyestrain?
10. How does digital light processing (DLP) technology work?

Lesson Labs ::

Complete the following exercises as directed by your instructor.

1. Examine your computer's monitor. First, look at the monitor attached to your computer. What brand and model is it? What other information can you get from the monitor by looking at its exterior? (Remember to look at the back.) Next, measure the monitor. What is the diagonal measurement of the monitor's front side? What is the viewing area, measured diagonally? Visit the manufacturer's Web site and see if you can find any additional information about your specific monitor.
2. If your PC has speakers attached to it, you can easily check or change the speaker volume. Move the mouse pointer to the Windows taskbar. Look for a small icon that looks like a speaker. If you see such an icon, click it. (If not, ask your instructor for assistance.) A small volume control will appear on the screen. You can use the mouse to drag the volume control up or down to change the volume setting, or select the Mute checkbox to silence the sound system. Click anywhere outside the volume control to close it.

LESSON // 4B

Printing

Overview: Putting Digital Content in Your Hands

Most computer users can't imagine working without a printer. Monitors and sound systems let you see and hear your work, but printers give you something you can touch, carry, and share with others. Printed documents are essential in most workplaces, where people must share reports, budgets, memos, and other types of information.

Over the past decade, the variety of available printing devices has exploded; however, three types of printers have become the most popular: dot matrix, ink jet, and laser. Within those three groups, consumers have hundreds of options, ranging widely in price and features. Several other types of special printing devices are available for users with special needs, such as large-format printouts or images with extremely accurate color and high resolution.

This lesson introduces you to the basics of hard-copy output devices. You will learn about the most common types of printers and see how each creates an image on paper. You will learn the criteria for evaluating different printers and examine some of the specialized printing devices designed for professional use.

OBJECTIVES ::

- List the three most commonly used types of printers.
- List the four criteria you should consider when evaluating printers.
- Describe how a dot matrix printer creates an image on a page.
- Explain how an ink jet printer creates an image on a page.
- Explain how a laser printer creates an image on a page.
- List four types of high-quality printing devices commonly used in business.

simnet™

Commonly Used Printers

Besides the monitor, the other important output device is the printer. Generally, printers fall into two categories: impact and nonimpact. An impact printer creates an image by using pins or hammers to press an inked ribbon against the paper. A simple example of an impact printer is a typewriter, which uses small hammers to strike the ribbon. Each hammer is embossed with the shape of a letter, number, or symbol; that shape is transferred through the inked ribbon onto the paper, creating a printed character.

Although it is seldom done today, many modern electric typewriters can be connected to a PC and used as a letter-quality printer (see Figure 4B.1). As a printer, however, even a good typewriter is slow and limited in the kinds of documents it can produce. The most common type of impact printer is the dot matrix printer (see Figure 4B.2). Other types of impact printers are line printers and band printers.

Nonimpact printers use other means to create an image. Ink jet printers, for example, use tiny nozzles to spray droplets of ink onto the page. Laser printers work like photocopiers, using heat to bond microscopic particles of dry toner to specific parts of the page (see Figure 4B.3).

In the early years of computing, dot matrix printers were the most commonly used printing devices. They are not as prevalent now, although dot matrix printers are still popular in business and academic settings because they are relatively fast and inexpensive to operate, and they do a good job of printing text and simple graphics. Ink jet printers now offer much higher quality for about the same price, and they have become more popular than dot matrix printers in homes and small businesses. Laser printers are also popular in homes and businesses, but they are more expensive to buy and operate than either ink jet or dot matrix devices.

FIGURE 4B.1

Although they are much slower than normal printers, many electronic typewriters can be connected to a PC and used to print documents such as letters or memos. This arrangement works well when the user does not need many different fonts or printing options or to print a high volume of documents.

Dot Matrix Printers

Dot matrix printers are commonly used in workplaces where physical impact with the paper is important, such as when the user is printing to carbon-copy or pressure-sensitive forms. These printers can produce sheets of plain text very quickly. They also are used to print very wide sheets, as data processing departments often use when generating large reports with wide columns of information.

A dot matrix printer creates an image by using a mechanism called a print head, which contains a cluster (or *matrix*)

FIGURE 4B.2

Many people think dot matrix printers are obsolete, but these printers are still widely sold and used. They are inexpensive compared to other kinds of printers and while they are not well suited to printing graphics, good dot matrix printers can produce high-quality text documents. Like other types of impact printers, dot matrix printers can be used with carbon-copy and other kinds of copy forms.

of short pins arranged in one or more columns. On receiving instructions from the PC, the printer can push any of the pins out in any combination. By pushing out pins in various combinations, the print head can create alphanumeric characters (see Figures 4B.4 and 4B.5).

When pushed out from the cluster, the protruding pins' ends strike a ribbon, which is held in place between the print head and the paper. When the pins strike the ribbon, they press ink from the ribbon onto the paper.

The more pins that a print head contains, the higher the printer's resolution. The lowest-resolution dot matrix printers have only nine pins; the highest-resolution printers have 24 pins.

The speed of dot matrix printers is measured in characters per second (cps). The slowest dot matrix printers create 50 to 70 characters per second; the fastest print more than 500 cps.

Although dot matrix printers are not commonly used in homes, they are still widely used in business, as are other types of impact printers:

- **Line Printers.** A line printer is a special type of impact printer. It works like a dot matrix printer but uses a special wide print head that can print an entire line of text at one time (see Figure 4B.6). Line printers do not offer high resolution but are incredibly fast; the fastest can print 3,000 lines of text per minute.
- **Band Printers** A band printer features a rotating band embossed with alphanumeric characters. To print a character, the machine rotates the band to the desired character, then a small hammer taps the band, pressing the character against a ribbon. Although this sounds like a slow process, band printers are very fast and very robust. Depending on the character set used, a good-quality band printer can generate 2,000 lines of text per minute.

FIGURE 4B.3

Laser printers produce the highest-quality text output, as well as graphics. Laser printers are commonly found in business settings where many people need to print documents. Sophisticated high-volume laser printers are often connected to networks and handle printing tasks for large workgroups.

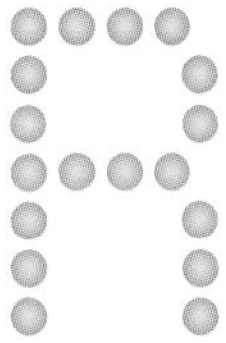

FIGURE 4B.4

A dot matrix printer forms a character by creating a series of dots.

Norton ONLINE

For more information on dot matrix printers, visit **http://www.mhhe.com/peternorton**.

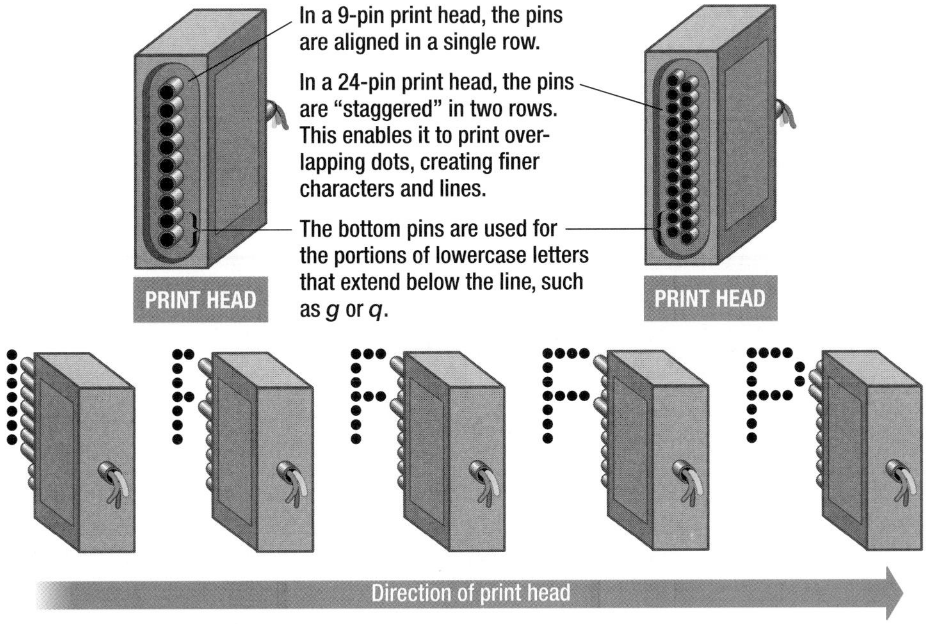

In a 9-pin print head, the pins are aligned in a single row.
In a 24-pin print head, the pins are "staggered" in two rows. This enables it to print overlapping dots, creating finer characters and lines.
The bottom pins are used for the portions of lowercase letters that extend below the line, such as *g* or *q*.
PRINT HEAD
PRINT HEAD
Direction of print head

FIGURE 4B.5

How a dot matrix printer creates an image.

Ink Jet Printers

Ink jet printers create an image directly on the paper by spraying ink through tiny nozzles (see Figure 4B.7). The popularity of ink jet printers jumped around 1990 when the speed and quality improved and prices plummeted. Today, good ink jet printers are available for less than $100. These models typically attain print resolutions of at least 300 dots per inch. These same models can print from two to four pages per minute (only slightly slower than the slowest laser printers).

Compared to laser printers, the operating cost of an ink jet printer is relatively low. Expensive maintenance is rare, and the only part that needs routine replacement is the ink cartridge, which ranges in price from $20 to $35. Many ink jet printers use one cartridge for color printing and a separate black-only cartridge for black-and-white printing. This feature saves money by reserving colored ink only for color printing.

Color ink jet printers have four ink nozzles: cyan (blue), magenta (red), yellow, and black. For this reason, they are sometimes referred to as CMYK printers, or as using the CMYK color process. These four colors are used in almost all color printing because it is possible to combine them to create any color. Notice that the colors are different from the primary additive colors (red, green, and blue) used in monitors. Printed color is the result of light bouncing off the paper, not color transmitted directly from a light source. Consequently, cyan, magenta, yellow, and black are sometimes called subtractive colors and color printing is sometimes called four-color printing. When used with special printing paper, many ink jet printers can produce photo-quality images. For this reason, they are often used to print pictures taken with a digital camera.

FIGURE 4B.6

Line printers use a special wide print head to print an entire line of text at one time.

Norton ONLINE

For more information on ink jet printers, visit **http://www.mhhe.com/peternorton**.

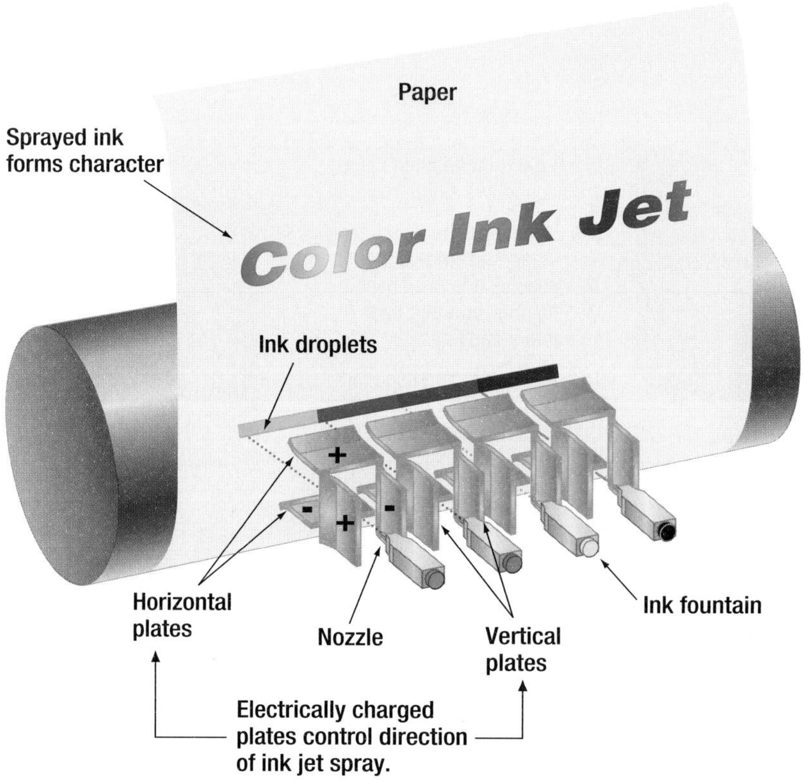

FIGURE 4B.7

How an ink jet printer creates an image.

Laser Printers

Laser printers are more expensive than ink jet printers, their print quality is higher, and most are faster. As their name implies, a laser is at the heart of these printers. A CPU and memory are built into the printer to interpret the data that it receives from the computer and to control the laser. The result is a complicated piece of equipment that uses technology similar to that in photocopiers. Figure 4B.8 shows how a laser printer works. The quality and speed of laser printers make them ideal for office environments, where several users can easily share the same printer via a network.

Just as the electron gun in a monitor can target any pixel, the laser in a laser printer can aim at any point on a drum, creating an electrical charge. Toner, which is composed of tiny particles of ink, sticks to the drum in the places the laser has charged. Then, with pressure and heat, the toner is transferred off the drum onto the paper. The amount of memory that laser printers contain determines the speed at which documents are printed.

A color laser printer works like a single-color model, except that the process is repeated four times and a different toner color is used for each pass. The four colors used are the same as in the color ink jet printers: cyan, magenta, yellow, and black.

Single-color (black) laser printers typically can produce between 4 and 16 pages of text a minute. If you are printing graphics, the output can be a great deal slower. The most common laser printers have resolutions of 300 or 600 dpi, both horizontally and vertically, but some high-end models have resolutions of 1,200 or 1,800 dpi. The printing industry stipulates a resolution of at least 1,200 dpi for top-quality professional printing. It is difficult to detect the difference between text printed at 600 dpi and at 1,200 dpi; the higher resolution is most noticeable in graphics reproduction such as photographs and artwork.

Laser printers start at about $150, and the price increases dramatically along with speed and resolution. Color laser printers are considerably more expensive than single-color printers. In addition, laser printers require new toner cartridges after a few thousand pages, and toner cartridges can cost anywhere from $40 to $200.

Norton ONLINE

For more information on laser printers, visit **http://www.mhhe.com/peternorton**.

FIGURE 4B.8

How a laser printer creates a printed page.

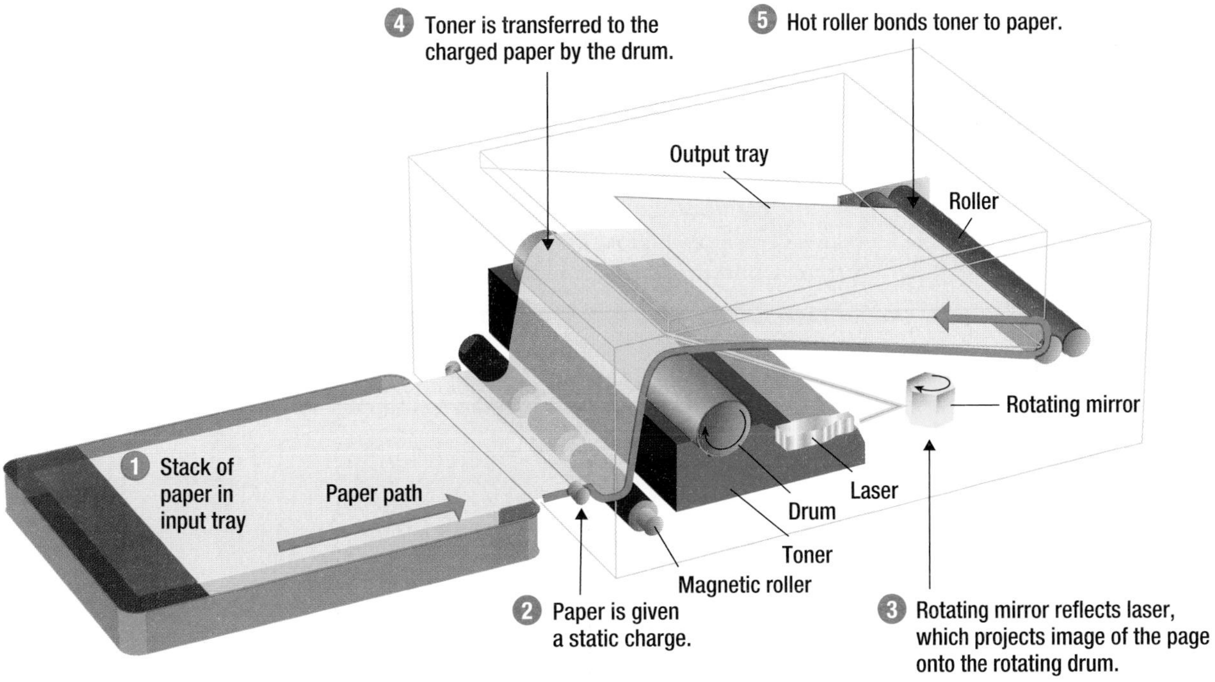
4 Toner is transferred to the charged paper by the drum.
5 Hot roller bonds toner to paper.
Output tray
Roller
Rotating mirror
1 Stack of paper in input tray
Paper path
Laser
Drum
Toner
Magnetic roller
2 Paper is given a static charge.
3 Rotating mirror reflects laser, which projects image of the page onto the rotating drum.

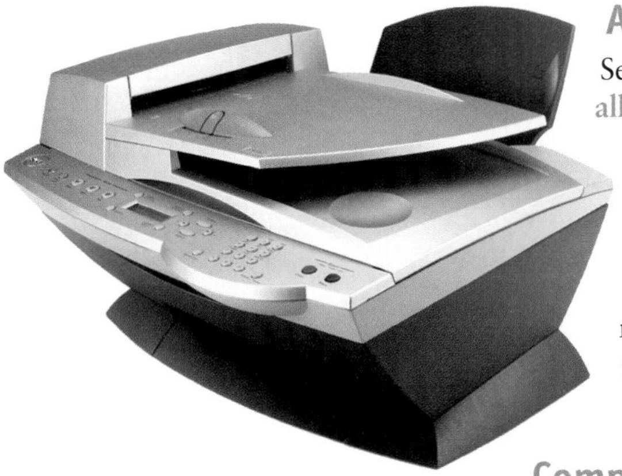

FIGURE 4B.9

All-in-one office machines, like this one, include a printer, copier, scanner, and fax.

All-in-One Peripherals

Several printer makers now use ink jet or laser printers as the basis for all-in-one peripherals (see Figure 4B.9). These devices combine printing capabilities with scanning, photocopying, and faxing capabilities. Small, lightweight, and easy to use, all-in-one devices are popular in home offices and small businesses, among users who cannot afford to buy several professional-quality devices for these tasks.

All-in-one peripherals are available in black-and-white and color models, at prices as low as $200. Laser-based models are significantly more expensive than ink jet models, especially when color printing is required.

Comparing Printers

When you are ready to buy a printer, you must consider how you plan to use it. Do you need to print only text, or are graphics capabilities also important? Do you need to print in color? Will you need to print a wide variety of fonts in many sizes? How quickly do you want your documents to be printed?

When evaluating printers, four additional criteria are important:

- **Image Quality.** Image quality, also known as print resolution, is usually measured in dots per inch (dpi). The more dots per inch a printer can produce, the higher its image quality. For example, most medium-quality ink jet and laser printers can print 300 or 600 dots per inch, which is fine for most daily business applications. If a printer's resolution is 600 dpi, this means it can print 600 columns of dots and 600 rows of dots in each square inch of the page, a total of 360,000 dots ($600 \times 600 = 360{,}000$) per inch, as shown in Figure 4B.10. Professional-quality printers, used for creating colorful presentations, posters, or renderings, offer resolutions of 1,800 dpi or even higher.
- **Speed.** Printer speed is measured in the number of pages per minute (ppm) the device can print. (As you learned earlier, however, the speed of dot matrix printers is measured in characters per second.) Most printers have different ppm ratings for text and graphics because graphics generally take longer to print. As print speed goes up, so does cost. Most consumer-level laser printers offer print speeds of 6 or 8 ppm, but high-volume professional laser printers can exceed 50 ppm.
- **Initial Cost.** The cost of new printers has fallen dramatically in recent years, while their capabilities and speed have improved just as dramatically. It is possible to buy a good-quality ink jet printer for personal use for less than $100; low-end laser printers can be found for less than $200. Professional-quality, high-output systems can range in price from $1,000 to tens of thousands of dollars. Color printers always cost more than black-and-white printers, and this is especially true of laser printers.

Norton ONLINE

For more information on all-in-one peripherals, visit **http://www.mhhe.com/peternorton**.

FIGURE 4B.10

The image quality of laser and ink jet printers is measured in dots per inch.

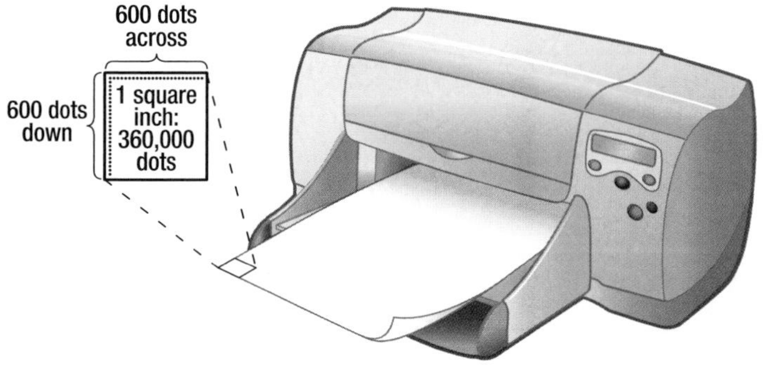

- **Cost of Operation.** The cost of ink or toner and maintenance varies with the type of printer (see Figure 4B.11). Many different types of printer paper are available, too, and the choice can affect the cost of operation. Low-quality recycled paper, for example, is fine for printing draft-quality documents and costs less than a penny per sheet. Glossy, thick, photo-quality stock, used for printing photographs, can cost several dollars per sheet depending on size.

SELF-CHECK ::

Circle the correct answer for each question.

1. When discussing printers, image quality is also known as this.
   a. output **b.** resolution **c.** ppm
2. In a dot matrix printer, this component contains a cluster (or matrix) of pins.
   a. print head **b.** cartridge **c.** drum
3. A laser printer's speed is measured in ____________ .
   a. cps **b.** ppm **c.** dpi

High-Quality Printers

Although most offices and homes use ink jet or laser printers, other types of printers are used for special purposes. These printers are often used by publishers and small print shops to create high-quality output, especially color output. The last type discussed in this section, the plotter, is designed specifically for printing large-format construction and engineering documents.

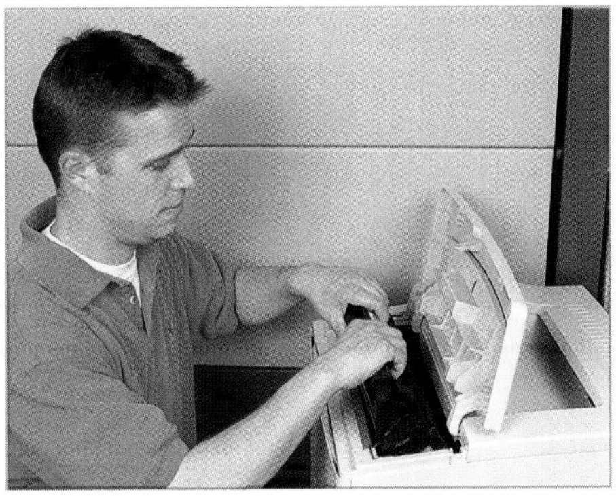

FIGURE 4B.11

For all their speed and convenience, high-volume printers can be costly to maintain. Toner cartridges for high-quality laser printers can cost well over $100 apiece.

Photo Printers

With digital cameras and scanners becoming increasingly popular, users want to be able to print the images they create or scan. While the average color ink jet or laser printer can handle this job satisfactorily, many people are investing in special photo printers (see Figure 4B.12). Many photo printers use ink jet technology, but a few use dye-sublimation technology. The best photo printers can create images that look nearly as good as a photograph printed using traditional methods.

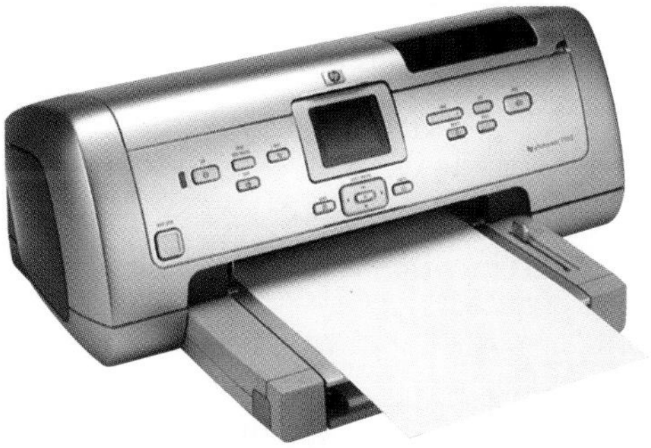

FIGURE 4B.12

Photo printers make it easy to print images taken with a digital camera.

Photo printers work slowly; some can take two to four minutes to create a printout. Several models create prints no larger than a standard 4 × 6-inch snapshot, although newer photo printers can produce 8 × 10-inch or even 11 × 14-inch prints. Many larger-format photo printers can print multiple images on a single sheet of paper (see Figure 4B.13).

FIGURE 4B.13

Many photo printers can output prints in a variety of sizes.

Productivity Tip

The Care and Feeding of Printers

Whether you own a $50 dot matrix printer or a $5,000 color laser printer, you want to get the most from your investment. Although today's printers are much more durable than those of a decade ago, they still work better and last longer if they are properly maintained. Luckily, most consumer-grade printers are easy to take care of. Here are some tips that will help you get years of service from your printer, no matter what kind of device it is.

Getting Basic Information

When maintaining your printer, the best place to start is the owner's manual. Check it for specific instructions on setting up, cleaning, clearing out paper jams, replacing components, and other maintenance-related tasks. You may be able to find these instructions on the manufacturer's Web site.

Always unplug your printer and let it cool down completely before doing any maintenance or cleaning. All printers—especially units that are used a lot—get hot inside, possibly hot enough to burn you. To avoid shock, disconnect the printer's cables from your computer or network. Also, be sure to remove the paper from the printer before working on it.

Positioning a Printer

Make sure your printer has room to breathe. This means setting up so there is space around it, to allow air to flow through the printer. This keeps down dust and avoids overheating. Avoid crowding objects (such as stacks of books or boxes) around the printer, or you may block air flow. Never stack anything on top of a printer; the weight can cause malfunctions.

Cleaning a Printer

Printers usually don't require heavy cleaning, but paper dust and airborne particles can collect inside a printer, adding to heat build-up and leading to mechanical problems. You can clean the outside surfaces of most printers with a dry or damp cloth, but don't use solvents or spray cleaners, which may be harmful to some printer parts.

To clean the inside of the printer, open it up and remove all paper. Remove the toner cartridge, ink cartridges, or ribbon as your owner's manual directs. Use a lint-free cloth or swabs to gently remove built-up dust and dirt. Do not use a wet cloth, and never spray any kind of liquid cleaner into your printer unless the manufacturer recommends doing so.

If the printer has a great deal of dust built up inside, you can use a vacuum cleaner with a narrow nozzle to pull out the dust. If dust appears to be stuck or is embedded in tiny spaces, use a can of compressed air to blast it loose, then vacuum it out.

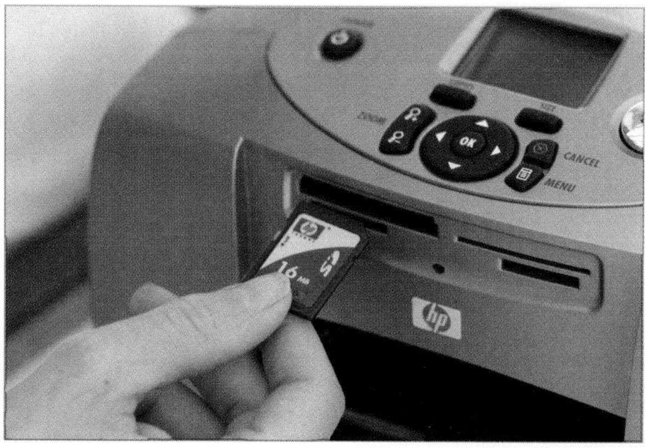

FIGURE 4B.14

Many photo printers accept the memory card from a digital camera, freeing you from connecting the printer to the camera or to a computer.

Because ink jet photo printers spray so much ink on the paper, it can take several minutes for a printout to dry, so smearing can be a problem. Still, these printers give digital photography enthusiasts a way to print and display their photos in hard-copy form. Photo printers range in price from $200 to more than $500, and the cost per print ranges from a few cents to a dollar (several times more expensive than traditional film processing).

One advantage of the newest photo printers is that they do not need a computer. These photo printers feature slots for memory cards used by many digital cameras (see Figure 4B.14). Instead of connecting the printer to a computer, the user can simply remove the memory card from the camera and plug it into the printer. Some photo printers can connect directly to a camera by a cable or even by an infrared connection.

Thermal-Wax Printers

Thermal-wax printers are used primarily for presentation graphics and handouts. They create bold colors and have a low per-page cost for printouts with heavy

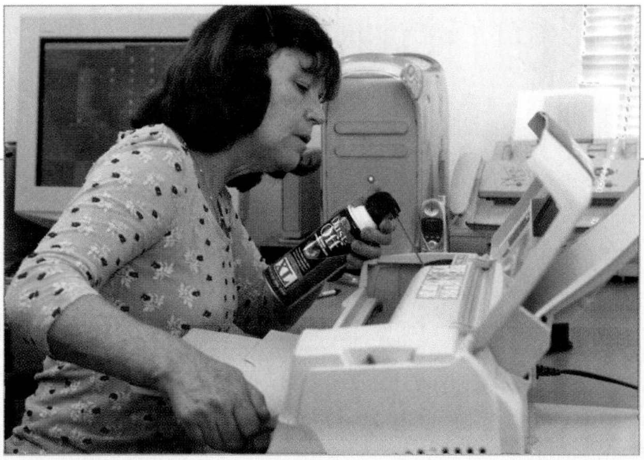

Compressed air is inexpensive and easy to use and can help keep your printer in top shape.

Dealing with Paper Jams

For years, paper jams have been the scourge of computer users. They strike at the worst times, and can take a long time to clear out. The best way to solve this problem is to prevent it:

- Make sure your paper is compatible with your printer. Some ink jet printers, for example, do not work well with thick, glossy paper. Check your manual to see what weights and sizes of paper will work best with your printer.
- Set the printer on an even, level surface. Tilting can encourage paper jams.
- Don't overfill the paper tray. Paper must be flat and able to slide freely through the mechanism. If the tray is crammed with paper, the sheets may be buckled or stuffed in too tightly to move.

If you experience a paper jam, see your owner's manual for instructions on clearing it. If paper jams are a common problem, contact the manufacturer for help.

Maintaining Your Drivers

Printers use special programs, called drivers, which enable them to communicate and exchange data with your PC and programs. If you use Windows 98, Me, NT, 2000, or XP, then there's a good chance that your printer's driver is built into the operating system. If not, you can install your printer's driver from the disk that comes with the printer.

Printer makers sometimes release updated versions of their printers' drivers, and it's a good idea to make sure that you are using the most current driver. To check for updated drivers, visit the manufacturer's Web site. If you use Microsoft's Windows Update service, your updated drivers may be available there. For more information on Windows Update, visit http://windowsupdate.microsoft.com.

PRODUCTIVITY TIP

color requirements, such as posters or book covers. The process creates vivid colors because the inks do not bleed into each other or soak the specially coated paper. Thermal-wax printers operate with a ribbon coated with panels of colored wax that melts and adheres to plain paper as colored dots when passed over a focused heat source.

Dye-Sublimation Printers

Desktop publishers and graphic artists get realistic quality and color for photo images using dye-sublimation (dye-sub) printers (see Figure 4B.15). In dye-sublimation technology, a ribbon containing panels of color is moved across a focused heat source capable of subtle temperature variations. The heated dyes evaporate from the ribbon and diffuse on specially coated paper or another

FIGURE 4B.15

Dye-sublimation printers come in a wide range of sizes and are used to print all kinds of high-resolution color documents, such as photographs, presentation graphics, posters, and t-shirts.

Computers In Your Career

Computer Training Specialist

Not everyone is proficient with computers, and not everyone wants to be. It's Karen Koenig's job to make sure that the students she's working with leave her classroom not only more knowledgeable about computers, but also more confident in their ability to use them in daily life.

"Once in a while I'll get a student who is afraid to touch the computer, for fear that he or she may delete files or mess something up," says Koenig, a computer training specialist in the Professional and Community Education area of Bowling Green State University's Continuing & Extended Education program located in Bowling Green, Ohio. "It's very rewarding when that same person walks out of my classroom feeling much more comfortable using technology."

A graduate of Bowling Green State University, Koenig earned her degree in business education and is a certified Microsoft Office User Specialist (MOUS). She began her career teaching a sole computer class, and later became a full-time instructor. Koenig spends her time teaching both day and evening classes of university faculty/staff and other adult students on how to use computers and specific applications like Microsoft Excel and Microsoft Word. Along the way, she's mastered applications such as HTML for Web site building and university-specific programs, such as a calendar-scheduling application used by faculty and staff.

Koenig sees future opportunities for computer trainers as good, based on how integrated computers are in our everyday lives. "It's amazing just how many people know nothing about computers, even though they've been around for so long," says Koenig, who is continually updating her own skills to meet her students' needs.

A successful trainer needs a strong background in general computer hardware and software. This means that a trainer should have a solid understanding of how a computer system functions and a mastery of current operating systems and common application software.

material, where they form areas of different colors. The variations in color are related to the intensity of the heat applied. Dye-sub printers create extremely sharp images, but they are slow and costly. The special paper they require can make the per-page cost as high as $3 to $4.

Plotters

A plotter is a special kind of output device. It is like a printer because it produces images on paper, but the plotter is typically used to print large-format images, such as construction drawings created by an architect.

Early plotters were bulky, mechanical devices that used robotic arms, which literally drew the image on a piece of paper. Table plotters (or flatbed plotters) use two robotic arms, each of which holds a set of colored ink pens, felt pens, or pencils. The two arms work in concert, operating at right angles as they draw on a stationary piece of paper. In addition to being complex and large (some are almost as big as a billiard table), table plotters are notoriously slow; a large, complicated drawing can take several hours to print.

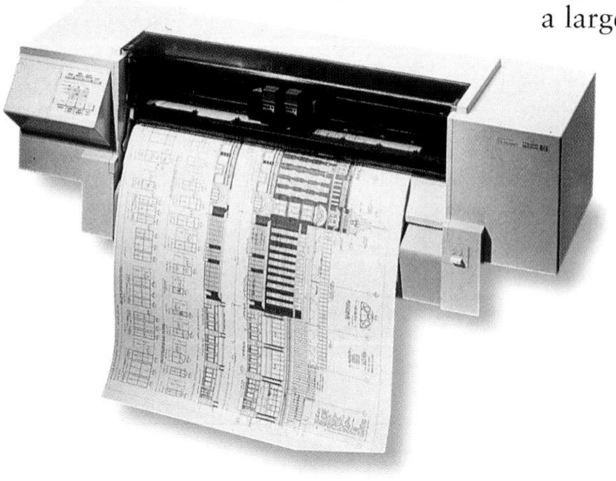

FIGURE 4B.16

A roller plotter uses a robotic arm to draw with colored pens on oversized paper. Here, an architectural drawing is being printed.

Often, trainers must get additional instruction or certification if they want to teach others to use certain programs. Companies such as Microsoft and Oracle, for example, offer trainer-certification programs that ensure employers that a trainer has mastered certain products and is qualified to teach others how to use them.

The pay scale for computer training specialists covers a wide range. Freelance trainers, for instance, may charge an hourly rate (ranging from $25 to $50, or higher), which goes up with the complexity of the programs being taught. The annual salary for full-time trainers can start out in the $18,000 to $30,000 range, but can go up with experience and expertise. Top-level trainers (who teach other trainers and develop training courses or materials) can earn $50,000 per year or more.

A variation on the table plotter is the roller plotter (also known as the drum plotter), which uses only one drawing arm but moves the paper instead of holding it flat and stationary (see Figure 4B.16). The drawing arm moves side to side as the paper is rolled back and forth through the roller. Working together, the arm and roller can draw perfect circles and other geometric shapes, as well as lines of different weights and colors.

In recent years, mechanical plotters have been displaced by thermal, electrostatic, and ink jet plotters, as well as large-format dye-sub printers. These devices, which also produce large-size drawings, are faster and cheaper to use than their mechanical counterparts. They also can produce full-color renderings as well as geometric line drawings, making them more useful than standard mechanical plotters (see Figure 4B.17).

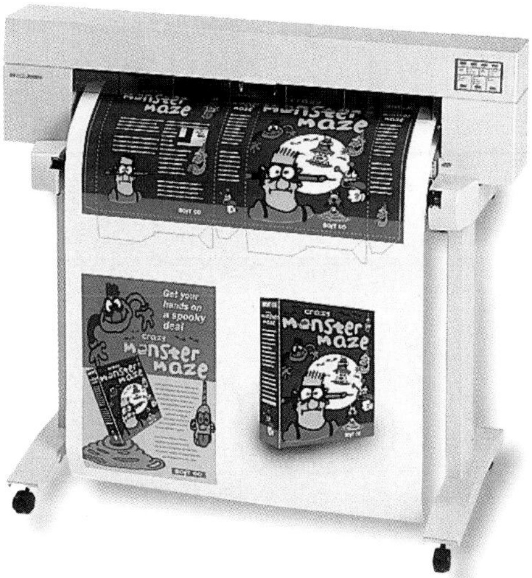

FIGURE 4B.17

Like desktop ink jet printers, an ink jet plotter uses a spray system to create either simple line drawings or detailed artistic renderings.

LESSON // 4B Review

Summary ::

- Printers fall into two general categories: impact and nonimpact.
- Impact printers create an image on paper by using a device to strike an inked ribbon, pressing ink from the ribbon onto the paper. Nonimpact printers use various methods to place ink on the page.
- When evaluating printers for purchase, you should consider four criteria: image quality, speed, initial cost, and cost of operation.
- A dot matrix printer is an impact printer. It uses a print head that contains a cluster of pins. The printer can push the pins out in rapid sequence to form patterns. The pins are used to press an inked ribbon against paper, creating an image.
- The speed of dot matrix printers is measured in characters per second. The fastest ones can print 500 characters each second.
- An ink jet printer is an example of a nonimpact printer. It creates an image by spraying tiny droplets of ink onto the paper.
- Ink jet printers are inexpensive for both color and black printing, have low operating costs, and offer quality and speed comparable to low-end laser printers.
- Laser printers are nonimpact printers. They use heat and pressure to bond tiny particles of toner (a dry ink) to paper.
- Laser printers produce higher-quality print and are fast and convenient to use, but they are also more expensive than ink jet printers. Laser printers are available in both color and black and white, and the highest-end laser printers provide resolutions of 1,200 dpi and greater.
- Thermal-wax and dye-sublimation printers are used primarily by print shops and publishers to create high-quality color images.
- Photo printers are specialized printers used to print color photographs taken with digital cameras.
- Plotters create large-format images, usually for architectural or engineering purposes, using mechanical drawing arms, ink jet technology, or thermal printing technology.

Key Terms ::

all-in-one peripheral, 166
band printer, 163
characters per second (cps), 163
dot matrix printer, 162
dots per inch (dpi), 166
dye-sublimation (dye-sub) printer, 169
impact printer, 162
ink jet printer, 164
laser printer, 165
line printer, 163
nonimpact printer, 162
pages per minute (ppm), 166
photo printer, 167
plotter, 170
print head, 162
thermal-wax printer, 168
toner, 165

Key Term Quiz ::

Complete each statement by writing one of the terms listed under Key Terms in each blank.

1. A(n) ____________ printer creates an image by using pins or hammers to press an inked ribbon against the paper.
2. A dot matrix printer creates an image by using a mechanism called a(n) ____________ .
3. The speed of dot matrix printers is measured in ____________ .
4. A laser printer is an example of a(n) ____________ printer.
5. A(n) ____________ printer creates an image by spraying ink through tiny nozzles.
6. A laser printer uses tiny particles of ink, called ____________ , to create an image.
7. A device that combines printing, scanning, faxing, and copying capabilities is called a(n) ____________ .
8. An ink jet printer's image quality is measured in ____________ .
9. A laser printer's speed is measured in ____________ .
10. A(n) ____________ printer creates vivid colors because the inks do not bleed into each other or soak the specially coated paper.

LESSON //4B Review

Multiple Choice ::

Circle the word or phrase that best completes each statement.

1. Which of the following is the most common type of impact printer?
   a. typewriter b. dot matrix printer c. line printer d. band printer
2. A laser printer works like this device.
   a. scanner b. dot matrix printer c. photocopier d. fax machine
3. A dot matrix printer's print head contains a cluster of ____________ .
   a. pins b. dots c. hammers d. characters
4. Which type of impact printer prints an entire line of text at one time?
   a. hammer printer b. ink jet printer c. band printer d. line printer
5. In ink jet printers, only this part needs routine replacement.
   a. ink jet b. ink well c. ink cartridge d. ink blot
6. Cyan, magenta, yellow, and black are sometimes called ____________ colors.
   a. multiplicative b. divisive c. additive d. subtractive
7. The term *dots per inch (dpi)* refers to a printer's ____________ .
   a. resolution b. speed c. output d. colors
8. Which printer's speed is *not* measured in pages per minute?
   a. ink jet b. dot matrix c. laser d. plotter
9. Most photo printers use this technology.
   a. plotter b. laser c. thermal-wax d. ink jet
10. To print out large-format copies of construction drawings, an architect might use this device.
   a. photo printer b. plotter c. line printer d. laser printer

Review Questions ::

In your own words, briefly answer the following questions.

1. What is the difference between an impact printer and a nonimpact printer?
2. How does a dot matrix printer create an image on paper?
3. How does a band printer work?
4. What kind of resolution and speed can you expect from a low-cost ink jet printer?
5. What four colors are used in color ink jet and laser printers?
6. How does a laser printer create an image on paper?
7. What four factors should you consider when evaluating printers?
8. If a printer is said to have a resolution of 600 dpi, what does this mean?
9. Describe a specific advantage of some new photo printers.
10. How does a dye-sublimation printer create an image on paper?

Lesson Labs ::

Complete the following exercises as directed by your instructor.

1. Find out what type of printer is connected to your computer. Open your PC's Printers window as directed by your instructor. If a printer is connected to your system, it will appear in this window. Right-click the printer's icon to open a shortcut menu. Then choose Properties to open the Properties dialog box for the printer. Write down the data in the dialog box. Do not make any changes in the dialog box, but leave it open for the next exercise.
2. With your printer's Properties dialog box open, click the General tab. Near the bottom of the tab, click the button labeled Print Test Page. A new dialog box appears, asking you to confirm that your printer produced a test page. If your printer produced a test page, click Yes (or Ok). If not, click No (or Troubleshoot) and ask your instructor for assistance. When you are finished, click Cancel to close the dialog box. Close all open windows.

Chapter Labs

Complete the following exercises using a computer in your classroom, lab, or home.

1. Change your display's color settings. By experimenting with your PC's color settings, you can determine the settings that work best for you. For example, if you do not plan to browse the World Wide Web or use multimedia products, you probably do not need to use the system's highest color settings; if you do, you need to make sure your monitor's settings are up to the task or you will not get the most from your computing experience. Before you take the following steps, close any running programs and make sure there is no disk in your system's floppy disk drive.
   a. Click the Start button to open the Start menu. Next, click Control Panel. The Control Panel window opens.
   b. Double-click the Display icon. The Display Properties dialog box opens.
   c. Click the Settings tab. Note the setting in the Color quality box and write it down.
   d. Click the Color quality drop-down list arrow and choose the lowest color setting. Then click Apply. Follow any instructions that appear on your screen. (Your computer may restart.)
   e. Open a program or two and look at the screen. How does it look? Note your impressions.
   f. Repeat steps A through E, this time choosing the highest color setting. Again, note your impressions.
   g. Repeat steps A through E, and select the system's original color setting.
2. What is your resolution? Like the color setting, your system's screen resolution can affect the quality of your computing experience. If your resolution is set too high, text and icons may be too small to view comfortably and you may strain your eyes. If the resolution is too low, you will spend extra time navigating to parts of your applications that do not fit on the screen. Try different settings to find what works best for you.
   a. Click the Start button to open the Start menu. Next, click Control Panel. The Control Panel window opens.
   b. Double-click the Display icon. The Display Properties dialog box opens.
   c. Click the Settings tab. Note the current setting in the Screen resolution box and write it down.
   d. Click the Screen resolution slider control and drag it to the lowest setting. Then click Apply. Follow any instructions that appear on your screen. (Your computer may restart.)
   e. Open a program or two and look at the screen. How does it look? Note your impressions.
   f. Repeat steps A through E, this time choosing the highest setting. Again, note your impressions.
   g. Repeat steps A through E, and select the system's original resolution setting.
3. Pick your dream printer. Visit these Web sites for information on various types of printers:

   Canon. http://www.usa.canon.com/consumer
   Epson. http://www.epson.com

Hewlett-Packard. http://www.hp.com
Lexmark. http://www.lexmark.com
NEC Technologies. http://www.nectech.com
Okidata. http://www.okidata.com
Tektronix. http://www.tek.com

When you are finished, decide which device would work best for you. Be prepared to tell your classmates about the device and to explain why you selected it.

Discussion Questions

As directed by your instructor, discuss the following questions in class or in groups.

1. When you think about the two most frequently used output devices for computers (monitors and printers), why will color technology for printers become more commonplace, more affordable, and more necessary to many users?
2. Think about your career plans. What type of output devices will be essential to your work?

Research and Report

Using your own choice of resources (such as the Internet, books, magazines, and newspaper articles), research and write a short paper discussing one of the following topics.

- Trends in monitor sizes, features, and prices.
- The most popular type of printer among home users.
- An in-depth discussion of dye-sublimation technology and its uses.

When you are finished, proofread and print your paper, and give it to your instructor.

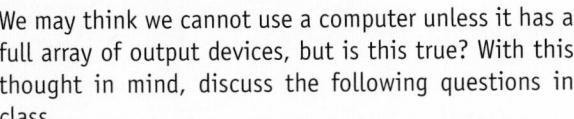

ETHICAL ISSUES

We may think we cannot use a computer unless it has a full array of output devices, but is this true? With this thought in mind, discuss the following questions in class.

1. The number of unneeded printouts is growing every year. This practice wastes paper, electricity, storage space, and natural resources. It also contributes to pollution and landfill use. If you could do one thing to reduce the practice of unnecessary printing, what would it be? Would you restrict paper use in offices? Would you ration paper? Would you take printers away from certain types of workers? Would you forbid the printing of certain types of documents (such as e-mail messages)? Are such radical actions needed? If you do not agree, what types of actions would you support?
2. Because PCs provide an ever-increasing variety of multimedia options, people are spending more and more time at their computers. Much of this time is spent playing games, downloading music from the Internet, Web surfing, and so on. In fact, recent studies indicate that many computer users are addicted to the Internet or to game playing. Do these facts bother you? Why or why not? Do you worry that you spend too much time at your computer? What would you do to help a friend or coworker if you thought he or she was devoting too much time to the computer?

Computing Keynotes

Buying your first computer can be just as challenging as buying your first car. Look at a few magazines or television advertisements and you will quickly see that there are hundreds of models and features to choose from. Sifting through all those options can be time-consuming and frustrating, and you may never feel certain that you are making the right choice or getting the best price.

With so many choices to make, what is the best way to buy a new PC? Very simply, the best thing you can do is plan ahead, understand your needs, and do your homework. This kind of preparation will help you find a PC that best meets your needs, at a price you can afford. That is what this *Computing Keynote* is all about: helping you decide what you need *before* you start shopping.

Many popular magazines feature dozens of advertisements for computers.

Think Before You Shop

If you have never bought a PC before, you are probably eager to get started. After all, you have a lot of shopping to do if you want to find the best deal! But before you hit the malls or go online, you need to make some decisions. That way, you will have a good idea of what you need, which may help you avoid looking at models or options that are not right for you.

So grab a pen and a piece of paper and answer some basic questions. The answers will help you decide what type of computer will best meet your needs, which options you must have, and which features you can live without.

1. **What will you use your computer for?** This is the most important question you can answer before buying a computer. Will you use a PC primarily for Internet surfing and word processing, or do you plan to develop programs? The more demanding your tasks are, the more powerful your computer should be. Be realistic: don't add "programming" or "database development" to your list unless you really plan to do those things. Use the following checklist to determine which activities you will use your computer for.

Task	Yes	No
Internet/e-mail/chatting	☐	☐
Word processing	☐	☐
Spreadsheet	☐	☐
Database management	☐	☐
Presentations	☐	☐
Recording or editing audio	☐	☐
Recording or editing video	☐	☐
Creating or editing graphics	☐	☐
Working with digital photos	☐	☐
Web design	☐	☐
Programming	☐	☐
Computer-aided design	☐	☐
Playing games	☐	☐

If your list includes a lot of tasks, or if you plan to work on a few demanding tasks, then you need a more powerful system. This means you will need the fastest processor, greatest amount of memory, and largest hard disk you can afford.

It's important to remember that some computing tasks are more processing-intensive than others. So, if you only plan to use your PC for word processing, e-mail, and Web surfing, you can easily get by with a lower-cost, lower-power processor, such as a Celeron. In this case, a PC with 128 MB of RAM will probably meet your needs. By choosing a system with a lower-power processor and minimal RAM, you can save hundreds of dollars.

Digital video editing and computer-aided design, however, require as much power and storage as your system can muster. Tasks such as these are very processing-intensive, requiring a system with the fastest processor and as much RAM as you can afford. Processing-intensive tasks also tend to be storage-intensive, too, so if you plan to use your new PC for chores like these, buy the fastest processor, the most RAM, and the biggest hard disk you can afford. If possible, make sure the PC has a built-in CD-RW or DVD-RW unit, so you can create high-volume backups of your work.

2. **What features or capabilities are most important to you?** If you want to use a PC mostly for game playing and listening to music, then good graphics and audio

Use the following checklist to help you decide which options you need and don't need. When you are ready to shop, use the list to help you compare options in the systems you consider buying.

Option	Yes	No	Details
Processor	☑	☐	Type: ________ Speed: ________ GHz
RAM	☑	☐	Type: ________ Amount: ________
Hard disk	☑	☐	Type: ________ Capacity: ________ Spin Rate: ________ Avg. Access Time: ________
Optical drive	☑	☐	Type: ________ Read Speed: ________ Write Speed: ________
Monitor	☐	☐	Type: ________ Size: ________ Special Features: ________
High-capacity floppy disk drive	☐	☐	Type: ________ Capacity: ________
Modem	☐	☐	Type: ________ Speed: ________
Keyboard	☑	☐	Type: ________ Special Features: ________
Pointing device	☑	☐	Type: ________ Special Features: ________
Video card	☑	☐	Type: ________ Amount of VRAM: ________
Sound card	☑	☐	Type: ________
Speakers	☐	☐	Type: ________
Microphone	☐	☐	Type: ________
Video camera	☐	☐	Type: ________
USB ports	☐	☐	Number: ________
IEEE 1394 ports	☐	☐	Number: ________
Special ports (MIDI, TV In/Out, Audio In/Out, multimedia memory cards, etc.)	☐	☐	Number: ________ Type(s): ________
Operating system	☑	☐	Type: ________ Version: ________
Antivirus software	☐	☐	Type: ________ Version: ________
Warranty	☐	☐	Type: ________ Duration: ________

CONTINUED >>>

capabilities may be more important to you than some other options. On the other hand, if you want to work with video, then a large hard disk and plenty of RAM may be most important to you.

3. **What features can you live without?** If you do not plan to watch DVD videos or record CDs on your system, then you probably shouldn't pay for a DVD player or CD-R/CD-RW drive. If you don't plan to install lots of software or hoard thousands of audio files, then you can save money by getting a smaller hard disk. If you do not plan to connect the computer to a network, then do not pay for a network interface card (although you do need one if you plan to connect to the Internet through a cable modem or DSL connection). By omitting features you do not need, the money you save can be applied toward the features you want.
4. **How much money can you afford to spend?** The answer to this question, of course, determines how much PC you can buy. But do not be disappointed if you cannot afford the biggest, fastest, most-power-packed PC in the store. Depending on your needs, you may be able to buy a system that is just right for you, for less than you imagined.

   Nearly every PC maker offers a line of home computers for $1,000 or less. Many of these machines feature processors with speeds of 1–2 GHz, 256 MB of RAM (or more), high-capacity hard drives, a fast system bus, and more. And remember: you don't have to buy everything at once. For example, if you already have a monitor, use it instead of buying a new one. The same applies to speakers, a printer, and other peripheral devices. If you already have a computer, you may get by just fine by buying a new system unit alone, saving hundreds of dollars in the process.

Don't worry if you don't have a lot of money to spend. You can easily find a fully equipped, powerful new PC for a few hundred dollars, if you do your homework.

Do Some Homework

Once you figure out why you want to use a PC and what basic features are most important, it's time to start learning about the different options that are available from most PC makers.

Check Out Processors Today's PCs are based on processors from two manufacturers—Intel and AMD—and you can learn the differences between their products by visiting their Web sites at http://www.intel.com and http://www.amd.com.

You can find even more detailed information by visiting some of the many Web sites that regularly review processors, such as

- **CNET Shopper.** http://shopper.cnet.com
- **MSN Technology.** http://tech.msn.com
- **PC Magazine.** http://www.pcmag.com
- **PC World.** http://www.pcworld.com

Know Your RAM Needs The rule of thumb is: "the more RAM you have, the better." Of course, this is not an *absolute* truth because it is possible to have more RAM than your system will use. On average, though, it is a good idea to have a reasonably high level of memory in your computer to enable your computer to run more efficiently.

If you can afford it, make sure that your new PC has at least 256 MB of RAM (this amount is standard on many lower-cost PCs, but not always); that should give you enough memory to run Windows and several applications at the same time. If the manufacturer gives you the option of installing faster RDRAM or DDR-SDRAM, and if you can afford it, take the option. Your system will perform better.

To best determine how much RAM you will actually need, check the system requirements for the operating system and application programs you plan to use. You can find this information on the side of the program's package or on the manufacturer's Web site. The more programs you plan to run simultaneously, the more RAM you need.

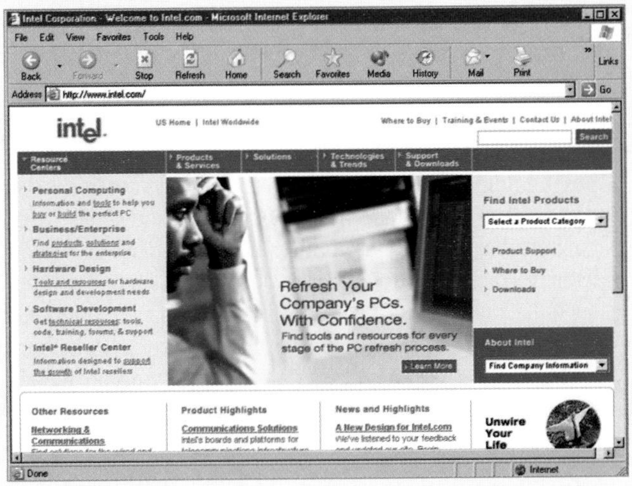

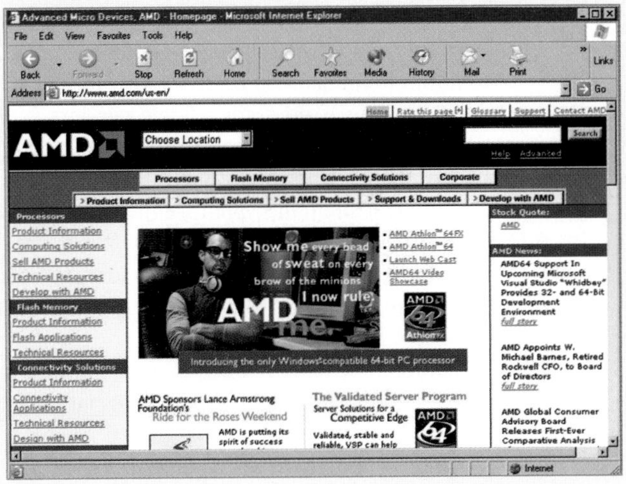

To learn the latest information on processors, visit the Web sites of the leading makers of CPUs.

Know Your Storage Needs Many new PCs come with enormous hard disks; it is easy to find models with 80 GB and larger drives. Of course, too little storage capacity will become a problem later on, forcing you to upgrade your system. On the other hand, too much storage capacity is simply a waste. Why pay for storage space you may never use?

As with RAM requirements, your operating system and application programs have specific storage requirements, which should be listed on the package. Check the package or the manufacturer's Web site to see how much disk space you will need for your operating system and applications. Double that amount and you will have a safe *minimum* requirement for your PC's storage. Be sure to allow room for programs you may install in the future, for your data files, and for the many temporary files that Windows creates as it runs.

Other Important Decisions

When you go computer shopping, you'll need to make decisions about many things—not just the computer itself. Give some thought to the following points before you shop:

- **PC or Macintosh?** If you talk to experienced PC and Mac users, you'll probably be surprised at how devoted they are to their favorite platforms. But personal preference is not always the best reason to decide whether to buy a PC or a Mac. If you need a system that is compatible with those used at your workplace or school, for example, it may be best to get that type of computer. Otherwise, you'll spend a lot of time trying to get programs and files to work together between the different computers.
- **Desktop or Portable?** Many people simply prefer the flexibility a notebook PC gives them. But you need to decide whether the portability of a notebook PC is worth the trade-offs. For example, if you check the prices of comparably equipped desktop and notebook PCs, you will find that the portable systems are usually more expensive. Further, they have smaller screens, and some people find them more cumbersome to use than a full-size computer. If you plan to use the system at home most of the time, you can buy a full-size keyboard, mouse, and monitor for about $200. But if you want to be able to take the system with you, a notebook or tablet PC can be a great investment.

To get an idea of how much RAM and storage space your new PC will need, check the requirements for the software you plan to run.

CONTINUED

- **To Bundle or Not to Bundle?** Nearly all consumer-level PCs come with lots of software already installed. This can be a great feature if you plan to use the software, but it also can drive up the system's cost. Some vendors will give you a choice of software bundles; for example, you may be able to choose from productivity-oriented programs, entertainment programs, photo-editing tools, or something else. If you are tempted to skip the bundle and save your money, remember: bundled software may be far cheaper than buying off-the-shelf programs later. Compare the prices before deciding.

  Some manufacturers like to bundle extra hardware with their PCs. These companies may offer special package prices for a PC and a printer, or a PC and a digital camera, or some other hardware combination. If you need the extra hardware anyway, then check the bundle's price against the cost of buying the devices separately. However, make sure the bundled hardware is comparable to the devices you would choose if you were to buy them separately.

- **To Extend or Not to Extend (the warranty)?** The majority of new PCs come with a one-year warranty that covers most problems you are likely to encounter. Some computers have a three-year manufacturer's warranty. The vendor will probably ask if you want to extend the warranty, and may give the option of stretching the warranty by one, two, or three years. You also may have the option of getting on-site service instead of shipping the computer off to be repaired. Extended warranties can cost anywhere from $50 to $250, depending on the options you choose. If you can't imagine opening a PC and trying to fix it yourself, then choose a vendor that offers a good basic warranty and extend it if you can afford to. If you aren't afraid to work on a PC yourself, then skip the extended warranty.

- **New or Used?** Granted, you can save big bucks by buying a used PC instead of a new one. However, you may be buying someone else's headaches. Has the system been damaged or upgraded? What kind of treatment has it received? Are all the components truly compatible? If you want to buy a used PC, stick with a brand-name system such as Compaq, IBM, Dell, or Gateway and try to find out as much as you can about the unit's history. Make sure the computer is not out of date; if it has a Pentium II processor, for example, you should consider it obsolete.

  Instead of buying a used PC, consider buying a factory-refurbished one from a major PC vendor. These computers are systems that were previously sold and then returned to the manufacturer. Often, these machines were never taken out of the box, or they were only slightly used. Manufacturers typically refurbish these systems by updating any outdated components and thoroughly testing them. Most refurbished PCs come with the same warranty as a new PC, but at a fraction of the cost.

Talking Turkey

Now that you know what you need (and don't need), it is time to start shopping. You can buy a computer in at least three ways; the method you choose depends on your comfort level:

- **At a Store.** If you live in or near a large town, you probably have access to stores that carry PCs, software, and

Macintosh computers make up about 5 percent of the total personal computer market, so compatibility may be an issue if you need to share files with other people.

Bundled hardware or software may be a good value, depending on your needs.

peripherals. It is a good idea to visit some of these stores so you can get a close-up look at different types of systems. While you are there, find out what kinds of services the store offers, what types of specials it runs, and what brands and models it carries.

Buying through a local computer store, office supply store, or electronics store has some advantages. For example, you can develop a relationship with the store personnel, which is important if you have problems later on. But there are downsides, too. If you work with a pushy salesperson, you may wind up paying for options you do not need or—worse—buying a PC that is not right for you. If the store sells PCs only as a sideline (as some department stores do), you may have trouble getting service later on.

- **By Phone.** Many major PC makers offer toll-free numbers, where sales representatives can help you configure a PC and give you an exact price. If you decide to shop by phone, you need to have a credit card handy (some vendors will not accept payment by check or money order unless you mail it to them first), along with a list of the options you want.
- **Online.** Online shopping is now the most popular way to buy a computer. Nearly every PC maker has a Web site that offers secure online shopping. Another bonus of online shopping is the availability of "configurators"—tools that let you select options for your system, then show how each option affects the total price. PC makers frequently offer "Internet-only" specials, which are not available if you order by phone or buy from a store. Again, however, you will need a credit card if you want to shop online; otherwise, you may have to call the vendor and arrange to pay by check or money order.

Remember, you get what you pay for. Thoroughly check out any used computer before buying it, and don't buy one that does not come with some kind of warranty.

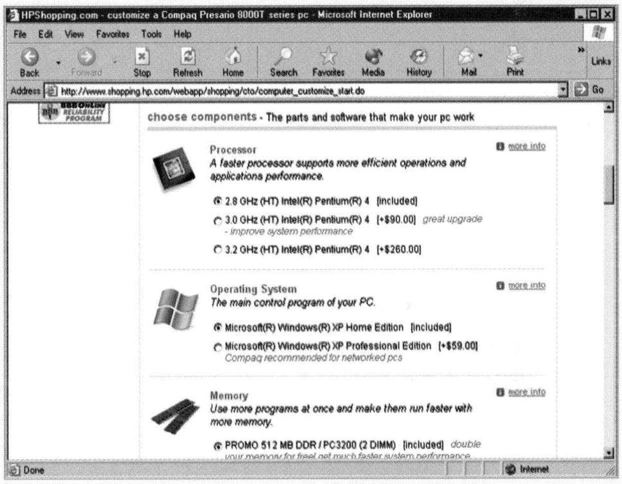

If you shop online, you can use a "configurator," like this one at the Hewlett Packard Web site, to select the exact options you want and see how they affect the system's price.

CHAPTER

5 Processing Data

CHAPTER CONTENTS ::

This chapter contains the following lessons:

LESSON // 5A

Transforming Data into Information

Overview: The Difference between Data and Information

It often seems as though computers must understand us because we understand the information they produce. However, computers cannot understand anything. Computers recognize two distinct physical states produced by electricity, magnetic polarity, or reflected light. Essentially, they understand whether a switch is on or off. In fact, the CPU, which acts like the "brain" of the computer, consists of several million tiny electronic switches, called transistors. A computer appears to understand information only because it operates at such phenomenal speeds, grouping its individual on/off switches into patterns that become meaningful to us.

In the world of computing, *data* is the term used to describe the information represented by groups of on/off switches. Although the words *data* and *information* often are used interchangeably, there is an important distinction between the two words. In the strictest sense, data consist of the raw numbers that computers organize to produce information.

You can think of data as facts out of context, like the individual letters on this page. Taken individually, most of them do not have much, if any, meaning. Grouped together, however, the data convey specific meanings. Just as a theater's marquee can combine thousands of lights to spell the name of the current show, a computer can group meaningless data into useful information, such as spreadsheets, charts, and reports.

OBJECTIVES ::

- >> Explain why computers use the binary number system.
- >> List the two main parts of the CPU and explain how they work together.
- >> List the steps that make up a machine cycle.
- >> Explain the difference between RAM and ROM.
- >> List three hardware factors that affect processing speed.

How Computers Represent Data

simnet™

From a very early age, we are introduced to the concept of numbers and counting. Toddlers learn early that they can carry two cookies, one in each hand. Kindergartners start counting by twos and fives. Invariably, we use the decimal number system. Our number system is based on 10, most likely because we have 10 fingers. A number system is simply a manner of counting. Many different number systems exist. Consider a clock. Clocks have 24 hours, each composed of 60 minutes. Each minute is composed of 60 seconds. When we time a race, we count in seconds and minutes.

Computers, like clocks, have their own numbering system, the binary number system.

Number Systems

To a computer, everything is a number. Numbers are numbers; letters and punctuation marks are numbers; sounds and pictures are numbers. Even the computer's own instructions are numbers. When you see letters of the alphabet on a computer screen, you are seeing just one of the computer's ways of representing numbers. For example, consider the following sentence:

Here are some words.

This sentence may look like a string of alphabetic characters to you, but to a computer it looks like the string of ones and zeros shown in Figure 5A.1.

FIGURE 5A.1

These 1s and 0s represent a sentence. The decimal system uses 10 symbols and multiple digits for the numbers 9 and higher.

H	0100 1000
e	0110 0101
r	0111 0010
e	0110 0101
	0010 0000
a	0110 0001
r	0111 0010
e	0110 0101
	0010 0000
s	0111 0011
o	0110 1111
m	0110 1101
e	0110 0101
	0010 0000
w	0111 0111
o	0110 1111
r	0111 0010
d	0110 0100
s	0111 0011
.	0010 1110

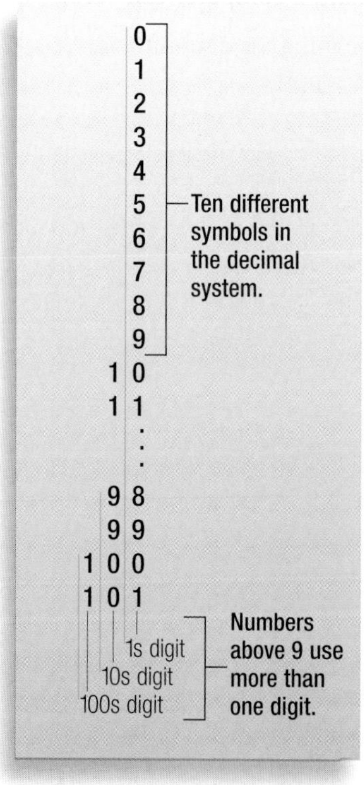

Computer data looks especially strange because people normally use base 10 to represent numbers. The decimal number system (*deci* means "10" in Latin) is called "base 10" because 10 symbols are available: 0, 1, 2, 3, 4, 5, 6, 7, 8, and 9. When you need to represent a number greater than 9, you use two symbols together, as in 9 + 1 = 10. Each symbol in a number is called a "digit," so 10 is a two-digit number. To build all the two-digit numbers (10–99) in the decimal number system, you use up all the possible pairings of the system's 10 symbols. After all 90 of the two-digit numbers are built, then you begin using three-digit numbers (100–999), and so on. This pattern can continue indefinitely, using only the 10 symbols you started with.

As the numbers start to become longer, the concept of place becomes important. Consider the number 1,325. Four places are represented in this number: the thousands, hundreds, tens, and ones. Thus, there is a 1 in the thousands place, a 3 in the hundreds place, a 2 in the tens place, and a 5 in the ones place. Figure 5A.2 illustrates the value of place.

FIGURE 5A.2

The decimal value 1,325 broken down into thousands, hundreds, tens, and ones places.

1325

= 1 * 1000 + 3 * 100 + 2 * 10 + 5 * 1

In a computer, however, all data is represented by the state of the computer's electronic switches. A switch has only two possible states—on and off—so it can represent only two numeric values. To a computer, when a switch is off, it represents a 0; when a switch is on, it represents a 1 (see Figure 5A.3). Because there are only two values, computers are said to function in base 2, which is also known as the binary number system (*bi* means "2" in Latin).

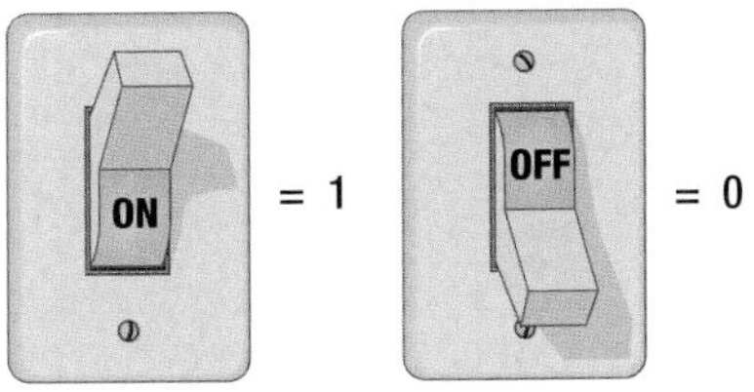

FIGURE 5A.3

Places in the decimal number system. In a computer, data are represented by the state of electronic switches. If a switch is on, it represents a 1. If a switch is off, it represents a 0.

When a computer needs to represent a quantity greater than one, it does the same thing you do when you need to represent a quantity greater than nine: it uses two (or more) digits. With only two digits to work with, there are many fewer two-digit pairings than in the decimal system. Binary has only two two-digit pairings. Once these two pairings are exhausted, four three-digit pairings are built. To familiarize yourself with the binary system, look at Table 5A.1.

In examining Table 5A.1 several trends become apparent. The first trend: notice that all odd numbers in decimal have a 1 as the last binary digit. A second trend: the pattern repeats. Consider the first four digits: 0, 1, 10, 11. The three-digit numbers repeat the pattern in order with a 1 (and filler zeros) placed at the beginning. The same is true of the eight four-digit numbers. They simply repeat the previous eight patterns in order, placing a 1 (and filler zeros) at the beginning. This pattern repeats indefinitely.

Norton ONLINE

For more information on number systems, visit **http://www.mhhe.com/peternorton**.

Bits and Bytes

When referring to computerized data, the value represented by each switch's state—whether the switch is turned on or off—is called a bit (a combination of *b*inary dig*it*). A bit is the smallest possible unit of data a computer can recognize or use. To represent anything meaningful (in other words, to convey information), the computer uses bits in groups.

A group of eight bits is called a byte (see Figure 5A.4). Half of a byte is called a nibble. With one byte, the computer can represent one of 256 different symbols or characters because the eight 1s and 0s in a byte can be combined in 256 different ways.

The value 256 is more than the number of symbols; it is the number of patterns of 0 and 1 that can be created using eight bits. This number can be obtained using a calculation: There are two possible states for a switch, on and off. In a byte there are eight switches. To calculate the number of patterns, raise 2 to the number of bits: $2^8 = 256$. Table 5A.2 shows the first 9 powers of 2.

The byte is an extremely important unit because there are enough different eight-bit combinations to represent all the characters on the keyboard, including all the letters (uppercase and lowercase), numbers, punctuation marks, and other symbols. If you look back at Figure 5A.1, you will notice that each of the characters (or letters) in the sentence *Here are some words.* is represented by one byte (eight bits) of data.

TABLE 5A.1

Counting in Base 10 and Base 2

Base 10	Base 2
0	0
1	1
2	10
3	11
4	100
5	101
6	110
7	111
8	1000
9	1001
10	1010
11	1011
12	1100
13	1101
14	1110
15	1111
16	10000

Text Codes

Early programmers realized that they needed a standard text code that was agreeable to all of them. In such a system, numbers would represent the letters of the alphabet, punctuation marks, and other symbols. This standard code system would enable any programmer or program to use the same combinations of numbers to represent the same individual pieces of data. The four most popular text code systems invented are the following:

- **EBCDIC.** EBCDIC (pronounced EB-si-dic) stands for Extended Binary Coded Decimal Interchange Code. EBCDIC is an eight-bit code that defines 256 symbols. It is still used in IBM mainframe and midrange systems, but it is rarely encountered in personal computers.

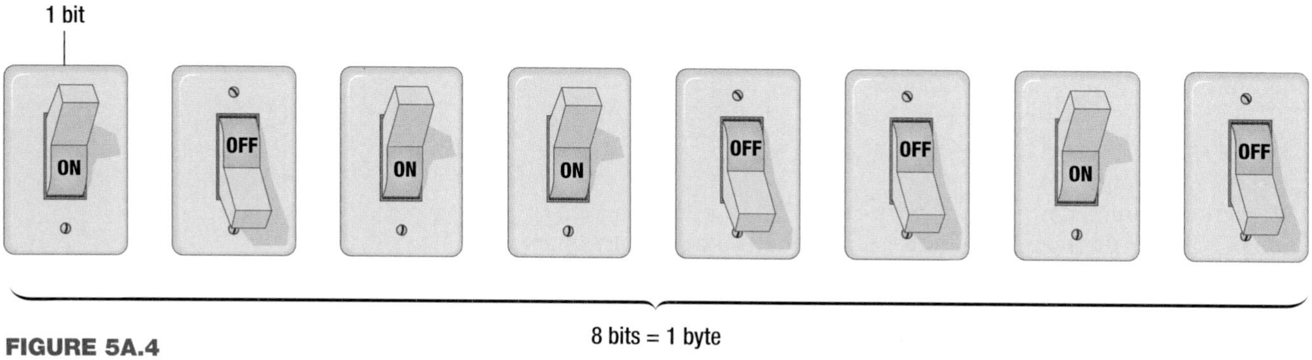

FIGURE 5A.4

One byte is composed of eight bits. A nibble is four bits.

TABLE 5A.2

Powers of 2

Power of 2	Value
0	1
1	2
2	4
3	8
4	16
5	32
6	64
7	128
8	256

simnet™

Norton ONLINE

For more information on text codes, visit **http://www.mhhe.com/peternorton**.

- **ASCII.** ASCII (pronounced AS-key) stands for the American Standard Code for Information Interchange. Today, the ASCII character set is by far the most commonly used in computers of all types. Table 5A.3 shows the 128 ASCII codes. ASCII is an eight-bit code that specifies characters for values from 0 to 127.
- **Extended ASCII.** Extended ASCII is an eight-bit code that specifies the characters for values from 128 to 255. The first 40 symbols represent pronunciation and special punctuation. The remaining symbols are graphic symbols.
- **Unicode.** The Unicode Worldwide Character Standard provides up to four bytes—32 bits—to represent each letter, number, or symbol. With four bytes, enough Unicode codes can be created to represent more than 4 billion different characters or symbols. This total is enough for every unique character and symbol in the world, including the vast Chinese, Korean, and Japanese character sets and those found in known classical and historical texts. In addition to world letters, special mathematical and scientific symbols are represented in Unicode. One major advantage that Unicode has over other text code systems is its compatibility with ASCII codes. The first 256 codes in Unicode are identical to the 256 codes used by the ASCII and Extended ASCII systems.

How Computers Process Data

Two components handle processing in a computer: the central processing unit, or CPU, and the memory. Both are located on the computer's motherboard (see Figure 5A.5).

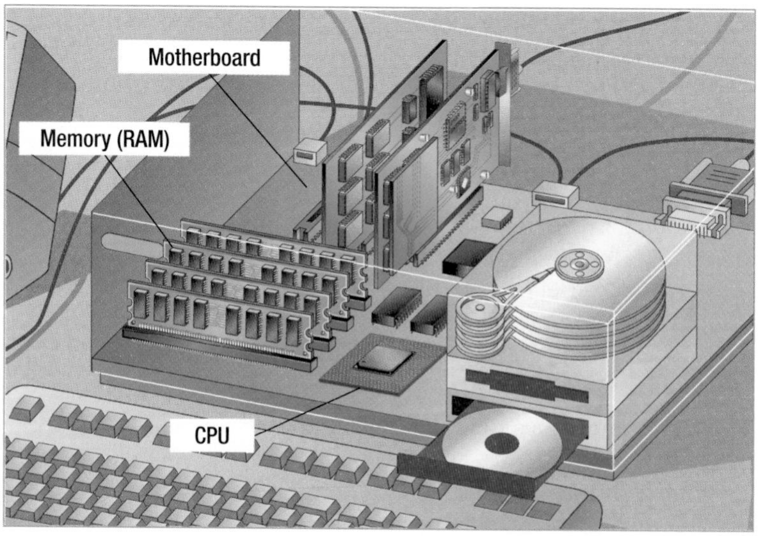

FIGURE 5A.5

Processing devices.

TABLE 5A.3

ASCII Codes

ASCII Code	Decimal Equivalent	Character	ASCII Code	Decimal Equivalent	Character	ASCII Code	Decimal Equivalent	Character
0000 0000	0	Null prompt	0010 1011	43	+	0101 0110	86	V
0000 0001	1	Start of heading	0010 1100	44	,	0101 0111	87	W
0000 0010	2	Start of text	0010 1101	45	-	0101 1000	88	X
0000 0011	3	End of text	0010 1110	46	.	0101 1001	89	Y
0000 0100	4	End of transmit	0010 1111	47	/	0101 1010	90	Z
0000 0101	5	Enquiry	0011 0000	48	0	0101 1011	91	[
0000 0110	6	Acknowledge	0011 0001	49	1	0101 1100	92	\
0000 0111	7	Audible bell	0011 0010	50	2	0101 1101	93	]
0000 1000	8	Backspace	0011 0011	51	3	0101 1110	94	^
0000 1001	9	Horizontal tab	0011 0100	52	4	0101 1111	95	_
0000 1010	10	Line feed	0011 0101	53	5	0110 0000	96	`
0000 1011	11	Vertical tab	0011 0110	54	6	0110 0001	97	a
0000 1100	12	Form feed	0011 0111	55	7	0110 0010	98	b
0000 1101	13	Carriage return	0011 1000	56	8	0110 0011	99	c
0000 1110	14	Shift out	0011 1001	57	9	0110 0100	100	d
0000 1111	15	Shift in	0011 1010	58	:	0110 0101	101	e
0001 0000	16	Data link escape	0011 1011	59	;	0110 0110	102	f
0001 0001	17	Device control 1	0011 1100	60	<	0110 0111	103	g
0001 0010	18	Device control 2	0011 1101	61	=	0110 1000	104	h
0001 0011	19	Device control 3	0011 1110	62	>	0110 1001	105	i
0001 0100	20	Device control 4	0011 1111	63	?	0110 1010	106	j
0001 0101	21	Neg. acknowledge	0100 0000	64	@	0110 1011	107	k
0001 0110	22	Synchronous idle	0100 0001	65	A	0110 1100	108	l
0001 0111	23	End trans. block	0100 0010	66	B	0110 1101	109	m
0001 1000	24	Cancel	0100 0011	67	C	0110 1110	110	n
0001 1001	25	End of medium	0100 0100	68	D	0110 1111	111	o
0001 1010	26	Substitution	0100 0101	69	E	0111 0000	112	p
0001 1011	27	Escape	0100 0110	70	F	0111 0001	113	q
0001 1100	28	File separator	0100 0111	71	G	0111 0010	114	r
0001 1101	29	Group separator	0100 1000	72	H	0111 0011	115	s
0001 1110	30	Record separator	0100 1001	73	I	0111 0100	116	t
0001 1111	31	Unit separator	0100 1010	74	J	0111 0101	117	u
0010 0000	32	Blank space	0100 1011	75	K	0111 0110	118	v
0010 0001	33	!	0100 1100	76	L	0111 0111	119	w
0010 0010	34	″	0100 1101	77	M	0111 1000	120	x
0010 0011	35	#	0100 1110	78	N	0111 1001	121	y
0010 0100	36	$	0100 1111	79	O	0111 1010	122	z
0010 0101	37	%	0101 0000	80	P	0111 1011	123	{
0010 0110	38	&	0101 0001	81	Q	0111 1100	124	|
0010 0111	39	’	0101 0010	82	R	0111 1101	125	}
0010 1000	40	(	0101 0011	83	S	0111 1110	126	~
0010 1001	41	)	0101 0100	84	T	0111 1111	127	Delete or rubout
0010 1010	42	*	0101 0101	85	U			

The CPU

The CPU is the "brain" of the computer, the place where data is manipulated. In large computer systems, such as supercomputers and mainframes, processing tasks may be handled by multiple processing chips. (Some powerful computer systems use hundreds or even thousands of separate processing units.) In the average microcomputer, the entire CPU is a single unit, called a microprocessor. Regardless of its construction, every CPU has at least two basic parts: the control unit and the arithmetic logic unit.

The Control Unit

All the computer's resources are managed from the control unit. Think of the control unit as a traffic signal directing the flow of data through the CPU, as well as to and from other devices. The control unit is the logical hub of the computer.

The CPU's instructions for carrying out commands are built into the control unit. The instructions, or instruction set, list all the operations that the CPU can perform. Each instruction in the instruction set is expressed in microcode—a series of basic directions that tell the CPU how to execute more complex operations.

The Arithmetic Logic Unit

Because all computer data is stored as numbers, much of the processing that takes place involves comparing numbers or carrying out mathematical operations. In addition to establishing ordered sequences and changing those sequences, the computer can perform two types of operations: arithmetic operations and logical operations. Arithmetic operations include addition, subtraction, multiplication, and division. Logical operations include comparisons, such as determining whether one number is equal to, greater than, or less than another number. Also, every logical operation has an opposite. For example, in addition to "equal to" there is "not equal to." Table 5A.4 shows the symbols for all the arithmetic and logical operations.

Many instructions carried out by the control unit involve simply moving data from one place to another—from memory to storage, from memory to the printer, and so forth. When the control unit encounters an instruction that involves arithmetic or logic, however, it passes that instruction to the second component of the CPU, the arithmetic logic unit, or ALU. The ALU actually performs the arithmetic and logical operations described earlier.

The ALU includes a group of registers—high-speed memory locations built directly into the CPU that are used to hold the data currently being processed. You can think of the register as a scratchpad. The ALU will use the register to hold the data currently being used for a calculation. For example, the control unit might load two numbers from memory into the registers in the ALU. Then it might tell the ALU to divide the two numbers (an arithmetic operation) or to see whether the numbers are equal (a logical operation). The answer to this calculation will be stored in another register before being sent out of the CPU.

TABLE 5A.4

Operations Performed by the Arithmetic Logic Unit

Arithmetic Operations		Logical Operations	
$+$	add	$=, \neq$	equal to, not equal to
$-$	subtract	$>, \ngtr$	greater than, not greater than
$\times$	multiply	$<, \nless$	less than, not less than
$\div$	divide	$\geqq, \ngeqq$	greater than or equal to, not greater than or equal to
$\wedge$	raise by a power	$\leqq, \nleqq$	less than or equal to, not less than or equal to

Machine Cycles

Each time the CPU executes an instruction, it takes a series of steps. The completed series of steps is called a machine cycle. A machine cycle itself can be broken down into two smaller cycles: the instruction cycle and the execution cycle. At the beginning of the machine cycle (that is, during the instruction cycle), the CPU takes two steps:

1. **Fetching.** Before the CPU can execute an instruction, the control unit must retrieve (or fetch) a command or data from the computer's memory.
2. **Decoding.** Before a command can be executed, the control unit must break down (or decode) the command into instructions that correspond to those in the CPU's instruction set. Figure 5A.6 shows how the CPU plays a sound.

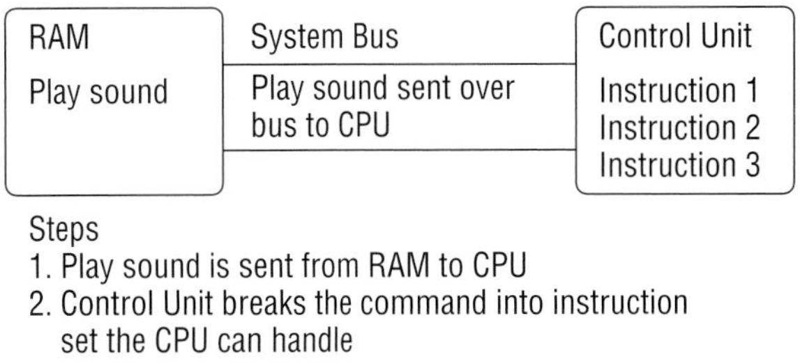

FIGURE 5A.6

Fetching and decoding an instruction to play a sound.

At this point, the CPU is ready to begin the execution cycle:

1. **Executing.** When the command is executed, the CPU carries out the instructions in order by converting them into microcode.
2. **Storing.** The CPU may be required to store the results of an instruction in memory (but this condition is not always required). Figure 5A.7 shows the result of the sound being played.

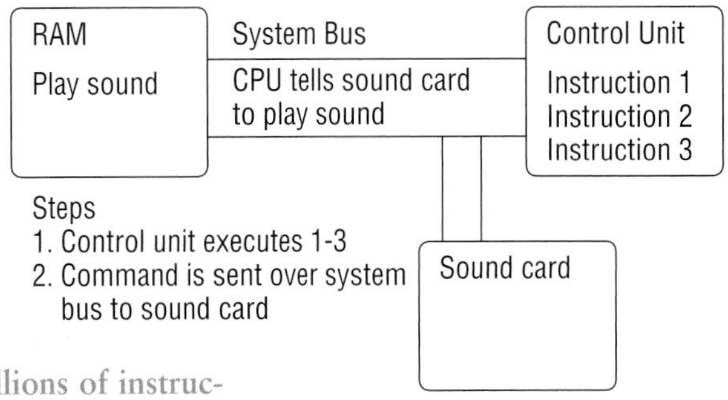

FIGURE 5A.7

The execution cycle plays the sound.

Although the process is complex, the computer can accomplish it at an incredible speed, translating millions of instructions every second. In fact, CPU performance is often measured in millions of instructions per second (MIPS). Newer CPUs can be measured in billions of instructions per second (BIPS).

Even though most microprocessors execute instructions rapidly, newer ones can perform even faster by using a process called pipelining (or pipeline processing). In pipelining, the control unit begins a new machine cycle—that is, it begins executing a new instruction—before the current cycle is completed. Executions are performed in stages: When the first instruction completes the "fetching" stage, it moves to the "decode" stage and a new instruction is fetched. It is helpful to think of a pipeline as an assembly line. Each instruction is broken up into several parts. Once the first part of an instruction is done, it is passed to the second part. Since the first step in the line is now idle, the pipeline then feeds a new step one. Using this technique, newer microprocessors can execute up to 20 instructions simultaneously.

Modern operating systems support the running of many programs, or multitasking. The CPU may be asked to perform tasks for more than one program. To make this work, the OS and the CPU create threads. A thread is one instruction from a program. The CPU will execute one thread from a program at one time. Since the CPU can perform each thread quickly, the user thinks that each program is being run at the same time. Newer processors support hyperthreading. Hyperthreading allows multiple threads to be executed at one time.

Norton ONLINE

For more information on machine cycles, visit **http://www.mhhe.com/peternorton**.

Memory

The CPU contains the basic instructions needed to operate the computer, but it cannot store entire programs or large sets of data permanently. The CPU needs to have millions (or even trillions, in some computers) of bytes of space where it can quickly read or write programs and data while they are being used. This area is called memory, and it consists of chips either on the motherboard or on a small circuit board attached to the motherboard. This electronic memory allows the CPU to store and retrieve data quickly.

There are two types of built-in memory: permanent and nonpermanent (see Figure 5A.8). Some memory chips retain the data they hold, even when the computer is turned off. This type of permanent memory is called nonvolatile. Other

FIGURE 5A.8

The CPU is attached to two kinds of memory: RAM, which is volatile, and ROM, which is nonvolatile.

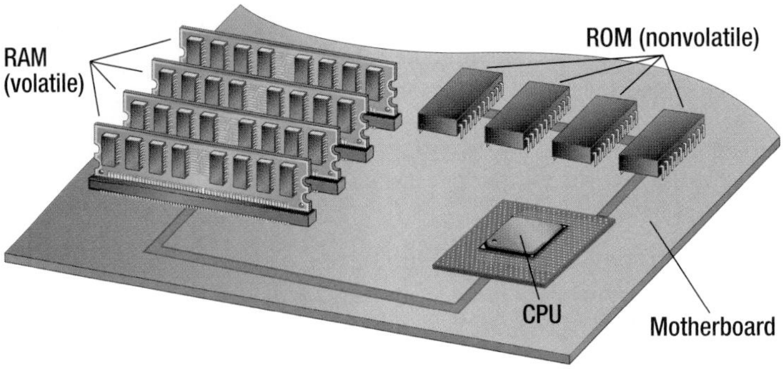

chips—in fact, most of the memory in a microcomputer—lose their contents when the computer's power is shut off. This type of nonpermanent memory is called volatile.

Nonvolatile Memory

Nonvolatile chips hold data even when the computer is unplugged. In fact, putting data permanently into this kind of memory is called "burning in the data," and it is usually done at the factory. During normal use, the data in these chips is only read and used—not changed—so the memory is called read-only memory (ROM). Specifically, chips that cannot be changed are called programmable read only memory (PROM). PROM chips are often found on hard drives and printers. They contain the instructions that power the devices. These instructions, once set, never need to be changed.

When a computer is turned on, it must know how to start. ROM contains a set of start-up instructions called the basic input output system (BIOS) for a computer. In addition to booting the machine, BIOS contains another set of routines, which ensure that the system is functioning properly and all expected hardware devices are present. This routine is called the power on self test (POST) .

FIGURE 5A.9

A 512MB CompactFlash card for a digital camera.

Flash Memory

Flash memory is a special type of nonvolatile memory. It is often used in portable digital devices for storage. Digital cameras, portable MP3 players, USB "keychain" storage devices, and game consoles all use flash memory. The flash memory works by having actual switches store the binary values that make up the data. Thus, on a camera with a flash card, the picture is stored on the card by turning millions of tiny switches on and off. Barring catastrophic damage to the card, the picture is stored indefinitely. Figure 5A.9 shows a typical flash memory card.

Volatile Memory

Volatile memory requires power to store data. The volatile memory in a computer is called random access memory (RAM). When people talk about computer memory in connection with microcomputers, they usually mean the RAM. RAM's job is to hold programs and data while they are in use. Physically, RAM consists of chips on a small circuit board (see Figure 5A.10). Single in-line memory modules (SIMMs) and dual in-line memory module (DIMM) chips are found in desktop computers, while the smaller, small outline DIMM (SO-DIMM) chips are found in laptop computers.

RAM is designed to be instantly accessible by the CPU or programs. The "random" in RAM implies that any portion of RAM can be accessed at any time. This helps make RAM very fast. Without the random abilities of RAM, the computer would be very slow.

Norton ONLINE

For more information on memory, visit **http://www.mhhe.com/peternorton**.

FIGURE 5A.10

Memory chips.

A computer does not have to search its entire memory each time it needs to find data because the CPU uses a memory address to store and retrieve each piece of data (see Figure 5A.11). A memory address is a number that indicates a location on the memory chips, just as a post office box number indicates a slot into which mail is placed. Memory addresses start at zero and go up to one less than the number of bytes of memory in the computer.

RAM is not used just in conjunction with the computer's CPU. RAM can be found in various places in a computer system. For example, most newer video and sound cards have their own built-in RAM (see Figure 5A.12), as do many types of printers.

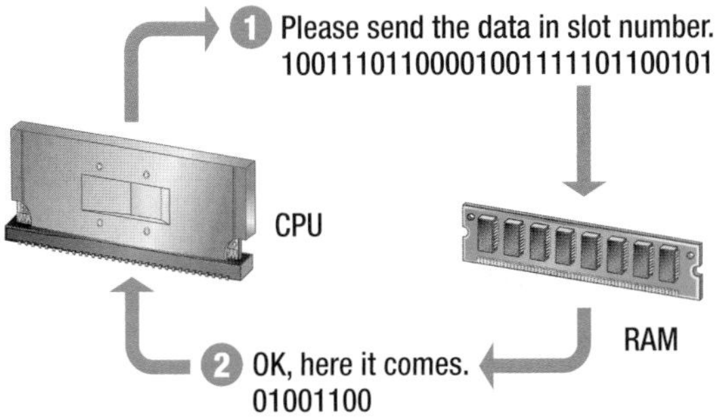
1 Please send the data in slot number.
10011101100001001111101100101
CPU
RAM
2 OK, here it comes.
01001100

FIGURE 5A.11

To request a byte of data, the CPU sends a memory address to RAM.

FIGURE 5A.12

Memory chips can be found in many parts of a computer system, such as this video card.

Factors Affecting Processing Speed

A CPU's design determines its basic speed, but other factors can make chips already designed for speed work even faster. You already have been introduced to some of these, such as the CPU's registers and memory. In this section, you will see how other factors—such as the cache memory, the clock speed, and the data bus—affect a computer's speed. Figure 5A.13 shows how these components might be arranged on the computer's motherboard.

Norton ONLINE

For more information on processing speeds, visit **http://www.mhhe.com/peternorton**.

Registers

The registers in the first PCs could hold two bytes—16 bits—each. Most CPUs sold today, for both PCs and Macintosh computers, have 32-bit registers. Many newer PCs, as well as minicomputers and high-end workstations, have 64-bit registers.

At Issue

Cyborgs Among Us: Wearable Technology

Cyborg: the melding of man and machine, organism and circuitry. Though no Robocop, metaphoric cyborgs are more than the stuff of media sci-fi. They are reality for the thousands who utilize a new generation of wearable computing device making intimate human–machine interaction now possible.

The term *wearable computer* refers to a wireless computer system worn on the user's body, either in a backpack, on a belt, or sewn into a piece of clothing such as a jacket or vest. Some are small enough to fit in the user's shirt pocket or have monitors worn as eyeglasses.

Wearable computers are designed specifically for mobile and mostly hands-free operations, often incorporating head-mounted displays and vocal recognition software. Most variations of wearable PCs are always on and always accessible. In this way, this new computing framework differs from that of other existing wireless technologies, such as laptop computers and personal digital assistants.

It is this "always ready" feature that is the true hallmark of wearables. Unlike other personal computers or handheld devices, a wearable computer is subsumed into the personal space of the user, becoming almost a part of him or her. This leads to a new form of synergy between human and computer, brought about by long-term adaptation through constancy of the user–computer interface. Over time, the user adapts to the computer to the point he or she no longer feels as if it is a separate entity. Often users report feeling uncomfortable—even "naked"—without their devices.

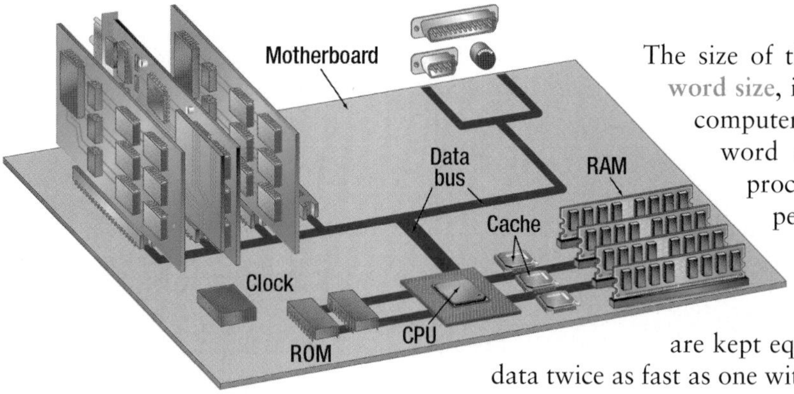

FIGURE 5A.13

Devices affecting processing speed.

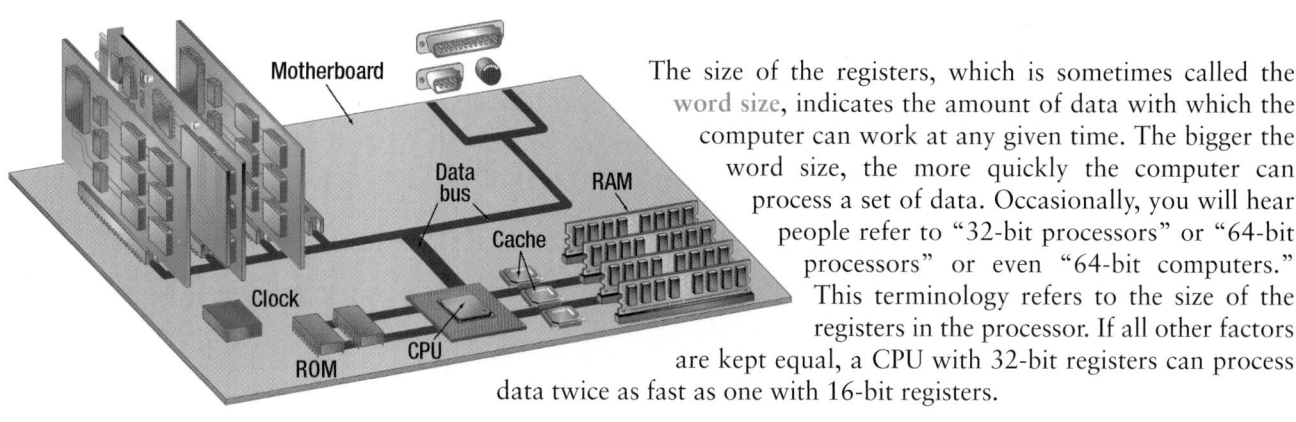

The size of the registers, which is sometimes called the word size, indicates the amount of data with which the computer can work at any given time. The bigger the word size, the more quickly the computer can process a set of data. Occasionally, you will hear people refer to "32-bit processors" or "64-bit processors" or even "64-bit computers." This terminology refers to the size of the registers in the processor. If all other factors are kept equal, a CPU with 32-bit registers can process data twice as fast as one with 16-bit registers.

Memory and Computing Power

The amount of RAM in a computer can have a profound effect on the computer's power. More RAM means the computer can use bigger, more powerful programs, and those programs can access bigger data files.

More RAM also can make the computer run faster. The computer does not necessarily have to load an entire program into memory to run it. However, the greater the amount of the program that fits into memory, the faster the program runs. To run Windows, for example, the computer usually does not need to load all its files into memory to run properly; it loads only the most essential parts into memory.

When the computer needs access to other parts of an operating system or a

SELF-CHECK ::

Complete each statement by filling in the blank(s).

1. A computer's CPU consists of millions of tiny switches called __________ .
   a. bits b. transistors c. registers
2. Base 2 is another name for the __________ .
   a. binary number system b. hexadecimal number system c. decimal number system
3. __________ can represent more than 4 billion different characters or symbols.
   a. ASCII b. Extended ASCII c. Unicode

Also unlike other portable devices, wearable PCs are full-featured computers, with all of the functionality of a traditional desktop or mainframe computer.

One company leading the way in the wearables space is Hitachi. The Hitachi wearable PC unit is small and lightweight enough to be carried in a pocket. It includes a head-mounted display that gives users the illusion that there is a 13-inch color screen in front of them. Users operate the machine via a tiny handheld optical mouse.

The Hitachi wearable PC runs on Microsoft's Windows CE operating system and contains a Hitachi 128 MHz RISC processor and 32 MB of RAM. It also comes with a Flash card and a USB slot. According to the firm, the unit measures 140 × 90 × 26 mm, and the whole device weighs a slight 500 g.

Though still on the cutting edge, many experts believe that wearables will someday soon supersede technologies such as mobile phones and PDAs, holding out the promise that wearable computers will improve the quality of day-to-day life for their Cyborg users.

AT ISSUE

program on the disk, it can unload, or swap out, nonessential parts from RAM to the hard disk. Then the computer can load, or swap in, the program code or data it needs. While this is an effective method for managing a limited amount of memory, the computer's system performance is slower because the CPU, memory, and disk are continuously occupied with the swapping process. Swapping unused contents of RAM to the hard disk is known as virtual memory. As shown in Figure 5A.14, if your PC has 128 MB of RAM (or more), you will notice a dramatic difference in how fast Windows runs because the CPU will need to swap program instructions between RAM and the hard disk much less often.

If you purchase a new computer system, it will probably come with at least 256 MB of RAM. Microsoft suggests 256 MB as the minimum recommended configuration for Windows XP. If you plan to play graphic-intensive games or develop complex graphics, you will need more RAM. The cost of upgrading the memory of a computer is very low, so upgrading RAM is the simplest and most cost-effective way to get more speed from

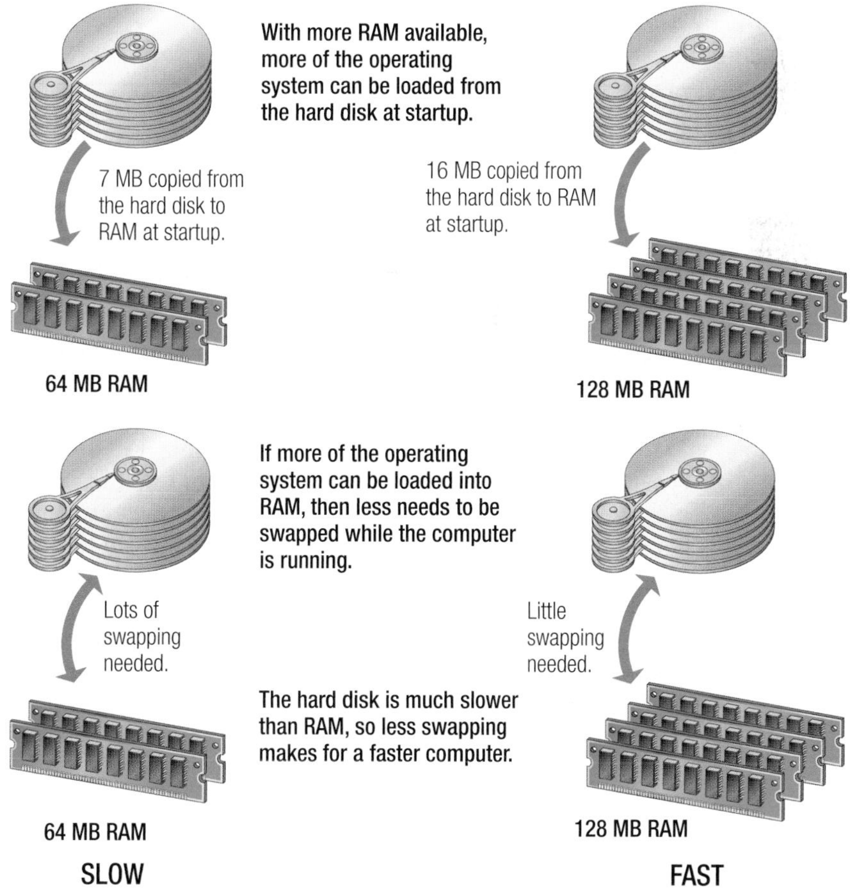
With more RAM available, more of the operating system can be loaded from the hard disk at startup.
7 MB copied from the hard disk to RAM at startup.
16 MB copied from the hard disk to RAM at startup.
64 MB RAM
128 MB RAM
If more of the operating system can be loaded into RAM, then less needs to be swapped while the computer is running.
Lots of swapping needed.
Little swapping needed.
The hard disk is much slower than RAM, so less swapping makes for a faster computer.
64 MB RAM
128 MB RAM
SLOW
FAST

FIGURE 5A.14

How RAM affects speed.

your computer. See the Productivity Tip, "Do You Need More RAM?" later in this chapter.

The Computer's Internal Clock

Every microcomputer has a system clock, but the clock's primary purpose is not to keep the time of day. Like most modern wristwatches, the clock is driven by a quartz crystal. When electricity is applied, the molecules in the crystal vibrate millions of times per second, a rate that never changes. The speed of the vibrations is determined by the thickness of the crystal. The computer uses the vibrations of the quartz in the system clock to time its processing operations.

Over the years, system clocks have become steadily faster. For example, the first PC operated at 4.77 megahertz. Hertz (Hz) is a measure of cycles per second. Megahertz (MHz) means "millions of cycles per second." Gigahertz (GHz) means "billions of cycles per second."

The computer's operating speed is tied to the speed of the system clock. For example, if a computer's clock speed is 800 MHz, it "ticks" 800 million times per second. A clock cycle is a single tick, or the time it takes to turn a transistor off and back on again. A processor can execute an instruction in a given number of clock cycles. As the system's clock speed increases, so does the number of instructions it can carry out each second.

Clock speeds greater than 1 GHz are now common, and processor speeds are increasing rapidly. At the time this book was written, processor speeds had eclipsed 3 GHz.

The Bus

A bus is a path between the components of a computer. There are two main buses in a computer: the internal (or system) bus and the external (or expansion) bus. The system bus resides on the motherboard and connects the CPU to other devices that reside on the motherboard. An expansion bus connects external devices, such as the keyboard, mouse, modem, printer, and so on, to the CPU. Cables from disk drives and other internal devices are plugged into the bus. The system bus has two parts: the data bus and the address bus (see Figure 5A.15).

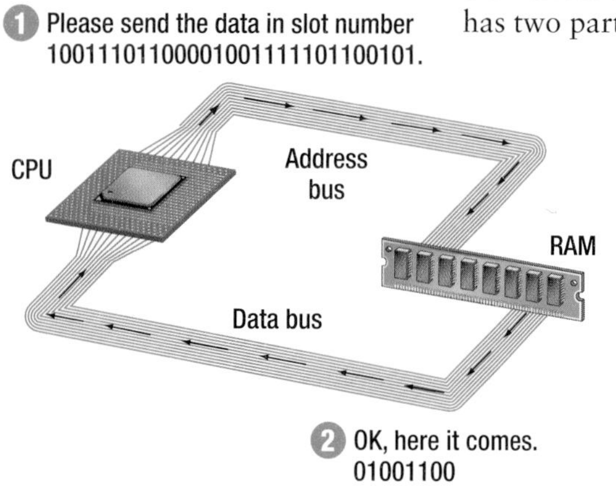

1 Please send the data in slot number 10011101100001001111101100101.
CPU
Address bus
RAM
Data bus
2 OK, here it comes. 01001100

FIGURE 5A.15

The system bus includes an address bus and a data bus. The address bus leads from the CPU to RAM. The data bus connects the CPU to memory, and to all the storage, input/output, and communications devices that are attached to the motherboard.

The Data Bus

The data bus is an electrical path that connects the CPU, memory, and the other hardware devices on the motherboard. Actually, the bus is a group of parallel wires. The number of wires in the bus affects the speed at which data can travel between hardware components, just as the number of lanes on a highway affects how long it takes people to reach their destinations. Because each wire can transfer one bit of data at a time, an eight-wire bus can move eight bits at a time, which is a full byte (see Figure 5A.16). A 16-bit bus can transfer two bytes, and a 32-bit bus can transfer four bytes at a time. Newer model computers have a 64-bit data bus called the FrontSide Bus that transfers eight bytes at a time.

Like the processor, the bus's speed is measured in megahertz (MHz) because it has its own clock speed. As you would imagine, the faster a bus's clock speed, the faster it can transfer data between parts of the computer. The majority of today's PCs have a bus speed of either 100 MHz or 133 MHz, but speeds of 800 MHz and higher are becoming more common.

The bus speed is directly tied into the CPU speed. All processors use a multiplier to make the CPU run faster. Here is how it works. Consider a system bus that runs at 400 MHz supporting a 1.6 GHz processor. The fastest the CPU can talk to external devices is 400 MHz. However, internally the processor runs at 1.6 GHz, or four times the bus speed. The multiplier in this system is four. Since the processor is so much faster than the bus, the processor spends most of the time idle.

The Address Bus

The address bus is a set of wires similar to the data bus (see Figure 5A.17). The address bus connects only the CPU and RAM and carries only memory addresses. (Remember, each byte in RAM is associated with a number, which is its memory address.)

Bus Standards

PC buses are designed to match the capabilities of the devices attached to them. When CPUs could send and receive only one byte of data at a time, there was no point in connecting them to a bus that could move more data. As microprocessor technology improved, however, chips were built that could send and receive more data at once, and improved bus designs created wider paths through which the data could flow. Common bus technologies include the following:

- The Industry Standard Architecture (ISA) bus is a 16-bit data bus. It became the de facto industry standard on its release in the mid-1980s and is still used in many computers to attach slower devices (such as modems and input devices) to the CPU.
- The Local bus was developed to attach faster devices to the CPU. A local bus is an internal system bus that runs between components on the motherboard. Most system buses use some type of local bus technology today and are coupled with one or more kinds of expansion bus.
- The Peripheral Component Interconnect (PCI) bus is a type of local bus designed by Intel to make it easier to integrate new data types, such as audio, video, and graphics.
- The Accelerated Graphics Port (AGP) bus incorporates a special architecture that allows the video card to access the system's RAM directly, greatly increasing the speed of graphics performance. The AGP standard has led to the development of many types of accelerated video cards that support 3-D and full-motion video. While AGP improves graphics performance, it cannot be used with all PCs. The system must use a chip set that supports the AGP standard. Most new computers feature AGP graphics capabilities in addition to a PCI system bus and an expansion bus.
- The Universal Serial Bus (USB) is a relatively new bus found on all modern machines. Unlike the PCI and AGP, USB is a hot swappable bus. This means that a user can connect then disconnect a USB device without affecting the machine. USB supports up to 127 devices connected in either a daisy chain or hub layout. In a daisy chain, each device is connected to the device before and after it in the line. The last device terminates the chain. Apple keyboards and mouse use USB daisy chain. The hub allows multiple devices to plug into one unit. Figure 5A.18 shows a Macintosh USB keyboard and mouse.

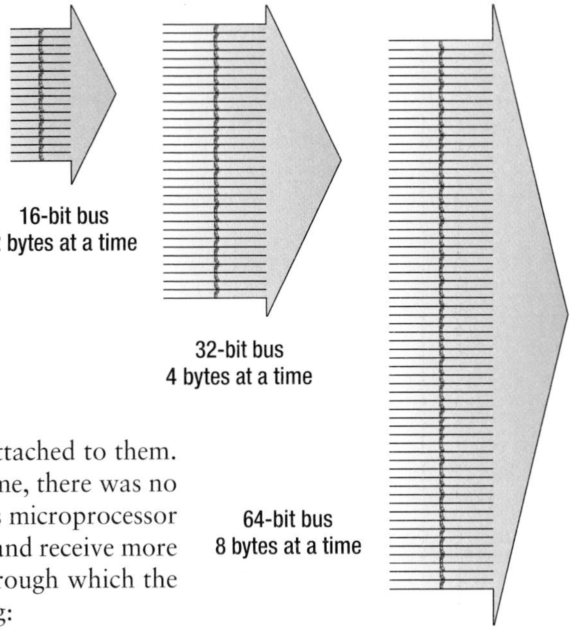

FIGURE 5A.16

With a wider bus, the computer can move more data in the same amount of time, or the same amount of data in less time.

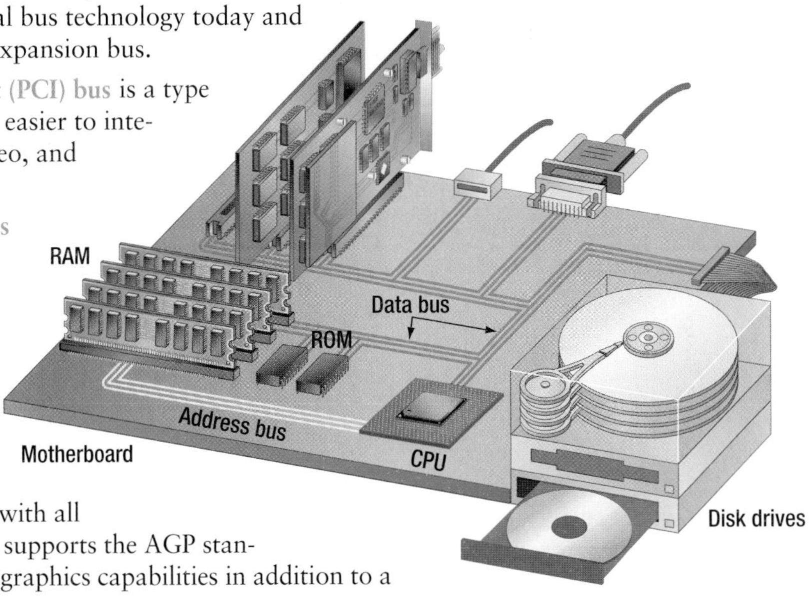

FIGURE 5A.17

Requests for data are sent from the CPU to RAM along the address bus. The request consists of a memory address. The data returns to the CPU via the data bus.

FIGURE 5A.18

Macintosh USB keyboard and mouse.

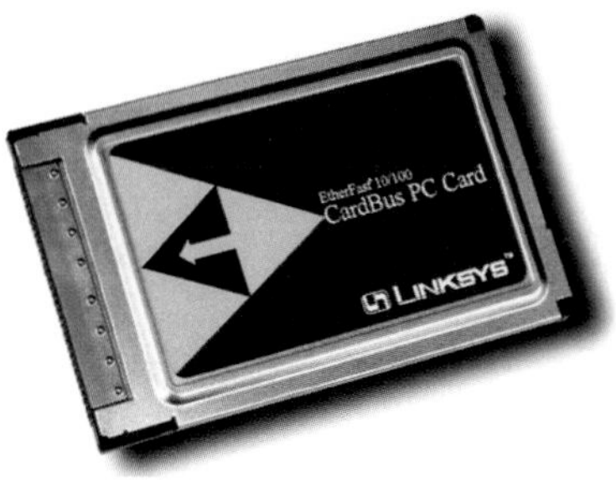

FIGURE 5A.19

A PC Card device.

- IEEE 1394 (FireWire) ports were once found only on Macintosh computers, but they are now increasingly common in IBM-compatible PCs. FireWire is used to connect video devices such as cameras and video cameras. Many digital TV connections also use FireWire.
- The PC Card bus is used exclusively on laptop computers. Like USB, PC Card is hot swappable. A PC Card is about the size of a stack of four credit cards. Common uses for PC Card include WiFi cards, network cards, and external modems. For secure notebooks, thumb scanners and other biometric security systems can be purchased. The most current form of PC Card is called CardBus and is mainly an external extension of an internal PCI bus. Figure 5A.19 shows a network interface card in the form of a PC Card.

Traditionally, the performance of computer buses was measured by the number of bits they could transfer at one time. Hence, the newest 64-bit buses are typically considered the fastest available. However, buses are now also being measured according to their data transfer rates—the amount of data they can transfer in a second—often measured in megahertz (MHz) or gigahertz (GHz). Hertz measures the number of times an electrical wave passes a fixed point on the bus. Higher numbers mean that more data can be transferred. Table 5A.5 lists the performance specifications of common buses.

Cache Memory

Moving data between RAM and the CPU's registers is one of the most time-consuming operations a CPU must perform, simply because RAM is much slower than the CPU. A partial solution to this problem is to include a cache memory in the CPU. Cache (pronounced *cash*) memory is similar to RAM except that it is extremely fast compared to normal memory and it is used in a different way.

Figure 5A.20 shows how cache memory works with the CPU and RAM. When a program is running and the CPU needs to read a piece of data or program instructions from RAM, the CPU checks first to see whether the data is in cache memory. If the data is not there, the CPU reads the data from RAM into its registers, but it also loads a copy of the data into cache memory. The next time the CPU needs the data, it finds it in the cache memory and saves the time needed to load the data from RAM.

TABLE 5A.5

Performance Specifications of Common Buses

Bus Type	Width (bits)	Transfer Speed	Hot Swappable
AGP 8	32	2.1 GHz	No
FireWire	32	400 MHz	Yes
ISA	16	8.33 MHz	No
PC Card	32	33 MHz	Yes
PCI	32	33 MHz	No
USB 2.0	32	480 MHz	Yes

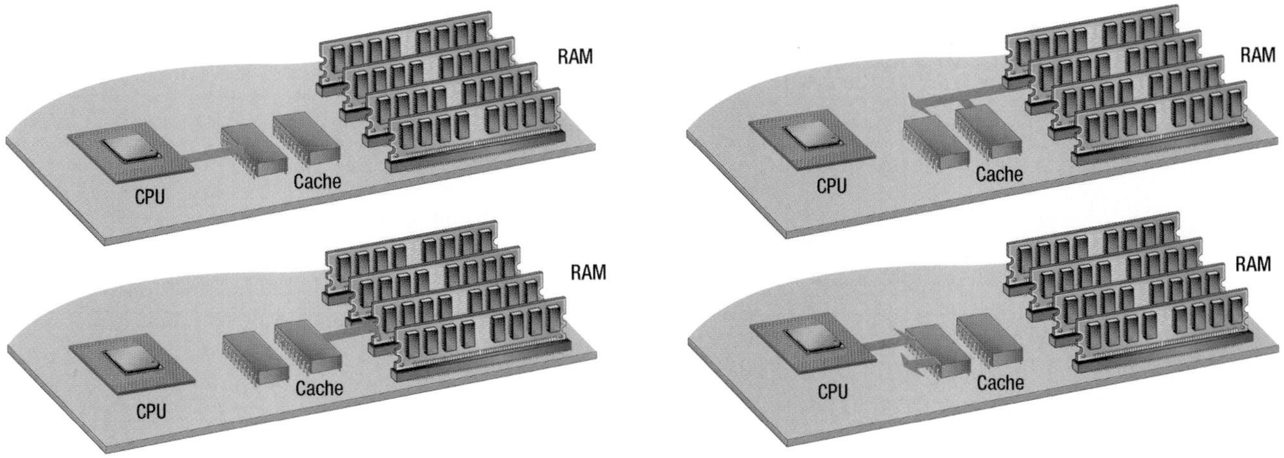

FIGURE 5A.20

The cache speeds processing by storing frequently used data or instructions in its high-speed memory. External (Level-2) cache is shown here, but most computers also have memory circuitry built directly into the CPU.

Cache is present in several places in a computer. Most hard drives and network cards have cache present to speed up data access. Without cache, your computer would be a much slower device.

Since the late 1980s, most PC CPUs have had cache memory built into them. This CPU-resident cache is often called Level-1 (L1) cache. Today, many CPUs have as much as 256 KB built in.

To add even more speed to modern CPUs, an additional cache is added to CPUs. This cache is called Level-2 (L2) cache. This cache used to be found on the motherboard. However, Intel and AMD found that placing the L2 cache on the CPU greatly increased CPU response. Many PCs being sold today have 512 KB or 1024 KB of motherboard cache memory; higher-end systems can have as much as 2 MB of L2 cache.

In addition to the cache memory built into the CPU, cache is also added to the motherboard. This motherboard-resident cache is now called Level-3 (L3) cache. L3 cache is found on very-high-end computers. It is not necessary for a computer to have L3 cache.

The three caches work like a assistant to a mechanic. First, the mechanic prepares a box containing all the tools he may need for the current job. Most likely, this is only a portion of his entire tool set. The mechanic slides under the car and uses a wrench to try to remove a nut. L2, seeing the mechanic use the wrench, figures that he will need either oil to loosen the nut or pliers to remove a bolt. L2 tries to predict what the mechanic will need and grabs these items from the box. Eventually, the mechanic finishes with the wrench and asks for the pliers. L1 holds on to the wrench in case the mechanic needs it again. L2 holds on to tools that might be needed soon. Eventually the mechanic will need the wrench again. L1 then hands the wrench to the mechanic who finishes the job. The process is made faster because the mechanic does not need to stop and root through the toolbox for each necessary tool.

L1, L2, and L3 all speed up the CPU, although in different ways. L1 cache holds instructions that have recently run. L2 cache holds potential upcoming instructions. L3 holds many of the possible instructions. In all cases, the cache memory is faster for the CPU to access, resulting in a quicker program execution.

Norton ONLINE

For more information on bus technologies, visit **http://www.mhhe.com/peternorton**.

Productivity Tip

Do You Need More RAM?

You've probably heard it a hundred times. RAM upgrades are cheap, easy, and fast—a great way to improve your PC's performance. But is it really as simple and inexpensive as the experts keep saying?

Well, yes and no. A lot of factors determine how costly or difficult a RAM upgrade can be, and other factors determine whether it will even do you any good. But make no mistake about it: if your computer is running slower than you like, adding RAM may give it some pep. If your PC is relatively new (say, no more than three years old), you may want to consider installing more RAM before trading up to a new system. The performance boost could make you want to keep that old PC a while longer.

If your PC is more than a couple of years old, and if you are becoming increasingly unhappy with its performance, then perhaps it is time to think about a memory upgrade. If that sounds like an overly simplistic approach to making the decision, ask yourself the following questions:

- Does your PC have less than 128 MB of RAM?
- Do you typically run more than one application at a time?
- Are you using a newer version of Windows, such as Windows Me, 2000, or XP?
- Does the system noticeably slow down during a long computing session, especially if you launch and close multiple programs or use the Internet?
- Do you need to reboot frequently?
- Do you ever see "insufficient memory" messages when you try to run a program or load a file?
- Does your hard disk light seem to flicker most of the time?

If you can answer "yes" to more than one of those questions, a RAM upgrade may be a good idea.

The decision to upgrade does not require a degree in computer science and you do not need to do much math. You should base your decision to upgrade on your satisfaction with the computer's performance. You should compare the cost and probable benefits of a RAM upgrade with the expense of a more thorough upgrade (such as replacing a processor, motherboard, and hard disk) or simply buying a new system.

A RAM upgrade may be the fastest, cheapest, and easiest way to improve your PC's performance.

Deciding to upgrade RAM offers two big advantages. First, it is less expensive than just about any other kind of upgrade you can do. Second, even if the upgrade does not improve your computer's performance a lot, it probably will not hurt anything, either.

You should not expect a RAM upgrade to speed up your system the way a new processor would. In fact, experts say that there is no reason to put more than 512 MB of RAM in most personal computers. Depending on the types of applications that are run, additional memory may not even be used because Windows allocates a certain amount of memory for itself and for each running application.

On the other hand, if your PC is short on RAM, it will not be able to run current software products very efficiently. For example, the practical minimum for a PC running a newer version of Windows 98 or Me is now considered to be 64 MB, and for running Windows 2000 or XP, the minimum is 128 MB. These requirements will give the PC enough memory to load essential operating system components and a couple of applications. Beyond that, however, the system has to rely on the hard disk as a source of "virtual memory," requiring the hard disk and RAM to spend time swapping data back and forth as it is needed. This process greatly reduces performance.

Realistically, the only way to answer this question is to do the upgrade. Chances are good that you will notice at least some improvement in your system's behavior.

PRODUCTIVITY TIP

LESSON // 5A Review

Summary ::

- Computer data is reduced to binary numbers because computer processing is performed by transistors that have only two possible states: on and off.
- The binary number system works the same way as the decimal system, except that it has only two available symbols (0 and 1) rather than ten (0, 1, 2, 3, 4, 5, 6, 7, 8, and 9).
- A single unit of data is called a bit; eight bits make up one byte.
- In the most common text-code set, ASCII, each character consists of one byte of data. In the Unicode text-code set, each character consists of up to four bytes of data.
- A microcomputer's processing takes place in the central processing unit, the two main parts of which are the control unit and the arithmetic logic unit (ALU).
- Within the CPU, program instructions are retrieved and translated with the help of an internal instruction set and the accompanying microcode.
- The CPU follows a set of steps for each instruction it carries out. This set of steps is called the machine cycle. By using a technique called pipelining, many CPUs can process more than one instruction at a time.
- The actual manipulation of data takes place in the ALU, which is connected to the registers that hold data and program instructions while they are being processed.
- Random access memory (RAM) is volatile (or temporary). Programs and data can be written to and erased from RAM as needed.
- Read only memory (ROM) is nonvolatile (or permanent). It holds instructions that run the computer when the power is first turned on.
- The CPU accesses each location in memory by using a unique number, called the memory address.
- The size of the registers, also called word size, determines the amount of data with which the computer can work at one time.
- The amount of RAM can affect speed because the CPU can keep more of the active program and data in memory, which is faster than storage on disk.
- The computer's system clock sets the pace for the CPU by using a vibrating quartz crystal. The faster the clock, the more instructions the CPU can process per second.
- The system bus has two parts—the data bus and the address bus—both of which are located on the motherboard.
- The width of the data bus determines how many bits can be transmitted at a time between the CPU and other devices.
- Peripheral devices can be connected to the CPU by way of an expansion bus.
- Cache memory is a type of high-speed memory that contains the most recent data and instructions that have been loaded by the CPU. The amount of cache memory has a tremendous impact on the computer's speed.

Key Terms ::

Accelerated Graphics Port (AGP) bus, 197
address bus, 197
American Standard Code for Information Interchange (ASCII), 188
arithmetic logic unit (ALU), 190
arithmetic operation, 190
basic input output system (BIOS), 192
billions of instructions per second (BIPS), 191
binary number system, 187
bit, 187
bus, 196
cache memory, 198
clock cycle, 196
clock speed, 196
control unit, 190
data bus, 196
data transfer rate, 198
decimal number system, 186

decode, 191
dual in-line memory module (DIMM), 192
execute, 191
execution cycle, 191
Extended ASCII, 188
Extended Binary Coded Decimal Interchange Code (EBCDIC), 187
fetch, 191
flash memory, 192
FrontSide Bus, 196
gigahertz (GHz), 196
hertz (Hz), 196
hyperthreading, 191
IEEE 1394 (FireWire), 198
Industry Standard Architecture (ISA) bus, 197
instruction cycle, 191
instruction set, 190
Level-1 (L1) cache, 199
Level-2 (L2) cache, 199
Level-3 (L3) cache, 199
local bus, 197
logical operation, 190
machine cycle, 190
megahertz (MHz), 196
memory address, 193
microcode, 190
millions of instructions per second (MIPS), 191
multitasking, 191
nonvolatile, 191
PC Card, 198
Peripheral Component Interconnect (PCI) bus, 197
pipelining, 191
power on self test (POST), 192
programmable read only memory (PROM), 192
register, 190
read only memory (ROM), 192
single in-line memory module (SIMM), 192
small outline DIMM (SO-DIMM), 192
store, 191
swap in, 195
swap out, 195
system clock, 196
text code, 187
thread, 191
transistor, 185
Unicode Worldwide Character Standard, 188
Universal Serial Bus (USB), 197
virtual memory, 195
volatile, 192
word size, 194

Key Term Quiz ::

Complete each statement by writing one of the terms listed under Key Terms in each blank.

1. People use the ____________ number system, but computers use the ____________ number system.
2. The term ____________ is a combination of the words *binary digit*.
3. The most widely used text code system among personal computers is ____________ .
4. A processor's built-in instructions are stored as ____________ .
5. ____________ are high-speed memory locations built directly into the CPU that hold data while they are being processed.
6. The ____________ is run when the system turns on and verifies that the hardware is working.
7. Digital cameras use ____________ to store pictures on removable cards.
8. The computer uses ____________ when it runs out of RAM, swapping program instructions or data out to the hard drive.
9. A ____________ is a portion of a computer program that is being run by a CPU.
10. The ____________ contains the list of all commands a CPU understands.

Review

Multiple Choice ::

Circle the word or phrase that best completes each statement.

1. The ________ standard promises to provide enough characters to cover all the world's languages.
   a. ASCII b. Unicode c. RAM d. EBCDIC
2. ________ may be built directly into a CPU or placed on the motherboard.
   a. RAM b. Parallel c. Cache memory d. Flash
3. The CPU uses a ________ to store and retrieve each piece of data in memory.
   a. control unit b. cache c. memory address d. POST
4. The computer can move data and instructions between storage and memory, as needed, in a process called ________ .
   a. swapping b. volatility c. pipelining d. exchanging
5. The bus's speed is directly tied to the speed of the computer's ________ .
   a. RAM b. CPU c. ROM d. DIMM
6. A laptop will most likely use ________ memory chips.
   a. DIMM b. SO-DIMM c. SIPP d. SIMM
7. Memory that loses its data when power is turned off is considered ________ memory.
   a. volatile b. static c. dynamic d. refreshed
8. The acronym ________ means billions of operations per second.
   a. GB b. MHz c. KHz d. GHz
9. A CPU that is following a series of steps to complete an instruction is using ________ technology.
   a. threading b. pipelining c. cache d. multitasking
10. This cache holds the most recently used data or instructions.
    a. L1 b. L2 c. L3 d. L4

Review Questions ::

In your own words, briefly answer the following questions.

1. What is the difference between data and information?
2. How many characters or symbols can be represented by one eight-bit byte?
3. What is meant by "word size"?
4. What is the difference between arithmetic operations and logical operations?
5. What is a data bus?
6. Describe how virtual memory works.
7. What is the difference between an L1 and an L2 cache?
8. Describe the role of a computer's system clock.
9. Why is a CPU often idle?
10. Why is it important to have a standard text code?

Lesson Labs ::

Complete the following exercises as directed by your instructor.

1. Using the list of ASCII characters in Table 5A.3, compose a sentence using ASCII text codes. Make sure the sentence includes at least six words and make it a complete sentence. Swap your ASCII sentence with a classmate, then translate his or her sentence into alphabetical characters. Time yourself. How long did it take you to translate the sentence? What does this tell you about the speed of a computer's processor?
2. Compare ASCII and EBCDIC. Create a table that lists the ASCII values and their corresponding EBCDIC values. Determine a mathematical formula to translate from one to another.

LESSON // 5B

Modern CPUs

Overview: The Race for the Desktop

How fast is fast enough? How powerful does a computer need to be? We may never know the ultimate answer to these questions because when it comes to computer performance, the bar continues to be raised.

Software developers and users constantly make greater demands of computers, requiring them to perform an ever-higher number of tasks. Processor developers respond with chips of ever-increasing speed and power. Chipmakers such as Intel, IBM, Freescale, Advanced Micro Devices (AMD), and others keep proving that there seems to be no end to the potential power of the personal computer.

This lesson looks at the processors most commonly found in personal computers and describes some of their most important features and distinguishing characteristics. You will learn how these CPUs are typically differentiated from one another and see how their performance is measured. You also will learn some of the ways you can extend the power of your PC's processor to other components by using its expansion capabilities.

OBJECTIVES ::

- >> Name the best-known families of CPUs.
- >> Differentiate the processors used in Macintosh and IBM-compatible PCs.
- >> Define the terms CISC and RISC.
- >> Identify one advantage of using multiple processors in a computer.
- >> Identify four connections used to attach devices to a PC.

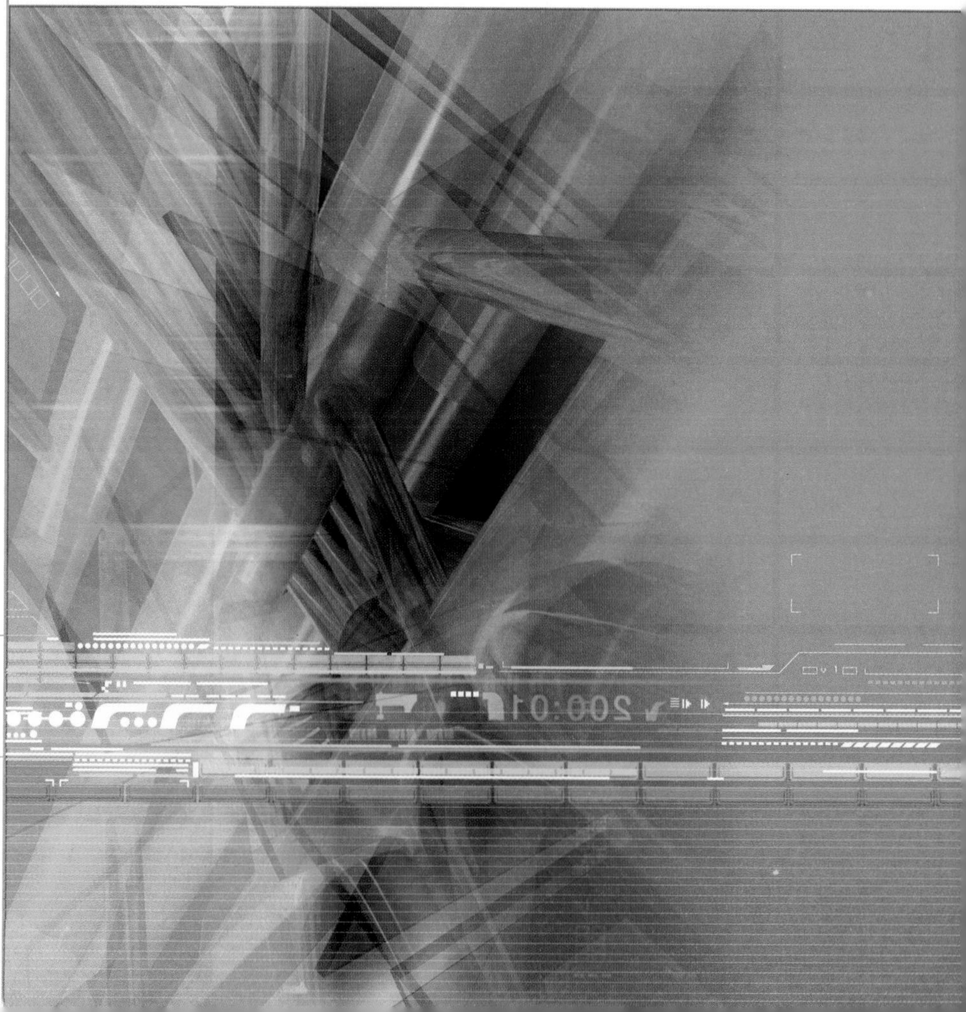

A Look Inside the Processor

You have already seen how a PC processes and moves data. For most people, the great mystery of the PC is what takes place inside its circuitry. How can this box of chips, wires, and other parts—most of which don't even move—do its work?

A processor's performance—even its capability to function—is dictated by its internal design, or architecture. A chip's architecture determines where its parts are located and connected, how it connects with other parts of the computer, and much more. It also determines the path that electricity (in the form of moving electrons) takes as it moves through the processor, turning its transistors on and off. There are many different chip architectures in use today, and each family of PC processors is based on its own unique architecture.

In fact, processors are differentiated by their architecture (see Figure 5B.1). The processors of IBM PCs and Macintosh computers have such different architectures, for example, that they cannot even run the same software; operating systems and programs must be written to run on each processor's specific architecture, to meet its requirements.

FIGURE 5B.1

Different processors have different architectures. In some cases, architectures are so different that processors cannot run the same software. For this reason, software must be written especially for Windows PCs, Macintosh computers, and workstations

A processor's architecture determines how many transistors it has, and therefore the processor's power (see Figure 5B.2). Simply stated, the more transistors in a processor, the more powerful it is. The earliest microprocessors had a few thousand transistors. The processors in today's PCs contain tens of millions. In the most powerful workstation and server computers, a processor may contain hundreds of millions of transistors. When a computer is configured to use multiple processors, it can ultimately contain billions of transistors.

A processor includes many other features that affect its performance. For example, a processor's performance is affected by the number of bits of data it can process at any one time. Currently, nearly all standard PC processors move data in 32-bit chunks; they are called "32-bit processors." In 2003 American Micro Devices (AMD) released a new generation of desktop PC processor that can handle 64 bits of data. (High-end workstations and many minicomputer systems have used 64-bit processors for about a decade.)

Microcomputer Processors

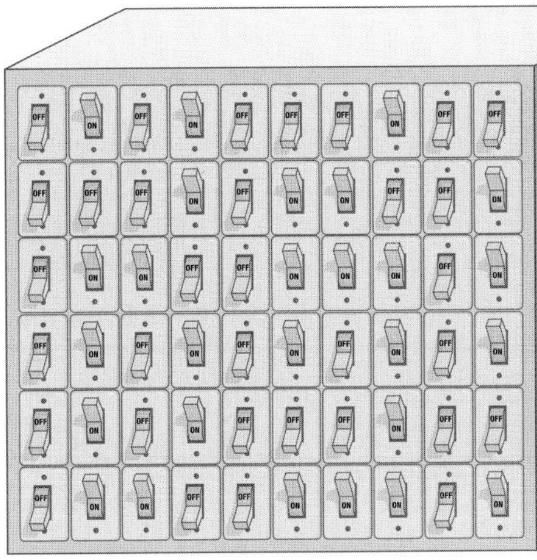

For two decades after the birth of the personal computer, the biggest player in the PC CPU market was Intel Corporation. This dominance began to change in 1998 when several leading computer makers began offering lower-priced systems using chips made by AMD and other chip manufacturers. Initially, these microprocessors offered less performance at a lower price. That situation has changed, however, as AMD made rapid advances in its products' capabilities. Today, Intel and AMD chips compete head to head, not only in performance, but also in price.

Intel and AMD are not the only manufacturers on the block. Motorola, now known as Freescale, manufactured the processors for all Macintosh computers up to and including the G4. They still make chips for communication devices. The newer Macintosh G5 boasts a chip made by IBM. Many other companies make specialized processors for workstations, minicomputers, handheld devices, automobile electronics, and kitchen appliances.

FIGURE 5B.2

Transistors are a key ingredient in any processor. The more transistors available, the more powerful the processor.

simnet™

Norton ONLINE

For more information on Intel's line of processors, visit **http://www.mhhe.com/peternorton**.

As you read the following sections, remember that performance specifications and features can change rapidly. Chip manufacturers make constant improvements to their products; as a result, the most popular PC processors now operate at speeds higher than 3 GHz, and they continue to be faster every month. By continuously refining chip designs and manufacturing processes, chip makers are always finding ways to add more transistors to chips.

Intel Processors

Intel is historically the leading provider of chips for PCs. In 1971, Intel invented the microprocessor—the so-called computer on a chip—with the 4004 model (see Figure 5B.3). This invention led to the first microcomputers that began appearing in 1975. Even so, Intel's success in this market was not guaranteed until 1981 when IBM released the first IBM PC, which was based on an Intel microprocessor.

A list of current Intel chips (see Figure 5B.4), along with their clock speeds and numbers of transistors, is shown in Table 5B.1.

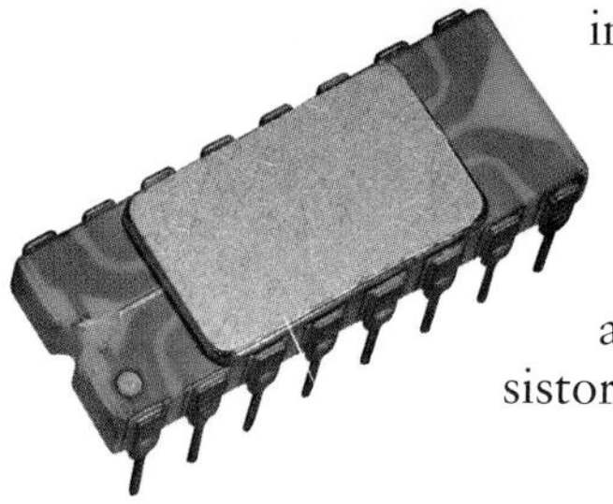

FIGURE 5B.3

Intel's first microprocessor, the 4004.

FIGURE 5B.4

The Pentium 4, Celeron, Xeon, and Itanium 2 processors.

Advanced Micro Devices (AMD) Processors

In 1998, Advanced Micro Devices (AMD) emerged as a primary competitor to Intel's dominance in the IBM-compatible PC market. Until that time, AMD processors were typically found in lower-performance, low-priced home and small business computers selling for less than $1,000. With the release of the K6 and Athlon processor series, AMD proved that it could compete feature for feature with many of Intel's best-selling products. AMD even began a new race for the fastest PC processor.

A list of current AMD chips (see Figure 5B.5), along with their clock speeds and numbers of transistors, is shown in Table 5B.2.

Norton ONLINE

For more information on AMD's line of processors, visit **http://www.mhhe.com/peternorton**.

TABLE 5B.1

Current Intel Processors

Model	Primary Use	Clock Speed	Number of Transistors
Itanium 2	Server	1.3 GHz and up	410 million
Pentium 4	PC	1.4 GHz and up	42–55 million
Pentium III Xeon	Server/Workstation	700 MHz and up	42–55 million
Pentium III	PC	650 MHz and up	28–44 million
Celeron	Budget PC	500 MHz and up	28–44 million

TABLE 5B.2

AMD Processors Used in Today's Personal Computers

Model	Clock Speed	Number of Transistors
Athlon FX 64	2.2 GHz and up	105.9 Million
Athlon XP	2.2 GHz and up	54.3 Million
Opteron for servers	1.4 GHz and up	106 Million
Athlon	1.0 GHz and up	37 million
Duron	600 MHz and up	25 million

FIGURE 5B.5

The Athlon and Duron processors.

Freescale Processors

Freescale Semiconductor, Inc., a subsidiary of Motorola, Inc., has a 50-year history in microelectronics. As mentioned earlier, many Apple computers use Freescale processors. Freescale processors were also an early favorite among companies that built larger, UNIX-based computers.

Through the years, Freescale offered two processor architectures that were used in Macintosh computers. The first is known as the 680*x*0 family. A new type of processor, which was developed by Freescale, Apple, and IBM, has replaced this family of processors. This new processor architecture, called the PowerPC architecture, is the basis for all new computers made by Apple. Freescale's MPC74*xx* processors can be found in Apple's G4 computers. PowerPC processors from Freescale are also ideal for Linux operating system implementations, which are growing in popularity among desktop users.

FIGURE 5B.6

MC680x0 die photograph and MPC7447A PowerPC processor from Freescale Semiconductor

IBM Processors

In addition to working with Apple and Freescale on the PowerPC line, IBM makes high-performance mainframe and workstation CPUs. In 2003, IBM partnered with Apple and released the G5 (see Figure 5B.7), advertised as the "fastest desktop processor ever." While most new chips can make this claim, the G5 delivered. The G5 delivered true workstation power at the cost of a standard desktop. As a demonstration, Pixar studios were provided with several G5-equipped computers. The Disney/Pixar movie *Finding Nemo* was created entirely on the G5 desktop computers. Previous releases from Pixar, including *Toy Story*, required high-end workstations.

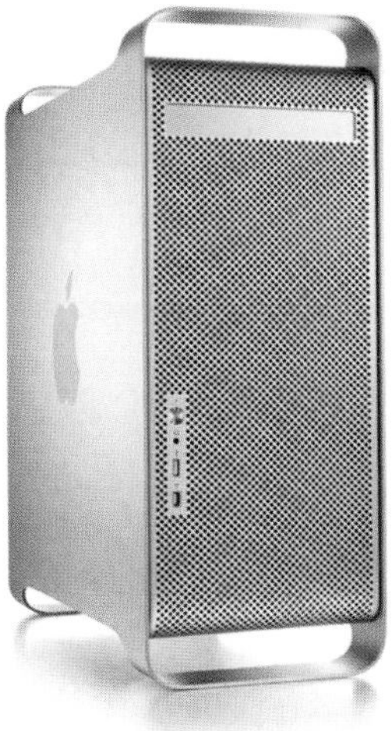

FIGURE 5B.7

The IBM/Apple G5 processor.

Norton Notebook

What *Is* a Computer Chip?

Throughout this book (and in any other information you read about computers), you see references to chips. Processors reside on chips, as do memory and other types of computer circuitry. But what does this mean? What is a computer chip?

To understand how chips work, you have to think small . . . very, very small. That's because the transistors, circuits, and connections that exist on a computer chip are so tiny that their dimensions are sometimes measured in terms of atoms rather than millimeters or inches.

Most computer chips are created on very thin wafers, which are made of nearly pure silicon. (Silicon is a mineral that is purified and refined for use in chips. It is used in many other products, too.) Some chips may be made from other materials, such as various types of plastic, but the chips commonly found in personal computers are silicon-based.

The Making of a Chip

Transistors and circuits exist as tiny channels on the surface of a chip, which means they must be carved out of the silicon. To do this, chip manufacturers use a process called photolithography to physically etch out the tiny grooves and notches that make up the chip's circuits. In the first step of this process, the silicon wafer's surface is covered with a gooey substance called photoresist, which is sensitive to certain types of light.

Next, a glass pattern (called a mask) is placed over the wafer. This pattern is marked with the precise lines where each transistor and circuit will lie on the chip's surface. The manufacturer then shines ultraviolet light through the pattern; the pattern's dark lines "mask" the silicon wafer from the light, protecting it. The exposed photoresist reacts to the light that touches it, softening the silicon beneath it. The exposed silicon is washed away, leaving a pattern of fine tracings on its surface.

The manufacturer then coats the wafer's surface with ions. This coating changes the way the silicon conducts electricity, making it more efficient at moving electrons through its circuits. (Moving electrons represent the binary 1s and 0s that make up data for the computer.) Because electrons are so small, the chip's circuitry can be very fine.

In the next step of the process, atoms of metal (such as aluminum or copper) are placed in the etched channels on

Comparing Processors

Most non–computer people only use the clock speed to compare two processors. This is a good comparison, but it is akin to comparing cars only by their top speed. There are many features of a car that are as important as rated speed. When comparing processors, many factors come into play. Larger cache and faster system bus speeds usually indicate more powerful processors. Table 5B.3 contrasts three powerful desktop processors.

TABLE 5B.3

CPUs' Performance Specifications

Specification	AMD Athlon 64 FX	Intel Pentium IV	PowerMac G5
Number of registers	16	16	80
Word size	64 bits	32 bits	64 bits
FrontSide or system bus speed	1.6 GHz	800 MHz	1 GHz
L1 cache	128 KB	na	na
L2 cache	1024 KB	512	512

the wafer's surface. These connections will conduct electrons as they move through the chip.

So Many Transistors, So Little Space

Today's manufacturing processes are so precise that they can squeeze millions of transistors onto a single chip not much larger than a person's thumbnail. One way to achieve this is by etching the chip's surface in separate layers, literally stacking sets of circuits on top of one another.

Another way is to place those circuits closer and closer together. Currently, chipmakers can place transistors so close that they are separated by less than a micron. (A micron is one-millionth of a meter.) Production technologies are constantly being refined. Today's popular PC processors contain tens of millions of transistors; in a few years, there may be as many as one billion transistors on a single processor chip.

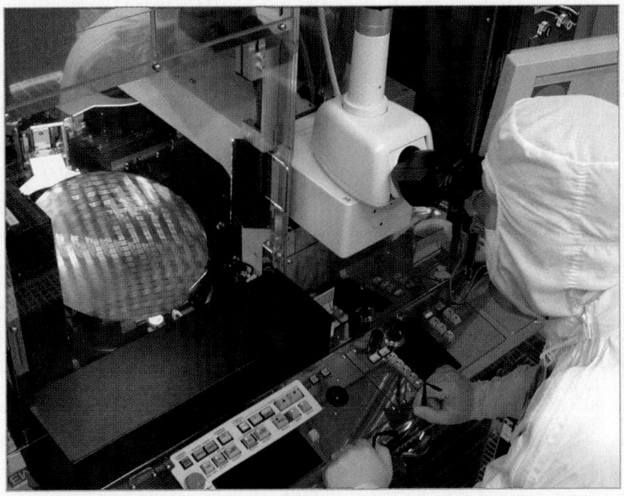

:: Chip designs are constantly evolving, making processors ever faster and more powerful.

NORTON NOTEBOOK

RISC Processors

The processors in IBM-compatible PCs are complex instruction set computing (CISC) processors. The instruction sets for these CPUs are large, typically containing 200 to 300 instructions.

Another theory in microprocessor design holds that if the instruction set for the CPU is kept small and simple, each instruction will execute in much less time, allowing the processor to complete more instructions during a given period. CPUs designed according to this theory are called reduced instruction set computing (RISC) processors. RISC instruction sets are considerably smaller than those used by CISC processors. The RISC design, which is used in the PowerPC processor but was first implemented in the mid-1980s, results in a faster and less expensive processor.

SELF-CHECK ::

Complete each statement by filling in the blanks.

1. The Itanium 2 processor has __________ transistors.
   - **a.** 45 million **b.** 105.9 million **c.** 410 million
2. The Athlon and Duron processors are made by ________.
   - **a.** Intel **b.** AMD **c.** Freescale
3. A joint effort of IBM, Freescale, and Apple produced the __________ processor.
   - **a.** G4 **b.** G5 **c.** G6

Parallel Processing

Another school of thought on producing faster computers is to build them with more than one processor. This type of system is said to be a multiprocessing (MP) system. The result is a system that can handle a much greater flow of data, complete more tasks in a shorter time, and deal with the demands of many input and output devices. A special form of MP that uses an even number of processors is symmetric multiprocessing (SMP). SMP's advantage is the number of processors is limited to a power of two. The limitation on the number of processors makes the systems easier to design.

Parallel processing is not a new idea in the minicomputer, mainframe, and supercomputer arenas. Manufacturers have developed computers with hundreds or even thousands of microprocessors— systems known as massively parallel processing (MPP) computers.

At the other end of the spectrum, multiple-processor versions of PCs are available today and are commonly used as network servers, Internet host computers, and stand-alone workstations. In fact, recent generations of standard PC microprocessors incorporate a measure of parallel processing by using pipelining techniques to execute more than one instruction at a time.

Norton ONLINE

For more information on parallel processing technologies, visit **http://www.mhhe.com/peternorton**.

simnet™

Extending the Processor's Power to Other Devices

You have already learned that all the components of a computer tie into the computer's CPU by way of the bus. When you need to add a new piece of hardware to your computer, you need to know how to connect it to the bus. In some cases, you can plug the device into an existing socket, or port, on the back of the computer. Most computers have several types of ports, each with different capabilities and uses. Older computers feature only three or four distinct types of ports, but new systems provide a wide array of specialized ports. When a port is not available, you need to install a circuit board that includes the port you need.

FIGURE 5B.8

Standard computer ports on modern computers.

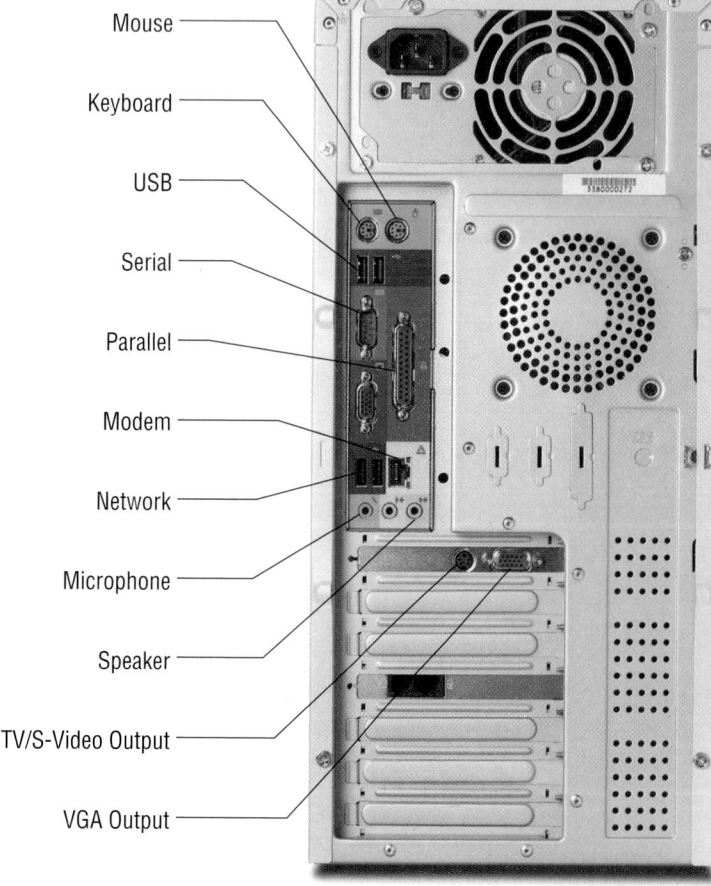

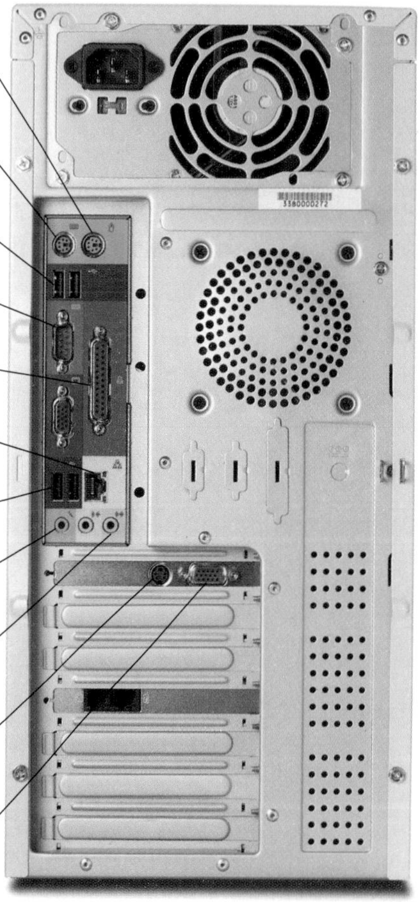

Standard Computer Ports

All modern computers come with the same basic set of ports. These allow you to connect common devices to your computer. Without these ports, your computer would not boot properly and if it did, you would be unable to interact with the software on the system.

Figure 5B.8 shows the back of a new computer. It contains several color-coded ports. At first glance, it can be overwhelming. However remember that most plugs only fit where they belong and a mistake is never catastrophic. The most commonly used ports are

- **Mouse and Keyboard Ports.** Accepts the keyboard and mouse plugs. The mouse is always the top port. If you make a mistake and plug the mouse into the keyboard port, the computer will not boot properly.
- **Two USB ports.** These accept any number of devices including cameras and joysticks.

- **Serial Port.** Serial ports are connected to external modems.
- **Parallel Port.** Most common uses are to connect older printers to the computer.
- **Audio Ports.** There are typically three audio ports on modern computers. The green speaker port is for your headphones or desktop speakers. The pink microphone port is for a small microphone. The yellow speaker out is designed for serious audiophiles to connect their computer to a home stereo system. Intense gamers or PC movie viewers may employ this option.
- **Network Port.** This port allows your computer to plug into a network or use a high-speed Internet connection. You will learn more about networking in Chapter 9, "Networks."
- **Modem Port.** It connects your computer to a phone line. The most common use for a modem is Internet access. You learned more about the Internet in Chapter 2, "Presenting the Internet."
- **Monitor Port.** Most monitors connect to the three-row port on the right side of the image. This can be found either by the serial port or with the expansion cards. Other monitor options may include connections to a TV.

Serial and Parallel Ports

A PC's internal components communicate through the data bus, which consists of parallel wires. Similarly, a parallel interface is a connection of eight or more wires through which data bits can flow simultaneously. Most computer buses transfer 32 bits simultaneously. However, the standard parallel interface for external devices such as printers usually transfers eight bits (one byte) at a time over eight separate wires.

With a serial interface, data bits are transmitted one at a time through a single wire (however, the interface includes additional wires for the bits that control the flow of data). Inside the computer, a chip called a universal asynchronous receiver-transmitter (UART) converts parallel data from the bus into serial data that flows through a serial cable. Figure 5B.9 shows how data flows through a nine-pin serial interface.

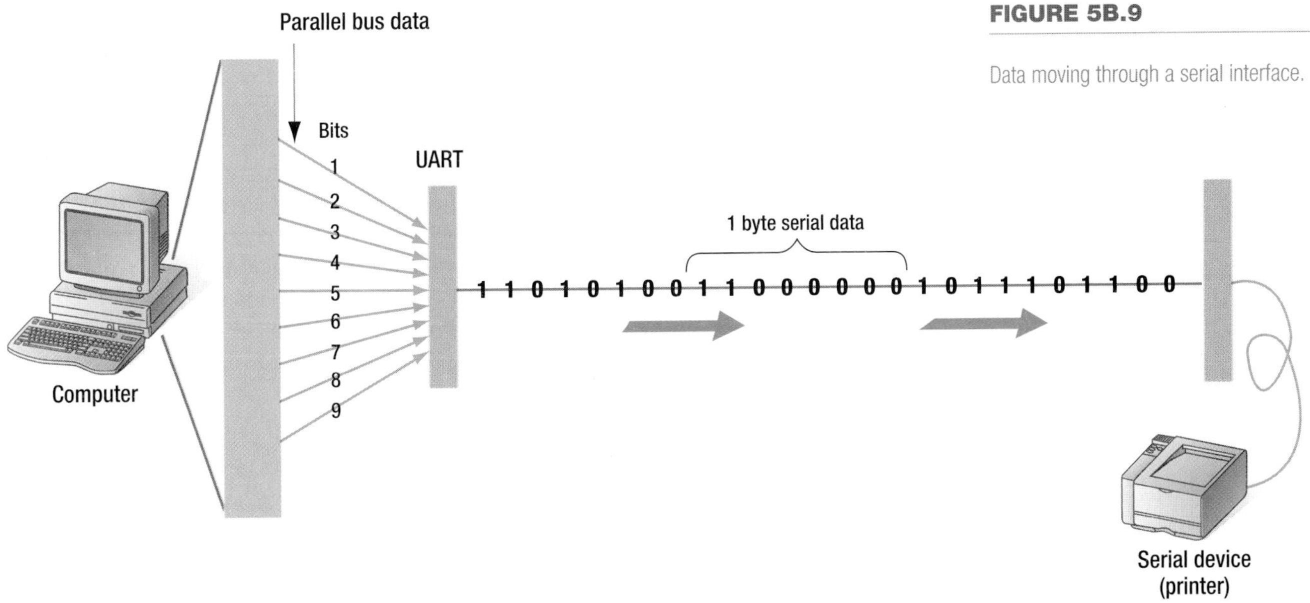

FIGURE 5B.9

Data moving through a serial interface.

FIGURE 5B.10

Data moving through a parallel interface.

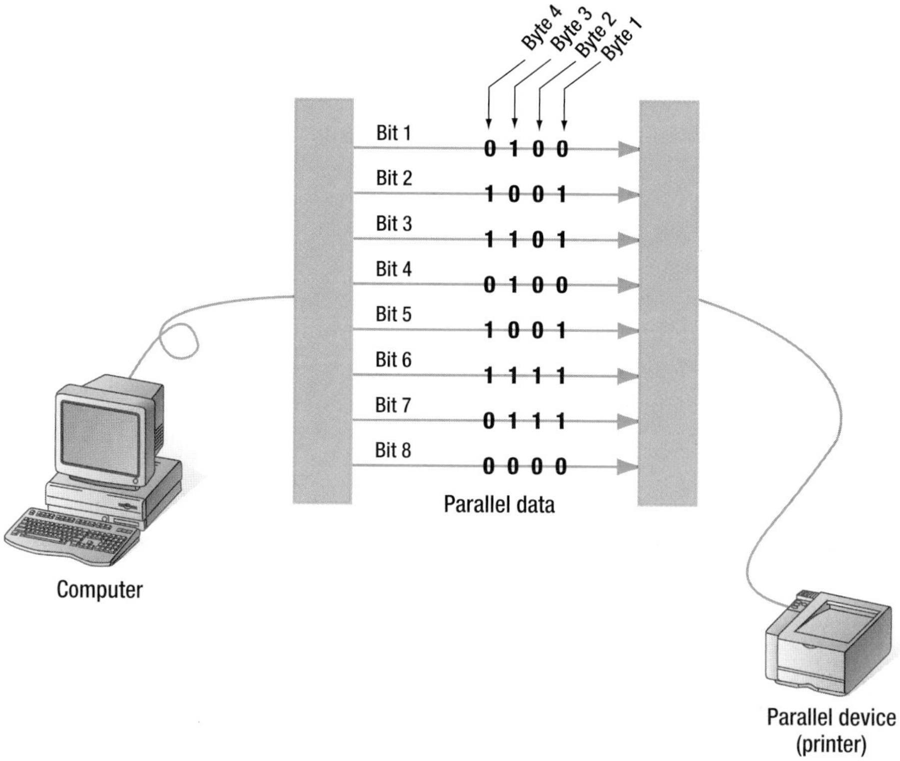

As you would expect, a parallel interface can handle a higher volume of data than a serial interface because more than one bit can be transmitted through a parallel interface simultaneously. Figure 5B.10 shows how data moves through a parallel interface.

Specialized Expansion Ports

In addition to the standard collection of expansion ports, many PCs include specialized ports. These ports allow the connection of special devices, which extend the computer's bus in unique ways.

SCSI

The Small Computer System Interface (SCSI, pronounced *scuzzy*) takes a different approach from standard parallel or serial ports. Instead of forcing the user to plug multiple cards into the computer's expansion slots, a single SCSI adapter extends the bus outside the computer by way of a cable. Thus, SCSI is like an extension cord for the data bus. Like plugging one extension cord into another to lengthen a circuit, you can plug one SCSI device into another to form a chain, as shown in Figure 5B.11. When devices are connected together this way and plugged into a single port, they are called a "daisy chain." Many devices use the SCSI interface. Fast, high-end hard disk drives often have SCSI interfaces, as do scanners, tape drives, and optical storage devices such as CD-ROM drives.

USB

The Universal Serial Bus (USB) has become the most popular external connection for PCs—both IBM-compatible and Macintosh systems. USB has several features that have led to its popularity. First, USB is a hot swappable bus. This means that users can switch USB devices without rebooting the PC. A second feature is its ease of use. Simply plugging the device in makes it ready to run. Finally, USB supports

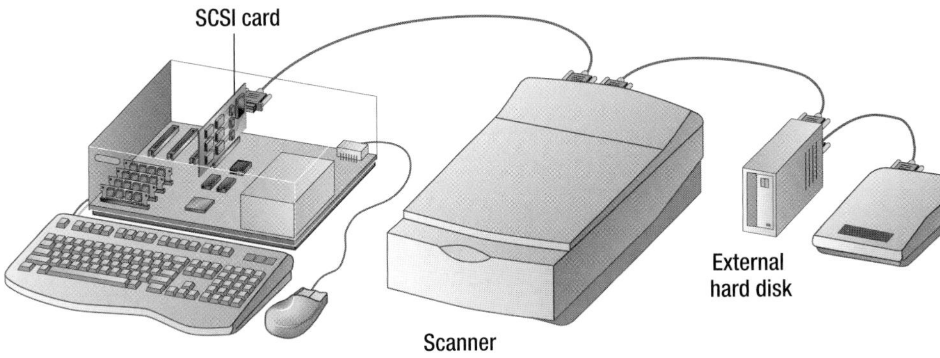

FIGURE 5B.11

SCSI peripherals daisy-chained together.

127 daisy-chained devices. Today, most new computers feature at least four USB ports, with two often in the front of the PC.

IEEE 1394 (FireWire)

Like the USB standard, the IEEE 1394 (FireWire) standard extends the computer's bus to many peripheral devices through a single port. Because IEEE 1394–compliant technology is so expensive, however, it is not expected to become the dominant bus technology, although it may gain wide acceptance as a standard for plugging video and other high-data-throughput devices to the system bus.

Musical Instrument Digital Interface (MIDI)

The Musical Instrument Digital Interface (MIDI) has been in use since the early 1980s, when a group of musical instrument manufacturers developed the technology to enable electronic musical instruments to communicate. Since then, MIDI has been adapted to the personal computer. Many sound cards are MIDI-compliant and feature a special MIDI port. Using a MIDI port, you can plug a wide variety of musical instruments and other MIDI-controlled devices into the computer. MIDI systems are widely used in recording and performing music to control settings for electronic synthesizers, drum machines, light systems, amplification, and more.

Norton ONLINE

For more information on SCSI, USB, FireWire, and MIDI technologies, visit **http://www.mhhe.com/peternorton**.

Expansion Slots and Boards

PCs are designed so that users can adapt, or configure, the machines to their own particular needs. PC motherboards have two or more empty expansion slots, which are extensions of the computer's bus that provide a way to add new components to the computer. The slots accept expansion boards, also called cards, adapters, or sometimes just boards. Figure 5B.12 shows a PC expansion board being installed. The board is being attached to the motherboard—the main system board to which the CPU, memory, and other components are attached.

Adapters that serve input and output purposes provide a port to which devices can be attached and act as translators between the bus and the device itself. Some adapters also do a significant amount of data processing. For example, a video controller

FIGURE 5B.12

An expansion board being inserted into an expansion slot.

Computers In Your Career

Computer Sales Professional

Computer-based phone systems were so revolutionary back in 1996 that few companies were interested in them. That reluctance made Mike Plumer's job as salesperson for AltiGen Communications, a Fremont, California, manufacturer of server-based phone systems, pretty challenging. "We were asking companies to buy something that they didn't even know existed," recalls Plumer, the firm's senior director of sales.

Plumer worked through the early challenges by finding other sales reps with a good mix of technical and business knowledge to join him, and by "knocking on a lot of companies' doors" to find those that were willing to purchase AltiGen's innovative products.

As with any new technology, AltiGen's products didn't stay unique for long as other companies began producing server-based systems. A public relations major who graduated from Iowa State University, Plumer continues to handle sales for the company while also overseeing its 14-person worldwide sales force. His day typically starts with a commute to work—time he uses to plan out the day ahead. Upon arriving at the office, he makes calls to his field sales reps and managers for a "status check."

In addition to selling and overseeing AltiGen's sales force, Plumer also handles myriad other tasks. When telecommunications companies are visiting for on-site sales training, for example, he may conduct a one-hour presentation on Voice over IP and networking. Such diversions keep the job interesting, says Plumer, who enjoys selling systems that range in price from $20,000 to $150,000.

"These sales require interaction not only with a company's tech personnel, but also with top decision makers," says Plumer. "You must be able to relate to people at the decision-making level while also displaying the technical aptitude needed to help them make those decisions." He sees future sales opportunities in the IT field as "very good," based on the fact that all high-tech companies rely on productive salespeople to push their products out to the masses.

Computer sales professionals like Plumer sell a wide variety of products and services. Here are just a few:

» **PC Hardware Sales.** This field includes personal computers—desktops, portables, network servers, network computers, and handheld computers.

is a card that provides a port on the back of the PC into which you can plug the monitor. It also contains and manages the video memory and does the processing required to display images on the monitor. Similar devices include sound cards, internal modems or fax/modems, and network interface cards.

PC Cards

Another type of expansion card is the PC Card (initially called a Personal Computer Memory Card International Association, or PCMCIA, card). It is a small device about the size of a credit card (see Figure 5B.13). This device was designed initially for use in notebook computers and other computers that are too small to accept a standard expansion card. A PC Card fits into a slot on the back or side of the notebook computer. PC Card adapters are also available for desktop computers, enabling them to accept PC Cards. Even some types of digital cameras accept PC Cards that store digital photographs. PC Cards are used for a wide variety of purposes and can house modems, network cards, memory, and even fully functioning hard disk drives.

FIGURE 5B.13

Small PC Card devices provide memory, storage, communications, and other capabilities.

- **Enterprise Hardware Sales.** The term *enterprise* usually means "big company," and big companies often have specialized, high-level computing needs.
- **Specialty Hardware Sales.** Nearly every kind of organization has some type of specialized hardware need, such as high-output color printers, storage subsystems, backup systems, and other peripherals.
- **Telecommunications Sales.** Telecommunications and computer technologies go hand in hand, and today's businesses are hungry for both.
- **Software Sales.** This industry extends beyond sales of operating systems and word processors; enterprise software includes massive database systems, network management software, data-mining tools, and other powerful and expensive packages.

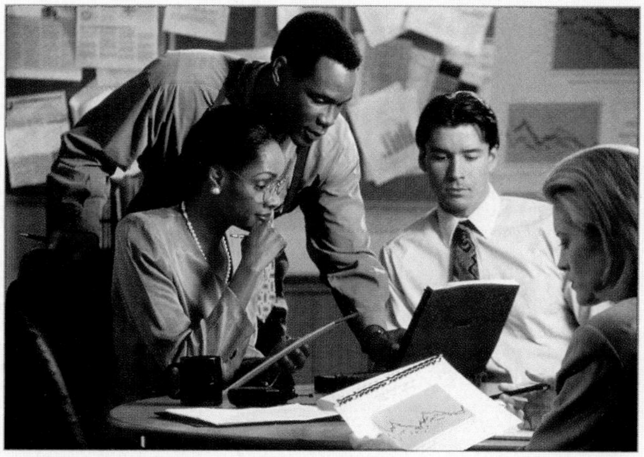

Sales professionals are compensated in different ways, including straight salary, commissions, bonuses, profit sharing, stock options, and other rewards. According to the Bureau of Labor Statistics, *Occupational Outlook Handbook, 2004–05 Edition*, the median annual earnings of sales representatives in the computer and data processing services field were $55,740. In addition to their earnings, sales representatives are usually reimbursed for expenses such as transportation costs, meals, hotels, and entertaining customers.

There are three categories of PC Card technologies: Type I, Type II, and Type III. The different types are typically defined by purpose. For example, Type I cards usually contain memory, Type II cards are used for network adapters, and Type III cards usually house tiny hard drives. Type I PC Cards are the thinnest available and have the fewest uses. Type III cards are the thickest and enable developers to fit disk storage devices into the card-size shell. Some PC Card adapters can hold multiple cards, greatly expanding the capabilities of the small computer.

Plug and Play

With the introduction of Windows 95, Intel-based PCs began supporting the Plug and Play standard, making it easier to install hardware via an existing port or expansion slot. Using hardware that complies with Windows' Plug and Play standard, the operating system can detect a new component automatically, check for existing driver programs that will run the new device, and load necessary files. In some cases, Windows will prompt you to install the needed files from a disk. Depending on how the new device is connected, this process may require restarting the system for the new hardware's settings to take effect. Still, this process is much simpler than the one required prior to Plug and Play technology, which usually forced the user to manually resolve conflicts between the new hardware and other components.

Norton ONLINE

For more information on Plug and Play, visit **http://www.mhhe.com/peternorton**.

LESSON // 5B Review

Summary ::

- A processor's architecture, or internal design, dictates its function and performance.
- A key to a processor's performance is the number of transistors it contains. Chip designers constantly look for new ways to place more transistors on microprocessor chips. Today's PC processors contain tens of millions of processors.
- Intel manufactured the processors used in the first IBM personal computers. Today, Intel's most popular PC processors are the Pentium 4, Pentium III Xeon, Pentium III, and Celeron. A newer Intel processor, the Itanium, is a 64-bit processor used in high-performance workstations and network servers.
- Advanced Micro Devices (AMD), which initially made lower-performance processors for low-cost PCs, now manufactures high-performance processors that compete directly with Intel. AMD's most popular PC processors are the Athlon and Duron.
- Freescale manufactured processors used in Apple's older Macintosh computers; its most popular processors are in the PowerPC family. Freescale also makes processors for other types of computing devices, such as minicomputers and workstations.
- IBM manufactures processors used in a variety of environments. IBM processors can be found in many models of mainframes. More recently IBM teamed with Freescale and Apple to develop the G5 processor.
- Most of the processors used in personal computers are based on complex instruction set computing (CISC) technology. PowerPC processors, and processors used in many other types of computers, are based on reduced instruction set computing (RISC) technology. Because they contain a smaller instruction set, RISC processors can run faster than CISC processors.
- A parallel processing system harnesses the power of multiple processors in a single system, enabling them to share processing tasks. In a massively parallel processor (MPP) system, many processors are used. Some MPP systems use thousands of processors at one time.
- External devices, such as those used for input and output, are connected to the system by ports on the back or front of the computer.
- Most computers come with a serial port and a parallel port. A serial port transmits one bit of data at a time; a parallel port transmits one byte (eight bits) of data at a time.
- If the computer does not have the right type of port for an external device (or if all the existing ports are in use), an expansion board can be installed into one of the PC's empty expansion slots.
- Bus technologies such as Small Computer System Interface (SCSI), Universal Serial Bus (USB), and IEEE 1394 (FireWire) enable the user to connect many devices through a single port.

Key Terms ::

adapter, 215
Advanced Micro Devices (AMD), 208
architecture, 207
board, 215
card, 215
complex instruction set computing (CISC), 211
configure, 215
expansion board, 215
expansion slot, 215
Freescale, 209
IBM, 209
Intel, 208
massively parallel processing (MPP), 212
multiprocessing (MP), 211
Musical Instrument Digital Interface (MIDI), 215
parallel interface, 213
Plug and Play, 217
reduced instruction set computing (RISC), 211
serial interface, 213
Small Computer System Interface (SCSI), 214
symmetric multiprocessing (SMP), 212
universal asynchronous receiver-transmitter (UART), 213

Key Term Quiz ::

Complete each statement by writing one of the terms listed under Key Terms in each blank.

1. A processor's internal design is called its ____________ .
2. ____________ and ____________ are the leading manufacturers of processors for IBM-compatible personal computers.
3. When you ____________ a PC, you are adapting it to best meet your needs.
4. With a(n) ____________ interface, data bits are transmitted one at a time through a single wire.
5. The ____________ enables electronic instruments and computers to communicate with one another.
6. The ____________ allows devices to be connected in a daisy chain.
7. ____________ ports can transmit eight bytes at a time.
8. In ____________ processors, the instruction sets are large, typically containing 200–300 instructions.
9. An expansion ____________ is plugged into a computer to provide additional connectivity or functionality.
10. A system that employs an even number of processors is said to use ____________ .

LESSON //5B Review

Multiple Choice ::

Circle the word or phrase that best completes each statement.

1. A computer system that uses a smaller instruction set is said to use ____________ technology.
   a. parallel processing b. RISC c. cache d. Zip
2. FireWire is another name for the ____________ interface.
   a. parallel b. IEEE 1394 c. MIDI d. USB
3. The ____________ processor is used in Apple's Macintosh computers.
   a. Celeron b. Athlon c. ThinkPad d. PowerPC
4. The more ____________ a processor has, the more powerful it is.
   a. microns b. transistors c. connections d. neurons
5. The instruction set for a ____________ processor usually contains 200 to 300 instructions.
   a. CISC b. SMP c. RISC d. IBM
6. You can connect an electronic instrument to your computer via the ____________ port.
   a. PS2 b. USB c. HDX d. MIDI
7. Older printers are likely to be connected through the ____________ interface.
   a. COM b. parallel c. modem d. network
8. Your phone line is connected to the ____________ on your computer.
   a. PS2 b. USB c. modem d. network
9. The green audio port is used to connect your ____________ .
   a. microphone b. speaker c. stereo d. guitar
10. Which of the following cannot be the number of processors in an SMP system?
    a. 4 b. 6 c. 8 d. 16

Review Questions ::

In your own words, briefly answer the following questions.

1. Describe the purpose of expansion slots in a PC.
2. What is the primary difference between a RISC processor and a CISC processor?
3. Why is a processor's architecture important?
4. What are the advantages of parallel processing?
5. What is the purpose of the UART?
6. Name the five processors currently available from Intel Corporation.
7. Name the five processors currently available from AMD.
8. The AMD Athlon 64 FX, the Intel Pentium 4, and the PowerMac G5 are the most powerful processors currently in use in PCs. What are the word sizes of these three processors?
9. Why can it be said that recent-generation PCs incorporate a measure of parallel processing, even though they have only one processor?
10. What is a "daisy chain"?

Lesson Labs ::

Complete the following exercise as directed by your instructor.

1. To view information about your computer's components, follow these steps:
   a. Open the Control Panel window. (The steps for opening the Control Panel vary, depending on the version of Windows you use. If you need help, ask your instructor.) In the Control Panel window, double-click the System icon.
   b. In the System Properties dialog box, select the Hardware tab and then open the Device Manager window to view the list of categories of devices attached to your system. If a category is preceded by a plus sign (+), click this symbol to display all the devices in that category.
   c. To read about a device, right-click its name, and then click Properties. A dialog box will appear displaying information about the selected device. *Warning*: Do not make any changes.
   d. Review the properties for your system's disk drives, ports, and system devices.
   e. Close any open windows or dialog boxes; then close the Control Panel window.

Chapter Labs

Complete the following exercises using a computer in your classroom, lab, or home.

1. Plug it in. With your instructor observing, turn your computer and monitor off and unplug them from their power source. Then take these steps:
   a. Move to the back of the computer and inspect all the cables plugged into it. Which devices are connected to the PC and by which cables? Which port is connected to each device? Make a chart of these connections.
   b. Unplug each connection. After all students have unplugged their devices for their computers, switch places with someone and reconnect all the devices to the computer. Does the other student's system have the same connections as yours? If not, can you reconnect all its devices correctly?
   c. Return to your PC. Use your chart to see whether your system has been reconnected correctly. If not, correct any connecting errors. When you are sure all devices are plugged into the right ports, reconnect the PC and monitor to the power source. Turn the PC on and make sure everything is working correctly.
2. Watch those files grow. The concept of bits and bytes may seem unimportant until you begin creating files on your computer. Then you can begin to understand how much memory and storage space your files take up (in bytes, of course). Create a file in Notepad, save it to disk, and take the following steps to add to the file to see how it grows:
   a. Launch Notepad. The steps to launch the program vary, depending on which version of Windows you use. If you need help, ask your instructor for directions.
   b. Type two or three short paragraphs of text. When you are done, click the File menu, and then click the Save As command.
   c. In the Save As dialog box, choose a drive and folder in which to save the new file, and give the file a short name you can remember easily, such as SIZE-TEST.TXT.
   d. With Notepad running, launch Windows Explorer. If you need help, ask your instructor for directions.
   e. Navigate to the drive and folder where you saved your Notepad file. When you find the file, look for its size in the Size column and write down the size. Close the Exploring window.
   f. Return to the Notepad window and add two or three more paragraphs of text. Then click the File menu and click the Save command to resave the file under the same name.
   g. Reopen Windows Explorer and look at the file's size again. Has it changed? By how much?
3. Learn more about Unicode. The Unicode text code system will become universally accepted in the next few years. All operating systems, application programs, data, and hardware architectures have started to conform to it. For this reason, learn as much as you can about Unicode and how it may affect your computing in the future. Visit the Unicode Consortium Web site: http://www.unicode.org.

Discussion Questions

As directed by your instructor, discuss the following questions in class or in groups.

1. Do you think the international interchange of data provided by the Unicode character set is a worthwhile goal for computing technology? Do you see any other benefits to Unicode's widespread implementation?
2. Why is the CPU commonly referred to as the computer's "brain"? Do you think it is a good idea to use this term to describe the CPU? Why?

Research and Report

Using your own choice of resources (such as the Internet, books, magazines, and newspaper articles), research and write a short paper discussing one of the following topics:

- The history of the Pentium family of processors.
- The uses of parallel processing computer systems in business.
- The USB and FireWire bus standards, and their possible impact on computers of the future.

When you are finished, proofread and print your paper, and give it to your instructor.

ETHICAL ISSUES

Computers are becoming more powerful all the time. Many people see this capability as a source of limitless benefits, but others view it as a threat. With this thought in mind, discuss the following questions in class.

1. As technology improves, processing becomes faster. It can be argued that computer technology has made Americans less patient than they were a decade ago. Do you agree? If so, do you see it as a benefit of our technological progress or a drawback? Should we restrain our urge to increase the pace of life? Be prepared to explain your position.
2. Computers are not only getting faster, but they also are becoming exponentially more powerful all the time. For example, many think that in the next decade artificial intelligence will be developed to the point that computers can begin reasoning—weighing facts, solving problems, perhaps even making decisions. Will people relinquish even a tiny bit of control to computers? If so, what kinds of decisions will we allow them to make for us? What risks do we run by enabling computers to become "smart" enough to solve problems or ultimately to think?

CHAPTER 6 Storing Data

CHAPTER CONTENTS ::

This chapter contains the following lessons:

Types of Storage Devices

Overview: An Ever-Growing Need

The earliest personal computers provided very little space for storing data. Some PCs did not feature disk drives at all. Instead, they stored programs and data on standard audio cassette tapes. Some PCs featured one or two floppy disk drives, but no hard disks. When the earliest PC hard disks came on the scene, they stored only 10 MB of data. Still, compared to a floppy disk (which then had a capacity of only 512 KB), 10 MB seemed like an infinite amount of space.

By contrast, even today's lowest-cost PCs feature hard disks with capacities of 40 GB, 80 GB, or more. You can easily find a hard drive that holds 180 GB of data for less than $200. Just as important, these large drives can transfer data at amazing speeds, and many are external—meaning they can connect to any computer via a USB or FireWire port.

In addition to floppy disks and hard drives, today's computer user can choose from a wide range of storage devices, from "key ring" devices that store hundreds of megabytes to digital video discs, which make it easy to transfer several gigabytes of data.

This lesson examines the primary types of storage found in today's personal computers. You'll learn how each type of storage device stores and manages data.

OBJECTIVES ::

- List four types of magnetic storage media commonly used with PCs.
- Explain how data is stored on the surface of a magnetic disk.
- List seven types of optical storage devices that can be used with PCs.
- Explain how data is stored on the surface of an optical disc.
- Name three types of solid-state storage devices.

Norton ONLINE

For more information on types of storage devices used in personal computers, visit **http://www.mhhe.com/peternorton**.

simnet™

Categorizing Storage Devices

The purpose of a storage device is to hold data—even when the computer is turned off—so the data can be used whenever it is needed. Storage involves two processes:

- Writing, or recording, the data so it can be found later for use.
- Reading the stored data, then transferring it into the computer's memory.

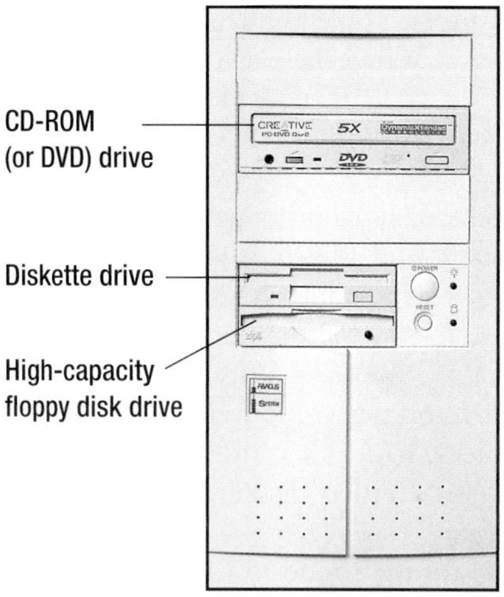

FIGURE 6A.1

Common storage devices found in today's PCs.

The physical materials on which data is stored are called storage media. The hardware components that write data to, and read data from, storage media are called storage devices (see Figure 6A.1). For example, a diskette is a storage medium (*medium* is the singular form of the word *media*); a diskette drive is a storage device.

The two main categories of storage technology used today are magnetic storage and optical storage. Although most storage devices and media employ one technology or the other, some use both. A third category of storage—solid-state storage—is increasingly being used in computer systems, but is more commonly found in devices such as digital cameras and media players.

Nearly every new PC comes with a diskette drive and a built-in hard disk, as shown in Figure 6A.1. Some PC makers now sell computers without built-in diskette drives, although they can be added to the system. Most new PCs also have a CD-ROM or DVD-ROM drive. For a little more expense, many consumers replace the optical drive with one that will let them record data onto an optical disc. A built-in drive for removable high-capacity floppy disks is another common feature in new PCs.

Magnetic Storage Devices

Norton ONLINE

For more information on magnetic storage devices and their operation, visit **http://www.mhhe.com/peternorton**.

simnet™

Because they all use the same medium (the material on which the data is stored), diskette drives, hard disk drives, high-capacity floppy disk drives, and tape drives use similar techniques for writing and reading data. The surfaces of diskettes, hard disks, high-capacity floppy disks, and magnetic tape are coated with a magnetically sensitive material, such as iron oxide, that reacts to a magnetic field (see Figure 6A.2).

Diskettes contain a single thin disk, usually made of plastic. This disk is flexible, which is why diskettes are often called floppy disks. A diskette stores data on both sides of its disk (numbered as side 0 and side 1), and each side has its own read/write head. High-capacity floppy disks contain a single disk, too, but their formatting enables them to store much more data than a normal floppy disk, as you will see later. Hard disks usually contain multiple disks, which are called platters because they are made of a rigid material such as aluminum.

How Data Is Stored on a Disk

You may remember from science projects that one magnet can be used to make another. For example, you can make a magnet by taking an iron bar and stroking it in one direction with a magnet. The iron bar becomes a magnet itself, because its iron molecules align themselves in one direction. Thus, the iron bar becomes polarized; that is, its ends have opposite magnetic polarity.

You also can create a magnet by using electrical current to polarize a piece of iron, as shown in Figure 6A.3. The process results in an electromagnet; you can control the polarity and strength of an electromagnet by changing the direction and strength of the current.

Magnetic storage devices use a similar principle to store data. Just as a transistor can represent binary data as "on" or "off," the orientation of a magnetic field can be used to represent data. A magnet has one important advantage over a transistor: that is, it can represent "on" and "off" without a continual source of electricity.

The surfaces of magnetic disks and tapes are coated with millions of tiny iron particles so that data can be stored on them. Each of these particles can act as a magnet, taking on a magnetic field when subjected to an electromagnet. The read/write heads of a magnetic disk or tape drive contain electromagnets that generate magnetic fields in the iron on the storage medium as the head passes over the disk or tape. As shown in Figure 6A.4, the read/write heads record strings of 1s and 0s by alternating the direction of the current in the electromagnets.

To read data from a magnetic surface, the process is reversed. The read/write head passes over the disk or tape while no current is flowing through the electromagnet. The head possesses no charge, but the storage medium is covered with magnetic fields, which represent bits of data. The storage medium charges the magnet in the head, which causes a small current to flow through the head in one direction or the other, depending on the field's polarity. The disk or tape drive

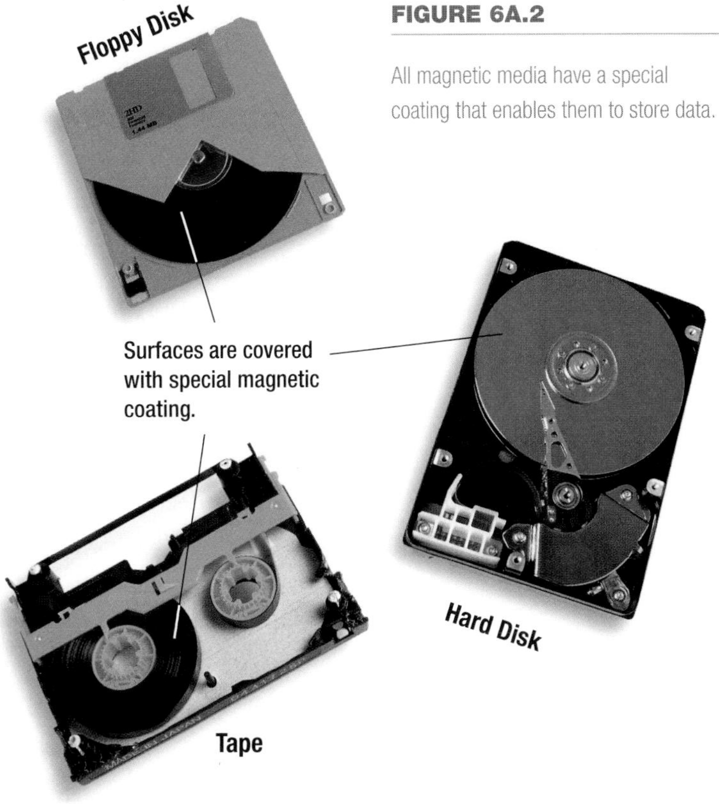

Surfaces are covered with special magnetic coating.

FIGURE 6A.2

All magnetic media have a special coating that enables them to store data.

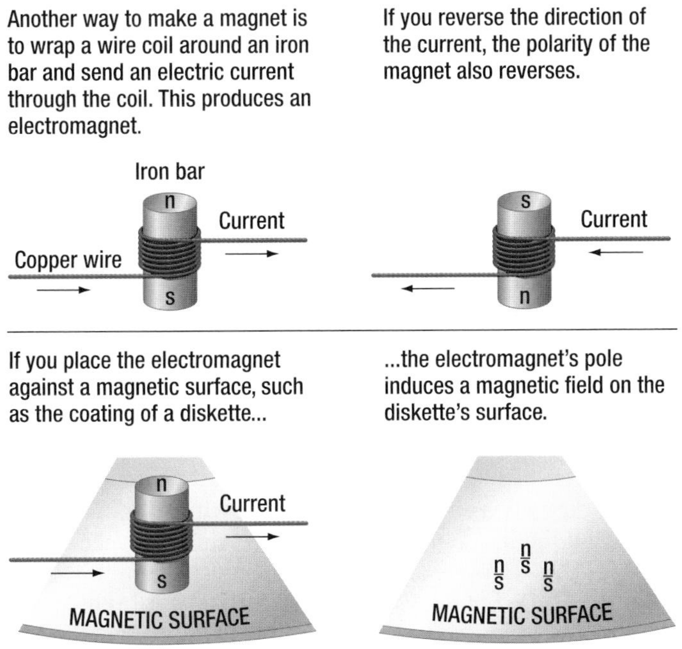

Another way to make a magnet is to wrap a wire coil around an iron bar and send an electric current through the coil. This produces an electromagnet.
If you reverse the direction of the current, the polarity of the magnet also reverses.
Iron bar
n
Current
Copper wire
s
s
Current
n
If you place the electromagnet against a magnetic surface, such as the coating of a diskette...
...the electromagnet's pole induces a magnetic field on the diskette's surface.
n
Current
s
MAGNETIC SURFACE
n
s
n
s
n
s
MAGNETIC SURFACE

FIGURE 6A.3

How an electromagnet creates a field on a magnetic surface.

FIGURE 6A.4

A read/write head recording data on the surface of a magnetic disk.

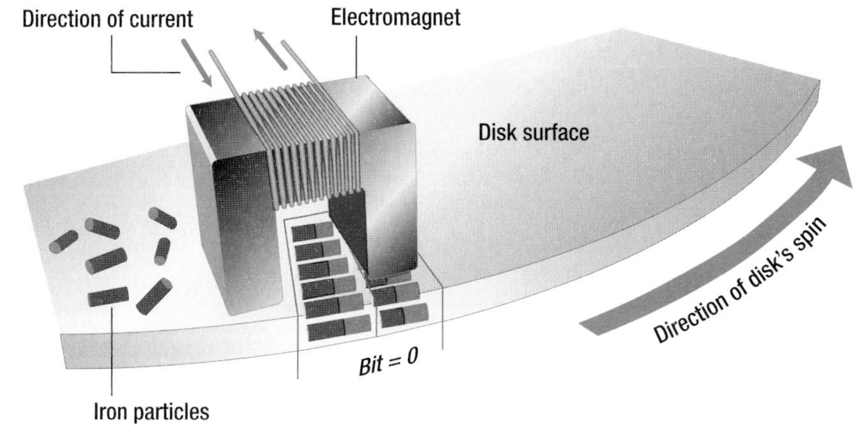

senses the direction of the flow as the storage medium passes by the head, and the data is sent from the read/write head into memory.

How Data is Organized on a Magnetic Disk

Before the computer can use a magnetic disk to store data, the disk's surface must be magnetically mapped so that the computer can go directly to a specific point on it without searching through data. (Because a magnetic disk drive's heads can go directly to any point on the disk's surface to read or write data, magnetic storage devices are also categorized as random access storage devices.) The process of mapping a disk is called formatting or initializing.

When you purchase new diskettes or high-capacity floppy disks, they should already be formatted and ready to use with your computer. In a new computer, the built-in hard disk is almost always already formatted and has software installed on it. If you buy a new hard disk by itself, however, you may need to format it yourself, but this is not difficult to do.

You may find it helpful to reformat diskettes from time to time, because the process ensures that all existing data is deleted from the disk. During the formatting process, you can determine whether the disk's surface has faulty spots, and you can copy important system files to the disk. You can format a floppy disk by using operating system commands (see Figure 6A.5).

Norton ONLINE

For more information on formatting disks, visit **http://www.mhhe.com/peternorton**.

FIGURE 6A.5

Formatting a diskette and a Zip disk (a high-capacity floppy disk).

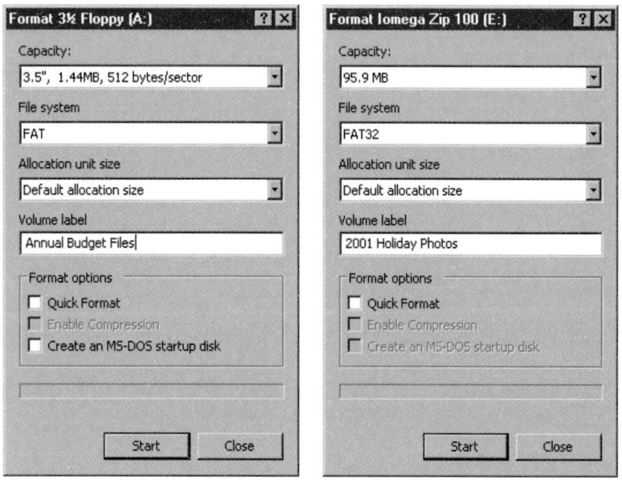

Tracks and Sectors

When you format a magnetic disk, the disk drive creates a set of concentric rings, called tracks, on each side of the disk. The number of tracks required depends on the type of disk. Most diskettes have 80 tracks on each side of the disk. A hard disk may have several hundred tracks on each side of each platter. Each track is a separate circle, like the circles on a bull's-eye target. The tracks are numbered from the outermost circle to the innermost, starting with 0, as shown in Figure 6A.6.

In the next stage of formatting, the tracks are divided into smaller parts. Imagine slicing a disk the way you slice a pie. As shown in Figure 6A.7, each slice would cut across all the disk's tracks, resulting in short segments called sectors. Sectors are where data is physically stored on the disk. In all diskettes and most hard disks, a sector can store up to 512 bytes (0.5 KB). All the sectors on a disk

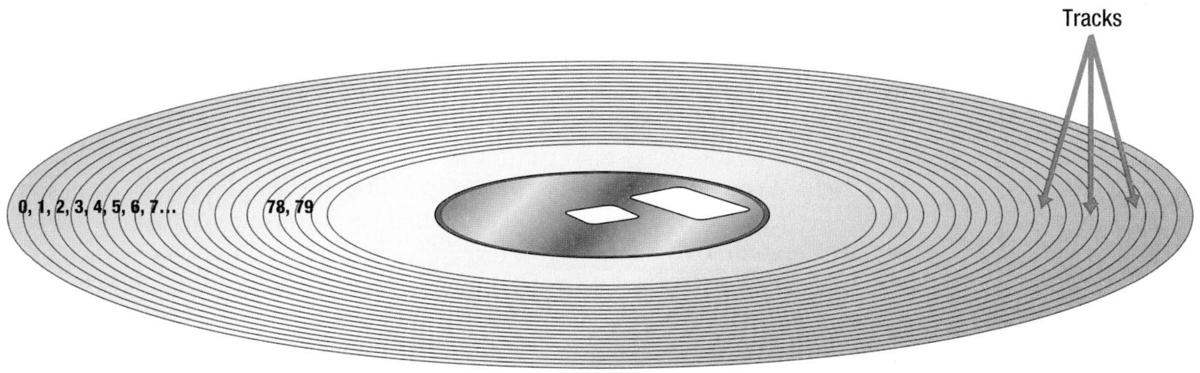

FIGURE 6A.6

Tracks are concentric circles on a disk's surface.

are numbered in one long sequence, so that the computer can access each small area on the disk by using a unique number.

A sector is the smallest unit with which any magnetic disk drive can work; the drive can read or write only whole sectors at a time. If the computer needs to change just one byte out of 512, it must rewrite the entire sector.

If a diskette has 80 tracks on each side, and each track contains 18 sectors, then the disk has 1,440 sectors (80×18) per side, for a total of 2,880 sectors. This configuration is true regardless of the length of the track. The disk's outermost track is longer than the innermost track, but each track is still divided into the same number of sectors. Regardless of physical size, all of a diskette's sectors hold the same number of bytes; that is, the shortest, innermost sectors hold the same amount of data as the longest, outermost sectors.

Of course, a disk's allocation of sectors per track is somewhat wasteful, because the longer outer tracks could theoretically store more data than the shorter inner tracks. For this reason, most hard disks allocate more sectors to the longer tracks on the disk's surface. As you move toward the hard disk's center, each subsequent track has fewer sectors. This arrangement takes advantage of the hard disk's potential capacity and enables a typical hard disk to store data more efficiently than a floppy disk. Because many hard disks allocate sectors in this manner, their sectors-per-track specification is often given as an average. Such hard disks are described as having "an average of *x* sectors per track."

As you will learn in Chapter 7, "Using Operating Systems," the computer's operating system (sometimes with help from utility programs) is responsible for managing all disk operations in a computer. It is up to the operating system to determine the precise locations where files are stored on the surface of a disk.

FIGURE 6A.7

Sectors on a disk, each with a unique number.

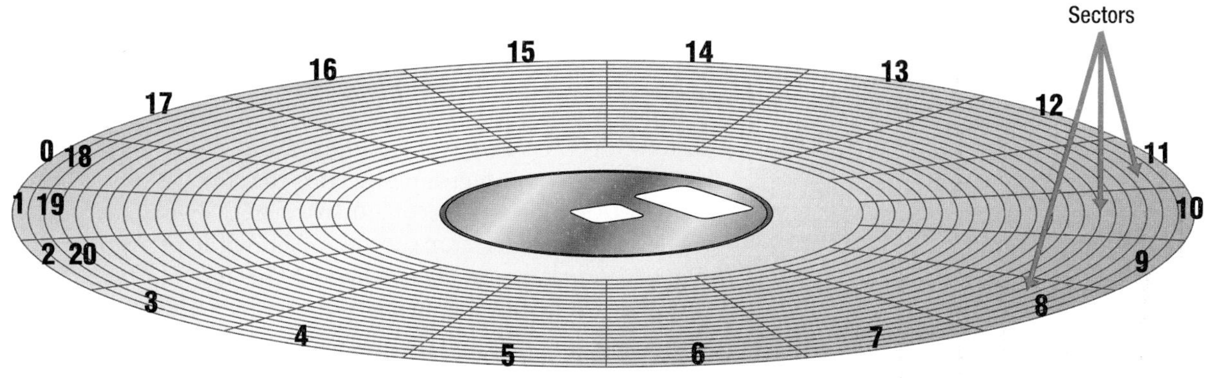

Norton ONLINE

For more information on file systems, visit **http://www.mhhe.com/peternorton**.

How the Operating System Finds Data on a Disk

A computer's operating system can locate data on a disk because each track and each sector are labeled, and the location of all data is kept in a special log on the disk. The labeling of tracks and sectors is called logical formatting.

Different operating systems can format disks in different ways. Each formatting method configures the disk's surface in a different manner, resulting in a different file system—a logical method for managing the storage of data on a disk's surface. A commonly used logical format performed by Windows is called the FAT file system because it relies on a standardized file allocation table (FAT) to keep track of file locations on the disk.

When a diskette is formatted with the FAT file system, four areas are created on the disk.

- The boot sector contains a program that runs when you first start the computer. This program determines whether the disk has the basic components that are necessary to run the operating system successfully. If the program determines that the required files are present and the disk has a valid format, it transfers control to one of the operating system programs that continues the process of starting up. This process is called booting, because the boot program makes the computer "pull itself up by its own bootstraps." The boot sector also contains information that describes other disk characteristics, such as the number of bytes per sector and the number of sectors per track—information that the operating system needs to access data on the disk.
- The file allocation table (FAT) is a log that records the location of each file and the status of each sector. When you write a file to a disk, the operating system checks the FAT to find an open area, stores the file, and then logs the file's identity and its location in the FAT. When a program needs to locate data on the disk, the operating system checks the FAT to see where that data is stored. During formatting, two copies of the FAT are created; both copies are always maintained to keep their information current.
- The root folder is the "master folder" on any disk. A folder (also called a directory) is a tool for organizing files on a disk. Folders can contain files or other folders, so it is possible to set up a hierarchical system of folders on your computer, just as you can have folders within other folders in a file cabinet. The topmost folder is known as the *root*, but may also be called the *root folder* or *root directory*. This is the folder that holds all the information about all the other folders on the disk. When you use the operating system to view the contents of a folder, the operating system lists specific information about each file in the folder, such as the file's name, its size, the time and date that it was created or last modified, and so on. Figure 6A.8 shows a typical folder listing on a Windows XP system.
- The data area is the part of the disk that remains free after the boot sector, the FAT, and the root folder have been created. This is where data and program files are actually stored on the disk.

FIGURE 6A.8

A folder listing in Windows XP.

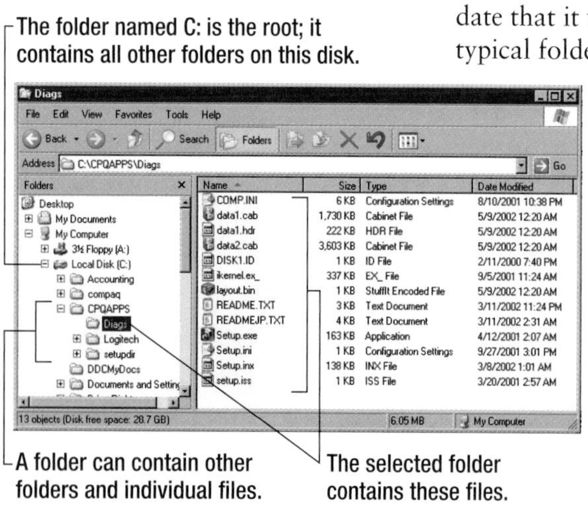
The folder named C: is the root; it contains all other folders on this disk.
A folder can contain other folders and individual files.
The selected folder contains these files.

During logical formatting, the operating system also groups sectors together, into storage units called clusters. A cluster, therefore, is simply a group of sectors that the OS sees as a single unit. A cluster is the smallest space an OS will allocate to a single file, and a cluster may store an entire file or just part of a file. Cluster sizes vary, depending on the size and type of the disk, but they can range from four sectors for diskettes to 64 sectors for some hard disks. Cluster usage is tracked in the file allocation table.

In the example shown earlier, you saw the results of formatting a floppy disk on a computer using the FAT file system. Different operating systems use different file systems:

- **File Allocation Table (FAT).** This file system, which is also known as FAT16, was used in MS-DOS and was the basis for the early Windows operating systems. In fact, all versions of Windows support FAT, although it is no longer the preferred file system; newer file systems offer better security and greater flexibility in managing files.
- **FAT32.** Introduced in Windows 95, FAT32 is an extended edition of the original FAT file system, providing better performance than FAT. It continues to be supported in Windows 2000 and Windows XP.
- **New Technology File System (NTFS).** Introduced with Windows NT and the basis for later operating systems, NTFS was a leap forward from FAT, offering better security and overall performance. NTFS also allowed Windows computers to use long file names (file names longer than eight characters) for the first time.
- **NTFS 5.** This updated version of NTFS is used in Windows 2000 and XP.
- **High-Performance File System (HPFS).** This was designed for use with IBM's OS/2.

Other operating systems (such as UNIX), and even some network operating systems (such as Novell NetWare), use their own file systems. Although each file system has different features and capabilities, they all perform the same basic tasks and enable a computer's disks and operating system to store and manage data efficiently.

Norton ONLINE

For more information on floppy disks, visit **http://www.mhhe.com/peternorton**.

Diskettes (Floppy Disks)

Figure 6A.9 shows a diskette and a diskette drive. The drive includes a motor that rotates the disk on a spindle and read/write heads that can move to any spot on the disk's surface as the disk spins. The heads can skip from one spot to another on the disk's surface to find any piece of data without having to scan through all of the data in between.

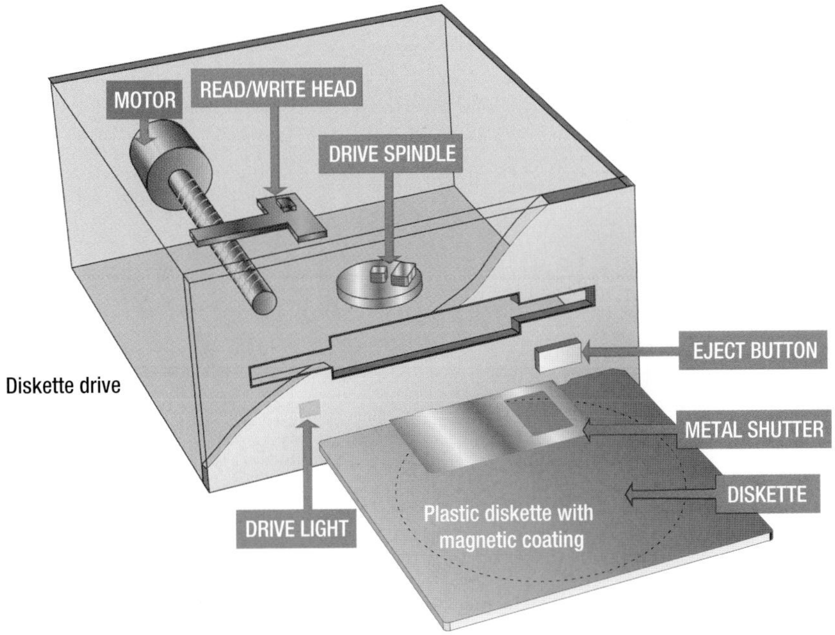

FIGURE 6A.9

Parts of a diskette and a diskette drive.

Diskettes spin at about 300 revolutions per minute. Therefore, the longest it can take to position a point on the diskette under the read/write heads is the amount of time required for one revolution—about 0.2 second. The farthest the heads have to move is from the center of the diskette to the outside edge (or vice versa). The heads can move from the center to the outside edge in even less time—about 0.17 second. Because both operations (rotating the diskette and moving the heads from the center to the outside edge) take place simultaneously, the maximum time to position the heads over a given location on the diskette—known as the maximum access time—remains the greater of the two times, or 0.2 second (see Figure 6A.10).

The maximum access time for diskettes can be longer, however, because diskettes do not spin when they are not being used. It can take about 0.5 second to rotate the disk from a dead stop.

A 3.5-inch diskette, as shown in Figure 6A.11, is encased in a hard plastic shell with a sliding shutter. When the disk is inserted into the drive, the shutter is slid back to expose the disk's surface to the read/write head.

A disk's **density** is a measure of its capacity—the amount of data it can store. To determine a disk's density, you can multiply its total number of sectors by the number of bytes each sector can hold. For a standard floppy disk, the equation looks like this:

```
    2,880 sectors
    × 512 bytes per sector
1,474,560 total bytes
```

FIGURE 6A.10

How maximum access time is determined for a diskette drive.

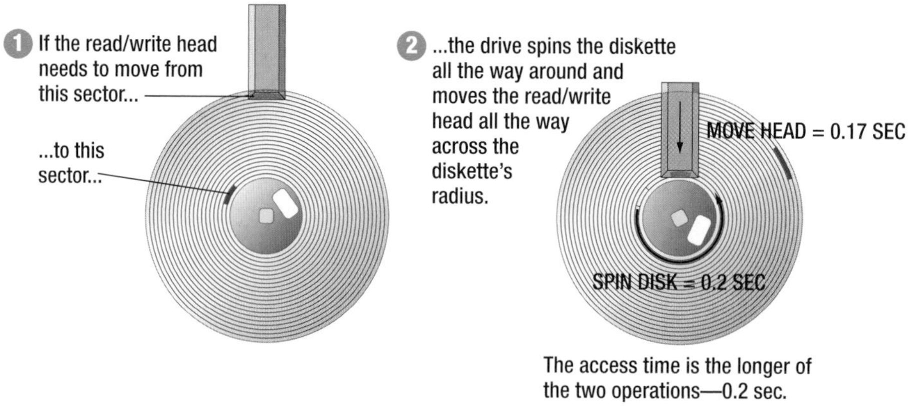

1 If the read/write head needs to move from this sector...
...to this sector...
2 ...the drive spins the diskette all the way around and moves the read/write head all the way across the diskette's radius.
MOVE HEAD = 0.17 SEC
SPIN DISK = 0.2 SEC
The access time is the longer of the two operations—0.2 sec.

FIGURE 6A.11

A 3.5-inch diskette.

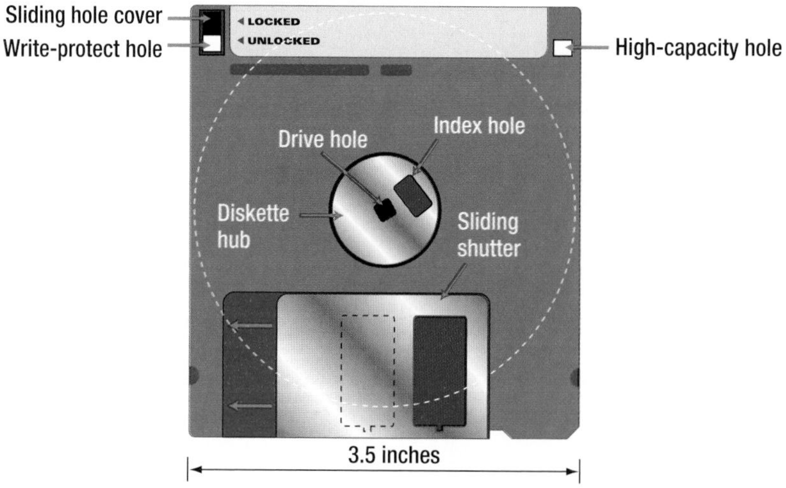

Sliding hole cover
Write-protect hole
LOCKED
UNLOCKED
High-capacity hole
Drive hole
Index hole
Diskette hub
Sliding shutter
3.5 inches

Hard Disks

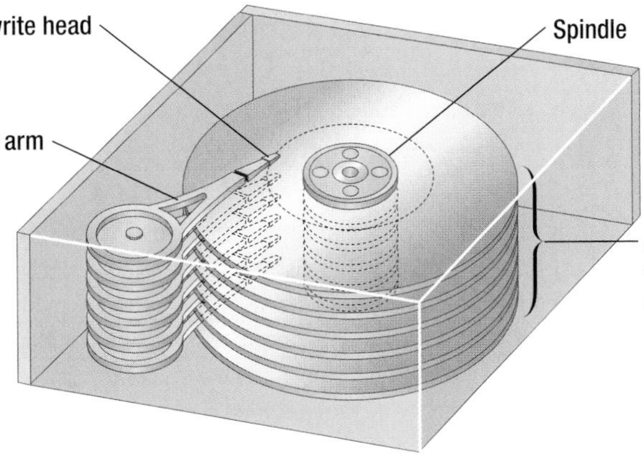

FIGURE 6A.12

Parts of a hard disk.

A hard disk includes one or more platters mounted on a central spindle, like a stack of rigid diskettes. Each platter is covered with a magnetic coating, and the entire unit is encased in a sealed chamber. Unlike diskettes, where the disk and drive are separate, the hard disk and drive are a single unit. It includes the hard disk, the motor that spins the platters, and a set of read/write heads (see Figure 6A.12). Because you cannot remove the disk from its drive (unless it is a removable hard disk), the terms *hard disk* and *hard drive* are used interchangeably.

The smallest hard disks available today can store several hundred megabytes; the largest store 200 GB or even more. Most entry-level consumer PCs now come with hard disks of at least 40 GB, but minimum capacities are continually increasing.

The hard disks found in most PCs spin at a speed of 3,600, 7,200, or 10,000 revolutions per minute (rpm). Very-high-performance disks found in workstations and servers can spin as fast as 15,000 rpm. (Compare these figures to a diskette's spin rate of 300 rpm). The speed at which the disk spins is a major factor in its overall performance. The hard disk's high rotational speed allows more data to be recorded on the disk's surface. This is because a faster-spinning disk can use smaller magnetic charges to make current flow through the read/write head. The drive's heads also can use a lower-intensity current to record data on the disk.

Hard disks pack data more closely together than floppy disks can, but they also hold more data because they include multiple platters. To the computer system, this configuration means that the disk has more than two sides: sides 0, 1, 2, 3, 4, and so on. Larger-capacity hard disks may use 12 or more platters.

Like diskettes, hard disks generally store 512 bytes of data in a sector, but hard disks can have more sectors per track—54, 63, or even more sectors per track are not uncommon.

Norton ONLINE

For more information on hard disks, visit **http://www.mhhe.com/peternorton**.

Removable High-Capacity Magnetic Disks

Removable high-capacity disks and drives combine the speed and capacity of a hard disk with the portability of a diskette. A wide variety of devices fall into this category, and each device works with its own unique storage medium. There are basically two types of removable high-capacity magnetic disks:

- **High-Capacity Floppy Disks.** Many computer makers now offer built-in high-capacity floppy disk drives in addition to a standard diskette drive. You can easily add a high-capacity floppy disk drive to a system that doesn't already have one. These drives use disks that are about the same size as a 3.5-inch diskette but have a much greater capacity than a standard diskette. The most commonly used high-capacity floppy disk system is the Zip drive and disks, made by Iomega Corp. (see Figure 6A.13). Zip disks come in capacities ranging from 100 MB to 750 MB.
- **Hot-Swappable Hard Disks.** At the high end in terms of price and performance are hot-swappable hard disks, also called removable hard disks. These disks are sometimes used on high-end

Norton ONLINE

For more information on removable high-capacity magnetic disks, visit **http://www.mhhe.com/peternorton**.

simnet™

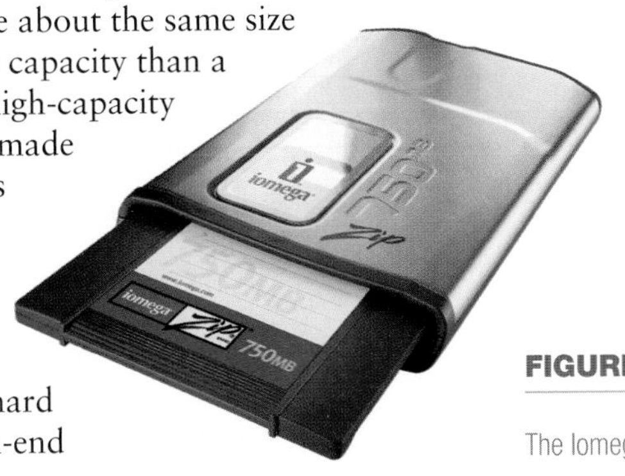

FIGURE 6A.13

The Iomega Zip system.

Productivity Tip

Backing Up Your Data

Backing up your data simply means making a copy of it, separate from the original version on your computer's hard disk. You can back up the entire disk, programs and all, or you can back up your data files. If your original data is lost, you can restore the backup copy, then resume your work with no more than a minor inconvenience. Here are some tips to help you start a regular backup routine.

Choose Your Medium

The most popular backup medium is the floppy disk, but you may need dozens of them to back up all your data files. A tape drive, removable hard disk, CD-RW, or DVD-RW drive may be a perfect choice if the medium provides enough storage space to back up your entire disk. When choosing your backup medium, the first rule is to make sure it can store everything you need. It also should enable you to restore backed-up data and programs with little effort. You can find medium-capacity tape drives and Zip drives for as little as \$100 to \$300. Prices increase with speed and capacity. Large-capacity disk cartridges, such as Iomega's Peerless system, start at around \$350 for the drive; 10 GB Peerless disks cost about \$150; and the 20 GB version costs about \$200.

Remote backup services are a growing trend. For a fee, such a service can connect to your computer remotely (via an Internet or dial-up connection) and back up your data to their servers. You can restore data remotely from such a system.

Make Sure You Have the Right Software

For backing up your entire hard disk to a high-capacity device, use the file-transfer software that came with the device. Your operating system also may have a built-in backup utility that works with several devices. The critical issue when choosing backup software is that it should enable you to organize your backups, perform partial backups, and restore selected files when needed.

Set a Schedule and Stick to It

Your first backup should be a full backup—everything on your hard disk—and it should be repeated once a week. Beyond that, you can do a series of partial backups—either

workstations or servers that require large amounts of storage. They allow the user to remove (swap out) a hard disk and insert (swap in) another while the computer is still running (hot). Hot-swappable hard disks are like removable versions of normal hard disks. The removable box includes the disk, drive, and read/write heads in a sealed container.

Norton ONLINE

For more information on tapes and tape drives, visit **http://www.mhhe.com/peternorton**.

Tape Drives

Tape drives read and write data to the surface of a tape the same way an audiocassette recorder does. The difference is that a computer tape drive writes digital data rather than analog data—discrete 1s and 0s rather than finely graduated signals created by sounds in an audio recorder.

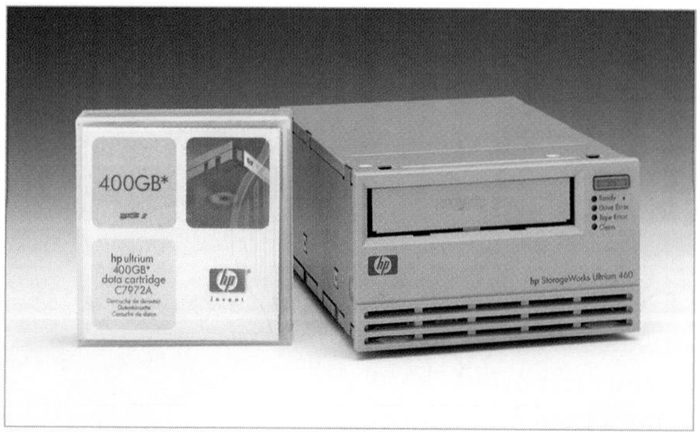

FIGURE 6A.14

New-generation tape drives feature data capacities of 200 GB and higher, and can transfer several megabytes of data per second.

Tape storage is best used for data that you do not use often, such as backup copies of your hard disk's contents. Businesses use tape drives for this purpose because they are inexpensive, reliable, and have capacities as high as 200 GB and greater (see Figure 6A.14).

PRODUCTIVITY TIP

incremental (files that have changed since the last partial backup) or differential (files that have changed since the last full backup).

Keep Your Backups Safe

Be sure to keep your disks or tapes in a safe place. Experts suggest keeping them somewhere away from the computer. If your computer is damaged or stolen, your backups will not suffer the same fate. Some organizations routinely ship their media to a distant location, such as a home office or a commercial warehouse, or store them in weather- and fireproof vaults. Home users may want to keep their backups in a fireproof box. Companies often keep three or more full sets of backups, all at different sites. Such prudence may seem extreme, but where crucial records are at stake, backups of files are vital to the welfare of a business.

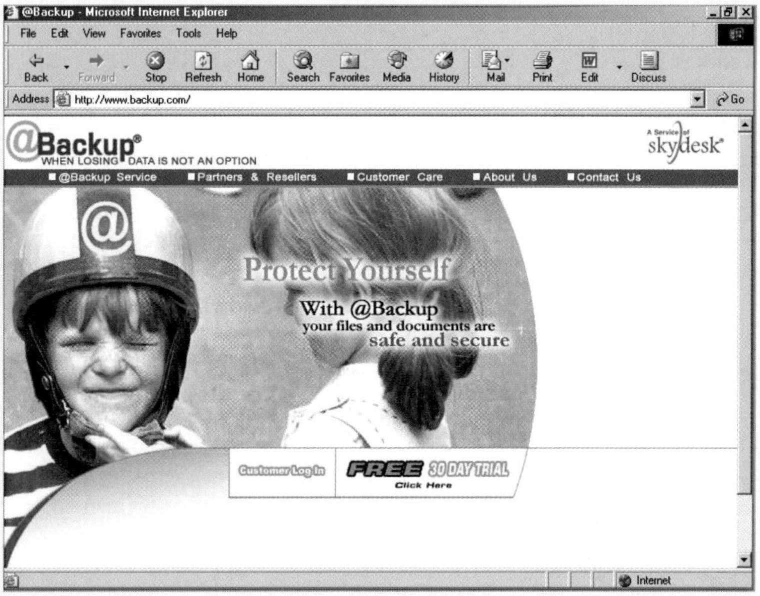

Tapes, however, are slow when it comes to accessing data. Because a tape is a long strip of magnetic material, the tape drive has to write data to it serially—one byte after another. To find a piece of data on a tape, the drive must scan through all the data in sequence until it finds the right item. For this reason, tape drives are often called sequential access devices. They locate data much more slowly than a random access storage device such as a hard disk.

SELF-CHECK ::

Circle the correct answer for each question.

1. A diskette is an example of a storage __________ .
   - a. mediator
   - b. media
   - c. medium
2. Unlike a transistor, a magnetic disk can store data without a continual source of __________ .
   - a. electricity
   - b. RPMs
   - c. polarity
3. Different operating systems use different __________ systems.
   - a. power
   - b. file
   - c. disk

Optical Storage Devices

The most popular alternatives to magnetic storage systems are optical systems, including CD-ROM, DVD-ROM, and their variants. These devices fall into the category of optical storage because they store data on a reflective surface so it can be read by a beam of laser light. A laser uses a concentrated, narrow beam of light, focused and directed with lenses, prisms, and mirrors.

Norton ONLINE

For more information on optical storage technologies, visit **http://www.mhhe.com/peternorton**.

Norton ONLINE

For more information on CD-ROM, visit **http://www.mhhe.com/peternorton**.

simnet™

CD-ROM

The familiar audio compact disc is a popular medium for storing music. In the computer world, however, the medium is called *compact disc–read-only memory (CD-ROM)*. CD-ROM uses the same technology used to produce music CDs. If your computer has a CD-ROM drive, a sound card, and speakers, you can play audio CDs on your PC (see Figure 6A.15).

A CD-ROM drive reads digital data (whether computer data or audio) from a spinning disc by focusing a laser on the disc's surface. Some areas of the disc reflect the laser light into a sensor, and other areas scatter the light. A spot that reflects the laser beam into the sensor is interpreted as a 1, and the absence of a reflection is interpreted as a 0.

FIGURE 6A.15

Real Networks, Inc., makes a variety of programs that let you record and play music on your PC. Here, the RealOne Player is being used to play music on an audio CD.

Data is laid out on a CD-ROM disc in a long, continuous spiral. Data is stored in the form of **lands**, which are flat areas on the metal surface, and **pits**, which are depressions or hollows. As Figure 6A.16 shows, a land reflects the laser light into the sensor (indicating a data bit of 1) and a pit scatters the light (indicating a data bit of 0). A standard compact disc can store 650 MB of data or about 70 minutes of audio. A newer generation of compact discs, however, can hold 700 MB of data or 80 minutes of audio.

Compared to hard disk drives, CD-ROM drives are slow. One reason has to do with the changing rotational speed of the disk. Like a track on a magnetic disk, the track of an optical disk is split into sectors. However, the sectors are laid out differently than they are on magnetic disks (see Figure 6A.17).

FIGURE 6A.16

How a CD-ROM drive reads data from the surface of a compact disc.

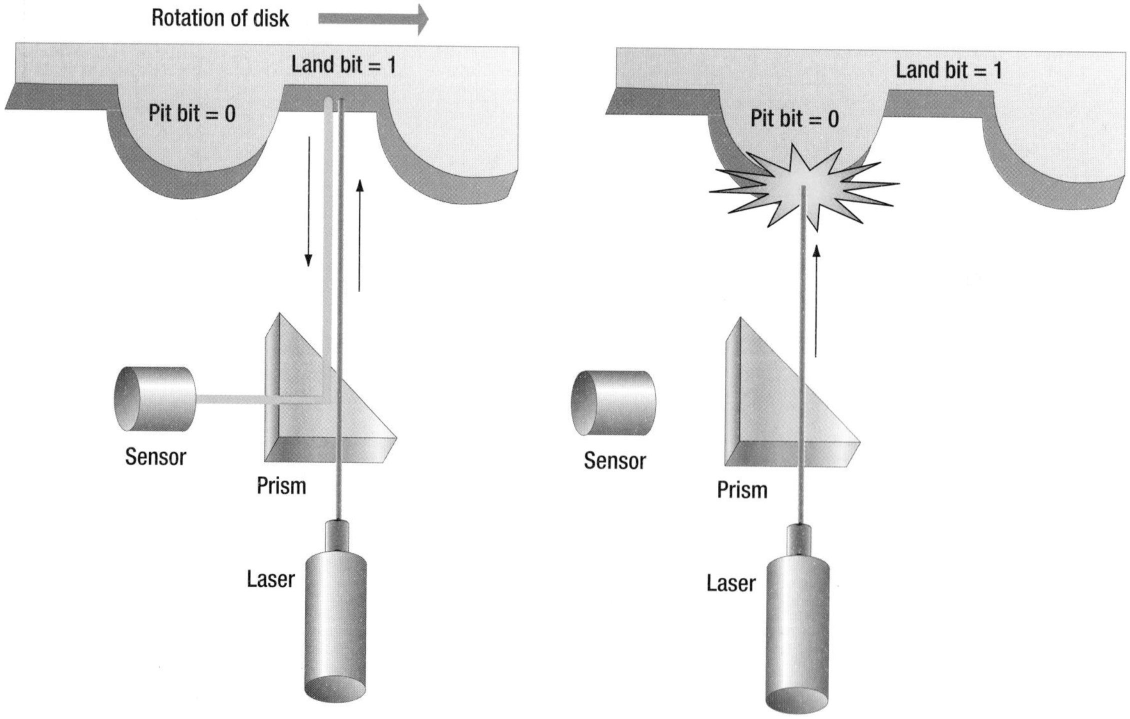

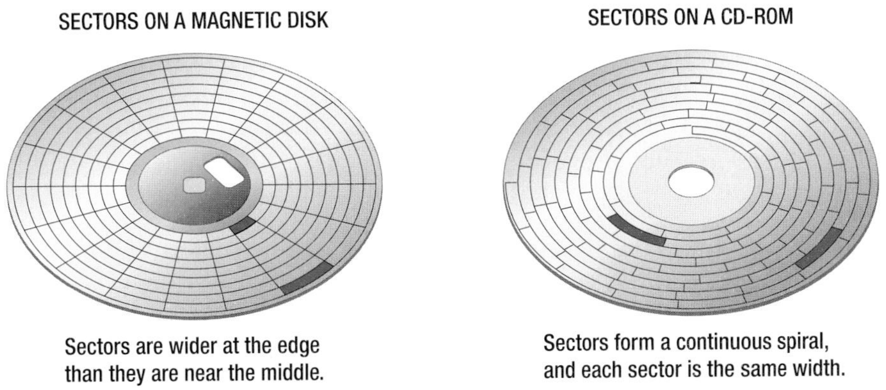

FIGURE 6A.17

The arrangement of sectors on a compact disc and a magnetic disk.

The sectors near the middle of the CD wrap farther around the disk than those near the edge. For the drive to read each sector in the same amount of time, it must spin the disc faster when reading sectors near the middle and slower when reading sectors near the edge. Changing the speed of rotation takes time—enough to seriously impair the overall performance of the CD-ROM drive.

The first CD-ROM drives could read data at 150 KBps (kilobytes per second) and were known as *single-speed* drives. Today, a CD-ROM drive's speed is expressed as a multiple of the original drive's speed—2x, 4x, 8x, and so on. A 2x drive reads data at a rate of 300 KBps (2 × 150). At the time this book was published, the fastest available CD-ROM drive was listed at a speed of 75x; it could read data at a rate of 11,250 KBps (or slightly more than 11 MBps).

Norton ONLINE

For more information on DVD-ROM, visit **http://www.mhhe.com/peternorton**.

simnet™

DVD-ROM

Many of today's new PCs feature a built-in digital video disc– read-only memory (DVD-ROM) drive rather than a standard CD-ROM drive. DVD-ROM is a high-density medium capable of storing a full-length movie on a single disk the size of a CD. DVD-ROM achieves such high storage capacities by using both sides of the disc and special data-compression technologies and by using extremely small tracks for storing data. (Standard compact discs store data on only one side of the disc.)

The latest generation of DVD-ROM disc actually uses layers of data tracks, effectively doubling their capacity. The device's laser beam can read data from the first layer and then look through it to read data from the second layer.

DVDs look like CDs (see Figure 6A.18). DVD-ROM drives can play ordinary CD-ROM discs (see Figure 6A.19). A slightly different player, the DVD movie player, connects to your

FIGURE 6A.18

If your PC features a DVD drive, you can watch movies on your computer.

FIGURE 6A.19

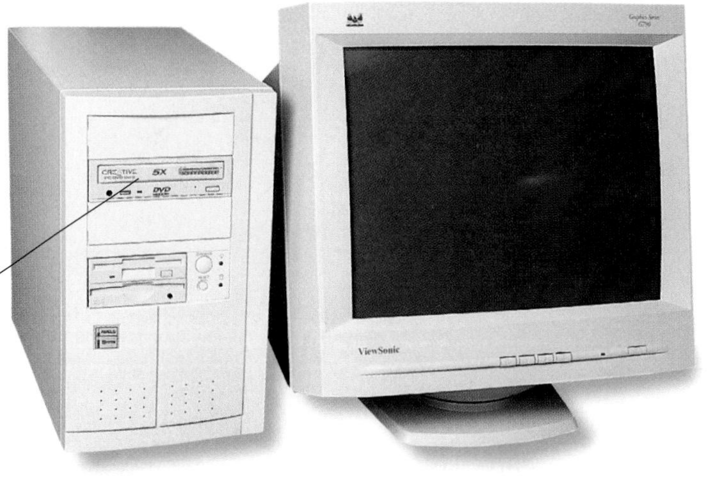

DVD-ROM movie players can read video, audio, and data from DVDs and CDs. In PC systems, built-in DVD-ROM drives look just like standard CD-ROM drives.

television and plays movies like a VCR. The DVD movie player also will play audio CDs as well as many types of data CDs, such as home-recorded audio discs, video CDs, and others.

Since each side of a standard DVD-ROM disc can hold 4.7 GB, these discs can contain as much as 9.4 GB of data. Dual-layer DVD-ROM discs can hold 17 GB of data.

Norton ONLINE

For more information on recordable optical storage, visit **http://www.mhhe.com/peternorton**.

Recordable Optical Technologies

The latest innovations in consumer-grade optical technologies allow home users to create their own DVDs, filled with audio and video, music, or computer data. Here are some popular "writable" CD and DVD technologies:

» **CD-Recordable.** A CD-Recordable (CD-R) drive allows you to create your own data or audio discs that can be read by most CD-ROM drives. Most CD-R discs can be played in audio CD players, too. After information has been written to part of the special recordable disc (called a CD-R disk), that information cannot be changed. With most CD-R drives, you can continue to record information to other parts of the disc until it is full.

» **CD-ReWritable (CD-RW).** Using a CD-ReWritable (CD-RW) drive, you can write data onto special rewritable compact discs (called CD-RW discs), then overwrite it with new data. In other words, you can change the contents of a CD-RW disc in the same manner as a floppy disk. CD-RW discs have the same capacity as standard compact discs, and most can be overwritten up to 100 times. CD-RW discs, however, will not play on every CD-ROM drive, and most CD-RW discs cannot store audio data.

» **PhotoCD.** Kodak developed the PhotoCD system to store digitized photographs on a recordable compact disc. Many film developing stores have PhotoCD drives that can record your photos on a CD. You can then put the PhotoCD in your computer's CD-ROM drive (assuming that it supports PhotoCD, and most do) and view the images on your computer as shown in Figure 6A.20. You also can paste them into other documents. With a PhotoCD, you can continue to add images until the disc is full. After an image has been written to the disc, however, it cannot be erased or changed.

» **DVD-Recordable (DVD-R).** After PC makers began adding DVD-ROM drives to computers, it did not take long for user demand to build for a recordable DVD system. The first to emerge is called DVD-Recordable (DVD-R).

Like CD-R, a DVD-R system lets you record data onto a special recordable digital video disc, using a special drive. Once you record data onto a DVD-R disc, you cannot change it.

FIGURE 6A.20

After your pictures have been processed and stored on a PhotoCD, you can see them on your computer screen and copy them into documents.

» **DVD-RAM.** The newest optical technology to reach consumers, sophisticated DVD-RAM drives let you record, erase, and rerecord data on a special disc. Using video editing software, you can record your own digitized videos onto a DVD-RAM disc, then play them back in any DVD player. DVD-RAM drives can read DVDs, DVD-R discs, CD-R discs, CD-RW discs, and standard CDs.

Solid-State Storage Devices

Solid-state storage devices are unique among today's storage devices because they do not use disks or tapes and have no moving parts. Solid-state storage is neither magnetic nor optical. Instead, it relies on integrated circuits to hold data. Some solid-state storage devices are nonvolatile, meaning they can retain their data even when the system's power is turned off. Others are volatile, meaning they require a constant supply of electricity or they will lose their data. The device's volatility depends on the type of memory circuits it uses.

Byte for byte, standard magnetic or optical storage is less expensive and more reliable than solid-state storage. However, solid-state storage devices have a big advantage over standard storage devices: speed. Memory devices can move data in much less time than any mechanical storage device. This is because solid-state devices have no moving parts and because they already store data electronically (the way it is used by the CPU). Unlike standard devices, solid-state devices do not need to move a head or sensor to find data or to convert it from magnetic or optical form into electronic form.

Norton ONLINE

For more information on solid-state storage devices, visit **http://www.mhhe.com/peternorton**.

Flash Memory

As you learned in Chapter 5, flash memory is a special type of memory chip that combines the best features of RAM and ROM. Like RAM, flash memory lets a user or program access data randomly. Also like RAM, flash memory lets you overwrite any or all of its contents at any time. Like ROM, flash memory is nonvolatile, so data is retained even when power is off.

Flash memory has many uses. For example, it is commonly used in digital cameras and multimedia players such as MP3 players. A new type of storage device for PCs, called the flash memory drive, is about the size of a car key (see Figure 6A.21). In fact, many users carry a flash memory drive on their keychain. These tiny devices usually connect to a computer's USB or FireWire port and can store 256 MB or more of data.

Norton ONLINE

For more information on flash memory and flash memory devices, visit **http://www.mhhe.com/peternorton**.

FIGURE 6A.21

Flash memory drives are small and easy to use but hold a lot of data.

Norton Notebook

Looking Back, Moving Forward

If there is any quality of a new technology that limits its adoption into the growing world of the PC, it's backwards compatibility. As the name suggests, backwards compatibility means that the technologies of tomorrow work with the technologies of today. (Similarly, forward compatibility means that today's technologies will work with the technologies of tomorrow.) Backwards compatibility (BC) is the point at which technological innovation meets economics. More simply: people will buy new stuff when they don't have to throw out all of their old stuff to use the new. Sometimes, even partial BC isn't enough. VCRs that supported the advanced SVHS video format could play traditional VHS tapes, but the higher-quality SVHS tapes they recorded couldn't be played on VHS VCRs. This meant consumers couldn't share SVHS home videos with grandparents and cousins unless the whole family bought SVHS machines. It never happened.

Having learned this and many similar lessons, the consortia that defined the various formats for recordable compact discs kept BC at the forefront of their work. The result? An audio CD-R burned in the world's fastest drive will still chug out tunes on Sony's original Discman from 1984. The importance of backwards compatibility was briefly lost, however, when many of the same companies worked together to develop the recordable DVD. In fairness, the issue wasn't just that manufacturers *chose* against BC. The technology didn't yet exist to make affordable, recordable DVDs that would work in the established base of DVD-ROM drives and home players. But, as late as 2003, many manufacturers continued to assume that purchasers of still-expensive DVD recorders wouldn't care if they could share home videos with grandparents and cousins. Sound familiar?

With no fewer than five major contenders for the "recordable DVD format crown," the matter seemed unlikely to resolve itself quickly. Then, home player makers realized they could provide compatibility with four of the five formats at no additional cost. Indeed, the price of home units has plummeted. This is supply and demand: Make your product usable by the most people, and you'll sell so many that you can lower the price. DVD recorder manufacturers have followed suit. Virtually all new DVD recorders can write discs in any of the four formats.

This might have been the end of the race were it not for two factors. First, recordable DVD discs are not just for video. They're used for PC backups, moving files, and so on. So they're subject to the same requirements of any other PC storage media. Briefly, these are ever-greater capacity, greater speed, lower cost, and BC. The second factor is that commercially released video DVDs have a higher storage capacity than first-generation recordables. Consumers couldn't easily back up the DVD movies they bought, and smaller video production houses couldn't produce DVDs with the same broad features consumers expect in commercial products.

Why do commercial discs have higher capacity? They implement two layers of recording material. The laser reads

Norton ONLINE

For more information on smart cards, visit **http://www.mhhe.com/peternorton**.

Smart Cards

Although it looks like an ordinary credit card, a smart card is a device with extraordinary potential (see Figure 6A.22). Smart cards contain a small chip that stores data. Using a special device, called a smart card reader, the user can read data from the card, add new data, or revise existing data.

Some smart cards, called intelligent smart cards, also contain their own tiny microprocessor, and they function like a computer. Although they have not yet come into widespread use, smart cards are finding many purposes—both current and future. For example, large hotels now issue guests a smart card instead of a key; the card not only allows guests to access their room, but it also allows them to charge other services and expenses to the card as well.

Someday, smart cards may be used to store digital cash that can be used to make purchases in stores or online (as long as the user has a reader connected to the PC). Smart cards could store a person's entire medical history, or they could be used as a source of secure ID.

the second, fully reflective layer by shining right through the first, semireflective/semitransparent layer. Dual-layer DVDs are economical—one disc costs less than two—and are convenient for users (no discs to turn over). Naturally, home players have supported dual layers for years.

Because the dual-layer idea already existed, it gave the DVD consortia a target for high-capacity recordable DVDs: backwards compatibility. This proved difficult. Commercially released DVD discs are made by completely different means than are recordables. The former are actually *pressed*, whereas most of the latter rely on phase changes in a crystalline layer. These simulate a pressed DVD's pits and lands. So any BC dual-layer system had to function like existing recordable discs *and* like commercial discs. The developers of the generally superior DVD+RW format were first to succeed, with the first drives available in 2004. Their achievement was both a technical and a political success; the motion-picture industry has attempted to stop the development of DVD technology because of fears that widespread copying of DVD movies will destroy their business model.

There comes a time in any technological chain, however, where backwards compatibility has too many drawbacks to make it cost-effective or even reasonable. This happened when the market embraced DVDs over CDs, so we could have full-length, high-quality digital movies on a single disc. Blu-Ray laser drives will likely be a similar successful break from BC. Announced in late 2003, Blu-Ray optical drives use a blue laser instead of the traditional red DVD laser or infrared CD laser. Blue lasers produce light at shorter wavelength than the others, so pits and lands can pack more densely. Blu-Ray provides 23 GB of storage on a 120 mm disc. That translates into 13 hours of standard video (conveniently, just over two hours of the forthcoming HDTV video). Planned improvements will take the capacity up to 100 GB, positioning these drives to replace the VCR and disk-based personal video recorders. Since a different laser type is required, Blu-Ray discs won't be playable in existing DVD players. However, DVDs and CDs of all current types should play in Blu-Ray drives with no trouble.

A Blu-Ray disc recorder

NORTON NOTEBOOK

FIGURE 6A.22

Smart cards may someday replace credit cards and drivers' licenses, or may be used as a form of portable storage for computer data.

Norton ONLINE

For more information on solid-state disks, visit **http://www.mhhe.com/peternorton**.

FIGURE 6A.23

Solid-state disk systems, like this one, can store vast amounts of data.

Solid-State Disks

A solid-state disk (SSD) is not a disk at all (see Figure 6A.23). Rather, this device uses very fast memory chips, such as synchronous dynamic RAM (SDRAM), to store data. SDRAM is much faster than standard RAM. Large-scale SSD systems can store a terabyte or more of data. An SSD may be a free-standing unit that connects to a server computer or a card that plugs into one of the server's expansion slots.

SSDs are gaining popularity among large organizations, which need instant access to constantly changing data. As mentioned already, solid-state storage devices allow much faster access to data, even while that data is being viewed and updated by other users. For this reason, SSDs are used primarily for enterprise-level network storage, to make data available to a large number of users at one time.

The biggest drawback of RAM-based SSDs (aside from their high cost) is volatility. RAM circuits need constant power to store data, or data will be lost. For this reason, many SSD systems feature built-in battery backups and a set of hard disks that "mirror" the memory. If power fails or a circuit goes bad, the system can still use backup data stored on its hard disks.

Summary ::

- Common storage devices can be categorized as magnetic, optical, or solid-state.
- The most common magnetic storage media are diskettes, hard disks, high-capacity floppy disks, and magnetic tape.
- The primary types of optical storage are compact disc–read-only memory (CD-ROM), digital video disc–read-only memory (DVD-ROM), CD-Recordable (CD-R), CD-ReWritable (CD-RW), DVD-Recordable (DVD-R), DVD-RAM, and PhotoCD.
- Magnetic storage devices work by polarizing tiny pieces of iron on the magnetic medium. Read/write heads contain electromagnets that create magnetic charges on the medium.
- Before a magnetic disk can be used, it must be formatted—a process that maps the disk's surface and creates tracks and sectors where data can be stored.
- Hard disks can store more data than diskettes because they contain more disks, rotate the disks at a higher speed, and can divide tracks into greater numbers of sectors.
- Removable hard disks combine high capacity with the convenience of diskettes.
- High-capacity floppy disks are a popular add-on for personal computers. They offer capacities up to 750 MB and the same portability as standard floppy disks.
- Magnetic tape systems offer slow data access; because of their large capacities and low cost, they are a popular backup medium.
- CD-ROM uses the same technology as a music CD does: a laser reads lands and pits on the surface of the disc.
- Standard CD-ROM discs can store up to 650 MB, although newer discs can hold 700 MB. Once data is written to the disc, it cannot be changed.
- DVD-ROM technology is a variation on the standard CD-ROM. DVDs offer capacities up to 17 GB.
- Other popular variations on the CD-ROM are CD-Recordable, CD-ReWritable, and PhotoCD. Popular variations of DVD-ROM are DVD-Recordable and DVD-RAM.
- Solid-state storage devices store data on memory circuits rather than disks or tapes. They store data electronically, not in a magnetic or optical form.
- Solid-state storage devices can use either volatile or nonvolatile memory. Examples of such devices include flash memory, smart cards, and solid-state disks.

LESSON //6A Review

Key Terms ::

boot sector, 230
booting, 230
cluster, 230
data area, 230
density, 232
directory, 230
DVD-RAM, 239
DVD-Recordable (DVD-R), 238
file allocation table (FAT), 230
file system, 230
flash memory drive, 239
folder, 230
formatting, 228
high-capacity floppy disk, 233
hot-swappable hard disk, 233
initializing, 228
intelligent smard card, 240
land, 236
logical formatting, 230
magnetic storage, 226
optical storage, 226
PhotoCD, 238
pit, 236
polarize, 227
random access storage device, 228
root folder, 230
sector, 228
sequential access device, 235
smart card, 240
solid-state disk (SSD), 242
solid-state storage, 226
storage device, 226
storage media, 226
Synchronous Dynamic RAM (SDRAM), 242
track, 228

Key Term Quiz ::

Complete each statement by writing one of the terms listed under Key Terms in each blank.

1. Floppy disks and compact discs are examples of ________ .
2. Because a hard disk can go directly to any piece of data stored on its surface, it is called a(n) ________ storage device.
3. When formatting a magnetic disk, the disk drive creates a set of concentric rings, called ________ , on its surface.
4. A(n) ________ is a group of sectors, which the operating system treats as a single storage unit.
5. A(n) ________ is a logical method for managing the storage of data on a disk's surface.
6. A magnetic disk's ________ is a measure of its storage capacity.
7. On the surface of an optical disc, data is stored as a series of ________ and ________ .
8. By using a(n) ________ drive, you can write data onto a special digital video disc, then erase or overwrite the data.
9. A(n) ________ hard disk can be removed and replaced while the computer is still running.
10. The ________ is the part of a magnetic disk that actually stores data and program files.

Multiple Choice ::

Circle the word or phrase that best completes each statement.

1. A(n) __________ is an example of a magnetic storage device.
   a. flash memory drive b. CD-ROM drive c. hard disk drive d. optical drive
2. Diskettes spin at about __________ revolutions per minute.
   a. 3 b. 30 c. 300 d. 3,000
3. The __________ of a hard disk contains a small program that runs when you start the computer.
   a. boot sector b. file allocation table c. file system d. file cluster
4. In a magnetic disk drive, the read/write heads generate __________ in the iron particles on the storage medium.
   a. polarized magnets b. electromagnetic pulses c. magnetic waves d. magnetic fields
5. The process of mapping a magnetic disk's surface is called __________ .
   a. polarizing b. charging c. formatting d. accessing
6. A magnetic disk's tracks are divided into smaller parts, called __________ .
   a. clusters b. sectors c. bytes d. slices
7. A(n) __________ is a tool for organizing the files on a disk.
   a. disk b. folder c. cluster d. record
8. A CD-ROM drive reads data from a spinning disc by focusing a(n) __________ on the disc's surface.
   a. laser b. read/write head c. magnetic field d. track
9. Each side of a standard DVD-ROM disc can hold up to __________ of data.
   a. 4.7 GB b. 9.4 GB c. 17 GB d. 140 GB
10. Intelligent smart cards contain their own __________ .
    a. read/write head b. microprocessor c. laser d. flash memory drive

LESSON //6A Review

Review Questions ::

In your own words, briefly answer the following questions.

1. List four types of magnetic storage media commonly used with PCs.
2. List seven types of optical storage devices that can be used with PCs.
3. Name three types of solid-state storage devices.
4. Why is a hard disk called a random access storage device?
5. Describe how a magnetic disk drive's read/write head can pass data to and from the surface of a disk.
6. What is the purpose of formatting a magnetic disk?
7. What is the storage capacity of a standard floppy disk?
8. Although magnetic tape can store a large quantity of data, it has one drawback when compared to other storage media, such as hard disks. Describe that drawback.
9. Describe the function of lands and pits on the surface of a compact disc.
10. How does a solid-state disk store data?

Lesson Labs ::

Complete the following exercises as directed by your instructor.

1. Format a blank floppy disk:
   a. Make sure the disk's write-protect tab is closed. Place the disk in the diskette drive.
   b. Launch Windows Explorer. (The steps to launch Windows Explorer depend on the version of Windows you use. Ask your instructor for specific directions.)
   c. Right-click the floppy disk icon in the left pane. Click Format on the shortcut menu.
   d. In the Format dialog box, choose a capacity for the disk. Click the Quick (Erase) option. Make sure the Display Summary When Finished option is checked. Click Start.
   e. Click Close twice. Remove the disk from the drive. Leave the Exploring window open.
2. Explore the contents of your hard disk. In the Exploring window's left pane, click the system's hard disk icon labeled (C:). Look at the status bar at the bottom of the window. How many "objects" (folders) are stored on the hard disk? How much free space is available? Click several folders and review their contents in the right pane. When finished, close the Exploring window.

LESSON // 6B

Measuring and Improving Drive Performance

Overview: The Need for Speed

An important factor in measuring overall system performance is the speed at which the computer's disk drives operate. Measures of drive performance generally are applied to the computer's hard disk but also can be applied to other types of drives.

When evaluating the performance of common storage devices, you need to be aware of two common measures: the average access time and the data transfer rate. For random-access devices (all the storage devices discussed, with the exception of magnetic tapes and solid-state devices), you generally want a low access time and a high data transfer rate.

Because tape drives are always slower than other types of storage devices, convenience and capacity are their best measures of performance. Solid-state devices typically access and transfer data much more rapidly than other types of storage devices so, again, convenience and capacity are usually your greatest concern when evaluating them.

These performance factors can be important when you are buying a new computer or upgrading your current system. You want to make sure that your drives operate at a speed that complements your processor's capabilities. You also want to make sure that the drive uses an interface that is compatible with any other devices you may add to the computer.

OBJECTIVES ::

- >> Define the term *average access time* and describe how it is measured.
- >> Explain why file compression is a factor in drive performance.
- >> Define the term *data transfer rate* and describe how it is measured.
- >> Explain two steps you can take to optimize the performance of your computer's hard disk.
- >> Identify four drive interface standards commonly used in PCs.

Norton ONLINE

For more information on determining a disk drive's average access time, visit **http://www.mhhe.com/peternorton**.

Average Access Time

For a storage device, average access time (or seek time) is the amount of time the device takes to move its read or read/write heads to any spot on the medium. It is important that the measurement be an average because access times can vary greatly, depending on how far the heads need to move. To measure the access time of a drive effectively, you must test many reads of randomly chosen sectors—a method that approximates the actual read instructions a disk drive would receive under normal circumstances.

Average access time is an important measure of performance for storage devices and memory. Even though memory chips have no moving read/write head, it is still critical to know how fast a memory system can locate a piece of data on a chip. For storage devices, access times are measured in milliseconds (ms), or one-thousandths of a second. For memory devices, access times are measured in nanoseconds (ns), or one-billionths of a second.

In a disk drive, access time depends on a combination of two factors: the speed at which a disk spins (revolutions per minute, or rpm) and the time it takes to move the heads from one track to another. The maximum access time for diskettes, as you learned in the previous lesson, is 0.2 second, or 200 milliseconds. The average access time is about one half the maximum, or 100 milliseconds.

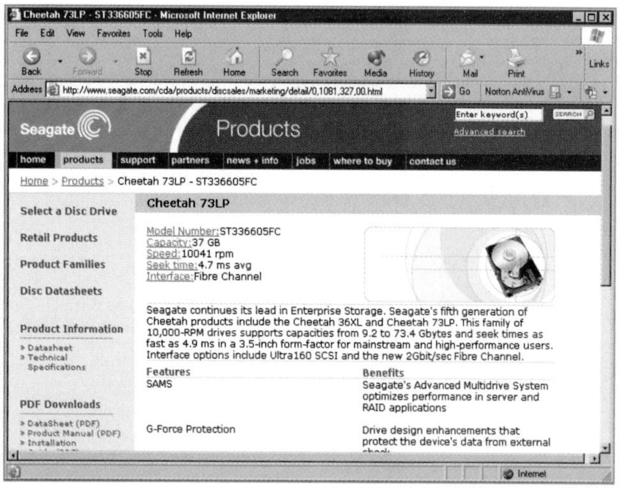

FIGURE 6B.1

Like many storage device manufacturers, Seagate Technology, Inc., provides product specifications on its Web site.

Average access times for hard drives can vary, but most good drives work at rates of 6 to 12 milliseconds, many times faster than diskette drives. Some very-high-performance hard disks have access times as fast as four or five milliseconds.

At 80 to 800 ms, access times for CD-ROM drives tend to be quite slow by hard disk standards, but tape drives offer the longest average access times of any storage device. Depending on the type of drive and format used, tape drives can take from a few seconds to a few minutes to find a specific piece of data on the tape's surface.

The easiest way to determine the average access time for a device is to check the manufacturer's specifications. You should be able to find the specifications for a device in its packaging or documentation, or you may be able to get them from the manufacturer's Web site (see Figure 6B.1). Popular computer-related magazines—such as *PC Magazine*, *Computer Shopper*, and others—regularly test new drives to measure various performance factors.

Data Transfer Rate

Norton ONLINE

For more information on determining a storage device's data transfer rate, visit **http://www.mhhe.com/peternorton**.

The other important statistic for measuring drive performance is the speed at which it can transfer data—that is, the amount of time it takes for one device to send data to another device. Speeds are expressed as a rate, or as some amount of data per unit of time. When measuring any device's data transfer rate (also called throughput), time is measured in seconds, but units of data may be measured in bytes, KB, MB, or GB. Figure 6B.2 illustrates data transfer rate.

As is the case with access times, data transfer rates can vary greatly from one device to another. Speeds for hard disks are generally high, from about 15 MBps for low-end home systems to 80 MBps and higher for the faster drives designed for high-performance workstations and servers. When buying a hard disk, the data transfer rate is at least as important a factor as the access time.

CD-ROMs and diskettes are the slowest storage devices. CD-ROMs range from 300 KBps for a double-speed player to 900 KBps for a 6x drive, to even higher speeds, with the data transfer rate corresponding to the drive's speed. Diskette drives average about 45 KBps. Removable hard disks range from about 1.25 MBps up into the hard disk range.

Some drive manufacturers and dealers advertise their drives' data transfer rates in units of megabytes per second (MBps); others express them in megabits per second (Mbps). When shopping, note if the rate specified is "MBps" or "Mbps."

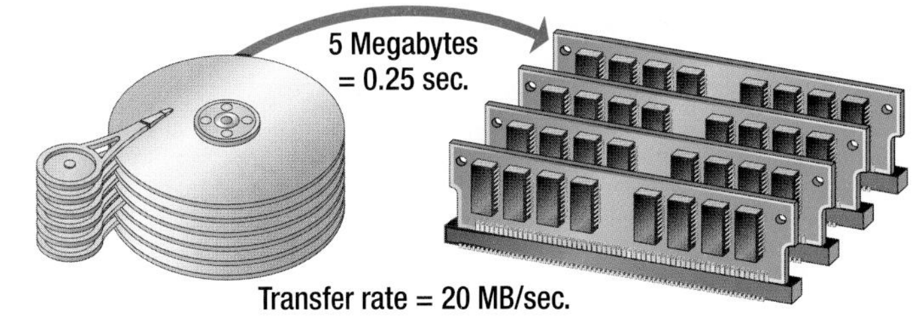

FIGURE 6B.2

Data transfer rate is the time required to move a specific amount of data (for example, 20 MB) from one device to another, such as from the hard disk to memory.

Optimizing Disk Performance

Over time, a PC's performance can slow down. This is especially true with older systems, but even newer PCs can suffer from occasional performance downturns. The computer may act sluggish in general or slow down when performing specific tasks such as loading or saving documents.

When a PC slows down in this manner, some hard-disk maintenance may fix the problem. Any PC that gets used a lot should get routine disk maintenance, or disk optimization. Using your operating system's built-in tools or other utilities, you can keep your computer's hard disk (or any other magnetic disk) running the best it can.

Norton ONLINE

For more information on disk optimization tools and methods, visit **http://www.mhhe.com/peternorton**.

Cleaning Up Unneeded Files

If your system has been in use for a while (even just a few months), hundreds of unneeded files may be cluttering up your hard disk. Windows accumulates all sorts of files during normal operations. Some of these files are meant to be stored only temporarily, but Windows does not always clean them out. If you ever shut down your computer improperly, Windows does not have a chance to delete these files, and they will stay put until you clear them out yourself. These files can really slow down your system because the hard disk has to deal with the unneeded files when looking for data or looking for space to store new files.

These files, called temporary (temp) files, are used by Windows to store various versions of documents in progress, files being sent to the printer, automatic backup files, and more. Windows usually stores these files with the filename extension .tmp in various locations on your disk. A hard disk also can get cluttered up by temporary Internet files, which are saved by your Web browser.

Newer versions of Windows feature a built-in utility called Disk Cleanup (see Figure 6B.3). Disk Cleanup and other disk-cleaning utilities can quickly find temporary files and remove them from your disk. The process takes only a few minutes and can free hundreds of megabytes of wasted space on an average hard disk.

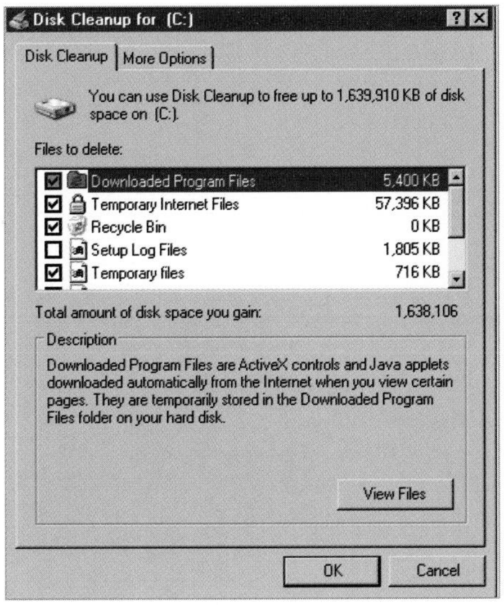

FIGURE 6B.3

This is the Disk Cleanup utility in Windows XP. It lets you choose the kinds of files you want to delete, then locates and removes them from the disk.

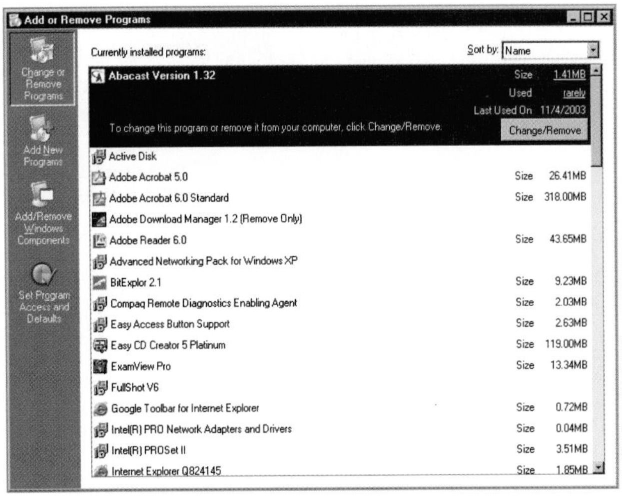

FIGURE 6B.4

The Add or Remove Programs utility in Windows XP. This window lets you select a program on your hard disk and remove it. The utility tells you how much disk space you will recover by removing a program.

Most computer users should clean the temporary files off their hard disks at least once a week.

If your hard disk contains programs that you do not plan to use, you can remove them—a process called uninstalling. To remove a program, start by checking its group in the Programs menu. If you see an Uninstall option, click it, and the program will uninstall itself. If you use a recent version of Windows, you also can use its Add or Remove Programs utility (see Figure 6B.4). There are a number of commercial software products that can uninstall programs from your system, too. Removing unneeded programs can improve your computer's performance.

Scanning a Disk for Errors

Another way to optimize disk performance is to scan the disk for errors, fix the errors, and possibly recover data that has been lost or corrupted because of a disk error. A disk error can be a bad spot on the disk's physical surface, or it can be a piece of data that cannot be accounted for in the FAT. Scanning a disk can be a time-consuming process, but if the disk has errors, scanning may be able to fix problems and improve performance.

Several (but not all) versions of Windows have a built-in disk-scanning utility (see Figure 6B.5), but you also can buy very sophisticated disk scanners.

Defragmenting a Disk

On the surface of a magnetic disk, fragmentation occurs when a file is stored in noncontiguous sectors on the disk's surface. In other words, pieces of files become scattered around on the disk. As you create, modify, copy, and delete files (and install and uninstall programs) over time, many files can become fragmented. Although your operating system keeps track of each fragment, a greatly fragmented disk can slow system performance because it can take longer to find and load all the pieces of files as they are needed by an application.

Windows features a built-in defragmentation utility, called Disk Defragmenter (see Figure 6B.6). You can use this utility—or one of several commercial utilities—to ensure that your files are stored as efficiently as possible on the disk. If your disk has never been defragmented before, you may notice a significant performance improvement after running this type of utility. (It is usually recommended that you run a disk-scanning utility before defragmenting the disk.)

Norton ONLINE

For more information on data compression, visit **http://www.mhhe.com/peternorton**.

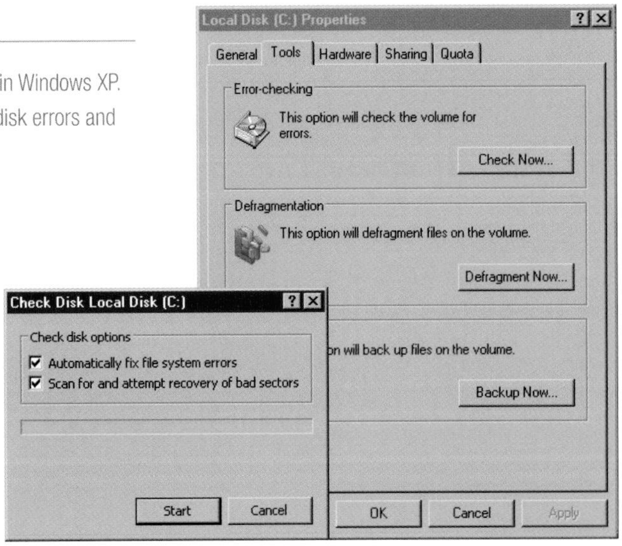

FIGURE 6B.5

The disk scanning utility in Windows XP. This tool attempts to fix disk errors and recover lost data.

File Compression

Even with the large storage devices available, many users still find themselves pushing the limits of their computer's storage capacity. One solution to this storage problem, besides upgrading to larger devices, is to compress data. File compression, or data compression, is the technology for shrinking the size of a file so it takes up less space on the disk. This frees up space for more data and programs to reside on the disk.

Compressing files will not necessarily improve a disk's performance; that is, compressing files will not reduce a disk's access time. However, file compression can enable you to store more data on a disk, effectively increasing the disk's capacity.

Entire hard disks, floppy disks, or individual files can be compressed by as much as a 3:1 ratio (so that 300 MB of data fill only 100 MB of space, for instance). File compression is performed by software that squeezes data into smaller chunks by removing information that is not vital to the file or data.

Some favorite compression programs for PCs include PKZIP and WinZip. StuffIT is a favorite compression utility among Macintosh enthusiasts.

Most file-compression utilities are useful for compressing one or more files to reduce their storage requirements. When you use a utility like WinZip, the program actually shrinks the selected files and then saves them together inside a new file, with its own name. The resulting file is called an archive file because it stores the compressed files inside it. Archive files are commonly used for exactly that purpose—archiving unneeded data files.

Figure 6B.7 shows an example of a file-compression utility at work. Depending on the circumstances (the compression software used, the data file's native program, and other factors), the user may need to extract the compressed files manually (that is, return them to their uncompressed state) before using them. Most file compression utilities enable the user to create self-extracting archive files—files that can extract themselves automatically.

Utilities such as WinZip, PKZIP, and StuffIT generally are not used to compress the contents of an entire hard disk. Because such files must be expanded manually, a lot of effort would be required to compress a disk's contents, select and expand files when you want to use them, and then recompress them. For this reason, programs such as DriveSpace are helpful. (DriveSpace is built into some versions of Windows, and you can purchase commercial utilities that perform full-disk compression. Windows XP includes its own utility for compressing disks.)

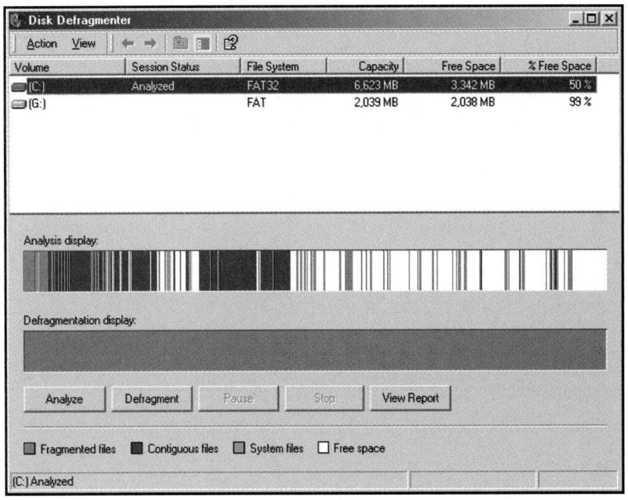

FIGURE 6B.6

The Disk Defragmenter utility in Windows XP.

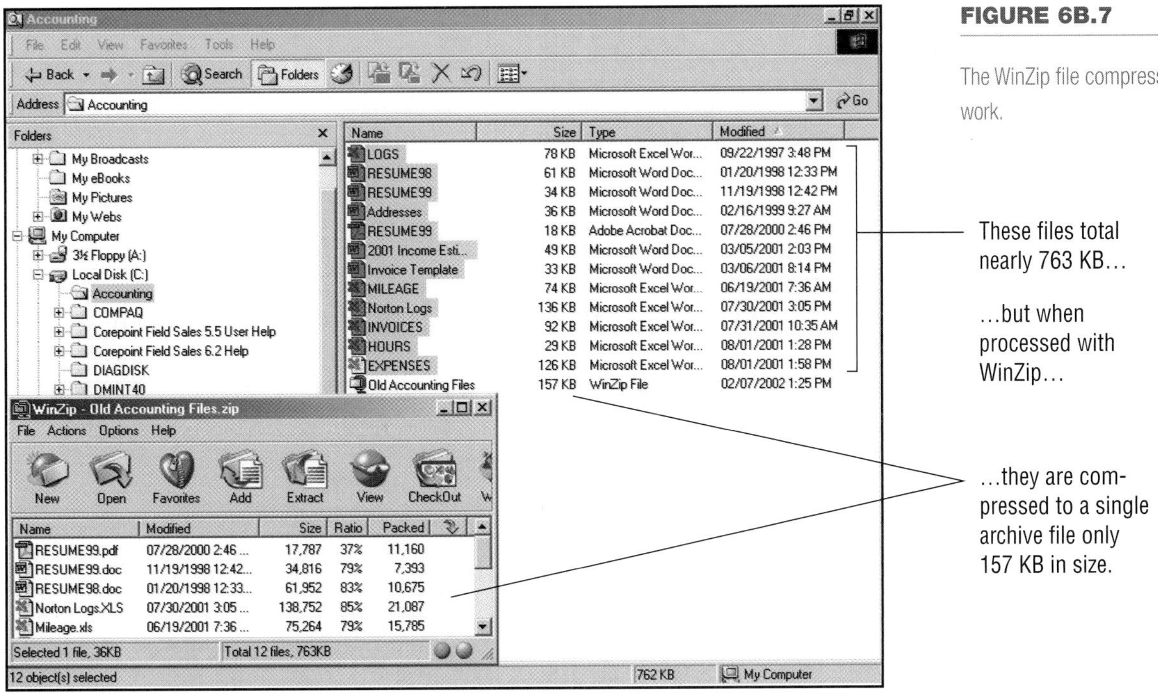

FIGURE 6B.7

The WinZip file compression utility at work.

At Issue

Digital Student Portfolios

The days of three-ring binders and spiral notebooks may be numbered. At a rising number of schools across the country, students record and share their school work not on paper but digitally.

Digital student portfolios are a selective collection of student work, chosen to present a personal learning history, posted to the World Wide Web or school intranet. Electronic portfolios can be an effective avenue for students to record personal learning, growth, and change. They can present documentation of students' abilities, provide information about what students have accomplished, as well as create a platform for students to share their work with parents, peers, and the public.

Work included in a student's portfolio may be about literature and writing, science, math, the arts, or any other subject area in the curriculum. Electronic portfolios can include varied media such as text, graphics, video, and sound, going far beyond what paper portfolios can produce and generating the capability for a wider audience.

Beyond the personal purpose of portfolios, portfolios bring together curriculum, instruction, and assessment. Creating a digital portfolio program within a school can have broader applications and can encourage schools to think about their systems and visions, and what the school wants students to be able to say about themselves.

The Coalition of Essential Schools (CES), a national affiliation of schools with a common set of beliefs about the purpose and practice of schooling, has implemented a student digital portfolio program as a school-wide innovation.

This program was activated with the understanding that the every school in the network would be involved in the preparation, planning, and implementation of a digital portfolio system. While this has been a more time-consuming and intricate process for CES than anticipated, it has allowed for more support for the program and more understanding about the schools' systems and their curriculum.

While CES uses custom-designed digital portfolio software, schools interested in working with digital portfolios can choose from a number of software products. These fall into two broad categories: software specifically designed for work with portfolios and general hypermedia software tools.

Drive-Interface Standards

Norton ONLINE

For more information on drive-interface standards, visit **http://www.mhhe.com/peternorton**.

Another important factor in determining how quickly a drive can read and write data is the type of controller that the drive uses. Just as a video monitor requires a controller to act as an interface between the CPU and the display screen, storage devices also need a controller to act as an intermediary between the drive and the CPU. A disk controller connects the disk drive to the computer's bus, acting as an interface between the two and enabling the drive to exchange data with other devices.

Currently, most personal computers use one of two drive-interface standards for built-in disk drives: EIDE or SCSI. A lot of confusion surrounds these two drive-interface standards because competing developers have introduced many variations of and names for these technologies. If you buy a PC today, it will almost certainly feature one of these two drive interfaces. If you plan to purchase a drive for an existing PC, be sure that the new drive is compatible with the computer's drive interface.

Two other types of interface—Universal Serial Bus (USB) and IEEE 1394 (also known as FireWire)—make it possible to attach additional disk drives and other devices to a computer. These interfaces

SELF-CHECK ::

Circle the correct answer for each question.

1. File compression works by removing __________ from a file.
   a. old data b. unsaved data c. unneeded data
2. What does the term *Mbps* stand for __________?
   a. megabits per second b. megabits per sector c. megabits per storage
3. What kind of storage device can be affected by fragmentation? __________
   a. optical b. magnetic c. solid-state

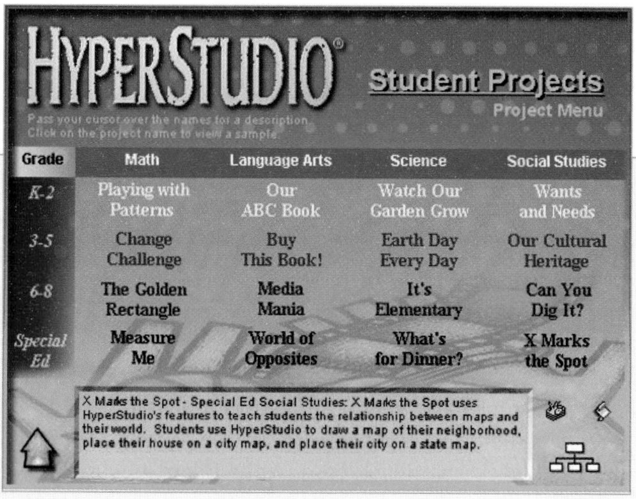

Both of these types of tools are exclusively engineered for assembling information about student work. The features vary, and schools should consider what end result is desired from a portfolio system and how each tool might help before making purchasing decisions. Electronic Portfolio by Learning Quest, Electronic Portfolio by Scholastic, and Persona Plus are examples of commercially available portfolio software.

A number of schools are opting to use hypermedia presentation tools to build portfolios from scratch. Digital Chisel (Pierian Spring Software), Director (Macromedia), and HyperStudio (Roger Wagner Publishing) are just a few examples of hypermedia software that can be utilized for digital portfolios. In addition, some schools create digital portfolios using Web-based tools.

One such school is Celebration School, a partnership between the Walt Disney Company, Stetson University, and the Osceola, Florida, school district. Using a network-based technology environment and Web-centric software, student data and information are not only platform independent, but also location independent—accessible at home and in the classroom, and across the 700-PC Celebration campus.

Says Scott Muri, Instructional Technology Specialist for the school, "As we look at the future direction of school, we're becoming increasingly Web-centric in order to effectively bridge the gap between school and home."

"Thanks to Web-based technology, in answering the parent's question 'What did you learn in school today?' the student can now say, 'Well, let me show you!'"

Source: http://www.essentialschools.org.

AT ISSUE

are not specifically drive-interface standards, because they are open and flexible enough to accommodate many kinds of devices.

Enhanced Integrated Drive Electronics (EIDE)

Enhanced integrated drive electronics (EIDE) is an improved version of an older drive-interface standard, called integrated drive electronics (IDE). While the IDE standard still exists and is the basis for several drive interfaces, the standard is known by many different names, and *EIDE* is widely regarded as the catchall term for drive interfaces based on this standard.

As a result, most new computer systems use the EIDE drive-interface standard, or one like it. The latest version of EIDE supports data transfer rates of 66 MBps. The EIDE standard's variants go by names such as Fast IDE, ATA, Fast ATA, ATA-2, ATA-3, ATA-4, Ultra ATA, and ATA66. Each offers somewhat different features and performance. For example, some EIDE disk controllers can host as many as four separate hard disks, providing access to more than 500 GB of data on a single system.

Small Computer System Interface (SCSI)

The history of the small computer system interface (SCSI) goes back to the 1970s. SCSI was originally developed as a way to connect third-party peripheral devices to mainframe computers—specifically, IBM mainframe computers. SCSI went through many transformations before the American National Standards Institute (ANSI) established a definition for the interface in 1986. Since then, the definition of SCSI has continued to evolve into SCSI-2, Wide SCSI, Fast SCSI, Fast Wide

Computers In Your Career

Careers in Outsourcing

There's no one looking over Barbara Odom's shoulder as she works on IT projects, and that's exactly how she likes it. As an independent technical writer based in Altamonte Springs, Florida, Odom has been running her own show, creating software documentation for high-tech companies since 1997. Her clients are concentrated in the financial arena and range from companies that develop financial software to companies that run ATM networks.

"Most of my clients tend to be small, entrepreneurial startups that don't have their own IT departments," says Odom, who charges those clients either $50 an hour or a flat fee to create how-to procedural guides that end users refer to when they need help installing, running, or troubleshooting their technology applications. Armed with a bachelor's degree in English from the State University of New York, Odom's job experience started in the 1980s when she served as a software support professional, conducted training classes, and wrote training materials.

Odom's work spans both online help systems and hardcopy manuals. Some projects require her to dial into a company's mainframe to access proprietary software for which she creates user manuals and documentation. Once completed, she edits the text and tweaks it to make sure it targets the proper audience, then submits the work and moves on to the next project.

When she's not writing, Odom is managing her company's technology needs, marketing herself to potential customers, upgrading hardware and software systems, and updating her own high-tech knowledge base. While Odom enjoys the independence that being an outsourcer provides, she's sometimes left out of the loop at the customer level and largely on her own when creating and completing projects.

"I don't get a lot of handholding or training," she says. "That in itself can be enjoyable, however, since it means I really have to sit down and figure out how the application works and how to convey that to the user."

As Odom has discovered, not every company can afford to staff a full-time IT department, but outsourcing isn't limited to small entrepreneurial types. Reston, Virginia–based market research firm Input reports that state and local

SCSI, Ultra SCSI, SCSI-3 (also known as Ultra-Wide SCSI), Ultra 2 SCSI, and Wide Ultra 2 SCSI.

SCSI allows even higher data transfer rates than are possible with EIDE. The Wide Ultra 2 SCSI interface, for example, supports a data transfer rate of 80 MBps. Because of its speed, flexibility, and high throughput rates, the SCSI drive interface standard is usually found in higher-end business systems, servers, and workstations (see Figure 6B.8).

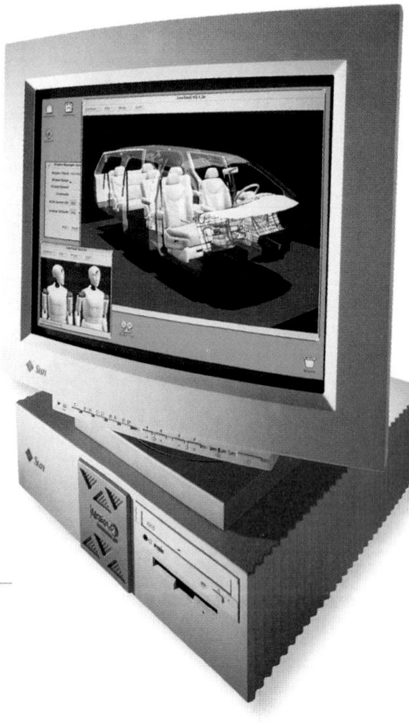

FIGURE 6B.8

SCSI drive interfaces are often found in high-performance desktop computers, workstations, and network servers.

USB and FireWire

As you learned in Chapter 5, "Processing Data," many newer computers feature Universal Serial Bus (USB) and IEEE 1394 (FireWire) interfaces. All sorts of peripherals can be attached to a computer through a USB or FireWire port, including storage devices (see Figure 6B.9).

COMPUTERS IN YOUR CAREER

governments also have jumped on the outsourcing bandwagon and will outsource $23 billion worth of information technology work by 2008.

Millions of skilled workers now work exclusively on an outsourced basis and make themselves available to any company that needs their skills for a given amount of time for fees that range from $25 to $100 an hour. Here are some of the most commonly outsourced positions for people with computer skills:

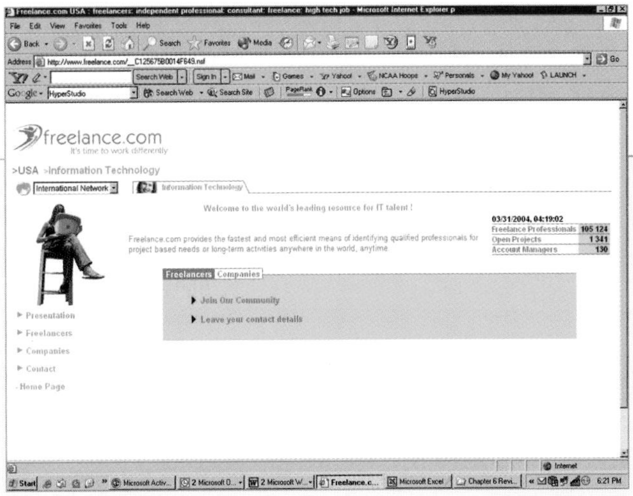

» **Programmers.** Software projects often get behind schedule or overwhelm a company's development staff. In either case, the company can fill the gaps by hiring a freelance programmer.

» **Network Administrators.** Nearly every American company has a computer network, but the vast majority of small- and medium-sized businesses cannot afford to keep a network administrator on staff. Instead, the business may outsource the work.

» **Hardware Technicians.** Successful freelance technicians have training (and certification, if possible) on many types of computer hardware, including desktop PCs, network servers, networking hardware, printers, and more.

Although USB and FireWire are not considered to be drive interfaces per se (they support many types of devices), they support high data transfer rates and provide connections that allow the host computer to control an external storage device just as if it were an internal one.

Like SCSI, USB and FireWire allow users to connect many peripherals at the same time. If your computer needs extra storage, this means you can simply purchase additional hard drives as you need them and connect them to your PC via a USB or FireWire connection.

FIGURE 6B.9

Many external storage devices, like this one from Maxtor, can be plugged into a PC's FireWire or USB port.

LESSON // 6B Review

Summary ::

- In storage devices, the average access time is the time it takes a read/write head to move to a spot on the storage medium.
- Diskette drives offer an average access time of 100 milliseconds. Hard drives are many times faster.
- Tape drives provide the slowest average access times of all magnetic storage devices; optical devices are also much slower than hard disks.
- The data transfer rate is a measure of how long it takes a given amount of data to travel from one device to another. Hard disks offer the fastest data transfer rates of any storage device.
- You can optimize the performance of a PC's hard disk by cleaning off unneeded files, scanning the disk for errors, and defragmenting the disk.
- File compression technology is used to shrink the size of files so that they take up less disk space.
- By using compression utilities, you can shrink multiple files into a single archive file. Some utilities enable you to compress the entire contents of a hard disk.
- Two drive-interface standards are commonly used today: EIDE and SCSI.
- Many storage devices can be connected to a PC's USB or FireWire port.

Key Terms ::

archive file, 251
average access time, 248
data compression, 250
data transfer rate, 248
defragmentation, 250
disk controller, 252
disk optimization, 249
enhanced integrated drive electronics (EIDE), 253
extract, 251
file compression, 250
fragmentation, 250
millisecond (ms), 248
nanosecond (ns), 248
seek time, 248
small computer system interface (SCSI), 253
temporary (temp) file, 249
throughput, 248
uninstalling, 250

Key Term Quiz ::

Complete each statement by writing one of the terms listed under Key Terms in each blank.

1. The amount of time a storage device takes to position its head over any spot on the medium is called ________ .
2. For storage devices, access times are measured in ________ .
3. For memory devices, access times are measured in ________ .
4. ________ may be measured in megabytes per second or megabits per second.
5. Any PC that gets used a lot should get routine disk maintenance, or ________ .
6. Over time, hundreds of ________ files can collect on your computer's hard disk.
7. ________ occurs when a file is stored in noncontiguous sectors on a disk's surface.
8. When you use a file compression utility to compress several files together, a special file, called a(n) ________ , is the result.
9. The term *EIDE* stands for ________ .
10. The term *SCSI* stands for ________ .

Multiple Choice ::

Circle the word or phrase that best completes each statement.

1. This lets you fit more data onto a magnetic disk.
   a. extraction b. defragmentation c. compression d. scanning
2. Which of the following connects a disk drive to the computer's bus?
   a. a hard disk b. a drive interface c. a sensor d. a standard
3. To remove a program from your computer, you can ________ it.
   a. uninstall b. delete c. store d. transfer
4. If a file is ________, its pieces are scattered across the surface of a disk.
   a. compressed b. archived c. defragmented d. fragmented
5. Which of the following is a common drive interface standard used in PCs?
   a. AEIOU b. ETC c. EIDE d. EIEIO
6. Which must you do to return compressed files to their uncompressed state?
   a. delete them b. extract them c. archive them d. Zip them
7. If a disk has a bad spot on its surface, the spot can be called a ________ .
   a. disk crash b. disk error c. disk scanner d. disk sector
8. Which drive-interface standard supports data transfer rates of 66 MBps?
   a. EIDE b. SCSI c. USB d. FireWire
9. What does the term *SCSI* stand for?
   a. small computer software interface b. small computer storage interface c. small computer system interface d. small computer standard interface
10. Although it is not a drive interface per se, this type of connection does support storage devices.
   a. EIDE b. USB c. SCSI d. MBps

Review Questions ::

In your own words, briefly answer the following questions.

1. What is the primary purpose of file compression utilities such as WinZip?
2. What is another name for the IEEE 1394 interface?
3. What is data transfer rate?
4. What is the most effective way to measure the average access time of a hard disk?
5. What is the average access time for a diskette drive?
6. What are average access times like for hard disks?
7. List three tasks you can perform that can improve the performance of a computer's hard disk.
8. How can fragmentation harm a system's performance?
9. Why is there confusion about the EIDE and SCSI drive-interface standards?
10. How are the SCSI, USB, and FireWire interfaces similar?

Lesson Labs ::

Complete the following exercise as directed by your instructor.

1. Learn what kind of hard disk controllers are installed in your computer.
   a. Open the Control Panel window, as directed by your instructor.
   b. Double-click the System icon to open the System Properties dialog box.
   c. Click the Device Manager tab. Click the plus sign (+) in front of Hard Disk Controllers. (Note: Depending on which version of Windows you use, you may need to access the Device Manager in a different way. Ask your instructor for specific directions.)
   d. Click to highlight an item listed under Hard Disk Controllers (depending on your OS, this item may be listed as one or more specific types of controllers); then click the Properties button. Write down the data for the selected controller, and then click Cancel.
   e. Repeat step D for each controller listed. When finished, click Cancel to close the System Properties dialog box. Then close the Control Panel window.

Chapter Labs

Complete the following exercises using a computer in your classroom, lab, or home.

1. Find your optimization tools. If you use Windows 98 or a later version, you can use the operating system's built-in disk optimization tools to remove unneeded files from a disk, to defragment a disk, and to scan a disk for errors.

   To use Disk Cleanup in Windows 98, Me, 2000, or XP:

   a. Click the Start button, open the Programs menu, click Accessories | System Tools | Disk Cleanup.
   b. When the Select Drive dialog box appears, click the drop-down arrow and select your primary hard disk. (This should be drive C:. If you are not sure which drive to select, ask your instructor for assistance.
   c. Click Ok.
   d. In the Disk Cleanup for dialog box, select all the check boxes in the Files to Delete list.
   e. If you want to see any of the files before deleting them, click the type of files you want to see, then click the View Files button. Close any windows that open to return to the Disk Cleanup for dialog box.
   f. Click Ok in the Disk Cleanup for dialog box.
   g. Windows may display a message box asking if you are sure you want to delete the files. If so, click the Yes button.
      Windows deletes the files.

   To scan your disk for errors:

In Windows 98 or Me:

A. Click Start button | Programs, click Accessories | System Tools | click ScanDisk.
B. When the ScanDisk dialog box opens, select your computer's primary disk drive. (This should be drive C:. If you are not sure which drive to choose, ask your instructor for help.)
C. Set other options in the ScanDisk dialog box, as directed by your instructor, then click Start.
D. Watch as Windows scans the disk for errors.
E. Click the CANCEL button when your instructor tells you to. Then click CLOSE to close the ScanDisk dialog box.

If you use Windows 2000 or XP:

A. Launch either Windows Explorer or My Computer, depending on your preference.
B. When the Windows Explorer or My Computer window opens, select your computer's primary disk drive. (This should be drive C:. If you are not sure which drive to choose, ask your instructor for help.)
C. Right-click the selected drive's icon. When the shortcut menu appears, click Properties.
D. When the Properties dialog box appears, click the Tools tab. Under Error-checking, click the Check Now button.
E. When the Check Disk dialog box appears, set options as directed by your instructor, then click Start.
F. Watch as Windows performs the scan. The actions Windows takes will depend on the options you selected in step E. When the scan is complete, close all open dialog boxes, then close the Windows Explorer or My Computer window.

CHAPTER SKILLS REVIEW

To defragment your hard disk with Windows' Disk Defragmenter:

In Windows 98 or Me:

A. Click Start button | Programs | Accessories | System Tools | Disk Defragmenter.

B. When the Select Drive dialog box opens, select your computer's primary disk drive. (This should be drive C:. If you are not sure which drive to choose, ask your instructor for help.)

C. Click the Settings button.

D. In the Disk Defragmenter Settings dialog box, select options as directed by your instructor, then click OK.

E. When the Select Drive dialog box reappears, click OK.

F. Windows begins defragmenting the disk. You can watch its progress by clicking the Show Details button.

G. Click the Stop button when your instructor tells you to. Then click Exit to close Disk Defragmenter.

If you use Windows 2000 or XP:

A. Click Start | Programs | Accessories | System Tools | Disk Defragmenter.

B. When the Disk Defragmenter window opens, select your computer's primary disk drive. (This should be drive C:. If you are not sure which drive to choose, ask your instructor for help.)

C. Click the Analyze button, and then watch the Analysis display pane as Windows determines the status of your disk drive.

D. When analysis is complete, click the Defragment button. Click the Stop button when your instructor tells you to.

E. Click the View Report button.

F. Review the report of your disk's status, and then click Close to close the report.

G. Click the Close button to close Disk Defragmenter.

Discussion Questions

As directed by your instructor, discuss the following questions in class or in groups.

1. Why do you think a basic truth in computing is that one never has enough storage space? What factors contribute to this situation? As hard disks get larger and larger, do you think we will reach a point where the standard desktop computer has more than enough storage space for the average user's needs? Have we reached that point already?
2. Suppose that your class is actually one department within a medium-sized company. You need to adopt a backup system for the department's data. As a group, what factors should you consider in making this decision? What backup technologies should you consider? What type of backup schedule should you follow?

Research and Report

Using your own choice of resources (such as the Internet, books, magazines, and newspaper articles), research and write a short paper discussing one of the following topics:

- The growth in capacity of PC storage devices, from the 1980s to the present.
- The consequences of compressing an entire hard disk's contents, using a utility such as DriveSpace.
- Holographic memory and its potential uses.

When you are finished, proofread and print your paper, and give it to your instructor.

ETHICAL ISSUES

Many storage device options are available. These choices are beneficial for many users, but they also can be drawbacks for software companies, music publishers, and others. With this thought in mind, discuss the following questions in class:

1. CD-R and CD-RW devices are getting cheaper and more popular. They let you create backups and store data in a safe format. However, people also use them to make illegal duplicates of software and audio CDs. If you had a CD-R or CD-RW device, would you consider making illegal duplicates? Do you think such copying should be illegal? Defend your answer.
2. You have seen that large companies store gigabytes of data about their customers. Do you know that many companies sell this information to other companies? As more organizations build databases about individuals, do you believe they should be free to exchange or sell this information? Why?

CHAPTER 7

Using Operating Systems

CHAPTER CONTENTS ::

This chapter contains the following lessons:

Lesson **7A:**
Operating Systems Basics

- >> Types of Operating Systems
- >> Providing a User Interface
- >> Running Programs
- >> Managing Hardware
- >> Enhancing an OS with Utility Software

Lesson **7B:**
Survey of PC and Network Operating Systems

- >> PC Operating Systems
- >> Network Operating Systems
- >> Embedded Operating Systems

Some other services that an operating system provides to programs, in addition to listing files, include

- Saving the contents of files to a disk.
- Reading the contents of a file from disk into memory.
- Sending a document to the printer and activating the printer.
- Providing resources that let you copy or move data from one document to another, or from one program to another.
- Allocating RAM among the running programs.
- Recognizing keystrokes or mouse clicks and displaying characters or graphics on the screen.

Sharing Information

Many types of applications let you move chunks of data from one place to another. For example, you may want to copy a chart from a spreadsheet program and place the copy in a document in a word processing program (see Figure 7A.13). Some operating systems accomplish this feat with a feature known as the Clipboard. The Clipboard is a temporary holding space (in the computer's memory) for data that is being copied or moved. The Clipboard is available for use by applications running under the operating system. For example, if you want to

Norton ONLINE

For more information on data sharing, visit **http://www.mhhe.com/peternorton**.

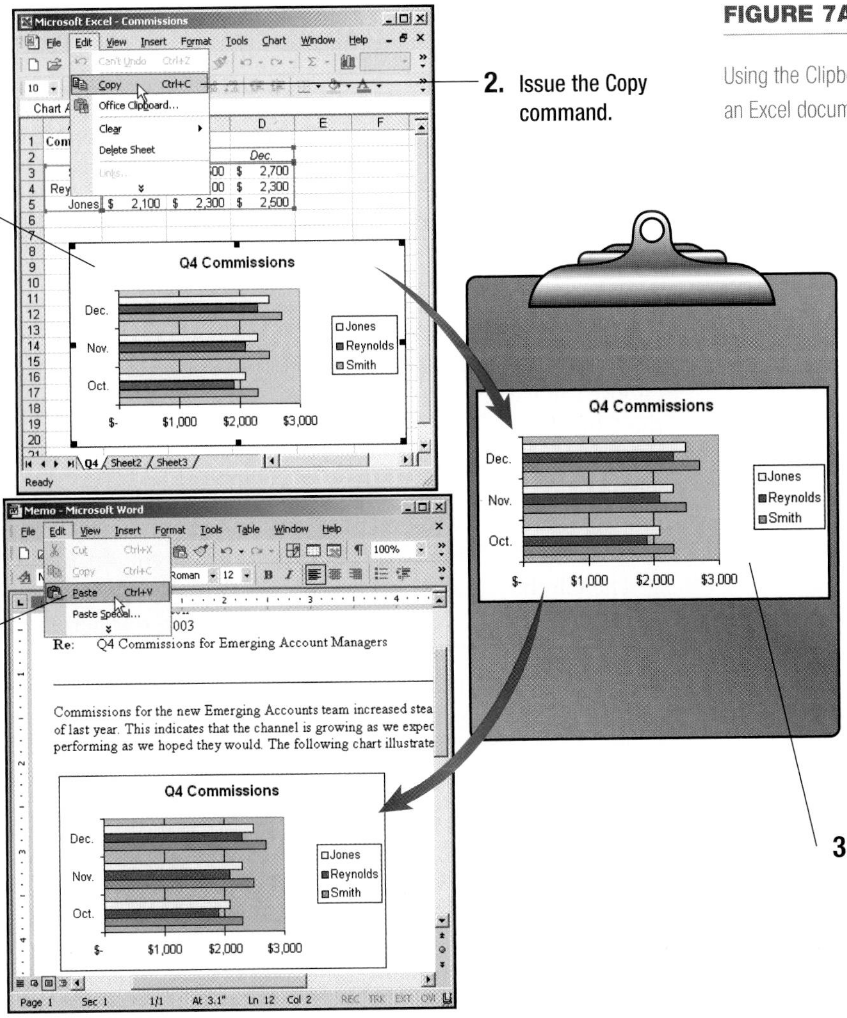

1. Select the desired data—in this case, a chart in Excel.
2. Issue the Copy command.
3. A copy of the data is placed on the Windows Clipboard.
4. Go to the destination document and issue the Paste command. The chart is placed in the Word document.
Q4 Commissions

FIGURE 7A.13

Using the Clipboard to copy a chart from an Excel document to a Word document.

Productivity Tip

Do-It-Yourself Tech Support

If you want to learn a new feature or need help solving a problem with a software program, the answers may be on your hard disk or the Internet.

Using Local Online Help

Most commercial operating systems and applications include an online help system that is installed on your computer along with the software. New-generation help systems include descriptions, tips, audio/video demonstrations, hyperlinks, and links to Internet-based resources.

To find help on your hard disk, open the help system and look for answers. To get help with the Windows XP operating system, for example, click the Start button and choose Help and Support from the Start menu. In any Windows application, click the Help menu and choose Contents or Help Topics. A Help window appears, providing tools that let you search for help in different ways. Remember the following tips:

» **Be Patient.** You may not find your answer immediately. Be prepared to try again.

» **Learn Different Search Options.** Most Windows-based help systems provide different options for finding help. For example, you may be able to browse a list of help topics that are organized by category. Or you may be able to search the help system for topics that contain certain terms or phrases. Some help systems let you type questions in plain English. If you need help printing a document, for example, you can type the question "How do I print a document?"

» **Think of the Problem in Different Ways.** For example, if you want help with setting up an Internet connection, the terms "Internet," "connection," "modem," and "Internet account" may bring up the right answers.

» **Use Bookmarks and Annotations.** Most help systems let you bookmark specific help topics so you can find them again quickly. You also can add your own notes to specific topics.

Using Remote Online Help

Many software makers provide help resources that you can access over the Internet.

» **Web-Based Technical Support.** Many software companies have a Support or Help link on their Web home page.

move a paragraph in a word processor document, select the paragraph, then choose the Cut command; the data is removed from the document and placed on the Clipboard. (If you want to leave the original data in place, you can use the Copy command; a copy is made of the data, and it is stored on the Clipboard but is not removed from the document.) After placing the insertion point in the document where you want to place the paragraph, you choose the Paste command; the data on the Clipboard is then placed into the document.

The Clipboard also can be used to move data from one document to another. For example, you can copy an address from one letter to another and thereby avoid rekeying the address. The real versatility of the Clipboard, however, stems from the fact that it is actually a part of the operating system and not a particular application. As a result, you can use the Clipboard to move data from one program to another.

The versatility of the Clipboard has been extended further with a feature known in Windows as OLE, which stands for Object Linking and Embedding. A simple cut and paste between applications results in object embedding. The data, which is known as an object in programming terms, is embedded in a new type of document. It retains the formatting that was applied to it in the original application, but its relationship with the original file is destroyed; that is, it is simply part of the new file. Furthermore, the data may be of a type that the open application

- **FAQs.** Most software companies have Web sites with lists of frequently asked questions (FAQs).
- **E-Mail Help.** At the company's Web site, you may find an option that lets you describe a problem and submit a request for help. A support technician will investigate the problem, or an automated system will send you a list of possible solutions.
- **Knowledge Bases.** A knowledge base is a sophisticated database containing detailed information about specific topics. To use a knowledge base, you type a term or phrase or describe a problem. After your text is matched against a database, you are presented with a list of possible solutions.
- **Newsgroups.** Large software companies sponsor newsgroups on the Internet. Using your newsreader, you can access these newsgroups, post questions for other users to answer, or participate in discussions about specific products and technical issues.

Before you use any remote online help resource, read all the information the company provides about it. Look for notices about fees, registration, and proof of product ownership.

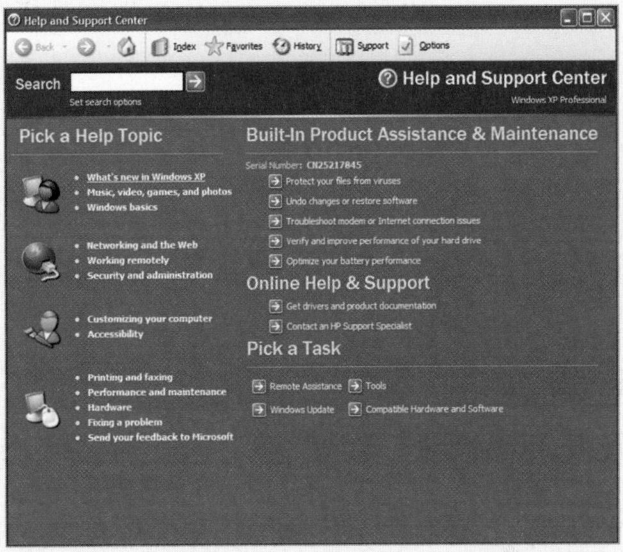

A program's help system is often the last place users turn for help, when it should be the first place.

cannot change. Therefore, if you want to edit embedded data, simply double-click the embedded object, and the original application that created the data is opened to allow editing of the embedded data.

Object linking adds another layer to the relationship: The data that is copied to and from the Clipboard retains a link to the original document so that a change in the original document also appears in the linked data. For example, suppose that the spreadsheet and memo shown in Figure 7A.13 are generated quarterly. They always contain the same chart updated with the most recent numbers. With object linking, when the numbers in the spreadsheet are changed, the chart in the report will automatically reflect the new figures. Of course, object linking is not automatic; you need to use special commands in your applications to create the link.

Managing Hardware

When programs run, they need to use the computer's memory, monitor, disk drives, and other devices, such as a printer. The operating system is the intermediary between programs and hardware. In a computer network, the operating system also mediates between your computer and other devices on the network.

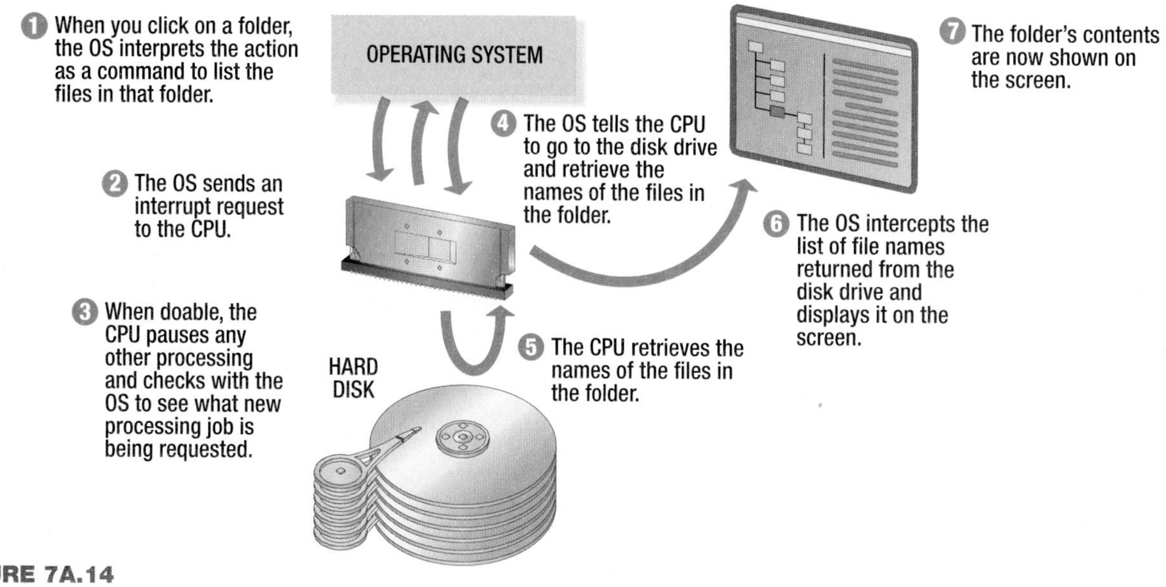
1 When you click on a folder, the OS interprets the action as a command to list the files in that folder.
OPERATING SYSTEM
2 The OS sends an interrupt request to the CPU.
3 When doable, the CPU pauses any other processing and checks with the OS to see what new processing job is being requested.
4 The OS tells the CPU to go to the disk drive and retrieve the names of the files in the folder.
HARD DISK
5 The CPU retrieves the names of the files in the folder.
6 The OS intercepts the list of file names returned from the disk drive and displays it on the screen.
7 The folder's contents are now shown on the screen.

FIGURE 7A.14

How the operating system communicates with the CPU.

Processing Interrupts

The operating system responds to requests to use memory and other devices, keeps track of which programs have access to which devices, and coordinates everything the hardware does so that various activities do not overlap causing the computer to become confused and stop working. The operating system uses interrupt requests (IRQs) to help the CPU coordinate processes. For example, Figure 7A.14 shows what happens if you tell the operating system to list the files in a folder.

Working with Device Drivers

In addition to using interrupts, the operating system often provides programs for working with special devices such as printers. These programs are called drivers because they allow the operating system and other programs to activate and use—that is, "drive"—the hardware device. Most new software you buy will work with your printer, monitor, and other equipment without requiring you to install any special drivers.

Enhancing an OS with Utility Software

Norton ONLINE

For more information on utility software, visit **http://www.mhhe.com/peternorton**.

Operating systems are designed to let you do most of the tasks you normally would want to do with a computer, such as managing files, loading programs, printing documents, and so on. But software developers are constantly creating new programs—called utilities—that enhance or extend the operating system's capabilities, or that simply offer new features not provided by the operating system itself. As an operating system is improved and updated, the functionality of popular utilities is included with subsequent releases of the OS. There are thousands of different utility programs, and you can find many on the Internet—some free and some at a price ranging from very inexpensive to hundreds of dollars.

While it is difficult to give a definitive list of utility software categories, the most common types that ordinary people use are disk and file management, Internet security, and OS customization tools. To complicate matters further, there are many packaged utility suites that combine two or more utilities into one bundle. The following sections describe a small selection of popular utilities.

Backup Utilities

For safekeeping, a backup utility can help you copy large groups of files from your hard disk to another storage medium, such as tape or a CD-R disc. Many newer operating systems feature built-in backup utilities (see Figure 7A.15), but feature-rich backup software is available from other sources. These utilities not only help you transfer files to a backup medium, they also help organize the files, update backups, and restore backups to disk in case of data loss.

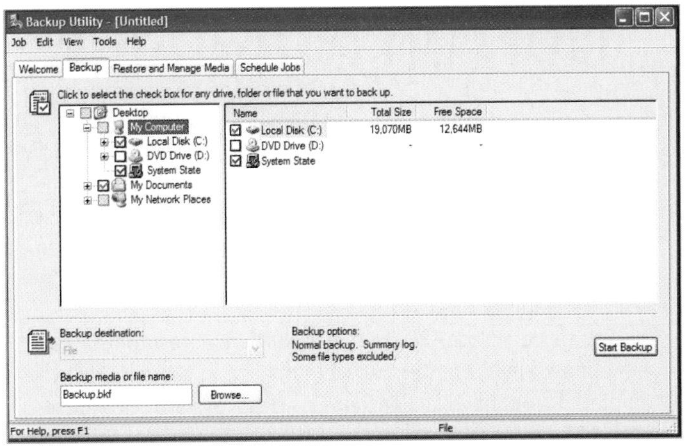

FIGURE 7A.15

The Windows Backup utility.

Antivirus

A virus is a parasitic program that can delete or scramble files or replicate itself until the host disk is full. As you will learn in "Computing Keynotes: Viruses," computer viruses can be transmitted in numerous ways, and users should be especially vigilant when downloading files over the Internet or reusing old diskettes that may be infected. An antivirus utility can examine the contents of a disk or RAM for hidden viruses and files that may act as hosts for virus code. Effective antivirus products not only detect and remove viruses; they also help you recover data that has been lost because of a virus.

Firewall

Your ISP and most corporations employ specialized computers on their Internet connections that are dedicated to examining and blocking traffic coming from and going to the Internet. Such a computer is called a firewall, and manufacturers such as Cisco, 3COM, and others offer these products at a very high price. These firewalls also require highly trained people to manage them. If you work in a corporation where a firewall is protecting the corporate network, leave the firewall function to the experts. At home, however, you will want to be sure to use either a smaller, less-expensive hardware firewall or install a software firewall utility on any computer directly connected to the Internet. Windows XP comes with a simple firewall that you can optionally turn on through the Properties dialog of each network connection. There are many third-party firewall programs, such as Kerio Winroute Pro, shown in Figure 7A.16.

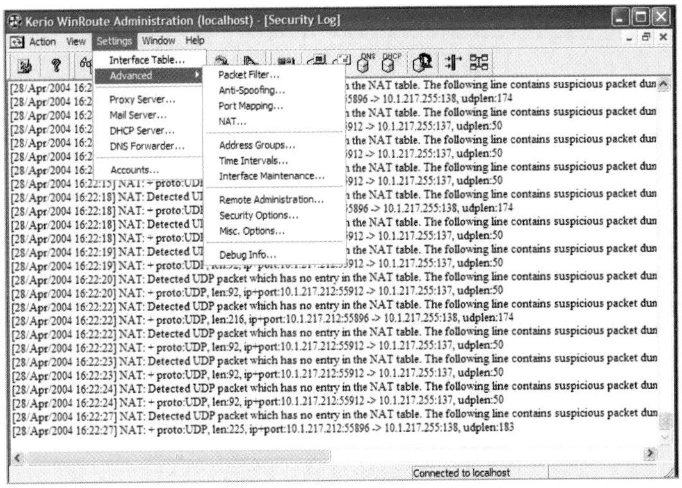

FIGURE 7A.16

Kerio Winroute Pro is one of many inexpensive personal firewall products available today.

Intrusion Detection

While a firewall offers protection from predictable intrusion, intrusion detection software reveals the types of attacks a firewall is thwarting, creating logs of the attempts and (depending on how you configure it) notifying you of certain types of intrusion attempts. In the competitive utility software field, intrusion detection is often added as a feature to firewall or bundled Internet security programs.

Screen Savers

Screen savers are popular utilities, although they serve little purpose other than to hide what would otherwise be displayed on the screen. A screen saver automatically appears when a keyboard or pointing device has not been used for a

Norton Notebook

Changing Your PC's Operating System

The operating system market has expanded over the past few years, freeing PC users to choose different operating systems. Users no longer feel locked into the OS provided by the PC's manufacturer.

Any newer-model PC (if it has sufficient resources) can run almost any currently available operating system. For example, if you have a Pentium II–class or later computer with 128 MB of RAM and a large hard disk, you do not necessarily need to run Windows 9*x*. Instead, you can use Windows NT or 2000, OS/2, Linux, and some versions of UNIX (but not the Mac OS). You might even be able to run Windows XP. If you have a Macintosh, you also may be able to run some versions of UNIX or Linux (but not Windows).

Consider Your Needs First

Consider your need for a new operating system. Do you need a different OS to use a specific application? Is the OS used in your workplace or school, or do you need to be OS-compliant with a workgroup? Do you plan to develop or test applications that run on a specific operating system? Or will a different operating system allow better performance from your computer? If you answer yes to any of these questions, a new OS may be a good idea.

Compatibility Is a Must

Before installing an OS, make sure that your hardware is completely compatible with it. If you have any doubts, check with the manufacturers of your computer and any devices attached to it. Check with the operating system's developer to see if a "hardware compatibility list" is available. This document may answer all your hardware-related questions and may be found on the developer's Web site. If you suspect a problem, weigh the costs of replacing the hardware against installing a new OS.

If your hardware is compatible, make sure you have adequate resources for the new OS. Having adequate resources can be a problem for some operating systems, such as Windows 2000 and XP, which consume a great deal of system resources. Make sure your PC has enough power, memory, and storage, not just for the OS, but also for your applications and data.

Next, make a list of all the applications you use or plan to use, and make sure they will run under the new OS. Be sure to include your utilities, Internet tools, and others. You may need to upgrade or replace some or all of your software to accommodate the new OS. Again, weigh this cost against the need for a new OS.

specified period of time. Screen savers display a moving image on the screen and were originally created to prevent displayed images from "burning" into the monitor. Today's monitors do not suffer from this problem, but screen savers remain a popular utility because they can add personality to the user's system. Figure 7A.17 shows a Windows screen saver that comes with the newer versions of Windows. Screen savers are available from many sources, and you can even use your own picture and graphic files with most screen saver programs.

FIGURE 7A.17

When the Windows 3D Pipes Screen Saver is active, it draws pipes with lots of bends.

Taking the Big Step

Before you install anything, take these precautions:

- **Back Up Your Hard Disk.** If you plan to install the OS on your existing hard disk, make a complete backup beforehand. If the installation goes wrong, you can restore the disk to its previous state. Before you back up, test the disk for errors (by using ScanDisk or a similar utility), defragment the drive, and run a full virus scan.
- **Decide Whether to Reformat.** You may want to reformat the disk completely before installing a new OS. Reformatting erases everything related to the previous operating system, and it may make installation easier. If you do not know how to format a hard disk, look in your current operating system's help system and follow the directions closely.
- **Call for Help If You Need It.** If you have never installed a new OS, you may not be prepared for all the pitfalls involved. If the upgrade is essential, then it is worth doing right, so get help from an experienced user or a computer technician before you start. Most computer manufacturers have extensive customer service support, but be prepared to wait some time before talking to a "real" person. If your questions are answered, then it is worth the wait.

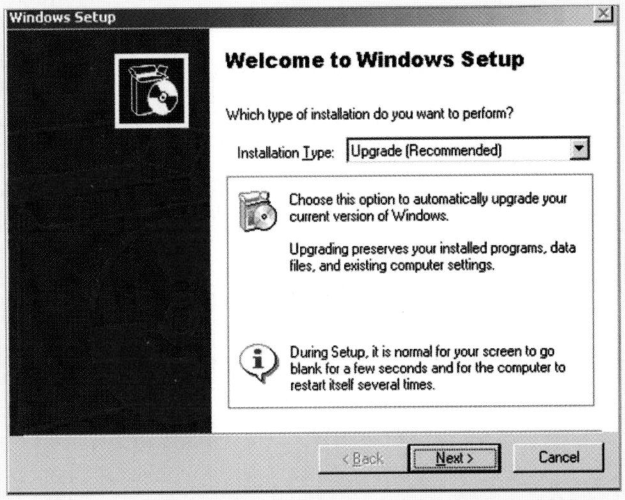

Many operating systems, such as Windows 2000 and XP, walk you through the upgrade process. They can even tell you if your existing hardware and software are compatible with the new OS.

LESSON // 7A Review

Summary ::

- An operating system is system software that acts as a master control program, controlling the hardware and interacting with the user and application software.
- An operating system performs the following functions:
  - Displays the on-screen elements with which you interact—the user interface.
  - Loads programs into the computer's memory so that you can use them.
  - Coordinates how programs work with the computer's hardware and other software.
  - Manages the way information is stored on and retrieved from disks.
- The four major types of operating systems are real-time operating systems, single-user/single-tasking operating systems, single-user/multitasking operating systems, and multi-user/multitasking operating systems.
- Most modern operating systems feature a graphical user interface (GUI). You control a GUI-based system by clicking graphical objects on the screen. In a typical GUI, all objects and resources appear on a background called the desktop.
- In a GUI, you access programs and other resources in rectangular frames called windows. Applications running under the same operating system use many of the same graphical elements, so you see a familiar interface no matter what program you are using.
- Some older operating systems use a command-line interface, which the user controls by typing commands at a prompt.
- The operating system manages all the other programs that run on the PC, and it provides services such as file management, memory management, and printing to those programs.
- Some operating systems enable programs to share information using a feature known as the Clipboard. This lets you create data in one program and use it again in other programs.
- The Object Linking and Embedding feature in Windows extends its data-sharing capabilities, allowing you to embed data into a document while working in an application that cannot, on its own, manipulate the data.
- The OS uses interrupt requests (IRQs) to maintain organized communication with the CPU and other hardware.
- Each hardware device is controlled by another piece of software, called a driver, that allows the OS to activate and use the device.
- A utility is a program that extends or enhances the operating system's capability. It may add a new capability to the operating system.

Key Terms ::

activate, 268
active window, 269
antivirus utility, 277
backup utility, 277
choose, 268
Clipboard, 273
command-line interface, 271
context menu, 269
Copy command, 274
Cut command, 274
desktop, 268
dialog box, 271
driver, 276
graphical user interface (GUI), 268
icon, 268
intrusion detection software, 277
menu, 270
menu bar, 269
multitasking, 266
multi-user/multitasking operating system, 267
Object Linking and Embedding (OLE), 274
Paste command, 274
pointer, 268
prompt, 271
Quick Launch bar, 269
real-time application, 266
real-time operating system, 266
screen saver, 277
scroll bar, 269
shortcut, 268
shortcut menu, 269
single-user/multitasking operating system, 266
single-user/single-tasking operating system, 266
Start button, 269
Start menu, 269
system call, 271
task switching, 270
taskbar, 269
terminal client, 267
terminal server, 267
title bar, 269
toolbar, 269
user interface, 268
user session, 267
utility, 276
window, 269

Key Term Quiz ::

Complete each statement by writing one of the terms listed under Key Terms in each blank.

1. The small pictures on the desktop—called __________—represent links to resources on the PC or network.
2. __________ is the ability to perform two or more tasks at the same time.
3. You interact with a command-line interface by typing strings of characters at a(n) __________ .
4. A running program may take up the whole screen or it may appear in a rectangular frame, called a(n) __________ .
5. A program that lets you back up data files is an example of a(n) __________ .
6. In a graphical user interface, you use a mouse (or other pointing device) to move a(n) __________ around the screen.
7. A(n) __________ supports an application that responds to certain input very, very quickly.
8. The process of moving from one open window to another is called __________ .
9. In Windows, when you right-click some objects on the screen, a special __________ appears.
10. In a GUI __________ let you view parts of a program or file that do not fit in the window.

LESSON // 7A Review

Multiple Choice ::

Circle the word or phrase that best completes each statement.

1. In a GUI, the window that is currently in use is called the ________ window.
   a. top b. active c. biggest d. framed
2. A list of command choices in an operating system or application is called a ________ .
   a. command line b. check box c. drop-down list d. menu
3. DOS and some versions of UNIX are examples of ________ interfaces.
   a. old-fashioned b. GUI c. command-line d. parallel
4. To remove data from one document and place it in another, you can use the ________ and ________ commands.
   a. Cut, Paste b. Copy, Paste c. File, Open d. Delete, Paste
5. In many GUI-based programs, a ________ displays buttons that let you issue commands quickly.
   a. command bar b. scroll bar c. menu bar d. toolbar
6. From what you learned in this chapter, select the type of operating system you would expect to be used in a computerized heart monitor.
   a. multi-user/multitasking b. real-time c. single-user/multitasking d. single-user/single tasking
7. Which of the following is *not* a type of utility software?
   a. customization tools b. disk and file management c. tabbed dialog box d. Internet security
8. The operating system is the intermediary between programs and ________ .
   a. user interface b. utilities c. ether d. hardware
9. An operating system keeps track of which programs have access to which hardware devices and uses ________ to help the CPU coordinate processes.
   a. interrupt requests (IRQs) b. disk drives c. multitasking d. user interface
10. What type of operating system allows multiple users to connect over the network to a special server and work with their programs in separate sessions, and allows each user to run multiple programs?
    a. single-user/multiple computers b. real time c. multi-user/multitasking d. single-user/single-tasking

Review Questions ::

In your own words, briefly answer the following questions.

1. What are the four primary functions that an operating system performs?
2. What device is used to work with graphical objects in a GUI?
3. When working with Windows, what happens when you right-click on most objects?
4. What is the function of windows in a GUI?
5. Why is task-switching a necessary feature of a multitasking operating system?
6. What is a dialog box?
7. Describe the Clipboard and its use.
8. What is the difference between object linking and object embedding?
9. Explain the value of running a screen saver.
10. Explain what a driver does.

Lesson Labs ::

Complete the following exercises as directed by your instructor.

1. Use your online help system to learn more about Windows. Click the START button, and then choose Help and Support from the Start menu. Explore the Help window to learn more about the tools provided by the help system in your particular version of the operating system. (The exact features vary from one version of Windows to another.) When you are comfortable with the Help window, use any method you prefer to search for information on these topics: *operating system, GUI, command, dialog box, menu,* and *multitasking*. When you are finished, close the Help window.
2. Practice using the DOS command prompt:
   a. Click the START button.
   b. If you use Windows 9*x* or 2000, point to Programs, then click the MS-DOS prompt on the Programs menu. If you use Windows XP, choose All Programs | Accessories | Command Prompt. Either way, the command prompt appears in a new window.
   c. At the prompt, type **DIR** and press ENTER. Review the results. Then type the **VER** command, press ENTER, and review the results. Close the window.

LESSON // 7B

Survey of PC and Network Operating Systems

OBJECTIVES ::

- >> List all the current PC operating systems.
- >> List and differentiate the various versions of Windows.
- >> Describe the role of network operating systems.
- >> Identify three current embedded operating systems.

Overview: Operating Systems Yesterday and Today

The personal computer (PC) has come a long way in a relatively short time, and much of the progress is due to the continuing advancements in operating systems. Over the past 30 years, the evolution in operating systems has made PCs easier to use and understand, more flexible, and more reliable. Today, in addition to the operating systems that consume hundreds of megabytes of disk space on personal computers, miniaturized operating systems fit into tiny handheld portable digital assistants (PDAs) and even cellular telephones.

Computer users have several choices when it comes to operating systems, although the choice is not always easy. The vast majority of new PCs are sold with some version of Windows installed, but many users (especially in business) are choosing to run UNIX or Linux. Apple Macintosh computers and the proprietary Mac OS have a small but important share of the desktop OS market.

This lesson is a survey of the primary operating systems used on personal computers and network servers today, describing the basic features of each.

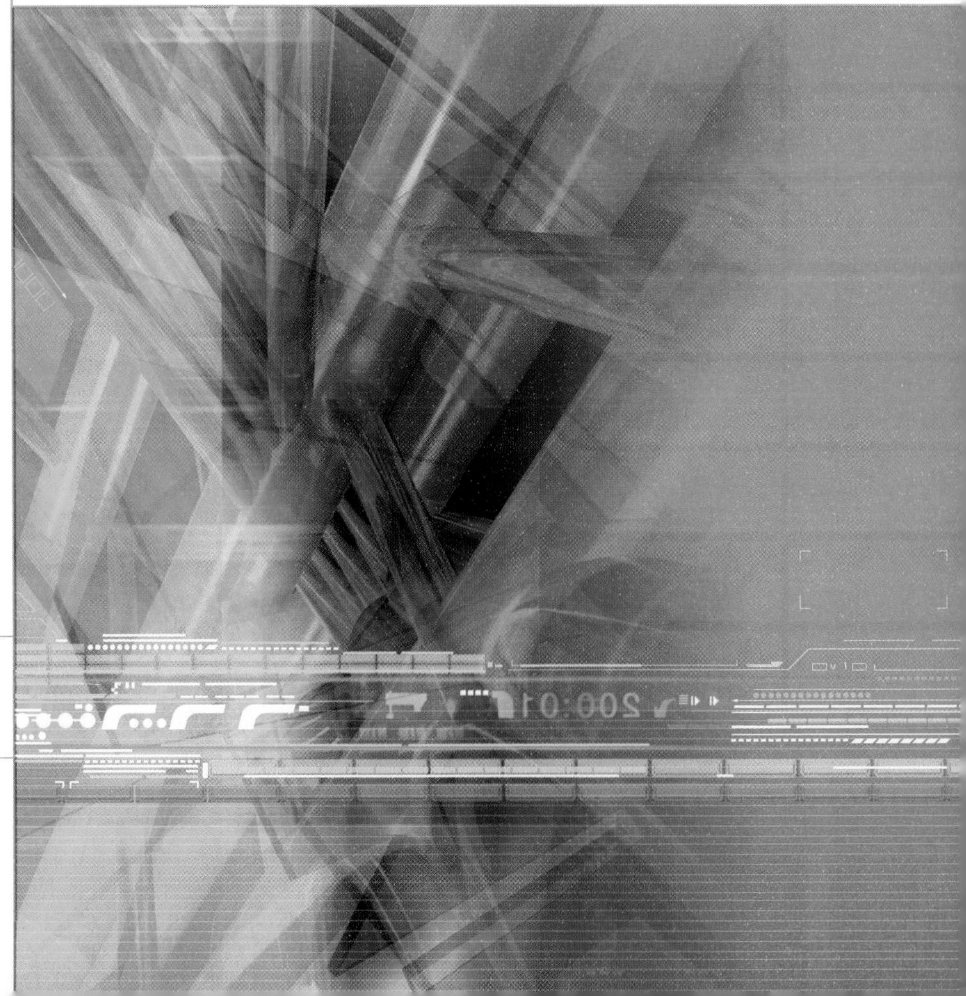

PC Operating Systems

Microsoft's Windows operating system continues to thrive on PCs all over the world and has the largest market share of any competitor. At this writing, even management at Apple Computers admits that the Macintosh has just 5 percent of the desktop OS market share, but Linux is making inroads on the desktop.

The following sections provide a brief survey of the many operating systems being used on desktop computers. Although some of these OSs—such as DOS and Windows 95—may seem out of date, they are still widely used and deserve to be included in this discussion.

Norton ONLINE

For more information on PC operating systems, visit **http://www.mhhe.com/peternorton**.

simnet™

DOS

Even though is has been around for decades, DOS (which stands for *disk operating system*) is still in use today for a variety of reasons. DOS originally came into widespread use in the 1980s, with the appearance of the IBM PC, which was the first personal computer to catch on with consumers and businesses.

Two versions of DOS reigned as the desktop operating system of choice throughout the 1980s. The first was PC DOS, which IBM released with its computers. The other was Microsoft's version of DOS, known as MS-DOS (Microsoft DOS), which was used on millions of "IBM-compatible" PCs, or "clones." (These terms describe any PC that is based on the same architecture used by IBM's personal computers.)

Despite its dominance in the PC market for more than a decade, DOS suffered some weaknesses. For example, it supported only one user at a time, and could run only one program at a time. It had no built-in support for networking, and users had to manually install drivers any time they added a new hardware component to their PC. DOS was also limited in the amount of RAM and storage space it could support. Finally, even today, DOS supports only 16-bit programs, so it does not take full advantage of the power of modern 32-bit (and 64-bit) processors. Finally, DOS used a command-line interface that forced users to remember cryptic command names.

So, why is DOS still in use? Two reasons are its size and simplicity. It does not require much memory or storage space for the system, and it does not require a powerful computer. Therefore, it is sometimes used as an embedded OS for devices that run very simple, single-tasking applications. Another reason for its continued use is that many businesses still have custom applications either written as a one-of-a-kind application for their business or written for their special needs and marketed to similar businesses. A restaurant may still be using the employee scheduling application written for it 10 or 15 years ago (see Figure 7B.1), or a small picture framing business may still use the same program to calculate the cost of the frames it builds and sells.

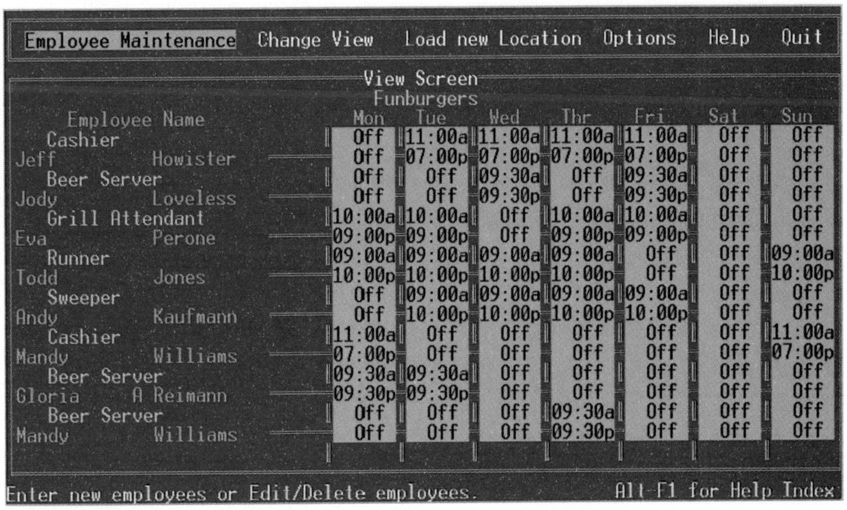

FIGURE 7B.1

DOS applications, like this one for employee scheduling, are still in use today. They are often custom applications written years ago for a certain industry or company.

Windows NT Workstation

Microsoft released Windows NT, a 32-bit operating system for PCs, in 1993. Windows NT (New Technology) was originally designed as the successor to DOS, but by the time it was ready for release, it had become too large to run on most of the PCs used by consumers at the time. As a result, Microsoft repositioned Windows NT to be a high-end operating system for powerful workstations and network servers used in business. (After releasing Windows NT, Microsoft went back to the drawing board to create a more consumer-oriented version of Windows to replace DOS on home and office PCs. Windows 95, which is discussed later, was the result.)

Because high-end networked computers fall into two primary categories, Microsoft separated Windows NT into two products: Windows NT Workstation and the first Windows version for network servers, Windows NT Server. The server product was optimized to run on dedicated network servers (see the discussion later in this chapter on NT Server).

FIGURE 7B.2

The interface for Windows NT Workstation 4.0, the last version of Windows to use "NT" in its name.

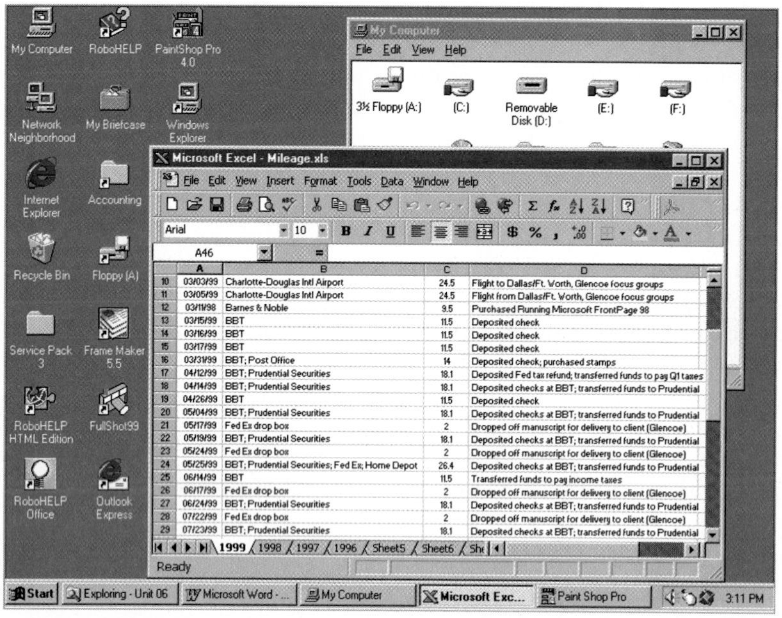

Although Windows NT Workstation 4.0 looks almost identical to Windows 95 (see Figure 7B.2), its underlying operating system is different; it's almost completely devoid of MS-DOS code that had been present in earlier versions of Windows. Windows NT Workstation is typically used on stand-alone PCs that may or may not be part of a network. While Windows NT Workstation supports networking and can be used as a server in peer-to-peer networks, it generally is not used on network servers. At first, "power users" made up a large part of the market for Windows NT Workstation. As a result, it can be found in such varied places as architectural firms, audio and video production studios, and graphics studios. Windows NT Workstation continues to be on desktops in large organizations, but it is being replaced by newer versions of Windows or by Linux.

Windows 9*x*

The term Windows 9*x* is used when referring to any member of the closely related threesome: Windows 95, Windows 98, and Windows Me. Although these versions of Windows are considered obsolete by many experts in the computer industry, they are still widely used, especially by consumers with older PCs. In fact, many businesses still run Windows 9*x* on their desktop PCs.

In 1995, Microsoft released Windows 95, a complete operating system that did not require MS-DOS to be installed separately before it was installed, unlike its predecessors (Windows 3.0, 3.1, and 3.11—collectively known as Windows 3.*x*). Windows 95 installs the necessary MS-DOS operating system components that it needs and has additional programming code that takes advantage of the more advanced capabilities of newer CPUs and maintains a GUI. Windows 3.x, by contrast, was an operating environment, which ran on top of DOS to provide a GUI and additional capabilities.

In addition to some MS-DOS program code that allows it to run DOS applications, Windows 95 contains 16-bit code that enables it to run programs originally designed for Windows 3.*x* (see Figure 7B.3). If a company had already invested in many such programs, it could continue to use its familiar programs while migrating to the new operating system.

Windows 95 has several other attractions as well. First, for programs designed with 32-bit processing, it can exchange information with printers, networks, and

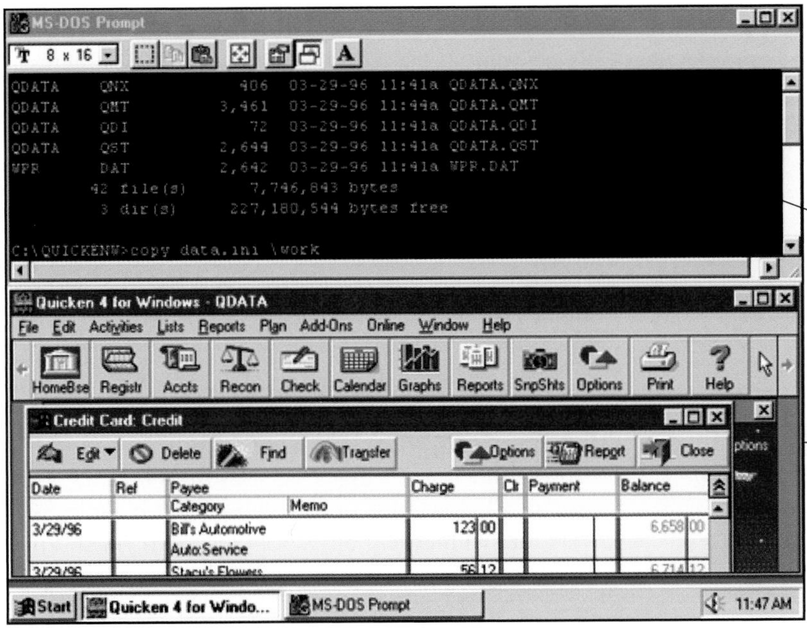

DOS, running in a window

A 16-bit application written for Windows 3.*x*

FIGURE 7B.3

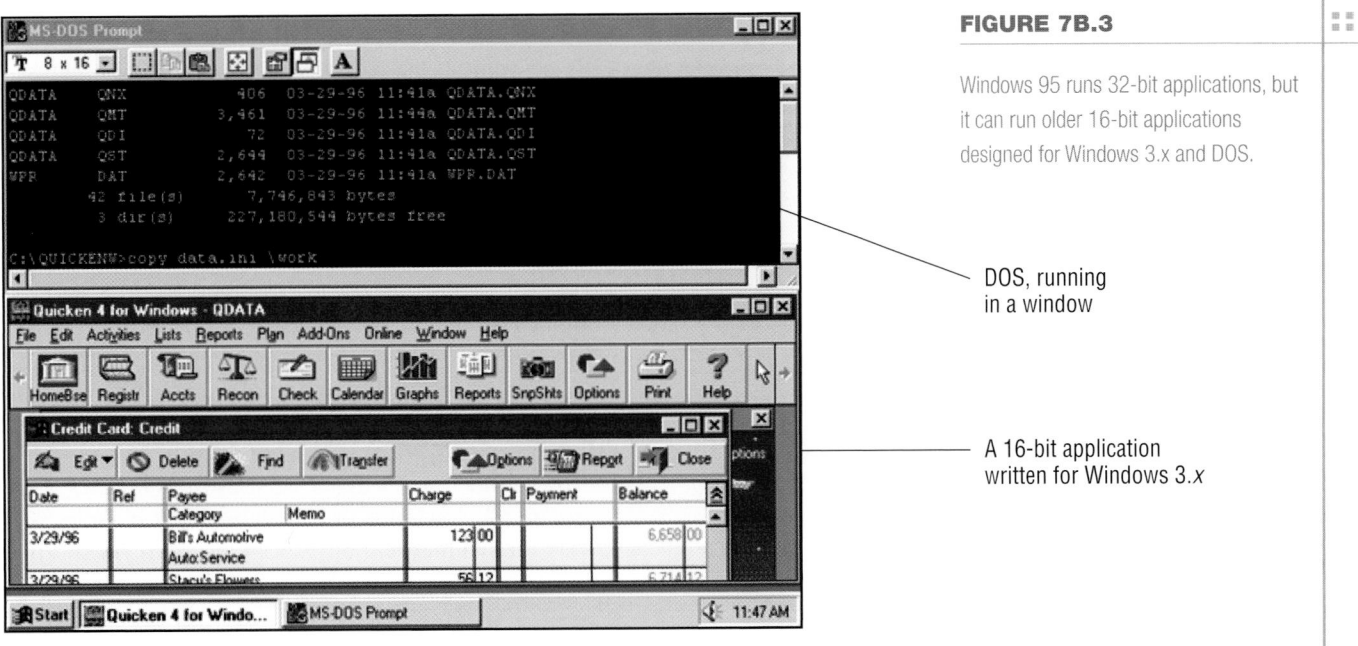

Windows 95 runs 32-bit applications, but it can run older 16-bit applications designed for Windows 3.x and DOS.

files in 32-bit pieces instead of 16-bit pieces (as in Windows 3.*x* and DOS). For moving information around in the computer, the effect was like doubling the number of lanes on an expressway. Windows 95 has improved multitasking, compared to previous versions of Windows, and it was the first version of Windows to support the Plug and Play standard for connecting new hardware. With integrated networking support and improvements to the GUI, such as the taskbar and START button, Windows 95 remains popular with individual users, in spite of newer versions with even more improvements.

Many experts considered Windows 98 (so-named for the year it was introduced—1998) to be an update to Windows 95 rather than a major Windows operating system upgrade. In other words, the differences from Windows 95 to Windows 98 are not as significant as the differences from Windows 3.*x* to Windows 95. However, one key change in Windows 98 is the inclusion of the Internet Explorer Web browser with a new feature, the Active Desktop, that lets users browse the Internet and local computer in a similar manner (see Figure 7B.4). Active Desktop enables users to integrate Internet resources such as stock tickers and news information services directly on the Windows desktop.

In 2000, Microsoft released Windows Me (Millennium Edition), the last member of the Windows 9*x* family of consumer-grade operating systems. Windows Me offers several notable enhancements over its predecessors, such as improved multimedia capabilities, built-in support for digital video editing, and enhanced Internet features. But like Windows 95 and 98, Windows Me still contains a lot of 16-bit code that supports old DOS and Windows 3.*x* applications. As a result, Windows Me was not much more stable or robust than Windows 95 or 98, and it was subject to frequent crashes.

FIGURE 7B.4

The Windows 98 Active Desktop lets the operating system function like a Web browser.

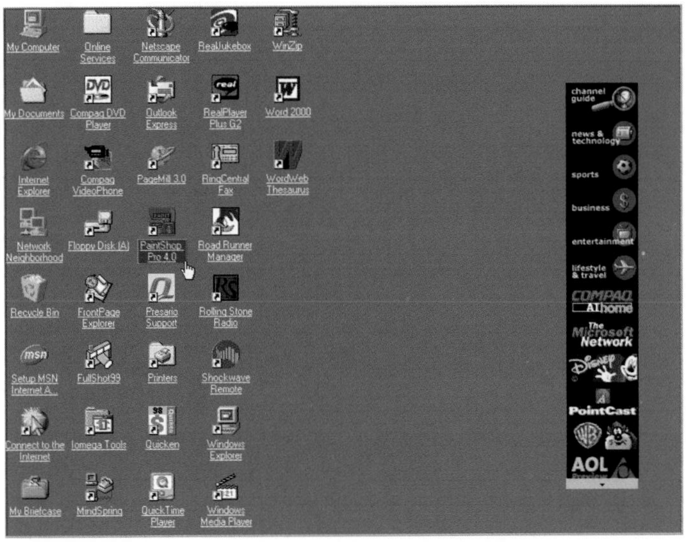

Windows 2000 Professional

Released in 2000, Windows 2000 combines the user-friendly interface and features of Windows 98 with the file system, networking, power, and stability of Windows NT and some new and improved features. This combination of features makes Windows 2000 both powerful and easy to use.

Microsoft developed four versions of Windows 2000: Windows 2000 Professional for the desktop and three versions especially for network servers, discussed later in this chapter (see Figure 7B.5).

Like its predecessor, Windows NT Workstation, Windows 2000 Professional is designed primarily for PCs in offices and small businesses. (Note that Microsoft did not release a version of Windows 2000 specifically for home or casual users.) It includes support for symmetric multiprocessing (SMP) with up to two processors.

FIGURE 7B.5

The Windows 2000 desktop is the same in all four versions of Windows 2000, including Windows 2000 Professional and the three server versions.

Windows XP

Windows XP, released in October 2001, is the latest in the Windows suite of PC operating system families. The desktop has a more three-dimensional look, with rounded corners and more shading. It also offers some brighter color choices (see Figure 7B.6). Windows XP is available in several different products: Windows XP Professional, Windows XP Home, Windows XP Media Center Edition, and Windows XP Embedded. Microsoft also created 64-bit Windows XP for use with AMD's Opteron and Athlon 64 CPUs. With Windows XP, Microsoft consolidated its consumer-grade and enterprise desktop operating systems into one environment. For home users, this means added security and an operating system that is far less likely to stall or crash than Windows 9*x*. Here are some of the features that have been upgraded in Windows XP:

- **Digital Media Support.** Through the use of Windows Media Player 9, users of XP can take advantage of digital broadcast support, as well as video and audio rendering for multimedia projects.
- **Advanced Networking and Communications.** Windows XP takes advantage of universal Plug and Play support, which enables the PC to find and use hardware connected via a network, without forcing the user to configure the system or install drivers. It also makes use of Internet Connection Sharing, which allows users to connect multiple computers to the Internet via a single connection.
- **Advanced Mobile Computing.** Through the use of features like Automatic Configuration, you can connect an XP-based laptop to a desktop PC without needing to know different types of network settings. XP's IrComm modem support lets you use a cellular telephone to connect to the Internet.

FIGURE 7B.6

The Windows XP desktop, shown here in its colorful default mode.

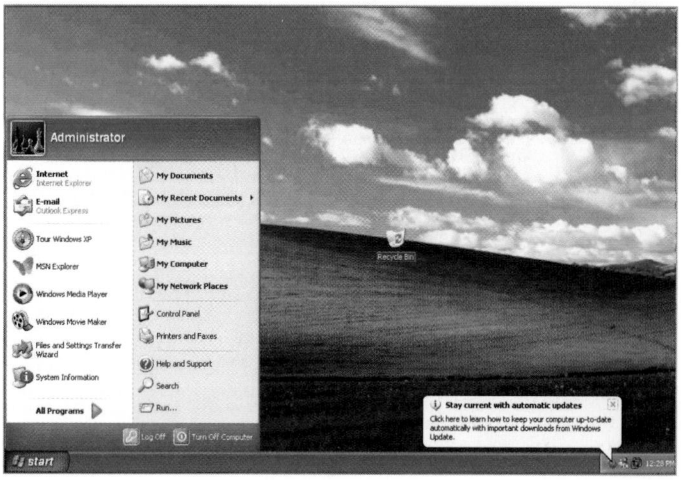

The Macintosh Operating System

The fact that the Macintosh operating system (or Mac OS) works only on Macintosh computers has long been considered one of the operating system's biggest drawbacks. Although it has a small market share, the Mac remains the first choice of many publishers, multimedia developers, graphic artists, and schools. The current version is called Mac OS System X (ten), which has had four major releases. The latest release is Mac OS X Panther, also called version 10.3. It has the same desktop, with upgrades to the OS and various components, such as the Finder, Mail, and Address Book. Figure 7B.7 shows the Mac OS X Panther desktop, customized by a user.

FIGURE 7B.7

The Mac OS System X desktop.

UNIX for the Desktop

It is difficult to pin UNIX down to one class of computer, because it runs on such a wide range, including supercomputers, notebook PCs, and everything in between. Although UNIX does not have an important place in the market for desktop operating systems, thanks to its power and its appeal to engineers and other users of CAD and CAM software, UNIX has been popular for high-powered workstations.

UNIX is not for the faint of heart because of its command-line interface, cryptic instructions, and the fact that it requires many commands to do even simple tasks. However, those who have worked with UNIX have found the power and stability of this OS worth the effort to learn the commands.

Linux for the Desktop

Even though Linux is considered a "freeware" operating system, industry experts have been impressed by its power, capabilities, and rich feature set. Linux is a full 32-bit, multitasking operating system that supports multiple users and multiple processors. Linux can run on nearly any computer and can support almost any type of application. Linux uses a command-line interface, but windows-based GUI environments, called shells, are available.

The biggest nontechnical difference between UNIX and Linux is price. Anyone can get a free copy of Linux on the Internet, and disk-based copies are often inserted in popular computer books and magazines. Commercial versions of Linux, which are inexpensive when compared to the cost of other powerful operating systems, are also available from a variety of vendors who provide the Linux code for free and charge for the extras, such as utilities, GUI shells, and documentation. At this writing, the most popular Linux vendors are Red Hat and Novell, and both offer special Linux bundles for desktop computers as well as for servers.

For all these reasons, Linux has become a popular OS in certain circles. Students and teachers have flocked to Linux not just for its technical advances but to participate in the global community that has built up around the operating system. This community invites Linux users and developers to contribute modifications and enhancements, and it freely shares information about Linux and Linux-related issues. Although Linux is typically considered to be a server platform, an increasing number of software companies are writing new desktop applications or modifying existing ones for Linux.

Norton ONLINE

For more information on the Macintosh operating system, visit **http://www.mhhe.com/peternorton**.

Norton ONLINE

For more information on UNIX and Linux, visit **http://www.mhhe.com/peternorton**.

At Issue

Controlling Computers with the Mind

The idea that humans could control computers with little more than their thoughts is the stuff of science fiction. Or is it?

Now a team of doctors, scientists, and programmers have developed a device that does exactly that. For the first time, a severely paralyzed—or "locked-in"—patient has the ability to control a computer directly with his or her thoughts.

The device, called the Brain Communicator, was created by Neural Signals, Inc., and allows a locked-in user (who is alert and intelligent but unable to move or speak due to stroke, disease, or injury) to control his or her personal computer without the need for a manual keyboard, voice recognition system, or other standard means of control. No voluntary movement is necessary.

Neural interface devices (NIDs) such as the Brain Communicator allow users to take advantage of small electrical signals generated spontaneously in the body. These signals can be obtained either directly or indirectly. Direct methods of collecting the signals involve surgical implantation in the user's body; indirect methods can utilize the user's muscle movements, eye movements, or EEG brain waves.

In the case of the Brain Communicator, a tiny, hollow glass cone filled with wires and chemicals approximately the size of the tip of a ballpoint pen is implanted onto the patient's brain. This "neurotrophic electrode" transmits the brain's electrical signals to a receiver that descrambles the signals and then translates them into corresponding digital outputs, so computer software can recognize them. This software, in turn, allows the user to control a cursor and special electronic devices that are attached to the computer.

With NIDs, simply by imagining movement, locked-in patients can use a word processor or speech synthesizer, surf the Internet, or access environmental controls such as lights, music, and TV. Medicine and computer technology combine to open the horizons of their locked-in world.

The idea for Neural Signals grew out of a research project of neural researcher and founder Dr. Phillip Kennedy. Today,

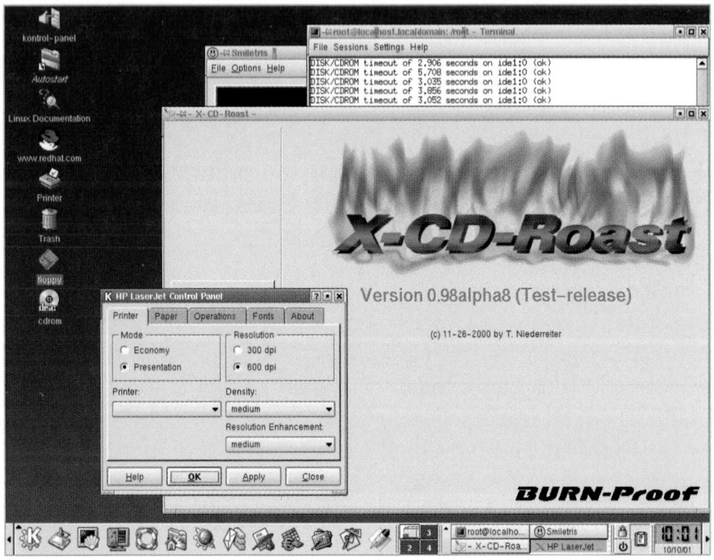

FIGURE 7B.8

Linux with an optional GUI desktop.

Figure 7B.8 shows the version of Linux released by Red Hat, with the KDE Desktop environment. Red Hat has grown into one of the most popular Linux releases, complete with its own community of followers, as well as their own Linux certification program, known as the Red Hat Certified Engineer (RHCE) program.

Network Operating Systems

A network operating system (NOS) is an OS that is designed to run on a network server dedicated to providing various services to other computers on the network. The "other" computers are called client computers, and each computer that connects to a network server must be running client software designed to request a specific service. If you are connecting to a server to store and retrieve files, your computer must have the client software that allows it to connect to that server for that purpose. Further, the specific client software needed varies based on the NOS running on the server.

All of today's desktop operating systems include support for some basic services, such as file and print sharing, over a network. But desktop operating systems are best reserved for the humdrum work of the average business or home user. They really don't work that well as servers. If you work in a small office and want to share a printer connected to your desktop computer with your coworkers, you can do this, whether you are running Windows, Linux, or Mac OS X, in the company develops its neural interfacing technology as a collaborative project with researchers at Georgia Tech, Emory University, and Georgia State University. Dr. Kennedy plans to use his brain-to-computer (BCI) technologies to help the over 125,000 quadriplegics in the United States as well as the 30,000 ALS patients immobilized on respirators. In addition, Neural Signals hopes to move into movement restoration and other markets for the technology.

Even as the future looks bright, the field of neural interfacing technology is still in its infancy and the practical applications of the technology have yet to be realized. Perhaps, someday soon, personal computers will come bundled with biological signal sensors and thought-recognition software just as commonly as the word processing and educational programs of today.

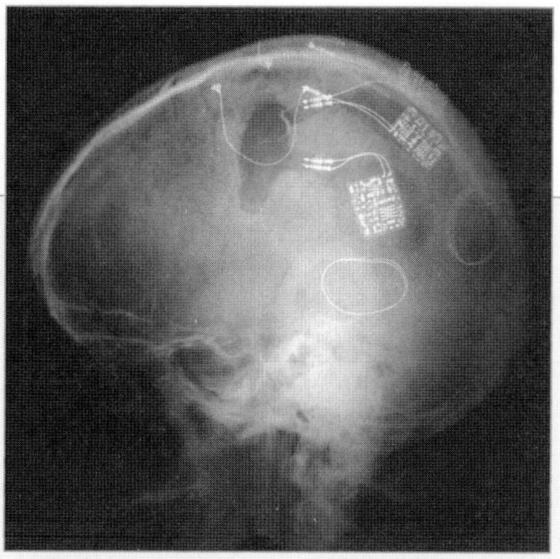

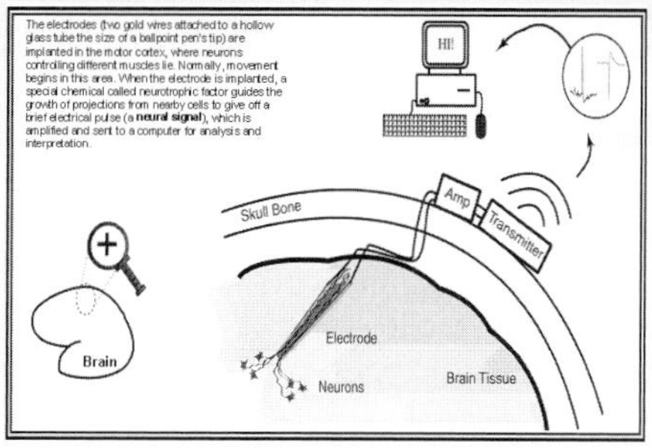

AT ISSUE

which case your computer is providing a network service.

Network operating systems are optimized to provide network services—with support for multiple processors and support for redundancy—both locally in the form of data redundancy on drives and specialized network redundancy, such as schemes in which one network server is a "mirror" of another server and is available immediately if the first server fails. There are many other "under-the-hood" enhancements that enable a NOS to provide reliable service.

SELF-CHECK ::

Circle the correct answer for each question.

1. Which operating system first appeared with the IBM PC?

   a. Windows b. DOS c. Linux

2. The START button appeared in this version of Windows.

   a. Windows 95 b. Windows 98 c. Windows Me

3. The biggest nontechnical difference between UNIX and Linux is _____.

   a. size b. price c. power

Norton ONLINE

For more information on network operating systems, visit **http://www.mhhe.com/peternorton**.

Windows NT Server

While it shares the same core as Windows NT Workstation, Windows NT Server has additional capabilities. Microsoft fine-tuned Windows NT Server so it would function as an operating system for servers. It has security features for grouping and authenticating users and controlling their access to network resources. It supports the use of many hard disks, working together to store huge amounts of data. It also can be configured to provide redundancy of data, writing the same data to multiple disks, so it is preserved in case one disk fails. All these features make it possible for Windows NT Server to ensure disk and data security even in the event of a catastrophic failure of a hard disk.

FIGURE 7B.9

The Windows 2000 Server GUI is identical to that of the Professional version.

Windows 2000 Server

Introduced in 2000, Microsoft Windows 2000 Server is available as three products, all of which support managing very large stores of data about the users of the network and the computer resources of the network. A generic term for such a specialized database is enterprise directory (not to be confused with the term *directory* sometimes used when talking about disk folders). One of the many things Windows 2000 Server can do that Windows 2000 Professional cannot is to manage a directory with a specialized service called Active Directory. All three server products have the same user interface as Windows 2000 Professional, as shown in Figure 7B.9.

- **Server Standard Edition.** This version is fine-tuned for use as a network server for the average business, with SMP support for up to two processors.
- **Advanced Server.** This is a more powerful version of the server edition. It includes support for SMP with up to four processors, enhanced balancing of network and component loads, and support for more RAM. Another important feature is print server clustering. With clustering, Windows 2000 can group print servers to provide alternate printers if one print server fails.
- **Data Center Server.** This version is the most powerful of the server editions, optimized for use as a large-scale application server, such as a database server. It includes the Advanced Server features, plus support for SMP with up to 32 processors. This product is not sold separately, but is sold through computer manufacturers, bundled with the very expensive, powerful servers.

Windows Server 2003

Microsoft extended its Windows Server system line with Windows Server 2003, introduced in April 2003 as two products:

- **Windows Server 2003 Standard Edition.** This version is fine-tuned for use as a network server for the average business, with SMP support for up to two processors.
- **Data Center Server.** This version is the most powerful of the server editions, optimized for use as a large-scale application server, such as a database server. It includes the Advanced Server features, plus support for SMP with up to 32 processors.

Windows Server 2003 has a Windows XP–style interface that hides a very beefed up server OS that Microsoft hopes will compete with UNIX, which dominates the very high-end enterprise network servers. This server OS was designed to support a set of technologies Microsoft dubbed the .NET Framework. In a nutshell, this means it is designed to support Web-based applications, large databases, e-commerce servers, and distributed applications, which are applications with parts that run on different computers, *distributing* the work and data across the network. The network, in this case, can be the Internet or a corporate intranet, or an extranet. (Intranets and extranets are discussed in Chapters 2, 9, and 10.)

Novell NetWare

NetWare (developed by Novell, Inc.) was one of the earliest and most popular network operating systems in terms of number of installations through the 1980s and into the 1990s. Although its market share has declined in recent years, Novell still has a strong following and continues to bring out new network products. NetWare server is now just one server operating system offered by Novell. Novell offers two Linux Server products, SuSE Enterprise and SuSE Standard, in addition to the Novell NetWare server product. The benefit of the NetWare server product is the long-term reliability of the product and the loyal network administrators of its installed base of servers that have been running earlier versions of NetWare servers for many years. The SuSE Linux products offer both a basic, department / small business NOS in SuSE Standard, and in SuSE Enterprise, a powerful operating system that can run on a broad range of computers, up to mainframes. The NetWare and SuSE Enterprise products support distributed applications.

UNIX for Servers

Because of its ability to work with so many kinds of hardware and its reliability (it rarely crashes), UNIX remains a very frequently chosen operating system for Internet host computers.

In the business world, UNIX remains a popular network operating system, especially among organizations that manage large databases shared by hundreds or thousands of users. Many types of specialized database-specific software programs have been developed for the UNIX platform and are deeply entrenched in industries such as insurance, medicine, banking, and manufacturing. The various versions of UNIX have collectively "owned" the market for very large, mission-critical servers in the largest of enterprises. UNIX is also widely used on Web servers, especially those that support online transactions and make heavy use of databases. In addition, UNIX has long been the OS of choice for the most critical servers of the Internet, such as those that maintain the lists of Internet domain names.

Linux for Servers

Linux has garnered a large share of the small business and home market as a server OS for providing Internet and networking services. An open operating system, it is a cost-effective alternative to other operating systems for sharing files, applications, printers, modems, and Internet services. There is a large number of Linux servers hosting Web sites and performing other roles on the Internet.

In the last few years, more and more vendors have brought out products bundled with Linux targeting large (enterprise) organizations; among them are Red Hat and Novell. Novell's venture into Linux products is expected to help bring about the eventual dominance of Linux on a wide range of servers, competing with both Microsoft and UNIX NOSs.

Embedded Operating Systems

An embedded operating system is one that is built into the circuitry of an electronic device, unlike a PC's operating system, which resides on a magnetic disk. Embedded operating systems are now found in a wide variety of devices, including appliances, automobiles, bar-code scanners, cell phones, medical equipment, and personal digital assistants. The most popular embedded operating systems for consumer products, such as PDAs, include the following:

- **Windows XP Embedded.** One of two embedded OSs currently available from Microsoft, Windows XP Embedded is based on the Windows XP Professional OS, but it is not an off-the-shelf operating system so much as it is a do-it-yourself kit for device manufacturers who wish to pick and choose the parts of the Windows XP Professional OS their products need.

Norton ONLINE

For more information on embedded operating systems, visit **http://www.mhhe.com/peternorton**.

Computers In Your Career

Help Desk and Technical Support Specialists

Mark Barry knows that when he picks up a phone line in his office, there's a good chance that the caller will be edgy, and possibly even on the verge of tears, over the fact that his or her hardware or software may never work properly again. Part-counselor, part-computer technician, Barry asks questions about the problem itself, positions himself in front of the same application or piece of hardware in his own office, then helps the caller find a workable solution.

"It's always great to be able to help someone take care of a technology problem," says Barry, president and owner of Configured PC in Whitinsville, Massachusetts. "There's a lot of personal satisfaction in befriending someone, and making their day." A graduate of Clark University's Computer Career Institute, Barry holds a CompTIA A+ certification. Prior to starting his own firm, which specializes in technical sales and support, he was a technical trainer for CompUSA.

With the assistance of one technical support professional and an office manager, Barry has made a career out of helping people work through their technology problems. He fills a gap in the industry where vendor technology support personnel often leave off: being able to communicate well with customers and walk them through diagnostic and repair steps via telephone. When he's not on the phone, Barry helps walk-in customers, makes house calls, and consults with clients in need of customized technology solutions.

Barry predicts a healthy demand for IT types who can communicate with customers—be they internal customers (those calling to an internal help desk) or outside customers (such as the ones he works with)—and walk them through technical problems with their hardware and software. Both help desk workers and technical support specialists share the same goal of helping others use their computers, but generally work in different environments:

- Help desk professionals are usually employed by a company to help its other employees with the computer systems they use at work. Suppose, for example, that you work for a large retailer and use its specialized order management or customer relationship management (CRM) software. If you need help using the program, you can call the company's internal help desk to ask for assistance.

- **Windows CE .NET.** The second Windows embedded product is Windows CE .NET. Also provided as a kit to manufacturers, it is not based on the Windows desktop products but is the latest version of Windows CE, which was designed especially for embedded devices requiring a real-time OS. Although a small OS, it supports wireless communications, multimedia, and Web browsing. It also allows for the use of smaller versions of Microsoft Word, Excel, and Outlook. Microsoft is positioning a version of Windows CE for the automotive market, calling it Windows Automotive.
- **Palm OS.** Palm OS is the standard operating system for Palm-brand PDAs as well as other proprietary handheld devices (see Figure 7B.10). For several years the Palm OS was the more popular option for handheld devices and there were many manufacturers offering PDAs with the Palm OS. More recently, only Palm and Sony continue to make PDAs that run the Palm OS, but they have a significant market share and, as a result, users have a large degree of choice in terms of software that can be used with this embedded system. The Palm OS continues to be used in other systems, such as cell phones and other small devices.

FIGURE 7B.10

Like many other handheld computing devices, the Palm line of personal digital assistants uses the Palm OS.

» Technical support specialists are usually employed by a company to help its customers use the products they have purchased from the company. If you have ever had trouble with a computer program and called the manufacturer for help, then you probably spoke with a technical support specialist.

According to the Bureau of Labor Statistics, computer support specialists are projected to be among the fastest-growing occupations over the 2000–2010 period, with job prospects being optimal for college graduates who are up to date with the latest skills and technologies; certifications and practical experience are essential for persons without degrees. Median annual earnings of computer support specialists were $36,460 in 2000, with the middle 50 percent earning between $27,680 and $48,440.

» **Pocket PC OS.** Pocket PC OS is a specific type of operating system that Microsoft developed to use in direct competition with the Palm OS on PDAs. These devices are targeted at the business and corporate market rather than consumers. The latest version gives users the ability to securely access data from a business network via a handheld device, and it gives system administrators the ability to manage and control a PC or server via a wireless network connection.

» **Symbian.** Symbian is an OS found in "smart" cell phones from Nokia and Sony Ericsson that feature options such as touch screens, games, multimedia functions, and Internet connectivity. In addition to the conventional cell phone functions, you can play games and view Web pages (in color) with a full browser over a high-speed mobile network.

LESSON // 7B Review

Summary ::

- Among the strengths of DOS are its small size, reliability, stability, simple command-line interface, and minimal system requirements.
- Windows NT was originally meant as a replacement for DOS. Microsoft issued two versions of the operating system: Windows NT Workstation and Windows NT Server.
- Windows 95 was Microsoft's first true GUI-based, 32-bit operating system for PCs. It supported multitasking and could run older programs that were written for DOS and Windows 3.*x*.
- Windows 2000 includes the interface and features of Windows 98, with the file system, networking, power, and stability of Windows NT. Microsoft released several versions of Windows 2000, each targeting a specific user or computing environment.
- Windows XP was released in 2001, and it marked the end of Microsoft's consumer-grade operating systems. This means that all computer users, including casual and home users, can have an operating system with enhanced security, networking support, and stability.
- The fact that the Mac OS works only on Macintosh computer hardware has long been considered one of the operating system's biggest drawbacks, but Mac remains the first choice of many publishers, multimedia developers, graphic artists, and schools.
- UNIX runs on a wide range of computers, including supercomputers, notebook PCs, and everything in between, but it does not have an important place in the market for desktop operating systems.
- Linux is a separate OS from UNIX, but it shows the UNIX influence and characteristics. Linux OS code is free, but it is also available through companies such as Novell and Red Hat, who bundle the OS code with utilities and documentation, charging for everything but the OS itself.
- Network operating systems are optimized to provide network services—with support for multiple processors and support for redundancy. This redundancy support occurs both locally in the form of data redundancy on drives and specialized network redundancy such as schemes in which one network server is a "mirror" of another server and is available immediately if the first server fails.
- Popular Network OSs include Microsoft server products, UNIX, Novell NetWare, and Linux.
- Embedded operating systems, such as the Palm OS, Symbian OS, and the Microsoft products—Windows XP Embedded, Windows CE .NET, and Pocket PC OS—are miniaturized OSs designed to run on small computing devices, such as handheld computers.

Key Terms ::

distributed application, 292
DOS, 285
embedded operating system, 293
enterprise directory, 292
Linux, 289
Macintosh operating system (Mac OS), 289
.NET Framework, 292
network operating system (NOS), 290
Palm OS, 294
Pocket PC OS, 295
shell, 289
Symbian, 295
UNIX, 289
Windows, 285
Windows 9*x*, 286
Windows 95, 286
Windows 98, 287
Windows 2000, 288
Windows CE .NET, 294
Windows Me, 287
Windows NT Server, 291
Windows NT, 285
Windows NT Workstation 4.0, 286
Windows XP, 288
Windows XP Embedded, 288
Windows XP Home, 288
Windows XP Media Center Edition, 288
Windows XP Professional, 288

Key Term Quiz ::

Complete each statement by writing one of the terms listed under Key Terms in each blank.

1. ________ was originally designed as the successor to DOS.
2. The term ________ is used when referring to Windows 95, Windows 98, and Windows Me.
3. Microsoft introduced the Active Desktop feature with the ________ operating system.
4. ________ is the latest in the Windows suite of desktop operating system families.
5. The ________ operating system runs only on Macintosh computers.
6. The ________ operating system runs on a wide range of computers, including supercomputers, notebook PCs, and everything in between.
7. ________ is considered to be a "freeware" operating system.
8. A(n) ________ is an OS that is designed to run on a network server dedicated to providing various services to other computers on the network.
9. A(n) ________ is a specialized database that contains data about the users of a network and the computer resources of the network.
10. A(n) ________ application is a program with parts that run on different computers, distributing the work and data across the network.

LESSON // 7B Review

Multiple Choice ::

Circle the word or phrase that best completes each statement.

1. The acronym DOS stands for __________ .
   a. distributed operating system
   b. driver operating system
   c. disk operating system
   d. diskless operating system
2. Windows NT was released as a __________-bit operating system in 1993.
   a. 8
   b. 16
   c. 32
   d. 64
3. One reason for the popularity of Windows 95 was its ability to run applications that were developed for this operating system.
   a. DOS
   b. UNIX
   c. Linux
   d. Mac OS
4. Windows 95 was the first version of Windows to support the __________ standard for connecting new hardware.
   a. GUI
   b. Plug and Play
   c. Enterprise Directory
   d. OS
5. Which feature of Windows 98 enables users to integrate Internet resources directly on the Windows desktop?
   a. Plug and Play
   b. Internet Explorer
   c. START button
   d. Active Desktop
6. Which version of Windows 2000 was intended for use on desktop computers?
   a. Professional
   b. Server
   c. Enterprise Edition
   d. Data Center Server
7. Microsoft has created a 64-bit version of this operating system, for use with AMD's Opteron and Athlon 64 CPUs.
   a. MS-UNIX
   b. Linux
   c. Windows XP
   d. DOS
8. The current version of the Macintosh operating system is called __________ .
   a. Max OS System I
   b. Mac OS System X
   c. Mac OS System Y
   d. Mac OS System N
9. How many processors are supported by the Data Center Server edition of Windows Server 2003?
   a. 8
   b. 16
   c. 32
   d. 64
10. Which network operating system has long been the OS of choice for the most critical servers of the Internet, such as those that maintain the lists of Internet domain names?
    a. DOS
    b. UNIX
    c. Windows NT Professional
    d. Mac OS

Review Questions ::

In your own words, briefly answer the following questions.

1. Name two versions of DOS that were popular during the 1980s.
2. What is a "clone"?
3. Explain why DOS is still in use.
4. Why didn't Windows NT replace DOS, as originally planned?
5. How is Windows NT Workstation different from Windows 95?
6. What was the primary use for Windows 2000 Professional?
7. UNIX may be described as being difficult to use. Why?
8. What purpose would a "shell" serve in Linux?
9. Windows Server 2003 supports the .NET Framework. What does this mean?
10. What is the Palm OS?

Lesson Labs ::

Complete the following exercise as directed by your instructor.

1. Use your operating system's search tools to find files on your computer's hard disk. Note that the following steps apply if you are using Windows XP. If you use a different version of Windows or a different operating system than Windows, ask your instructor for directions.
   a. Click Start | Search. The Search Results window opens.
   b. Click All files and folders.
   c. Click in the All or part of the file name text box, and type ***.txt**. This tells windows to search for all files with the filename extension *txt*.
   d. From the Look in drop-down list, select your computer's hard disk (typically C:).
   e. Click Search. Windows conducts the search and displays the results in the right-hand pane of the Search Results window.
   f. Repeat the search, specifying ***.html**, ***.doc**, and ***.gif** as your search criteria. When you are finished, close the Search Results window.

Chapter Labs

Complete the following exercises using a computer in your classroom, lab, or home.

1. Create a file system. Suppose that you work for a soft drink company. Your manager has asked you to create a business proposal for a new product—a fun, caffeine-free soda for kids under the age of eight. The proposal will be about 50 pages in length and will include several supporting documents, such as reports, memos, budgets, customer lists, research on the product's safety, focus group results, taste tests, and so on. These different documents will be created in several forms, including word processing documents, spreadsheet files, databases, presentations, and so on.

   Your first task is to create a file system on your computer's hard disk where you can store and manage all these files. Using a piece of paper, design a set of folders (and subfolders, if needed) to store all the files in a logical manner. Be prepared to share your file system with the class and to discuss the logic behind your file system.

2. Get the latest on Windows XP. If you do not have Windows XP yet, chances are good that you will be using it in the future. Get a jump on the OS by finding the latest information about it on the Web.

   Visit the following Web sites for more information:

   Microsoft Corporation. Visit Microsoft's main Windows XP page at http://www.microsoft.com/windowsxp/default.asp.

   PC Magazine. For a series of articles and reviews about Windows XP, visit http://www.pcmag.com/winxp.

3. Learn more about Linux. If you are curious about Linux, or want to install Linux on your system, you can find everything you need on the Internet. Visit the following Web sites for more information on Linux and learn where you can get a free copy. (*Note:* Do *not* download any files from the Internet without your instructor's permission.)

   Linux Online. Hosted by Linux.Org, this site provides a comprehensive array of resources. Visit http://www.linux.org.

   The Linux Gazette. An online newsletter for Linux users of all levels can be found at http://www.linuxgazette.com/.

   Linux Planet. For articles, reviews, technical information, and links to Linux resources, visit http://www.linuxplanet.com/.

CHAPTER SKILLS REVIEW

Discussion Questions

As directed by your instructor, discuss the following questions in class or in groups.

1. Discuss the benefits of using the object linking and embedding (OLE) capabilities of newer operating systems. Can you think of a task where OLE would be helpful? What types of documents can someone create using OLE? Give examples.
2. What does multitasking mean to the average computer user?

Research and Report

Using your own choice of resources (such as the Internet, books, magazines, and newspaper articles), research and write a short paper discussing one of the following topics:

- The benefits of using a command-line interface rather than a graphical user interface.
- The story behind the creation of the Linux operating system.
- A cost comparison of currently available desktop operating systems.

When you are finished, proofread and print your paper, and give it to your instructor.

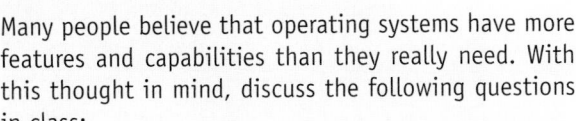

ETHICAL ISSUES

Many people believe that operating systems have more features and capabilities than they really need. With this thought in mind, discuss the following questions in class:

1. The Windows Update feature has been part of the Windows operating system since the release of Windows 98. This tool enables the operating system to notify the user when updated features are available for downloading on the Internet. Some observers think that future operating systems will be able to update themselves automatically without first notifying the user. How do you feel about this possibility? What dangers could it pose to users?
2. Many observers believe that by including so many features (such as disk defragmenters, file management tools, and Internet applications) in its operating systems, Microsoft has taken market share away from other companies that might develop and sell such tools to Windows users. Do you agree with this criticism, or do you feel that an operating system should include such "extras"?

CHAPTER

8 Working with Application Software

CHAPTER CONTENTS ::

This chapter contains the following lessons:

Lesson **8A:**
Productivity Software

- >> Acquiring Software
- >> Word Processing Programs
- >> Spreadsheet Programs
- >> Presentation Programs
- >> Personal Information Managers

Lesson **8B:**
Graphics and Multimedia

- >> Understanding Graphics File Formats
- >> Getting Images into Your Computer
- >> Graphics Software
- >> Multimedia Basics

LESSON // 8A

Productivity Software

Overview: Software to Accomplish the Work of Life

You have seen that hardware alone doesn't do much of anything. PC hardware must work under the control of the operating system in order to accomplish work. The work that the hardware or operating system can do on its own is very limited, however. Their jobs are focused mostly on running the computer itself, not helping the user perform tasks.

Application software shifts this focus from the computer to humans. Application software is designed to help users be productive, which is why one class of it is called productivity software. There are as many different types of application software as there are different tasks to accomplish on a PC.

This lesson introduces you to some of the most commonly used types of application software—the programs that millions of people use each day to accomplish routine tasks. Although you might think of a computer as being a highly specialized machine, in fact it is most often used for basic, everyday tasks at home, school, and work. By applying computers and application programs to these mundane tasks, people can be more productive, creative, and efficient.

OBJECTIVES ::

- Identify four different ways to acquire software.
- Name three kinds of formatting you can perform with word processing software.
- Identify four types of data that can be used by spreadsheet programs.
- Explain what presentation programs are used for.
- List two key tasks that people perform with PIM applications.

Acquiring Software

Norton ONLINE

For more information on acquiring software, visit **http://www.mhhe.com/peternorton**.

As there are hundreds of different types of software applications, there are a number of different ways for users to obtain the software they need. Sometimes, individuals create the special software they need, but commercial products are what the vast majority of people use. These products are designed to perform the work that most people need to do.

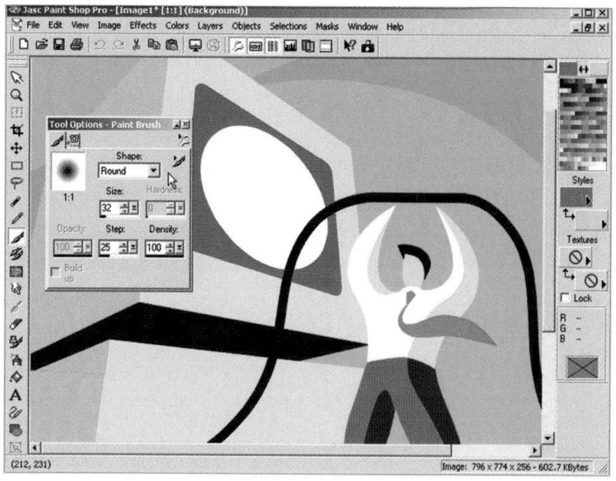

FIGURE 8A.1

Paint Shop Pro is an example of a popular stand-alone graphics program.

Commercial Software

The term commercial software refers to any software program that must be paid for in some way. Commercial software programs come in several different forms:

- **Stand-Alone Programs.** A stand-alone program is an application that performs only one type of task, such as a word processing program, a graphics program, or an e-mail program (see Figure 8A.1). Of course, such a program might have many tools and features, but it basically focuses on one type of task or a range of related tasks.
- **Software Suites.** Software programs that are very commonly used—such as word processing software, spreadsheets, Web-authoring tools, and e-mail programs—are often packaged together and sold as software suites. A software suite is a set of carefully integrated tools that are designed to work together seamlessly (see Figure 8A.2). This includes the popular Microsoft Office family of products—Word, Excel, Outlook, PowerPoint, Access—as well as more special-purpose suites, like the Corel family of graphics software.
- **Shareware Programs.** One very popular type of commercial software is called shareware (see Figure 8A.3). Shareware gets its name from the fact that its developers encourage users to share it with one another, and to try out the software before purchasing it. Typically, the user is allowed a certain number of days to work with the software before registering and/or paying for it. (Many shareware authors ask for payment, but many others only require the user to register the program.)

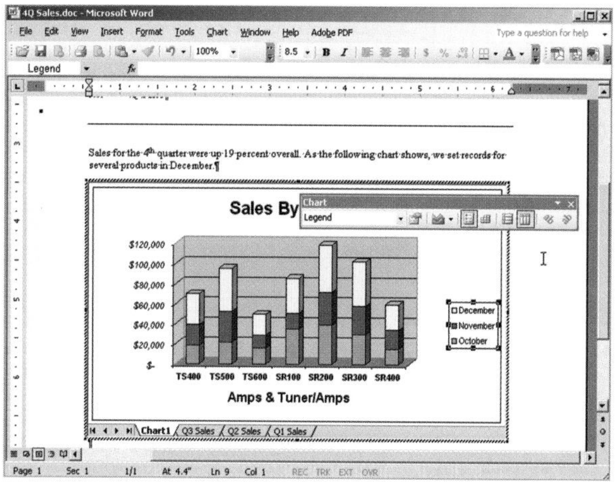

FIGURE 8A.2

In a carefully designed software suite, programs can share data and tools, so users can work with many different types of data in one program when necessary.

Freeware and Public Domain Software

A close cousin to shareware is freeware. Freeware is any software that is made available to the public for free; the developer does not expect any payment from users. This may sound like public domain software, but it is not.

In the case of shareware and freeware, the original author maintains an ownership interest in the product, even though the software may be given away at no charge. If you use shareware or freeware programs, you must abide by the terms of a license that prohibits you from making changes to the software or selling it to someone else.

In the case of public domain software, no compensation is usually expected and the source code is free for anyone to use for any purpose whatever. (Source code is the underlying instructions that make a program work. You'll learn about source code and programming in Chapter 13, "Software Programming and Development.") You may be familiar with the concept of public domain from literature. If a publisher determines that a market exists for a new book of classic fairy tales, there is no need to hunt down the heirs of Mother

Goose to negotiate a royalty, or to get permission to change the stories. It is the same with public domain software.

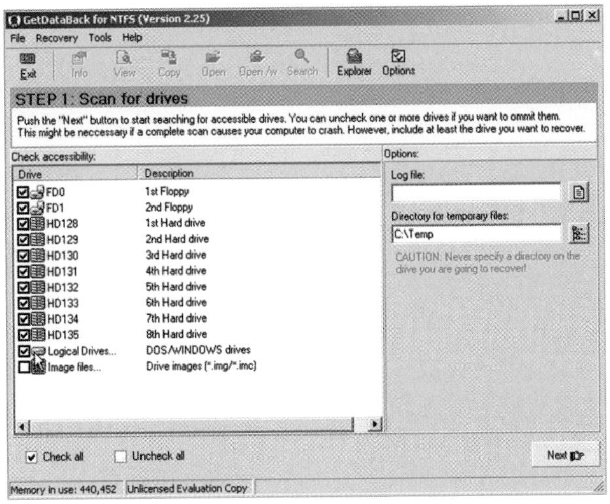

FIGURE 8A.3

Many popular utilities are shareware programs. This one, called GetDataBack, can help you recover files that have been accidentally deleted.

Open-Source Software

Sometimes software is designed for users who need to customize the programs they use. This special need is often met by open-source software. Open-source software is software of any type whose source code is available to users. Source code is available in editable formats, as are the many development libraries that are used to create applications. Users or other software developers can modify this code and customize it, within certain guidelines set forth by the application's creator. Open-source software is often sold commercially, although it is sometimes available for free. A company may release an open-source version of a product it's developing to build interest in the product before it is sold. The developer also may benefit from the comments and experience of many users who don't work for the company but freely give their thoughts in an informal exchange for the software being available.

Many kinds of open-source programs are available, from standard productivity programs to high-level network administration tools (see Figure 8A.4).

FIGURE 8A.4

OpenOffice.org is an open-source application suite that runs on many different platforms. It is available for free and is used by about 16 million people worldwide.

Word Processing Programs

A word processing program (also called a word processor) provides tools for creating all kinds of text-based documents, as shown in Figures 8A.5 and 8A.6. Word processors are not limited to working with text; they enable you to add images to your documents and design documents that look like products of a professional print shop. Using a word processor, you can create long documents with separate chapters, a table of contents, an index, and other features.

A word processor can enhance documents in other ways; you can embed sounds, video clips, and animations into them. You can link different documents together—for example, link a chart from a spreadsheet into a word processing report—to create complex documents that update themselves automatically. Word processors can even create documents for publishing on the World Wide Web, complete with hyperlinked text and graphics.

Norton ONLINE

For more information on word processing programs, visit **http://www.mhhe.com/peternorton**.

FIGURE 8A.5

This simple birthday card was created in a word-processing program. It features colors, rotated text, and graphics.

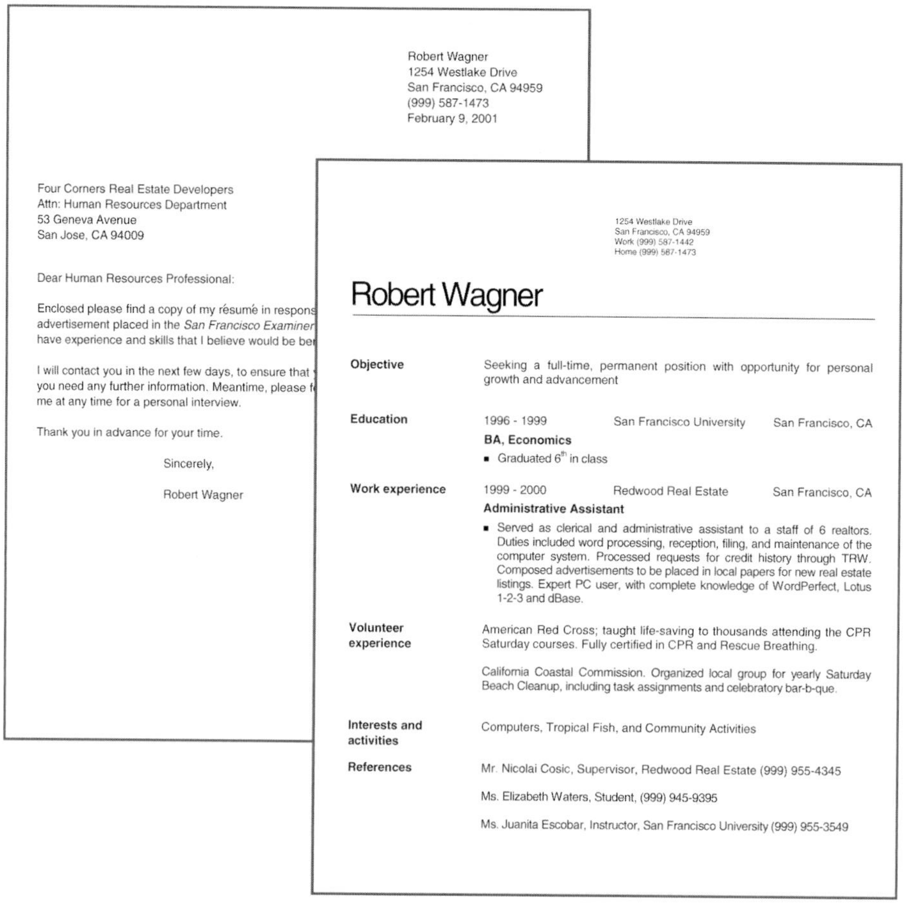

Robert Wagner
1254 Westlake Drive
San Francisco, CA 94959
(999) 587-1473
February 9, 2001

Four Corners Real Estate Developers
Attn: Human Resources Department
53 Geneva Avenue
San Jose, CA 94009

Dear Human Resources Professional:

Enclosed please find a copy of my résumé in respons
advertisement placed in the *San Francisco Examiner*
have experience and skills that I believe would be be

I will contact you in the next few days, to ensure that
you need any further information. Meantime, please f
me at any time for a personal interview.

Thank you in advance for your time.

Sincerely,

Robert Wagner

1254 Westlake Drive
San Francisco, CA 94959
Work (999) 587-1442
Home (999) 587-1473

Robert Wagner

Objective — Seeking a full-time, permanent position with opportunity for personal growth and advancement

Education — 1996 - 1999 San Francisco University San Francisco, CA
BA, Economics
- Graduated 6th in class

Work experience — 1999 - 2000 Redwood Real Estate San Francisco, CA
Administrative Assistant
- Served as clerical and administrative assistant to a staff of 6 realtors. Duties included word processing, reception, filing, and maintenance of the computer system. Processed requests for credit history through TRW. Composed advertisements to be placed in local papers for new real estate listings. Expert PC user, with complete knowledge of WordPerfect, Lotus 1-2-3 and dBase.

Volunteer experience — American Red Cross; taught life-saving to thousands attending the CPR Saturday courses. Fully certified in CPR and Rescue Breathing.

California Coastal Commission. Organized local group for yearly Saturday Beach Cleanup, including task assignments and celebratory bar-b-que.

Interests and activities — Computers, Tropical Fish, and Community Activities

References — Mr. Nicolai Cosic, Supervisor, Redwood Real Estate (999) 955-4345

Ms. Elizabeth Waters, Student, (999) 945-9395

Ms. Juanita Escobar, Instructor, San Francisco University (999) 955-3549

FIGURE 8A.6

Word processors are used frequently to create business letters and resumes. The formatting can be simple (as demonstrated by the cover letter) or more elaborate (as in the resume).

simnet™

The Word Processor's Interface

The word processor's main editing window displays a document and several tools, as illustrated in Figure 8A.7. In addition to a document area (or document window), which is where you view the document, a word processor provides several sets of tools, including

- A menu bar, which displays titles of menus (lists of commands and options).
- Toolbars, which display buttons that represent frequently used commands.
- Rulers, which show you the positions of text, tabs, margins, indents, and other elements on the page.
- Scroll bars, which let you scroll through a document that is too large to fit inside the document area.
- A status bar, which displays information related to your position in the document, the page count, and the status of keyboard keys.

Entering and Editing Text

You create a document by typing on the keyboard—a process known as entering text. In a new document, the program places a blinking insertion point (also called a cursor) in the upper-left corner of the document window. As you type, the insertion point advances across the screen, showing you where the next character will be placed (see Figure 8A.8).

Word processing software lets you change text without retyping the entire page; you retype only the text that needs to be changed. Changing an existing document is called editing the document.

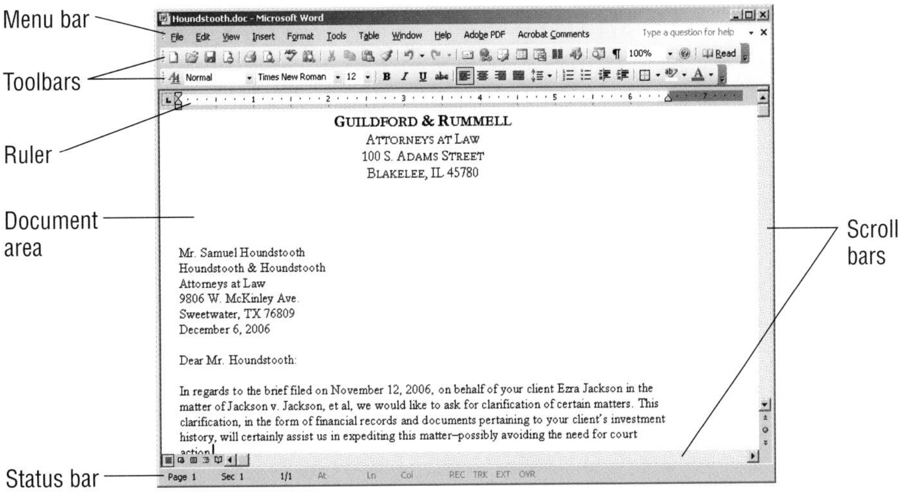

FIGURE 8A.7

Microsoft Word's interface features tools that are commonly found in word processing programs.

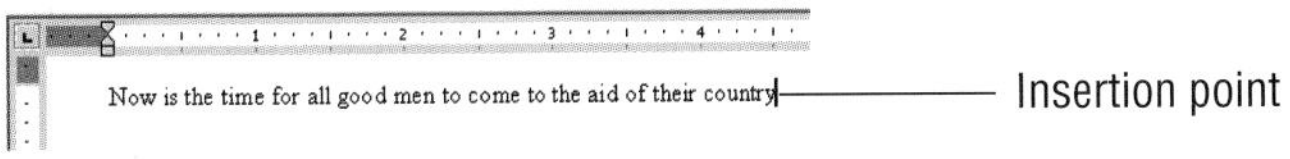

FIGURE 8A.8

The insertion point shows your place in a document as you type.

The word processor's real beauty is its ability to work with blocks of text. A block is a contiguous group of characters, words, lines, sentences, or paragraphs in your document that you mark for editing or formatting. To mark text for editing or formatting, you select it. You can select text by using the mouse, the keyboard, or both. When you select text, it changes color—becoming highlighted, as shown in Figure 8A.9—to indicate that it is selected. You can erase an entire selected block by pressing the DELETE key or by typing other text over the selected block. You can change the formatting of the selection by making it bold or underlined, for example, or by changing the font or font size. To deselect a selected block of text, click the mouse anywhere on the screen or press any arrow key. The text is displayed again as it normally would be.

It's important to understand that these same data-entry and data-editing concepts apply to many other types of programs, including spreadsheets, databases, presentation programs, and others. If you can enter, edit, and select text in one program, then you know how to do it in other programs.

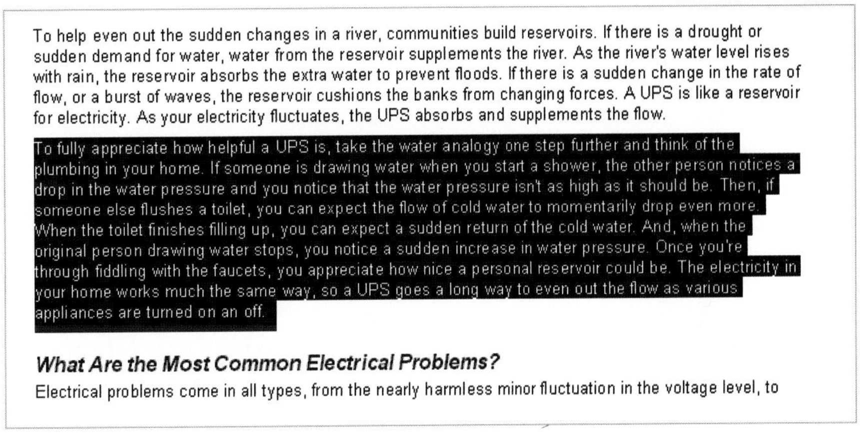

To help even out the sudden changes in a river, communities build reservoirs. If there is a drought or sudden demand for water, water from the reservoir supplements the river. As the river's water level rises with rain, the reservoir absorbs the extra water to prevent floods. If there is a sudden change in the rate of flow, or a burst of waves, the reservoir cushions the banks from changing forces. A UPS is like a reservoir for electricity. As your electricity fluctuates, the UPS absorbs and supplements the flow.

To fully appreciate how helpful a UPS is, take the water analogy one step further and think of the plumbing in your home. If someone is drawing water when you start a shower, the other person notices a drop in the water pressure and you notice that the water pressure isn't as high as it should be. Then, if someone else flushes a toilet, you can expect the flow of cold water to momentarily drop even more. When the toilet finishes filling up, you can expect a sudden return of the cold water. And, when the original person drawing water stops, you notice a sudden increase in water pressure. Once you're through fiddling with the faucets, you appreciate how nice a personal reservoir could be. The electricity in your home works much the same way, so a UPS goes a long way to even out the flow as various appliances are turned on an off.

What Are the Most Common Electrical Problems?

Electrical problems come in all types, from the nearly harmless minor fluctuation in the voltage level, to

FIGURE 8A.9

The paragraph that appears as white text against a black background is highlighted. The user has selected the text for editing or formatting.

Formatting Text

Most word processing features are used to format the document. The process of formatting a document includes controlling the appearance of text, the layout of text on the page, and the use of pictures and other graphic elements. Most formatting features fall into one of three categories:

» Character formatting includes settings that control the attributes of individual text characters such as fonts, font size, and type style. A font is a named set of characters that have the same characteristics. Popular fonts include Courier, Times New Roman, and Arial, but popular word processors feature dozens of different fonts (see Figure 8A.10). A font's size (its height) is measured in points. One point equals 1/72 of an inch, so 72 points equal one inch. Type styles are effects applied to characters such as boldface, underline, or italic.

FIGURE 8A.10

Basic character-formatting tools in Microsoft Word.

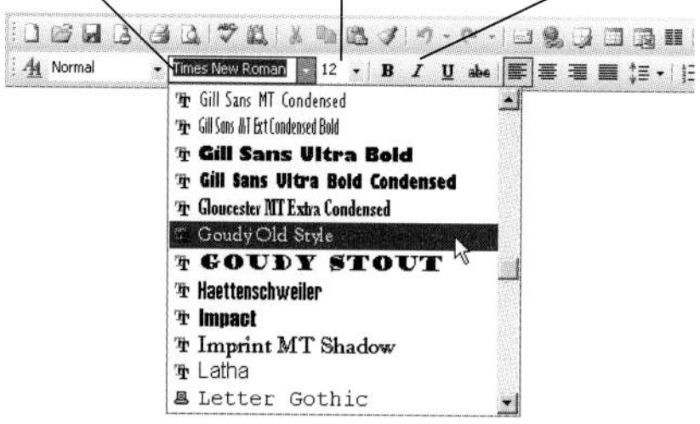

» **Paragraph formatting** includes settings applied only to one or more entire paragraphs, such as line spacing, paragraph spacing, indents, alignment, tabs, borders, or shading. In a word processor, a **paragraph** is any text that ends with a special character called a paragraph mark. You create a paragraph mark when you press the ENTER key.

FIGURE 8A.11

A newsletter, such as this one, has many different formats, including sections, columns, fonts, borders, and others. This newsletter was created in a standard word processing program.

» **Document formatting** includes the size of the page, its orientation, and headers or footers. Word processing software also lets you apply special formats, such as columns, to documents. You also can divide a document into sections and give each section its own unique format (see Figure 8A.11).

Spreadsheet Programs

A **spreadsheet** program is a software tool for entering, calculating, manipulating, and analyzing sets of numbers. Spreadsheets have a wide range of uses—from family budgets to corporate earnings statements. As shown in Figure 8A.12, you can set up a spreadsheet to show information in different ways, such as the tradi-

FIGURE 8A.12

Spreadsheet users usually set up their information to display in a classic row-and-column format. However, spreadsheet programs also enable you to create elaborate reports with charts, text, colors, and graphics.

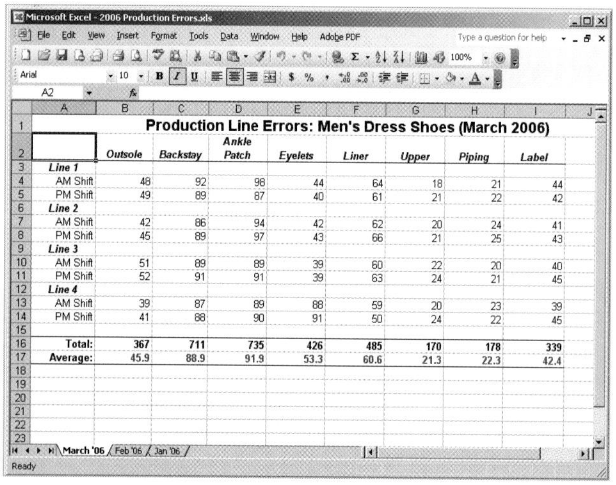

Microsoft Excel - 2006 Production Errors.xls

Production Line Errors: Men's Dress Shoes (March 2006)

	Outsole	Backstay	Ankle Patch	Eyelets	Liner	Upper	Piping	Label
Line 1								
AM Shift	48	92	98	44	64	18	21	44
PM Shift	49	89	87	40	61	21	22	42
Line 2								
AM Shift	42	86	94	42	62	20	24	41
PM Shift	45	89	97	43	66	21	25	43
Line 3								
AM Shift	51	89	89	39	60	22	20	40
PM Shift	52	91	91	39	63	24	21	45
Line 4								
AM Shift	39	87	89	88	59	20	23	39
PM Shift	41	88	90	91	50	24	22	45
Total:	**367**	**711**	**735**	**426**	**485**	**170**	**178**	**339**
Average:	**45.9**	**88.9**	**91.9**	**53.3**	**60.6**	**21.3**	**22.3**	**42.4**

March '06 / Feb '06 / Jan '06

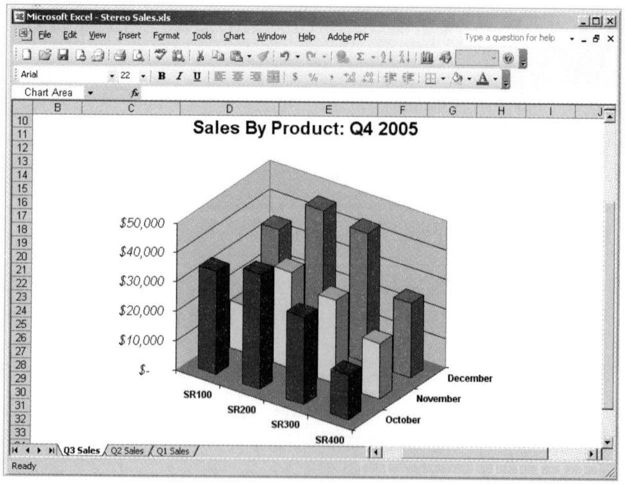

tional row-and-column format (the format used in ledger books) or a slick report format with headings and charts.

The Spreadsheet's Interface

Like a word processor, spreadsheets provide a document area, which is where you view the document. In a spreadsheet program, you work in a document called a worksheet (or sheet, as it is also called), and you can collect related worksheets in a workbook (called a notebook in some programs). Worksheets can be named, and a workbook can contain as many individual worksheets as your system's resources will allow.

A typical spreadsheet interface provides a menu bar, toolbars, scroll bars, and a status bar. Spreadsheet programs also display a special formula bar, where you can create or edit data and formulas in the worksheet.

An empty worksheet (one without any data) looks like a grid of rows and columns. The intersection of any column and row is called a cell, as shown in Figure 8A.13. You interact with a spreadsheet primarily by entering data into individual cells. A typical worksheet contains thousands of individual cells.

Norton ONLINE

For more information on spreadsheet programs, visit **http://www.mhhe.com/peternorton**.

simnet™

Entering Data in a Worksheet

Entering data in a worksheet is simple. Using the mouse or arrow keys, you select a cell to make it active. The active cell is indicated by a cell pointer, a rectangle that makes the active cell's borders look bold (see Figure 8A.14).

To navigate the worksheet, you need to understand its system of cell addresses. All spreadsheets use row and column identifiers as the basis for their cell addresses. If you are working in the cell where column B intersects with row 3, for example, then cell B3 is the active cell.

When you have selected a cell, you simply type the data into it. When a cell is active, you also can type its data into the formula bar. The formula bar is handy because it displays much more data than the cell can. If a cell already contains data, you can edit it in the formula bar.

A worksheet's cells can hold several types of data, but the four most commonly used kinds of data are

» **Labels.** Worksheets can contain text—called labels (names for data values)—as well as numbers and other types of data. In spreadsheets, text is usually used to identify a value or series of values (as in a row or column heading) or

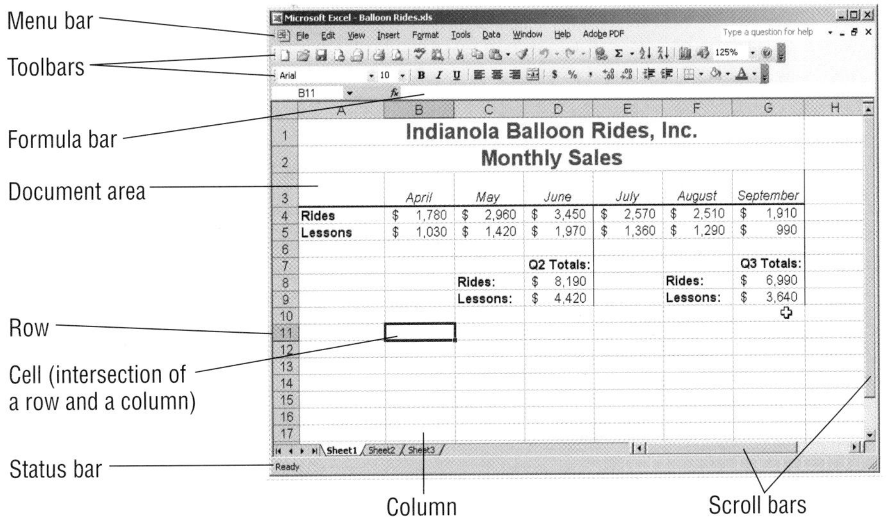

FIGURE 8A.13

Microsoft Excel's interface features tools common to nearly all Windows and Macintosh spreadsheets.

FIGURE 8A.14

Cell addresses help you navigate a worksheet.

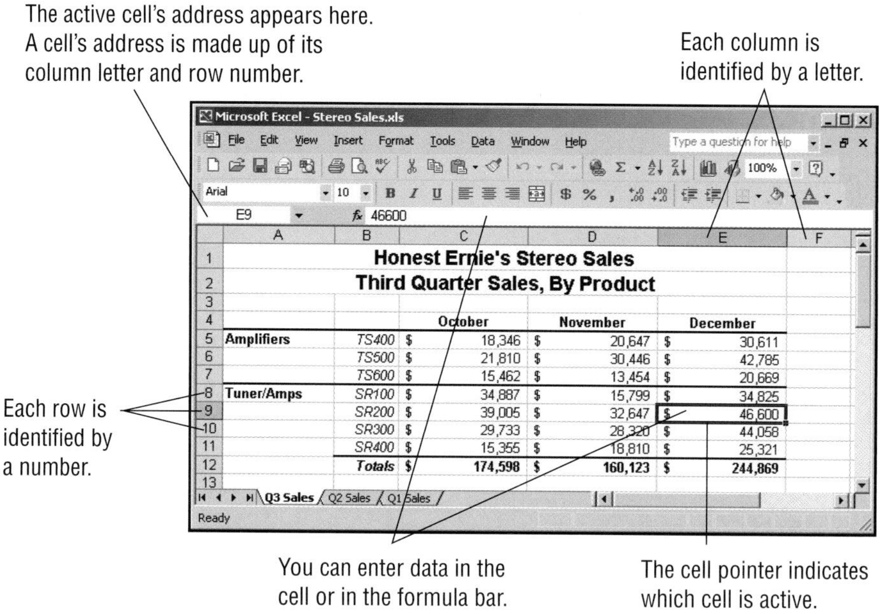
The active cell's address appears here. A cell's address is made up of its column letter and row number.
Each column is identified by a letter.
Microsoft Excel - Stereo Sales.xls
Honest Ernie's Stereo Sales
Third Quarter Sales, By Product
October
November
December
Amplifiers
Tuner/Amps
Totals
Q3 Sales
Q2 Sales
Q1 Sales
Ready
Each row is identified by a number.
You can enter data in the cell or in the formula bar.
The cell pointer indicates which cell is active.

to describe the contents of a specific cell (such as a total). Labels help you make sense of a worksheet's contents (see Figure 8A.15).

» **Values.** In a spreadsheet, a value is any number you enter or that results from a computation. You might enter a series of values in a column so that you can total them. Or you might enter several different numbers that are part of an elaborate calculation. Spreadsheets can work with whole numbers, decimals, negative numbers, currency, and other types of values, including scientific notation.

» **Dates.** Dates are a necessary part of most worksheets, and spreadsheet programs can work with date information in many ways. A date may be added to a worksheet simply to indicate when it was created. Spreadsheets also can use dates in performing calculations, as when calculating late payments on a loan. If the spreadsheet knows the payment's due date, it can calculate late fees based on that date.

» **Formulas.** The power of the spreadsheet lies in formulas, which calculate numbers based on values or formulas in other cells. You can create many kinds of formulas to do basic arithmetic operations, calculus or trigonometric operations, and so on. Suppose, for example, that the manager of a real estate office wants to calculate the commissions paid to agents over a specific time period. Figures 8A.16 and 8A.17 show a simple formula that takes the total sales for each agent and calculates the commission for that total. If any part of the formula (either the sales total or the commission percentage) changes, the formula can automatically recalculate the resulting commission.

Cells also can hold graphics, audio files, and video or animation files. To the spreadsheet program, each type of data has a particular use and is handled in a unique manner.

SELF-CHECK ::

Circle the correct answer for each question.

1. You can __________ shareware before you have to register or pay for it.
   a. modify   b. try out   c. distribute
2. Word processors contain tools for creating __________-based documents.
   a. text   b. number   c. chart
3. In a spreadsheet, __________ can help you make sense of a worksheet's contents.
   a. formulas   b. values   c. labels

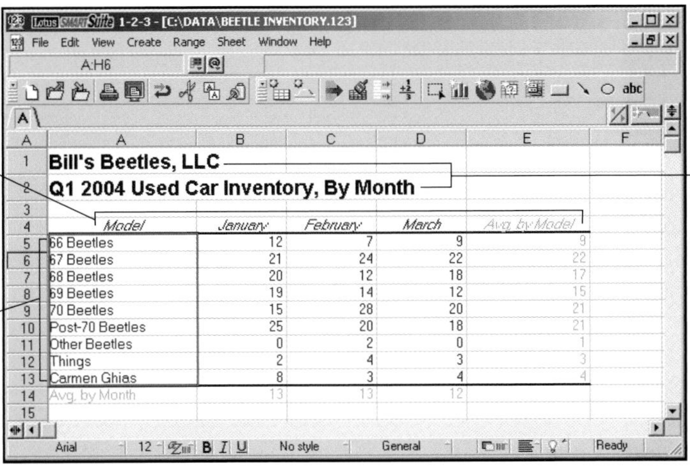
These labels are column headings that describe the contents of the cells below them.
These labels identify the data in the cells to their right.
These labels are used as titles for the sheet.
Bill's Beetles, LLC
Q1 2004 Used Car Inventory, By Month

FIGURE 8A.15

Labels help organize the information in a worksheet.

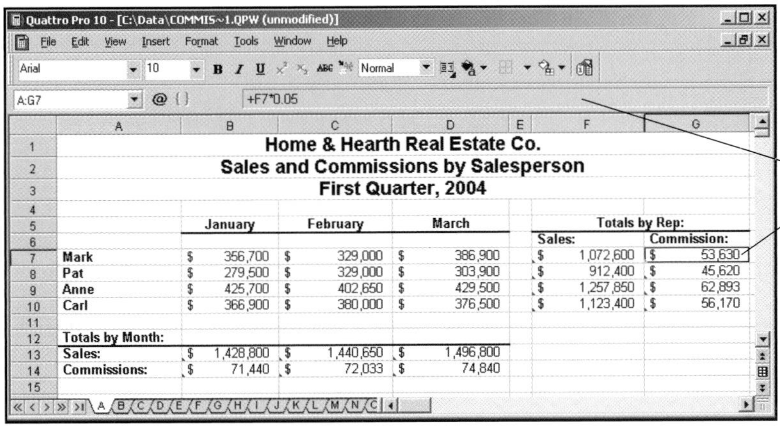
Home & Hearth Real Estate Co.
Sales and Commissions by Salesperson
First Quarter, 2004
This cell contains a simple formula that multiplies total sales by a commission percentage. Notice that the cell displays the results of the formula, rather than the formula itself.

FIGURE 8A.16

An example of a formula used to calculate simple percentages.

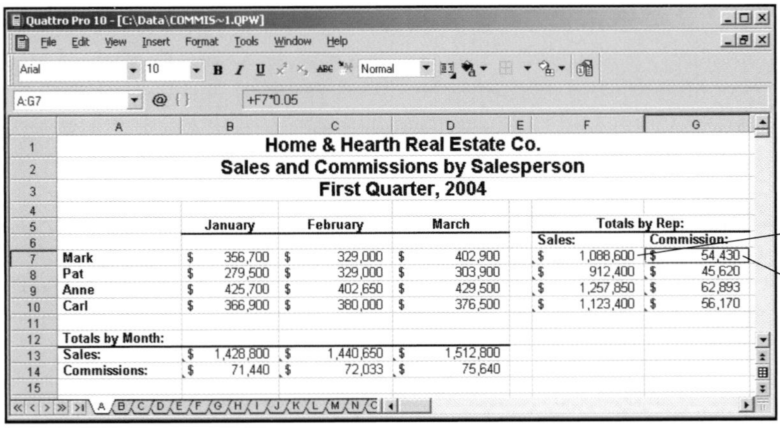
Home & Hearth Real Estate Co.
Sales and Commissions by Salesperson
First Quarter, 2004
When this agent's sales total changes...
...the commission is automatically recalculated.

FIGURE 8A.17

Spreadsheet formulas can recalculate automatically if any of their base data changes.

Presentation Programs

If you have ever attended a seminar or lecture that included slides or overhead transparencies that were projected on a wall screen or displayed on a computer screen or video monitor, then you probably have seen the product of a modern presentation program. Presentation programs enable the user to create and edit colorful, compelling presentations that can be displayed in various ways and used to support any type of discussion.

Norton ONLINE

For more information on presentation programs, visit **http://www.mhhe.com/peternorton**.

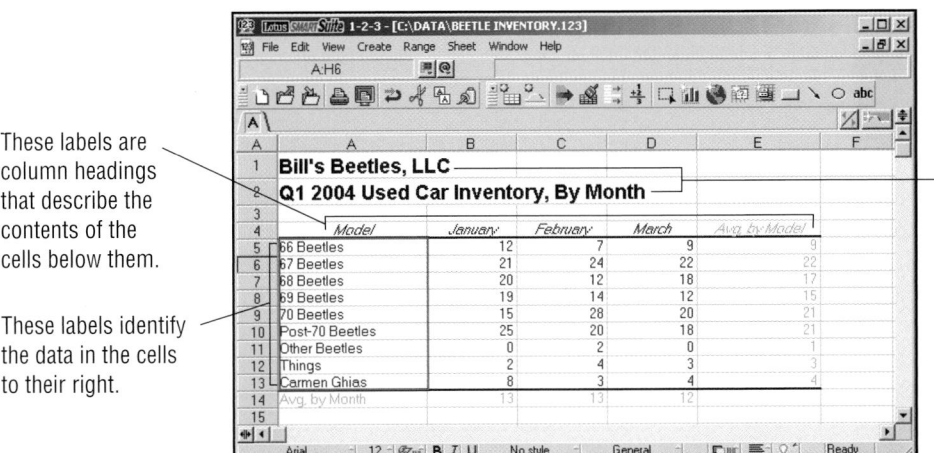

At Issue

Who Really Owns the Software on Your PC?

Once you start using a computer, it does not take long to learn that software can be very expensive. If you use your PC a lot, especially if you use it for work, you can spend hundreds or even thousands of dollars on software in a very short time.

But even though you pay a lot for software, you do not necessarily *own* the programs on your PC. This fact surprises a lot of people, but it is true just the same.

What happens, then, when you pay for a piece of software? That depends on the software maker, but very few developers grant you actual ownership of a program, even after you "purchase" it. Instead of buying the software itself, you really pay for a license that grants you permission to install and use the software.

Why a License?

In very simple terms, a license is an agreement between you and the software's maker. Under most software license agreements, the developer grants you a few rights to the program, but keeps all the remaining rights.

Most licenses allow the user to install the program on a single computer and to make one backup copy of the installation disk(s). If you want to install the software on a different computer, the agreement may state that you must uninstall it from the first computer. If you install the program on multiple PCs or make multiple duplicates of it, you may be violating the terms of the license. If the software developer catches you, it can take the software away from you and even press charges under applicable laws.

Software developers have good reasons for licensing software instead of selling it outright:

» **Piracy.** Software piracy is the act of copying software without the developer's consent (and, more important, without paying the developer), then selling or giving away the copies. If you use the original installation disks to install the program on multiple computers at the same time, that is piracy too. Software developers lose billions of dollars every year because of piracy. By licensing their products and maintaining some ownership of them, however, developers can take action against pirates. If a developer actually sold the software itself, it might be giving away all its rights to it, and piracy would be an even greater problem.

simnet™

Presentation programs allow the user to design slides—single-screen images that contain a combination of text, numbers, and graphics (such as charts, clip art, or pictures) often on a colorful background. A series of slides, displayed in a specific order to an audience, is called a presentation. Usually, the person showing the slides (the presenter) speaks to the audience while the slides are being displayed. The slides themselves show unique, specific pieces of information; the presenter fills in the details with his or her speech.

Slides can be simple or sophisticated. Depending on your needs, you can turn a basic slide show into a multimedia event using the built-in features of many presentation programs.

The Presentation Program's Interface

The typical presentation program displays a slide in a large document window and provides tools for designing and editing slides. Presentation programs provide many of the features found in word processors (for working with text), spreadsheets (for creating charts), and graphics programs (for creating and editing simple graphics). You can add elements to the slide simply by typing, making menu or toolbar choices, and dragging. As you work on the slide, you see exactly how it will look when it is shown to an audience.

Figure 8A.18 shows a slide in Microsoft PowerPoint, a popular presentation program. Note that the status bar says that the presentation contains five slides. A presentation can contain a single slide or hundreds. Presentation programs let

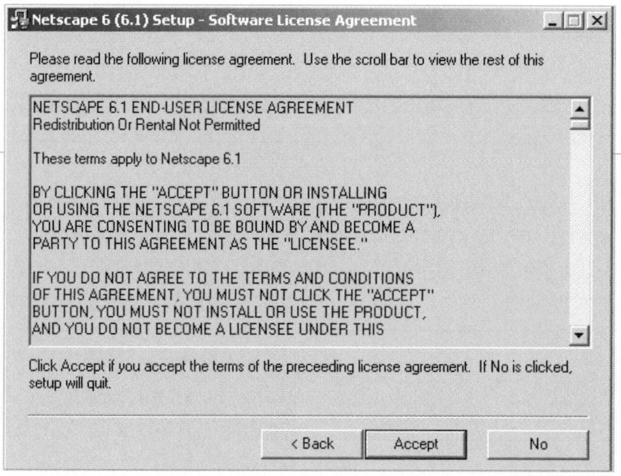

A software license agreement. This agreement appears on the screen when you install the program. You can accept or decline the agreement.

» **Modifications.** Most license agreements state that you cannot make modifications to a program's source code. If developers allowed this, it would be an easy matter for others to make changes to a program, then try to claim the modified program as their own.

Even though the developer keeps most rights to a program, however, you still have some rights, too. If the program does not perform as you expected, you have the right to return or exchange it. You also should be able to expect reasonable customer support from the developer.

Where Will I Find the License?

In many cases, the license agreement and its terms may be printed on the software's packaging; when you open the package and install the program, you are bound by the license's terms. More and more developers, however, are adding the agreement to the software installation process. This means that when you install the program, the agreement appears on the screen so you can read it. You then can click a button to indicate whether you accept or decline the agreement. If you accept, the installation continues. If you decline, the installation aborts.

Either way, you should always read the license agreement carefully and decide if you want to accept it. If you do not accept the license agreement, you may be able to return the software. (Note, however, that many stores may not accept opened software packages for a refund, although you may be able to exchange it for a store credit or a different program.) If you accept a license agreement, however, you should honor its terms.

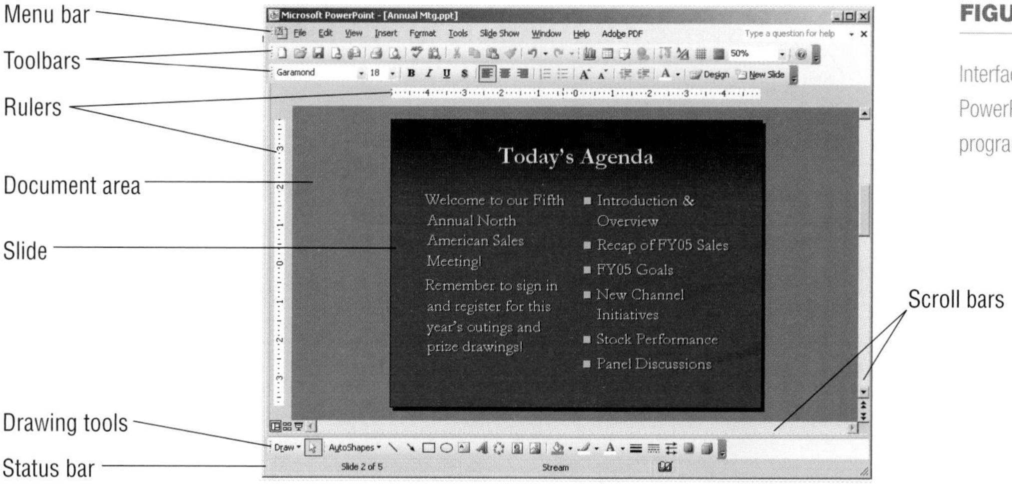

FIGURE 8A.18

Interface features of Microsoft PowerPoint, a popular presentation program.

you save a group of slides in one file so that you can open the related slides and work with them together.

A presentation program includes a menu bar, one or more toolbars (for managing files, formatting, drawing, and doing other tasks), rulers, slide-viewing or navigation buttons that let you move from one slide to another, a status bar, and other tools.

Creating a Presentation

Creating a presentation is simple; just choose the type of slide you want to create and then start adding the content. A complete presentation usually includes multiple slides arranged in a logical order. As you go, you can insert new slides anywhere, copy slides from other presentations, and reorder the slides.

You can create slides from scratch (starting with a blank slide), but it is easier and faster to work with one of the presentation program's many templates. A **template** is a predesigned document that already has coordinating fonts, a layout, and a background. Your presentation program should provide dozens of built-in templates, as shown in Figure 8A.19.

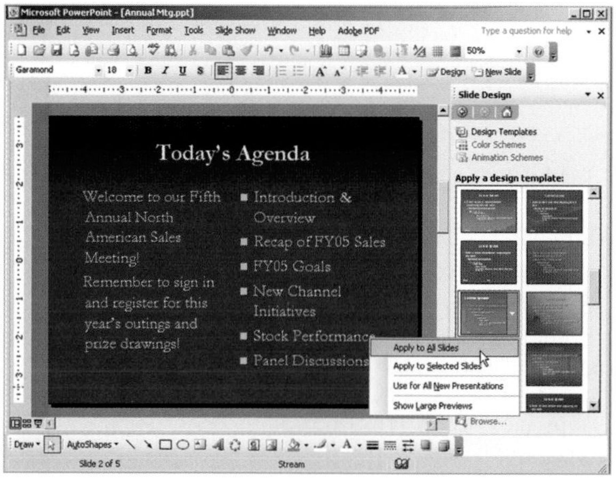

FIGURE 8A.19

Choosing a template in PowerPoint.

FIGURE 8A.20

Choosing a layout for a new slide. The new slide will be inserted after the slide that is on the screen.

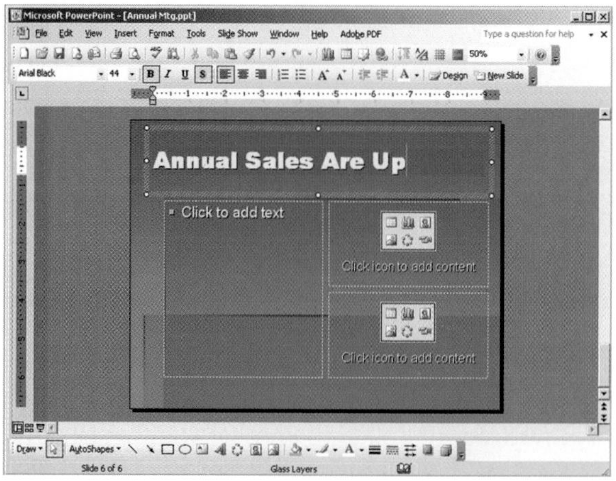

FIGURE 8A.21

Adding text to a slide.

After you select a template, you can quickly assemble a presentation by creating individual slides. To create a slide, you choose a layout for it, as shown in Figure 8A.20. Presentation programs provide many slide layouts that hold varying combinations of titles, text, charts, and graphics. You can choose a different layout for each slide in your presentation, if you want.

After you select a layout, the blank slide appears in the document window, ready for you to add text, charts, or graphics. The program provides special **text boxes** and **frames** (special resizable boxes for text and graphical elements, respectively) to contain specific types of content. These special boxes often contain instructions telling you exactly what to do. To add text to a text box, simply click in the box and type your text, as shown in Figure 8A.21. The text is formatted automatically, but you can easily reformat the text later, using many of the same formatting options that are available in word processors.

Adding charts, tables, clip art, or other graphics is nearly as easy (see Figure 8A.22). When you choose a slide layout that contains a chart, for example, you enter the chart's data in a separate window, called a *datasheet*. The program uses the data to create a chart.

To insert clip art or another type of graphic in a slide, you can select an image from your software's collection of graphics (as shown in Figure 8A.23) or import an image file such as a scanned photograph or clip art. Built-in paint tools also enable you to draw simple graphics and add them to your slides. These tools are handy if you want to add callouts to specific elements of a slide.

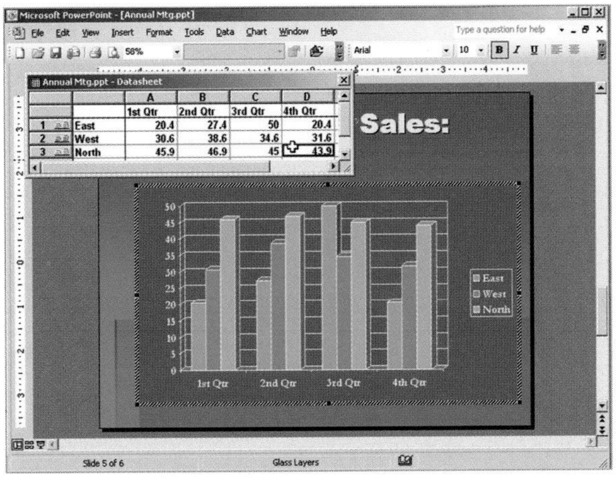

FIGURE 8A.22

Creating a chart in PowerPoint. You type the chart's data in the datasheet window, which resembles a spreadsheet program. The program uses the data to create a chart, which appears on your slide.

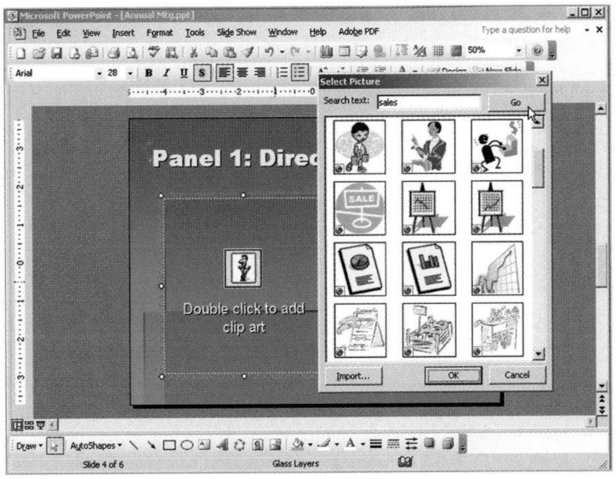

FIGURE 8A.23

Selecting a graphic to insert into a slide.

Presenting Slide Shows

You can present slides directly from your computer's disk, along with any audio or video files that you embed in your slides. Your audience can view slides in several ways:

» **On the PC's Screen.** If you are presenting slides to a few people, your PC's monitor might be adequate for an informal slide show. Of course, the larger the monitor, the better your audience can see the slides.

» **On a Large-Format Monitor.** Large-format CRT and plasma monitors can display your slides at the proper resolution and large enough for a sizable audience to view comfortably (see Figure 8A.24). These devices are expensive and more difficult to transport than a standard monitor, but they may be the best solutions for some presentation settings.

» **On a Television Screen.** Using a PC-to-TV converter, you can connect your computer to a standard television and view the PC's video output on the television monitor. This solution may sound convenient, but compatibility issues must be considered (not all converters work with all televisions, for example), and televisions do not display images at the same resolution as a PC monitor. Image quality may suffer when a PC-to-TV converter is used.

» **From a Data Projector.** Portable, high-resolution data projectors are expensive, but they can display slides to a large audience. These projectors plug into one of the PC's ports and accept the system's video output.

FIGURE 8A.24

You can get the best results from your slide shows if you present them directly from the PC's disk using a display device that is appropriate for the audience and room size.

Productivity Tip

Automating Your Work with Macros

Although you may think your favorite software program saves you a great deal of time and energy, it could probably save you a great deal more if you used its most powerful tools—macros.

What Is a Macro?

Simply put, a macro is a list of commands, keystrokes, or other actions that have been saved and given a name. When you create a macro, you record a series of actions. When you replay the macro, it repeats those actions for you. You can use macros to automate nearly any task that requires multiple steps—no matter how many steps are involved.

Many commercial applications support macros, and some even feature an array of built-in, predefined macros that you can use right away or customize to suit your own work style. These applications usually allow you to create your own macros to automate tasks that you perform frequently or that require several steps (making them difficult to do manually).

Creating a Macro

Suppose, for example, that you are using a word processor to clean up a collection of old documents that were keyed by someone who always inserted two blank spaces after every period. Today, it is more common to insert only one blank space after a period. One of your tasks is to eliminate all the extra blank spaces from the documents. To make this change to a document, you can scan through the document one line at a time, replacing the extra spaces as you find them. Or you can use the word processor's Find and Replace commands to automate the process. This function can search the document; when it finds a period followed by two spaces, it replaces them with a period followed by one space. Manually running the Find and Replace feature, however, can still take a lot of time.

If your word processor supports macros, you can create a new macro that does the job for you. Just open one of the documents, start the word processor's macro-recording feature, and manually perform the Find and Replace process

Regardless of the method you use to project your slides, navigating a slide show is a simple process. You can move from one slide to the next by clicking the mouse button or pressing ENTER. Or you can automate the presentation by setting a display time for each slide. Presentation programs make it easy to take slides out of sequence or rearrange slides during a presentation. You can even use the program's drawing tools to draw on a slide while it is being displayed.

Norton ONLINE

For more information on PIMs, visit **http://www.mhhe.com/peternorton**.

Personal Information Managers

It's harder than ever to keep track of people. You probably know several people who have a home phone number, a cell phone number, one or two e-mail addresses, an instant messenger address, and a fax machine number, all in addition to their "snail mail" address. (The term **snail mail** refers to the U.S. Postal Service.) To make matters more difficult, some people also have a Web page, a special number for voice mail messages, a pager, and even a second mailing address!

It is very common for businesspersons to have multiple contact points. Of course, these many means of contacting people are supposed to make it easier to reach them. But keeping track of all those names, numbers, and addresses—called **contact information**—can be frustrating.

The explosion of contact information has given rise to a special type of software, called the **personal information manager**, or **PIM**. A personal information manager is designed to keep track of many different kinds of contact information, for many different people. PIMs are sometimes referred to as **contact managers** or

PRODUCTIVITY TIP

while the recorder runs. You can then save the macro, give it a name (such as "Period_and_One_Space"), and assign it to a shortcut key (such as ALT+1) or a toolbar button, depending on your program's macro capabilities. Afterward, you can run the macro with the click of a mouse or by pressing a simple key combination instead of manually repeating all the steps yourself.

Macros can be as simple or as complex as necessary, and you can create macros for nearly any task. In a spreadsheet, for example, you might create a macro that selects a column of data, applies a specific format, sorts the data, and inserts a function (like SUM) at the bottom. In a graphics program, you might create a macro that opens a group of image files, sizes them and adjusts their color settings, and prints them out on individual sheets, each identified by its file name. A macro can even include other macros, enabling you to perform multiple tasks at one time.

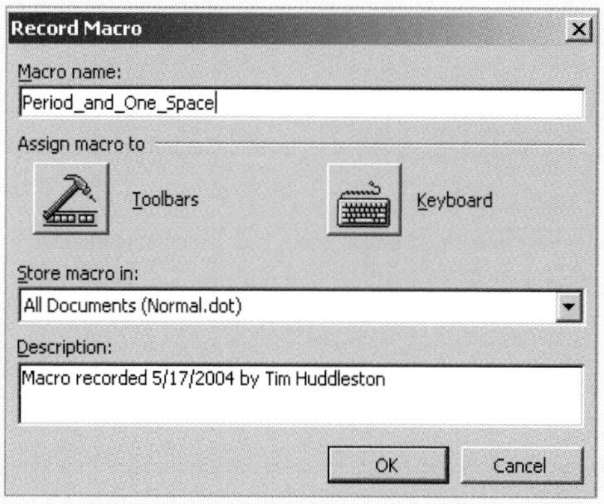

Preparing to record a new macro, in Microsoft Word.

contact-management software. One of the most popular PIMs is Microsoft Outlook, shown in Figure 8A.25.

PIMs make contact management easy, because they provide special placeholders for all kinds of contact information—everything from phone numbers and e-mail addresses to Web pages and regular mail addresses. To manage contact information for a person, you add him or her to your contact list. (Most PIMs store and arrange contacts by first name or last name, according to your preference.) Then you simply type all the contact points into the appropriate boxes in that person's contact sheet (see Figure 8A.26).

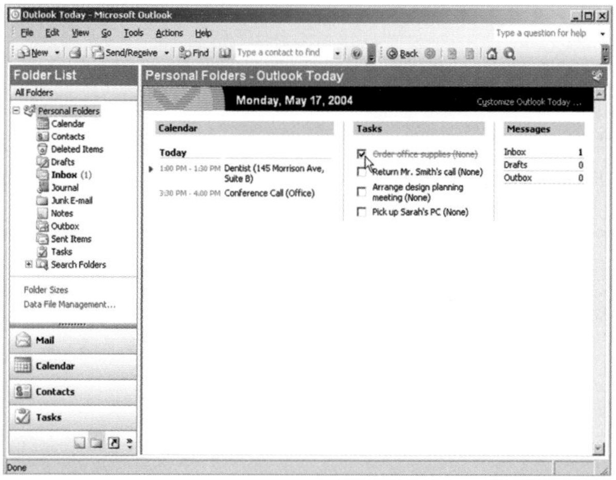

FIGURE 8A.25

Microsoft Outlook lets you manage contact lists, your schedule, and other important information. It is also a powerful e-mail program.

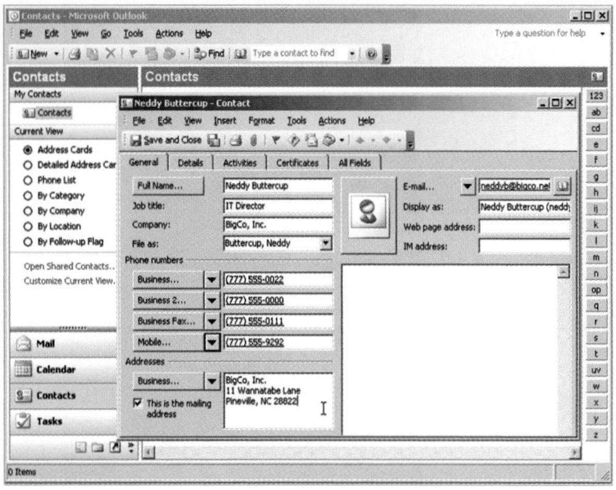

FIGURE 8A.26

Adding contact information for a person in Microsoft Outlook.

Like many other PIMs, Outlook stores much more than just contact information. You also can use a PIM to manage your schedule, create reminders, and set up to-do lists. Outlook is also a powerful e-mail program that you can use to send messages to anyone in your contact list (see Figure 8A.27). Contact lists are often called address books in e-mail programs and PIMs.

Many professionals, especially salespeople, use a PIM as their primary software tool. This is because they can manage their calendar and associate specific events with specific contacts. For example, if you schedule a meeting, you can place it in your PIM's calendar; note the time, place, and purpose of the meeting; and create a list of attendees from your contact list. This capability not only lets you manage your schedule down to the last detail, but gives you a permanent record of your activities. (See Figure 8A.28.)

FIGURE 8A.27

Sending an e-mail message in Outlook.

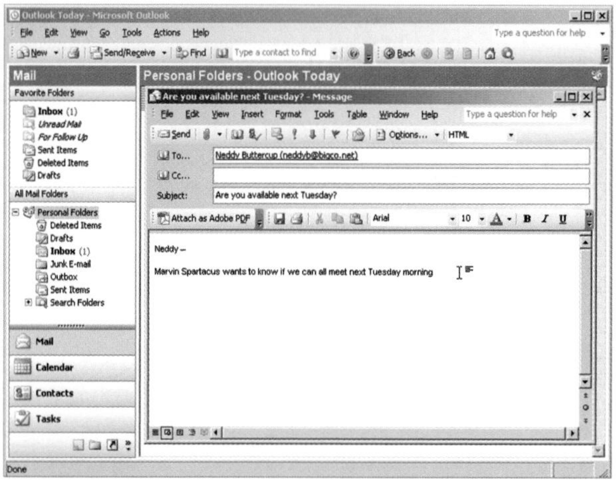

FIGURE 8A.28

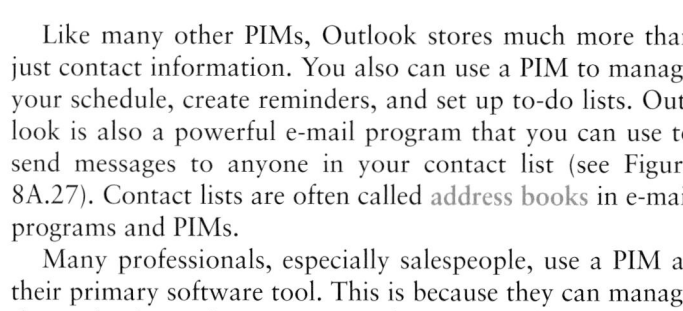

A PIM's scheduling capabilities let you manage meetings, deadlines, appointments, and special events.

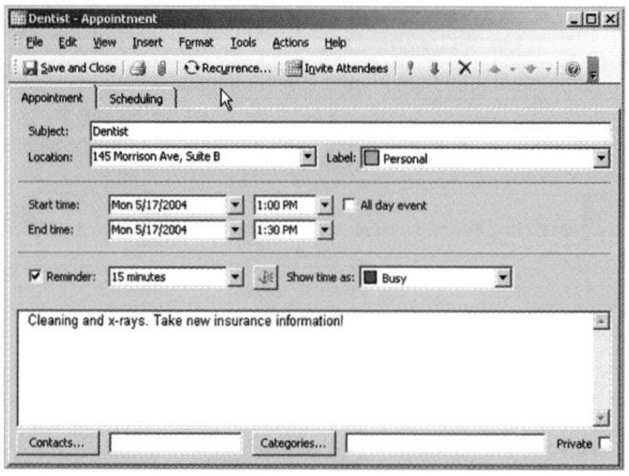

Summary

- Commercial software is any program you must purchase. Commercial software is sold in the form of stand-alone programs, software suites, and shareware.
- Some software does not have to be purchased, such as freeware, public domain software, and open-source software.
- Word processing programs are used to create and format text-based documents, such as letters and reports.
- Word processors feature on-screen tools found in most kinds of productivity applications. These tools include a menu bar, toolbars, rulers, scroll bars, and a status bar.
- Most of a word processor's tools are used for formatting documents. You can format characters, paragraphs, and entire documents using these tools.
- Spreadsheet programs are used to create numerically based documents, such as budgets.
- Spreadsheets work with four basic kinds of data: labels, numbers, dates, and formulas. A spreadsheet can perform complex calculations on the numbers in its cells.
- Presentation programs let you create presentations, which are collections of single-screen images called slides. A presentation may also be called a slide show.
- Presentation programs include tools found in word processors, spreadsheets, and graphics programs, so you can combine all manner of text and images on your slides. You can present slides directly from your computer's disk.
- Personal information managers (PIMs) are special programs designed to manage contact information, schedules, and other personal or business information.
- Many PIMs also are e-mail programs, making it easy to send e-mail messages to anyone in the program's address book.

LESSON //8A Review

Key Terms ::

address book, 318
block, 307
cell, 309
cell address, 309
cell pointer, 309
character format, 307
commercial software, 304
contact information, 316
contact-management software, 317
contact manager, 316
deselect, 307
document area, 306
document format, 308
document window, 306
edit, 306
font, 307
format, 307
formula, 310
formula bar, 309
frame, 314
freeware, 304
label, 309
menu bar, 306
open-source software, 305
paragraph, 308
paragraph format, 308
PC-to-TV converter, 315
personal information manager (PIM), 316
point, 307
presentation, 312
presentation program, 312
public domain software, 304
ruler, 306
scroll bar, 306
select, 307
shareware, 304
slide, 312
snail mail, 316
software suite, 304
spreadsheet, 308
stand-alone program, 304
status bar, 306
template, 314
text box, 314
toolbar, 306
type style, 307
value, 310
word processing program, 305
word processor, 305
workbook, 309
worksheet, 309

Key Term Quiz ::

Complete each statement by writing one of the terms listed under Key Terms in each blank.

1. You can try out a(n) ________ program before you must purchase or register it.
2. ________ is software of any type whose source code is available to users.
3. Changing an existing document is called ________ the document.
4. Word processors enable you to perform three basic types of formatting: ________ , ________ , and ________ .
5. In a spreadsheet program, you actually work in a document called a(n) ________ .
6. A column letter and a row number combine to form a(n) ________ .
7. A spreadsheet program uses ________ to calculate numbers based on the contents of a worksheet's cells.
8. You use a presentation program to design ________ , which are single-screen images containing a combination of text, numbers, and graphics.
9. In a slide, you enter text in a special placeholder, which is called a(n) ________ .
10. The term ________ refers to the U.S. Postal Service.

Multiple Choice ::

Circle the word or phrase that best completes each statement.

1. A word processing program or an e-mail program is an example of a ________ program.
   a. system b. spreadsheet c. template d. stand-alone
2. Most word processors feature one or more ________ , which provide buttons that issue commands.
   a. menu bars b. toolbars c. status bars d. scroll bars
3. In a word processor, you ________ text to mark it for editing or formatting.
   a. block b. delete c. move d. select
4. To navigate a worksheet, you should understand its system of ________ .
   a. cell addresses b. spreadsheets c. formulas d. labels
5. ________ can help you make sense of a worksheet's contents.
   a. Cell pointers b. Labels c. Cell references d. Values
6. In a spreadsheet program, a ________ is a set of worksheets in the same file.
   a. formula b. label c. workbook d. value
7. In a worksheet, a ________ is the intersection of a row and a column.
   a. formula bar b. cell c. ruler d. frame
8. To create a chart in a slide, you enter data in a separate window called a ________ .
   a. datasheet b. spreadsheet c. worksheet d. rapsheet
9. A ________ is designed to keep track of many different kinds of contact information, for many different people.
   a. workbook b. program c. PIM d. stand-alone program
10. In a personal information manager, a contact list may be called a(n) ________ .
    a. black book b. contact book c. address book d. contact point

LESSON //8A Review

Review Questions ::

In your own words, briefly answer the following questions.

1. List three forms in which commercial software can be acquired.
2. In a word processor, what makes a block of text?
3. What happens when you press ENTER in a word processor?
4. What is the purpose of a formula bar in a spreadsheet program?
5. What is the difference between a spreadsheet and a worksheet?
6. What does a formula do in a spreadsheet?
7. What is a presentation?
8. Describe two ways you can create slides in a presentation program.
9. List four ways you can display a slide show to an audience.
10. What is contact information?

Lesson Labs ::

Complete the following exercises as directed by your instructor.

1. Practice some basic formatting:
   a. In your word processor's document area, type a few lines of text, allowing the lines to wrap when they reach the right edge of the screen. Press ENTER and type a new paragraph. Create several more paragraphs. (If you have trouble thinking of text to type, just copy a few paragraphs of text from this book.)
   b. Using the mouse, select a word. (Double-click the word or drag the mouse pointer across it.) Click the Bold tool. Then deselect the word by pressing an arrow key on the keyboard. Select the word again and click the Bold tool to turn off the effect.
   c. Select different words, lines, and paragraphs and practice using other tools such as a Font tool, a Font size tool, Italic, and Underline.
   d. Close the program by clicking the Close button (the button marked with an X on the title bar). If the program prompts you to save the file, choose No.
2. Practice using a worksheet:
   a. In your worksheet's document area, type numbers in cells A1 through A5.
   b. Using the mouse, select all the values in this range. (Click in cell A1, then drag the mouse pointer down through cell A5.)
   c. Click in cell A6 and type **=SUM(A1:A5)**. Press ENTER. The total of the values in cells A1 to A5 should appear in cell A6. If it does not, ask your instructor for help.
   d. Click in cell A3 and press DELETE. The value in the cell disappears and the total in cell A6 changes.
   e. Issue the Undo command. (There should be an Undo tool on the toolbar. If not, ask your instructor for assistance.) The value is returned to cell A3 and the total in cell A6 updates once more.
   f. Click in cell B6 and type **=A6*0.05**. Press ENTER. The formula's result appears in cell B6.
   g. Close the spreadsheet program by clicking the Close button. If the program prompts you to save the worksheet, choose No.

LESSON // 8B

Graphics and Multimedia

Overview: Graphics, Graphics Everywhere

You may not realize that many of the images you see are created on a computer. From postage stamps to magazine illustrations, from billboards to television programs, all kinds of graphics are created and edited using computers and graphics software. Graphics programs—and the designers who use them—have become so polished that it is often impossible to tell a photograph or hand-drawn illustration from a computer-generated graphic.

With the computer's capability to mimic traditional artists' media, graphics software allows artists to do with a computer what they once did with brushes, pencils, and darkroom equipment. Similarly, architects and engineers now do most of their design and rendering work on computers—although many were trained in traditional paper-based drafting methods. By using the computer, they produce designs and renderings that are highly accurate and visually pleasing.

Graphics software has advanced a great deal in a short time. In the early 1980s, most graphics programs were limited to drawing simple geometric outlines, usually in one color. Today, graphics software offers advanced drawing and painting tools and almost unlimited color control. You can see the products of these powerful tools everywhere you look. Their results can be subtle or stunning, obviously artificial, or amazingly lifelike.

OBJECTIVES ::

- Define the terms *bitmap* and *vector* and differentiate these file types.
- List some of the most commonly used file formats for bitmap and vector images.
- Identify four ways to load graphic files into a computer.
- List five types of graphics software and their uses.
- Define the terms *multimedia* and *interactivity*.

Understanding Graphics File Formats

Norton **ONLINE**

For more information on graphic files and formats, visit **http://www.mhhe.com/peternorton**.

Computers can create many, many kinds of graphics—from simple line drawings to three-dimensional animations. But all graphics files fall into one of two basic categories, known as bitmapped and vector files.

Bitmap and Vector Graphics

Graphics files are made up of either

» A grid, called a **bitmap**, whose cells are filled with one or more colors, as shown in Figure 8B.1. The individual cells in the grid can all be filled with the same color or each cell can contain a different color. The term **raster** is sometimes used to describe bitmap images. Bitmap images also may be referred to as *bitmapped images*. The easiest way to imagine how bitmaps work is to think of your computer's monitor. It displays images as collections of individual colored pixels. Each pixel is a cell in the grid of a bitmapped image. In fact, the individual pieces that make up a bitmapped image are often called *pixels*.

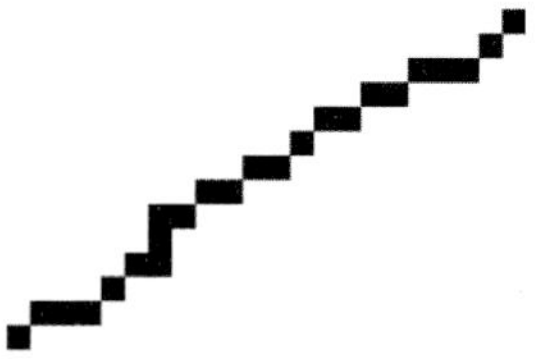

FIGURE 8B.1

If you magnify a bitmap, you can see its individual pixels.

» A set of **vectors**, which are mathematical equations describing the size, shape, thickness, position, color, and fill of lines or closed graphical shapes (see Figure 8B.2).

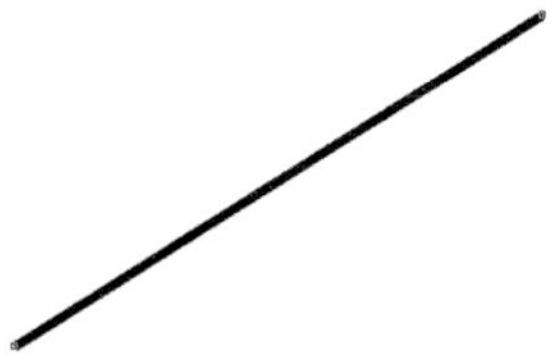

FIGURE 8B.2

This vector is defined as a line stretching between two endpoints, rather than as a set of pixels.

Some types of graphics programs work with bitmaps; some work with vectors; and some can work with both. Each type of graphics file has its own advantages and disadvantages. Whether you use a bitmap- or vector-based program depends on what you are trying to do. For example, if you want to be able to retouch a photo, create seamless tiling textures for the Web or for 3-D surfaces, or create an image that looks like a painting, you will choose bitmap-based software (see Figure 8B.3).

Vector-based software is your best choice if you want the flexibility of resizing an image without degrading its sharpness, the ability to reposition elements easily in an image, or the ability to achieve an illustrative look as when drawing with a pen or pencil.

FIGURE 8B.3

Working with a digitized photograph in Paint Shop Pro, a popular bitmap-based graphics program.

Strictly speaking, vectors are lines drawn from one point to another, as shown in Figure 8B.4. Vector-based software can use mathematical equations to define the thickness and color of a line, its pattern or fill, and other attributes. Although a line on the screen is still displayed as a series of blocks (because that is how all monitors work), it is an equation to the computer. Thus, to move the line from location A to location B, the computer substitutes the coordinates for location A with those for location B. This substitution saves the effort of calculating how to change the characteristics of thousands of individual pixels.

File Formats and Compatibility Issues

Perhaps more than other types of computer-generated documents, graphics files require users to understand and work with different types of file formats. A **file format** is a standardized method of encoding data for storage. File formats are important because they tell the program what kind of data is contained in the file and how the data is organized.

File formats may be proprietary or universal. The structure of a proprietary file format is under the sole control of the software developer who invented the format. Universal file formats are based on openly published specifications and are commonly used by many different programs and operating systems. For example, Adobe Photoshop, by default, saves images in its proprietary PSD format, but it also can save files in several universal formats, such as TIF, GIF, JPEG, PICT, and TGA. Word processing programs can read and save files in specific formats such as DOC or RTF, or TXT.

Nearly all bitmap-based graphics programs can use any of the file formats listed in Table 8B.1. For this reason, these formats are said to be compatible with such programs. For example, most bitmap-based programs can open, read, and save a file in GIF format and convert it to a different bitmap format, such as TIF.

Most vector-based programs create and save files in a proprietary file format. These formats are either incompatible with (cannot be used by) other programs, or they are not totally supported by other programs. The problem with incompatibility led developers to create universal file formats for vector-based programs. Only a handful of common file formats, such as DXF (Data Exchange Format) and IGES (Initial Graphics Exchange Specification) exist for vector graphics.

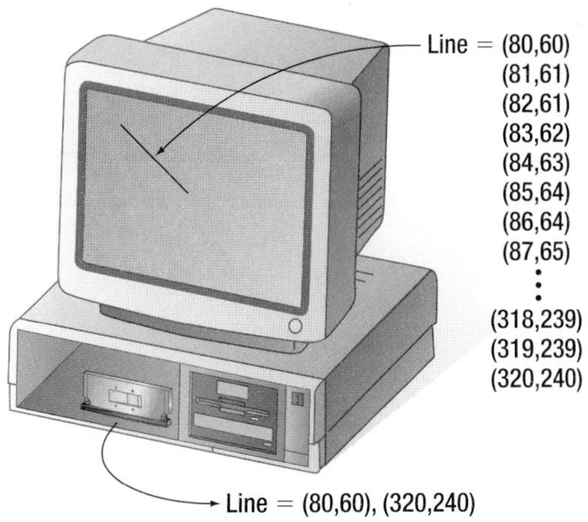

FIGURE 8B.4

To the monitor, a line is just a long list of individual pixels. With vector-based software, the CPU can represent the same line using just the endpoints.

TABLE 8B.1

Standard Formats for Bitmap Graphics

Format	Description
BMP	(BitMaP) A graphics format native to Microsoft Windows, BMP is widely used on PCs for icons and wallpaper. Some Macintosh programs also can read BMP files. The BMP file format supports up to 24-bit depth color, or over 16 million different colors.
PICT	(PICTure) This is the native format defined by Apple for use on Macintosh computers. It is widely used on Macs but is not usually used on PCs.
TIFF	(Tagged Image File Format) TIFF is a bitmap format defined in 1986 by Microsoft and Aldus (now part of Adobe) and widely used on both Macs and PCs. This format is usually the best to use when exchanging bitmap files that will be printed or edited further.
JPEG	(Joint Photographic Experts Group) JPEG is often abbreviated as JPG (pronounced JAY-peg). This bitmap format is common on the World Wide Web and is often used for photos and other high-resolution (24-bit or millions of colors) images that will be viewed on screen.
GIF	(Graphic Interchange Format) Like JPEG images, GIF images are often found on World Wide Web pages. Unlike JPEG images, GIF images can contain only 256 or fewer unique colors.
EMF	(Windows Enhanced Metafile) This format was originally developed for the Microsoft Office suite of applications. It uses the Windows built-in graphics device interface, or GDI, to create images that can be scaled to display at the highest-possible resolution on any device selected—screen or printer. This technology creates something of a hybrid between the vector graphics and bitmap types, since EMF bitmaps can be resized without any loss of quality.

Getting Images into Your Computer

Nearly all graphics programs let you create images from scratch by building lines and shapes into complex graphics. But artists and designers do not always start from scratch; they often begin with an existing image and then edit or enhance it by using graphics software. There are several ways to load images into a computer for editing, but the most common methods are

- **Scanners.** An image scanner is like a photocopy machine, but instead of copying an image onto paper, it transfers the image directly into the computer (see Figure 8B.5). A scanned image is usually a bitmap file, but software tools are available for translating images into vector format.

FIGURE 8B.5

Scanning an image into a computer for editing.

- **Digital Cameras.** A digital camera stores digitized images for transfer into a computer. The resulting file is generally a bitmap.
- **Digital Video Cameras.** A digital video camera captures and stores full-motion video on small tapes or optical discs. You can copy the content onto a computer for editing or transfer to another storage medium, such as DVD.
- **Clip Art.** The term clip art originated with large books filled with professionally created drawings and graphics that could be clipped from the pages and glued to a paper layout. Today, clip art provides an easy way to enhance digital documents. Many software programs (especially word processors) feature built-in collections of clip art, and collections are also available on CD-ROM and the Internet (see Figure 8B.6). Clip art can be in either bitmap or vector format.

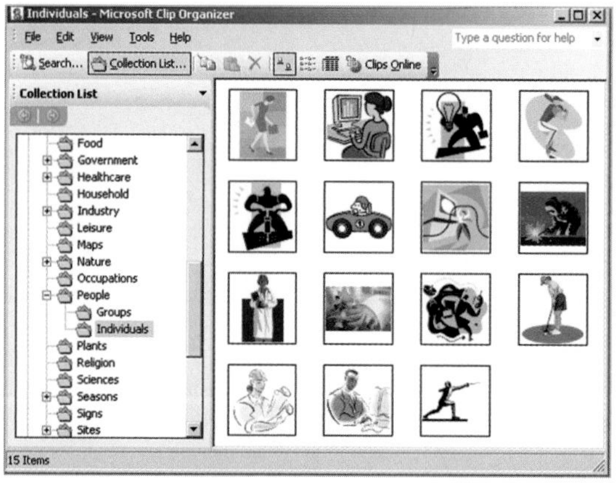

FIGURE 8B.6

The clip art collection from Microsoft Word 2003.

Graphics Software

Creating a digital image or manipulating an existing image can involve a complex array of processes. Since even the most sophisticated graphics program cannot perform all the operations that may be required for some types of graphics, designers frequently use more than one of the five major categories of graphics software to achieve their goals, including

- Paint programs.
- Photo-editing programs.
- Draw programs.
- Computer-aided design (CAD) programs.
- 3-D modeling and animation programs.

Of the five, the first two are bitmap-based paint programs; the rest are vector-based draw programs (although 3-D programs commonly work with vectors or bitmaps).

Norton ONLINE

For more information on all types of graphics software, visit **http://www.mhhe.com/peternorton**.

Paint Programs

Paint programs are bitmap-based graphics programs. You already may be familiar with a paint program, like Windows Paint. Paint programs range from the very simple (with only a handful of tools) to the very complex, with tools that have names such as paintbrush, pen, chalk, watercolors, airbrush, crayon, and eraser. Because paint programs keep track of each and every pixel placed on a screen, they also can perform tasks that are impossible with traditional artists' tools—for example, erasing a single pixel or changing every pixel in an image from one color to another color.

Paint programs provide the tools for creating some spectacular effects. More sophisticated paint programs can make brush strokes that appear thick or thin, soft or hard, drippy or neat, opaque or transparent. Some programs allow you to change media with a mouse click, turning your paintbrush into chalk or a crayon or giving your smooth "canvas" a texture such as rice paper or an eggshell (see Figure 8B.7).

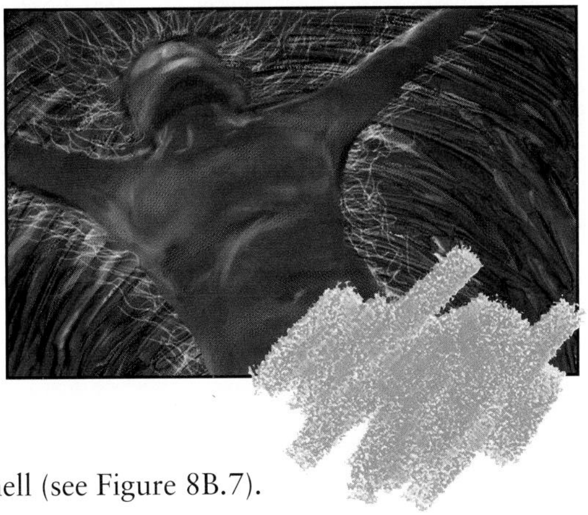

FIGURE 8B.7

Watercolors and textures are a few of the effects available in sophisticated paint programs.

Draw Programs

Draw programs are vector-based graphics programs that are well suited for work when accuracy and flexibility are as important as coloring and special effects. You see the output of draw programs in everything from cereal box designs to television show credits.

Simply by clicking and dragging in a draw program, you can change a shape into a different shape, move it, or copy it (see Figure 8B.8). Paint programs don't provide this flexibility because they do not recognize lines, shapes, and fills as unique objects.

Draw programs are sometimes referred to as object-oriented programs because each item drawn—whether it is a line, square, rectangle, or circle—is treated as a separate and distinct object from all the others. (Some designers and draw programs use the term *entity* rather than *object*, but the concept is the same.) All objects created in draw programs consist of an outline and a fill. The fill can be nothing at all, a solid color, a vector pattern, a photo, or something else. For example, when you draw a square with a draw program, the computer remembers your drawing as a square of a fixed size at a specific location, which may or may not be filled—not as a bunch of pixels in the shape of a square.

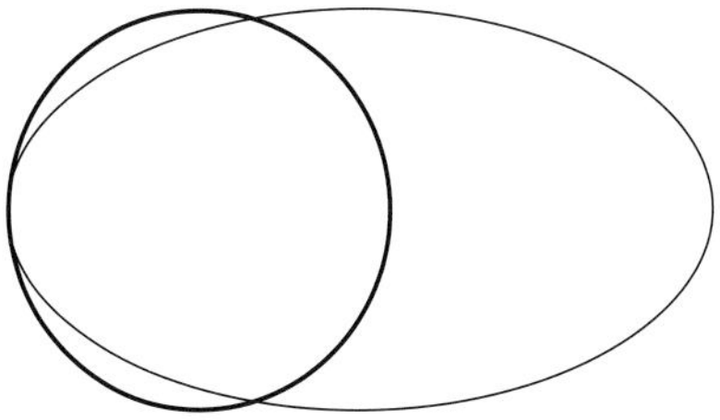

FIGURE 8B.8

Changing a circle into an oval by dragging, in a draw program.

Photo-Editing Programs

When scanners made it easy to transfer photographs to the computer at high resolution, a new class of software was needed to manipulate these images on the screen. Cousins to paint programs, photo-editing programs now take the place of a photographer's darkroom for many tasks. Because photo-editing programs (like paint programs) edit images at the pixel level, they can control precisely how a

FIGURE 8B.9

Repairing a scratched image with an airbrush tool.

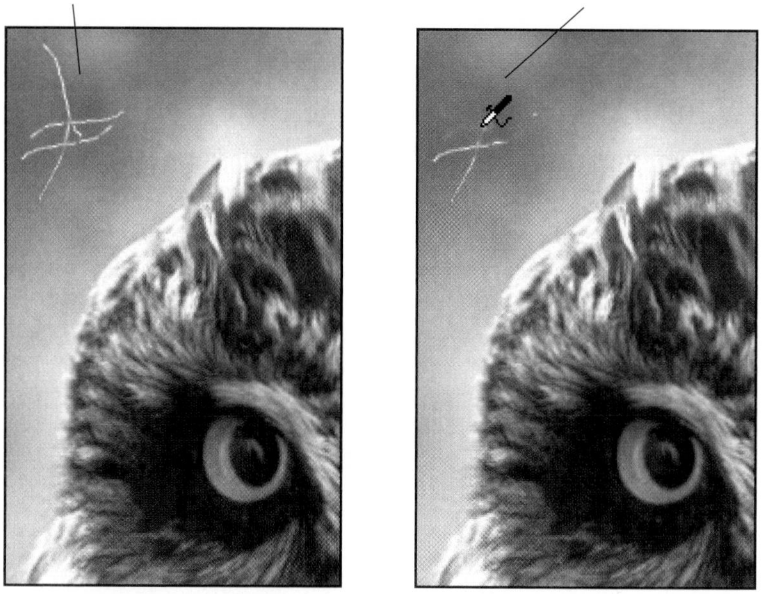
White lines come from scratches on the original film.
Using the airbrush tool, the artist can blend them into the background.

picture will look. They also are used to edit nonphotographic images and to create images from scratch.

FIGURE 8B.10

This image demonstrates how a photo-manipulation program can be used to combine two photos together to create a striking effect.

Photo-editing programs are used most often for simple jobs such as sharpening focus, adjusting contrast, or removing flaws from digitized images. In Figure 8B.9, for example, software is being used to hide a scratch in a scanned photo. But photo-editing programs are also used to modify photographs in ways far beyond the scope of a traditional darkroom, as shown in Figure 8B.10.

Computer-Aided Design Programs

Computer-aided design (CAD), also called *computer-aided drafting* or *computer-aided drawing*, is the computerized version of the hand-drafting process that used to be done with a pencil and ruler on a drafting table (see Figure 8A.11). CAD is used extensively in technical fields such as architecture and in mechanical, electrical, and industrial engineering. CAD software also is used in other design disciplines, such as textile and clothing design and product and package design.

FIGURE 8B.11

Construction documents—commonly known as blueprints—are commonly created in CAD programs and used as the basis for buildings, engineering projects, and countless manufactured products.

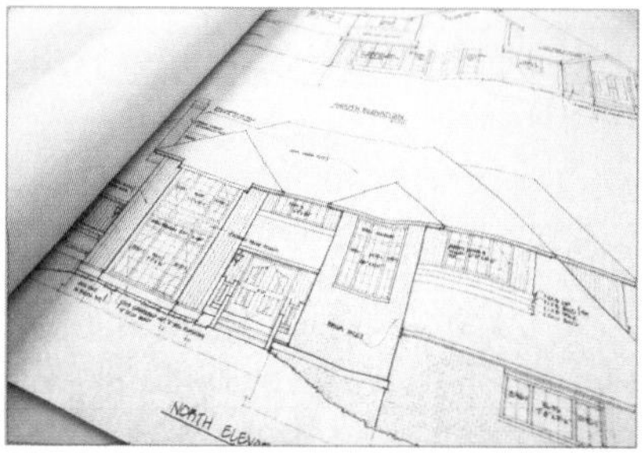

Vector-based CAD drawings are usually the basis for the actual building or manufacturing process of houses, engine gears, or electrical systems, for example.

To satisfy the rigorous requirements of manufacturing, CAD programs provide a high degree of precision. If you want to draw a line that is 12.396754 inches long or a circle with a radius of 0.90746 centimeter, a CAD program can fulfill your needs. In fact, CAD programs are so precise, they can produce designs accurate to the micrometer—or one-millionth of a meter.

3-D and Animation Software

You are constantly exposed to elaborate 3-D imaging in movies, television, and print. Many of these images are now created with a special type of graphics software, called 3-D modeling software. Fast workstations or PCs coupled with 3-D modeling programs can lend realism to even the most fantastic subjects.

Digital 3-D objects can be modified to any shape using electronic tools much like those used in woodworking. For example, holes can be drilled into computer-based 3-D objects, and corners can be made round or square by selecting the appropriate menu item. Three-dimensional objects also can be given realistic textures and patterns (see Figure 8B.12), or they can be animated or made to fly through space.

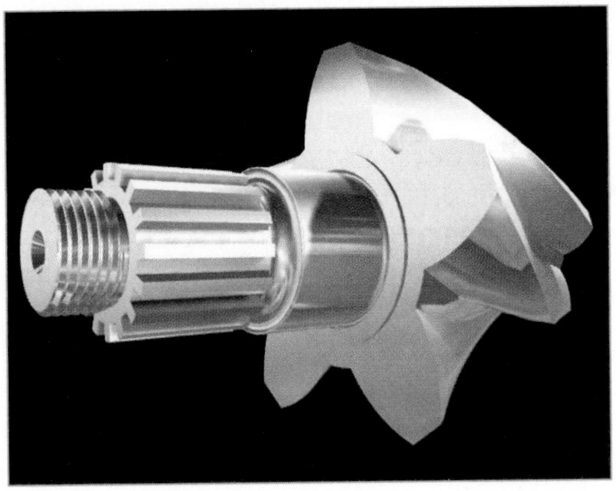

FIGURE 8B.12

A three-dimensional gear, created in a 3-D modeling program.

An outgrowth of the 3-D explosion is computer-based animation. Since the creation of filmmaking, animation was possible only through a painstaking process of hand-drawing a series of images (called cells), as shown in Figure 8B.13, and then filming them one by one. Each filmed image is called a frame. When the film is played back at high speed (usually around 30 frames per second for high-quality animation), the images blur together to create the illusion of motion on the screen. The process of manually creating a short animation—even just a few seconds' worth—can take weeks of labor.

Computer-generated imaging (CGI) has changed the world of animation in many ways. Although computer animation works on the same principles as traditional animation (a sequence of still images displayed in rapid succession), computer animators now have highly sophisticated tools that take the drudgery out of the animation process and allow them to create animation more quickly than ever. Computer animators also have the advantage of being able to display their animation on the computer screen or output them to CD-ROM, videotape, or film.

An added bonus of computer animation is the ability to animate three-dimensional characters and create photorealistic scenes. (The computer-generated image looks so realistic that it could be mistaken for a photograph of a real-life object.) These capabilities make computer-generated characters difficult to distinguish from real ones. Some examples are the character Gollum in *The Lord of the*

FIGURE 8B.13

Images from a traditional, manually drawn animation. Although computers speed up the animation process tremendously, they still work on the same idea: generate hundreds or thousands of individual frames and then display them in rapid succession to create the illusion of motion.

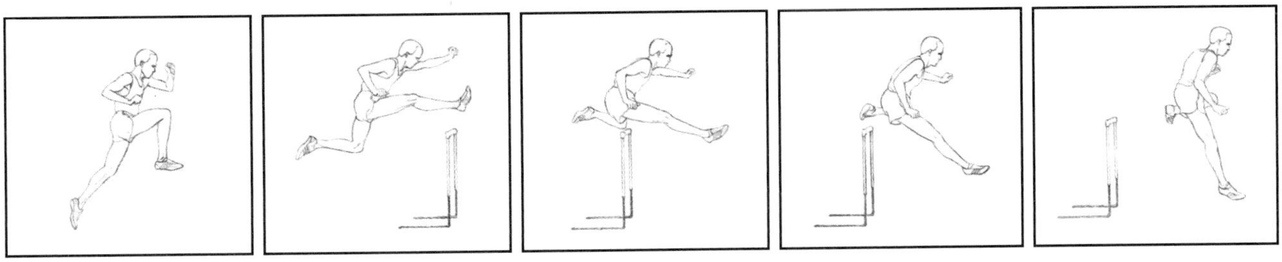

Norton Notebook

Why Own When You Can Rent?

At some point in the lives of many adults, someone older and in a position of supposed wisdom will ask, "Why rent an apartment when you can own a house?" While responsive answers to the question are usually forthcoming, the fact remains that the question is fundamentally rhetorical. The person speaking isn't seriously inquiring about anything; they're simply waiting for an opportunity to provide their young listener with a viewpoint. The question rings in the mind with that "used car salesman on television" intonation: *But wait! There's more!* But the question has taken on real meaning, thanks to the development of broadband technologies that stand ready to turn the future into the past.

In the past, for almost all companies, owning a computer was simply out of the question. You've heard the history: Computers filled whole buildings, needed their own support staff, and so forth. What you may not know is that most, if not all, of the private companies that *did* purchase computers before the evolution of the PC leveraged the tremendous purchase and support cost by providing time-sharing computer services to other companies. For example, a small chain of grocery stores might have had no need for a computer of its own, but computational power would really help with weekly inventory, monthly financial reports, and so on. The store chain would rent time on a mainframe computer, during which time its inventories and so forth would be run. This time-sharing scheme was so successful, it wasn't uncommon for a mainframe owner to not be the primary user of the computer.

All this changed with the development of the PC and, in time, the cheap availability of tremendous computing power on the desktop. (Based strictly on the number of instructions a computer can perform in one second, modern desktop PCs are well in excess of 7,000 times faster than mainframe computers from the 1980s. Relative to work accomplished, PCs are considerably faster still.) You've seen elsewhere in this chapter how application software, run on a local PC, changed the face of computing and the whole world. However, there are drawbacks to running programs and processing data in this way. Of the many problems we could talk about, the greatest has almost always been the nature of personal computers themselves. Programs and data stored on a PC are just that: on *a* PC. Simple sharing of files used to be anything but simple, and an entire genre of software used to exist to make it possible. Digital collaboration was simply out of the question.

Eventually, local area networks and Microsoft Windows made moving and sharing files simple, and collaboration became possible through special multi-user versions of application software. With all of this data being shared successfully across high-speed networks, one of the remaining major drawbacks to companywide computing (often called "enterprise" computing) was the cost of installing all

FIGURE 8B.14

Computer-generated animation is often so lifelike that it is hard to distinguish from the real thing.

Rings: The Two Towers and the eerie landscapes of *The Matrix* series of movies. Using computers and special animation software, artists and designers can create many types of animation, from simple perspective changes to complex full-motion scenes that incorporate animated characters with real-life actors and sound (see Figure 8B.14).

Norton ONLINE

For more information on multimedia, visit **http://www.mhhe.com/peternorton**.

Multimedia Basics

For much of history, information was presented via a single, unique medium. A *medium* is simply a way of sharing information. Sound, such as the human voice, is one type of medium; for centuries before written language came into widespread use, speech was the primary way of sharing knowledge (see Figure 8B.15). People also told stories (and left a record of their lives) through drawings and paintings.

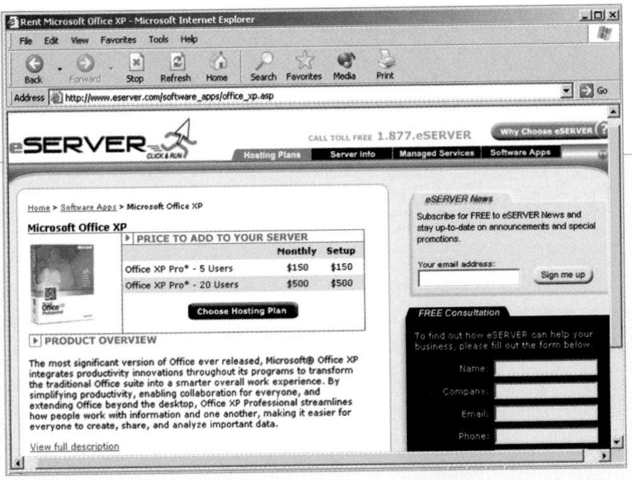

the necessary applications on each desktop. In order for employees all over the world to work together on a project, each employee needed the creator application for the project. Even if a particular user only worked with a particular program twice a year, the company had to purchase a full-cost user license for the product. A possible solution to this rather central concern may be a new twist on the old idea of time-shared computing: application service providers, or ASPs. As the name implies, ASPs are for application software what ISPs are for the Internet itself.

ASPs provide access to an application over a network connection to a central application server. On an as-needed basis, application components are downloaded to user workstations. Companies can subscribe to specific applications and, in most cases, pay fees based on actual employee usage. In principle, access to an application through an ASP program should be dramatically less expensive than purchasing a full user license for each employee who has occasional need for the software. Additionally, companies receive customer and technical support from the ASP, not from the application manufacturer and not through the costly maintenance of in-house technical support staff. Since the customer company doesn't own the application software—the ASP does—the direct cost of software updates is included in the subscription fees, and the indirect update costs, such as unproductive downtimes and the aforementioned technical support staff, are borne by the ASP as part of its own costs of doing business. The most significant difference between time-sharing and ASP use, of course, is that all of the actual computing—except in the case of database servers—is done on the user's desktop. This means that online applications run much the same as do locally installed ones. Applications need not be installed on every PC, so many desktop units need only minimal internal storage. The ASP business model is a new idea for the 21st century, but its basis lies in time-tested efficient use of resources—money, time, bandwidth, and people.

NORTON NOTEBOOK

The creation of written language gave people yet another medium for expressing their thoughts. Today, people commonly use speech, sounds, music, text, graphics, animation, and video to convey information. These are all different types of media (the term *media* is the plural of *medium*), and each has traditionally been used to present certain types of information.

SELF-CHECK ::

Circle the correct answer for each question.

1. The individual pieces that make up a bitmapped image are often called ________.
   a. vectors b. pixels c. graphics
2. A ________ tells a program what kind of data is contained in a file and how the data is organized.
   a. file format b. utility c. document
3. A ________ program's drawings are often used as the basis for construction documents.
   a. paint b. CAD c. draw

Long ago, people discovered that messages are more effective (that is, the audience understands and remembers them more easily) when they are presented through a combination of different media. This combination is what is meant by the term multimedia—using more than one type of medium at the same time.

The computer has taken multimedia to a high level by enabling us to use many different media simultaneously. A printed encyclopedia, for example, is basically

Computers In Your Career

Careers in Multimedia

No two workdays are alike for Corby Simpson, senior programmer at Toronto-based creativePOST Inc., a post-production facility offering creative solutions for broadcast television and interactive media that has worked with clients such as The Discovery Channel and General Motors.

Simpson may start the day programming a CD-ROM filled with video content and then switch to designing a CD-ROM label for distribution, authoring a DVD, or developing content for use on a personal digital assistant (PDA) later in the day.

When he's not handling one of those projects, he's updating his skills and learning about new technologies.

"Keeping up with the new trends can be a full-time job in itself," says Simpson, who completed a three-year media arts program and a one-year interactive multimedia postgraduate program at Sheridan College.

For Simpson, the multimedia field is most enjoyable for the creative outlet it provides. "It's one of the only industries where you can invent things with no cost attached to them, just time," says Simpson. "You can also invent other people's ideas, and if they're successful, you get a piece of that pie too."

Sometimes, the creative aspect also can pose challenges for Simpson, who recently was under pressure to learn how to change the way 50,000 lines of computer code worked. "The application was our own invention, so we couldn't outsource it," says Simpson. "Under normal conditions somebody would go to school for three years to learn what we did in less than a month." Simpson sees opportunities in the multimedia field as growing, thanks to an increase in Web-based applications and wireless development.

Careers in multimedia are as varied and as numerous as multimedia products, with the workload typically shared by a team, helmed by a creative director who is responsible for developing and refining the overall design process from start to finish. The creative director is also responsible for integrating that design process into the developmental process of the company. The team members of a multimedia project usually include some or all of the following:

- **Art Director** Directs the creation of all art for the project.
- **Technical Lead** Ensures that the technological process of a project works and that it accommodates all project components and media.

pages of text and pictures. In a multimedia version, however, the encyclopedia's pictures can move, a narrator's recorded voice can provide the text, and the user can move around at will by clicking hypertext links and using navigational tools. By combining different types of media to present the message, the encyclopedia's developer improves the chances that users will understand and remember the information.

FIGURE 8B.15

Speech is the most basic and universal medium for communicating thoughts and ideas. After centuries of practice, people find speech a natural and effective way to communicate.

Of course, the same point can be made about television programming because it uses various media at the same time. Computer technologies, however, enable PC-based multimedia products to go one step further. Because the computer can accept and respond to input from the user, it can host interactive multimedia events, involving the user unlike any book, movie, or television program.

Interactivity has been defined in many ways, but in the realm of multimedia, the term means that the user and program respond to one another: the program contin-

- **Interface Designer** Directs the development of the user interface for a product, which includes not only what users see but also what they hear and touch.
- **Instructional Designer** Designs the instructional system for the product, which determines how material is taught, if the product is educational.
- **Visual Designer** Creates the various art forms, usually within a specialized area.
- **Interactive Scriptwriter** Weaves the project's content among various media and forms of interactivity.
- **Animator** Uses 2-D and 3-D software to create animation and effects.
- **Sound Producer** As a manager, creative artist, and programmer, a sound producer designs and produces all the audio in a product.
- **Videographer** Creates the video footage that interfaces with the interactive technology of the product.
- **Programmer/Software Designer** Designs and creates the underlying software that runs a multimedia program and carries out the user's commands.

The Bureau of Labor Statistics reports that job opportunities for multimedia professionals are expected to grow as fast as average for all occupations through the year 2010. Median annual earnings of salaried multimedia artists and animators were $41,130 in 2000, with the middle 50 percent earning between $30,700 and $54,040.

ually provides the user with a range of choices that the user selects to direct the flow of the program. This level of interactivity is the primary difference between computer-based multimedia programs and other kinds of multimedia events. Most television programs, for example, require the viewer only to sit and observe. Computers, however, make it possible to create interactive media, which enable people to respond to—and even control—what they see and hear. By using the PC to control the program, the user can make choices, move freely from one part of the content to another, and in some cases customize the content to suit a specific purpose.

Interactive media are effective (and successful) because they provide this give-and-take with the user. You will find this level of interactivity in practically any popular multimedia product, whether the program is a video game, a digital reference tool, an electronic test bank, or a shopping site on the Web (see Figure 8B.16).

FIGURE 8B.16

Because they provide the user with different types of content and options for navigating and displaying that content, computer-based games and references are highly interactive.

LESSON // 8B Review

Key Terms ::

3-D modeling software, 329
bitmap, 324
BMP, 325
clip art, 326
compatible, 325
computer-aided design (CAD), 328
computer-generated imaging (CGI), 329
draw program, 327
DXF, 325
EMF, 325
file format, 324
frame, 329
GIF, 325
IGES, 325
incompatible, 325
interactive, 332
interactivity, 332
JPEG, 325
multimedia, 331
paint program, 327
photo-editing program, 327
photorealistic, 329
PICT, 325
raster, 324
TIFF, 325
vector, 324

Key Term Quiz ::

Complete each statement by writing one of the terms listed under Key Terms in each blank.

1. The term ________ is sometimes used to describe bitmap images.
2. A(n) ________ is a standardized method of encoding data for storage.
3. If a program can use a specific file format, the two are said to be ________ .
4. The ________ bitmap file format is often used for photos and other high-resolution images that will be viewed on screen.
5. The ________ and ________ file formats are two of the common file formats used for vector graphics.
6. ________ programs keep track of each and every pixel on the screen.
7. ________ programs are cousins to paint programs and now take the place of a photographer's darkroom for many tasks.
8. High-quality animation is usually played at a speed of 30 ________ per second.
9. The term ________ refers to the use of more than one medium at a time to present information.
10. If a multimedia program can accept and respond to input from the user, it is said to be ________ .

Multiple Choice ::

Circle the word or phrase that best completes each statement.

1. A(n) __________ image is defined as a grid whose cells are filled with color.
   a. bitmap b. vector c. printed d. interactive
2. A __________ image consists of mathematical equations describing the size, shape, thickness, position, color, and fill of lines or closed graphical shapes.
   a. raster b. large c. vector d. complex
3. Graphics __________ can be proprietary or universal.
   a. images b. file formats c. bitmaps d. programs
4. A __________ can convert a printed image into digital format.
   a. photocopier b. digital camera c. scanner d. computer
5. The __________ graphics file format was defined for use on Macintosh computers.
   a. JPEG b. TIFF c. IGES d. PICT
6. If a program and a file format cannot work together, they are said to be __________ .
   a. incompatible b. compatible c. universal d. proprietary
7. You can use a paint program to change every _____ in an image from one color to another color.
   a. frame b. pixel c. CAD d. format
8. __________ is the computerized version of the hand-drafting process.
   a. Multimedia b. Interactivity c. CAD d. Painting
9. The term *media* is the plural form of __________ .
   a. medium b. multimedia c. multimedium d. multimediocre
10. Although television is an example of multimedia, it is not __________ .
    a. plural b. interactive c. active d. passive

Review Questions ::

In your own words, briefly answer the following questions.

1. Name the two primary categories of graphics files.
2. List four popular methods you can use to get images into a computer.
3. Where does the term *clip art* come from?
4. List six common file formats used for bitmap images.
5. Identify one difference between GIF-format images and JPEG-format images.
6. Name five key types of graphics software.
7. Define the term *multimedia*.
8. What is interactivity, in the context of multimedia?
9. What is special about a photorealistic image?
10. What are photo-editing programs most commonly used for?

Lesson Labs ::

Complete the following exercises as directed by your instructor.

1. If your computer came with Windows installed, it may have one or more graphics programs such as Windows Paint, Microsoft Image Composer, or some other program installed. Check your Programs menu for programs that might be used for graphics. If the product's name does not make its use clear, ask your instructor for help. List the graphics programs installed on your system.
2. Launch Windows Paint and draw a picture. Windows Paint is a basic bitmap-based paint program that is almost always installed with Windows. To launch the program, click the Start button, open the Programs menu, point to Accessories, and click Paint. Experiment with the program's drawing tools to create a simple image. Print and save the image, if your instructor approves, then close Paint.
3. If your school's computer lab or library has multimedia products on CD-ROM, check one out and use it. What type of application did you select? Determine what types of media it uses. What sorts of navigational tools does it provide? How easy is the product to use? Does it serve its purpose? Write a one-page report on the product and summarize its strengths and flaws.

Chapter Labs

Complete the following exercises using a computer in your classroom, lab, or home.

1. Find some fonts. The Internet is a good place to find and acquire fonts. Some fonts can be downloaded from various Web sites at no cost. Other fonts can be purchased over the Web. Visit the following Web sites and study the available fonts, but do not download any fonts without your instructor's permission.

    Microsoft Typography. http://www.microsoft.com/typography/default.asp. (You won't actually find fonts here, but you will find a tremendous amount of information about fonts and links to non-Microsoft sites where fonts can be downloaded.)

    CNet. http://www.cnet.com. Use the Search tool to search on the term "fonts."

    ZDNet. http://www.zdnet.com. Use the Search tool to search on the term "fonts."

2. Check out some audio/video players. Several audio and video players are available for use on the PC, and each provides a unique set of features in addition to supporting various multimedia file types. Visit these Web sites for information on a few players, but do not download any software without your instructor's permission:

    Real Networks, Inc. For information about the RealOne Player, visit http://www.real.com.

    Microsoft. For information about Windows Media Player, visit http://www.microsoft.com/windows/windowsmedia.

    Apple Computer, Inc. For information on the QuickTime player, visit http://www.quicktime.com.

Discussion Questions

As directed by your instructor, discuss the following questions in class or in groups.

1. Do you think that using a spell checker and a grammar checker for all your final documents is a sufficient substitute for proofreading? Explain why.
2. Suppose that you were asked to give a presentation on a subject you understand well. To support your presentation, you must prepare a 20-minute slide show using presentation software. Describe the slide presentation you would create. How many slides would you use? How would you organize them? What types of content would you use in each? What features of the presentation program would you use to enhance the presentation?

Research and Report

Using your own choice of resources (such as the Internet, books, magazines, and newspaper articles), research and write a short paper discussing one of the following topics:

- The ways spreadsheet programs are used in business.
- Basic design principles you should follow when creating a slide show.
- Copyright protection as it applies to graphics.

When you are finished, proofread and print your paper, and give it to your instructor.

ETHICAL ISSUES

Software programs have made traditional tools such as typewriters and film obsolete. But like any powerful tool, they can be used and abused. With this thought in mind, discuss the following questions in class.

1. Word processors make it easy to create documents. They also make it easy to copy documents created by others. Copying other people's work is a growing concern because more people are downloading others' creations from the Internet and disks and then using the documents as their own. Would you use this tactic, say, to create a term paper for school? Do you think it is legally or morally right? Why or why not?
2. Magazines commonly retouch photographs before printing them, especially on covers. In some cases, editors make the subjects look very different from what they look like in reality, and not always for the better. Should this type of retouching be regulated, or do you see it as a harmless practice? Support your position.

CHAPTER 9 Networks

CHAPTER CONTENTS ::

This chapter contains the following lessons:

LESSON // 9A

Networking Basics

Overview: Sharing Data Anywhere, Anytime

When PCs first appeared in businesses, software programs were designed for a single user. There were few obvious advantages to connecting PCs, and the technology was not adequate for doing so. As computers spread throughout business, developers began offering complex software designed for multiple users. Many organizations quickly learned the importance of connecting PCs. Data communications—the electronic transfer of information between computers—became a major focus of the computer industry. During the past decade, networking technology has become the most explosive area of growth in the entire computer industry. The demand for larger and faster high-capacity networks has increased as businesses have realized the value of networking their computer systems.

Networks come in many varieties. When most people think of a network, they imagine several computers in a single location sharing documents and devices such as printers. But a network can include all the computers and devices in a department, a building, or multiple buildings spread over a wide geographic area, such as a city or even a country. By interconnecting many individual networks into a massive single network, people around the world can share information as though they were across the hall from one another. The information they share can be much more than text documents. Many networks carry voice, audio, and video traffic, enabling videoconferencing and types of collaboration that were not possible just a few years ago. The Internet is an example of one such network and is possibly the single largest network in existence today.

OBJECTIVES ::

- Identify at least three benefits of using a network.
- Differentiate between LANs and WANs.
- Identify at least three common network topologies.
- Name two common network media.
- Identify network hardware and linking devices.

FIGURE 9A.1

Most office PCs are connected together to form a network.

The Uses of a Network

A network is a set of technologies—including hardware, software, and media—that can be used to connect computers together, enabling them to communicate, exchange information, and share resources in real time (see Figure 9A.1).

You should think of a network as a group of technologies. Nearly all networks require hardware, software, and media—such as wires—to connect computer systems together.

Networks allow many users to access shared data and programs almost instantly. When data and programs are stored on a network and are shared, individual users can substantially reduce the need for programs on their own computers. Networks open up new ways to communicate, such as e-mail and instant messaging. By allowing users to share expensive hardware resources such as printers, networks reduce the cost of running an organization.

Simultaneous Access

There are moments in any business when several workers may need to use the same data at the same time. A good example is a company's quarterly sales report, which needs to be viewed and updated by several managers. Without a network that allows workers to share files, workers must keep separate copies of data stored on different disks by each worker who accesses the data. When the data is modified on one computer, data on the other computers becomes outdated. It becomes difficult to determine which copy of the data is the most current.

Norton ONLINE

For more information on networks, visit **http://www.mhhe.com/peternorton**.

simnet™

Companies can solve this problem by storing commonly used data at a central location, usually on a network server (also called a server). A network server is a central computer with a large storage device and other resources that all users can share. You learned about the kinds of computers that can function as network servers in Chapter 1.

If the server stores data files for users to access, it is commonly called a file server. The business can store a single copy of a data file on the server that employees can access whenever they want (see Figure 9A.2). Then, if one user makes a change to the file, other users will see the change when they use the file, and no one needs to figure out who has the latest copy of the data. Advanced software is needed to allow simultaneous access to the same file.

In addition to using many of the same data files, most office workers also use the same programs. In an environment where PCs are not networked, a separate copy of each program must be installed on every computer. This setup can be

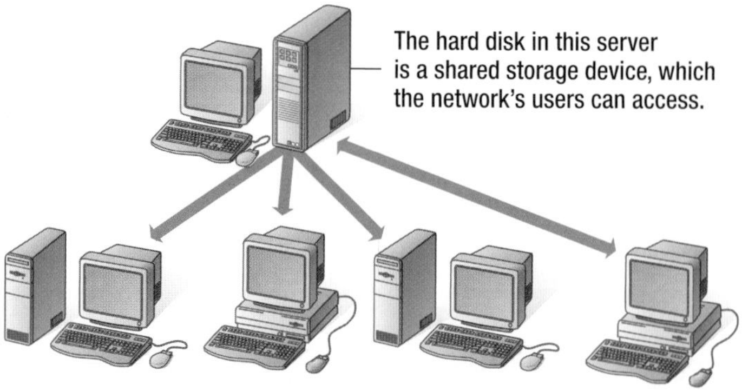

The hard disk in this server is a shared storage device, which the network's users can access.

FIGURE 9A.2

Users can share data stored on a central file server.

costly for two reasons. First, software can be expensive, especially when you must buy many dozens or hundreds of copies. Second, installing and configuring a program on many different computers can take a lot of time and labor, and maintaining many separate installations of a program is an ongoing expense. There are two basic solutions to this problem:

» **Site Licenses.** One solution to this problem is to purchase a site license for an application. Under a site license, a business buys a single copy (or a few copies) of an application and then pays the developer for a license to copy the application onto a specified number of computers. Under a site license, each user has a complete, individual copy of the program running on his or her PC, but the business generally pays less money than it would by purchasing a complete copy of the software for each user.

» **Network Versions.** Another solution is to connect users' computers to a central network server and enable users to share a network version of a program. In a network version, only one copy of the application is stored on the server, with a minimum number of supporting files copied to each user's PC. When workers need to use a program, they simply load it from the server into the RAM of their own desktop computers, as shown in Figure 9A.3.

There are trade-offs with placing applications on a centrally located server. In some networks, and with certain types of programs, the user's computer handles all the processing tasks required by the application, even though the application's core files are stored on the network. In other cases, the network server also handles some or all of the processing tasks. In these cases, the network server may be called an application server because it handles some application processing as well as storage.

Shared Peripheral Devices

The ability to share peripheral devices (especially expensive ones such as high-volume laser printers, which can cost thousands of dollars) is one of the best reasons for small businesses to set up a network. Although printers are more affordable than they were a few years ago, it is still too expensive to provide every worker with a personal printer. Aside from the cost of buying multiple printers, maintenance contracts and supplies increase the total cost of ownership. When several people can share a printer on a network, printing becomes less expensive and easier to manage (see Figure 9A.4).

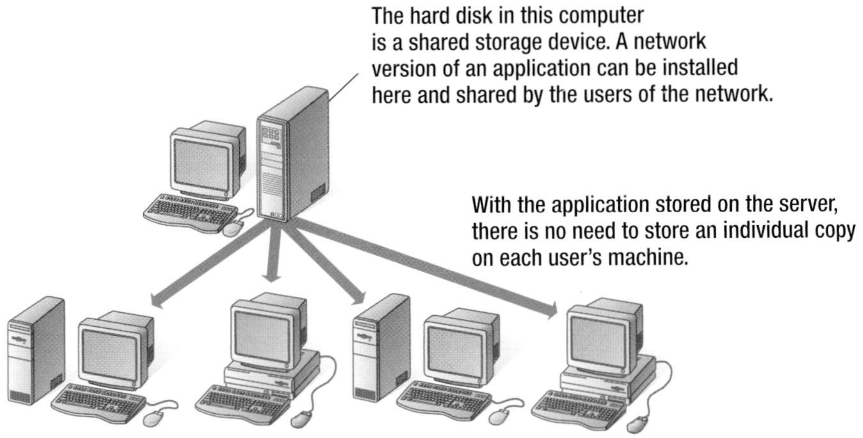

The hard disk in this computer is a shared storage device. A network version of an application can be installed here and shared by the users of the network.
With the application stored on the server, there is no need to store an individual copy on each user's machine.

FIGURE 9A.3

Using a network version of an application.

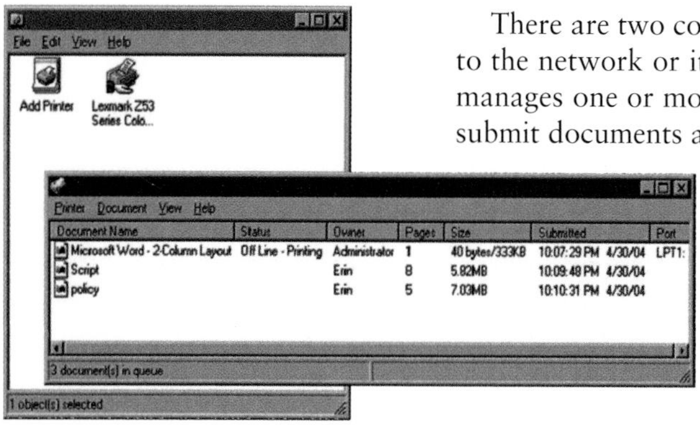

FIGURE 9A.4

This print server is displaying a queue where a user named Erin is waiting to print two documents behind the user named Administrator.

Norton ONLINE

For more information on e-mail and network conferencing technologies, visit **http://www.mhhe.com/peternorton**.

There are two common ways to share a printer. A printer can connect directly to the network or it can be attached to a print server, which is a computer that manages one or more printers. Either way, users on desktop PCs will be able to submit documents across a network to a printer.

Personal Communications

One of the most far-reaching applications of data communications is electronic mail (e-mail), a system for exchanging written messages (and, increasingly, voice and video messages) through a network.

In Chapter 2, you learned how e-mail travels over the Internet. An e-mail system in a company's network functions in much the same way (see Figure 9A.5). Such systems may be purely internal, but many companies connect their private networks to the Internet so workers can send messages to and receive messages across the Internet from people outside the company's network.

In addition to e-mail, the spread of networking technology is adding to the popularity of teleconferencing. A teleconference is any kind of multiway communication carried out in real time using telecommunications or computer networks and equipment. In a teleconference, audio and video signals travel across a local area network through the use of cables and switches or across the network's Internet connections to remote sites located throughout the world. Subcategories of teleconferencing include

- **Videoconferencing.** Videoconferencing enables real-time communication over a distance by allowing people at two or more sites to communicate with each other by seeing a video picture of the people at the other sites. Each site has one or more cameras, microphones, loudspeakers, and monitors, as well as a CODEC (compressor/decompressor), which processes the audio and video. It aims to create a sense of a person at a distant site appearing to be there in the same room, an effect that has been called virtual presence.
- **Audio-conferencing.** Audio-conferencing provides an audio link similar to that of a conventional telephone, except that it offers much higher-quality audio and enables more than two sites to be linked together. Using hands-free audio units with sensitive microphones and sophisticated echo-cancellation software, audio-conferencing enables communication between groups of participants.
- **Data-conferencing.** Data-conferencing enables participants at two or more sites to have a shared workspace on their computer desktops. This might be a shared "whiteboard" where they can draw, write, or import and manipulate images collaboratively in real time. Or it might be "application sharing," where a piece of software can be run and controlled by both users.

FIGURE 9A.5

Sending and receiving e-mail over a typical network.

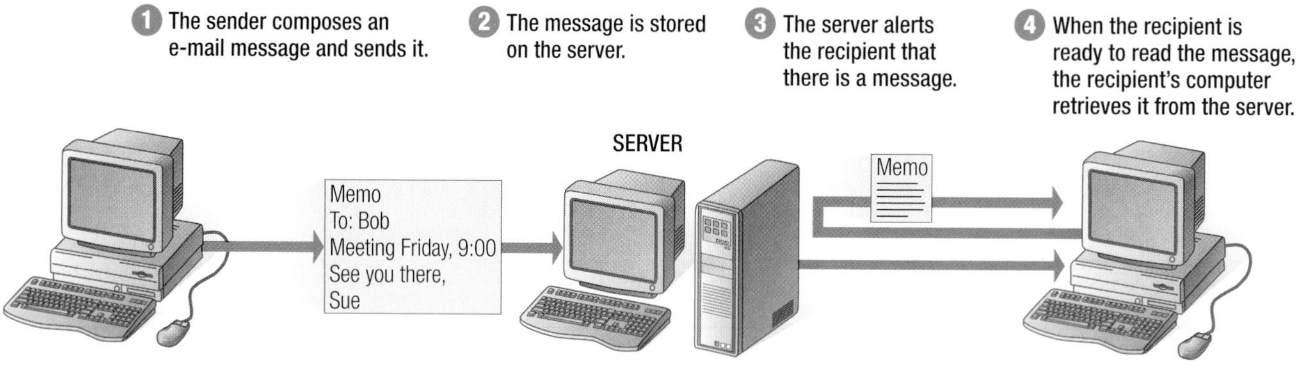

Data-conferencing is often used in conjunction with video- or audio-conferencing and can be useful when users at different sites want to work together on documents.

Another developing area of integrated communication is Voice over Internet Protocol (VoIP). VoIP systems bypass the need for the cost of regular telephone service by using the company's internal network to send and receive phone calls. VoIP transmits the sound of your voice over a computer network using the Internet Protocol (IP) rather than sending the signal over traditional phone wires. The PC that sits on a user's desk will share the same wire as a VoIP phone. This can work on a private network for interoffice calls or over the Internet.

The interoffice type of connection is called pure VoIP (see Figure 9A.6). The destination computer is identified by its IP address or by a name, which the company translates into an IP address. With the other method, VoIP-to-POTS, there exist special-purpose servers called plain old telephone service (POTS) gateways (see Figure 9A.7). These servers have one foot in the IP world (i.e., they are servers on the Internet or the intranet) and one foot in the POTS world (i.e., they have POTS line circuitry). POTS gateways allow phone calls to jump the gap between the POTS and the Internet.

Norton ONLINE

For more information on Voice over Internet Protocol, visit **http://www.mhhe.com/peternorton**.

Easier Data Backup

In business, data is extremely valuable, so it is important that employees back up their data. One way to assure that data is backed up is to keep it on a shared

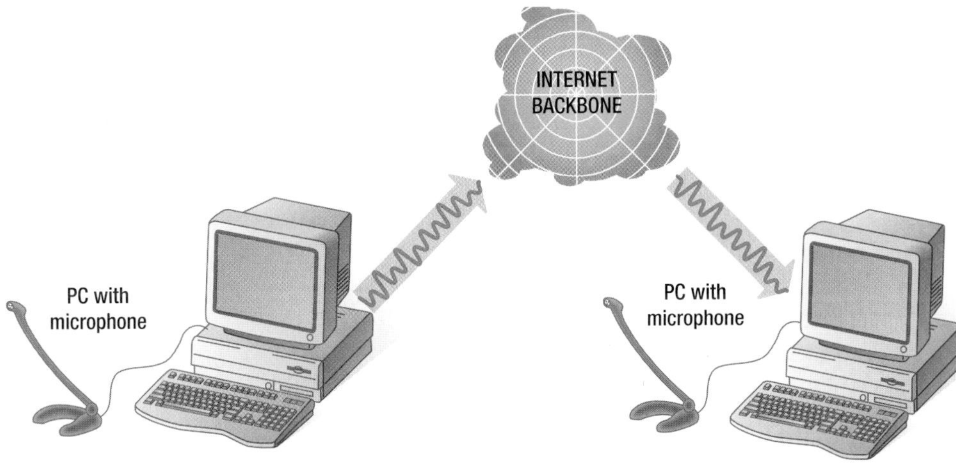

FIGURE 9A.6

Pure VoIP (Voice over IP) system; there's no cost for the telephone call, only a cost for the Internet connection.

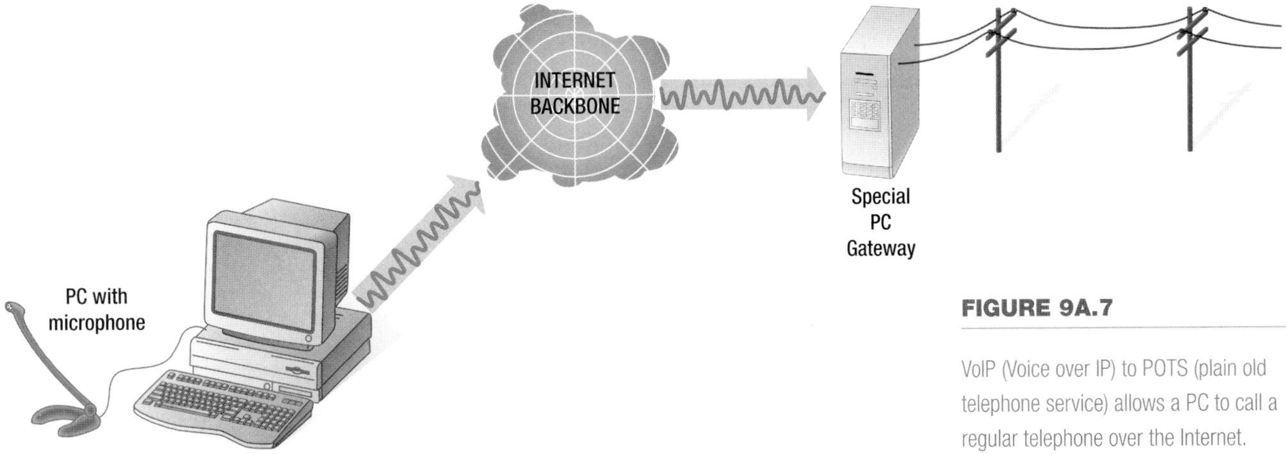

FIGURE 9A.7

VoIP (Voice over IP) to POTS (plain old telephone service) allows a PC to call a regular telephone over the Internet.

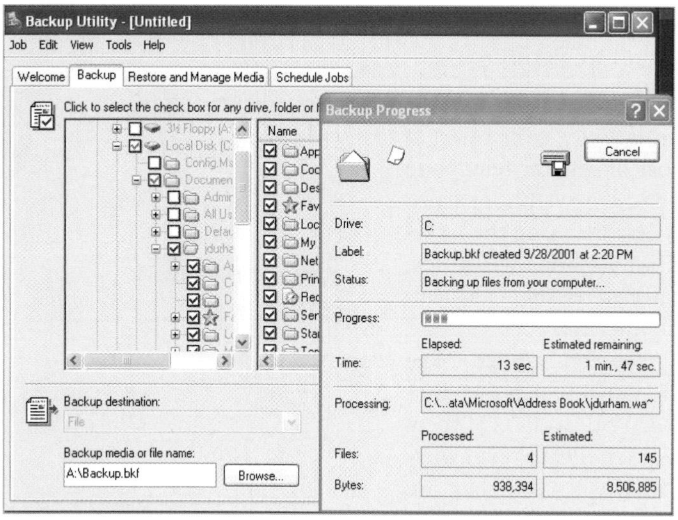

FIGURE 9A.8

Backup systems like this one can be used to back up a server and individual personal computers on the network.

Norton ONLINE

For more information on local LANs, WANs, and other common types of networks, visit **http://www.mhhe.com/peternorton**.

simnet™

storage device that employees can access through a network. Often the network manager makes regular backups of the data on the shared storage device (see Figure 9A.8).

Managers also can use special software to back up files stored on employees' hard drives from a central location. With this method, files do not have to be copied to the server before they can be backed up.

Common Types of Networks

If you want to understand the different types of networks and how they operate, you need to know how networks are structured. There are two main types of networks: local area networks (LANs) and wide area networks (WANs).

Local Area Networks (LANs)

A local area network (LAN) is a data communication system consisting of several devices such as computers and printers. This type of network contains computers that are relatively near each other and are physically connected using cables, infrared links, or wireless media. A LAN can consist of just two or three PCs connected together to share resources, or it can include hundreds of computers of different kinds. Any network that exists within a single building, or even a group of adjacent buildings, is considered a LAN. A LAN is not a system that connects to the public environment (such as the Internet) using phone or data lines.

It is often helpful to connect separate LANs together so they can communicate and exchange data. In a large company, for example, two departments located on the same floor of a building may have their own separate LANs, but if the departments need to share data, then they can create a link between the two LANs.

Wide Area Networks (WANs)

Typically, a wide area network (WAN) is two or more LANs connected together, generally across a wide geographical area. For example, a company may have its corporate headquarters and manufacturing plant in one city and its marketing office in another. Each site needs resources, data, and programs locally, but it also needs to share data with the other sites. To accomplish this feat of data communication, the company can attach devices that connect over public utilities to create a WAN. (Note, however, that a WAN does not have to include any LAN systems. For example, two distant mainframe computers can communicate through a WAN, even though neither is part of a local area network.)

These remote LANs are connected through a telecommunication network (a phone company) or via the Internet through an Internet service provider (ISP) that contracts with the telecommunication networks to gain access to the Internet's backbone.

Hybrid Networks

Between the LAN and WAN structures, you will find hybrid networks such as campus area networks (CANs) and metropolitan area networks (MANs). In addition, a new form of network type is emerging called home area networks (HANs). The need to access corporate Web sites has created two classifications known as intranets and extranets. The following sections introduce these networks.

Campus Area Networks (CANs)

A campus area network (CAN) follows the same principles as a local area network, only on a larger and more diversified scale. With a CAN, different campus offices and organizations can be linked together. For example, in a typical university setting, a bursar's office might be linked to a registrar's office. In this manner, once a student has paid his or her tuition fees to the bursar, this information is transmitted to the registrar's system so the student can enroll for classes. Some university departments or organizations might be linked to the CAN even though they already have their own separate LANs.

Metropolitan Area Networks (MANs)

The metropolitan area network (MAN) is a large-scale network that connects multiple corporate LANs together. MANs usually are not owned by a single organization; their communication devices and equipment are usually maintained by a group or single network provider that sells its networking services to corporate customers. MANs often take the role of a high-speed network that allows for the sharing of regional resources. MANs also can provide a shared connection to other networks using a WAN link. Figure 9A.9 shows the relationship between LANs, MANs, and WANs.

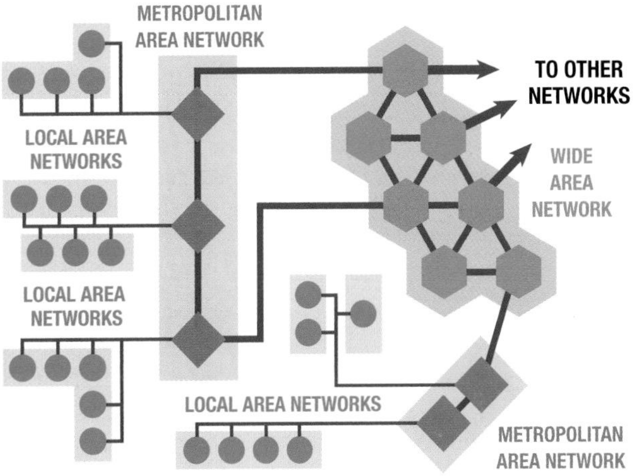

FIGURE 9A.9

The relationship between LANs, MANs, and WANs.

Home Area Networks (HANs)

A home area network (HAN) is a network contained within a user's home that connects a person's digital devices, from multiple computers and their peripheral devices, such as a printer, to telephones, VCRs, DVDs, televisions, video games, home security systems, "smart" appliances, fax machines, and other digital devices that are wired into the network.

Intranets and Extranets

Much of the technology available on the Internet is also available for private network use. The company's internal version of the Internet is called an intranet. As you learned in Chapter 2, an intranet uses the same Web server software that gives the public access to Web sites over the Internet. The major difference is that an intranet usually limits access to employees and selected contractors having ongoing business with the company.

Web pages have become very popular and, using integrated software, many operating systems offer complete Web server software or at least a personal Web server. This gives users the ability to create Web pages on their local computers that can be viewed by other members of the same network. Just like on the Internet, users can allow others (again, usually employees) to browse their Web site and to upload or download files, video clips, audio clips, and other such media. Users also can set controls and limit who may access the Web site.

Extranets are becoming a popular method for employees to exchange information using the company's Web site or e-mail while traveling or working from home. An extranet is a partially accessible internal company Web site for authorized users physically located outside the organization. Whereas an intranet resides completely within the company's internal network and is accessible only to people that are members of the same company or organization, an extranet provides various levels of accessibility to outsiders. You can access an extranet only if you have a valid username and password, and your identity determines which parts of the extranet you can view.

How Networks Are Structured

Norton ONLINE

For more information on common network structures, visit **http://www.mhhe.com/peternorton**.

simnet™

Networks can be categorized by the roles the servers and PCs play in terms of hierarchical and security interaction. Some networks use servers (server-based networks) and some do not (peer-to-peer networks). These terms are defined in detail in the following sections.

Server-Based Networks

To understand a server-based network, it is important to know the meaning of the term *node* in a network. A **node** is a processing location that can be a PC or some other device such as a networked printer. Usually, server-based networks include many nodes and one or more servers, which control user access to the network's resources.

As described earlier, this central computer is known as the file server, network server, application server, or just the server. Files and programs used by more than one user (at different nodes) are often stored on the server.

A **file server network** (see Figure 9A.10) is a fairly simple example of this kind of nodes-and-server network. This arrangement gives each node access to the files on the server, but not necessarily to files on other nodes. When a node needs information from the server, it requests the file containing the information. The server simply stores files and forwards (sends) them to nodes that request them.

One way to identify a server-based network is the point at which network resources such as files are made available to users. In this environment, users gain access to files, printers, and other network-based objects by obtaining rights and permissions given through a centrally controlled server or groups of servers. Users must "log on" to the network to gain access to its resources.

Client/Server Networks

One popular type of server-based network is the **client/server network**, where individual computers share the processing and storage workload with a central server. This arrangement requires special software for the nodes and the server. It does not, however, require any specific type of network. Client/server software can be used on LANs or WANs, and a single client/server program can be used on a LAN where all the other software is based on a simple file server system.

The most common example of client/server computing involves a database that can be accessed by many different computers on the network. The database is stored on the network server, along with a portion of the database management

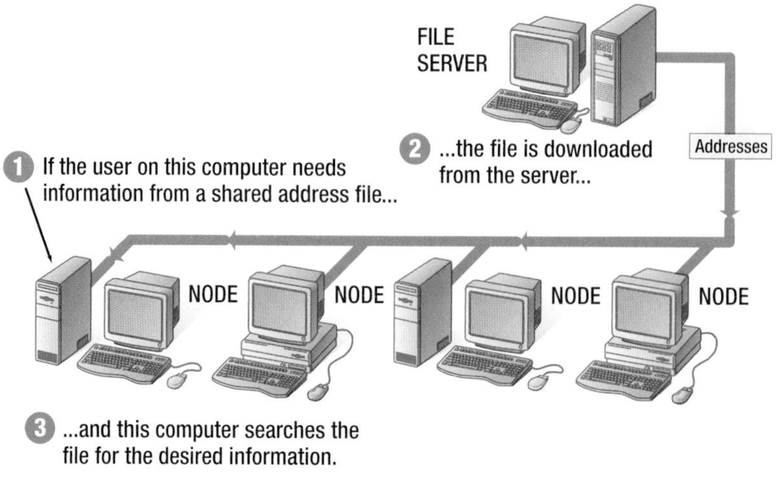
FILE SERVER
1 If the user on this computer needs information from a shared address file...
2 ...the file is downloaded from the server...
Addresses
NODE
NODE
NODE
NODE
3 ...and this computer searches the file for the desired information.

FIGURE 9A.10

A simple LAN with a file server.

system (DBMS)—the program that allows users to work with the database. The user's computer (which can be called the node, workstation, or client) stores and runs the client portion of the DBMS. When a user needs to find information in the database, he or she uses client software to send a query to the server, which searches the database and returns the information to the user's PC (see Figure 9A.11).

Peer-to-Peer Networks

In a peer-to-peer network (abbreviated as "P2PN" and sometimes called a workgroup), all nodes on the network have equal relationships to all others, and all have similar types of software that support the sharing of resources (see Figure 9A.12). In a typical peer-to-peer network, each node has access to at least some of the resources on all other nodes. If they are set up correctly, many multi-user operating systems give users access to files on hard disks and to printers attached to other computers in the network. Many client operating systems, such as Windows 9*x*, Windows 2000 Professional, Windows Me, Windows XP, and the Macintosh OS, feature built-in support for peer-to-peer networking. This enables users to set up a simple peer-to-peer network using no other software than their PCs' own operating systems.

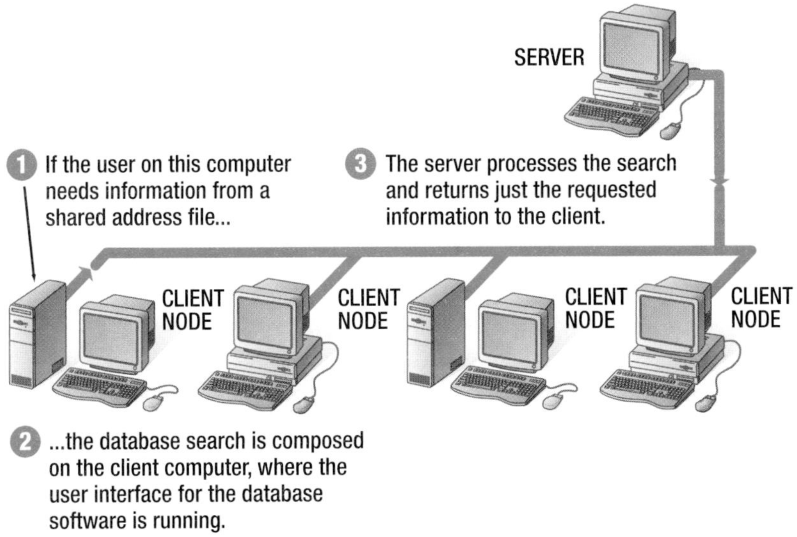
SERVER
1 If the user on this computer needs information from a shared address file...
3 The server processes the search and returns just the requested information to the client.
CLIENT NODE
CLIENT NODE
CLIENT NODE
CLIENT NODE
2 ...the database search is composed on the client computer, where the user interface for the database software is running.

FIGURE 9A.11

Processing information in a client/server computing model.

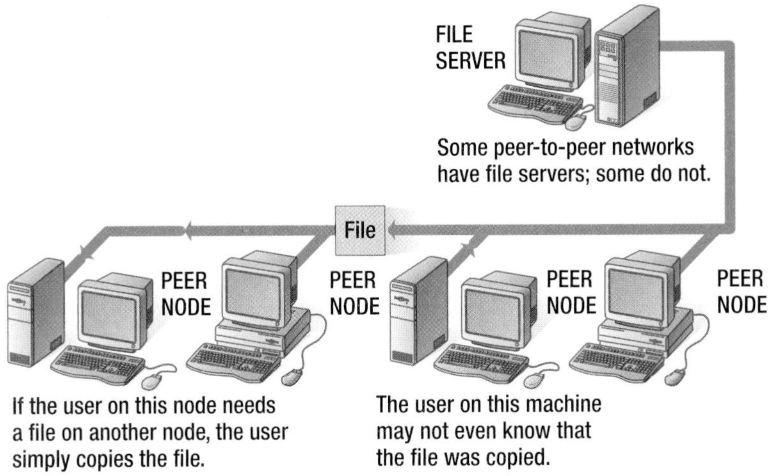
FILE SERVER
Some peer-to-peer networks have file servers; some do not.
File
PEER NODE
PEER NODE
PEER NODE
PEER NODE
If the user on this node needs a file on another node, the user simply copies the file.
The user on this machine may not even know that the file was copied.

FIGURE 9A.12

A peer-to-peer network.

At Issue

Catching "Cyberslackers" on the Job

Imagine that you run a small company that has 12 employees. To make the workers more productive, you invest in cutting-edge computers, network services, and Internet connections for each of them.

One day, you learn that two of your employees are using their PCs and Internet access a great deal, but not for work-related purposes. One employee, you learn, is using the system to collect pornographic pictures on the Internet and is e-mailing them to friends. The other employee has started her own real estate business on the side and is using your company's computers to run her new business.

Such on-the-job behaviors are called "cyberslacking"—using company computers for personal or recreational purposes instead of work. It is a growing problem in the United States, and many companies are taking a stand against cyberslacking employees. Here's why:

- Some kinds of cyberslacking can lead to lawsuits. If a worker is using the company's computers to distribute pornography, the company can be implicated because it "supported" the person's activities. If someone sees or receives one of the images and is offended by it, a lawsuit could result.
- Careless use of the Internet can invite viruses and hacking.
- A company's reputation is put at risk by such activities. How would clients and the community react if you are sued? It could take years to recover from the embarrassment and regain trust.
- If the two employees devote just one hour a day to their "hobbies," that's 10 hours per week of lost productivity. As the employer, you are paying for those hours, but no work for your company is getting done; in fact, you may be paying the cyberslackers to harm your company.

Companies Taking Action

Companies can institute policies against all kinds of computer use. For example, an employer can forbid workers from

- Visiting Web sites not directly related to their job.
- Using the company's e-mail system to send or receive personal messages.
- Participating in chat rooms or newsgroups.
- Downloading or installing any type of software on a company computer.
- Creating or storing certain types of documents on corporate systems.

One of the main distinguishing characteristics of the peer-to-peer network is the management and control point of access to shared resources such as files and printers. With peer-to-peer networks, access is controlled on the local PC by the user setting passwords on shared folders and printers. For example, if a user wants to gain access to a shared resource such as a Word document stored on another user's PC, the requesting user must ask the user with the document to share the file. The user sharing the Word document also may require that the requesting user utilize a password to access it.

A peer-to-peer network also can include a network server. In this case, a peer-to-peer LAN is similar to a file server network. The only difference between them is that the peer-to-peer network gives users greater access to the other nodes than a file server network does.

Some high-end peer-to-peer networks allow distributed computing, which enables users to draw on the processing power of other computers in the network.

SELF-CHECK ::

Circle the word or phrases that best complete each statement.

1. __________ is one of the benefits of using a network.
   - **a.** File security
   - **b.** Peripheral sharing
   - **c.** Protection from viruses
2. If a server stores data files for users to access, it is commonly called a(n) __________ .
   - **a.** file server
   - **b.** application server
   - **c.** folder server
3. A(n) __________ generally does not connect to the public environment using phone or data lines.
   - **a.** WAN
   - **b.** Internet
   - **c.** LAN

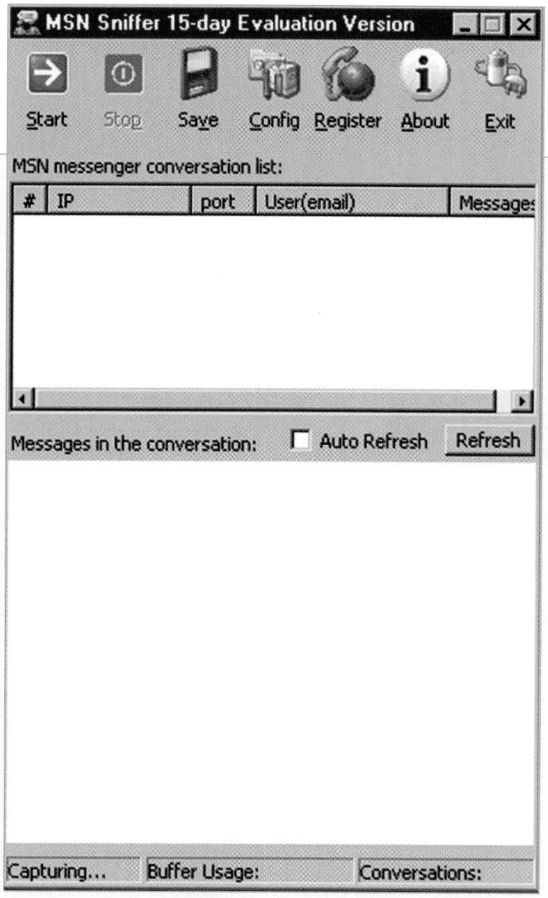

Be careful when using an employer's computer. Misusing it can lead to trouble.

Policies alone, however, may not be enough to protect businesses. For this reason, managers are using sophisticated tools to combat cyberslacking, especially involving the Internet. Such tools include

- **Web Filters.** Filtering software enables companies to block employee access to certain Web sites.
- **Surveillance Software.** This type of software enables managers to review an employee's Internet activities in real time. If the user visits any Web sites, uploads or downloads files, lurks in newsgroups, or joins chat discussions, the software logs the actions.
- **Proxy Servers.** While not its primary purpose, this type of software (or hardware/software combination) can be configured to trap network traffic that is coming from or going to an unauthorized source.
- **Packet Sniffers.** Packet sniffers examine all packets being transmitted over a network. Packet sniffers are effective at detecting traffic bound for Internet services such as Usenet, IRC, and FTP, among others.

Some employers go so far as to purchase "keystroke capturing" software. When installed on a PC, the program actually captures each keystroke as the user types and directs the keystroke to a hidden file on the user's disk or network.

For example, a user can transfer tasks that take a lot of CPU power—such as creating computer software or rendering a 3-D illustration—to other computers on the network. This leaves the user's machines free for other work.

Network Topologies and Protocols

An important feature of any LAN is its topology—the logical layout of the cables and devices that connect the nodes of the network. Network designers consider several factors when deciding which topology or combination of topologies to use: the type of computers and cabling (if any) in place, the distance between computers, the speed at which data must travel around the network, and the cost of setting up the network.

Data moves though the network in a structure called packets. Packets are pieces of a message broken down into small units by the sending PC and reassembled by the receiving PC. Different networks format packets in different ways, but most packets have two parts: the header and the payload. The header is the first part of the packet, which contains information needed by the network. The header identifies the node that sent the packet (the source), and provides the address of the node that will receive the packet (the destination). The network reads each packet's header to determine where to send the packet and, in some cases, to determine the best way to get it to its destination. The header also holds

Norton ONLINE

For more information on network topologies and protocols, visit **http://www.mhhe.com/peternorton**.

control data that helps the receiving node reassemble a message's packets in the right order. The payload is the actual data that is being transmitted between the two nodes. (In the Internet environment, packets are called datagrams.)

A network's topology and related technologies are important for two reasons. First, a correctly designed network, using the most appropriate topology for the organization's needs, will move data packets as efficiently as possible. Second, the network's topology plays a role in preventing collisions, which is what happens when multiple nodes try to transmit data at the same time. Their packets can collide and destroy each other.

FIGURE 9A.13

In a bus topology network, one cable connects all the devices together.

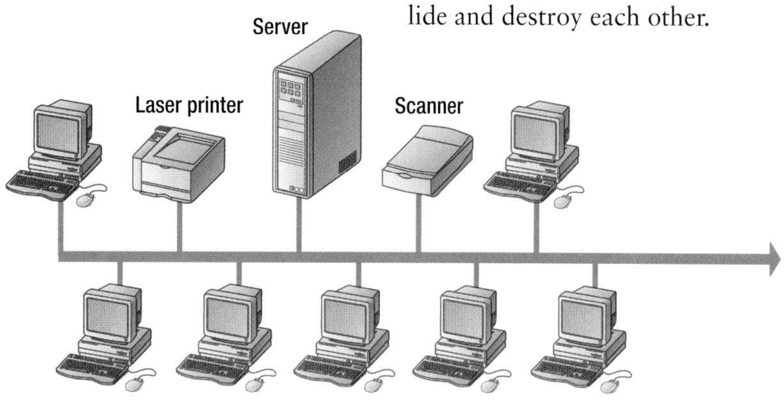

A bus topology network uses one cable (see Figure 9A.13). All the nodes and peripheral devices are connected in a series to that cable. A special device, called a terminator, is attached at the cable's start and end points, to stop network signals so they do not bounce back down the cable. This topology's main advantage is that it uses the least amount of cabling of any topology. In a bus topology network, however, extra circuitry and software are used to keep data packets from colliding with one another. A broken connection can bring down all or part of the network.

FIGURE 9A.14

The star topology connects all nodes to a hub or switch.

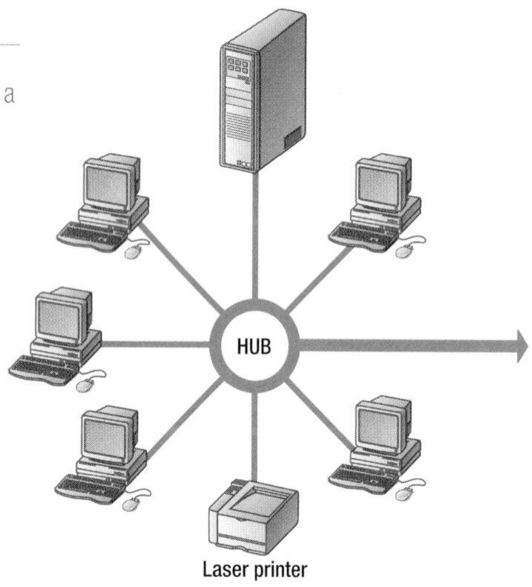

The star topology (see Figure 9A.14) is probably the most common topology. In a star network, all nodes are connected to a device called a hub and communicate through it. Data packets travel through the hub and are sent to the attached nodes, eventually reaching their destinations. Some hubs—known as intelligent hubs—can monitor traffic and help prevent collisions. In a star topology, a broken connection between a node and the hub does not affect the rest of the network. If the hub is lost, however, all nodes connected to that hub are unable to communicate.

FIGURE 9A.15

The ring topology is a linked circular chain.

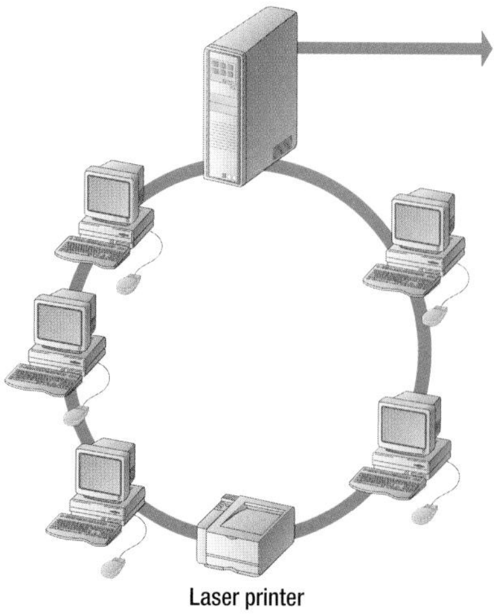

The ring topology (see Figure 9A.15) connects the network's nodes in a circular chain, with each node connected to the next. The last node connects to the first, completing the ring. Each node examines data as it travels through the ring. If the data—known as a token—is not addressed to the node examining it, that node passes it to the next node. There is no danger of collisions because only one packet of data travels the ring at a time. If the ring is broken, however, the entire network is unable to communicate.

The mesh topology (see Figure 9A.16) is the least-used network topology and the most expensive to implement. In a mesh environment, a cable runs from every computer to every other computer. If you have four computers, you must have six cables—three coming from each computer to the other computers. The big advantage to this arrangement is that data can never fail to be delivered; if one connection goes down, there are other ways to route the data to its destination.

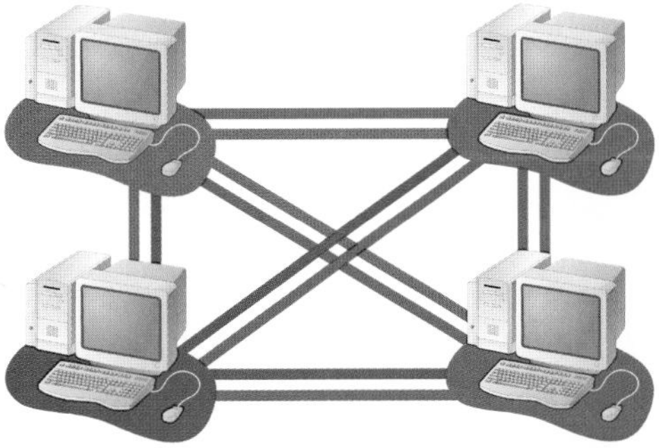

FIGURE 9A.16

In a meshed topology, all nodes are connected to each other.

Network Media

With computer networks, *media* refers to the means used to link a network's nodes together. There are many different types of transmission media, the most popular being twisted-pair wire (normal electrical wire), coaxial cable (the type of cable used for cable television), and fiber optic cable (cables made out of glass). In wireless networks, the atmosphere itself acts as the medium because it carries the wireless signals that nodes and servers use to communicate. The following sections examine wire-based and wireless media.

Norton ONLINE

For more information on network media, visit **http://www.mhhe.com/peternorton**.

simnet™

Wire-Based Media

Twisted-pair cable (see Figure 9A.17) normally consists of four pairs of wires. The individual pairs have two wires that are separately insulated in plastic, then twisted around each other and bound together in a layer of plastic. (Our telephone system uses this type of wiring, usually containing only two or three pairs for the most part.) Except for the plastic coating, nothing shields this type of wire from outside interference, so it is also called unshielded twisted-pair (UTP) wire. Some twisted-pair wire is encased in a metal sheath and therefore is called shielded twisted-pair (STP) wire. Twisted-pair wire was once considered a low-bandwidth medium, but networks based on twisted-pair wires now support transmission speeds up to 1 Gbps (gigabit per second).

FIGURE 9A.17

Twisted-pair cable wires are insulated and twisted around each other. They are usually used to connect hubs/switches to PCs in a star topology.

Like the cabling used in cable television systems, coaxial cable (see Figure 9A.18) has two conductors. One is a single wire in the center of the cable, and the other is a wire mesh shield that surrounds the first wire, with an insulator between. Because it supports transmission speeds up to 10 Mbps (megabits per second), coaxial cable can carry more data than older types of twisted-pair wiring. However, it is also more expensive and became less popular when twisted-pair technology improved.

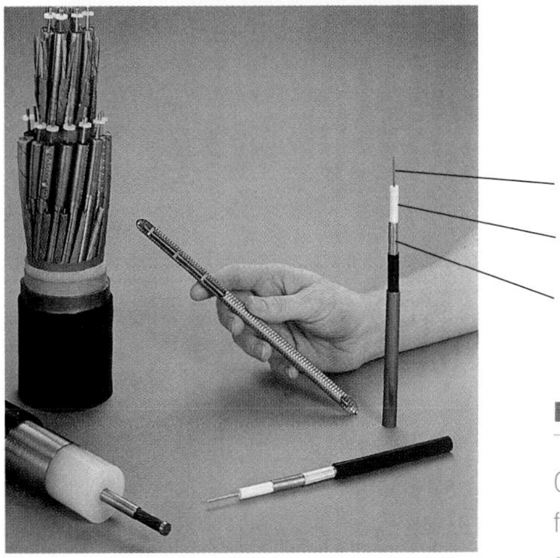

FIGURE 9A.18

One-inch coaxial cables are usually found in older networks. The large cables shown here are used for crossing greater distances such as the ocean.

A fiber-optic cable (see Figure 9A.19) is a thin strand of glass that transmits pulsating beams of light rather than electric current. Fiber-optic cable can carry data at more than a billion bits per second. Because of improvements in transmission hardware, however, fiber-optic transmission speeds now approach 100 Gbps. Fiber-optic cable is immune to the

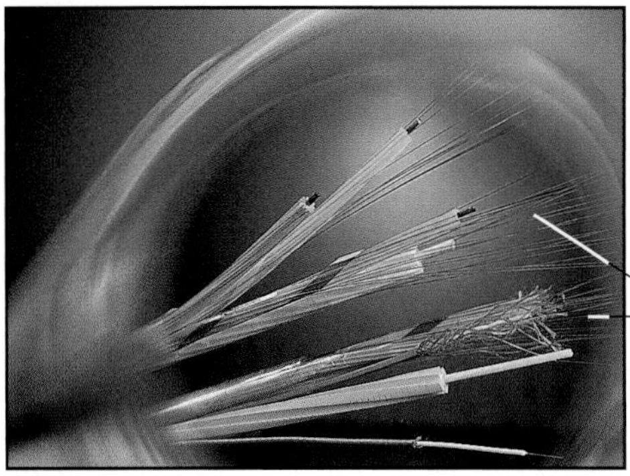

FIGURE 9A.19

Although very fast, fiber-optic cables are not easy to cut and cannot be bent to accommodate sharp angles.

electromagnetic interference that is a problem for copper wire. Fiber-optic cable not only is extremely fast and can carry an enormous number of messages simultaneously, but it is a very secure transmission medium.

Wireless Media

Wireless networks use radio or infrared signals that travel through the air (called *ether*) for transmitting data. Office LANs can use radio signals to transmit data between nodes in a building. Laptops equipped with cellular modems allow users to connect to the office network when they travel. Corporate WANs often use microwave transmission to connect LANs within the same metropolitan area (see Figure 9A.20). WANs that cover long distances often use satellites and microwave communication.

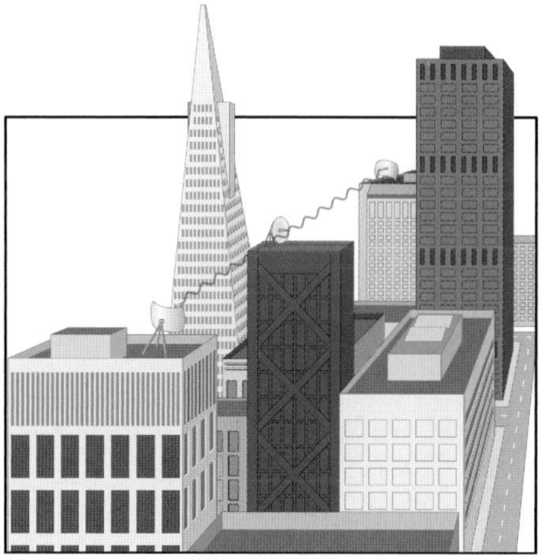

FIGURE 9A.20

This wireless network is using line-of-site dishes to link locations together.

Network Hardware

As data moves between PCs, it needs to be channeled properly to reach its final destination. To make this possible, the proper hardware must be attached to and between all PCs.

Network Interface Cards (NICs)

Regardless of the wiring and topology used, each computer on the network needs a hardware component to control the flow of data. The device that performs this function is the network interface card (NIC) (see Figure 9A.21), also known as a network adapter card or network card. This printed circuit board fits into one of the computer's expansion slots and provides a port where the network cable is attached.

In the case of a wireless NIC, there will not be a port, an antenna will be showing, or a light will indicate that an internal antenna is activated (see Figure 9A.22). Network software works with the operating system and tells the computer how to use the NIC. Both the network software and the NIC must adhere to the same network protocols, which are explored later in this chapter.

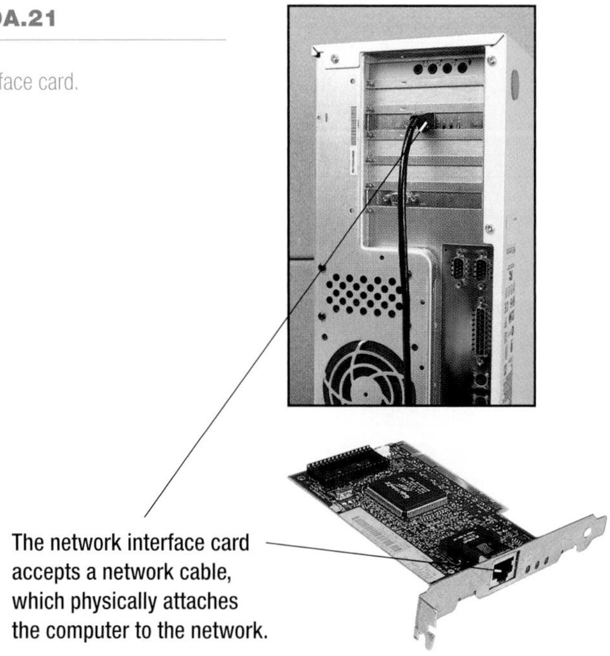

The network interface card accepts a network cable, which physically attaches the computer to the network.

FIGURE 9A.21

Network interface card.

Network Linking Devices

To create a network, some type of linking mechanism is needed to interconnect at least two computers. Sometimes this device can be as simple as a special cable, called a crossover cable, that is attached to two computers (NIC to NIC). Although now you have a network, it is barely a network. If you want to add more devices, then something more than a crossover cable is required. Most servers, nodes, and printers are attached by a linking device or a series of linking devices. These linking devices are connected together using cables such as the Category 5 cable, which is discussed in more detail below. Linking devices have ports where cables connect them to the nodes, printers, or other devices that have ports or NICs installed. The various linking devices that are available include

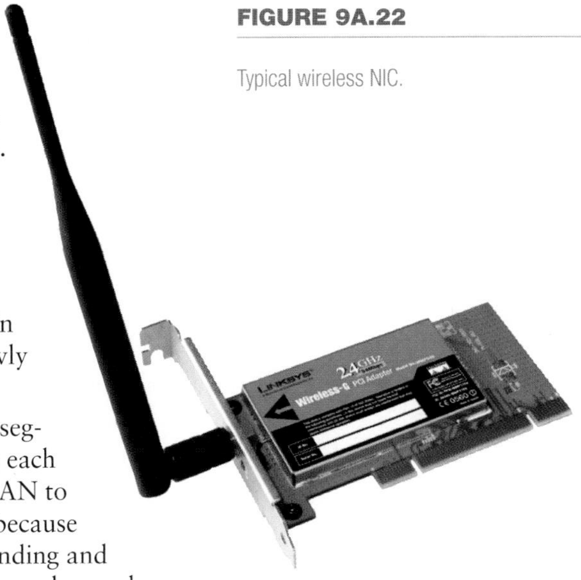

FIGURE 9A.22

Typical wireless NIC.

- **Hubs.** A hub is an affordable connection point for different types of devices on a network. This is not a particularly fast connection because it broadcasts the packets it receives to all nodes attached to its ports. Due to the substantial reduction in the cost of switches (explained below), this technology is slowly becoming obsolete.
- **Bridges.** A bridge is a device that connects two LANs or two segments of the same LAN. A bridge looks at the information in each packet header and forwards data that is traveling from one LAN to another. Bridges are becoming a less-relied-upon technology because they use an older method for determining which nodes are sending and receiving data and their functions are now integrated into more advanced devices.
- **Switches.** A switch is a device that learns which machine is connected to its port by using the PC, printer, or other devices' IP address. This is a very popular and sought-after device used to connect a LAN. A switch substantially reduces the amount of broadcast traffic and is currently the most popular network-linking device. Modern switches can even function as routers (see below), allowing multiple LANs to be interconnected by linking each LAN's switches together. This is called an uplink.
- **Routers.** A router is a complicated device that stores the routing information for networks (see Figure 9A.23). A router looks at each packet's header to determine where the packet should go and then determines the best route for the packet to take toward its destination. A router will not allow broadcast traffic to cross the device unless modified to do so. Thus, a packet must be addressed to a specifically identified destination to pass through the router. A router is connected to at least two networks, commonly two LANs or WANs or a LAN and its ISP's network. Routers are located at gateways, the places where two or more networks connect. Today, routers can come with a built-in hub or switch, which also allows computers on the small company's network, or intranet, to share files without having to buy multiple pieces of equipment. Routers also provide a security element as well. They can include several forms of firewall security. One form of protection comes from the NAT (Network Address Translation) table, which hides the company's internal node IP addresses from the Internet. Usually, an ISP will provide the company or home user with an IP address for the WAN side of the router that will serve as the port connecting to the Internet.

FIGURE 9A.23

A router.

To create a connection between different types of networks, you need a gateway, placed at a junction (gateway) between two or more networks (see Figure 9A.24). Gateways have several meanings within the networking environment. In its simplest form, a gateway is a node on a network that serves as an entrance to another network. In the small business or home network, the gateway is the device that routes data from a local PC to an outside network such as the Internet. The router intercepts then redirects and filters (if necessary) any data packets passing through. Packets from different types of networks have different kinds of information in their headers, and the information can be in various formats. The gateway can take a packet from one type of network, read its header, and then

Norton ONLINE

For more information on network linking devices, visit **http://www.mhhe.com/peternorton**.

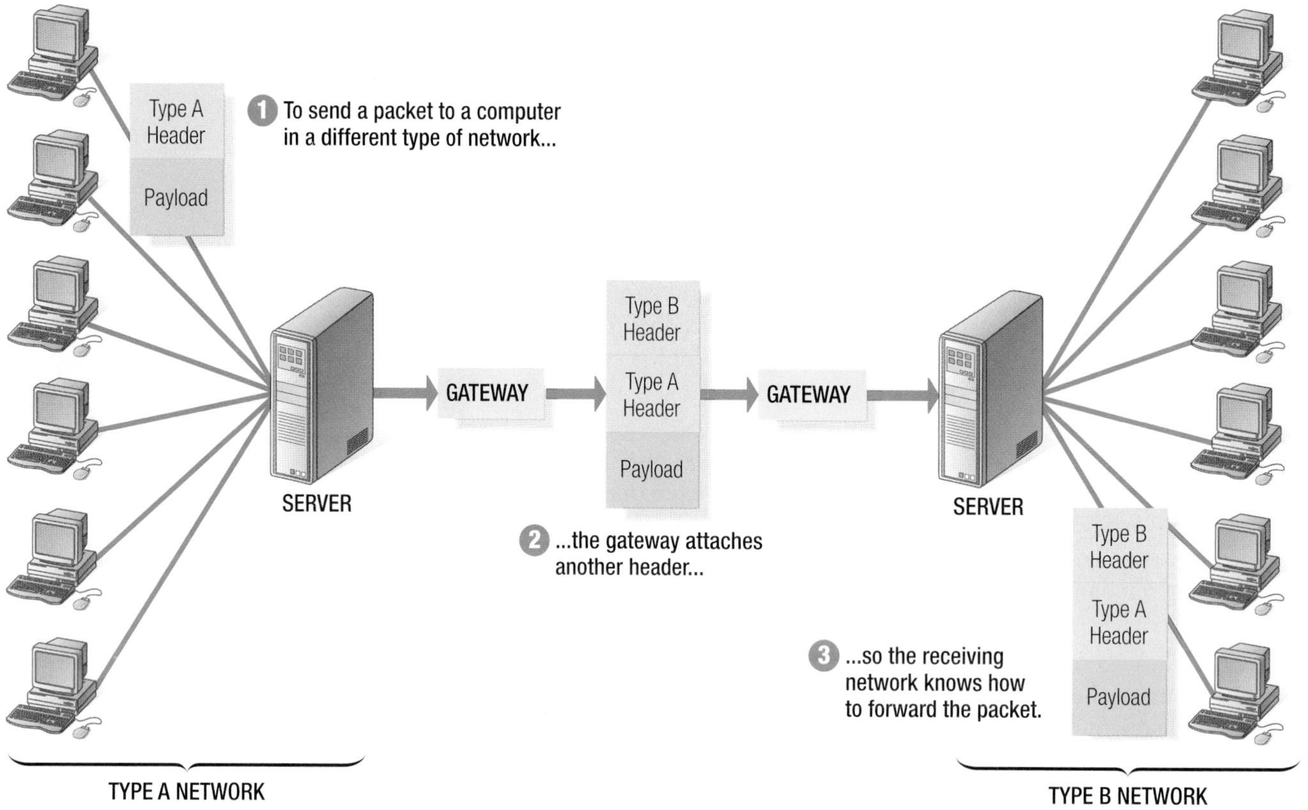

FIGURE 9A.24

This is an example of the simplest form of gateway. The gateway forwards a packet from one type of network to a different type of network.

add a second header that is understood by the second network. When configuring your internal network to allow an Internet connection, you need to point the PC to the gateway's IP address.

This gateway address does not have to be manually added to each computer thanks to advances with server and router software. Today, users can simply enable Dynamic Host Control Protocol (DHCP) on the computer and the LAN port of the router (or server acting as a router) and the device will automatically assign all necessary Internet configurations. DHCP is also referred to as dynamic addressing.

Building a typical network is possible by bringing together many of the components presented in this section. Figure 9A.25 shows an example of the connections needed to complete a network.

Cabling Equipment

Tying together the linking devices, servers, nodes, printers, and other network equipment into an actual LAN is the cabling equipment. Cabling equipment is designed to work with a certain kind of network topology, and each one has certain standard features.

In network communications, the quality of media refers to the distance and speed data can travel down wires, cables, fiber optics, or other communication media. For example, consider Category 5 (Cat5) cable, a popular type of twisted-pair wiring that contains four twisted pairs. A Cat5 cable can carry data 100 meters without attenuation; this means that for up to 100 meters, the signal will not drop off enough so that that data packet cannot be read properly. Sometimes network media are compared by the amount of data they can carry, a factor commonly referred to as bandwidth. Simply stated, the higher a medium's bandwidth, the more data it can transmit at any given time. Bandwidth is expressed in cycles per second (Hertz) or in bits per second. With Cat5 cable, data can move at a speed up to 100 Mbps. Data can only move as fast as the narrowest point will

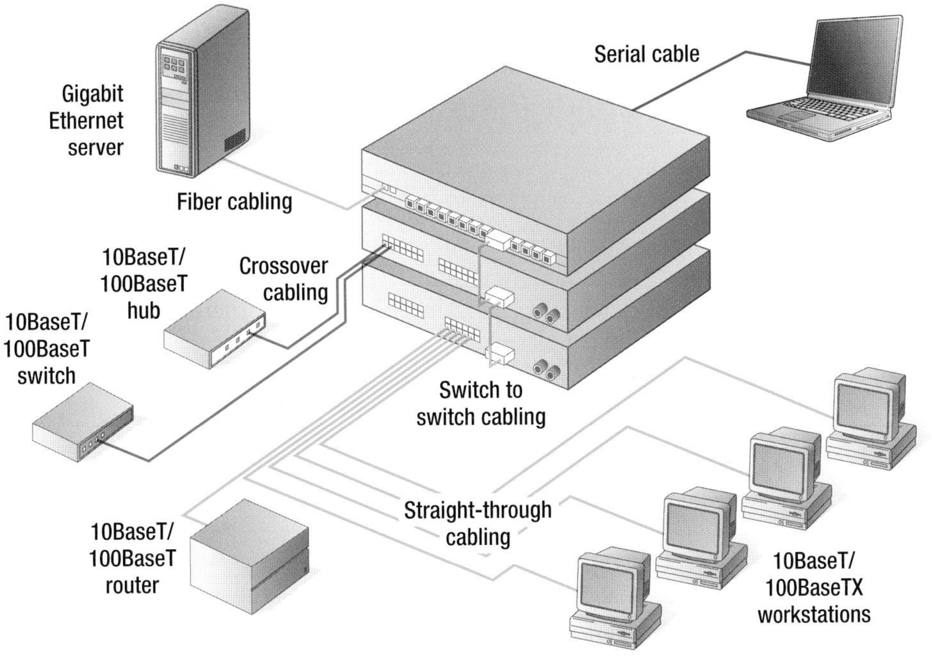

FIGURE 9A.25

Bringing all the connections together.

allow. If all nodes are using Cat5 100 Mbps cable and 100 Mbps network adapter cards but are attached to a 10 Mbps hub, then they will receive data at the rate of 10 Mbps.

The most common types of network technologies include

- **Ethernet.** The most common network technology in use. The original implementations of Ethernet used coaxial cable and were called 10Base-5 and 10Base-2. The most popular implementation of Ethernet—called 10Base-T—uses a star topology and twisted-pair wires and can achieve transmission speeds up to 10 Mbps (megabits per second). Most new network installations use an Ethernet star topology with either twisted-pair or fiber-optic cables as the medium. With Ethernet, if two nodes transmit data at the same instant, the collision is detected and the nodes retransmit one at a time.
- **Fast Ethernet.** Fast Ethernet (also called 100Base-T) is available using the same media and topology as Ethernet, but different NICs are used to achieve speeds of up to 100 Mbps. This type of network commonly uses the Category 5 network cable described previously. (Figure 9A.26 shows a typical Cat5 cable with the RJ45 connector.) A new standard is called Category 6 (Cat6). The general difference between Cat5 and Cat6 is in the transmission performance. This improvement provides a higher signal-to-noise ratio, allowing higher reliability for current applications and higher data rates for future applications.

FIGURE 9A.26

A typical Cat5 cable with the RJ45 connector.

- **Gigabit Ethernet.** Gigabit Ethernet is a version of Ethernet technology that supports data transfer rates of one gigabit per second. It evolved from the same 10 Mbps Ethernet technology that was created in the 1970s. Although capable of transferring 10 Gbps, a standard that became more affordable and popular is 1000Base-T or 1 Gbps. Another standard that is popular is the 5 Gbps fiber-optic cable that is used to connect switches together (see Figure 9A.27). The Ethernet protocol can allow

Norton Notebook

Fighting Hackers

It may sound too alarming, but experts say there is a good chance that your home computer has already been visited by hackers via the Internet. In fact, if your home computer has broadband, always-on Internet access through a high-speed connection—such as an ISDN, DSL, or cable modem connection—it is almost certain that hackers have found your system and determined whether it can be invaded. Because these connections are always "on" (meaning your system remains connected to the Internet as long as the power is on), they give hackers plenty of time to find your system on the Internet and look for ways to get inside.

Networking experts say that home PCs have a number of vulnerabilities that can grant a hacker easy access. These include security holes in Windows itself, as well as Internet applications such as browsers. Further, most users fail to password-protect any part of their systems.

Hackers, Crackers

Malicious hackers (sometimes called "crackers") spend a great deal of time mapping the Internet; that is, trying to identify as many vulnerable computers as they can. To accomplish this, they use a variety of software tools.

At the very least, a hacker or cracker can "ping" your computer to see if it is turned on and connected to the Internet. This is like walking through a neighborhood and trying to open the front door to each house. In pinging, someone sends a message to your computer; if it responds, the sender knows your computer is active and connected to the network. Pinging is usually the first step in the invasion process, and experts say that a typical PC gets pinged several times each week.

Once an invader finds a way to access your system's resources, there may be no limit to the damage that can be done. Files containing important data can be moved, renamed, deleted, or copied. Hackers may try to use your PC's resources without your knowledge.

Keeping Invaders at Bay

If you connect to the Internet through a standard modem and a dial-up connection, and if you stay connected for only short periods, then you may not need to worry about an invader getting into your system. However, if you leave your dial-up connection active for long periods, or if you have a perpetual connection through a high-speed link,

FIGURE 9A.27

A fiber optic switch connector.

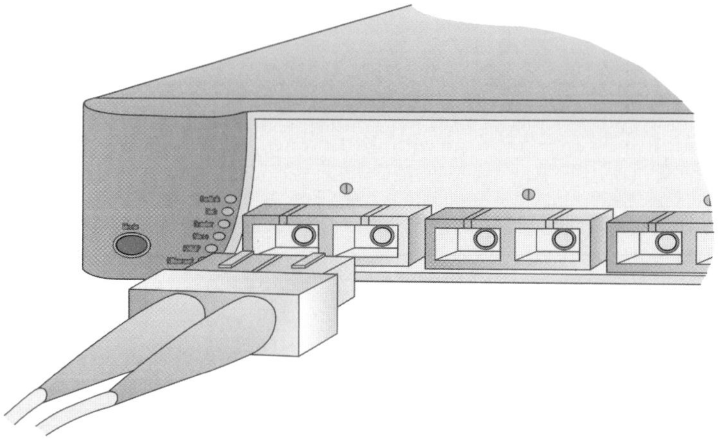

a network administrator to back up 2 TB (terabytes) of data in about 27 minutes. Gigabit Ethernet also can carry approximately 900 video signals at once, at about 1.5 Mbps of digital video. With advanced audio, video, and telephone applications coming into the market every day, it will not be long before the Gigabit Ethernet standard will become the norm for high-bandwidth tasks and processes.

» **Token Ring.** The controlling hardware in a Token Ring network transmits an electronic token—a small set of data—to each node on the network many

If you connect to the Internet through a high-speed connection, a personal firewall is one of your best defenses against hackers.

then you should take a serious look at your system's security.

Here are a few basic steps you can take to keep crackers out of your system:

» **Plug Windows' Security Holes.** This means turning off file and printer sharing, at the very least, unless you need these features to be activated for a LAN or home network connection. To learn more about these features, open the Windows help system and look for information on file sharing and printer sharing.

» **Use Passwords and Manage Them Effectively.** Windows enables you to password-protect a variety of resources. If you use any network features, you should password-protect them and change your passwords frequently. Experts advise that you use long passwords (more than eight characters), and do not use passwords that could be easily guessed. Never use a "blank" password.

» **Get a Personal Firewall.** As you may recall, a firewall is a hardware and/or software tool that prohibits unauthorized access to a network, especially over the Internet. Personal firewalls are available in a wide range of prices and features, but you can get a good one for about $50. Some are even available for free.

» **Ask Your Internet Service Provider (ISP) for Help.** Check your ISP's Web site for security-related information. If you still have questions, call the ISP and talk to a technical support person. List your concerns about security and see what kind of answers you get.

times each second if the token is not already in use by a specific node. A computer can copy data into the token and set the address where the data should be sent. The token then continues around the ring, and each computer along the way looks at the address until the token reaches the computer with the address that was recorded in the token. The receiving computer then copies the contents of the token and sends an acknowledgment to the sending computer. When the sending computer receives the acknowledgment from the receiving computer, it resets the token's status to "empty" and transmits it to the next computer in the ring. The hardware for a Token Ring network is expensive; Token Ring adapter cards can cost as much as five times more than other types of network adapters. Token Ring networks once operated at 4 or 16 Mbps, but like Ethernet, new standards for Token Ring have increased the transmission rate, which is now up to 100 Mbps.

Protocols

Each LAN is governed by a protocol, which is an agreed-upon format for transmitting data between two devices. There are many standard protocols. Each has particular advantages and disadvantages. Some protocols are simpler than others, some are more reliable, and some are faster. To effectively communicate, a user must have the same protocol installed on the local PC and the remote PC to make a connection.

Protocols take the form of software or hardware that must be installed on every computer on the network. For an Ethernet network, usually the operating system software tells the computer exactly how to break up, format, send, receive, and reassemble data using the TCP/IP, NetBIOS/NetBEUI, or IPX/SPX protocols. Without such software installed, a computer cannot participate in the network.

Protocols, using their own methods, break data down into small packets in preparation for transportation. Linking devices pass these packets to the various pieces of equipment, including other computers and printers that are attached to the network. As discussed earlier in this chapter, a packet is a data segment that includes a header, payload, and control elements that are transmitted together (see Figure 9A.28). The receiving computer reconstructs the packets into their original structure. A typical Ethernet packet is structured as in Figure 9A.29.

A single LAN may utilize more than one protocol. Some of the most common protocols in use today include

- **TCP/IP.** Originally associated with UNIX hosts, TCP/IP is the protocol of the Internet and is required on any computer that must communicate across the Internet. TCP/IP is now the default networking protocol of Windows 2000 Professional (client) and Server editions, Windows XP, Windows Server 2003, and many other operating systems.
- **IPX/SPX.** A proprietary protocol of Novell, IPX/SPX has been used in most versions of the NetWare network operating system for networking offices throughout the world. Newer versions of NetWare also support TCP/IP.
- **NetBIOS/NetBEUI.** A relatively simple protocol that has no real configurable parameters, NetBIOS/NetBEUI sends messages to every computer that can receive them. It is an excellent protocol for networking small offices or homes, but it does not expand well into larger environments.

FIGURE 9A.28

An e-mail message is divided up into packets.

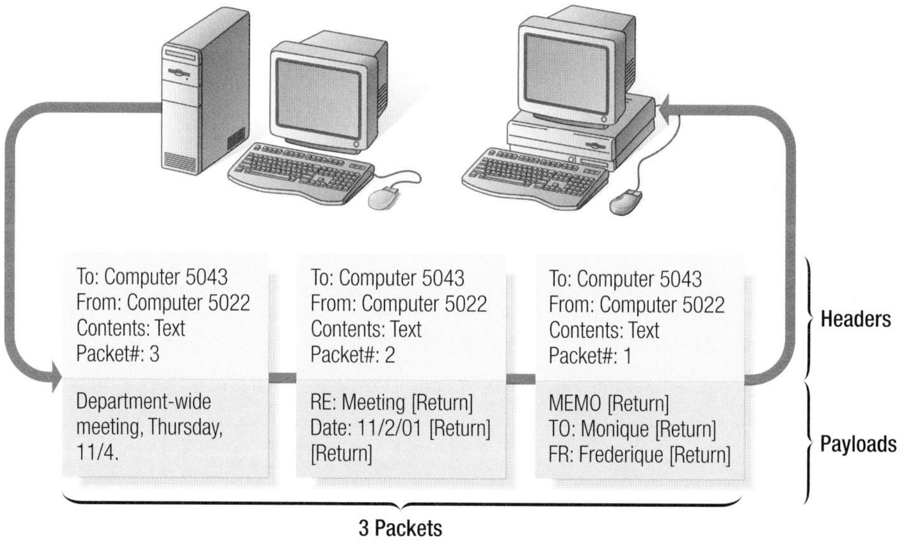

FIGURE 9A.29

Standard Ethernet packets are made up of 0s and 1s—called bits—that are combined in groups of eight bits to form a byte.

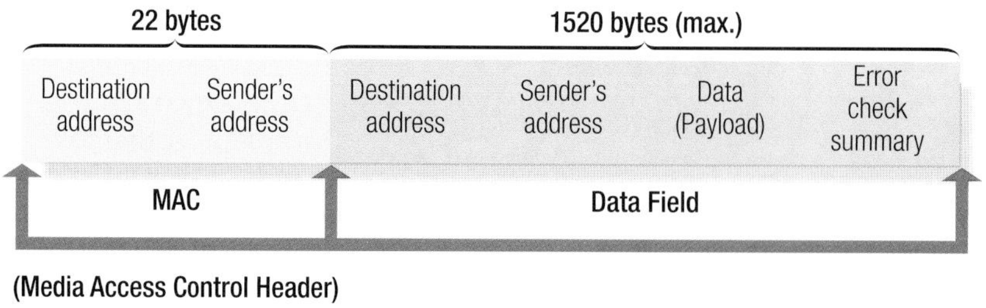

Summary ::

- A network is a way to connect computers for communication, data exchange, and resource sharing.
- Many networks are built around a central computer called a server, which provides storage and other resources that users can share.
- A local area network (LAN) consists of computers that are relatively close to one another. A LAN can have a few PCs or hundreds of them in a single building or several buildings.
- A wide area network (WAN) results when multiple LANs are connected through public utilities such as phone lines or microwave systems.
- Many networks are built around a central server. The PCs and other devices that connect to the server are called nodes.
- In a file server network, the server provides storage and file-sharing services for the nodes.
- An application server is a server that is used to run applications from a centralized location on the network to free up resources on the nodes.
- In a client/server network, nodes and the server share the storage and processing tasks.
- A peer-to-peer network is a small network that usually does not include a central server. In a peer-to-peer network, users can share files and resources on all the network's nodes.
- A topology is the physical layout of the cables and devices that connect the nodes of a network. Topologies get their names—such as bus, star, or ring—from the shape of the network they create.
- When used in the context of networks, the term *media* refers to the wires, cables, and other means by which data travels from its source to its destination.
- The most common media for data communications are twisted-pair wire, coaxial cable, fiber-optic cable, and wireless links.
- The performance of network media is measured by the amount of data they can transmit each second. This value is called bandwidth. The higher a network's bandwidth, the more data it can carry.
- A protocol is an agreed-upon format for transmitting data between two devices. Some popular protocols include TCP/IP (the Internet protocol), IPX/SPX, and NetBIOS/NetBEUI.

LESSON //9A Review

Key Terms ::

10Base-T Ethernet, 357
application server, 343
attenuation, 356
bandwidth, 356
bridge, 355
bus topology, 352
campus area network (CAN), 347
client/server network, 348
coaxial cable, 353
datagrams, 352
distributed computing, 350
dynamic addressing, 356
Dynamic Host Control Protocol (DHCP), 356
Ethernet, 357
Fast Ethernet (100Base-T), 357
fiber-optic cable, 353
file server, 342
file server network, 348
gateway, 355
Gigabit Ethernet, 357
home area network (HAN), 347
header, 351
hub, 355
local area network (LAN), 346
mesh topology, 352
metropolitan area network (MAN), 347
network, 342
network interface card (NIC), 354
network server, 342
network version, 343
node, 348
packet, 351
payload, 352
peer-to-peer network, 349
print server, 344
protocol, 359
ring topology, 352
router, 355
server, 342
site license, 343
star topology, 352
switch, 355
teleconference, 344
terminator, 352
token, 352
Token Ring, 358
topology, 351
twisted-pair cable, 353
videoconference, 344
Voice over Internet Protocol (VoIP), 345
wide area network (WAN), 346
wireless networks, 354
wireless NIC, 354

Key Term Quiz ::

Complete each statement by writing one of the terms listed under Key Terms in each blank.

1. A(n) __________ is a network of computers that serves users located relatively near each other.
2. If you connect computers together to communicate and exchange information, the result is called a(n) __________ .
3. The physical layout of wires and devices that connect the network's nodes is called the network's __________ .
4. In a bus topology network, a special deviced called a(n) __________ is placed on each end of the cable.
5. A(n) __________ is a thin strand of glass that transmits pulsating beams of light at speeds that approach 100 Gbps.
6. A(n) __________ is the device that is added to a PC that allows it to connect to a LAN.
7. A centralized computer that allows multiple remote users to share the same printing device is referred to as a __________ .
8. __________ cables have two conductors: one is a single wire in the center and the other is a wire mesh shield that surrounds the first wire.
9. A(n) __________ is a popular device used to connect a LAN. It substantially reduces broadcast traffic.
10. High-end peer-to-peer networks allow for __________ . This lets users access the power of multiple computers to process programs such as 3-D illustration software.

Multiple Choice ::

Circle the word or phrase that best completes each sentence.

1. Companies store data on a network server because it is ________ .
   a. easier to track changes made to important data
   b. less convenient for the user to access the data from home
   c. easier to download or retrieve large video files
   d. more difficult for users to access programs
2. In a ________ network, all devices are connected to a device called a hub and communicate through it.
   a. bus
   b. star
   c. ring
   d. mesh
3. A solution that connects users' computers to a central network server that enables them to share programs is called ________ .
   a. single-user version programs
   b. PC license programs
   c. site license programs
   d. network version programs
4. When software is stored and run from a centralized location, the computer containing such software is called a(n) ________ .
   a. file server
   b. print server
   c. application server
   d. CD server
5. A ________ is an agreed-upon format for transmitting data between two devices.
   a. protopology
   b. protoplasm
   c. prototype
   d. protocol
6. ________ means any kind of multiway communication carried out in real time using telecommunications or computer network equipment.
   a. Videoconferencing
   b. Data-conferencing
   c. Teleconferencing
   d. Serial-conferencing
7. A ________ is two or more LANs connected together, generally across a large geographical area.
   a. WAN
   b. SAN
   c. CAN
   d. HAN
8. An extranet is like an intranet except that it allows company employees access to corporate Web sites from the ________ .
   a. employee's desktop PC
   b. supervisor's PC
   c. employee's fax/printer device
   d. Internet
9. A ________ is a type of network usually found where students and school administrators have a need to share files across several buildings.
   a. wide area network (WAN)
   b. metropolitan area network (MAN)
   c. campus area network (CAN)
   d. local area network (LAN)
10. An arrangement where user accounts are centralized on a server and PCs gain access to network resources by accessing this server is called a ________ .
   a. client/server network
   b. peer-to-peer network
   c. server-to-server network
   d. client/client network

LESSON //9A Review

Review Questions ::

In your own words, briefly answer the following questions.

1. List four benefits that networks provide to their users.
2. How can a network help a small business save money on printing?
3. Name four types of media used to link networks.
4. List four types of network topologies used in wire-based networks.
5. Name three common LAN protocols.
6. A network is a set of technologies that can be used to connect computers together. What three general components are needed to set up a network?
7. What are packets and how do they work?
8. What distinguishes a peer-to-peer network?
9. Companies use their own Web sites to support operations. What is the distinction between an intranet and an extranet?
10. Companies are attempting to save telephone communication costs by implementing this technology. What is the technology called?

Lesson Labs ::

Complete the following exercise as directed by your instructor. (Note: This exercise assumes you are using Windows XP or Windows 2000. If you have a different version of Windows, ask your instructor for specific directions.)

1. Explore your network.
   a. On your Windows desktop, double-click the My Network Places icon. The My Network Places window opens. This window lets you access all the computers, folders, files, and devices on the network.
   b. Find the icon named Entire Network and double-click it. What do you see? Because every network is unique, the contents of this window will vary from network to network.
   c. Following your instructor's directions, click icons and open new windows to explore your network. How many network resources can you access?
   d. When you finish exploring, close all open windows.

LESSON // 9B

Data Communications

Overview: The Local and Global Reach of Networks

Networks were once used mainly by the military, universities, and large government agencies, but today networks span the globe and reach into the average home. Today, millions of small businesses have set up connections to the Internet, enabling users to browse the World Wide Web and exchange e-mail.

Medium-sized and large businesses typically use networks to connect users for the same reasons as small businesses, but they also may use a large-scale LAN or WAN to connect departments or divisions that may be located in different buildings, regions, or even continents. Many businesses use a direct connection to the Internet to provide Internet access to their users.

Even a home computer user can be part of a truly global network. A connection to the Internet makes your home computer one of the millions of nodes on the vast Internet network. You can share files, collaborate, communicate, and conference with people on the other side of the globe. This lesson examines some of the most common ways of transmitting data via networks and the Internet.

OBJECTIVES ::

- Explain how computer data travels over telephone lines.
- Explain a modem's function.
- Explain how a modem's transmission speed is measured.
- Differentiate four types of digital data connections.
- Describe how wireless networks function.

simnet™

Data Communications with Standard Telephone Lines and Modems

Data communications usually take place over media (such as cables or wireless links) that are specifically set up for the network, and thus are known as dedicated media. The alternative to using dedicated media is to use the telephone system—called the plain old telephone system (POTS)—for data communications. This option is possible because the telephone system is really just a giant network owned by the telephone companies.

As we know it, the telephone network is designed to carry the two-way transmission of electronic information, but it is very different from a typical computer network. Remember, the telephone system was originally designed to carry voice messages, which are analog signals (see Figure 9B.1). Telephone lines, however, can also be used to transmit digital data. By connecting a computer to the telephone line, you can send data to potentially anyone else in the world who has a computer and phone service, and you do not need to set up a network to do it since you can use the world's largest network, the Internet.

FIGURE 9B.1

The telephone system was designed to handle voice transmissions, rather than digital data.

However, regular analog phone lines are not very well suited for carrying data. They transmit data at a much, much slower rate than a typical Ethernet network—so slowly, in fact, that standard phone lines are simply impractical for many kinds of data transmissions. Also, computers and analog phone lines cannot work directly with one another; they require special hardware and software to "translate" data between the digital computer and the analog phone line. As a result, telephone companies now offer digital lines along with special connecting equipment specifically designed for data communications.

Modems

Norton ONLINE

For more information on modems, visit **http://www.mhhe.com/peternorton**.

Although digital telephone lines are gaining popularity, millions of homes and businesses still have only analog telephone lines. Attaching a computer to an analog telephone line requires a modem, so it is important to know something about how modems work and what to look for when you buy one.

In standard telephone service, a telephone converts the sound of your voice into an electric signal that flows through the telephone wires. The telephone at the other end converts this electric signal back into sound so that the person you are talking to can hear your voice. Both the sound wave and the telephone signal are analog signals, electrical waves that vary continuously with the volume and pitch of the speakers' voices.

A computer's "voice" is digital; that is, it consists of on/off pulses representing 1s and 0s. A device called a modem (short for *mod*ulator-*dem*odulator) is needed to translate these digital signals into analog signals that can travel over standard telephone lines. In its modulation phase, the modem turns the computer's digital signals into analog signals, which are then transmitted across the phone line. The reverse takes place during its demodulation phase, as the modem receives analog signals from the phone line and converts them into digital signals for the computer. Figure 9B.2 shows how computers communicate through modems and a telephone connection.

A modem's transmission speed (the rate at which it can send data) is measured in bits per second (bps). Today's fastest modems for dial-up connections on standard phone lines have a maximum theoretical transmission speed of 56,000 bits per second, or 56 kilobits per second (Kbps), and are called 56K modems. The 56K modem's speed is due to several factors, such as the modem's use of the V.90 or newer V.92 data communications standards. These standards allow modems to communicate more efficiently over analog phone lines. These modems seldom actually achieve their highest potential transmission rate, however, because of bad

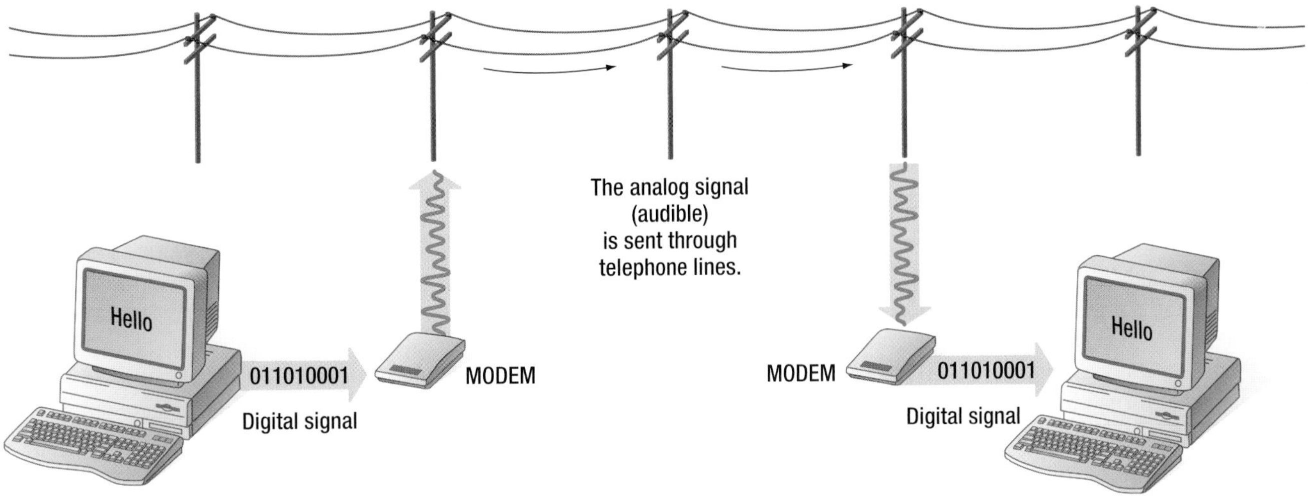

connections and noise in the telephone lines. Still, if you must use a standard phone line for data communications, a 56K modem will give you the fastest data transmission speeds available for PCs.

Data moves through the line so quickly that even the smallest amount of static can introduce significant errors. Noise you could not hear if you were using the telephone line for a conversation can wreak havoc with computer data. As a result, modems and communications software use error-correction protocols to recover from transmission errors. These protocols enable a modem to detect errors in the data it is receiving and to request that error-ridden data be resent from its source.

An external modem is a box that houses the modem's circuitry outside the computer (see Figure 9B.3). It connects to the computer using a serial, USB, or FireWire port, and then connects to the telephone system with a standard telephone jack. An internal modem is a circuit board that plugs into one of the computer's expansion slots (see Figure 9B.4). An internal modem saves desktop space but occupies an expansion slot. Modems also come in the form of a PC Card for use with laptop computers and with newer models, are likely to be built into the laptop appearing as a port in one of the sides (see Figure 9B.5). Some use standard telephone lines, but others include a cellular phone, which enables completely wireless transmissions.

Most modems used with personal computers also can emulate a fax machine. Called fax modems, these devices can exchange faxes with any other fax modem or fax machine. With the proper software, users can convert incoming fax files into files that can be edited with a word processor—something that stand-alone fax machines cannot do.

FIGURE 9B.2

How modems connect computers through telephone lines.

FIGURE 9B.3

On the back of this external modem are connections for attaching it to the computer, a telephone jack, and a telephone.

FIGURE 9B.4

An internal modem plugs into one of the computer's expansion slots.

FIGURE 9B.5

This notebook computer is equipped with a modem in the form of a PC Card. The modem comes equipped with a cellular unit, so the user can log into a network without using a telephone line.

Productivity Tip

The Telecommuter's Checklist

Today, many people have the opportunity to work at home or on the road with the help of computers, telecommunications equipment, and the Internet. These workers are called *telecommuters* because they work at a remote location rather than their employer's office.

Companies are supporting efforts to allow employees from time to time to work from home. Some employees who travel often also are using home offices because it can be less expensive to equip a home worker than to pay for onsite office space. Employers also can reduce workplace-related hazards by minimizing the number of workers on site. Another benefit of telecommuting is that some workers are more productive in a home office where they can spend more time actually working on assignments and less time commuting.

To be effective, telecommuters must be just as well equipped as someone working in the company's office headquarters. The home offices need to be set up for creating and processing data, exchanging data with others, and communicating with colleagues and clients. A typical telecommuter's equipment checklist might look like this:

- **A Reliable Computer.** Because of the remoteness from the main office, telecommuters may need more powerful computers, or at least more reliable equipment, to complete the necessary tasks. Often the telecommuter needs to have important programs and data files stored on a local disk. This is because the off-site worker may not always be able to access all programs and data files he or she needs by remotely logging into the company's network. In this case, the telecommuter needs to have important programs and data files stored on a local disk. Because the telecommuter's computer may need to perform additional tasks, such as remotely connecting to other systems, faxing, and printing to a local printer, the more power and storage space the computer system has, the better.
- **Data Communications Media.** Although most computers have a modem, dial-up connections are too slow and inefficient for many business uses. For this reason, many employers equip telecommuters' PCs with a network card, enabling them to use a cable modem or DSL connection. Oftentimes with these high-speed connections, multiple PC connections may be made using switches or hubs, or a wireless access point. Telecommuters usually use the Internet to connect with the office's network or they may dial up over a phone line that attaches directly to the company's private network. It is critical that the Internet connection be fast enough to meet all access demands needed for proper productivity.

Uses for a Modem

File transfer is the process of exchanging files between computers, either through telephone lines or a network. If you use your computer to send a file to another person's computer, you are said to be uploading the file. If you use your computer to copy a file from a remote computer, you are said to be downloading the file. For a file to be transferred from one computer to another through a pair of modems, both computers must use the same file transfer protocol. The most common file transfer protocols for modems are called Kermit, Xmodem, Ymodem, Zmodem, and MNP.

SELF-CHECK ::

Circle the word or phrase that best completes each statement.

1. The term *modem* is short for ________ .
   a. modulate/demodulate   b. network interface card   c. modal/demodal
2. If a modem detects an error in data it has received from another computer, it can request that the data be ________ .
   a. deleted   b. resent   c. changed
3. Most PC modems can emulate a ________ .
   a. scanner   b. keyboard   c. fax machine

PRODUCTIVITY TIP

- » **Faxing Alternatives.** Rather than purchasing an expensive fax machine that takes up space and ties up a phone line, many telecommuters use the more affordable scanner instead. Using fax software, they can send and receive faxes directly from their PC. If they need to fax a document with a signature, they can scan the document first and then fax it. Multifunction "all-in-one" printer/copier/scanner/fax machines are ideal for telecommuters.
- » **Wireless Communications.** With the use of access points offered by hotels and cafes, having a wireless NIC for a laptop can allow mobile users access to the company's private network via the Internet at any time. Today, handheld devices offer the same type of access. A farther-reaching technology is the use of various cellular phone devices that allow Internet connections via the cell phone connection.
- » **Service Accounts.** Telecommuters are often responsible for setting up and maintaining their own accounts for communications and Internet services, especially when their home is in a different city than their employer's office. A conscientious employer will reimburse the worker for reasonable expenses, but the employee may be expected to seek out, set up, and maintain communication accounts and Internet services.

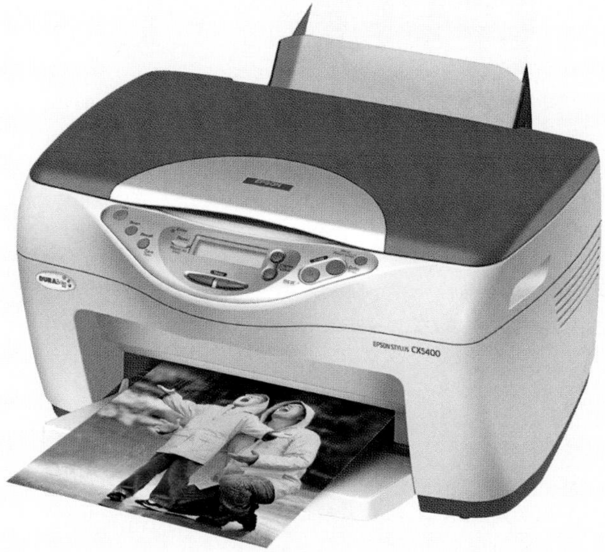

With the help of PCs and communications equipment, millions of people have found that they can be more productive working at home than at the company's office.

Using Digital Data Connections

simnet™

As you learned earlier, standard telephone lines transmit analog signals in which sound is translated into an electrical current. As a result, you need a modem to translate data into a form that can be sent over telephone lines. Modems can sometimes transmit data at rates as high as 56 kilobits per second (56 Kbps). Still, when you consider that most cable modems or DSL connections can transmit data at speeds up to and sometimes exceeding 1.5 Mbps, phone lines and modems seem like a poor alternative.

The telephone companies recognized this problem several years ago and began the long process of converting an analog system into a digital system. The massive data channels that connect major geographical regions are already digital cables, but the telephone lines running under or above most city streets are still analog. This combination of digital and analog lines makes for an extremely confusing system, especially when you are transmitting data through a modem (see Figure 9B.6). However, when the telephone companies complete the transition and digital lines are installed to every building, the data transmission system will be a lot simpler.

FIGURE 9B.6

Sending data requires the computer to transmit a digital signal to a modem, which transmits an analog signal to the switching station, which in turn transmits a digital signal to another switching station. The receiving computer gets a digital signal from the modem, which received an analog signal from the last switching station in the chain.

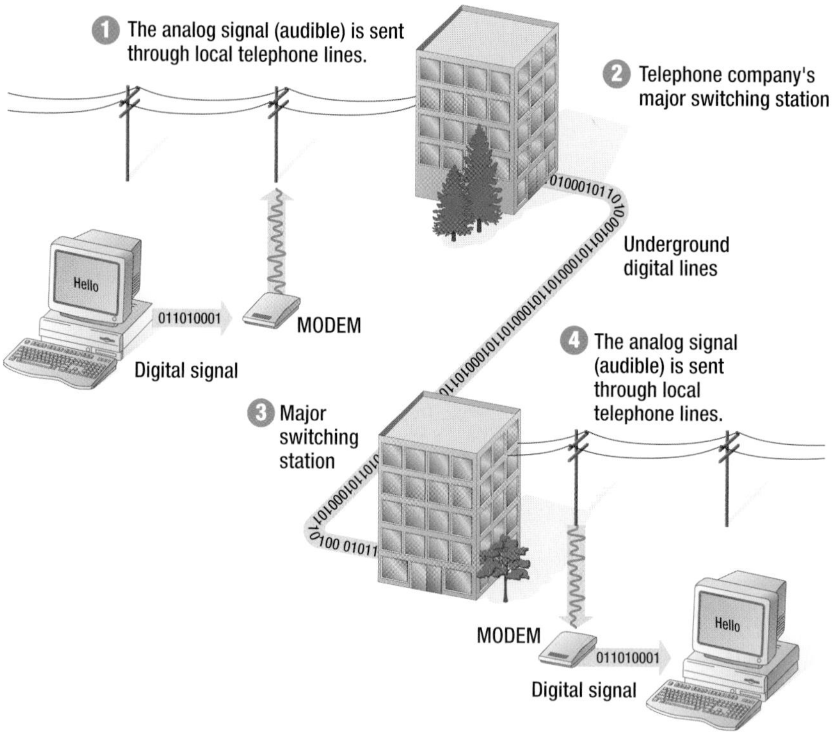

The transformation from analog to digital lines will affect most users in three simple ways:

- A different phone will be needed. A digital phone that translates voice into bits rather than an analog signal is needed.
- There will be no more need for a modem. An adapter that simply reformats the data so that it can travel through the telephone lines is needed.
- Data can be sent very quickly.

Broadband Connections

Several broadband technologies are being offered by the telecommunication industry today. The term broadband is used to describe any data connection that can transmit data faster than is possible through a standard dial-up connection using a modem. Some of the better known are called integrated services digital network (ISDN), T1, T3, DSL, cable modems, and ATM.

To get an understanding of the increments in bandwidth, you need to know that a basic rate integrated services digital network (basic rate ISDN or BRI) connection combines two 64 Kbps data channels and one 19 Kbps error-checking channel (see Figure 9B.7). In the United States, a primary rate ISDN (PRI) connection provides 24 channels at 64 Kbps each for a total bandwidth increase of 1.544 Mbps. This level of bandwidth is also known as Fractional T1 service. It is also possible to purchase lines from telephone companies that offer even more bandwidth. For example, a T3 line offers 672 channels of 64 Kbps each (plus control lines) for a total of 44.736 Mbps. The cost of this technology remains high, so many telecommunication companies offer services between the levels of BRI and PRI.

Norton ONLINE

For more information on broadband technologies for data communications, visit **http://www.mhhe.com/peternorton**.

DSL Technologies

Another type of digital telephone service—called digital subscriber line (DSL)—is very popular, especially with home users. This is because DSL service is typically

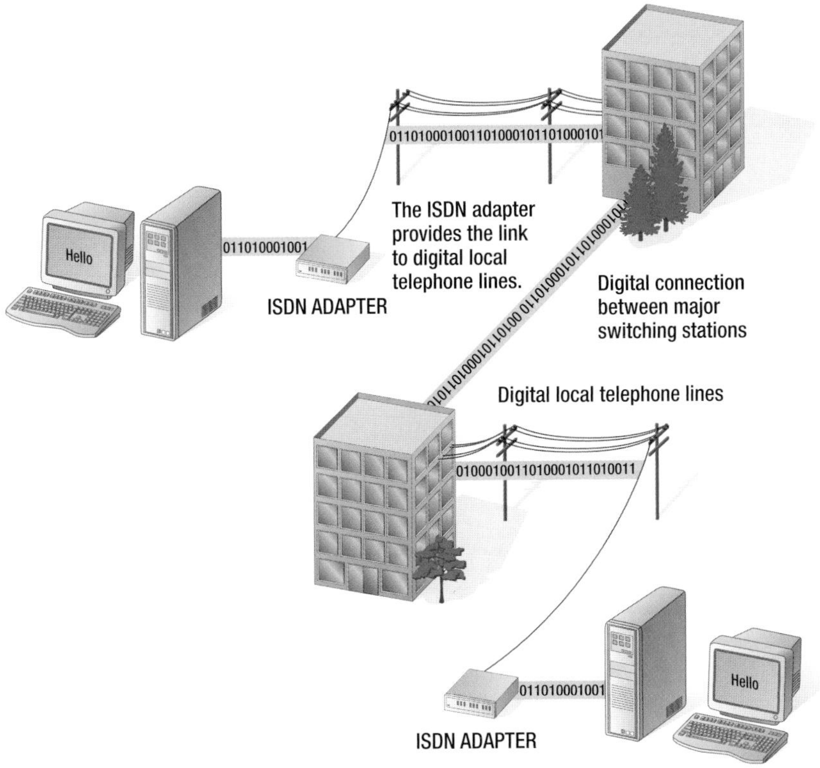

FIGURE 9B.7

With local digital telephone lines, data transmissions can remain in a digital form from the sending computer to the receiving computer.

less expensive than T1 services in terms of hardware, setup, and monthly costs. In fact, many local telephone companies offer only DSL services in their markets, forgoing other broadband technologies altogether.

Several types of DSL, including the following, are available in different markets, each offering different capabilities and rates ranging from 100 Kbps to over 30 Mbps:

- Asymmetrical DSL (ADSL)
- Rate adaptive DSL (RADSL)
- High-bit-rate DSL (HDSL)
- ISDN DSL (IDSL)
- Symmetric DSL (SDSL)
- Very-high-bit-rate DSL (VDSL)

The actual performance you can achieve with DSL depends on the type of DSL service you choose, the distance between the DSL modem and the telephone company's switch, and many other factors.

Cable Modem Connections

Cable modem service is a technology that enables home computer users to connect to the Internet through their cable TV connection with higher speeds than those offered by dial-up connections (see Figure 9B.8). However, cable modems also are finding acceptance in small- to medium-sized businesses as an alternative to other technologies such as DSL. Cable modems usually achieve download speeds of about 27 Mbps but are capable of speeds equal to T1. These speeds are substantial increase over dial-up connections. The only limitations on speed are the number of users in the local neighborhood sharing the same connections.

In a typical cable network, a facility called a "head end" serves as the primary point where the television signals enter the system through satellite and standard

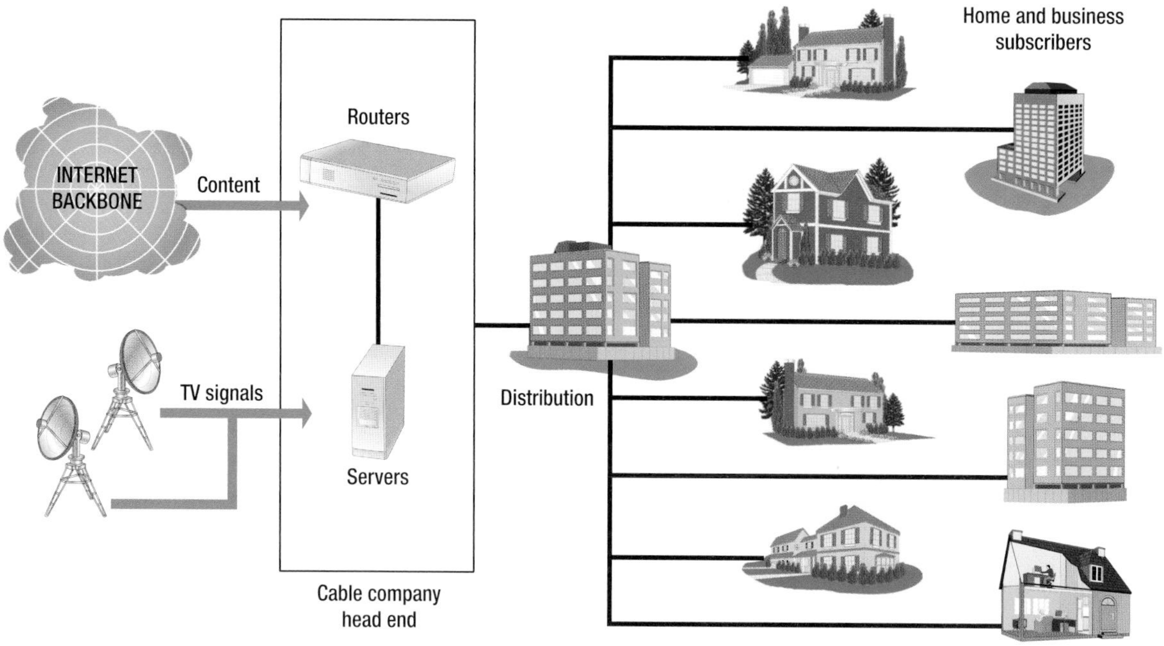

FIGURE 9B.8

A cable modem system combines a typical cable television network with a wide area network, which is connected to the Internet.

over-the-air broadcast means. The head end is also where the dedicated Internet connection occurs, connecting the cable TV network to the Internet. From the head end, the network branches out to subscriber locations using combinations of fiber-optic and copper cable, typically terminating at each end-user location as coax cable. Because a transmission must often traverse several miles from the head end to the end user, amplifiers are used to keep the signal strong. The greater the distance from the head end, the more amplifiers are required.

ATM

DSL, cable modems, T1, and T3 can all be used effectively to set up WANs as long as the networks are used primarily for transferring the most common types of data—files, e-mail messages, and so on. However, these types of services are not always well suited for transmitting live video and sound. As a result, communications companies offer a service called ATM, which stands for asynchronous transfer mode.

ATM is a protocol designed by the telecommunications industry as a more efficient way to send voice, video, and computer data over a single network. It was originally conceived as a way to reconcile the needs for these different kinds of data on the telephone system, but the proponents of ATM argue that it also can be implemented on computer LANs and WANs. In fact, ATM is a network protocol. To install ATM, the purchase of special network adapter cards for every networked device and special higher-level switches is required.

Norton ONLINE

For more information on wireless networks, visit **http://www.mhhe.com/peternorton**.

simnet™

Wireless Networks

Most companies rely heavily on cabling. However, small awkward areas and older buildings make the use of wires very difficult. Also, although this situation is changing with newer homes, most older houses are not wired with network cabling. Rather than removing walls and spending many hours pulling cables or paying an electrician to do it, home owners are opting for wireless networks. In addition, wireless technology allows connectivity so that portable and handheld computers can move around while being continuously connected to a network.

Wireless: 802.11

The wireless standard that is becoming very popular follows the family of specifications called 802.11 or Wi-Fi. The 802.11b standard describes specifications for wireless speeds up to 11 Mbps, which is a little faster than the slowest form of Ethernet (10 Mbps) but much faster than the typical 1.5Mbps high-end DSL connection. The 802.11g standard describes specifications for wireless LANs that provide 20+ Mbps connection speeds.

Wireless Access Point

To create a wireless LAN, a wireless access point is needed. In a wireless environment, single or multiple PCs can connect through a single wireless access point (WAP). In larger wireless topologies, multiple wireless machines can roam through different access points and stay on the same network domain with the same level of security. If the network must grow to handle more users, or expand its range, extension points can be added.

The WAP connects to an Ethernet LAN like any other device and allows computers with wireless NICs to function in the Ethernet LAN environment. In addition, some wireless access points come with built-in routers, firewalls, and switches so that you do not have to buy multiple hardware devices (see Figure 9B.9).

FIGURE 9B.9

Wireless firewall switch router.

A very important limitation with wireless devices is distance. The distance a wireless access point can reach depends on the antenna and the obstacles between devices that weaken the signal. Depending on the quality of the device, a typical antenna can reach between 50 and 150 meters.

Wireless Adapter

A PC or laptop needs a wireless adapter card (wireless NIC) that meets 802.11b or 802.11g standards to make contact with the WAP (see Figure 9B.10). Many wireless NICs come with utility software that allows you to monitor signal strength and download speeds.

FIGURE 9B.10

A wireless NIC

Computers In Your Career

Careers in Networking

With the increased attention to national and corporate security in the United States, Michael French is well positioned for a long and successful career in computer networking, particularly when it comes to protecting those systems from hackers.

As a senior security consultant for IBM, French has conducted and managed projects for leading firms in the insurance, banking, investment, and educational industries. A typical workday will find him on the road at a client's location, working to improve security on company networks, SUN Solaris servers, or PCs running Microsoft Windows.

French is living proof that networking professionals have a wide range of career paths to choose from. Before joining IBM, for example, French ran his own consulting firm focused on mobile computing and voice/data networks and previously served as vice president of e-commerce for Bank of America.

A graduate of Brown University and Long Island University, where he earned a Master of Science in management science, French is IBM certified in IT security, was awarded two patents for electrical designs, and was a co-inventor on four other patents. He typically works a 10-hour day, with much of it spent assessing network security for individual IBM clients.

Keeping up to date on the latest developments in the networking space is French's biggest job challenge, and one he overcomes by reading, studying, and attending trade conferences and seminars. "There's a constant need to upgrade your knowledge," says French. "The current buzzword, for example, is Voice over IP and it's unleashing a flood of new products and problems that we never knew we had."

Most rewarding about the IT networking field, says French, is that it's always interesting and never boring. The job also comes with a degree of autonomy, since many networking professionals manage their own projects and are considered competent and capable of making decisions and attaining goals. He sees future prospects in networking as "exciting" and doesn't predict any drop-off in demand for good networking professionals. "It's a fast-growing and fast-changing field," he adds.

Other careers relating to networking and data communications include

- **Customer Service Support.** Many entry-level jobs are coming from the customer support areas of software, operating systems, and telecommunication systems industries. This involves troubleshooting issues with customers over the phone or sometimes providing mobile on-site support. Customer support comes in various levels. Front-line support is usually called level 1. The support levels can go all the way back to the developers of the software or hardware. Support at this level is usually very technical and the salaries are high.

- **Network Administrators.** These individuals are responsible for managing a company's network infrastructure. Some of the jobs in this field include designing and implementing networks, setting up and managing users' accounts, installing and updating network software and applications, and backing up the network.
- **Information Systems (IS) Managers.** IS managers are responsible for managing a team of information professionals, including network administrators, software developers, project managers, and other staff. Jobs in the IS management field differ according to the needs of the company.
- **Data Communications Managers.** These managers are responsible for setting up and maintaining Internet, intranet, and extranet sites. Often they are also responsible for designing and establishing an organization's telecommuting initiative.

The Bureau of Labor Statistics calls networking one of the most rapidly growing fields in the computing industry. Median annual earnings of network and computer systems administrators were $51,280 in 2000, with the middle 50 percent earning between $40,450 and $65,140.

Although the networking fields are facing a slight economic downturn for upper-level jobs, the industry is expected to grow faster than other industries, especially at the skilled support or entry levels.

LESSON // 9B Review

Summary ::

- Networks, and especially home users, commonly transmit data across telephone lines.
- Telephone companies are offering more digital lines (which are better suited to data transmission). While homes and businesses are still served by analog telephone lines, the use of cable modems and DSL is rapidly growing.
- To transfer digital data over analog telephone lines, computers must use modems. When a computer sends data, its modem translates digital data into analog signals for transmission over standard telephone lines. At the receiving end, the computer's modem converts the analog signals back into digital data.
- Modem transmission speeds are measured in bits per second (bps). Currently the preferred standard for modems is 56 Kpbs.
- Using digital connections, businesses and homes can transmit data many times faster than is possible over standard phone lines.
- The most popular digital lines offered by telephone companies include T1, T3, and DSL. They offer faster data transfer rates and higher bandwidths than standard phone lines.
- Another type of digital service is called ATM (asynchronous transfer mode). ATM is adapted for transmitting high-volume data files such as audio, video, and multimedia files.
- Many cable companies now offer Internet connections to homes and businesses through the same lines that carry cable television service. Cable modem service can be as fast as T1 and some types of DSL services.
- Wireless technology follows a standard called 802.11. The two most popular standards in use are 802.11b and 802.11g. In addition to other requirements, each governs the standards for wireless speeds. The 802.11b standard describes specifications for speeds up to 11 Mps and 802.11g, for 20+ Mbps connections.
- To gain access to an Ethernet LAN wirelessly, you need a wireless NIC and a wireless access point (WAP) needs to be added to the Ethernet LAN.

Key Terms ::

802.11b, 373
802.11g, 373
asynchronous transfer mode (ATM), 372
basic rate integrated services digital network (basic rate ISDN or BRI), 370
bits per second (bps), 366
broadband, 370
cable modem service, 371
dedicated media, 366
digital subscriber line (DSL), 370
download, 368
error-correction protocol, 367
extension points, 373
external modem, 367
fax modem, 367
file transfer, 368
integrated services digital network (ISDN), 370
internal modem, 367
modem, 366
plain old telephone system (POTS), 366
T1, 370
T3, 370
upload, 368
Wi-Fi, 373
wireless access point (WAP), 373

Key Term Quiz ::

Complete each statement by writing one of the terms listed under Key Terms in each blank.

1. The process of copying a file from a remote computer onto your computer is called ________ .
2. The process of sending a file to another user's computer over a network is called ________ .
3. There are several different versions of ________ service, each offering its own capabilities and rates.
4. A modem's transmission speed is measured in ________ .
5. A device that is added into an expansion slot that allows users to connect the PC to the telephone line is called a(n) ________ .
6. ________ service is a good choice for businesses that need to transmit very large files, such as live audio or video feeds.
7. The term ________ describes any data connection that can transfer data faster than a standard dial-up connection.
8. Your telephone connects to an "old-fashioned" network, called the ________ .
9. Modems and communications software use ________ protocols to recover from transmission errors.
10. ________ is another name to describe 802.11 technology.

LESSON //9B Review

Multiple Choice ::

Circle the word or phrase that best completes each statement.

1. You should consider ________ when purchasing a modem.
   a. transmission speed and data length
   b. error correction and transmission speed
   c. fastest error correction method
   d. bus speed of PC
2. The abbreviation *bps* stands for ________ .
   a. bytes per second
   b. bits per second
   c. bandwidth per second
   d. baudrate per second
3. A(n) ________ enables a modem to determine whether data has been corrupted and to request that it be retransmitted.
   a. TCP protocol
   b. file transfer protocol
   c. Internet protocol
   d. error-protection protocol
4. ________ service offers a total of 44.736 Mbps of bandwidth.
   a. ATM
   b. T1
   c. T2
   d. T3
5. In a cable network, the ________ is where the cable TV network connects to the Internet.
   a. head end
   b. switching station
   c. cable modem
   d. RJ45 jack
6. If you want to connect to a remote network or the Internet using a modem, you need to connect the modem to a(n) ________ .
   a. analog telephone line
   b. digital telephone line
   c. teleconferencing line
   d. ATM line
7. The expression *Mbps* stands for ________ .
   a. ten thousand bits per second
   b. megabits per second
   c. gigabits per second
   d. microbits per second
8. The basic rate ISDN service provides ________ .
   a. one 256 Kbps data channel and one 64 Kbps error-checking channel
   b. two 64 Kbps data channels and one 19 Kbps error-checking channel
   c. 13 communication channels
   d. two 13 communication channels
9. ________ is possible though a network or telephone lines.
   a. cellular data transfer
   b. Internet access and file transfer
   c. analog file updating
   d. digital signaling
10. A modem converts the computer's digital data into analog signals in the ________ phase of its operation.
    a. modularization
    b. modulification
    c. modulation
    d. modularitization

Review Questions ::

In your own words, briefly answer the following questions.

1. Why are modems required when two computers need to exchange data over standard telephone lines?
2. What factors should you consider when purchasing a modem?
3. If digital telephone lines completely replace analog lines, how will data communications be simplified?
4. Name three different versions of DSL service.
5. What is the difference between the 802.11b standard and the 802.11g standard?
6. Why don't 56K modems usually achieve their highest potential data transmission rate?
7. What are two popular types of modem devices that can be attached to or installed in a PC?
8. Most modems used with PCs also can emulate this type of office machine. What is the machine and what is the device called?
9. File transferring usually involves two types of processes; what are they?
10. BRI and basic rate ISDN have the same meaning. What do these acronyms mean and how are they the same?

Lesson Labs ::

Complete the following exercises as directed by your instructor.

1. Determine if your PC has a modem and view its settings. Open the Control Panel window and then double-click the Modems icon (Phone and Modem Options icon if using Windows XP) to open the Modems Properties dialog box. If any modems are listed, select them one at a time and click the Properties button. Review the properties for each modem. Be careful not to change any settings. Close all open windows and dialog boxes.
2. HyperTerminal is a Windows utility that enables your computer to "call" another computer directly and exchange data over a telephone line. Choose Start | Programs | Accessories | Communications | HyperTerminal. When HyperTerminal launches, open the Help menu and study the Help topics to learn more about the program and its capabilities. When you are finished, close all open windows and dialog boxes.

Chapter Labs

Complete the following exercises using a computer in your classroom, lab, or home. (*Note:* These exercises assume you are using Windows XP or Windows 2000 and that your computer is connected to a network. If not, ask your instructor for assistance.)

1. Learn more about networking in Windows. Windows provides many networking-related options and services. To learn more about the networking capabilities that are built into your version of Windows, use the Help system to find information. Here's how:
   a. Click the Start button to open the Start menu and then click Help (Help and Support if using Windows XP). Depending on which version of Windows you use, a different kind of Help window will appear.
   b. If you use Windows XP, skip to step C. If you use Windows 2000, click the Show button on the Help window's toolbar to open the left-hand pane of the Help window. Click the Contents tab and then click the Networking link. The category expands, revealing more than a dozen Help topics dealing with networking. Click each topic in the Contents tab and read the information that appears in the right-hand pane of the Help window.
   c. If you use Windows XP, click the heading Network and the Web; then select the Network options and begin the tour by clicking the Getting Started option.
   d. When you are finished, close all open windows and dialog boxes.
2. Want to set up a home network? If you have more than one computer at home, you may want to set up a home network so they can share a printer, an Internet connection, or other kinds of resources. Creating a home network is a lot easier and cheaper than you might think. The Internet is a good place to learn about all types of home networks, to shop for the hardware and software you need, and to get step-by-step instructions for building your own network. Visit the following sites to learn more:

   2Wire Support. http://www.2wire.com/?p=72

   About.com's Home Networking Tutorial. http://compnetworking.about.com/cs/homenetworking/a/homenetguide.htm

   Actiontec Home Computer Networking Info Center. http://www.homenethelp.com

   International Engineering Consortium On-Line Education: Home Networking http://www.iec.org/online/tutorials/home_net
3. Check out videoconferencing. Several affordable videoconferencing applications are available, all of which enable you to join online videoconferences on a private network or the Internet. You can learn more about some of these products at these Web sites:

   iVisit. http://www.ivisit.com

   ClearPhone. http://www.clearphone.com

   First Virtual Communications. http://www.fvc.com

   Microsoft Windows NetMeeting. http://www.microsoft.com/windows/netmeeting

Discussion Questions

As directed by your instructor, discuss the following questions in class or in groups.

1. Create a list of ways in which companies can save money by setting up a network. Look beyond issues such as printing and sharing programs. Can you imagine other ways to save money by using a network?
2. How practical do you think home networks really are? Do you see a practical use for them, besides playing games or sharing printers? In your opinion, will people really connect their PCs, home appliances, and utilities with a home network someday? Why or why not? Share your views with the group, and be prepared to support them.

Research and Report

Using your own choice of resources (such as the Internet, books, magazines, and newspaper articles), research and write a short paper discussing one of the following topics:

- The growth of telecommuting in American business.
- The largest private LAN or WAN in the United States.
- Recent advances in small-switch technology.

When you are finished, proofread and print your paper, and give it to your instructor.

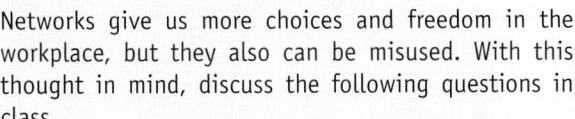

ETHICAL ISSUES

Networks give us more choices and freedom in the workplace, but they also can be misused. With this thought in mind, discuss the following questions in class.

1. Telecommuters enjoy working at home because it gives them more control over their schedules while removing the distractions that are part of the workplace. Realizing that they are no longer under the watch of a supervisor, however, some workers abuse their telecommuting privileges. What are the risks to business of allowing employees to telecommute? At what point is an employee abusing the freedom afforded by telecommuting? In your view, what kinds of activities or behaviors constitute such abuse?
2. It is estimated that most occurrences of hacking are conducted by employees who pilfer data from their employers' networks and then sell or misuse that information. How far should companies go to prevent such abuse? What kinds of punishments are appropriate?

10

CHAPTER

Working in the Online World

CHAPTER CONTENTS ::

This chapter contains the following lessons:

LESSON // 10A

Connecting to the Internet

Overview: Joining the Internet Phenomenon

As more businesses and people join the Internet community, they are finding that the Internet is enhancing their work lives. Thanks to communications technologies, many businesspeople now work from home instead of commuting to an office each day.

Before you can do anything online, however, you must connect your PC to the Internet. There are several ways to do this. For most people, choosing a type of Internet connection is pretty easy. But if you live in a remote area or have a special need, the choice may be more difficult. Regardless, it's a good idea to understand all your options for getting online so you can pick the one that will work best for you.

This lesson provides an overview of the options for connecting a computer to the Internet. It also shows how the wireless Internet works, and discusses the need for wireless security.

OBJECTIVES ::

- List two primary methods for connecting to the Internet.
- Identify the high-speed data links commonly used to connect individuals and small businesses to the Internet.
- Describe how satellite communications can be used for Internet connections.
- Understand the need for wireless security.

Connecting to the Internet through Wires

Norton ONLINE

For more information on dial-up connections, visit **http://www.mhhe.com/peternorton**.

There are many ways to obtain access to the Internet. The method varies according to the type of computer system being used and the types of connections offered. Some connections, such as dial-up, must be initiated every time you desire Internet access. Other connection types remain available 24/7; these "always-on" or "full-time" connections make Internet access as simple as opening your browser or e-mail program.

Dial-up Connections

In many homes and small businesses, individual users connect to the Internet by using a telephone line and a 56 Kbps modem. The easiest way to create this kind of connection is by setting up an inexpensive account with an Internet service provider (ISP). The ISP maintains banks of modems at its facility to process the incoming dial-up requests from customers. The ISP's servers route traffic between customers' computers and the Internet.

FIGURE 10A.1

The New Connection Wizard in Windows XP guides you through the process of configuring a dial-up or other type of network or Internet connection.

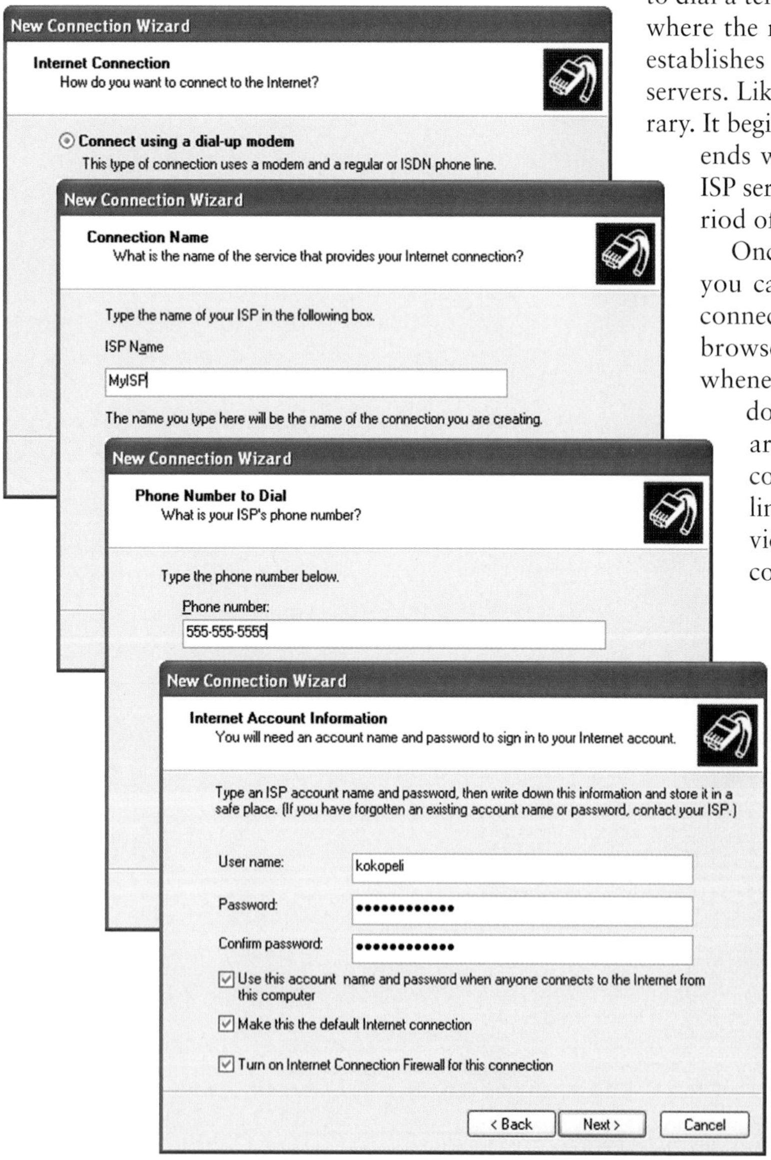

New Connection Wizard
Internet Connection
How do you want to connect to the Internet?
Connect using a dial-up modem
This type of connection uses a modem and a regular or ISDN phone line.
New Connection Wizard
Connection Name
What is the name of the service that provides your Internet connection?
Type the name of your ISP in the following box.
ISP Name
MyISP
The name you type here will be the name of the connection you are creating.
New Connection Wizard
Phone Number to Dial
What is your ISP's phone number?
Type the phone number below.
Phone number:
555-555-5555
New Connection Wizard
Internet Account Information
You will need an account name and password to sign in to your Internet account.
Type an ISP account name and password, then write down this information and store it in a safe place. (If you have forgotten an existing account name or password, contact your ISP.)
User name:
kokopeli
Password:
Confirm password:
Use this account name and password when anyone connects to the Internet from this computer
Make this the default Internet connection
Turn on Internet Connection Firewall for this connection
< Back
Next >
Cancel

In a dial-up connection, your computer uses its modem to dial a telephone number given to you by the ISP. (This is where the name "dial-up connection" comes from.) This establishes the connection between your PC and the ISP's servers. Like any phone call, the connection is only temporary. It begins when the ISP's server "answers" the call, and ends when your PC or the server "hangs up." Most ISP servers disconnect automatically after a certain period of inactivity.

Once a connection is configured on your computer, you can use the connection applet for that specific connection or configure your applications, such as a browser and e-mail client, to open the connection whenever you open the application. If you use Windows XP, you can run the New Connection Wizard to set up all the required information for the connection (see Figure 10A.1). If you use an online service such as AOL or CompuServe, the service provides client software that dials the connection for you.

High-Speed Broadband Connections

When many users share an Internet connection through a LAN, the connection between the network and the ISP must be adequate to meet all needs. This often means supporting the traffic created by all the users at the same time. Fortunately, dedicated high-speed data circuits are available from telephone companies, cable TV services, and other suppliers such as large networking companies and satellite service providers. These high-speed services are sometimes called broadband connections, because they use media that can handle multiple signals at once, such as fiber optics, microwave, and other technologies.

To be considered broadband, the connection must be able to transmit data at a rate faster than is possible with the fastest dial-up connection.

If you connect through a LAN at school or work, the LAN's connection to the Internet may be through a high-speed connection such as a T1 or T3 line. Even with hundreds of users on the network, these ultra-fast connections allow large files and complex Web pages to download quickly.

Not too long ago, people found a huge difference between the experience of browsing Web pages and downloading files on the Internet over high-speed connections at school or work versus doing the same from their home computer. Now that broadband technologies for the home or small business are becoming available in many areas, and are priced within the reach of many individuals, it is entirely practical to establish an Internet connection at home that is at least 10 times as fast as a standard 56K modem link.

Integrated Services Digital Network (ISDN) Service

Integrated services digital network (ISDN) is a digital telephone service that simultaneously transmits voice, data, and control signaling over a single telephone line. ISDN service operates on standard telephone lines but requires a special modem and phone service, which adds to the cost. An ISDN data connection can transfer data at up to 128,000 bits per second (128 Kbps). Most telephone companies offer ISDN at a slightly higher cost than the standard dial-up service that it replaces. In some areas, especially outside of the United States, it may be all that is available.

The benefits of ISDN (beyond the faster speed compared to a dial-up connection) include being able to connect a PC, telephone, and fax machine to a single ISDN line and use them simultaneously. Many ISPs and local telephone companies that offer Internet access services support ISDN connections.

However, ISDN is dropping out of favor because of the increasing availability of higher-performance broadband options, such as the cable modem and DSL connections discussed next. Especially in remote parts of the world, another optional broadband service, satellite communications (discussed later in this chapter), may be a more viable option than ISDN.

Norton ONLINE

For more information on ISDN service, visit **http://www.mhhe.com/peternorton**.

Digital Subscriber Line (DSL) Services

Digital Subscriber Line (DSL) service is similar to ISDN in its use of the telephone network, but it uses more advanced digital signal processing and algorithms to compress more signals through the telephone lines. DSL also requires changes in components of the telephone network before it can be offered in an area. Like ISDN, DSL service can provide simultaneous data, voice, and fax transmissions on the same line.

DSL technologies are used for the "last mile" between the customer and a telephone company's central office. From there, the DSL traffic destined for the Internet travels over the phone company network to an Internet exchange point (IXP) and onto the Internet (see Figure 10A.2).

Several versions of DSL services are available for home and business use. Each version provides a different level of service, speed, bandwidth, and distance, and they normally provide full-time connections. The two most common are Asynchronous DSL (ADSL) and Synchronous DSL (SDSL). Others include High-data-rate DSL (HDSL) and Very High-data-rate DSL (VDSL). The abbreviation used to refer to DSL service in general begins with an *x* (*x*DSL), reflecting the variation of the first character in the DSL versions.

Across the standards, data transmission speeds range from 128 Kbps for basic DSL service through 8.448 Mbps for high-end service. When DSL speeds are described, they are usually the speed of traffic flowing "downstream"—that is, from the Internet to your computer. ADSL's downstream speed is much faster than its

Norton ONLINE

For more information on DSL services, visit **http://www.mhhe.com/peternorton**.

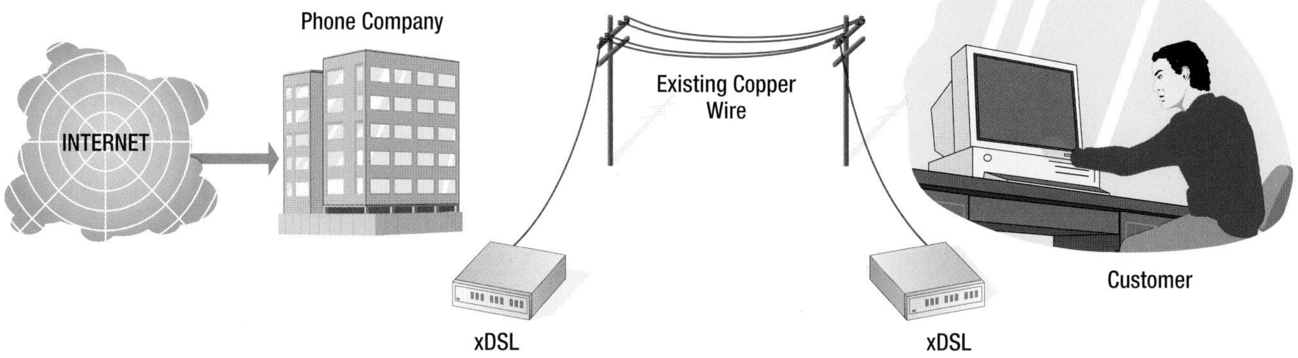

FIGURE 10A.2

DSL provides broadband communications between the customer and the phone company. From there, customers access the Internet through the phone company network.

upstream speed, while SDSL provides the same speed in each direction but is usually more expensive. Most people only require the higher speeds for downloads (browsing the Internet, downloading multimedia files, and so on), so SDSL service is only recommended for customers who must upload a great deal of data.

Even when you subscribe to a certain DSL service, transmission speeds can vary greatly and are affected by several factors, including distance, wire and equipment type, service provider capabilities, and more. It also should be noted that different providers may use DSL terms differently, and apply different usage standards in delivering DSL services. These variations often create great confusion among customers and cause delays in the acceptance of DSL in some markets.

Norton ONLINE

For more information on cable modem service, visit **http://www.mhhe.com/peternorton**.

Cable Modem Service

Many cable television (CATV) companies now use a portion of their network's bandwidth to offer Internet access through existing cable television connections. This Internet connection option is called cable modem service because of the need to use a special cable modem to connect (as shown in Figure 10A.3).

Cable television systems transmit data over coaxial cable, which can transmit data as much as 100 times faster than common telephone lines. Coaxial cable allows transmission over several channels simultaneously—the Internet data can be transmitted on one channel while audio, video, and control signals are transmitted separately. A user can access the Internet from his or her computer and watch cable television at the same time, over the same cable connection, and without the two data streams interfering with one another.

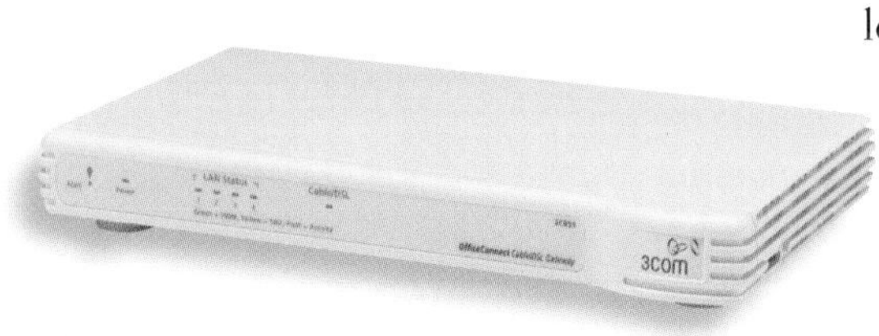

FIGURE 10A.3

Cable modems provide fast data-transfer speeds at costs comparable to a standard ISP account.

How PC Applications Access the Internet

Connecting a desktop computer to the Internet actually involves two separate issues: software and the network connection. With the variety of software applications that may be used to access an Internet service, and the huge variety of networking hardware available, as well as the network drivers—including both the NIC driver and protocols—the industry has developed standards for software that acts as an interface between the applications and the network drivers. Such a software interface is called an application programming interface (API). Like a puzzle, in which adjacent pieces must fit to create the whole picture, an API provides a puzzle piece that fits neatly between the applications and the drivers. Only the driver must understand and interact directly with the hardware. Sockets is the name of an API for UNIX computers, while Windows Sockets, or Winsock, is an adaptation of Sockets for Microsoft Windows operating systems.

Norton ONLINE

For more information on Winsock, visit **http://www.mhhe.com/peternorton**.

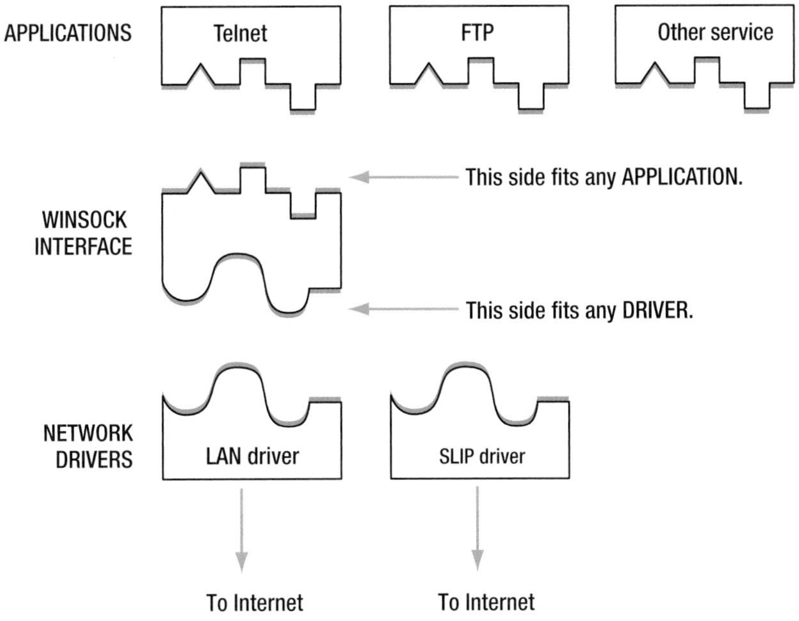

FIGURE 10A.4

How Winsock provides an interface between applications and networks.

These APIs make it possible to mix and match application programs from more than one developer, and to allow those applications to work with each other and with any type of networking hardware. Figure 10A.4 shows how applications, the Winsock interface, and network drivers fit together. The drivers shown include a LAN (most often for an Ethernet NIC) and the driver used for a dial-up connection.

SELF-CHECK ::

Circle the correct answer for each question.

1. This type of connection needs to be initiated every time the computer needs to access the Internet.
   a. cable modem service b. DSL c. dial-up
2. DSL service is provided by this type of organization.
   a. telephone company b. cable company c. IPX
3. Cable television systems send data over _____.
   a. antennaes b. coaxial cable c. DSL connections

Connecting to the Internet Wirelessly

The concept of a wireless network that would cover a very wide area is not a recent phenomenon. Radio technology has been around for over 100 years and was used to send information before wired telephone networks were common. For example, Morse code was used by ships at sea even before the *Titanic* sank in 1912. But as radio technology progressed, the use of radio transmissions for voice became dominant. Like wired communications, wireless technologies have moved from analog to digital over the years. Today, you can connect to the Internet through cellular networks, wireless wide area networks (WWANs), wireless LAN (WLAN) connections, and by satellite.

New wireless handheld devices take advantage of WWAN technology, allowing users to surf the Internet from any location offering the required signal. Enhanced personal digital assistants have cellular communications features and Internet software, but they are being overshadowed by smart phones that have added many of the features of PDAs plus screens and software for working on the Internet.

Norton ONLINE

For more information on wireless Internet connections, visit **http://www.mhhe.com/peternorton**.

Wireless WAN (WWAN) Connections

A wireless wide area network (WWAN) is a digital network that extends over a large geographical area. A WWAN receives and transmits data using radio signals

At Issue

On the Beat with Techno-Cops

The newest addition to the Sacramento California Police Department (SACPD) just sits in the car all day, doesn't write tickets, and doesn't wear a badge. But the "new guy" might just be the most effective member of the force at catching the bad guy.

This rookie is Versadex, a wireless mobile computer and public safety software system, complete with mobile records management and linked to computer-aided dispatch and radio systems.

Mobile computer systems such as the Versadex Computer Aided Dispatch (CAD) and Records Management System (RMS)—created by Versaterm—are the latest weapon in law enforcement's high-tech arsenal. They result in reduced workload, better information, and increased safety for officers in the field.

These systems give in-the-field access to all of the records and information an officer back at a desk at headquarters has, allowing police officers to get down to their real job: fighting crime.

The Versaterm CAD and RMS, Northrop Grumman mobile computers, and other components of the solution save officers a significant amount of time and make them—and the public—safer because of the information that is now available and the speed at which it can be accessed. According to the SACPD, with the new integrated hardware and software in place, officers saw improvements almost immediately.

For example, under the new system, officers can query both the central and national police computers about questionable license plates or suspects directly from the safety of the patrol car. Access to the county's mainframe system, which hosts local warrant information and parolee probation status, is credited with saving officers time and equipping them with critical information about whom they are handling.

This type of information used to be accessed over the radio, often taking up to 20 minutes to get warrant information and from 60 to 90 minutes for data from parole officers. This data is now accessible almost instantly.

over cellular sites and satellites, which make the network accessible to mobile computer systems. At the switching center, the WWAN splits off into segments and then connects to either a specialized public or private network via telephone or other high-speed communication links. The data then is linked to an organization's existing LAN/WAN infrastructure (see Figure 10A.5). The coverage area for a WWAN is normally measured in miles (or kilometers) and it is therefore more susceptible to environmental factors, like weather and terrain, than wired networks.

A WWAN is a fully bidirectional wireless network capable of data transfer at speeds in excess of 100 Mbps for a cost comparable with most DSL connections. Usually, basic WWAN services offer connection speeds between 1 and 10 Mbps. With dedicated equipment, the speeds can reach 100 Mbps. A WWAN system requires an antenna tuned to receive the proper radio frequency (RF). Through the use of intelligent routing, the user's data travels to the Internet and then to the appropriate Web sites or e-mail addresses.

With a WWAN system, a signal originates from the provider at a centralized transmission unit. The company will interface with the carrier using a dish antenna connected to a transceiver device through a coaxial cable. The other side of the transceiver is a port for a typical CAT5 Ethernet cable that connects to a LAN bridge that also contains a multiport hub. The hub will allow speeds of 100 Mbps for use by the LAN.

Satellite Services

Satellite services provide two-way data communications between the customer and the Internet. Many places in the world do not have a telephone network that can support broadband, nor do they have cellular coverage. For these locations, and for those who require Internet access while traveling, satellite connections are

The NEC notebooks are used extensively out of the car as well. Officers take them into homes and businesses to take witness statements and incident reports.

Northrop Grumman Mission Systems (NGMS) provided the car-mounted mobile data computers used by Versaterm. In addition to the Sacramento installation, NGMS has successfully overseen the activation of E-911 systems in several other major cities, including Atlanta, Baltimore, Chicago O'Hare Airport, and Los Angeles, as well as a statewide system in Ohio.

Radio IP's RadioRouter is the wireless network solution selected by the SACPD, offering TCP/IP connectivity from the base station to patrol cars. PC devices running a secure, encrypted wireless IP network are deployed through Radio Router, enabling officers access to any of the SACPD's local area network–based applications.

In the future, the department plans to integrate other useful technologies into the network, including automatic vehicle location (AVL) software and the ability to interface directly with a mug-shot system the Sacramento Police Department shares with Sacramento County. Eventually mug shots, identifying information, and fingerprints will be available in the patrol car, giving officers immediate access to a suspect's criminal history.

Worldwide, police departments are adopting mobile computer technologies to assist officers on the job.

AT ISSUE

FIGURE 10A.5

A WWAN includes devices that retransmit the wireless signal.

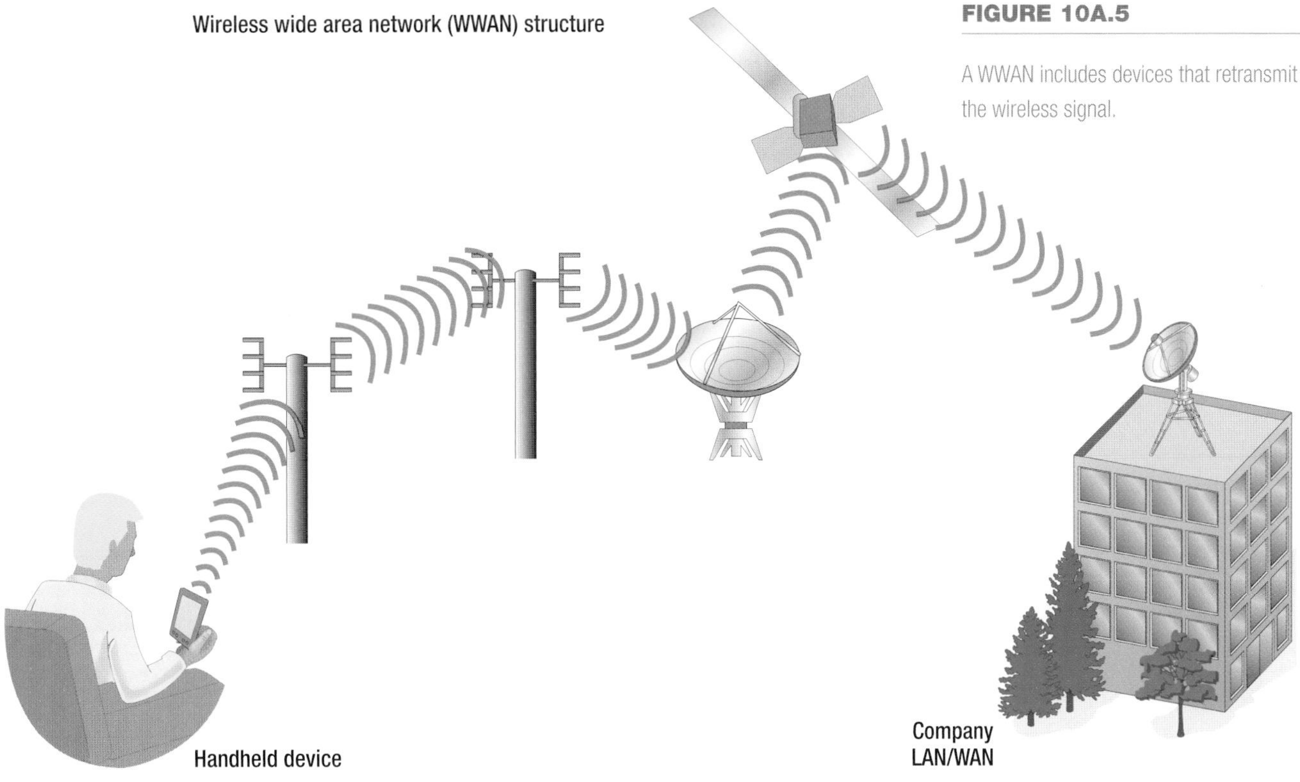

the answer, and they are becoming more affordable. Worldwide, 13 percent of ISP links to the Internet backbone and to customers use satellite communications. In fact, it is estimated that 10 percent of the worldwide broadband traffic in 2003 involved satellite communications.

Satellite connections are suitable for large businesses and for small offices, cyber-cafes, and homes. They also are used by the armed forces, business, and individuals for mobile communications. This wireless service is always on, unlike dial-up connections.

When an individual or organization contracts with an ISP for a satellite server, an earth-based communications station is installed. The generic name for this station is very small aperture terminal (VSAT). It includes two parts: a transceiver (a satellite dish) that is placed outdoors in direct line of sight to one of several special data satellites in geostationary orbit around the earth and a modem-like device that is connected to the dish, placed indoors, and connected to a computer or LAN. In a mobile implementation, the dish may be mounted on a land- or water-based vehicle. When a satellite travels in a geostationary orbit, it moves at the same speed as the earth's rotation and it is always positioned over the same place on the earth. Therefore the dish can be focused precisely on the satellite.

The satellite links to large hub stations where the VSAT operators, and now various ISPs, are located along with their very-high-speed backbones for cross-country network connectivity (see Figure 10A.6).

WLAN Connections

Wireless LANs are very common now, and are based on a technology that is often referred to as Wi-Fi (short for wireless fidelity). The distance covered by a wireless local area network (WLAN) is usually measured in feet (or meters) rather than miles. Therefore, this is not a technology that connects directly to an ISP (as a WWAN or satellite connection will) but can be used to connect to another LAN or device through which Internet access is achieved.

FIGURE 10A.6

A signal travels from a VSAT to a satellite, then back to earth to a large hub station where it is connected to the Internet. Return signals make a similar trip.

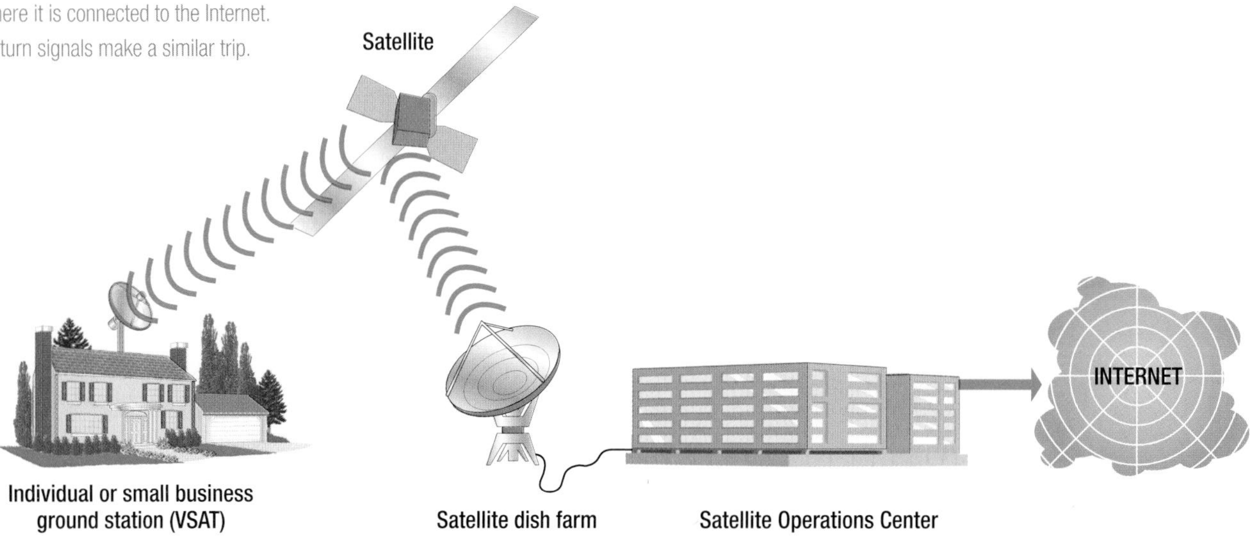

On a WLAN, a wireless access point acts as a wireless hub or switch. The most common implementations of WLANs involve using a wireless access point to link wireless computers to a wired LAN so they can use resources on the LAN and/or connect through a router to the Internet (see Figure 10A.7).

To connect to the Internet, the wireless access point is connected to a wired LAN like any other device, and then computers with wireless NICs can access the LAN. The wireless access point may be purchased in combination with other features such as firewalls, routers, and switches. A wireless access point may be attached to a port on a standard hub or switch being used by the LAN.

To connect to the wireless access point, the PC or laptop will need a wireless NIC. This device can be a PCI card NIC, an external USB NIC, or a Type II card that goes into the slot on the side of the laptop.

More security on WLANs is necessary because of a growing practice, called war driving, in which people travel around a city carrying a specialized device, or simple notebook computer equipped with a wireless NIC, searching for unprotected WLANs. These are often referred to as hot spots. The intent is to publicize these locations by marking buildings with symbols that tell others in-the-know that the marked building is a hot spot. This advertising of an unprotected WLAN gives access to a private network, which opens up the possibility of all types of threats.

If you plan to connect to the Internet via a wireless LAN connection, you should enable encryption on the wireless access point and on all computers you wish to have connect. You will first need to ensure that the access point, your wireless NICs on each computer, and your operating systems all support the same level of encryption, and that you understand how to configure it properly on each device. Most WLAN devices and OSes support an encryption standard called Wire Equivalent Privacy (WEP). This encryption method has proven easy to defeat by war drivers and others. As a consequence, another standard, Wi-Fi Protected Access (WPA), was created. It works with existing hardware and software that have been upgraded and new devices that are WEP-enabled out of the box.

FIGURE 10A.7

A WLAN connected via an access point to a wired LAN

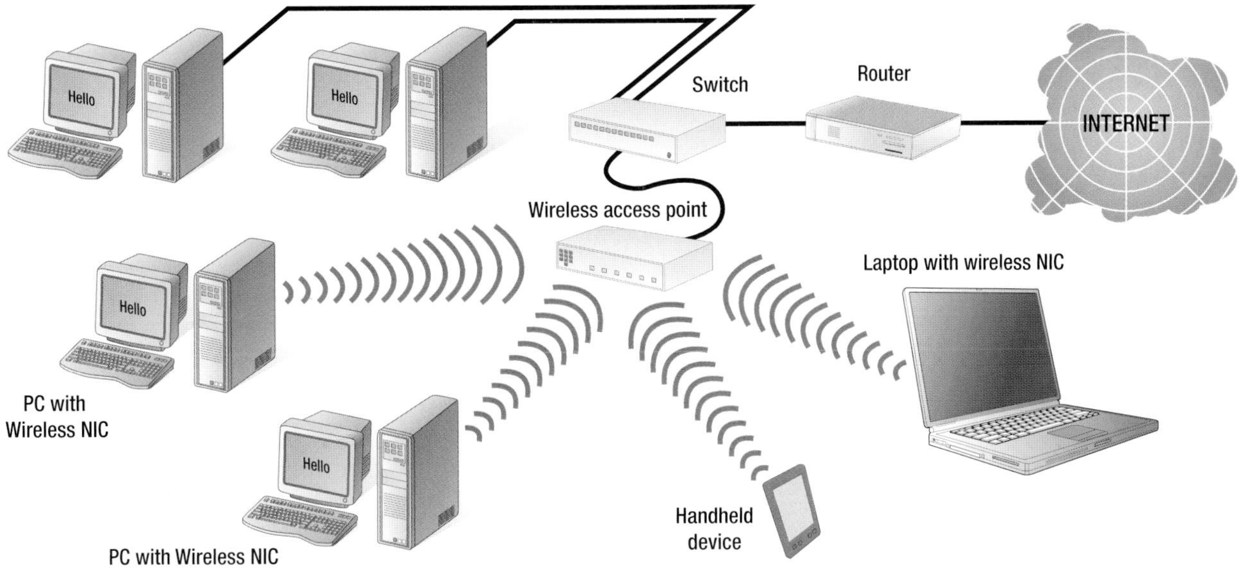

Productivity Tip

Sharing an Internet Connection

If you have just one PC at home, you can probably think of many reasons to set up another computer. One of the best reasons to have multiple PCs is to allow two or more people to access the Internet at one time.

But that kind of convenience comes with a catch. Even if you plan on installing multiple computers, your home probably has only one Internet connection. This means you need to find a way for all those PCs to share that single connection.

If this news is enough to make you rethink that second PC, it shouldn't be. Once your computers are set up to share an Internet connection, they'll be able to share just about anything else. How's that for convenience?

First, You Need a Network

There are two different ways to share an Internet connection, but both require that the computers be networked together. (For more information on networking, see Chapter 9, "Networking.") The idea of setting up a home network might seem intimidating, but it shouldn't be. If your needs are simple, you can easily find home networking kits that contain all the hardware and software you need to do the job, for surprisingly little money.

If your computers are in the same room or are separated only by a wall, then you should be able to set up a wire-based network without too much effort. Otherwise, consider installing a wireless network. Although wireless networks are a bit more expensive, they give you greater flexibility than wired networks. With a wireless LAN, for example, you can move your computers to different rooms and still stay connected to the network.

Of course, it's beyond the scope of this article to teach you how to set up a network...even a very small one. But there are plenty of resources that can help you get started. Your instructor should be able to recommend some helpful books and Web sites. You can also visit this book's site (http://www.mhteched.com/Norton) for an up-to-date list of Web sites geared toward networking basics.

Sharing a Broadband Connection

If your home's Internet connection is broadband, using a cable modem or DSL connection, then it should be easy to share. The first PC should already be connected to the cable or DSL modem via a network interface card and cable. To add another computer to this type of Internet connection, install an inexpensive router (sometimes called a "hub/router" or even a "residential gateway"). For about $50, these devices allow two or more PCs to share a connection.

Connect the modem to the router, and then connect each of the PCs to the router by running the appropriate type of cable from each PC's network interface card to one of the router's available ports. For standard wire-based networks, Category-5 cabling is commonly used. (Of course, wireless options are available as well, but your PCs will need wireless NICs that are compatible with a wireless router. Again, look for a kit or a set of products that are made to work together.)

When you share a broadband connection this way, it's usually a "plug-and-play" affair. If your components are well matched, and if you are using Windows XP, your PCs should be online as soon as the connections are established. There should be little, if any, software configuring to do.

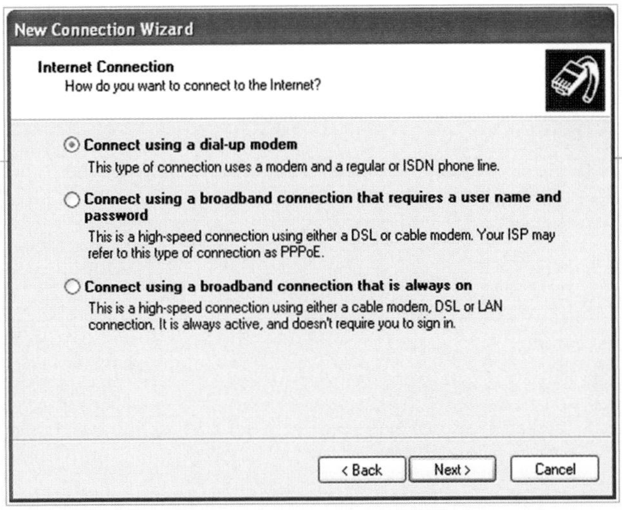

The New Connection Wizard.

Sharing a Dial-Up Connection

If your first computer accesses the Internet through a dial-up connection (using a standard modem and telephone line), sharing a connection can be a bit trickier. You need to connect your computers together using an Ethernet hub or switch. Once your network is established, you can use the Internet Connection Sharing (ICS) feature in Windows to set up the shared connection. ICS is available in Windows 98 Second Edition, Windows Me, Windows 2000, and Windows XP.

ICS provides an easy-to-use wizard to walk you through the process of sharing the connection. Before you start, make sure that your network is set up and all computers are on. Back up your data, and study the ICS information in Windows' help system. Then, launch the ICS wizard and follow the instructions that appear on your screen.

If ICS doesn't work for you, or if you prefer to try a different connection-sharing program, other software tools are available. For example, you might try WinGate or WinProxy as an alternative to ICS. Be warned, however, that these tools work in a slightly different manner than ICS and can be more difficult to configure, especially if you are not familiar with networking.

PRODUCTIVITY TIP

LESSON // 10A Review

Summary

- The two primary means of connecting a computer to the Internet are through wires or through wireless means.
- There are several ways to connect to the Internet through wires. The most common way is through a standard 56 Kbps modem and telephone line. This establishes a dial-up connection.
- A dial-up connection works like other kinds of phone calls, because the computer's modem must dial a telephone number to contact the ISP's servers. The connection lasts until the user's computer or ISP's server hangs up.
- Broadband connections are an increasingly popular way to access the Internet. To be considered broadband, a connection must be faster than a dial-up connection. Using a broadband connection, it is possible to transmit data as much as 10 times faster than is possible through a standard dial-up connection.
- Integrated services digital network (ISDN) service can transmit data up to 128 Kbps using a standard phone line, but the service is falling out of favor because faster services are available.
- There are several types of Digital Subscriber Line (DSL) services, each with a different name and different level of service. DSL services transmit data at speeds ranging from 128 Kbps to 8.448 Mbps.
- Subscribers to cable television services can use a special cable modem to access the Internet through their cable TV connection.
- To communicate with the Internet, PC applications use a special type of program, called an application programming interface. The API for Windows is called Winsock.
- Wireless Internet connections are increasingly popular, and take several forms.
- A wireless WAN (WWAN) allows users to connect over a large geographic area, as long as their wireless devices can transmit and receive the proper signals. Some WWANS can transmit data at speeds higher than 100 Mbps.
- Many high-speed Internet connections make use of satellite technologies. Satellite connections are the answer for users living in remote areas with limited or no telephone service.
- A wireless LAN (WLAN) is like a wired LAN in that it covers a small geographic area. Typically, the wireless portion of the LAN connects to a wired portion, which makes the physical connection with the Internet.
- Wireless LANs require additional security measures to prevent unauthorized users from tapping into the network and gaining access to servers or other users' systems. Security schemes such as WEP and WPA are designed to prevent unauthorized access to wireless networks.

Key Terms ::

Asynchronous DSL (ADSL), 385
broadband, 384
cable modem service, 386
dial-up connection, 384
Digital Subscriber Line (DSL), 385
hot spot, 391
integrated services digital network (ISDN), 385
Sockets, 386
Synchronous DSL (SDSL), 385
very small aperture terminal (VSAT), 390
war driving, 391
Wi-Fi Protected Access (WPA), 391
Winsock, 386
Wire Equivalent Privacy (WEP), 391
wireless local area network (WLAN), 390
wireless wide area network (WWAN), 387

Key Term Quiz ::

Complete each statement by writing one of the terms listed under Key Terms in each blank.

1. In a(n) __________ connection, your computer uses its modem to dial a telephone number given to you by the ISP.
2. To be considered a(n) __________ connection, a connection must be able to transmit data at a rate faster than is possible with a dial-up connection.
3. A(n) __________ data connection can transfer data up to 128 Kbps.
4. __________ service is similar to ISDN, but uses more advanced digital signal processing and algorithms to compress more signals through the telephone lines.
5. __________ provides downstream speeds that are much faster than its upstream speeds.
6. Because of its costs __________ service is only recommended for customers who must upload a great deal of data.
7. __________ service transmits data through coaxial cable.
8. The adaptation of the Sockets API for Windows is called __________ .
9. The distance covered by a(n) __________ is usually measured in feet (or meters).
10. An unprotected wireless LAN is sometimes called a(n) __________ .

Multiple Choice ::

Circle the word or phrase that best completes each statement.

1. This type of Internet connection might be compared to a regular telephone call, in terms of its duration.
   a. satellite b. broadband c. dial-up d. dish
2. Many homes and small businesses connect to the Internet by using a telephone line and this.
   a. A 5.6 Kbps modem b. A 56 Kbps modem c. A 560 Kbps modem d. A 5,600 Kbps modem
3. High-speed Internet connections are sometimes called __________ connections.
   a. broadband b. highband c. bigband d. wideband
4. A broadband connection may provide a home computer user with data transfer speeds that are __________ times faster than a standard 56K modem link.
   a. 10,000 b. 1,000 c. 100 d. 10
5. Which high-speed service is now dropping out of favor, because higher-performance services are becoming increasingly available?
   a. T1 b. dial-up c. ISDN d. ADSL
6. Several different versions of this service are available, each offering a different level of performance.
   a. ISDN b. DSL c. cable modem d. satellite
7. Which abbreviation is used to refer to DSL service in general?
   a. *a*DSL b. *x*DSL c. *y*DSL d. *n*DSL
8. Sockets and Winsock are examples of this type of software.
   a. VCR b. DSL c. IPX d. API
9. Which of the following is a network that extends over a large geographical area?
   a. WLAN b. WWAN c. WEP d. WSAT
10. Wi-Fi Protected Access was created as a replacement for this encryption standard.
    a. WEP b. WPA c. WLAN d. WWAN

LESSON // 10A Review

Review Questions ::

In your own words, briefly answer the following questions.

1. What are the two primary methods for connecting a computer to the Internet?
2. In basic terms, how does a dial-up Internet connection work?
3. Who commonly provides high-speed Internet connections?
4. Describe the type of service provided by ISDN.
5. List four variations of DSL service.
6. What range of data transmission speeds are available for the various types of DSL service?
7. Identify two significant drawbacks to DSL services.
8. How is a wireless WAN's coverage area measured?
9. What is a very small aperture terminal (VSAT)?
10. What is war driving?

Lesson Labs ::

Complete the following exercises as directed by your instructor.

1. Determine whether your computer has a modem. (You may need your instructor's assistance to complete this exercise.) Open the Control Panel. If you see a Phone and Modem Options icon, select the icon to open the Phone and Modem Options dialog box. (Depending on which version of Windows you use, this icon may have a different name.) Write down the information about your modem. Close the Phone and Modem Options dialog box.
2. Use Control Panel to see whether your PC has a network interface card installed. In Control Panel, select the System icon to open the System Properties dialog box. Select the Device Manager tab, and then select the plus sign (+) next to Network adapters. (In Windows XP, you can access the Device Manager through the Hardware tab.) If any adapters are installed, the list expands to show them. Select each adapter in turn, and select Properties to display the Properties dialog box. Write down the information for each adapter, and then select Cancel. Close the Control Panel window.

LESSON // 10B

Doing Business in the Online World

Overview: Commerce on the World Wide Web

The World Wide Web has become a global vehicle for electronic commerce (e-commerce), creating new ways for businesses to interact with one another and their customers. E-commerce means doing business online, such as when a consumer buys a product over the Web instead of going to a store to buy it.

E-commerce technologies are rapidly changing the way individuals and companies do business. You can go online to buy a book, lease a car, shop for groceries, or rent movies. You can even get a pizza delivered to your door without picking up the phone.

But these kinds of transactions are only the tip of the e-commerce iceberg. In fact, the vast majority of e-commerce activities do not involve consumers at all. They are conducted among businesses, which have developed complex networking systems dedicated to processing orders, managing inventories, and handling payments.

This lesson introduces you to the basics of e-commerce at the consumer and business levels. You will learn how to make sure your online shopping and browsing activities are secure, and how to protect your personal information when using the Internet.

OBJECTIVES ::

- Explain, in basic terms, what *e-commerce* is.
- Describe two e-commerce activities that are important to consumers.
- Describe one important way businesses use e-commerce technologies.
- Explain the role of intranets and extranets in business-to-business e-commerce.
- List two ways to make sure you are shopping on a secure Web page.

Norton ONLINE

For more information on e-commerce for consumers, visit **http://www.mhhe.com/peternorton**.

simnet™

E-Commerce at the Consumer Level

Tens of thousands of online businesses cater to the needs of consumers. These companies' Web sites provide information about products and services, take orders, receive payments, and provide on-the-spot customer service. Consumer-oriented e-commerce Web sites take many forms and cover the gamut of products and services, but can be divided into two general categories: shopping sites and personal-finance sites.

Online Shopping

Online shopping means buying a product or service through a Web site. (Another term for online shopping is business-to-consumer (B2C) transaction.) Even if you have never shopped online, you probably have heard of Web sites such as Amazon.com and Buy.com (see Figure 10B.1). They are just two of the many popular Web sites where consumers can buy all sorts of things.

What can you buy online? The list is almost limitless—including everything from cars to appliances, electronics to jewelry, clothes to books, fine wines to old-fashioned candies. You can subscribe to your favorite newspaper or magazine online, hunt for antiques, and order complete holiday meals for delivery to your door. You can even buy and sell items of all kinds on auction sites like eBay—a one-time fad that has turned into a full-time business for thousands of eBay users (see Figure 10B.2)

There are thousands of consumer Web sites and each has its own look, feel, and approach to customer satisfaction. But effective online shopping sites share a few essential features:

- A catalog where you can search for information about products and services.
- A "checkout" section where you can securely pay for the items you want to purchase.
- A customer-service page, where you can contact the merchant for assistance.

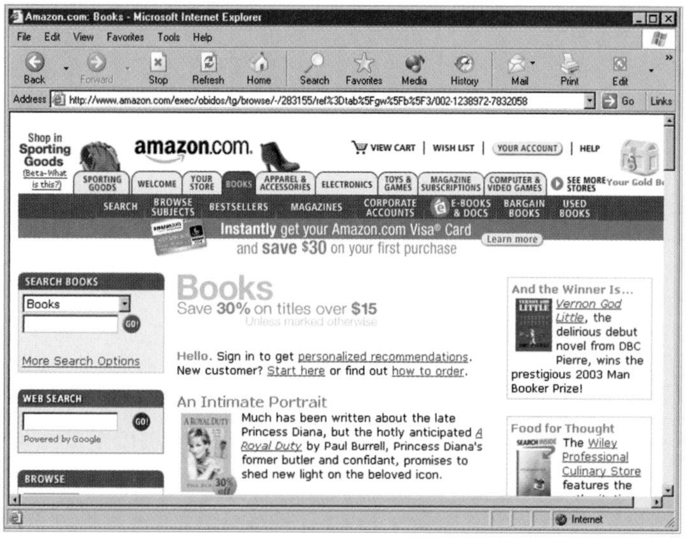

FIGURE 10B.1

Like many e-commerce sites that target consumers, Amazon.com offers a catalog, extensive help, secure purchasing, customer service, and other features.

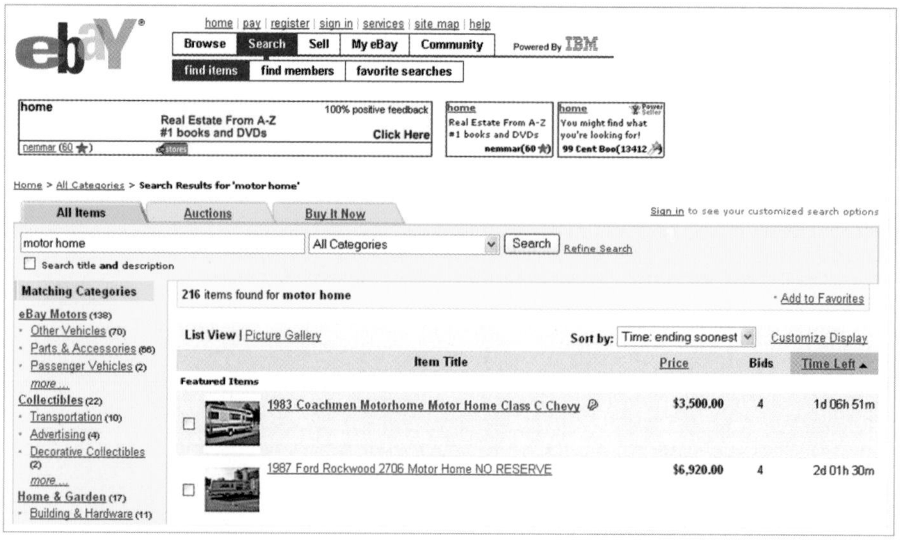

FIGURE 10B.2

At auction sites like eBay, you can bid on just about any kind of item imaginable.

Online Stores versus Physical Locations

In a brick-and-mortar store (that is, a physical store that you can visit in person to do your shopping), you can wander the aisles and see the merchandise for yourself (see Figure 10B.3). If the store is too big or the layout too confusing, you can ask a clerk or a customer service representative for guidance. This is one big advantage of going to the store yourself.

In an online store (that is, a store that exists only on the Web, with no physical locations you can visit), you don't have that advantage. You can't walk the aisles, pick up the merchandise, or grab some free samples. You have to do all your shopping in your browser window. Amazon.com and PCConnection.com are examples of online stores, because they have no "real" store you can go to.

A hybrid merchant is called a click-and-mortar store—a physical store that also has a Web site where you can shop. Best Buy and Nordstrom are examples of click-and-mortar stores because they have physical locations in many cities, as well as Web sites where you can view and purchase their products (see Figure 10B.4). Some click-and-mortar retailers let customers buy items online, then pick them up or return them at the store. This arrangement offers the best of both worlds in convenience and customer service.

FIGURE 10B.3

Sometimes there is no substitute for shopping in a real store.

Using Online Catalogs

Online shopping would be very difficult if merchants did not provide easy-to-use catalogs on their Web sites. In the early days of e-commerce, many retailers struggled to come up with catalogs that were user-friendly for customers and easy to manage. Retail-oriented Web sites need to be maintained and updated on a continuing basis, so that prices and descriptions are always correct. Site managers and designers must be careful to balance their own needs against those of consumers, or they risk losing business.

Many e-commerce Web sites are set up like directories (see Figure 10B.5). These catalogs lump products or services into categories and subcategories. If you

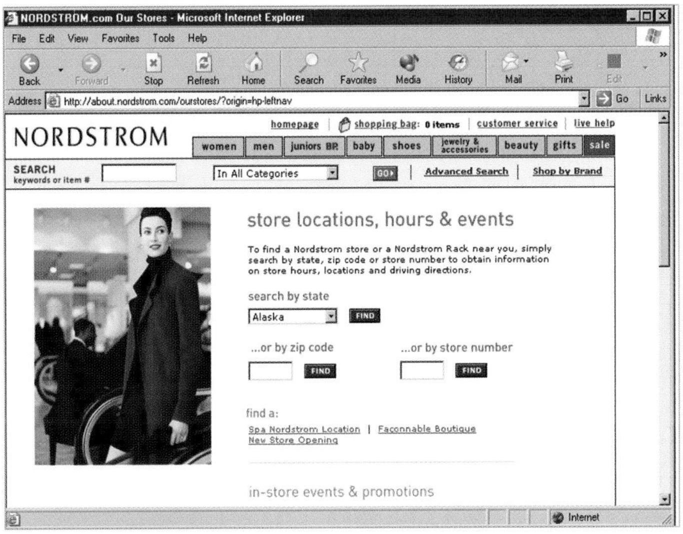

FIGURE 10B.4

Nordstrom is an example of a "click-and-mortar" store, with physical locations and an online presence.

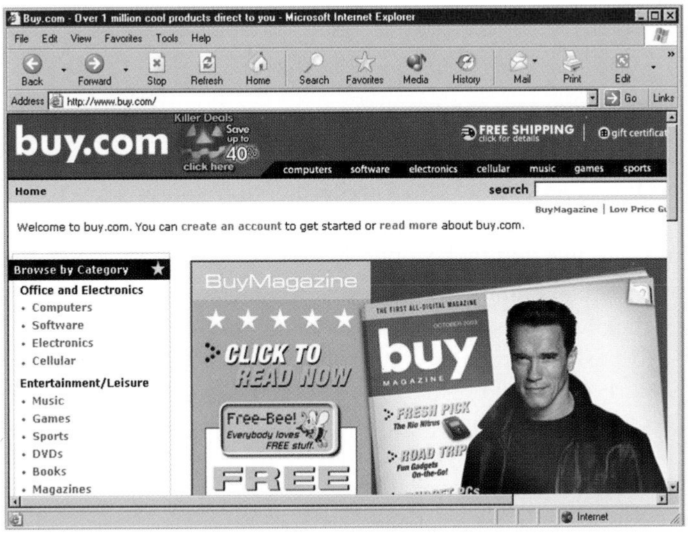

FIGURE 10B.5

Like many online merchants, Buy.com categorizes its products, making it easy to find anything in its online catalog.

are shopping for an MP3 player at the Web site of an electronics vendor, for example, you might click the Electronics category first, then the Personal Electronics subcategory, then Personal Audio, then Handheld Devices, and then MP3 Players.

Along with a directory of product categories, you may find a Search tool at your favorite online shopping site. Like any Web search engine, this tool lets you conduct a keyword search, but the search occurs only on the merchant's site instead of the entire Web. So, if you are shopping for boots on a site that sells outdoor gear, you should be able to click in the Search box, type **boots**, and press ENTER. The site will then display a list of products or pages that match your interest (see Figure 10B.6).

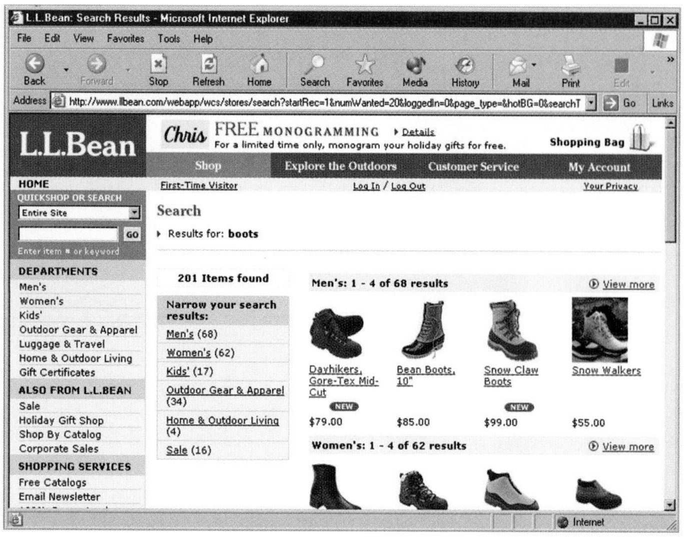

FIGURE 10B.6

Searching for boots at the L.L. Bean Web site.

Paying for Purchases

Online merchants usually try to make online shopping as similar as possible to shopping at a real store. One way they do this is by letting shoppers fill a shopping cart—an electronic holding area that stores information about items that the customer has chosen for purchasing (see Figure 10B.7).

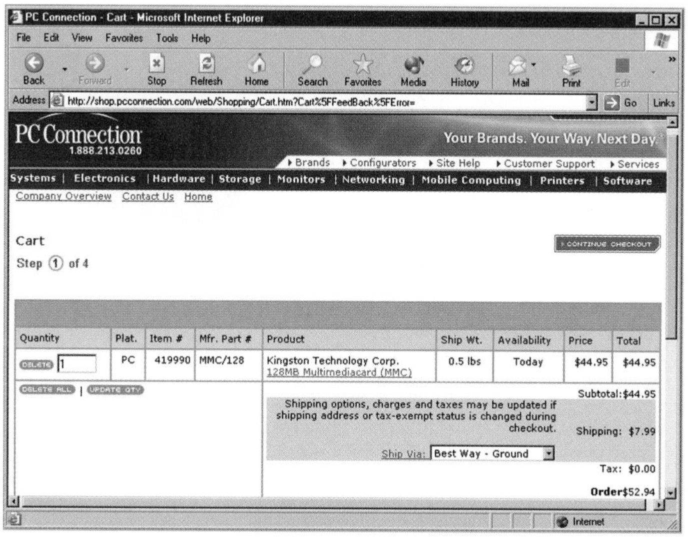

FIGURE 10B.7

An example of an electronic shopping cart at the PC Connection Web site. This user is preparing to purchase a memory upgrade for a computer. The cart shows the product, model information, price, quantity, in-stock status, shipping charges, and more.

When you are ready to make your purchase, you can pay for it in several ways. Two of the most common payment methods include the following:

» **One-Time Credit Card Purchase.** If you do not want to set up an account with the seller, you can provide your personal and credit card information each time you make a purchase.

» **Set Up an Online Account.** If you think you will make other purchases from the online vendor, you can set up an account at the Web site (see Figure 10B.8). The vendor stores your personal and credit card information on a secure server, and then places a special file (called a cookie) on your computer's disk. Later, when you access your account again by typing a user ID and password, the site uses information in the cookie to access your account. Online accounts are required at some vendors' Web sites, such as brokerage sites that provide online investing services.

Getting Customer Service

Would you buy clothes at a department store that had no Customer Service counter? Probably not. When you spend your money, you want to make sure that someone will be available to help if you have a problem. This is just as true on the Web as in any store.

Before you buy anything from a Web site, check its customer service resources (see Figure 10B.9). Look for the following information:

- **Contact Information.** You should be able to contact a customer service representative by telephone and by regular mail—not just by e-mail. If the site does not display at least one customer service number and one mailing address, consider shopping elsewhere.
- **Return Policies.** If you want to return a product that you bought online, you will probably be responsible for packing it up and shipping it. You may need to get an authorization number or take other steps to ensure that the return is handled correctly.
- **Shipping Policies.** Before ordering, find out what your shipping options are. Many online vendors use the least expensive means of shipping unless you ask for something else. Always check the shipping charges before checking out, and make sure they are reasonable.
- **Charges and Fees.** Some online vendors charge processing fees or other "hidden" fees, which that may not be described when you purchase something. Look for signs that the seller charges such fees.

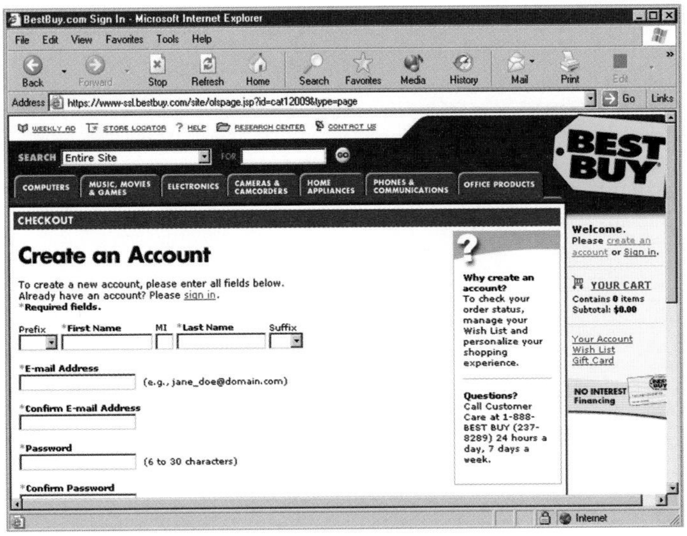

FIGURE 10B.8

Setting up an account at the Best Buy Web site.

Online Banking and Finance

simnet™

Retailers are not the only businesses reaching out to consumers over the Web. No matter where you live in the United States, there's a good chance that your local bank has a Web site where you can manage your accounts. If you are interested in investing, borrowing money, buying insurance, applying for a credit card, or doing some other task involving personal finance, you can do that online, too.

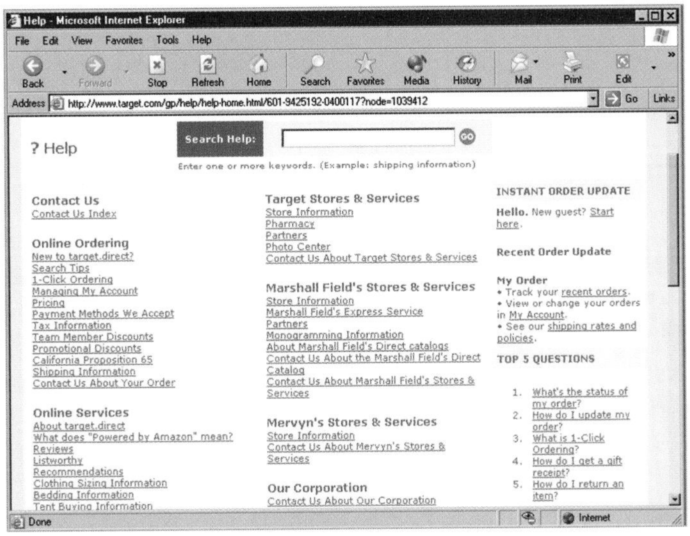

FIGURE 10B.9

Always look for customer service information before buying anything through a Web site. This is the main Help page at Target's Web site.

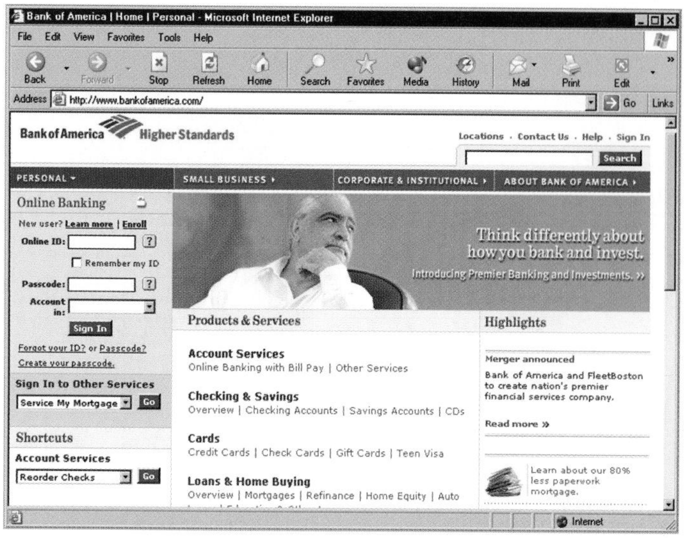

FIGURE 10B.10

Like many banks' Web sites, the Bank of America site lets customers create and manage accounts, pay bills, and do other banking.

Online Banking

The term online banking refers to using a bank's Web site to handle banking-related tasks (see Figure 10B.10). Individuals and businesses alike can visit any bank's Web site and do the following:

- Create an account
- Transfer funds
- Record or view transactions
- Reconcile statements
- Pay bills

If you use a personal-finance program at home (such as Microsoft Money or Quicken), it can use your Internet connection to access your bank accounts online. This feature makes it easy to manage your accounts and keep your checkbook balanced.

Online Finance

The term online finance refers to any kind of personal financial transaction you can conduct online, other than managing your bank accounts (see Figure 10B.11). These activities include:

- Investing
- Applying for loans
- Applying for credit cards
- Buying insurance
- Preparing tax returns and paying taxes
- Doing financial research or seeking financial advice

SELF-CHECK ::

Circle the correct answer for each question.

1. Which of the following is not an essential feature of an effective e-commerce Web site?

   a. catalog b. customer service c. great graphics

2. Which of the following is making it easy for companies to handle huge volumes of transactions?

   a. protocols b. Web-based technologies c. online catalogs

3. You should avoid shopping at a Web site if its customer service department can be reached only by this means.

   a. e-mail b. telephone c. regular mail

E-Commerce at the Business Level

Beyond individual consumer transactions, e-commerce has given companies an entirely different way to conduct business. Using powerful Web sites and online databases, companies not only sell goods to individual customers, but also track inventory, order products, send invoices, and receive payments. Using e-commerce technologies (ranging from standard networks to supercomputers), companies are rapidly forming online partnerships to collaborate on product designs, sales and marketing campaigns, and more. By giving one another access to their private networks, corporate partners access vital information and work together more efficiently.

Norton ONLINE

For more information on business-to-business e-commerce, visit **http://www.mhhe.com/peternorton**.

simnet™

Business-to-Business (B2B) Transactions

Although millions of consumer transactions take place each day on the Web, business-to-business (B2B) transactions actually account for most of the money that is spent online. As its name implies, a business-to-business transaction is one that takes place between companies; consumers are not involved.

The concept of B2B transactions did not arrive with the Internet. In fact, companies were doing business electronically long before the rise of the Web, by using

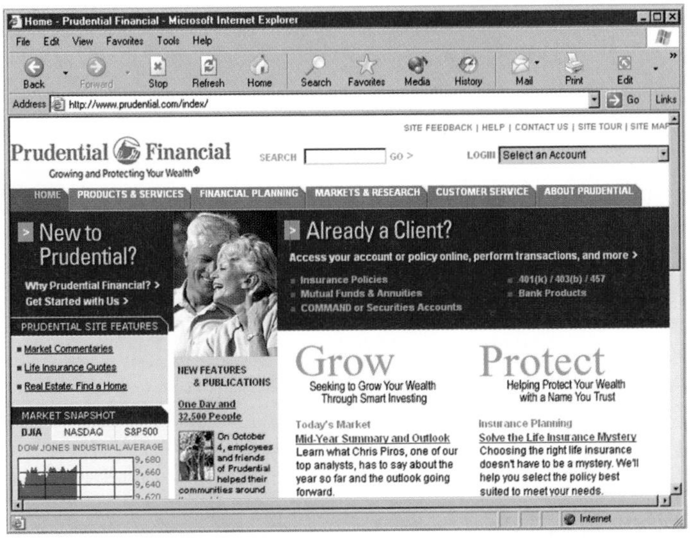

FIGURE 10B.11

At Prudential Financial's Web site, clients can investigate insurance options, make investments, get advice, and do other financial tasks.

private networks and computer systems to handle transactions. But Internet technologies have made the process easier, more efficient, and available to virtually all businesses.

Any financial transaction between two companies can be considered a B2B transaction, and probably can be handled over the Internet (see Figure 10B.12). Consider some examples:

- A store orders an out-of-stock product from a distributor.
- A car manufacturer orders parts from a wide range of suppliers.
- A stock broker buys shares for a client by using an electronic exchange.
- A bank requests credit information from a major credit-reporting agency.

FIGURE 10B.12

Ordering parts or products from a supplier is one of the most common types of B2B transaction.

You can probably think of other examples, too. In any case, the transaction occurs whether it is handled on paper, through a private network, or via the Internet. It does not necessarily have to take place on the Web. However, Web-based technologies are making it easy for companies to handle huge volumes of transactions.

Intranets and Extranets

Businesses use many different means to handle transactions electronically. For example, two companies may have their own networks, but may link them together so they can share certain resources and exchange certain types of data. Using this kind of link, for example, a design firm and a building contractor can collaborate on designs, quickly make changes to shared documents, update schedules, conduct online meetings, and transmit invoices to one another.

But most companies do business with many other companies, not just one. For this reason, they need to have systems that are flexible enough to handle an ever-changing array of partners or customers. An effective way to do this is to create corporate networks that look and function like the Internet, and which grant access to authorized external users through the Internet. These specialized business networks are called intranets and extranets.

An **intranet** is a corporate network that uses the same protocols as the Internet, but which belongs exclusively to a corporation, school, or some other organization. The intranet is accessible only to the organization's workers. If the intranet is connected to the Internet, then it is secured by a special device called a firewall, which prevents unauthorized external users from gaining access to it.

Norton ONLINE

For more information on intranets and extranets, visit **http://www.mhhe.com/peternorton**.

simnet™

Norton Notebook

Business, the Internet, and Everything

When the Internet was first developed by scientists and academics, its purpose was to share research and communication more effectively. At the time, fax machines and overnight express delivery were still years away, and moving data electronically across the country was a revolutionary opportunity. The problem with revolutions, as Maximilien Robespierre could certainly attest, is that, once you've got them started, they tend to take on a life of their own far beyond the imaginings and ideals of their founders. No one involved with the early development of Internet technologies started out thinking, "We're going to make a packet of money with this." It wasn't until nearly 20 years after initial work on what became the Internet that the World Wide Web was developed, and businesspeople suddenly came to the conclusion that the Internet was some kind of idealized television. That is to say, a new medium where, for the small cost of producing a little lowest-common-denominator entertainment or news, companies could get customers to willingly sit through endless streams of product advertisements—with the added bonus that you could actually *sell* your products directly over the Internet, and even get people to *pay you* to ship them out. On television, it was necessary to create engaging advertisements that motivated people out of their homes and into the stores. On the Web, everything available for sale could be turned into a high-profile impulse buy.

Riding high on this wave of idealistic consumerism, thousands of people with a little technical savvy—some of them, very little—created initial public offerings of stock (IPOs) for tech companies that were going to do amazing things. Nobody was sure what those amazing things would be, but everyone knew that someone else was doing the actual work, developing actual products to solve actual problems. All you had to do was put up a Web page with a cool animated logo and keep your eyes open for the right coattails to ride all the way to the bank. The stock market found itself littered—and I use that word with precision—with thousands of "dot com" companies. Even respectable, established corporations were taken in by the charade, investing their employees' 401(k) retirement plans in these promising newcomers with no products, no profits, but stratospheric stock prices: "So the word *must* be that they're about to come out with the next must-have thing!" But they weren't, and they didn't. In an atmosphere of general economic downturn, hundreds of thousands of jobs and billions of dollars simply evaporated. Magazines and books from 1995 to 2001 were stuffed with messages that the Internet had created a new economy in which old business methods and rules simply no longer applied. They were wrong. At the end of the day, by which I mean around the middle of 2001, it remained true that one must spend less than one makes, one must satisfy one's customers, and one must actually produce or provide something of value in order for one to make a profit. Business is still business-as-usual.

Or is it? Despite the disappearance of the majority of "Internet companies," the Internet remains, and online technology continues to evolve in areas of tangible products and services. That technology is real, and it has changed more about us than we may initially realize. Consider, by way of example, the motion picture industry. This century-old industry has spread from Thomas Edison's lab in New Jersey to

An **extranet** is an intranet that can be accessed by authorized outside users over the Internet. To gain entrance to the extranet's resources, an external user typically must log on to the network by providing a user name and a password.

Intranets and extranets are popular for several reasons:

- Because they use the same protocols as the Internet, they are simpler and less expensive to install than many other kinds of networks.
- Because they enable users to work in standard (and usually free) Web browsers, they provide a consistent, friendly interface (see Figure 10B.13).
- Because they function with standard security technologies, they provide excellent security against unauthorized access.

Telecommuters

A **telecommuter** is someone who normally works in a location other than the company's office or factory (see Figure 10B.14). Most telecommuters work from their homes, while many are constantly moving from one location to another. Either way, telecommuters rely on computers and Internet connections to do their jobs.

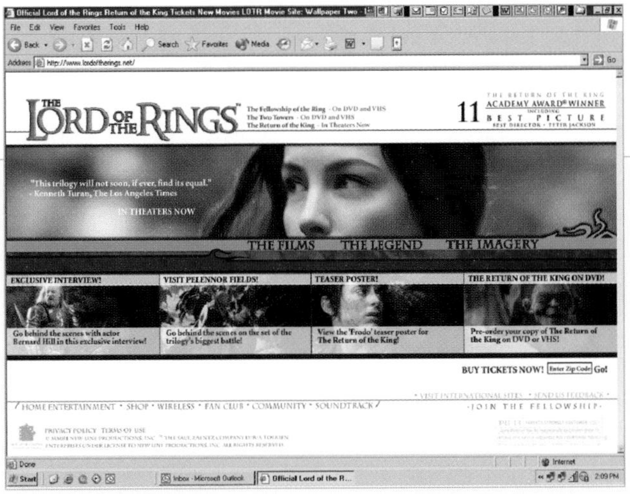

Hollywood, and on to "Bollywood" in India. Thanks to the development of DVD technology, it's often no longer vital that a movie earn a profit at the box office. Films that are financial flops can be repackaged, repositioned, and sold on DVD to an ever-thriving movie rental industry and home purchasers. Profits from DVD sales are so great that motion picture studios have begun to instruct directors to think from the beginning in terms of the two movies she or he wants to make—the first to be shown in theatres, the second to be available exclusively on a multidisc DVD package including "never-before-seen" footage. At first, most of these never-before-seen add-ins were nothing more than scraps from the cutting room floor—material that the director had deemed of insufficient quality to be shown in the theatre. Now, however, additional viable footage is intentionally shot and budgeted, never to be shown in theatres . . . but you can purchase it for private viewing. The Internet comes into this equation with the realization that the same digital video and broadband technologies developed in the hope of creating profitable "interactive television" made it possible for consumers to copy and share DVD content without paying for it. That technology also enables small production houses to create, market, and sell their motion pictures, circumventing traditional distribution channels and, sometimes, retailers. And the open forum provided by the worldwide Internet has led to the dissemination of instructions and tools for defeating copy protection methodologies.

So, traditional businesses that weren't damaged in the vast failure of Internet companies may find themselves damaged by the vast success of the Internet itself. Most media companies have retaliated by wasting millions of taxpayer dollars clogging the courts with questions like "What is ownership?" and "What do we actually mean when we say 'purchase'?" These are desperate attempts to turn back time and undo what is already sitting in millions of offices and homes. To survive, these businesses will have to redefine themselves and move forward in a post-Internet world, embracing the individual's ownership of powerful technology. They must spend less than they make, satisfy their customers, and produce something of value in order to make a profit—business as usual!

NORTON NOTEBOOK

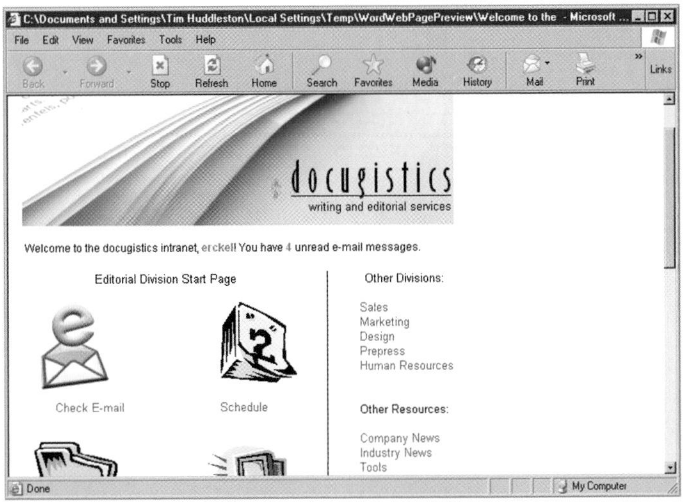

FIGURE 10B.13

An intranet's interface can look and work like any other Web page, allowing users to access resources and perform tasks in a browser window.

Computers In Your Career

Career Opportunities and the Internet

As customer relationship management (CRM) supervisor for Jenny Craig Inc., in Carlsbad, California, Jon Kosoff starts his day when he clicks on his e-mail box in the morning to check his messages, and then prioritizes the day's projects. After that it's anything goes, and Kosoff wouldn't have it any other way.

"My job is very project-oriented, so no two days are ever the same," says Kosoff, who holds a degree in economics from the University of California Santa Barbara. He says the technical training he's learned along the way, combined with a solid financial foundation, has helped him not only to use technology, but to also understand the return on investment that his employer gains from its use.

Kosoff oversees Jenny Craig's e-mail and Web site as well as the integration of customer data into the company's database and marketing efforts. That means using the Internet in conjunction with the firm's internal database to reach customers worldwide. "When I started here four years ago, we were sending out 4,000 text-based e-mails a month," says Kosoff. "Today we send out about 700,000 Flash and HTML messages a month."

Other key duties include updating Jenny Craig's Web site content to ensure that it represents the firm's current business objectives. That's not as easy as it sounds, says Kosoff, who explains that the firm has gone through a number of leadership changes over the last few years. Such changes lead to business objective changes and can have a profound effect on a firm's overall Web site and marketing strategy.

Perhaps the most satisfying aspect of working with the Internet, Kosoff adds, is the instant gratification that it provides. "You can see what you've done almost instantly, and share it not only with the company," he says, "but also with your friends and family 24/7."

Internet careers are among those expected to be the fastest growing occupations through 2010, according to the Bureau of Labor Statistics. Robert Half International reports

FIGURE 10B.14

Today, many people work at home and use a PC to access their company's network through the Internet. Companies must take measures to ensure that this kind of access is secure.

Telecommuters usually use their home computer to access the Internet, which in turn lets them connect to their employers' private network. This connection may take place through an extranet, but other kinds of networking techniques can be used to give telecommuters access to the network while keeping everyone else out.

Security

Until 1998, e-commerce was slow to gain acceptance among consumers who were concerned about security. Many people feared that it was not safe to provide personal or credit card information over the Internet because it was possible for criminals to intercept the data and use it, or to steal it from unprotected Web servers. Those fears have largely been eliminated, however, with improved security measures and public perception of the Internet's safety.

It is actually very easy to make sure that you are surfing safely and keeping your personal information secure while online, even when you are giving credit card numbers to a Web merchant.

Reputable e-commerce Web sites (especially those run by well-known companies) use sophisticated measures to ensure that customer information cannot fall into the hands of criminals. Online merchants typically protect customers by providing secure Web pages where customers can enter credit card and account numbers, passwords, and other personal information.

Norton ONLINE

For more information on online security, visit **http://www.mhhe.com/peternorton**.

simnet™

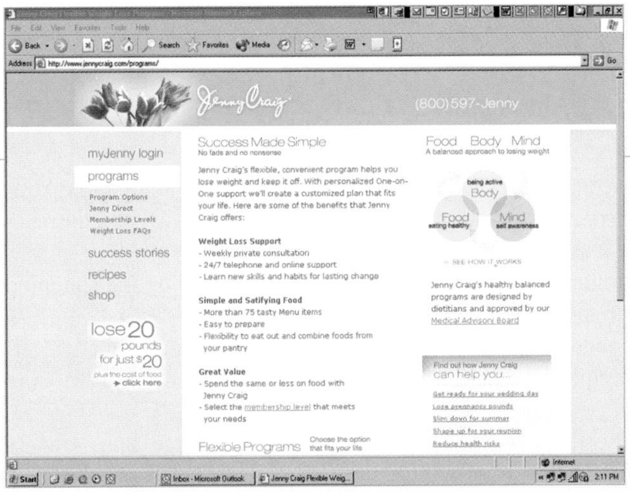

starting salaries in 2001 for Internet-related occupations ranged from $58,000 to $82,500 for Web masters, and $56,250 to $76,750 for Internet/intranet developers.

In the Internet age, there is a growing demand for network administrators, information system professionals, and data communications managers. Aside from careers that focus on architecture and administration of the Internet, many other professions require not only a working knowledge of the Internet but also a mastery of the tools used to create and distribute content across it. Here are a few such careers:

» **Web Designers and Web Masters.** Corporate Web, intranet, and extranet sites are developed, designed, and maintained most often by teams of professionals. At the helm of such teams are experienced designers and Web masters.

» **Multimedia Developers.** As more people connect to the Internet, companies face increasing competition to provide highly visual, interactive content that enables them to capture and retain visitors to their Web sites.

» **Programmers.** Programmers are finding all sorts of opportunities in Internet development because Web sites are commonly used to support high-level functions such as interactivity, searches, data mining, and more.

To secure the data you transmit to a Web site, online merchants can encode pages using secure sockets layer (SSL) technology, which encrypts data. (Encryption technology secures data by converting it into a code that is unusable by anyone who does not possess a key to the code.) If a Web page is protected by SSL, its URL will begin with https:// rather than http://.

When using an e-commerce site, you can determine if the current page is secure in two ways (see Figure 10B.15):

» **Check the URL.** If the page's URL begins with https://, the page is secure. The letter *s* indicates security measures.

» **Check Your Browser's Status Bar.** If you use Microsoft Internet Explorer or Netscape Navigator, a closed padlock symbol will appear in the browser's status bar when a secure Web page is open.

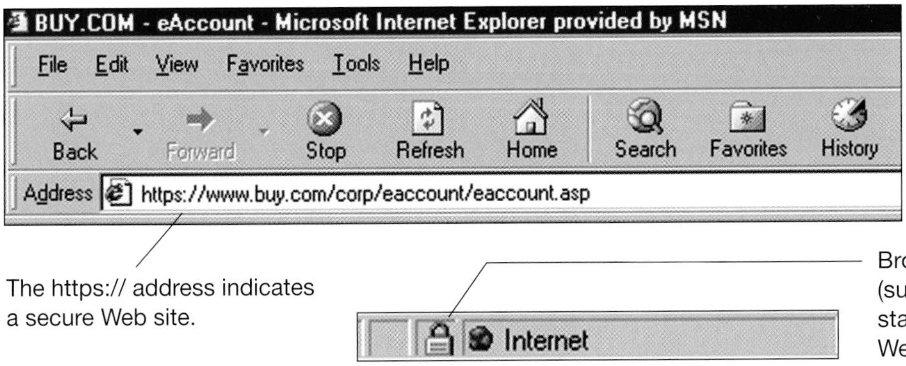

Browsers display special symbols (such as a closed padlock on the status bar) to indicate a secure Web site.

FIGURE 10B.15

Verifying that a Web page is secure.

LESSON // 10B Review

Summary ::

- Electronic commerce (e-commerce) means doing business online, and can be conducted between consumers and businesses, or among businesses with no consumer involvement.
- Two primary types of consumer-oriented e-commerce activities are online shopping and online banking and finance.
- Businesses have been conducting transactions electronically for years, but the advent of Internet technologies has made the process easier and accessible to more businesses.
- Businesses use many networking technologies to support e-commerce, but intranets and extranets make e-commerce easier by utilizing Internet technologies.
- An intranet is a corporate network that works like the Internet, but belongs exclusively to an organization.
- An extranet is an intranet that allows access by some authorized external users, usually through the Internet.
- Telecommuters are workers who work somewhere besides a company location, such as from home. They rely on computers and Internet technologies to access the company's network resources.
- Security is an important aspect of e-commerce, and enhanced security measures have contributed to the explosion of e-commerce transactions in recent years.
- Consumers can take steps to make sure they are using secure Web pages when doing business online.

Key Terms ::

brick-and-mortar store, 397
business-to-business (B2B) transaction, 402
business-to-consumer (B2C) transaction, 398
click-and-mortar store, 399
cookie, 400
electronic commerce (e-commerce), 397
encryption, 407
extranet, 404
intranet, 403
online banking, 402
online finance, 402
online shopping, 398
online store, 399
secure sockets layer (SSL), 407
secure Web page, 406
shopping cart, 400
telecommuter, 404

Key Term Quiz ::

Complete each statement by writing one of the terms listed under Key Terms in each blank.

1. ________ means doing business online.
2. ________ means buying a product or service through a Web site.
3. Another term for online shopping is ________ .
4. A(n) ________ is a store that exists only on the Web, with no physical location you can visit.
5. A(n) ________ is an electronic holding area, provided by an online merchant, that stores information about items the customer has chosen for purchasing.
6. The term ________ refers to any kind of personal financial transaction you can conduct online, other than managing your bank accounts.
7. A(n) ________ transaction is one that takes place between companies, and does not involve consumers.
8. A(n) ________ is an intranet that can be accessed by outside users over the Internet.
9. A(n) ________ is someone who normally works in a location other than the company's office or factory.
10. To secure the data you transmit to a Web site, online merchants can encode pages using ________ technology.

LESSON // 10B Review

Multiple Choice ::

Circle the word or phrase that best completes each statement.

1. This one-time fad has turned into a full-time business for thousands of online shoppers.
   a. buying groceries online b. managing bank accounts online c. buying and selling items through online auctions d. paying taxes online
2. Which part of an online store's Web site can you use to contact the merchant for assistance?
   a. catalog b. customer-service page c. checkout section d. home page
3. This type of store lets you wander the aisles and see the merchandise for yourself.
   a. catalog store b. clicks-and-bricks store c. online- only store d. brick-and-mortar store
4. Many e-commerce Web sites' catalogs are set up like ________, lumping products or services into categories and subcategories.
   a. directories b. search engines c. brick-and-mortar stores d. vendor
5. Online merchants usually try to make online shopping as similar as possible to this.
   a. shopping by mail b. shopping at a real store c. shopping by phone d. shopping in a different country
6. When you set up an account with an online merchant, the Web site may place one of these on your computer's disk.
   a. catalog b. shopping cart c. cookie d. encryption
7. Which of the following can *not* be done when banking online?
   a. create an account b. buy a sweater c. view transactions d. pay bills
8. Which type of transaction between companies can be considered a B2B transaction?
   a. any financial transaction b. buying parts c. ordering products d. purchasing stocks
9. This is a corporate network that uses the same protocols as the Internet, but which belongs to an organization, and which prohibits access by external users.
   a. network b. intranet c. extranet d. internalnet
10. This technology secures data by converting it into a code that is unusable by anyone who does not possess a key to the code.
    a. shopping cart b. B2B c. user name d. encryption

Review Questions ::

In your own words, briefly answer the following questions.

1. If an e-commerce Web site's catalog is set up like a search engine, how does it work?
2. What are the two most common payment methods used when making purchases from online merchants?
3. What purpose does a cookie serve, when you set up an online account with a merchant?
4. What is one advantage of using a personal-finance program, such as Microsoft Money or Quicken?
5. List two personal-financial transactions you can conduct online, other than managing your bank accounts.
6. Which type of transaction accounts for most of the money that is spent online?
7. What is the purpose of a firewall in an intranet or extranet?
8. What is a telecommuter?
9. How do online merchants typically protect customers?
10. When using an e-commerce site, how can you determine if the current page is secure?

Lesson Labs ::

Complete the following exercises as directed by your instructor.

1. Do some shopping. Visit the Web site of one popular online merchant. (Your instructor may ask you to visit a specific site.) Without purchasing anything or providing any personal information, inspect the site. What products does it sell? How does its catalog function? Is it easy to navigate the site and find products? Check the site's customer-service and help options. Describe your findings in a one-page report, to share with the class.
2. Can you bank online? Visit the Web site of one of your local banks, or a site chosen by your instructor. Without setting up an account or providing any personal information, inspect the site. What kinds of banking-related tasks can you do at the site? How easy is it to find the services you need at the site? Does the site require you to visit a bank branch to conduct certain transactions? Describe your findings in a one-page report, to share with the class.

Chapter Labs

Complete the following exercises using a computer in your classroom, lab, or home.

1. Learn more about getting connected to the Internet. One of the best places to learn about connecting to the Internet is on the Internet. Dozens of reliable Web sites provide technical support as well as tutorials for connecting with the various services explained in this chapter. To find more information about connecting to the Internet, visit these Web sites:

   http://www.centerspan.org/tutorial/connect.htm CenterSpan is an online toolbox providing transplant surgeons and physicians with essential information and resources, but it also has a great tutorial on getting connected.

   http://www.restartoffice.com/windowsXP1.htm#start This site focuses on setting up Windows XP. Restart Office Services is an Information Services Company in Houston, Texas, that builds business and personal Websites.

   http://www.intra-connect.net/Support/How-Do-I-Setup-My-Dial-Up-Account.php This site focuses on many types of operating systems that want to connect to the Internet via modem and telephone line. Founded in 1997, Intra-Connect is in the business of providing fast and reliable Internet services to clients all over the United States.

   http://www.ibuybroadband.com/ibb2/know-xdsl.asp#B ibuybroadband.com is a consumer-oriented service dedicated to helping individuals. They are primarily an online service to find the best way to upgrade to high-speed Internet access.

2. Stopping spam mail is not an easy job since it is difficult for a program to decide what e-mail is legitimate and what e-mail is junk. Visit the following sites to learn more about spam-preventing software. Find affordable software that offers the most protection for the cost.

   http://everythingemail.net/email_unsolicited.html

   http://spam.abuse.net/

   http://www.cauce.org/

   http://www.ftc.gov/bcp/conline/pubs/online/inbox.htm

Discussion Questions

As directed by your instructor, discuss the following questions in class or in groups.

1. Initially, the Web was built for the purpose of allowing one site to hyperlink to another. Linking was both accepted and encouraged when the Internet was a research network. However, with the introduction of the public to the Internet, some site owners have contended that before making a link, the linking site must ask for permission from the Web site owner. Should it be made illegal for one site to list a link to another without consent of the owner?
2. What makes society civilized are the norms by which it lives. Cellular phones have introduced a new challenge for the civilized world. Now that we can call anyone at any time, should we call or take a call while in restrooms, at meetings, eating dinner, or on a train? List 10 rules that we should apply to the use of cell phones.

Research and Report

Using your own choice of resources (such as the Internet, books, magazines, and newspaper articles), research and write a short paper discussing one of the following topics:

» The growth of the handheld computer market and how it has been affected by multifeatured cell phones.

» The cost and availability of DSL and cable modem services in your area.

» The ways to overcome the limitations of wireless technology.

When you are finished, proofread and print your paper, and give it to your instructor.

ETHICAL ISSUES

1. What ethical issues are involved in the practice of war riding? Are network administrators at fault for not protecting their networks? Or are war riders ethically responsible for their actions?
2. Online masquerading is the concept of presenting one's self in an idealized fashion while dealing with others over the Internet. Is there an ethical issue when users represent themselves as younger (or even older), or as being more attractive, or possibly as having great wealth? What if the person masquerading is a convicted child molester? What if the person masquerading was only convicted of a minor crime?

Computing Keynotes

When personal computers first came to the American workplace—and for years afterward—very few corporate computer users specialized in any one area of technology. The workforce was roughly divided into two groups:

- **End Users.** People who were expected to know very little beyond the basic operation of the programs they used.
- **"Computer Guys."** People with a broad general knowledge of computers, who could install systems, troubleshoot problems, and perhaps even manage a network.

Today, however, the world of information technology (IT) has evolved into many specialized areas of processes and applications. You would be hard-pressed to go into any medium-sized or large company and find a single "computer guy" who is in charge of running the entire system. This evolution has created many different, highly specialized jobs for IT professionals. Depending on the company and the type of business it does, you can find people filling dozens of varied and equally important IT-related jobs. Examples include network administrators, programmers, Web developers, graphics professionals, help system authors, trainers, and many others. Of course, each of these jobs requires a unique kind of training and the special skills needed to operate the tools used in a particular job.

With so many people involved in specialized roles, employers now face a difficult question. That is, how do you verify someone's skills to make sure that he or she is right for the job? While a four-year or two-year degree is important, many companies now look for computing professionals who have completed one of the many IT certification programs that now exist.

Certifications have become an extremely important type of credential in today's IT-oriented workplace. Depending on the type of job and skills required, a certification may be almost as important as a college degree to your employer. Whether you complete a certification program by itself or as part of your college or vocational training, your IT certification proves that you have received specialized training in a specific area of computing technology. By demonstrating that you have the skills required for a certain job, a certification differentiates you from other job seekers in a crowded and competitive marketplace. Certification can improve your chances of getting the job you want, earning promotions, and increasing your earnings.

Types of Computer Certifications

If you are interested in an IT-related career, you can choose from a multitude of computer certification programs. You may have heard of certifications from such companies as Microsoft or Oracle, but they are just the tip of the iceberg; many manufacturers—such as IBM, Cisco Systems, Citrix, and others—offer certifications related to their particular products.

In addition to product-specific certifications, there are also vendor-independent certifications that are sponsored by various professional groups. One of the more popular vendor-independent certifications is the A+ Service Technician certification. This certification does not come from any single manufacturer, but it is overseen by the Computer Technology Industry Association (CompTIA), and it covers a variety of products and technologies.

Many independent training companies also offer certification programs. One example is Prosoft, a training company that sponsors the Certified Internet Webmaster (CIW) certification.

The following sections describe some of the various certifications that apply to information technology. While this list is not complete, it should give you an idea of the many kinds of certifications that are available.

Application Certifications An application certification is basically what the name implies: a certification that proves your knowledge of a certain program or application. Two popular application certification programs are:

- **Microsoft Office Specialist (Office Specialist).** The program certifies your skill as a user of the applications in the Microsoft Office suite of programs, including Word, Excel, PowerPoint, Access, and Outlook. Certifications are available for Office 2000, Office XP, and Office 2003. You can earn one of three types of certification—Master,

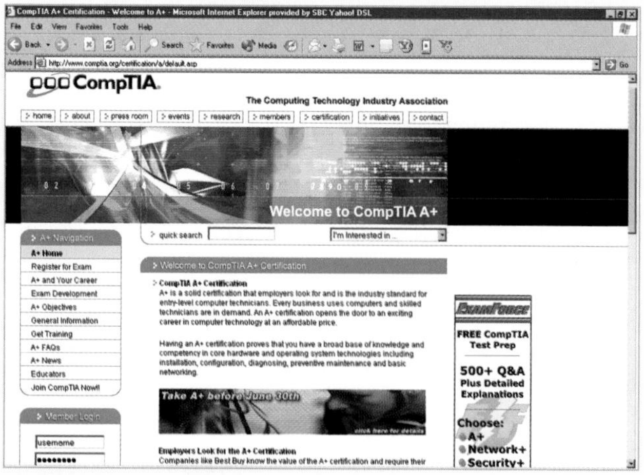

CompTIA offers certifications on a variety of computer-related disciplines, including networking, Internet technologies, and computer security. Its most popular certification is A+, which verifies that PC repair technicians have knowledge equivalent to six months' experience in the field.

Expert, or Specialist—in any or all of the Office programs. To earn an Office Specialist certification, you must pass a set of core- or expert-level examinations. For details on the Office Specialist certification program, visit http://www.microsoft.com/learning/mcp/officespecialist/default.asp.

- **Corel Certification.** The program offers certifications for users of Corel products, including the most recent versions of CorelDRAW and WordPerfect. Corel offers three types of certification: Proficient, Expert, and Instructor. To earn a certification, you must pass an examination, which can be taken online. For more information, visit the Corel home page at http://www.corel.com and click the Training link.

Entry-Level PC Repair and Networking Certifications

In addition to calling the following certifications *entry-level*, you could also call them *vendor-neutral*, because this is how they are known in the certification arena. But these certifications qualify as entry-level because they typically require only six months of computing experience. These certifications have given hundreds of thousands of people the chance to enter a new area of employment, in spite of the fact that many of them have little computing experience. Two of the most popular entry-level certifications are these:

- **A+ Service Technician Certification.** A testing program sponsored by the CompTIA. It certifies the experience of entry-level computer service technicians on a wide range of hardware, software, and networking technologies. Through CompTIA, applicants can find resources to help prepare for exams, register for exams, and learn about hundreds of different certification programs. For more information on CompTIA and its certification programs, visit http://www.comptia.com and click the Certification link.

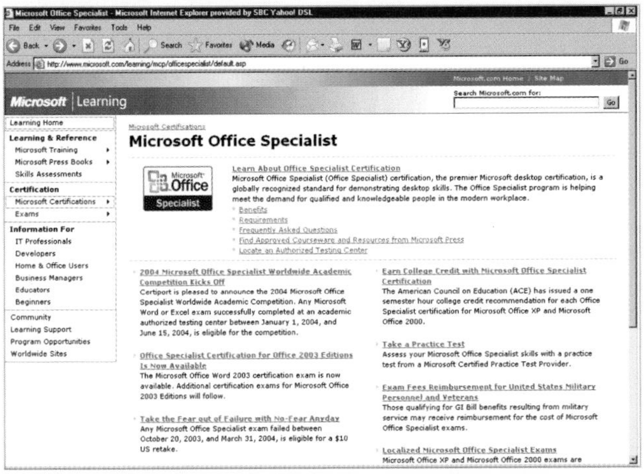

The home page of the Microsoft Office Specialist certification program.

- **Network+ Certification.** An entry-level exam that focuses on the skills that would be needed by any general networking practitioner. It is considered entry-level because it measures the technical knowledge of networking professionals with 18 to 24 months of experience in the IT industry. The exam covers a wide range of vendor- and product-neutral networking technologies. This means you don't have to be expert in any single networking product to pass the exam. Many industry leaders were involved in the creation and development of Network+ certification, such as 3Com, IBM, Microsoft, and Novell. There is only one test to take and pass to become Network+ certified, so the program continues to grow in popularity for individuals looking to earn a certification for their entry-level general networking knowledge. You can learn all about the Network+ certification program by visiting the CompTIA Web site at http://www.comptia.com, clicking the Certification link, and then clicking the Network+ link.

Internet and Web Development Certifications

Local area networks helped businesses by enhancing the way employees worked, processed business, and interacted with one another. What the LAN did for small to mid-sized companies 10 years ago, the Internet is doing for them now: allowing them to expand their business presence and client base, and again, to change the core way they do business. From the Internet's explosion have grown a host of different Web-related careers such as Web development, Web administration, and Web security. There are certifications for all types of Web professionals. Two of the most popular Web-related certifications are:

- **Certified Internet Webmaster (CIW).** This program offers vendor-neutral certifications, which help networking professionals use their existing IT skills to move into Internet-based technologies. The CIW program lets you follow different tracks based on the skills you want to acquire. CIW tracks cover a range of professional roles, including application developer, e-commerce designer, enterprise developer, and internetworking and security professional.
- **Macromedia Certified Professional.** This designation qualifies candidates who are skilled at Web development and implementation using various Macromedia products. Macromedia offers developer certifications on Dreamweaver MX, ColdFusion MX, and Flash MX. The Macromedia developer certifications measure a professional

CONTINUED >>>

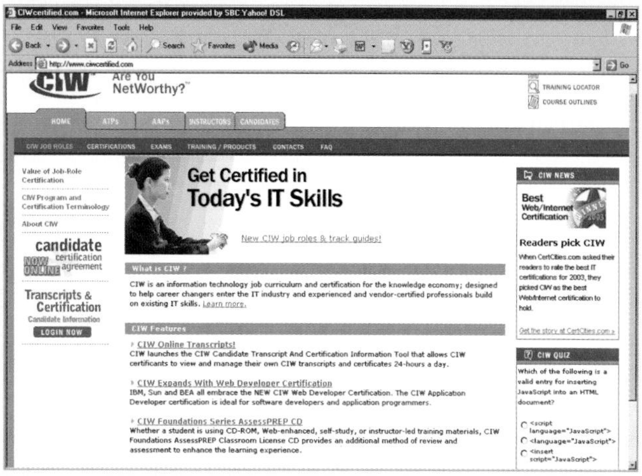

To learn more about CIW certification, visit the CIW home page at http://www.ciwcertified.com.

Web developer's ability to identify requirements and strategies for Web site design and develop, implement, test, deploy solutions, and maintain Web sites.

Networking and Operating System Certifications Networking and operating system certifications prove your ability to implement, manage, and administer certain operating systems and network operating systems. There is a variety of manufacturer-sponsored certifications in this area, and each vendor offers certifications in several tracks.

- **Microsoft Certified System Administrator (MCSA)** and **Microsoft Certified Systems Engineer (MCSE).** Certifications prove that you are skilled with the Microsoft suite of network server and operating system products, such as Windows 2003 Server, Windows Server 2000, and Windows XP. An MCSA designation certifies that you have the ability to successfully manage and troubleshoot computers and networks that run on the Windows operating systems. MCSA is an easier certification to achieve than MCSE because it requires that you pass three core exams, one elective exam, and one upgrade exam. To earn an MCSE Windows Server 2003 certification, which proves you can design and implement a Windows Server 2003 environment for business, you must pass *six* core exams, one elective exam, and two upgrade exams. Fortunately, the required MCSA core exams count toward MCSE certification, so once you've made it to MCSA, you are nearly halfway to achieving an MCSE certification. The core exams cover such topics as installing, configuring, and administering the operating system, as well as understanding the network infrastructure and the corresponding directory services component.

For complete information on Macromedia's certification programs, visit http://www.macromedia.com/support/training/certified_professional_program/.

- **Certified Novell Administrator (CNA)**, **Certified Novell Engineer (CNE)**, **Master Certified Novell Engineer,** and its newest certification, the **Certified Linux Engineer (CLE).** Novell, which is a company that specializes in network operating systems and servers, offers several certifications. These programs verify your knowledge of Novell's network server products—including Netware and Novell Nterprise Linux Services—as well as your ability to plan, implement, configure, and administer these products.
- **Cisco Certified Network Administrator (CCNA).** Cisco Systems is one of the largest manufacturers of hardware and software that runs the Internet. It offers a variety of

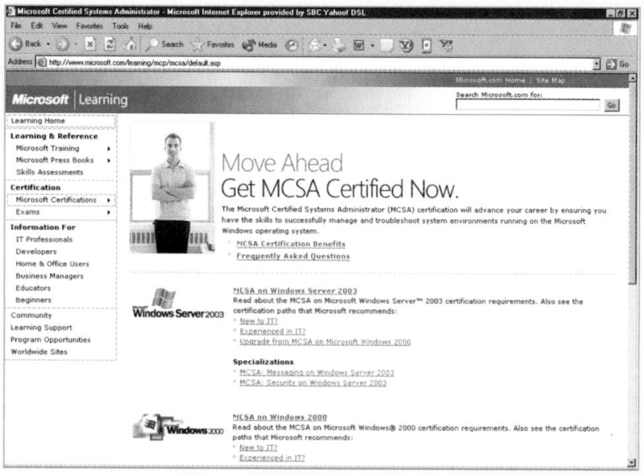

For more information about the MCSA certification, visit http://www.microsoft.com/learning/mcp/mcsa/windows2003.

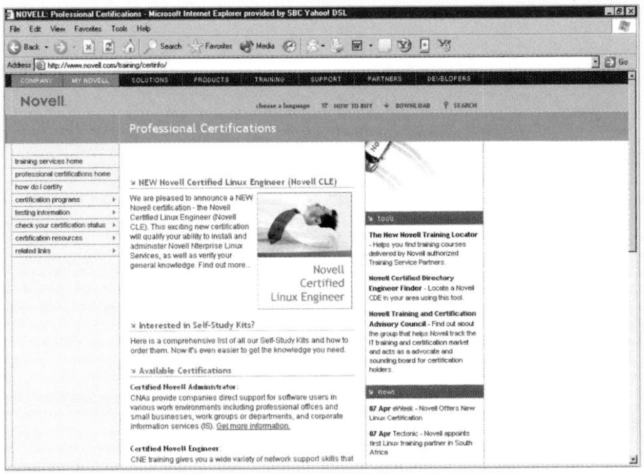

For more information on Novell's certification programs, visit http://www.novell.com/training/certinfo.

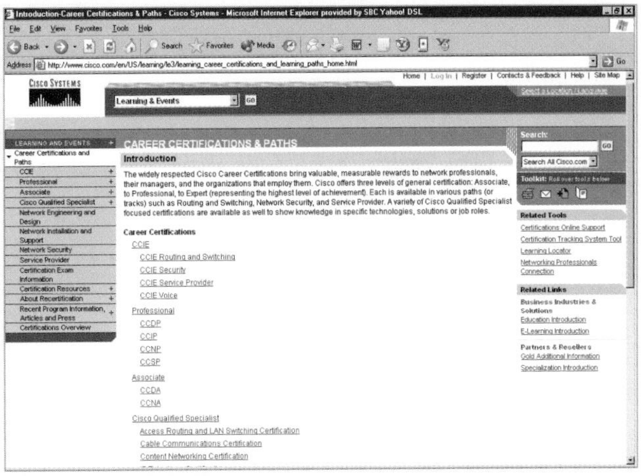

To learn about Cisco's certification programs, visit http://www.cisco.com/en/US/learning/le3/learning_career_certifications_and_learning_paths_home.htm.

certifications that test different levels of knowledge about the use of its products. The Cisco Certified Network Administrator (CCNA) is Cisco's entry-level certification and it verifies your ability to implement, configure, and operate local area and wide area network services, as well as dial-up services for small networks. To earn a CCNA certification, you need a good understanding of networking protocols, such as IP, IPX, RIP, Ethernet, and IGRP. Cisco offers two basic certification tracks in the CCNA program: basic and advanced. You must pass a single exam to earn a CCNA certification.

Database Certification Database certifications typically verify your ability to administer databases, develop applications using databases, and run Web services using databases.

Oracle, one of the largest developers of database programs, offers several certification paths for its Oracle9i and Oracle10g database systems. In the Oracle database administrator path, you can receive three certifications: **Oracle Database Administrator Certified Associate** (two exams), **Oracle Database Administrator Certified Professional** (two exams), and **Oracle Database Administrator Certified Master** (one exam). The Oracle developers track has two certifications: **Oracle PL/SQL Developer Certified Associate** (two exams) and **Oracle Forms Developer Certified Professional** (one exam).

Programming and Application Development Certifications Programming or application development certifications prove your ability to work within a particular development environment. To earn one of these certifications, you must pass examinations that test your product knowledge, your understanding of the actual development environment or language on which the product is based, and your ability to use the product to develop a custom solution.

- **Microsoft Certified Solution Developer (MCSD).** One of the more popular application development certifications is the MCSD for Microsoft .NET program. This certification is for programmers who design and implement custom business solutions with Microsoft .NET development platforms, such as VisualBasic.NET and C# .NET. To qualify, you must pass four core exams and one elective exam. The core exams consist of a Web Application Development test, a Windows Application Development test, an XML

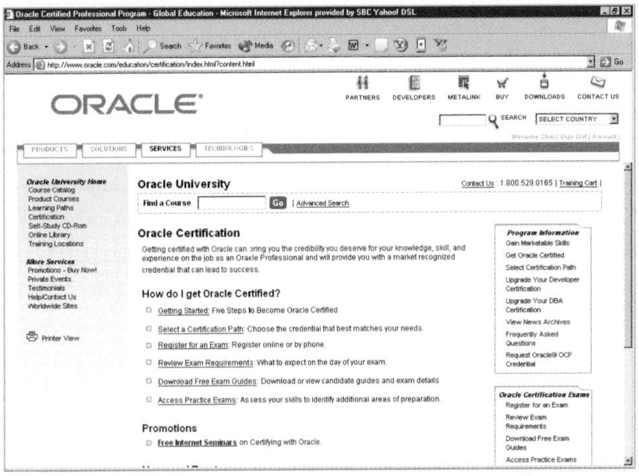

To learn more about Oracle certification, visit http://www.oracle.com/education/certification/index.html

CONTINUED

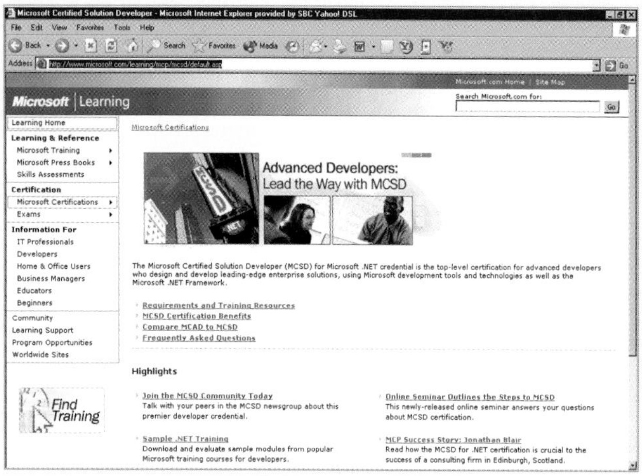

The home page of the MSCD certification program.

Web Services and Server Components Development test, and a Solutions Architecture exam. You also must pass one elective, which you can choose from a list of options. For the elective exams, you can choose tests that cover Microsoft SQL Server 2000 Enterprise Edition, Microsoft BizTalk Server 2000 Enterprise, or Microsoft Commerce Server 2000. For more information on the MCSD program, visit http://www.microsoft.com/learning/mcp/mcsd/default.asp.

- **Certified Lotus Professional (CLP)—Collaborative Solutions Application Developer.** This program is also a vendor-specific certification, which verifies your expertise in the use of Lotus application development tools. This certification focuses on knowledge of products such as Lotus Notes, Lotus Domino, Lotus Sametime, Quickplace, and Lotus Workflow. Candidates must hold a Certified Lotus Specialist designation and also be able to pass three separate exams: Developing Applications Using Lotus Workflow, Developing Web Applications in Sametime3, and Domino.Doc 3.0 Customization.

Certification Resources If you are interested in earning one or more technology-related certifications, here are some Web sites that can provide helpful, general information:

- **Go Certify.** This site offers information on a wide range of IT certifications. Certifications are grouped by both vendor and type. Go Certify provides information about each certification, such as the certification vendor, the skill level, the initial and continuing requirements, and the exam pricing. It is a great place to start when deciding on what certification to pursue. Visit http://www.gocertify.com.

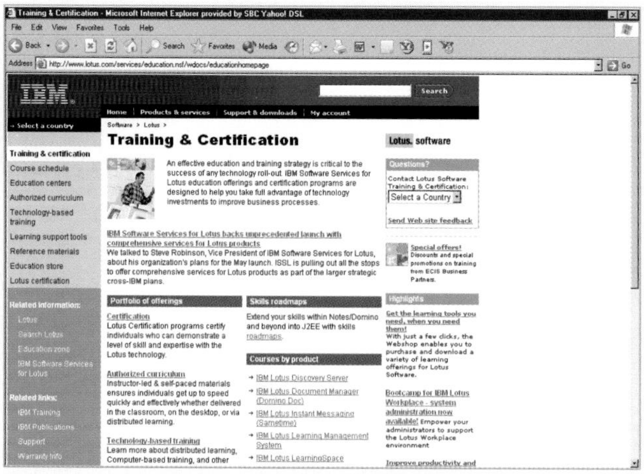

For more information about Lotus certifications, visit http://www.lotus.com/services/education.nsf/wdocs/educationhomepage.

- **Cert Cities.** An online subsidiary of *MCP Magazine*, this site is completely devoted to news and events in the world of IT certification. Within this site, you will find certification information, articles on different certifications, as well as study tips and reference material guides. The publisher also offers an annual salary survey of individuals who hold various certifications. Visit http://www.certcities.com.

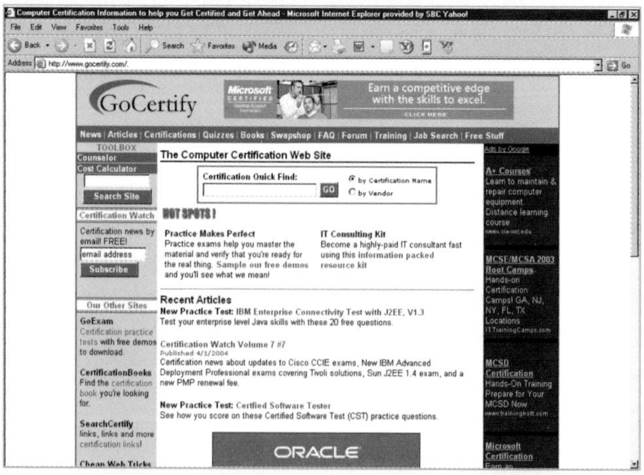

The Go Certify home page.

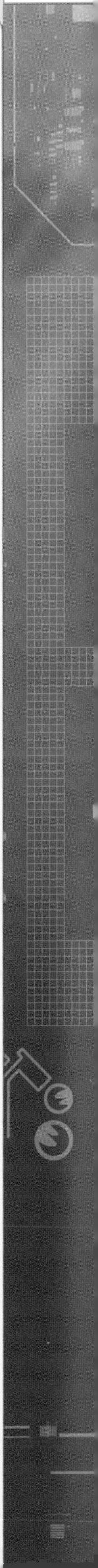

CHAPTER 11

Database Management

CHAPTER CONTENTS ::

This chapter contains the following lessons:

LESSON // 11A

Database Management Systems

Overview: The Mother of All Computer Applications

People need data, so we create all kinds of lists to store and organize it. A grocery list, a phone book, a library's card catalog, and an instructor's list of students are all organized lists of data. Likewise, computers can be used to store and manage lists of data, and this is the reason for the computerized database. In fact, many early attempts to build and program computers grew out of a need to manage large lists of data. That's why you probably have heard the phrase *data processing*—computers manipulate (or *process*) data. And that data is usually stored in databases.

Today's computers are much more sophisticated than early computers, but they still need an organized data source. This need applies to just about every type of computer program. For example, a word processor maintains several databases—such as a dictionary of words for the spell checker and thesaurus, a list of available fonts, and other types of data.

Practically every application—even if it has nothing to do with words or organized lists—has grown from earlier programs that stored and processed data. Large commercial applications (such as facilities management or sales support software) may look very different from a common word processor, but there is still a database at the heart of each operation. In short, you can think of the database as the mother of all computer applications. This lesson introduces you to the basics of computerized databases and database management systems.

OBJECTIVES ::

- Define the terms *database* and *database management system* (DBMS).
- List at least three tasks that a DBMS enables users to do.
- Differentiate between flat-file databases and relational databases.
- List three steps needed to create a database.
- Explain the purpose of filters and forms.
- List three examples of query languages.

Databases and Database Management Systems

To make large collections of data useful, people and organizations use computers and an efficient data management system. A **database** is a collection of related data or facts. A **database management system (DBMS)** is a software tool that allows people to store, access, and process data or facts into useful information.

Many large companies and organizations rely heavily on a commercial or custom DBMS to handle immense data resources. Often, a DBMS is custom-programmed to fit the exact needs of a company; it may be designed to run on a large mainframe computer system or a large client–server network.

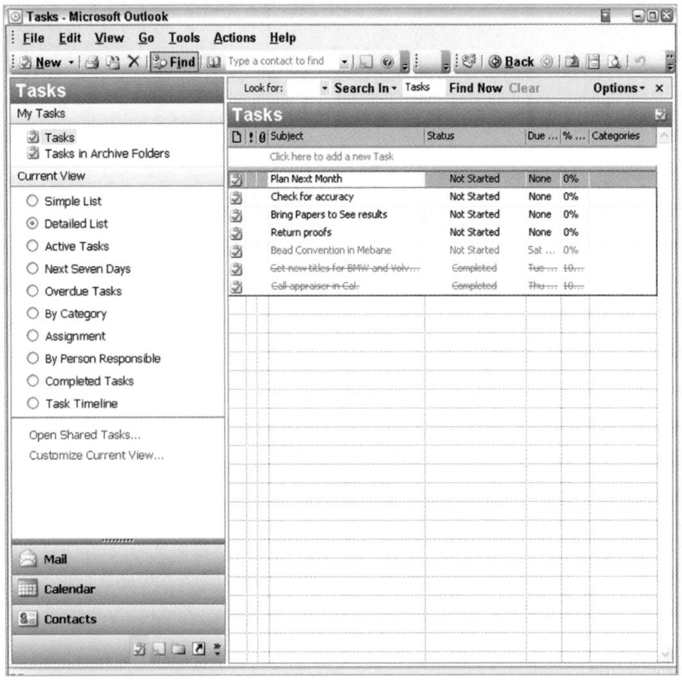

FIGURE 11A.1

Microsoft Outlook uses databases to help you manage contact and schedule information. Outlook also provides e-mail and other functions, but at its core it is a complex database and DBMS.

Personal computers bring database management to the desktops of individuals in businesses and homes. Although the casual computer user doesn't need an inventory-tracking system, home users utilize commercial DBMS products for such tasks as maintaining address lists, managing household budgets, and storing data for home businesses.

Many small database programs that run on personal computers are not referred to as databases or database management programs; instead they are called personal information managers (PIMs), personal organizers, and other names. Behind their interfaces, however, these PC programs have the heart of a database management system. For example, Figure 11A.1 shows Microsoft Outlook, a popular personal information manager that uses databases. As you learned in Chapter 8, a PIM lets you store and manage your schedules, e-mail addresses, and other types of information.

A DBMS makes it possible to do many routine tasks that would otherwise be tedious and time-consuming without a computer. For example, a DBMS can

- Sort thousands of addresses by ZIP code.
- Find all records of people who live in a certain state.
- Print a list of selected records, such as all real estate listings that closed escrow last month.

In other words, a DBMS not only stores data, it also allows users to easily make use of that data. The DBMS can sift through thousands or even millions of pieces of data, returning only the data you need. And it can find relationships between data, such as giving you a list of all accounts that are two months overdue.

The Database

A database contains a collection of related items or facts arranged in a specific structure. The most obvious example of a noncomputerized database is a telephone directory. Telephone companies use electronic database programs to produce their printed phone books. Sometimes you will see a specialized phone book that is arranged not only by last name, but by other items such as phone number or street address. These books are easy to produce because the telephone company's electronic database can rapidly reorganize the data in many different ways.

Before learning more about the powers of electronic databases, you need to learn how data is organized within a database and some common database terms. To help you visualize how a database stores data, think about a typical address book like the one shown in Figure 11A.2.

Norton ONLINE

For more information on databases, visit **http://www.mhhe.com/peternorton**.

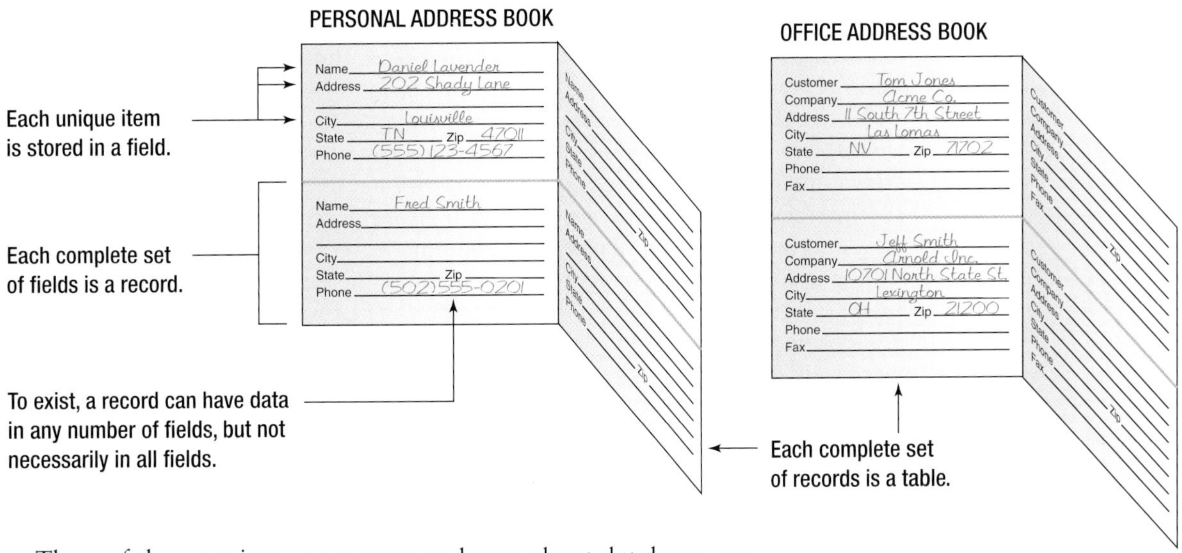
PERSONAL ADDRESS BOOK
OFFICE ADDRESS BOOK
Each unique item is stored in a field.
Each complete set of fields is a record.
To exist, a record can have data in any number of fields, but not necessarily in all fields.
Each complete set of records is a table.

FIGURE 11A.2

Data is stored in tables. A table is divided into records, and each record is divided into fields.

Three of the most important terms to know about databases are

- **Fields.** Notice in Figure 11A.2 that each piece of data in the address book is stored in its own location, called a field. For example, each entry has a field for Name, as well as fields for Address, City, State, ZIP code, and Phone. Each unique type of data is stored in its own field. (The term *column* is sometimes used instead of *field*. IBM uses *column* fairly consistently, and Microsoft now uses it increasingly.)
- **Records.** One full set of fields—that is, all the related data about one person or object—is called a record. Therefore, all the information for the first person is record 1, all the information for the second person is record 2, and so on. (The term *row* is sometimes used instead of *record* by IBM and Microsoft.)
- **Tables.** A complete collection of records makes a table.

Once you have a structure for storing data, you can add new data, create reports, and perform other tasks with the data. For example, you might create a customer report that groups customers by ZIP code. These extra documents—forms and reports—along with the tables, collectively form a database, as shown in Figure 11A.3. Two of the most common elements of a database are forms and reports:

- Forms are documents that are filled in to create records.
- Reports are documents that display a select portion of a database's information in an easily read format. Such a report might list all overdue accounts.

FIGURE 11A.3

A database consists of tables and all the supporting documents.

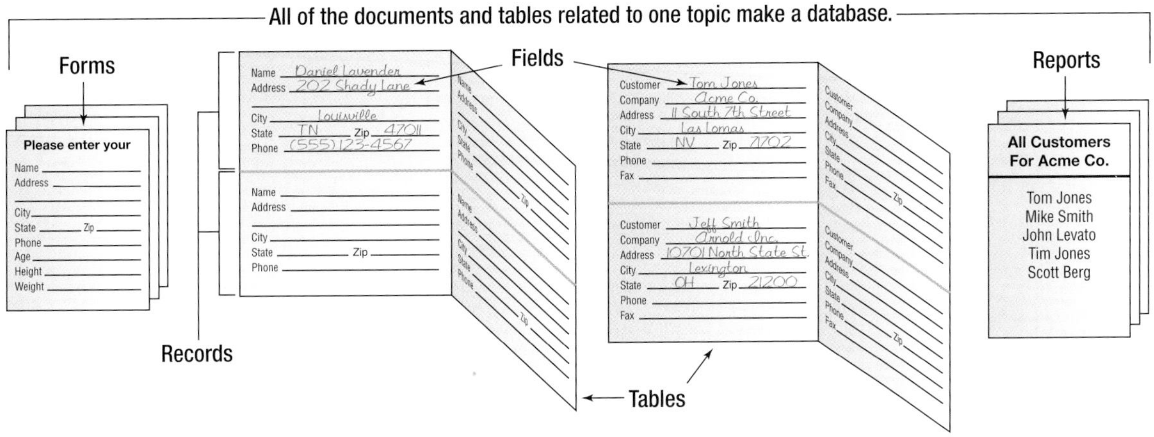
All of the documents and tables related to one topic make a database.
Forms
Fields
Reports
Please enter your
All Customers For Acme Co.
Tom Jones
Mike Smith
John Levato
Tim Jones
Scott Berg
Records
Tables

Now that you have a better understanding of database terms, you can begin exploring an electronic database. Figure 11A.4 shows a customer information table as it appears in the PC database application Lotus Approach.

Notice that the table arrangement consists of a set number of named columns (fields) and an arbitrary number of unnamed rows (records). Perhaps you can see why some people are abandoning the traditional terms *field* and *record* and replacing them with *column* and *row*. Visually, each record looks like a horizontal row, and the fields look like vertical columns.

A table organizes each record's data by the same set of fields, but in most database applications, a table can store any number of records. For example, if you are storing employee data, the table can expand as necessary to include as many employees as you hire. The only limit to the table's size is the storage capacity of the computer system.

However, the fields in a table remain fixed; they normally remain as they were defined when the table was created. There is a finite number of "facts" or fields about each employee.

Each record in the table does not necessarily have data in every field. For a record to exist, however, it must have data in at least one field. For example, a record for an employee must include the person's name. The employee's name is not an optional fact about an employee; it will always be present in the record for each employee. A record may or may not include the person's home phone number or date of birth; these types of data may be considered optional facts about an employee and therefore may not always be included in the record.

The order of fields in a table strictly defines the location of each type of data in every record. For example, a phone number field must contain a record's phone number—it cannot contain a person's name or ZIP code. Similarly, the set of fields in any one table provides a sensible definition of the database for those who must access its data. For instance, you would expect to find the part number for a radiator in an inventory of auto parts, but you should not expect to view an employee's payroll record in the same table.

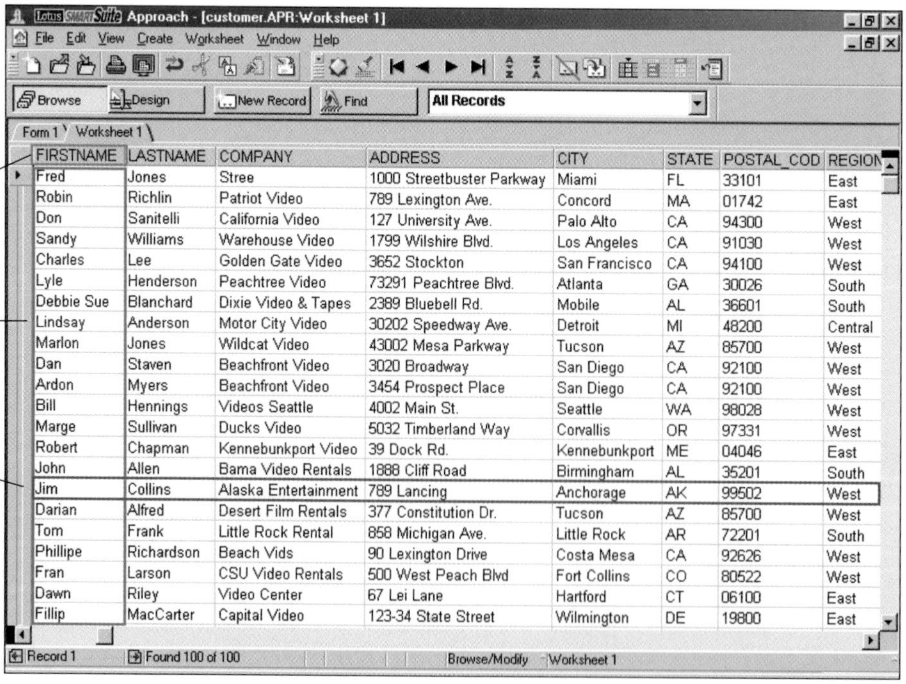

FIRSTNAME	LASTNAME	COMPANY	ADDRESS	CITY	STATE	POSTAL_COD	REGION
Fred	Jones	Stree	1000 Streetbuster Parkway	Miami	FL	33101	East
Robin	Richlin	Patriot Video	789 Lexington Ave.	Concord	MA	01742	East
Don	Sanitelli	California Video	127 University Ave.	Palo Alto	CA	94300	West
Sandy	Williams	Warehouse Video	1799 Wilshire Blvd.	Los Angeles	CA	91030	West
Charles	Lee	Golden Gate Video	3652 Stockton	San Francisco	CA	94100	West
Lyle	Henderson	Peachtree Video	73291 Peachtree Blvd.	Atlanta	GA	30026	South
Debbie Sue	Blanchard	Dixie Video & Tapes	2389 Bluebell Rd.	Mobile	AL	36601	South
Lindsay	Anderson	Motor City Video	30202 Speedway Ave.	Detroit	MI	48200	Central
Marlon	Jones	Wildcat Video	43002 Mesa Parkway	Tucson	AZ	85700	West
Dan	Staven	Beachfront Video	3020 Broadway	San Diego	CA	92100	West
Ardon	Myers	Beachfront Video	3454 Prospect Place	San Diego	CA	92100	West
Bill	Hennings	Videos Seattle	4002 Main St.	Seattle	WA	98028	West
Marge	Sullivan	Ducks Video	5032 Timberland Way	Corvallis	OR	97331	West
Robert	Chapman	Kennebunkport Video	39 Dock Rd.	Kennebunkport	ME	04046	East
John	Allen	Bama Video Rentals	1888 Cliff Road	Birmingham	AL	35201	South
Jim	Collins	Alaska Entertainment	789 Lancing	Anchorage	AK	99502	West
Darian	Alfred	Desert Film Rentals	377 Constitution Dr.	Tucson	AZ	85700	West
Tom	Frank	Little Rock Rental	858 Michigan Ave.	Little Rock	AR	72201	South
Phillipe	Richardson	Beach Vids	90 Lexington Drive	Costa Mesa	CA	92626	West
Fran	Larson	CSU Video Rentals	500 West Peach Blvd	Fort Collins	CO	80522	West
Dawn	Riley	Video Center	67 Lei Lane	Hartford	CT	06100	East
Fillip	MacCarter	Capital Video	123-34 State Street	Wilmington	DE	19800	East

FIGURE 11A.4

A customer information table in Lotus Approach. One of the fields in this table is outlined in green; one of the records is outlined in purple.

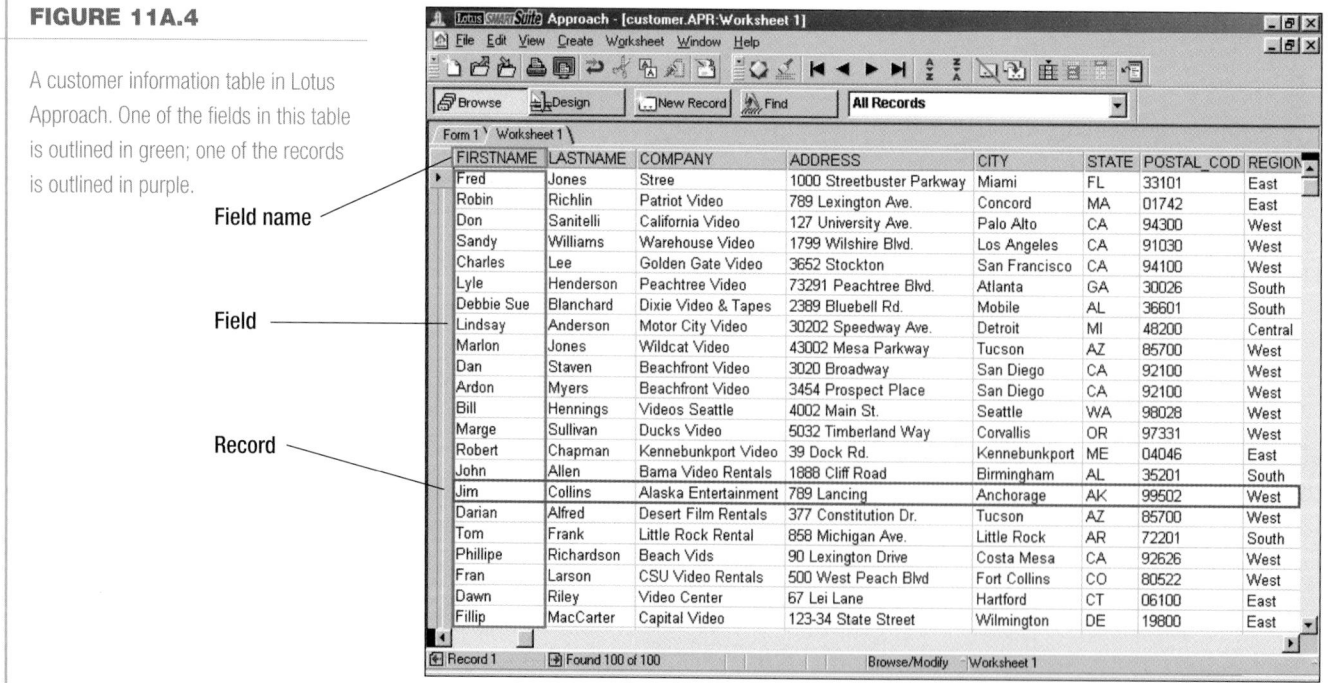

Flat-File and Relational Database Structures

Many early database applications and some current low-end applications access and manipulate only one table at a time. These applications store each table in its own file. When dealing with such databases, there is no reason to use the term *table* because the table and the database are one and the same. Very often, the table is simply called a file or just "the database."

To be more precise, however, a database file that consists of a single data table is called a flat-file database. Flat-file databases are useful for certain single-user or small-group situations, especially for maintaining lists such as address lists or inventories. Data that is stored, managed, and manipulated in a spreadsheet is similar to a flat-file database. (Notice that the table in Figure 11A.4 looks like a spreadsheet. If this table were stored by itself or not associated with any other database tables, it would be a flat-file database.)

Although they are easy to learn and use, flat-file database systems can be difficult to maintain and are limited in their power. When numerous files exist (one for each table or related document), there is often a lot of data redundancy, which increases the chance for errors, wastes time, and uses excess storage space. Adding, deleting, or editing any field requires that you make the same changes in every file that contains the same field.

In a relational database—a database made up of a set of tables—a common field existing in any two tables creates a relationship between the tables. As shown in Figure 11A.5, a Customer ID field in both the Customers table and the Orders table links the two tables, while a Product ID field links the Orders and Products tables.

The relational database structure is easily the most prevalent in today's business organizations. In a business, a typical relational database would likely contain separate tables with information on customers, employees, vendors, orders, and inventory.

Multiple tables in this kind of database make it possible to handle many data management tasks, for example:

» The customer, order, and inventory tables can be linked to process orders and billing.
» The vendor and inventory tables can be linked to maintain and track inventory levels.
» The order and employee tables can be linked to control scheduling.

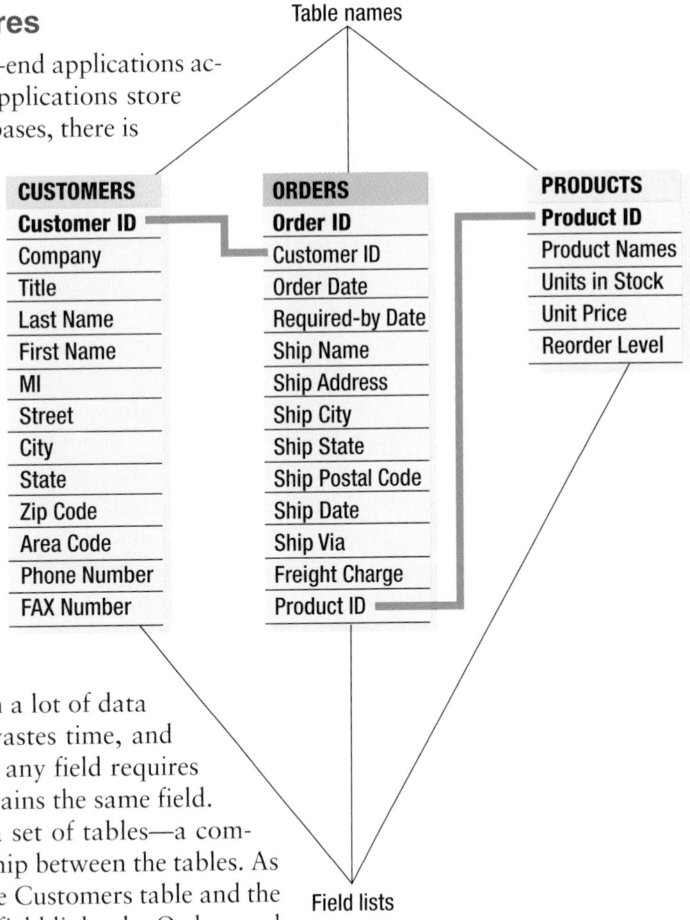

FIGURE 11A.5

Linked fields in relational database tables are indicated by red lines.

The DBMS

As you have seen, a database is basically a collection of data. A database management system is a program, or collection of programs, that allows any number of users to access and modify the data in a database. A DBMS also provides tools that enable users to construct special requests (called queries) to find specific records in the database. Data management tasks fall into one of four general categories:

» Entering data into the database.
» Housekeeping tasks, such as updating data, deleting obsolete records, and backing up the database.

Norton ONLINE

For more information on database management systems, visit **http://www.mhhe.com/peternorton**.

Norton Notebook

Data Warehouses

For years, companies have gathered and managed vast amounts of data of every imaginable kind. Because data truly is the lifeblood of a corporation, you can think of the corporation's data storage system as its heart. The bigger and stronger that system is, the more information it can handle and the more effectively it will operate.

Large and medium-sized companies are taking new approaches to storing and managing their huge collections of data. On the storage side of the equation is the data warehouse—a massive collection of corporate information, often stored in gigabytes or terabytes of data. Setting up a data warehouse is much more complicated than simply dumping all kinds of data into one storage place. Companies must consider several factors such as the following before investing in a data warehousing structure:

- **Storage Space.** One of the most popular mass-storage schemes is based on a redundant array of independent disks (RAID). RAID is a storage system that links any number of disk drives so that they act as a single disk. In this system, information is written to two or more disks simultaneously to improve speed and reliability, and to ensure that data is available to users at all times. Large-scale RAID systems offer up many terabytes of storage and incredibly fast access and data transfer times.
- **Processing Scheme.** Generally, two technologies are used to control data warehouses: symmetrical multiprocessing (SMP) and massively parallel processing (MPP). Using special RAID controllers, such systems can rapidly collect data, check it for errors, and retrieve a backup copy of the data if necessary.
- **Backup Strategy.** RAID's capabilities are based on three basic techniques: (1) mirroring, (2) striping, and (3) striping-with-parity. In a mirrored system, data is written to two or more disks simultaneously, providing a complete copy of all the information on a drive in the event one drive should fail. Striping provides the user with a speedy response by spreading data across several disks. Striping alone, however, does not provide backup if one of the disks in an array fails. Striping-with-parity provides the

- Sorting the data—that is, arranging or reordering the database's records.
- Obtaining subsets of the data.

The last type of data-management task—finding records—is extremely important. Because database files can grow very large (many gigabytes—millions of records—on large systems), finding data quickly is not a trivial matter. A DBMS, especially when it is running on powerful hardware, can find any speck of data in an enormous database in minutes, sometimes even in seconds or fractions of a second. Equally important, a DBMS provides the means for multiple users to access and share data in the same database by way of networked computer systems.

SELF-CHECK ::

Circle the correct answer for each question.

1. Flat-file databases are most useful for __________ .
   - a. Large-scale databases
   - b. Banking
   - c. Single-user or small-group situations
2. In most database applications, a table can __________ .
   - a. Hold only one field
   - b. Store any number of records
   - c. Never be updated
3. A relational database includes __________ .
   - a. More than one table
   - b. A single, large table
   - c. A table with large records

Working with a Database

The DBMS interface presents the user with data and the tools required to work with the data. You work with the interface's tools to perform these data management functions:

- Creating tables
- Viewing records
- Sorting records
- Creating queries
- Generating reports

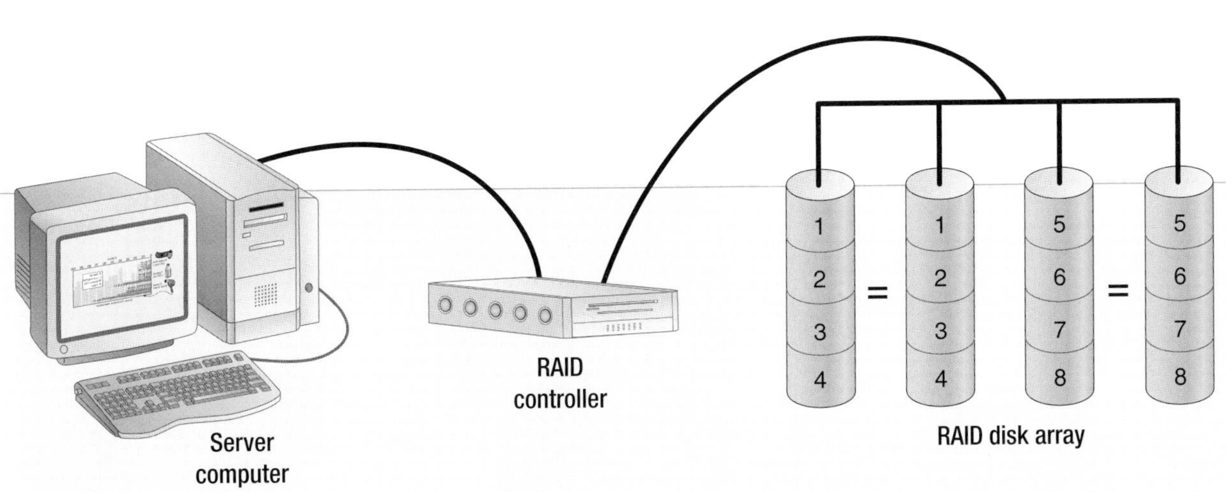

In a simple RAID array like this, data is written to two or more disks at once, resulting in multiple copies. This protects the data in case one disk fails. In more sophisticated RAID configurations, data from a single file is spread over multiple disks, and duplicates are made. Error-checking is also provided in such arrays.

speed of striping with the reliability of mirroring; in this scenario, the system stores parity information that can be used to reconstruct data if a disk drive fails.

» **Speed.** Newer data-warehousing systems not only incorporate huge disk drives, but some interconnect the drives with fiber-optic lines rather than standard wire-based buses. Fiber-optic lines use beams of pulsing light to transmit data and operate many times faster than standard data-bus technologies.

Huge data warehouses can supply the data requirements for tens of thousands of users in a large organization. They also are used to store and support thousands or millions of transactions per day on active Web sites, such as the popular electronic auction and retail Web sites.

Creating Database Tables

The first step in building any database is to create one or more tables. To create a new database, you must first determine what kind of data will be stored in each table. In other words, you must define each field in the table by following a three-step process:

1. Name the field.
2. Specify the field type.
3. Specify the field size.

Understanding Field Types

When naming a field, indicate as briefly as possible what the field contains. Figure 11A.6 shows a database table with clearly named fields.

Specifying the field type requires knowledge of what kind of data the DBMS can understand. Most modern database systems can work with various predefined field types. Figure 11A.7 shows examples of several common field types.

FIGURE 11A.6

Clearly named fields in a database table.

Table : C:\...\stock.db

	Stock No	Vendor No	Equipment Class	Model	Part No	Description
1	900.00	3,820.00	Vehicle	DV-100	T-5100	Underwater Diver Vehicle
2	912.00	2,014.00	Vehicle	18-DV	7160-00	Underwater Diver Vehicle
3	1,313.00	3,511.00	Air Regulators	MK-200/G200	12-200-000	Regulator System
4	1,314.00	5,641.00	Air Regulators	TR-200	6832-14A	Second Stage Regulator
5	1,316.00	3,511.00	Air Regulators	MK-10/G200 B	12-502-000	Regulator System

Field name

FIGURE 11A.7

Field types.

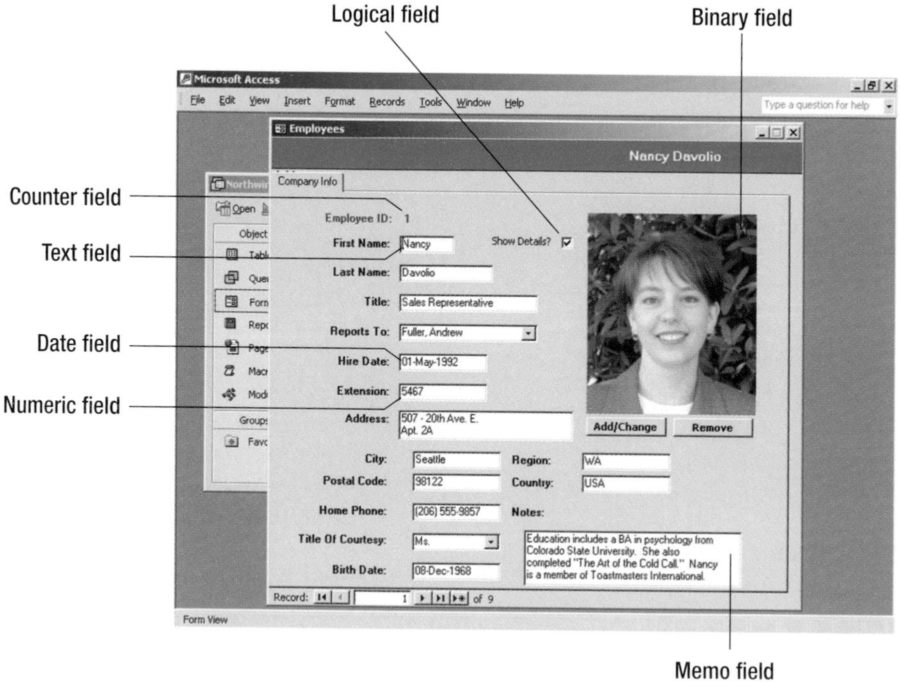

Text fields (also called string fields, character fields, or alphanumeric fields) accept any string of letters or numbers that are not used in calculations. Such an entry might be a person's name, a company's name, an address, a phone number, or any other textual data.

Numeric fields store purely numeric data. The numbers in a numeric field might represent currency, percentages, statistics, quantities, or any other value that can be (but is not necessarily) used in calculations. The data itself is stored in the table strictly as a numeric value, even though the DBMS can display the value with formatting characters such as dollar or percent signs, decimal points, or commas. Sometimes a numeric data field is required to have certain mathematical characteristics, such as integer (whole numbers), floating point (fractions), and so on.

A date field or time field stores date or time entries. These field types convert a date or time entry into a numeric value, just as dates and times are stored internally as serial numbers in spreadsheet cells. In most database systems, a date value represents the number of days that have elapsed since a specific start date. When you enter a date in a date field, the DBMS accepts your input, displays it in the format of a date (such as 9/9/2003), and converts it to a number (such as 37873) that it stores in the database. Date and time fields typically include automatic error-checking features. For instance, date fields can verify a date's accuracy and account for the extra day in a leap year. Date and time fields are handy for calculating elapsed time periods, such as finding records for invoices 31 days overdue.

Logical fields (also called Boolean fields) store one of only two possible values. You can apply almost any description for the data (yes or no, true or false, on or off, and so forth). For example, a Catalog field in a Customer table can tell a customer service representative whether a customer has ordered a new catalog (Yes) or not (No).

Binary fields store binary objects, or BLOBs. A BLOB (binary large object) can be a graphic image file such as clip art, a photograph, a screen image, a graphic, or formatted text. A BLOB also can be an audio file, video clip, or other object, as shown in Figure 11A.8.

In some DBMSs, counter fields (sometimes called index or autonumber fields) store a unique numeric value that the DBMS assigns to each record. Because it is

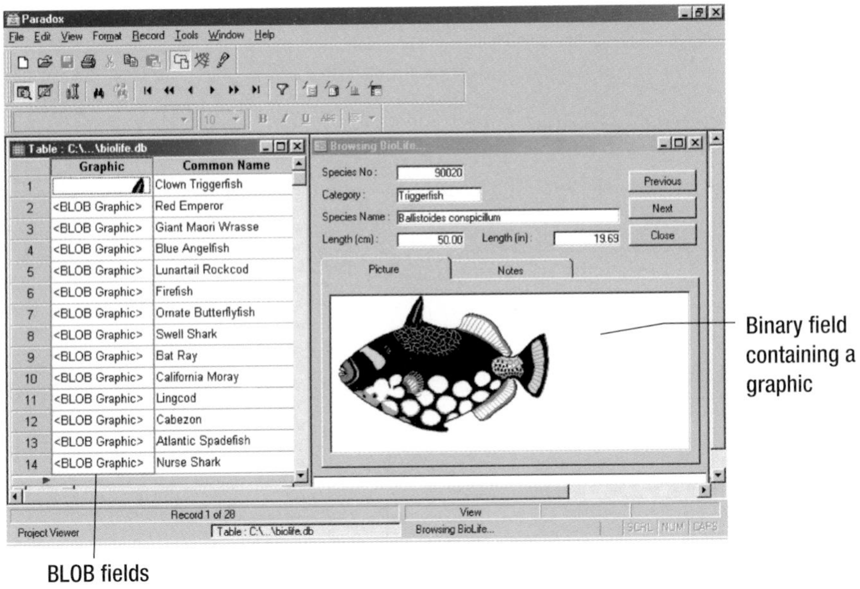

FIGURE 11A.8

Binary fields allow graphics and other nontext items to be stored in a database.

possible for two records to have identical data in some tables (such as two employees with the same name), a counter field ensures that every record will contain at least one completely unique piece of data. Counter fields also may be used for creating records that number sequentially, such as invoices.

Because most field types have fixed lengths that restrict the number of characters in an entry, memo fields (also called description fields) provide fields for entering notes or comments of any length. With a memo field, you don't specify the size of the data.

Entering Data in a Table

After the table has been set up, data can be entered. In most cases, entering data is a matter of typing characters at the keyboard. Entering data in a database table is much like entering data in a spreadsheet program. The process can have more pitfalls than you might expect, however, especially if it is being carried out by someone other than the table's designer. For example, the DBMS might not handle a number correctly if the user enters it with a dollar sign—even though the number will be displayed as a dollar amount. If the data is entered with an inconsistent mix of upper- and lowercase letters, the DBMS may not be able to sort the data or locate specific records.

Most DBMSs allow you to create a data entry form to make data entry easier (see Figure 11A.9). A form is nothing more than a custom view of the table that typically shows one record at a time and includes special controls and labels that make data entry less confusing. For example, the form's designer can include controls that automatically move the insertion point to the next field when the typist presses the ENTER or TAB key. This makes it easy for a typist to move from one field to the next without having to take a hand off the keyboard and reach for the mouse. Or the form can convert all the input into capital letters to maintain data consistency. A form can even direct input into multiple tables, which really makes life easier for a typist who does not know about the underlying structure of the DBMS and database tables.

Viewing Records

The way data appears on screen contributes to how easily users can work with it. You have already seen examples of data presented in two-dimensional, worksheet-style tables. With many DBMS products, you use the table view (sometimes

FIGURE 11A.9

Forms make data entry easier.

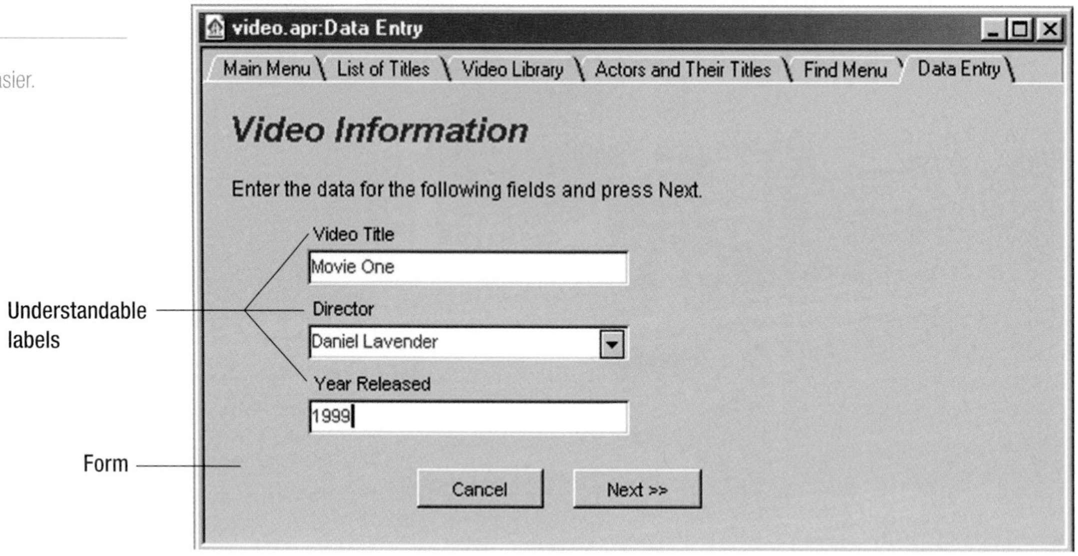

called the datasheet view) to create a database table and to modify field specifications. This view is also suitable for seeing a list of records that you request to view in some meaningful way, such as all customers who live in the same city.

Sometimes viewing the entire table is unwieldy because there are too many entries. Filters are a DBMS feature for displaying a selected list or subset of records from a table. The visible records satisfy a condition that the user sets. It is called a filter because it tells the DBMS to display those records that satisfy the condition while hiding—or filtering out—those that do not. For example, you can create a filter that displays only those records that have the data "Gold" in the Status field, as shown in Figure 11A.10.

As shown in Figure 11A.11, a DBMS also allows you to create forms for viewing records. These forms are similar in design to those used in data entry, but they are used to display existing data instead of receiving new data. By using forms, you can create simple, easily understood views of your data that show just one record at a time. You also can create complex forms that display related information from multiple tables.

FIGURE 11A.10

When you view a data table in datasheet view, you can see all records and fields at the same time—or as many as will fit on the screen.

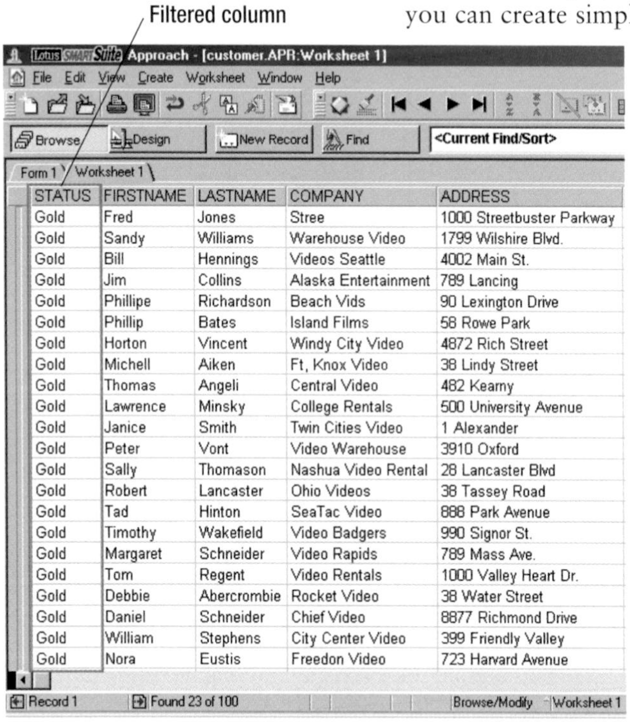

STATUS	FIRSTNAME	LASTNAME	COMPANY	ADDRESS
Gold	Fred	Jones	Stree	1000 Streetbuster Parkway
Gold	Sandy	Williams	Warehouse Video	1799 Wilshire Blvd.
Gold	Bill	Hennings	Videos Seattle	4002 Main St.
Gold	Jim	Collins	Alaska Entertainment	789 Lancing
Gold	Phillipe	Richardson	Beach Vids	90 Lexington Drive
Gold	Phillip	Bates	Island Films	58 Rowe Park
Gold	Horton	Vincent	Windy City Video	4872 Rich Street
Gold	Michell	Aiken	Ft, Knox Video	38 Lindy Street
Gold	Thomas	Angeli	Central Video	482 Kearny
Gold	Lawrence	Minsky	College Rentals	500 University Avenue
Gold	Janice	Smith	Twin Cities Video	1 Alexander
Gold	Peter	Vont	Video Warehouse	3910 Oxford
Gold	Sally	Thomason	Nashua Video Rental	28 Lancaster Blvd
Gold	Robert	Lancaster	Ohio Videos	38 Tassey Road
Gold	Tad	Hinton	SeaTac Video	888 Park Avenue
Gold	Timothy	Wakefield	Video Badgers	990 Signor St.
Gold	Margaret	Schneider	Video Rapids	789 Mass Ave.
Gold	Tom	Regent	Video Rentals	1000 Valley Heart Dr.
Gold	Debbie	Abercrombie	Rocket Video	38 Water Street
Gold	Daniel	Schneider	Chief Video	8877 Richmond Drive
Gold	William	Stephens	City Center Video	399 Friendly Valley
Gold	Nora	Eustis	Freedon Video	723 Harvard Avenue

Sorting Records

One of the most powerful features of a DBMS is the ability to sort a table of data, either for a printed report or for display on the screen. Sorting arranges records according to the contents of one or more fields. For example, in a table of products, you can sort records into numerical order by product ID or into alphabetical order by product name. To obtain the list sorted by product name, you define the condition for the Product Name field that tells the DBMS to rearrange the records in alphabetical order for this data (see Figure 11A.12). You can sort the same list on another field, such as Supplier, as shown in Figure 11A.13.

When sorting records, one important consideration is determining the sort order. An ascending sort order arranges records in alphabetical order (from A to Z), numerical order (from 0 to 9), or chronological order (from

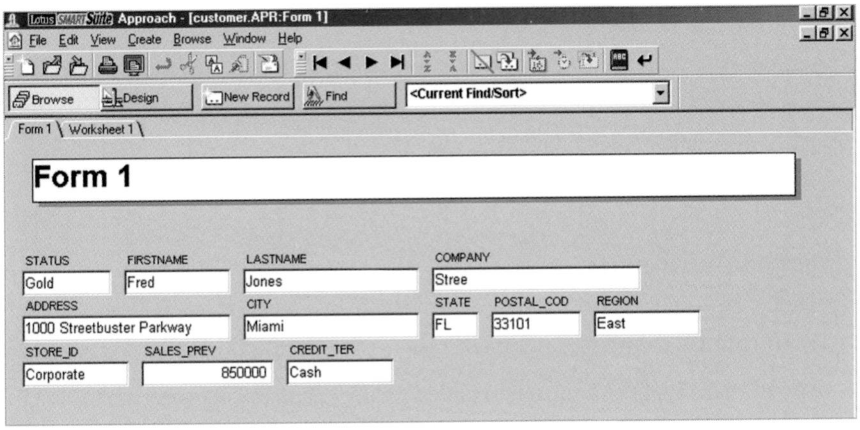

FIGURE 11A.11

A form lets the user work with information for a single record.

Here, the records are sorted according to entries in this field.

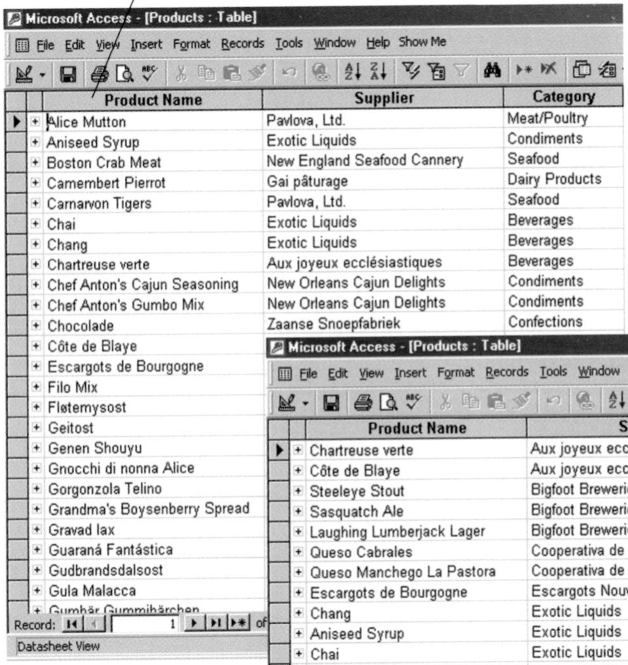

FIGURE 11A.12

Records arranged alphabetically by product name.

Now the records are sorted according to entries in this field.

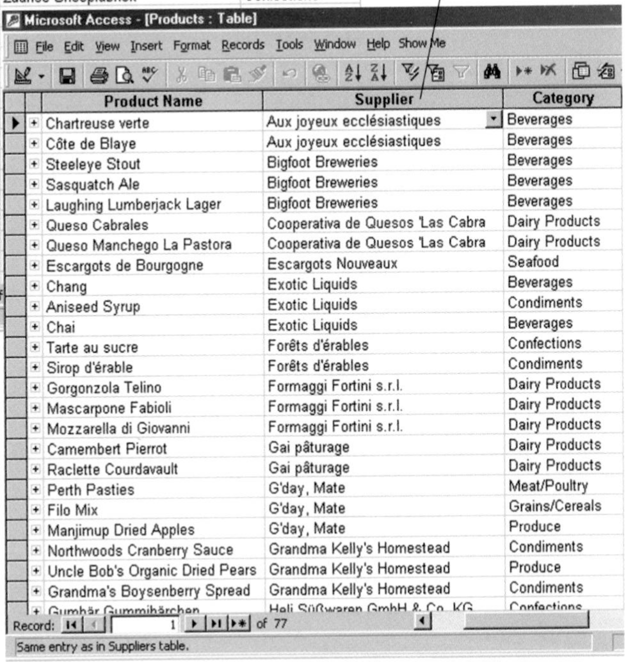

FIGURE 11A.13

The records have now been arranged alphabetically according to the contents of the Supplier field.

1/1/1900 to 12/31/1999). For example, if you base an ascending sort on a Last Name field, the records will be arranged in alphabetical order by last name. Conversely, a descending sort order arranges records in the opposite order—that is, from Z to A, or from 9 to 0.

Querying a Database

Norton ONLINE

For more information on database queries and query languages, visit **http://www.mhhe.com/peternorton**.

In a manner similar to entering sort conditions, you can enter expressions or criteria that

- » Allow the DBMS to locate records.
- » Establish relationships or links between tables to update records.
- » List a subset of records.
- » Perform calculations.
- » Delete obsolete records.
- » Perform other data management tasks.

Any of these types of requests is called a query, a user-constructed statement that describes data and sets criteria so that the DBMS can gather the desired data and construct specific information. In other words, a query is a more powerful type of filter that can gather information from multiple tables in a relational database.

For example, a sales manager might create a query to list orders by quarter. The query can include field names such as Customer and City from a Customers table, and Order Date from an Orders table. To obtain the desired information, the query requires the specific data or criteria that will isolate those records (orders received during a given period) from all the records in both tables. In this case, the sales manager includes a range of dates during which the orders shipped.

Some database systems provide special windows or forms for creating queries. Generally, such a window or form provides an area for selecting the tables the query will work with and columns for entering the field names where the query will obtain or manipulate data.

It should be possible to generate a single language that can, in theory, query any database. If such a language were developed, a user who knew the language could query any database, regardless of who created the database or what software was used in the creation. Mainframe database developers created the Structured English QUEry Language (SEQUEL) in the mid 1970s to solve this dilemma. SEQUEL, and its later variant SQL, are English-like query languages that allow the user to query a database without knowing much about the underlying database structure (see Figure 11A.14).

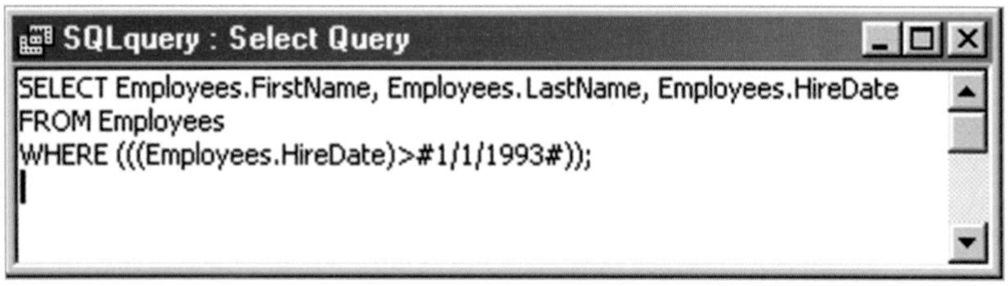
SQLquery : Select Query
SELECT Employees.FirstName, Employees.LastName, Employees.HireDate
FROM Employees
WHERE (((Employees.HireDate)>#1/1/1993#));

FIGURE 11A.14

This SQL query opens the Employees table and extracts a list of all employees whose hire date is after 01/01/1993.

SQL (Structured Query Language, pronounced "ess-cue-el" or "sequel") is a powerful tool and nearly all PC-based database management systems include it. Because each DBMS application has its own special features, however, developers have a tendency to create dialects of SQL that do not quite meet the standard for a universal database querying language. Sometimes the developers add commands; other times they limit the commands or some of the command options. Nevertheless, SQL is useful and you will see it available in relational DBMSs such as SQL Server, Oracle, DB2, Microsoft Access, and others.

In addition to SQL, PC-based databases sometimes use a query/programming language called Xbase (see Figure 11A.15). Like SQL, Xbase is somewhat English-like, but it is more complicated because its commands cover the full range of database activities, not just queries. As with SQL, software developers have a

FIGURE 11A.15

An Xbase query to generate a list of employees hired after 01/01/1993.

```
Use Employees
List FirstName, LastName for HireDate >"01/01/93"
```

tendency to create dialects of Xbase to suit their software's needs, so each version of Xbase may be a little different from its peers.

Some DBMS programs provide an interface, like a form or a grid, that collects the facts about a query from the user and composes the SQL or query statements behind the scenes. This feature allows a user to query by example (QBE) or to perform "intuitive" queries. With QBE, you specify the search criteria by typing values or expressions into the fields of a QBE form or grid (see Figure 11A.16).

Field:	LastName	FirstName	HireDate
Table:	Employees	Employees	Employees
Sort:			
Show:	☑	☑	☑
Criteria:			>#1/1/93#
or:			

FIGURE 11A.16

A QBE query to generate a list of employees hired after 01/01/1993.

Whether a DBMS uses SQL, Xbase, or QBE, or offers all three, the results of a query are always the same (see Figure 11A.17).

Hire Dates Post 1-1-93 : Sele...

Last Name	First Name	Hire Date
Peacock	Margaret	03-May-93
Buchanan	Steven	17-Oct-93
Suyama	Michael	17-Oct-93
King	Robert	02-Jan-94
Callahan	Laura	05-Mar-94
Dodsworth	Anne	15-Nov-94

Record: 1 of 6

FIGURE 11A.17

The results of the SQL, Xbase, or QBE query showing a list of employees hired after 01/01/1993.

Generating Reports

Not all DBMS operations have to occur on screen. Just as forms can be based on queries, so can reports. A report is printed information that, like a query result, is assembled by gathering data based on user-supplied criteria. In fact, report generators in most DBMSs create reports from queries.

Reports can range from simple lists of records to customized formats for specific purposes, such as invoices. Report generators can use selected data and criteria to carry out automated mathematical calculations as the report is printed. For example, relevant data can be used to calculate subtotals and totals for invoices or sales summaries. Reports are also similar to forms because their layout can be customized with objects representing fields and other controls, as shown in Figure 11A.18.

Marine Adventures and Sunken Treasures

Listing of Customer Dive Shops Worldwide

Bahamas

Customer No.	Name	Street	City	State/Prov.	ZIP/Postal Code
1,231.00	Unisco	PO Box Z-547	Freeport		
2,163.00	SCUBA Heaven	PO Box Q-8874	Nassau		
2,165.00	Shangri-La Sports Center	PO Box D-5495	Freeport		
5,384.00	Tora Tora Tora	PO Box H-4573	Nassau		

Belize

Customer No.	Name	Street	City	State/Prov.	ZIP/Postal Code
1,984.00	Adventure Undersea	PO Box 744	Belize City		

Bermuda

Customer No.	Name	Street	City	State/Prov.	ZIP/Postal Code
6,215.00	Underwater SCUBA Comp	PO Box Sn94	Somerset		SXBN
6,582.00	Norwest'er SCUBA Ltd.	PO Box 6834	Paget		PSBZ

British West Indies

Customer No.	Name	Street	City	State/Prov.	ZIP/Postal Code
1,354.00	Cayman Divers World Unl.	PO Box 541		Grand Cayman	
3,151.00	Fisherman's Eye	PO Box 7542		Grand Cayman	
5,163.00	Safari Under the Sea	PO Box 7456		Grand Cayman	

Canada

Customer No.	Name	Street	City	State/Prov.	ZIP/Postal Code
1,551.00	Marmot Divers Club	827 Queen St.	Kitchner	Ontario	G3N 2E1
2,156.00	Davy Jones' Locker	246 S. 16th Place	Vancouver	British Columbia	K8V 9P1
4,531.00	On-Target SCUBA	7-73763 Nakanawa	Winnipeg	Manitoba	J2R 5T3

FIGURE 11A.18

This polished-looking summary is a relatively simple database report.

At Issue

Play Ball! Baseball Enters the Information Age

What if a batter knew the probability pitcher Curt Shilling would throw a high-and-inside fast ball on a 3 and 2 count in the third inning? What if the pitcher knew player Bernie Williams swings at curve balls that are high and outside 62 percent of the time when he's behind the count and hits .033 when he does? What if Major League Baseball coaches and players could access such information—all while playing a game?

Now they can. Using a complex database of baseball statistics and special software, teams today have a new, high-tech weapon in the highly competitive world of MLB.

Software company Tendu has created a complex archival database system for use by professional ball players and their coaches and managers. With the software, a coach can check his laptop for exactly the info he needs to instruct his players before taking the field, including a player's ZR (zone rating) and RF (range factor), a hitter's OPS (on-base percentage plus slugging percentage), and a pitcher's WHIP (walks and hits allowed per inning pitched).

Not that keeping and tracking statistics is anything new. Baseball stats are an almost sacred part of the national pastime. Computer-generated analysis has been part of the game for at least a decade, with the industry leader STATS, Inc., dominating the market. But the Washington-based Tendu is working to bring a level of precision and detail to stat-keeping as yet unseen.

Tendu relies on a team of 17 former collegiate and professional ballplayers who spend hours reviewing games off satellite feeds and inputting everything that happens into Tendu's computers. *Everything*: type, speed, movement, and location of each pitch; where and how hard the ball was hit; player performance; and the results of every play. Each of the season's 2,400 games takes up to 12 hours to log. Overnight, teams are updated on the most complex statistical minutiae imaginable.

Tendu's application consists of a data-collection interface, an application architect, a developer, swing components, a flat-file database, a homegrown app server, an

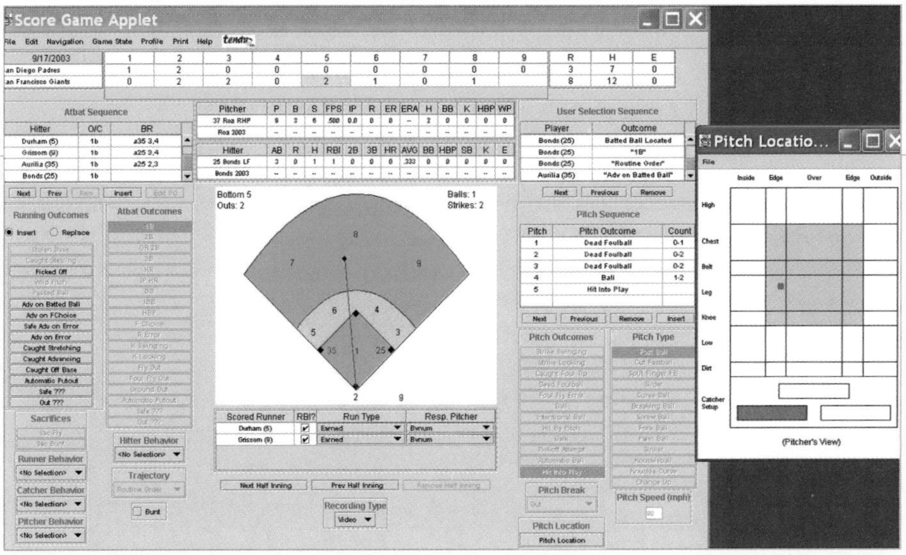

Tendu software can keep track of every baseball statistic imaginable.

Apache Web server, TiVo systems for data input, and the Java runtime environment.

So far, only the NY Mets and the Oakland A's have adopted the new system, but Tendu promises many more teams will do so next season.

The question is, will Tendu and similar start-ups revolutionize the way baseball is played? Or are they just high-tech toys to be utilized by a few pioneers? Some question whether technology has a role in the tradition of baseball, where hunches and judgment calls are the rule.

But Tendu and other high-tech advocates hope to convince teams that using advanced technology is the future of the game. As Boston Red Sox president Larry Lucchino said, "We've lived through an information revolution that has affected every aspect of our lives. Why shouldn't baseball be similarly impacted by the sea of change?"

LESSON // 11A Review

Summary ::

- A database is a repository for collections of related data or facts.
- A database management system (DBMS) is a software tool that enables many users to add, view, and work with the data in a database.
- Flat-file databases are two-dimensional tables of fields and records. They cannot form relationships with other tables.
- Relational databases are powerful because they can form relationships among different tables.
- To create a database, you must first set up its tables and define the types of fields each table will contain.
- Forms are custom screens for displaying and entering data that can be associated with database tables and queries.
- Filters let you browse through selected records that meet a set of criteria.
- Sorting arranges records in a table according to specific criteria.
- Queries are user-constructed statements that set conditions for selecting and manipulating data.
- Reports are user-generated sets of data usually printed as a document.

Key Terms ::

binary field, 428
binary large object (BLOB), 428
counter field, 428
database, 422
database management system (DBMS), 422
date field, 428
field, 423
filter, 430
flat-file database, 425
form, 429
logical field, 428
memo field, 429
numeric field, 428
query, 432
query by example (QBE), 433
record, 423
relational database, 425
report, 433
sort, 430
SQL, 432
table, 423
text field, 428
time field, 428
Xbase, 432

Key Term Quiz ::

Complete each statement by writing one of the terms listed under Key Terms in each blank.

1. In a database table, each row represents a(n) __________ .
2. In a record, it is not necessary for every __________ to contain data.
3. A(n) __________ contains a single table.
4. Index or autonumber fields are also called __________ .
5. __________ is an English-like query language used by nearly all PC-based database management systems.
6. A(n) __________ is a DBMS feature used to display a selected list or subset of records from a table.
7. A(n) __________ field allows you to enter text of any length.
8. You can create printed __________ from the data in a database.
9. DBMS means __________ .
10. The term *column* is sometimes used instead of the more popular term __________ .

LESSON // 11A Review

Multiple Choice ::

Circle the word or phrase that best completes each statement.

1. A __________ is an example of a database.
   a. telephone book b. form c. field d. report
2. A __________ is a complete collection of records.
   a. table b. field c. DBMS d. row
3. A __________ database is made up of a set of tables where a common field in any two tables creates a relationship between the tables.
   a. flat-file b. large c. relational d. DBMS
4. A __________ can store an object, such as a picture, rather than text or numeric data.
   a. counter field b. binary field c. logical field d. numeric field
5. A __________ tells the DBMS to display records that satisfy a condition while hiding those that do not.
   a. form b. column c. filter d. report
6. Clerks or other data entry personnel fill in a __________ .
   a. filter b. report c. SQL d. form
7. You use a(n) __________ sort order to arrange records alphabetically, from A to Z.
   a. rising b. falling c. ascending d. descending
8. A unique numeric value that the DBMS assigns to each record is called a __________ .
   a. counter field b. query c. binary field. d. time field
9. A __________ field can hold only one of two values, such as Yes or No.
   a. two-way b. binary c. logical d. counter
10. Characters that are not used in calculations are usually stored in a __________ .
    a. database b. text field c. date field d. binary field

Review Questions ::

In your own words, briefly answer the following questions.

1. What is the difference between a database and a database management system?
2. In a database table, what does each column represent?
3. What is a form?
4. What is a filter?
5. What is a query?
6. Why are records sometimes called "rows"?
7. What is special about a memo field?
8. What are counter fields used for?
9. When should a BLOB be used?
10. Logical fields hold what kind of data?

Lesson Labs ::

Complete the following exercises as directed by your instructor.

1. Determine whether a database management program is installed on your computer. If you have an application suite (such as Microsoft Office, Corel WordPerfect Office, or Lotus SmartSuite) installed, a database application may be installed as part of the suite. Otherwise, a stand-alone DBMS package may be installed. Locate your DBMS and launch it. What steps must you take to start the program?
2. Create a sample database by using a database application, a spreadsheet program, or your word processor's table feature.
   a. Launch the program.
   b. Set up the following field names: Last Name, First Name, Street Address, City, State, ZIP Code, and Phone Number. If you are using a database program, you may need to specify whether these fields should be text, numeric, or other types of fields.
   c. Enter data in each field for six people. When you are finished, save the new file to disk. Name it My First Database, and then close the program.

LESSON // 11B

Survey of Database Systems

Overview: When Applications Grow Huge

You've probably used a variety of computer applications: a word processor, an Internet browser, games, and so on. These are relatively small programs, designed to be installed on a single computer's hard drive, to run within that computer, and generally to interact with only a single user at any one time. That's the traditional computer application model, and it's still the largest category of computer programs.

But there's another category—called *enterprise software*—and it's becoming ever more popular. Enterprise software can be any type of large-scale program that is meant to handle the needs of many users. One hallmark of enterprise software is that it is almost always networked—made available to users via a large private network or the Internet. Another characteristic of many enterprise applications is the fact that they are based on very large, complex databases. In some organizations, thousands of users may access the same enterprise application, but for a wide range of different purposes.

This lesson introduces you to enterprise software and discusses its importance in today's organizations. You will also learn about the various types of database management systems that lie at the heart of these applications.

OBJECTIVES ::

- >> Define the terms *enterprise*, *distributed application*, and *tier*.
- >> Provide at least two examples of how software can handle many users at once.
- >> Explain how databases are used by businesses and individuals.
- >> Compare the four most popular corporate database management systems.

Enterprise Software

You could use the word *enterprise* to describe any organization. However, people who work with computers use the term enterprise to mean organizations with large hardware installations running large software applications. In other words, an enterprise system is a very large-scale computer system. Enterprise software is typically a suite of applications used by hundreds, or even thousands, of people at the same time, which handles millions of records, or both.

Sometimes an enterprise application looks very much like the DBMS that drives it, as is the case with many inventory management programs. Other times the underlying database is mostly hidden, as is the case in many order entry systems.

Because enterprise systems are so large, it is tempting to think of them as mainframe tools and not a major concern for PC users. However, today's PCs are as powerful as mainframes were a few years ago, and many large-scale DBMS applications—such as Oracle, IBM's DB2, and Microsoft's SQL Server—run just fine on PC servers and networks. So it is possible that, in a business or educational environment, you might run into enterprise software, particularly where a network is used. And even if a single PC does not have a huge application running on it, that PC might be part of a group of PCs working together to execute various parts of a single huge application. The Internet, and improvements in communications and security, make it possible for applications to be divided into parts that reside on different PCs—even if those PCs are in separate locations around the world. An application that executes on separate PCs like this is called a distributed application.

The word tier is another term used to describe distributed applications. For instance, if you divide the job of managing a database between two computers (a client and server), it is called a two-tier application. You also find three-tier applications: one computer displays a visible user interface for data entry; a second computer executes the business logic (figuring out what data is needed from the database, how to connect to the database, and so on); and a third computer holds the database itself. Some database applications—called *n*-tier applications—divide among even more than three machines.

Norton ONLINE

For more information on enterprise software, visit **http://www.mhhe.com/peternorton**.

Meeting the Needs of Many Users

Some enterprise applications must be able to handle a great deal of traffic, from users who may be located all over the place. For example, two users with identical software can access the same data source and perform the same tasks, even if they are on opposite sides of town—or opposite sides of the world. It is also possible for users to work with different software but still access the same central data source. One example of this is when people using different Internet browsers place orders from the same online database, as shown in Figure 11B.1.

Here's another example. One popular type of enterprise software is called an electronic document management (EDM) system. It tracks documents, keeps related ideas together, and aids in facilities management. Using such an application, a maintenance worker can display line drawings of a factory floor to see what changes are necessary for an impending project. The same software also allows a secretary to record text notes from a project meeting and link them to the line drawings of the factory

FIGURE 11B.1

Enterprise applications may need to service many thousands of users simultaneously, such as the database system underlying eBay.

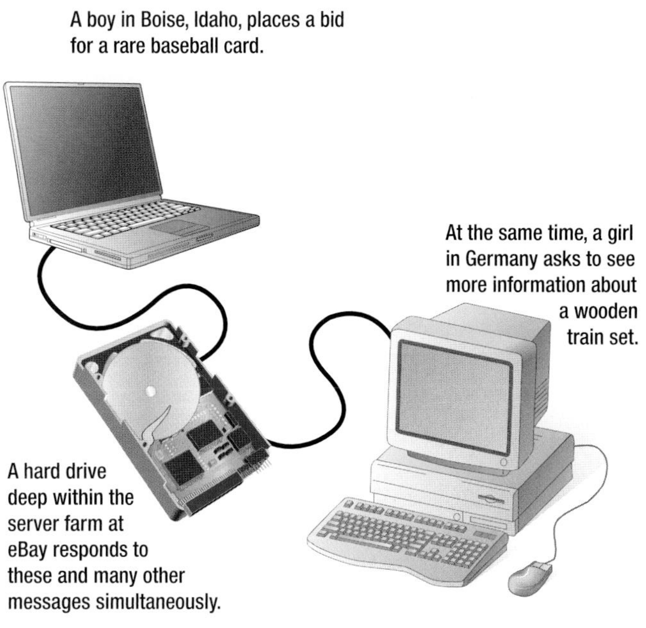
A boy in Boise, Idaho, places a bid for a rare baseball card.
At the same time, a girl in Germany asks to see more information about a wooden train set.
A hard drive deep within the server farm at eBay responds to these and many other messages simultaneously.

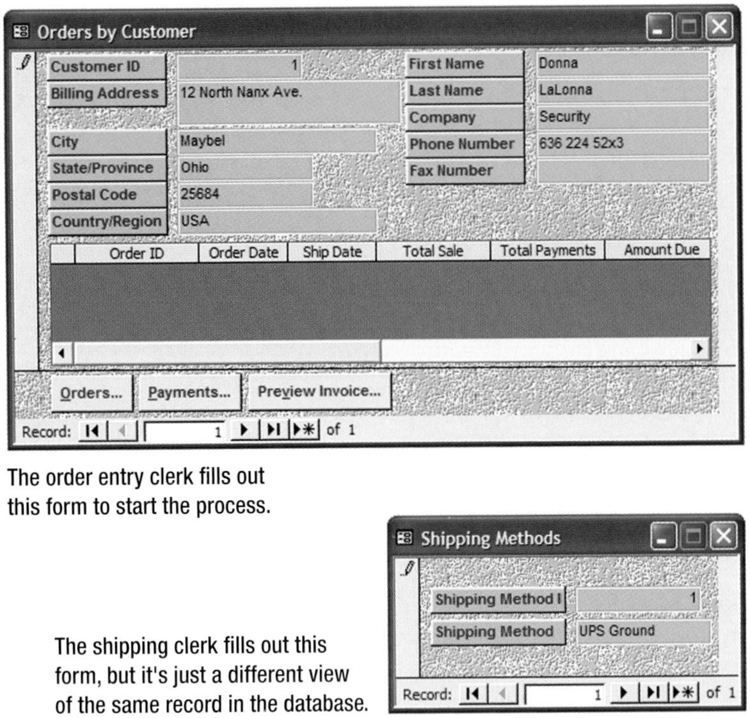

FIGURE 11B.2

Although these two users are typing into different forms, they are simultaneously interacting with the same record in the database.

floor. Engineers using the software can add redline corrections to the factory floor drawings, and project supervisors can display the meeting notes. As work on the project progresses, an engineer may use the software to add a bill of materials while a company purchasing agent tracks inventory as it is consumed.

The idea of one application meeting the needs of many diverse users applies even if the users are doing different kinds of work. Consider an EDM system that is used to manage patient records in a hospital. A receptionist may use the software to record appointments and patient insurance claims, while a doctor may use the same patient records to find X-rays and medical histories. In another part of the hospital, an administrator can monitor the number of beds in use and determine staffing needs accordingly. In other words, enterprise software is large and each user interface may look different depending on the needs of the particular user, but it is all tied together underneath by a DBMS (see Figure 11B.2).

There's another issue to consider when many people need to use the same database: High traffic can potentially slow things down to a crawl, just like rush hour in Atlanta. One popular solution: If someone wants to view a table of data, it's often best to detach that table from the database and send this disconnected table to the user.

For example, many thousands of people surf the Amazon product catalog at any given time, so it would be impractical to maintain a direct open connection between each of them and the Amazon database. The popular Microsoft Access database application (described later in this chapter) can only efficiently maintain between 10 and 30 simultaneous updating user connections. Database administrators can solve this bottleneck to a degree by using **disconnected datasets**. An example of a disconnected dataset is shown in Figure 11B.3.

FIGURE 11B.3

This disconnected dataset is a table that was copied from a sample grocer's database, but the connection to that database is no longer active.

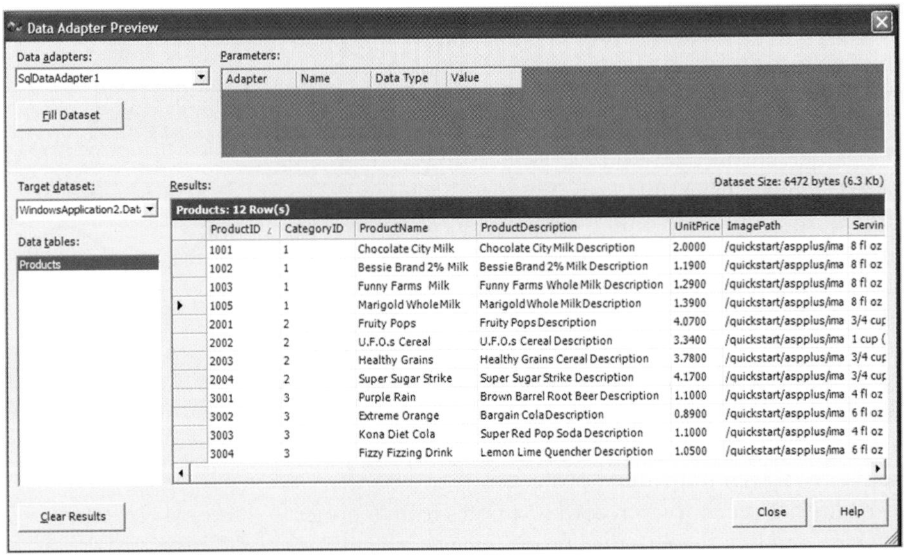

Here's how it works: The user connects to the database, but only long enough to "check out" the list of products he or she is interested in reviewing. The connection to the database is broken, but the user can spend as long as he or she wants viewing the dataset, the portion of the database the user requested. Finally, if you've made any changes to the database (such as typing in a review of a product), a new brief connection is established with the server and your review is submitted. After being examined for appropriateness by an employee, your review is then formally added to the database. During all this activity, connections to the database itself are only maintained briefly, only for as long as it takes to extract a set of data, or update a table with new data.

Regardless of the tasks performed by a particular piece of enterprise software, there is a good chance that a database is at work somewhere down in the system. The fact that a database lurks at the heart of most enterprise software does not mean the software looks or acts like a database—at least not from the end user's perspective. In fact, you usually find user-friendly, nontechnical interfaces that deliberately hide the underlying database from the users. Often these user interfaces—the screens that the users interact with—are designed to look like familiar, existing paper forms that the user once filled out by hand.

Databases at Work

No matter what kind of work you do, you're almost certain to use a computer in at least some aspect of your job. And if you use a computer, you'll also be using databases often. Databases replace, or supplement, many traditional information storage systems. Everything from file cabinets to dictionaries is disappearing from today's workplace. After all, why thumb through a dictionary when it's so much easier to type in a word at Webster's online site at http://www.m-w.com/netdict.htm (see Figure 11B.4). As soon as a dictionary appears on the Internet, it's no longer just a dictionary, a book full of words—it's a database of words, as you can see in Figure 11B.5.

Norton ONLINE

For more information on data mining, visit **http://www.mhhe.com/peternorton**.

Databases in Business

Databases have become essential to most modern businesses—to the point that most companies cannot remain competitive if they don't computerize at least

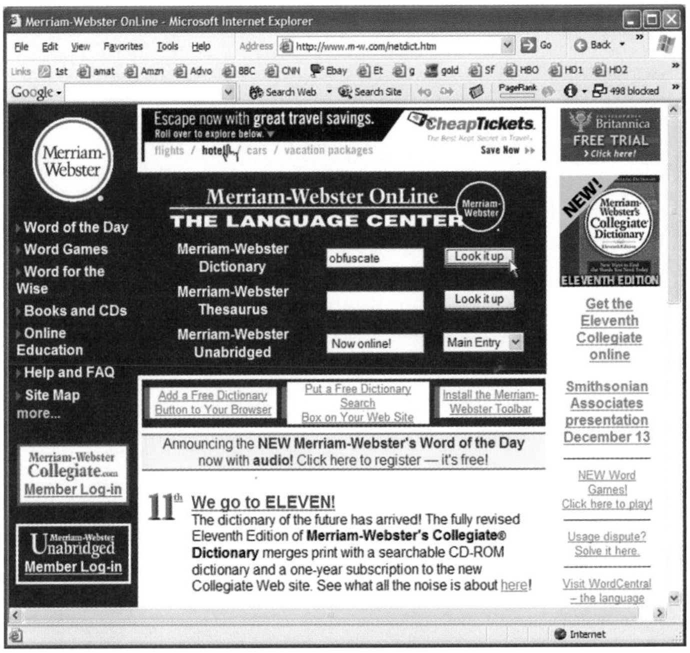

FIGURE 11B.4

Many Internet sites are simply entry forms for database queries. Here you can query the Merriam-Webster dictionary.

FIGURE 11B.5

After you click the Look It Up button, the dictionary's database is searched and results are displayed instantly.

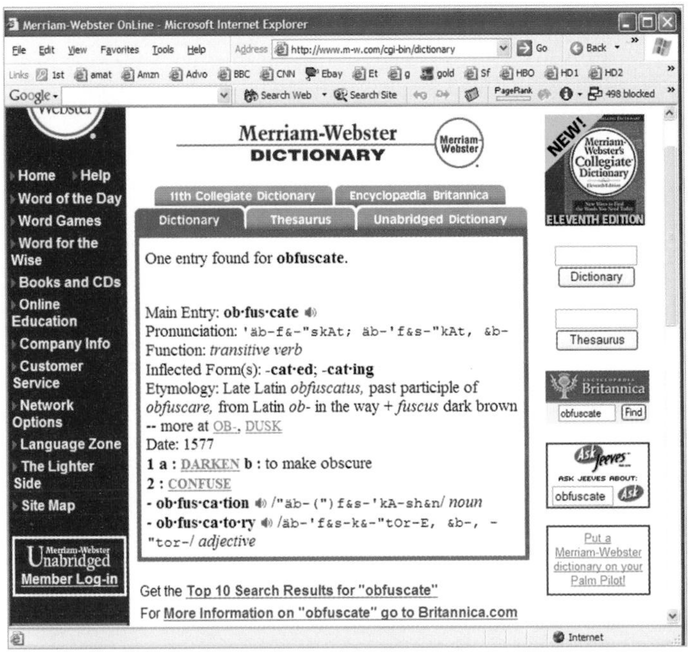

some of their operations. Obvious productivity boosts result from using databases for inventory management, payroll, order fulfillment, and other clerical tasks. Perhaps less obvious are the sometimes startling ideas that bubble up when the new database analysis technique called data mining is used.

Knowledge discovery is a type of database utility designed to analyze data and report back with useful information. Data mining is one type of knowledge discovery where a program searches a database, discovering hidden information. Using statistics, artificial intelligence, modeling techniques, and other tools, data mining can predict trends or relationships that likely would never be noticed by a human analyst—even a really skilled, hardworking analyst.

Data mining can provide a company with suggestions about improving efficiency, predict trends, and otherwise offer wise and useful ideas. Notice that data mining doesn't just provide *facts*; it provides actual *ideas*—and there is a difference.

For example, data mining can give you answers to questions you didn't ask. Traditional data analysis requires that you first ask a question, such as "give me a list of all overdue accounts." SQL can get answers to practically any specific question you want to ask of a database.

Data mining, however, works differently. It searches a database all by itself, discovering "gems" of information and bringing them to your attention.

For example, data mining might tell you that 78 percent of the people who bought your tea kettle returned to your Web site within two weeks to buy a tea strainer. With information like this, you can store these items together in the warehouse, saving your company some money. And you can modify your catalog to suggest to your tea kettle customers that they might want to purchase the strainer at the same time, saving your customers shipping and handling costs. Everybody wins.

Organizations accumulate huge amounts of data, and usually within that giant collection of information are relationships that—once revealed via data mining—can be used to improve efficiency. Traditionally, you had to know what to look for before you could begin an analysis of a database. You had to know what questions to ask of the data. Data mining discovers subtle, sophisticated, and sometimes essential information that nobody would have noticed. It can alert you, for example, that your customers in California are increasingly purchasing from a competitor. What's more, it can tell you why they're abandoning your product line, and what you can do about it. And it can make these recommendations early on, before the problem becomes impossible to solve.

Databases on the Internet

Many ordinary Web sites, and nearly every commercial site, run on top of a database. Any site that provides a search feature is offering you access to their database. And, of course, whenever you view a catalog or place an online order, you're interacting with a database. Amazon and eBay are perhaps the most famous online database-driven sites.

FIGURE 11B.6

Google has become the most popular Internet search engine.

Beyond commerce, the Internet also offers all kinds of other databases: collections of art, movie reviews, science articles, genealogy records, newspaper stories, and millions of other subjects. You'll find databases offering information as general as world geography and as specific as photos of aardvark feeding habits. Without a doubt, the Internet is the world's greatest research tool. It is filled with millions of databases—on every topic under the sun—just waiting for you to mine them.

In a larger sense, the entire Internet itself can be considered one huge database. Or perhaps a more accurate term would be *super-database*, a database of databases. True, it's not structured into tables, records, and fields, but you can use Google or other search engines and nearly always find the information you're looking for.

Search engines work by sending out crawlers, or "spiders" (to travel the "web," get it?). These little "robot agents" continually look for new Web pages and send their Internet addresses back to the search engine's database. If you're interested in finding out how large or fresh each search engine's database is, you can find that information at http://searchenginewatch.com/reports.

And what a whopping collection of data the Internet offers. For example, Google (its query page is shown in Figure 11B.6), is reported to contain an index to over 3.3 billion documents. No wonder you can find out all you need to know about aardvarks, as shown in Figure 11B.7.

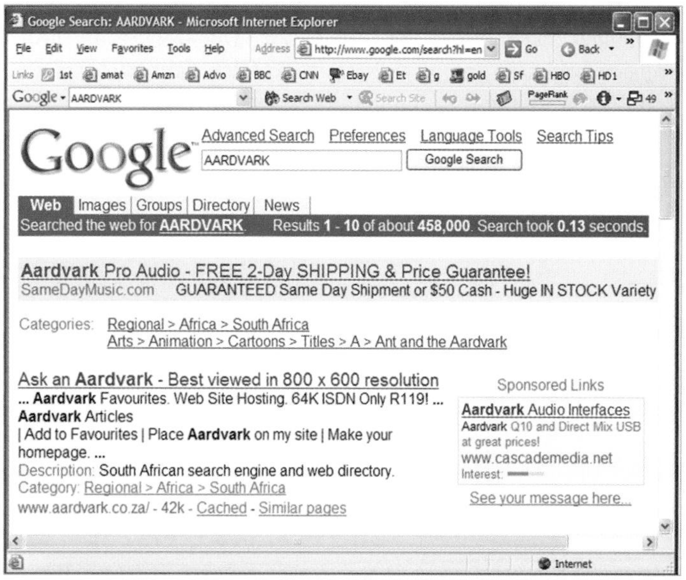

FIGURE 11B.7

Ask Google to see Web pages with information about aardvarks, and you get 458,000 results in thirteen-hundredths of a second. That's a very swift database search!

Databases for Individuals

Personal databases are useful for managing various aspects of your life. They're good, for example, if you like collecting things. If you enjoy cooking, you'll find definite benefits from entering all your recipes into a cookbook application. True, the initial data-entry process is tedious. You have to type everything into the program's database, which certainly gives you an appreciation of how tough a job data entry can be. But once you've finished, you'll be able to "import" recipes from Internet cooking sites—just copy and paste them right into your personal database.

Productivity Tip

Database Macros

If you often use Access—or indeed most other applications—it's sometimes useful to create macros. If there's some task that you frequently repeat, consider creating a macro to do that job for you quickly and automatically. For example, instead of having to move the mouse around, clicking down through a series of menus, you can simply create a macro that does the job for you. In this section, you see how to display a personal message showing any information you want.

In many Microsoft applications, you can turn on a "recorder" that watches you as you accomplish some task, and then memorizes the steps you followed. Access doesn't offer this recorder option, but you can easily create Access macros nonetheless.

To see how to create a macro, start Access and choose File | New. Then click Blank Database to create a new, empty database. Click the Create button in the File New Database dialog box. The dialog box closes. Click Macros in the left pane of the database window. This highlights the Macros option, as shown here.

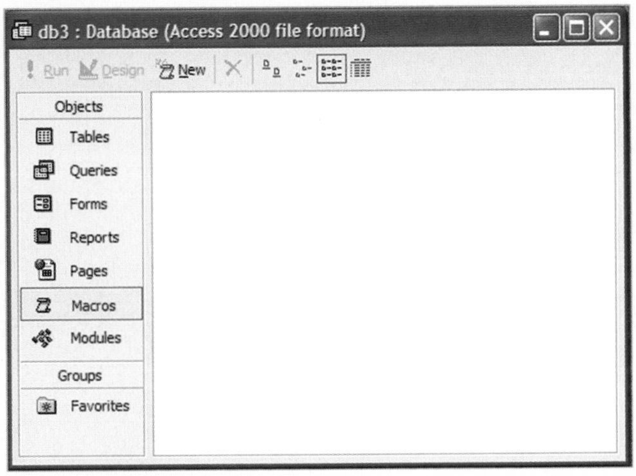

This is where you can start building a macro.

Click the New button in the database window. A macro window opens where you can specify the steps that the macro will take to complete its task. Click the down-arrow button in the Action column in the macro window and you see a list of the available steps and tasks a macro can accomplish. You can choose 58 different behaviors—from simple beeping to running an entire application.

Click the Msgbox option in the Action drop-down list. Notice that a description of this action appears in the lower right pane of the macro window. (To add additional behaviors for this macro, just move down one line by clicking the line below the word MsgBox.)

After you've built your personal database, you can then reap the benefits of computerization:

- Search your collection by a variety of criteria (by particular ingredients, or combinations of ingredients; calorie content; ethnic cuisine; appliance used such as crock pot; category such as desserts; preparation time; and so on).
- Print out a list of ingredients to take to the supermarket.
- Easily adjust a recipe that feeds four to make it feed eight—with a click of the mouse.

You'll get similar benefits from building databases for other kinds of collections: coins, books, CDs, or whatever your hobby is. And don't forget that today's databases can include photos as well as text—so you can make your personal database even more useful. Figure 11B.8 shows a personal cookbook database.

Microsoft Access is the clear leader for personal databases—it's easy to use and comes bundled with some versions of Microsoft Office (see Figure 11B.9). However, Access isn't really usable for large-scale, enterprise databases because it can host only, in the worst case, 10 users simultaneously, and the biggest database it can manage is two billion bytes. That might seem like a lot, but recall that *enterprise* means *huge* in the DBMS world, and enterprise database software such as Oracle (discussed later in this section) can handle trillions of bytes (terabytes) and

PRODUCTIVITY TIP

Your personal message macro can be used to display any information you wish.

A MsgBox is designed to display a message, so you see a list of available "arguments" (qualities) you can give to your message box. Find the set of Action Arguments on the lower left of the macro window and type **Be sure to save your work often!** in the Message field. Leave the Beep argument as is; it will cause the computer to beep whenever this message box is displayed. Click the Type field and notice that you can choose a variety of message box styles from a drop-down list. Choose the Information style, which adds a little icon to the message. In the Title field, type **Alert.** All these arguments are optional. But a message box with no message isn't too useful.

Now save your macro by choosing File | Save and when asked what Macro name you want to give it, replace the default Macro1—which isn't very descriptive—by typing **SaveWarning.** Click Ok and notice that the top of your macro window has changed to display the new name for this macro.

It's time to test your creation! Choose Run | Run and you see your excellent custom message box, as shown here. You can make the message quite large if you want to. For example, you might want to type in a list of frequently used phone numbers, macros, shortcut keys, or whatever. Then, any time you run this macro, you can see your list.

You can run macros several ways. One quick way is to click the Macros option in the database window. Look at the database window now—you'll see that Access has listed your SaveWarning macro, ready for you to double-click to execute it. You also can execute macros from the Tools menu, or even assign a shortcut key combination, such as CTRL+M, that when pressed runs the macro. Look in Access Help for details on how to assign keys.

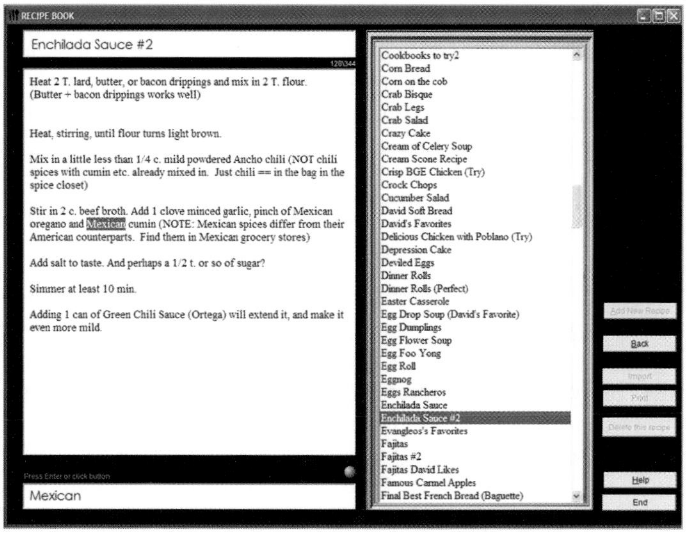

FIGURE 11B.8

Track, manage, and search any collection you enjoy. Here's a personal cookbook database.

FIGURE 11B.9

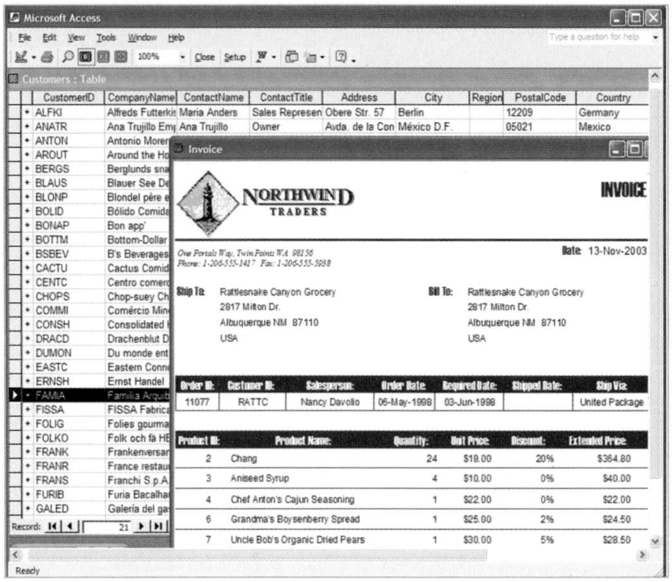

Microsoft Access is the most popular personal and small business database system.

SELF-CHECK ::

Circle the correct answer for each question.

1. Enterprise software means __________ .
   - **a.** a very large-scale computer system
   - **b.** business software
   - **c.** personal software
2. The data analysis technique that can give you answers to questions you didn't even ask is called __________ .
   - **a.** database management
   - **b.** data diving
   - **c.** data mining
3. Microsoft Access can efficiently accommodate __________ simultaneous updating users.
   - **a.** 3
   - **b.** 10 to 30
   - **c.** 2,000

simultaneously handle thousands of users. *Your* personal collection doesn't need this power, but eBay does.

Nonetheless, for home and small business database management, Access is likely to be your DBMS of choice.

Common Corporate Database Management Systems

Over the years, database management systems have come and gone. In the early 1980s, dBASE was the dominant commercial database system, but today enterprise systems dominate the scene: Oracle Corp.'s Oracle Database, IBM Corp.'s DB2, and Microsoft Corp.'s SQL Server. Each has its strengths; in this section, you learn the primary differences between these three traditional DBMSs. Also, MySQL is introduced; it can be used for free, and is especially popular for new Internet database work.

simnet™

Norton ONLINE

For more information on Oracle, visit **http://www.mhhe.com/peternorton**.

Oracle

First introduced more than 25 years ago, the Oracle database system has become the most popular enterprise-level DBMS in the world, with around 40 percent of this market. Oracle—like DBMS competitors Microsoft and IBM—offers a large suite of applications, utilities, and languages that can be used together to solve business problems and manage data. However, Oracle is losing market share to rivals IBM and Microsoft. Oracle has a reputation as the most flexible enterprise DBMS, but with this flexibility comes its equally famous complexity. In addition, Oracle is capable of running on various operating systems—Windows, UNIX, Macintosh, and Linux—a capability sometimes known as platform independence.

DB2

IBM's DB2 has versions that run on Windows, Linux, and various versions of UNIX operating systems and currently enjoys second place in popularity with around 34 percent of installed DBMSs. IBM is the most venerable of computer companies and has been developing relational database systems since 1970. IBM also developed SQL, the language now used almost universally for database queries and, in some cases, even commands that manipulate data.

As with Oracle and Microsoft, IBM offers a family of DBMS software, called DB2 Universal Database, and a suite of associated applications to assist with data mining, analysis, and integration, as well as enterprise management and data warehousing. DB2—like Oracle and SQL Server—offers a stable, robust system that's capable of high-volume activity, and includes the guarantees and support that you would expect from a major company like IBM.

Norton ONLINE

For more information on DB2, visit **http://www.mhhe.com/peternorton**.

SQL Server

Microsoft's SQL Server is the fastest-growing DBMS, though it currently has only about 11 percent of the enterprise-level database management market. In many ways, it's similar to Oracle, though a key difference is SQL Server's requirement that it run on Windows operating systems, where Oracle runs on various OSs.

Nonetheless, SQL Server is gaining in popularity because it offers improved language features and greater speed and efficiency on some benchmark tests. SQL Server 2000 currently comes in eight different versions, offering various performance and price levels to meet the needs of various organizations. Some versions are designed to manage huge data loads and they go all the way down to one that runs on tiny devices like Pocket PCs. The ability to adjust to changes in *scale*—to offer stability and efficiency when expanding from, say, only 100 to 1 million transactions—is known as scalability.

Norton ONLINE

For more information on SQL Server, visit **http://www.mhhe.com/peternorton**.

MySQL

MySQL is the most popular enterprise DBMS for the "open source" community. Some estimates range as high as four million installed MySQL applications. Many businesses enterprises embrace Linux (an "open source" operating system) and MySQL is the leading DBMS for the Linux platform. MySQL is generally simpler to use, but has fewer features than the competition, such as DB2 or SQL Server. Also, an important consideration for many businesses is MySQL's lower cost. However, MySQL isn't sitting still: It has added interfaces for Microsoft's .NET system and also now offers transactional features as well. MySQL is often recommended for new Web applications, particularly where cost is a major factor. MySQL works less well with legacy (older technology) databases. Also, MySQL isn't as scalable as alternative DBMSs. So if you expect your Web site to have surges of hundreds of simultaneous visitors interacting with your database, you need more power than MySQL currently offers. In that case, you're better off choosing Oracle or SQL Server.

Norton ONLINE

For more information on MySQL, visit **http://www.mhhe.com/peternorton**.

Computers In Your Career

Database Careers

Whether she's checking to make sure the nightly backups ran smoothly, updating data for one of her employer's 15,000 member companies, or importing new member data into the systems, Jennifer Case says she's "never bored" with her job as database administrator for CompTIA, an Oak Brook Terrace, Illinois–based global trade association representing the business interests of the information technology industry.

Case, who has a bachelor's degree in business and a master's degree in management information systems from the University of Illinois Springfield, works a 35-hour week that's spent monitoring, updating, and upgrading CompTIA's massive database, which includes members from 89 countries. One of her first stops in the morning is a special e-mail box dedicated to "user concerns," such as abnormal data or a record that's malfunctioned.

Other key duties include importing and exporting data for CompTIA's membership team, ironing out any system glitches that may occur when Case exports or imports to another firm's system, and tracking membership data (from basic information like name and address, to more complex information like the type of events members attended during the last 12 months). Case also designs and publishes the documentation for the database and related processes on the Internet, where CompTIA's staff can access them.

Fielding data from a large number of sources can be challenging at times, says Case, who is charged with making sure member data is consistent with CompTIA's data. It's not always easy, particularly when her firm's system is different than that of its members (for example, required fields on data forms may not match). "It's an ongoing issue because every new member has their own data set, and we have to develop new solutions to handle that," says Case.

Job opportunities in database-related careers are very good, says Case, who points to companies' use of knowledge management to reduce information overload as proof. Who

better than a database administrator to narrow down the information into useful chunks? To be most useful, Case says, database professionals will need to keep their technology and people skills polished and up to date, while constantly thinking of ways to enhance and maximize their systems.

Database technologies touch the work lives of millions of people each day, including secretaries, clerks, help desk and product support specialists, software engineers, and database programmers and developers who work with databases on a daily basis. Database administrators work with database management systems software and determine ways to organize and store data. They determine user requirements, set up computer databases, and test and coordinate changes.

In 2000, the Bureau of Labor Statistics reported median annual earnings of database administrators of $51,990, with the middle 50 percent earning between $38,210 and $71,440. The median annual earnings of database administrators employed in computer and data processing services were $63,710, and in telephone communication, $52,230.

Because they also may design and implement system security, database administrators often plan and coordinate security measures. With the volume of sensitive data generated every second growing rapidly, data integrity, backup, and keeping databases secure have become increasingly important aspects of the job for database administrators.

LESSON // 11B Review

Summary ::

- Enterprise software is a relatively large software system of interacting applications and one or more databases.
- Today's enterprise software usually splits its tasks among two or more applications, running on different PCs. This is known as a distributed application.
- The parts of a distributed application are known as *tiers*, so there are now two-tier, three-tier, and even *n*-tier (*n* meaning *any* number) applications.
- One of the best ways to handle heavy user traffic is to allow users to "check out" parts of a database. These disconnected datasets are a copy of a table or query, and they solve the problem of too many users simultaneously interacting with a database.
- Data mining is a sophisticated utility that searches a database, discovering hidden information. It often provides surprising results; it can give you useful answers to important questions that you didn't even think to ask.
- The Internet itself is a huge, super-database: a searchable database containing millions of other databases—a good portion of all human knowledge.
- Personal databases can be useful for organizing collections, keeping track of anniversaries, managing recipes, and many other tasks.
- The major business database systems—Oracle, SQL Server, and DB2—may someday face competition from "open source" software such as MySQL. However, MySQL isn't scalable enough—at least at this point in its development—to service high-traffic installations.

Key Terms ::

Access, 446
business logic, 441
crawler, 445
data mining, 444
DB2, 449
disconnected dataset, 441
distributed application, 441
EDM (electronic document management), 441
enterprise software, 441
enterprise system, 441
knowledge discovery, 444
MySQL, 449
n-tier application, 441
Oracle, 448
platform independence, 448
scalability, 449
SQL Server, 449
tier, 441
two-tier application, 441

Key Term Quiz ::

Complete each statement by writing one of the terms listed under Key Terms in each blank.

1. When an application is divided into several parts running on different computers, it's called a(n) ________ .
2. If a program can run on various operating systems, it is described as having ________ .
3. A(n) ________ is a portion of a database that a user can "check out" without maintaining a connection to the database.
4. A distributed application with two components is described as being a(n) ________ application.
5. A program's ability to adjust in drastic changes in usage levels is known as ________ .
6. ________ is the most popular enterprise DBMS for the "open source" community.
7. Automated programs that roam the Internet, gathering information such as the addresses of active Web sites, are called ________ .
8. ________ is IBM's suite of database programs used mostly for high-volume, enterprise systems.
9. ________ refers to an application that either manages large amounts of data or handles large numbers of users simultaneously, or both.
10. In a three-tier application, one computer may be responsible for executing the ________ which is figuring out what data is needed from the database, and other issues.

LESSON //11B Review

Multiple Choice ::

Circle the word or phrase that best completes each statement.

1. Applications that can handle high-volume traffic are called ________ .
   a. *n*-tier b. SQL c. enterprise d. DBMS
2. An application's ability to successfully manage changes in scale is known as ________ .
   a. scalability b. durability c. efficiency d. robustness
3. ________ is the most popular enterprise DBMS for the "open source" community.
   a. SQL Server b. Oracle c. DB2 d. MySQL
4. If a distributed application is divided among more than three machines, it is called a(n) ________ application.
   a. multi-tier b. *x*-tier c. *n*-tier d. *y*-tier
5. The Internet can be seen as one huge ________ .
   a. Google b. database c. enterprise d. application
6. When a user "checks out" a disconnected dataset, the connection to the database is ________ .
   a. maintained b. reversed c. sped up d. broken
7. Today's three most popular enterprise DBMSs are DB2, Oracle, and ________ .
   a. SQL Server b. MySQL c. Access d. EDM
8. Database programs often provide ________ that resemble familiar paper forms.
   a. tables b. interfaces c. filters d. datasets
9. ________ is a type of database utility designed to analyze data and report back with useful information.
   a. Knowledge discovery b. Expert discovery c. Answer discovery d. Solution discovery
10. Many commercial Web sites access a ________ .
    a. mainframe computer b. macro c. disconnected dataset d. database

Review Questions ::

In your own words, briefly answer the following questions.

1. Explain why data mining is often useful in making business decisions.
2. What is business logic?
3. What is data mining?
4. How do disconnected datasets help improve database performance?
5. What is platform independence?
6. Explain why Access is not a good choice for high-volume, large-scale enterprise systems.
7. What is an EDM system?
8. Why might you call the Internet a super-database?
9. What's the difference between MySQL and SQL Server?
10. Why do some database professionals favor platform-independent DBMSs such as Oracle?

Lesson Labs ::

Complete the following exercises as directed by your instructor.

1. Learn more details about the features offered by today's powerhouse enterprise DBMSs. Look at Oracle Corp.'s Oracle Database at this Web site: http://www.oracle.com/database. What is the latest version Oracle offers? Locate links on the Oracle Web site that offer demos, comparisons with other DBMSs, reviews by database experts, performance analysis, migration information, and so on. Explore these topics with a view to making a recommendation about why Oracle would, or would not, be a good choice for a small company that averages three visitors per day to its Web site. (*Note*: Don't download any files from the Internet without your instructor's permission.)
2. Compare the features offered by Microsoft's SQL Server (http://www.microsoft.com/sql) with the features offered by Oracle. Which system do you think seems best suited to a company that plans to move from Windows to Linux within the next five years? Explain your reasoning.

Chapter Labs

Complete the following exercises using a computer in your classroom, lab, or home.

1. Design a database. You can create an outline for a database by using a word processor. Imagine that you own a small business that sells gourmet coffees. You want to create a database system to store information about products, vendors, customers, employees, accounts paid and received, and so on. Open your word processor and, in a blank document, list the tables you would include in your database. Under the name of each table, create a list of the fields the table should contain. Use your word processor's drawing tools to show the relationships between the tables. When you are finished, print the document and save the file under the name "Design." Close the word processor.
2. Create user documentation for the database you designed in the previous exercise. Assume that your database will be used on an Internet site, so some of its tables and fields will be displayed on the site's pages for customers to see. Open a word processor and write a paragraph explaining to a database professional how to implement your database. Then list the data type of each field in the database. Describe which tables and fields should be made public on the Web site and which should be hidden from the public and used only internally by the company.
3. Explore privacy issues. Given that the Internet is the greatest research tool the world has ever known, answers to your questions are often only a few seconds away. Try searching for "Patriot Act" to see what the ACLU and others are saying about the potential dangers in today's database-driven world. See if you can find the actual document that Congress passed: H.R. 3162 (October 25, 2001). It begins like this: "To deter and punish terrorist acts in the United States and around the world, to enhance law enforcement investigatory tools, and for other purposes."

Discussion Questions

As directed by your instructor, discuss the following questions in class or in groups.

1. Describe a scenario in which a large organization might use a database management system. What types of tables would the organization's database contain? What kinds of relationships would exist among the tables? What types of forms would be needed, and by what users? What types of queries and reports would managers want to run on this database?
2. Discuss the advantages of using a database in your personal life. What hobbies would benefit from computerization? How hard would it be to type in all the data for various kinds of collections—stamps, buttons, coins, books, and so on? When designing a personal database, how would you divide the data into tables, and then divide the tables into fields?

Research and Report

Using your own choice of resources (such as the Internet, books, magazines, and newspaper articles), research and write a short paper discussing one of the following topics:

- SQL and its uses in business.
- The advantages of relational databases, compared to flat-file databases.
- Explain several ways that XML is used in business databases today.

When you are finished, proofread and print your paper, and give it to your instructor.

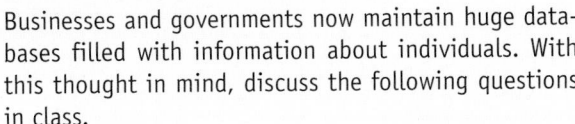

ETHICAL ISSUES

Businesses and governments now maintain huge databases filled with information about individuals. With this thought in mind, discuss the following questions in class.

1. You submit information about yourself whenever you apply for a credit card, subscribe to a magazine, or register a product that you have purchased. Should businesses and government agencies be allowed to keep this data permanently? How much information should they be allowed to collect about individuals? Do you feel the practice of maintaining—and even selling—your personal data is wrong or should be illegal? Why or why not?
2. Credit agencies, banks, and other institutions commonly sell information about their customers, which is then used to create direct-marketing lists. Some people feel only you should decide whether or not to sell your private information. Do you share this view? Why or why not?

CHAPTER 12

Development of Information Systems

01 02 03 04 05 06 07 08 09 10 11 12 13 14

CHAPTER CONTENTS ::

This chapter contains the following lessons:

LESSON // 12A

The Basics of Information Systems

Overview: What Is an Information System?

In its most basic form, an information system (often abbreviated as IS) is a mechanism that helps people collect, store, organize, and use information. The basic purpose of any information system is to help its users get a certain type of value from the information in the system, regardless of the type of information that is stored or the type of value desired. Information systems, therefore, can be designed to help people harness many kinds of information in countless ways. Ultimately, the information system is the computer's reason for being.

Information systems have become such a normal part of the modern business world that we do not notice them anymore. For example, do you realize that the process of making an ATM withdrawal is managed by a huge financial information system?

As you study information systems, remember that they do much more than store and retrieve data—they help people *use* information, whether that involves sorting lists, running a factory's computer-controlled machining system, printing reports, matching a single fingerprint against a national database of millions of prints, or tracking planes in the night sky.

OBJECTIVES ::

- Define the term *information system*.
- Name five types of information systems.
- Explain the purpose of each major type of information system.
- Distinguish between intranets, extranets, and virtual private networks.
- Discuss technologies for storing and managing data.

FIGURE 12A.1

Computer storage systems are often compared to file cabinets, and for good reason: They give people a way to organize and store large amounts of information.

The Purpose of Information Systems

Information systems consist of three basic components:

- The physical means for storing data, such as a file cabinet or hard disk. A notebook may meet the data storage requirements of a very small organization. For many businesses, data storage is an enormous requirement that involves terabytes of disk space (see Figure 12A.1).
- The procedures for handling information to ensure its integrity. Regardless of the size of the information system, data-management rules must be followed to eliminate duplicate entries, validate the accuracy of data, and avoid the loss of important data.
- The rules regarding data's use and distribution. In any organization, data is meant to be used for specific purposes in order to achieve a desired result. By establishing rules governing the use of its information, an organization preserves its resources rather than wasting them on manipulating data in useless ways. To ensure the security of their mission-critical data, many organizations set rules that limit the information that can be made available to certain workers, enabling workers to access only the most appropriate types of information for their jobs. Different people require different information to perform their jobs. The rules of the system govern what information should be distributed to whom, at what time, and in what format.

These basic components may seem simple, but a large information system can be very complicated. In addition to the three components listed earlier, it is important that the system have a means for distributing information to different users, whether it is a system of desk trays or a modern network. Most of today's information systems also include tools for sorting, categorizing, and analyzing information—further adding to their complexity, but also making them much more useful to people.

Types of Information Systems

As more and more business functions have been automated, information systems have become increasingly specialized. One of a company's systems, for example, may help users gather and store sales orders. Another system may help managers analyze data. These specialized systems can operate alone or they can be combined to create a larger system that performs different functions for different people.

Office Automation Systems

An office automation system uses computers and/or networks to perform various operations, such as word processing, accounting, document management, or communications. Office automation systems are designed to manage information and—more important—to help users handle certain information-related tasks more efficiently. In large organizations, simple tasks such as project scheduling, record keeping, and correspondence can become extremely time-consuming and labor-intensive. By using office automation tools, however, workers at all levels can spend less time and effort on the mundane tasks, allowing time for handling more mission-critical jobs such as planning, designing, and selling. For this reason, nearly any complete information system has an office automation component.

Norton ONLINE

For more information on office automation systems, visit **http://www.mhhe.com/peternorton**.

Office automation systems can be built from off-the-shelf applications. There are several suites of office automation programs, such as Microsoft Office, WordPerfect Office, and Lotus SmartSuite. Each of these includes several applications, such as a word processor, a spreadsheet program, a presentation program, an e-mail client, and a database management system. The programs can be used interchangeably to facilitate office tasks (see Figure 12A.2).

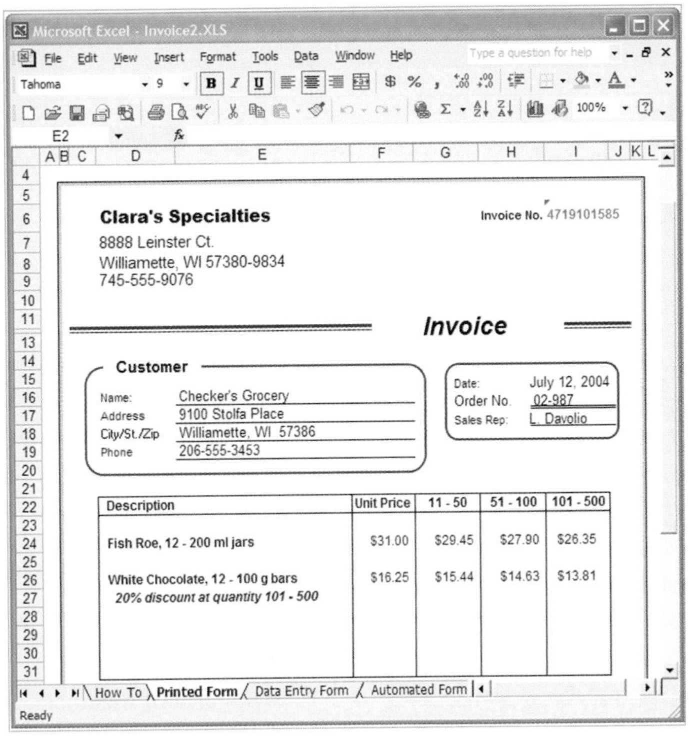

FIGURE 12A.2

Companies often automate standard tasks, such as the creation of correspondence or invoices. Here, Microsoft Excel is used to create an invoice based on an existing template and information from a customer database.

Transaction Processing Systems

A transaction is a complete event, which may occur as a series of many steps, such as taking an order from a customer. Although you may conduct business transactions frequently, you may have never considered the steps that make up a typical transaction. All these steps can be processed through an information system. A system that handles the processing and tracking of transactions is called a transaction processing system (TPS).

Consider the process for ordering a product from a catalog by telephone. The transaction typically begins when a customer service representative collects information about you, such as your name, address, credit card number, and the items you want to purchase. The customer service representative may enter the data into a database through an on-screen form, which ensures that the data is saved in the appropriate data tables. On the other hand, if you order or purchase a product in person, a sales clerk might "swipe" your credit card through a card reader and enter other information about you into a point-of-sales (POS) system. Either way, the critical data must be entered into the information system before the transaction's steps can be completed.

The human order taker is bypassed if you purchase merchandise from Amazon.com or one of countless other sites that offer online shopping. Otherwise it's basically the same. You select the items you wish to purchase, place them into a virtual shopping cart, and when you have finished selecting items you move to the checkout area, a page where you see the total price of the items, select the method of payment and delivery, and specify the delivery address.

No matter whether you use the telephone or the Web, after taking your order, the company verifies your credit card information, checks its inventory to determine whether the items are available, "picks" the items from inventory, ships them to you, and bills your credit card. At each step, the order must be passed to the appropriate department (see Figure 12A.3).

It is important that the right people review the data at the appropriate times. Suppose, for example, that an item you order is out of stock. In a well-designed system, a customer service representative receives an alert about this information and notifies you, giving you the option of placing the item on back-order and ensuring that your credit card will not be billed until the item is actually shipped to you. If you receive a product and want to return it, the information from your order also is used to process the return so you do not need to restart the process with the vendor.

Norton ONLINE

For more information on transaction processing systems, visit **http://www.mhhe.com/peternorton**.

Norton ONLINE

For more information on management information systems, visit **http://www.mhhe.com/peternorton**.

Management Information Systems

Within any business, workers at different levels need access to the same type of information, but they may need to view the information in different ways. At a call

FIGURE 12A.3

An example of a transaction processing system. The order information is used to manage the processes of inventory control, shipping, billing, payments, and more.

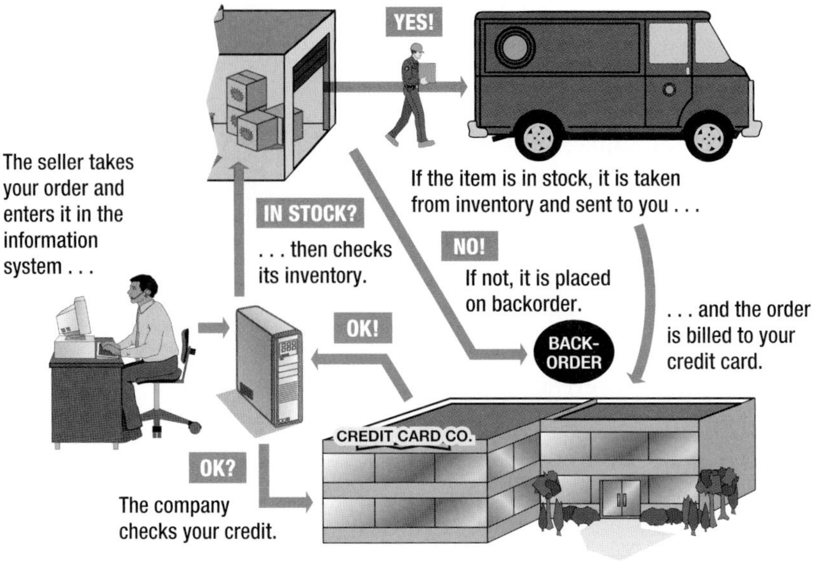
YES!
The seller takes your order and enters it in the information system . . .
IN STOCK?
. . . then checks its inventory.
If the item is in stock, it is taken from inventory and sent to you . . .
NO!
If not, it is placed on backorder.
BACK-ORDER
. . . and the order is billed to your credit card.
OK!
CREDIT CARD CO.
OK?
The company checks your credit.

center, for example, a supervisor may need to see a daily report detailing the number of calls received, the types of requests made, and the production levels of individual staff members. A midlevel manager, such as a branch manager, may need to see only a monthly summary of this data shown in comparison to previous months, with a running total or average.

Managers at different levels also may need very different types of data. A senior manager, such as a vice president of finance or chief financial officer, could be responsible for a company's financial performance; he or she would view the company's financial information (usually in detail) regularly. But a front-line manager who oversees daily production may receive little or no financial data, except when it specifically affects his or her area of responsibility.

FIGURE 12A.4

Management information systems generate reports for managers at different levels.

Milltown Manufacturing, Inc.
Sales Analysis
Q4 2002

	Sales	Backorders	Shipments
October	$ 87,542.00	$ 13,921.00	$ 73,621.00
November	$ 98,451.00	$ 10,188.00	$ 88,263.00
December	$ 96,444.00	$ 14,769.00	$ 81,675.00
	$ 282,437.00	$ 38,878.00	$ 243,559.00

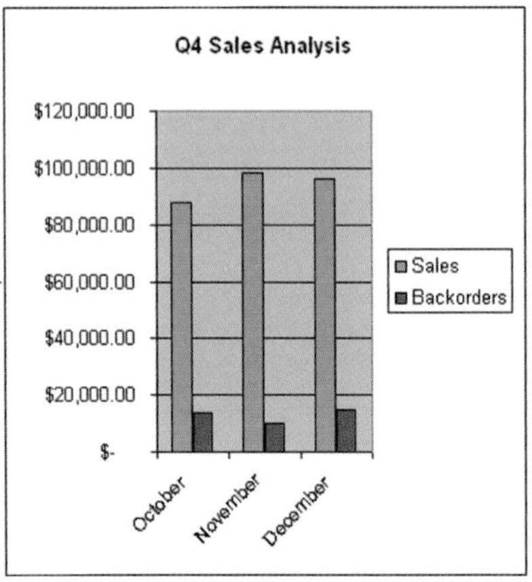
Q4 Sales Analysis
$120,000.00
$100,000.00
$80,000.00
$60,000.00
$40,000.00
$20,000.00
$-
October
November
December
Sales
Backorders

A management information system (MIS) is a set of software tools that enables managers to gather, organize, and evaluate information about a workgroup, department, or entire organization. These systems meet the needs of three different categories of managers—executives, middle managers, and front-line managers—by producing different kinds of reports drawn from the organization's database. An efficient management information system summarizes vast amounts of business data into information that is useful to each type of manager (see Figure 12A.4).

Decision Support Systems

A decision support system (DSS) is a special application that collects and reports certain types of business data that can help managers make better decisions (see Figure 12A.5). Business managers often use decision support systems to access and analyze data in the company's transaction processing system. In addition, these systems can include or access other types of data, such as stock market reports or data about competitors. By compiling this kind of data, the decision support system can generate specific reports that managers can use in making mission-critical decisions.

Norton **ONLINE**

For more information on decision support systems, visit **http://www.mhhe.com/peternorton**.

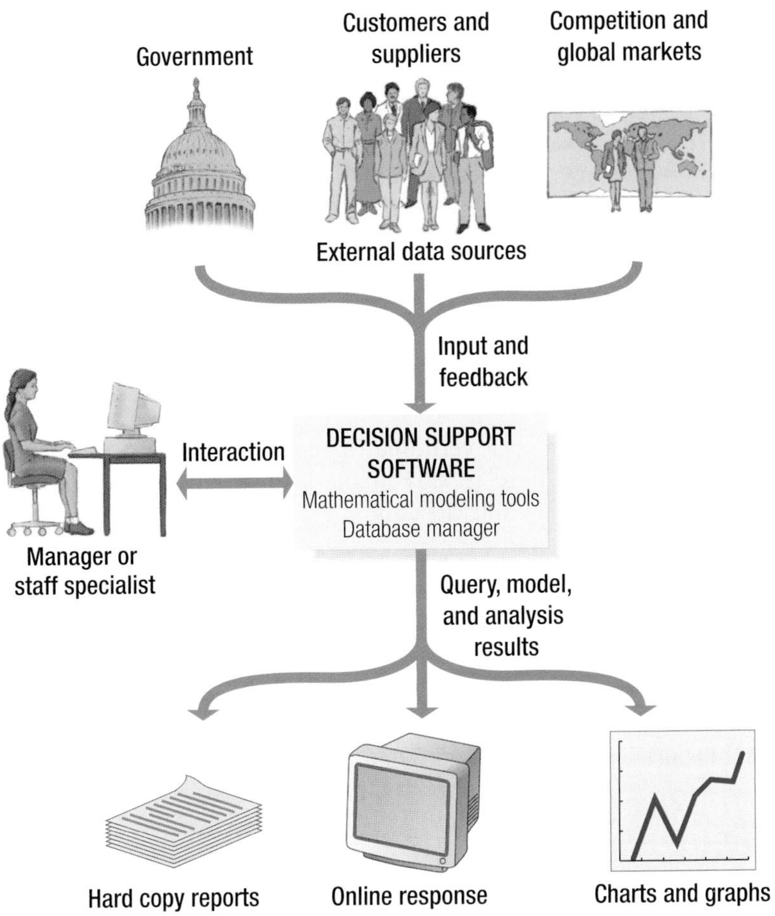

FIGURE 12A.5

A simple example of a decision support system.

Decision support systems are useful tools because they give managers highly tailored, highly structured data about specific issues. Many decision support systems are spreadsheet or database applications that have been customized for a certain business. These powerful systems can import and analyze data in various formats, such as flat database tables or spreadsheets, two-dimensional charts, or multidimensional "cubes" (meaning that several types of data and their interrelationships can be graphically shown). They can quickly generate reports based on existing data and update those reports instantly as data changes.

Expert Systems

An expert system performs tasks that would normally be done by a human, such as medical diagnoses or loan approvals. After analyzing the relevant data, some expert systems recommend a course of action, which a person can then consider taking. For example, a diagnostic system might review a patient's symptoms and medical history and then suggest a diagnosis and possible treatments. A doctor can then consider the system's recommendations before treating the patient. In fact, an expert system called Mycin was developed at Stanford University in the 1970s in order to diagnose and recommend treatment for specific blood infections. It was only used experimentally, due to ethical and legal issues at that time related to the use of computers in medicine. Nevertheless, it was an important step in the design and eventual acceptance of commercial expert systems.

Some expert systems are empowered to make decisions and take actions. An example is an expert system that monitors inventory levels for a grocery store chain. When the system determines that inventory of a product falls below a given

Norton ONLINE

For more information on expert systems, visit **http://www.mhhe.com/peternorton**.

level, it can automatically order a new shipment of the product from a supplier. Another good example is the type of expert system used in air traffic control. If the system detects that two aircraft are on a collision course or flying too near one another, it can issue a warning without human intervention.

An expert system requires a large collection of human expertise in a specific area. This information is entered into a highly detailed database, called a knowledge base, which is refined as new information becomes available. A program called an inference engine then examines a user's request in light of that knowledge base and selects the most appropriate response or range of possible responses (see Figure 12A.6).

Information Systems Technologies

Information systems rely on a veritable three-dimensional puzzle managed by professionals who work hard to stay at the leading edge of technology while keeping current IS services stable. Just about every technological advance in communications, computing, and data storage is harnessed for the vast needs of information systems.

FIGURE 12A.6

The basic structure of an expert system.

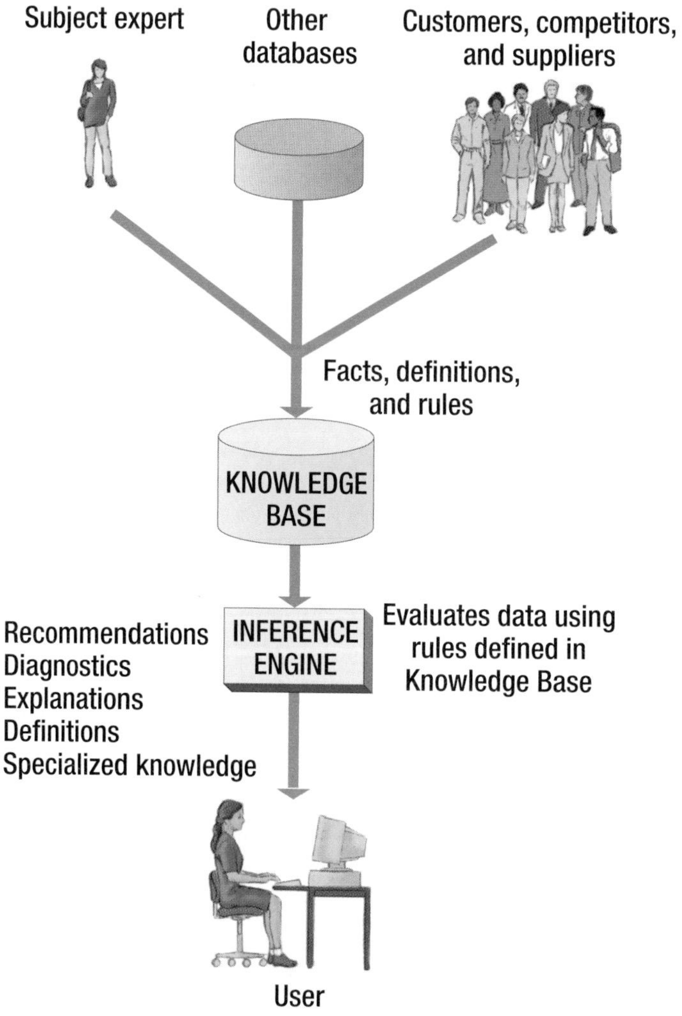

Intranets

As you learned in Chapters 9 and 10, an intranet is a private network employing Internet technologies (Web sites, FTP sites, e-mail, etc.) dedicated to the use of people who are authorized to use it, such as employees or members. They may connect from computers on the private network or over the Internet. When an intranet is connected to the Internet, the services on the intranet are protected by a firewall and visitors are required to log on (through a network authorization server) with a valid user name and password.

Any client computer with a Web browser can participate in an intranet. Figure 12A.7 shows an intranet offering several services to various types of client computers.

Norton ONLINE

For more information on intranets, visit **http://www.mhhe.com/peternorton**.

Extranets

Each manufacturing company (and other types of organizations, too) must maintain important links in what is referred to as a supply chain. The links in a supply chain connect the various processes that must be accomplished from establishing a need for a product, through creating it, to the final distribution or delivery to the customer. The interim links include ordering raw materials, taking delivery of the raw materials, moving the materials through the manufacturing process, and, finally, shipping the product to distributors or the final customer. Today's business markets are fast-paced and very competitive. To control costs and improve efficiency, manufacturers and retailers don't want to do expensive warehousing of materials and products, but still require that these things be available to them when they are needed. Such just-in-time inventory requires the best communications between each of the organizations participating in the supply chain—something that can be done when they have access to each others' networks. Therefore, two or more private networks (that in turn may be intranets) are connected, and the resulting combined network is called an extranet. Figure 12A.8 shows an extranet between a customer company and a vendor. Communication between the companies may occur over the Internet or over a special communications line leased from the phone company.

Norton ONLINE

For more information on extranets, visit **http://www.mhhe.com/peternorton**.

FIGURE 12A.7

In an intranet, the Web sites, FTP sites, and other Internet-style resources are reserved for the use of authorized users, who may gain access from within the private network or from the Internet. Only valid traffic passes the firewall and a user name and password are required before gaining access to the intranet services.

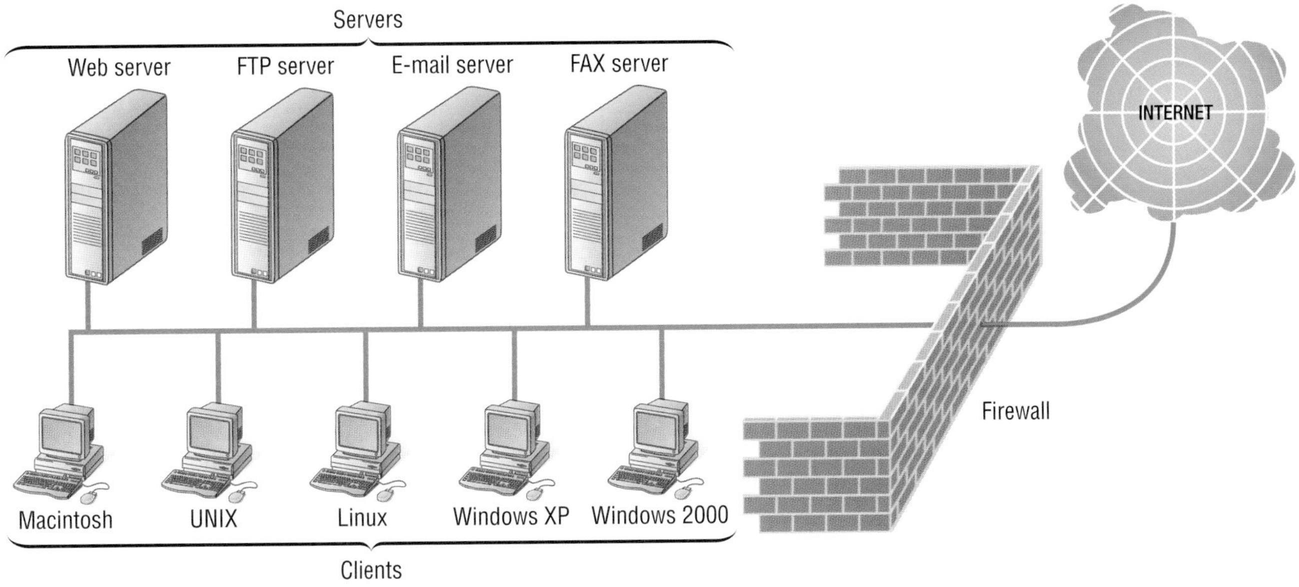

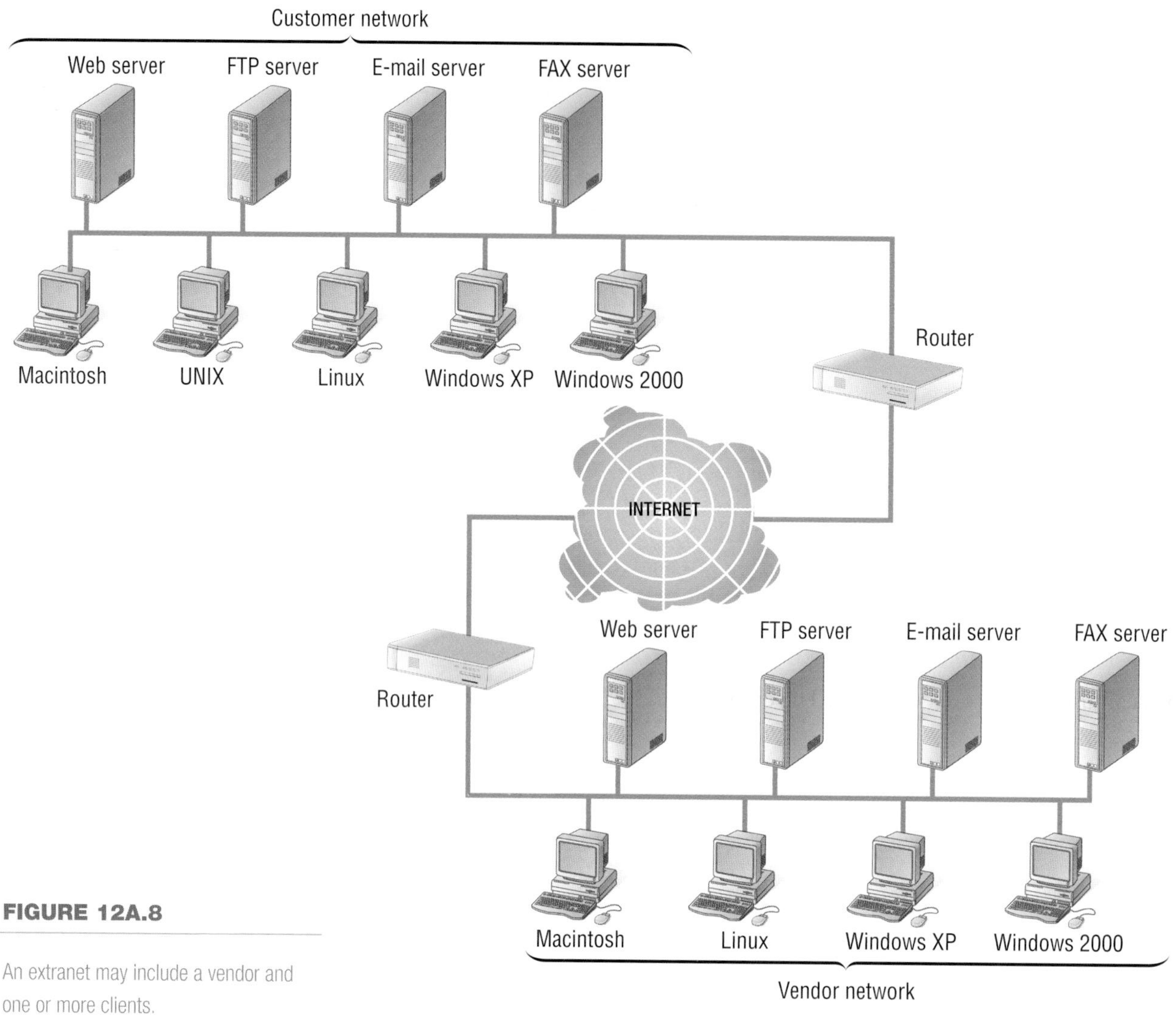

FIGURE 12A.8

An extranet may include a vendor and one or more clients.

Norton ONLINE

For more information on virtual private networks, visit **http://www.mhhe.com/peternorton**.

Virtual Private Networks

For many years, organizations have connected geographically separated network sites and the most common method of doing this was by leasing a dedicated line, a telecommunications service for carrying data. An IS manager could select speeds ranging from 56 Kbps for low-end services, through medium-level services like T1 at 1.54 Mbps, all the way up to an extremely high-end fiber-optic cable service called OC-192 at 9.952 Gbps. The many options for making WAN connections using dedicated leased lines are expensive—and, generally, the faster the service, the more costly.

The transition of the Internet into the public domain in the early 1990s gave managers another option for connecting their geographically separated networks. They had two major concerns: reliability of the Internet and the security risk of using a public network to connect private networks. Managers gradually gained confidence in the reliability of the Internet and when a technique called virtual private network (VPN) was developed, they could use a public network (the Internet) to provide WAN connections that were previously achieved over dedicated, and therefore assumed secure, lines. In recent years, many companies have moved away from leasing lines for WAN connections to using VPNs to connect geographically separated private networks over the Internet.

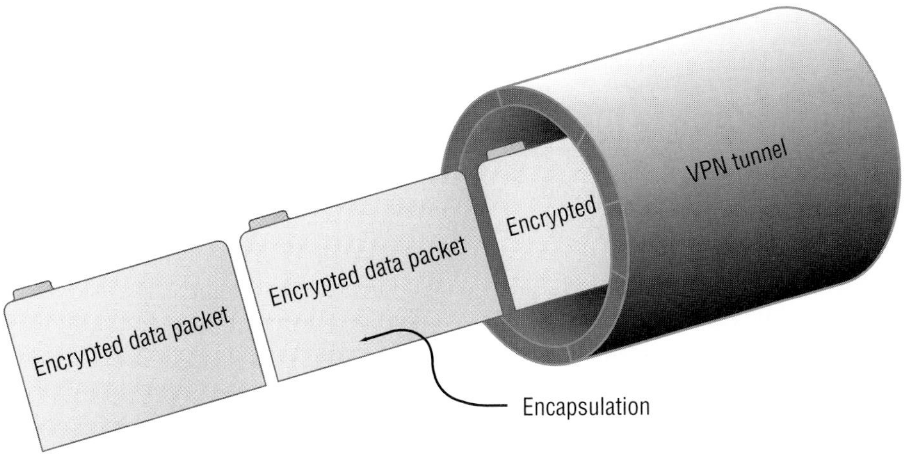

FIGURE 12A.9

For secure communications, the data packets are encrypted within the encapsulation of the VPN.

Today VPNs connect private networks to other networks, or individuals, such as sales people, to a private network. A VPN employs a method called tunneling, in which each packet from the sending network is encapsulated within another packet and sent over the Internet. A VPN is often made more secure by adding encryption of the data within each encapsulated packet (see Figure 12A.9). Authentication of both ends of the tunnel adds further security.

An employee who needs to connect to a network from other geographical locations can use a remote access VPN. The employee makes a normal dial-up connection to the Internet and then, using special VPN client software, connects to a VPN server (also called a *network access server*) that provides the tunnel between the client and the VPN server, using a predetermined level of security. The employee logs into and accesses the corporate network through that server. Figure 12A.10 shows a laptop connecting to a network using a remote access VPN. The actual use of the VPN is transparent to the user once the laptop has been properly configured. An IS employee can configure it so that the user just has to click an icon with a simple label like "Home office" to initiate the entire process.

A VPN used to connect two networks is called a site-to-site VPN. Both networks may be part of the same private intranet or they may be networks of partner companies participating in an extranet. The VPN servers at each end establish and maintain the VPN.

Many organizations still use expensive leased lines, but now they can pick and choose just how and when they use them.

FIGURE 12A.10

A single user can use a remote access VPN for a secure connection to a corporate network.

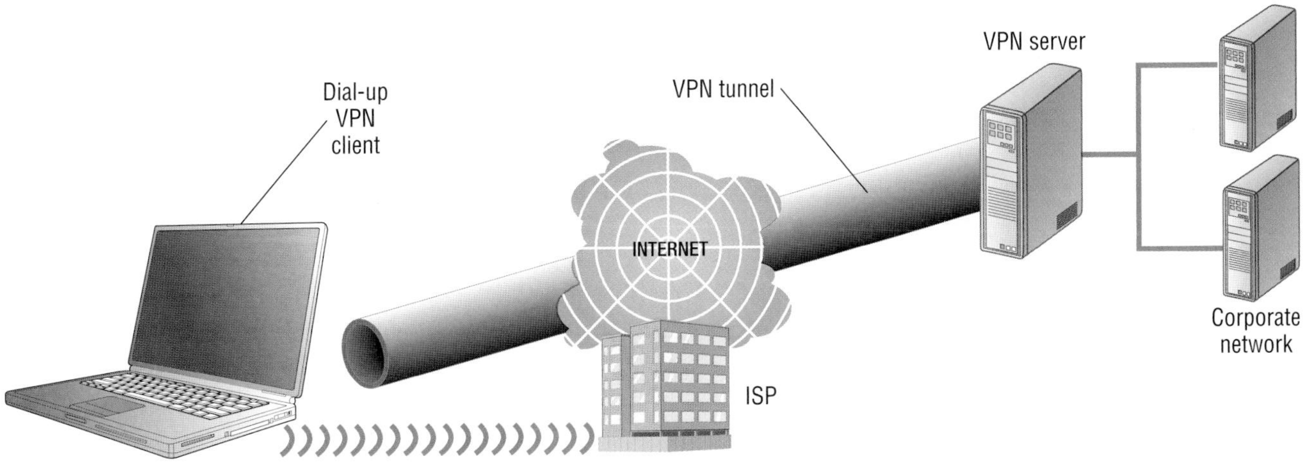

Electronic Data Interchange

Electronic data interchange (EDI) is the electronic transfer of information between companies over networks. EDI can occur between companies over extranets or the Internet. EDI is a form of e-commerce, and the data exchanged is usually in a format that complies with a standard defined by one of the several international standardization and conformity assessment organizations. By using such standards, organizations are guaranteed that the data exchanged will be in a usable format.

EDI data ranges from purchase orders and invoices through very sensitive patient medical records. But EDI differs from other transfers of data between organizations in an important way. Consider e-mail: An employee of a vendor company may send an e-mail to a customer's employee, but this e-mail is not EDI because e-mail is free-format textual data between individuals. EDI is data delivered electronically in a predetermined format between applications running in each organization, as shown in Figure 12A.11, which shows EDI servers in two organizations. In this case, the client company has an order entry system that goes through the EDI server, where it is formatted and transferred to the vendor company's EDI server, which feeds the data to the order processing application. When a student authorizes the transfer of his or her transcript from one university to another, that transfer may well be done via an EDI system. The data is transferred directly from software in one company's network to software on another company's network. EDI may be transferred directly between organizations or they may use a third-party service provider. Implementing EDI between organizations is usually very expensive.

Norton ONLINE

For more information on electronic data interchange, visit **http://www.mhhe.com/peternorton**.

Storing and Managing Data

For years companies have gathered and managed vast amounts of data of every imaginable kind. Because data truly is the lifeblood of a corporation, you can think of the corporation's data storage system as its heart. The bigger and stronger that system is, the more information it can handle, and the more effectively it will operate.

Large and medium-sized companies are taking new approaches to storing and managing their huge collections of data. On the storage side of the equation is the

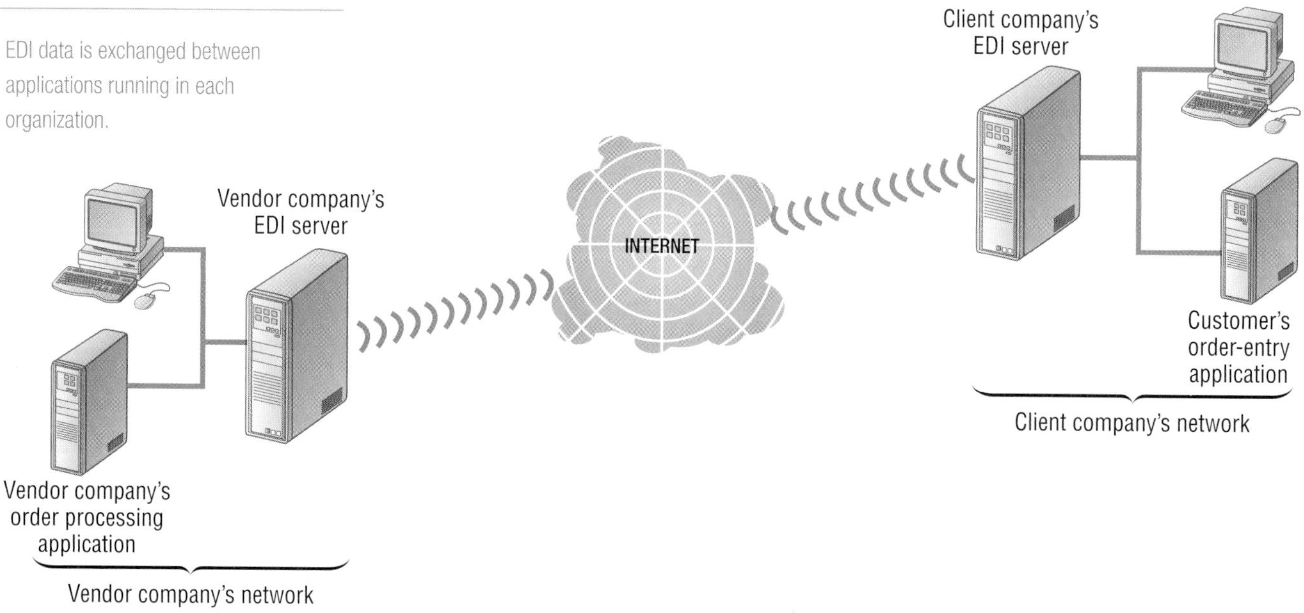

FIGURE 12A.11

EDI data is exchanged between applications running in each organization.

data warehouse, a massive collection of corporate information. On the management side is a process called data mining.

Data Warehouses

Setting up a data warehouse is much more complicated than simply dumping all kinds of data into one storage place. Often, a data warehouse will include a variety of data stored in many databases throughout the enterprise. Companies must consider factors such as the following before investing in a data warehousing structure:

The amount of data required today to do business, and which must be archived for reporting and historical reasons, is growing. To add to the burden, the data must be available when needed. If data is not available—or worse, is lost—a company loses money and may be breaking laws.

Now that most companies have some sort of Internet presence, perhaps selling their wares 24/7 or maintaining offices around the world, absolutely no downtime is tolerated. Since systems will fail, the solution is to provide as much fault tolerance as possible. Fault tolerance is the ability to continue as if nothing has happened, even after a major component (such as a hard disk) or a complete computer system has failed. Fault tolerance can be provided many ways—and it can be provided at the disk level, the computer level, or the network level.

The fault tolerant storage hardware may be a mainframe system or a disk array attached to nonmainframe servers. A disk array consists of multiple disk drives used in combination to provide better performance and/or fault tolerance. These disk arrays provide gigabytes or terabytes of storage space (see Figure 12A.12). To provide computer-level fault tolerance, a redundant disk system may be connected to two different computers, and if one computer fails, the second automatically takes over. An organization may even have an entire duplicate of their data warehouse maintained on servers at a second network site and kept up-to-date with the primary servers. Then, in the event of a network failure, all traffic is diverted to the backup servers.

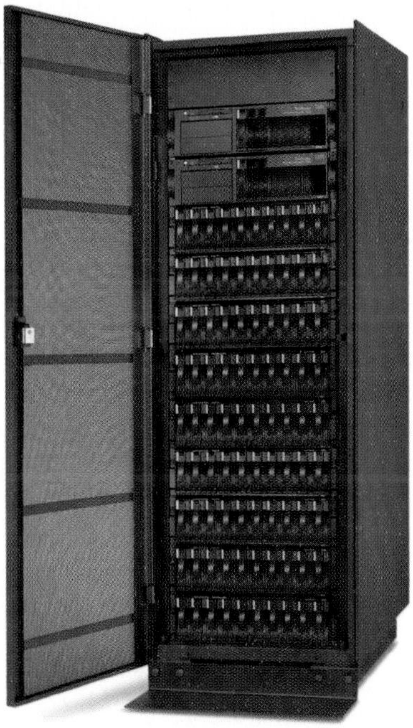

FIGURE 12A.12

A large-scale disk array allows an organization to store huge amounts of data while providing fault tolerance to ensure fast recovery from the failure of one or more disk drives.

While data must be available when required, it also must be kept secure from unauthorized access. IS personnel must apply all necessary measures to protect data from loss—accidental or intentional—and to protect data from being gathered by individuals for illegal or competitive purposes. To protect the data from loss, they back up the data frequently and install nonstop and redundant systems. To protect data from being accessed by unauthorized people, users must be authenticated with a user name and password.

Data Mining

Huge data warehouses can supply the data requirements for tens of thousands of users in a large organization. They also are used to store and support thousands or millions of transactions per day on active Web sites, such as the popular electronic auction and retail Web sites.

Norton ONLINE

For more information on data warehousing and data mining, visit **http://www.mhhe.com/peternorton**.

At Issue

Mapping Military Movement

The science of war involves more than just battles and bullets. Even with the best troops, training, and tactics, nothing happens until something *moves*. That's where the military's Traffic Management Command Transportation Engineering Agency (TEA) comes in.

As the primary Department of Defense (DoD) deployment engineering and analysis center, TEA uses state-of-the-art analytical systems and advanced information-system technologies to satisfy the logistics of getting people, munitions, and equipment to where it's needed—timely, efficiently, and safely.

To accomplish this, TEA has tapped into cutting-edge Geographic Information System (GIS) technology. The TEA's GIS database manages all of the geographic data necessary for deployments, including information about U.S. highway networks, bridges, railways, traffic patterns, weather, military installations, and seaports.

Attached to these databases are GIS-based models that TEA uses to conduct transportation engineering studies of highways, railroads, ports, intermodal facilities, and installations. These studies determine the transportation infrastructure requirements needed to ensure that personnel and equipment move safely and efficiently from origin to destination, whether during peacetime or war.

But despite the success of the military's GIS logistics information, Military Traffic Management Command needed a way to provide easier and less-costly GIS access to the military community. Using its current system, it cost $50,000 to $100,000 to train and equip an operator to use TEA's proprietary system. Partnering with GeoDecisions, a division of Gannett Fleming Inc., the DoD recently moved to take its GIS system to the World Wide Web.

The TEA and GeoDecisions have developed a prototype Internet-based Military Road and Rail Status Reporting System. The pilot focuses on transportation routes between the military command center at Fort Hood and the port of Beaumont, Texas. The new system will allow military personnel to log into a single Web site to search, browse, and display all of the needed logistical information.

Having a place to store lots of data, however, leads to another question: How do you find what you need in all that data? This may be accomplished with large-scale enterprise database management systems and tools that enable users to add and work with the raw data in the database, converting it into useful information. The process of searching and sorting data to find relationships within it is called *data mining*, and it is possible only with the proper tools and approaches to managing large volumes of data. (You were introduced to database management systems and data mining in Chapter 11.)

An important step in making all the data useful is called **data scrubbing**. Data scrubbing or data validation is the process of safeguarding against erroneous or duplicate data. In the case of Federal Express's database, for example, imagine the problems that could result if multiple packages were assigned the same tracking number. A data-scrubbing procedure prevents this mishap from occurring.

Data scrubbing can be handled in many ways. For example, during the data-entry process, the DBMS may refuse to accept data that does not conform to a certain format, or that is not spelled in a specific way, or that is duplicated in another record. This ensures that all customer IDs, ZIP codes, and telephone

SELF-CHECK ::

Circle the correct answer for each question.

1. In an information system, the procedures for handling information help ensure its ________ .
   a. value b. integrity c. size
2. By using ________ tools, workers reduce the time and effort spent on some tasks.
   a. office automation b. GUI c. search
3. A(n) ________ system provides different types of information for different types of managers.
   a. office automation b. decision support c. management information system (MIS)

Maj. Chris Holinger tracks an ongoing Operation Southern Watch mission inside the Combined Air Operations Center at a forward-deployed base. Spanning nearly 30,000 square feet, the CAOC is the nerve center for all U.S. Central Command air operations. With crews operating around the clock, CAOC officials plan, control, and track all coalition missions throughout the region

Populating the GIS Internet database are real-time traffic reports for the areas between the fort and the port, supplied by the Texas Transportation Institute. A series of sensors embedded in road surfaces by the TTI give immediate conditions on traffic speed and congestion. The Texas Department of Transportation provides daily reports on road construction, and AccuWeather will make meteorological maps available to the project on an hourly basis from a file transfer protocol (FTP) site.

To train drivers in the routes' topography, the Federal Highway Administration provides video logging of the primary convoy route between Fort Hood and Beaumont. The video is captured by vehicle-mounted digital cameras and then linked to a Global Positioning System receiver for latitude and longitude geo-referencing. Aerial photographs from the Texas DOT and digital topographic maps from the U.S. Geological Survey give an overhead perspective of terrain, road conditions, cultural features, and landmarks.

If the new system proves successful, the Department of Defense plans to implement it nationwide. A national GIS system would include all of the major deployment sites and other equipment support bases, ports, and the routes in between.

numbers are formatted in the same manner, which guarantees consistency throughout the database.

Information Systems Hardware

While many of an organization's information resources may be distributed around various sites, medium to large organizations will still have at least one building or campus of buildings dedicated to information systems. If you were to look inside one of these facilities, you would find a variety of computer systems serving the needs of the organization. The majority of them, hundreds or even thousands in some organizations, would be network servers—but you also would find minicomputers and mainframe computers. You might even find a supercomputer if the organization has some extraordinary processing need, such as scientific research.

While the type of computer systems used says a lot about the processing needs of information systems, there are other critical needs. In this section, we'll look at the storage needs of an enterprise, then hardware for ensuring reliability, and, finally, systems that can grow with the company and allow operating in a heterogeneous environment.

Enterprise Storage

Enterprise storage includes both the methods and technologies an organization uses to store data. For most, this term also conjures an image of storage of vast amounts of data, the processing of that data, and the ability to access what is needed when it is needed.

Norton ONLINE

For more information on enterprise storage systems, visit **http://www.mhhe.com/peternorton**.

Storage Systems

Information systems are based on the gathering and managing of data. Any interruption in access to this data, or loss of the data, is extremely costly to organizations. Some organizations would suffer huge financial losses if their data were unavailable for even seconds. Others may have a threshold of hours or days before the loss of access to data becomes significant. Therefore, the storage systems store large amounts of data efficiently, while maintaining accessibility of the data in terms of both speed of access and the ability to recover from a failure. Storage system hardware technologies designed with these needs in mind include various implementations of RAID and a group of technologies that provide network storage.

RAID A redundant array of independent disks (RAID) is a storage system that links any number of disk drives (a disk array) so that they act as a single disk. This is done for better performance and/or redundancy.

RAID's capabilities are based on many different techniques, but there are three basic ones: striping, mirroring, and striping-with-parity. Each technique was assigned a number, and there are more variations of these, also assigned numbers.

- Striping, called RAID 0, provides the user with rapid access by spreading data across several disks. Striping alone, however, does not provide redundancy. If one of the disks in a striped array fails, the data is lost.
- In a mirrored system, called RAID 1, data is written to two or more disks simultaneously, providing a complete copy of all the information on multiple drives in the event one drive should fail. This improves reliability and availability, and if one disk fails, the mirrored disk continues to function, thus maintaining reliability and availability. Figure 12A.13 shows a simple RAID array using RAID 1.
- Striping-with-parity, or RAID 4, is a more sophisticated RAID configuration in which data is spread over multiple disks. It provides the speed of striping with the safety of redundancy because the system stores parity information that can be used to reconstruct data if a disk drive fails. Such arrays also provide error-checking.

In many implementations of RAID 1 or 4, the failed disk can be replaced without powering down the system. This process is called hot-swapping.

Large-scale RAID systems can offer many terabytes of storage and incredibly fast access and data transfer times.

Network Storage Network storage is a general term describing a variety of hardware devices for storing data on a network—and it's based largely on disk storage. When we think of disk storage, we usually think of a desktop or laptop

FIGURE 12A.13

The four cylinders each represents a single disk system in the array. The volumes, numbered 1 through 8, are mirrored to separate physical disks in the array.

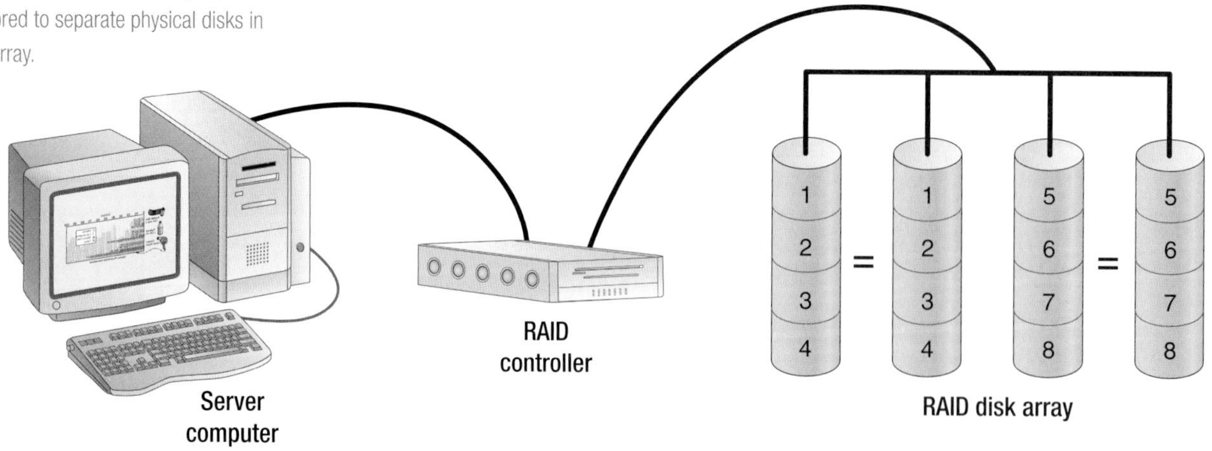

computer with a single hard disk system installed. Even network servers often fit this model, although they may have multiple disks and/or an external disk system, such as a RAID array. These storage devices are categorized as direct attached storage (DAS) because each storage device is directly attached to the computer and, with the exception of an external disk array, dependent on the computer's processing power.

A storage device that is connected directly to a network is an example of network attached storage (NAS). Consider such a free-standing disk system, containing many disk drives, that is shared by multiple network servers or minicomputers, as shown in Figure 12A.14. The network servers can each devote their processing power to the task at hand and let the processors in the storage systems take care of data storage services. Now, take it even further and place many such storage devices on a single high-speed network, dedicated to storage. Now you have a storage area network (SAN), such as that shown in Figure 12A.15.

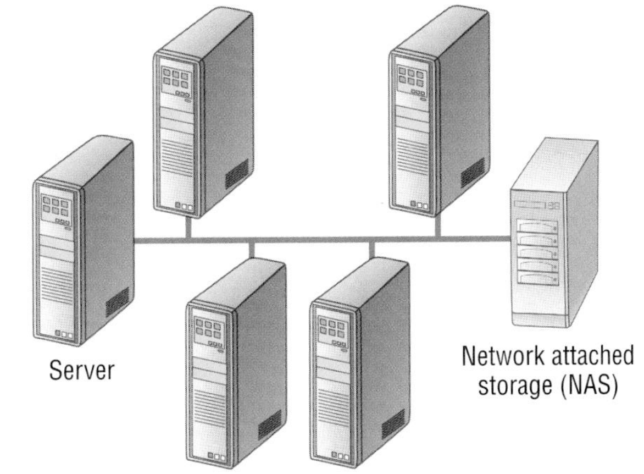

FIGURE 12A.14

An example of network attached storage in which the storage hardware is attached directly to the network and one or more network servers access the data over the network.

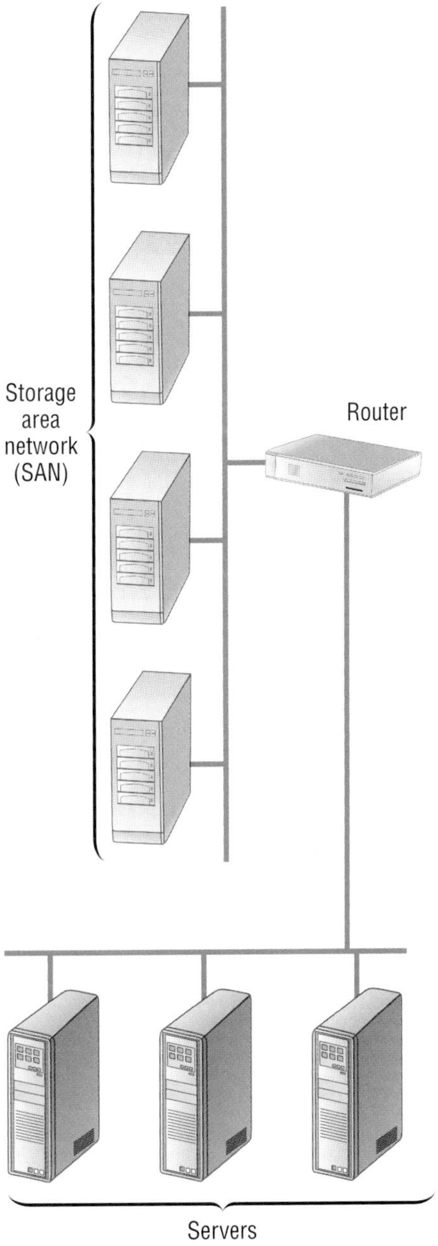

FIGURE 12A.15

A storage area network with four storage devices on a high-speed network segment. The network servers can access the data on any of these devices.

Backup

A crucial component of successful enterprise storage is a backup strategy. Several of the hardware technologies described earlier address backup needs. A RAID 1 mirrored drive is constantly duplicated—a form of backup—while the striping-with-parity of a RAID 4 system only provides fault tolerance, not an actual backup. Neither of these methods addresses the need to be able to take your data back to a previous point in time.

Most transaction processing systems can be configured to create transaction logs that will allow an administrator to roll back the database to a previous point in time. However, corrupted data may predate the saved transaction logs and it may not be possible to roll back to a point that does not include the corrupted data. That is why even those systems are still supplemented by more conventional

Productivity Tip

Understanding Online Help Systems

For several reasons, online help systems have almost completely replaced printed manuals for many types of computer products. First, they are cheaper to produce than printed materials. Second, they can be updated and distributed much more quickly. Third, they can be interactive and intuitive, making them far more instructive and easier to use than any printed manual.

Online help can take several forms, which can be used in any combination:

- **Electronic Documents.** An electronic document is a computer-based version of a printed manual. It may be included with software even when no printed manuals are provided. Such documents look like printed books but are used on-screen, using a viewer such as Adobe's Acrobat Reader. Electronic documents may feature hyperlinked index and contents entries, as well as hyperlinked cross-references. You can click a heading, page number, or reference to jump to the desired section. Electronic documents also may feature search tools, bookmarking tools, and other helpful resources.
- **Application Help Systems.** Most software applications feature an online help system installed with the product. Windows-based application help systems use a standard interface; after you learn how to use one help system, you can use another with ease. Application help systems can include audio, animation, video-based demonstrations, links to Internet resources, and much more.
- **Web Help.** Newer-generation help systems can be used over the World Wide Web or a corporate intranet through a standard Web browser. The advantage of Web help is that it is centralized—located on a single server—instead of being stored on each user's system. This enables administrators to update the information quickly.
- **FAQs.** Many companies post electronic documents containing frequently asked questions (FAQs) on their Web or intranet sites, on newsgroups, and on bulletin boards. As their name implies, FAQs provide answers to the most commonly asked questions about a product, and a FAQ may be the first place to look when you have a problem with a product.

FIGURE 12A.16

A tape library system provides automated backup, tape changing, and tape storage.

backup systems. There is a great deal of important data that is not managed by a transaction-based system, and new regulations mandating the types of information that must be stored also increase the burden on IS personnel to perform regular point-in-time data backups and maintain them for a period of time—indefinitely for some types of data. The most common hardware for these backup systems is based on tape drives.

Like hard drives, there are tape devices suitable for the needs of any size organization. For businesses with data storage and backup needs well within the gigabyte range, there are direct-attached tape devices, installed at one or more servers. For the medium to large organizations whose data stores run well into the terabytes, there are tape libraries, a large tape system that fits into a console the size of a large refrigerator (see Figure 12A.16). A tape library will use a robotic component called an auto loader to change and store multiple tape cartridges.

A tape backup system can be added to the same high-speed network segment as the disk storage, and therefore allow for high-speed backup that will not interfere with other network traffic.

Nonstop and Redundant Systems

The term "mission-critical" describes a system that must run without failure, or with nearly instant recovery from failure—a fault-tolerant system. A decade ago systems described as mission-critical were in such areas as finance, medicine, national defense, and emergency services. Today the numbers of applications that are considered mission-critical have expanded as more organizations participate in the global economy through the Internet, offering services to customers and employees across time zones and thus beyond normal local business hours.

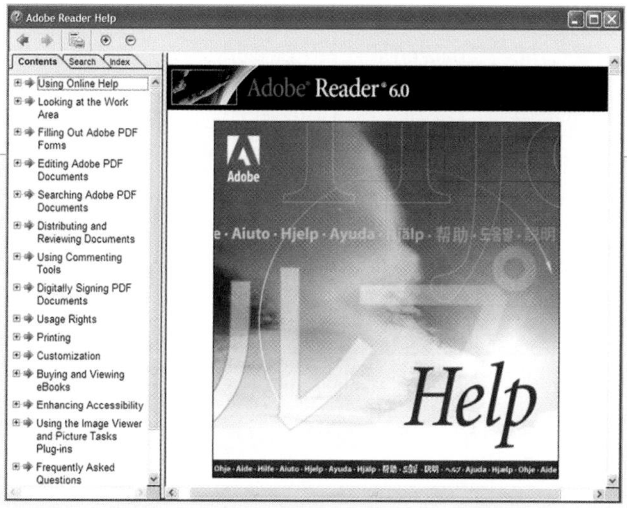

Most computer products, especially those sold to consumers, feature extensive online help systems installed with the application, as well as Web-based help.

PRODUCTIVITY TIP

» **Knowledge Bases.** As described elsewhere in this unit, knowledge bases can help you find information and technical support online. You can find many knowledge bases at the Web sites of companies that produce software and hardware products. To use a knowledge base, type a question or a term into the site's search box. The knowledge base will then provide you with one or more possible solutions to your problem.

» **E-Mail Support.** Some software companies provide technical support via e-mail. You compose an e-mail message describing your question or problem and submit it to the manufacturer. You receive a response within 24 hours, in most cases. Depending on the nature of your problem, you may receive a standard document or a customized response from a technical support person.

These systems require nonstop service, meaning that business can continue "as usual" even though some component is down due to planned service or a failure. Fail-over is the process of switching to a standby, redundant component or system in the event of failure.

Redundancy can be as simple as mirrored drives and as complex as redundant servers, usually configured as clusters and redundant networks. (See Figure 12A.17.)

Scalable and Interoperable Systems

A system that is scalable can be incrementally expanded as the need occurs. Scalability is the capability to be scaled, and is now expected in information systems, as businesses offering products and services worldwide must be ready to grow with the market. Scalability is required at both the software and hardware levels.

Interoperability also is required of information systems to allow partnership and customer–vendor relationships between organizations using a variety of systems. Interoperability is the ability of each organization's information system to work with the other, sharing data and services.

The Information Systems Department

Over the years, as large companies began automating tasks with computers and information systems, a new type of department was created to service those rapidly growing and changing systems. Initially, these departments—and the people who worked in them—were isolated from the rest of a company's operations.

Norton ONLINE

For more information on IS departments, visit **http://www.mhhe.com/peternorton**.

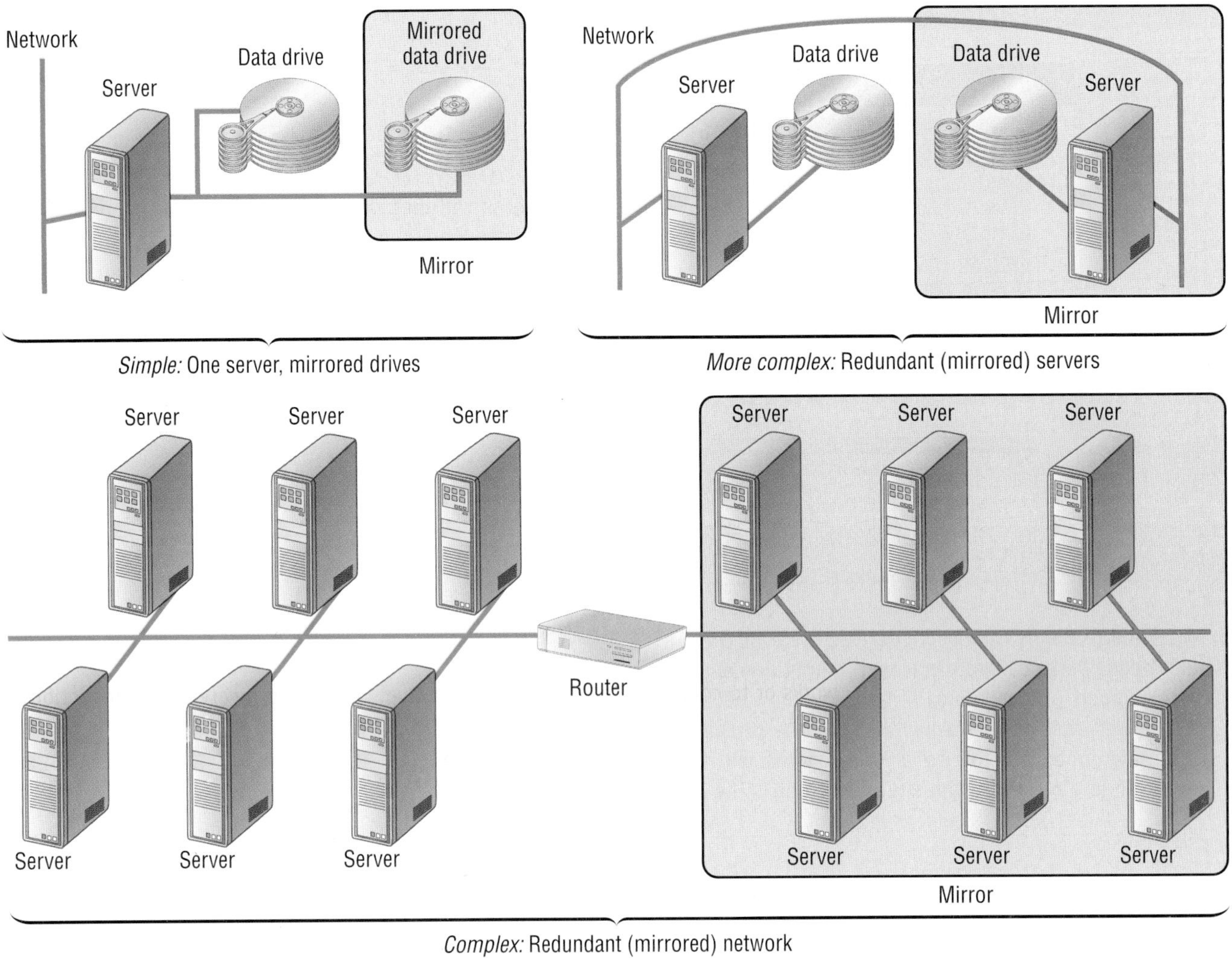

FIGURE 12A.17

Redundancy can be accomplished with mirrored drives, servers, or networks. These and other methods also can be combined.

These specialized departments were in charge of creating the systems (typically using the corporate mainframe or minicomputers) that collected data from the operations level and turning it into information for managers.

Eventually, however, the rise of the PC and PC-based networks changed these departments and the systems they serviced. As people other than managers became information workers, the **Information Systems (IS) department** started serving entire organizations and became an integral part of the business operation.

The size of a company's IS department usually is relative to the company's size. In very large companies, these departments may employ hundreds or even thousands of people. The names of these departments vary, as well as their size. The organization chart of one company may include an Information Systems (IS) department, while another company may use the name Management Information Systems (MIS) or Information Technology (IT).

Summary ::

- An information system includes a means of storing information, procedures for handling information, and rules that govern the delivery of information to people in the organization.
- All information systems, regardless of their type, serve the same purpose: to help users get value from their information.
- Office automation systems automate routine office tasks such as correspondence and invoicing.
- Transaction processing systems not only store information about individual events but also provide information that is useful in running an organization.
- Management information systems produce reports for different types of managers.
- Decision support systems can produce highly detailed, custom reports based on the information in an organization's transaction processing system and data from other sources. These reports can assist managers in making decisions.
- Expert systems include, in a knowledge base, the knowledge of human experts in a particular subject area. They analyze requests from users in developing a course of action.
- Virtual private networks (VPNs) are used to connect a private network to other networks or to connect individuals to a private network. In both cases, the connection is made over a public network, usually the Internet.
- One or more organizations can transfer data in a predetermined format directly between electronic data interchange (EDI) applications,
- A data warehouse is the large store of data required by an organization.
- Data mining involves using and manipulating data so that it is useful to an organization.
- Enterprise storage employs a variety of technologies such as RAID disk systems for redundancy and fault tolerance at the disk level and the use of storage systems on a network.
- Network storage includes a variety of hardware technologies to provide data to network users.
- A storage area network is a single high-speed network, containing NAS systems.
- A critical component of storage management is a backup system. Large data stores require sophisticated, robotic tape systems, called tape libraries.
- IS systems must have built-in scalability to accommodate the needs of quickly expanding businesses.
- A well-structured IS department not only supports an organization's information systems, but also supports the organization's overall mission.

LESSON // 12A Review

Key Terms ::

auto loader, 474
data scrubbing, 470
data warehouse, 469
decision support system (DSS), 462
direct attached storage (DAS), 473
electronic data interchange (EDI), 468
enterprise storage, 471
expert system, 463
fault tolerance, 469
hot-swapping, 472
inference engine, 464
information system (IS), 459
Information Systems department, 476
knowledge base, 464
management information system (MIS), 462
mirrored, 472
network attached storage (NAS), 473
network storage, 472
off-the-shelf applications, 461
office automation system, 460
RAID 0, 472
RAID 1, 472
RAID 4, 472
redundant array of independent disks (RAID), 472
remote access VPN, 467
scalability, 475
scalable, 475
site-to-site VPN, 467
storage area network (SAN), 473
striping, 472
striping-with-parity, 472
transaction, 461
transaction processing system (TPS), 461
tunneling, 467
virtual private network (VPN), 466

Key Term Quiz ::

Complete each statement by writing one of the terms listed under Key Terms in each blank.

1. Many office automation systems can be built from ________ , like those found in any computer store.
2. Managers commonly use ________ systems to assist in the decision-making process.
3. A(n) ________ analyzes data and produces a recommended course of action.
4. In many organizations, a(n) ________ is responsible for creating and maintaining information systems.
5. A(n) ________ helps an organization automate routine tasks, such as correspondence and billing, so workers can focus on more important tasks.
6. A device called a(n) ________ can be used to automatically change and store multiple tapes in an enterprise backup library.
7. In the processes known as ________ , a disk can be replaced without powering down the computer system.
8. A(n) ________ has NAS devices connected to a dedicated, high-speed network segment.
9. A data storage technique known as ________ (or RAID 0), spreads data across several disks.
10. A(n) ________ is a massive collection of corporate information.

Multiple Choice ::

Circle the word or phrase that best completes each statement.

1. Many organizations set up ________ that limit the information that is available to certain workers.
   a. rules b. help systems c. information systems d. card files
2. 2. A(n) ________ system is one that must run without failure or with nearly instant recovery from failure.
   a. system b. record c. mission critical d. transaction
3. Management information systems create different types of ________ for different types of managers in an organization.
   a. information b. transactions c. reports d. data
4. The process of validating the data in a database is called ________.
   a. data scouring b. data scrubbing c. data washing d. data cleaning
5. ________ is the electronic transfer of information between companies over networks.
   a. Electronic data exchange b. Electronic data sharing c. Electronic data swapping d. Electronic data interchange
6. A(n) ________ is a private network that employs Internet technologies.
   a. storage area network b. intranet c. LAN d. P2PN
7. A computer system that is ________ can be incrementally expanded as the need occurs.
   a. scalable b. interoperable c. redundant d. transparent
8. When you purchase an item over the Internet, the several steps you take are considered to be a(n) ________ .
   a. decision support system (DSS) b. process c. application d. transaction
9. An office automation system can be built from a(n) ________ .
   a. off-the-shelf application b. transaction processing system (TPS) c. expert system d. management information system (MIS)
10. An information system that can be used by a variety of client computer systems running in different network environments is said to be ________ .
    a. nonstop b. interoperable c. fault-tolerant d. RAID 4

LESSON // 12A Review

Review Questions ::

In your own words, briefly answer the following questions.

1. What is an information system?
2. What are the three basic components of an information system?
3. What is the basic purpose of any information system?
4. Why do organizations use office automation systems?
5. What is a transaction?
6. Why is a decision support system a useful tool?
7. Why would an organization perform data mining?
8. Describe the difference between network attached storage (NAS) and a storage area network (SAN).
9. If your information systems are primarily transaction-based with transaction logging turned on, why would you employ a separate backup system?
10. How is data stored in a mirrored (RAID 1) storage system?

Lesson Labs ::

Complete the following exercises as directed by your instructor.

1. Determine what kinds of information systems are in place at your school. You may need to interview members of the school's IS department, or your instructor may divide the class into groups and assign each group to investigate the systems used in different departments in the school. What types of services does each system provide to its users?
2. Find out which types of IS employees work in your town. Pick a business or organization in your town and make an appointment to talk to its IS manager. Who works in that organization's IS department? Does the staff include managers, technology analysts, database specialists, programmers, or other types of specialists? Find out exactly what functions each person performs and how the organization benefits from each person's work.

LESSON // 12B

Building Information Systems

Overview: The Importance of Well-Built Information Systems

As you learned in Lesson 12A, "The Basics of Information Systems," a well-designed information system can be an important factor in an organization's success. The system not only provides mission-critical information to its users but also enables users to input information quickly and efficiently.

In any organization, crucial decisions may be based on the reports produced by an information system. For this reason, developers must ensure that the system works accurately and leaves out no details as it sorts, queries, and analyzes its data. Customer satisfaction also may rely on an information system's performance, as is the case when support technicians use an expert system to help customers solve problems.

To create effective information systems, corporations will spend millions of dollars on development in a process that can take months and involve input from dozens or even hundreds of people. Along the way, IS professionals analyze the organization, its internal processes, the needs of its employees and customers, technologies already in place, and much more. All these factors are crucial to understanding the business and how an information system will help it achieve its goals. The following sections offer a brief introduction to the process that IS professionals follow in developing information systems—a process called the systems development life cycle.

OBJECTIVES ::

- Define the term *systems development life cycle (SDLC)*.
- Identify the five phases in the SDLC.
- Name some of the IS professionals involved in each phase of the SDLC.
- Describe four ways an organization can convert from an old information system to a new one.
- Describe two evolving system development methods.

Norton ONLINE

For more information on information systems development, visit **http://www.mhhe.com/peternorton**.

The Systems Development Life Cycle

To help create successful information systems, the systems development life cycle (SDLC) was developed. The SDLC is an organized way to build an information system. As Figure 12B.1 illustrates, the SDLC is a series of five phases:

- Needs analysis
- Systems design
- Development
- Implementation
- Maintenance

Together, the phases are called a life cycle because they cover the entire "life" of an information system.

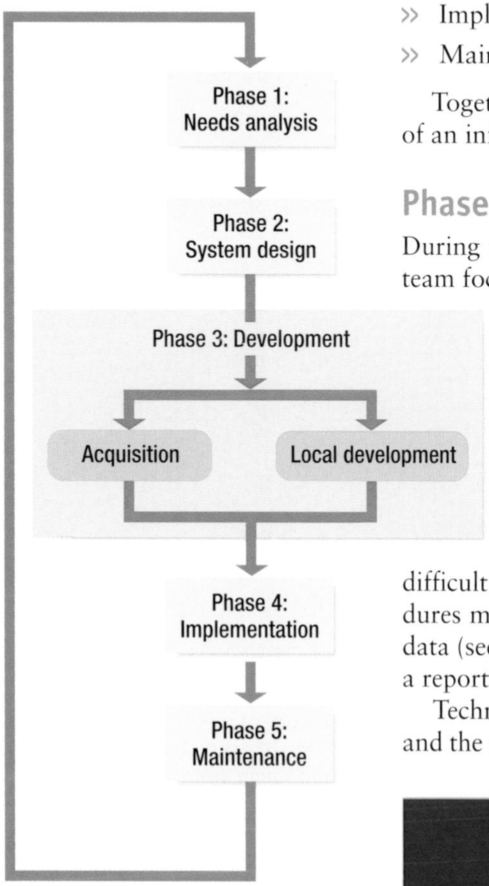

FIGURE 12B.1

The systems development life cycle.

Phase 1: Needs Analysis

During the needs analysis phase, the first phase of the SDLC, the development team focuses on completing three tasks:

- Defining the problem and deciding whether to proceed.
- Analyzing the current system in depth and developing possible solutions to the problem.
- Selecting the best solution and defining its function.

Phase 1 begins when the organization identifies a need, which can be met by creating a new information system or modifying the existing one. Users may complain, for example, that the current system is too difficult to use or that it does not meet some business requirement. Simple procedures may require too many steps, or the system may crash repeatedly and lose data (see Figure 12B.2). A manager may approach the IS department and request a report that is not currently produced by the system.

Technology analysts then begin a preliminary investigation, talking with users and the managers of the departments that are to be affected. The first challenge is

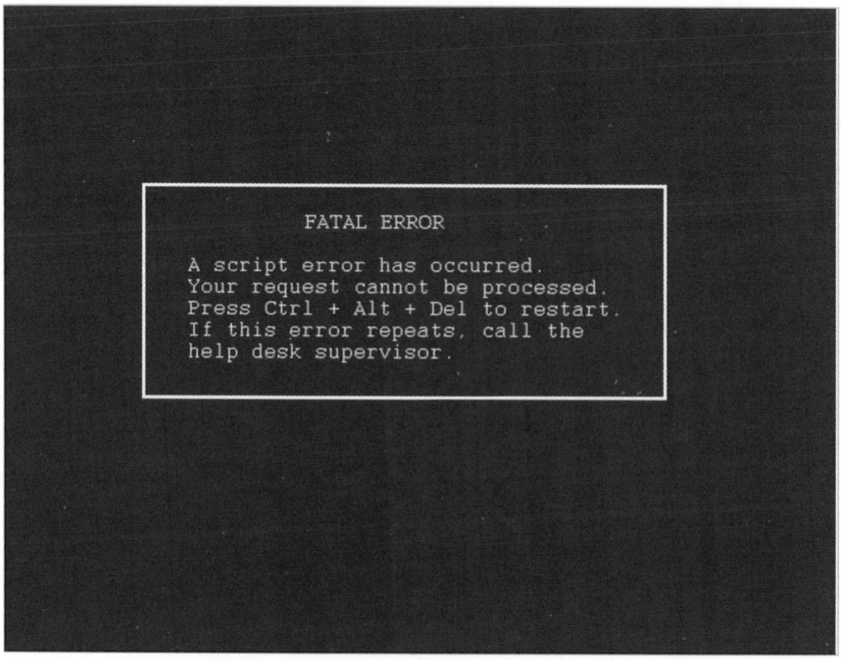

FIGURE 12B.2

If users see a lot of messages like this, there may be a problem with the system that needs attention from the IS department.

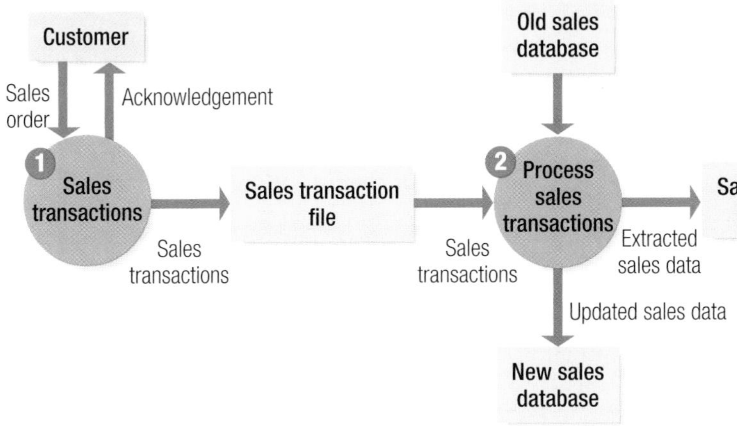

FIGURE 12B.3

A data flow diagram.

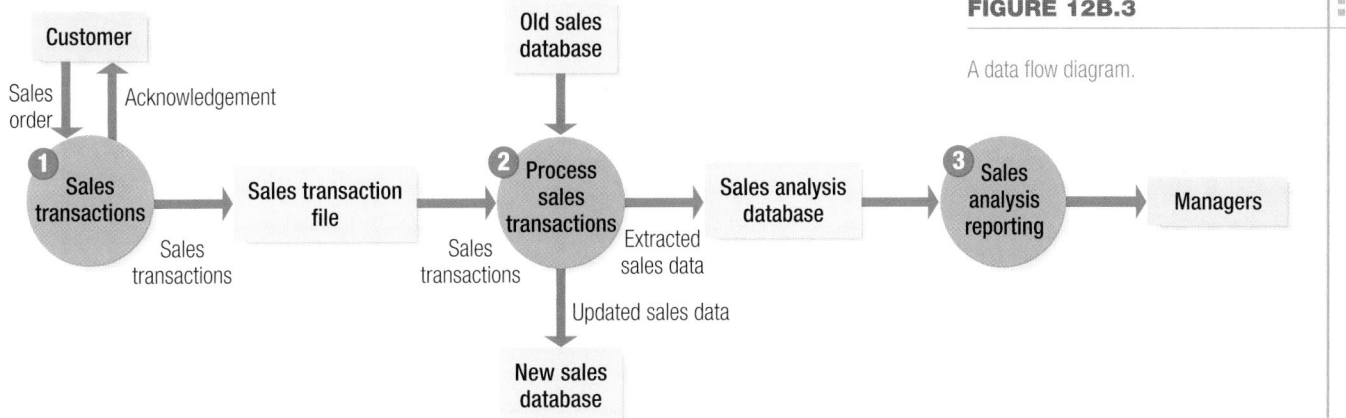

to define the problem accurately. In many situations, the actual problem may not be the one that was reported initially to the team. Rather, it may be only a symptom of a different, underlying problem. Thus, accurately defining the problem is crucial to moving on with subsequent phases of the project.

When the problem is defined, the IS department can decide whether to start the project (the "go/no go" decision). When a decision to proceed is made, technology analysts begin a thorough investigation of the current system and its limitations. They work with the people directly involved with the problem to document how it can be solved.

```
If item is received and
        the invoice date is over 30 days old
                If supplier is on payment hold status
                        indicate status on invoice
                        issue pending/future payment transaction

                Else issue payment voucher transaction

        Else calculate payment date
                issue pending/future payment transaction

Else issue invoiced/not received transaction
```

FIGURE 12B.4

Structured English.

Analysts can document a problem or an entire system in several different ways. Some analysts use data flow diagrams, which show the flow of data through a system, as shown in Figure 12B.3. Analysts also may use structured English—a method that uses English terms and phrases to describe events, actions, and alternative actions that can occur within the system, as shown in Figure 12B.4. Another option is to present the actions taken under different conditions in a decision tree, which graphically illustrates the events and actions that can occur in the system, as shown in Figure 12B.5.

At the end of phase 1, the team recommends a solution. The analysts use information they have already gathered from system users to determine which features must be included in the solution (what reports should be generated, in what form they will be put out, and what special tools are needed). Throughout the needs analysis phase, the team remains focused on what the system must do, not on how the features will be implemented.

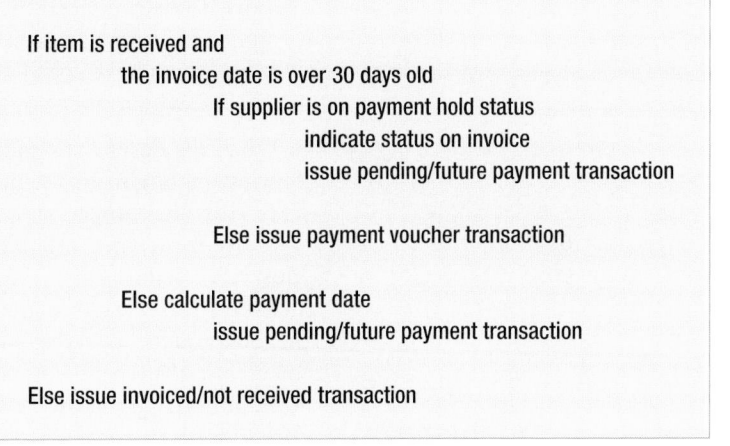

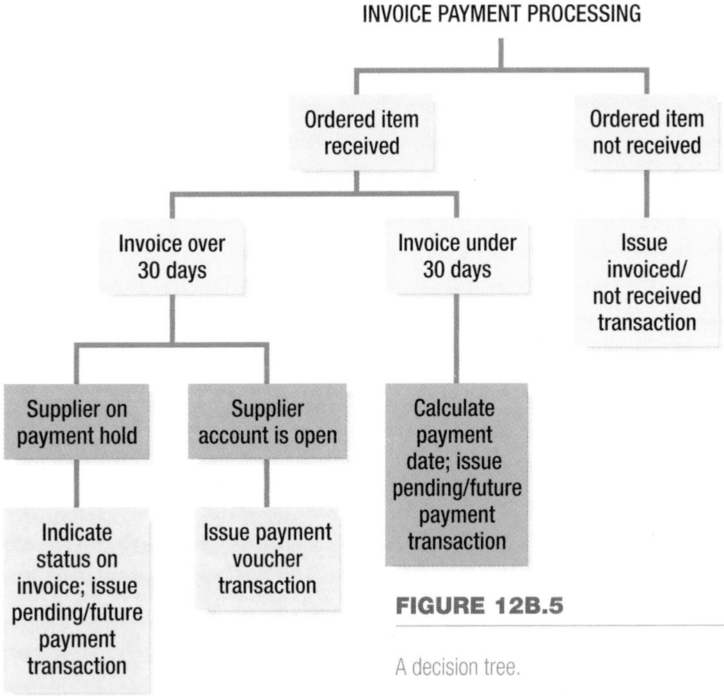

FIGURE 12B.5

A decision tree.

Phase 2: Systems Design

During the systems design phase, the project team tackles the "how" of the selected solution. For example, a database application must be able to accept data from users and store it in a database. These are general functions, but how will the team implement them? How many input screens are necessary, for example, and what will they look like? What kind of menu options must be available? What kind of database will the system use?

The analysts and programmers involved at this point often use a combination of top-down and bottom-up designs to answer these questions:

- In top-down design, team members start with the big picture and move to the details. They look at major functions that the system must provide and break these down into smaller and smaller activities. Each of these activities then will be programmed in the next phase of the SDLC.
- In bottom-up design, the team starts with the details (for example, the reports to be produced by the system) and then moves to the big picture (the major functions or processes). This approach is particularly appropriate when users have specific requirements for output—for example, payroll checks, which must contain certain pieces of information.

When the design passes inspection, development begins. Sometimes, however, a review highlights problems with the design, and the team must return to analysis or stop altogether.

Many tools are available to help teams through the steps of system design. Most of these tools also can be used during development (phase 3) or even during analysis (phase 1). Many teams use working models called prototypes to explore the look and feel of screens with users. They also use special software applications for creating these prototypes quickly as well as for building diagrams, writing code, and managing the development effort. These applications fall into the category of computer-aided software engineering (CASE) tools. In other words, computer software is used to develop other computer software more quickly and reliably.

Phase 3: Development

During the development phase, programmers play the key role, creating or customizing the software for the various parts of the system. There are two alternative paths through phase 3: the acquisition path and the local development path.

- **Acquisition.** As early as phase 1, the team may decide that some or all of the necessary system components are available as off-the-shelf hardware or software and may decide to acquire, rather than develop, these components. Buying off-the-shelf components means that the system can be built faster and cheaper than if every component is developed from scratch. Another advantage of acquired components is that they have already been tested and proven reliable, although they may need to be customized to fit into the overall information system.
- **Local Development.** When an off-the-shelf solution is not available or will not work with other parts of the system, the project team may need to develop a solution themselves. On the software side, this means writing program code from scratch or making changes to existing software in the system. On the hardware side, it may mean physically constructing a portion of the information system, typically using purchased components.

In many cases, project teams buy some components and develop others. Thus, they follow both acquisition and local development paths at the same time through the SDLC (see Figure 12B.6).

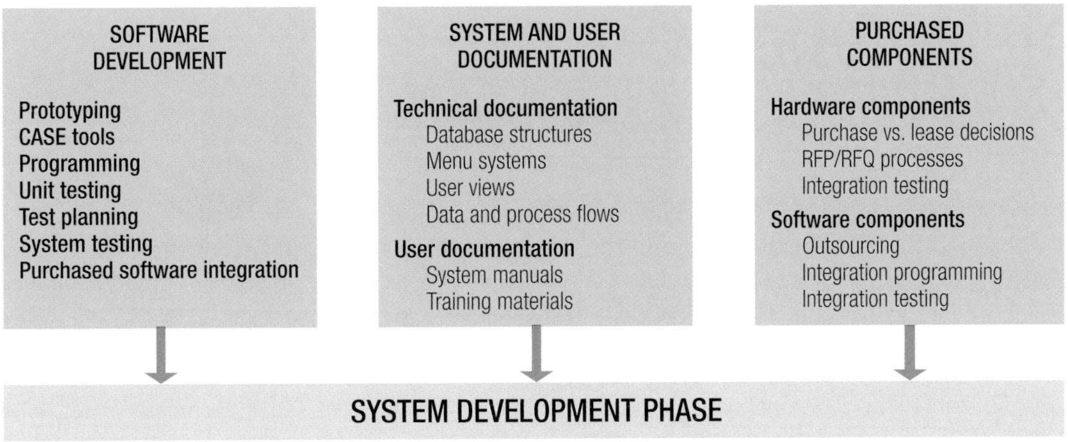

FIGURE 12B.6

These parts are created or acquired during phase 3.

During this phase, technical writers and/or online help authors work with the project team to produce the technical documentation and online help for the system. Testing is also an integral part of phases 3 and 4 (development and implementation). The typical approach to testing is to move from an individual component to the system as a whole. The team tests each component separately (unit testing) and then tests the components of the system with each other (system testing). Errors are corrected, the necessary changes are made, and the tests are then run again. The next step is installation testing, when the system is installed in a test environment and tested with other applications used by the business. Finally, acceptance testing is done; the end users test the installed system to make sure that it meets their criteria.

Phase 4: Implementation

In the implementation phase, the project team installs the hardware and software in the user environment. The users start using the system to perform work, rather than just to provide feedback on the system's development.

The process of moving from the old system to the new is called conversion. IS professionals must handle this process carefully to avoid losing or corrupting data or frustrating users trying to perform their work. As shown in Figure 12B.7, there are several different ways to convert a department or an organization, including the following:

- **Direct Conversion.** All users stop using the old system at the same time and then begin using the new. This option is fast, but it can be disruptive; pressure on support personnel can be excessive.
- **Parallel Conversion.** Users continue to use the old system while an increasing amount of data is processed through the new system. The outputs from the two systems are compared; if they agree, the switch is made. This option is useful for additional live testing of the new system, but it is fairly time-intensive because both systems are operating at the same time.
- **Phased Conversion.** Users start using the new system, component by component. This option works only for systems that can be compartmentalized.
- **Pilot Conversion.** Personnel in a single pilot site use the new system, and then the entire organization makes the switch. Although this approach may take more time than the other three, it gives support personnel the opportunity to test user response to the system thoroughly; then the support team will be better prepared when many people make the conversion.

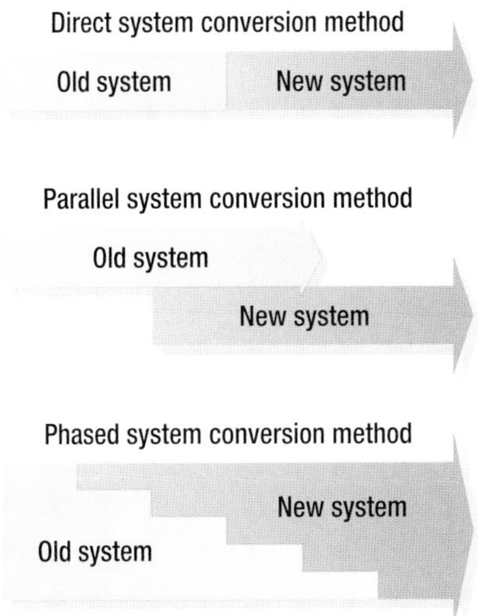

FIGURE 12B.7

Implementation methods.

Norton Notebook

The Knowledge Worker

As you will see in this lesson, there are plenty of career opportunities for people who want to work directly in an information systems department. Beyond those specialized careers, however, many other professions have been changed because of information systems. People in these jobs (many of which are not technical in nature) work differently than they ever did before; the tools and skills required by these jobs have changed dramatically, thanks to the growing use of information systems. These people are the knowledge workers, and their ranks have increased by untold numbers in the past decade.

What Is a Knowledge Worker?

The term *knowledge worker* dates back to the mid-1990s when—thanks to the proliferation of the Internet, corporate networks, and computerized information systems—people began sharing information on an unprecedented scale. As more people and organizations became connected and exchanged data electronically, many experts saw a great societal shift occurring. We were moving, they said, from the "information age" to the "knowledge age."

The knowledge worker, therefore, was any person whose work involved the use or development of knowledge of any kind. The knowledge worker's tasks might include researching, verifying, analyzing, organizing, storing, distributing, or selling knowledge. Although this may sound like a specialized field of endeavor, it really is not when you consider that any type of information may be considered knowledge, especially if it can be used in any way within a business. Therefore, a knowledge worker might be anyone from a financial strategist who uses expert systems for economic forecasts, to a technical writer, who amasses information about a particular program for use in the product's documentation.

As a result, *knowledge worker* has become a catch-all term, referring to any worker whose job involves the processing of information. A knowledge worker can be anyone who handles information in an organization, whether it includes mission-critical reports or involves a simple appointment book.

Even though the term *knowledge worker* has been diluted by overuse, it does not diminish the knowledge worker's role in the enterprise, especially when the knowledge at hand has real value. For example, consider the demographic data used by companies to market their products or services, or the financial information crucial to helping a business overcome its accumulated debt. When analyzed and used properly, such knowledge can mean the difference between success and failure. For this reason, knowledge workers of all types should recognize the potential value of the information they handle and treat it accordingly.

Trainers and support personnel play a significant role during the conversion. Training courses usually involve classroom-style lectures, hands-on sessions with sample data, and computer-based training that users can work with on their own time.

Phase 5: Maintenance

After the information systems are implemented, IS professionals continue to provide support during the maintenance phase. They monitor various indices of system performance, such as response time, to ensure that the system is performing as intended. They also respond to changes in users' requirements. These changes occur for various reasons. As users work with the system on a daily basis, they may recognize instances where a small change in the system would allow them to work more efficiently. In addition, management may request changes due to a change in state or federal regulations of the industry.

Errors in the system also are corrected during phase 5. Systems are often installed in a user environment with known programming or design errors. Typically, these errors have been identified as noncritical or not important enough to delay installation. Programmers have lists of such errors to correct during the maintenance phase. In addition, daily use of the system may highlight more serious errors for the programmers to fix.

NORTON NOTEBOOK

Becoming an Effective Knowledge Worker

Regardless of your actual job title, your employability increases if you can prove your skills as an effective knowledge worker. Here are some tips:

- **Master Your Organization's Knowledge Management Tools.** The actual tools vary from one organization to another, but they often include file management; word processing, database, and spreadsheet applications; and analytical tools.
- **Develop Your Information-Finding Skills.** You may not be expected to know everything, but you will be respected for your ability to find information quickly and effectively. Practice using information-finding tools such as Internet search engines, reference books, and others that apply to your profession.
- **Prove Your Trustworthiness.** Knowledge can include trade secrets, market feedback, contracts, licenses, and other types of proprietary information. Employers expect their workers not to share this information with anyone who should not see it. Learn to recognize private information and keep it confidential.

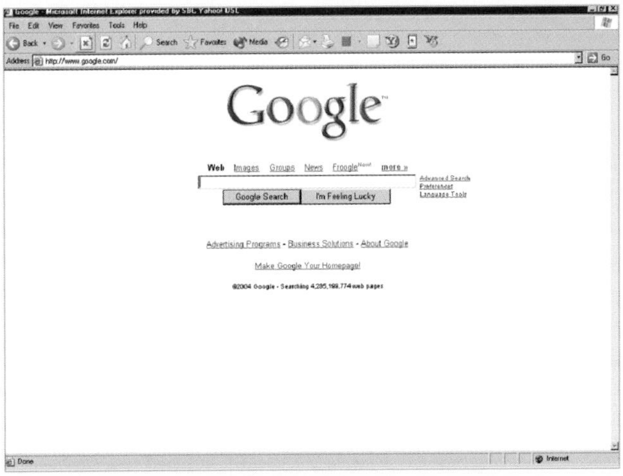

Internet search engines such as Google can be valuable for any knowledge worker who needs to find information on the Internet. Google can perform basic or advanced searches, making it a good choice for many kinds of information-seeking tasks.

Changes or upgrades to the system are made regularly during the remaining life of the system. At some point, however, making patch repairs to the system may not meet user requirements—particularly if radical changes have been made since the system was installed. The IS professionals or managers in a user department might then begin calling for a major modification or new system. At this point, the SDLC has come full circle, and the analysis phase begins again.

SELF-CHECK ::

Circle the correct answer for each question.

1. A well-designed information system can be an important factor in an organization's ________ .

   a. help desk b. hiring practices c. success

2. The systems development life cycle is an organized way to ________ .

   a. mirror data b. build an information system c. create forms

3. During the development phase, the programmers may take either the local development or the ________ path.

   a. acquisition b. direct conversion c. straight and narrow

Evolving Systems Development Methods

The traditional SDLC described above has been around for a long time. While it has many proponents, it has garnered some criticism over the years—primarily that it takes so long to do that the needs may have changed significantly before a new system is implemented. To compete in the current global economy, businesses must react quickly to changing business needs and have sought ways to create and modify information systems quickly enough to stay competitive. The answer to this need is contained in several methodologies. We'll look at two of these evolving methods: rapid application development and object-oriented systems analysis.

Rapid Application Development

Norton ONLINE

For more information on rapid application development, visit **http://www.mhhe.com/peternorton**.

Rapid application development (RAD) is a term that has been assigned to a variety of evolving methods for shortening the conventional SDLC. Because there are so many different RAD implementations, we will focus on just one representative description. It is important to remember that RAD is used to develop IS systems very quickly, even requiring that the deadline be met at the expense of some of the functionality.

The phases of a typical RAD are

1. Requirements planning
2. User design
3. Rapid construction
4. Transition
5. Maintenance

While these phases appear to be similar to those of the traditional SDLC, the intensity and the level of commitment required in the first two phases of RAD are expected to shorten the entire development process. These two phases are usually implemented in structured workshops, with participants isolated from day-to-day tasks and required to make commitments to the project and to each workshop (see Figure 12B.8).

FIGURE 12B.8

The RAD system development life cycle.

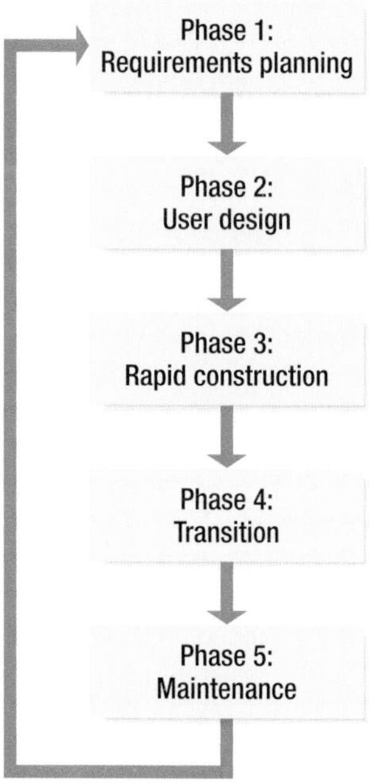

Phase 1: Requirements Planning

During this first phase, the requirements of the project are defined. Many organizations employ a method called joint requirements planning (JRP) to identify high-level, strategic management requirements. At the heart of JRP are highly structured workshops in which senior managers participate in defining the goals and strategy of the organization and defining the goals and priorities of the new system. New systems may require cooperation between departments or business units that do not always have common goals and that normally are under different managers. Therefore, it is important that all decision makers participate in these workshops.

Phase 2: User Design

The user design phase of RAD actually includes both system analysis—but now from a user perspective—and design of the system. It may use a method called joint applications design (JAD), which, like JRP, also centers on structured workshops. But now the participants are the actual business users (both managers and end-users) of the proposed system. IS personnel are always present to assist in technical details, but not as decision makers. JAD evolved out of the realization that user requirements are often challenging for a third party to understand through the traditional tools of observation, interviews, and questionnaires. JAD works to determine the correct requirements that also meet the business needs established in the requirements planning phase. While JAD was created for use in the development of large mainframe systems, it has more recently been applied to RAD and Web development.

Participants in the JAD workshops use prototyping tools and various diagramming techniques to create the design. A CASE tool may be used to illustrate the resulting design, which then can be used to accurately move into the construction phase.

Phase 3: Rapid Construction

During the rapid construction phase, IS professionals create a detailed design based on the results of the previous phase. All prototypes created during this phase must be approved by the users. Using CASE tools, they move from detailed design to the creation of the code for the system. The project may be broken up into smaller chunks and assigned to small teams. The components are tested and approved.

As with the conventional SDLC, the technical documentation and online help for the new system also are created during this phase.

Phase 4: Transition

The transition phase involves further comprehensive testing using simulated data. Users are trained on the system, and any organizational changes required by the new system are implemented. Finally, the old and new systems are run in parallel, until the new system has proved itself and the old system is phased out.

Phase 5: Maintenance

The maintenance phase is often missing in descriptions of RAD, but ongoing maintenance is required of any information system. As with the conventional SDLC, IS personnel support the use of the new system and monitor its performance. They also respond to changes in users' requirements and changes requested by management.

Maintenance also is required to detect and correct errors and continue to make any necessary changes and upgrades throughout the life of the system.

Object-Oriented Systems Analysis (OOSA)

Another systems development method is object-oriented systems analysis (OOSA), a method that is applied to the findings of the needs analysis and affects the subsequent phases. OOSA departs from the conventional methods by creating entities called objects and then establishing relationships between the objects. For example, as a result of the needs analysis of a point-of-sale system, it is clear that each item to be sold is an entity and when using OOSA, each item is defined as an object. Other objects in the point-of-sale system could be sales associate, store ID, and department. Each object is assigned attributes. In the case of the product object, the attributes could include price, color, description, size, manufacturer, and any other characteristic that has significance for the users. Next, relationships are established between the objects. For example, the item must be moved into inventory once it comes into the store and must be moved out of inventory when it is sold. At the time of sale, a sales associate performs the sales transaction. Such relations are established for all defined objects, creating a model of the entire project. Once the relationships between the objects are fully understood, it becomes clear how best to break up the project into smaller pieces that can be assigned to different development teams. Following OOSA, the development teams may use conventional programming tools, or they can use tools such as Java that enable developers to write programming code based on object-orientation rules.

Norton ONLINE

For more information on object-oriented systems analysis, visit **http://www.mhhe.com/peternorton**.

Computers In Your Career

COMPUTERS IN YOUR CAREER

Careers in Information Systems

He may have been an English major, but the fact that Seth Miller put himself through college by working in the computer lab paved a clear path to a successful career in information systems. Having attended college when the desktop publishing and PC revolution was taking off, Miller says he started out learning how to build small networks and gradually worked his way up to larger, more complex IT projects.

When working as a system administrator for a digital prepress house, Miller not only gained network infrastructure experience—including how to build and connect large networks—but he also learned a thing or two about customer service and the Internet. "I registered my first domain name back in 1993," says Miller, who today heads up Miller Systems, Inc., a Boston-based Web development and information technology firm that handles technology projects for small to midsize companies.

As president and CEO of his own firm, Miller plans his schedule on a week-to-week or month-to-month basis, depending on what type of projects his firm has taken on. When a client needs a new enterprisewide software solution or an e-commerce-enabled Web site, for example, he handles the client relations and much of the strategic problem solving.

"I assist with the technical architecture, but my key role is helping clients organize their content and design their user experience," says Miller, who works one-on-one with clients to uncover business problems and design technology solutions to alleviate those challenges. The most exciting aspect of the job, says Miller, is solving "very big" IT problems for a wide range of companies. "When you can remove a significant number of steps—particularly mundane, tedious tasks—and shave time off of someone's day," says Miller, "it's very satisfying."

Looking ahead, Miller says the information systems professionals in most demand will be those network and development engineers who are both tech-savvy and business-savvy and who can apply their knowledge and expertise in "real-world" business environments.

The need for organizations to incorporate existing and future technologies in order to remain competitive has

IS professionals spend much of their time interacting with end users.

become a more pressing issue over the last several years, according to the Bureau of Labor Statistics. As electronic commerce becomes more common, how and when companies use technology are critical issues. Computer and information systems managers play a vital role in the technological direction of their organizations, handling everything from constructing the business plan to overseeing network and Internet operations.

Computer and information systems managers plan, coordinate, and direct research and design the computer-related activities of firms. They determine technical goals in consultation with top management and make detailed plans for the accomplishment of these goals. For example, working with their staff, they may develop the overall concepts of a new product or identify computer-related problems standing in the way of project completion.

The BLS reports that employment of computer and information systems managers is expected to increase much faster than the average for all occupations through the year 2010. Earnings for computer and information systems managers vary by specialty and level of responsibility, but the BLS reports median annual earnings of $78,830 for 2000, with the middle 50 percent earning between $59,640 and $100,820.

LESSON // 12B Review

Summary ::

- The systems development life cycle (SDLC) is an organized method for building an information system.
- The SDLC includes five phases: needs analysis, systems design, development, implementation, and maintenance.
- The needs analysis phase includes (1) defining the problem and deciding whether to proceed with the project, (2) analyzing the current system, and (3) selecting a solution.
- During systems design, the project team decides how the solution will work.
- During development, programmers create or customize software for the system.
- During implementation, the hardware and software are installed in the user environment.
- The process of moving from an old system to a new one is called conversion. The project team may follow four different conversion methods: direct, parallel, phased, and pilot.
- During the maintenance phase, IS professionals provide ongoing training and support to the system's users. Fixes or improvements to the system are made during its remaining life.
- The need for businesses to react quickly to changing business requirements has resulted in newer, faster methods for systems development.
- An evolving alternative to the conventional SDLC is rapid application development (RAD), which relies on intense workshops in two of the phases to shorten the development life cycle.
- Object-oriented systems analysis (OOSA) is another evolving method that fits into the conventional SDLC at the needs analysis phase but that affects all other phases.

Key Terms ::

- acceptance testing, 485
- bottom-up design, 484
- computer-aided software engineering (CASE), 484
- conversion, 485
- data flow diagram, 483
- decision tree, 483
- development phase, 484
- implementation phase, 485
- installation testing, 485
- joint applications design (JAD), 488
- joint requirements planning (JRP), 488
- maintenance phase, 486
- needs analysis phase, 482
- object-oriented systems analysis (OOSA), 489
- prototype, 484
- rapid application development (RAD), 488
- structured English, 483
- system testing, 485
- systems design phase, 484
- systems development life cycle (SDLC), 482
- top-down design, 484
- unit testing, 485

Key Term Quiz ::

Complete each statement by writing one of the terms listed under Key Terms in each blank.

1. The abbreviation *SDLC* stands for __________ .
2. The phases of the __________ represent the entire life of an information system from conception through the end of its usefulness.
3. In __________ , the IS team starts with the big picture and moves to the details.
4. Programmers play the key role in the __________ of the SDLC.
5. The final phase of the SDLC is called the __________ .
6. During the SDLC, one or more teams may use a working model called a(n) __________ to explore the look and feel of the screens with users.
7. One of the ways that analysts can document a problem or an entire system is by using a(n) __________ , which graphically illustrates the events and actions that can occur in the system.
8. The __________ system-development method focuses on structured workshops, but includes actual business users of the proposed system.
9. __________ is a term that has been assigned to a variety of methods for shortening the time required to develop an information system using conventional SDLC.
10. Using __________ , developers take the result of the analysis and design phases and define objects and relationships between objects.

LESSON // 12B Review

Multiple Choice ::

Circle the word or phrase that best completes each statement.

1. During needs analysis, the development team must __________ .
   a. define the problem   b. implement the system   c. decide how to implement the system   d. create applications
2. By using __________ , developers can verbally describe the events, actions, and alternative actions that can occur within an information system.
   a. data flow diagrams   b. structured English   c. prototypes   d. decision trees
3. In __________ , developers look at major system functions and break them into smaller and smaller activities.
   a. top-down design   b. bottom-up design   c. acquisition   d. parallel conversion
4. When programmers take the __________ path, they elect to create system components.
   a. acquisition   b. maintenance   c. local development   d. structured English
5. The process of moving from an old system to a new one is called __________ .
   a. implementation   b. acquisition   c. systems design   d. conversion
6. Which of the following is computer software used to develop other computer software quickly and reliably?
   a. prototyping   b. data flow diagrams   c. computer-aided software engineering (CASE) tools   d. decision trees
7. When users have specific requirements for output that must contain certain pieces of information, the development team will likely use a __________ .
   a. bottom-up design   b. top-down design   c. conversion   d. pilot
8. During RAD requirements planning, an organization may use __________ to identify high-level, strategic management requirements.
   a. joint application design (JAD)   b. rapid construction   c. OOSA   d. joint requirements planning (JRP)
9. JRP and JAD both use highly structured __________ .
   a. programming   b. objects   c. workshops   d. rules
10. Object-oriented systems analysis defines objects that are assigned __________ and the relationships between the objects are defined.
    a. developers   b. tools   c. attributes   d. numbers

Review Questions ::

In your own words, briefly answer the following questions.

1. Why is it so important that information systems be well designed and structured?
2. What is the main focus of the systems design phase of the SDLC?
3. Describe the differences between top-down and bottom-up design.
4. What is the difference between the acquisition path and the local development path in the development phase of the SDLC?
5. What are the four types of conversion methods that may be used in the implementation phase of the SDLC?
6. In general terms, what is achieved during the implementation phase?
7. What type of events during the maintenance phase of an information system life cycle might call for a return to the needs analysis phase.
8. What is the primary criticism of the traditional SDLC?
9. The phases of the traditional SDLC and the phases of RAD appear similar. Describe what distinguishes the two.
10. How does object-oriented systems analysis differ from convention SDLC?

Lesson Labs ::

Complete the following exercises as directed by your instructor.

1. Using a sheet of paper, draw a decision tree that shows the actions and alternatives (such as order input, customer support, billing, and so on) that can occur in one portion of a transaction processing system. Your instructor may divide the class into groups and ask each group to design a tree for a specific part of the system.
2. Create some user documentation. Open a word processor, write a single paragraph of text on any subject, and then format the text. Now create a one-page document that explains the process of creating and formatting that paragraph. Write the documentation for someone who has never used a word processor. Be sure to include numbered steps and explain the procedure in detail.

Chapter Labs

Complete the following exercises using a computer in your classroom, lab, or home.

1. Create your own IS department. Suppose that your city has just been granted an NFL expansion team. The team's owner is in the process of building a new stadium and hiring office staff; the team owner has hired you to be the organization's CIO. Your first task is to determine the types of information systems the team will need, and then you must hire IS professionals to build and maintain those systems. Follow these steps:
   a. Using two pieces of paper, map the information systems you think will be needed.
   b. List the IS department positions you want to fill.
   c. Describe the role you want each IS staff member to play.
   d. When you are finished with your diagrams and lists, share them with the class. Be prepared to support your design and hiring decisions.
2. Chart the flow. On a piece of paper (or several pieces, if necessary), create a data flow diagram that maps the flow of data for a transaction processing system of a business that sells tickets to events such as concerts or ball games.
3. Get a job. Visit the following Web sites and see if you can find job listings for IS professionals such as technology analysts, network administrators, or technical writers:
   a. **NationJob Network.** http://www.nationjob.com/
   b. **Monster.com.** http://www.monster.com/
   c. **EDP Professionals.** http://www.misjobs.com/
4. Search for knowledge. The Microsoft Knowledge Base is an excellent example of an online expert system. You can use it to obtain technical support and answer questions about any Microsoft product. Access the Microsoft Knowledge Base:
   a. Visit the Microsoft Web site at http://www.microsoft.com/.
   b. Click the Support link, and then click the Knowledge Base link.
   c. When the Knowledge Base page appears, click the drop-down arrow next to the Select a Microsoft Product box and select a product, such as Internet Explorer or a version of Windows.
   d. Click in the Search For box and type a term that relates to the product you selected. For example, if you selected Windows XP as the product, you could type in **security** to find documents pertaining to security features and known security problems in Windows XP.
   e. Click the Go button. If the knowledge base contains any documents that match your search criteria, they are listed in the window. Click a link to view a document.
   f. Once you get the hang of using the knowledge base, search for information on at least two more products.

Discussion Questions

As directed by your instructor, discuss the following questions in class or in groups.

1. Suppose that you run a manufacturing facility that produces automotive parts. Discuss the types of information that would be important to the operation of the plant. What kind of information system or systems would you want to use at the facility?
2. Discuss the issues addressed during the needs analysis phase of the SDLC for a new hospital. What are the biggest challenges during this phase?

Research and Report

Using your own choice of resources (such as the Internet, books, magazines, and newspaper articles), research and write a short paper discussing one of the following topics:

- Ownership of data on a corporate network. (For example, if you receive an e-mail message at work, who owns that message?)
- What type of information system is used by online retailers such as Amazon.com or Orbitz.com? How do these retailers make use of their information systems?
- Pick one of the IS department jobs listed earlier in this unit and do a more in-depth analysis of it. What is the salary range for that position? What kind of educational background is required for such a job?

When you are finished, proofread and print your paper, and give it to your instructor.

ETHICAL ISSUES

Information systems can make it easier for workers at many levels to access information within an organization. With this thought in mind, discuss the following questions in class.

1. In some organizations, managers insist that certain classes of employees be prevented from accessing some types of information, such as financial data. In your view, is this practice fair? Why or why not? What business reasons would managers have for limiting access to certain types of information?
2. You have become tired of your job so, while at work, you use a company PC and printer to create a new resume and cover letter. You store these files on the company's network and they are found by a manager, who threatens to fire you for your actions. Is the manager correct in following this course of action? Support your views on this issue.

CHAPTER 13

Software Programming and Development

CHAPTER CONTENTS ::

This chapter contains the following lessons:

LESSON // 13A

Creating Computer Programs

Overview: What Is a Computer Program?

Software, as you learned in Chapter 1, provides the instructions that run the hardware in a computer. Without software, the computer cannot function—it is nothing more than a bunch of parts. Some software commands may be built into select pieces of hardware (like CPUs and ROM chips), but even in these cases, the programming is simply a "hard-coded" version of software. An example of such hard-coding can be found in something as typical as a digital watch. Although you may not even think of it, some kind of software is built into the watch's circuitry that makes it work. Because software is such an integral part of any computer system, it is important to understand what software is and where it comes from.

The term *software* can be used generically, as in the statement "Software tells the computer what to do." The term can be used more specifically to describe an operating system or application. For example, you might say, "Windows XP is a piece of software," or "PhotoShop is a piece of software." On any one computer, the software usually consists of the operating system, various utilities (sometimes considered part of the operating system), and applications.

The following sections explain what programs are and how they function. They describe some of the processes and tools that software developers use when creating computer programs.

OBJECTIVES ::

- Define the term *computer program*.
- Describe the use of flowcharts and pseudocode in programming.
- Identify two ways in which a program can work toward a solution.
- Differentiate the two main approaches to computer programming.
- List and describe three elements of object-oriented programming.

simnet™

What Is a Computer Program?

A computer program is a set of instructions or statements (also called *code*) to be carried out by the computer's CPU. Programs, or software, come in many forms. These can be broken down into three major categories: operating systems, utilities, and applications (see Figure 13A.1).

A program is typically composed of a main module and submodules. These modules are stored as a collection of files; large programs can contain thousands of individual files, each serving a specific purpose. Some of the files contain instructions for the computer, while other files contain data. For Windows-based PCs, some common extensions for program files include the following:

- **Executable Files.** An executable (.exe, .com) file is the part of a program that actually sends commands to the processor. In fact, when you run a program, you are running the executable file. The processor executes the commands in the file—thus the name *executable file*. Executable files usually (but do not always) have the filename extension .exe.
- **Dynamic Link Library Files.** A dynamic link library (.dll) file is a partial .exe file. A .dll file will not run on its own; instead, its commands are accessed by another running program. Because .dll files can contain parts of an executable program, they provide programmers with an effective way of breaking large programs into small, replaceable components. This feature makes the entire program easier to upgrade. In addition, .dll files also can be shared by several programs at one time.
- **Initialization Files.** An initialization (.ini) file contains configuration information, such as the size and starting point of a window, the color of the background, the user's name, and so on. Initialization files help programs start running or contain information that programs can use as they run. Although initialization files are still in use, many newer programs store user preferences and other program variables in the Windows Registry—a special database that holds information about the computer's user, installed programs, and certain hardware devices.
- **Help Files.** A help (.hlp, .chm) file contains information in an indexed and cross-linked format. By including a help file, programmers can provide the user with online help information.

Norton ONLINE

For more information on executable, dynamic link library, initialization, and help files, visit **http://www.mhhe.com/peternorton**.

FIGURE 13A.1

The major categories of software include operating systems, utilities, and applications.

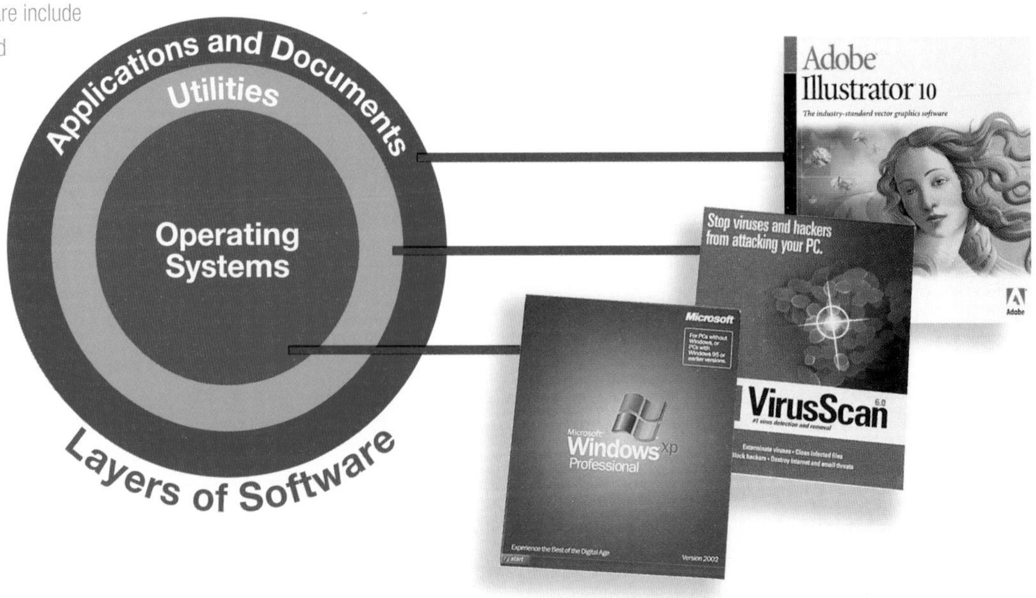

» **Batch Files.** A batch (.bat) file automates common or repetitive tasks. A batch file is a simple program that consists of an unformatted text file containing one or more operating system commands. If you type a batch file's name at a command prompt, your operating system will execute the commands in the file.

By default, most program files are stored in a folder that bears the application's name or an abbreviation of it. However, some programs' files may be placed in other folders. For example, the .dll files on Windows XP are usually stored in the c:\windows\system32 folder. To view a list of most of the files needed to run an application, you can open that application's folder. Figure 13A.2 shows a typical software directory, in this case, for a hypothetical program called CoolToys version 1.3.

Hardware/Software Interaction

Software is the reason people purchase computers. A program's instructions execute at the hardware level, mainly on the CPU. The program, for example, may tell the CPU to retrieve a specific piece of information from memory. If the program tells the CPU to play a sound file, then the program generates an interrupt. An interrupt is a signal to the CPU to execute a series of preprogrammed steps as a response to the interrupt. In this case the hardware would send the sound file to the audio output device.

A highly trained individual called a computer programmer creates this list of instructions. The list is often called code, and the process of writing the list is usually called coding.

Code

The term code refers to statements that are written in any programming language, as in machine code or higher-level code. As you saw in Chapter 5, computers think and speak in the binary number system. Of course, binary is too cryptic for humans to deal with for any length of time. This is why computer-programming languages

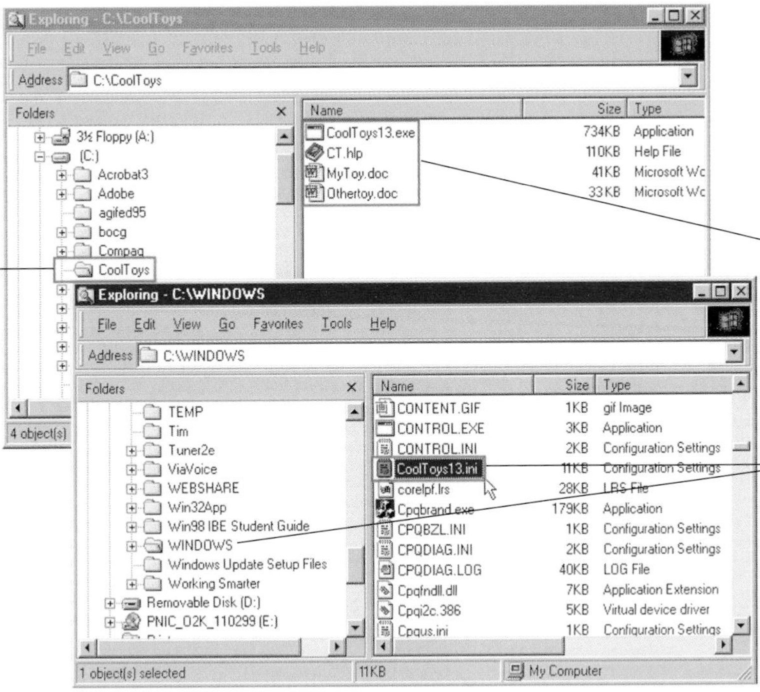

FIGURE 13A.2

Applications usually have executable, help, initialization, and document files.

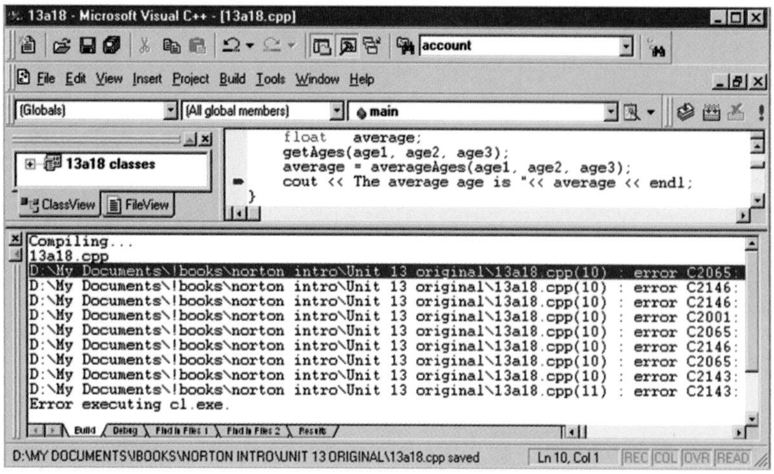

FIGURE 13A.3

The missing quotation mark (") in front of "The" is a syntax error that causes several other fictitious errors.

were created—to simplify the process of writing instructions that computers can use.

Programming is both tedious and exciting. It is tedious because all programming languages, like spoken languages, have a series of demanding rules. Speakers of English can make several grammatical mistakes and still communicate with their listener. However, a piece of code must be perfect before it will run. No grammatical mistakes or syntax errors are allowed in programming. The programmer must fix these errors before the program can be tested. Figure 13A.3 shows a syntax error in a C++ program.

Programming is exciting on many levels. First and foremost, writing code provides the programmer with the chance to create something new. The developer gets to exercise his or her creative muscles. Second, excitement comes from the challenge of solving a problem. The problem can be as simple as calculating a value or as complex as determining the path of a satellite in orbit. Being able to solve problems, however minor, with a piece of code is a lure that many programmers find hard to resist.

Norton ONLINE

For more information on machine code, visit **http://www.mhhe.com/peternorton**.

Machine Code

As you learned in Chapter 1, the computer's memory and processing switches use the binary number system, which consists of 1s and 0s. Any software commands that directly affect hardware must be written in the binary number system. Because these 1s and 0s form the language of computer hardware, this code is often called machine code or machine language. Machine language consists entirely of 1s and 0s. While this format would not make sense to you, it would make perfect sense to the computer and could be explained as the lowest-level computer language. Figure 13A.4 shows an example of machine code.

FIGURE 13A.4

An example of machine code.

11010010	10101010	10100010	01100111	10100010
01000110	10111000	10111100	01101101	10111100
10100010	10101101	00011001	01010110	00011001
10111100	11010010	10000100	10111101	10000100
00011001	01000110	10111010	11101100	10111010
10000100	10100010	10010110	00011000	10010110
10111010	10111100	01100111	10111010	01100111
10010110	00011001	01101101	01101011	01101101
01100111	10000100	01010110	01110010	01010110
01101101	10111010	10111101	10011001	10111101
01010110	10010110	11101100	00110101	11101100
10111101	01100111	00011000	01010110	10100010
11101100	01101101	10111010	10111101	10111100
00011000	01010110	01101011	11101100	00011001
10111010	10111101	01110010	11010010	10000100
01101011	11101100	10011001	01000110	10111010
01110010	11010010	00110101	10100010	10010110
10011001	01000110	10101010	10111100	01100111
00110101	10100010	10111000	00011001	01101101
10101010	10111100	10101101	10000100	01010110
11010010	10101010	10100010	01100111	10100010
01000110	10111000	10111100	01101101	10111100
10100010	10101101	00011001	01010110	00011001
10111100	11010010	10000100	10111101	10000100
00011001	01000110	10111010	11101100	10111010
10000100	10100010	10010110	00011000	10010110
10111010	10111100	01100111	10111010	01100111
10010110	00011001	01101101	01101011	01101101
01100111	10000100	01010110	01110010	01010110
01101101	10111010	10111101	10011001	10111101
01010110	10010110	11101100	00110101	11101100
10111101	01100111	00011000	01010110	10100010
11101100	01101101	10111010	10111101	10111100
00011000	01010110	01101011	11101100	00011001
10111010	10111101	01110010	11010010	10000100
01101011	11101100	10011001	01000110	10111010
01110010	11010010	00110101	10100010	10010110
10011001	01000110	10101010	10111100	01100111
00110101	10100010	10111000	00011001	01101101
10101010	10111100	10101101	10000100	01010110

Norton ONLINE

For more information on programming languages, visit **http://www.mhhe.com/peternorton**.

simnet™

Programming Languages

Although a computer's code must consist of nothing but 1s and 0s, computer programmers do not work (or think) that way. Programmers use programming languages instead of binary. Programming languages enable the programmer to describe a program using a variation of basic English. The results are saved in a file and called source code. As an example, Figure 13A.5 shows the Visual Basic.NET source code for a program.

You will learn more about specific programming languages later in this chapter.

Compilers and Interpreters

After creating a piece of source code, the programmer must convert the source code into machine code (break it down into a series of 1s and 0s) before it can run on a computer. The job of converting the source code is handled by one of two types of programs:

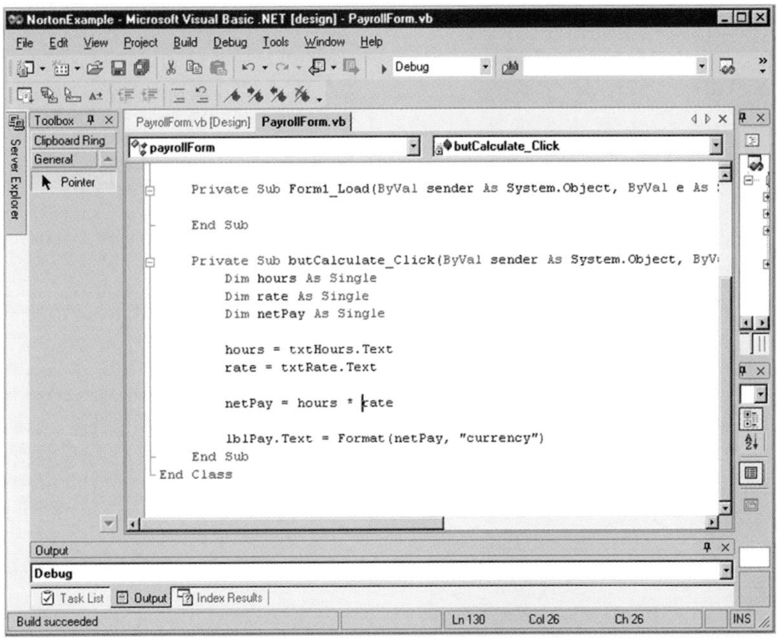

FIGURE 13A.5

An example of source code for an application created in Visual Basic.NET.

- A compiler converts all the source code into machine code, creating an executable file. The output of the compiler is called object code. In some languages the object code must then be linked to produce a true executable file. In other languages the object code itself is directly executable. The programmer can copy the executable object code onto any similar system and run the program. In other words, once compiled, the program is a stand-alone executable file that no longer needs the compiler to run. Of course, each programming language requires its own compiler to translate code written in that language. For example, the programming language C++ requires a C++ compiler, while the language Pascal requires a Pascal compiler. Figure 13A.6 shows an example of a compiler.
- An interpreter also converts source code to machine code. Instead of creating an executable object code file, however, the interpreter translates and then executes each line of the program, one line at a time. Interpreters translate code on the fly, so they have a certain flexibility that compilers lack. The interpreted code runs slower than compiled code because the code must be interpreted each time it is run, and a copy of the interpreter must accompany the

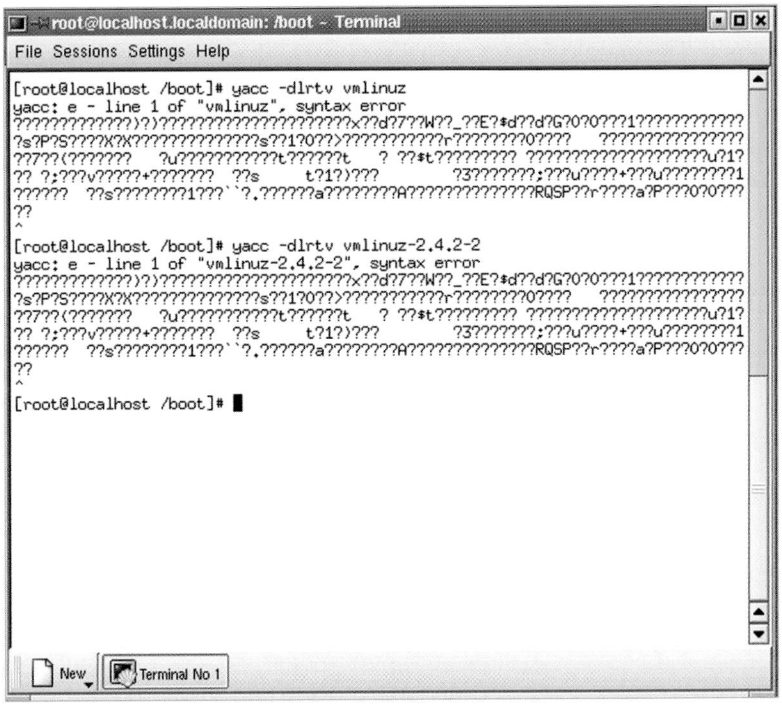

FIGURE 13A.6

The Yet Another C Compiler (YACC), which is found in many versions of Linux.

FIGURE 13A.7

An example of a Perl clock script.

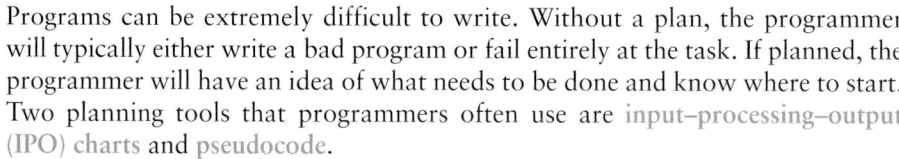

```
sub divide {@months = ('January','February','March','April','May','June','July','August','Se
@days = ('Sunday','Monday','Tuesday','Wednesday','Thursday','Friday','Saturday');
($sec,$min,$hour,$day,$month,$year,$day2) = (localtime(time))[0,1,2,3,4,5,6];
if ($sec < 10) { $sec = "0$sec"; }
if ($min < 10) { $min = "0$min"; }
if ($hour < 10) { $hour = "0$hour"; }
if ($day < 10) { $day = "0$day"; }
$year += "1900";
if ($order) { &time; &divide; &date; }
else { &date; &divide; &time; }
sub date {
        if ($dateformat) {
                if ($weekday) { print "$days[$day2], "; }
                if ($dateformat == 1) { print "$months[$month] $day, $year"; }
                else {
                        $month++;
                        print "$month/$day/$year";
                }
        }
}
sub time {
        if ($timeformat == 2) { print "$hour:$min:$sec"; }
        elsif ($timeformat == 1) {
                if ($hour >= 12) { $ex = "P.M."; }
                else { $ex = "A.M."; }
                if ($hour == 0) { $hour = 12; }
                if ($hour > 12) { $hour -= 12; }
                print "$hour:$min:$sec $ex";
        }
}
sub divide {
```

code everywhere it goes. Therefore, every system that needs the program must have a copy of the interpreter as well as the source code. Some popular interpreted languages include LISP, BASIC, and Visual Basic. Figure 13A.7 illustrates a clock program written in Perl.

Planning a Computer Program

Programs can be extremely difficult to write. Without a plan, the programmer will typically either write a bad program or fail entirely at the task. If planned, the programmer will have an idea of what needs to be done and know where to start. Two planning tools that programmers often use are input–processing–output (IPO) charts and pseudocode.

The IPO chart helps the programmer determine what is needed to write the program. It consists of three columns. In the first column, the programmer lists what data is needed to solve the task. In the last column, the programmer lists the desired output. The middle column is the hard part. Here the programmer lists the steps needed to get the desired output. Typically the steps are written in pseudocode.

Pseudocode is natural language statements that look like programming code. The idea is to write in English what needs to happen in code. Quite often the programmer is unsure how to write each step of the program. At least in describing the code, the programmer has a head start and can start thinking about how to implement the code.

Table 13A.1 shows an IPO chart detailing a payroll application. The program will calculate gross pay for an hourly employee. For simplicity's sake, overtime wages are ignored.

To solve the problem, the programmer must determine how many hours the employee worked and his or her hourly pay. This is handled in steps 1 and 2 of the processing section. A wise programmer will then check to ensure that this data makes sense. Step 3 performs this check. Valid hours could be between 0 and 40 hours. A person claiming to work more than 100 hours in a week is an example of invalid data. The program must respond to this error. Step 4 calculates the answer. Finally, step 5 prints the answer on the screen.

Norton ONLINE

For more information on planning a computer program, visit **http://www.mhhe.com/peternorton**.

TABLE 13A.1

The IPO Chart for a Program that Calculates Gross Pay for an Hourly Employee

Input	Processing	Output
Hours worked	Input hours worked	Gross pay
Hourly wage	Input hourly wage	
	Validate data	
	Pay = hours worked * hourly wage	
	Display gross pay	

How Programs Solve Problems

You already know that a program is a set of steps for controlling a computer, but you may not know what the steps look like. Their appearance or structure depends a little on the programming language, but the overall concept is the same regardless of the language. Each step in the code is an instruction that performs a single task in a sequence of steps that perform a more complex task.

Program Control Flow

When you launch a program, the computer begins reading and carrying out statements at the executable file's main entry point. Typically, this entry point is the first line (or statement) in the file, although it may be located elsewhere. After execution of the first statement, program control passes (or flows) to another statement, and so on, until the last statement of the program has been executed. Then the program ends. The order in which program statements are executed is called program control flow.

Algorithms

The steps represented in an IPO chart usually lead to some desired result. Collectively, these steps are called an algorithm. An algorithm is a series of step-by-step instructions that, when followed, produce a known or expected result. The steps to finding a solution remain the same, whether you are working out the solution by computer or by hand—which is why you can have both a working program and a hand-drawn IPO chart for completing the same task.

Figure 13A.8 shows a flowchart algorithm for finding the highest peak on a topographical map. Flowcharts are a very structured way to design programs.

Norton ONLINE

For more information on algorithms, visit **http://www.mhhe.com/peternorton**.

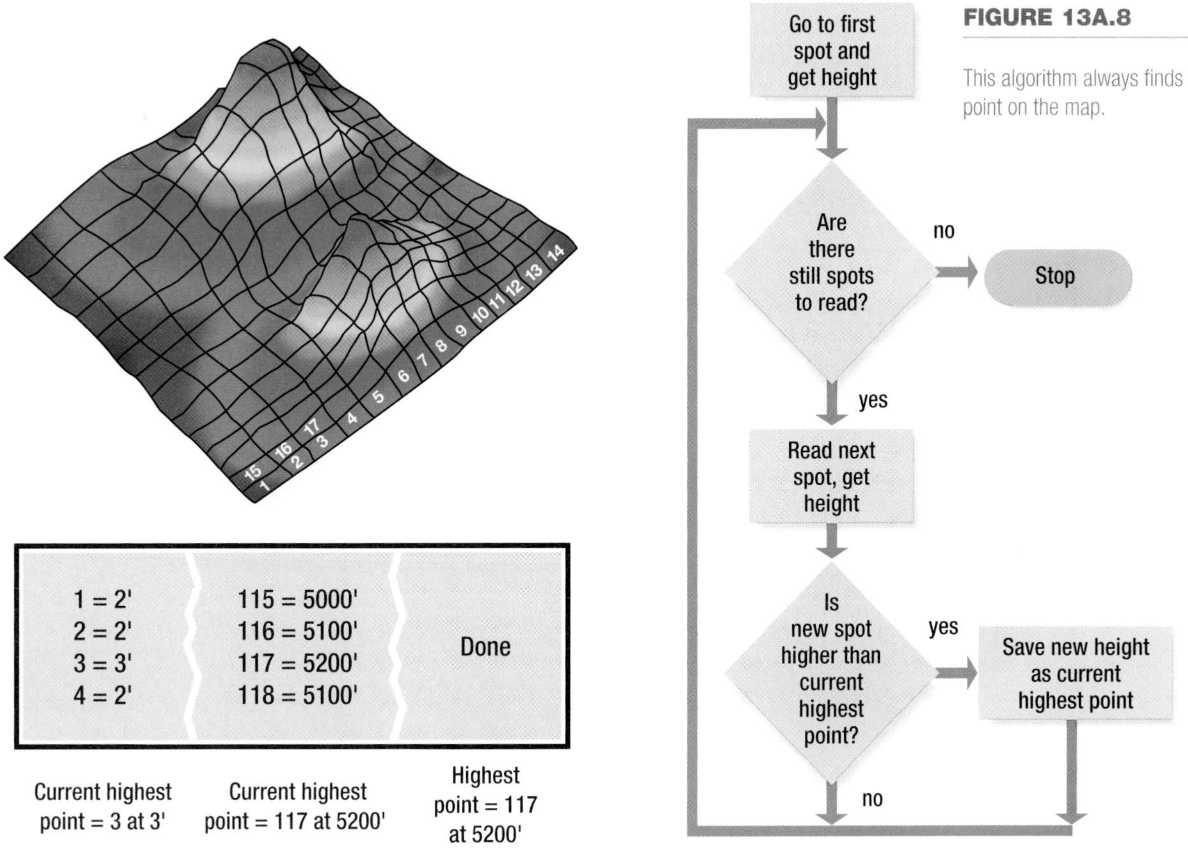

FIGURE 13A.8

This algorithm always finds the highest point on the map.

The algorithm simply samples each square on the grid—one square at a time—and compares the results with the current highest peak. The process is slow, but it always finds the highest point.

Algorithms have many other uses. A spreadsheet program, for instance, might contain an algorithm to display the sum of cells highlighted by the user. Such an algorithm would allow the user to highlight cells, read the numbers in those cells, total the numbers, and display them on the screen. Another algorithm within the spreadsheet program might look for the longest word in a column and then adjust the width of the column to fit the text.

Heuristics

Norton ONLINE

For more information on heuristics, visit **http://www.mhhe.com/peternorton**.

Sometimes, no algorithm exists to solve a problem, or the algorithm is so complex or time-consuming that it cannot be coded or run. In these cases, programmers rely on heuristics to help solve problems or perform tasks. **Heuristics** are like algorithms; they are a set of steps for finding the solution to a problem. But unlike an algorithm, a heuristic does not come with a guarantee of finding the best possible solution. Heuristics offer a good chance of finding a solution, although not necessarily the best one.

Figure 13A.9 shows a heuristic for finding the highest peak on a topographical map. The heuristic works under the assumption that mountains build up from

FIGURE 13A.9

Heuristics provide a best-guess approach to problem solving.

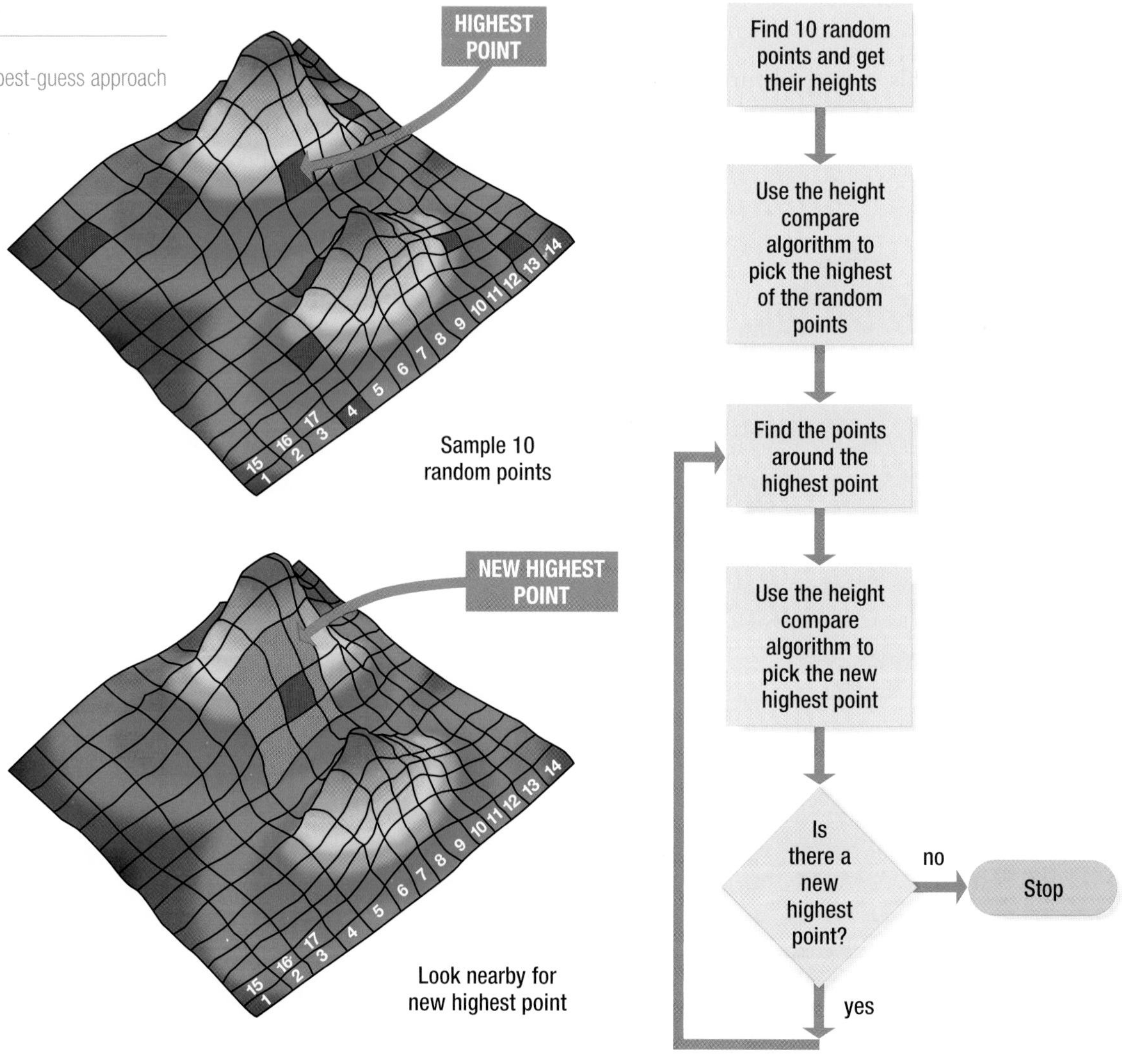
HIGHEST POINT
Sample 10 random points
NEW HIGHEST POINT
Look nearby for new highest point
Find 10 random points and get their heights
Use the height compare algorithm to pick the highest of the random points
Find the points around the highest point
Use the height compare algorithm to pick the new highest point
Is there a new highest point?
no
Stop
yes

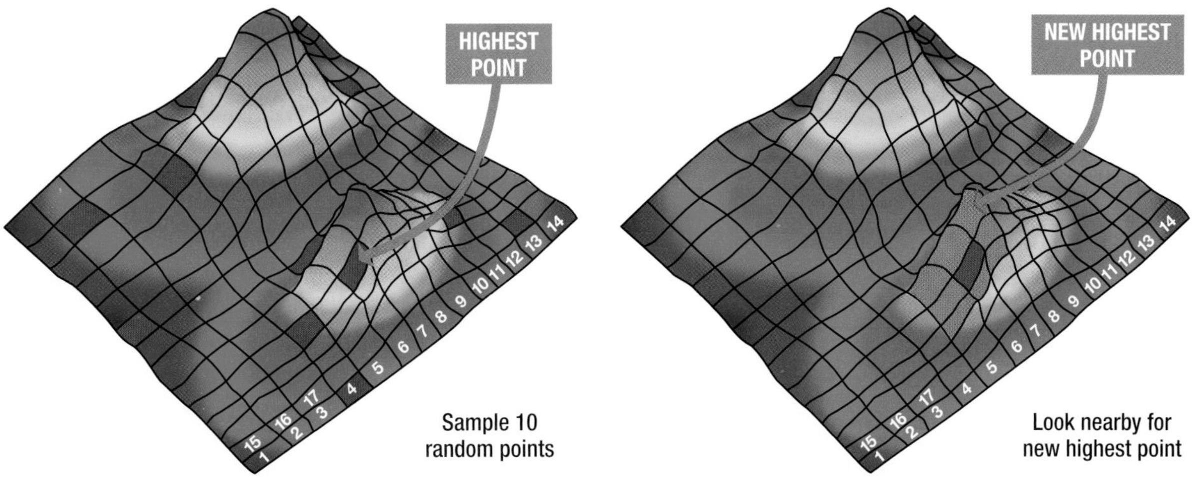

FIGURE 13A.10

Heuristics are not always guaranteed to find the best possible answer.

foothills and that the peak cannot be standing in a square by itself in the middle of a valley. Following this heuristic, the program samples 10 random spots on the map and compares them to see which is the highest.

The heuristic assumes that, because you have to go up to reach the peak, the current highest point must lead up to the peak. To find the next step to the peak, the program samples a few spots immediately around the current highest point and compares them. Once the program has found a new highest point, it repeats the process of sampling around the current high point and looking for a new highest point. In this way, the heuristic climbs the mountain to the peak. As you can see, the heuristic always climbs up—and only up. It is possible that, based on the original starting points, the heuristic may climb the shorter mountain. While the heuristic supplies a solution, it may not supply the best solution every time. Figure 13A.10 shows the heuristic climbing the wrong peak.

Heuristics are less likely to appear in ordinary applications (such as a spreadsheet or word processor) because these applications rarely require a task to be performed for which there is no definite solution. Heuristics are extremely common in more advanced programs that track vast quantities of data in complex ways. For example, software that helps forecasters predict the weather cannot possibly process every piece of available data in every possible form. Even if the program could process all the data, it still could not hope to accurately predict something as complex as the weather. By using heuristics, however, the programs can cull the weather-related data to find useful information and then create a reasonably accurate guess at the weather based on that data.

Some programs use both heuristics and algorithms. Antivirus software utilizes algorithms to find well-known viruses like MS Blaster and CodeRed. Newer viruses are caught using heuristics that look for virus-like patterns. These include files that attempt to write to portions of the hard drive or that open Outlook. The nastier viruses are those that know how the heuristics work and avoid them. Figure 13A.11 shows the configuration screen for Norton AntiVirus's Bloodhound Heuristics.

FIGURE 13A.11

Norton AntiVirus includes heuristics to protect your machine from new viruses.

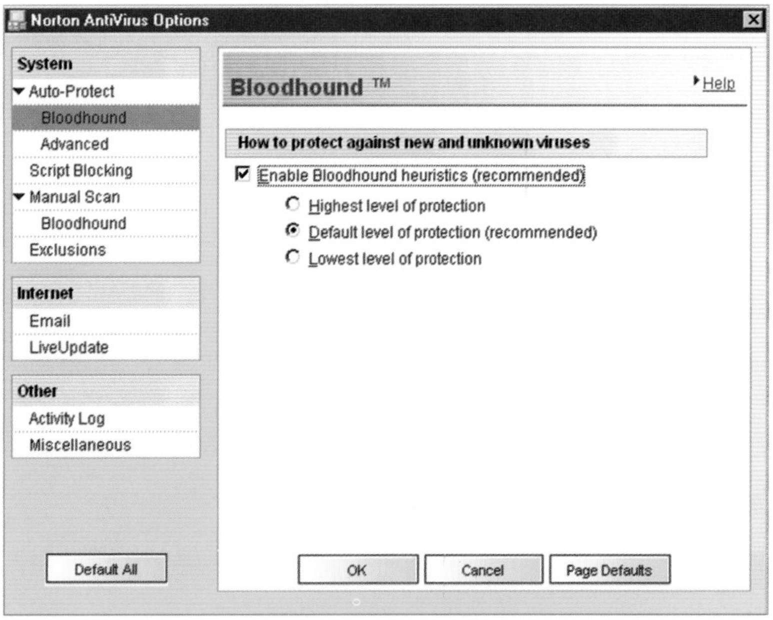

Productivity Tip

Finding Faster Algorithms

At first, the study of algorithm complexity might not seem important—especially with today's fast computers. Nevertheless, programmers and mathematicians have developed an entire field of study dedicated to understanding algorithm complexity and its effects on computer performance. A simple demonstration called The Traveling Salesman shows how a complex algorithm can get out of control.

In this problem, a salesman wants to visit all the cities in his route following the shortest possible path. With just a few cities, the problem seems quite simple; there are few possible combinations and the salesman can compare the distances easily. If another city is added, however, the number of steps to compare all of the possible different routes grows exponentially. After a few more cities are added, the number of comparisons makes the problem too time-consuming to attempt to solve.

How Is Complexity Determined?

Determining complexity is relatively simple in theory, although math skills are required if you want exact numbers. Roughly speaking, you can determine the complexity of an algorithm by creating a run-time equation that is a function of the input into the algorithm. The equation looks at the size of the algorithm's input—such as the size of a list to be sorted or the number of digits in a number to be factored—and determines the number of steps needed to reach a solution. In effect, you are creating an artificial run-time based on input size. In real life, the algorithm may not have to perform every step every time, so the equation represents a worst-case input. Once you have the run-time equation, you can test various input sizes and see how the run-time grows. If the run-time grows dramatically faster than the input size, you have a problem.

Categorizing Algorithms

To discuss algorithm complexity, mathematicians categorize algorithms as either tractable or intractable:

» **Tractable Problems.** These problems (which are also called fast, efficient, or easy) have a run-time that grows

Structured and Object-Oriented Programming

When writing a program, a programmer first creates an IPO of the algorithm or heuristic to be followed. Once the programmer is ready, he or she uses a programming language to create the code that will produce the desired result. To create a program's source code, programmers generally follow one of two programming methods—structured programming or object-oriented programming.

Structured programming evolved in the 1970s. The name refers to the practice of building programs out of small modules which were easy to read and understand. Each module had a single entrance and exit, and performed a single task. Structured programming practices can be used with any programming language. One goal of structured programming is the creation of easy-to-read code. Prior coding techniques resulted in "spaghetti code" that was nearly impossible to read, understand, and maintain. Software developers have found that structured programming results in improved efficiency, but they continue to struggle with the process of building software quickly and correctly.

Reuse is recognized as the best solution to these software development problems. Reusing code allows programs to be built quickly and correctly. In the 1980s, computing took another leap forward with the

SELF-CHECK ::

Circle the correct answer for each question.

1. The term __________ refers to statements that are written in a language the computer can understand.
   a. process   b. syntax   c. code
2. Which portion of an IPO chart describes the data that is to be entered by the user?
   a. input   b. processing   c. output
3. Which of the following is false about programming?
   a. it can be exciting   b. you do not need to worry about syntax   c. there are rules to programming

at a slow rate when compared to the input size. Technically, a tractable problem is one where the time equation is a polynomial function of the input size. You can solve a tractable problem in a reasonable amount of time or with a reasonable amount of computer resources.

- **Intractable Problems.** These problems (which are also called slow, inefficient, or hard) have a run-time that grows rapidly when compared to the input size. To be exact, an intractable problem has a time equation that is an exponential function of the input size. Occasionally you cannot solve these problems, but more often, they simply take lots of time or huge computer resources to reach a solution.

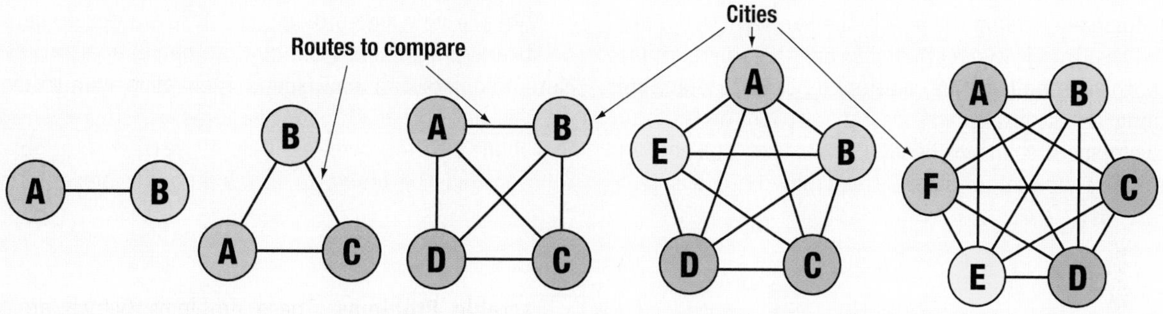

The addition of each city increases the number of route comparisons exponentially for The Traveling Salesman.

PRODUCTIVITY TIP

development of object-oriented programming (OOP). The building blocks of OOP, called objects, are reusable, modular components (which are explained in detail later).

OOP builds on and enhances structured programming. You do not leave structured programming behind when you work with an object-oriented language. Objects are composed of structured program pieces, and the logic of manipulating objects is also structured.

Programming Structures

Researchers in the 1960s demonstrated that programs could be written with three control structures:

- Sequence structure defines the default control flow in a program. Typically, this structure is built into programming languages. Unless directed otherwise, a computer executes lines of code in the order in which they are written.
- Selection structures are built around special program flow constructs called conditional statements. A conditional statement is simply a test that determines what the program will do next. Such tests typically can have only two results—true or false. If the condition statement is true, certain lines of code are executed. If the condition statement is false, those lines of code are not executed. When the program makes a decision using a conditional statement, the program flow can often go in one of two different directions depending on the outcome of the decision. These different sequences of code are called branches. For this reason, selection structures are sometimes called branching structures (see Figure 13A.12).

Norton ONLINE

For more information on structured programming, visit **http://www.mhhe.com/peternorton**.

At Issue

Hot and Oh-So-Cool: Technology Forecasts the Weather

Even though weather conditions can change in an instant, forecasting the weather hadn't changed much since World War II.

It took cutting-edge Java programming and Internet connectivity to break free of tradition to re-create the meteorology model and allow meteorologists to get the most out of today's new technologies. Gone are the paper-based weather map and charts. In their place are highly scaleable dynamic graphical interfaces and information systems.

One company leading the way is the San Francisco–based WeatherLabs, Inc. (www.weatherlabs.com). WeatherLabs provides both meteorology information services to electronic publishing industries, as well as the software architecture and development solutions needed to analyze, present, and disseminate this weather data. Its weather content is delivered through broadcast on the Internet, via wireless and mobile technologies, and over satellite broadcast.

WeatherLabs' success is based on a proprietary Java technology–based weather forecasting and content creation system. In fact, the central, server-side engine permeates every aspect of WeatherLabs, responsible for weather and climate forecasting intelligence, numerical analysis, and forecasting algorithms, packaged directly inside JavaBeans components.

With the new meteorology model, just a dozen meteorologists and programmers can now do the job of a staff of 100. Meteorologists can now spend their time monitoring the weather data for quality-control purposes rather than worrying about pouring over the tons of weather data observed from around the globe, or developing the presentation of

FIGURE 13A.12

In structured programming, control follows the code sequentially along a branch of code.

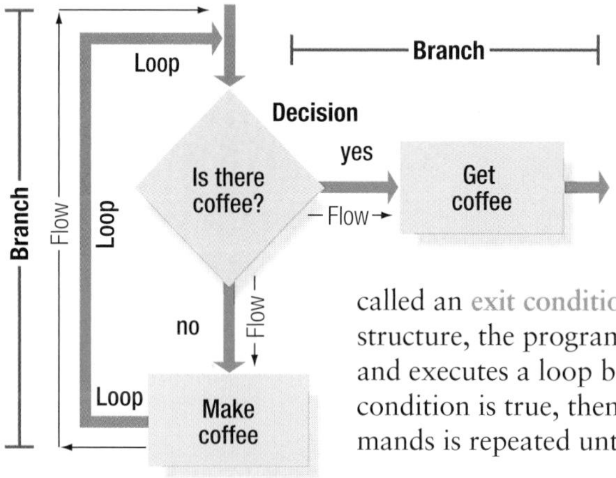

» Repetition structures (or looping structures) are based on constructs called loops. A loop is a piece of code that repeats again and again until some condition—called an exit condition—is met. In a repetition structure, the program checks a condition statement and executes a loop based on the condition. If the condition is true, then a block of one or more commands is repeated until the condition is false.

Norton ONLINE

For more information on object-oriented programming, visit **http://www.mhhe.com/peternorton**.

Object-Oriented Programming

Concepts of object-oriented programming, such as objects and classes, can seem abstract at first, but many programmers claim that an object orientation is a natural way of thinking about the world. Because OOP gives them an intuitive way to model the world, they say, programs become simpler, programming becomes faster, and the burden of program maintenance is lessened.

Objects

Look around you—you are surrounded by objects. Right now, the list of objects around you might include a book, a computer, a light, walls, plants, pictures, and so on.

Think for a moment about what you perceive when you look at a car on the street. Your first impression is probably of the car as a whole. You do not focus on the steel, chrome, and plastic elements that make up the car. The entire unit, or object, is what registers in your mind.

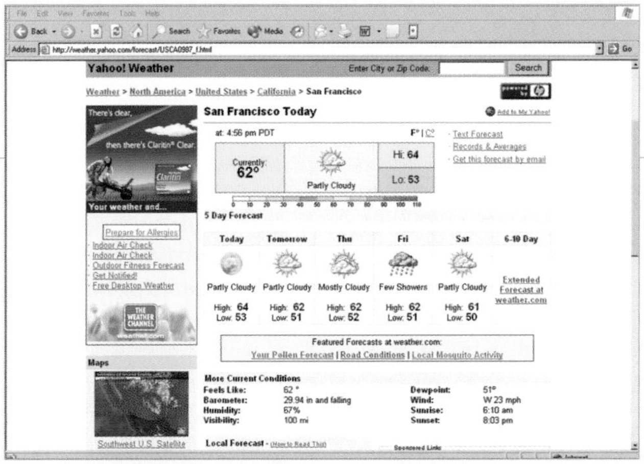

the weather data. The server-side technology does it for them.

The WeatherLabs' system is highly automated and created to be user-friendly. Based on HTML templates, basic weather content is transmitted to all customers, "cookie-cutter" fashion. Then, users edit and personalize the templates as desired to create unique user interfaces, wrapping their custom content around the core weather data. The end result is weather content as varied as satellite and Doppler radar imagery, ski reports, airport delay forecasts, anecdotes from historical weather almanacs, search tools, and personalized editorial content from around the globe. This allows CondéNet's chic travel weather center to have its own look and feel, very different than the family-oriented Prodigy or Netscape, or the highly graphical interface used by Excite.

So, while many online providers may look as if each has its own in-house staff of meteorologists, under the covers, all these sites are based on the same server-side Java technology–based applications.

Now, how would you describe that car to someone sitting next to you? You might start with its attributes, such as the car's color, size, shape, top speed, and so on. An attribute describes the characteristics of an object. You might then talk about what the car can do; that is, you describe its functions. For example, the car moves forward, moves backward, opens its windows, and so on. Together, the attributes and the functions define the object. In the language of OOP, every object has attributes and functions that may encapsulate (contain) other objects.

When you look more closely at the car, you may begin to notice many smaller component objects. For example, the car has a chassis, a drive train, a body, and an interior. Each component is, in turn, composed of other objects. The drive train includes an engine, transmission, rear end, and axle. So an object can be either a whole unit or a component of other objects. Objects can include other objects. Figure 13A.13 shows a car replete with attributes, functions, and encapsulated objects.

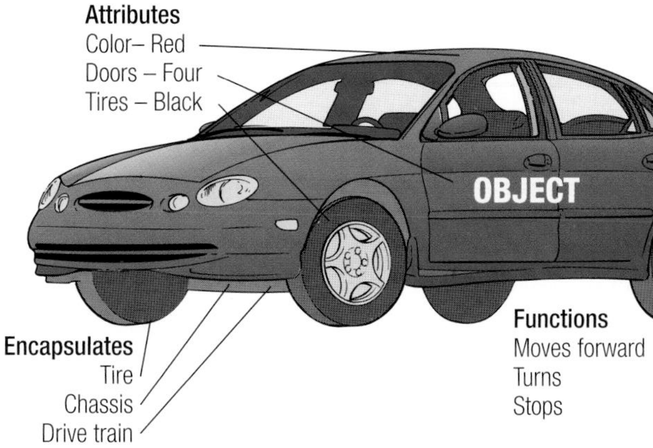

FIGURE 13A.13

The car object has both attributes and functions; the car also encapsulates other objects, such as tires, chassis, and drive train—each with its own unique attributes and functions.

LESSON // 13A Review

Summary ::

- Software contains the commands that run the hardware in a computer.
- A computer program is a set of commands that tell the CPU what to do. Software may contain only an executable program file, or it may have several other supporting files such as dynamic link library (.dll), initialization (.ini), and help (.hlp) files.
- To create a program, a programmer writes source code, which is compiled or interpreted to create object code.
- Object code, also known as machine code, is the binary language file that tells the CPU what to do.
- The order in which program statements are executed is called program control flow.
- Programmers translate algorithms and heuristics into programs designed to solve problems.
- Structured programming uses functions built up along a logical program flow to perform each task in the algorithm or heuristic.
- Object-oriented programming allows a programmer to think modularly because programs are assembled into components, called objects.
- In programming, an object is a self-contained unit that includes functions and attributes.

Key Terms ::

algorithm, 505
attribute, 511
batch (.bat) file, 501
branch, 509
code, 501
compiler, 503
conditional statement, 509
dynamic link library (.dll) file, 500
encapsulate, 511
executable (.exe, .com) file, 500
exit condition, 510
flowchart, 505
help (.hlp, .chm) file, 500
heuristic, 506
initialization (.ini) file, 500
interpreter, 503
interrupt, 501
input–processing–output (IPO) chart, 504
loop, 510
looping structure, 510
machine code, 502
machine language, 502
object, 509
object code, 503
object-oriented programming (OOP), 509
program control flow, 505
programming language, 502
pseudocode, 504
repetition structure, 510
selection structure, 509
sequence structure, 509
source code, 502
structured programming, 508

Key Term Quiz ::

Complete each statement by writing one of the terms listed under Key Terms in each blank.

1. A(n) __________ file contains configuration information that helps a program run.
2. Programmers use __________ to convert all the source code for a program into machine code, thus creating an executable file.
3. To plan a program, a programmer might use a(n) __________ chart.
4. A(n) __________ is a set of steps that always leads to a solution.
5. __________ programming arose in the 1960s as a way to help developers avoid creating "spaghetti code."
6. A(n) __________ does not come with a guarantee of finding the best possible solution.
7. A(n) __________ converts source code to machine code, but does not create an executable object code file.
8. A(n) __________ is a statement that determines what the program should do next.
9. The building blocks of object-oriented programming are reusable blocks of code called __________ .
10. C++ and BASIC are examples of a __________ .

LESSON // 13A Review

Multiple Choice ::

Circle the word or phrase that best completes each statement.

1. A computer program is a collection of ________ that are carried out by the computer's CPU.
   a. instructions b. loops c. steps d. algorithms
2. Programming languages enable programmers to describe programs. This description is called ________ .
   a. an OOP b. source code c. an interpreter d. an object
3. ________ is a simplified natural-language version of a program.
   a. Pseudocode b. Control flow c. Algorithm d. A flowchart
4. A loop repeats until a(n) ________ is met.
   a. object b. error c. exit condition d. syntax
5. One goal of ________ is development of readable code.
   a. programming languages b. interpreters c. compilers d. structured programming
6. ________ builds on and enhances structured programming.
   a. A compiler b. A programming language c. Object-oriented programming d. Program control flow
7. A(n) ________ is steps to solve a problem that is not guaranteed to provide an answer.
   a. algorithm b. IPO chart c. heuristic d. flowchart
8. The 1s and 0s that CPUs can understand is called its ________.
   a. syntax b. interrupt c. interpreter d. machine language
9. A(n) ________ file is a partial .exe file that has its commands accessed by other programs.
   a. .ini b. .dll c. .bat d. .dat
10. The order in which program statements are executed is called ________ .
    a. program control flow b. program syntax c. programming language d. program execution

Review Questions ::

In your own words, briefly answer the following questions.

1. What goes into the three columns of an IPO chart?
2. Describe the difference between a compiler and an interpreter.
3. Why were programming languages developed?
4. Conditional statements and loops are examples of what?
5. What is an executable file?
6. Describe how reusing code can simplify a programmer's job.
7. What is the benefit of planning code before trying to write it?
8. What are the advantages of using dynamic link library (.dll) files in a program?
9. What is a flowchart?
10. What is the difference between an algorithm and a heuristic?

Lesson Labs ::

Complete the following exercise as directed by your instructor.

1. Take the following steps to see how many executable files are stored in your computer's Windows folder:
   a. Launch Windows Explorer. (The procedure for doing this depends on which version of Windows is installed on your computer. Ask your instructor for assistance, if necessary.)
   b. In the left pane of the Exploring window, find and click the Windows folder. The folder's contents appear in the window's right pane.
   c. In the right pane, click the Type column heading. This action arranges the pane's contents by file or folder types.
   d. List all the executable (.exe) files in the folder. The exact number of executable files may vary from system to system. Compare the number of executable files on your system to other students'.
   e. Find the Notepad.exe file in the Windows folder and double-click the file. The Notepad text editing program will open on your screen.
   f. Close Notepad, and then close the Exploring window.

LESSON // 13B

Programming Languages and the Programming Process

OBJECTIVES ::

- Identify the three main categories of programming languages.
- Describe the five generations of programming languages.
- Name at least five major programming languages.
- Describe a visual programming environment and how it is used.
- List the five phases of the systems development life cycle for programming.

Overview: The Keys to Successful Programming

Programming can be a complex process; it requires training, planning, and some specialized tools. If you think this task sounds like any other construction process, you are right; creating a software program is like building an office building or a shopping center. You have to study the market, create a plan, hire a crew, get special tools, and then (finally) build the building. But the work does not stop there. You must continually update your creation to meet the changing needs of the people who use it.

Successful programmers are knowledgeable in two key areas: programming tools (the software and languages used to develop applications) and the programming process (the step-by-step procedures that programmers follow to ensure consistent, well-developed products). Software developers of all backgrounds—and in many different working environments—follow a uniform set of procedures in their work. Thus, programmers can work together more easily on large projects and they can accurately predict how their programs will work. You will learn more about the development process later in this lesson. First, you will learn about the programmer's special tools: programming languages.

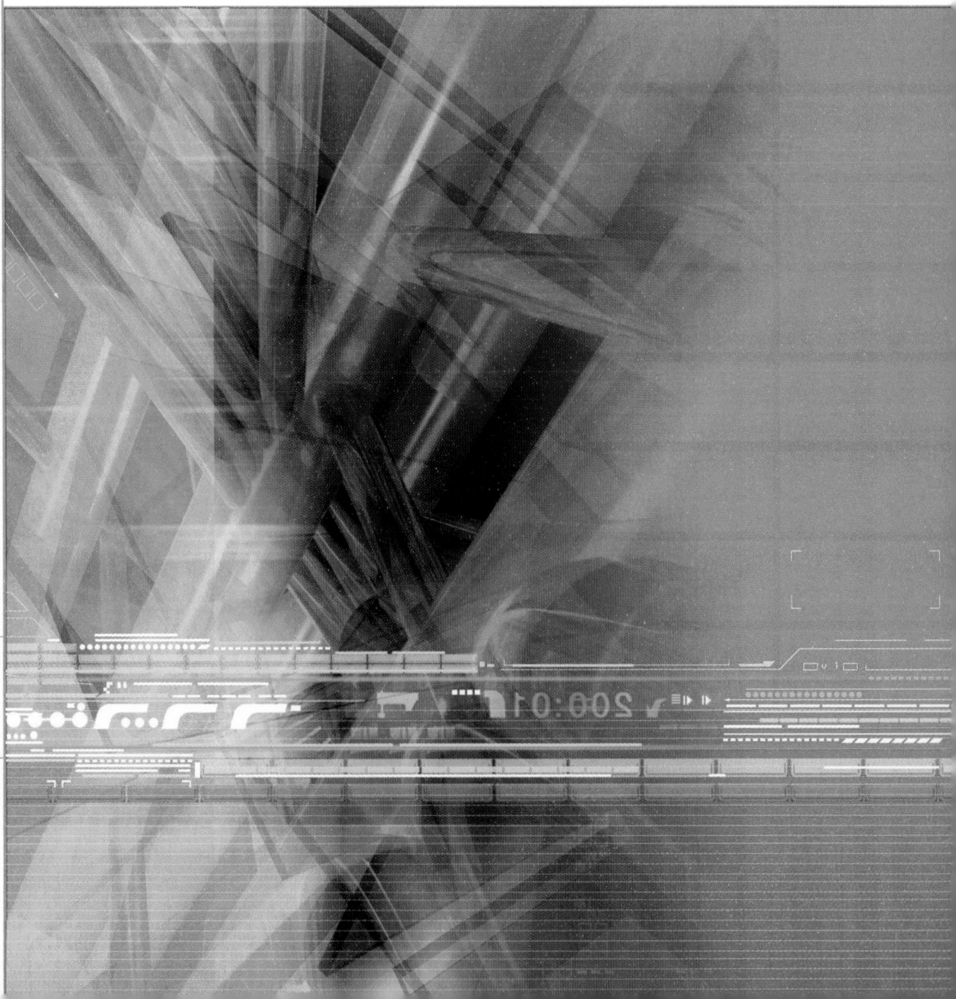

The Evolution of Programming Languages

As you learned earlier in this chapter, programming is a way of creating a set of instructions for the computer. To create these instructions, programmers use rigidly defined programming languages to create source code; then they convert the source code into machine (or object) code for the computer.

Machine code—those 1's and 0's—is the only language that a computer understands. People, however, have difficulty understanding machine code. To make software development easier, researchers developed progressively more sophisticated programming languages. This evolution in development tools allowed programmers to focus less on strings of numbers and more on command sequences. In other words, developers could think about their programs in human terms rather than the computer's terms. As a result, today's programmers can create command sequences that you can read like any other language. The programming tools handle the tedious chore of converting the humanlike instructions into strings of numbers that computers can understand.

As you will learn in this lesson, programmers can choose from many development tools that differ greatly in capability, flexibility, and ease of use. Despite their differences, however, most programming languages share one characteristic: each programming language requires the programmer to follow some very strict rules. For example, programming languages require developers to

- Provide information in a certain order and structure.
- Use special symbols.
- Use punctuation (sometimes).

These rules are called the syntax of the programming language, and they vary a great deal from one language to another. Figure 13B.1 shows a piece of source code written in a programming language called C++.

Notice that in Figure 13B.1, each line of code includes special abbreviations, spacing, or punctuation. This special writing style is the syntax of the C++ programming language. If the code were written in a different language, you would see differences in spacing, phrasing, punctuation, and so on. Regardless of which language the programmer uses, however, he or she must follow the correct syntax for that language. If the syntax is not correct, the compiler or interpreter will issue errors and warnings and will not be able understand the source code. It also will either fail or create incorrect object code.

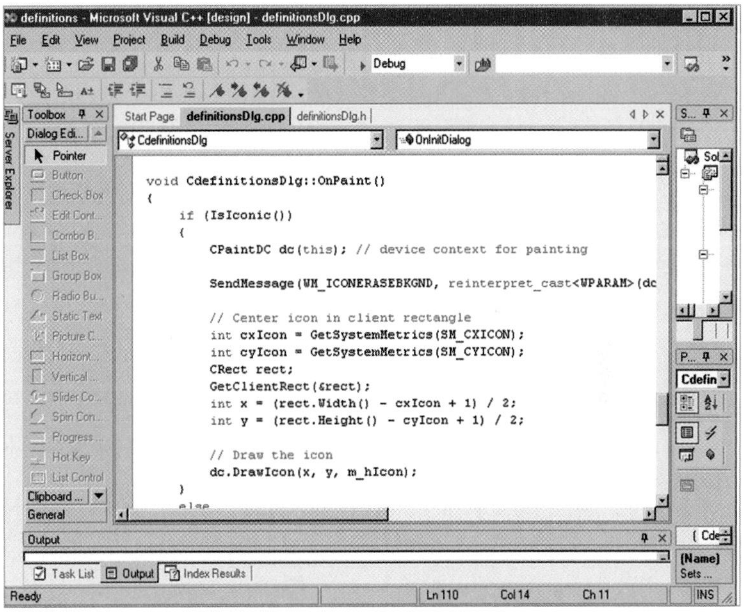

FIGURE 13B.1

The syntax of each programming language dictates the exact spacing, symbols, words, and punctuation used in the code.

Categories of Programming Languages

Hundreds of programming languages are currently in use around the world. Some are highly specialized and used in only one branch of science or industry, while others are well known and used almost everywhere. Some languages are obsolete and used only to maintain older systems, while others are so new that many programmers do not even know that they exist.

You can group programming languages in several different ways. For example, you might group them into those that use structured programming and those that do not. Or you might group them by those used in business versus those used in scientific circles. Programming languages are usually grouped, however, by their

Norton ONLINE

For more information on the history of programming languages, visit **http://www.mhhe.com/peternorton**.

place in the evolution of programming languages. Based on evolutionary history, programming languages are divided into three broad categories:

» Machine languages
» Assembly languages
» Higher-level languages

Machine and Assembly Languages

Machine languages are the most fundamental of languages. Using a machine language, a programmer creates instructions in the form of machine code (1's and 0's) that a computer can follow. Machine languages are defined by hardware design. In other words, the machine language for a Macintosh is not the same as the machine language for a Pentium PC. In fact, the machine language for different Pentium versions is slightly different. A computer understands only its native machine language—the commands in its instruction set. These commands instruct the computer to perform elementary operations such as loading, storing, adding, and subtracting.

Assembly languages were developed by using short, English-like, abbreviations to represent common elements of machine code. To develop software with an assembly language, a programmer uses a text editor (a simple word processor) to create source files. To convert the source files into object code, the developer uses a special translator program, called an assembler, to convert each line of assembler code into one line of machine code. This is where the name *assembly language* comes from. Although assembly languages are highly detailed and cryptic, they are still much easier to use than machine language. About the only time programmers write programs of significant size in an assembly language is when then are concerned with the code being efficient and fast. (One example of this rule is action games, where the program's speed is critical.) Instead, programmers use assembly languages to fine-tune important parts of programs written in a higher-level language.

There is not much you can tell by looking at machine code (1s and 0s), and you would have to know a huge amount of specialized information before you could write it. Assembly code, however, is a bit less cryptic . . . but only a bit. As you can see in Figure 13B.2, assembly code uses specialized English-like phrases along with hardware-specific numbers.

Higher-Level Languages

Higher-level languages were developed to make programming easier. These languages are called higher-level languages because their syntax is more like human

Norton ONLINE

For more information on machine and assembly languages, visit **http://www.mhhe.com/peternorton**.

FIGURE 13B.2

Machine code is just 1s and 0s, but assembly code is a step closer to English.

Assembly Code

```
;CLEAR SCREEN USING BIOS
CLR: MOV AX,0600H       ;SCROLL SCREEN
     MOV BH,30          ;COLOUR
     MOV CX,0000        ;FROM
     MOV DX,184FH       ;TO 24,79
     INT 10H            ;CALL BIOS;
;INPUTTING OF A STRING
KEY: MOV AH,0AH         ;INPUT REQUEST
     LEA DX,BUFFER      ;POINT TO BUFFER WHERE STRING STORED
     INT 21H            ;CALL DOS
     RET                ;RETURN FROM SUBROUTINE TO MAIN PROGRAM;
; DISPLAY STRING TO SCREEN
SCR: MOV AH,09          ;DISPLAY REQUEST
     LEA DX,STRING      ;POINT TO STRING
     INT 21H            ;CALL DOS
     RET                ;RETURN FROM THIS SUBROUTINE;
```

Machine Code

```
000101001011010101010101
111011010101010101011100
001010010100101111010111
100101001011010101010101
011010010011001011110111
000100010101110101010001
101010010101001010110111
000101001011010101010101
```

language than either assembly or machine language code. Higher-level programming languages use familiar words rather than the detailed strings of digits that make up machine instructions. To express computer operations, these languages use operators such as the plus and minus signs that are the familiar components of mathematics. As a result, people can read, write, and understand computer programs much more easily when using a higher-level language. Still, the instructions must be translated into machine language before the computer can understand and carry them out. One line of a higher-level language usually translates into many lines of machine language. This makes it faster to write in a higher-level language, but you sacrifice some control over the actual code produced.

Programming languages are sometimes discussed in terms of generations. Later generations include languages that are both easier to use and more powerful than those in earlier generations. Machine languages, therefore, are called first-generation languages and assembly languages are second-generation languages. The higher-level languages began with the third generation.

Norton ONLINE

For more information on higher-level languages, visit **http://www.mhhe.com/peternorton**.

Third-Generation Languages

Third-generation languages (3GLs) make it easier to write structured programs. Because they are the first languages to use true English-like phrasing, they also make it easier for programmers to share in the development of programs. Team members can read each other's source code and understand the logic and program control flow. Figure 13B.3 shows two pieces of source code from third-generation languages—one written in BASIC, the other in C. Notice that while these third-generation languages are different from one another in their syntax, they are both fairly English-like and not too hard to follow.

FIGURE 13B.3

Despite their special syntax rules, 3GLs use English-like words and phrases.

BASIC code

```
IF D& > 15 THEN
   DO WHILE D& > 1
      D& = D& - 1
   LOOP
END IF
```

C code

```
if (d > 15)
{
   do
   {
      d--;
   } while (d > 1);
}
```

Another important point to remember about third-generation languages is that these languages are portable. If you have a compiler or interpreter for a particular computer and operating system, you can use it to create an executable from the source code. (This procedure is called porting the code to another system.) You might have to modify the source code a little when porting, especially if you are porting to a completely different kind of computer (for example, from a PC to a mainframe). As long as you have a compiler or interpreter for a given type of system, you can usually convert your source code to object code for that machine. In contrast, machine code and assembly code are highly processor-specific and must be specially written for each type of computer on which they run.

There are many high-level languages and there is no reason why you should have to know the details of each. However, it is always helpful to know a little about the more common languages you may hear about in programming circles. Some of the currently popular languages include the following:

- **C.** Often regarded as the thoroughbred of programming languages, C produces programs with fast and efficient executable code. C is also a powerful language. With it, you can make a computer do just about anything it is possible for a computer to do. Because of this programming freedom, C is extremely popular with professional developers, although it is now being replaced by C++.
- **C++.** C++ is the object-oriented implementation of C. Like C, C++ is an extremely powerful and efficient language. Learning C++ means learning everything about C and then learning about object-oriented programming and its implementation with C++. Nevertheless, more C programmers move to C++ every year, and the newer language has replaced C as the language of choice among software development companies.
- **Java.** Java is an object-oriented programming environment for creating cross-platform programs. When the Internet became popular in the mid-1990s, Java's developer, Sun Microsystems, developed Java to become a programming

environment for the Internet. Later, Sun added on the ability to write programs that did not run inside a browser. With Java, Web designers can create interactive and dynamic programs (called applets) for Web pages.

» **ActiveX.** Microsoft's answer to Java is ActiveX. ActiveX code creates self-contained functions similar to Java applets that may be accessed and executed by any other ActiveX-compatible program on any ActiveX system or network. ActiveX can create signed applications. A signed application is one that has been verified as being safe to run on a computer. At present, ActiveX is implemented on Windows 9*x*, Windows NT, Windows 2000, Windows XP, and Macintosh systems, and there are plans for supporting UNIX also.

Fourth-Generation Languages

Fourth-generation languages (4GLs) are easier to use than third-generation languages. Generally, a 4GL uses either a text environment, much like a 3GL, or a visual environment.

In the text environment, the programmer uses English-like words when generating source code. Typically, a single statement in a 4GL may perform the same tasks as many lines of a 3GL.

In a 4GL visual environment, the programmer uses a toolbar to drag and drop various items like buttons, labels, and text boxes to create a visual definition of an application. Once the programmer has designed the program's appearance, he or she can assign various actions to the objects on the screen. For example, a programmer may place a button on the screen and assign an action like "Open Customer table." Figure 13B.4 shows a visual development environment, in this case, Visual Basic.NET.

Most 3GLs and 4GLs allow the programmer to work in an integrated development environment, or IDE. IDEs provide the programmer with all of the tools needed to develop applications in one program. Compilers and run-time support for their applications are present. Microsoft's Visual Studio and Sun's Java Studio are two professional IDEs.

Fourth-generation languages include the following:

» **.NET.** .NET is Microsoft's newest entry into the programming arena. It combines several programming languages into one IDE. Included are Visual Basic, C++, C#, and J#. .NET is poised to be the developers' only environment. Using .NET, developers can write programs for Windows, the World Wide

FIGURE 13B.4

Creating a form using visual tools. For example, to place a box on a form, Visual Basic programmers simply drag the box from a toolbox onto the form. They can adjust the length of the box by dragging its borders.

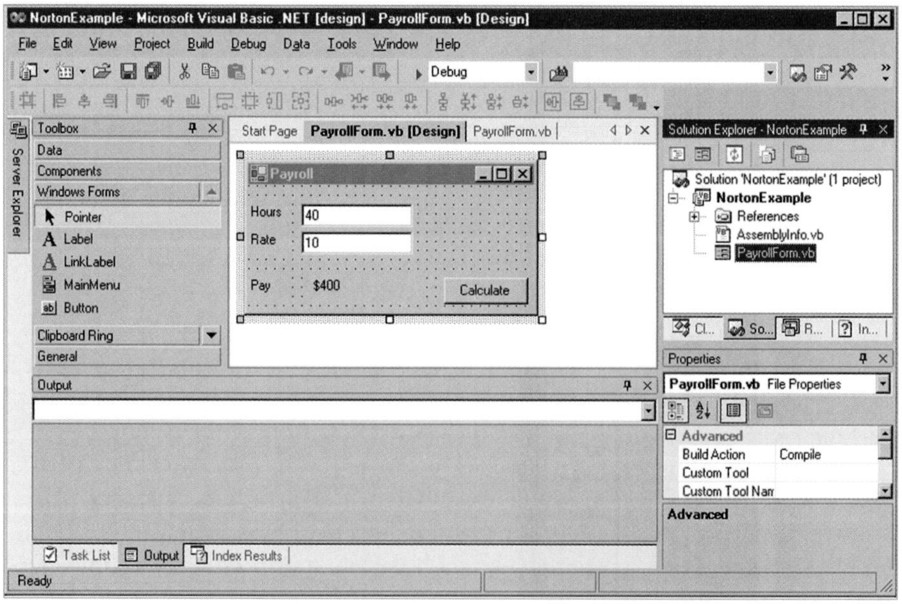

Web, and PocketPC. (As discussed in Chapter 7, PocketPC is a version of Windows designed for PDAs.) .NET makes authoring programs for all of these environments easier. Figure 13B.5 lists some of the application types that can be created in the Educational version of Visual Studio .NET.

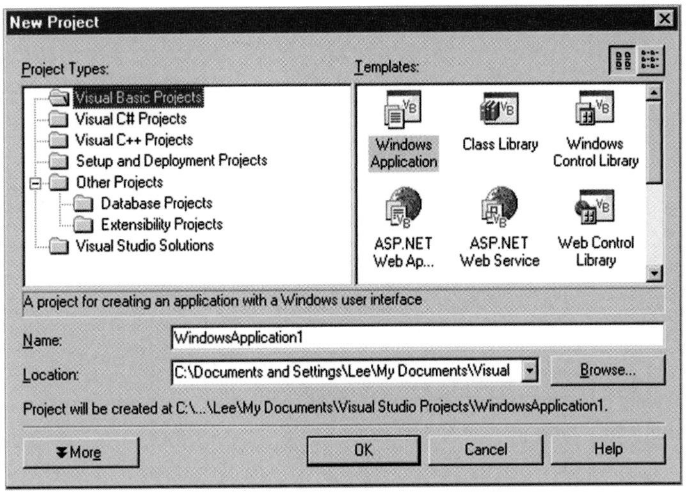

FIGURE 13B.5

Visual Studio .NET is a very flexible environment, supporting most programmers' needs.

- **Authoring Environments.** Authoring environments are special-purpose programming tools for creating multimedia applications, computer-based training programs, Web pages, and so on. One example of an authoring environment is Macromedia Director (which uses the Lingo scripting language). You can use it to create multimedia titles combining music clips, text, animation, graphics, and so forth. As with other visual development environments, much of the code is written automatically. However, most of the robust authoring environments also include their own languages, called scripting languages, which provide tools for added control over the final product. The programs used to create World Wide Web pages fall into another category of tools that are often lumped together with authoring environments. Some of these programs include Microsoft FrontPage, Netscape Visual JavaScript, and NetObjects Fusion.
- **Sun Studio One.** Sun Studio One is a visual editor for Java and Swing applets. An applet is a program that runs inside of a Web page. Studio One provides a complete IDE as well as several wizards to automate common tasks such as creating an applet. Studio One has an advantage over other Java environments: it is developed by Sun, the creators of Java.

Fifth-Generation Languages

Fifth-generation languages (5GLs) are actually something of a mystery. Depending on which expert you ask, they may or may not even agree that 5GLs exist. Some experts consider the more advanced authoring environments to be 5GLs, while others do not. In principle, a 5GL would use artificial intelligence to create software based on your description of what the software should do. This type of system is proving more difficult to invent than the code it was intended to create.

World Wide Web Development Languages

Few technology components of late have affected our culture like the Internet and the World Wide Web. The Internet has evolved from simple text-based messages to complex Web sites that are visual, interactive, and responsive. Likewise, Web-related development tools have evolved in power and capabilities. Therefore, it is impossible to talk in a contemporary context about programming and development without talking about tools that make Web development possible.

- **Hypertext Markup Language (HTML).** Hypertext Markup Language is the programming language used to create documents for the World Wide Web. Using HTML, you define a Web document's structure by using such components as attributes and tags. Tags, as you will recall from the earlier discussion of Web pages, provide links to other points of the document, to other documents on the same site, or to documents on other sites. HTML tags also are used to format a Web page's look, to position graphics and multimedia elements, and to incorporate components created in other programming languages such as Java or Flash.

Norton ONLINE

For more information on World Wide Web development languages, visit **http://www.mhhe.com/peternorton**.

simnet™

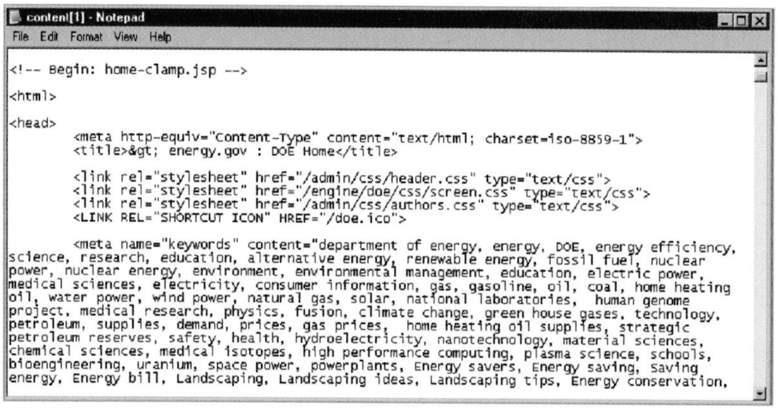
content[1] - Notepad
File Edit Format View Help
<!-- Begin: home-clamp.jsp -->
<html>
<head>
<meta http-equiv="Content-Type" content="text/html; charset=iso-8859-1">
<title>> energy.gov : DOE Home</title>
<link rel="stylesheet" href="/admin/css/header.css" type="text/css">
<link rel="stylesheet" href="/engine/doe/css/screen.css" type="text/css">
<link rel="stylesheet" href="/admin/css/authors.css" type="text/css">
<LINK REL="SHORTCUT ICON" HREF="/doe.ico">
<meta name="keywords" content="department of energy, energy, DOE, energy efficiency, science, research, education, alternative energy, renewable energy, fossil fuel, nuclear power, nuclear energy, environment, environmental management, education, electric power, medical sciences, electricity, consumer information, gas, gasoline, oil, coal, home heating oil, water power, wind power, natural gas, solar, national laboratories, human genome project, medical research, physics, fusion, climate change, green house gases, technology, petroleum, supplies, demand, prices, gas prices, home heating oil supplies, strategic petroleum reserves, safety, health, hydroelectricity, nanotechnology, material sciences, chemical sciences, medical isotopes, high performance computing, plasma science, schools, bioengineering, uranium, space power, powerplants, Energy savers, Energy saving, Saving energy, Energy bill, Landscaping, Landscaping ideas, Landscaping tips, Energy conservation,

FIGURE 13B.6

An example of HTML code from the U.S. Department of Energy Web site.

Because HTML lacks several critical features of formal programming languages, such as the ability to make selections, most programmers don't feel HTML is a true programming language.To a programming novice, however, HTML can be made to do wondrous things in a Web page. One fact about HTML that makes it so easy to use is that you can write HTML code in a simple text editor (such as Notepad) or any word processing program. In fact, many word processors have an HTML option where you can save your document as HTML for placement on the Web. Many other types of common application programs, such as spreadsheets and presentation programs, also can automatically convert a standard document into HTML format, complete with hyperlinks and other navigation tools. Professional Web designers, however, usually use HTML editing programs such as Microsoft FrontPage to create Web pages. Figure 13B.6 shows an example of HTML tags in a Web document.

» **Extensible Markup Language (XML).** A next-generation Web content development language, Extensible Markup Language (XML) typically refers to a new markup language that allows developers to describe a page in such a way that one source document can be presented in several different formats such as a Web page, a printable document, and a PDF file. In structure, XML looks like HTML, but the developer is free to create new tags. XML is not a replacement for HTML. XML needs HTML and other technologies to properly display its data. Figure 13B.7 shows an XML database of multiple-choice questions. Each question has four choices. The correct tag describes which of the choices is correct; 0 is the first choice.

FIGURE 13B.7

This XML database holds multiple-choice questions. Notice that the tags are easy to understand.

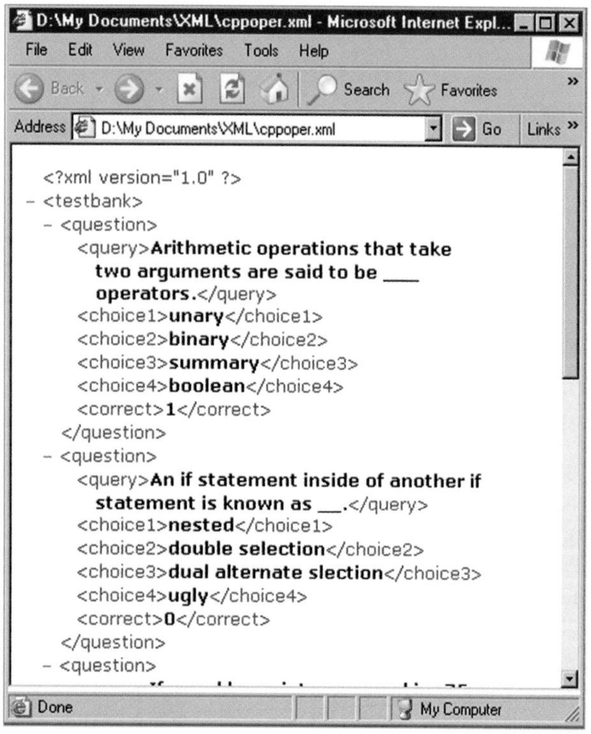
D:\My Documents\XML\cppoper.xml - Microsoft Internet Expl...
File Edit View Favorites Tools Help
Back
Search
Favorites
Address D:\My Documents\XML\cppoper.xml
Go
Links
<?xml version="1.0" ?>
- <testbank>
- <question>
<query>Arithmetic operations that take two arguments are said to be ___ operators.</query>
<choice1>unary</choice1>
<choice2>binary</choice2>
<choice3>summary</choice3>
<choice4>boolean</choice4>
<correct>1</correct>
</question>
- <question>
<query>An if statement inside of another if statement is known as __.</query>
<choice1>nested</choice1>
<choice2>double selection</choice2>
<choice3>dual alternate slection</choice3>
<choice4>ugly</choice4>
<correct>0</correct>
</question>
- <question>
Done
My Computer

» **Extensible HTML (XHTML).** XHTML is the newer version of HTML. It is very similar in all aspects to HTML. However, the rules are more strict. HTML allows for very "loose" coding. XHTML requires that all items be "well formed." This means the developer must write perfect XHTML code every time. XHTML is becoming the standard language of Web developers.

» **Extensible Style Sheet Language (XSL).** Extensible Style Sheet Language (XSL) is one of the XML technologies. Its purpose is to display and format XML documents for HTML browsers like Internet Explorer. The XSL document is composed of several rules that dictate how the document should be formatted. Once the XML document is opened in a browser, the XSL rules are applied. The user sees only a normal HTML page. Using XSL it is relatively simple to have one XML document with several different views.

» **Extensible Markup Language Mobile Profile (XHTML MP).** In recent years, more and more people have begun using tiny devices (such as PDAs) to connect to the Internet using a wireless technology, such as cellular modems. This demand has created the need for new development environments such as Extensible Markup Language Mobile Profile (XHTML MP), formerly known as Wireless Markup Language (WML). Web designers can use WML to create documents that can be viewed by handheld devices such as Web-enabled cell phones, PDAs, and even digital pagers. As miniature hardware makes greater gains in display quality and bandwidth-processing capabilities, languages such as XHTML MP will become commonly used.

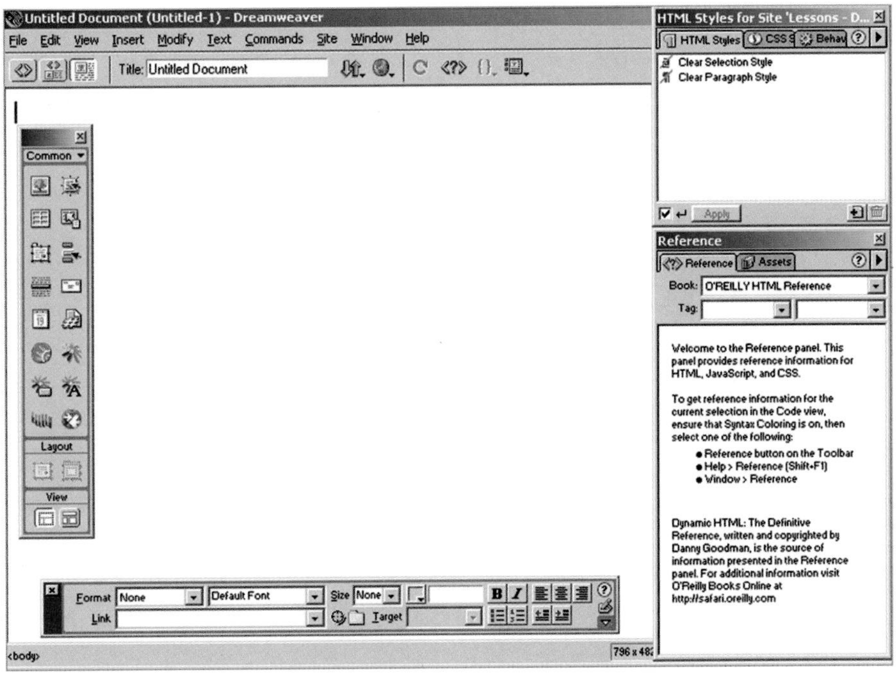

FIGURE 13B.8

The Dreamweaver development environment.

- **Dreamweaver.** Macromedia Dreamweaver is an HTML editor that allows the developer to visually write Web pages. Developers can use Dreamweaver to create forms, tables, and other components for HTML pages. Dreamweaver goes beyond standard HTML editors, however, by utilizing Dynamic HTML (DHTML) to add such functionality as timeline animation and absolute positioning of content. Like many HTML editors, Dreamweaver can do most of the coding tasks behind the scenes; the user does not need to know DHTML to create powerful Web pages. Figure 13B.8 shows the Dreamweaver development environment.
- **Flash.** Macromedia's Flash is a development tool for creating very sophisticated Web pages, which can include moving graphics, animation, sound, and interactivity. Figure 13B.9 shows a simple example of Flash in use.
- **Director.** Macromedia's Director is a full-fledged multimedia authoring environment that is part of the Macromedia Shockwave Studio suite of programs. Director gives multimedia program and Web developers the ability to create

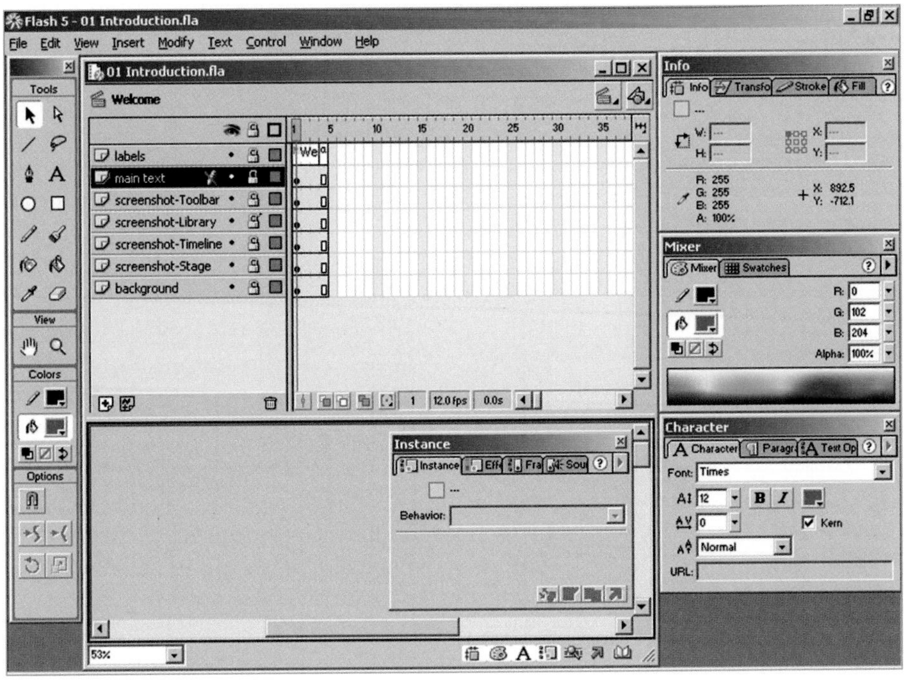

FIGURE 13B.9

The Flash 5 authoring tool in use.

FIGURE 13B.10

Macromedia Director.

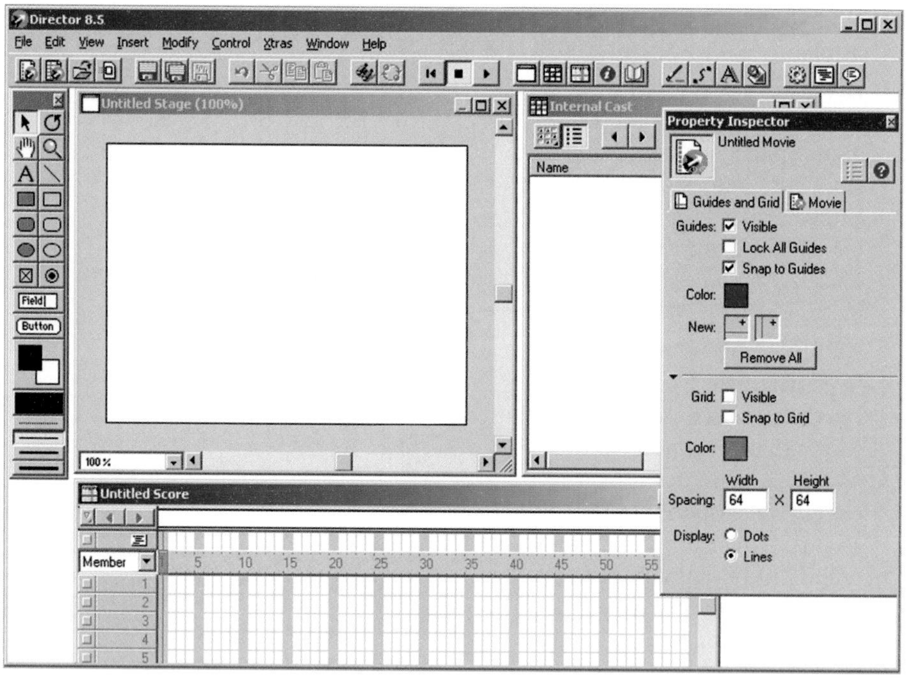

three-dimensional and interactive components, utilizing full-motion video, animation, navigation tools, audio, and much more. Director is commonly used to create graphically rich online training tools and product demos that can be viewed from a disk, CD-ROM, or the Internet. Figure 13B.10 shows Director in use.

Norton ONLINE

For more information on scripting languages, visit **http://www.mhhe.com/peternorton**.

Scripting Languages

HTML is fine for creating visually stunning documents on the Web. However, HTML is a static technology. This means that once a Web page is created, it does not change until someone edits the HTML. This scenario is fine for documents that rarely change. But consider a Web page that displays the current temperature for Pittsburgh, Pennsylvania. This page cannot be static; the temperature changes too often. Web scripting languages satisfy this need.

Several scripting languages exist for the Web. The main characteristic of scripting languages is the ability to create a dynamic Web page. Dynamic pages can change based on user input. A common example is online stores. The customer selects the desired types of products and the Web page is displayed. For most stores, it would be impossible to maintain a static page for all products. Instead, a script is written that reads from a database of products. This script then writes the necessary HTML to display the products. Figure 13B.11 displays the output from a search for caffeine on www.thinkgeek.com.

FIGURE 13B.11

A scripted response to a search for caffeine. Notice the .cgi extension in the Web page. This often signifies a Perl script.

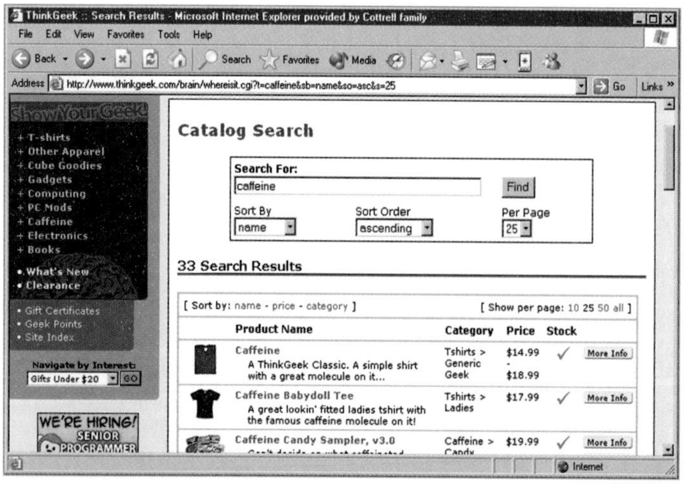

» **JavaScript.** JavaScript, originally developed by Netscape, is designed to work within HTML. It allows for page verification, simple animation, and calculations. JavaScript was initially called Livescript, and has no relationship to the programming language Java except in name. It can run inside nearly any modern browser. Figure 13B.12 shows a JavaScript script that displays the appropriate greeting based on time of day.

» **Active Server Pages (ASP).** Active Server Pages (ASP) is Microsoft's entry into the Web scripting arena. Based on Visual Basic, ASP is particularly good at accessing Microsoft databases. This makes it a good candidate for online storefronts. ASP can only work if the Web site is hosted on a Windows server. The most current version is ASP.NET

» **Practical Extraction and Reporting Language** (Perl), one of the first scripting languages, originating on UNIX systems as a way to automate administrative tasks. It has morphed into a Web scripting language. Perl, an open source language, is found on most UNIX/Linux–based Web providers and most Windows servers as well. Since Web sites using Perl can be hosted on both platforms, Perl is a good language for a Web developer to learn.

» **Hypertext Preprocessor (PHP).** Hypertext Preprocessor (PHP) is a very popular scripting language. It runs on UNIX/Linux or Windows servers. PHP is especially good at reading databases such as Oracle and MySQL. The compiler and code are offered to the general public as open source software, making it free to use. PHP is offered at most Web hosting sites. Like Perl, PHP is a good language for a Web developer to learn.

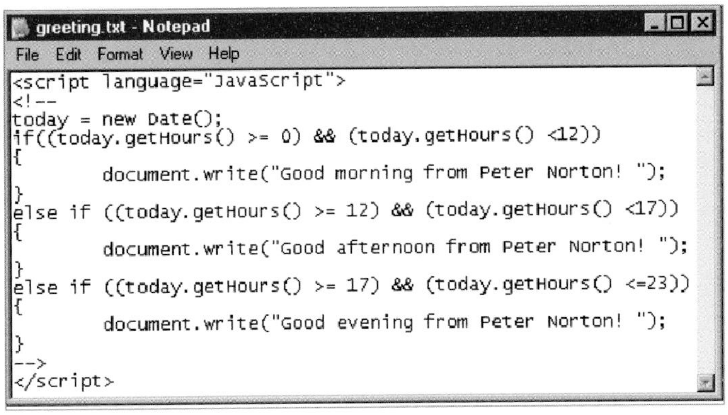

greeting.txt - Notepad

File Edit Format View Help

```
<script language="JavaScript">
<!--
today = new Date();
if((today.getHours() >= 0) && (today.getHours() <12))
{
        document.write("Good morning from Peter Norton! ");
}
else if ((today.getHours() >= 12) && (today.getHours() <17))
{
        document.write("Good afternoon from Peter Norton! ");
}
else if ((today.getHours() >= 17) && (today.getHours() <=23))
{
        document.write("Good evening from Peter Norton! ");
}
-->
</script>
```

FIGURE 13B.12

The greeting changes based on the time of day.

SELF-CHECK ::

Circle the correct answer for each question.

1. All programming languages require users to follow certain rules of ________ .
   a. style b. syntax c. grammar
2. The process of making object code from one system work on another type of system is called ________ .
   a. porting b. designing c. developing
3. Dreamweaver goes beyond standard HTML editors by using ________ .
   a. Dynamic Perl b. Dynamic XML c. Dynamic HTML

The Systems Development Life Cycle for Programming

Programs are the building blocks of information systems. When they create software products, programmers follow a process—or life cycle—that is similar to the life cycle for entire information systems. The systems development life cycle (SDLC) is detailed in Chapter 12. The similar software development life cycle is discussed here.

Norton ONLINE

For more information on the SDLC for programming, visit **http://www.mhhe.com/peternorton**.

» **Phase 1: Needs Analysis.** Needs analysis is the stage when a need or problem is identified and understood. At this early stage, the programmer looks at the program design to see what the user needs for an interface and starting point and what the user needs the program to do. Typically, the end-user should have a lot of input in the needs analysis stage. Once the programmer has determined the program's starting and stopping points, he or she can begin to design the code.

» **Phase 2: Program Design.** Program design is the stage at which programmers begin roughing out the logic they will use when the actual coding begins. Many tools are used in the program design process, although programmers often rely on whiteboards and the backs of napkins. Three of these design tools are IPO charts (for structured programming), circles and message pipes (object-oriented programming), and pseudocode. Figure 13B.13 shows a simple set of objects and message pipes, like those a programmer might develop when designing an object-oriented program.

Norton Notebook

Artificial Intelligence: Will Computers Ever Think?

Artificial intelligence (AI) can be defined as a program or machine that can solve problems or recognize patterns. A more "pure" definition of AI might be a computer or program that can fool a human into thinking he or she is dealing with another human. Such a computer could both learn and reason; thus, another definition of artificial intelligence might be a computer that can learn and reason.

Artificial intelligence software is used in many real-world applications, from determining if banks should grant loans to voice recognition and terrain-following missile guidance systems. Even applications such as word processors and e-mail make use of AI concepts. For example, a word processor's grammar checker attempts to understand and correct a language concept that most users cannot fully explain themselves. Regardless of the actual task, artificial intelligence is used in two basic areas:

- **Problem Solving.** In problem solving, the artificial intelligence program must look at a problem or collection of data and determine what to do next. For example, a bank may use an artificial intelligence system to look at your credit history and lifestyle before deciding whether or not to lend you money. This type of system is called an expert system.
- **Pattern Recognition.** In pattern recognition, the artificial intelligence program must look for repeated or known occurrences of data. Examples include artificial vision and speech recognition.

Of course, many artificial intelligence programs combine elements of both areas to solve a problem. For example, a data compression utility must look for repeated patterns in the data and then decide how to rewrite the data to eliminate the duplications.

Some Examples of AI Techniques

Artificial intelligence may be applied in many different ways depending on the problem to be solved and the resources available. Some common techniques include the following:

- **Decision Trees.** These software guides are simply maps that tell the computer what to do next based on each decision it makes. Each decision leads to a new branch with new decisions and consequences.

FIGURE 13B.13

In the design phase, object-oriented programmers use objects and message pipes to design their programs.

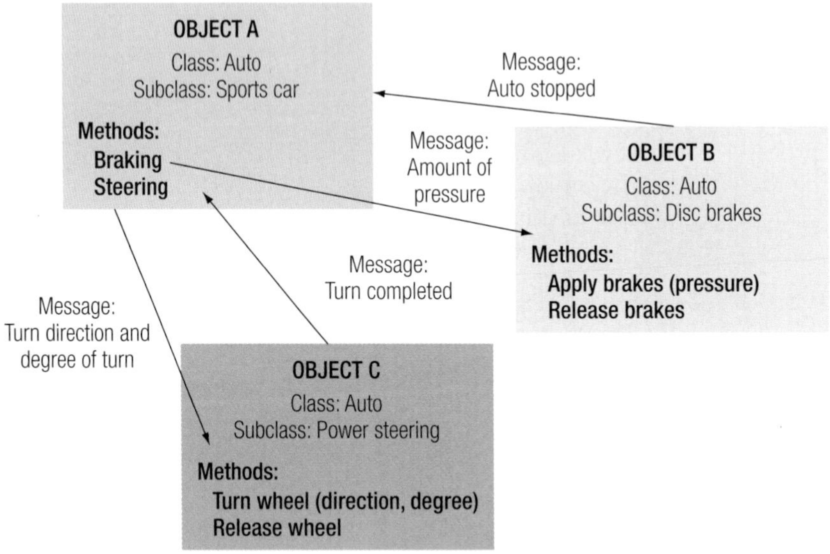

- **Phase 3: Development.** Development (also called coding) involves writing and testing source code. The software development phase is similar to the system life cycle's development phase, but instead of determining the system's overall layout, the programmer writes the code that implements the user's requirements. The programmer might write source code in a text editor and

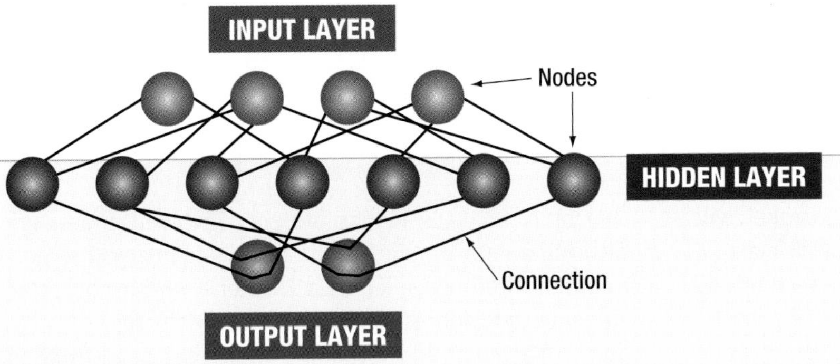

Neural networks are modeled after real neural connections in the human brain.

» **Rules-Based Systems.** These systems work by following a set of rules given by the programmer. So long as the programmer has anticipated every possible circumstance that the program may encounter, it can solve any problem.

» **Feedback.** This technique is used to modify programs. Basically, a feedback system monitors the results of a solution to see if the solution worked or in what areas it failed.

» **Knowledge-Based Systems.** These systems are similar to a rules-based system, but they use feedback to learn from their mistakes. As a result, knowledge-based systems can actually learn to solve new problems.

» **Heuristics.** This software technique is something like a recipe for a problem-solving approach rather than an algorithm that solves a specific problem.

Building an Artificial Brain

To create a true artificial intelligence, scientists could try building an artificial brain called a neural network. The human brain consists of billions and even trillions of neurons, each with as many as a million connections to other neurons. Scientists have identified hundreds of different types of neurons and more than 50 different patterns of neuron connections. This level of complexity is simply beyond any computer currently in existence. Even the most powerful parallel computers with tens of thousands of processors do not come close to equaling the number or variety of connections in a human brain.

NORTON NOTEBOOK

then compile the code, or he or she may use a visual editor and create a picture of the application before compiling the code. Most of the effort required to complete a program is spent in this phase using the programming languages you have been learning about.

Despite their best efforts, programmers inevitably create errors, or bugs, in their programs. There are two main types of errors: syntax errors and logic errors. Syntax errors violate the rules of the programming language. Finding syntax errors is relatively easy because the compiler or interpreter will point them out to the programmer. Logic errors, actual mistakes in the algorithm, are more difficult to find and may not even show up until weeks or months after the program has been implemented. The process of identifying and eliminating these errors is called debugging. Figure 13B.14 shows a list of syntax errors found by a C++ compiler. You can see by their cryptic nature that the programmer has to have some special knowledge to understand the errors and fix them.

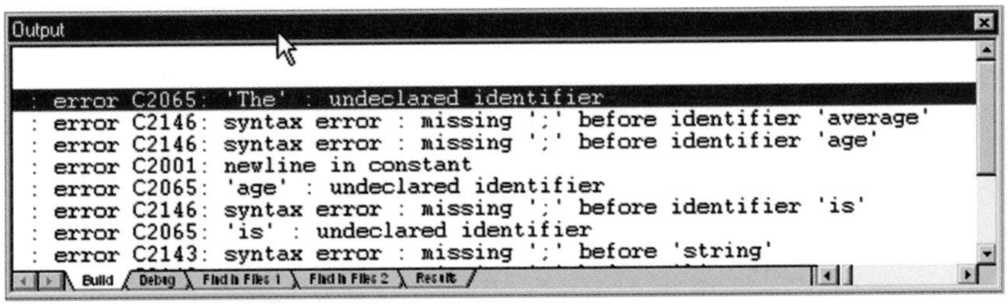

FIGURE 13B.14

Compilers help programmers locate and fix syntax errors.

Computers In Your Career

Careers in Programming

In Douglas McDowell's world, a few simple keystrokes will tweak an application or software program and make a client's eyes light up, knowing that his or her technology problems are solved. A principal consultant with IT consulting firm Intellinet in Atlanta, McDowell works one-on-one with customers, using his programming and business intelligence expertise to create technology solutions.

"As a programmer, I'm solving problems that bring high value to companies almost instantaneously," says McDowell, a professional chef who graduated from Wheaton College and earned his Masters in information technology. He changed careers after a back injury sidelined his restaurant career and says he was drawn to the analytical problem solving and business problem evaluation that a career in programming served up.

McDowell spends his 10-hour days handling the project management side of database development by working one-on-one with Intellinet's clients. He first conducts business analysis to figure out what technology the company already has in place and how he can create and integrate new systems or solutions that will help the infrastructure run more productively.

One of McDowell's recent projects involved a network monitoring a data warehouse for a cable company. The project earned Intellinet a Certified Partner Award for business intelligence solution using Microsoft technologies.

"It's a matter of understanding what they need from an application or solution that I will build, and figuring out what problem it needs to solve," says McDowell, whose certifications include .NET architecture and development; Windows, Windows Exchange, Security, and Systems; business intelligence with a focus on SQL Server; MCP; and MCSE. "Then, I complete the solution according to those requirements."

The growth in the economy and the popularity of graphics games and the Internet are driving a programming boom. Not only are programming jobs available, but also they are getting more and more interesting. Programming jobs tend to be grouped into the following broad categories:

» **Scientific Programmer.** These programmers use a specialized knowledge of science and engineering to develop high-tech programs. Scientific programmers work in fields like aerospace engineering, meteorology, oceanography, and astronomy.

» **Phase 4: Implementation.** Implementation involves installing software and allowing users to test it. This step often includes a lot of documenting, both inside the code and in the form of manuals for the users. Many programmers also will tell you that they do most of their debugging at this stage. Certainly the implementation stage is when any misconceptions the programmer had about the code are found and fixed.

» **Phase 5: Maintenance.** Maintenance starts as soon as the program is installed. Work continues on products for several reasons. Some minor bugs may not have been fixed at the time the program was released. The programmers also may add major new functioning, in response to either market demands or user requests. This is the longest phase of the program development life cycle, sometimes spanning many years.

» **Business Programmer.** Almost every business has a need for computers, and every computer needs programs. Thus, there is a strong demand for programmers who combine a knowledge of programming with a knowledge of business operations.

» **Operating System Programmer.** Of course, every computer and computer-controlled machine needs an operating system and some kind of programmed control. In some cases, such as PCs, the programmers develop operating systems like DOS, Windows, or UNIX.

» **Entertainment Programmer.** Game programmers develop everything from educational software to video games. In every case, the programmers must combine a strong knowledge of game theory with graphics and multimedia programming.

» **Web Programmer.** The World Wide Web has created a whole new programming field. Naturally, the existence of the Web has created a demand for HTML and Java programmers. However, the Web also fuels a demand for programmers who can develop tools that allow the Web to provide multimedia content. Because the Web is still in its infancy, no one can predict what Web content is likely to develop or what will be popular and what will fail.

The Bureau of Labor Statistics expects the programming field to grow about as fast as the average for all occupations through 2010, with jobs for both systems and applications programmers most plentiful in data processing service firms, software houses, and computer consulting businesses. Median annual earnings of computer programmers were $57,590 in 2000, with the middle 50 percent earning between $44,850 and $74,500 a year.

LESSON // 13B Review

Summary ::

- The only real computer language is machine language, which is a series of 1s and 0s that is understood by computers but meaningless to people.
- Programming languages can be placed into one of three basic categories: machine languages, assembly languages, and high-level languages.
- Higher-level languages allow the programmer to create programs using English-like words and phrases. Some fourth-generation languages include visual environments that allow the programmer to draw a program's interface and then assign actions to the interface's components.
- Many newer development environments have been created for Web design and multimedia programming, and some are very sophisticated. These range from basic HTML editors to feature-rich multimedia environments like Flash and Director, which allow the developer to merge animations and sound with interactive elements.
- Pure HTML creates static Web pages. Dynamic pages are created by using a scripting language like JavaScript or Perl.
- XML is a series of technologies that allow the storage and view of data on Web pages. XML holds the data. XSL and its subsets format the document for view.
- When creating software programs, developers follow a development cycle that is modeled on the systems development life cycle used in information systems development. The software development life cycle is broken into the same five stages.
- Needs analysis is the stage when a need or problem is identified or understood.
- During program design, programmers use pseudocode and message pipes to plan the programming process.
- Program development includes writing and testing the actual software code, compiling or interpreting, and debugging.
- During the implementation phase, the software is installed and users are allowed to test it.
- After implementation, the maintenance phase begins. During this stage of the software development life cycle, programs are maintained with bug fixes and updates.

Key Terms ::

Active Server Pages (ASP), 525
applet, 520
assembler, 518
assembly language, 518
bug, 527
Director, 523
Dreamweaver, 523
dynamic, 524
Extensible Markup Language (XML), 522
Extensible Markup Language Mobile Profile (XHTML MP), 522
Extensible Stylesheet Language (XSL), 522
fifth-generation language (5GL), 521
first-generation language, 518
Flash, 523
fourth-generation language (4GL), 520
higher-level language, 518
Hypertext Preprocessor (PHP), 525
integrated development environment (IDE), 520
JavaScript, 524
logic error, 527
.NET, 520
Perl, 525
port, 519
portable, 519
second-generation language, 518
static, 524
syntax, 517
syntax error, 527
third-generation language (3GL), 518
Wireless Markup Language (WML), 522

Key Term Quiz ::

Complete each statement by writing one of the terms listed under Key Terms in each blank.

1. In historical terms, assembly languages are referred to as ________ languages.
2. A(n) ________ is a mistake that can cause a program to run in an unexpected or incorrect way.
3. Animation for Web sites is often handled using Macromedia ________ .
4. ________ languages are so called because their syntax is closer to human language than either machine or assembly language.
5. The XML technology ________ is designed to format XML documents for display on the Web.
6. The newer version of WML is ________ .
7. Initially developed by Netscape, ________ allows scripting within the HTML document.
8. Microsoft's entry into the Web scripting market is ________ .
9. Visual Studio .NET and Dreamweaver are examples of an ________ , which simplifies the development of a program or Web site.
10. The ________ language is especially good at developing Web sites from databases.

LESSON // 13B Review

Multiple Choice ::

Circle the word or phrase that best completes each statement.

1. The newest version of HTML is ________.
   a. WML b. XHTML c. XML d. XSL
2. ________ are seldom used except to fine-tune important parts of programs written in a high-level language.
   a. Compilers b. Assembly languages c. Interpreters d. Front ends
3. C++ and Java are examples of ________ languages.
   a. first-generation b. third-generation c. fourth-generation d. fifth-generation
4. ________ programming languages use familiar words rather than the detailed strings of digits that make up machine instructions.
   a. Machine b. Assembly c. Higher-level d. All
5. Programmers begin roughing out the logic they will use in the ________ stage of the software SDLC.
   a. program design b. development c. implementation d. testing
6. Which of the following is a language that is commonly used to write .cgi scripts for web pages?
   a. JavaScript b. C++ c. Visual Basic d. Perl
7. Applets for the Web are written in the ________ language.
   a. Java b. .NET c. PHP d. C++
8. In a 4GL ________ environment, the programmer uses a toolbar to drag and drop items like buttons and text boxes to create a definition of an application.
   a. visual b. text c. scripting d. coding
9. ________ looks like HTML, but the developer is free to create new tags.
   a. Perl b. XML c. Java d. CGI
10. This product is an IDE for Java.
    a. Visual Studio b. Netscape Visual JavaScript c. Macromedia Director d. Sun Studio One

Review Questions ::

In your own words, briefly answer the following questions.

1. What is meant by "porting" code from one type of computer system to another?
2. How do XML and HTML work together?
3. Describe the disagreement that some programmers have, regarding fifth-generation programming languages.
4. What are the five phases of the systems development life cycle as applied to software development?
5. What happens during the implementation phase of the software SDLC?
6. Describe the difference between HTML and XHTML.
7. Why is object-oriented programming considered to be a very natural manner of programming?
8. What would a developer build using PHP?
9. What are the keys to being a successful programmer?
10. How does an IDE make it easier for a developer to write a program?

Lesson Labs ::

Complete the following exercises as directed by your instructor.

1. Using a text editor like Notepad (or a piece of paper) and the given commands, write a pseudocode algorithm that goes through a short list of numbers and places all the even numbers into one list and all the odd numbers in another list. Use the following commands: While, get number, if/then/else, put number in even list, put number in odd list.
2. Using Notepad (or another piece of paper), review the pseudocode you created in the first exercise and create documentation to explain what the pseudocode does. Remember, the more documentation you add, the easier it will be for others to understand your logic.

Chapter Labs

Complete the following exercise using a computer in your classroom, lab, or home.

1. Create a Web page trick. Web pages can be filled with lines of simple code that create special effects or cause the page to behave in certain ways. In many cases, you do not need to be a programmer or even use a real programming language to build "tricks" into a Web page. This exercise shows you an example of a cool trick you can add to any Web page by typing a few lines of code. It may not be actual programming, but you will feel like a programmer when you're done. In the following steps, you will create a small HTML page that displays the word *mhhe.* What is the trick? When you view the page in a browser, and your mouse pointer touches the text, the word *mhhe* will change color and font and the background color behind the text will also change. Once you create the file, you will test it in your Web browser. (*Note*: This exercise assumes that you use Microsoft Internet Explorer 5.0 or later, or Netscape Navigator 5.0 or later. If you use an older version of either browser, the mouseover may not work.)

a. Open Notepad and type in the following code, exactly as shown here, including the blank spaces:

```
<html>
<head>
<title>Mouse Rollover</title>

</head>
<body>
<p>
<a href="http://www.mhhe.com">mhhe</a></p>
</body>
</html>
```

b. Save the file as Test.html in any folder you like.

c. Launch Internet Explorer or Netscape Navigator and open the Test.html file. You should see the word *mhhe* on your screen.

d. Click mhhe and watch your screen change to the mhhe Online Web site.

e. Now we will insert the code to write the rollover trick. Position your cursor on the line between </title> and </head>. Enter the following code exactly as it appears here.

```
<style>
<!-
a: link  {
font-family: arial, sans-serif;
font-weight: normal;
            }
a:hover {
color:#FF0000;
background:#00FF00;
font-family: arial, sans-serif;
font-weight: bold;
            }
-->
</style>
```

f. Reopen your file in your browser. Move your mouse pointer to the word Hello! and let it rest there. Notice that the word changes from a normal font to bold. This change is caused by the special code you typed into the HTML file.
g. Try adding other hyperlinks. Repeat the lines starting at the <p> and ending with the </p>. Change http://www.mhhe.com to a Web site of your choosing. Refresh your browser screen and test both links.
h. When you are finished testing your page, close your Web browser.

Discussion Questions

As directed by your instructor, discuss the following questions in class or in groups.

1. Do you think it would be easier to write programs with a structured or an object-oriented programming language? Why?
2. Programmers are encouraged to create crash-proof programs. Why is this so important? What are some possible reasons a program could crash from user error?

Research and Report

Using your own choice of resources (such as the Internet, books, magazines, and newspaper articles), research and write a short paper discussing one of the following topics:

- The impact of Java on the Internet and application development.
- The techniques of making a program crash proof.
- The debate over fifth-generation programming languages.

When you are finished, proofread and print your paper, and give it to your instructor.

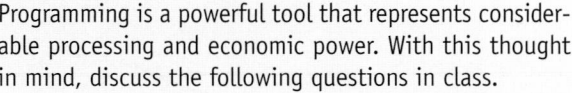

ETHICAL ISSUES

Programming is a powerful tool that represents considerable processing and economic power. With this thought in mind, discuss the following questions in class.

1. Assume a programmer is attempting to develop a true artificial intelligence system. If the programmer is successful, what are the ethical implications? Should the program be considered alive? If so, does the program have basic human rights? Is it ethical to turn the program on and off? Should the program be allowed to interact with other artificially intelligent systems? Can the program be guilty of a crime or the victim of one? What responsibility does the programmer bear for the system's actions, in this scenario?
2. Discuss the implications of computer piracy. What happens to the economy when users pirate software (copy them without paying for them)? Do not just consider the giants like Microsoft. Include the small developers in your discussion. What happens to software innovation when piracy is commonplace? What other problems can arise due to software piracy? Who suffers most from software piracy? What role, if any, should the government play in combating piracy?

14

CHAPTER

Protecting Your Privacy, Your Computer, and Your Data

CHAPTER CONTENTS ::

This chapter contains the following lessons:

Lesson **14A:**
Understanding the Need for Security Measures

- Basic Security Concepts
- Threats to Users
- Threats to Hardware
- Threats to Data

Lesson **14B:**
Taking Protective Measures

- Protecting Yourself
- Keeping Your Data Secure
- Safeguarding Your Hardware

Understanding the Need for Security Measures

Overview: The Need for Computer Security

While reading this book, you have discovered how important computers and their contents are to everyone. Safeguarding your computer and its valuable information is important. Just imagine what your life would be like if all your financial records, schoolwork, and personal correspondence were suddenly changed, destroyed, or made public. What would you be willing to do to prevent this from happening?

You are aware that cars are stolen every day, so you probably take measures such as locking the doors, parking in a garage, or using a car alarm. In the same way, you should be aware of the threats facing your computer and data, and take measures to protect them as well. By taking some precautionary steps, you can safeguard not only your hardware, software, and data, but yourself.

The first step to good computer security is awareness. You should understand *all* the dangers that specifically threaten your computer system. You need to know how each threat can affect you and prioritize them accordingly. This lesson introduces you to some of the most common threats to your privacy, data, and hardware. The following lesson shows you how to protect yourself and your system.

OBJECTIVES ::

- Define the terms *threat*, *vulnerability*, and *countermeasure* in the context of computer security.
- Describe four specific threats that computer users face.
- Describe three specific threats to computer hardware.
- Describe three specific threats to data.

FIGURE 14A.1

A vacant house with an open window is not only vulnerable to threats, but invites them. Is your home burglar-proof?

Basic Security Concepts

You will see certain terms throughout this chapter, so it is best to become familiar with them before going any further.

Threats

The entire point of computer security is to eliminate or protect against threats. A threat is anything that can cause harm. In the context of computer security, a threat can be a burglar, a virus, an earthquake, or a simple user error.

By itself, a threat is not harmful unless it exploits an existing vulnerability. A vulnerability is a weakness—anything that has not been protected against threats, making it open to harm (see Figure 14A.1). For instance, an unlocked car is vulnerable to theft. The vulnerability is meaningless unless a thief is in the neighborhood. But you probably always lock your car or park it in a safe place anyway . . . just in case a thief should happen to come along.

Degrees of Harm

That said, it's important to realize that threats, and the harm they can cause, are a matter of degree. If you live on top of a mountain, for example, there is probably no threat of flooding. If you don't use antivirus software, however, there is a very good chance that your computer will become infected, especially if it stays connected to the Internet. Because you can gauge the degree of harm that different threats can cause, you can prioritize them. That is, you can decide which threats are more likely to "get you" and take precautions against them.

When people think of the ways their computer system can be damaged, they may think only of damage to the hardware or the loss of data. In reality, computer systems can be damaged in many ways. And remember, as you learned in Chapter 1, you (the user) are part of the computer system. You, too, can suffer harm of various kinds, from the loss of important data, to the loss of privacy, to actual physical harm.

When protecting your computer system, it pays to think in the broadest possible terms about the types of harm that could affect you. A nasty virus or hacker can wipe out your programs as well as your data. If your PC is connected to a network, other systems on the network could suffer similar problems. Damages to your home or office—such as a fire or flood—can easily extend to your computer and everything stored on it (see Figure 14A.2).

FIGURE 14A.2

If your home were to catch fire, what would happen to your important data? How can you protect data from a fire or flood?

Countermeasures

A countermeasure is any step you take to ward off a threat—to protect yourself, your data, or your computer from harm. For example, regularly backing up your data is a countermeasure against the threat of data loss. A firewall is a countermeasure against hackers.

There are two classes of countermeasures. The first shields the user from personal harm, such as threats to personal property, confidential information, financial records, medical records, and so forth. The second safeguard protects the computer system from physical hazards such as theft, vandalism, power problems, and natural disasters or attacks on the data stored and processed in computers.

Threats to Users

Networks and the Internet have created limitless possibilities for people to work, communicate, learn, buy and sell, play games, and interact with others around the world. These possibilities come from the openness of networks—especially the Internet, which is available to virtually everyone, for virtually any kind of use. However, the very openness that makes the Internet so valuable also has made it a conduit for many types of threats.

Still, we cannot blame the Internet for all computer-related problems. Some issues, such as identity theft, are still best accomplished with little or no help from a computer. Others, such as injuries stemming from computer use, are often the fault of poor design or poor work habits.

Norton ONLINE

For more information on identity theft, visit **http://www.mhhe.com/peternorton**.

Identity Theft

Identity (ID) theft occurs when someone impersonates you by using your name, Social Security number, or other personal information to obtain documents or credit in your name. With the right information, an identity thief can virtually "become" the victim, obtaining a drivers license, bank accounts, mortgages, and other items in the victim's name.

Identity theft cost the U.S. economy $53 billion in 2002. That year alone, 10 million Americans became victims of ID theft. According to the Federal Trade Commission, identity theft rose by nearly 41 percent from 2001 to 2002 and shot up 81 percent between 2002 and 2003 (see Figure 14A.3).

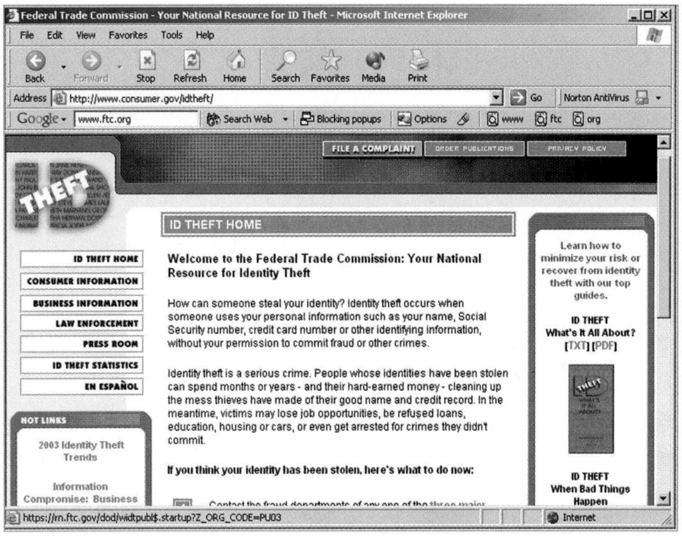

FIGURE 14A.3

The Federal Trade Commission's ID Theft Web site is a clearinghouse of information on ID theft.

Beyond monetary losses, however, victims of ID theft pay in other ways, spending many hours trying to repair the financial damages and regain their good reputation.

Identity thieves can use several methods—low-tech as well as high-tech—to obtain the information they need:

- **Shoulder Surfing.** A trick known as shoulder surfing is as simple as watching someone enter personal identification information for a private transaction, such as an ATM machine.
- **Snagging.** In the right setting, a thief can try snagging information by listening in on a telephone extension, through a wiretap, or over a cubicle wall while the victim gives credit card or other personal information to a legitimate agent.
- **Dumpster Diving.** Other techniques are as simple as stealing mail containing personal information. A popular low-tech approach is dumpster diving. Thieves can go through garbage cans, dumpsters, or trash bins to obtain cancelled checks, credit card statements, or bank account information that someone has carelessly thrown out (see Figure 14A.4).

FIGURE 14A.4

Be careful not to throw away documents that contain valuable information. An ID thief may find what he needs in your own trash can.

The thief wins when he finds items that have account numbers or personal information.

Some ID thieves are brazen enough to swipe documents right out of your mailbox. Some of the most important documents you use come to you in the mail every month: bills, account statements, credit card offers, financial records, and many others. On a good day, a thief could snag everything he needs right from your mailbox.

- **Social Engineering.** This method is not as sophisticated as it sounds, but can still be effective. In social engineering, the ID thief tricks victims into providing critical information under the pretext of something legitimate. The thief can call an unwary victim, for example; claim to be a system administrator at the Web site of the victim's bank; and ask for the victim's user ID and password for a system check. With this information in hand, the thief can go online and access the victim's account information directly through the bank's Web site.
- **High-Tech Methods.** Sophisticated ID thieves can get information using a computer and Internet connection. For instance, Trojan horses can be planted on a system or a person's identity may be snagged from unsecured Internet sites. Although not common, it happens. One reason it is not common is because of the general use of security technologies such as Secure Sockets Layer (SSL) and Secure HTTP (S-HTTP) to ensure the integrity and confidentiality of credit card and financial transactions. Because so much attention is paid to protecting transmitted data, social engineering and low-tech swindles are the predominant sources of identity theft.

Loss of Privacy

Did you know that your buying habits are tracked electronically, in a range of commercial systems? This doesn't apply just to online transactions either. Any time you use a "store loyalty" card to rent movies or buy groceries, the purchases are logged in a database (see Figure 14A.5). Your medical, financial, and credit records are available to anybody authorized to view them.

FIGURE 14A.5

Many of the purchases you make are logged in corporate databases.

Many of the companies you deal with every day—from your local supermarket to your insurance company—maintain databases filled with information about you. You might expect these firms to know your name and address, but you might be surprised to learn that they know how many times each month you put gas in your car or buy a magazine. And a lot of companies do not keep this information confidential; they may sell it to other companies who are interested in knowing about you.

Personal information is a business commodity that supports a huge shadow industry called data mining. Data mining is a business-intelligence-gathering process that every large organization, from banks to grocery stores, employs to sift through computerized data. Companies spot useful patterns in overall behavior to target individuals for special treatment. Data mining is a $200-million-a-year industry, and it is growing rapidly because it pays big dividends.

Public Records on the Internet

Norton ONLINE

For more information on accessing public records, visit **http://www.mhhe.com/peternorton**.

Your personal information is available to anybody who has the few dollars required to buy it from commercial public record services. For a minimal price, companies such as Intelius and WhoWhere.com will give you detailed reports about most people. These reports contain such detailed information as

- **Criminal records,** including sex offender registry, felonies, misdemeanors, and federal and county offenses

» **Background information,** including marriage records, divorce records, adoption records, driving records, credit history, bankruptcies in the past 20 years, tax liens, small claims, past address history, neighbors, property ownership, mortgages, and licenses.

Records such as marriage licenses and divorce records are public records. This means that they, along with many other kinds of legal records, are available to anybody who wants to view them. There are a number of companies that collect public records, package them, and sell them to anyone who wishes to purchase them (see Figure 14A.6).

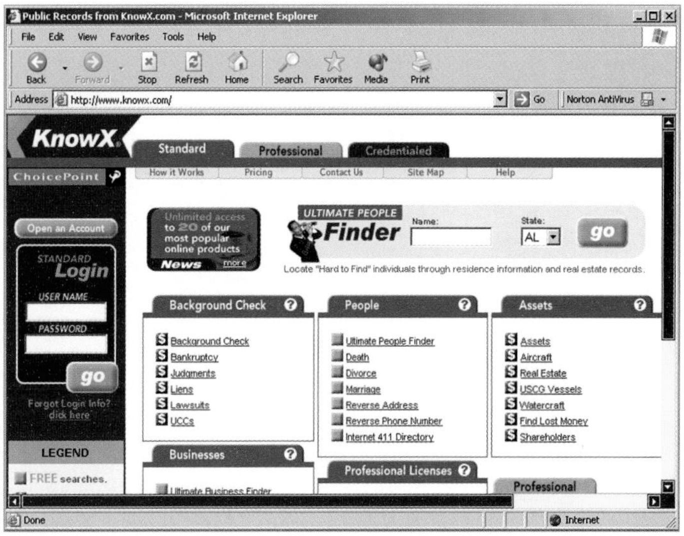

FIGURE 14A.6

You can obtain background information on most people in the United States by accessing an Internet public records source.

Internet Monitoring, Profiling, and Spying

When using the Internet, you should be aware that your interests and habits are being monitored automatically (see Figure 14A.7). The monitoring activity can be carried out by programs running on your own computer or a connected server. This might not seem to be a problem since "if you aren't doing anything wrong you have nothing to fear." However, the interpretation of why you visit a particular site is in the eye of the beholder. You may not be aware of how your browsing habits are interpreted by others. A single visit to one of the ubiquitous advertiser banner ads at the top of your browser identifies you as someone with an interest in related products.

Data about when you visited, what you looked at, and how long you stayed is used by most commercial Web sites. Use of this data is called "online profiling" and is done to build a profile of your interests and habits. It is analyzed to learn more about you. There are commercial profiles for most people in the United States based on the browsing activity of a particular IP address. This address is tied to the name of the owner of that address no matter who is doing the actual browsing. The reports contain information about browsing habits and may contain accompanying marketing conclusions, called psychographic data. This data makes guesses about who you really are based on your surfing behavior and elaborate inferences are drawn about your interests, habits, associations, and other traits. These guesses are available to any organization willing to pay for access to the profile. Online marketers, commercial information service providers, and, in some cases, federal agencies may have access.

FIGURE 14A.7

Even if your online activities are completely innocent, they may be tracked. This tracking allows companies to build profiles of your interests, so they can market products in ways that are most likely to interest you.

Online Spying Tools

Software developers have created a number of ways to track your activities online. Although many of these tools were created for benign purposes—such as helping legitimate Webmasters determine who visits their sites most often—they are also being used in ways most consumers do not appreciate. These tools are described in the following sections. In the next lesson, you will learn some techniques for managing these threats to your privacy.

Cookies

A cookie is a small text file that a Web server asks your browser to place on your computer. The cookie contains information that identifies your computer (its IP address), you (your user name or e-mail address), and information about your visit to the Web site. For instance, the cookie might list the last time you visited the site, which pages you downloaded, and how long you were at the site before

Norton ONLINE

For more information on online spying tools, visit **http://www.mhhe.com/peternorton**.

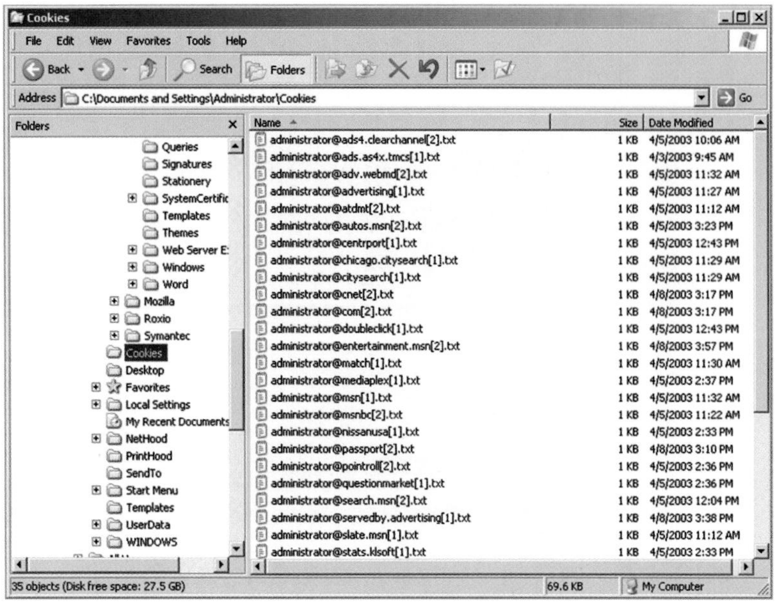

FIGURE 14A.8

A collection of cookies on a typical PC. Windows actually stores copies of cookies in several different folders, making it difficult to find them all. This is why you need special software to manage them.

leaving. If you set up an account at a Web site such as an e-commerce site, the cookie will contain information about your account, making it easy for the server to find and manage your account whenever you visit.

Despite their helpful purpose, cookies are now considered a significant threat to privacy. This is because they can be used to store and report many types of information. For example, a cookie can store a list of *all* the sites you visit. This data can be transferred to the site that placed the cookie on your system, and that information can be used against your wishes. For example, the cookie's maker might use the cookie to determine what kinds of advertisements will appear on your screen the next time you visit the Web site. Many Webmasters use information from cookies to determine the demographic makeup of their site's audience. Even worse, cookies can be used as the basis of hacker attacks.

At any time, your PC may be storing hundreds or thousands of cookies (see Figure 14A.8). If you could examine them, you probably would decide that you didn't want to keep many of them on your system. For this reason, tools have been developed to help users manage cookies and limit the damage they can do.

Web Bugs

A Web bug is a small GIF-format image file that can be embedded in a Web page or an HTML-format e-mail message. A Web bug can be as small as a single pixel in size and can easily be hidden anywhere in an HTML document.

Behind the tiny image, however, lies code that functions in much the same way as a cookie, allowing the bug's creator to track many of your online activities. A bug can record what Web pages you view, keywords you type into a search engine, personal information you enter in a form on a Web page, and other data. Because Web bugs are hidden, they are considered by many to be eavesdropping devices. Upon learning about Web bugs, most consumers look for a way to defeat them. A number of anti–Web bug programs now exist.

Spyware

The term spyware is used to refer to many different kinds of software that can track a computer user's activities and report them to someone else. There are now countless varieties of spyware programs. Another common term for spyware is adware, because Internet advertising is a common source of spyware.

Some types of spyware operate openly. For example, when you install and register a program, it may ask you to fill out a form. The program then sends the information to the developer, who stores it in a database. When used in this manner, spyware-type programs are seen as perfectly legitimate because the user is aware that information is being collected.

More commonly, however, spyware is installed on a computer without the user's knowledge and collects information without the user's consent. Spyware can land on your PC from many sources: Web pages, e-mail messages, and pop-up ads are just a few. Once on your machine, spyware can track virtually anything you do and secretly report your activities to someone else. Spyware can record individual keystrokes, Web usage, e-mail addresses, personal information, and other types of data. Generally, the program transmits the collected data via e-mail or to a Web page.

The average computer user may have a dozen or more spyware programs on his or her PC at any given time, according to some reports (see Figure 14A.9). This means that any number of companies can be using spyware to track your online activities. For this reason, anti-spyware software development has exploded, with dozens of spyware-killing products on the market.

FIGURE 14A.9

Cleaning spyware applications from a PC with X-Cleaner, a spyware-removal tool.

Spam

Although the availability of your private information might be troubling, the consequence for most users is something called spam. Spam is Internet "junk mail." After all, your e-mail address is often included in the personal information that companies collect and share. The correct term for spam is unsolicited commercial e-mail (UCE). Almost all spam is commercial advertising (see Figure 14A.10). According to reports filed with Congress in early 2004, about two-thirds of all e-mail traffic was spam messages. In the United States, nearly 80 percent of all e-mail was spam.

Norton ONLINE

For more information on spam, visit **http://www.mhhe.com/peternorton**.

You might think that the answer to spam e-mail is simple: just delete the messages when they arrive. But for many computer users, spam is much too big a problem for such a simple solution. Some people receive dozens, even hundreds, of spam messages daily. The problem is huge for businesses, where corporate e-mail servers needlessly store and transfer countless spam messages each month. At the personal level, spam recipients spend time reviewing unwanted messages, in fear they may accidentally delete legitimate mail. This alone costs untold hours of wasted time. The real solution to spam, therefore, is to control it before it reaches all the people who don't want it.

Defining spam is important to controlling it. One person's important message, after all, is another person's spam. This difference makes it hard to establish a legal basis for prevention. Since 2003, the legally accepted definition of the characteristics of spam is commercial e-mail, bulk transmitted to millions of people at a time. The volume and the fact that each message contains substantially the same content define spam.

People who send out these endless streams of spam (spammers) get e-mail addresses in three ways:

- Purchasing lists of e-mail addresses through brokers.
- "Harvesting" e-mail addresses from the Internet.
- Generating random strings of characters in an attempt to match legitimate addresses.

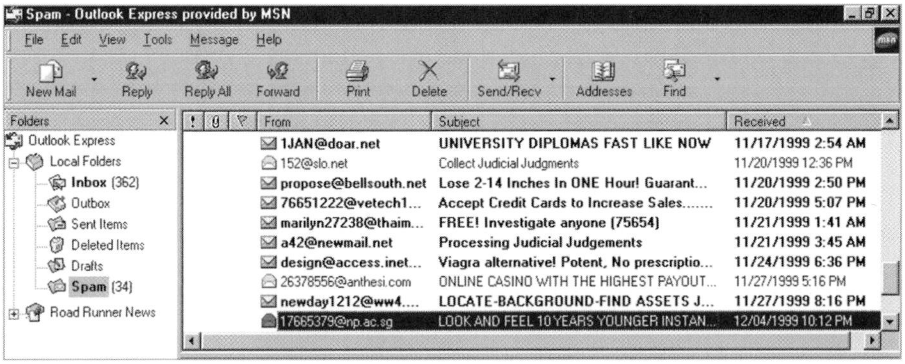

FIGURE 14A.10

A collection of spam messages. For millions of computer users, spam is a vexing, daily problem that robs them of productive time.

FIGURE 14A.11

You can learn more about anti-spam laws and citizen movements by visiting anti-spam Web sites such as The SpamCon Foundation's site, at http://spamcon.org.

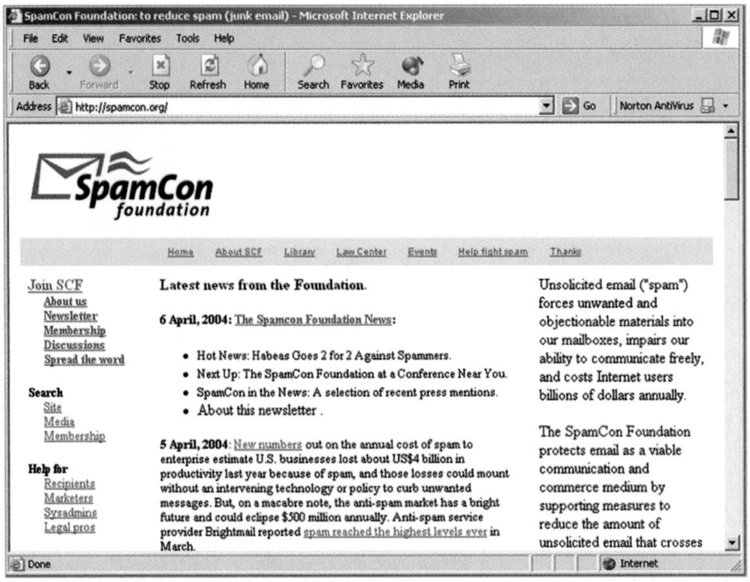

The U.S. law regulating spam is the Controlling the Assault of Non-Solicited Pornography and Marketing Act of 2003, or the CAN-SPAM Act of 2003 (see Figure 14A.11). It took effect on January 1, 2004, and is based on the concept of affirmative consent. This means that the recipient of the message must give explicit consent to receive a commercial e-mail message. Under this law, it is illegal to

- Send a commercial e-mail message with header information that is false or misleading (such as a subject line that does not state the message's true purpose).
- Spoof the originating address, or relay a message from another computer in order to disguise its point of origin. Spoofing is a social engineering term that describes an attempt by the sender of the message to convince the recipient that the message is from someone else.
- Not clearly identify that the message is an advertisement or solicitation.

The message must provide a conspicuous opportunity to decline further messages. If the recipient declines additional messages, it is illegal to send one that falls within the scope of the request. It is illegal for anyone acting on behalf of the sender to send such a message or for the sender to transfer the address to anybody else.

Computer-Related Injuries

Computer use can cause physical injuries to the user. Prolonged mouse and keyboard use, staring at a monitor for too long, and poor seating conditions are the primary causes of such injuries. For more information on specific computer-related ailments and ways to avoid them, see Chapter 3, "Interacting with Your Computer," and Chapter 4, "Seeing, Hearing, and Printing Data."

Threats to Hardware

Threats to your computer's hardware involve incidents that have an effect on the operation or maintenance of the computer. They range from such routine things as system breakdown and misuse to malicious actions of individuals including theft and vandalism of the equipment. Disasters such as fire and flood are also threats.

Power-Related Threats

Power problems affect computers in two ways:

- Power fluctuations, when the strength of your electrical service rises or falls, can cause component failures.
- Power failure, when power is lost altogether, causes systems to shut down.

Both power failure and fluctuations can result in a loss of data.

Power problems can arise for many reasons. People commonly think that electrical storms are the primary cause of power interruptions, but storms are actually one of the least likely causes. A more likely source is the house or building itself. Disturbances from high-demand equipment such as air conditioners, space heaters, dryers, and copy machines produce fluctuations, for example.

As a countermeasure against power-related problems, you can equip your system with one of the following devices:

- Surge suppressors protect against voltage spikes. These inexpensive plugs can be bought in most hardware stores.
- Line conditioners provide additional functions. Not only do they protect against spikes, but they also safeguard against the line noise from high-demand electrical equipment operated near your computer. This protects the computer against voltage drops, called *sags*. Because of their additional features, line conditioners cost more than surge suppressors. They are available in some high-end hardware stores and in most electronics stores.
- Uninterruptible power supplies (UPS) are essentially a battery backup for your computer (see Figure 14A.12). A UPS protects the system from electrical events including a total loss of power. One important function of a UPS is the "soft landing" feature. It ensures that the computer will be shut down normally if the device's battery runs out before power is restored. You can buy a UPS for a home computer for less than $100. Prices increase with the extra functions, capacity, and battery life.

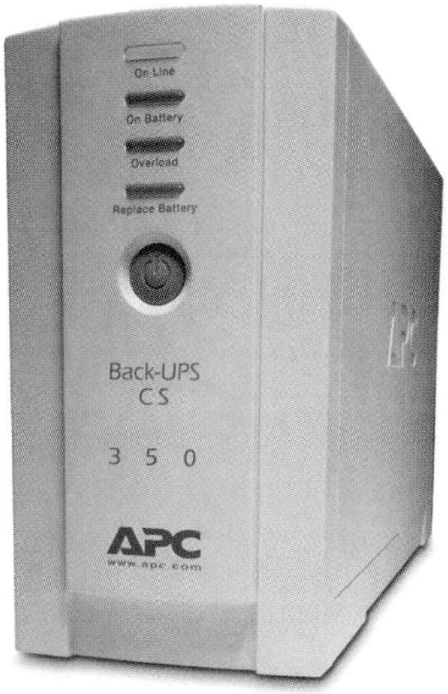

FIGURE 14A.12

A UPS is your best defense against power fluctuations or outages.

Theft and Vandalism

A burglar or vandal can do tremendous damage to a computer, resulting in total loss of the system and the data it stores. While this fact may seem obvious, very few homeowners and students take precautions to protect their PCs from intentionally destructive acts.

The best way to keep thieves and vandals at bay is to keep your system in a secure area. Special locks are available that can attach a system unit, monitor, or other equipment to a desk, making it very difficult to move (see Figure 14A.13). Home alarm

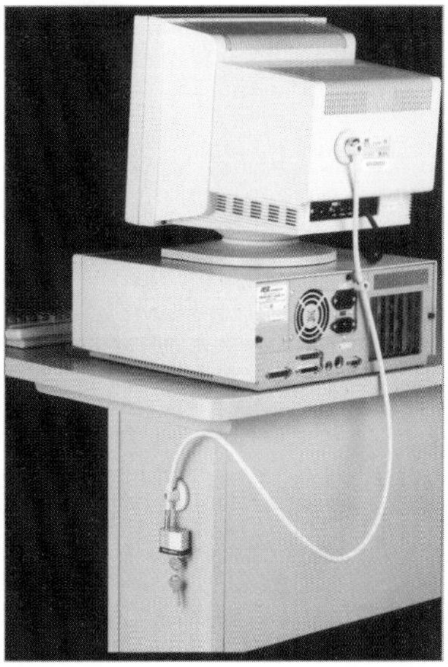

FIGURE 14A.13

A special locking cable can anchor expensive equipment to a desk.

Norton ONLINE

For more information on power-related problems and their solutions, visit **http://www.mhhe.com/peternorton**.

Norton ONLINE

For more information on anti-theft devices for computing equipment, visit **http://www.mhhe.com/peternorton**.

Productivity Tip

Keeping Your PC Up to Date

Because PC hardware and software are becoming increasingly complex, it is becoming increasingly important to do regular maintenance on them. At the very minimum, this means defragmenting your hard disk, checking for viruses, and performing other basic housekeeping chores to keep your machine humming along. You learned several of these techniques in Chapter 6, "Storing Data." But routine system maintenance includes another step that many users ignore: updating important system and program files.

By making sure that your system software is kept up to date, you reduce the risk of system failures and keep your programs running as well as possible. Device drivers provide a good example. Suppose you update your operating system, then your CD-ROM drive begins functioning poorly. You might be able to fix this problem by installing an updated device driver that is more compatible with your new OS.

Fortunately, you don't need to call a PC technician (or become one yourself) to update critical system files. Thanks to a new breed of automated Web sites, you can sit back and let your PC update itself.

If you are a registered user of Microsoft Windows or Microsoft Office, for example, you can visit Microsoft's product update Web sites and download bug fixes, patches, updated system files, templates, security-related files, and much more. You can visit the Windows Update site at http://windowsupdate.microsoft.com. You can find the Office Update site at http://officeupdate.microsoft.com.

Users of Windows 2000 and Windows XP can configure their operating system to automatically update files. These versions of Windows can find and install updates in the background, whenever the PC is connected to the Internet.

Companies such as Symantec (http://www.symantec.com/downloads), McAfee (http://software.mcafee.com/centers/download/default.asp), and other makers of popular antivirus software and utility programs host product-update sites, too. At these sites, users can download up-to-the-minute versions of virus databases, utilities, drivers, and other products. This updating is extremely important; without the latest virus definitions, your

systems are a good investment, as well, especially when expensive equipment and priceless data are at stake.

Accidental harm is much harder to address, but no less of a threat. Something as simple as spilling a cup of coffee into your system unit provides a spectacular example. This is why most computer rooms have a sign saying "no food or drinks." There are so many ways a human can accidentally damage a computer that it is pointless to attempt to list them all. However, a sound set of safety procedures can handle the typical ones. These procedures are formulated from a thorough threat analysis, conducted under the dictates of Murphy's Law—"whatever can go wrong, will go wrong."

Norton ONLINE

For more information on dealing with natural disasters, visit **http://www.mhhe.com/peternorton**.

Natural Disasters

Disaster planning addresses natural and man-made disasters. It is not called "disaster prevention" because things like earthquakes and hurricanes are hard to predict and impossible to prevent. However, you can plan for them. A well thought-out plan can minimize the loss of information and interruption of work should a disaster occur.

Because natural disasters vary by location, your first step is to make a list of all of the disasters that you think could happen in your area, then prioritize that list. For instance, no matter where you live, fires at home are more likely to happen than tornados. Even though tornados are more destructive, you should have plans for handling the more frequent disasters. Table 14A.1 lists three categories of disasters.

No matter what disasters you include in your list, your countermeasures should include awareness, anticipation, and preparation. The first two are simple:

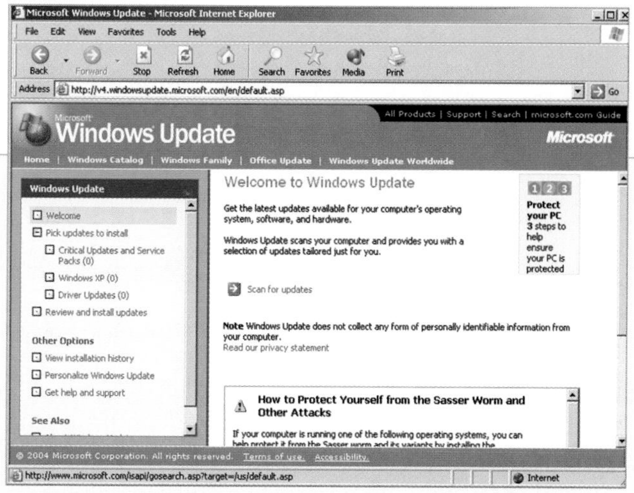

The Windows Update Web site, seen in the Microsoft Internet Explorer browser.

antivirus software cannot protect your system against the latest viruses.

If you use any kind of high-capacity storage device—such as a Zip drive, a CD-RW drive, or a DVD-R/RW drive—you can probably visit the manufacturer's Web site for updated drivers and utilities that can make your drive easier to use or more functional.

If you have purchased a new computer, operating system, application, or peripheral, and if the product is from a major manufacturer, there's a good chance the product offers online support of some kind. To learn what options are available for your specific products, check your online help systems and printed documentation. Look for Web addresses for software update, download, or support pages.

How often should you update? It depends on the software. If you use a new version of Windows, you should configure to check for updates whenever you're online. That way, you won't miss a critical update, which could compromise your system's security. Check for updates to your antivirus software definitions at least once a week; if your antivirus program can receive updates automatically, set it to do so. Otherwise, it's a good idea to check for updated device drivers and support files occasionally, to keep your peripheral devices and other programs running as well as possible.

PRODUCTIVITY TIP

TABLE 14A.1

Examples of Natural, Site, and Civil Disasters

Natural Disasters	Site Disasters	Civil Disasters
Localized or area floods	Building and forest fires	Car, plane, or train crash
Lightning storms	Water and sewer emergencies	Civil disturbance
Snowstorms and/or extreme cold	Telephone or cable service interruptions	Disease outbreak and quarantine
Tornado	Chemical and gas leaks or spills (both in and external to the building)	War or terrorism
Hurricane	Explosions (both in and external to the building)	
Earthquake	Failure of the building structure	

be aware that a disaster could strike and anticipate it when conditions are right. For example, if you live on the East Coast of the United States, you know when to anticipate a hurricane.

Preparation can mean many steps, and you probably have a lot of options—too many to list here. But ask yourself what you can do quickly to protect your PC and data in a disaster. Could you move the PC to a safe place quickly, without putting yourself in danger? Could you get to your backup disks or tapes quickly, so they could be saved? Is fire protection available? Do you know how to turn off the gas, electric, and water services to your home? Having answers to questions like these can make a huge difference when minutes count.

SELF-CHECK ::

Circle the word or phrase that completes each statement.

1. Threats are not harmful unless they exploit an existing __________ .
   a. danger b. vulnerability c. computer
2. A backup is a __________ against data loss.
   a. threat b. security c. countermeasure
3. To assume your identity, an ID thief needs only the right __________ .
   a. information b. computer c. software

Threats to Data

The purpose of a computer is to process data in some way to create information. The goal of computer security is to protect this process. Because data and information are intangible, this mission is difficult. Despite this, you should try to protect everything of value from every threat you can identify. There are three general categories of threat: malicious code and malware, criminal acts, and cyberterrorism.

Malware, Viruses, and Malicious Programs

Norton ONLINE

For more information on malware, visit **http://www.mhhe.com/peternorton**.

The term malware describes viruses, worms, Trojan horse attack applets, and attack scripts. These virulent programs represent the most common threat to your information.

Viruses are pieces of a computer program (code) that attach themselves to host programs. Worms are particular to networks, spreading to other machines on any network you are connected to and carrying out preprogrammed attacks on the computers. Trojan horses, like their namesake, introduce malicious code under the guise of a useful program. Another form of malware is an attack script that is specifically written, usually by expert programmers, to exploit the Internet. Another threat is posed by Java applets that hide in Web pages. They are launched when the user's browser visits that site.

For more detailed information on combating viruses, worms, Trojan horses, and other types of malicious programs, see the Computing Keynote section "Computer Viruses," which follows this chapter.

Cybercrime

Norton ONLINE

For more information on cybercrime, visit **http://www.mhhe.com/peternorton**.

Computer crime is aimed at stealing the computer, damaging information, or stealing information. Computer crime is not necessarily technical in origin. Most criminal acts against computers do not directly involve technology. In fact, 72 percent of the computer crimes reported to the FBI in 2003 involved simple hardware theft.

The use of a computer to carry out any conventional criminal act, such as fraud, is called cybercrime and is a growing menace. Cybercrime is growing so rapidly, in fact, that the federal government has created a handful of agencies to deal with computer-related crimes (see Figure 14A.14). Instances of Internet fraud increased in 2002 as compared to 2001. In that year alone, federal officials arrested 135 cybercriminals and seized over $17 million in assets. Criminal actions included setting up fraudulent bank Web sites to steal account information from unsuspecting customers, auction fraud, and nondelivery of merchandise. Credit and debit card fraud were significant in 2002. The losses reported by the victims totaled $54 million, versus $17 million the year before, and complaints referred to law enforcement totaled 48,252, compared to 16,755 in 2001.

Hacking

Hacking remains the most common form of cybercrime, and it continues to grow in popularity. A hacker is someone who uses a computer and network or Internet connection to intrude into another computer or system to perform an illegal act (see Figure 14A.15). This may amount to simple trespassing or acts that corrupt, destroy, or change data.

In another form, hacking can be the basis for a distributed denial of service (DDOS) attack, in which a hacker hides malicious code on the PCs of many unsuspecting victims. This code may enable the hacker to take over the infected PCs, or simply use them to send requests to a Web server. If the hacker controls enough PCs, and can get them to send enough requests to the targeted Web server, the server essentially becomes jammed with requests and stops functioning. Successful DDOS attacks can cost targeted companies millions of dollars. The extent of the problem is not known simply because it is so widespread. PricewaterhouseCoopers estimates that viruses and hacking alone cost the world economy upwards of $1.6 trillion in 2003.

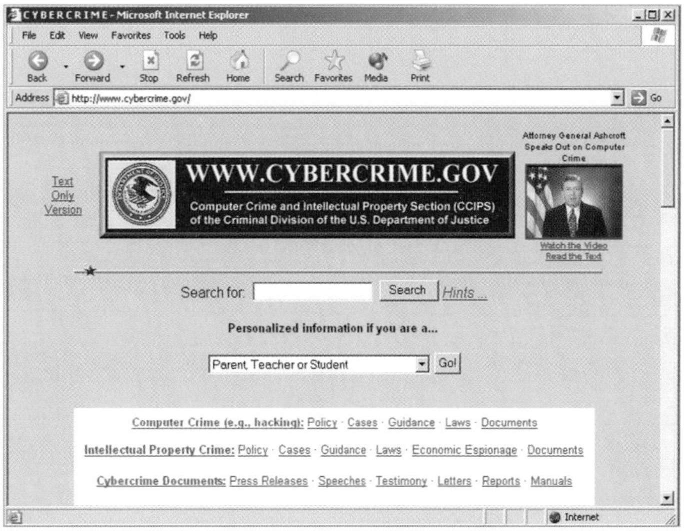

FIGURE 14A.14

The federal government tracks computer crime in all its forms. You can learn more about cybercrime and the government's responses to it at Web sites like this one.

At one time, a hacker was just a person who understood computers well; however, hacking now refers to criminal or antisocial activity. Today, hackers' activities are usually categorized by their intent:

- Recreation attacks.
- Business or financial attacks.
- Intelligence attacks.
- Grudge and military attacks.
- Terrorist attacks.

FIGURE 14A.15

Hackers are commonly thought of as young, antisocial people who prefer to stay in the shadows. This is not necessarily true, however. There is a large, thriving network of hackers around the world, some of whom operate in the open.

Other than posing an invasion of privacy, recreational hacking is relatively harmless. In most cases, recreational hackers just attempt to prove their abilities without doing any damage. In business, financial, or intelligence attacks, however, hackers often engage in data diddling—forging or changing records for personal gain, or attempting to copy the data from the penetrated system. Grudge attacks are carried out by hackers with a grievance against an individual or organization, and such attacks are frequently destructive. The harm from terrorist attacks could be catastrophic. The industrial world is highly dependent on its computers and there is evidence that this type of attack may be the tool of future war.

Norton ONLINE

For more information on hacking and hacking methods, visit **http://www.mhhe.com/peternorton**.

Common Hacking Methods

Hackers use a variety of methods to break into computer systems. These methods fall into three broad categories:

- **Sniffing.** The term sniffing refers to finding a user's password. There are three ways to sniff a password: password sharing, password guessing, and password capture. Password sharing is the most common and occurs when a victim simply discloses his or her password to a hacker. Passwords are shared out of simple ignorance, when victims do not realize that the password might be used against their wishes or in ways they would never intend. Password guessing is done exactly as the term implies: a hacker tries to guess a user's password and keeps trying until he or she gets it right. Users can safeguard against password guessing by using complex passwords. Network

At Issue

Software Piracy

One of the biggest legal issues facing the computer industry is software piracy, which is the illegal copying of computer software. Each year, software companies lose billions of dollars in sales because of piracy, as people illegally copy and use programs instead of paying for them.

Piracy is such a big problem because it is so easy to do. In most cases, it is no more difficult to steal a program than it is to copy a music CD. Software pirates give up the right to receive upgrades and technical support, but they gain the use of the program without paying for it.

You learned about the different ways to acquire software in Chapter 8, "Working with Application Software," and that nearly all software programs come with a license agreement of some sort that defines how the software can be used. Most licenses—especially for commercial programs—place restrictions on copying the program, and many forbid the user to make any copies at all.

Software pirates, however, pay no attention to such restrictions. The vast majority of pirates are actually casual computer users who copy a program as a favor to a friend or family member. These pirates may not even be aware that what they are doing is illegal. At the other end of the spectrum, professional pirates make hundreds or thousands of copies of expensive programs and sell them or distribute them freely over the Internet.

Since licensing agreements don't stop pirates, software developers take other approaches to copy protection. (Copy protection is a device, program, or agreement that attempts to prevent users from illegally copying a program.) A few developers who sell very expensive, special-purpose software require the user to install a device called a hardware lock before installing the program. Such programs won't run if the lock isn't present. Since each lock is uniquely matched to the software, a pirated copy of the program won't run on an unlocked computer.

More commonly, developers require the user to enter a password, a serial number, or some other code when installing the program. Most developers print a code on the

administrators can prevent guessing by limiting the number of attempts anyone can make to log into the network. In password capture, a password is obtained by some type of malware program and forwarded to the hacker. Passwords may be captured electronically if they are sent as text that is not encrypted. For example, during a login session, a hacker may intercept the password data when it is sent to a server even if it is encrypted within the system itself.

- **Social Engineering.** Social engineering used to be called "running a confidence game." The hacker may use any number of frauds to "con" victims out of their passwords. It might be as simple as dumpster diving. Just as in identity theft, a password thief searches the victim's trash in order to find useful access information. Another form of social engineering is the "phone survey," the "application," and the "emergency situation." In these situations, a hacker may contact potential victims by phone or e-mail, and ask the victims to provide password information for an apparently legitimate reason (see Figure 14A.16). This method is sometimes referred to as phishing.
- **Spoofing.** Hackers may alter an e-mail header to make it appear that a request for information originated from another address. This is called spoofing. They can gain electronic entry by pretending to be at a legitimate computer, which is called IP spoofing. Using this technique, the hacker intercepts a message or gains access to the system by posing as an authorized user. On a network, this is done by altering the message information to make it appear that it originated from a trusted computer.

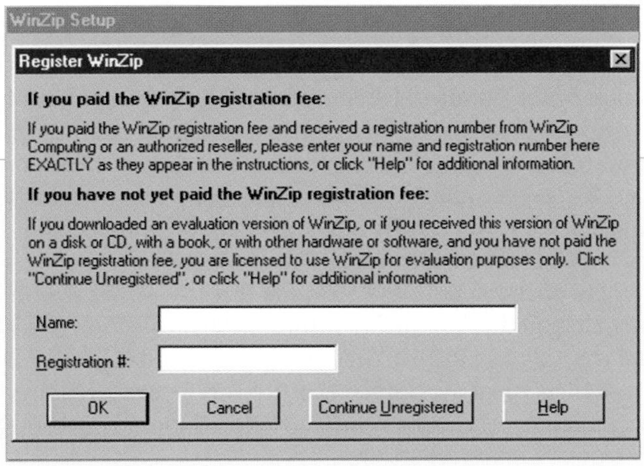

Many programs require you to provide a password, special code, or serial number during installation.

program's packaging. Anyone who does not have code may not be able to install the software. Some programs can be installed without the code but they may have some features crippled or may "nag" the user to register the software or provide the code when the program runs.

No antipiracy scheme, however, is foolproof. Sophisticated pirates have found ways to defeat hardware locks, and it's easy to copy an installation code onto a CD case when you copy the CD itself.

With the release of Windows XP and Office XP, Microsoft began a new approach to copy protection: product activation. When you use Windows or Office XP (or Office 2003) for the first time, you are prompted to "activate" it. During the activation process, the software contacts Microsoft via your Internet connection. The Microsoft server checks its records to determine whether anyone else activated your specific copy of the program. If not, the program becomes active and you can use it freely. If not, you need to contact the company and explain yourself. The program will run for only 30 days without being activated; after that, it locks up.

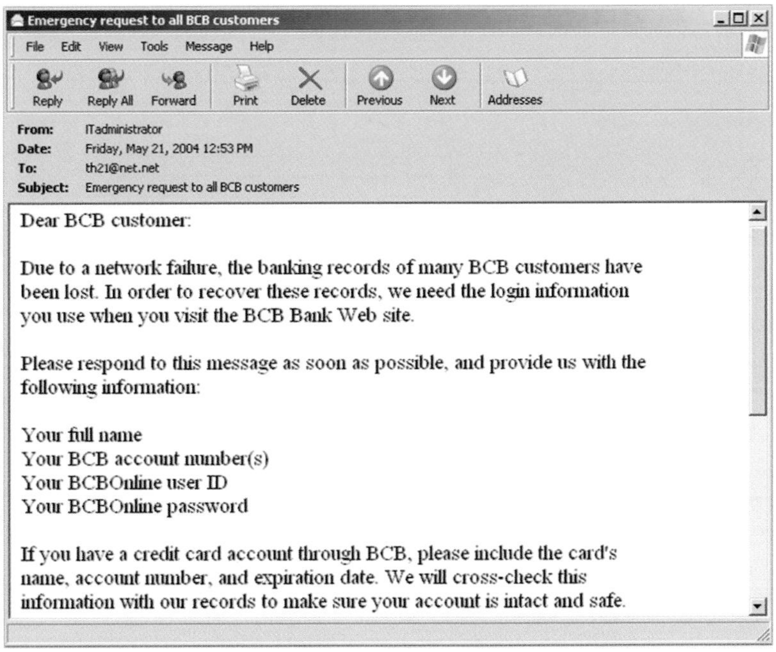

FIGURE 14A.16

If you ever receive a "phish" message from a password thief, it might contain a request like this one.

Norton ONLINE

For more information on cyberterrorism, visit **http://www.mhhe.com/peternorton**.

Cyberterrorism

Cyberwarfare and cyberterrorism are new forms of warfare; they attack the critical information infrastructure of the nation. The conventional goal in the case of **cyberterrorism** is to harm or control key computer systems, or digital controls. It is done to accomplish an indirect aim such as to disrupt a power grid or telecommunications. Typical targets are power plants, nuclear facilities, water treatment plants, and government agencies. However, any site with network-based monitoring and control systems is vulnerable if it is hooked to the Internet.

Cyberterrorism is not a new phenomenon. In 1996, the threat was so credible that the federal government created the Critical Information Protection Task Force, which later became the Critical Infrastructure Protection Board (CIPB). The Information Security Management Act of 2002 set basic security requirements for all government systems; at the same time, the White House issued the first coherent national strategy to secure cyberspace.

This strategy provides an overall direction for the effort to combat cyberterrorism. Solutions need to be formulated by individual businesses and the federal and state agencies designated to deal with this problem. There are many state and federal agencies devoted to developing effective responses to cyberterrorism. In 2002, coordination of this effort became the responsibility of the Department of Homeland Security (DHS) with a budget of more than $2.6 billion for cyberterrorism in 2003. Other effective responses include government-sponsored clearinghouses such as the Computer Emergency Response Team (CERT) Coordination Center (http://www.cert.org) at Carnegie Mellon University and the National Information Assurance Training and Education Center (http://niatec.info) at Idaho State University. These agencies provide essential information and guidance for practitioners and educators (see Figure 14A.17).

FIGURE 14A.17

The CERT Web site and others like it are excellent sources of information on cyberterrorism, viruses, and other technological threats.

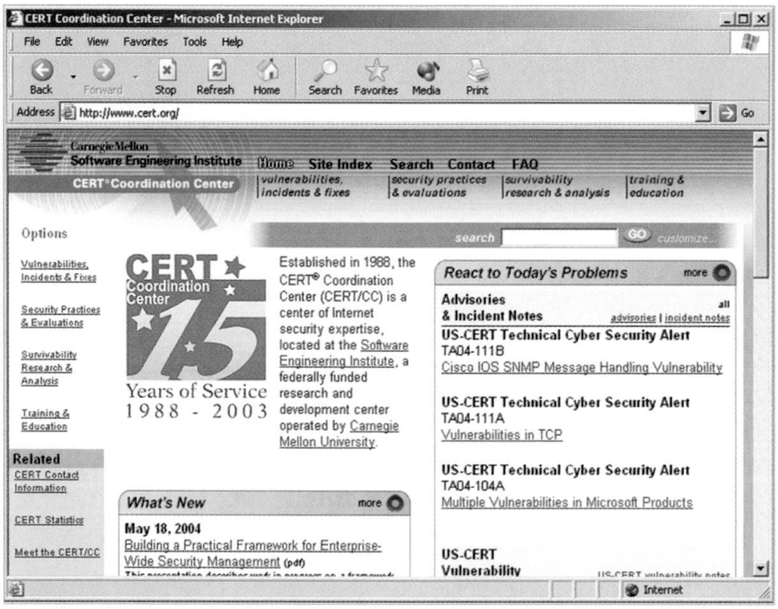

Summary ::

- The goal of computer security is to eliminate or protect against threats. A threat is anything that can cause harm.
- A countermeasure is any step taken to ward off a threat. Countermeasures are meant to protect data and systems from damage.
- Computer use poses several kinds of threats to users. These include the risk of identity theft, the loss of privacy, the exposure to spam, and even physical injuries.
- In identity theft, an ID thief impersonates someone else by using the victim's name and personal information. A successful ID thief can obtain documents and conduct business transactions in the victim's name.
- Many companies monitor the activities of consumers each day and compile this information for various reasons. The growing amount of personal data that is sold and traded among companies—and which is available for individuals to access—raises concerns about the loss of personal privacy.
- Spam is unwanted, or "junk," e-mail messages. Spam messages are usually commercial in nature and may arrive by the dozens or hundreds in a person's inbox. There are a variety of steps you can take to avoid receiving spam.
- Computer hardware is vulnerable to physical harm from power-related problems, theft, vandalism, and natural disasters. Users can take precautions against some hardware threats, and should plan for others.
- Data may be the most valuable part of a computer system, so it faces many unique threats. These include loss due to malware, viruses, and other malicious programs, as well as hackers, cybercrime, and cyberterrorism.
- Cybercrime is any criminal act that is carried out via a computer. Cybercrime is a growing problem.
- Hacking is a form of cybercrime. A hacker uses a computer and network connection to gain access to other computer systems. Hackers infiltrate systems for many different reasons.
- Cyberterrorism is a form of warfare in which terrorists attempt to harm or gain control of important computer systems, such as the systems that run electrical or communications systems.

LESSON // 14A Review

Key Terms ::

adware, 542
cookie, 541
countermeasure, 538
cybercrime, 548
cyberterrorism, 552
data diddling, 549
distributed denial of service (DDOS) attack, 549
dumpster diving, 539
hacker, 549
hacking, 549
identity (ID) theft, 539
IP spoofing, 550
line conditioner, 545
line noise, 545
malware, 548
password capture, 550
password guessing, 549
password sharing, 549
phishing, 550
power failure, 545
power fluctuation, 545
public record, 541
shoulder surfing, 539
snagging, 539
sniffing, 549
social engineering, 540
spam, 543
spammer, 543
spoofing, 544
spyware, 542
surge suppressor, 545
threat, 538
uninterruptible power supply (UPS), 545
unsolicited commercial e-mail (UCE), 543
vulnerability, 538
Web bug, 542

Key Term Quiz ::

Complete each statement by writing one of the terms from the Key Terms list in each blank.

1. A(n) ________ is a weakness—anything that has not been protected against threats, making it open to harm.
2. ________ occurs when someone impersonates you by using your name, Social Security number, or other personal information.
3. A low-tech ID thief might resort to ________ , searching for personal information in garbage cans.
4. In ________ , an ID thief tricks victims into providing critical information under the pretext of something legitimate.
5. If a legal record is available to anyone who wants to see it, the record is said to be a(n) ________ .
6. The correct term for spam is ________ .
7. In ________ , the sender of an e-mail message tries to convince the recipient that the message is from someone else.
8. A special device, called a(n) ________ , protects equipment from line noise.
9. The term ________ describes viruses, worms, Trojan horses, and attack scripts.
10. The use of a computer to carry out any conventional criminal act, such as fraud, is called ________ .

Multiple Choice ::

Circle the word or phrase that best completes each sentence.

1. Burglars, viruses, and earthquakes are all examples of ________ because they can harm a computer or its data.
   a. countermeasures b. threats c. vulnerabilities d. cybercrimes
2. It's important to realize that threats, and the harm they can cause, are a matter of ________ .
   a. degree b. trust c. time d. fact
3. If you regularly back up your data, this is a ________ against the threat of data loss.
   a. firewall b. class c. security d. countermeasure
4. In the right setting, a thief can try ________ information by listening in while the victim gives credit card or other personal information to a legitimate agent.
   a. sniffing b. spoofing c. snagging d. slipping
5. Because of the attention paid to the protection of ________ , social engineering and low-tech swindles are the predominant sources of identity theft.
   a. garbage b. transmitted data c. personal information d. hackers
6. Anytime you use a "store loyalty" card to rent movies or buy groceries, the purchases are logged in a ________ .
   a. spam b. transaction c. directory d. database
7. The use of data about your Web-surfing habits is called ________ .
   a. online profiling b. IP profiling c. user profiling d. surfer profiling
8. A ________ is a small text file that a Web server can place on your computer.
   a. cupcake b. cookie c. brownie d. twinkie
9. A ________ protects your computer system against voltage spikes.
   a. plug b. line drive c. battery backup d. surge suppressor
10. A ________ is someone who uses a computer and a network or Internet connection to intrude into another computer or system to perform an illegal act.
    a. hacker b. programmer c. terrorist d. spammer

LESSON // 14A Review

Review Questions ::

In your own words, briefly answer the following questions.

1. By itself, is a threat harmful?
2. Are all threats, and the damage they can cause, equal?
3. Describe the two classes of countermeasures.
4. List five methods that identity thieves can use to obtain the personal information they need to impersonate someone.
5. What is spyware?
6. What is the purpose of data mining?
7. What is a Web bug?
8. List three methods spammers use to get e-mail addresses.
9. What are three categories of disasters that can strike your home or workplace?
10. What is a distributed denial of service attack?

Lesson Labs ::

Complete the following exercises as directed by your instructor.

1. Open your e-mail program and look at your Inbox. Does it contain any messages that you would describe as spam? If so, review the messages. What, if anything, do the messages have in common? For example, do the subject lines honestly represent the messages' contents? Do the messages appear to have been sent from an actual person or from phony addresses? Are the messages commercial in nature? Are any obscene? Do any contain pictures? Do any contain links to Web sites? Do any contain an "opt-out" link, which states that you can be removed from the source's mailing list? Compile your analysis in a one-page report and be prepared to deliver it to the class.
2. How much personal information do you give away? Do a self-survey to answer this question. In the past six months, have you given away any information about yourself? Think about purchases you've made online, over the phone, and in stores. You also may give out information when registering at a Web site, setting up an account, registering a product, or subscribing to a magazine. List all the personal information you've given out and estimate the number of times you have willingly released it.

LESSON // 14B

Taking Protective Measures

Overview: Keeping Your System Safe

In the preceding lesson, you learned about some of the many threats that can affect you, your privacy, your data, and your computer. Although these threats range from mild to severe, you need to take each of them seriously. This means evaluating the chance that each one might strike you, prioritizing likely threats by severity, and taking the appropriate precautions.

In this lesson, you will learn about specific steps you can take to secure your computer system and your data from a variety of threats. You might be surprised to learn that computer security is not primarily a technical issue, and is not necessarily expensive. For the most part, keeping your system and data secure is a matter of common sense. By mastering a few basic principles and some easy-to-use software programs, you can virtually guarantee the safety of your hardware, software, data, and privacy.

OBJECTIVES ::

- List three ways you can protect your identity from theft.
- Name two precautions you can take to guard your personal information.
- Identify seven federal laws designed to protect an individual's privacy and personal information.
- Describe methods for managing spyware and cookies on your computer.
- List three steps you can take to avoid spam.
- Explain the purpose of a firewall and why you may need one.
- Describe four ways to protect hardware and storage media.

Protecting Yourself

The only part of your computer system that needs protection more than your data is you. Remember that if an identity thief strikes or a malicious Webmaster gets hold of your personal information, your computer will keep right on working, but other aspects of your life will be affected.

The following sections revisit some of the threats that computer users face and tell you how to prevent them from becoming a reality.

Avoiding Identity Theft

Victims of identity theft stand to lose large sums of money, suffer damage to their credit and reputation, and can possibly even lose possessions if the situation is not handled properly. It's important to remember that even if you don't make transactions yourself, you may still be held responsible for them unless you take action quickly.

Recall that ID thieves mainly use nontechnical methods to get the information they need to impersonate someone. Likewise, most of the precautions you can take against ID theft are "low-tech." Further, they all are matters of common sense; you should do these things anyway, even if ID theft were not even possible.

Norton ONLINE

For more information on avoiding ID theft, visit **http://www.mhhe.com/peternorton**.

Managing Your Papers

From the moment they enter your mailbox until they reach the landfill, many of your most valuable documents are vulnerable. These include account statements, financial records, bills, credit card applications, and other documents that you receive and handle every week. By handling them wisely, you can keep them out of the hands of an ID thief:

- **Guard Your Mail.** Pick up your mail as soon as possible after it arrives. Never allow mail to sit for a long time in your mailbox. If ID theft is a problem in your area, get a P.O. box and have sensitive documents delivered there. Also, put important outgoing mail in a public mailbox or take it to the post office, where no one can steal it.
- **Check Your Statements Immediately.** Open and check your bank and credit card statements as soon as you get them. Look for suspicious charges, ATM transactions, or checks you did not write; if you find one, report it immediately. The sooner you report suspicious activity, the greater the chance that the company will be able to help you. Some financial institutions place a time limit on reporting unauthorized transactions; after the time limit, your bank or credit card company may ask you to pay for the charge.
- **Discard Important Documents Wisely.** Some documents need to be kept on file for some time. For example, you should keep pay stubs and credit card statements for at least three years, in case you need them for tax purposes. But when you are ready to get rid of any important document, do it right. Shred any document that contains sensitive information such as your Social Security number, account numbers, or passwords (see Figure 14B.1).

FIGURE 14B.1

Shredders are inexpensive and easy to use and render documents useless to an ID thief.

Guarding Personal Information

In the course of a normal week, you probably give away all sorts of information about yourself without even thinking about it. It pays to be careful when sharing personal information, to make sure it doesn't fall into the wrong hands:

- Never give anyone an account number over the phone unless you are sure he or she is a legitimate agent. Remember, a bank or legitimate business will never call you and ask for an account number. They should already have this information; if they need it, they will notify you by mail.
- Never give out account numbers, passwords, or other personal information via e-mail. E-mail is not a secure way to transmit data. It can be intercepted, or the recipient can forward it to someone else. Banks and legitimate businesses won't ask you to provide such information via e-mail.
- When buying something online, make sure the Web site is secure before entering any personal information into a form. (For more information on secure online shopping, see Chapter 2, "Presenting the Internet.")

Looking at the Big Picture

You can take additional steps to protect your credit as well as your personal information:

- **Check your credit report at least once a year.** A credit report is a document that lists all your financial accounts that can be a source of credit or that you can use for making purchases or for other transactions. These include bank accounts, mortgages, credit cards, and others. Under certain circumstances, you may be entitled to get a free copy of your credit report one or more times a year. Even if you need to pay for a copy of your credit report, you should get one from each of the three major credit reporting bureaus (Equifax, Experian, and Trans Union) at least once each year. Check each report not just to learn your overall credit rating but to find and report any errors they may contain.
- **Maintain a good filing system.** Carefully file all important papers and keep them for at least three years. You may need them to dispute errors on a credit report or when reporting unauthorized activity to your credit card company or bank.
- **Check with your bank and credit card company.** Make sure you are protected against unauthorized charges (see Figure 14B.2). In most states, your liability is limited if someone else accesses your bank account or uses your credit card without your knowledge. But you may be required to report the incident quickly. Contact these agencies and ask what protections they offer against fraud and ID theft.

FIGURE 14B.2

This page, at the VISA Web site, explains the company's "zero liability" policy. Many credit cards carry similar protections, but you may be responsible for reporting unauthorized activity on your card.

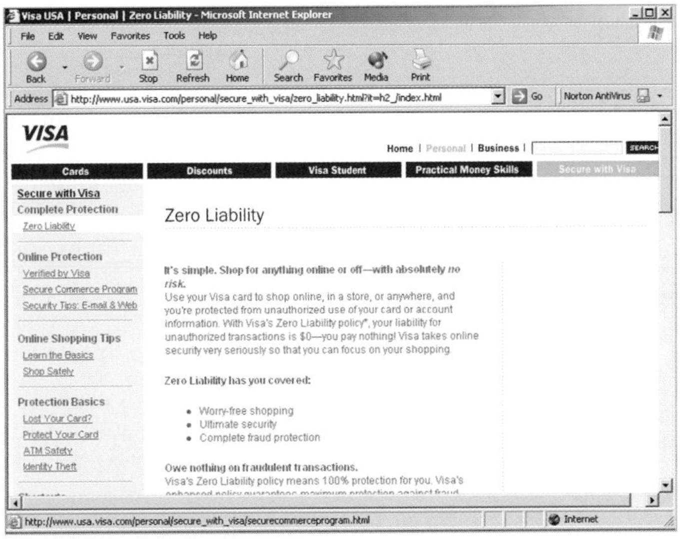

Protecting Your Privacy

If you take precautions to guard against ID theft, you'll be going a long way toward protecting your privacy in general, but there are a few other steps you should take to keep your private information out of the wrong hands.

Keeping Marketers at Bay

One of the main reasons for guarding your personal information is to avoid the attention of marketers,

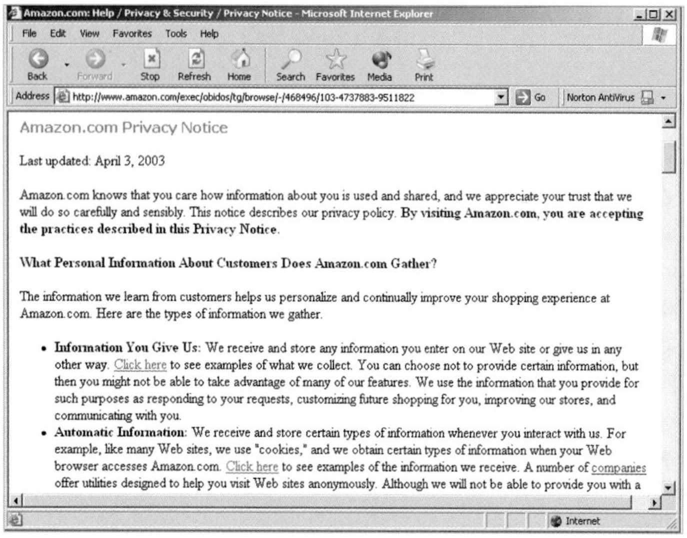
Amazon.com: Help / Privacy & Security / Privacy Notice - Microsoft Internet Explorer
File Edit View Favorites Tools Help
Back Forward Stop Refresh Home Search Favorites Media Print
Address http://www.amazon.com/exec/obidos/tg/browse/-/468496/103-4737883-9511822
Go
Norton AntiVirus
Amazon.com Privacy Notice
Last updated: April 3, 2003
Amazon.com knows that you care how information about you is used and shared, and we appreciate your trust that we will do so carefully and sensibly. This notice describes our privacy policy. By visiting Amazon.com, you are accepting the practices described in this Privacy Notice.
What Personal Information About Customers Does Amazon.com Gather?
The information we learn from customers helps us personalize and continually improve your shopping experience at Amazon.com. Here are the types of information we gather.
• Information You Give Us: We receive and store any information you enter on our Web site or give us in any other way. Click here to see examples of what we collect. You can choose not to provide certain information, but then you might not be able to take advantage of many of our features. We use the information that you provide for such purposes as responding to your requests, customizing future shopping for you, improving our stores, and communicating with you.
• Automatic Information: We receive and store certain types of information whenever you interact with us. For example, like many Web sites, we use "cookies," and we obtain certain types of information when your Web browser accesses Amazon.com. Click here to see examples of the information we receive. A number of companies offer utilities designed to help you visit Web sites anonymously. Although we will not be able to provide you with a
Internet

FIGURE 14B.3

The privacy notice at Amazon.com.

who want to know as much about you as possible so they can target marketing campaigns to people of your demographic status or interests. The following tips can help you keep them off your back:

- » **Be Wary about Filling Out Forms.** Whenever you fill out a form on a Web page, send in a subscription card for a magazine, or submit a warranty card for a product, you give out information about yourself. Some of these forms ask for much more than your name and address. As a general rule, don't submit such forms (either online or by mail) unless you have read the company's privacy policy (see Figure 14B.3). This policy will tell you how the company handles private information and what they will do with your information. Many companies provide an opt-out option on their registration or warranty forms. If you select this option, the company promises either not to share your information with anyone else or not to send you advertisements.
- » **Guard Your Primary E-Mail Address.** As you will read later in this lesson, you can avoid spam by having two e-mail addresses. Give your primary address only to people you trust and use the second address for everything else. The secondary address will receive most of the spam, leaving your main inbox relatively clean.

Norton ONLINE

For more information on laws that protect your privacy and personal information, visit **http://www.mhhe.com/peternorton**.

Knowing Your Rights

You can protect yourself further by knowing your legal rights (see Figure 14B.4). Consumers have the right to control access to their information. The control is based on a set of laws that have evolved over the past 40 years, including

- » In 1966, the Freedom of Information Act (5 U.S.C. § 552) allowed each individual to view and amend personal information kept about them by any governmental entity.
- » The Privacy Act of 1974 (5 U.S.C. § 552a) places universal restrictions on sharing of information about you by federal agencies without written consent.
- » The Fair Credit Reporting Act (1970) mandates that personal information assembled by credit reporting agencies must be accurate, fair, and private. It allows you to review and update your credit record as well as dispute the entries.
- » The Electronic Communications Privacy Act (1986) prevents unlawful access to voice communications by wire. It originally regulated electronic wiretaps and provided the basis for laws defining illegal access to electronic communications, including computer information. It is the basis for protection against unreasonable governmental intrusion into Internet usage, stored electronic communications, and e-mail.
- » The Right to Financial Privacy Act of 1978 and the Financial Modernization Act of 1999 (Gramm-Leach-Bliley) require companies to give consumers notice of their privacy and information-sharing practices.

In response to terrorist attacks on September 11, 2001, the federal government took actions aimed at modifying these protections. Specifically, the Uniting and Strengthening America by Providing Appropriate Tools Required to Intercept and Obstruct Terrorism Act was enacted. It is commonly known as the USA Patriot Act and extends the authority of law enforcement and intelligence agencies in monitoring private communications and access to your personal information.

Managing Cookies, Spyware, and Other "Bugs"

Unlike most of the countermeasures you have read about previously, high-tech methods are required to deal with threats such as cookies and spyware. Luckily, there are many options to choose from, including some that can find and eradicate just about any type of spyware that might find its way onto your system.

Dealing with Cookies

Most Web browsers feature built-in settings that give you some control over cookies (see Figure 14B.5). Internet Explorer, for example, gives you the option of refusing all cookies, accepting all cookies, or requiring notification before allowing a cookie onto your PC. If you actually use these tools, however, they can make browsing difficult. If you refuse all cookies, some Web sites simply won't function in your browser. If you set your browser to notify you before accepting a cookie, you can expect to see a notification (in the form of a pop-up message) every few seconds. This is because most Web sites use cookies in some manner.

Making things more difficult is the fact that there are multiple types of cookies, including the following:

- » **Session cookies** are temporary cookies that are automatically deleted when you close your browser (ending your browsing session). Session cookies can be essential for viewing some Web pages, and they generally are not used to store any type of personal information. Session cookies are also known as **transient cookies**.
- » **Persistent cookies** are stored on your computer's hard disk until they expire or you delete them. (Persistent cookies usually have expiration dates, at which time they are deleted.) Persistent cookies are used to store information about you or to remember settings you have made for a Web site you visit often. Persistent cookies are also called **stored cookies**.
- » **First-party cookies** come from the Web site you are currently viewing. First-party cookies are persistent and usually store preferences you have set for viewing the site. Some first-party cookies store information that can personally identify you.
- » **Third-party cookies** come from a different Web site than the one you are currently viewing. This is possible because some Web sites get content from other sites. Banner ads are an example. Third-party cookies are often used to track your browsing history for marketing purposes. These cookies are usually session cookies but can be persistent.

If you don't manage cookies, thousands can build up on your hard disk. Although persistent cookies are set to expire, their expiration date may be years away.

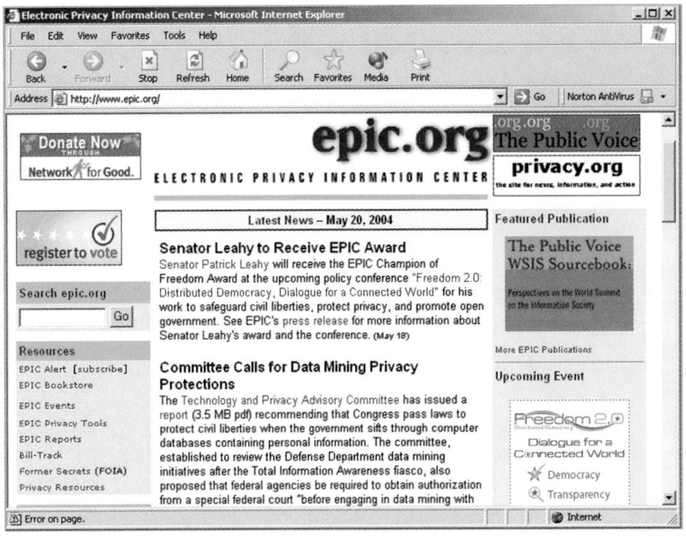

FIGURE 14B.4

You can learn more about the laws regarding public records by visiting Web sites such as the Electronic Privacy Information Center at http://www.epic.org.

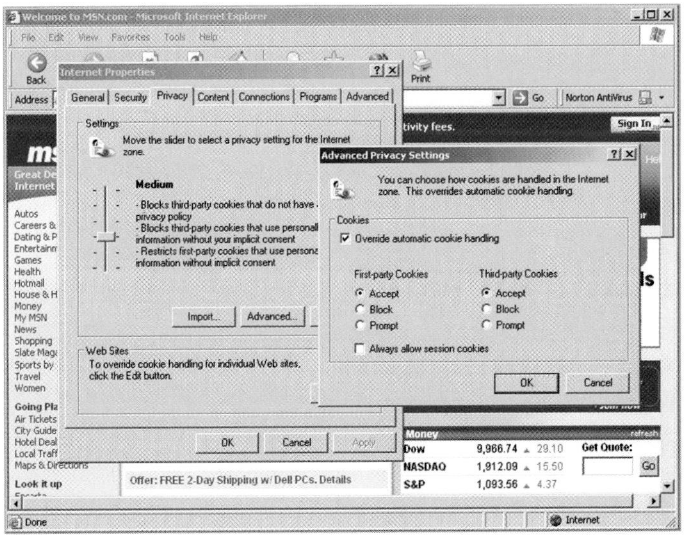

FIGURE 14B.5

Cookie-control settings in Microsoft Internet Explorer.

Norton ONLINE

For more information on cookie-management and anti-spyware utilities, visit **http://www.mhhe.com/peternorton**.

Further, you may decide you just don't want all these cookies on your system gathering information about you. There are two ways to manage cookies:

- **Manually Delete Them.** Your Web browser should have a tool that lets you erase cookies. Figure 14B.6 shows cookies being manually deleted in Internet Explorer.
- **Use Cookie Management Software.** A cookie-management utility can locate and delete all the cookies on your PC, either automatically or when you tell it to. Some utilities will let you decide which cookies to remove and which ones to keep. This is a good idea, because it lets you keep cookies for Web sites you trust while getting rid of the rest. Some programs, such as Cookie Crusher, focus primarily on handling cookies. More feature-filled programs such as Windows Washer can remove cookies and other types of files from your system, making it difficult for anyone to track your surfing habits.

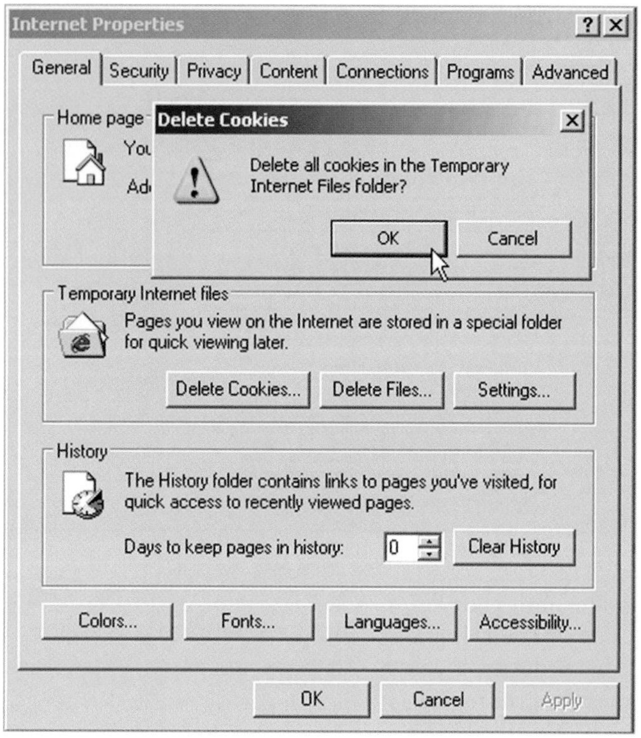

FIGURE 14B.6

Deleting cookies in Microsoft Internet Explorer.

Removing Web Bugs and Spyware

Most software developers classify Web bugs and spyware together. For this reason, most anti-spyware utilities (or anti-adware utilities, as they may be called) can detect both types of programs. The key to successfully dealing with these nuisances is to find an anti-spyware program you like, run it frequently, and keep it up-to-date according to the developer's directions. Popular anti-spyware programs include SpyGuard, NoAdware, and XoftSpy, but there are many others (see Figure 14B.7). Many antivirus programs can find and remove Web bugs and spyware in addition to viruses, worms, and other malicious files.

Another key to avoiding spyware is to be careful about downloading files and programs from the Internet. Shareware and freeware programs are popular sources of spyware, because many spyware developers pay other software developers to include spyware code in their programs.

Also, be sure to install a pop-up blocker on your PC (see Figure 14B.8). These small utilities prevent secondary browser windows (called pop-up windows, because they "pop up" on your screen) from appearing when you are on the Web. The majority of pop-ups are advertisements, many of which carry spyware.

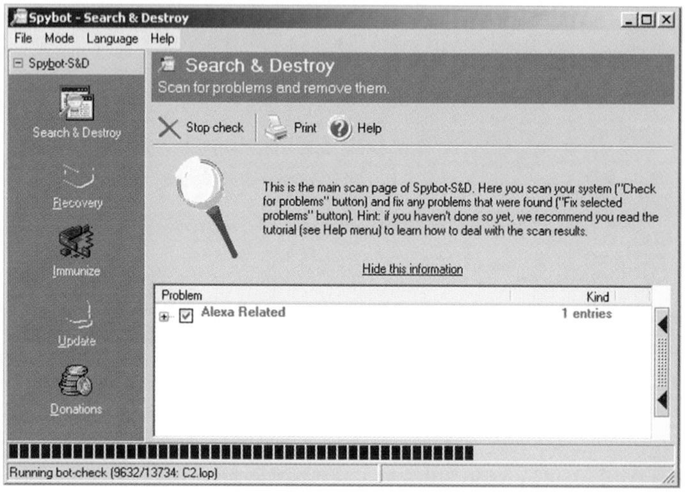

FIGURE 14B.7

Scanning for spyware with Spybot – Search & Destroy.

Evading Spam

You can take several countermeasures against spam, all of which are simple. First, if you receive a great deal of spam, contact your Internet service provider. Have a list of messages ready and be prepared to give your ISP information about the messages. Many ISPs have the ability to block messages from known spammers or messages that appear to be spam. Your ISP can tell you how to take advantage of these services, which are typically free.

As mentioned earlier, you should never give your primary e-mail address to any person or business you don't know. (Your primary e-mail account is the one you set up with your ISP as part of your Internet access package.) Instead, give that address only to people and businesses you trust, and ask them not to give it to anyone else. Then, set up a secondary e-mail account using a free, Web-based e-mail service such as Hotmail or Yahoo (see Figure 14B.9). Use this address when you must provide an e-mail address when making a purchase or registering for a service. The secondary address can collect the spam, while your primary address stays out of the hands of spammers.

You also can protect yourself by setting up filters in your e-mail program. A filter is a rule you establish that the program must follow when receiving mail. (For this reason, e-mail filters are sometimes called rules.) For example, you can tell the program to ignore messages from a specific sender or to automatically store certain messages in a specific folder. In Microsoft Outlook, filters are configured from the Tools menu (see Figure 14B.10).

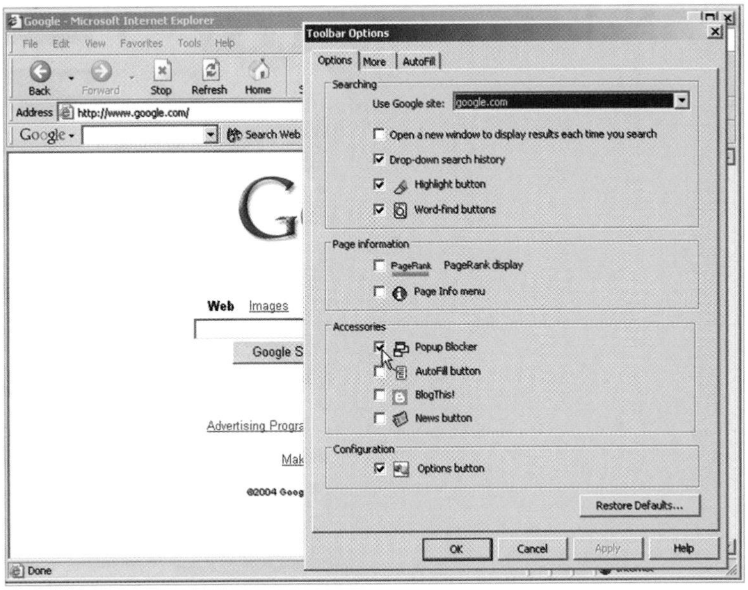

FIGURE 14B.8

Configuring the Google toolbar in Microsoft Internet Explorer. This toolbar, which you can download for free from the Google Web site (http://www.google.com), can block pop-up windows.

Protection that is more robust is provided by special programs called spam blockers. These programs monitor e-mail messages as you receive them, can block messages from known spammers, and can mark suspicious messages. Spam-blocking software is available from many reputable vendors, such as McAfee and Symantec.

Finally, never respond to a spam message, even if it includes a link that purports to "remove you" from the sender's address list. Most such "remove me" options are phony. If you respond, the spammer knows that your e-mail account is active and you are a good target.

To get onto the Internet equivalent of a "do not spam" list, you may choose to opt out of any kind of targeted advertising by going to http://www.networkadvertising.org (see Figure 14B.11). This site is operated by the Network Advertising Initiative (NAI) and it is that industry's voluntary response to the objections to secretive tracking and spamming of Internet users.

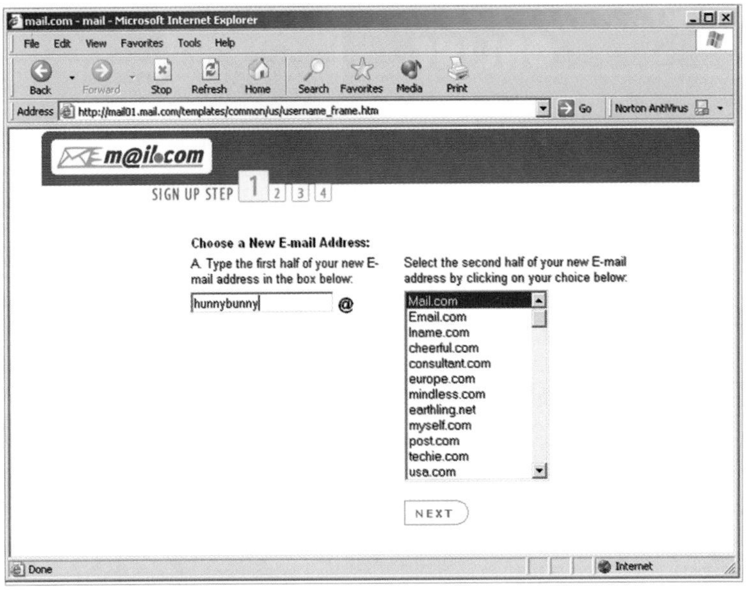

FIGURE 14B.9

Setting up a free e-mail account on the Mail.com Web site. There are dozens of free, Web-based e-mail services to choose from.

Keeping Your Data Secure

Threats to your data are numerous, but the most ominous threat comes from malware in its various forms: viruses, worms, Trojan horses, and others. Viruses, in fact, are such a significant problem that an entire Computing Keynote feature, "Computer Viruses," is devoted to them following this chapter. Refer to that feature for detailed information on viruses of all types and the best methods for dealing with them.

FIGURE 14B.10

Setting up an e-mail filter in Microsoft Outlook.

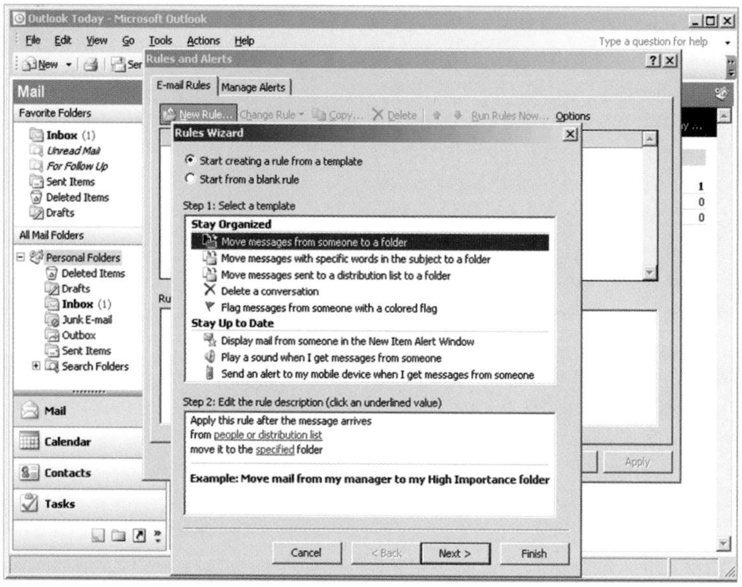

FIGURE 14B.11

The "opt out" page at the Network Advertising Initiative's Web site.

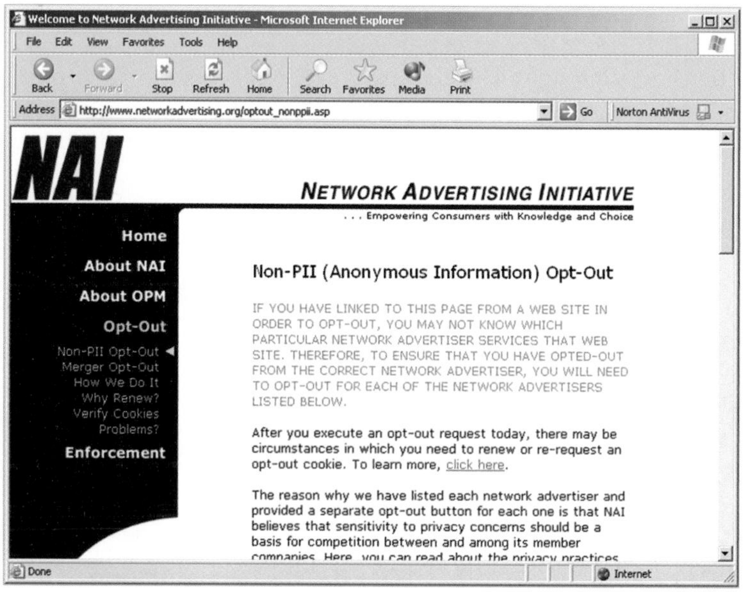

Norton ONLINE

For more information on avoiding spam, visit **http://www.mhhe.com/peternorton**.

The following sections discuss two important countermeasures you can take to protect your data from a variety of threats.

Restricting Access to Your System

Aside from viruses, disk failures, and natural disasters, the worst thing that can happen to your data is when someone else gains access to it. And it doesn't take a professional hacker to ruin all the data on your PC. A member of your own family can do it just as well, if unintentionally. This is why it's critical to restrict access to your system, to keep other people away from your data.

Limiting Physical Access

If other users have physical access to your PC, you still may be able to limit their ability to find your data. Most newer operating systems, such as Windows XP, allow users to set up "accounts" on a shared PC. In his or her account, each user can set up a unique set of preferences, such as the desktop's appearance, passwords, and more. Your operating system may allow you to hide folders and files, or make them private so that no one else can open them while using your computer.

Some applications can lock files so they can be opened only with a password (see Figure 14B.12). If others frequently use your computer, you may want to take advantage of these features. If your PC is part of a network, you can turn off sharing of entire disks or of individual files and folders. You also can encrypt data so no one else can use it via a network connection.

If other people have physical access to your computer, but you don't want them to use it, configure your operating system to require a password when starting up. As an extra precaution, set up a password-protected screen saver. (A screen saver is a blank screen or a moving image that appears on the screen after the computer has gone unused for several minutes.) Configure the screen saver to ask for a password before going off; this way, no one will be able to use your system if you leave it running.

For specific instructions on configuring these privacy tools, refer to the help system or documentation for your operating system and applications.

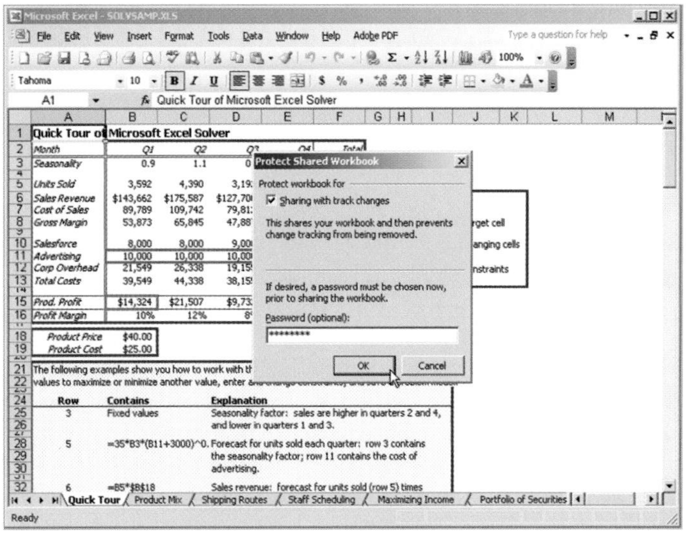

FIGURE 14B.12

Protecting a document in Microsoft Excel. The document cannot be edited unless the user provides a password.

Using a Firewall

You have seen the term *firewall* used several times already in this book. That's because firewalls have become an essential part of any network that is connected to the Internet. A firewall's main purpose is to prohibit unauthorized access to your computer via the Internet.

A functioning firewall is your best defense against hackers or anyone else who might try to reach your PC via the Internet. There are various kinds of firewalls—both hardware and software—and they can use different methods to keep intruders away from your system. Many firewalls work, for example, by effectively "hiding" your computer from other computers on the Internet. The only computers that can find your computer are the ones with which you have initiated communications.

If your PC connects to the Internet through an always-on connection—that is, a connection that is always active, such as a cable modem or DSL connection—then you should use a firewall. Without one, your computer is virtually unprotected from intruders, who can easily find your system and break into it.

If you do not yet have a firewall, you should get one. Many network hubs and hub/router units have firewalls built in and can be purchased for as little as $50 (see Figure 14B.13). Hardware firewalls are easy to use, especially those designed for home and small network use. Just connect it and you're done.

If you prefer a software firewall, there are plenty to choose from. In fact, Windows XP has a basic firewall built in that you can activate in less than a minute (see Figure 14B.14). For more sophisticated protection, you can purchase a full-featured firewall program such as ZoneAlarm, BlackICE PC Protection, or Norton Personal Firewall.

Norton ONLINE

For more information on personal firewalls, visit **http://www.mhhe.com/peternorton**.

FIGURE 14B.13

Many routers, such as this one by Linksys, feature built-in firewalls.

Backing Up Data

You never know when or how data may be lost. A simple disk error can do just as much damage as a hacker might do. And even the most experienced computer user occasionally deletes a file or folder by accident. When such events happen, you'll be in the clear if you keep your data backed up (see Figure 14B.15).

Norton Notebook

Nexus: Converging Technologies

I was recently asked what word I would select if I had to use only one to describe the entire phenomena of the personal computer. These "sound bite" moments tend to be more annoying than they are edifying, but then it occurred to me: Convergence. If there's one thing that personal computing has been "about" for the roughly half-century of its existence, convergence is that thing. That fact makes the personal computer a tool unique in human history—and not just because no one had seen a dancing hamster previously. Even if we didn't recognize it consciously early in the process, every development, every improvement to the PC and its related technologies has been about bringing everything together. What do I mean by "everything"?

Everything.

Let's start with the PC itself. You've already seen how the very notion of developing a personal computer was an act of divergence. Before PCs came on the scene, bank central computers did finance, Wang and IBM word processing machines created letters and other documents, and mainframes at MIT did whatever it was that MIT was doing at the time. The very first personal computers brought separate functions together in a single multipurpose unit. (And we've already talked about how, today, your personal computer can contribute to the work going on at MIT and other institutions.) As the PC developed, it gained the capability to work with music, then graphical images, then digital sound and digital video. Today's media-centered PCs are the nexus of almost everything we do or enjoy, creatively speaking. When marketing, technology, and economy all come together to put $100,000 worth of dedicated digital video power into a desktop PC that can still do all those other things we do, how could it be otherwise?

As we humans have embraced the PC, it, in turn, has gathered us to it. While there certainly are valid socioeconomic arguments that computing is anything but ubiquitous—in the broadest sense of that word—it remains true that some significant number of humans have found themselves enabled by the presence of the PC. Our world has today the potential—if nothing more—to be a smaller place, if we choose for it to be so. In the very long run, the specific choices we make collectively about how computing will, or won't, bring us together as a species may be less important than the ways that the simple presence of those options changes us.

On the most personal scale, the PC has crushed economic barriers, eliminating something as simple yet pervasive as long-distance telephone charges, helping more families stay in regular contact. Those for whom a daily newspaper might be a luxury—or an impossibility—can use public access PCs in schools and libraries to stay abreast of news and look for opportunities to improve their own lives. Perhaps even more than the free public libraries themselves, it is the PC that is our point of connection to history, to new ideas and disparate cultures.

For almost every person in the industrialized parts of the world, our very lives are converging on personal computing. Financial records have moved from the file folder to the hard disk folder. Communication has transitioned from telephone to microphone and from postage stamps to—somewhat ironically, perhaps—telephone (or network cable). Crayons and

FIGURE 14B.14

Activating the firewall in Windows XP Professional.

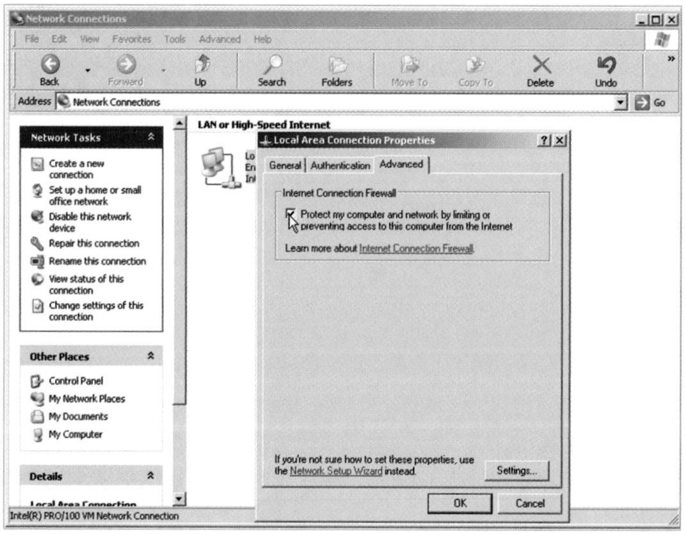

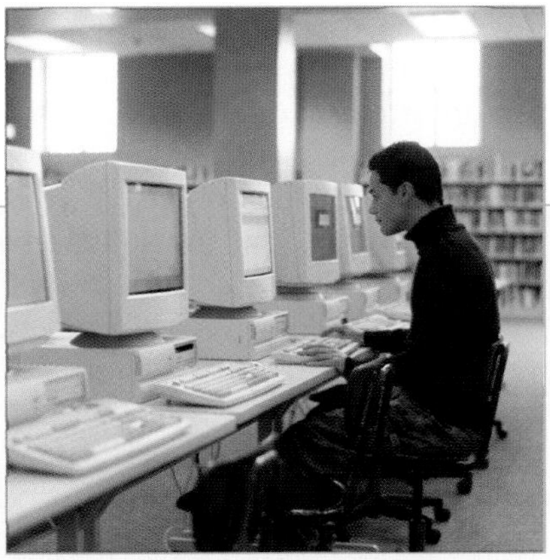

Personalizing a portal on the MSN Web site

paint have been joined by keyboard, tablet, and mouse. Even "little black books" are now password-protected PDAs and contact lists. However far you see your future career as being from the world of "computer science," you will unquestionably find computers in your world. You may be ordering parts, billing a customer, checking shelf stock, arguing over a commission, researching medications, reviewing lesson plans, or colonizing Mars, but the computer will never be far away.

Even aspects of our lives that have never had anything to do with spreadsheets and databases are congregating around the PC. Consider property. I don't mean real estate; I mean personal property—your stuff. I can assure you, when I was a child, no one—not even record companies—gave much thought to the somewhat surreal question "After a customer buys our vinyl record, who owns it?" On the mere face of it, that question would have been ridiculous. You bought it—you owned it. But did you? New questions about intellectual property abound: Who owns a CD that you buy? What do we really mean by "owns," and is it possible to own the physical CD without owning the music on it, even though that music is the CD's only purpose for being? More broadly, does having your home electronically connected to the world impact what freedoms you should have "in the privacy of your own home"? These will undoubtedly be some of the most important types of questions answered in the coming decades. They don't seem as ridiculous today. Why not? The PC is out there; that's why not. The PC and all of its related technologies have made it possible for the sale of a single CD to be shared by a limitless number of individuals who otherwise would have had to purchase it. DVD movies that are region-coded because of financial arrangements beneficial to the distributor can be viewed anywhere—and can be copied and shared simultaneously. Perfect digital copies cost about a buck for each blank disc.

You have already read how the PC industry tries to address these and similar converging issues of property, privacy, and ethics. Trusted Computing, DRM, proposed limitations to the PC's operating system and device drivers—all these are attempts to return the genie to the bottle. These problems and their possible solutions have driven scores of people such as civil liberties activists, academics, judges, religious leaders, and government officials toward the heretofore-foreign world of computing. Consequently, it is extremely important that people in these and related fields understand not only their own issues, but technology, too. You are already well on your way to becoming a technology-aware citizen. On behalf of the past, congratulations. On behalf of the future, thank you.

All roads once led to Rome. Today, they lead to a more metaphoric place—a place as big as the world but as nearby as that box under your desk.

NORTON NOTEBOOK

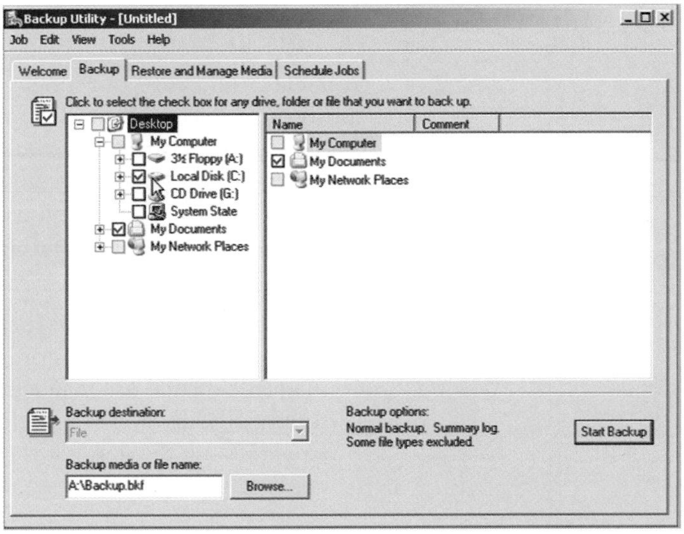

FIGURE 14B.15

Using the backup utility in Windows XP.

Norton **ONLINE**

For more information on backing up data, visit **http://www.mhhe.com/peternorton**.

SELF-CHECK ::

Circle the correct word or phrase that best completes each statement.

1. To avoid ID theft, you should __________ your mail as soon as it arrives.

   a. shred **b.** hide **c.** pick up

2. E-mail is not a __________ way to transmit data.

   a. secure **b.** legal **c.** practical

3. The __________ places restrictions on the sharing of information about you by federal agancies.

   a. Fair Credit Act **b.** Privacy Act of 1974 **c.** Freedom of Information Act

You can use a backup copy of your data to restore lost files to your PC. Backups are useful for lots of reasons. If you save changes to a file, then decide the changes should not have been made, you can return to the previous version of the file by using the backup. If you buy a new computer, having a complete backup makes it easy to move your data and programs.

For details on performing regular backups, see Chapter 6, "Storing Data."

Safeguarding Your Hardware

Hardware is actually easy to secure. As mentioned already, you can limit physical access to your computer system. If necessary, you can even anchor it to a desk, making it difficult to steal.

But even if theft is unlikely, there are still steps you should take to keep your PC hardware safe and functioning. These are countermeasures against hardware failures that not only can be costly, but can result in lost data.

Using Automated Warnings

Some operating systems, such as Windows XP Professional, create an information log that lists important or unusual events that occur within the system. In Windows XP, this tool is called the Event Viewer. You can use the event viewer to see events relating to your system's applications, security, and hardware devices.

Windows' Event Viewer automatically generates information, error, and warning messages. You need to use the Event Viewer to see them (see Figure 14B.16). You also can use the Event Viewer to configure your own warnings, although that probably is not necessary. Still, it is a good idea to review the logs' contents occasionally, to see if any recurring events or warnings require attention. For this purpose, the Event Viewer can be very helpful to a technician if your computer needs repair.

FIGURE 14B.16

Viewing a message about a system error, in the Windows XP Event Viewer.

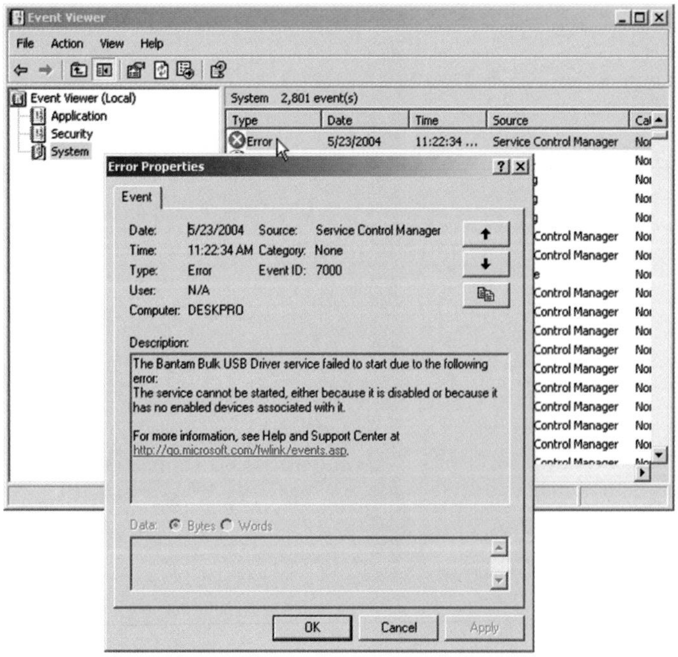

Handling Storage Media

You may think of your floppy disks and CDs as sturdy little objects. After all, they have your data encased in hard plastic. But storage media are a great deal more vulnerable than you might think. You should take precautions to protect your loose storage media (and the data they hold) from

» **Magnetism.** Floppy disks should always be kept away from sources of magnetism. Remember, floppy disks (as well as storage tapes and other magnetic media) are magnetically sensitive. A floppy disk drive uses tiny electromagnets to store data on the disk's surface. If the disk is exposed to another magnet, degaussing can occur. Degaussing occurs when a magnetic medium is close enough to a magnetic source to erase its contents. Magnets are everywhere, and many electrical appliances generate magnetic fields. Loudspeakers, your computer's monitor, and fluorescent light fixtures are common examples.

- **Heat and Cold.** Never store disks where they can be exposed to extreme heat or cold. If you leave a disk in front of a window on a sunny day (or, worse, in a car), it may warm up enough to melt a little. Extreme cold can cause media to shrink or crack. In either case, the data may be lost or the disk may not be able to spin properly when you insert it in a drive. Storage media survive best and last longer if you store them in a dry place, at room temperature, and away from direct light (see Figure 14B.17).
- **Moisture.** Don't allow disks to get wet, especially floppy disks. You can dry a CD off with a clean towel, but that isn't possible with a floppy disk.
- **Dust, Dirt, and Fingerprints.** Dust and dirt can make it impossible for a disk drive to read data on the disk's surface. Even a small smudge or fingerprint can interfere with a disk's operation. Keep disks as clean as possible, and always handle them by the edges.

FIGURE 14B.17

Keep your disks in a storage unit designed to hold them, away from sources of heat and light.

Storing Computer Equipment

To reduce wear and tear on computer equipment and to protect it from possible theft and damage, it is important to store computer hardware properly:

- Never store your equipment near large electrical equipment, such as refrigerators or generators.
- Store your equipment in climate- and heat-controlled environments (see Figure 14B.18). Heat and humidity will deteriorate delicate boards and other delicate components. Like storage media, computers and other hardware components fare better in dry, room-temperature environments where dust and moisture are minimal.
- Determine whether natural hazards such as fire and flood might affect the storage area, then take appropriate actions.
- Ensure that the stored equipment is properly stacked. Don't store equipment in piles or stack computers on top of one another.

FIGURE 14B.18

If you need to store your computer equipment, it's best to put it back in the original boxes. Otherwise, be sure to cover it and store it off the floor to avoid water damage.

Keeping Your Computer Clean

Although it appears robust, the computer is a precision instrument and should be kept spotless. You should not place liquids on or near a computer or its media. In addition you should not eat or smoke while operating it. Even if you have not contaminated it with food or smoke, the computer requires regular cleaning using the commercial tools and products that are sold in most computer stores. Physical parts are subject to wear and tear; it is important to keep them clean and well maintained. A common cause of component failure is dust buildup, which affects everything from the mechanics of your drives to the integrity of your circuit

Computers In Your Career

Computer Scientist

Dr. Michael Young is not the average computer scientist. Sure, he's well versed in the ways of technology and excellent at problem solving, but he knows a really good video game when he sees one. That's why this assistant professor of computer science at North Carolina State University in Raleigh allocates 40 percent of his time to Liquid Narrative Group, a group of computer science students who are creating software tools that will improve the artificial intelligence (AI) of games and educational software.

Specifically, Dr. Young and his team are investigating ways that the software allows users to both interact with the narrative, or storyline, and feel like an active participant in the way the story unfolds. "We want to open games up so players have more of a role in how games unfold," says Dr. Young. "We're trying to build general software tools that can understand both what's going on in a game and what makes for an interesting game or a good story."

When Dr. Young isn't exploring new ways to improve the gaming experience, you can find him teaching in the classroom or laboratory, or handling project management and administrative tasks like proposal writing. He holds a PhD from the University of Pittsburgh in Intelligence Systems, a Masters degree from Stanford University in Computer Science, and a Bachelors in Computer Science from California State University Sacramento.

Dr. Young says future opportunities for computer scientists are "quite strong" because of how deeply embedded information technology has become in our everyday lives. In fact, he says making people's lives easier and/or better is the biggest reward of his job. In addition to academia, computer scientists like Dr. Young work in government and private industry as theorists, researchers, or inventors.

The higher level of theoretical expertise and innovation they apply to complex problems and the creation or application of new technology distinguishes computer scientists' jobs. Dr. Young advises students interested in the field to focus not only on core computer science concepts, but to

FIGURE 14B.19

Special tools such as "canned air" and a small vacuum can keep your PC clean.

boards and the reliability of the power supplies. Dust worsens heating problems by blanketing components and clogging vents. You should maintain the fans and filters that ventilate the inside of your CPU cabinet (see Figure 14B.19). If you do not feel capable of changing filters and "dusting" the internal components, you should schedule regular visits to commercial computer maintenance services.

educate themselves on specific industries where opportunities exist for computer scientists.

For example, scientists working for an automobile manufacturer need to have a good understanding of that specific business and its needs. This knowledge helps the scientist understand the business's problems and more intelligently create solutions to those problems. The same is true whether the scientist works for NASA, the Department of Defense, or a large university.

Computer scientists employed by academic institutions work in areas ranging from complexity theory, to hardware, to programming language design. Some work on multidisciplinary projects such as developing and advancing uses of virtual reality, in human-computer interaction, or in robotics. Their counterparts in private industry work in areas such as applying theory, developing specialized languages or information technologies, or designing programming tools, knowledge-based systems, or computer games.

According to the Bureau of Labor Statistics, median annual earnings of computer and information scientists, research, were $70,590 in 2000. The group expects demand for qualified computer scientists to grow in the future as people become more and more dependent on computer systems for their livelihood.

LESSON // 14B Review

Summary ::

- You can protect your privacy and avoid identity theft by handling important documents carefully—especially those that contain personal information such as your Social Security number or account numbers.
- Another important step to protecting your privacy is to be careful about giving out personal information. It is never a good idea, for example, to give out account numbers or passwords via e-mail. Do so over the phone only if you are sure you are dealing with a legitimate business.
- You should check your credit report once a year, to look for suspicious transactions and errors. The report can provide clues if someone else is making transactions in your name.
- A variety of laws exist to protect your personal information from being misused. By learning more about these laws, you can better safeguard your privacy.
- Your Web browser may provide tools for managing cookies, but a cookie-management utility will offer more options for identifying and removing unwanted cookies from your PC.
- Similarly, you can use special anti-spyware software to find and delete spyware from your system. Some antivirus programs also target spyware.
- To avoid receiving spam, avoid giving out your e-mail address. Otherwise, you can reduce spam by setting up a secondary e-mail account, using e-mail filters, and working with your ISP to block spam messages.
- To secure your data, you must keep other people away from it. This means limiting physical access to your computer so other people cannot get to your data. It also means using a firewall to prevent hackers from accessing your system via the Internet.
- Regular data backups are an effective countermeasure against threats to your data. Should any of your data become lost or damaged, you can restore it to you computer by using a backup copy.
- By protecting your hardware, you are also protecting your data and avoiding the expense of replacing your PC. Make sure others cannot get to your PC and damage or steal it.
- Take care when handling computer hardware and storage media, to avoid damaging them. If a disk becomes damaged, the data it stores may be lost.
- Another way to protect your PC hardware and data is by keeping the system clean and avoiding exposure to magnetism or extreme temperatures. Dust can also cause system components to fail, so it is important to keep your PC clean.

Key Terms ::

always-on connection, 565
anti-adware utility, 562
anti-spyware utility, 562
cookie-management utility, 562
credit report, 559
degaussing, 569
Electronic Communications Privacy Act, 560
Event Viewer, 568
Fair Credit Reporting Act, 560
filter, 563
Financial Modernization Act of 1999, 560
first-party cookie, 561
Freedom of Information Act, 560
opt-out option, 560
persistent cookie, 561
pop-up blocker, 562
pop-up window, 562
primary e-mail account, 563
Privacy Act of 1974, 560
restore, 568
Right to Financial Privacy Act of 1978, 560
rule, 563
screen saver, 565
secondary e-mail account, 563
session cookie, 561
spam blocker, 563
stored cookie, 561
third-party cookie, 561
transient cookie, 561
USA Patriot Act, 560

Key Term Quiz ::

Complete each statement by writing one of the terms from the Key Terms list in each blank.

1. A(n) ________ is a document that lists all your financial accounts that can be a source of credit or that you can use to make purchases or other transactions.
2. If you select the ________ on a company's Web page or warranty form, the company promises either not to share your information or not to send you advertisements.
3. The ________ Act of 1970 mandates that personal information assembled by credit reporting agencies must be accurate, fair, and private.
4. A(n) ________ cookie is temporary; it is automatically deleted when you close your browser.
5. A(n) ________ cookie comes from a different Web site than the one you are viewing.
6. A(n) ________ window is a secondary browser window that may contain an advertisement and carry spyware.
7. Your ________ e-mail account is the one you set up with your ISP as part of your Internet access package.
8. By creating a(n) ________ in your e-mail program, you can tell the program to ignore messages from a specific sender.
9. A(n) ________ is a blank screen or a moving image that appears on the screen after the computer has gone unused for several minutes.
10. You can use a backup copy of your data to ________ lost files to your PC.

Review

Multiple Choice ::

Circle the word or phrase that best completes each sentence.

1. From the moment they enter your mailbox until they reach the landfill, many of your most valuable documents are ________ .
   a. yours b. vulnerable c. missing d. shredded
2. Before discarding them, you should ________ any document that contains sensitive information such as your Social Security number, account numbers, or passwords.
   a. read b. hide c. throw away d. shred
3. A bank or legitimate business will never ask for your account number by ________ .
   a. law b. itself c. e-mail d. any means
4. You should check your ________ at least once a year.
   a. credit report b. e-mail filters c. shredder d. privacy laws
5. If a company asks you to complete a form on its Web site, you should first check the company's ________ .
   a. URL b. privacy policy c. security settings d. warranty
6. Most Web browsers feature built-in settings that give you some control over ________ .
   a. Web bugs b. cookies c. ads d. spyware
7. If the Web site you are viewing places a cookie on your system, the cookie is called a ________ cookie.
   a. session b. third-party c. first-party d. expired
8. A key to avoiding ________ is to be careful about downloading files and programs from the Internet.
   a. spam b. cookies c. spyware d. pop-ups
9. An e-mail program's filters also may be called ________ .
   a. spams b. blockers c. accounts d. rules
10. ________ occurs when magnetic media is close enough to a magnetic source to erase its contents.
    a. Desensitizing b. Demagnetizing c. Defragmenting d. Degaussing

Review Questions ::

In your own words, briefly answer the following questions.

1. Why should you tell your bank or credit card company about suspicious transactions or charges immediately?
2. List two methods you should not use to give out personal information such as an account number or a password.
3. How can you avoid spam by having two e-mail addresses?
4. Name two laws that require companies to give consumers notice of their privacy and information-sharing practices.
5. List four types of cookies that can be placed on your computer by a Web site.
6. What is the best way to deal with spyware and Web bugs?
7. What is a spam blocker?
8. How might your operating system help you protect the privacy of your files if you share your PC with other users?
9. When is it especially important to use a firewall?
10. Why is it important to protect storage media from dust, dirt, and fingerprints?

Lesson Labs ::

Complete the following exercise as directed by your instructor.

1. Check your cookie-management settings. To do this, launch your browser. If you use Internet Explorer, open the Tools menu, then click Internet Options. When the Internet Properties dialog box appears, click the Privacy tab, and then click the Advanced button. When the Advanced Privacy Settings dialog box appears, check the cookie-management settings. Close both dialog boxes by clicking Cancel.

   If you use Netscape Navigator, open the Edit menu, then click Preferences. When the Preferences dialog box appears, double-click the Privacy & Security category, then click Cookies. Check the settings that appear, and then close the dialog box by clicking Cancel.

   Do not change the settings unless your instructor directs you to do so.

Chapter Labs

Complete the following exercises using a computer in your classroom, lab, or home.

1. Learn more about pop-up blockers. Pop-up windows can make Web surfing a maddening experience. A good pop-up blocker can save you a lot of time and aggravation by preventing pop-up windows from appearing on your screen, while letting you decide if you want specific pop-ups to open.
   To learn more about pop-up blockers, visit your favorite search engine and conduct a search on the key words "pop-up blocker". Visit several sites and compare at least three programs. (Do not download or install any software without your instructor's consent.) Summarize the comparison in a one-page report, and be prepared to present your findings to the class.
2. Back up a folder. Use your operating system's Help system to find out if your OS has a built-in backup utility. If so, launch the utility and learn how it works. With your instructor's permission, use the program to back up at least one file or folder. You may be able to back up the data to a floppy disk, Zip disk, network drive, or recordable CD. Next, use the program's Help system to learn how to restore the backed-up data, in case it were accidentally deleted from the hard disk.
3. Learn more about CAN-SPAM. Go online and research the CAN-SPAM law, which took effect at the beginning of 2004. What measures does the law take to limit the amount of spam messages that consumers receive? What penalties does it assess spammers who violate the law? What recourse does the law give to consumers who continue to receive a lot of spam? Your instructor may ask you to focus on one aspect of the law, or to work with a group. Compile your findings into a one-page report, and be prepared to share it with the class.

Discussion Questions

As directed by your instructor, discuss the following questions in class or in groups.

1. Laws such as CAN-SPAM hope to curb the amount of junk e-mail by imposing restrictions on spammers. Do you think these laws go far enough? Should unsolicited commercial e-mail messages be banned altogether? Why or why not? If the government attempted to ban spam completely, what hurdles would it face?
2. Before you read this chapter, what steps (if any) were you taking to protect your personal information? How will you change your approach to guarding your privacy? Compare your thoughts and ideas with those of your classmates.

Research and Report

Using your own choice of resources (such as the Internet, books, magazines, and newspaper articles), research and write a short paper discussing one of the following topics:

- The various methods firewalls use to protect a computer or network.
- The extent to which spyware is being used online, and the reasons for it.
- The effects the environment can have on a computer.

When you are finished, proofread and print your paper, and give it to your instructor.

ETHICAL ISSUES

1. One of the primary reasons why it is easy to violate the rights of others is because of the relative anonymity that the Internet allows. Rather than having to go out and steal, or trespass, all you have to do is execute a programming routine in your own home. For instance, if you had to steal the software by going to the store and shoplifting a CD, you would get a sense that you were committing a crime. But if you download a file containing all of the same material, it is hard to get a sense that you are doing something wrong. Discuss the impact that the "virtuality" of the Internet has on our perception of ethical violations. In particular, what other areas of ethics might need a new set of definitions besides file sharing?
2. Many people who think about those sorts of things believe that the Internet will force us to define a new legal framework to embody the new powers it bestows. Specifically, where does the Internet blur the legal definitions? Consider issues of pornography, intellectual property, sabotage, government regulation, and taxation.

You may have seen the TV commercial: a bored-looking office worker sits in her cubicle, checking her e-mail. She perks up when she sees a message with an exciting subject line, then unthinkingly opens the message. Instantly, a menacing-looking character appears on her computer screen, "eats" the program icons on her desktop, and announces that she has just unleashed a virus. Within seconds, the same chaos erupts in the surrounding cubicles, and it becomes clear that the worker has made a horrible mistake.

In reality, computer viruses aren't so dramatic. In fact, most viruses are designed to hide, do their work quietly, and avoid detection for as long as possible. But a virus's damage can be dramatic in the extreme, causing untold losses to data and productivity.

Because of their ability to cause damage and disruption, viruses have been big news in recent years, especially with the outbreak of e-mail viruses beginning in the late 1990s. These viruses alone have accounted for billions of dollars in downtime and lost data in the past few years. Experts predict that virus attacks will only increase in the future.

Even so, many computer users are unaware of the dangers posed by viruses and make no effort to protect their computers and data from viruses. This is the primary reason viruses continue to be so successful.

What Is a Computer Virus?

A virus is a parasitic program that infects another legitimate program, which is sometimes called the host. To infect the host program, the virus modifies the host to store a copy of the virus. Many viruses are programmed to do harm once they infect the victim's system. As you will see later, a virus can be designed to do various kinds of damage. But the ability to do damage is not what defines a virus.

To qualify as a virus, a program must be able to replicate (make copies of) itself. This can mean copying itself to different places on the same computer or looking for ways to reach other computers, such as by infecting disks or traveling across networks. Viruses can be programmed to replicate and travel in many ways.

Here are some common ways to pick up a virus:

- Receiving an infected file attached to an e-mail message, or a virus hidden within the message itself. E-mail has become the single most common method for spreading viruses, especially now that so many people use the Internet to exchange messages and files. Viruses can even be spread through online chat rooms and instant messenger programs.

Viruses may not look menacing, but they can do all kinds of damage.

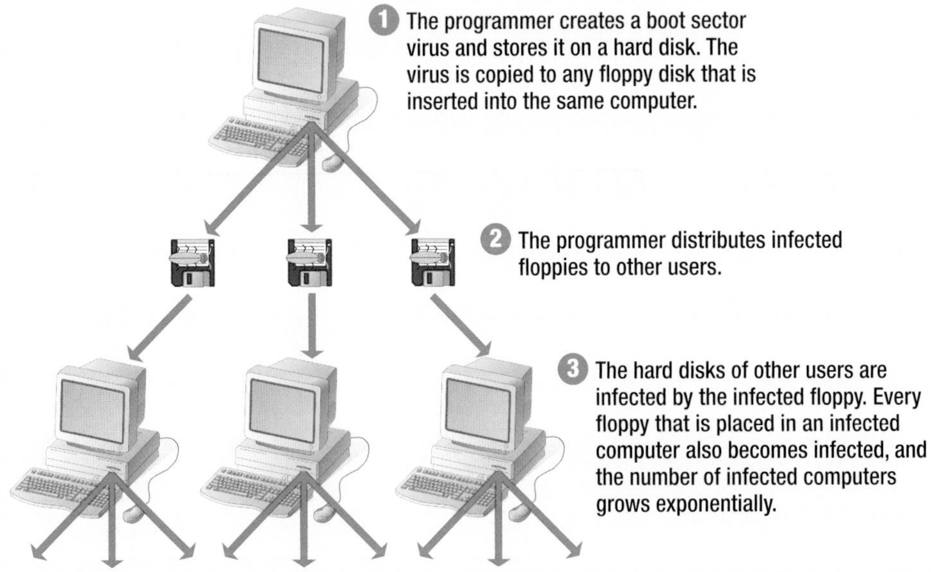

1 The programmer creates a boot sector virus and stores it on a hard disk. The virus is copied to any floppy disk that is inserted into the same computer.
2 The programmer distributes infected floppies to other users.
3 The hard disks of other users are infected by the infected floppy. Every floppy that is placed in an infected computer also becomes infected, and the number of infected computers grows exponentially.

Many viruses can spread by copying themselves to floppy disks or recordable CDs. As shown here, each time an infected machine's user gives someone else a disk, a copy of the virus goes with it.

>> Downloading an infected file to your computer across a network, an online service, or the Internet. Unless you have antivirus software that inspects each incoming file for viruses, you probably will not know if you have downloaded an infected file.

>> Receiving an infected disk (a diskette, a CD created by someone with a CD-R drive, a high-capacity floppy disk, and so on) from another user. In this case, the virus could be stored in the boot sector of the disk or in an executable file (a program) on the disk.

>> Copying to your disk a document file that is infected with a macro virus. An infected document might be copied from another disk or received as an attachment to an e-mail message.

What Can a Virus Do?

The majority of computer viruses are relatively harmless; their purpose is to annoy their victims rather than to cause specific damage. Such viruses are described as benign. Other viruses are indeed malicious, and they can do great damage to a computer system if permitted to run.

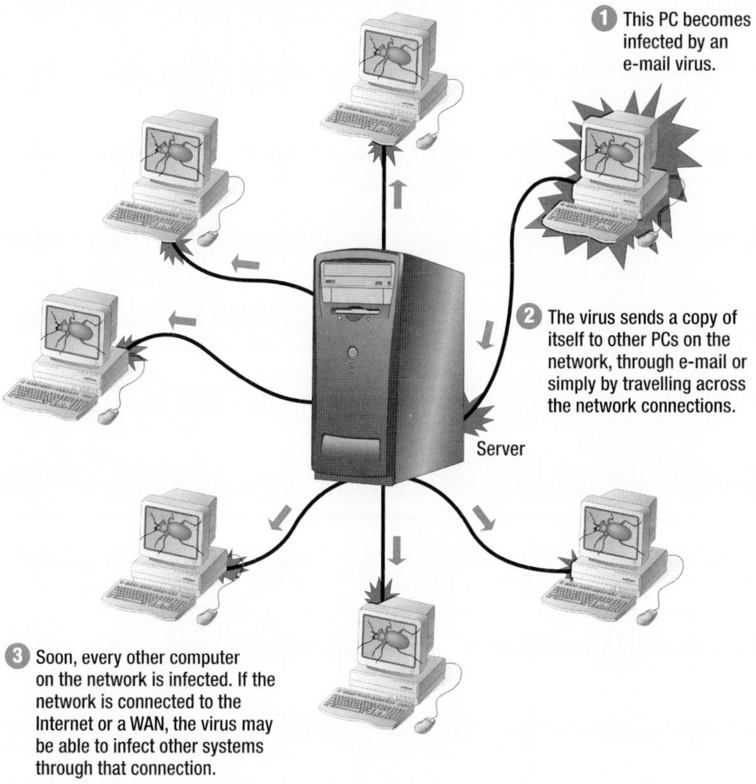

1 This PC becomes infected by an e-mail virus.
2 The virus sends a copy of itself to other PCs on the network, through e-mail or simply by travelling across the network connections.
Server
3 Soon, every other computer on the network is infected. If the network is connected to the Internet or a WAN, the virus may be able to infect other systems through that connection.

Viruses also can spread through a network connection, as shown here. In this simple example, one PC has been infected by a virus, which quickly spreads to other computers on the network.

Viruses can be programmed to do many kinds of harm, including the following:

>> Copy themselves to other programs or areas of a disk.

>> Replicate as rapidly and frequently as possible, filling up the infected system's disks and memory, rendering the system useless.

>> Display information on the screen.

>> Modify, corrupt, or destroy selected files.

>> Erase the contents of entire disks.

>> Lie dormant for a specified time or until a given condition is met, and then become active.

>> Open a "back door" to the infected system that allows someone else to access and even take control of the system through a network or Internet connection. This type of virus may actually be a type of program called a Trojan Horse, and can be used to turn an infected system into a "zombie," which the virus's author can use to attack other systems. For example, by using viruses to create a large number of zombie systems, the author can use the zombies to send thousands of requests to a specific Web server, effectively shutting it down. Such an attack is sometimes called a "denial of service (DOS) attack" or a "distributed denial of service (DDOS) attack," because it prevents the server from providing services to users.

This list is by no means comprehensive. Virus programmers can be extremely creative, and many create viruses to perform a specific type of task, sometimes with a specific victim in mind. Regardless, you need to protect your system against all kinds of viruses, because nearly any one can strike at any time, given the right circumstances.

Viruses may seem like major problems for individual computer users. For corporations, however, viruses can be devastating in terms of lost data and productivity. U.S. companies lose billions of dollars every year to damage caused by viruses. Most of the expenses come from the time and effort required to locate and remove viruses, restore systems, rebuild lost or corrupted data, and ensure against future attacks. But companies also lose valuable work time—millions of person-hours each year—as workers sit idle, unable to use their computers.

CONTINUED >>>

Categories of Viruses

Depending on your source of information, different types of viruses may be described in slightly different ways. Some specific categories of viruses include the following:

- **Bimodal, Bipartite, or Multipartite Viruses.** This type of virus can infect both files and the boot sector of a disk.
- **Bombs.** The two most prevalent types of bombs are time bombs and logic bombs. A time bomb hides on the victim's disk and waits until a specific date (or date and time) before running. A logic bomb may be activated by a date, a change to a file, or a particular action taken by a user or a program. Many experts do not classify bombs as viruses, but some do. Regardless, bombs are treated as viruses because they can cause damage or disruption to a system.
- **Boot Sector Viruses.** Regarded as one of the most hostile types of virus, a boot sector virus infects the boot sector of a hard or floppy disk. This area of the disk stores essential files the computer accesses during start-up. The virus moves the boot sector's data to a different part of the disk. When the computer is started, the virus copies itself into memory where it can hide and infect other disks. The virus allows the actual boot sector data to be read as though a normal start-up were occurring.
- **Cluster Viruses.** This type of virus makes changes to a disk's file system. If any program is run from the infected disk, the program causes the virus to run as well. This technique creates the illusion that the virus has infected every program on the disk.
- **E-mail Viruses.** E-mail viruses can be transmitted via e-mail messages sent across private networks or the Internet. Some e-mail viruses are transmitted as an infected attachment—a document file or program that is attached to the message. This type of virus is run when the victim opens the file that is attached to the message. Other types of e-mail viruses reside within the body of the message itself. To store a virus, the message must be encoded in HTML format. Once launched, many e-mail viruses attempt to spread by sending messages to everyone in the victim's address book; each of those messages contains a copy of the virus.
- **File-Infecting Viruses.** This type of virus infects program files on a disk (such as .exe or .com files). When an infected program is launched, the virus's code is also executed.
- **Joke Programs.** Joke programs are not viruses and do not inflict any damage. Their purpose is to frighten their victims into thinking that a virus has infected and damaged their system. For example, a joke program may display a message warning the user not to touch any keys or the computer's hard disk will be formatted.

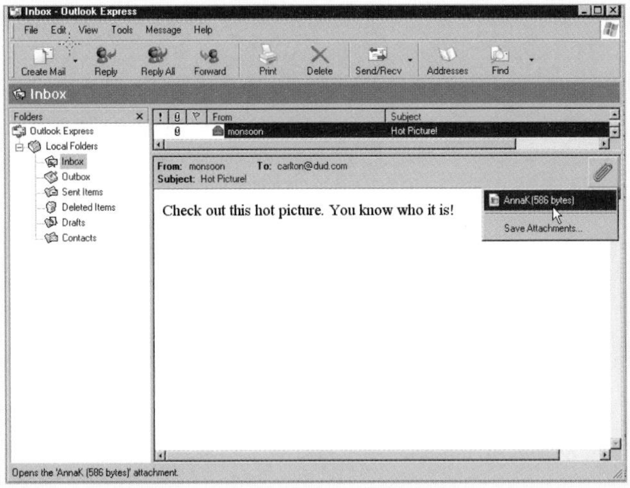

An e-mail attachment may look harmless, but opening it could unleash a virus onto your PC.

- **Macro Viruses.** A macro virus is designed to infect a specific type of document file, such as Microsoft Word or Excel files. These documents can include macros, which are small programs that execute commands. (Macros are typically used to issue program-specific commands, but they also can issue certain operating-system commands.) A macro virus, disguised as a macro, is embedded in a document file and can do various levels of damage to data, from corrupting documents to deleting data.
- **Polymorphic, Self-Garbling, Self-Encrypting, or Self-Changing Viruses.** This type of virus can change itself each time it is copied, making it difficult to isolate.
- **Stealth Viruses.** These viruses take up residence in the computer's memory, making them hard to detect. They also can conceal changes they make to other files, hiding the damage from the user and the operating system.
- **Trojan Horses.** A Trojan Horse is a malicious program that appears to be friendly. For example, some Trojan Horses appear to be games. Because Trojan Horses do not make duplicates of themselves on the victim's disk (or copy themselves to other disks), they are not technically viruses. But, because they can do harm, many experts consider them to be a type of virus. Trojan Horses are often used by hackers to create a "back door" to an infected system as described earlier.
- **Worms.** A worm is a program whose purpose is to duplicate itself. An effective worm will fill entire disks with

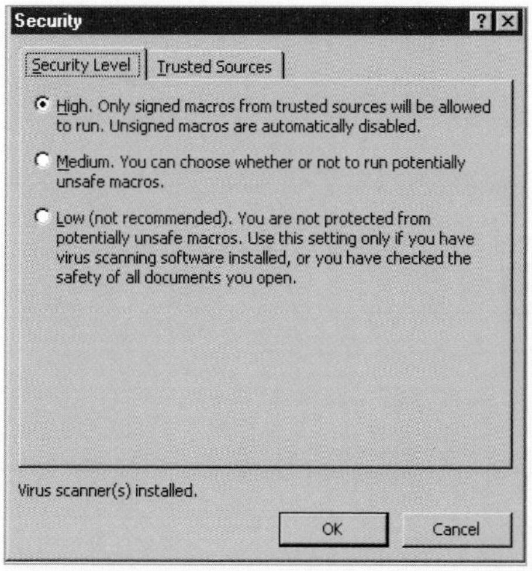

Macro viruses have become such a problem that many software programs now provide built-in security measures against them. This screen shows Microsoft Word's macro security settings, which can disable any macro to prevent it from running.

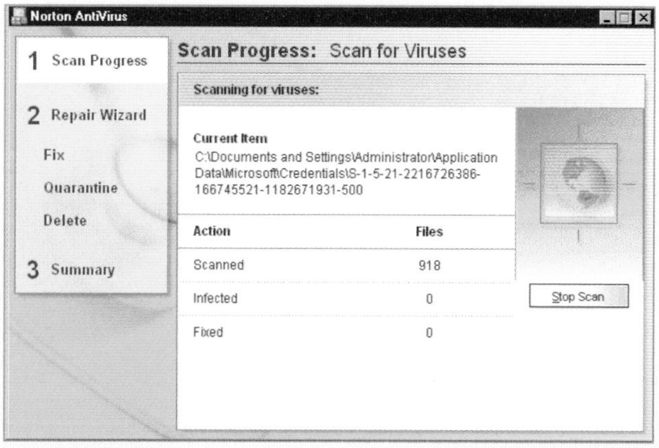

Scanning a computer's memory and hard disk with Norton AntiVirus.

copies of itself and will take up as much space as possible in the host system's memory. Many worms are designed to spread to other computers. An entire LAN or corporate e-mail system can become totally clogged with copies of a worm, rendering it useless. Worms are commonly spread over the Internet via e-mail message attachments and through Internet Relay Chat (IRC) channels. Technically, a worm is not the same as a virus. Because worms have become so prevalent in recent years, however, and because they can do considerable damage, worms are treated as though they were viruses.

Preventing Infection

Safeguarding a system against viruses is not difficult if you have a little knowledge and some utility software.

Start by being aware that viruses can come from many sources—even sources you trust. For example, an e-mail virus may arrive in your inbox disguised as a message from a friend or colleague because it has already infected that person's computer. A homemade data CD or floppy disk can be infected, too. In fact, even programs purchased in shrink-wrapped packages from reputable stores have been known to harbor viruses on rare occasions. The best precaution is to treat all e-mail messages and disks as potential carriers of infection.

Checking for viruses requires antivirus software, which scans your computer's memory and disks for known viruses and eradicates them. After it is installed on your system and activated, a good antivirus program checks for infected files automatically every time you insert any kind of disk or download a file via a network or Internet connection. Most antivirus utilities can also scan e-mail messages and attached files as you receive or send them. Sophisticated virus scanners can also alert you if a Web page attempts to load suspicious code onto your PC.

Some popular antivirus programs include

- McAfee VirusScan
- Norton AntiVirus
- Virex
- PC-cillin
- Avast!

However, simply having antivirus software on your computer is not enough to keep viruses away. This is where many casual computer users slip up and allow their systems to be infected.

Once you install the software, be sure to read its documentation thoroughly and master all of its functions. Most antivirus programs allow you to make various settings, such as activating automatic e-mail scanning. All these options may not be active by default, so you may need to activate them yourself and choose settings to control their operation. Make sure that you understand all the program's options and set them to give you maximum protection. Once the program is in place, scan your computer's disks at least once every week to check for viruses; your program may include a scheduling function that can automate disk-scanning for you.

Because new viruses are released almost daily, no antivirus program can offer absolute protection against them all. Many antivirus software vendors allow users to download updated virus definitions or virus patterns (databases

CONTINUED

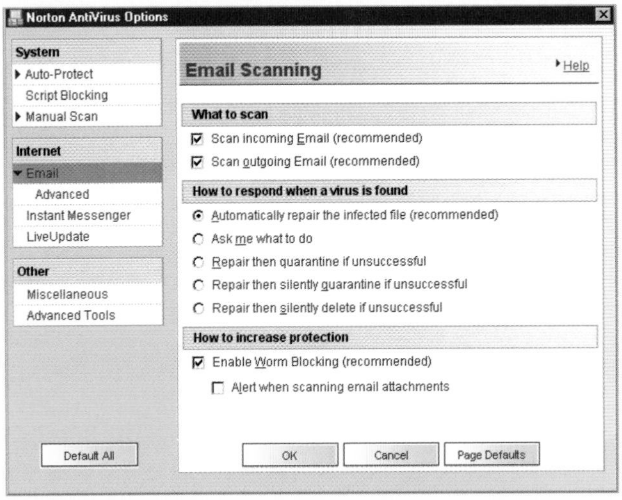

Setting options in Norton AntiVirus.

of information about viruses and code that can eradicate them) to their programs over the Internet. The newest-generation antivirus programs can find, download, and install updated virus definitions by themselves, automatically, whenever your computer is connected to the Internet. Whether you choose to update your antivirus software manually or automatically, you should do it at least once a week, to make sure you are protected against the latest viruses.

It's also a good idea to stay up to date on the latest news about viruses. A good way to do that is to visit the Web site of your antivirus software program's developer. A few other sources of general virus-related information are

- **Computer Security Institute (CSI).** http://www.gocsi.com
- **IBM Antivirus Research.** http://www.research.ibm.com/antivirus
- **Vmyths.com.** http://www.vmyths.com
- **Symantec Security Response.** http://www.symantec.com/avcenter
- **F-Secure Security Information Center.** http://www.f-secure.com/vir-info
- **CERT Coordination Center Computer Virus Resources.** http://www.cert.org/other_sources/viruses.html

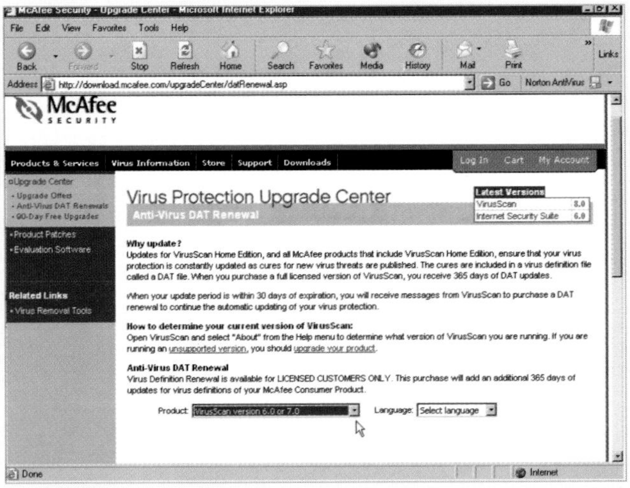

Downloading updated virus definitions from the McAfee VirusScan Web site.

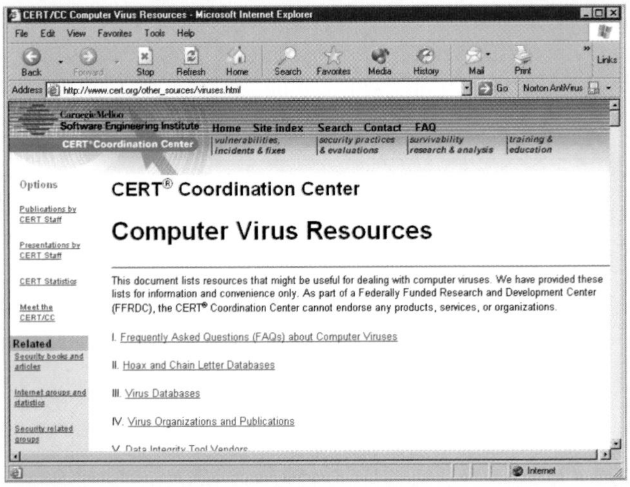

Many reputable Web sites, such as the CERT Coordination Center, provide up-to-the-minute information on viruses and virus prevention.

Appendix A

History of Microcomputers

1965

Honeywell corporation introduces the H316 "Kitchen Computer." This is the first home computer and is offered in the Neiman Marcus catalog for $10,600.

1970

Ken Thompson and Denis Ritchie create the UNIX operating system at Bell Labs. UNIX will become the dominant operating system for critical applications on servers, workstations, and high-end microcomputers.

1971

In 1971, Dr. Ted Hoff puts together all the elements of a computer processor on a single silicon chip slightly larger than one square inch. The result of his efforts is the Intel 4004, the world's first commercially available microprocessor. The chip is a four-bit computer containing 2,300 transistors (invented in 1948) that can perform 60,000 instructions per second. Designed for use in a calculator, it sells for $200. Intel sells more than 100,000 calculators based on the 4004 chip. Almost overnight, the chip finds thousands of applications, paving the way for today's computer-oriented world, and for the mass production of computer chips now containing millions of transistors.

Steve Wozniak and Bill Fernandez create a computer from chips rejected by local semiconductor companies. The computer is called the Cream Soda Computer because its creators drank Cragmont cream soda during its construction.

1972

Dennis Ritchie and Brian Kernighan create the C programming language at Bell Labs. The UNIX operating system is re-written in C. C becomes one of the most popular programming languages for software development.

5.25-inch floppy diskettes are introduced, providing a portable way to store and move data from machine to machine.

1973

IBM introduces new mass storage devices: the eight-inch, two-sided floppy disk that can hold 400 KB of data and the Winchester eight-inch, four-platter hard drive that can hold an amazing 70 MB of data.

Bob Metcalfe, working at Xerox PARC, creates a methodology to connect computers called Ethernet.

1974

Intel announces the 8080 chip. This is a 2-MHz, eight-bit microprocessor that can access 64 KB of memory using a two-byte addressing structure. It has over 6000 transistors on one chip. It can perform 640,000 instructions per second.

Motorola introduces the 6800 microprocessor. It is also an eight-bit processor and is used primarily in industrial and automotive devices. It will become the chip of choice for Apple computers sparking a long-running battle between fans of Intel and Motorola chips.

1975

The first commercially available microcomputer, the Altair 880, is the first machine to be called a "personal computer." It has 64 KB of memory and an open 100-line bus structure. It sells for $397 in kit form or $439 assembled. The name "Altair" was suggested by the 12-year-old daughter of the publisher of *Popular Electronics* because Altair was the destination that evening for the *Enterprise*, the *Star Trek* space ship.

Two young college students, Paul Allen and Bill Gates, unveil the BASIC language interpreter for the Altair computer. During summer vacation, the pair formed a company called Microsoft, which eventually grows into one of the largest software companies in the world.

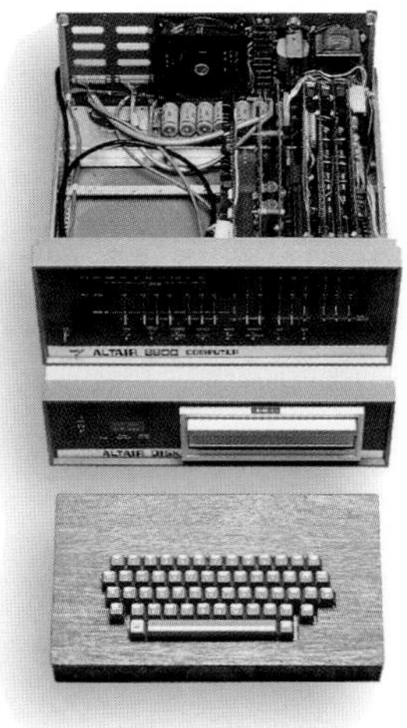

1976

Steve Wozniak and Steve Jobs build the Apple I computer. It is less powerful than the Altair, but also less expensive and less complicated. Users must connect their own keyboard and video display, and have the option of mounting the computer's motherboard in any container they

choose—whether a metal case, a wooden box, or a briefcase. Jobs and Wozniak form the Apple Computer Company together on April Fool's Day, naming the company after their favorite snack food.

1977

The Apple II computer is unveiled. It comes already assembled in a case, with a built-in keyboard. Users must plug in their own TVs for monitors. Fully assembled microcomputers hit the general market, with Radio Shack, Commodore, and Apple all selling models. Sales are slow because neither businesses nor the general public know exactly what to do with these new machines.

Datapoint Corporation announces Attached Resource Computing Network (ARCnet), the first commercial LAN technology intended for use with microcomputer applications.

1978

Intel releases the 8086 microprocessor, a 16-bit chip that sets a new standard for power, capacity, and speed in microprocessors.

Epson announces the MX-80 dot-matrix printer, coupling high performance with a relatively low price. (Epson from Japan set up operations in the United States in 1975 as Epson America, Inc., becoming one of the first of many foreign companies to contribute to the growth of the PC industry. Up until this point, it has been U.S. companies only. According to Epson, the company gained 60 percent of the dot-matrix printer market with the MX-80.)

1979

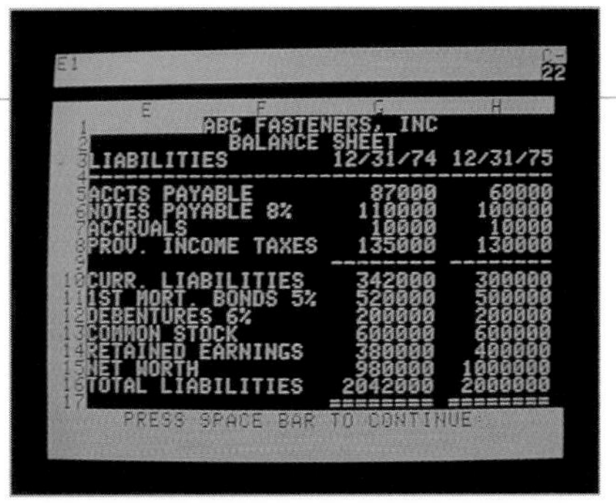

Intel introduces the 8088 microprocessor, featuring 16-bit internal architecture and an eight-bit external bus.

Motorola introduces the 68000 chip; it contains 68,000 transistors, hence the name. It will be used in early Macintosh computers.

Software Arts, Inc., releases VisiCalc, the first commercial spreadsheet program for personal computers. VisiCalc is generally credited as being the program that paved the way for the personal computer in the business world.

Bob Metcalf, the developer of Ethernet, forms 3Com Corp. to develop Ethernet-based networking products. Ethernet eventually evolves into the world's most widely used network system.

MicroPro International introduces WordStar, the first commercially successful word-processing program for IBM-compatible microcomputers.

1980

IBM chooses Microsoft (co-founded by Bill Gates and Paul Allen) to provide the operating system for its upcoming PC. Microsoft purchases a program developed by Seattle Computer Products called Q-DOS (for Quick and Dirty Operating System), and modifies it to run on IBM hardware.

Bell Laboratories invents the Bellmac-32, the first single-chip microprocessor with 32-bit internal architecture and a 32-bit data bus.

Lotus Development Corporation unveils the Lotus 1-2-3 integrated spreadsheet program, combining spreadsheet, graphics, and database features in one package.

1981

Adam Osborne creates the world's first "portable" computer, the Osborne 1. It weighs about 22 pounds, has two 5.25-inch floppy drives, 64 KB of RAM, and a five-inch monitor but no hard drive. It is based on the z80 processor, runs the CP/M operating system, and sells for $1,795. The Osborne 1 comes with WordStar (a word processing application) and SuperCalc (a spreadsheet application). It is a huge success.

IBM introduces the IBM-PC, with a 4.77 MHz Intel 8088 CPU, 16 KB of memory, a keyboard, a monitor, one or two 5.25-inch floppy drives, and a price tag of $2,495.

Hayes Microcomputer Products, Inc., introduces the SmartModem 300, which quickly becomes the industry standard.

Xerox unveils the Xerox Star computer. Its high price eventually dooms the computer to commercial failure, but its features inspire a whole new direction in computer design. Its little box on wheels (the first mouse) can execute commands on screen (the first graphical user interface).

1982

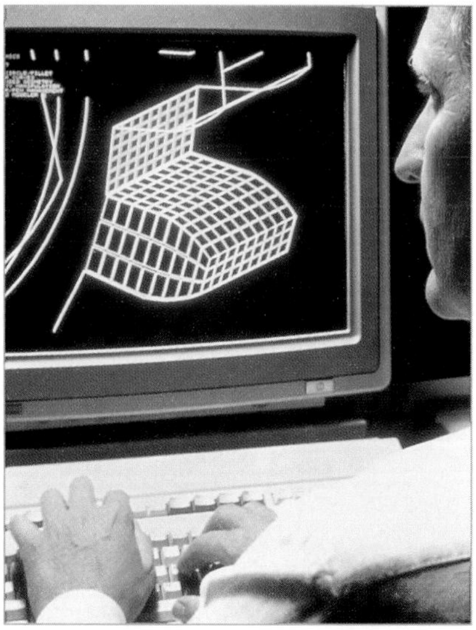

Intel releases the 80286, a 16-bit microprocessor.

Sun Microsystems is formed and the company begins shipping the Sun-1 workstation.

AutoCAD, a program for designing 2-D and 3-D objects, is released. AutoCAD will go on to revolutionize the architecture and engineering industries.

Work begins on the development of TCP/IP. The term *Internet* is used for the first time to describe the worldwide network of networks that is emerging from the ARPANET.

1983

Time magazine features the computer as the 1982 "Machine of the Year," acknowledging the computer's new role in society.

Apple introduces the Lisa, a computer with a purely graphical operating system and a mouse. The industry is excited, but Lisa's $10,000 price tag discourages buyers.

IBM unveils the IBM-PC XT, essentially a PC with a hard disk and more memory. The XT can store programs and data on its built-in 10MB hard disk.

The first version of the C++ programming language is developed, allowing programs to be written in reusable independent pieces, called objects.

The Compaq Portable computer is released, the first successful 100 percent PC-compatible clone. (The term *clone* refers to any PC based on the same architecture as the one used in IBM's personal computers.) Despite its hefty 28 pounds, it becomes one of the first computers to be lugged through airports.

1984

Adobe Systems releases its PostScript system, allowing printers to produce crisp print in a number of typefaces, as well as elaborate graphic images.

Richard Stallman leaves MIT to start the GNU (GNU's not Unix) free software project. This project will grow adding thousands of programs to the library of free (open-source, available under a special license), software. This movement is supported by the Free Software Foundation, an alternative to expensive, closed-source software.

Apple introduces the "user-friendly" Macintosh microcomputer, which features a graphical interface.

IBM ships the IBM-PC AT, a 6 MHz computer using the Intel 80286 processor, which sets the standard for personal computers running DOS.

IBM introduces its Token Ring networking system. Reliable and redundant, it can send packets at 4 Mbps; several years later it speeds up to16 Mbps.

Satellite Software International introduces the WordPerfect word processing program.

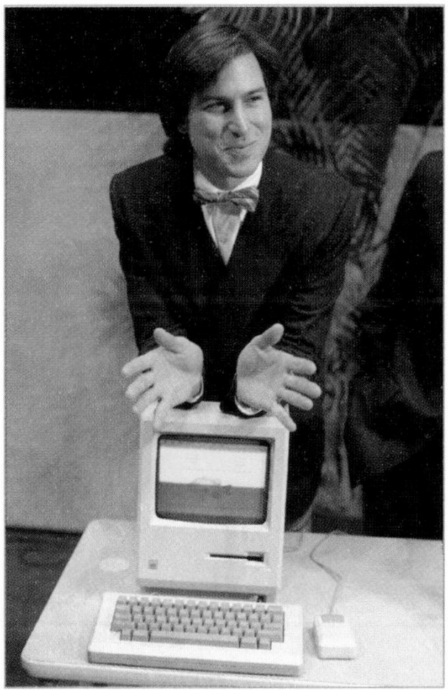

1985

Intel releases the 80386 processor (also called the 386), a 32-bit processor that can address more than four billion bytes of memory and performs 10 times faster than the 80286.

Aldus releases PageMaker for the Macintosh, the first desktop publishing software for microcomputers. Coupled with Apple's LaserWriter printer and Adobe's PostScript system, PageMaker ushers in the era of desktop publishing.

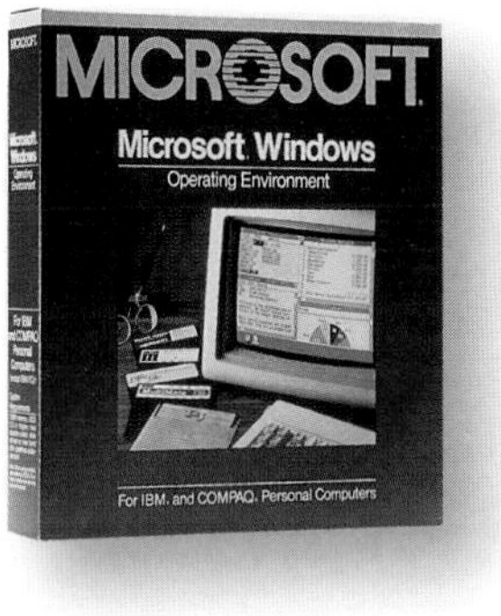

Microsoft announces the Windows 1.0 operating environment, featuring the first graphical user interface for PCs mirroring the interface found the previous year on the Macintosh.

Hewlett-Packard introduces the LaserJet laser printer, featuring 300 dpi resolution.

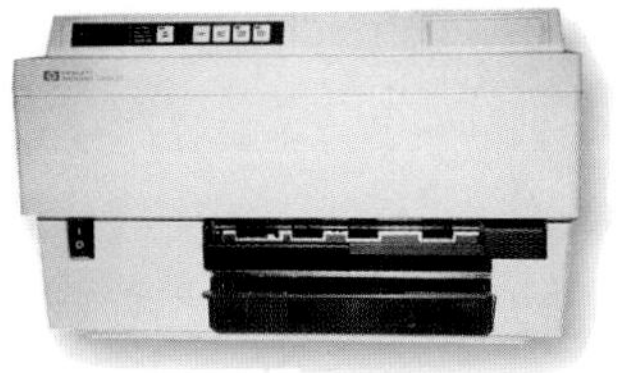

1986

IBM delivers the PC convertible, IBM's first laptop computer and the first Intel-based computer with a 3.5-inch floppy disk drive.

Microsoft sells its first public stock for $21 per share, raising $61 million in the initial public offering.

The First International Conference on CD-ROM technology is held in Seattle, hosted by Microsoft. Compact discs are seen as the storage medium of the future for computer users.

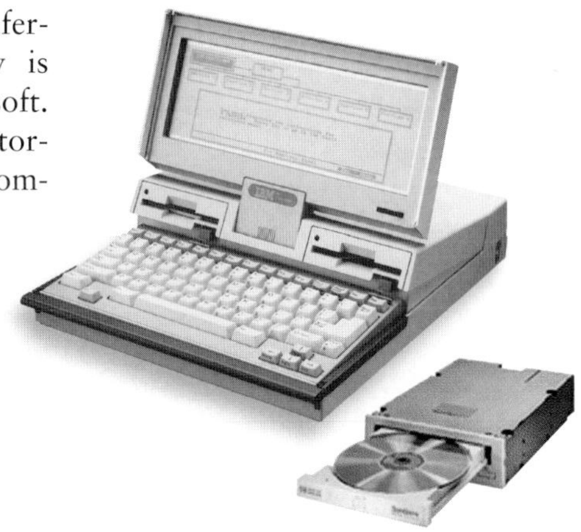

1987

IBM unveils the new PS/2 line of computers, featuring a 20-MHz 80386 processor at its top end. This product line includes the MicroChannel bus, but is not a great success because consumers do not want to replace industry standard peripherals. To compete with IBM's MicroChannel architecture, a group of other computer makers introduces the EISA (Extended Industry Standard Architecture) bus.

IBM introduces its Video Graphics Array (VGA) monitor offering 256 colors at 320 × 200 resolution, and 16 colors at 640 × 480.

The Macintosh II computer, aimed at the desktop publishing market, is introduced by Apple Computer. It features an SVGA monitor. Apple Computer introduces HyperCard, a programming language for the Macintosh, which uses the metaphor of a stack of index cards to represent a program—a kind of visual programming language. HyperCard allows linking across different parts of a program or across different programs; this concept will lead to the development of HTML (hypertext markup language).

Motorola unveils its 68030 microprocessor.

Novell introduces its network operating system, called NetWare.

1988

IBM and Microsoft ship OS/2 1.0, the first multitasking desktop operating system. Its high price, a steep learning curve, and incompatibility with existing PCs contribute to its lack of market share.

Apple Computer files the single biggest lawsuit in the computer industry against Microsoft and Hewlett-Packard, claiming copyright infringement of its operating system and graphical user interface.

Hewlett-Packard introduces the first popular ink jet printer, the HP Deskjet.

Steve Jobs' new company, NeXT, Inc., unveils the NeXT computer, featuring a 25-MHz Motorola 68030 processor. The NeXT is the first computer to use object-oriented programming in its operating system and an optical drive rather than a floppy drive.

Apple introduces the Apple CD SC, a CD-ROM storage device allowing access to up to 650 MB of data.

A virus called the "Internet Worm" is released on the Internet, disabling about 10 percent of all Internet host computers.

1989

Intel releases the 80486 chip (also called the 486), the world's first one-million-transistor microprocessor. The 486 integrates a 386 CPU and math coprocessor onto the same chip.

Tim Berners-Lee develops software around the hypertext concept, enabling users to click on a word or phrase in a document and jump either to another location within the document or to another file. This software provides the foundation for the development of the World Wide Web, and is the basis for the first Web browsers.

The World Wide Web is created at CERN, the European Particle Physics Laboratory in Geneva, Switzerland, for use by scientific researchers.

Microsoft's Word for Windows introduction begins the Microsoft Office suite adoption by millions of users. Previously, Word for DOS had been the second-highest-selling word processing package behind WordPerfect.

1990

Microsoft releases Windows 3.0, shipping one million copies in four months.

A multimedia PC specification setting the minimum hardware requirements for sound and graphics components of a PC is announced at the Microsoft Multimedia Developers' Conference.

The National Science Foundation Network (NSFNET) replaces ARPANET as the backbone of the Internet.

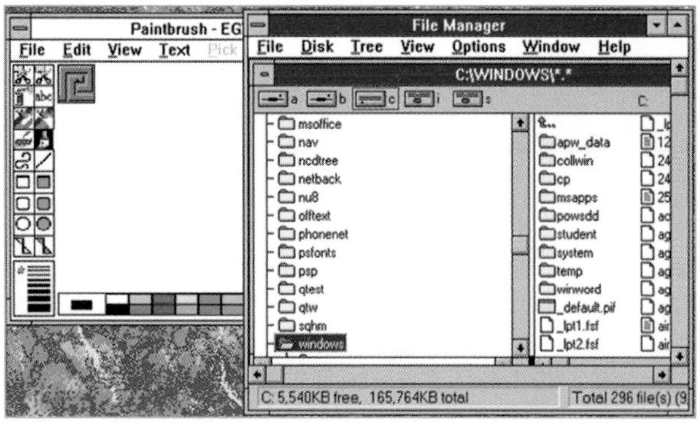

Motorola announces its 32-bit microprocessor, the 68040, incorporating 1.2 million transistors.

1991

Linus Torvalds releases the source code for Linux 0.01 (a clone of UNIX for the 80386 personal computer) on the Internet. It quickly becomes the base operating system of the open-source movement. Linux will grow to become one of the most widely used open-source PC operating systems.

Apple Computer launches the PowerBook series of battery-powered portable computers.

Apple, IBM, and Motorola sign a cooperative agreement to design and produce RISC-based chips, integrate the Mac OS into IBM's enterprise systems, produce a new object-oriented operating system, and develop common multimedia standards. The result is the PowerPC microprocessor.

1992

With an estimated 25 million users, the Internet becomes the world's largest electronic mail network.

In Apple Computer's five-year copyright infringement lawsuit, Judge Vaughn Walker rules in favor of defendants Microsoft and Hewlett-Packard, finding that the graphical user interface in dispute is not covered under Apple's copyrights.

Microsoft ships the Windows 3.1 operating environment, including improved memory management and TrueType fonts.

IBM introduces its ThinkPad laptop computer.

1993

Mosaic, a point-and-click graphical Web browser, is developed at the National Center for Supercomputing Applications (NCSA), making the Internet accessible to those outside the scientific community.

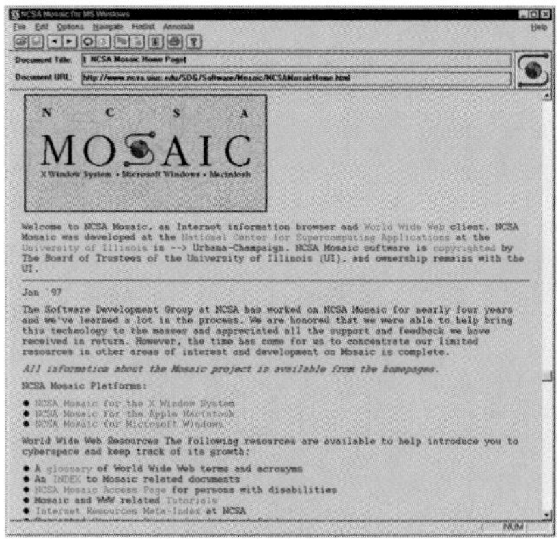

Intel, mixing elements of its 486 design with new processes, features, and technology, delivers the long-awaited Pentium processor. It offers a 64-bit data path and more than 3.1 million transistors.

Apple Computer expands its entire product line, adding the Macintosh Color Classic, Macintosh LC III, Macintosh Centris 610 and 650, Macintosh Quadra 800, and the Powerbooks 165c and 180c.

Apple introduces the Newton MessagePad at the Macworld convention, selling 50,000 units in the first 10 weeks.

Microsoft ships the Windows NT operating system.

IBM ships its first RISC-based RS/6000 workstation, featuring the PowerPC 601 chip developed jointly by Motorola, Apple, and IBM.

1994

Apple introduces the Power Macintosh line of microcomputers based on the PowerPC chip. This line introduces RISC to the desktop market. RISC was previously available only on high-end workstations.

Netscape Communications releases the Netscape Navigator program, a World Wide Web browser based on the Mosaic standard, but with more advanced features.

Online service providers CompuServe, America Online, and Prodigy add Internet access to their services.

After two million Pentium-based PCs have hit the market, a flaw in the chip's floating-point unit is found by Dr. Thomas Nicely. His report is made public on CompuServe.

Red Hat Linux is introduced and quickly becomes the most commonly used version of Linux.

1995

Intel releases the Pentium Pro microprocessor.

Motorola releases the PowerPC 604 chip, developed jointly with Apple and IBM.

Microsoft releases its Windows 95 operating system with a massive marketing campaign, including prime-time TV commercials. Seven million copies are sold the first month, with sales reaching 26 million by year's end.

Netscape Communications captures more than 80 percent of the World Wide Web browser market, going from a start-up company to a $2.9 billion company in one year.

A group of developers at Sun Microsystems create the Java development language. Because it enables programmers to develop applications that will run on any platform, Java is seen as the future language of operating systems, applications, and the World Wide Web.

Power Computing ships the first-ever Macintosh clones, the Power 100 series with a PowerPC 601 processor.

eBay, the premier online auction house, is formed.

1996

Intel announces the 200 MHz Pentium processor.

U.S. Robotics releases the PalmPilot, a personal digital assistant that quickly gains enormous popularity because of its rich features and ease of use.

Microsoft adds Internet connection capability to its Windows 95 operating system.

Several vendors introduce Virtual Reality Modeling Language (VRML) authoring tools that provide simple interfaces and drag-and-drop editing features to create three-dimensional worlds with color, texture, video, and sound on the Web.

The U.S. Congress enacts the Communications Decency Act as part of the Telecommunications Act of 1996. The act mandates fines of up to $100,000 and prison terms for transmission of any "comment, request, suggestion, proposal, image or other communication which is obscene, lewd, lascivious, filthy, or indecent" over the Internet. The day the law is passed, millions of Web page backgrounds turn black in protest. The law is immediately challenged on constitutional grounds, ultimately deemed unconstitutional, and repealed.

Sun Microsystems introduces the Sun Ultra workstation that includes a 64-bit processor.

1997

Intel announces MMX technology, which increases the multimedia capabilities of a micro-processor. Also, Intel announces the Pentium II microprocessor. It has speeds of up to 333 MHz and introduces a new design in packaging, the Single Edge Contact (SEC) cartridge. It has more than 7.5 million transistors.

AMD and Cyrix step up efforts to compete with Intel for the $1000-and-less PC market. Their competing processors are used by PC makers such as Dell, Compaq, Gateway, and even IBM.

The U.S. Justice Department files an antitrust lawsuit against Microsoft, charging the company with anticompetitive behavior for forcing PC makers to bundle its Internet Explorer Web browser with Windows 95.

Netscape Communications and Microsoft release new versions of their Web browser. Netscape's Communicator 4 and Microsoft's Internet Explorer 4 provide a full suite of Internet tools, including Web browser, newsreader, HTML editor, conferencing program, and e-mail application.

Digital Video/Versatile Disc (DVD) technology is introduced. Capable of storing computer, audio, and video data, a single DVD disc can hold an entire movie. DVD is seen as the storage technology for the future, ultimately replacing standard CD-ROM technology in PC and home entertainment systems.

1998

Microsoft releases the Windows 98 operating system. Seen mainly as an upgrade to Windows 95, Windows 98 is more reliable and less susceptible to crashes. It also offers improved Internet-related features, including a built-in copy of the Internet Explorer Web browser.

Netscape announces that it will post the source code to the Navigator 5.0 Web browser on the Internet. This is a major step in the open-source software movement.

The Department of Justice expands its actions against Microsoft, attempting to block the release of Windows 98 unless Microsoft agrees to remove the Internet Explorer browser from the operating system. Microsoft fights back and a lengthy trial begins in federal court, as the government attempts to prove that Microsoft is trying to hold back competitors such as Netscape.

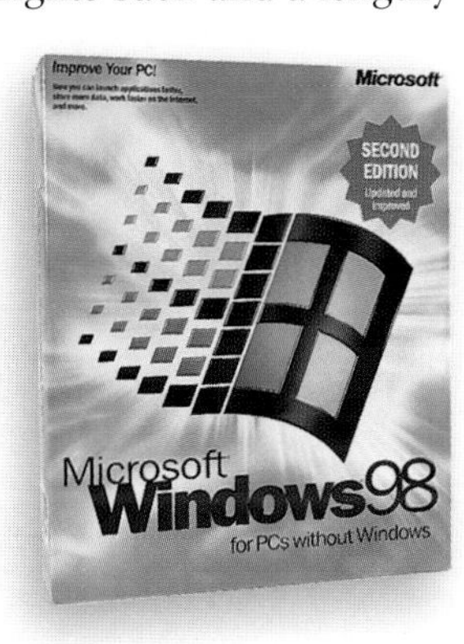

Intel releases two new versions of its popular Pentium II chip. The Pentium II Celeron offers slower performance than the standard PII, but is aimed at the $1,000-and-less PC market, which quickly embraces this chip. At the high end, the Pentium II Xeon is designed for use in high-performance workstations and server systems, and it is priced accordingly. Both chips boost Intel's market share, reaching deeper into more vertical markets.

Apple Computer releases the colorful iMac, an all-in-one system geared to a youthful market. The small, lightweight system features the new G3 processor, which outperforms Pentium II-based PCs in many respects. The iMac uses only USB connections, forcing many users to purchase adapters for system peripherals, and the computer does not include a floppy disk drive.

The new Internet Protocol, version 6 (IPv6), draft standard is released by the Internet Engineering Task Force.

1999

Intel unveils the Pentium III processor, which features 9.5 million transistors. Although the Pentium III's performance is not vastly superior to the Pentium II, it features enhancements that take greater advantage of graphically rich applications and Web sites. A more powerful version of the chip (named Xeon) is also released, for use in higher-end workstations and network server systems.

With its Athlon microprocessor, Advanced Micro Devices finally releases a Pentium-class chip that outperforms the Pentium III processor. The advance is seen as a boon for the lower-price computer market, which relies heavily on chips from Intel's competitors.

Sun Microsystems acquires Star Division Corporation and begins free distribution of StarOffice, a fully featured alternative to Microsoft Office and other proprietary office productivity products.

Apple Computer introduces updated versions of its popular iMac computer, including a laptop version, as well as the new G4 system, with performance rated at one gigaflop, meaning the system can perform more than one billion floating point operations per second.

The world braces for January 1, 2000, as fears of the "Millennium Bug" come to a head. As airlines, government agencies, financial institutions, utilities, and PC owners scramble to make their systems "Y2K-compliant," some people panic, afraid that basic services will cease operation when the year changes from 1999 to 2000.

Peter Merholz coins the term *blog*, a contraction of Web-log. In early 1999, there are already 50 recognized blog sites on the Web. By 2005 the sites will number in the hundreds of thousands.

The Internet Assigned Number Agency begins assigning Internet Protocol addresses using the new IPv6 addressing structure.

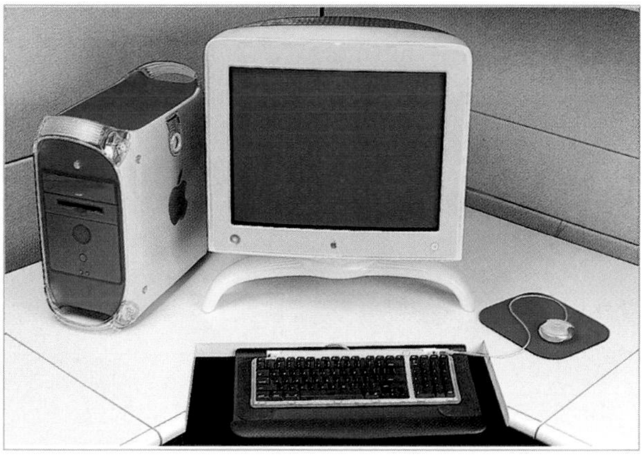

2000

Shortly after the new year, computer experts and government officials around the world announce that no major damage resulted from the "millennium date change," when computer clocks rolled over from 1999 to 2000. Immediately, a global debate begins to rage: had the entire "Y2K bug" been a hoax created by the computer industry, as a way to reap huge profits from people's fears? Industry leaders defend their approach to the Y2K issue, stating that years of planning and preventive measures had helped the world avoid a global computer-driven catastrophe that could have brought the planet's economy to a stand-still.

Microsoft introduces Windows 2000 on February 17. It is the biggest commercial software project ever attempted and one of the largest engineering projects of the century, involving 5,345 full-time participants, over half of them engineers. The final product includes almost 30 million lines of code.

On March 6, Advanced Micro Devices (AMD) announces the shipment of a 1GHz version of the Athlon processor, which will be used in PCs manufactured by Compaq and Gateway. It is the first 1GHz processor to be commercially available to the consumer PC market. Within days, Intel Corp. announces the release of a 1GHz version of the Pentium III processor.

In April, U.S. District Judge Thomas Penfield Jackson rules that Microsoft is guilty of taking advantage of its monopoly in operating systems to hurt competitors and leverage better deals with its business partners. Soon after the finding, the Department of Justice recommends that the judge break Microsoft into two separate companies: one focused solely on operating systems, the other focused solely on application development. Microsoft quickly counters by offering to change a number of its business practices. The judge rules to divide the software giant into two companies.

IBM (International Business Machines) announces that it will being selling computers running the Linux operating system. As with other Linux vendors, the IBM version of Linux will be open source.

2001

Microsoft releases the Windows XP operating system, with versions for home computers and business desktops. The XP version of Microsoft Office also is unveiled.

After blaming digital music pirates for lost revenue, the Recording Industry Association of America (RIAA) files lawsuits against purveyors of MP3 technology—most notably Napster, an online service that enables users to share MP3-format files freely across the Internet. The suits effectively shut down Napster, but do not stop individuals and other file-sharing services from exchanging music, text, and other files.

Apple introduces OS X, a new operating system for Macintosh computers that is based on BSD (Berkley Software Distribution) Unix with a beautiful graphical interface. It is an immediate success.

Several versions of recordable DVD discs and drives hit the market. Users instantly adopt the devices to store digitized home movies, data, and software; even though movie pirates soon begin copying and distributing movies on DVD, most users find the large capacity discs a wonderful storage and backup medium.

After several years of explosive growth, the "dot-com" revolution goes in to sudden reverse. As thousands of Web-based companies go out of business (giving rise to the phrase "dot-bomb"), tens of thousands of workers lose their jobs, shareholders suffer billions of dollars in losses, and the world's financial markets learn a valuable lesson.

Apple introduces the iPod, the premier music player with a 5 GB internal hard disk that will store 1,000 CD-quality songs.

Technology takes an important new role in society after the United States is attacked by terrorists on September 11, 2001. Government agencies, the military, and airlines place a new emphasis on security, recruiting new high-tech methods to monitor travelers and inspect people and baggage for dangerous items. Almost immediately, billions of dollars are invested in the development of new bomb-detection technologies and the creation of a huge, multinational database that can allow airlines to track the movements of passengers through the flight system.

Europe and Asia adopt the new Internet Protocol standard IPv6, the United States has not yet moved to adopt the new standard.

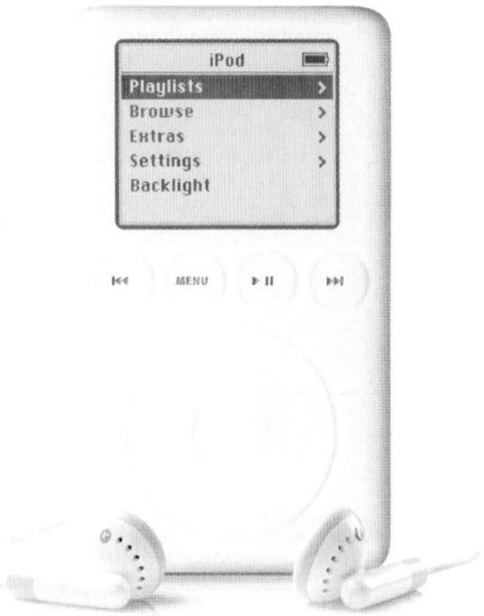

2002

Because of to the high cost of flying and concerns about security, many American businesses drastically reduce business travel. Increasingly, companies rely on technologies such as video-conferencing, teleconferencing, and online document sharing to work with partners and customers.

After a year of devastating shakeouts, the dot-com world begins to pick itself up again. The new breed of online entrepreneur bases companies on sound business practices, rather than the glamour of simply being "new economy." Investments in new online ventures slow to a trickle, enabling only those companies with the best ideas and real promise of profits to flourish.

The wireless networking boom continues with an emphasis on enabling handheld computers and telephones to access the Internet via wireless connections. Products such as digital two-way pagers, wireless phones, and combination telephone/PDAs sell at unprecedented levels.

Michael Robertson releases Lindows, a Linux-based operating system that has a full graphical user interface and comes with Open Office software. Wal-Mart and Fry's, two large retail chains, market Lindows-based computer systems for as little as $199. Microsoft immediately sues Robertson to try to prevent the product from reaching the market but loses.

XML (eXtensible Markup Language) and Web-based applications take center stage in many businesses.

Microsoft releases Windows XP Server Edition and the .NET Framework.

OpenOffice.org announces the release of OpenOffice.org 1.0, a free, full-featured suite of productivity applications compatible with the file formats used by Microsoft Office and many other office suites. An open-source alternative to expensive application suites, OpenOffice.org runs under Windows, Solaris, Linux, the Mac OS, and other operating systems.

2003

The National Center for Supercomputing Applications announces that Mike Showerman and Craig Steffen created a supercomputer based on 70 Sony PlayStation 2 gaming systems. The supercomputer cost about $50,000 to build, uses the Linux operating system and a Hewlett-Packard high-speed switch, and can perform 6.5 billion mathematical operations per second.

The Slammer worm does over $1 billion in damage and demonstrates that no network is truly secure.

Lindows explodes across the globe with several countries opting for this powerful and inexpensive alternative to high-priced proprietary software.

Microsoft releases Office 2003, the latest in the Office suite series.

Intel and AMD release 64-bit processors targeted for the home computer market.

Apple introduces the Power Macintosh G5, a 64-bit processor.

In a continuing attempt to control file sharing, the Recording Industry Association of America begins suing individuals who share files.

Apple opens an online music store, iTunes, offering more than 200,000 titles at $0.99 each.

Wi-Fi (Wireless Fidelity) or 802.11b/g comes to the consumer market with hot spots springing up both in home networking and in some commercial locations such as Starbucks. With this new technology comes the new technique called "war driving," where individuals drive around in automobiles with laptop computers looking for wireless networks that will allow them access.

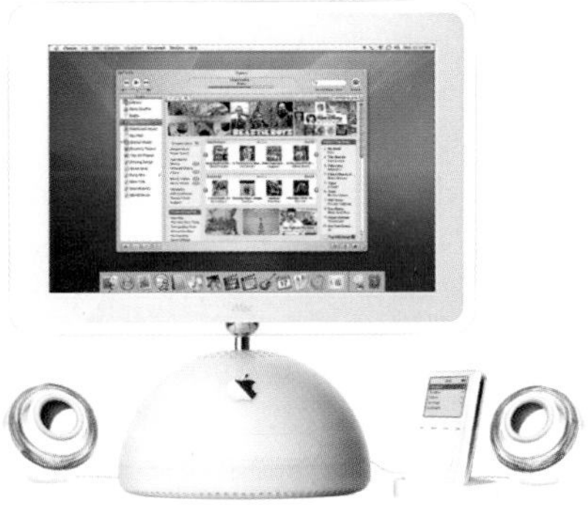

2004

Spam (unsolicited e-mail) and malware (programs such as viruses, Trojan Horses, and worms) cause major problems across the Internet. Crackers use viruses to generate spam and attack companies. One example is Mydoom, which takes control of more than 250,000 personal computers and uses them to attack the SCO Group Inc. Web site. Some estimates made in mid-2004 show that nearly 85 percent of all e-mail messages can be classified as spam.

By March, Apple's Itunes store has sold 50 millions songs.

Centralized computing makes a resurgence in both home and business environments with mainframe-like servers feeding "stateless devices" formerly known as dumb terminals.

RFID (Radio Frequency Identification) tags, common on some products, are seen as an invasion of privacy when shoppers are scanned to see what brands they buy.

2005

The last of the old Internet Protocol addresses (IPv4) is assigned and now all Net devices worldwide must support the new standard, IPv6.

Microsoft releases the next version of Windows, code named Longhorn.

"Disposable computers" move into home computing. People no longer try to repair a broken personal computer; they simply throw away the old one and buy a new one that is quickly updated to contain everything on the old machine.

Bluetooth-enabled devices allow sharing of files, text, data, images, and music across a wide range of personal devices, allowing you to play tunes from your iPod on your cell phone or as background on your PDA.

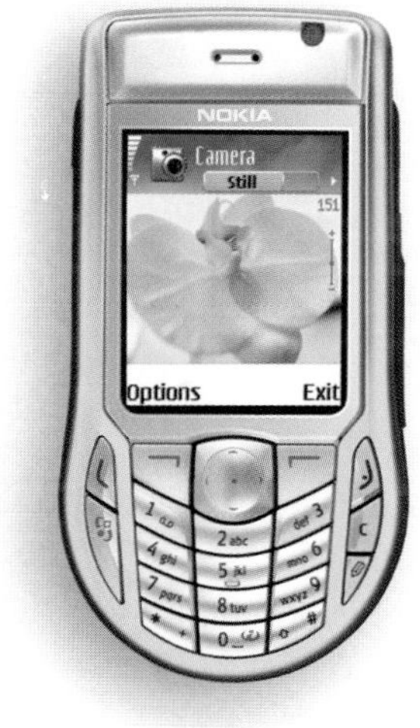

Appendix B

Self-Check Answers

Chapter 1, Lesson A, page 10
1. C
2. A
3. B

Chapter 1, Lesson B, page 36
1. B
2. A
3. C

Chapter 2, Lesson A, page 57
1. B
2. A
3. C

Chapter 2, Lesson B, page 79
1. B
2. A
3. C

Chapter 3, Lesson A, page 113
1. B
2. A
3. B

Chapter 3, Lesson B, page 127
1. B
2. A
3. B

Chapter 4, Lesson A, page 153
1. C
2. A
3. B

Chapter 4, Lesson B, page 167
1. B
2. A
3. B

Chapter 5, Lesson A, page 194
1. B
2. A
3. C

Chapter 5, Lesson B, page 211
1. C
2. B
3. B

Chapter 6, Lesson A, page 235
1. C
2. A
3. B

Chapter 6, Lesson B, page 252
1. C
2. A
3. B

Chapter 7, Lesson A, page 272
1. B
2. A
3. B

Chapter 7, Lesson B, page 291
1. B
2. A
3. B

Chapter 8, Lesson A, page 310
1. B
2. A
3. C

Chapter 8, Lesson B, page 331
1. B
2. A
3. B

Chapter 9, Lesson A, page 350
1. B
2. A
3. C

Chapter 9, Lesson B, page 368
1. A
2. A
3. C

Chapter 10, Lesson 0A, page 387
1. C
2. A
3. B

Chapter 10, Lesson 0B, page 402
1. C
2. A
3. B

Chapter 11, Lesson A, page 426
1. C
2. B
3. A

Chapter 11, Lesson B, page 448
1. A
2. C
3. B

Chapter 12, Lesson A, page 470
1. B
2. A
3. C

Chapter 12, Lesson B, page 487
1. C
2. B
3. A

Chapter 13, Lesson A, page 508
1. C
2. A
3. B

Chapter 13, Lesson B, page 525
1. B
2. A
3. C

Chapter 14, Lesson A, page 548
1. B
2. C
3. A

Chapter 14, Lesson B, page 568
1. C
2. A
3. B

Glossary

Numerals

10Base-T See *Ethernet.*

100Base-T See *Fast Ethernet.*

3-D modeling software Graphics software used to create electronic models of three-dimensional objects.

3GL See *third-generation language.*

4GL See *fourth-generation language.*

5GL See *fifth-generation language.*

802.11b A wireless networking standard that describes specifications for data transmission speeds up to 11 Mbps.

802.11g A wireless networking standard that describes specifications for data transmission speeds of 20 Mbps and higher.

A

Accelerated Graphics Port (AGP) bus A bus standard that incorporates a special architecture that allows the video card to access the system's RAM directly, greatly speeding up graphics performance. Most new computers feature AGP graphics capabilities in addition to a PCI system bus and an expansion bus.

acceptance testing Testing performed during the development phase of the systems development life cycle. In acceptance testing, end users work with the installed system to ensure that it meets their criteria.

Access A database management program.

activate (1) To initiate a command or load a program into memory and begin using it. (2) To *choose*; for example, you can activate a resource by choosing its icon, toolbar button, or filename.

active matrix LCD A liquid crystal display (LCD) technology that assigns a transistor to each pixel in a flat-panel monitor, improving display quality and eliminating the "submarining" effect produced by some types of flat-panel monitors. Also called a *thin-film transistor (TFT)* display.

Active Server Pages (ASP) A specialized Web-scripting language that enables a Web page to access and draw data from databases.

active window On the computer screen, the window in which the user's next action will occur. The active window's title bar is highlighted, while the title bars of inactive windows appear dimmed.

adapter See *expansion board.*

address book A database that stores information about people, such as their names, addresses, phone numbers, e-mail addresses, and other details. Commonly part of a personal information management or e-mail program.

address bus A set of wires connecting the computer's CPU and RAM, across which memory addresses are transmitted.

Address Resolution Protocol (ARP) A specialized protocol that resolves logical IP addresses into physical addresses.

ADSL See *Asynchronous DSL.*

Advanced Micro Devices (AMD) A chip manufacturer that makes processors for PC-compatible computers.

adware See *spyware.*

AGP See *Accelerated Graphics Port.*

algorithm A set of ordered steps or procedures necessary to solve a problem.

all-in-one peripheral A device that combines the functions of printing, scanning, copying, and faxing. All-in-one peripherals can be based on either laser or ink jet printing technology and may operate in black and white, color, or both.

alphanumeric field See *text field.*

alphanumeric keys On a computer keyboard, the keys that include the letters of the alphabet, numerals, and commonly used symbols.

ALU See *arithmetic logic unit.*

always-on connection An Internet connection that is always active, as long as the computer is running. Cable modem and DSL connections are examples of always-on connections.

AMD See *Advanced Micro Devices.*

American Standard Code for Information Interchange An eight-bit binary code developed by the American National Standards Institute (ANSI) to represent symbolic, numeric, and alphanumeric characters. The ASCII character set is the most commonly used character set in PCs.

anonymous FTP archive An FTP site with files available to the general public. The user types the word "anonymous" as the account name in order to access the files.

anti-adware utility See *anti-spyware utility.*

antiglare screen A device that fits over a computer monitor and reduces glare from light reflecting off the screen.

anti-spyware utility A program that can locate and remove spyware programs from a user's computer. Some anti-spyware utilities can "immunize" a computer against known types of spyware, to prevent them from infecting the system.

antivirus utility A program that scans a computer's disks and memory for viruses; when it detects viruses, it removes them. Some antivirus programs can help the user recover data and program files that have been damaged by a virus and can actively scan files as they are being copied from a disk or downloaded from the Internet.

Apache HTTP Server A Web server product developed by the Apache Group. A robust and commercial-grade Web server that is maintained and improved upon as free, open-source software, Apache is the most popular Web server and runs on UNIX, Linux, and Windows servers.

APIPA See *automatic private IP address.*

applet A small program that can be run from within a Web page. Many Web-based applets are written in the Java programming language.

application server A network server that hosts shared application files, enabling multiple users to use a network version of a software program. Generally, an application server performs some or all of the processing tasks required by users of the application.

application software Any computer program used to create or process data, such as text documents, spreadsheets, graphics, and so on. Examples include database management software, desktop publishing programs, presentation programs, spreadsheet programs, and word processing programs.

architecture The design of any part of a computer system, or of an entire system, including software and hardware. The design of a microprocessor's circuits, for example, is called its architecture.

archive file A file that stores one or more compressed files, which have been shrunk by a data-compression program.

arithmetic logic unit (ALU) The component of the CPU that handles arithmetic and logical functions.

arithmetic operation One of two types of operations a computer can perform, which are handled by the arithmetic logic unit (ALU). Arithmetic operations include addition, subtraction, multiplication, and division. See also *logical operation*.

ARP See *Address Resolution Protocol*.

ARPANET Acronym for *Advanced Research Projects Agency Network*. An early network developed by the Department of Defense to connect computers at universities and defense contractors. This network eventually became part of the Internet.

article A message posted to an Internet newsgroup. A series of related articles and responses is called a *thread*.

ASCII See *American Standard Code for Information Interchange*.

assembler A computer program that converts assembly language instructions into machine language.

assembly language A second-generation programming language that uses simple phrasing in place of the complex series of binary numbers used in machine language.

Asynchronous DSL (ADSL) A variation on Digital Subscriber Line (DSL) service that provides different data transmission speeds for uploading and downloading data.

Asynchronous Transfer Mode (ATM) A network protocol designed to send voice, video, and data transmissions over a single network. ATM provides different kinds of connections and bandwidth on demand, depending on the type of data being transmitted.

ATM See *Asynchronous Transfer Mode*.

attenuation The loss of signal strength as analog or digital data travels through a network medium.

attribute (1) An enhancement or stylistic characteristic applied to text characters in a font, such as bold or italic. (2) In object-oriented programming, a component of the overall description of an object.

auto loader In a large tape backup system, a robotic device that can automatically load and eject tapes in tape drives.

automatic private IP address (APIPA) A special group of private IP addresses. If a computer is configured to obtain an address automatically (as a DHCP client) on a TCP/IP network but does not receive an address from a DHCP server, it will automatically give itself an address within the APIPA range, first making sure that no other host on the network has that address.

autonumber field See *counter field*.

average access time The average amount of time a storage or memory device requires to locate a piece of data. For storage devices, average access time is usually measured in milliseconds (ms). Average time is measured in nanoseconds (ns) in memory devices. Also called *seek time*.

B

B2B transaction See *business-to-business transaction*.

B2C transaction See *business-to-consumer transaction*.

back up To create a duplicate set of program or data files in case the originals become damaged. (A duplicate file made for this purpose is called a *backup* file.) Files can be backed up individually, by entire folders, and by entire drives. Backups can be made to many types of storage media, such as diskettes, optical discs, or tape. Verb—two words ("I am going to back up the files on the server."); noun or adjective—one word ("He used a backup utility to make a backup of that file.")

backbone The central structure of a network that connects other elements of the network and handles the major traffic.

backup utility A program that enables the user to copy one or more files from a hard disk to another storage medium (such as a floppy disk, tape, or compact disc) for safekeeping or use in case the original files become damaged or lost.

band printer A type of impact printer that uses a rapidly moving, circular band embossed with characters. A hammer strikes the band to press a character against an inked ribbon.

bandwidth The amount of data that can be transmitted over a network at any given time. Bandwidth may be measured in bits per second (bps) or in hertz (Hz).

bar code A pattern of bars printed on a product or its packaging. A device called a *bar code reader* can scan a bar code and convert its pattern into numeric digits. After the bar code reader has converted a bar code image into a number, it transfers that number to a computer, just as though the number had been typed on a keyboard.

bar code reader An input device that converts a pattern of printed bars (called a *bar code*) into a number that a computer can read. A beam of light reflected off the bar code into a light-sensitive detector identifies the bar code and converts the bar patterns into numeric digits that can be transferred to a computer. Bar code readers are commonly used in retail stores.

basic input output system (BIOS) A set of instructions, stored in ROM, that help a computer start running when it is turned on.

basic rate integrated services digital network (basic rate ISDN or BRI) The simplest and slowest type of ISDN connection. A basic rate ISDN connection combines two 64 Kbps data channels and one 19 Kbps error-checking channel.

basic rate ISDN See *basic rate integrated services digital network.*

batch (.bat) file An executable file that can be used to automate common or repetitive tasks. A batch file is a simple program that consists of an unformatted text file containing one or more commands. If you type a batch file's name in at a command prompt, your operating system will execute the commands in the file. A batch file can have a .com extensions instead of a .bat extension.

billions of instructions per second (BIPS) A common unit of measure when gauging the performance of a computer's processor.

binary field A database field that stores binary objects (such as clip art, photographs, screen images, formatted text, sound objects, and video clips) or OLE objects (such as charts or worksheets created with a spreadsheet or word processor).

binary large object (BLOB) (1) A graphic image file such as clip art, a photograph, a screen image, formatted text, a sound object, or a video clip. (2) An OLE object such as a chart or worksheet created with a spreadsheet or word processor; frequently used with object-oriented databases.

binary number system A system for representing the two possible states of electrical switches, which are on and off. (The binary number system is also known as *base 2*.) The binary number system gets its name from the fact that it includes only two numbers: 0 and 1. In computer storage and memory systems, the numeral 0 represents off and a 1 represents on.

BIOS See *basic input output system.*

BIPS See *billions of instructions per second.*

bit The smallest unit of data that can be used by a computer, represented by a 1 or a 0.

bitmap A binary representation of an image in which each part of the image, such as a pixel, is represented by one or more bits in a coordinate system. Also called a *raster.*

bits per second (bps) A measure of data transmission speed. This unit may be used to measure the data transmission rate of a specific device—such as a modem or disk drive—or for the components of a network. May be modified as kilobits per second (Kbps), megabits per second (Mbps), or gigabits per second (Gbps).

BLOB See *binary large object.*

block A contiguous series of characters, words, sentences, or paragraphs in a word processing document. This term is also sometimes used to describe a range of cells in a spreadsheet. Once a block of text or cells has been selected, the user can perform many different actions on it, such as moving, formatting, or deleting.

BMP Abbreviation for *bitmap*. BMP is a graphic-file format native to Windows and OS/2. BMP is widely used on PCs for icons and wallpaper.

board See *expansion board.*

Boolean field See *logical field.*

Boolean operator Special words—such as AND, OR, and NOT—that can be used to modify a keyword search in a Web-based search engine. These operators are commonly used in standard database queries.

boot To start a computer. The term comes from the expression "pulling oneself up by one's own bootstraps."

boot sector The portion of a disk that contains the master boot record—a program that runs when the computer is first started and determines whether the disk has the basic operating system components required to run successfully.

bottom-up design A design method in which system details are developed first, followed by major functions or processes.

bps See *bits per second.*

branch One of several directions that flows from a condition statement or function call within a sequence structure.

BRI See *basic rate integrated services digital network.*

brick-and-mortar store A business, such as a retail store, that has a physical location but does not have an online presence such as a Web site.

bridge A device that connects two LANs and controls data flow between them.

broadband Describes a high-speed network connection or data connection to the Internet. To qualify as broadband, a connection must transmit data faster than is possible with a dial-up connection through a standard modem and telephone line. Cable modems and DSL are common examples of broadband Internet connections.

browser See *Web browser.*

buddy list A list of people who can participate in chats, using instant messaging software.

buffer A dedicated space in memory or on a disk that temporarily stores data until it is needed by a program. Once the data has been used, it is deleted from the buffer.

bug An error in a computer program.

bus The path between components of a computer. The bus's width determines the speed at which data is transmitted. When used alone, the term commonly refers to a computer's data bus.

bus topology A network topology in which all network nodes and peripheral devices are attached to a single conduit.

business logic The process executed by one computer in a three-tier distributed application. This process can include determining what data is needed from a database, the best way to connect to the database, and other tasks.

business-to-business (B2B) transaction A transaction (such as the placing of an order or the paying of an invoice) conducted by two businesses. A B2B transaction can be conducted in many ways, with or without the use of computers, but the term *B2B* is commonly used to describe transactions that occur online or through a private corporate network such as an extranet.

business-to-consumer (B2C) transaction A transaction (such as the ordering of a product or the paying of a bill) conducted between an individual consumer and a business. A B2C transaction can be conducted in many ways, with or without the use of computers, but the term *B2C* is commonly used to describe transactions that occur via the Internet.

byte The amount of memory required to store a single character. A byte is comprised of eight bits.

C

cable modem service A technology that provides an Internet connection using cable television wiring. To connect to the Internet, a special device called a *cable modem* is required. The modem connects the user's PC or network to the cable television system.

cache memory High-speed memory that resides between the CPU and RAM in a computer. Cache memory stores data and instructions that the CPU is likely to need next. The CPU can retrieve data or instructions more quickly from cache than it can from RAM or a disk.

CAD See *computer-aided design*.

campus area network (CAN) A larger version of a *local area network (LAN)*, usually used to connect adjacent buildings such as those found on college campuses.

CAN See *campus area network*.

card See *expansion board*.

carpal tunnel syndrome A form of repetitive stress injury. Specifically, an injury of the wrist or hand commonly caused by repetitive motion, such as extended periods of keyboarding.

CASE See *computer-aided software engineering*.

cathode ray tube (CRT) A type of monitor that uses a vacuum tube as a display screen. CRTs are most commonly used with desktop computers.

CD See *compact disc*.

CD-R See *CD-Recordable drive*.

CD-Recordable (CD-R) An optical disc drive that enables the user to create customized CD-ROM discs. Data that has been written to a CD-R disc cannot be changed (overwritten). CD-R discs can be read by any CD-ROM drive. CD-R drives are commonly used to create backup copies of program or data files, or to create duplicates of existing compact discs.

CD-ReWritable (CD-RW) An optical disc drive that enables the user to create customized CD-ROM discs. Unlike a CD-R disc, a CD-RW disc's data can be overwritten, meaning the data can be updated after it has been placed on the disc.

CD-ROM See *compact disc read-only memory*.

CD-ROM drive An optical disc drive that enables a computer to read data from a compact disc. Using a standard CD-ROM drive and compact disc, the computer can only read data from the disc and cannot write data to the disc.

CD-RW See *CD-ReWritable drive*.

cell In a spreadsheet or database table, the intersection of a row and a column, forming a box into which the user enters numbers, formulas, or text. The term also is used to refer to the individual blocks in a table created in a word processing program.

cell address In a spreadsheet, an identifier that indicates the location of a cell in a worksheet. The address is composed of the cell's row and column locations. For example, if the cell is located at the intersection of column B and row 3, then its cell address is B3.

cell pointer A square enclosing one cell of a worksheet, identifying that cell as the active cell. The user positions the cell pointer in a worksheet by clicking the cell or by using the cursor movement keys on the keyboard.

central processing unit (CPU) The computer's primary processing device, which interprets and executes program instructions and manages the functions of input, output, and storage devices. In personal computers, the CPU is composed of a control unit, an arithmetic logic unit, built-in memory, and supporting circuitry such as a dedicated math processor. The CPU may reside on a single chip on the computer's motherboard or on a larger card inserted into a special slot on the motherboard. In larger computers, the CPU may reside on several circuit boards.

CGI See *computer-generated imaging*.

channel Discussion group where chat users convene to discuss a topic.

character field See *text field*.

character formatting In a word processor, settings that control the attributes of individual text characters, such as font, type size, type style, and color.

characters per second (cps) A measure of the speed of impact printers such as dot matrix printers.

chat One of the services available to users of the Internet and some online services. Using special chat software or Web-based chatting tools, users can exchange messages with one another in real time.

choose See *activate*.

circuit board A rigid rectangular card—consisting of chips and electronic circuitry—that ties the processor to other hardware. In a personal computer, the primary circuit board (to which all components are attached) is called the *motherboard*.

CISC See *Complex Instruction Set Computing*.

click To select an object or command on the computer screen (for example, from a menu, toolbar, or dialog box) by pointing to the object and then pressing and releasing the primary mouse button once.

click-and-mortar store A business such as a retail store that has one or more physical locations as well as an online presence such as a Web site. Customers can conduct transactions with such a business by visiting a physical location or using its Web site.

client An application program on a user's computer that requests information from another computer, such as a network server or Web host, over a network or the Internet. The term also may be used to refer to the computer itself, as it requests services via a network.

client/server network A hierarchical network strategy in which the processing is shared by a server and numerous clients. In this type of network, clients provide the user interface, run applications, and request services from the server. The server contributes storage, printing, and some or all processing services.

clip art Predrawn or photographed graphic images that are available for use by anyone. Some clip art is available through licensing, some through purchase, and some for free.

Clipboard A holding area maintained by the operating system in memory. The Clipboard is used for storing text, graphics, sound, video, or other data that has been copied or cut from a document. After data has been placed in the Clipboard, it can be inserted from the Clipboard into other documents, in the same application, or in a different application.

clock cycle In a processor, the amount of time required to turn a transistor off and back on again. Also called a *tick*. A processor can execute an instruction in a given number of clock cycles, so as a computer's clock speed (the number of clock cycles it generates per second) increases, so does the number of instructions it can carry out each second.

clock speed A measure of a processor's operating speed, currently measured in megahertz (MHz, or millions of cycles per second) or gigahertz (GHz, or billions of cycles per second). A computer's operating speed is based on the number of clock cycles, or ticks, it generates per second. For example, if a computer's clock speed is 800 MHz, it "ticks" 800 million times per second.

cluster On a magnetic disk (such as a hard disk), a group of sectors that are treated as a single data-storage unit. The number of sectors per disk can vary, depending on the type of disk and the manner in which it is formatted.

coaxial cable (coax) A cable composed of a single conductive wire wrapped in a conductive wire mesh shield with an insulator in between.

code The instructions or statements that are the basis of a computer program.

color monitor A computer monitor whose screen can display data in color. A color monitor's capabilities are based on a variety of factors. Current high-resolution color monitors can display more than 16 million colors, but they also can be set to display as few as 16 colors or varying shades of gray.

command An instruction issued to the computer. The user can issue commands, usually by choosing from a menu, clicking an on-screen tool or icon, or pressing a combination of keys. Application programs and the operating system also issue commands to the computer.

command-line interface A user interface that enables the user to interact with the software by typing strings of characters at a prompt.

command prompt See *prompt*.

commercial software Software that a manufacturer makes available for purchase. The consumer usually pays for a license to use the software, instead of purchasing the software itself.

communications device An input/output device used to connect one computer to another to share hardware and information. This family of devices includes modems and network interface cards.

compact disc (CD) A type of optical storage medium, identical to audio CDs. The type of CD used in computers is called *compact disc read-only memory (CD-ROM)*. As the device's name implies, you cannot change the information on the disc, just as you cannot record over an audio CD. Standard compact discs can store either 650 MB or 700 MB of computer data, or 70 minutes or 80 minutes of audio data.

compact disc read-only memory (CD-ROM) The most common type of optical storage medium. In CD-ROM, data is written in a series of lands and pits on the surface of a compact disc (CD), which can be read by a laser in a CD-ROM drive.

compatible Describes the capability of one type of hardware, software, or data file to work with another. See also *incompatible*.

compiler A program that translates a file of program source code into machine language.

Complex Instruction Set Computing (CISC) Describes a type of processor designed to handle large and comprehensive instruction sets. CISC processors are commonly used in IBM-compatible PCs.

computer An electronic device used to process data, converting the data into information that is useful to people.

computer-aided design (CAD) Software used to create complex two- or three-dimensional models of buildings and products, including architectural, engineering, and mechanical designs.

computer-aided software engineering (CASE) Software used to develop information systems. CASE automates the analysis, design, programming, and documentation tasks.

computer-generated imaging (CGI) The process of using powerful computers and special graphics, animation, and compositing software to create digital special effects or unique images. CGI is frequently used in filmmaking, game design, animation, and multimedia design.

computer system A four-part system that consists of hardware, software, data, and a user.

conditional statement A feature of selection structure programming that directs program flow by branching to one part of the program or another depending on the results of a comparison.

configure To adapt a computer to a specific need by selecting from a range of hardware or software options. Configuration may include installing new or replacement hardware or software or changing settings in existing hardware or software.

contact information Data that can help communicate with individuals or businesses, such as names, mailing addresses, phone numbers, e-mail addresses, and other details. This kind of information is often stored and managed in special software, such as contact-management software, personal information managers, or e-mail programs.

contact-management software See *personal information manager*.

contact manager See *personal information manager*.

context menu In Windows 95 and later operating systems, a brief menu that appears when the user right-clicks certain items.

The menu contains commands that apply specifically to the item that was right-clicked. Also called a *shortcut menu.*

control unit The component of the CPU that contains the instruction set. The control unit directs the flow of data throughout the computer system. See also *instruction set.*

conversion The process of replacing an existing system with an updated or improved version. Information systems (IS) professionals may use one or more different conversion methods when changing an organization's system.

cookie A special text file that a Web server places on a visitor's computer. A cookie may store information about your visit at a Web site, or it may store personal information such as credit card data. Web sites create cookies and store them on the user's computer.

cookie-management utility A program that allows the user to control the handling of cookies on the PC. Using a cookie-management program, you can determine what types of cookies to allow on your system and can selectively remove cookies at any time.

Copy command An application command that makes a duplicate of data selected from a document and stores it in the Clipboard without removing the data from the original document. The data then can be used in other documents and other applications.

counter field A database field that stores a unique incrementing numeric value (such as an invoice number) that the DBMS automatically assigns to each new record. Also called *autonumber field.*

countermeasure Any step that is taken to avoid or protect against a threat.

cps See *characters per second.*

CPU See *central processing unit.*

crawler A special software program, commonly used by search engines, that travels the Internet looking for new Web pages and recording their addresses. Also called *spiders.*

credit report A document that lists all your financial accounts that can be a source of credit or that you can use for making purchases or for other transactions. These include bank accounts, mortgages, credit cards, and others.

CRT See *cathode ray tube.*

cursor A graphic symbol on the screen that indicates where the next keystroke or command will appear when entered. Also called the *insertion point.*

cursor-movement keys On a computer keyboard, the keys that direct the movement of the on-screen cursor or insertion point, including the up, down, left, and right arrows and the HOME, END, PAGE UP, and PAGE DOWN keys.

Cut command An application command that removes data selected from a document and stores it in the Clipboard. The data is no longer a part of the original document. While in the Clipboard, the data can be used in other documents or applications.

cybercrime The use of a computer to carry out any conventional criminal act, such as fraud.

cyberterrorism A form of warfare in which terrorists attack a nation's critical information infrastructure. The conventional goal is to harm or control key computer systems or digital controls in order to disrupt utilities or telecommunications. Typical targets are power plants, nuclear facilities, water treatment plants, and government agencies.

cylinder A vertical stack of tracks, one track on each side of each platter of a hard disk.

D

daisy wheel printer A now-obsolete type of impact printer that uses a spinning wheel embossed with alphanumeric characters, which are pressed against an inked ribbon to create an image.

DAS See *direct attached storage.*

data Raw facts, numbers, letters, or symbols that the computer processes into meaningful information.

data area The part of the disk that remains free to store information after the logical formatting process has created the boot sector, file allocation table (FAT), and root folder.

data bus An electrical path composed of parallel wires that connect the CPU, memory, and other hardware on the motherboard. The number of wires determines the amount of data that can be transferred across the bus at one time.

data compression The process of reducing data volume and increasing data-transfer rates by using mathematical algorithms to analyze groups of bits and encode repeating sequences of data.

data compression utility A program that reduces the volume of data by manipulating the way the data is stored.

data diddling The copying or altering of data on an infiltrated system by a hacker.

Data Exchange Format (DXF) An open file format for vector graphics files.

data flow diagram A method of documenting how data moves through a system, including input, processing, and output.

data mining A method of searching large databases for specific types of information, used by large organizations. For example, companies with large databases of customer information may use data mining technologies to search for purchasing trends or very specific kinds of demographic data.

data projector An output device that can project a computer's display onto a screen or wall.

data scrubbing The process of ensuring the integrity and usefulness of data in a database. Data scrubbing can ensure, for example, that all telephone numbers are formatted a specific way, duplicate entries are identified, and inappropriate data is not allowed in the database. Also called *data validation.*

data transfer rate The rate at which a data storage device can transfer data to another device; expressed as either bits per second (bps) or bytes per second (Bps). Also called *throughput.*

data validation See *data scrubbing.*

data warehouse Refers to a huge collection of data in one or more databases, of the kind often used by large businesses.

database A collection of related data organized with a specific structure.

database management system (DBMS) A computer program used to manage the storage, organization, processing, and retrieval of data in a database.

datagram The term for data packets when traversing the Internet. A datagram (or packet) is a piece of a larger message that has been broken up for transmission over the Internet.

date field A database field that stores a date.

DB2 An enterprise-level database management system, developed and sold by IBM Corp.

DBMS See *database management system.*

DDOS attack See *distributed denial of service attack.*

debugging The process of tracking down and correcting errors (called *bugs*) in a software program.

decimal number system The system that uses 10 digits to represent numbers; also called *base 10.*

decision support system (DSS) A specialized application used to collect and report certain types of business data, which can be used to aid managers in the decision-making process.

decision tree A graphical representation of the events and actions that can occur in a program or information system under different conditions.

decoding (1) In a machine cycle, the step in which the control unit breaks down a command into instructions that correspond to the CPU's instruction set. (2) During file compression, the process of reinserting bits stripped away during encoding.

dedicated media Media (such as cables or wireless links) that are specifically set up for use in a network.

defragmentation The process of locating file fragments (parts of a file that are stored in noncontiguous sectors) on the surface of a magnetic disk, then storing them in contiguous sectors. This process can help optimize a disk's performance by allowing it to locate and load files in less time.

degaussing The process of disrupting a magnetic field. If a floppy disk become degaussed, for example, the data stored on it can be corrupted or destroyed.

density A measure of the quality of a magnetic disk's surface. The higher a disk's density, the more data the disk can store.

description field See *memo field.*

deselect The opposite of *select*. In many applications, the user can select, or highlight, blocks of text or objects for editing. By clicking the mouse in a different location or pressing a cursor-movement key, the user removes the highlighting and the text or objects are no longer selected.

desktop In a computer operating system, a graphical workspace in which all of the computer's available resources (such as files, programs, printers, Internet tools, and utilities) can be easily accessed by the user. In such systems, the desktop is a colored background on which the user sees small pictures, called *icons*. The user accesses various resources by choosing icons on the desktop.

desktop computer A full-size personal computer whose system unit is designed to sit on top of a desk or table; such computers are not considered to be portable. One variation of the desktop model is the *tower model,* whose system unit can stand upright on the floor.

development phase Phase 3 of the systems development life cycle, in which programmers create or customize software to fit the needs of an organization, technical documentation is prepared, and software testing is begun.

device Any electronic component attached to or part of a computer; hardware.

DHCP See *Dynamic Host Control Protocol.*

dial-up connection An Internet connection between a client computer and an Internet service provider's (ISP's) server computer, which takes place over a standard telephone line, using a standard modem. Such connections are called "dial-up" because the client computer's modem must dial a telephone number in order to connect to the ISP's server computer.

dialog box A special-purpose window that appears when the user issues certain commands in a program or graphical operating system. A dialog box gets its name from the "dialog" it conducts with the user as the program seeks the information it needs to perform a task.

digital The use of the numerals 1 and 0 (digits) to express data in a computer. The computer recognizes the numeral 1 as an "on" state of a transistor, whereas a 0 represents an "off" state.

digital camera A camera that converts light intensities into digital data. Digital cameras are used to record images that can be viewed and edited on a computer.

digital light processing (DLP) A technology used in some types of digital projectors to project bright, crisp images. DLP devices use a special microchip, called a *digital micromirror device,* that uses mirrors to control the image display. DLP projectors can display clear images in normal lighting conditions.

digital pen See *pen.*

Digital Subscriber Line (DSL) A form of digital telephone service used to transmit voice and data signals. There are several varieties of DSL technology, which include Asymmetrical DSL, High bit-rate DSL, and others.

Digital Video Disc (DVD) A high-density optical medium capable of storing a full-length movie on a single disc the size of a standard compact disc (CD). Unlike a standard CD, which stores data on only one side, a DVD-format disc stores data on both sides. Using compression technologies and very fine data areas on the disc's surface, newer-generation DVDs can store several gigabytes of data.

Digital Video Disc-RAM (DVD-RAM) A type of optical device that allows users to record, erase, and re-record data on a special disc. Using video editing software, you can record your own digitized videos onto a DVD-RAM disc, then play them back in any DVD player. (However, special encoding makes it impossible to copy movies from commercial DVD onto a DVD-RAM disc.) DVD-RAM drives can read DVDs, DVD-R discs, CD-R discs, CD-RW discs, and standard CDs.

digitize To convert an image or a sound into a series of binary numbers (1s and 0s) that can be stored in a computer.

DIMM See *Dual In-Line Memory Module.*

direct attached storage (DAS) A storage device that is attached directly to a computer and that depends on the computer's processor.

Director A multimedia authoring program, developed by Macromedia, Inc.

directory See *folder.*

disconnected datasets Information that is temporarily copied from a central database to a user's computer and resides on the user's system only for as long as the user needs it. During that time, the connection with the database is broken.

disk A storage medium commonly used in computers. Two types of disks are used: magnetic disks, which store data as charged particles on the disk's surface; and optical discs, which use lasers to read data embossed on the disc in a series of lands and pits.

disk controller A device that connects a disk drive to the computer's bus, enabling the drive to exchange data with other devices.

disk defragmenter A utility program that locates the pieces of fragmented files saved in noncontiguous sectors on a magnetic disk and rearranges them so they are stored in contiguous sectors. Defragmenting a disk can improve its performance because the operating system can locate data more efficiently.

disk drive A storage device that holds, spins, reads data from, and writes data to a disk.

disk optimization One or more disk-management procedures that can improve a disk's performance. Disk optimization procedures include defragmentation, deletion of unneeded files, compression, and others.

diskette A removable magnetic disk encased in a plastic sleeve. Also called *floppy disk* or *floppy.*

diskette drive A device that holds a removable floppy disk when in use; read/write heads read and write data to the diskette.

display adapter See *video card.*

distributed application A program that is divided into parts, each of which executes on a different computer. In essence, the program's execution is distributed across multiple systems.

distributed computing A system configuration in which two or more computers in a network share applications, storage, and processing power. Also called *distributed processing.*

distributed denial of service (DDOS) attack A type of hacking attack in which a hacker hides malicious code on the PCs of many victims. This code may enable the hacker to take over the infected PCs, or simply use them to send requests to a Web server. If the hacker controls enough PCs, and can get them to send enough requests to the targeted Web server, the server essentially becomes jammed with requests and stops working.

distributed processing See *distributed computing.*

DLL See *dynamic link library file.*

DLP See *digital light processing.*

DNS See *domain name system.*

docking station A base into which a portable computer can be inserted, essentially converting the portable computer into a desktop system. A docking station may provide connections to a full-size monitor, keyboard, and mouse, as well as additional devices such as speakers or a digital video camera.

document A computer file consisting of a compilation of one or more kinds of data. There are many types, including text documents, spreadsheets, graphics files, and so on. A document, which a user can open and use, is different from a program file, which is required by a software program to operate.

document area In many software applications, the portion of the program's interface in which the active document appears. In this part of the interface, the user can work directly with the document and its contents. Also called *document window.*

document format In productivity applications, a setting that affects the appearance of the entire document, such as page size, page orientation, and the presence of headers or footers.

document window See *document area.*

domain name A name given to a computer and its peripherals connected to the Internet that identifies the type of organization using the computer. Examples of domain names are .com for commercial enterprises and .edu for schools. Also called *top-level domain.*

domain name system (DNS) A naming system used for computers on the Internet. This system provides an individual name (representing the organization using the computer) and a domain name, which classifies the type of organization.

dot matrix printer A type of impact printer that creates characters on a page by using small pins to strike an inked ribbon, pressing ink onto the paper. The arrangement of pins in the print head creates a matrix of dots—hence the device's name.

dot pitch The distance between phosphor dots on a monitor. The highest-resolution monitors have the smallest dot pitch.

dots per inch (dpi) A measure of resolution commonly applied to printers, scanners, and other devices that input or output text or images. The more dots per inch, the higher the resolution. For example, if a printer has a resolution of 600 dpi, it can print 600 dots across and 600 down in a one-inch square, for a total of 360,000 dots in one square inch.

double-click To select an object or activate a command on the screen by pointing to an object (such as an icon) and pressing and releasing the mouse button twice in quick succession.

download To retrieve a file from a remote computer. The opposite of *upload.*

dpi See *dots per inch.*

drag To move an object on the screen by pointing to the object, pressing the primary mouse button, and holding down the button while dragging the object to a new location.

drag and drop To move text or graphics from one part of the document to another by selecting the desired information, pressing and holding down the primary mouse button, dragging the selection to a new location, and releasing the mouse button. Also called *drag-and-drop editing*.

draw program A graphics program that uses vectors to create an image. Mathematical equations describe each line, shape, and pattern, allowing the user to manipulate all elements of the graphic separately.

Dreamweaver A Web-authoring environment, developed by Macromedia, Inc.

driver A small program that accepts requests for action from the operating system and causes a device, such as a printer, to execute the requests.

DSL See *Digital Subscriber Line*.

DSS See *decision support system*.

Dual In-Line Memory Module (DIMM) One type of circuit board containing RAM chips.

dual-scan LCD An improved passive-matrix technology for flat-panel monitors in which pixels are scanned twice as often, reducing the effects of blurry graphics and submarining (an effect that occurs when the mouse pointer blurs or disappears when it is moved).

dumpster diving The act of searching through trash in hopes of finding valuable personal information such as account numbers, passwords, or Social Security numbers; commonly practiced by identity thieves.

DVD See *digital video disc*.

DVD-R See *DVD-Recordable*.

DVD-RAM See *Digital Video Disc-RAM*.

DVD-Recordable (DVD-R) An optical disc drive that can record data onto the surface of a special, recordable DVD disc. Once data has been written to the disc, it cannot be overwritten.

DXF See *Data Exchange Format*.

dye-sublimation (dye-sub) printer A printer that produces photographic-quality images by using a heat source to evaporate colored inks from a ribbon, transferring the color to specially coated paper.

dynamic Describes anything that can be changed. For example, a computer's IP address may be dynamic, meaning that it changes each time the user connects to the Internet. Similarly, a Web page's content can be dynamic, changing in response to user inputs.

dynamic addressing Another name for *Dynamic Host Control Protocol (DHCP)*.

Dynamic Host Control Protocol (DHCP) An Internet protocol that automatically assigns all necessary Internet configurations to a computer that connects to the Internet.

dynamic IP address The address given to a computer by a DHCP server.

dynamic link library (.dll) file A partial executable file. A .dll file will not run all on its own; rather, its commands are accessed by another running program.

E

EBCDIC See *Extended Binary Coded Decimal Interchange Code*.

e-commerce See *electronic commerce*.

EDI See *Electronic Data Interchange*.

edit To make modifications to an existing document file.

EDM See *electronic document management*.

EIDE See *Enhanced Integrated Drive Electronics*.

ELD See *electroluminescent display*.

electroluminescent display (ELD) A monitor that is similar to an LCD monitor but uses a phosphorescent film held between two sheets of glass. A grid of wires sends current through the film to create an image.

electromagnetic field (EMF) A field of magnetic and electrical forces created during the generation, transmission, and use of low-frequency electrical power. EMFs are produced by computers.

electronic commerce The practice of conducting business transactions online, such as selling products from a World Wide Web site. The process often involves the customer's providing personal or credit card information online, presenting special security concerns. Also called *e-commerce*.

Electronic Communications Privacy Act A federal law (enacted in 1986) that prevents unlawful access to voice communications by wire. It originally regulated electronic wiretaps and provided the basis for laws defining illegal access to electronic communications, including computer information. It is the basis for protection against unreasonable governmental intrusion into Internet usage, stored electronic communications, and e-mail.

Electronic Data Interchange (EDI) The transfer of information electronically between companies over networks.

electronic document management A popular type of enterprise software that tracks documents, keeps related ideas together, and aids in facilities management.

electronic mail A system for exchanging written, voice, and video messages through a computer network. Also called *e-mail*.

e-mail See *electronic mail*.

e-mail address An address that identifies an individual user of an electronic mail system, enabling the person to send and receive e-mail messages. The e-mail address consists of a user name, the "at" symbol (@) and the DNS address.

e-mail client See *e-mail program*.

e-mail program Software that lets you create, send, and receive e-mail messages. Also called an *e-mail client*.

embedded operating system A computer operating system that is built into the circuitry of an electronic device—unlike a PC's operating system, which resides on a magnetic disk. Embedded operating systems are typically found in devices such as PDAs.

EMF See *electromagnetic field*.

encapsulate To include characteristics or other objects within an object in an object-oriented program.

encryption The process of encoding and decoding data, making it useless to any system that cannot decode (decrypt) it.

Enhanced Integrated Drive Electronics (EIDE) An enhanced version of the IDE interface.

enterprise directory A collection of data about the users of a network and the computer resources of the network. This database typically is managed by the network operating system, which resides on a network server.

enterprise software Software that is used by hundreds or thousands of people at the same time, or that handles millions of records, or both.

enterprise storage A large-scale system of data storage, connected to the computer system of a large organization.

enterprise system A very large-scale computer system, such as one used by a large organization.

ergonomics The study of the physical relationship between people and their tools. In the world of computing, ergonomics seeks to help people use computers correctly to avoid physical problems such as fatigue, eyestrain, and repetitive stress injuries.

error-correction protocol A standard for correcting errors that occur when static interferes with data transmitted via modems over telephone lines.

Ethernet The most common network protocol. Also called *10Base-T*.

Event Viewer In later versions of Windows, a program that records certain conditions, such as errors, and creates a log that is usable by the system's user or administrator.

executable (.exe, .com) file The core program file responsible for launching software.

execute To load and carry out a program or a specific set of instructions. Executing is also called *running*.

execution cycle The second portion of the machine cycle, which is the series of steps a CPU takes when executing an instruction. During the execution cycle, the CPU actually carries out the instruction by converting it into microcode. In some cases, the CPU may be required to store the results of an instruction in memory; if so, this occurs during the execution cycle.

exit condition In programming, a condition that must be met in order for a loop to stop repeating.

expansion board A device that enables the user to configure or customize a computer to perform specific tasks or to enhance performance. An expansion board—also called a *card*, *adapter*, or *board*—contains a special set of chips and circuitry that add functionality to the computer. An expansion board may be installed to add fax/modem capabilities to the computer, for example, or to provide sound or video-editing capabilities.

expansion slot The area of the motherboard into which expansion boards are inserted, connecting them to the PC's bus.

expert system An information system in which decision-making processes are automated. A highly detailed database is accessed by an inference engine, which is capable of forming an intelligent response to a query.

Extended ASCII An extension of the ASCII character set, which specifies the characters for values from 128 to 255. These characters include punctuation marks, pronunciation symbols, and graphical symbols.

Extended Binary Coded Decimal Interchange Code (EBCDIC) An eight-bit code that defines 256 symbols. It is still used in IBM mainframe and midrange systems, but it is rarely encountered in personal computers.

Extensible Hypertext Markup Language (XHTML) An outgrowth of HTML, XHTML is a superset of the HTML commands, including the capabilities of HTML and adding to them. XHTML allows for the execution of programs written in Extensible Markup Language (XML) and it is itself extensible, meaning that it allows for new commands and features to be added.

Extensible Markup Language (XML) An outgrowth of HTML, it is a markup language that allows data to be stored in a human-readable format. The language also allows users to create unique tags or other elements.

Extensible Markup Language Mobile Profile (XHTML MP) A new development environment formerly known as Wireless Markup Language (WML) used to create documents that can be viewed by handheld devices such as Web-enabled cell phones, PDAs, and even digital pagers.

Extensible Stylesheet Language (XSL) An XML technology that allows XML documents to be formatted for display in HTML-based browsers.

extension point A device that allows a greater number of users to access a wireless network.

external cache See *Level-2 cache*.

external modem A communications device used to modulate data signals. This type of device is described as "external" because it is housed outside the computer and connected to the computer through a serial port and to the telephone system with a standard telephone jack.

extract To uncompress one or more compressed files that have been stored together in an archive file.

extranet A network connection that enables external users to access a portion of an organization's internal network, usually via an Internet connection. External users have access to specific parts of the internal network but are forbidden to access other areas, which are protected by firewalls.

eyestrain Fatigue of the eyes, caused by staring at a fixed object for too long. Extended computer use can lead to eyestrain.

F

Fair Credit Reporting Act A federal law (enacted in 1970) that mandates that personal information assembled by credit reporting agencies must be accurate, fair, and private. It allows individuals to review and update their credit record as well as dispute the entries.

FAQ See *frequently asked questions*.

Fast Ethernet A networking technology, also called *100Base-T*, that uses the same network cabling scheme as Ethernet but uses different network interface cards to achieve data transfer speeds of up to 100 Mbps.

FAT See *file allocation table.*

fault tolerance The ability of a computer system to continue functioning, even after a major component has failed.

fax modem A modem that can emulate a fax machine.

fetching The first step of the CPU's instruction cycle, during which the control unit retrieves (or fetches) a command or data from the computer's memory.

fiber-optic cable A thin strand of glass wrapped in a protective coating. Fiber-optic cable transfers data by means of pulsating beams of light.

field The smallest unit of data in a database; used to group each piece or item of data into a specific category. Fields are arranged in a column and titled by the user.

fifth-generation language (5GL) A high-level programming language that theoretically would use artificial intelligence techniques to create software, based on the programmer's description of the program.

file A set of related computer data (used by a person) or program instructions (used by an application or operating system) that has been given a name.

file allocation table (FAT) In a diskette or hard disk, a log created during the logical formatting process that records the location of each file and the status of each sector on the disk.

file compression See *data compression.*

file compression utility See *data compression utility.*

file format A standardized method of encoding data for storage.

file server The central computer of a network; used for shared storage. A server may store software applications, databases, and data files for the network's users. Depending on the way a server is used, it also may be called a *network server, application server,* or *server.*

file server network A hierarchical network strategy in which the server is used to store and forward files to the nodes. Each node runs its own applications.

file system In an operating system, a logical method for managing the storage of data on a disk's surface.

file transfer The process of sending a file from one computer to another by modem or across a network. See also *download* and *upload.*

file transfer protocol (FTP) A set of rules that dictate the format in which data is sent from one computer to another.

filter (1) A DBMS tool that enables the user to establish conditions for selecting and displaying a subset of records that meet those criteria. (2) In an e-mail program, a tool that allows the user to decide how messages are handled. For example, you can create a filter that automatically deletes messages from a certain sender or that stores certain messages in a specific folder. In e-mail programs, a filter also may be called a *rule.*

Financial Modernization Act of 1999 A federal law that requires companies to give consumers notice of their privacy and information-sharing practices.

firewall An antipiracy method for protecting networks. A firewall permits access to public sections of the network while protecting proprietary areas.

FireWire See *IEEE 1394.*

first-generation language A term applied to machine languages, which were the earliest and crudest programming languages used with personal computers.

first-party cookie A cookie placed on a user's computer by the Web site he or she is currently viewing. First-party cookies are persistent and usually store preferences the user has set for viewing the site. Some first-party cookies store information that can personally identify the user.

Flash A development tool for creating very sophisticated Web pages; it can include moving graphics, animation, sound, and interactivity.

flash memory A special type of memory chip that combines the best features of RAM and ROM. Like RAM, flash memory lets a user or program access data randomly. Also like RAM, flash memory lets the user overwrite any or all of its contents at any time. Like ROM, flash memory is nonvolatile, so it retains data even when power is off.

flash memory drive A small-format storage device that uses flash memory to hold data. This highly portable storage device is small enough to be carried on a keychain.

flat-file database A database file consisting of a single data table that is not linked to any other tables.

flat-panel display A thin, lightweight monitor used in laptop and notebook computers. Most flat-panel displays use LCD technology.

floppy See *diskette.*

floppy disk See *diskette.*

flowchart A diagram of the program control flow.

folder A tool for organizing data stored on a disk. A folder contains a list of files and other folders stored on the disk. A disk can hold many folders, which can in turn store many files and other folders. Also called a *directory.*

font A family of alphanumeric characters, symbols, and punctuation marks that share the same design. Modern applications provide many different fonts and enable users to use different fonts in the same document. Also called a *typeface.*

form A custom screen created in a database management system (DBMS) for displaying and entering data related to a single database record.

format (1) As relating to magnetic storage devices, the layout of tracks and sectors in which data is stored. (2) In productivity applications, a setting that affects the appearance of a document or part of a document.

formatting (1) The process of magnetically mapping a disk with a series of tracks and sectors where data will be stored. Also called *initializing*. (2) The process of applying formatting options (such as character or paragraph formats) to a document.

formula A mathematical equation within a cell of a spreadsheet. To identify it and distinguish it from other spreadsheet entries, a formula begins with a special symbol, such as a plus sign or an equal sign.

formula bar In spreadsheet programs, a special text box that displays the active cell's address and the data or formula entered in that cell. The user may be able to enter or edit data or formulas in this box.

fourth-generation language (4GL) An advanced programming language used to create an application.

fragmentation Describes the state of a file that has been broken into sections that are stored on noncontiguous sectors of a disk.

frame (1) In networking, a small block of data to be transmitted over a network. A frame includes an identifying header and the actual data to be sent. Also called a *packet*. (2) In animation, a single still image that, when viewed with many other images in rapid succession, creates the illusion of motion. (3) In many software applications, a special tool that enables the user to place an object—such as a text box or an image from a separate file—in a document. The frame surrounds the object in the document, enabling the user to position and resize the object as needed.

Freedom of Information Act A federal law (enacted in 1966) that allows individuals to view and amend personal information kept about them by any governmental entity.

Freescale A subsidiary of Motorola, Inc., that produces microprocessors used in many Apple computers, as well as in large-scale UNIX-based systems.

freeware Software that is made freely available to the public by the publisher. Freeware publishers usually allow users to distribute their software to others, as long as the software's source files are not modified and as long as the distributor charges no fees or does not profit from the distribution.

frequently asked questions (FAQs) A document routinely developed by a newsgroup; it lists questions most commonly asked in the newsgroup, along with their answers. FAQs help a newsgroup's members avoid the repeated posting of the same information to the group.

FrontSide Bus Found in many newer model computers, a 64-bit data bus that transfers eight bytes at a time.

FTP See *file transfer protocol.*

FTP client software Programs that enable users to download files from an FTP site.

FTP server A computer used to store FTP sites, many containing thousands of individual programs and files.

FTP site A collection of files stored on an FTP server; users can copy files from and to their own computer.

function (1) In a spreadsheet, a formula used to perform complex operations, such as adding the contents of a range or finding the absolute value of a cell's contents. (2) In programming, a block of statements designed to perform a specific routine or task.

function key The part of the keyboard that can be used to quickly activate commands; designated F1, F2, and so on.

G

game controller A specialized type of input device that enables the user to interact with computer games. Two popular types of game controllers are game pads and joysticks.

game pad A type of game controller that usually provides two sets of controls—one for each hand. These devices are extremely flexible and are used to control a wide variety of game systems.

gateway A computer system that can translate one network protocol into another so that data can be transmitted between two dissimilar networks.

GB See *gigabyte.*

GHz See *gigahertz.*

GIF Acronym for *graphics interchange format*. A graphics file format supported by many graphics programs. GIF files are commonly used in Web pages.

Gigabit Ethernet The newest addition to Ethernet technology; capable of transferring 10 Gb of data per second.

gigabyte (GB) Equivalent to approximately one billion bytes; a typical measurement of data storage.

gigahertz (GHz) Equivalent to one billion cycles per second; a common measure of processor clock speed.

graphical user interface (GUI) A user interface in which actions are initiated when the user selects an icon, a toolbar button, or an option from a pull-down menu with the mouse or other pointing device. GUIs also represent documents, programs, and devices on screen as graphical elements that the user can use by clicking or dragging.

grayscale monitor A monitor that displays up to 256 shades of gray, ranging from white to black.

GUI See *graphical user interface.*

H

hacker An expert in computer technology who uses skill and innovative techniques to solve complex computing problems. Hackers are more notorious, however, for creating problems such as invading private or governmental computer networks, accessing data from corporate databases, online extortion, and other activities.

hacking Describes an activity performed by a *hacker*, such as invading a computer system through a network or Internet connection.

HAN See *home area network.*

handheld personal computer A personal computer that is small enough to be held in one hand. Also called *palmtop computer.*

hard disk A nonremovable magnetic storage device included in most PCs that stores data on a stack of aluminum platters, each coated with iron oxide, enclosed in a case. The device includes the hard disk platters, a spindle on which the platters spin, a read/write head for each side of each platter, and a sealed chamber that encloses the disks and spindle. Many hard disks also include the drive controller, although the controller is a separate unit on some hard disks. Also called a *hard drive*.

hard drive See *hard disk*.

hardware The physical components of a computer, including processor and memory chips, input/output devices, tapes, disks, modems, and cables.

header (1)The initial part of a data packet being transmitted across a network. The header contains information about the type of data in the payload, the source and destination of the data, and a sequence number so that data from multiple packets can be reassembled at the receiving computer in the proper order. See *frame*. (2) A recurring line or paragraph of text appearing at the top of each page in a document. Headers often include page numbers, the document's title, the name of the current chapter, or other information.

headphones A small pair of speakers attached to a headband for wearing on the head. A type of output device that allows the user to listen to audio output without disturbing others.

headset An input/output device that features a microphone and one or two speakers mounted on a headband for wearing on the head.

help (.hlp, .chm) file A file included with most software programs; it provides information for the user, such as instructions for using the program's features.

helper application A program that must be added to your browser in order to play special content files—especially those with multimedia content—in real time. Also called *plug-in application*.

hertz (Hz) The frequency of electrical vibrations, or cycles, per second.

heuristics A programming technique for solving a problem or performing a task; it does not always find the best possible solution.

high-capacity floppy disk A small, removable disk that resembles a standard diskette, but provides much higher data storage capacity. Typically, high-capacity floppy disks have data densities of 100 MB or greater.

higher-level language A language designed to make programming easier through the use of familiar English words and symbols.

holographic memory A futuristic type of storage device that stores enormous amounts of data within the structure of a crystal; it uses special lasers to read and write data.

home area network (HAN) A local area network that exists within a home, used to connect the computers and peripheral devices in the home. A HAN is commonly used to allow multiple users to share a single Internet connection.

home page An organization's principal Web page, which may provide links to other Web pages having additional information.

host A computer that provides services to other computers that connect to it. Host computers provide file transfer, communications services, and access to the Internet's high-speed data lines.

hot-swappable hard disk A magnetic storage device similar to a removable hard disk. A removable box encloses the disk, drive, and read/write heads in a sealed container. This type of hard disk can be added to or removed from a server without shutting down the server.

hot swapping The process of removing a device (such as a storage device) from a computer and replacing it without shutting down the system first and without disrupting the system's operations. Devices that can be changed in this manner are called *hot-swappable*.

HTML See *Hypertext Markup Language*.

HTML tag A code used to format documents in Hypertext Markup Language (HTML) format.

HTTP See *Hypertext Transfer Protocol*.

HTTPS See *Secure Hypertext Transfer Protocol*.

hub In a network, a device that connects nodes and servers together at a central point.

hyperlink See *hypertext link*.

hypertext A software technology that provides fast and flexible access to information. The user can jump to a topic by selecting it on screen; used to create Web pages and help screens.

hypertext link A word, icon, or other object that when clicked jumps to another location on the document or another Web page. Also called *hyperlink* or *link*.

Hypertext Markup Language (HTML) A page-description language used on the World Wide Web that defines the hypertext links between documents.

Hypertext Preprocessor (PHP) A scripting language commonly used in Web development. Applications developed in PHP are useful for obtaining data from online databases.

Hypertext Transfer Protocol (HTTP) A set of file transfer rules used on the World Wide Web; it controls the way information is shared.

hyperthreading A technology supported by some newer processors that allows multiple threads to be executed at the same time.

Hz See *hertz*.

I

I/O See *input/output*.

IANA See *Internet Assigned Numbers Authority*.

IBM Refers to the IBM Corporation, a leading maker of computer hardware, software, and technologies.

ICANN See *Internet Corporation for Assigned Names and Numbers*.

ICMP See *Internet Control Message Protocol*.

icon A graphical screen element that executes one or more commands when clicked with a mouse or other pointing device.

IDE See *integrated development environment.*

identity (ID) theft A type of crime in which a thief uses someone else's identity to obtain money or conduct business transactions. This crime usually involves the theft of the victim's personal information, such as a Social Security number, credit card number, or bank account information.

IEEE 1394 An expansion bus technology that supports data-transfer rates of up to 400 Mbps. Also called *FireWire.*

IETF See *Internet Engineering Task Force.*

IGES See *Initial Graphics Exchange Specifications.*

IIS See *Internet Information Server.*

IM See *instant messaging.*

image scanner An input device that digitizes printed images. Sensors determine the intensity of light reflected from the page, and the light intensities are converted to digital data that can be viewed and manipulated by the computer. Sometimes called simply a *scanner.*

IMAP4 See *Internet Mail Access Protocol Version 4.*

impact printer A type of printer that creates images by striking an inked ribbon, pressing ink from the ribbon onto a piece of paper. Examples of impact printers are dot-matrix printers and line printers.

implementation phase Phase 4 of the systems development life cycle. In this phase, new software and hardware are installed in the user environment, training is offered, and system testing is completed.

incompatible The opposite of *compatible.* Describes the inability of one type of hardware, software, or data file to work with another.

Industry Standard Architecture (ISA) bus A PC bus standard developed by IBM, extending the bus to 16 bits. An ISA bus can access 8-bit and 16-bit devices.

inference engine Software used with an expert system to examine data with respect to the knowledge base and to select an appropriate response.

information processing cycle The set of steps a computer follows to receive data, process the data according to instructions from a program, display the resulting information to the user, and store the results.

information system A mechanism that helps people collect, store, organize, and use information. An information system does not necessarily include computers; however, a computer is an important part of an information system.

Information Systems department The people in an organization responsible for designing, developing, implementing, and maintaining the systems necessary to manage information for all levels of the organization.

INI file See *initialization file.*

Initial Graphics Exchange Specifications (IGES) One of a few universal file formats for vector graphics.

initialization (.ini) file A file containing configuration information, such as the size and starting point of a window, the color of the background, the user's name, and so on. Initialization files help programs start running or they contain information that programs can use as they run.

initializing See *formatting.*

ink jet printer A type of nonimpact printer that produces images by spraying ink onto the page.

input device Computer hardware that accepts data and instructions from the user. Examples of input devices include the keyboard, mouse, joystick, pen, trackball, scanner, bar code reader, microphone, and touch screen.

input/output (I/O) Communications between the user and the computer or between hardware components that result in the transfer of data.

input/output (I/O) device A device that performs both input and output functions. Modems and network interface cards are examples of input/output devices.

input–processing–output (IPO) chart A programming tool used in the planning of a software development project, an IPO chart contains three columns that list the program's required inputs, processes, and outputs.

insertion point See *cursor.*

installation testing During the development phase of the systems development life cycle (SDLC), the installation of a new system in a test environment where it is tested by the business.

instant messaging (IM) Chat software that enables users to set up buddy lists and open a window to "chat" when anyone on the list is online.

instruction A command that the computer must execute so that a specific action can be carried out.

instruction cycle The first portion of the machine cycle, which is the series of steps a CPU takes when executing an instruction. During the instruction cycle, the CPU's control unit fetches a command or data from the computer's memory, enabling the CPU to execute an instruction. The control unit then decodes the command so it can be executed.

instruction set Machine language instructions that define all the operations a CPU can perform.

integrated development environment (IDE) A programming tool that provides the programmer with all of the tools needed to develop applications in one program; most commonly used with 3GLs and 4GLs.

integrated pointing device A pointing device built into the computer's keyboard; consists of a small joystick positioned near the middle of the keyboard, typically between the *g* and *h* keys. The joystick is controlled with either forefinger. Two buttons that perform the same function as mouse buttons are just beneath the spacebar and are pressed with the thumb. One type of integrated pointing device, developed by IBM, is called *TrackPoint.*

integrated services digital network (ISDN) A digital telecommunications standard that replaces analog transmissions and transmits voice, video, and data.

Intel A leading manufacturer of microprocessors. Intel invented the first microprocessor, which was used in electronic calculators.

Intel's product line includes the *x*86 processors and the Pentium processor family.

intelligent smart card A type of smart card that contains its own processor and memory.

interactive Refers to software products that can react and respond to commands issued by the user or choices made by the user.

interactivity In multimedia, a system in which the user and program respond to one another. The program gives the user choices, which the user selects to direct the program.

interface See *user interface*.

internal modem A communications device used to modulate data signals. This type of modem is described as "internal" because it is a circuit board that is plugged into one of the computer's expansion slots.

Internet Originally, a link between ARPANET, NSFnet, and other networks. Today, a worldwide network of networks.

Internet Assigned Numbers Authority (IANA) An organization responsible for distributing IP addresses to regional Internet registries, coordinating with the IETF and others to assign protocol parameters, and other tasks.

Internet Control Message Protocol (ICMP) A special protocol used by Internet hosts (computers and routers) to report errors in transmission. A companion protocol to IP, ICMP also is used for managing, testing, and monitoring the network.

Internet Corporation for Assigned Names and Numbers (ICANN) A nonprofit corporation that oversees the domain name system.

Internet Engineering Task Force (IETF) An international technical body concerned with developing protocol standards, mostly involving TCP/IP.

Internet Information Server (IIS) A popular Web server product, developed by Microsoft Corporation.

Internet Mail Access Protocol Version 4 (IMAP4) An advanced e-mail protocol used on the Internet.

Internet Protocol (IP) Part of the TCP/IP protocol suite, a protocol that maintains the network addresses for the logical internetwork overlaying the physical network. Just as there is a physical address for every computer connected to a network, in a TCP/IP network there is also a specific logical address assigned to each computer or device that functions at the network layer. These addresses are called *IP addresses*, and each computer, router, and network printer, and all other devices that function at the network layer, must have an IP address.

Internet Protocol (IP) address A unique four-part numeric address assigned to each computer on the Internet, containing routing information to identify its location. Each of the four parts is a number between 0 and 255.

Internet relay chat (IRC) A multiuser system made up of channels that people join for exchanging messages either publicly or privately. Messages are exchanged in real time, meaning the messages are transmitted to other users on the channel as they are typed in.

Internet service provider (ISP) An intermediary service between the Internet backbone and the user, providing easy and relatively inexpensive access to shell accounts, direct TCP/IP connections, and high-speed access through dedicated data circuits.

internetworking The process of connecting separate networks together.

interpreter In programming, a software tool that converts source code to machine code. Instead of creating an executable file (as a compiler does), however, an interpreter executes each bit of machine code as it is converted. Interpreters, therefore, are said to translate code on the fly.

interrupt A preprogrammed set of steps that a CPU follows.

intranet An internal network whose interface and accessibility are modeled after an Internet-based Web site. Only internal users are allowed to access information or resources on the intranet; if connected to an external network or the Internet, the intranet's resources are protected from outside access by firewalls.

intrusion detection software Software that works with (or is built into) a firewall, which reveals the types of attacks a firewall is thwarting. The program creates logs of the attacks and may notify the user or administrator of certain types of intrusion attempts.

IP *See Internet Protocol.*

IP address See *Internet Protocol address.*

IP spoofing A method used by hackers and spammers to send messages to a victim from what appears to be a trusted computer.

IPO chart See *input–processing–output chart.*

IRC See *Internet relay chat.*

IS department See *Information Systems department.*

ISA bus See *Industry Standard Architecture bus.*

ISDN See *integrated services digital network.*

ISP See *Internet service provider.*

J

JAD See *joint applications design.*

Java A programming language used for creating cross-platform programs. Java enables Web page designers to include small applications (called *applets*) in Web pages.

Java applet A Java-based program included in a Web page.

JavaScript A Java-based scripting language, commonly used to create applets.

joint applications design (JAD) A process—sometimes used during the user design phase of the rapid application development (RAD) systems development cycle—in which users and developers work together to create applications. The JAD process focuses on structured workshops, in which developers and business users can collaborate.

Joint Photographic Experts Group (JPEG) format A bitmap file format commonly used to display photographic images.

joint requirements planning (JRP) A process—often used during the requirements planning phase of the rapid application development (RAD) systems development cycle—to identify high-level, strategic management requirements. At the heart of JRP are highly structured workshops in which senior managers participate in defining the goals and strategy of the organization and defining the goals and priorities of the new system.

joystick An input device used to control the movement of on-screen components; typically used in video games.

JPEG See *Joint Photographic Experts Group format*.

JRP See *joint requirements planning*.

K

KB See *kilobyte*.

keyboard The most common input device, used to enter letters, numbers, symbols, punctuation, and commands into the computer. Computer keyboards typically include numeric, alphanumeric, cursor-movement, modifier, and function keys, as well as other special keys.

keyboard buffer A part of memory that receives and stores the scan codes from the keyboard controller until the program can accept them.

keyboard controller A chip within the keyboard or the computer that receives the keystroke and generates the scan code.

keyboarding Touch typing using a computer keyboard.

keyword A term or phrase used as the basis for a search when looking for information on the World Wide Web.

kilobyte (KB) Equivalent to 1,024 bytes; a common measure of data storage.

knowledge base A highly specialized database used with an expert system to intelligently produce solutions.

knowledge discovery Describes a type of database utility designed to analyze data and report useful information.

L

L1 cache See *Level-1 cache*.

L2 cache See *Level-2 cache*.

L3 cache See *Level-3 cache*.

label Descriptive text used in a spreadsheet cell to describe the data in a column or row.

LAN See *local area network*.

land A flat area on the metal surface of a optical disc that reflects the laser light into the sensor of an optical disc drive. See also *pit*.

laptop computer See *notebook computer*.

laser printer A quiet, fast printer that produces high-quality output. A laser beam focused on an electrostatic drum creates an image to which powdered toner adheres, and that image is transferred to paper.

LCD monitor See *liquid crystal display monitor*.

LDAP See *Lightweight Directory Access Protocol*.

Level-1 (L1) cache A type of cache memory built directly into the microprocessor. Also called *on-board cache*.

Level-2 (L2) cache A type of cache memory that is external to the microprocessor but is positioned between the CPU and RAM. Also called *external cache*.

Level-3 (L3) cache A type of cache memory that is built into the computer's motherboard.

Lightweight Directory Access Protocol (LDAP) A set of protocols used for accessing information directories such as e-mail names and addresses stored on a mail server. The advantages of LDAP are that it is very fast, it is simpler, and it is constructed to work with TCP/IP. LDAP eventually should make it possible for almost any application running on virtually any computer platform to obtain directory information such as e-mail addresses.

line conditioner A device that protects hardware from electrical surges and line noise.

line noise Power disturbances that can be caused by high-demand electrical equipment such as air conditioners.

line printer A type of impact printer that uses a special, wide print head to print an entire line of characters at one time.

link See *hypertext link*.

Linux A freely available version of the UNIX operating system. Developed by a worldwide cooperative of programmers in the 1990s, Linux is a feature-rich, 32-bit, multiuser, multiprocessor operating system that runs on virtually any hardware platform.

liquid crystal display (LCD) monitor A flat-panel monitor on which an image is created when the liquid crystal becomes charged; used primarily in notebook computers.

listserv An e-mail server that contains a list of names and enables users to communicate with others on the list in an ongoing discussion.

local area network (LAN) A system of PCs located relatively near to one another and connected by wire or a wireless link. A LAN permits simultaneous access to data and resources, enhances personal communication, and simplifies backup procedures.

local bus An internal system bus that runs between components on the motherboard.

logic error A bug in which the code directs the computer to perform a task incorrectly.

logical field A database field that stores only one of two values: yes or no, true or false, on or off, and so on. Also called a *Boolean field*.

logical formatting An operating system function in which tracks and sectors are mapped on the surface of a disk. This mapping creates the master boot record, FAT, root folder (also called the *root directory*), and the data area. Also called *soft formatting* and *low-level formatting*.

logical operation One of the two types of operations a computer can perform. Logical operations usually involve making a comparison, such as determining whether two values are equal. See also *arithmetic operation*.

loop A program or routine that executes a set of instructions repeatedly while a specific condition is true, or until a new event (called an *exit condition*) occurs.

looping structure See *repetition structure.*

low-level formatting See *logical formatting.*

M

machine code See *machine language.*

machine cycle The complete series of steps a CPU takes in executing an instruction. A machine cycle itself can be broken down into two smaller cycles: the instruction cycle and the execution cycle.

machine language The lowest level of computer language. Machine language includes the strings of 1s and 0s that the computer can understand. Although programs can be written in many different higher-level languages, they all must be converted to machine language before the computer can understand and use them. Also called *machine code.*

Mac OS See *Macintosh operating system.*

Macintosh operating system (Mac OS) The operating system that runs on machines built by Apple Computer.

macro A series of commands and other actions, recorded and saved with a name for later use. Many programs support macros, which enable users to automate repetitive or common tasks.

magnetic disk A round, flat disk covered with a magnetic material (such as iron oxide), the most commonly used storage medium. Data is written magnetically on the disk and can be recorded over and over. The magnetic disk is the basic component of the diskette and hard disk.

magnetic storage A storage technology in which data is recorded when iron particles are polarized on a magnetic storage medium.

mail merge The process of combining a text document, such as a letter, with the contents of a database, such as an address list; commonly used to produce form letters.

mail server In an e-mail system, the server on which messages received from the post office server are stored until the recipients access their mailboxes and retrieve the messages.

mainframe A large, multiuser computer system designed to handle massive amounts of input, output, and storage. A mainframe is usually composed of one or more powerful CPUs connected to many input/output devices, called *terminals*, or to personal computers. Mainframe systems are typically used in businesses requiring the maintenance of huge databases or simultaneous processing of multiple complex tasks.

maintenance phase Phase 5 of the systems development life cycle. In this phase, the new system is monitored, errors are corrected, and minor adjustments are made to improve system performance.

malware Describes a variety of malicious software programs such as viruses, spyware, and Web bugs.

MAN See *metropolitan area network.*

management information system (MIS) A set of software tools that enables managers to gather, organize, and evaluate information about a workgroup, department, or an entire organization. These systems meet the needs of three different categories of managers—executives, middle managers, and front-line managers—by producing a range of standardized reports drawn from the organization's database. A good management information system summarizes vast amounts of business data into information that is useful to each type of manager.

massively parallel processing (MPP) A processing architecture that uses hundreds or thousands of microprocessors in one computer to perform complex processes quickly.

mb See *megabit.*

MB See *megabyte.*

mbps See *megabits per second.*

MBps See *megabytes per second.*

mechanical mouse A mouse that tracks motion mechanically, using a ball, a set of rollers, and built-in sensors. As the mouse is moved across a flat surface, the ball's rolling motion is detected by the rollers and sensors, which send data about the mouse's direction and speed to the computer.

media The plural form of the word *medium*. See *medium*.

medium (1) In storage technology, a medium is material used to store data, such as the magnetic coating on a disk or tape, or the metallic platter in a compact disc. (2) In networking, a medium is a means of conveying a signal across the network, such as a cable. (3) In multimedia, a medium is a single means of conveying a message, such as text or video.

megabit (mb) Equivalent to approximately one million bits. A common measure of data transfer speeds.

megabits per second (mbps) Equivalent to one million bits of data per second.

megabyte (MB) Equivalent to approximately one million bytes. A common measure of data storage capacity.

megabytes per second (MBps) Equivalent to one million bytes of data per second.

megahertz (MHz) Equivalent to millions of cycles per second. A common measure of clock speed.

memo field A database field that stores text information of variable length. Also called *description field.*

memory A collection of chips on the motherboard, or on a circuit board attached to the motherboard, where all computer processing and program instructions are stored while in use. The computer's memory enables the CPU to retrieve data quickly for processing.

memory address A number used by the CPU to locate each piece of data in memory.

menu A list of commands or functions displayed on screen for selection by the user.

menu bar A graphical screen element—located above the document area of an application window—that displays a list of the types of commands available to the user. When the user selects an option from the menu bar, a list appears displaying the commands related to that menu option.

mesh topology An expensive, redundant cabling scheme for local area networks, in which each node is connected to every other node by a unique cable.

message header Information that appears at the beginning of an e-mail message, providing details about the sender and the message.

metasearch engine A Web-based search engine that compiles the search results from several other engines, allowing for a wider range of results.

metropolitan area network (MAN) A larger version of a local area network (LAN); it can be used to connect computer systems in buildings in the same town or city.

MHz See *megahertz*.

microcode Code that details the individual tasks the computer must perform to complete each instruction in the instruction set.

microcomputer See *personal computer (PC)*.

micron A unit of measure equivalent to one-millionth of a meter.

microphone An input device used to digitally record audio data, such as the human voice. Many productivity applications can accept input via a microphone, enabling the user to dictate text or issue commands orally.

microprocessor Integrated circuits on one or more chips that make up the computer's CPU. Microprocessors are composed of silicon or other material etched with many tiny electronic circuits.

MIDI See *Musical Instrument Digital Interface*.

midrange computer See *minicomputer*.

millions of instructions per second (MIPS) A common unit of measure when gauging the performance of a computer's processor.

millisecond (ms) Equivalent to one-thousandth of a second; used to measure access time of storage devices such as hard disks. See also *nanosecond*.

minicomputer A midsize, multiuser computer capable of handling more input and output than a PC but with less processing power and storage than a mainframe. Also called a *midrange computer*.

MIPS See *millions of instructions per second*.

mirrored See *RAID 1*.

MIS See *management information system*.

mobile computer Any type of computer system that can the user can carry. Examples include notebook computers and PDAs.

modem Abbreviation for *modulator/demodulator*. An input/output device that allows computers to communicate through telephone lines. A modem converts outgoing digital data into analog signals that can be transmitted over phone lines and converts incoming analog signals into digital data that can be processed by the computer.

modifier keys Keyboard keys that are used in conjunction with other keys to execute a command. The IBM-PC keyboard includes SHIFT, CTRL, and ALT modifier keys.

monitor A display screen used to provide computer output to the user. Examples include the cathode ray tube (CRT) monitor, flat-panel monitor, and liquid crystal display (LCD).

monochrome monitor A monitor that displays only one color (such as green or amber) against a contrasting background.

motherboard The main circuit board of the computer; it contains the CPU, memory, expansion slots, bus, and video controller. Also called the *system board*.

Motorola A maker of computer chips.

mouse An input device operated by rolling across a flat surface. The mouse is used to control the on-screen pointer by pointing and clicking, double-clicking, or dragging objects on the screen.

MP See *multiprocessing*.

MPP See *massively parallel processing*.

ms See *millisecond*.

MS-DOS Acronym for *Microsoft–Disk Operating System*. The command-line interface operating system developed by Microsoft for PCs. IBM selected DOS as the standard for early IBM and IBM-compatible machines.

multimedia Elements of text, graphics, animation, video, and sound combined for presentation to the consumer.

multiprocessing (MP) See *parallel processing*.

multitasking The capability of an operating system to load multiple programs into memory at one time and to perform two or more processes concurrently, such as printing a document while editing another.

multi-user/multitasking operating system A powerful operating system that supports more than one user at a time, performing more than one task at a time. UNIX is an example of a multi-user/multitasking operating system.

Musical Instrument Digital Interface (MIDI) A specialized category of input/output devices used in the creation, recording, editing, and performance of music.

MySQL A popular, open-source database management program.

N

name server A special server that functions as part of the domain name system (DNS). DNS name servers store domain names that are mapped to IP addresses. The main Internet DNS name servers are located on one of the Internet backbones, while others are located at ISP facilities and within many large organizations.

nanosecond (ns) One-billionth of a second. A common unit of measure for the average access time of memory devices.

NAS See *network attached storage*.

needs analysis phase Phase 1 of the systems development life cycle. In this phase, needs are defined, the current system is analyzed, alternative solutions are developed, and the best solution and its functions are selected.

.NET A development environment that combines several programming languages, including Visual Basic, C++, C#, and J#. Using .NET, developers can write programs for Windows, the World Wide Web, and PocketPC.

.NET Framework A set of technologies that support Web-based applications, large databases, e-commerce servers, and distributed applications.

Netscape Fast Track A popular Web server program, developed by Netscape Communications.

network (1) A system of interconnected computers that communicate with one another and share applications, data, and hardware components. (2) The act of connecting computers together in order to permit the transfer of data and programs between users.

network attached storage (NAS) A large, dedicated storage device that is attached directly to a network rather than being part of a server.

network interface card (NIC) A circuit board that controls the exchange of data over a network.

network news transfer protocol (NNTP) A set of rules that enable news servers to exchange articles with other news servers.

network operating system (NOS) A group of programs that manage the resources on a network.

network operations center (NOC) A professionally managed facility that houses high-volume Web servers.

network protocol A set of standards used for network communications.

network server See *file server*.

network storage Refers to one or more shared storage devices attached to a network.

network version An application program especially designed to work within a network environment. Users access the software from a shared storage device.

news A public bulletin board service on the Internet; organized into discussion groups representing specific topics of interest.

news server A host computer that exchanges articles with other Internet servers.

newsgroup An electronic storage space where users can post messages to other users, carry on extended conversations, and trade information.

newsreader A software program that enables the user to post and read articles in an Internet newsgroup.

NIC See *network interface card*.

NNTP See *network news transfer protocol*.

NNTP server Another name for news servers using the network news transfer protocol.

NOC See *network operations center*.

node An individual computer that is connected to a network.

nonimpact printer A type of printer that creates images on paper without striking the page in any way. Two common examples are ink jet printers, which spray tiny droplets of ink onto the page, and laser printers, which use heat to adhere particles of toner to specific points on the page.

nonvolatile The tendency for memory to retain data even when the computer is turned off (as is the case with ROM).

NOS See *network operating system*.

notebook computer A small, portable computer with an attached flat screen; typically powered by battery or AC and weighing less than 10 pounds. Notebook computers commonly provide most of the same features found in full-size desktop computers, including a color monitor, a fast processor, a modem, and adequate RAM and storage for business-class software applications. Also called *laptop computer*.

ns See *nanosecond*.

NSFnet Acronym for *National Science Foundation Network*. A network developed by the National Science Foundation (NSF) to accommodate the many users attempting to access the five academic research centers created by the NSF.

***n*-tier application** A distributed database application that is divided among more than three computers.

numeric field A database field that stores numeric characters.

numeric keypad The part of a keyboard that looks and works like a calculator keypad; it has 10 digits and mathematical operators.

O

object In object-oriented programming, a data item and its associated characteristics, attributes, and procedures. An object's characteristics define the type of object—for example, whether it is text, a sound, a graphic, or video. Attributes might be color, size, style, and so on. A procedure refers to the processing or handling associated with the object.

object code The executable file in machine language that is the output of a compiler.

object embedding The process of integrating a copy of data from one application into another, as from a spreadsheet to a word processor. The data retains the formatting applied to it in the original application, but its relationship with the original file is destroyed.

object linking The process of integrating a copy of data from one application into another so that the data retains a link to the original document. Thereafter, a change in the original document also appears in the linked data in the second application.

Object Linking and Embedding (OLE) A Windows feature that combines object embedding and linking functions. OLE allows the user to construct a document containing data from a single point in time or one in which the data is constantly updated.

object-oriented programming (OOP) A programming technology that makes use of reusable, modular components, called *objects*.

object-oriented systems analysis (OOSA) A systems development methodology.

OCR See *optical character recognition*.

octet Refers to a common format for IP addresses, in which addresses are 32 bits long, in four eight-bit fields.

off-the-shelf application A software product that is packaged and available for sale; installed as-is in some system designs.

office automation system A system designed to manage information efficiently in areas such as word processing, accounting, document management, or communications.

OLE See *Object Linking and Embedding.*

on-board cache See *Level-1 cache.*

online (1) The state of being connected to, served by, or available through a networked computer system or the Internet. For example, when a user is browsing the World Wide Web, that person's computer is said to be online. (2) Describes any computer-related device that is turned on and connected, such as a printer or modem that is in use or ready for use.

online banking The use of Web-based services to conduct transactions with a bank, such as managing accounts or paying bills.

online finance The use of Web-based services to conduct financial transactions such as investing or buying insurance.

online service A telecommunications service that supplies e-mail and information search tools.

online shopping The use of Web-based services to make purchases from online retailers, such as Web-based bookstores or clothing stores.

online store A business that operates only online, such as through a Web site, and has no physical location.

OOP See *object-oriented programming.*

OOSA See *object-oriented systems analysis.*

open-source software Software that is available for free and whose source code can be modified by users.

Open System Interconnection Reference Model (OSI Model) A theoretical networking model that describes how the various parts of a network system should work together to format and transmit data. The Internet, as well as many private networks, is based on this model.

operating environment An intuitive graphical user interface that overlays the operating system but does not replace it. Microsoft Windows 3.*x* is an example.

operating system (OS) The master control program that provides an interface for a user to communicate with the computer; it manages hardware devices, manages and maintains disk file systems, and supports application programs.

opt-out option An option available on many Web sites and registration forms. By selecting this option, the user affirms that he or she does not want to be contacted by the company or its partners, and that he or she does not want the company to sell or share information about him or her.

optical character recognition (OCR) software Technology that enables a computer to translate optically scanned data into character codes, which then can be edited.

optical drive A storage device that writes data to and reads data from an optical storage medium such as a compact disc.

optical mouse A pointing device that tracks its location (and the pointer's location on the screen) by using a beam of light, such as a laser, bounced off a reflective surface.

optical storage Refers to storage systems that use light beams to read data from the surface of an optical disc. Data is stored as a series of lands and pits on the disc's reflective surface. Generally speaking, optical storage systems provide higher storage capacities than typical magnetic storage systems, but they operate at slower speeds.

Oracle A popular database management system, developed by Oracle Corp.

OS See *operating system.*

OSI Model See *Open System Interconnection Reference Model.*

output device A hardware component, such as a monitor or printer, that returns processed data to the user.

P

P2P See *peer-to-peer network.*

packet A small block of data transmitted over a network that includes an identifying header and the actual data to be sent. Also called a *frame.*

page-white display The LCD version of the paper-white display, which produces a very high contrast between the monitor's white background and displayed text or graphics, which usually appear in black. This high-contrast, black-and-white monitor is sometimes used by graphic designers and page-layout technicians.

pages per minute (ppm) A common measure for printer output speed. Consumer-grade laser printers, for example, typically can print from 6 to 10 pages per minute depending on whether text or graphics are being printed. See also *characters per second.*

paint program A graphics program that creates images as bitmaps, or a mosaic of pixels.

Palm OS The operating system used by Palm handheld devices.

palmtop computer See *handheld personal computer.*

paper-white display A specialized CRT monitor that produces a very high contrast between the monitor's white background and displayed text or graphics, which usually appear in black. This high-contrast, black-and-white monitor is sometimes used by graphic designers and page-layout technicians.

paragraph In a word processing program, any series of letters, words, or sentences followed by a hard return. (A hard return is created by pressing the ENTER key.)

paragraph format A setting that affects the appearance of one or more entire paragraphs, such as line spacing, paragraph spacing, indents, alignment, tab stops, borders, and shading.

parallel interface A channel through which eight or more data bits can flow simultaneously, such as a computer bus. A parallel interface is commonly used to connect printers to the computer; also called a *parallel port.*

parallel port See *parallel interface.*

parallel processing The use of multiple processors to run a program. By harnessing multiple processors, which share the processing workload, the system can handle a much greater flow of data, complete more tasks in a shorter period of time, and deal with the demands of many input and output devices. Also called *multiprocessing (MP)* or *symmetric multiprocessing (SMP)*.

passive matrix LCD Liquid crystal display technology used for flat-panel monitors; it relies on a grid of transistors arranged by rows and columns. In a passive matrix LCD, the color displayed by each pixel is determined by the electricity coming from the transistors at the end of the row and the top of the column.

password A word or code used as a security checkpoint by an individual computer system or a network to verify the user's identity.

password capture A technique used by hackers and identity thieves to learn passwords or other personal information from a victim. In password capture, the thief listens to or records telephone conversations or intercepts network transmissions in hopes of gathering the right information.

password guessing A technique used by hackers and identity thieves to learn passwords or other personal information from a victim. In password guessing, the thief attempts to log into a network or Web site by guessing the victim's password.

password sharing A technique used by hackers and identity thieves to learn passwords or other personal information from a victim. In password sharing, the victim unwittingly gives his or her password to the thief by writing it down in a conspicuous place or telling it to someone else.

Paste command An application command that copies data from the Clipboard and places it in the document at the position of the insertion point. Data in the Clipboard can be pasted into multiple places in one document, multiple documents, and documents in different applications.

payload In a packet, the actual data being transmitted across a network or over telephone lines. Also refers to the executable portion of a computer virus or the output produced by a virus.

PC See *personal computer*.

PC Card A specialized expansion card the size of a credit card; it fits into a computer and is used to connect new components.

PC DOS A version of the disk operating system marketed by IBM Corp.

PC-to-TV converter A hardware device that converts a computer's digital video signals into analog signals for display on a standard television screen.

PC video camera A small video camera that connects to a special video card on a PC. When used with videoconferencing software, a PC video camera enables users to capture full-motion video images, save them to disk, edit them, and transmit them to other users across a network or the Internet.

PCI See *Peripheral Component Interconnect bus*.

PDA See *personal digital assistant*.

peer-to-peer (P2P) network A network environment in which all nodes on the network have equal access to at least some of the resources on all other nodes.

peer-to-peer (P2P) service A special type of connection provided via the Internet, which allows connected client computers to communicate and exchange data directly instead of using server computers.

pen An input device that allows the user to write directly on or point at a special pad or the screen of a pen-based computer, such as a PDA. Also called a *stylus*.

Peripheral Component Interconnect (PCI) bus A PC bus standard developed by Intel; it supplies a high-speed data path between the CPU and peripheral devices.

Perl A scripting language commonly used in the development of Web-based applications.

persistent cookie A cookie that remains on the user's hard disk after the current browsing session is ended. Persistent cookies are usually set to "expire" on a certain date; until then, they remain active.

personal computer (PC) The most common type of computer found in an office, classroom, or home. The PC is designed to fit on a desk and be used by one person at a time; also called a *microcomputer*.

personal digital assistant (PDA) A very small portable computer designed to be held in one hand; used to perform specific tasks, such as creating limited spreadsheets or storing phone numbers.

personal information manager (PIM) A software program used for collecting and refining information about people, schedules, and tasks. PIMs are also called *contact-management software* or *contact managers*, because these programs are used primarily for managing information about people the user commonly contacts.

phishing A technique used by hackers and identity thieves to learn passwords and other important information from victims. In phishing, the thief contacts victims via phone or e-mail, pretending to be a legitimate business such as a bank, then asks the victim for private information.

photo-editing program A multimedia software tool used to make modifications, including adjusting contrast and sharpness, to digital photographic images.

photo printer A special color printer used for outputting photo-quality images. These printers are typically used to print images captured with a digital camera or an image scanner.

PhotoCD A special optical disc technology, developed by Kodak, for digitizing and storing standard film-based photographs.

photorealistic Describes computer-generated images that are lifelike in appearance and not obviously models.

PICT Abbreviation for *picture*. A graphics file format developed for and commonly used on the Macintosh platform, but seldom used on the PC platform.

PIM See *personal information manager*.

pipelining A technique that enables a processor to execute more instructions in a given time. In pipelining, the control unit begins executing a new instruction before the current instruction is completed.

pit A depressed area on the metal surface of an optical disc that scatters laser light. Also see *land*.

pixel Contraction of *picture element*. One or more dots that express a portion of an image on a computer screen.

plain old telephone system (POTS) Refers to the standard, existing system of telephone lines that has been in use for decades in the United States. The system includes millions of miles of copper wiring and thousands of switching stations, which ensure that analog telephone signals are routed to their intended destination. This system is now also commonly used to transmit digital data between computers; however, the data must be converted from digital form to analog form before entering the telephone line, then reconverted back to digital form when it reaches the destination computer. This conversion is handled at the computer by a device called a *modem*.

plasma display A type of flat-panel monitor in which a special gas (such as neon or xenon) is contained between two sheets of glass. When the gas is electrified via a grid of small electrodes, it glows. By controlling the amount of voltage applied at various points on the grid, each point acts as a pixel to display an image.

platform independence The capability of a program to run under different operating systems and/or hardware platforms.

plotter An output device used to create large-format hard copy; generally used with CAD and design systems.

Plug and Play An operating system feature that enables the user to add hardware devices to the computer without performing technically difficult configuration procedures.

plug-in application See *helper application*.

Pocket PC OS An operating system designed to run on some types of handheld computers and other small computing devices.

point (1) A standard unit used in measuring fonts. One point equals 1/72 inch in height. (2) To move the mouse pointer around the screen by manipulating the mouse or another type of pointing device.

point-of-presence (PoP) Describes a connection point to the Internet, such as the connection points used by Internet service providers.

pointer An on-screen object used to select text; access menus; move files; and interact with programs, files, or data represented graphically on the screen.

pointing To move the mouse pointer around the screen by mainipulating the mouse or another type of pointing device.

pointing device A device that enables the user to freely move an on-screen pointer and to select text, menu options, icons, and other onscreen objects. Two popular types of pointing devices are mice and trackballs.

polarized The condition of a magnetic bar with ends having opposite magnetic polarity.

PoP See *point-of-presence*.

POP See *post office protocol*.

POP server A server computer on an e-mail system that manages the flow of e-mail messages and attachments, using the post office protocol.

pop-up See *pop-up window*.

pop-up blocker A software program that prevents unwanted pop-up windows from appearing on the user's screen when browsing the Web.

pop-up window A secondary browser window that unexpectedly appears when browsing the Web. Pop-up windows commonly contain advertisements and often host spyware.

port (1) A socket on the back of the computer used to connect external devices to the computer. (2) To transfer a software application from one platform to another.

portable Describes software applications that are easily transferred from one platform to another, or hardware that can be easily moved.

post To publish a document on the Internet by using one of its services, such as news, FTP, or the World Wide Web.

POST See *power on self test*.

post office protocol (POP) A networking protocol used by e-mail servers to manage the sending and receiving of e-mail messages and attachments.

Post Office Protocol Version 3 (POP3) A commonly used protocol that controls the handling of e-mail messages over the Internet.

POTS See *plain old telephone system*.

power failure The loss of electrical power.

power fluctuation A sudden, unexpected increase or decrease in electrical power. Power fluctuations have various causes; extreme fluctuations can be harmful to computer hardware and data.

power on self test (POST) A routine stored in a computer's BIOS that runs whenever the computer is started. This routine conducts checks to determine whether various parts of the system are functioning properly.

ppm See *pages per minute*.

presentation A collection of slides that can be shown to an audience. Presentations are created using special software, called a *presentation program*.

presentation program Software that enables the user to create professional-quality images, called *slides*, that can be shown as part of a presentation. Slides can be presented in any number of ways, but they are typically displayed on a large screen or video monitor while the presenter speaks to the audience.

primary e-mail account An individual's main e-mail account, which is usually established as part of an account with an Internet service provider.

print head In impact printers, a device that strikes an inked ribbon, pressing ink onto the paper to create characters or graphics.

print server A special network server that is devoted to managing printing tasks for multiple users. A print server makes it easy for many users to share a single printer.

printer An output device that produces a hard copy on paper. Two types are impact and nonimpact.

Privacy Act of 1974 A federal law that restricts federal agencies from sharing information about individuals without their written consent.

private IP address An IP address that is reserved for use by a specific organization's computer.

processing A complex procedure by which a computer transforms raw data into useful information.

processor See *central processing unit (CPU)*.

program (1) A set of instructions or code to be executed by the CPU; designed to help users solve problems or perform tasks. Also called *software*. (2) To create a computer program. The process of computer programming is also called *software development*.

program control flow The order in which a program's statements are executed when the program is run.

programmable read-only memory (PROM) A type of computer chip whose contents cannot be changed. PROM chips are often found on hard drives and printers. They contain the instructions that power the devices. These instructions, once set, never need to be changed.

programmer The person responsible for creating a computer program, including writing new code and analyzing and modifying existing code.

programming language A higher-level language than machine code for writing programs. Programming languages use variations of basic English.

PROM See *programmable read-only memory*.

prompt In a command-line interface, the on-screen location where the user types commands. A prompt usually provides a blinking cursor to indicate where commands can be typed. Also called a *command prompt*.

protocol A set of rules and procedures that determine how a computer system receives and transmits data.

prototype A working system model used to clarify and refine system requirements.

pseudocode "Fake" code; a text version of the program control flow; similar to the program code but lacking the exact syntax and details.

public domain software Software that is freely available to anyone, free of charge. Generally, users can modify the source code of public domain software.

public IP address An IP address that is available for use by any computer on the Internet.

public record A legal document, such as driving records or marriage licenses, that is available for viewing by anyone.

publish See *post*.

Q

QBE See *query by example*.

query In a database management system (DBMS), a search question that instructs the program to locate records that meet specific criteria.

query by example (QBE) In a database management system (DBMS), a tool that accepts a query from a user and then creates the SQL code to locate data requested by the query. QBE enables the user to query a database without understanding SQL.

Quick Launch bar A customizable area of the Windows taskbar that lets you launch programs with a single click.

R

RAD See *rapid application development*.

RAID 0 A data storage technology (also called *striping*) that provides the user with rapid access by spreading data across several disks in a disk array. Striping alone, however, does not provide redundancy. If one of the disks in a striped array fails, the data is lost.

RAID 1 A data storage technology (also called *mirroring*) in which data is written to two or more disks simultaneously, providing a complete copy of all the information on multiple drives in the event one drive should fail. This improves reliability and availability, and if one disk fails, the mirrored disk continues to function, thus maintaining reliability and availability.

RAID 4 A data storage technology (also called *striping-with-parity*) in which data from each file is spread over multiple disks. It provides the speed of striping with the safety of redundancy because the system stores parity information that can be used to reconstruct data if a disk drive fails. Such arrays also provide error-checking.

RAM See *random access memory*.

random access memory (RAM) A computer's volatile or temporary memory, which exists as chips on the motherboard near the CPU. RAM stores data and programs while they are being used and requires a power source to maintain its integrity.

random access storage device A storage device that can locate data at any point on the storage medium without going through all the data up to that point. Floppy disks, hard disks, and optical discs are examples of random access storage devices.

rapid application development (RAD) A method used in systems development that allows for fast creation of computer systems and applications in an organization.

raster See *bitmap*.

read/write head The magnetic device within the disk drive that reads, records, and erases data on the disk's surface. A read/write head contains an electromagnet that alters the polarity of magnetic particles on the storage medium. Most disk drives have one read/write head for each side of each disk in the drive.

read-only memory (ROM) A permanent, or nonvolatile, memory chip used to store instructions and data, including the computer's startup instructions.

real-time application An application that responds to certain inputs extremely quickly—thousandths or millionths of a second (milliseconds or microseconds, respectively). Real-time applications are needed to run medical diagnostics equipment, life-support systems, machinery, scientific instruments, and industrial systems.

real-time operating system An operating system designed to support real-time applications.

record A database row composed of related fields; a collection of records makes up the database.

Reduced Instruction Set Computing (RISC) Refers to a type of microprocessor design that uses a simplified instruction set; it uses fewer instructions of constant size, each of which can be executed quickly.

redundant array of independent disks (RAID) a storage system that links any number of disk drives (a disk array) so that they act as a single disk. This is done for better performance and/or redundancy.

refresh rate The number of times per second that each pixel on the computer screen is scanned; measured in hertz (Hz).

register High-speed memory locations built directly into the ALU and used to hold instructions and data currently being processed.

relational database A database structure capable of linking tables; a collection of tables that share at least one common field.

Remote Access VPN Special networking software that allows a user to create a secure connection to a private network via the Internet.

repeat rate A keyboard setting that determines how rapidly the character is typed and how long an alphanumeric key must be held down before the character will be repeated.

repetition structure A control structure in which a condition is checked and a loop is executed based on the result of the condition. Also called *looping structure*.

repetitive stress injury (RSI) An injury to some part of the body caused by continuous movement. Computer-related injuries include strain to the wrist, neck, and back.

report A database product that displays data to satisfy a specific set of search criteria presented in a predefined layout, which is designed by the user.

resolution The degree of sharpness of an image, determined by the number of pixels on a screen; expressed as a matrix.

resolver A network device that converts logical IP addresses into physical addresses.

restore To replace a damaged or missing file on a hard disk with a copy from a backup.

right-click To use the right mouse button of a two-button mouse to select an object or command on the screen.

Right to Financial Privacy Act of 1978 A federal law that requires companies to give consumers notice of their privacy and information-sharing practices.

ring topology A network topology in which network nodes are connected in a circular configuration. Each node examines the data sent through the ring and passes on data not addressed to it.

RISC See *Reduced Instruction Set Computing.*

ROM See *read-only memory.*

root folder The top-level folder on a disk. This primary folder contains all other folders and subfolders stored on the disk. Also called the *root directory*, or sometimes just the *root*.

router A computer device that stores the addressing information of each computer on each LAN or WAN; it uses this information to transfer data along the most efficient path between nodes of a LAN or WAN.

RSI See *repetitive stress injury.*

rule See *filter.*

ruler An on-screen tool in a word processor's document window. The ruler shows the position of lines, tab stops, margins, and other parts of the document.

run See *execute.*

S

SAN See *storage area network.*

scalability A program's capability to adjust to changes in scale—the number of users it must support or the numbers of tasks it must perform.

scanner See *image scanner.*

screen saver A utility program that displays moving images on the screen if no input is received for several minutes; originally developed to prevent an image from being burned into the screen.

scroll To move through an entire document in relation to the document window in order to see parts of the document not currently visible on screen.

scroll bar A vertical or horizontal bar displayed along the side or bottom of a document window that enables the user to scroll horizontally or vertically through a document by clicking an arrow or dragging a box within the scroll bar.

SCSI See *Small Computer System Interface.*

SDLC See *systems development life cycle.*

SDSL See *Synchronous DSL.*

search engine A Web site that uses powerful data-searching techniques to help the user locate Web sites containing specific types of content or information.

second-generation language Refers to assembly language, which is slightly more advanced and English-like than machine languages (which are considered first-generation languages).

second-level domain (SLD) A domain name given to an organization. In the URL www.government.org, for example, *government* is the second-level domain.

secondary e-mail account A backup e-mail account that can be used as a collection place for spam and other unwanted e-mail messages.

sector A segment or division of a track on a disk.

Secure Hypertext Transfer Protocol (HTTPS) An Internet protocol used to encrypt individual pieces of data transmitted between a user's computer and a Web server, making the data unusable to anyone who does not have a key to the encryption method.

secure sockets layer (SSL) An Internet protocol that can be used to encrypt any amount of data sent over the Internet between a client computer and a host computer.

secure Web page A Web page that uses one or more encryption technologies to encode data received from and sent to the user.

seek time See *average access time.*

select (1) To highlight a block of text (in a word processor) or range (in a spreadsheet), so the user can perform one or more editing operations on it. (2) To click once on an icon.

selection structure A control structure built around a conditional statement.

sequence structure A type of control structure in which a computer executes lines of code in the order in which they are written.

sequential access device A storage device that must search a storage medium from beginning to end in order to find the data that is needed. Such devices cannot access data randomly. A tape drive is an example of a sequential access device.

serial interface A channel through which data bits flow one at a time. Serial interfaces are used primarily to connect a mouse or a communications device to the computer. Also called a *serial port.*

serial port See *serial interface.*

server See *file server.*

session cookie A cookie that remains on the user's hard disk only during a Web-browsing session. The cookie is deleted when the session ends. Also called a *transient cookie.*

shadow mask In a cathode ray tube (CRT) monitor, a fine mesh made of metal fitted to the shape and size of the screen. The holes in the shadow mask's mesh are used to align the electron beams to ensure that they strike the correct phosphor dot. In most shadow masks, these holes are arranged in triangles.

shareware Software that can be used without paying a fee or registering for a specified time period. After that time, the user is obligated to purchase and/or register the product.

shell Refers to a GUI environment that can run on top of a command-line operating system, such as Linux or UNIX.

shopping cart At many e-commerce Web sites, a feature that lets the shopper store, review, and edit items to be purchased before checking out.

shortcut Any means that enables the user to quickly execute an action or issue a command. On the Windows desktop, for example, icons serve as shortcuts by allowing you to quickly launch programs. Within programs, you may be able to click buttons or press specific keys to quickly perform tasks; these buttons and keystrokes are also shortcuts.

shortcut menu See *context menu.*

shoulder surfing A method used by hackers and identity thieves to learn passwords and other personal information from their victims. In shoulder surfing, the thief watches as the victim enters a password or other information at a computer, ATM, phone, or other device.

S-HTTP See *Secure Hypertext Transfer Protocol.*

SIMM See *Single In-Line Memory Module.*

Simple Mail Transfer Protocol (SMTP) A common protocol for sending e-mail between servers on the Internet. It also often is used for sending e-mail from an e-mail client to a server.

Single In-Line Memory Module (SIMM) One type of circuit board containing memory chips.

single-user/multitasking operating system An operating system that supports only one user at a time, but allows the user to perform multiple tasks simultaneously, such as running several programs at the same time. Examples include Windows and the Macintosh operating system.

single-user/single-tasking operating system An operating system that supports only one user at a time and allows the user to perform only one task at a time. Examples include MS-DOS and some operating systems designed for use on handheld computers.

site license An agreement in which an organization purchases the right to use a program on a limited number of machines. The total cost is less than would be required if individual copies of the software were purchased for all users.

site-to-site VPN A special type of networking software that can be used to connect two networks together in a secure manner. Both networks may be part of the same private intranet or they may be networks of partner companies participating in an extranet.

SLD See *second-level domain.*

slide An individual graphic that is part of a presentation. Slides are created and edited in presentation programs.

Small Computer System Interface (SCSI) A high-speed interface that extends the bus outside the computer, permitting the addition of more peripheral devices than normally could be connected using the available expansion slots.

small outline DIMM (SO-DIMM) A small-format memory chip found in portable computers.

smart card A plastic card—about the same size as a standard credit card—that contains a small chip that stores data. Using a special device, called a smart card reader, the user can read data from the card, add new data, or revise existing data.

smart card reader A device that can read data from or write data to a smart card.

smart phone A digital cellular phone that includes many of the features found in a personal digital assistant (PDA), such as schedule management, e-mail, Web access, and others.

SMP Acronynm for *symmetric multiprocessing*. See *parallel processing*.

SMTP See *Simple Mail Transfer Protocol.*

snagging A method used by identity thieves to gather passwords or other personal information from a victim. In snagging, the thief listens in on a telephone extension, through a wiretap, or over a cubicle wall while the victim gives credit card or other personal information to a legitimate agent.

snail mail A term used to describe the U.S. Postal Service.

sniffing Describes a variety of methods used by hackers and identity thieves to gather passwords or other personal information from victims.

social engineering Describes a variety of methods used by hackers and identity thieves to gather passwords or other personal information from victims. Social engineering usually involves tricking a victim into divulging personal information.

Sockets An application programming interface (API) for the UNIX operating system that assists in connecting a UNIX computer to the Internet.

SO-DIMM See *small outline DIMM*.

soft formatting See *logical formatting*.

software See *program*.

software license An agreement between a software program's developer and its user. Most licenses grant the user certain rights related to the program's use, but they do not give the user actual ownership of the program.

software piracy The illegal duplication and/or use of software.

software suite A set of software programs that are sold and installed together, and that have been developed so that their interfaces are common and they can easily exchange data with one another.

solid-state disk (SSD) A high-speed, high-capacity storage device based on random access memory (RAM) circuits rather than disks.

solid-state storage Describes any type of storage device that uses memory chips rather than disks to store data.

sort To arrange database records in a particular order—such as alphabetical, numerical, or chronological order—according to the contents of one or more fields.

sound card An expansion card that records and plays back sound by translating the analog signal from a microphone into a digitized form that the computer can store and process, and then translating the data back into analog signals or sound.

source code Program statements created with a programming language.

spam (1) Another term for junk e-mail. (2) To distribute unrequested messages across the Internet or an online service. Spammers often flood newsgroups with messages and send e-mail messages to thousands of individuals. Spam messages often attempt to sell a product or service (like regular junk mail) but frequently carry negative, indecent, or obscene material.

spam blocker A software program that is designed to prevent unwanted e-mail messages from reaching the user.

spammer A person who distributes junk e-mail messages.

spawn To launch a program from within another program. For example, to allow the user to view streaming multimedia content, a Web browser may spawn a second application, such as the QuickTime Player.

speech recognition An input technology that can translate human speech into text. Some speech-recognition systems enable the user to navigate application programs and issue commands by voice control, as well as to create documents by dictating text; also called *voice recognition*.

spider See *crawler.*

sponsored link In a page of results created by a search engine, a link that has been purchased by a merchant. Sponsored links usually appear before nonsponsored links in search results, or may appear separately from nonsponsored links.

spoof To distribute unrequested e-mail messages while concealing the sender's identity. In spoofing, the spoofer's message identifies the sender as someone else or shows no sender's identity at all. This method protects the spoofer from retaliation from those who receive unwanted messages. See also *spam*.

spreadsheet A grid of columns and rows used for recording and evaluating numbers. Spreadsheets are used primarily for financial analysis, record keeping, and management, as well as to create reports and presentations.

spyware Software that tracks a computer user's activities and reports the activities back to someone else. Spyware can be used to monitor Internet use, e-mail, and keyboard or mouse actions.

SQL See *Structured Query Language*.

SQL Server A database management system, developed by Microsoft Corp.

SSD See *solid-state disk*.

SSL See *secure sockets layer*.

stand-alone program A software application that is designed to perform one type of task, such as word processing or photo editing. Stand-alone programs typically are purchased and installed by themselves.

star topology A network topology in which network nodes connect to a central hub through which all data is routed.

START button A Windows 95/98/2000/NT/XP screen element—found on the taskbar—that displays the Start menu when selected.

Start menu A menu in the Windows 95/98/2000/NT/XP operating systems; the user can open the Start menu by clicking the START button; the Start menu provides tools to locate documents, find help, change system settings, and run programs.

start page The page that opens automatically when a Web browser launches.

static Describes anything that does not change. If a computer has a static IP address, for example, the address never changes.

static IP address An IP address that never changes. A computer with a static IP address always uses the same address.

status bar An on-screen element that appears at the bottom of an application window and displays the current status of various parts of the current document or application, such as the page number, text entry mode, and so on.

storage The portion of the computer that holds data or programs while they are not being used. Storage media include magnetic disks, optical discs, tape, and cartridges.

storage area network (SAN) A network that is devoted to a storage system. In a very large enterprise, for example, storage requirements may be so great, and storage devices so numerous, that a complete network is required for the storage system itself.

storage device The hardware components that write data to and read data from storage media. For example, a diskette is a type of storage medium, whereas a diskette drive is a storage device.

storage media The physical components or materials on which data is stored. Diskettes and compact discs are examples of storage media.

stored cookie See *persistent cookie*.

storing The second step of the CPU's execution cycle.

streaming audio/video Multimedia content that is sent to the user's desktop in a continuous "stream" from a Web server. Because audio and video files are large, streaming content is sent to the user's disk in pieces; the first piece is temporarily buffered (stored on disk), then played as the next piece is stored and buffered.

striping See *RAID 0*.

striping-with-parity See *RAID 4*.

structured English A programming design tool and a method of documenting a system using plain English terms and phrases to describe events, actions, and alternative actions that can occur.

structured programming A programming process that uses a set of well-defined structures, such as condition statements and loops.

Structured Query Language (SQL) The standard query language used for searching and selecting records and fields in a relational database.

stylus See *pen*.

submarining In older passive-matrix LCD displays, a problem caused by the monitor's inability to refresh itself fast enough. One characteristic of submarining is the disappearance of the mouse pointer when it moves across the screen.

subscribe To select a newsgroup so the user can regularly participate in its discussions. After subscribing to a newsgroup in a newsreader program, the program automatically downloads an updated list of articles when it is launched.

Super VGA (SVGA) An IBM video display standard capable of displaying resolutions up to 1024 × 768 pixels, with 16 million colors.

supercomputer The largest, fastest, and most powerful type of computer. Supercomputers are often used for scientific and engineering applications and for processing complex models that use very large data sets.

surge supressor A device that protects electrical equipment from sudden spikes (surges) in electrical service.

SVGA See *Super VGA*.

swap in To load essential parts of a program into memory as required for use.

swap out To unload, or remove, nonessential parts of a program from memory to make room for needed parts.

switch A networking device that learns which machine is connected to its port by using the device's IP address.

Symbian An operating system designed for use on handheld computers.

symmetric multiprocessing (SMP) See *parallel processing*.

Synchronous DSL (SDSL) A type of Digital Subscriber Line (DSL) technology that provides the same data transmission speeds for both uploading and downloading data.

syntax The precise sequence of characters required in a spreadsheet formula or in a programming language.

syntax error A bug in which the code is incorrectly entered so that the computer cannot understand its instructions.

sysop See *system operator*.

system board See *motherboard*.

system call A feature built into an application program that requests a service from the operating system, as when a word processing program requests the use of the printer to print a document.

system clock The computer's internal clock, which is used to time processing operations. The clock's time intervals are based on the constant, unchanging vibrations of molecules in a quartz crystal; currently measured in megahertz (MHz).

system operator (sysop) In an online discussion group, the person who monitors the discussion.

system software A computer program that controls the system hardware and interacts with application software. The designation includes the operating system and the network operating system.

system testing During the development phase of the systems development life cycle, the testing of an entire system that is conducted prior to installation.

system unit In a personal computer, the case that contains the system's essential hardware components, including the processor, disk drives, and motherboard.

systems design phase Phase 2 of the systems development life cycle. In this phase, the project team researches and develops alternative ways to meet an organization's computing needs.

systems development life cycle (SDLC) A formal methodology and process for the needs analysis, system design, development, implementation, and maintenance of an information system.

T

T1 A communications line that represents a higher level of the ISDN standard service and supplies a bandwidth of 1.544 Mbps.

T3 A communications line capable of transmitting a total of 44.736 Mbps.

table A grid of data, set up in rows and columns.

tablet PC A newer type of portable PC, similar in size to a notebook PC; it allows the user to input data and commands with a pen rather than a standard keyboard or pointing device.

tag In a markup language such as HTML, a marker that indicates where formatting or some other attribute begins or ends.

tag pair The tags of the same purpose that appear at the beginning and the end of a formatted element in a markup language.

tape drive A magnetic storage device that reads and writes data to the surface of a magnetic tape. Tape drives are generally used for backing up data or restoring the data of a hard disk.

task switching The process of moving from one open window to another.

taskbar A Windows 95/98/2000/NT/XP screen element—displayed on the desktop—that includes the START button and lists the programs currently running on the computer.

TB See *terabyte*.

TCP See *Transmission Control Protocol*.

TCP/IP See *Transmission Control Protocol/Internet Protocol*.

telecommute To work at home or on the road and have access to a work computer via telecommunications equipment, such as modems and fax machines.

telecommuter A person who works at home or on the road and requires access to a work computer via telecommunications equipment, such as modems and fax machines.

teleconference A live, real-time communications session involving two or more people in different locations, using computers and telecommunications equipment.

temporary (.tmp) file A file created by an operating system or application that is needed only temporarily. Such files are usually deleted from the disk when they are no longer required.

terabyte (TB) Equivalent to one trillion bytes of data; a measure of storage capacity.

terminal An input/output device connected to a multiuser computer such as a mainframe.

terminal client Networking software that creates a user session when a user runs a program from a network server (the terminal server).

terminal server In multi-user/multitasking networked environments, a server that gives multiple users access to shared programs and other resources.

terminator In a bus topology network, a special device that is placed at the end of the network cable. The device prevents data signals from "bouncing back" after reaching the end of the cable, thus preventing data collisions.

text box In word processing and presentation software, a special frame that enables the user to contain text in a rectangular area. The user can size and position the text box like a frame by dragging the box or one of its handles. Also see *frame*.

text code A standard system in which numbers represent the letters of the alphabet, punctuation marks, and other symbols. A text code enables programmers to use combinations of numbers to represent individual pieces of data. EBCDIC, ASCII, and Unicode are examples of text code systems.

text field A database field that stores a string of alphanumeric characters; also called *alphanumeric field* or *character field*.

TFT Acronym for *thin-film transistor*. See *active matrix LCD*.

thermal-wax printer A printer that produces high-quality images by using a heat source to evaporate colored wax from a ribbon, which adheres to the paper.

thin-film transistor (TFT) See *active matrix LCD*.

third-generation language (3GL) A category of programming languages that supports structured programming and enables programmers to use true English-like phrasing when writing program code.

third-party cookie A cookie that is placed on the user's computer by a Web server other than the one hosting the page being viewed.

thread A series of related articles and responses about a specific subject, posted in a newsgroup.

threat Anything that can cause harm to a computer system, its data, or its user.

throughput See *data-transfer rate*.

tier One of the application servers in a distributed application.

TIFF Acronym for *tagged image file format*. A graphics file format widely used on both PCs and Macintosh computers. Commonly used when exchanging bitmap files that will be printed or edited, the TIFF format can faithfully store images that contain up to 16.7 million colors without any loss of image quality.

time field A database field that stores a time.

title bar An on-screen element displayed at the top of every window that identifies the window contents. Dragging the title bar changes the position of the window on the screen.

TLD See *top-level domain*.

token In a network using ring topology, any piece of data that is being transferred across the network. Each node examines the data and passes it along until it reaches its destination.

Token Ring IBM's network protocol, based on a ring topology in which linked computers pass an electronic token containing addressing information to facilitate data transfer.

toner A substance composed of tiny particles of charged ink that is used in laser printers. The ink particles stick to charged areas of a drum and are transferred to paper with pressure and heat.

toolbar In application software, an on-screen element appearing just below the menu bar. The toolbar contains multiple tools, which are graphic icons (called *buttons*) representing specific actions the user can perform. To initiate an action, the user clicks the appropriate button.

top-down design A systems design method in which the major functions or processes are developed first, followed by the details.

top-level domain (TLD) See *domain name*.

topology The physical layout of wires that connect the computers in a network; includes bus, star, ring, and mesh.

touch screen An input/output device that accepts input directly from the monitor. To activate commands, the user touches words, graphical icons, or symbols displayed on screen.

touchpad See *trackpad*.

track An area used for storing data on a formatted disk. During the disk-formatting process, the operating system creates a set of magnetic concentric circles on the disk; these are the tracks. These tracks are then divided into sectors, with each sector able to hold a given amount of data. By using this system to store data, the operating system can quickly determine where data is located on the disk. Different types of disks can hold different numbers of tracks.

trackball An input device that functions like an upside-down mouse, consisting of a stationary casing containing a movable ball that is operated by hand. Trackballs are used frequently with laptop computers.

trackpad A stationary pointing device that the user operates by moving a finger across a small, touch-sensitive surface. Trackpads are often built into portable computers. Also called a *touchpad*.

TrackPoint See *integrated pointing device*.

transaction A series of steps required to complete an event, such as taking an order or preparing a time sheet.

transaction processing system (TPS) A type of information system that handles the processing and tracking of transactions.

transient cookie See *session cookie*.

transistor An electronic switch within the CPU that exists in two states: conductive (on) or nonconductive (off). The resulting combinations are used to create the binary code that is the basis for machine language.

Transmission Control Protocol (TCP) One of the key protocols of the Internet and many private networks, TCP manages the delivery of data through a network.

Transmission Control Protocol/Internet Protocol (TCP/IP) The set of commands and timing specifications used by the Internet to connect dissimilar systems and to control the flow of information.

tunneling The process of creating a secure, private connection over the public Internet. The connection may exist between individual computers, a single computer and a private network, or two private networks.

twisted-pair cable Cable used in network connections. Twisted-pair cable consists of copper strands, individually shrouded in plastic, twisted around each other in pairs and bound together in a layer of plastic insulation; also called *unshielded twisted-pair (UTP) wire*. Twisted-pair wire encased in a metal sheath is called *shielded twisted-pair (STP) wire*.

two-tier application A distributed database application, portions of which are executed on two separate computers.

type style An attribute applied to a text character, such as underlining, italic, and bold, among others. Most application programs provide a wide variety of type styles that the user can freely apply to text anywhere in a document.

typeface See *font*.

U

UART See *Universal Asynchronous Receiver Transmitter*.

UCE See *unsolicited commercial e-mail*.

UDP See *User Datagram Protocol*.

Unicode Worldwide Character Standard A character set that provides 16 bits to represent each symbol, resulting in 65,536 different characters or symbols, enough for all the languages of the world. The Unicode character set includes all the characters from the ASCII character set.

uniform resource locator (URL) An Internet address used with HTTP in the format *type://address/path*.

uninstall To remove an installed program from a computer's disk.

uninterruptible power supply (UPS) A device that supplies electrical power even after electrical service has failed. A UPS can allow a computer system to keep running, at least temporarily, after power to the building fails. At the very least, a UPS will allow the system to keep running long enough to save data and shut down safely.

unit testing During the development phase of the systems development life cycle, the testing of components of a new system, which takes place prior to system testing.

Universal Asynchronous Receiver-Transmitter (UART) A chip that converts parallel data from the bus into serial data that can flow through a serial cable, and vice versa.

Universal Serial Bus (USB) A new expansion bus technology that currently enables the user to connect 127 different devices into a single port.

UNIX A 32-bit, fully multitasking, multithreading operating system developed by Bell Labs in the 1970s. A powerful, highly scalable operating system, UNIX (and variants of it) is used to operate supercomputers, mainframes, minicomputers, and powerful PCs and workstations. UNIX generally features a command-line interface, although some variants of UNIX feature a graphical operating environment as well.

unsolicited commercial e-mail (UCE) The official term for *spam*. UCE is any e-mail message that is sent to multiple recipients, which contains commercial content.

upload To send a file to a remote computer. The opposite of *download*.

UPS See *uninterruptible power supply*.

URL See *uniform resource locator*.

USA Patriot Act A federal law (enacted in 2001) that extends the authority of law enforcement and intelligence agencies in monitoring private communications and access to your personal information.

USB See *Universal Serial Bus.*

user The person who inputs and analyzes data using a computer; the computer's operator.

User Datagram Protocol (UDP) A transport protocol that is sometimes used instead of the more common TCP (Transport Control Protocol) for sending messages across a network.

user ID See *user name.*

user interface The on-screen elements that enable the user to interact with the software.

user name A code that identifies the user to the system; often the user's full name, a shortened version of the user's name, or the user's e-mail name. Also called a *user ID.*

user session The period during which a user interacts with a terminal server, using a shared program on a network.

utility A software program that may be used to enhance the functionality of an operating system. Examples of utility software are disk defragmenters and screen savers.

V

value A numerical entry in a spreadsheet—representing currency, a percentage, a date, a time, a fraction, and so on—that can be used in calculations.

vector A mathematical equation that describes the position of a line.

very small aperture terminal (VSAT) An earth-based communications station that allows an individual or organization to connect to the Internet via satellite.

VGA See *Video Graphics Array.*

video capture card A specialized expansion board that enables the user to connect video devices—such as VCRs and camcorders—to the PC. This enables the user to transfer images from the video equipment to the PC, and vice versa. Many video cards enable the user to edit digitized video and to record the edited images on videotape.

video card A circuit board attached to the motherboard that contains the memory and other circuitry necessary to send information to the monitor for display on screen. This controller determines the refresh rate, resolution, and number of colors that can be displayed. Also called the *display adapter.*

Video Graphics Array (VGA) An IBM video display standard capable of displaying resolutions of 640 × 480, with 16 colors.

video RAM (VRAM) Memory on the video controller (sometimes called *dual-ported memory*) that can send a screen of data to the monitor while receiving the next data set.

videoconference A live, real-time video communications session involving two or more people using computers, video cameras, telecommunications and videoconferencing software.

viewing angle The widest angle from which a display monitor's image can be seen clearly. Generally speaking, cathode ray tube (CRT) monitors provide a wider viewing angle than liquid crystal display (LCD) monitors do.

viewing area The actual portion of a computer monitor that displays an image.

virtual memory Space on a computer's hard drive that acts as a backup to system RAM. Programs can store instructions or data in virtual memory that is not needed immediately; when an instruction or data is needed, it can quickly be moved into RAM, where the processor can access it.

virtual private network Technologies that allow data to be exchanged securely and privately over a public network, such as the Internet.

virus A parasitic program that infects another legitimate program, sometimes called the *host.* To infect the host program, the virus modifies the host so that it contains a copy of the virus.

virus definition A database of information about specific viruses that enables an antivirus program to detect and eradicate viruses. Also called a *virus pattern.*

virus pattern See *virus definition.*

Voice over Internet Protocol (VoIP) A protocol that allows voice data to travel over the Internet.

voice recognition See *speech recognition.*

VoIP See *Voice over Internet Protocol.*

volatile The tendency for memory to lose data when the computer is turned off, as is the case with RAM.

VPC Acronym for *virtual private connection.* See *virtual private network.*

VPN See *virtual private network.*

VRAM See *video RAM.*

VSAT See *very small aperture terminal.*

vulnerability Any aspect of a system that is open to harm. For example, if a computer does not have antivirus software, this is a vulnerability because the system can easily become infected by a virus.

W

WAN See *wide area network.*

WAP See *wireless access point.*

war driving The act of searching an area covered by a Wi-Fi network to locate spots where wireless Internet access is available.

Web browser A program that enables the user to view Web pages, navigate Web sites, and move from one Web site to another. Also called a *browser.*

Web bug A GIF-format graphic file, placed in a Web page or HTML-format e-mail message, that can be used to track a person's online activities. Web bugs are commonly considered to be a form of spyware.

Web page A document developed using HTML and found on the World Wide Web. Web pages contain information about a particular subject with links to related Web pages and other resources.

Web server An Internet host computer that may store thousands of Web sites.

Web site A collection of related Web pages.

Webcam An inexpensive video camera that connects directly to a PC and captures video images that can be broadcast over the Internet or through a network connection.

Webmaster A person or group responsible for designing and maintaining a Web site.

WEP See *Wire Equivalent Privacy*.

wheel mouse A pointing device that features a wheel, located between its two buttons. The user can spin the wheel to scroll through a document.

wide area network (WAN) A computer network that spans a wide geographical area.

Wi-Fi Stands for Wireless Fidelity. A networking standard that supports data communications without the use of wire-based media.

Wi-Fi Protected Access (WPA) An encryption method designed to protect data and private information as it is being transmitted over a wireless network.

window An area on the computer screen in which an application or document is viewed and accessed.

Windows A family of operating system products developed and produced by Microsoft Corp. The vast majority of personal computers run Windows, with versions including Windows 3.*x*, 95.*x*, NT, 2000, and XP. Windows versions 3.*x* and earlier were actually operating environments—graphical interfaces that ran on top of the DOS operating system. In versions 95 and later, Windows is a full-fledged operating system.

Winsock An application programming interface (API) for the Windows operating system that assists in connecting a Windows computer to the Internet.

Wire Equivalent Privacy (WEP) A networking standard that provides wireless networks a level of security similar to that found in secure wire-based networks.

wireless access point (WAP) See *access point*.

wireless local area network (WLAN) A local area network that uses wireless means rather than wires or cabling for data transmission.

Wireless Markup Language (WML) A development language used to create Web pages that can be displayed on small-format Web-enabled devices such as PDAs or cell phones.

wireless network A network that transmits data without the use of wires or cables. Such networks typically transmit data via radio waves or infrared signals.

wireless NIC A network interface card that connects a computer to a wireless network.

wireless wide area network (WWAN) A wide area network that uses wireless means rather than wires or cabling for data transmission.

WLAN See *wireless local area network*.

WML See *Wireless Markup Language*.

word processing program Software used to create and edit text documents such as letters, memos, reports, and publications. Also called a *word processor*.

word processor See *word processing program*.

word size The size of the registers in the CPU, which determines the amount of data the computer can work with at any given time. Larger word sizes lead to faster processing; common word sizes include 16 bits, 32 bits, and 64 bits.

workbook A data file created with spreadsheet software, containing multiple worksheets.

worksheet The data file created with spreadsheet software.

workstation A fast, powerful microcomputer used for scientific applications, graphics, CAD, CAE, and other complex applications. Workstations are usually based on RISC technology and operated by some version of UNIX, although an increasing number of Intel/Windows-based workstations are coming into popular use.

World Wide Web (the Web or WWW) An Internet service developed to incorporate footnotes, figures, and cross-references into online hypertext documents.

WPA See *Wi-Fi Protected Access*.

WWAN See *wireless wide area network*.

WWW See *World Wide Web*.

X-Z

Xbase A generic database language used to construct queries. Xbase is similar to SQL but more complex because its commands cover the full range of database activities beyond querying.

XHTML See *Extensible Hypertext Markup Language*.

XHTML MP See *Extensible Hypertext Markup Language Mobile Profile*.

XML See *Extensible Markup Language*.

XSL See *Extensible Stylesheet Language*.

Photo Credits

xxiv Aaron Haupt; **xxv** Aaron Haupt; **xxvi** Amanita Pictures; **xxvii** Courtesy Microsoft.

Chapter 1

1A.1 Photo courtesy of Acer America; **1A.2** Courtesy MIT Museum; **1A.3** Photodisc Green/Getty Images; **1A.4** Walter Hodges/Stone/Getty Images; **1A.5** RF/Corbis; **1A.6 left** LWA-Dann Tardiff/Corbis; **1A.6 center** Jose Luis Pelaez/Corbis; **1A.6 right** Richard T. Nowitz/Corbis; **1A.7** CMCD/Getty Images; **1A.8** Ryan McVay/Getty Images; **1A.9** Courtesy Sun Microsystems, Inc.; **1A.10** Ariel Skelley/Corbis; **1A.11** Courtesy IBM Corporation; **1A.12** Anthony P. Bolante/Getty Images; **1A.13** Courtesy palmOne, Inc.; **1A.14** Courtesy Nokia; **1A.15** Javier Pierini/Getty Images; **1A.16** Bob Stefko/The Image Bank/Getty Images; **1A.17** Ed Lallo/Index Stockq; **1A.18** Jon Riley/Stone/Getty Images; **1A.19** Yellow Dog Productions/Getty Images; **1A.20** Bruce Ando/Index Stock; **1A.21** Courtesy of Cray, Inc.; **1A.22 left** Bettmann/Corbis; **1A.22 right** Walter Hodges/Corbis; **1A.23 left** Javier Pierini/Corbis; **1A.23 center** Jason Homa/The Image Bank/Getty Images; **1A.23 right** Ken Glaser/Index Stock; **1A.27** Ed Bock/Corbis; **1A.29** Michael Rosenfeld/Stone/Getty Images; **1A.30** Thinkstock LLC/Index Stock; **1A.31** Frank Pedrick/Index Stock; **p. 13 top** David Pollack/Corbis; **p. 19 top** Courtesy Apple Computer; **1B.2** Ariel Skelley/Corbis; **1B.3** Bonnie Kamin/Index Stock; **1B.7** Aaron Haupt; **1B.8** Photo courtesy of Intel Corporation; **1B.9** Kingston Technology Company, Inc.; **1B.10** Courtesy IBM Corporation; **1B.11** Amanita Pictures; **1B.12 left** Courtesy Sony; **1B.12 top right** Courtesy IBM Corporation; **1B.12 bottom right** Mark Steinmetz; **1B.13** Teri Stratford; **1B.14 both** Mark Steinmetz; **1B.22** Spencer Grant/Photoedit; **1B.23** David Young Wolff/Photoedit; **1B.24** John Madere/Corbis.

Chapter 2

2A.1 Bettmann/Corbis; **2A.2** Salus, CASTING THE NET: FROM ARPANET TO INTERNET AND BEYOND, p. 64, © 1995 Addison-Wesley Publishing Company Inc. Reprinted by permission of Pearson Education, Inc. Publishing as Pearson Addison Wesley.; **p. 69 top** Dennis Degnan/Corbis; **2B.1** Courtesy Research in Motion.

Chapter 3

3A.8 both Courtesy Microsoft; **3A.10** Courtesy Microsoft; **3A.14** Photo courtesy of Logitech.; **3A.22** Courtesy Microsoft; **3A.24** Aaron Haupt; **3A.25** Siede Preis/Getty Images; **3A.26** Courtesy IBM Corporation.; **3A.27** Jose Luis Pelaez/Corbis; **3A.29** The M1 Workstation found at www.Microsphere.com; **3A.30** Aaron Haupt; **3A.31** C. Sherburne/PHotoLink/Getty Images; **p. 117** Don Wright/AP Wide World; **3B.1** Pete Pacifica/The Image Bank/Getty Images; **3B.2** Anthony P. Bolante/Microsoft/Getty; **3B.3** Courtesy UPS; **3B.4** Bob Daemmrich/The Image Works; **3B.5** Jose Luis Pelaez/Corbis; **3B.6** Matt Meadows; **3B.7** Courtesy IBM Corporate Archives; **3B.8** Courtesy FedEx; **3B.9** Mak-1; **3B.12** William Tauffic/Corbis Stock Market; **3B.15** Steve Cole/Getty Images; **3B.16** Patrick Durand/Corbis; **3B.17** David Young Wolff/Photoedit; **3B.18** B. Busco/Getty Images; **3B.19** Photos of DC-CAM 3200Z and Sound Blaster Audigy 2 ZS provided courtesy of Creative Technology Ltd.; **3B.20 both** Digital Stock; **p. 96** Doug Martin; **p. 129 top** Roger Ball/Corbis Stock Market; **p. 133 top** David Kelly Crow/Photoedit.

Chapter 4

4A.1 left Silicon Graphics R F220 Flat Panel Display: © 2004 Silicon Graphics, Inc. Used by permission. All rights reserved. Image courtesy of Engineering Animation, Inc.; **4A.1 center** Ryan McVay/Getty Images; **4A.1 right** Courtesy IBM; **4A.3** Courtesy Audiovox; **4A.8 both** Photo courtesy Acer America; **4A.9** palmOne, Zire, Tungsten, Treo, logos, stylizations, and design marks associated with all the preceding, and trade dress associated with palmOne, Inc.'s products, are among the trademarks or registered trademarks owned by or exclusively licensed to palmOne, Inc.; **4A.11, 4A.12** Ryan McVay/Getty Images; **4A.14 both** Applied Optical Company; **4A.20** Courtesy NVIDIA Corporation; **4A.22** Humanscale Glare Filter; **4A.23** Courtesy IBM; **4A.24** Courtesy Altec Lansing; **4A.26** Photo of Sound Blaster Audigy 2 ZS provided courtesy of Creative Technology Ltd.; **4A.28** Joaquin Palting/Getty Images; **p. 153** Courtesy Panasonic; **p. 157** Copyright IFAW/D.; **4B.1** Aaron Haupt; **4B.2** Courtesy Epson America, Inc.; **4B.3** Photo courtesy of Hewlett-Packard.; **4B.6** Aaron Haupt; **4B.9** Courtesy of Dell Inc.; **4B.11** Aaron Haupt; **4B.12, 4B.13, 4B.14** Photo courtesy of Hewlett-Packard.; **4B.15** Courtesy © Eastman Kodak Company. KODAK is a trademark.; **4B.16, 4B.17** Photo courtesy of Hewlett-Packard.; **p. 169 top** David Young Wolff/Photoedit; **p. 171 top** Burgum Boorman/Getty Images; **p. 178** Doug Martin; **p. 180** Ted Horowitz/Corbis; **p. 181** Courtesy Microsoft; **p. 182 left** Michael Newman/Photoedit; **p. 182 right** Susan Van Etten/Photoedit; **p. 183** Ross Anania/Photodisc Green/Getty Images.

Chapter 5

5A.9 Sandisk Corporation 2004; **5A.10 both** Kingston Technology Company, Inc.; **5A.12** Courtesy Sun Microsystems, Inc.; **5A.18** Courtesy Apple Computer, Inc.; **5A.19** Courtesy Linsys.; **p. 195** Photo courtesy of Xybernaut Corporation; **p. 201** Tony Freeman/Photoedit; **5B.1 left** Photo courtesy of Intel Corporation; **5B.1 top right** Courtesy Freescale Semiconductor, Inc.; **5B.1 bottom right** Photo courtesy of Intel Corporation; **5B.4 all** Photo courtesy of Intel Corporation; **5B.5 both** Photo Courtesy of AMD 2004.; **5B.6 left** Courtesy Freescale Semiconductor, Inc.; **5B.6 right** Matt Meadows; **5B.7 both** Courtesy Apple Computer, Inc.; **5B.8** Photo courtesy of Acer America; **5B.12** Mark Burnett; **5B.13** Courtesy 3Com; **p. 211** Photo courtesy of Intel Corporation; **p. 217** Jose Luis Pelaez/Corbis.

Chapter 6

6A.2 all Aaron Haupt; **6A.13** Courtesy IOMEGA Corporation; **6A.14** Photo courtesy Hewlett-Packard; **6A.18** Matt Meadows; **6A.19** Mark Burnett; **6A.20** Bigshots/Photodisc Red/Getty Images; **6A.21** Sandisk Corporation 2004; **6A.22** Photo courtesy of Hitachi, Ltd.; **6A.23** Aaron Martz, courtesy Teaxas Memory Systems, Inc.; **p. 241 top** Blue-ray Disc Recorder with built-in BS Digital Tuner. Courtesy Sony Electronics Inc.; **6B.8** Courtesy Sun Microsystems; **6B.9** Courtesy Seagate Technology.

Chapter 7

p. 291 both Photo courtesy of Neural Signals, Inc.; **7B.10** palmOne, Zire, Tungsten, Treo, logos, stylizations, and design marks associated with all the preceding, and trade dress associated with palmOne, Inc.'s products, are among the trademarks or registered trademarks owned by or exclusively licensed to palmOne, Inc.; **p. 295 top** Photographers Choice/Getty Images; **p. 295 bottom** Jose Luis Pelaez/Corbis.

Chapter 8

8A.24, p. 333 top Mark Burnett; **8B.5** Amanita Pictures; **8B.11** RF/Corbis; **8B.14** Kobal Collection; **8B.15** Aaron Haupt; **p. 96** Doug Martin.

Chapter 9

9A.1 Christian Hoehn/Getty Images; **9A.17, 9A.18, 9A.19, 9A.21** Aaron Haupt; **9A.22, 9A.23** Photo courtesy of Linksys; **9A.26** Courtesy TrippLite; **p.359** Courtesy Symantec; **9B.1** Javier Pierini/Corbis; **9B.3** Courtesy U.S. Robotics; **9B.4** Courtesy Zoom Technologies; **9B.5** Courtesy IBM; **9B.9** Photo courtesy of Linksys; **9B.10** D-Link Systems, Inc.; **p. 369** Epson America, Inc.; **p. 375** Jim Craigmyle/Corbis.

Chapter 10

10A.1 Michael Newman/Photoedit; **10A.3** Courtesy 3Com; **10B.2** DiMaggio/Kalish/Corbis; **10B.3** David Young Wolff/Photoedit; **10B.12** Walter Hodges/Corbis; **10B.14** John Henley/Corbis.

Chapter 11

p. 451 Charles Gupton/Corbis.

Chapter 12

12A.1 Lawrence Manning/Corbis; **12A.12** Courtesy IBM; **12A.16** Courtesy IBM; **p. 471** U.S. Air Force; **p. 491** Ed Honowitz/Getty Images.

Chapter 14

14A.1 VCL/Getty Images; **14A.2** Michael S. Yamashita/Corbis; **14A.4** Kevin R. Morris/Corbis; **14A.5** Chuck Savage/Corbis; **14A.7** RF/Corbis; **14A.12** Courtesy American Power Conversion; **14A.13** Courtesy Computer Products, Inc.; **14A.15** RF/Comstock/Getty Images; **14B.1** Spencer Grant/Photoedit; **14B.13** Photo courtesy of Linksys; **14B.17** Property of Fellowes; **14B.18, 14B.19** David Young Wolff/Photoedit; **p. 567** Photodisc Red/Getty Images; **p. 571** Paul Sakuma/AP Wide World.

TIMELINE

p. 584-1965 Computer History Museum; **p. 584-1970** Lucent Technologies Inc./Bell Labs; **p. 584-1971** Photo courtesy of Intel Corporation; **p. 585-1972** W. Cody/Corbis; **p. 585-1973** Courtesy IBM; **p. 585-1974** Photo courtesy of Intel Corporation; **p. 586-1975, 1976** Computer History Museum; **p. 586-1977** Courtesy Apple Inc.; **p.587-1978** Photo courtesy of Intel Corporation; **p. 587-1980 left** Courtesy Microsoft; **P. 587-1980 right** Box shot of Lotus 1-2-3 (copyright 1980) IBM Corporation. Used with permission of IBM Corporation. Lotus and 1-2-3 are trademarks of IBM Corporation.; **p. 588-1981 top** Computer History Museum; **p. 588-1981 bottom** Courtesy of IBM Corporate Archives; **p. 588-1982** Photo courtesy Hewlett-Packard; **p. 589-1983** Photo courtesy Hewlett-Packard; **1984** Paul Sakuma/AP Wide World; **1985 left** Courtesy Microsoft; **1985 right** Photo courtesy Hewlett-Packard; **1986, 1987 left** Courtesy of IBM Corporate Archives; **1987 right** Courtesy Apple Inc.; **1988** Shahn Kermani/Getty Images; **1989 left** Photo courtesy of Intel Corporation; **1989 right** Donna Coveny/MIT News; **1990 left** Courtesy Microsoft; **1990 right** Courtesy IBM; **1991 left** Paul Sakuma/AP Wide World; **1991 right** Courtesy of Apple Inc.; **1992** Courtesy IBM; **1993 left** Courtesy National Center for Supercomuting Applications and the Board of Trustees of the University of Illinois.; **1993 right** Reproduced with Permission of Motorola, Inc.; **1994 bottom** RED HAT is a registered trademark of Red Hat, Inc.; **1995 left** Courtesy Microsoft; **1995 right** eBay™ is a trademark of eBay Inc.; **1996 left** Amanita Pictures; **1996 right** Paul Sakuma/AP Wide World; **1997 left** Photo courtesy of Intel Corporation; **1997 right, 1998 left** Amanita Pictures; **1998 right, 1999** Aaron Haupt; **2000 left** Amanita Pictures; **2000 center** Photo courtesy AMD 2004; **2000 right** Photo courtesy of Intel Corporation; **2001 left** Courtesy Microsoft; **2001 center** Courtesy Apple, Inc; **2001 right** AP Wide World; **2002 top** Steve Chenn/Corbis; **2002 bottom left** Courtesy Handspring. palmOne, Zire, Tungsten, Treo, logos, stylizations, and design marks associated with all the preceding, and trade dress associated with palmOne, Inc.'s products, are among the trademarks or registered trademarks owned by or exclusively licensed to palmOne, Inc.; **2002 center** Denis Poroy/AP Wide World; **2002 bottom right** Open Office.org; **2003 left** © Robin Scholtz; **2003 right** Courtesy Apple, Inc.; **2005** Photo courtesy of Nokia.

Index

C

D

F

G

J

K

L

M

N

O

P

Q

R

S

T

U

X

Y

Z